CONSTITUTIONAL LAW FOR A CHANGING AMERICA

RIGHTS, LIBERTIES, AND JUSTICE

CONSTITUTIONAL LAW FOR A CHANGING AMERICA

RIGHTS, LIBERTIES, AND JUSTICE

FOURTH EDITION

LEE EPSTEIN
Washington University

THOMAS G. WALKER
Emory University

CQ PRESS

A DIVISION OF
CONGRESSIONAL QUARTERLY INC.
WASHINGTON, D.C.

CQ Press
A Division of Congressional Quarterly Inc.
1414 22nd Street, N.W.
Washington, DC 20037
(202) 822-1475; (800) 638-1710
www.cqpress.com

∞ The paper used in this publication meets the minimum requirements of the American National Standard for Information Sciences—Permanence of Paper for Printed Library Materials, ANSI Z39.48-1992.

Printed and bound in the United States of America.

04 03 02 01 00   5 4 3 2 1

Interior Design: Kachergis Book Design, Pittsboro, North Carolina
Cover Design: Gary Gore, Nashville, Tennessee

Library of Congress Cataloging-in-Publication Data
Epstein, Lee, 1958–
    Constitutional Law for a changing America : rights, liberties, and
    justice / Lee Epstein, Thomas G. Walker.— 4th ed.
        p.   cm.
    Includes bibliographical references and index.
    ISBN 1-56802-542-4 (alk. paper)
    1. Civil rights—United States—Cases. 2. Constitutional law—United
    States—Cases. I. Walker, Thomas G. II. Title.
    KF4748 .E67 2001
    342.73'085—dc21
                                                        00-010997

In honor of our parents
Ann and Kenneth Spole
Josephine and George Walker

CONTENTS

CHRONOLOGICAL TABLE OF CASES

TABLES, FIGURES, AND BOXES

CHAPTER 5

CHAPTER 6

CHAPTER 7

CHAPTER 8

CHAPTER 9

PREFACE

Nine years have passed since *Constitutional Law for a Changing America: Rights, Liberties, and Justice* made its debut in a discipline already supplied with many fine casebooks by law professors, historians, and social scientists. We believed then, as we do now, that there was a need for a fresh approach because, as political science professors who regularly teach courses on public law, and as scholars concerned with judicial processes, we saw a growing disparity between what we taught and what our research taught us.

We had adopted books for our classes that focused primarily on Supreme Court decisions and how the Court applied the resulting legal precedents to subsequent disputes, but as scholars we understood that to know the law is to know only part of the story. A host of political factors—internal and external—influence the Court's decisions and shape the development of constitutional law. Among the more significant forces at work are the ways lawyers and interest groups frame legal disputes, the ideological and behavioral propensities of the justices, the politics of judicial selection, public opinion, and the positions elected officials take, to name just a few.

Because we thought no existing book adequately combined the lessons of the legal model with the influences of the political process, we wrote one. In most respects, our book follows tradition: readers will find, for example, that we include the classic cases that best illustrate the development of constitutional law. But our focus is different, as is the appearance of this volume. We emphasize the arguments raised by lawyers and interest groups and include tables and figures on Court trends, profiles of influential justices and organizations, and other materials that bring out the rich political context in which decisions are reached. As a result, students and instructors will find this work both similar to and different from casebooks they may have read before.

Integrating traditional teaching and research concerns was only one of our goals. Another was to animate the subject of public law. As instructors, we find our subject inherently interesting—to us public law is exciting stuff. The typical constitutional law book, however, could not be less inviting in design, presentation, or prose. That kind of book seems to dampen enthusiasm. We have written a book that we hope mirrors the excitement we feel for our subject. Along with cases excerpted in the traditional manner, we have included descriptions of the events that led to the suits, photographs of litigants, and relevant exhibits from the cases. We hope these materials demonstrate to students that Supreme Court cases are more than just legal names and citations, that they involve real people engaged in real disputes. Readers will also find material designed to enhance their understanding of the law, such as information on the Supreme Court decisionmaking process, the structure of the federal judiciary, and briefing court cases. Also included are a glossary of legal terms and brief biographical information on each justice.

In preparing this fourth edition, we have strengthened the distinctive features of the earlier versions by making changes at all three levels of the book—organization, chapters, and cases. In response to the comments of many instructors and questions from our students, we added a new chapter on the Second Amendment, which the Supreme Court has all but neglected. Considering the renewed scholarly interest and battles in the political arena over gun control, we too found ourselves scrambling in class to address students' questions and were forced to rely on supplemental material. The new chapter eliminates that problem.

The most significant changes are in the individual chapters. All have been thoroughly updated to include significant opinions handed down during the 1997–1998, 1998–1999, and 1999–2000 terms. Where relevant, we also updated the narrative to take into account recent events in the legal and political environments. The chapter on criminal rights, for example, now includes a discussion of the Court's reaffirmation of *Miranda v. Arizona;* the chapter on discrimination describes recent events surrounding debates over affirmative action and gay and lesbian rights; and the chapters discussing freedom of expression, obscenity and libel, and privacy delve even deeper into legal issues associated with the "information age," especially the astronomical growth of the World Wide Web.

Finally, we made two kinds of changes in our presentation of the case material. First, to broaden students' perspective on the U.S. legal system, we added boxes on the laws and legal practices of other countries. Students and instructors now will be able to compare and contrast U.S. Supreme Court decisions over a wide range of issues—including the death penalty, prayer in school, and libel—with policies developed in other countries. This material already has provided fodder for lively debates in our classes, and we hope it will in yours as well. Second, finding ourselves increasingly confronted with questions from students about the fate of particular litigants—for example, what happened to Ernesto Miranda?—and hearing the same from colleagues elsewhere, we decided to attach "Aftermath" boxes to a select set of cases. In addition to providing human interest material, they can lead to interesting discussions about the impact of decisions on the lives of "ordinary" Americans.

Also worth noting, we retained and enhanced the changes we made in the third edition pertaining to case presentation. We continue to excerpt concurring and dissenting opinions; in fact, virtually all cases analyzed in the text now include one or the other or both. Although these opinions lack the force of precedent, they are useful in helping students to see alternative points of view. We also provide universal resource locators (URLs) to the full text of the opinions and, where available, to a Web site containing oral arguments in many landmark cases. We took this step because we recognize how rewarding it can be to read decisions in their entirety and to listen to oral arguments. Doing so, we believe, helps students to develop an important skill—differentiating between viable and less-viable arguments. Finally, we continue to retain the historical flavor of the decisions, reprinting verbatim the original language used in the *U.S. Reports* to introduce the justices' writings. Students will see that during most of its history the Court used the term "Mr." to refer to justices, as in "Mr. Justice Holmes delivered the opinion of the Court" or "Mr. Justice Harlan, dissenting." In 1980 the Court dropped the "Mr." This point may seem minor, but we think it is evidence that the justices, like other Americans, updated their usage to reflect fundamental changes in American society—in this case, the emergence of women as a force in the legal profession and shortly thereafter on the Court itself.

One thing has not changed—our intention to keep the text up to date. Each year we will produce a print supplement containing the important opinions issued by the Court since this book's publication. The first supplement for this volume, with cases from the 2000–2001 term, will appear in October 2001. (Contact the Marketing Department at CQ Press, 202-887-6363, for further information.) To make the most recent opinions available before publication of the print supplement, we also maintain a Web site—navigate to: *http://clca.cqpress.com*—that includes excerpts of cases from the Court's current term or the term just ended.

ACKNOWLEDGMENTS

Although the first edition of this volume was published only nine years ago, it had been in the works for many more. During those developmental years, numerous people provided guidance, but none as much as Joanne Daniels, a former editor at CQ Press. It was Joanne who conceived of a constitutional law book that would be accessible, sophisticated, and contemporary. And it was Joanne who brought that concept to our attention and helped us develop it into a book. We are forever in her debt.

Because this new edition charts the same course as the first three, we remain grateful to all of those who had a hand in the previous editions. They include David Tarr and Jeanne Ferris at CQ Press, Joseph A. Kobylka of Southern Methodist University, and our many colleagues who reviewed and commented on them: Judith A. Baer, Ralph Baker, Lawrence Baum, John Brigham, Gregory A. Caldeira, Bradley C. Canon, Robert A. Carp, Phillip J. Cooper, Sue Davis, John Fliter, John B. Gates, Edward V. Heck, Kevin McGuire, Wayne McIntosh, John A. Maltese, Susan Mezey, Richard J. Pacelle Jr., C. K. Rowland, Donald R. Songer, and Harry P. Stumpf. Most of all, we wish to acknowledge the contributions of our editor at CQ Press, Brenda Carter, who has seen *Constitutional Law for a Changing America* through three editions. There are many things we could say about Brenda—all positive—but perhaps this best summarizes our feelings: we cannot think of one editor, not one, in this business with whom we would rather work. Somehow she knows exactly when to steer us and when to steer clear.

We also remain extremely grateful to our copy editor, Carolyn Goldinger. She has worked with us since the first edition, and her imprint is, without exaggeration, *every-where*. She continues to make our prose more accessible, to question our interpretation of certain events and opinions—and is all too often right—and to make our tables and figures understandable. We thank Talia Greenberg, Scott Kuzner, and Tom Roche for tracking down new illustrations for this edition and Gwenda Larsen for her superior organizational skills.

Many thanks also go to Jeffrey A. Segal for his frank appraisal of the earlier works and his willingness to discuss even half-baked ideas for changes; to Judith Baer and Leslie Goldstein for their help with the revision of the Discrimination chapter and their answers to innumerable e-mail messages; to Jack Knight for his comments on the drafts of several chapters; and to Harold J. Spaeth for his wonderful data set.

Our home institutions provided substantial support, not complaining when presented with astronomical telephone bills, postal fees, and copying expenses. For this and all the moral support they provide, we thank all of our colleagues and staffs.

Finally, we acknowledge the support of our friends and families. We are forever grateful to our former professors for instilling in us their genuine interest in and curiosity about things judicial and legal, and to our parents for their unequivocal support. Walker expresses his special thanks to Aimee and Emily for always being there, and Epstein to her husband, Jay, for enduring all that he does not have to (but does, anyway), without complaining (much).

Any errors of omission or commission remain our sole responsibility. We encourage students and instructors alike to comment on the book and to inform us of any errors. Contact us at: *epstein@artsci.wustl.edu* or *polstw@emory.edu.*

TWO BUILDING BLOCKS undergird virtually every book on rights, liberties, and justice: the U.S. Supreme Court and the amendments to the U.S. Constitution. No matter which approach these volumes take, their purpose is to help you understand how the Court has interpreted the Bill of Rights and other amendments to the Constitution.

Constitutional Law for a Changing America is no different. Although we also develop some unique themes, including the legal and political factors that explain why the Court reaches the decisions it does, our primary goal is to provide the narrative and opinion excerpts necessary for you to develop a firm understanding of the Supreme Court's approach to the Constitution's provisions concerning rights, liberties, and justice.

We devote the first part of the book to the two building blocks: the Court and the amendments to the Constitution. In what follows, we consider the events leading up to the drafting of the Bill of Rights and some of the debates over its adoption. Chapter 1 looks at the Court, examining both the procedures it uses to decide cases and its approaches to decisionmaking. In the next two chapters, we begin to put the two building blocks together by considering how the Court has interpreted its own power (Chapter 2) and how it has analyzed the general nature and applicability of the Bill of Rights (Chapter 3).

THE ROAD TO THE BILL OF RIGHTS

Before the adoption of the Declaration of Independence, the Continental Congress selected a group of delegates to make recommendations for the formation of a national government. Composed of representatives of each of the thirteen colonies, this committee proposed a national charter, the Articles of Confederation, which Congress approved and submitted to the states for ratification in November 1777. Ratification was achieved in March 1781.

This document, the Articles of Confederation, was the nation's first written charter, but it changed the way the government operated very little: the articles merely formalized practices that had developed prior to 1774. For example, rather than provide for a compact between the people and the government, the charter institutionalized "a league of friendship" among the states, and its guiding principle was state sovereignty. This is not to suggest that the charter failed to provide for a central government; in fact, the articles created a national governing apparatus. There was a one-house legislature, but no formal federal executive or judiciary. The legislature had some power, most notably in the area of foreign affairs, but it derived its authority from the states that had created it, not the people.

The weaknesses in the system soon became apparent, and the Continental Congress issued a call for a convention to meet in May 1787 in Philadelphia "for the sole and express purpose of revising the Articles of Confederation." Within a month, however, the fifty-five delegates had dramatically altered their mission. Viewing the articles as unworkable, they decided to start afresh. What emerged just four months later, on September 17, was an

TABLE 1-1 The Ratification of the Constitution

State	Date of Action	Decision	Margin
Delaware	December 7, 1787	Ratified	30:0
Pennsylvania	December 12, 1787	Ratified	46:23
New Jersey	December 18, 1787	Ratified	38:0
Georgia	December 31, 1787	Ratified	26:0
Connecticut	January 8, 1788	Ratified	128:40
Massachusetts	February 6, 1788	Ratified with amendments	187:168
Maryland	April 26, 1788	Ratified	63:11
South Carolina	May 23, 1788	Ratified with amendments	149:73
New Hampshire	June 21, 1788	Ratified with amendments	57:47
Virginia	June 25, 1788	Ratified with amendments	89:79
New York	July 26, 1788	Ratified with amendments	30:27
North Carolina	August 2, 1788	Rejected	184:84
	November 21, 1789	Ratified with amendments	194:77
Rhode Island	May 29, 1790	Ratified with amendments	34:32

SOURCE: Daniel A. Farber and Suzanna Sherry, *A History of the American Constitution* (St. Paul, Minn.: West Publishing, 1990), 216.

entirely new government scheme embodied in the U.S. Constitution.

Pleased with their handiwork, the Framers "adjourned to City Tavern, dined together and took cordial leave of each other."[1] Most of the delegates were more than ready to go home after the long, hot summer in Philadelphia, and they departed with confidence that the new document would receive speedy approval by the states. At first, their optimism appeared justified. As Table 1-1 depicts, before the year was out four states had ratified the Constitution—three by unanimous votes. But after January 1788 the pace began to slow. By this time, an opposition movement was marshaling arguments to persuade state convention delegates to vote against ratification. What these opponents, the so-called Anti-Federalists, feared most of all was the Constitution's new balance of power. They believed that strong state governments provided the best defense against the concentration of too much power in the national government, and that the proposed Constitution tipped the scales the other way. These fears were countered by the Federalists, who favored ratification. The Federalists' arguments and writings took many forms, but among the most important was a series of eighty-five articles published in New York newspapers, under the pen name Publius. Written by John Jay, James Madison, and Alexander Hamilton, *The Federalist Papers* continues to provide insight into the objectives and intent of the Founders.[2]

Debates between the Federalists and their opponents were often highly philosophical, with emphasis on the appropriate roles and powers of national institutions. In the states, however, ratification drives were marked by the stuff of ordinary politics—deal making. Massachusetts provides a case in point. After three weeks of debate among delegates, Federalist leaders realized that they would never achieve victory without the support of Gov. John Hancock. They went to his house and proposed that he endorse ratification on condition that a series of amendments be tacked on for consideration by Congress. The governor agreed, but in return he wanted to become president of the United States if Virginia failed to ratify or George Washington refused to serve. Or he would accept the vice presidency. With the deal cut, Hancock went the state convention to propose a compromise—the ratification of the Constitution with amend-

1. *1787*, compiled by historians of the Independence National Historical Park (New York: Exeter Books, 1987), 191.

2. *The Federalist Papers* are available on the Internet at: *http://lcweb2. loc.gov/const/fedquery.html.*

ments. The delegates agreed, making Massachusetts the sixth state to ratify.

This compromise—the call for a bill of rights— caught on, and Madison began to advocate it whenever close votes were likely. As it turned out, he and other Federalists needed to mention it quite often: as Table 1-1 indicates, of the nine states ratifying after January 1788, seven recommended that the new Congress consider amendments. New York and Virginia probably would not have agreed to the Constitution without such additions, and Virginia called for a second constitutional convention for that purpose. Other states began devising their own wish lists—enumerations of specific rights they wanted put into the document.

Why were states so reluctant to ratify the Constitution without a bill of rights? Some viewed the new government scheme with downright suspicion because of the extensive powers granted to the proposed national government. But more tended to agree with Thomas Jefferson, who, in a letter to James Madison, argued that "a bill of rights is what the people are entitled to against every government on earth, general and particular, and what no just government should refuse, or rest on inference."

What Jefferson's remark suggests is that, although many people thought well of the new system of government, they were troubled by the lack of a declaration of rights. At the time, Americans clearly understood concepts of *fundamental* and *inalienable* rights, those that inherently belonged to them and that no government could deny. Even England, the country with which they had fought a war for their freedom, had such guarantees. The Magna Carta of 1215 and the Bill of Rights of 1689 gave Britons the right to a jury trial, to protection against cruel and unusual punishments, and so forth. Moreover, after the Revolution, almost every state constitution included a philosophical statement about the relationship between citizens and their government and/or a list of fifteen to twenty inalienable rights, such as religious freedom and electoral independence. Small wonder that the call for such a statement or enumeration of rights became a battle cry. If it was so widespread, we might ask why the Framers failed to include a bill of rights in the original document. Did they not anticipate the reaction?

Records of the 1787 constitutional debates indicate that, in fact, the delegates considered specific individual guarantees on at least four separate occasions.[3] On August 20 Charles Pinckney submitted a proposal that included several guarantees, such as freedom of the press and the eradication of religious tests, but the various committees never considered his plan. On September 12, 14, and 16, just before the close of the convention, some tried, again without success, to convince the delegates to enumerate specific guarantees. At one point, George Mason said that a bill of rights "would give great quiet to the people; and with the aid of the state delegations, a bill might be prepared in a few hours." This motion was unanimously defeated by those remaining in attendance. On the convention's last day, Edmund Randolph made a desperate plea that the delegates allow the states to submit amendments and then convene a second convention. Although he favored a bill of rights, Pinckney responded, "Conventions are serious things, and ought not to be repeated."

Why these suggestions received such unwelcome receptions by the majority of delegates is a matter of scholarly debate. Some suggest that the pleas came too late, that the Framers wanted to complete their mission by September 15 and were simply unwilling to stay in Philadelphia even one day longer. Others disagree, arguing that the Framers were more concerned with the structure of government than with individual rights and that the plan they devised—one based on enumerated, not unlimited powers—would foreclose the need for a bill of rights. Hamilton wrote, "The Constitution is itself . . . a Bill of Rights."[4] Under it the government could exercise only those functions specifically bestowed upon it; all remaining rights belonged to the people. He also asserted that "independent of those which relate to the structure of government," the Constitution did, in fact, contain some of the more necessary specific guarantees.[5]

---

3. The following discussion comes from Daniel A. Farber and Suzanna Sherry, *A History of the American Constitution* (St. Paul, Minn.: West Publishing, 1990), 221–222. This book reprints verbatim debates over the Constitution and the Bill of Rights.

4. *The Federalist Papers*, No. 84, Isaac Kramnick, ed. (New York: Penguin Books, 1987), 477.

5. Ibid., 473.

For example, Article I, Section 9, prohibits bills of attainder, ex post facto laws, and the suspension of writs of habeas corpus. Hamilton and others further argued that the specification of rights was not only unnecessary, but also could even be dangerous because no list could contain everything.

Despite these misgivings, the reality of the political environment caused many Federalists to change their views on including a bill of rights. They realized that if they did not accede to state demands, either the Constitution would not be ratified or a new convention would be necessary. As neither alternative was particularly attractive, they agreed to amend the Constitution as soon as the new government came into power.

In May 1789, one month after the start of the first Congress, Madison announced to the House of Representatives that he would draft a bill of rights and submit it within the coming month. As it turned out, the task proved more difficult than Madison thought; the state conventions had suggested to Congress more than two hundred amendments, some of which would have significantly decreased the power of the national government. After sifting through these lists, Madison at first thought it might be best to incorporate the amendments into the Constitution's text, but he soon changed his mind. Instead, he presented the House with the following statement, echoing the views expressed in the Declaration of Independence:

That there be prefixed to the Constitution a declaration—That all power is originally vested in, and consequently derived from, the people.[6]

The legislators rejected this proposal, preferring a catalogue of rights to a philosophical statement. Madison returned to his task, eventually fashioning a list of seventeen amendments. When he took it back to the House, however, the list was greeted with suspicion and opposition. Some members of Congress, even those who had argued for a bill of rights, now did not want to be bothered with the proposals, insisting that they had more important business to settle. One suggested that other nations would not see the United States "as a serious trading partner as it was still tinkering with its constitution instead of organizing its government."[7]

Finally, in July, after Madison had prodded and even begged, the House considered his proposals. A special committee scrutinized them and reported a few days later, and the House adopted, with some modification, Madison's seventeen amendments. The Senate approved some and rejected others so that by the time the Bill of Rights was submitted to the states on October 2, only twelve remained.[8]

The states ended up ratifying ten of the twelve. The amendments that did not receive approval were the original Articles I and II. Article I dealt with the number of representatives:

After the first enumeration required by the first article of the Constitution, there shall be one Representative for every thirty thousand, until the number shall amount to one hundred, after which the proportion shall be so regulated by Congress, that there shall be not less than one hundred Representatives, nor less than one Representative for every forty thousand persons, until the number of Representatives shall amount to two hundred; after which the proportion shall be so regulated by Congress, that there shall not be less than two hundred Representatives, nor more than one Representative for every fifty thousand persons.

Article II contained the following provision:

No law varying the compensation for the services of the Senators and Representatives shall take effect, until an election of Representatives shall have intervened.

This article also failed to garner sufficient support from the states in the 1790s and did not become a part of the Bill of Rights. Unlike the original Article I, however, this provision eventually took its place in the Constitution. In 1992, more than two hundred years after it was proposed, the states ratified it as the Twenty-seventh Amendment to the U.S. Constitution.

Why the states originally refused to pass this amendment, along with the original Article I, is a mystery, for few records of state ratification proceedings exist. What we do know is that on December 15, 1791, when Virginia

---

6. The full text of Madison's statement is available in *Contexts of the Constitution: A Documentary Collection on Principles of American Constitutional Law* by Neil H. Cogan (New York: Foundation Press, 1999), 813–815.

7. Quoted in Farber and Sherry, *American Constitution*, 231.

8. Among those rejected was the one Madison "prized above all others": that the states would have to abide by many of the enumerated guarantees. See Chapter 3 on incorporation of the Bill of Rights.

TABLE 1-2 Methods of Amending the Constitution

Proposed By	Ratified By	Used For
Two-thirds vote in both houses of Congress	State legislatures in three-fourths of the states	26 amendments
Two-thirds vote in both houses of Congress	Ratifying conventions in three-fourths of the states	21st Amendment
Constitutional convention (called at the request of two-thirds of the states)	State legislatures in three-fourths of the states	Never used
Constitutional convention (called at the request of two-thirds of the states)	Ratifying conventions in three-fourths of the states	Never used

ratified, the Bill of Rights became part of the U.S. Constitution.

THE AMENDMENT PROCESS

It is truly remarkable that Congress proposed and the states ratified ten amendments to the Constitution in three years: since then only seventeen others have been added! Undoubtedly, such reticence would have pleased the writers of the Constitution. They wanted to create a government that would have permanence, even though they also recognized the need for flexibility. One of the major flaws in the Articles of Confederation, some thought, was the amending process: changing that document required the approval of all thirteen states. The Framers imagined an amending procedure that would be "bendable but not trendable, tough but not insurmountable, responsive to genuine waves of popular desire, yet impervious to self-serving campaigns of factional groups."[9] Therefore, in Article V, they spelled out the procedures for altering the Constitution (see Table 1-2). The Constitution can be amended in one of four ways. But, perhaps because the First Congress chose a particular method—it approved the amendments and the state legislatures ratified them—that way has been used most often. Indeed, all but the Twenty-first Amendment, which repealed prohibition, followed that route.

That only twenty-seven amendments have made it through Congress and the states and that twenty-six have taken the same path does not mean that other proposals

have not been offered. In fact, through 1996 Congress had considered more than ten thousand amendments and sent thirty-three of them to the states. Among those thirty-three were the Child Labor Amendment (proposed in 1924), prohibiting the "labor of persons under 18 years of age" and the Equal Rights Amendment (proposed 4in 1972), stating that "equality of rights under law shall not be denied or abridged by the United States or any State on account of sex." In both instances, an insufficient number of states agreed to their ratification.

Attempts to use other proposal methods are not unusual.[10] At present, the states are only two votes short of requesting Congress to call a national convention to consider a balanced budget amendment—although the country's robust fiscal health, among other factors, makes it unlikely that more states will join this movement any time soon. An effort also persists to persuade Congress to propose an amendment limiting the number of terms that U.S. representatives and senators can serve.

THE SUPREME COURT AND THE AMENDMENT PROCESS

So far, our discussion of the amendment process has not mentioned the president or the Supreme Court. The reason is that neither has any formal constitutional role in it. We do not mean to suggest, however, that these institutions have nothing to do with the process: both have

9. J. T. Keenan, *The Constitution of the United States: An Unfolding Story,* 2d ed. (Chicago: Dorsey Press, 1988), 41.

10. Perhaps the most widely reported was the effort by Everett Dirksen, R-Ill., (Senate, 1951–1969) to get the states to request a national convention with the purpose of overturning *Reynolds v. Sims,* the Supreme Court's 1964 reapportionment decision. He failed, by one state, to do so.

BOX 1-1   FOUR AMENDMENTS THAT OVERTURNED SUPREME COURT DECISIONS

THE ELEVENTH

When Chisholm sued Georgia in 1793 and the Supreme Court dropped a bombshell on states-righters by agreeing to hear the case, Anti-Federalists were outraged. Congress responded swiftly by proposing the Eleventh Amendment, which was ratified by the requisite three-fourths of the states within a year, though not declared ratified until 1798. The amendment protects states against suits by citizens of another state or of another country.

THE FOURTEENTH

Congress and the High Court tangled again after the *Dred Scott v. Sandford* (sometimes spelled Dread Scott by abolitionists) case of 1857. Nine separate decisions were rendered on this case, but Chief Justice Roger B. Taney spoke for the "majority" in declaring that slaves could not be citizens and that Congress had exceeded its purview in prohibiting slavery in the territories. A Civil War and a few years of Reconstruction intervened before the Fourteenth Amendment, which conferred citizenship on all persons born or naturalized in the United States, could correct the *Scott* ruling.

THE SIXTEENTH

Congress next "got around the Supreme Court" through the passage of the Sixteenth Amendment, which legalized the income tax. In 1895 the Court turned down a federal income tax law on grounds that the Constitution requires taxes to be apportioned among the states proportionately according to population. But, in a spirit of cooperation, the Court invited Congress to overthrow the objection by means of an amendment. Congress proposed the Sixteenth Amendment in 1909, and the states ratified it in 1913.

THE TWENTY-SIXTH

President Richard Nixon, although signing a change in the Voting Rights Act that allowed eighteen-year-olds to vote in federal, state, and local elections, expressed doubt that the law was constitutional. Suit was speedily arranged, and the Court confirmed the president's misgivings in a 5–4 rejection that said, in effect: "The Congress does not have jurisdiction over state and local elections."

At a time when eighteen-year-olds were losing their lives in Vietnam, the Twenty-sixth Amendment had wide popular approval. In record time it was proposed by Congress in March 1971 and ratified in June, giving eighteen-year-olds the right to vote in national, state, and local elections.

SOURCE: From *The Constitution of the United States: An Unfolding Story*, 2d ed., by J. T. Keenan, 42–43. Copyright © 1988 by The Dorsey Press. Reprinted by permission of the publisher, Brooks/Cole, Pacific Grove, Calif.

---

significant, albeit informal, functions. Presidents often instigate and support proposals for constitutional amendments. Indeed, virtually every chief executive has wanted some alteration to the Constitution. In his first inaugural address, George Washington urged adoption of a bill of rights; two hundred years later, George Bush urged quick ratification of an amendment to prohibit flag desecration. The Court also has played two important roles in the process.

First, it has served as an "instigator." Of the seventeen additions to the Constitution after the Bill of Rights, Congress proposed four specifically to overturn Supreme Court decisions (*see Box 1-1*). Many consider one of these—the Fourteenth—the single most important amendment since 1791.

A healthy portion of the ten thousand or so proposals Congress has considered were aimed at similar objectives, among them the failed Child Labor and Equal Rights Amendments, both of which emanated, at least in part, from Supreme Court rulings rejecting their premises.[11] More recently, Congress has considered the following amendments, all of which were aimed at overturning Court decisions: a human life amendment that would make abortions illegal (in response to *Roe v. Wade*, 1973); a school prayer amendment that would allow public

11. In 1916 Congress passed a child labor law that prohibited the shipment in interstate commerce of anything made by children under age fourteen. When the Court struck down this act (and another like it) as an unconstitutional use of congressional power (*Hammer v. Dagenhart*, 1918), Congress proposed a Child Labor Amendment. See Clement E. Vose, *Constitutional Change* (Lexington, Mass.: Lexington Books, 1972).

school children to engage in prayer (in response to *Engel v. Vitale,* 1962, and *School District of Abington Township v. Schempp,* 1963); and a flag desecration amendment that would prohibit mutilation of the American flag (in response to *Texas v. Johnson,* 1989). The term limits amendment, noted above, would overturn the Supreme Court's ruling in *U.S. Term Limits v. Thornton* (1994).

Second, the Court has been asked to interpret Article V, which deals with the amendment process, but it has been hesitant to do so. One example is *Coleman v. Miller* (1939), which involved the actions of the Kansas legislature over the Child Labor Amendment, Proposed by Congress in 1924, the amendment stated: "The Congress shall have power to limit, regulate, and prohibit the labor of persons under eighteen years of age." In January 1925 Kansas legislators rejected the amendment. The issue arose again, however, when the state senate reconsidered it in January 1937. At that time, the legislative body split, 20–20, with the lieutenant governor casting the decisive vote to approve it. Members of the Kansas legislature (mostly those who had opposed the proposal) challenged the 1937 vote on two grounds: they questioned the ability of the lieutenant governor to break the tie and, more generally, they questioned the reconsideration of an amendment that previously had been rejected. Writing for the Court, Chief Justice Charles Evans Hughes refused to address these points. Rather, he asserted that the suit raised questions, particularly those pertaining to recision, that were political and, therefore, nonjusticiable, meaning that a court was not appropriate place to settle them. In his words, the "ultimate authority" over the amendment process was Congress, not the Court.

Over the years, the Court has followed the *Coleman* approach, leaving questions regarding the interpretation of Article V to Congress. Consider how it treated its most recent Article V case, *NOW v. Idaho* (1982). At issue was a 1978 act of Congress that extended the original deadline for state ratification of the Equal Rights Amendment from 1979 to 1982; the act also rejected a clause that would have permitted state legislatures to rescind their prior approval. In the wake of a strong anti-ERA movement, Idaho, which had passed the amendment in the early 1970s, decided to ignore federal law and retract its original vote.[12] The National Organization for Women challenged the state's action, and in 1982 the Court docketed the case for argument. But, upon the request of the United States, it dismissed the suit as moot: the congressionally extended time period for ratification had run out, and the controversy was no longer viable.

The Court might be confronted with even more difficult questions in the near future. For example, if the drive for a balanced budget amendment succeeded in attaining the support of two-thirds of the states, the Court might have to consider issues relating to the creation of a second constitutional convention. Would the delegates to such a convention deliberate only the amendments under consideration or would they be free to take up any or all parts of the Constitution? Addressing this question might be one of the most significant tasks the Supreme Court has ever faced. Remember that the 1787 delegates met to amend the Articles of Confederation, but instead reframed the entire system of government. Perhaps that is why those same men were so vehemently opposed to the notion of holding another convention to propose a bill of rights. Jefferson, for one, believed that a second convention could significantly weaken the government.

In any event, it may be a while before the Court must address this delicate issue. Since 1983 no state has passed the balanced budget amendment, a situation we might now credit to present-day budget surpluses. At that time, however, analysts attributed the amendment's failure to the formation of an anticonvention movement that strongly opposes any tinkering with the original document. To appreciate the seriousness of such an enterprise, we need only remind ourselves that the U.S. Constitution is the world's oldest surviving ruling charter and that the Bill of Rights is its heart.

---

12. Three other states, Kentucky, Nebraska, and Tennessee, also rescinded.

CHAPTER 1

UNDERSTANDING THE U.S. SUPREME COURT

THIS BOOK is devoted to narrative and opinion excerpts showing how the U.S. Supreme Court has interpreted many of the amendments to the Constitution. As a student approaching civil rights, civil liberties, and justice, perhaps for the first time, you may think it is odd that the subject requires 794 pages of text. After all, in length, the Constitution and the amendments to it could fit easily into many Court decisions. Moreover, the document itself—its language—seems so clear.

First impressions, however, can be deceiving. Even apparently clear constitutional scriptures do not necessarily lend themselves to clear constitutional interpretation. For example, according to the First Amendment, "Congress shall make no law . . . prohibiting the free exercise" of religion. Sounds simple enough, but could you, based on those words, answer the following questions, all of which have been posed to the Court?

• May a state refuse to give unemployment benefits to an individual who quits her job because her employer wants her to work on Saturdays, the day of rest in her religion?
• May the military retain a policy that forbids Jews in service from wearing yarmulkes?
• May a city prohibit the sacrificing of animals for religious purposes?

What these and other questions arising from the different guarantees contained in the Constitution illustrate is that a gap sometimes exists between the document's words and reality. Although the language seems explicit, its meaning can be elusive and difficult to follow. Accordingly, justices have developed various approaches to resolving disputes.

But, as Figure 1-1 shows, a great deal happens before the justices actually decide cases. We begin our discussion with a brief overview of the steps depicted in the figure. Next, we consider explanations for the choices justices make at the final and most important stage, the resolution of disputes.

PROCESSING SUPREME COURT CASES

During the 1999 term more than 7,300 cases arrived at the Supreme Court's doorstep, but the justices decided, with a written opinion, only 81.[1] The disparity between the number of parties that want the Court to resolve their disputes and the number the Court agrees to resolve raises some important questions: How do the justices decide which cases to hear? What happens to the cases it rejects? Those it agrees to resolve? We address these and other questions by describing how the Court processes its cases.

Deciding to Decide: The Supreme Court's Caseload

As the figures for the 1999 term indicate, the Court heard and decided only 1 percent of the cases it received. This percentage is low even by contemporary standards (more typically the Court decides about 5 percent of the

1. Data courtesy of the clerk of the U.S. Supreme Court.

FIGURE 1-1 The Processing of Cases

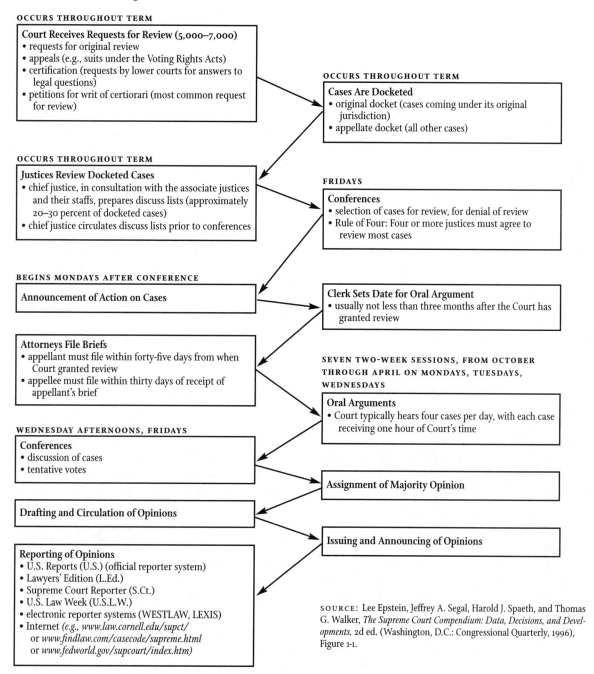

OCCURS THROUGHOUT TERM

Court Receives Requests for Review (5,000–7,000)
- requests for original review
- appeals (e.g., suits under the Voting Rights Acts)
- certification (requests by lower courts for answers to legal questions)
- petitions for writ of certiorari (most common request for review)

OCCURS THROUGHOUT TERM

Cases Are Docketed
- original docket (cases coming under its original jurisdiction)
- appellate docket (all other cases)

OCCURS THROUGHOUT TERM

Justices Review Docketed Cases
- chief justice, in consultation with the associate justices and their staffs, prepares discuss lists (approximately 20–30 percent of docketed cases)
- chief justice circulates discuss lists prior to conferences

FRIDAYS

Conferences
- selection of cases for review, for denial of review
- Rule of Four: Four or more justices must agree to review most cases

BEGINS MONDAYS AFTER CONFERENCE

Announcement of Action on Cases

Clerk Sets Date for Oral Argument
- usually not less than three months after the Court has granted review

Attorneys File Briefs
- appellant must file within forty-five days from when Court granted review
- appellee must file within thirty days of receipt of appellant's brief

SEVEN TWO-WEEK SESSIONS, FROM OCTOBER THROUGH APRIL ON MONDAYS, TUESDAYS, WEDNESDAYS

Oral Arguments
- Court typically hears four cases per day, with each case receiving one hour of Court's time

WEDNESDAY AFTERNOONS, FRIDAYS

Conferences
- discussion of cases
- tentative votes

Assignment of Majority Opinion

Drafting and Circulation of Opinions

Issuing and Announcing of Opinions

Reporting of Opinions
- U.S. Reports (U.S.) (official reporter system)
- Lawyers' Edition (L.Ed.)
- Supreme Court Reporter (S.Ct.)
- U.S. Law Week (U.S.L.W.)
- electronic reporter systems (WESTLAW, LEXIS)
- Internet (e.g., *www.law.cornell.edu/supct/* or *www.findlaw.com/casecode/supreme.html* or *www.fedworld.gov/supcourt/index.htm*)

SOURCE: Lee Epstein, Jeffrey A. Segal, Harold J. Spaeth, and Thomas G. Walker, *The Supreme Court Compendium: Data, Decisions, and Developments,* 2d ed. (Washington, D.C.: Congressional Quarterly, 1996), Figure 1-1.

cases it receives), but it follows the general trend in Supreme Court decisionmaking: the number of requests for review has increased dramatically over the century, but the number of cases the Court formally decides each year has not increased. So, for example, in 1930 the Court agreed to decide 159 of the 726 disputes pending before it. Six decades later, in 1990, the number of cases granted review fell to 141, but the sum total of pending disputes had risen to 6,302—or nearly 9 times greater than the 1930 figure.[2]

How do these cases get to the Supreme Court? How does the Court decide which will get a formal review and which will be rejected? Why does the Court make the choices that it does? Let us consider each of these questions, for they are fundamental to an understanding of judicial decisionmaking.

How Cases Get to the Court: Jurisdiction and the Routes of Appeal. Cases come to the Court in one of four ways: either by a request for review under the Court's original jurisdiction or by three appellate routes—appeals, certification, and petitions for writs of certiorari *(see Figure 1-1).* Chapter 2 explains more about the Court's original jurisdiction, as it is central to understanding the landmark case of *Marbury v. Madison* (1803). Here, it is sufficient to note that original cases are those that have not been heard by any other court. Article III of the Constitution authorizes such suits in cases involving ambassadors from foreign countries and those to which a state is a party. But, because congressional legislation permits lower courts to exercise concurrent authority over most cases meeting Article III requirements, the Supreme Court does not have exclusive jurisdiction over them. Consequently, the Court normally accepts, on its original jurisdiction, only those cases in which one state is suing another (usually over a disputed boundary) and sends the rest back to the lower courts for an initial ruling. That is why, in recent years, original jurisdiction cases comprise only a tiny fraction of the Court's overall docket—between one and five cases per term.

2. Data are from Lee Epstein, Jeffrey A. Segal, Harold J. Spaeth, and Thomas G. Walker, *The Supreme Court Compendium: Data, Decisions, and Developments,* 2d ed. (Washington, D.C.: Congressional Quarterly, 1996), Tables 2-5 and 2-6.

Most cases reach the Court under its appellate jurisdiction, meaning that a lower federal or state court has already rendered a decision and one of the parties is asking the Supreme Court to review that decision. As Figure 1-2 shows, such cases typically come from one of the U.S. courts of appeals or state supreme courts. The U.S. Supreme Court, the nation's highest tribunal, is the court of last resort.

To invoke the Court's appellate jurisdiction, litigants can take one of three routes, depending on the nature of their dispute: appeal as a matter of right, certification, and certiorari. Cases falling into the first category (normally called "on appeal") involve issues Congress has determined are so important that a ruling by the Supreme Court is necessary. Before 1988 these included cases in which a lower court declared a state or federal law unconstitutional or in which a state court upheld a state law challenged as violating the U.S. Constitution. Although the justices were supposed to decide such appeals, they often found ways to deal with them more expediently—by either failing to consider them or issuing summary decisions (shorthand rulings). Finally, in 1988, at the Court's urging, Congress virtually eliminated "mandatory" appeals. Today the Court is legally obliged to hear only those few cases (typically involving the Voting Rights Act) appealed from special three-judge district courts.

A second, rarely used, route to the Court is certification. Under the Court's appellate jurisdiction and by an act of Congress, lower appellate courts can file writs of certification, asking the justices to respond to questions aimed at clarifying federal law. Because only judges may use this route, very few cases come to the Court this way. Moreover, the justices may accept a question certified to them or dismiss it.

That leaves the third and most common appellate path, a request for a writ of certiorari (from the Latin meaning "to be informed"). In a petition for a writ of certiorari, the litigants desiring Supreme Court review ask the Court, literally, to become "informed" about their cases by requesting the lower court to send up the record. Most of the eight thousand or so cases that arrive each year come as requests for certiorari. The Court, ex-

FIGURE 1-2 The American Court System

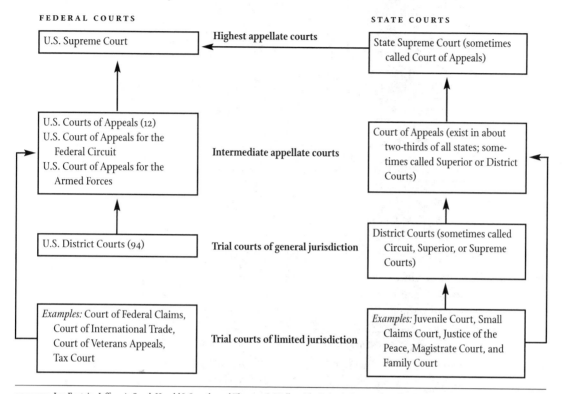

FEDERAL COURTS

| | | **STATE COURTS** |

U.S. Supreme Court — Highest appellate courts — State Supreme Court (sometimes called Court of Appeals)

U.S. Courts of Appeals (12)
U.S. Court of Appeals for the Federal Circuit
U.S. Court of Appeals for the Armed Forces

Intermediate appellate courts

Court of Appeals (exist in about two-thirds of all states; sometimes called Superior or District Courts)

U.S. District Courts (94)

Trial courts of general jurisdiction

District Courts (sometimes called Circuit, Superior, or Supreme Courts)

Examples: Court of Federal Claims, Court of International Trade, Court of Veterans Appeals, Tax Court

Trial courts of limited jurisdiction

Examples: Juvenile Court, Small Claims Court, Justice of the Peace, Magistrate Court, and Family Court

SOURCE: Lee Epstein, Jeffrey A. Segal, Harold J. Spaeth, and Thomas G. Walker, *The Supreme Court Compendium: Data, Decisions, and Developments,* 2d ed. (Washington, D.C.: Congressional Quarterly, 1996), Figure 7–2.

ercising its ability to choose the cases to review, grants "cert" to less than 5 percent of the petitions. Granting cert means that the justices have decided to give the case full review; denying cert means that the decision of the lower court remains in force.

How Does the Court Decide? The Case Selection Process. "Deciding to decide" presents something of a mixed blessing to the justices. Selecting the approximately hundred cases to review from the large number of requests is an arduous task that requires the justices or their law clerks to look over hundreds of thousands of pages of briefs and other memoranda. However, the ability to exercise discretion frees the Court from one of the major constraints on judicial bodies: the lack of agenda control. The justices may not be able to reach out and propose cases for review the way members of Congress

can propose legislation, but the enormous number of petitions ensures that they can resolve at least some issues important to them.

Many scholars have tried to determine what makes a case "certworthy," that is, worthy of review by the Supreme Court. Before we review some of their findings, let us consider the case selection process itself. The original pool of about eight thousand petitions faces several checkpoints along the way *(see Figure 1-1),* which significantly reduce the amount of time the Court, acting as a collegial body, spends on deciding what to decide. The staff members in the office of the Supreme Court clerk act as the first gatekeepers. When a petition for certiorari arrives, the clerk's office examines it to make sure it is in proper form, that it conforms to the Court's precise rules. For example, briefs must "be produced on paper

FIGURE 1-3 A Page from Justice Brennan's Docket Books

	HOLD FOR	CERT.		JURISDICTIONAL STATEMENT				MERITS		MOTION		ABSENT	NOT VOTING
		G	D	N	POST	DIS	AFF	REV	AFF	G	D		
Burger, Ch. J..................			✓					✓	✓				
Brennan, J.....................		✓	✓										
Stewart, J.....................		✓						✓					
White, J.......................								✓	✓				
Marshall, J....................			✓										
Blackmun, J...................		✓	✓					✓					
Powell, J......................		✓						✓					
Rehnquist, J..................								✓	✓				
Stevens, J.....................			✓										

SOURCE: Dockets of Justice William J. Brennan Jr., Manuscript Division, Library of Congress, Washington, D.C.
NOTE: In the CERT. column, G = grant the petition; D = deny the petition. In the MERITS column, REV = reverse the decision of the court below; AFF = affirm the decision of the court below.

that is opaque, unglazed, 6⅛ by 9¼ inches in size, and not less than 60 pounds in weight, and shall have margins of at least three fourths of an inch on all sides." Exceptions are made for litigants who cannot afford to pay the Court's fees. The rules governing these petitions, known as in forma pauperis briefs, are somewhat looser, allowing indigents to submit briefs on 8½- by 11-inch paper. The Court's major concern, or so it seems, is that the document "be legible."[3] The clerk's office gives all acceptable petitions an identification number, called a "docket number," and forwards copies to the chambers of the individual justices. Each justice reviews the petitions, making independent decisions about which cases he or she feels are worthy of a full hearing. Some have their clerks read and summarize all the petitions; most use the "certiorari pool system" in which clerks from different chambers collaborate in reading and then writing memoranda on the petitions.[4] Either way, the justices use their clerks' reports as a basis to make case selection decisions.

During this process, the chief justice plays a special role, serving as yet another checkpoint on petitions. Be-fore the justices meet to make case selection decisions, the chief circulates a "discuss list," containing those cases he feels worthy of full Court consideration; any justice may add cases to this list, but may not subtract any. About 20 percent to 30 percent of the cases that come to the Court make it to the list and are actually discussed by the justices in conference. The rest are automatically denied review, and the lower court decision stands.[5]

This much we know. Because the Court's conferences are attended only by the justices and held in private, we cannot say precisely what transpires. We can offer only a rough picture based on scholarly writings, the comments of justices, and our examination of the private papers of a few retired justices. These sources tell us that the discussion of each petition begins with the chief justice presenting a short summary of the facts and, typically, stating his vote. The associate justices, who sit at a rectangular table in order of seniority, then comment on each petition, with the most senior justice speaking first and the newest member last. The associate justices usually provide some indication of how they will vote on the merits of the case if it is accepted. Indeed, as Figure 1-3 shows, the justices record certiorari and merits votes in their

3. Rules 33 and 39 of the Rules of the Supreme Court of the United States. All Supreme Court rules are available at: *www.law.cornell.edu/rules/supct/*.

4. Supreme Court justices are authorized to hire four law clerks each. Typically, these clerks are outstanding recent graduates of the nation's top law schools.

5. For information on the discuss list, see Gregory A. Caldeira and John R. Wright, "The Discuss List: Agenda Building in the Supreme Court," *Law and Society Review* 24 (1990): 807–836.

docket books. But, given the large number of petitions, the justices apparently discuss few cases in detail.

By tradition, the Court adheres to the so-called Rule of Four: it grants certiorari to those cases receiving the affirmative vote of at least four justices. The Court identifies the cases accepted and rejected on a "certified orders list," which is released to the public. For cases granted certiorari or in which probable jurisdiction is noted, the clerk informs participating attorneys, who then have specified time limits in which to turn in their written legal arguments (briefs), and the case is scheduled for oral argument.

Considerations Affecting Case Selection Decisions. In this section, we consider the path of the cases the Court agrees to decide. But first, we take up an equally intriguing issue—two sets of factors scholars have identified as affecting the Court's review decision: legal considerations and political considerations.[6]

Legal considerations are listed in Rule 10, which the Court has established to govern the certiorari decision-making process:

Review on a writ of certiorari is not a matter of right, but of judicial discretion. A petition for a writ of certiorari will be granted only for compelling reasons. The following, although neither controlling nor fully measuring the Court's discretion, indicate the character of the reasons the Court considers:

(a) a United States court of appeals has entered a decision in conflict with the decision of another United States court of appeals on the same important matter; has decided an important federal question in a way that conflicts with a decision by a state court of last resort; or has so far departed from the accepted and usual course of judicial proceedings, or sanctioned such a departure by a lower court, as to call for an exercise of this Court's supervisory power;

(b) a state court of last resort has decided an important fed-

eral question in a way that conflicts with the decision of another state court of last resort or of a United States court of appeals;

(c) a state court or a United States court of appeals has decided an important question of federal law that has not been, but should be, settled by this Court, or has decided an important federal question in a way that conflicts with relevant decisions of this Court. A petition for a writ of certiorari is rarely granted when the asserted error consists of erroneous factual findings or the misapplication of a properly stated rule of law.

To what extent do the considerations outlined in Rule 10 affect the Court? The answer is mixed. On the one hand, the Court seems to follow its dictates. In particular, the presence of actual conflict between or among federal courts, a major concern of Rule 10, substantially increases the likelihood of review; if actual conflict is present in a case, there is a 33 percent chance that the Court will grant review—as compared with the usual 5 percent certiorari rate.[7] On the other hand, as political scientists Gregory A. Caldeira and John R. Wright explain, Rule 10 is not all that helpful in understanding "how the Court makes gatekeeping decisions."[8] The Court may use the existence of actual conflict as a threshold (cases that do not present conflict *may* be rejected); it does not accept all cases with conflict because there are too many.[9]

The legal considerations listed in Rule 10 may act as constraints on the justices' behavior, but they do not necessarily further our understanding of what occurs in cases meeting the criteria. That is why scholars have looked elsewhere—to *political* factors that may influence the Court's case selection process. Three are particularly important. The first is the U.S. solicitor general (SG), the attorney who represents the U.S. government before the Supreme Court. Simply stated, when the SG files a petition, the Court is very likely to grant certiorari. In fact, the Court accepts about 70 percent to 80 percent of the cases in which the federal government is the petitioning party.

---

6. Some scholars have noted a third set: procedural considerations. These emanate from Article III, which—under the Court's interpretation—places constraints on the ability of federal tribunals to hear and decide cases. These constraints are reviewed in Chapter 2. Here we note the two that are particularly important for the review decision: the case must be appropriate for judicial resolution in that it presents a real "case" and "controversy" (justiciability) and the appropriate person must bring the case (standing). Unless these procedural criteria are met, the Court—at least theoretically—will deny review. It is worth noting, however, that because most petitions meet these criteria, they are not especially useful in helping the justices make their case selection decisions.

7. See Gregory A. Caldeira and John R. Wright, "Organized Interests and Agenda Setting in the U.S. Supreme Court," *American Political Science Review* 82 (1988): 1109–27.

8. Ibid., 1115.

9. In fact, during any given term, the Court rejects hundreds of cases in which real conflicts exist. See Lawrence Baum, *The Supreme Court,* 7th ed. (Washington, D.C.: CQ Press, 2001), 111.

BOX 1-1   THE AMICUS CURIAE BRIEF

IN THE
Supreme Court of the United States
OCTOBER TERM, 1994
JUNE 26, 1995
NO. 94-1941

———— • ————

UNITED STATES OF AMERICA, *Petitioner*

— v. —

COMMONWEALTH OF VIRGINIA, et al., *Respondents.*

ON PETITION FOR A WRIT OF CERTIORARI TO THE UNITED STATES
COURT OF APPEALS FOR THE FOURTH CIRCUIT

**BRIEF OF AMICI CURIAE NATIONAL WOMEN'S LAW CENTER, AMERICAN
CIVIL LIBERTIES UNION, THE AMERICAN ASSOCIATION OF UNIVERSITY WOMEN,
B'NAI B'RITH WOMEN, CENTER FOR ADVANCEMENT OF PUBLIC POLICY,
CENTER FOR WOMEN POLICY STUDIES, COALITION OF LABOR UNION WOMEN,
CONNECTICUT WOMEN'S EDUCATION AND LEGAL FUND, EQUAL RIGHTS ADVOCATES,
FEDERALLY EMPLOYED WOMEN, INC., NATIONAL COUNCIL OF JEWISH WOMEN, INC.,
NATIONAL COUNCIL OF NEGRO WOMEN, NATIONAL EDUCATION ASSOCIATION, THE NATIONAL
GAY AND LESBIAN TASK FORCE, NATIONAL ORGANIZATION FOR WOMEN, THE NATIONAL
WOMAN'S PARTY, NATIONAL WOMEN'S CONFERENCE COMMITTEE, NATIONAL WOMEN'S
POLITICAL CAUCUS, NOW LEGAL DEFENSE AND EDUCATION FUND, TRIAL LAWYERS FOR
PUBLIC JUSTICE, WOMEN EMPLOYED, WOMEN'S LAWPROJECT, AND THE WOMEN'S
LEGAL DEFENSE FUND IN SUPPORT OF THE PETITION**

MARCIA D. GREENBERGER, DEBORAH L. BRAKE
National Women's Law Center, 11 Dupont Circle, Suite 800,
Washington, D.C. 20036

SARA L. MANDELBAUM, STEVEN R. SHAPIRO, JANET GALLAGHER
American Civil Liberties Union, 132 W. 43rd Street, New York, NY 10036

ROBERT N. WEINER, *Counsel for Record*, WALTER J. ROCKLER,
PETER G. NEIMAN, MARK ECKENWILER, ARNOLD & PORTER
555 12th Street, N.W., Washington, D.C. 20004
(202) 942-5000
Counsel for Amici Curiae

The amicus curiae practice probably originates in Roman law. A judge would often appoint a *consilium* (officer of the court) "to advise him on points on which he [was] in doubt."[1] That may be why the term amicus curiae translates from the Latin as "friend of the court." But today it is the rare amicus who is a friend of the court. Rather, contemporary briefs almost always are a friend of a party, supporting one side over the other at the certiorari and merits stages. Consider the brief filed in *United States v. Virginia* (1996), the cover of which is reprinted here. In that case, the National Women's Law Center and other organizations supported the federal government's request to have the Court hear the case. They, along with the United States, believed that the court below erred when it allowed the state of Virginia to maintain a single-sex admissions policy at Virginia Military Institute. These groups were anything but neutral participants.

How does an organization become an amicus curiae participant in the Supreme Court of the United States? Under the Court's rules, groups wishing to file an amicus brief at the cert or merits stage must obtain the written consent of the parties to the litigation (the federal and state governments are exempt from this requirement). If the parties refuse to give their consent, the group can file a motion with the Court asking for its permission. The Court today almost always grants these motions.

1. Frank Covey Jr., "Amicus Curiae: Friend of the Court," *De Paul Law Review* 9 (1959): 33.

Scholars have posited a number of reasons for the solicitor general's success as a petitioner. One is that the Court is cognizant of the SG's special role. A presidential appointee whose decisions often reflect the administration's philosophy, the SG also represents the interests of the United States. As the nation's highest court, the Supreme Court cannot ignore these interests. In addition, the justices rely on the solicitor general to act as a filter; that is, they expect the SG to examine carefully the cases to which the government is a party and bring only the most important to their attention. Finally, because solicitors general are involved in so much Supreme Court litigation, they acquire a great deal of knowledge about the Court that other litigants do not. They are "repeat players" who know the "rules of the game" and can use them to their advantage. For example, they know how to structure their petitions to attract the attention and interest of the justices.

The second political factor is the amicus curiae (friend of the court) brief. These briefs may be filed by interest groups at the certiorari stage before the Court makes its selection decision *(see Box 1-1)*. Research by Caldeira and Wright shows that amicus briefs significantly enhance a case's chance to be heard, and multiple briefs have a greater effect.[10] Another interesting finding of their study is that even when groups file *in opposition* to granting certiorari, they increase—rather than decrease—the probability that the Court will hear the case.

What can we make of these findings? Most important is this: although the justices may not be strongly influenced by the arguments contained in these briefs (if they were, why would briefs in opposition to certiorari have the opposite effect?), they seem to use them as cues. In other words, because amicus curiae briefs filed at the certiorari stage are somewhat uncommon—less than 10 percent of all petitions are accompanied by amicus briefs—they single out a case, to draw the justices' attention. If major organizations are sufficiently interested in an appeal to file briefs in support of (or against) Court review, then the petition for certiorari is probably worth the justices' serious consideration.

In addition, we have strong reasons to suspect that a third political factor—the ideology of the justices—affects actions on certiorari petitions. Researchers tell us that the justices of the liberal Warren Court were more likely to grant review to cases in which the lower court reached a conservative decision so that they could reverse, while those of the moderately conservative Burger Court took liberal results to reverse. It would be difficult to believe that the current justices would be any less likely than their predecessors to vote on the basis of their ideology. Scholarly studies also suggest that justices engage in strategic voting behavior at the cert stage. In other words, justices are forward thinking; they consider the implications of their cert vote for the later merits stage, asking themselves: If I vote to grant a particular petition, what are the odds of my position winning down the road? As one justice explained his calculations, "I might think the Nebraska Supreme Court made a horrible decision, but I wouldn't want to take the case, for if we take the case and affirm it, then it would become precedent."[11]

The Role of Attorneys

Once the Supreme Court agrees to decide a case, the clerk of the Court informs the parties. The parties have two methods of presenting their side of the dispute to the justices—written and oral arguments.

Written Arguments. Written arguments, called briefs, are the major vehicles for parties to Supreme Court cases to document their positions. Under the Court's rules, the appealing party (known as the appellant or petitioner) must submit its brief within forty-five days of the time the Court grants certiorari; the opposing party (known as the appellee or respondent) has thirty days after receipt of the appellant's brief to respond with arguments urging affirmance of the lower court ruling.

The Court has specific rules covering the presentation and format of the briefs. For example, the briefs of both parties must be submitted in forty copies and not exceed fifty pages in length. Rule 24 outlines the material that briefs must contain:

10. Caldeira and Wright, "Organized Interests and Agenda Setting."

11. Quoted in H. W. Perry, *Deciding to Decide* (Cambridge: Harvard University Press, 1991), 200.

1. A description of the questions presented for review.

2. A list of the parties to the proceeding.

3. A table of contents and list of authorities.

4. Citations to the opinions and judgments issued by the courts below.

5. A statement describing the Supreme Court's jurisdiction over the case.

6. A description of the constitutional provisions, treaties, statutes, ordinances, and regulations relevant to the case.

7. A concise statement of the case, including the relevant facts and other matter material to the appeal.

8. A summary of the argument.

9. The detailed argument, including the points of fact and law presented.

10. A conclusion stating the relief the party is seeking.

The clerk sends the briefs to the justices, who normally study them before oral argument. Written briefs are important because the justices may use them to formulate the questions they ask the lawyers representing the parties. The briefs also serve as a permanent record of the positions of the parties, available to the justices for consultation after oral argument when they decide the case outcome. A well-crafted brief can place into the hands of the justices arguments, legal references, and suggested remedies that later may be incorporated into the opinion.

In addition to the briefs submitted by the parties to the suit, Court rules allow interested persons, organizations, and government units to participate as amici curiae on the merits—just as they are permitted to file such briefs at the review stage. Those wishing to submit friend of the court briefs must obtain the written permission of the parties or the Court. Only the federal government and state governments are exempt from this requirement (*see Box 1-1*).

Oral Arguments. Attorneys also have the opportunity to present their cases orally before the justices. Each side has thirty minutes to convince the Court of the merits of its position and to field questions the justices may raise. The justices are allowed to interrupt the attorneys at any time with comments and questions, as an exchange between Justice Byron White and Sarah Weddington, the attorney representing Jane Roe in *Roe v. Wade* (1973), indicates. White got the ball rolling when he asked Weddington to respond to an issue her brief had not addressed: whether abortions should be performed during all stages of pregnancy or should somehow be limited. The following discussion ensued:

WHITE: And the statute doesn't make any distinction based upon at what period of pregnancy the abortion is performed?

WEDDINGTON: No, Your Honor. There is no time limit or indication of time, whatsoever. So I think—

WHITE: What is your constitutional position there?

WEDDINGTON: As to a time limit—

WHITE: What about whatever clause of the Constitution you rest on—Ninth Amendment, due process . . . —that take you right up to the time of birth?

WEDDINGTON: It is our position that the freedom involved is that of a woman to determine whether or not to continue a pregnancy. Obviously I have a much more difficult time saying that the State has no interest in late pregnancy.

WHITE: Why? Why is that?

WEDDINGTON: I think that's more the emotional response to a late pregnancy, rather than it is any constitutional—

WHITE: Emotional response by whom?

WEDDINGTON: I guess by persons considering the issue outside the legal context, I think, as far as the State—

WHITE: Well, do you or don't you say that the constitutional—

WEDDINGTON: I would say constitutional—

WHITE: —right you insist on reaches up to the time of birth, or—

WEDDINGTON: The Constitution, as I read it . . . attaches protection to the person at the time of birth.

In the Court's early years, there was little doubt about the importance of such exchanges, of oral arguments in general. Because attorneys did not always prepare written briefs, the justices relied on orals to learn about the cases and to help them marshal their arguments for the next stage. Moreover, orals were considered important public events, with the most prominent attorneys of the day participating. Arguments often went on for days: *Gibbons v. Ogden* (1824), the landmark Commerce Clause case, was argued for five days, and *McCulloch v. Maryland* (1819), the litigation challenging the constitutionality of the national bank, took nine days to argue.

Scholars, lawyers, and judges have questioned the effectiveness of oral argument and its role in decision making. Chief Justice Earl Warren maintained that they made little difference to the outcome. Once the justices have read the briefs and studied related cases, most have relatively firm views on how the case should be decided, and orals change few minds. Justice William J. Brennan Jr., however, maintained that they were extremely important as they help justices to clarify core arguments. Orals may not be good predictors of the Court's final votes, but they provide some indication of what the justices believe to be the central issues of the case. In addition, we should not forget the symbolic importance of the oral argument stage: it is the only part of the Court's decision-making process that occurs in public.

It is unlikely that this debate will ever be resolved, but you now have the opportunity to form your own opinion. Political scientist Jerry Goldman has made the oral arguments of many cases available on the World Wide Web (*oyez.nwu.edu*). Throughout the book, you will find the URLs (universal resource locators) of the specific pages to which you can navigate to listen to arguments in the cases you are reading.

The Supreme Court Decides: Some Preliminaries

After the Court hears oral arguments, it meets in a private conference to discuss the case and to take a preliminary vote. Following is a description of the Court's conference procedures, along with two events that happen after the conference: the assignment of the opinion of the Court and the opinion circulation period.

The Conference. In these days of "government in the sunshine" the Court stands alone in its insistence that its decisions take place in a private conference, with no one in attendance except the justices. Congress has agreed to this by exempting the federal courts from open government and freedom of information legislation. There are two basic reasons. First, the Supreme Court—which, unlike Congress, lacks an electoral connection—is supposed to base its decisions on factors other than public opinion. Opening up deliberations to press scrutiny, for example, might encourage the justices to take notice of popular sentiment, which is not supposed to influence

them. Or so the argument goes. Second, although in conference the Court reaches tentative decisions on cases, the opinions explaining the decisions remain to be written. This process can take many weeks or even months, and it is not until the opinions have been written, circulated, and approved that the decision is final. Because the decisions can have a major impact on politics and the economy, any party having advance knowledge of case outcomes could use that information for unfair business and political advantage.

The system works so well that, with only a few exceptions, the justices have not experienced information leaks, and it is impossible to know precisely what occurs in the deliberation of any particular case. We can, however, piece together the procedures and the general nature of the Court's discussions from the papers of retired justices and the comments of others. We have learned the following. First, we know that the chief justice presides over the deliberations. He calls up the case for discussion and then presents his views on the issues and how the case should be decided. The remaining justices state their views and votes in order of seniority.

The level and intensity of discussion, as Justice Brennan's notes from conference deliberations reveal, differ from case to case. In some, it appears that the justices had very little to say. The chief presented his views, and the rest noted their agreement. In others, every Court member had something to add. Whether the discussion is subdued or lively, it is unclear to what extent conferences affect the final decisions. It would be unusual for a justice to enter the conference room without having reached a tentative position on the cases to be discussed; after all, he or she has read the briefs and listened to oral arguments. But the conference is the first opportunity the justices have to review cases as a group and size up the positions of their colleagues. This sort of information, as we shall see, may be important as the justices begin the process of crafting and circulating opinions.

Opinion Assignment. The conference typically leads to a tentative outcome and vote. What happens at this point is critical because it determines who assigns the writing of the opinion of the Court—the Court's only authoritative policy statement, the only one that establishes precedent. Under Court norms, the chief justice assigns the writing of the opinion when he votes with the majority. The chief may decide to write the opinion or assign it to one of the other justices who voted with the majority. When the chief justice votes with the minority, the assignment task falls to the most senior member of the Court who voted with the majority.

In making these assignments, the chief justice (or the senior associate in the majority) takes many factors into account. Forrest Maltzman and Paul J. Wahlbeck examined the opinion assignments of Chief Justice Rehnquist.[12] These scholars discovered that the chief tries to equalize the distribution of the Court's workload. This concern makes sense: the Court will not run efficiently, given the burdensome nature of opinion writing, if some justices are given many more assignments than others. The research also suggests that Rehnquist takes into account the justices' particular areas of expertise. He recognizes that some of his colleagues have more knowledge of particular areas of the law than others, and he tends to assign accordingly. By encouraging specialization, Rehnquist may be increasing the quality of opinions and reducing the time to write them. Finally, Maltzman and Wahlbeck noted that when a case was decided by a one-vote margin, Rehnquist assigns the opinion to a moderate member of the majority rather than to an extreme member. His reasoning seems clear: if the writer in a close case drafts an opinion with which other members of the majority are uncomfortable, the opinion may drive justices to the other side, causing the majority to become a minority. Rehnquist tries to minimize this risk by asking justices squarely in the middle of the majority coalition to write.

Opinion Circulation. Regardless of the factors the chief considers in making assignments, one thing is clear: the opinion writer is a critical player in the opinion circulation phase, which eventually leads to the final decision of the Court. The writer begins the process by circulating an opinion draft to the others.

Once the justices receive the first draft of the opinion, they have many options. First, they can join the opinion,

meaning that they agree with it and want no changes. Second, they can ask the opinion writer to make changes, that is, *bargain* with the writer over the content of and even the disposition—to reverse or affirm the lower court ruling—offered in the draft. The following memo sent from Brennan to White is exemplary: "I've mentioned to you that I favor your approach to this case and want if possible to join your opinion. If you find the following suggestions . . . acceptable, I can join you."[13]

Third, they can tell the opinion writer that they plan to circulate a dissenting or concurring opinion. A dissenting opinion means that the writer disagrees with the disposition the majority opinion reaches and with the rationale it invokes; a concurring opinion generally agrees with the disposition but not with the rationale. Finally, justices can tell the opinion writer that they await further writings, meaning that they want to study various dissents or concurrences before they decide what to do.

As justices circulate their opinions and revise them—the average majority opinion undergoes three to four revisions in response to colleagues' comments—many different opinions on the same case, at various stages of development, will be floating around the Court over the course of several months. Because this process is replicated for each case the Court decides with a formal written opinion, it is possible that scores of different opinions may be working their way from office to office at any point in time.

Eventually, the final version of the opinion is reached, and each justice expresses a position in writing or by signing an opinion of another justice. This is how the final vote is taken. When all of the justices have declared themselves, the only remaining step is for the Court to announce its decision and the vote to the public.

All of these procedures have evolved over time. Some have been codified into the Supreme Court's rules; others are norms. But there are other ways to design a court system. While the U.S. system can be described as diffuse or decentralized—a lower court can declare a law unconstitutional—other systems are characterized by the existence of one constitutional court (*see Box 1-2*).

12. "May it Please the Chief? Opinion Assignments in the Rehnquist Court," *American Journal of Political Science* 40 (1996): 421–443.

13. Memorandum from Justice Brennan to Justice White, 12/9/76, re: 75-104, *United Jewish Organizations v. Carey.*

BOX 1-2   THE AMERICAN LEGAL SYSTEM IN GLOBAL PERSPECTIVE

THE AMERICAN legal system can be described as *dual, parallel,* and (for the most part) *three tiered.* It is dual because both one federal system and fifty state systems coexist, each ruling on disputes falling under their particular purviews. This does not mean, however, that state courts never hear cases involving claims made under the U.S. Constitution or that federal courts necessarily shun cases arising out of state law. In fact, the U.S. Supreme Court can review cases involving federal questions on which state supreme courts have ruled and can strike down state laws if they are incompatible with the U.S. Constitution. Similarly, many cases arising from state law and heard in state courts also contain federal issues that must be resolved.

Differences exist among the states, but most today roughly parallel the federal system. Trial courts—the lowest rungs on the ladder—are the entry points into the system *(see Figure 1-2).* In the middle of the ladder are appellate courts, those that upon request review the records of trial court proceedings. Finally, both have supreme courts, bodies that provide final answers to legal questions in their own domains.

Although a supreme court sits atop each ladder, the U.S. Supreme Court plays a unique role—it is the apex of both state and federal court systems. Because it can hear cases and ultimately overturn the rulings of federal and state court judges. It is presumably *the* authoritative legal body in the United States.

Many nations have created legal systems that, to greater or lesser extents, resemble the American system. For example, Japan, whose constitutional document was largely drafted by Americans, also has a three-tiered structure. Cases begin at the district (trial) court level, move to high courts (Japan's version of mid-level appellate courts) and, finally to the Supreme Court.[1] But other nations—first Germany and Italy, and later Belgium, Portugal, South Africa, Spain, and most of the countries of Eastern Europe—took a much different approach. In these countries, the highest court is not a supreme court but a single constitutional court, which has a judicial monopoly on interpreting matters of constitution-al law. These constitutional courts are not a part of the "ordinary" court system; litigants do not typically petition the justices to review decisions of lower courts. Rather, when judges confront a law whose constitutionality they doubt, they are obliged to send the case directly to the constitutional court. This tribunal receives evidence on the constitutional issue, sometimes gathers evidence on its own, hears arguments, perhaps consults sources that counsel overlooked, and hands down a decision. But, unlike in the United States, the constitutional court does not decide the case because it has not heard a case; it has only addressed a question of constitutional interpretation. Although the court publishes an opinion justifying its ruling and explaining the controlling principles, the case still must be decided by regular tribunals. In some countries—for example, Germany, Italy, and Russia—public officials also may bring suits in their constitutional court to challenge the legitimacy of legislative, executive, or judicial acts, and, under some circumstances, private citizens may start similar litigation. Where judicial action is challenged, the constitutional court in effect reviews a decision of another court, but the form of the action is very different from an appeal in the United States.

This type of court system is often called "centralized" because the power of judicial review—that is, the power to review government acts for their compatibility with the nation's constitution and strike down those acts that are not compatible—rests in one constitutional court; other courts are typically barred from exercising judicial review, although they may refer constitutional questions to the constitutional tribunal. In contrast, the U.S. system is deemed "decentralized" because ordinary courts—not just supreme courts—can engage in judicial review, We shall return to this distinction in Chapter 2 *(see Box 2-1).*

---

1. Japan has summary courts with jurisdiction over minor civil and criminal cases. District courts (trial courts of general jurisdiction) can hear civil appeals from summary courts. For more details, see Herbert Jacob, ed., *Courts, Law, and Politics* (New Haven: Yale University Press, 1996), chap. 6.

SUPREME COURT DECISIONMAKING: LEGALLY RELEVANT APPROACHES

So far, we have examined the processes the justices follow to reach decisions on the disputes brought before them. We answered basic questions about the institutional procedures the Court uses to carry out its responsibilities. The questions we did not address were why the justices reach particular decisions and what forces play a role in determining their choices. As you might imagine, there is no shortage of explanations for Court decisions, but they can be categorized into two groups: the legally relevant and the extralegal *(see page 32)*. You will detect strains of these approaches in the justices' opinions throughout the book.

Legally relevant approaches to U.S. Supreme Court decision making emanate from expectations of how Americans expect justices to behave, particularly what they should and should not consider to reach decisions. Jurists are supposed to shed all their personal biases, preferences, and partisan attachments when they take their seats on the bench, for those things, it is argued, should have no bearing on Court decisions. Rather, justices ought to reach decisions in accord with factors that are grounded in the law.

In some sense, then, legally relevant approaches originated to answer the question of how justices *should* decide pending disputes. But, for several reasons, we ask you to think about this question: Do the justices invoke legally relevant approaches to reach decisions, or do they reach their decisions first and then use legally relevant approaches to justify them? One reason is that the justices themselves often say they use legally relevant factors to resolve disputes because they consider them appropriate criteria for reaching decisions. Another is that some scholars express agreement with the justices, arguing that Court members cannot follow their own personal preferences, the whims of the public, or other non–legally relevant factors "if they are to have the continued respect of their colleagues, the wider [legal] community, citizens, and leaders." Rather they "must be principled in their decision-making process."[14] Whether they are prin-

cipled in their decisionmaking is for you to determine as you read the cases to come. First, however, it is necessary to have some sense of specific factors that comprise the legally relevant category. We offer five of the most important and describe the judicial philosophies that support their use in decisionmaking.

The Doctrine of Original Intent

It was more than two hundred years ago that the Supreme Court first invoked the term *the intention of the Framers.* In *Hylton v. United States* (1796) the Court said, "It was . . . obviously the intention of the framers of the Constitution, that Congress should possess full power over every species of taxable property, except exports. The term taxes, is generical, and was made use of to vest in Congress plenary authority in all cases of taxation."[15] In *Hustler Magazine v. Falwell* (1988) the Court used the same grounds to find that cartoon parodies, however obnoxious, constitute expression protected by the First Amendment.

Undoubtedly, justices over the years have frequently looked to the intent of the Framers to reach conclusions about the disputes before them.[16] But why? What possible relevance could the Framers' intentions have for today's controversies? Advocates of this approach offer several answers. First, they assert that the Framers acted in a calculated manner; that is, they knew what they were doing, so why should we disregard their precepts? One adherent said, "Those who framed the Constitution chose their words carefully; they debated at great length the most minute points. The language they chose meant something. It is incumbent upon the Court to determine what that meaning was."[17]

Second, if they scrutinize the intent of the Framers, justices can deduce "constitutional truths," which they

14. Ronald Kahn, "Institutional Norms and Supreme Court Decision-Making: The Rehnquist Court on Privacy and Religion," in *Supreme Court*

Decision-Making: New Institutionalist Approaches, ed. Cornell W. Clayton and Howard Gillman (Chicago: University of Chicago Press, 1999), 176.

15. Example cited by Boris I. Bittker in "The Bicentennial of the Jurisprudence of Original Intent: The Recent Past," *California Law Review* 77 (1989): 235.

16. Given the subject of this volume, we deal here exclusively with the intent of the Framers of the U.S. Constitution and its amendments, but one also could apply this approach to statutory construction by considering the intent of those who drafted the laws in question.

17. Edwin Meese III, Address Before the American Bar Association, July 9, 1983, Washington, D.C.

can apply to cases. Doing so, proponents argue, would produce neutral principles of law and eliminate value-laden decisions.[18] Consider, for example, speech advocating the violent overthrow of the government. Suppose the government enacted a law prohibiting such expression and arrested members of a radical political party for violating it. Justices could scrutinize this law in several ways. A liberal might conclude, solely because of his liberal values, that the First Amendment prohibits a ban on such expression. Conservative jurists might reach the opposite conclusion. Neither would be proper jurisprudence in the opinion of those who advocate an original intent approach, because both are value laden, and ideological preferences should not creep into the law. Rather, justices should examine the Framers' intent as a way to keep the law value free. Applying this approach to free speech, one adherent argues, leads to a clear, unbiased result:

Speech advocating violent overthrow is . . . not [protected] "political speech" . . . as that term must be defined by a Madisonian system of government. It is not political speech because it violates constitutional truths about processes and because it is not aimed at a new definition of political truth by a legislative majority.[19]

Finally, supporters of this mode of analysis argue that it fosters stability in law. They assert that the law today is far too fluid; it changes with the ideological whims of the justices, creating havoc for those who must implement and interpret Court decisions. Lower court judges, lawyers, and even ordinary citizens do not know if today's rights will exist tomorrow. Following a jurisprudence of original intent would eliminate such confusion because it provides a principle that justices would consistently follow.

Although many Supreme Court opinions contemplate the original intent of the Framers, and arguments in favor of such an approach seem to have merit, this view also has critics. One reason for the controversy is that the doctrine became quite politicized in the 1980s. Those who advocated it, particularly Edwin Meese, an at-

torney general in President Ronald Reagan's administration, and defeated Supreme Court nominee Robert Bork, were widely viewed as conservatives who were using the doctrine to attain their own ideological ends.

Others, however, have raised several more concrete objections to this jurisprudence. Justice Brennan in 1985 argued that if the justices employed only this approach, the Constitution would lose its applicability and be rendered useless:

We current Justices read the Constitution in the only way that we can: as Twentieth Century Americans. We look to the history of the time of the framing and to the intervening history of interpretation. But the ultimate question must be, what do the words of the text mean in our time. For the genius of the Constitution rests not in any static meaning it might have had in a world that is dead and gone, but in the adaptability of its great principles to cope with current problems and current needs. What the constitutional fundamentals meant to the wisdom of other times cannot be their measure to the vision of our time. Similarly, what those fundamentals mean for us, our descendants will learn, cannot be the measure to the vision of their time.[20]

Another criticism is that the Constitution embodies not one intent, but many. Political scientists Jeffrey A. Segal and Harold J. Spaeth pose some interesting questions: "Who were the Framers? All fifty-five of the delegates who showed up at one time or another in Philadelphia during the summer of 1787? Some came and went. . . . Some probably had not read [the Constitution]. Assuredly, they were not all of a single mind."[21]

Finally, from which sources should justices divine the original intentions of the Framers? They could look at the records of the constitutional debates and at the Founders' journals and papers, but some of what passes for "records" of the Philadelphia convention are jumbled, even forged.[22] During the debates, the secretary became confused and thoroughly botched the minutes; and

18. See, for example, Robert Bork, "Neutral Principles and Some First Amendment Problems," *Indiana Law Journal* 47 (1971): 1–35.

19. Ibid., 31.

20. William J. Brennan Jr., Address to the Text and Teaching Symposium, Georgetown University, October 12, 1985, Washington, D.C.

21. Jeffrey A. Segal and Harold J. Spaeth, *The Supreme Court and the Attitudinal Model* (New York: Cambridge University Press, 1993), 39. See also William Anderson, "The Intention of the Framers: A Note on Constitutional Interpretation," *American Political Science Review* 49 (1955): 340.

22. We adopt the next few sentences from C. Herman Pritchett, Walter F. Murphy, and Lee Epstein, *Courts, Judges, and Politics,* 5th ed. (New York: McGraw-Hill, 2000).

James Madison, who took the most complete and probably the most reliable notes on what was said, edited them after the convention adjourned.

Those who rely on the original intent might claim that the condition of the historic record is less a barrier to their approach. The popular debate on ratification was full; millions of pamphlets (heavily outnumbering the entire population) argued for and against the new political system. This mass of literature, however, demonstrates not one but dozens of understandings of what the new constitution would mean. In other words, they often fail to provide a single clear message. Justice Robert H. Jackson made this point when he wrote:

Just what our forefathers did envision, or would have envisioned had they foreseen modern conditions, must be divined from materials almost as enigmatic as the dreams Joseph was called upon to interpret for Pharaoh. A century and a half of partisan debate and scholarly specification yields no net result but only supplies more or less apt quotations from respected sources on each side of any question. They largely cancel each other.[23]

Textualism I: Literalism

On the surface, textualism resembles the doctrine of original intent: it puts a premium on the Constitution. But this is where the similarity ends. In an effort to prevent the infusion of new meanings from sources outside the text of the Constitution, adherents of original intent seek to deduce constitutional truths by examining the *intended* meanings behind the words. Textualists look no further than the words of the Constitution to reach decisions. Justice Antonin Scalia explained the differences between the approaches in a 1996 speech:

I belong to a school, a small but hardy school, called "textualists" or "originalists." That used to be "constitutional orthodoxy" in the United States. The theory of originalism treats a constitution like a statute, and gives it the meaning that its words were understood to bear at the time they were promulgated. You will sometimes hear it described as the theory of original intent. You will never hear me refer to original intent, because as I say I am first of all a textualist, and secondly an

originalist. If you are a textualist, you don't care about the intent, and I don't care if the framers of the Constitution had some secret meaning in mind when they adopted its words. I take the words as they were promulgated to the people of the United States, and what is the fairly understood meaning of those words.[24]

Under Scalia's brand of textualism, it is fair game for justices to go beyond the literal meaning of the words and consider what they would have ordinarily meant to the people of that time—a type of textual analysis to which we return momentarily. To other textualists, who we might call pure textualists or *literalists*, it is only the words in the constitutional text, and the words alone that justices ought consider.

And it is this distinction—between original intent and literalism—that can lead to some extraordinary differences in case outcomes. If we use again the example of speech aimed at overthrowing the U.S. government, original intent advocates would hold that the meaning behind the First Amendment prohibits such expression. Those who consider themselves *pure* literalists, on the other hand, might scrutinize the words of the First Amendment—"Congress shall make no law . . . abridging freedom of speech"—and read them literally: *no law* means *no law*. Hence, any statute infringing on speech, even a law that prohibits expression advocating the overthrow of the government, would violate the First Amendment.

Original intent and literalism sometimes overlap. When it comes to the right to privacy, particularly its use to create other rights, such as legalized abortion, *some* original intent adherents and literalists would reach the same conclusion: it does not exist. The former would argue that it was not the intent of the Framers to confer privacy; the latter, that because the Constitution fails to guarantee explicitly this right, Americans do not automatically possess it.

Although strains of literalism run through the opinions of many justices, Hugo Black is most closely associated with this view *(see Box 1-3)*. During his thirty-four-

---

23. *Youngstown Sheet & Tube Co. v. Sawyer* (1952).

24. Antonin Scalia, "A Theory of Constitutional Interpretation," Remarks at The Catholic University of America, Washington, D.C., October 18, 1996.

year tenure on the Court, Justice Black reiterated the literalist philosophy. His own words best describe his position:

My view is, without deviation, without exception, without any ifs, buts, or whereases, that freedom of speech means that government shall not do anything to people . . . either for the views they have or the views they express or the words they speak or write. Some people would have you believe that this is a very radical position, and maybe it is. But all I am doing is following what to me is the clear wording of the First Amendment. . . . As I have said innumerable times before I simply believe that "Congress shall make no law" means Congress shall make no law. . . . Thus we have the absolute command of the First Amendment that no law shall be passed by Congress abridging freedom of speech or the press.[25]

Why did Black advocate literalism? Like original intent adherents, he viewed it as a value-free form of jurisprudence. If justices looked only at the words of the Constitution, their decisions would not reflect ideological or political values, but rather those of the document. Black's opinions provide good illustrations. Although he almost always supported claims of free *speech* against government challenges, he refused to extend constitutional protection to *expression* that was not precisely speech. For example, he asserted that activities such as flag burning and the wearing of arm bands, even if designed to express political views, fell outside of the speech protected by the First Amendment.

Moreover, literalists maintain that their approach is superior to the doctrine of original intent. They say that some provisions of the Constitution are so transparent that, were the government to violate them, justices could "almost instantaneously and without analysis identify the violation"; they would not need to undertake an extensive search to uncover the Framers' understanding.[26] Often cited examples include the "mathematical" provisions of the Constitution, such as the command that the president's term be four years, and that the president be at least thirty-five years old.

Despite the seeming logic of these justifications and the high regard scholars have for Black, many have actively attacked his brand of jurisprudence. Some assert that it led him to take some rather odd positions, particularly in cases involving the First Amendment. For example, most analysts and justices—even those considered liberal—agree that obscene materials fall outside of First Amendment protection and that states can prohibit their dissemination. But, in opinion after opinion, Black clung to the view that no publication could be banned on the grounds that it was obscene.

A second objection is that literalism can result in inconsistent outcomes. For example, is it really sensible for Black to hold that obscenity is constitutionally protected, while other types of expression, such as the desecration of the flag, are not?

Segal and Spaeth raise yet a third problem with literalism: it supposes a precision in the English language that does not exist. Not only may words, including those used by the Framers, have multiple meanings, but also the meanings themselves may be contrary. For example, the common legal word *sanction,* as Segal and Spaeth note, means to punish *and* to approve.[27] How, then, would a literalist construe it?

Finally, even when the words are crystal clear, literalism may not be on firm ground. Despite the precision of the mathematical provisions, Frank Easterbrook has suggested that they, like all the others, are loaded with "reasons, goals, values, and the like."[28] The Framers might have imposed the presidential age limit "as a percentage of average life expectancy"—to ensure that presidents have a good deal of practical political experience before ascending to the presidency and little opportunity to engage in politicking after they leave—or "as a minimum number of years after puberty"—to guarantee that they are sufficiently mature but not to unduly limit the pool of eligible candidates. Seen in this way, the words "thirty-five Years" in the Constitution may not have much value: they may be "simply the framers' shorthand for their more complex policies, and we could replace

25. Hugo L. Black, *A Constitutional Faith* (New York: Knopf, 1969), 45–46.

26. We draw this material and the related discussion to follow from Mark V. Tushnet, "A Note on the Revival of Textualism," *Southern California Law Review* 58 (1985): 683.

27. Segal and Spaeth, *The Supreme Court and the Attitudinal Model,* 34.

28. Frank Easterbrook, "Statutes' Domains," *University of Chicago Law Review* 50 (1983): 536.

BOX 1-3   HUGO LAFAYETTE BLACK (1937–1971)

THE EIGHTH child of a Baptist store-keeper and farmer, Hugo Black was born February 27, 1886, in Harlan, Alabama, and spent the first years of his life in the hill country near there. When he was still a youngster, his family moved to Ashland, a larger community where his father's business prospered. Black attended the local schools in Ashland and, after trying one year at Birmingham Medical College, decided to study law. At eighteen he entered the University of Alabama Law School at Tuscaloosa.

Receiving his LL.B. in 1906, Black returned to Ashland and set up his first law practice. The following year a fire destroyed his office and library, and Black decided to move to Birmingham. There he quickly established a relationship with labor by defending the United Mine Workers strikers in 1908. Black also developed an expertise for arguing personal injury cases.

BLACK was named a part-time police court judge in Birmingham in 1910 and was elected county solicitor (public prosecutor) for Jefferson County in 1914. As solicitor, he gained a measure of local fame for his investigation of reports of the brutal means police employed while questioning suspects at the notorious Bessemer jail. When he left the solicitor's post in 1917 to join the World War I effort, Black had succeeded in emptying a docket that had once held as many as three thousand pending cases.

His brief military career kept him within the borders of the United States. He returned to practice law in Birmingham in 1918 and continued to expand his practice, still specializing in labor law and personal injury cases. He married Josephine Foster, February 23, 1921. They had two sons and one daughter. In 1923 Black joined the Ku Klux Klan, but resigned from the organization two years later just before he ran for the Democratic nomination for the Senate seat held by Democrat Oscar Underwood. Campaigning as the poor man's candidate, Black won the party's endorsement and the subsequent election. He entered the Senate in 1927 and immediately began to study history and the classics at the Library of Congress to compensate for his lack of a liberal education.

During his two terms in the Senate, Black used committee hearings to investigate several areas, including abuses of marine and airline subsidies and the activities of lobbying groups. In 1933 he introduced a bill to create a thirty-hour workweek. This legislation, after several alterations, was finally passed in 1938 as the Fair Labor Standards Act. One of the Senate's strongest supporters of President Franklin Roosevelt, Black spoke out in favor of his 1937 Court-packing scheme and the New Deal programs.

Black's support for the administration and his strong liberal instincts led the president to pick him as his choice to fill the Supreme Court seat vacated by the retirement of Willis Van Devanter. Black was confirmed by the Senate, 63–16, on August 17, 1937.

Black's previous affiliation with the Ku Klux Klan was widely reported in the national news media after his confirmation. The furor quickly died down, however, when the new justice admitted in a dramatic radio broadcast that he had indeed been a member of the Klan but added that he had resigned many years before and would comment no further. During his Court career, Black always carried in his pocket a copy of the United States Constitution.

Black's first wife died in 1951, and he married Elizabeth Seay DeMerritte, September 11, 1957. He retired from the Court September 17, 1971, after suffering an impairing stroke. He died eight days later in Washington.

SOURCE: Adapted from Joan Biskupic and Elder Witt, *Guide to the U.S. Supreme Court*, 3d ed. (Washington, D.C.: Congressional Quarterly, 1997), 930.

them by 'fifty years' or 'thirty years' without impairing the integrity of the constitutional structure."[29] More generally, as Justice Oliver Wendell Holmes Jr. once put it, "A word is not a crystal, transparent and unchanged, it is the skin of a living thought and may vary greatly in color and content according to the circumstances and the time in which it is used."[30]

Textualism II: Meaning of the Words

As we noted above, advocates of textual approaches suggest that justices need look no further than the words of the Constitution to reach decisions. But as we also suggested, adherents do not necessarily approach the task of interpreting the "words" in the same way. While Black claimed to be loath to go beyond the literal meaning of the words, Scalia is not so reticent. Indeed, under his "meaning of the words" brand of textualism, it is appropriate for justices to ask what the words would have ordinarily meant to the people of that time.[31]

Seen in this way, the "meaning of the words" approach to constitutional interpretation has its roots in both literalism and originalism: it emphasizes the words of the Constitution at the time the Framers wrote them. But there are differences. While literalists stress the words themselves, this mode highlights their meaning; and while originalism focuses on the intent behind phrases, at least some variants of the meaning of the words approach emphasize "lexicographic skill"—asking justices to interpret the words of the Constitution according to their meaning at the time they were written.[32]

The merits of this approach are similar to those of literalism and originalism. By focusing on how the Framers defined their own words and then applying their definitions to disputes over those constitutional provisions containing them, this approach seeks to generate value-free and ideology-free jurisprudence. Indeed, one of the most important developers of this approach, William W. Crossley, specifically embraced it to counter "sophis-

tries" of the "living-document" view of the Constitution.[33]

Chief Justice Rehnquist's opinion in *Nixon v. United States* (1993) provides a particularly good illustration of the value of this approach. Here, the Court considered a challenge to the procedures the Senate used to impeach a federal judge, Walter L. Nixon Jr. Rather than having the entire Senate try the case, a special twelve-member committee heard it and reported to the full body. Nixon argued that this procedure violated Article I of the Constitution, which states, "The Senate shall have the sole power to try all Impeachments." But before he addressed Nixon's claim, Rehnquist sought to determine whether courts had any business resolving such disputes. He used a meaning of the words approach to consider the word *try* in Article I:

Petitioner argues that the word "try" in the first sentence imposes by implication an additional requirement on the Senate in that the proceedings must be in the nature of a judicial trial. . . . There are several difficulties with this position which lead us ultimately to reject it. The word "try," both in 1787 and later, has considerably broader meanings than those to which petitioner would limit it. Older dictionaries define try as "[t]o examine" or "[t]o examine as a judge." See 2 S. Johnson, A Dictionary of the English Language (1785). In more modern usage the term has various meanings. For example, try can mean "to examine or investigate judicially," "to conduct the trial of," or "to put to the test by experiment, investigation. . . ." Webster's Third New International Dictionary (1971).

Like the other modes we have examined, the meaning of the words approach is not without its critics. One objection is similar to that leveled at originalism: it is too static. Political scientist C. Herman Pritchett noted that like originalism, it can "make a nation the prisoner of its past, and reject any constitutional development save constitutional amendment."[34]

Another criticism is that it may be just as difficult for justices to establish the meaning of words as it is to establish the original intent behind them. Attempting to understand what the Framers meant by each word can

29. Tushnet, "A Note on the Revival of Textualism," 686.

30. *Towne v. Eisner* (1918).

31. See his "Originalism: The Lesser Evil," *University of Cincinnati Law Review* 849 (1989).

32. David W. Rohde and Harold J. Spaeth, *Supreme Court Decision Making* (San Francisco: W. H. Freeman, 1976), 41.

33. W. W. Crossley, *Politics and the Constitution in the History of the United States* (Chicago: University of Chicago Press, 1953), 1172–3.

34. C. Herman Pritchett, *Constitutional Law of the Federal System* (Englewood Cliffs, N.J.: Prentice-Hall, 1984), 37.

be a far more daunting task in the run-of-the-mill case than it was for Rehnquist in *Nixon*. It might even require the development of a specialized dictionary, which could take years of research to compile and still not have any value—determinate or otherwise.

This last criticism becomes even more poignant when we consider that Crosskey did, in fact, develop "a specialized dictionary of the eighteenth-century word-usages, and political and legal ideas." He believed that such a work was "needed for a true understanding of the Constitution." But some scholars have been skeptical of the understandings, many of which were highly "unorthodox," to which it led him.[35] The same charge has been leveled at a more recent work on textualism, *The Bill of Rights: Creation and Reconstruction* by Akhil Reed Amar.[36]

Where does Professor Amar's textualism lead him? It should make us a bit suspicious that it leads him to disagree with what he calls "mainstream scholars" on almost every controversial constitutional question. Indeed, in some areas—especially criminal procedure—he stands virtually alone against a broad consensus. Can conventional wisdom have been so wrong for so long? Perhaps it was, and perhaps it takes Professor Amar's strong textualism to expose the errors. But . . . law is an incrementalist discipline, and we ought to mistrust a thesis that blinds us with its novelty and brilliance.[37]

Logical Reasoning

Unlike originalism or the meaning of the words approach, logical reasoning is not necessarily dependent on historical interpretations of particular constitutional provisions. Rather, it suggests that judges should engage in reasoned analysis. Such an analysis often takes the form of a syllogism—a type of logic in which justices draw a conclusion from two assumed premises, major and minor.

Chief Justice John Marshall's opinion in *Marbury v. Madison* provides an often-cited example of logical reasoning in action:

MAJOR PREMISE: A law repugnant to the Constitution is void.
MINOR PREMISE: This law is repugnant to the Constitution.
CONCLUSION: Therefore, this law is void.

The beauty of logical analysis, as this example illustrates, is that the resulting decision takes on an objective, perhaps even a scientific, aura. In other words, Marshall's syllogism suggests that anybody with a logical mind would reach the same conclusion. But is this necessarily so? Consider another syllogism:

MAJOR PREMISE: Sweden has many storks.
MINOR PREMISE: Storks deliver babies.
CONCLUSION: Therefore, Sweden has many babies.

We know that storks do not deliver babies, and therein lies the major problem with logical reasoning: because it can be undertaken in the absence of any factual analysis, almost any conclusion can result. To see this, compare the two syllogisms. If we assume that the major premises of both are accurate, then the soundness of their conclusions rests with the factual accuracy of the minor premises. Obviously, storks do not deliver babies, but is Marshall's minor premise any more believable or logically driven? Put another way, can logic reveal whether a particular law is repugnant to the Constitution?

To many the answer is no. As Justice Holmes put it:

The life of the law has not been logic: it has been experience. The felt necessities of the time, the prevalent moral and political theories, intuitions of public policy, avowed or unconscious, even the prejudices which judges share with their fellow-men, have had a good deal more to do than the syllogism in determining the rules by which men should be governed.[38]

35. Bittker, "The Bicentennial of the Jurisprudence of Original Intent," 237–238. Some applauded Crosskey's conclusions. Charles E. Clark, for example, in "Professor Crosskey and the Brooding Omnipresence of Erie-Tompkins," *University of Chicago Law Review* 21 (1953): 24, called it "a major scholastic effort of our times." Others were appalled. See Julius Goebel Jr., "Ex Parte Clio," *Columbia Law Review* 54 (1954): 450, who wrote, "[M]easured by even the least exacting of scholarly standards, [the work] is in the reviewer's opinion without merit."

36. Yale University Press (1998).

37. Suzanna Sherry, "Textualism and Judgment," *George Washington Law Review* 66 (1998): 1148.

38. *The Common Law*, quoted by Max Lerner in *The Mind and Faith of Justice Holmes* (New York: Modern Library, 1943), 51–52.

Stare Decisis

Translated from Latin, stare decisis means "let the decision stand." What the term suggests is that, as a general rule, jurists should decide cases on the basis of previously established precedent. In shorthand terms, judicial tribunals should honor prior rulings.

The benefits of this approach are fairly evident. If justices rely on past cases to resolve current cases, some scholars argue, the law they generate becomes predictable and stable. Justice Harlan F. Stone acknowledged the value of precedent in a somewhat more ironic way: "The rule of stare decisis embodies a wise policy because it is often more important that a rule of law be settled than that it be settled right."[39] The message, however, is the same: if the Court adheres to past decisions, it provides some direction to all who labor in the legal enterprise. Lower court judges know how they should and should not decide cases; lawyers can frame their arguments in accord with the lessons of past cases; legislators understand what they can and cannot enact or regulate, and so forth.

Precedent, then, can be an important and useful factor in Supreme Court decisionmaking. Along these lines, it is interesting to note that the Court rarely reverses itself—it has done so less than three hundred times over its entire history. Even modern-day Courts, as Table 1-1 shows, have been loath to overrule precedents. In the forty-six terms covered in the table, the Court has overturned only 122 precedents, or about 2.7 per term. What is more, the justices almost always cite previous rulings in their decisions; indeed, it is the rare Court opinion that does not mention other cases.[40] Finally, several scholars have verified that precedent helps to explain Court decisions in some areas of the law. In one study, analysts found that the Court reacted quite consistently to legal doctrine presented in more than fifteen years of death penalty litigation. Put differently, using precedent from past cases, the researchers could correctly categorize the outcomes (for or against the death penalty) in 75

TABLE 1-1 Precedents Overruled, 1953–1998 Terms

Court Era (Terms)	Number of Terms	Number of Overruled Precedents	Average Number of Overrulings Per Term
Warren Court (1953–1968)	16	41	2.6
Burger Court (1969–1985)	17	47	2.8
Rehnquist Court (1986–)	13	34	2.6

SOURCE: U.S. Supreme Court Data Base, with orally argued citation as the unit of analysis. The table includes cases in which the majority opinion formally altered precedent, as well as those in which the Court claimed that a precedent was no longer good law. For more details on the data, see Harold J. Spaeth's documentation to the U.S. Supreme Court Judicial Data Base, available at: www.ssc.msu.edu/~pls/pljp/databases.html.

percent of sixty-four cases decided since 1972.[41] Scholarly work considering precedent in search and seizure litigation had similar success.[42]

Despite these data, we should not conclude that the justices necessarily follow this approach. Many allege that judicial appeal to precedent often is mere window dressing, used to hide ideologies and values, rather than a substantive form of analysis. There are several reasons for this allegation.

First, the Supreme Court has generated so much precedent that it is usually possible to find support for any conclusion. By way of proof, turn to any page of any opinion in this book and you probably will find the writers—both for the majority and the dissenters—citing precedent.

Second, it may be difficult to locate the rule of law emerging in a majority opinion. To decide whether a previous decision qualifies as a precedent, judges and commentators often say, one must strip away the nonessentials of a case and expose the basic reasons for the

39. *United States v. Underwriters Association* (1944).
40. See Jack Knight and Lee Epstein, "The Norm of Stare Decisis," *American Journal of Political Science* 40 (1996): 1018–35.
41. Tracey E. George and Lee Epstein, "On the Nature of Supreme Court Decision Making," *American Political Science Review* 86 (1992): 323–337.
42. Jeffrey A. Segal, "Predicting Supreme Court Cases Probabilistically: The Search and Seizure Cases, 1962–1984," *American Political Science Review* 78 (1984): 891–900.

Supreme Court's decision. This process is generally referred to as "establishing the principle of the case," or the ratio decidendi. Other points made in a given opinion—obiter dicta (any expression in an opinion that is unnecessary to the decision reached in the case or that relates to a factual situation other than the one actually before the court)—have no legal weight, and judges are not bound by it. It is up to courts to separate the ratio decidendi from dicta. This task can be difficult, but it provides a way for justices to skirt precedent with which they do not agree. All they need to do is declare parts of it to be dicta. Or justices can brush aside even the ratio decidendi when it suits their interests. Because the Supreme Court, at least today, is so selective about the cases it decides, it probably would not take a case for which clear precedent existed. Even in the past, two cases that were precisely identical probably would not be accepted. What this means is that justices can always deal with "problematic" ratio decidendi by distinguishing the case at hand from those that have already been decided.

A scholarly study of the role of precedent in Supreme Court decisionmaking analyzes a third reason. Two political scientists hypothesized that if precedent matters, it ought to affect the subsequent decisions of members of the Court. If a justice dissented from a decision establishing a particular precedent, the same justice would not dissent from a subsequent application of the precedent. But that was not the case. Of the eighteen justices included in the study, only two occasionally subjugated their preferences to precedent.[43]

Finally, and most interesting, many justices recognize the limits of stare decisis in cases involving constitutional interpretation. As Justice William O. Douglas once wrote, a judge should support the Constitution, "not the gloss which his predecessors may have put on it."[44] But Justice Black may have said it best:

Ordinarily it is sound policy to adhere to prior decisions but this practice has quite properly never been a blind, inflexible rule. Courts are not omniscient. Like every other human agency, they too can profit from trial and error, from experience and reflection. As others have demonstrated, the principle commonly referred to as stare decisis has never been thought to extend so far as to prevent the courts from correcting their own errors. . . . Indeed, the Court has a special responsibility where questions of constitutional law are involved to review its decisions from time to time and where compelling reasons present themselves to refuse to follow erroneous precedents; otherwise mistakes in interpreting the Constitution are extremely difficult to alleviate and needlessly so.[45]

In fact, of the 122 precedents overruled between the 1953 and 1998 terms (see Table 1-1), 67 percent involved constitutional issues.[46]

Balancing Approaches

So far we have examined five modes of analysis that are not case specific, meaning that conclusions reached by literalists and original intent advocates, for example, on points of law would not waiver with the facts of a given case. The original intent advocates would always hold that the First Amendment does not protect speech advocating the violent overthrow of the government, and the literalists would always reach the opposite conclusion, regardless of the controversy at hand. Supporters of a balancing approach take a position that is more case specific than philosophical; that is, in each case they balance the interests of the individual against those of the government. Their decisions can vary because at times an individual's activity outweighs the government's interest in prohibiting it, while at other times the reverse holds true.

The balancing approach, however, is not monolithic. Some justices take a strict view of balancing, giving the interests of individuals and governments equal weight. They justify doing so on constitutional and philosophical grounds, saying, for example, that while the First Amendment protects individual speech, the text of the Constitution gives legislatures the power to enact laws that may sometimes interfere with speech. The Court, according to this view, should initially give equal weight to

43. Jeffrey A. Segal and Harold J. Spaeth, "The Influence of Stare Decisis on the Votes of U.S. Supreme Court Justices," *American Journal of Political Science* 40 (1996): 971–1002.

44. William O. Douglas, "Stare Decisis," *Columbia Law Review* 49 (1949): 736.

45. *Green v. United States* (1958).

46. We computed this figure from the U.S. Supreme Court Judicial Data Base.

both and then balance them to determine which should fall. Justice John Marshall Harlan's opinion in *Barenblatt v. United States* (1959) demonstrates this theory in practice. Among the issues raised was whether a congressional committee could question an individual about his political beliefs and associations. Lloyd Barenblatt alleged that he could refuse to answer such questions because they infringed on his First Amendment rights. Harlan wrote:

Where First Amendment rights are asserted to bar governmental interrogation, resolution of the issue always involves a balancing by the courts of the competing private and public interests at stake in the particular circumstances shown.

He held that, in this instance, the scale favored the government over Barenblatt.

Balancing also can take at least two other forms. While some opinions, such as Harlan's in *Barenblatt*, weigh equally the claims of governments and individuals, others give preference to one above the other. In accordance with a philosophy of judicial restraint, Justice Felix Frankfurter often balanced government interests versus individual interests but with a finger on the scale: he gave preference to the state over the individual. He did so in the belief that a body made up of unelected judges should not lightly overturn laws passed by legislatures composed of representatives elected by the populace. In his view,

the framers of the Constitution denied . . . legislative powers to the federal judiciary. They chose instead to insulate the judiciary from the legislative function. They did not grant to this Court supervision over legislation. . . . The removal of unwise laws from the statute books . . . lies not to the court but to the ballot and to the processes of democratic government.[47]

In contrast to Frankfurter's perspective is the preferred freedoms position, which also balances interests, but tips the scale to favor the individual's rights and liberties. According to this view, "freedom of expression is so vital in its relationship to the objectives of the Constitution that inevitably it must stand in a preferred position . . . [and, therefore,] legislation claimed to impinge

on rights of free speech and thought should be inspected more critically by the judiciary."[48] In other words, the Court should regard any laws touching upon First Amendment rights with a good deal of suspicion. Why? Justice Jackson provides some reasons:

The very purpose of a Bill of Rights was to withdraw certain subjects from the vicissitudes of political controversy, to place them beyond the reach of majorities and officials and to establish them as legal principles to be applied by the courts. One's right to life, liberty, and property, to free speech, a free press, freedom of worship and assembly, and other fundamental rights may not be submitted to vote: they depend on the outcome of no elections.[49]

Debates over this mode of analysis generally have centered on views about the role of the Supreme Court in a democratic society.[50] Those opposed to the equal balancing of Harlan and to the judicial restraint of Frankfurter contend that each ignores the Court's role of protecting minority interests. According to this argument, the Court, because it is not elected, is in the best position to protect groups and individuals who hold unpopular views. As Justice Brennan wrote in *NAACP v. Button* (1963),

Groups which find themselves unable to achieve their objectives through the ballot frequently turn to the courts. . . . And, under the conditions of modern government, litigation may well be the sole practicable avenue open to a minority to petition for redress of grievances. . . . For such a group, association for litigation may be the most effective form of political association.

Brennan opposed doctrines like absolute balancing because they almost always lead to decisions in favor of the majority. Consider the outcome in *Barenblatt:* Would it have been possible for Justice Harlan to weigh the interests of all against those of one man and reach any other conclusion?

Frankfurter and others chastise adherents of a posi-

47. *West Virginia Board of Education v. Barnette* (1943). For a fuller version of Frankfurter's dissent in this case, see pages 284–285.

48. Robert B. McKay, "The Preference for Freedom," *New York University Law Review* 34 (1959): 1182.

49. *West Virginia Board of Education v. Barnette* (1943).

50. For more specific criticisms of balancing, see Laurent B. Frantz, "The First Amendment in the Balance," *Yale Law Journal* 71 (1962): 1424–50. On the preferred freedoms approach, see Frankfurter's dissent in *Kovacs v. Cooper* (1949).

tion giving special treatment to individual rights and liberties. In Frankfurter's view, that posture is "mischievous" because its application gives the Court too much power. When Congress and other legislative bodies enact laws that reflect the will of the people, why should the Court—composed of unelected officials—strike them down? In this light, the Court should be seen as part of the ruling regime, willing to reflect its wishes.

SUPREME COURT DECISIONMAKING: EXTRALEGAL APPROACHES

So far in our discussion we have not mentioned the justices' ideologies, their political party affiliations, or their personal views on various public policy issues. The reason is that legally relevant approaches to Supreme Court decisionmaking do not admit that these factors play a role in the way the Court arrives at its decisions. Instead, they suggest that justices divorce themselves from their personal and political biases and settle disputes based upon the law. Extralegal approaches posit a quite different vision of Supreme Court decisionmaking. They argue that the forces that drive the justices are anything but legal in composition. Put in different terms, extralegal approaches suggest that it is unrealistic to expect justices to shed all their preferences and values and to ignore public opinion when they put on their black robes. Rather, under the black robes there is a person like all of us whose biases and partisan attachments are strong and pervasive.

Justices usually do not admit that they are swayed by the public or that they vote according to their ideologies. Therefore, our discussion of extralegal approaches is distinct from that of legally relevant factors. Here you will find little in the way of supporting statements from Court members, for it is an unusual justice indeed who admits to following anything but legally relevant criteria in deciding cases. Instead, we have included the results of decades of research by scholars who think that nonlegally relevant forces shape judicial decisions. We organize these approaches into three categories: preference based, strategic, and political. See if you think these scholarly accounts are persuasive.

Preference-Based Approaches

As a class, preference-based approaches see the justices as rational decisionmakers who hold certain values they would like to see reflected in the outcomes of Court cases. The two most prevalent preference-based approaches stress the importance of judicial attitudes and roles.

Judicial Attitudes. Attitudinal approaches emphasize the importance of the justices' ideologies. Typically, scholars examining the ideologies of the justices discuss the degree to which a justice is conservative or liberal— as in "Justice X holds conservative views on issues of criminal law" or "Justice Y holds liberal views on free speech." This school of thought holds that when a case comes before the Court each justice evaluates the facts of the dispute and arrives at a decision consistent with his or her personal ideology.

One of the first scholars to study the importance of the justices' personal attitudes was Pritchett.[51] Examining the Court during the 1930s and 1940s, Pritchett observed that dissent had become an institutionalized feature of judicial decisions *(see Figure 1-4)*. If precedent and other legal factors drove Court rulings, why did various justices interpreting the same legal provisions consistently reach different results? Pritchett concluded that the justices were not following precedent but were "motivated by their own preferences."[52]

Pritchett's findings touched off an explosion of research on the influence of attitudes on Supreme Court decisionmaking.[53] Much of this scholarship describes how liberal or conservative the various justices were and attempts to predict their voting behavior based on their attitudinal preferences. To understand some of these differences, consider Table 1-2, which presents the voting records of the present chief justice, William Rehnquist,

51. C. Herman Pritchett, *The Roosevelt Court* (New York: Macmillan, 1948); and Pritchett, "Divisions of Opinion Among Justices of the U.S. Supreme Court, 1939–1941," *American Political Science Review* 35 (1941): 890–898.

52. Ibid, xiii.

53. The classic works in this area are Pritchett, *The Roosevelt Court;* Glendon Schubert, *The Judicial Mind* (Evanston, Ill: Northwestern University Press, 1965); and Rohde and Spaeth, *Supreme Court Decision Making.* For a lucid, modern-day treatment, see Segal and Spaeth, *The Supreme Court and the Attitudinal* Model, chap. 6.

FIGURE 1-4 Percentage of U.S. Supreme Court Cases with at Least One Dissenting Opinion, 1800–1998 Terms

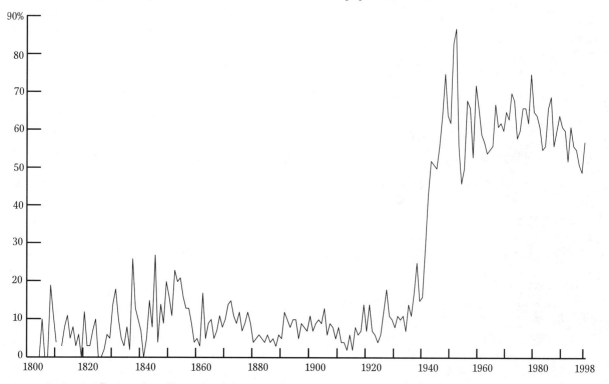

SOURCES: Lee Epstein, Jeffrey A. Segal, Harold J. Spaeth, and Thomas G. Walker, *The Supreme Court Compendium*, 2d ed. (Washington, D.C.: Congressional Quarterly, 1996), Table 3-2. Updated from the U.S. Supreme Court Judicial Data Base.

and his two immediate predecessors, Warren Burger and Earl Warren. The data report the percentage of times each voted in the liberal direction in two different issue areas: civil liberties and economic liberties.

The data show dramatic differences among these three important jurists, especially in civil liberties. Cases in this category include disputes over issues such as the First Amendment freedoms of religion, speech, and press, the right to privacy, the rights of the criminally accused, and illegal discrimination. The liberal position is a vote in favor of the individual who is claiming a denial of these basic rights. Warren supported the liberal side almost 80 percent of the time, but Burger and Rehnquist did so in less than 30 percent of such cases. Economics cases involve challenges to the government's authority to regulate the economy. The liberal position supports an active role by the government in controlling business

and economic activity. Here, too, the three justices show different ideological positions. Warren is the most liberal of the three, ruling in favor of government regulatory activity in better than 80 percent of the cases, while Burger and Rehnquist support such government activity in less than half. These data are typical of the findings of most such studies. Within given issue areas, individual justices tend to show consistent ideological predispositions.

Moreover, we often hear that a particular Court is ideologically predisposed toward one side or the other. For example, on October 5, 1999, the *New York Times* described Justice Anthony Kennedy as "a member of the Court's conservative majority" on certain kinds of criminal justice disputes; on July 7, 1996, the *Denver Post* ran a story entitled, "Supreme Court Sharpens its Conservative Edge." Sometimes an entire Court era is described in terms of its political preferences, such as the "liberal"

TABLE 1-2 Liberal Voting of the Chief Justices, 1953–1998 Terms

| | Issue Areas | | | |
| | Civil Liberties | | Economics | |
	Number of Cases	Percentage Liberal	Number of Cases	Percentage Liberal
Warren	763	78.9%	441	81.6%
Burger	1,415	29.6	423	42.6
Rehnquist	1,918	21.6	619	43.8

SOURCES: U.S. Supreme Court Data Base, with orally argued citation as the unit of analysis. For more details on the data, see Harold J. Spaeth's documentation to the U.S. Supreme Court Judicial Data Base, available at: *www.ssc.msu.edu/~pls/pljp/databases.html.*

NOTE: The data in this table are based on decisions reached during the following tenures: Earl Warren, 1953–1968; Warren Burger, 1969–1985; William Rehnquist, 1986– .

Warren Court or the "conservative" Rehnquist Court. Figure 1-5 confirms that these labels have some basis in fact. Looking at the two lines from left to right, from the 1950s through the 1990s, note the downward trend, indicating the increased conservatism of the Court in economics and civil liberties cases.

How valuable are the ideological terms used to describe particular justices or Courts in helping us understand judicial decisionmaking? On the one hand, knowledge of justices' ideologies can lead to fairly accurate predictions about their voting behavior. Suppose, for example, that the Rehnquist Court hands down a decision dealing with the death penalty and that the vote in the case is 7–2 in favor of the criminal defendant. The most conservative members of the Court on death penalty cases are Justices Antonin Scalia and Clarence Thomas—they almost always vote against the defendant. If we predicted that Scalia and Thomas cast the dissenting votes in our hypothetical death penalty case, we would almost certainly be right.[54]

On the other hand, preference-based approaches are not foolproof. First, how do we know if a particular justice is liberal or conservative? The answer typically is that we know a justice is liberal or conservative because

he or she casts liberal or conservative votes. Scalia favors conservative positions on the Court because he is a conservative, and we know he is a conservative because he favors conservative positions in the cases he decides. This is circular reasoning indeed. Second, knowing that a justice is liberal or conservative or that the Court decided a case in a liberal or conservative way does not tell us much about the Court's (or the country's) policy positions. To say that *Roe v. Wade* is a liberal decision is to say little about the policies governing abortion in the United States. If it did, this book would be nothing more than a list of cases labeled liberal or conservative. But such labels would give us no sense of two hundred years of constitutional interpretation.

Finally, we must understand that ideological labels are occasionally time dependent, that they are bound to particular historical eras. In *Muller v. Oregon* (1908) the Supreme Court upheld a state law that set a maximum number on the hours women (but not men) could work. How would you, as a student at the turn of the twenty-first century, view such an opinion? You probably would classify it as conservative because it seems to patronize and protect women. But in the early 1900s most considered *Muller* a liberal ruling because it allowed the government to regulate business.

A related problem is that some decisions do not fall neatly on a single conservative-liberal dimension. Exemplary is *Wisconsin v. Mitchell* (1993), in which the Court upheld a state law that increased the sentence for crimes if the defendant "intentionally selects the person against whom the crime is committed" on the basis of race, religion, national origin, sexual orientation, and other similar criteria. Is this ruling liberal or conservative? If you view the law as penalizing racial or ethnic hatred, you would likely see it as a liberal decision. However, if you see the law as treating criminal defendants more harshly and penalizing a person because of what he or she believes or says, the ruling is conservative.

Judicial Role. Another concept within the preference-based category is the judicial role, which scholars have defined as norms that constrain the behavior of jurists.[55]

54. We adopt this example from Segal and Spaeth, *The Supreme Court and the Attitudinal Model*, 223.

55. See James L. Gibson, "Judges' Role Orientations, Attitudes, and Decisions," *American Political Science Review* 72 (1978): 917.

FIGURE 1-5   Court Decisions on Economics and Civil Liberties, 1953–1997 Terms

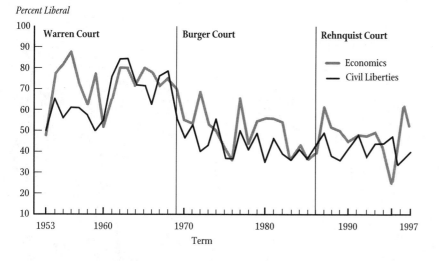

Percent Liberal

SOURCES: Lee Epstein, Jeffrey A. Segal, Harold J. Spaeth, and Thomas G. Walker, *The Supreme Court Compendium: Data, Decisions, and Developments*, 2d ed. (Washington, D.C.: Congressional Quarterly, 1996), Table 3-8. Updated from the U.S. Supreme Court Judicial Data Base.

Some students of the Court argue that each justice has a view of his or her role, a view that is based upon fundamental beliefs of what a good judge should do or what the proper role of the Court should be. The belief is that jurists vote in accordance with these role conceptions.

Analysts typically discuss judicial roles in terms of activism and restraint. An activist justice believes that the proper role of the Court is to assert independent positions in deciding cases, to review the actions of the other branches vigorously, to strike down unconstitutional acts willingly, and to impose far-reaching remedies for legal wrongs whenever necessary. Restraint-oriented justices take the opposite position. Courts should not become involved in the operations of the other branches unless absolutely necessary. The benefit of the doubt should be given to actions taken by elected officials. Courts should impose remedies that are narrowly tailored to correct a specific legal wrong.

Based on these definitions, we might expect to find activist justices more willing than their opposites to strike down legislation. Therefore, a natural question to ask is this: To what extent have specific jurists practiced judicial activism or restraint? The data in Table 1-3 address this question by reporting the votes of justices on the current Court in cases in which the majority declared federal, state, or local legislation unconstitutional. Note the wide variation among the justices, even for those who sat together and therefore heard many of the same cases. For example, compare Justice John Paul Stevens' rate of nearly 85 percent (meaning that he almost always voted with the majority to strike down laws) with Chief Justice Rehnquist's 39 percent—a difference of over 45 percentage points, despite the fact that Stevens' and Rehnquist's service on the Court has overlapped by twenty-five years.

Even more interesting may be the behavior of Justice Frankfurter, who served on the Court between 1939 and 1962. In many Supreme Court opinions, Frankfurter declared his adherence to the doctrine of judicial restraint. But relevant data suggest otherwise. During his last nine years on the bench, Frankfurter voted with the majority to overturn federal laws in 76.6 percent of the sixty-four cases in which he participated.

The Frankfurter example should make clear that what justices say they do and what they actually do may be two different things. It also illustrates a less obvious point: judicial activism and restraint do not necessarily equal

TABLE 1-3 Votes in Support of and Opposition to Decisions Declaring Legislation Unconstitutional: The Current Court

Justice	All Laws	%	Federal Laws Only	%
Breyer	20/8	71.4	8/5	61.5
Ginsburg	26/9	74.3	7/6	53.8
Kennedy	70/4	94.6	13/1	92.9
O'Connor	103/37	73.6	20/3	87.0
Rehnquist	98/155	38.7	20/13	56.5
Scalia	59/24	71.1	15/1	93.8
Souter	43/9	82.7	8/5	61.5
Stevens	166/32	83.8	15/12	55.6
Thomas	35/13	72.2	13/0	100.0
TOTALS	620/291	68.1	119/46	72.1

SOURCE: U.S. Supreme Court Data Base, with orally argued citation as the unit of analysis. For more details on the data, see Harold J. Spaeth's documentation to the U.S. Supreme Court Judicial Data Base, available at: *www.ssc.msu. edu/~pls/pljp/databases.html*.
    NOTE: Figures to the left of the slash indicate the number of votes cast in favor of striking down legislation; figures to the right indicate the number of votes in favor of upholding the legislation. Percentages indicate the percentage of cases in which the justice voted with the majority to declare legislation unconstitutional.

FIGURE 1-6 Provisions of Federal, State, and Local Laws and Ordinances Held Unconstitutional by the Supreme Court, 1789–1989

Number Held Unconstitutional

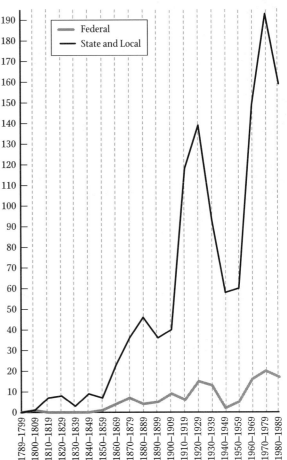

SOURCE: Harold W. Stanley and Richard G. Niemi, *Vital Statistics on American Politics,* 5th ed. (Washington, D.C.: CQ Press, 1995), 286.
    NOTE: We do not include data for the most recent decade as it is not complete. Stanley and Niemi report that the Court struck down three federal laws and thirty-one state and local laws between 1990 and 1994.

judicial liberalism and conservatism. An activist judge need not be liberal, and a judge who practices restraint need not be conservative. As for Frankfurter, scholars argue that in his voting behavior he was "a staunch economic conservative" who was willing to strike down laws that impinged on his policy preferences.[56] Among the twenty-seven justices who served on the Court between 1953 and 1996, only three—Harlan, Whittaker, and Thomas—supported liberal outcomes in economic cases at a rate lower than Frankfurter's 39 percent. In other words, in some areas of the law, Frankfurter was a conservative activist.

It is also true that so-called liberal Courts are no more likely to strike down legislation than are conservative Courts. Figure 1-6 shows the number of federal, state, and local laws struck down since 1789. Note the relatively high numbers of statutes declared unconstitutional during the 1920s, 1970s, and 1980s, all periods of relative conservatism on the Court. Such activism calls into ques-

56. See Segal and Spaeth, *The Supreme Court and the Attitudinal Model,* 236–237.

tion a strong relationship between ideology and judicial role.

We have shown that one can use measures, such as the number of laws struck down, to assess the extent to which justices practice judicial activism or restraint. But does this information help us understand Supreme

Court decisionmaking? This question is difficult to answer because few scholars have studied the relationship between roles and voting in a systematic way.

The paucity of scholarly work on judicial roles leads to a criticism of the approach: it is virtually impossible to separate roles from attitudes. When Justice Frankfurter voted to uphold an economically conservative law, can we conclude that he was practicing restraint? The answer, quite clearly, is no. It may have been his conservative attitude toward economic cases—not restraint—that led him to uphold the law. Another criticism of role approaches is similar to that leveled at attitudinal factors—they tell us very little about the resulting policy in a case. Again, to say that *Roe v. Wade* was an activist decision because it struck down abortion laws nationwide is to say nothing about the policy content of the opinion.

Strategic Approaches

Strategic accounts of judicial decisions rest on a few simple propositions: justices may be primarily seekers of legal policy (as the attitudinal adherents claim) or they may be motivated by jurisprudential principles (as legally relevant approaches suggest), but they are not unconstrained actors who make decisions based solely on their own ideological attitudes or own jurisprudential desires. Rather, justices are strategic actors who realize that their ability to achieve their goals—whatever those goals might be—depends on a consideration of the preferences of other relevant actors (such as their colleagues and members of other political institutions), the choices they expect others to make, and the institutional context in which they act. Scholars have termed this a "strategic" account because the ideas it contains are derived from the rational choice paradigm, on which strategic analysis is based and as it has been advanced by economists and political scientists working in other fields. Accordingly, we can restate the strategic argument in this way: we can best explain the choices of justices as strategic behavior and not merely as a response to ideological or jurisprudential values.[57]

Such arguments about Supreme Court decisionmaking seem to be sensible: a justice can do very little alone. It takes a majority vote to decide a case and a majority agreeing on a single opinion to set precedent. Under such conditions, human interaction is important, and case outcomes—not to mention the rationale of decisions—can be influenced by the nature of relations among the members of the group.

Although scholars have not considered strategic approaches to the same degree that they have studied judicial attitudes, a number of influential works point to their importance. Research started in the 1960s and continuing today into the private papers of the former justices consistently has shown that through intellectual persuasion, effective bargaining over opinion writing, informal lobbying, and so forth, justices have influenced the actions of their colleagues.[58]

How does strategic behavior manifest itself? One possibility is in the frequency of vote changes. During the deliberations that take place after oral arguments, the justices discuss the case and vote on it. These votes do not become final until the opinions are completed and the decision is made public (*see Figure 1-1*). Research has shown that between the initial vote on the merits of cases and the official announcement of the decision at least one vote switch occurs more than 50 percent of the time.[59] This figure indicates that justices change their minds—inexplicable phenomena if we believe that justices are simply liberals or conservatives and always vote in accord with their preferences.

Consider an example unearthed from the papers of

57. For more details on this approach, see Lee Epstein and Jack Knight, *The Choices Justices Make* (Washington, D.C.: CQ Press, 1998).

58. Walter F. Murphy, *Elements of Judicial Strategy* (Chicago: University of Chicago Press, 1964); David J. Danelski, "The Influence of the Chief Justice in the Decisional Process of the Supreme Court," in *The Federal Judicial System*, ed. Thomas P. Jahnige and Sheldon Goldman (New York: Holt, Rinehart, and Winston, 1968); J. Woodford Howard, "On the Fluidity of Judicial Choice," *American Political Science Review* 62 (1968): 43–56; Epstein and Knight, *The Choices Justices Make;* Forest Maltzman, Paul J. Wahlbeck, and James Spriggs, *Crafting Law on the Supreme Court: The Collegial Game* (New York: Cambridge University Press, 2000).

59. Saul Brenner, "Fluidity on the Supreme Court, 1956–1967," *American Journal of Political Science* 26 (1982): 388–390; Brenner, "Fluidity on the United States Supreme Court: A Re-examination," *American Journal of Political Science* 24 (1980): 526–535; Forest Maltzman and Paul J. Wahlbeck, "Strategic Considerations and Vote Fluidity on the Burger Court," *American Political Science Review* 90 (1996): 581.

Justice Thurgood Marshall. During the 1990 term the justices unanimously voted in conference to affirm the lower court judgment in *Owen v. Owen,* a bankruptcy case, and Chief Justice Rehnquist assigned the majority opinion to Justice Scalia. Scalia circulated his draft on December 3 with an accompanying memo: "I was as firm as any of you in my opinion that the judgment in this case had to be an affirmance. I found it impossible, however, to write it that way. . . . I hope that you may agree with me, but otherwise the opinion will have to be reassigned." In other words, Scalia was telling his colleagues that he had changed his mind and written to reverse the lower court opinion.

Justice Marshall scribbled "NO!!!" and "WAIT" in large letters across the Scalia draft. The chief justice responded with a rather curt note to Scalia, asserting that he should not have written the opinion if he had changed his mind; rather, he should have asked to have it reassigned immediately. Rehnquist decided to have a go at it himself. In the meantime, just four days later Justice O'Connor indicated that she could "join something along [the] lines" Scalia proposed. Suddenly, the nine-person majority to affirm had dwindled to seven.

Another defection from the majority came in February, when Rehnquist sent the following memo to the others: "After Nino [Scalia] circulated his draft opinion coming out to 'reverse' rather than to 'affirm,' I reassigned this case to myself. . . . After having made this effort, I have decided that Nino was correct. . . . Anyone else wishing to do so, of course, is free to try their hand at the same task which I attempted. . . . I therefore assign the case back to Nino and join his revised opinion." By the end of March every justice except John Paul Stevens had agreed to sign Scalia's opinion, and Stevens was open to persuasion. During the early days of April he and Scalia exchanged several memos on possible revisions to the opinion. In the end, Scalia could not accommodate him, and Stevens wrote a lone dissent taking the position all nine originally had expressed.

Over a few short months, a 9–0 vote to affirm became an 8–1 decision to reverse. Surely, such a large vote shift is unusual, but our perusal of Marshall's papers leads us to conclude, like earlier scholars, that it is not unusual

for justices to reevaluate their initial positions or to succumb to the persuasion of their colleagues. Nor is it atypical for colleagues to attempt to persuade each other of the merits of their positions.

Vote shifts are just one manifestation of the interdependence of the Court's decision-making process. Another is the revision of opinions that occurs in almost every Court case.[60] As opinion writers try to accommodate their colleagues' wishes, their drafts may undergo five, ten, even fifteen revisions. Bargaining over the content of an opinion is important because it can significantly alter the policy ultimately expressed. A clear example is *Griswold v. Connecticut* (1965), in which the Court considered the constitutionality of a state law that prohibited the dissemination of birth control devices and information, even to married couples. In his initial draft of the majority opinion, Justice Douglas struck down the law on the grounds that it interfered with the First Amendment's right of association. A memorandum from Justice Brennan convinced Douglas to alter his rationale and to establish the foundation for a right to privacy. "Had the Douglas draft been issued as the *Griswold* opinion of the Court, the case would stand as a precedent on the freedom of association," rather than serve as the landmark ruling it became.[61]

Although strategic approaches have their uses, *Griswold* points to a problem. To date, scholarly treatments have been ad hoc or case specific—we do not know whether a case like *Griswold* represents the rule or the anomaly. Until analysts begin to study interdependent decision making more systematically, which manuscript collections such as Marshall's, Brennan's, and Lewis F. Powell's make possible, the general value of this approach will remain unknown.

Political Factors

In addition to internal bargaining, strategic approaches (as well as others) also take account of political pressures that come from outside the Court. We consider three sources of such influence: public opinion, partisan

60. Epstein and Knight, *The Choices Justices Make,* chap. 3.
61. See Bernard Schwartz, *The Unpublished Opinions of the Warren Court* (New York: Oxford University Press, 1985), chap. 7.

politics, and interest groups. While reading about these sources of influence, keep in mind that one of the fundamental differences between the Supreme Court and the political branches is that there is no direct electoral connection between the justices and the public. Once appointed, justices may serve for life. They are not accountable to the public and are not required to undergo any periodic reevaluation of their decisions. So why would they let the stuff of ordinary partisan politics, such as public opinion and interest groups, influence their opinions?

Public Opinion. To address this question, let us first look at public opinion as a source of influence on the Court. We know that the president and members of Congress are always trying to find out what the people are thinking. Conducting and analyzing public opinion polls is a never-ending task, and there is good reason for this activity. The political branches are supposed to represent the people, and the incumbents' reelection prospects can be jeopardized by straying too far from what the public wants. But federal judges—including Supreme Court justices—are not dependent upon pleasing the public to stay in office, and they do not serve in the same kind of representative capacity that legislators do.

Does that mean that the justices are not affected by public opinion? Some scholars claim that the answer, for at least three reasons, is no. First, because justices are political appointees, nominated and approved by popularly elected officials, it is logical that they reflect, however subtly, the views of the majority. It is probably true that an individual radically out of step with either the president or the Senate would not be nominated, much less confirmed. Second, the Court, at least occasionally, views public opinion as a legitimate guide for decisions. It has even gone so far as to incorporate that dimension into some of its jurisprudential standards. For example, in evaluating whether certain kinds of punishments violate the Eighth Amendment's prohibition against cruel and unusual punishment, the Court proclaimed that it would look toward "evolving standards of decency," as defined by public sentiment.[62] The third reason relates to the Court as an institution. Put simply, the justices have no

mechanism for enforcing their decisions. Instead, they depend on other political officials to support their positions and on general public compliance, especially when controversial Court opinions have ramifications beyond the particular concerns of the parties to the suit.

Certainly, we can think of particular cases that lend support to these claims—cases in which the Court seems to have embraced public opinion, especially under conditions of extreme national stress. One example occurred during World War II. In *Korematsu v. United States* (1944) the justices endorsed the government's program to remove all Japanese Americans from the Pacific Coast states and relocate them to inland detention centers. It seems clear that the justices were swept up in the same wartime apprehensions as the rest of the nation. But it is equally as easy to summons examples of the Court handing down rulings that fly in the face of what the public wants. The most obvious example occurred after Franklin D. Roosevelt's 1932 election to the presidency. By choosing Roosevelt and electing many Democrats to Congress, the voters sent a clear signal that they wanted the government to take vigorous action to end the Great Depression. The president and Congress responded with many laws—the so-called New Deal legislation—but the Court remained unmoved by the public's endorsement of Roosevelt and his legislation. In case after case, at least until 1937, the justices struck down many of the laws and administrative programs designed to get the nation's economy moving again.

More systematic research, scrutinizing the correspondence between various measures of public opinion and trends in Court decisions, have yielded equally mixed results. On one end of the spectrum are studies by political scientists Thomas Marshall and William Mishler and Reggie Sheehan. Marshall finds that, at the very least, Court rulings do not deviate significantly from the views of the citizenry: "When a clear-cut poll majority or plurality exists, over three-fifths of the Court's decisions reflect the polls. By all arguable evidence the modern Supreme Court appears to reflect public opinion about as accurately as other policy makers."[63] Mishler and

---

62. *Trop v. Dulles* (1958).

63. Thomas Marshall, *Public Opinion and the Supreme Court* (New York: Unwin Hyman, 1989), 97.

Sheehan go even further, suggesting that changes in the public's ideological mood have a causal effect on Court decisions: The justices "are broadly aware of fundamental trends in the ideological tenor of public opinion, and . . . at least some justices, consciously or not, may adjust their decisions at the margins to accommodate such fundamental trends."[64]

On the other end of the spectrum are those scholars who remain unconvinced of the role of public opinion in Court decisionmaking. In part, this disbelief emanates from a concern about the nature of the research that has been conducted. Helmut Norpoth and Jeffrey Segal, for example, criticized Mishler and Sheehan's research.[65] In reexamining that study's methodology, they reasoned as follows: "Does public opinion influence Supreme Court decisions? If the model of influence is of the sort where the justices set aside their own (ideological) preferences and abide by what they divine as the vox populi, our answer is a resounding no." What Norpoth and Segal find instead is that Court appointments made by Richard Nixon in the early 1970s caused a "sizable ideological shift" in the direction of Court decisions *(see Figure 1-5)*. The entry of conservative justices created the illusion that the Court was echoing public opinion; it was not that sitting justices modified their voting patterns to conform to the changing views of the public.

This finding reinforces yet another criticism of this approach: that public opinion affects the Court only indirectly through presidential appointments, and not through the justices' reading of public opinion polls. This distinction is important, for if justices were truly influenced by the public, their decisions would change with the ebb and flow of opinion. But if they merely share their appointing president's ideology, which must mirror the majority of the citizens *at the time of the president's election*, their decisions will remain constant over time. They would not fluctuate, as public opinion often does.

At the end of the day, the question of whether public opinion affects Supreme Court decisionmaking remains an open one. This is reinforced by the most recent research, which tends to reach conclusions somewhat between Mishler and Sheehan on one side and Segal and Norpoth on the other. As the authors of one of these studies note, "Commenting on Mishler and Sheehan, Norpoth and Segal argue that the role of public opinion on Court decisions is wholly indirect through the election-nomination-confirmation process. Mishler and Sheehan claim a direct public opinion influence. Our results . . . leave us in the middle of this debate. We believe that there is a trace of influence for both processes, but our results are too weak to leave us confident about the matter."[66]

Partisan Politics. Public opinion is not the only political factor that some allege influence the justices. As Jonathan Casper wrote, we cannot overestimate "the importance of the political context in which the Court does its work." In his view, the statement that the Court follows the election returns "recognizes that the choices the Court makes are related to developments in the broader political system."[67] In other words, the political environment has an effect on Court behavior. In fact, many assert that the Court is responsive to the influence of partisan politics, both internally and externally.

On the inner workings of the Court, social scientists long have argued that political creatures inhabit the Court, that justices are not simply neutral arbiters of the law. Since 1789, the beginning of constitutional government in the United States, those who have ascended to the bench have come from the political institutions of government or, at the very least, have affiliated with a particular political party. Judicial scholars recognize that justices bring with them the philosophies of those partisan attachments. Just as the members of the present Court tend to reflect the views of the Republican Party or

64. William Mishler and Reginald S. Sheehan, "The Supreme Court as a Counter-Majoritarian Institution? The Impact of Public Opinion on Supreme Court Decisions," *American Political Science Review* 87 (1993): 89.

65. Helmut Norpoth and Jeffrey A. Segal, "Popular Influence in Supreme Court Decisions," *American Political Science Review* 88 (1994): 711–716.

66. James A. Stimson, Michael B. MacKuen, and Robert S. Erikson, "Dynamic Representation," *American Political Science Review* 89 (September 1995): 556. For a succinct review of this literature, see Bradley C. Canon and Charles A. Johnson, *Judicial Policies*, 2d ed. (Washington, D.C.: CQ Press, 1999), 196–197.

67. Jonathan Casper, *The Politics of Civil Liberties* (New York: Harper and Row, 1972), 293.

Democratic Party, so too did the justices who came from the ranks of the Federalists and Jeffersonians. As one might expect, justices who affiliate with the Democratic Party tend to be more liberal in their decisionmaking than those who are Republicans.

The Court also faces political pressure from the outside. Although the justices have no electoral connection or mandate of responsiveness, the other institutions of government have some influence on judicial behavior, and, naturally, the direction of that influence reflects the partisan composition of those branches. The Court has always had a complex relationship with the president, a relationship that provides the president with several possible ways to influence judicial decisions. The president has some direct links with the Court, including (1) the power to nominate justices and shape the Court; (2) personal relationships with sitting justices, including Franklin Roosevelt's with James Byrnes, Lyndon Johnson's with Abe Fortas, and Richard Nixon's with Warren Burger; and (3) the notion that the president, having been elected within the previous four years, may carry a popular mandate, reflecting the preferences of the people, which would affect the environment within which the Court operates.

A less direct source of influence is the executive branch, which operates under the president's command. The bureaucracy can assist the Court in implementing its policies, or it can hinder the Court by refusing to do so, a fact of which the justices are well aware. As a judicial body, the Supreme Court cannot implement or execute its own decisions. It often must depend on the executive branch to give its decisions legitimacy through action. The Court, therefore, may act strategically, anticipating the wishes of the executive branch and responding accordingly to avoid a confrontation that could threaten its legitimacy. *Marbury v. Madison,* in which the Court enunciated the doctrine of judicial review, is the classic example *(see Chapter 2 for an excerpt).* Some scholars suggest that the justices knew if they ruled a certain way, the Jefferson administration would not carry out their orders. Because the Court felt that such a failure would threaten the legitimacy of judicial institutions, it crafted its opinion in a way that would not force the administration to take any action, but would send a message about its displeasure with the administration's politics.

Another indirect source of presidential influence is the U.S. solicitor general. We have already discussed the SG's success as a petitioning party, and the office can have an equally pronounced effect at the merits stage. In fact, data indicate that, whether acting as an amicus curiae or as a party to a suit, the SG's office is generally able to convince the justices to adopt its preferred positions.[68]

Presidential influence is also demonstrated in the kinds of arguments a solicitor general brings into the Court. That is, solicitors general representing Democratic administrations tend to present more liberal arguments; those from the ranks of the Republican Party, more conservative arguments. The transition from the Bush administration to the Clinton administration provides an interesting illustration. Bush's solicitor general had filed amicus curiae briefs—many of which took a conservative position—in a number of cases heard by the Court during the 1993–1994 term. Drew S. Days III, Clinton's first solicitor general, rewrote at least four of those briefs to reflect the new administration's more liberal posture. For example, Days argued that the Civil Rights Act of 1991 should be applied retroactively, whereas the Bush administration suggested that it should not be. In another case, Days claimed that jurors cannot be dismissed on the basis of sex; his predecessor argued that such dismissals were constitutional.

Congress, too—or so some argue—can influence Supreme Court decisionmaking. Like the president, the legislature has many powers over the Court the justices cannot ignore.[69] Some of these resemble presidential powers—the Senate's role in confirmation proceedings, the implementation of judicial decisions—but there are others. Congress can restrict the Court's jurisdiction to hear cases, enact legislation or propose constitutional amendments to recast Court decisions, and hold judicial salaries constant. To forestall a congressional attack, the Court might accede to legislative wishes. Often-cited examples include the Court's willingness to defer to the

---

68. See Epstein et al., *Supreme Court Compendium,* Tables 7-15 and 7-16.
69. See William N. Eskridge Jr., "Overriding Supreme Court Statutory Interpretation Decisions," *Yale Law Journal* 101 (1991): 331.

Radical Republican Congress after the Civil War and to approve New Deal legislation after Roosevelt proposed his Court-packing plan in 1937. Some argue that these examples represent anomalies, not the rule. The Court, they say, has no reason to respond strategically to Congress because it is so rare that the legislature threatens, much less takes action, against the judiciary. Only once has Congress retaliated against the Court by removing its jurisdiction over a class of cases—and that occurred more than a hundred years ago. This argument needs to be kept in mind as you read the cases that pit the Court against Congress and the president.

Interest Groups. In *The Federalist Papers*, No. 78, Alexander Hamilton wrote that the U.S. Supreme Court was "to declare the sense of the law" through "inflexible and uniform adherence to the rights of the constitution and individuals." Despite this expectation, Supreme Court litigation has become political over time. We see manifestations of politics in virtually every aspect of the Court's work, from the nomination and confirmation of justices to the factors that influence their decisions, but perhaps the most striking example of this politicization is the incursion of organized interest groups into the judicial process.

Naturally, interest groups may not attempt to persuade the Supreme Court the same way lobbyists deal with Congress. It would be grossly improper for the representatives of an interest group to approach a Supreme Court justice directly. Instead, as already mentioned, interest groups try to influence Court decisions by submitting written legal arguments called amicus curiae briefs *(see Box 1-1)*. This procedure allows interest groups to make their views known to the Court, even when the group is not a direct party to the litigation.

These days, it is a rare case before the U.S. Supreme Court that does not attract such submissions. On average, organized interests filed at least one amicus brief in 75.5 percent of all cases decided by full opinion between 1986 and 1996.[70] In fact, during a typical term in the 1990s, 4.5 amici co-signed each friend of the court brief, for a total of about 1,800 organizational participants.

Some cases, particularly those involving such controversial issues as abortion and affirmative action, have attracted even wider participation. In *Regents of the University of California v. Bakke* (1978; *for an excerpt, see pages 721–727*), involving admission of minority students to medical school, more than one hundred organizations filed fifty-eight amici briefs: forty-two backed the university's admissions policy, and sixteen supported Bakke. In addition to participating as amici, groups are sponsoring cases—that is, providing litigants with attorneys and the money necessary to pursue their cases—in record numbers.

The explosion of interest group participation in Supreme Court litigation raises two questions. First, why do groups go to the Court? The answer is obvious: they want to influence the Court's decisions. But groups also go to the Supreme Court to achieve other, more subtle, ends. One is the setting of institutional agendas: by filing amicus curiae briefs at the case-selection stage or by bringing cases to the Court's attention, organizations seek to influence the justices' decisions on which disputes to hear. Group participation also may serve as a counterbalance to other interests that have competing goals. So, for example, if Planned Parenthood, a pro-choice group, observes Life Legal Defense Foundation, a pro-life group, filing an amicus curiae brief in an abortion case (or vice versa), it too may enter the dispute to ensure that its side is represented in the proceedings. Finally, groups go to the Court to publicize their causes and their organizations. The NAACP Legal Defense Fund's legendary litigation campaign to end school segregation provides an excellent example. It resulted not only in a favorable policy decision in *Brown v. Board of Education* (1954; *for an excerpt, see pages 638–641*), but also it established the LDF as the foremost organizational litigant of this issue.

The second question is this: Can groups influence the outcomes of Supreme Court decisions?[71] This question has no simple answer. When interest groups participate on both sides, it is reasonable to speculate that one or

---

70. Lee Epstein et al., *Supreme Court Compendium*, Table 7-26.

71. We adopt some of this material from Pritchett, Murphy, and Epstein, *Courts, Judges, and Politics*, chap. 6.

more of them exerted some intellectual influence or at least that intervention of groups on the winning side neutralized the arguments of those who lost. To be sure of how much influence any group or private party exerted, a researcher would have to interview all the justices who participated in the decision—and they do not grant such interviews—because a citation to a brief may indicate only that a justice is seeking support for a conclusion he or she had already reached.

We can be more certain that many cases would not get into any court, much less the U.S. Supreme Court, without the help of an interest group. Therefore, we can say that, because judges have to wait for cases to come before them, groups help set the judicial agenda. It may be that many judges, especially judges on appellate courts, look on interest groups as sources of important information that otherwise would not come to their attention. Gregory A. Caldeira and John R. Wright's research on amici participation at the agenda-setting stage supports this contention.[72] The growing percentage of U.S. Supreme Court opinions that cite amici's arguments reinforces the point. During the Warren Court, the justices cited briefs amicus curiae in about 40 percent of their opinions; that figure rose to 66 percent for Burger Court justices; and to 68 percent for the Rehnquist Court.[73] It thus seems clear is that the justices—now more than ever—are at least learning enough from amici briefs to cite them in their opinions.

Once having gained the attention of a court, attorneys for some groups, such as the Women's Rights Project of the American Civil Liberties Union and the NAACP, are often more experienced and their staffs are more adept at research than counsel for what Marc Galanter calls "one-shotters."[74] For the NAACP, Thurgood Marshall would orchestrate help from allied groups, allocating the task of making specific arguments to each, and enlisting sympathetic social scientists to muster supporting data. Before going to the Supreme Court for oral argument, he would sometimes have a practice session with friendly law professors, each one playing the role of a particular justice

and trying to pose the sorts of question that justice would be likely to ask. That sort of preparation can pay off, but it need not be decisive. In oral argument, Allan Bakke's attorney showed ignorance of constitutional law and curtly told one justice who tried to help him that he would like to argue the case his own way. Despite this poor performance, Bakke won.

On the other hand, there is strong evidence suggesting that attorneys working for interest groups are no more successful than private counsel. One study paired similar cases decided by the same district court judge, the same year, with the only major difference being that one case was sponsored by a group, the other brought by attorneys unaffiliated with an organized interest. Despite Galanter's contentions about the obstacles confronting one-shotters, the study found no major differences between the two.[75]

In short, the debate over the influence of interest groups continues, and it is a debate that you will have ample opportunity to consider. Within the case excerpts we often provide information on the arguments of amici and attorneys so that you can compare these points with the justices' opinions.

CONDUCTING RESEARCH ON THE SUPREME COURT

As you can see, there is considerable disagreement in the scholarly and legal communities about why justices decide cases the way they do, and the various approaches show up in many of the Court's opinions in this book. Remember that the opinions here are excerpts, designed to highlight the most important points of the various majority, dissenting, and concurring opinions. Occasionally, you may want to read the decisions in their entirety. Following is an explanation of how to locate opinions and other kinds of information on the Court and its members.

Locating Supreme Court Decisions

U.S. Supreme Court decisions are published by various reporters. The four major reporters are: *U.S. Reports*,

72. Caldeira and Wright, "Organized Interests and Agenda Setting."

73. See Epstein et al., *Supreme Court Compendium*, Table 7-26.

74. "Why The 'Haves' Come Out Ahead: Speculations on the Limits of Social Change," *Law and Society Review* 9 (1974): 95.

75. Lee Epstein and C. K. Rowland, "Debunking the Myth of Interest Group Invincibility in the Court," *American Political Science Review* 85 (1991): 205–217.

TABLE 1-4 Reporting Systems

Reporter/Publisher	Form of Citation (terms)	Description
United States Reports Government Printing Office	Dall. 1–4 (1790–1800) Cr. 1–15 (1801–1815) Wheat. 1–12 (1816–1827) Pet. 1–16 (1828–1843) How. 1–24 (1843–1861) Bl. 1–2 (1861–1862) Wall. 1–23 (1863–1875) U.S. 91– (1875–)	Contains official text of opinions of the Court. Includes tables of cases reported, cases and statutes cited, miscellaneous materials, and subject index. Includes most of the Court's decisions. Court opinions prior to 1875 are cited by the name of the Reporter of the Court. For example, Dall. stands for Alexander J. Dallas, the first reporter.
United States Supreme Court Reports, *Lawyers' Edition* West Group	L. Ed. L. Ed. 2d	Contains official reports of opinions of the Court. Additionally, provides per curiam and other decisions not found elsewhere. Summarizes individual majority and dissenting opinions and counsel briefs.
Supreme Court Reporter West Publishing Company	S. Ct.	Contains official reports of opinions of the Court. Contains annotated reports and indexes of case names. Includes opinions of justices in chambers. Appears semi-monthly.
United States Law Week Bureau of National Affairs	U.S.L.W.	Weekly periodical service containing full text of Court decisions. Includes four indexes: topical, table of cases, docket number table, and proceedings section. Contains summary of cases filed recently, journal of proceedings, summary of orders, arguments before the Court, argued cases awaiting decisions, review of Court's work, and review of Court's docket.

SOURCES: Lee Epstein, Jeffrey A. Segal, Harold J. Spaeth, and Thomas G. Walker, *The Supreme Court Compendium: Data Decisions, and Developments*, 2d ed. (Washington, D.C.: Congressional Quarterly, 1996), Table 1-5. Dates of reporters are from Joan Biskupic and Elder Witt, *Guide to the U.S. Supreme Court*, 3d ed. (Washington, D.C.: Congressional Quarterly, 1997), 826.

Lawyers' Edition, Supreme Court Reporter, and *U.S. Law Week.* All contain the opinions of the Court, but vary in the kinds of ancillary material they provide. For example, as Table 1-4 shows, the *Lawyers' Edition* contains excerpts of the briefs of attorneys submitted in orally argued cases, *U.S. Law Week* provides a topical index of cases on the Court's docket, and so forth.

Locating cases within these reporters is easy if you know the case *citation.* Case citations, as the table shows, take different forms, but they all work in roughly the same way. To see how, turn to page 252 to find an excerpt of *Texas v. Johnson* (1989). Directly under the case name is a citation: 491 U.S. 397, which means that *Texas v. Johnson* appears in volume 491, page 397, of *U.S. Reports.*[76] The first set of numbers is the volume number; the U.S. is the

form of citation for *U.S. Reports;* and the second set of numbers is the starting page of the case.

Texas v. Johnson also can be located in the three other reporters. The citations are as follows:

Lawyers' Edition: 105 L. Ed. 2d 342 (1989)
Supreme Court Reporter: 109 S. Ct. 2533 (1989)
U.S. Law Week: 57 U.S.L.W. 4770 (1989)

Note that the abbreviations vary by reporter, but they parallel the *U.S. Reports* in that the first set of numbers is the volume number, and the second set is the starting page number.

If you do not know the citation, try to find out the year the case was decided. With this information, you

76. In this book, we list only the *U.S. Reports* cite because it is the official record of Supreme Court decisions. It is the only reporter pub-

lished by the federal government; the three others are privately printed. Almost every law library has *U.S. Reports.* If your college does not have a law school, check with your librarians. If they have any Court reporter, it is probably *U.S. Reports.*

can check the index of the appropriate volume of the *U.S. Reports (see Appendix 6)* or of the other reporters.

In addition to these print volumes, Supreme Court opinions are available in various electronic forms. First, several companies maintain data bases of the decisions of federal and state courts, along with a wealth of other information. In some institutions these services—LEXIS-NEXIS and Westlaw—are available only to law school students. Check with your librarians to see if your school provides access to other students, perhaps via Academic Universe (a subset of the LEXIS-NEXIS service), Second, the Legal Information Institute (LII) at Cornell Law School *(www.law.cornell.edu),* FindLaw *(www.findlaw. com/casecode/supreme.html),* and FedWorld *(www. fedworld.gov/supcourt/index.htm)*—to name just three—index Supreme Court opinions and offer an array of indices and search capabilities. You can read the opinions from your browser (for example, Netscape Navigator), have them e-mailed to you, or download them immediately. The LII site contains cases decided since 1990; it also houses an archive of selected historically important Court opinions *(http://supct.law.cornell.edu/supct/cases/ name.htm);* Findlaw's site contains Supreme Court opinions dating back to 1893; FedWorld has more than seven thousand cases from 1937 to 1975. If a case we have excerpted is located in these archives, we have noted the URL after the case citation.

Locating Other Information on the Supreme Court and Its Members

As you might imagine, there is no shortage of reference material on the Court. Four good (print) starting points are:

1. *The U.S. Supreme Court: A Bibliography* is an annotated bibliography of scholarly writings on the Court.[77] Entries cover the development of the Court, its work, various areas of the law, and the justices.

2. *The Supreme Court Compendium: Data, Decisions, and Developments,* second edition, contains information on the following dimensions of Court activity: the

Court's development, review process, opinions and decisions, judicial background, voting patterns, and impact.[78] You will find data as varied as the number of cases the Court decided during a particular term, the votes in the Senate on Supreme Court nominees, and the law schools the justices attended.

3. *Guide to the U.S. Supreme Court,* third edition, provides a fairly detailed history of the Court. It also summarizes the holdings in landmark cases and provides brief biographies of the justices.[79]

4. *The Oxford Companion to the Supreme Court of the United States* is an encyclopedia, containing entries on the justices, important Court cases, the amendments to the Constitution, and so forth.[80]

The U.S. Supreme Court also gets a great deal of attention on the World Wide Web. The Legal Information Institute *(www.law.cornell.edu)* is particularly useful. In addition to Supreme Court decisions, the LII contains links to various documents (such as the U.S. Code and state statutes) and to a vast array of legal indexes and libraries. If you are unable to find the material you are looking for here, you may locate it by clicking on one of the links.

Another worthwhile site is the Home Page of the Law and Courts Section of the American Political Science Association *(www.artsci.wustl.edu/~polisci/lawcourt.html).* Devoted to promoting interest in teaching and research in the areas of law and the judicial process, this site contains links to papers, data sources, and other web sites relating to law and courts.

As already mentioned, you can listen to selected oral arguments of the Court at the Oyez Project site *(oyez.nwu. edu).* Oyez contains audio files of Supreme Court oral arguments for selected constitutional cases decided between 1955 and 1999. For those cases included in the archive, we provide the URLs.

Finally, in 2000 the Court put up its own Web site *(www.supremecourtus.gov).* There you will find historical

78. Epstein et al., *Supreme Court Compendium.*
79. Joan Biskupic and Elder Witt, *Guide to the U.S. Supreme Court,* 3d ed. (Washington, D.C.: Congressional Quarterly, 1997).
80. Kermit Hall, ed., *The Oxford Companion to the Supreme Court of the United States* (New York: Oxford University Press, 1992).

77. Fenton S. Martin and Robert U. Goehlert, *The U.S. Supreme Court: A Bibliography* (Washington, D.C.: Congressional Quarterly, 1990).

information about the Court, as well as opinions, orders, and the Court's current calendar.

These are just a few of the many sites—perhaps hundreds—that contain information on the federal courts. To find others, invoke search engines, such as Yahoo (www.yahoo.com) or AltaVista (www.altavista.com), which are vehicles for locating legal and other resources that the sites listed above may not contain. Enter the search word(s), and the engine will match the term against its data base of web sites. If you want to limit your search to legal resources, invoke one of Yahoo's or AltaVista's specific search index mechanisms—for example, Government: Law, Legal Research (www. yahoo.com/Government/ Law/Legal_Research). From there, you can conduct general searches or further limit your search to one of the following categories: Academic Papers, Cases, Companies, Institutes, Journals, or Libraries.

There is at least one other important electronic source of information on the Court—Harold Spaeth's computer-dependent U.S. Supreme Court Judicial Databases. They provide a wealth of data beginning with the Vinson Court (1946 term) to the present. Among the many attributes of Court decisions coded by Spaeth are the names of the courts making the original decision, the identities of the parties to the cases, the policy context of a case, and the votes of each justice. You can obtain the databases and accompanying documentation, free of charge (www.ssc.msu.edu/~pls/pljp). The data bases also are available to faculty, staff, and students at colleges and universities that are members of the Inter-University Consortium for Political and Social Science Research in Ann Arbor, Michigan.

In this chapter, we have examined Supreme Court procedures and attempted to shed some light on how and why justices make the choices they do. Our consideration of preference-based factors, for example, highlighted the role ideology plays in Court decisionmaking, and our discussion of political explanations emphasized public opinion and interest groups. After reading this chapter, you may have concluded that the justices are relatively free to go about their business as they please. But, as we shall see in the next chapter, that is not necessarily so.

Although Court members have a good deal of power and the freedom to exercise it, they also face considerable institutional obstacles. It is to the subjects of judicial power and constraints that we now turn.

READINGS

Ackerman, Bruce. *We the People.* Cambridge: Harvard University Press, 1991.

Amar, Akhil Reed. *The Bill of Rights: Creation and Reconstruction.* New Haven: Yale University Press, 1998.

Baum, Lawrence. *The Supreme Court,* 7th ed. Washington, D.C.: CQ Press, 2000.

———. *The Puzzle of Judicial Behavior.* University of Michigan Press, 1997.

Biskupic, Joan, and Elder Witt. *Guide to the U.S. Supreme Court,* 3d ed. Washington, D.C.: Congressional Quarterly, 1997.

Bobbitt, Philip. *Constitutional Interpretation.* Cambridge: Basil Blackwell, 1991.

Bork, Robert. "Neutral Principles and Some First Amendment Problems," *Indiana Law Journal* 47 (1971): 1–35.

Brenner, Saul, and Harold J. Spaeth. *Stare Indecisis: The Alteration of Precedent on the Supreme Court, 1946–1992.* New York: Cambridge University Press, 1995.

Burt, Robert A. *The Constitution in Conflict.* Cambridge: Belknap Press, 1992.

Caldeira, Gregory A., and John R. Wright. "The Discuss List: Agenda Building in the Supreme Court." *Law and Society Review* 24 (1990): 807–836.

———. "Organized Interests and Agenda Setting in the U.S. Supreme Court." *American Political Science Review* 82 (1988): 1109–27.

Canon, Bradley C., and Charles A. Johnson. *Judicial Policies: Implementation and Impact,* 2d ed. Washington, D.C.: CQ Press, 1998.

Carter, Lief H. *Reason in Law,* 4th ed. New York: HarperCollins, 1994.

———. *An Introduction to Constitutional Interpretation: Cases in Law and Religion.* New York: Longman, 1991.

———. *Contemporary Constitutional Lawmaking.* New York: Pergamon Press, 1985.

Casper, Jonathan. *The Politics of Civil Liberties.* New York: Harper and Row, 1972.

Clayton, Cornell W., and Howard Gillman, eds. *Supreme Court Decision-Making: New Institutionalist Approaches.* Chicago: University of Chicago Press, 1999, 176.

Crosskey, W. W., and William Jeffrey Jr. *Politics and the Constitution in the History of the United States.* Chicago: University of Chicago Press, 1980.

Duxbury, Neil. *Patterns of American Jurisprudence.* Oxford: Clarendon Press, 1995.

Dworkin, Ronald. *Taking Rights Seriously.* Cambridge: Harvard University Press, 1977.

Epstein, Lee, and Jack Knight. *The Choices Justices Make.* Washington, D.C.: CQ Press, 1998.

Epstein, Lee, Jeffrey A. Segal, Harold J. Spaeth, and Thomas G. Walker. *The Supreme Court Compendium: Data, Decisions, and Developments*, 2d ed. Washington, D.C.: Congressional Quarterly, 1996.

Epstein, Lee, Thomas G. Walker, and William Dixon. "On the Mysterious Demise of Consensual Norms in the United States Supreme Court." *Journal of Politics* 50 (1988): 361–389.

Fisher, Louis. *Constitutional Dialogues*. Princeton: Princeton University Press, 1988.

Gibson, James L. "Judges' Role Orientations, Attitudes, and Decisions." *American Political Science Review* 72 (1978): 911–924.

Gillman, Howard. *The Constitution Besieged: The Rise and Demise of Lochner Era Police Powers Jurisprudence*. Durham: Duke University Press, 1993.

Goldstein, Leslie Friedman. *In Defense of the Text*. Savage, Md.: Rowman and Littlefield, 1991.

Goodhart, Arthur L. "Determining the Ratio Decidendi of a Case." *Yale Law Journal* 40 (1930): 161.

Halpern, Stephen C., and Charles M. Lamb, eds. *Supreme Court Activism and Restraint*. Lexington, Mass.: D. C. Heath, 1982.

Howard, J. Woodford. "On the Fluidity of Judicial Choice." *American Political Science Review* 62 (1968): 43–56.

Kahn, Ronald. "Institutional Norms and Supreme Court Decision-Making: The Rehnquist Court on Privacy and Religion." In *Supreme Court Decision-Making: New Institutionalist Approaches*. Ed. Cornell W. Clayton and Howard Gillman. Chicago: University of Chicago Press, 1999.

———. *The Supreme Court and Constitutional Theory*. Lawrence: University Press of Kansas, 1994.

Knight, Jack, and Lee Epstein, "The Norm of Stare Decisis." *American Journal of Political Science* 40 (1996): 1018–35.

Lawrence, Susan E. *The Poor in Court*. Princeton: Princeton University Press, 1990.

Lee, Thomas R. "Stare Decisis in Historical Perspective: From the Founding Era to the Rehnquist Court." *Vanderbilt Law Review* 52 (1999): 647–734.

Levinson, Sanford V. *Constitutional Faith*. Princeton: Princeton University Press, 1988.

Levy, Leonard W. *Origins of the Bill of Rights*. New Haven: Yale University Press, 1999.

Lynch, Joseph M. *Negotiating the Constitution: The Earliest Debates over Original Intent*. Ithaca: Cornell University Press, 1999.

Maltzman, Forrest, and Paul J. Wahlbeck. "May It Please the Chief? Opinion Assignments in the Rehnquist Court." *American Journal of Political Science* 40 (1996): 421–443.

———. "Strategic Policy Considerations and Voting Fluidity on the Burger Court." *American Political Science Review* 90 (1996): 581–592.

Maltzman, Forest, Paul J. Wahlbeck, and James Spriggs. *Crafting Law on the Supreme Court: The Collegial Game*. New York: Cambridge University Press, 2000.

Marshall, Thomas. *Public Opinion and the Supreme Court*. New York: Unwin Hyman, 1989.

Marshall, Thurgood. "Reflections on the Bicentennial of the United States Constitution." *Harvard Law Review* 101 (1987): 1.

Martin, Fenton S., and Robert U. Goehlert. *The U.S. Supreme Court: A Bibliography*. Washington, D.C.: Congressional Quarterly, 1990.

McCloskey, Robert G. *The American Supreme Court*. Chicago: University of Chicago Press, 1960.

McGuire, Kevin T. *The Supreme Court Bar: Legal Elites in the Washington Community*. Charlottesville: University Press of Virginia, 1993.

Mishler, William, and Reginald S. Sheehan. "The Supreme Court as a Counter-Majoritarian Institution? The Impact of Public Opinion on Supreme Court Decisions." *American Political Science Review* 87 (1993): 87–101.

Murphy, Walter J. *Elements of Judicial Strategy*. Chicago: University of Chicago Press, 1964.

Norpoth, Helmut, and Jeffrey A. Segal. "Popular Influence in Supreme Court Decisions." *American Political Science Review* 88 (1994): 711–716.

Pacelle, Richard L., Jr. *The Transformation of the Supreme Court's Agenda*. Boulder: Westview Press, 1991.

Perry, H. W., Jr. *Deciding to Decide: Agenda Setting in the United States Supreme Court*. Cambridge: Harvard University Press, 1991.

Perry, Michael J. *The Constitution in the Courts: Law or Politics?* New York: Oxford University Press, 1994.

Porto, Brian L. *The Craft of Legal Reasoning*. Fort Worth: Harcourt Brace, 1998.

Posner, Richard. *The Problems of Jurisprudence*. Cambridge: Harvard University Press, 1990.

Powell, Lewis F., Jr. "What Really Goes on at the Supreme Court." *American Bar Association Journal* 66 (1980): 721.

Pritchett, C. Herman. *The Roosevelt Court*. New York: Macmillan, 1948.

Provine, Doris Marie. *Case Selection in the United States Supreme Court*. University of Chicago Press, 1980.

Rehnquist, William. "The Notion of a Living Constitution. *Texas Law Review* 54 (1976): 693.

Segal, Jeffrey A. "Predicting Supreme Court Cases Probabilistically: The Search and Seizure Cases, 1962–1984." *American Political Science Review* 78 (1984): 891–900.

Segal, Jeffrey A., and Harold J. Spaeth. *The Supreme Court and the Attitudinal Model*. New York: Cambridge University Press, 1993.

Sherry, Suzanna. "Textualism and Judgment." *George Washington Law Review* 66 (1998): 1148–52.

Slotnick, Elliot F. "Who Speaks for the Court? Majority Opinion Assignment from Taft to Burger." *American Journal of Political Science* 23 (1979): 60–77.

Smith, Rogers M., "Political Jurisprudence, The 'New Institutionalism,' and the Future of Public Law." *American Political Science Review* 82 (1988): 89–108.

Spaeth, Harold J., and Jeffrey A. Segal. *Majority Rule or Minority Will*. New York: Cambridge University Press, 1999.

Stearns, Maxwell L. *Constitutional Process: A Social Choice Analysis of Supreme Court Decision Making*. Ann Arbor: University of Michigan Press, 2000.

Sunstein, Cass R. *The Partial Constitution*. Cambridge: Harvard University Press, 1993.

Tribe, Laurence H., and Michael C. Dorf. *On Reading the Constitution.* Cambridge: Harvard University Press, 1991.

Tushnet, Mark V. "A Note on the Revival of Textualism." *Southern California Law Review* 58 (1985): 683–700.

van Geel, T. R. *Understanding Supreme Court Opinions.* New York: Longman, 1991.

Wahlbeck, Paul J., James F. Spriggs, and Forrest Maltzman. "Marshalling the Court: Bargaining and Accommodation on the United States Supreme Court." *American Journal of Political Science* 42 (1998): 294–315.

Walker, Thomas G., and Lee Epstein. *The Supreme Court of the United States: An Introduction.* New York: St. Martin's Press, 1992.

Wasby, Stephen L. *The Supreme Court in the Federal Judicial System,* 4th ed. Chicago: Nelson-Hall, 1993.

Wechsler, Herbert. "Toward Neutral Principles of Constitutional Law." *Harvard Law Review* 43 (1959): 1–35.

Wellington, Harry H. *Interpreting the Constitution: The Supreme Court and the Process of Adjudication.* New Haven: Yale University Press, 1990.

Whittington, Keith E. *Constitutional Interpretation: Textual Meaning, Original Intent, and Judicial Review.* Lawrence: University Press of Kansas, 1999.

CHAPTER 2

THE JUDICIARY: INSTITUTIONAL POWERS AND CONSTRAINTS

I N 1989 Congress passed the Flag Protection Act, which penalized by a one-year jail sentence and a thousand dollar fine anyone who "knowingly mutilates, defaces, physically defiles, burns, maintains on the floor or ground, or tramples upon any flag of the United States." Just one year later, in *United States v. Eichman,* the U.S. Supreme Court struck down the law as a violation of the First Amendment. What the Court did was a rare, but not unexpected, act. For nearly two centuries federal courts have exerted the power of judicial review, the power to review acts of government to determine their compatibility with the U.S. Constitution. Despite the fact that the Constitution does not explicitly give them such power, the courts' authority to do so has been challenged only occasionally. Today, we take for granted the notion that federal courts may review government actions and strike them down if they violate constitutional mandates.

Nevertheless, when courts exert this power, as the U.S. Supreme Court did in *Eichman,* they provoke controversy. Look at it from this perspective: Congress, composed of officials we *elect,* passed the Flag Protection Act, which was then rendered invalid by a Supreme Court of *unelected* judges. Such an occurrence strikes some people as odd, perhaps even antidemocratic. Why should we Americans allow a branch of government, over which we have no electoral control, to review and nullify the actions of the government officials we elect to represent us?

As we shall see throughout the book, the alleged anti-democratic nature of judicial review is just one of many controversies surrounding the practice. To appreciate them fully, it is important to have a firm grasp of the development of judicial review in the United States. Many of the early justifications for its practice are still fueling disputes.

Judicial review is the primary weapon that federal courts have to keep the other branches of government in check. Because the power could be awesome in scope, many critics tend to emphasize it to the neglect of factors that constrain its use. In the second part of this chapter, we explore the limits on judicial power. An appreciation of both aspects of judicial power is necessary to understand the cases in this chapter and those to come.

JUDICIAL REVIEW

Even though judicial review is the most powerful tool of federal courts and there is evidence that the Framers intended for courts to have it, it is not mentioned in the Constitution. Early in U.S. history, federal courts claimed it for themselves. In *Hylton v. United States* (1796) Daniel Hylton challenged the constitutionality of a 1793 federal tax on carriages. According to Hylton, the act violated the constitutional mandate that direct taxes must be apportioned on the basis of population. With only three justices participating, the Court upheld the act. But by even considering it, the Court in effect used its authority to review acts of Congress.

Not until 1803, however, did the Court invoke judicial

William Marbury

John Marshall

review to strike down legislation deemed incompatible with the U.S. Constitution. That decision came in the landmark case *Marbury v. Madison*. How does Chief Justice John Marshall justify the Court's power to strike down legislation when the newly framed Constitution failed to confer judicial review on the Court?

Marbury v. Madison

1 CR. (5 U.S.) 137 (1803)
www.law.cornell.edu/supct/cases/name.htm
Vote: 4 (Chase, Marshall, Paterson, Washington)
    0
Opinion of the Court: Marshall
Not participating: Cushing, Moore

When voting in the presidential election of 1800 was over, it was apparent that President John Adams, the Federalist candidate, had lost after a long and bitter campaign, but it was not clear who the winner was. In those days voters did not elect a single ticket consisting of a candidate for president and a candidate for vice president; rather, the person with the most votes became president, and the second place person became vice president. In 1800 the voting had resulted in a tie between Republican candidate Thomas Jefferson and his running mate, Aaron Burr, and the election had to be settled in the House of Representatives. In February 1801 the House elected Jefferson. Because the Federalists had lost both the presidential election and their majority in Congress, they took steps to maintain control of the third branch of government, the judiciary.

The lame-duck Congress enacted the Circuit Court Act of 1801, which created six new circuit courts and several district courts to accommodate the new states of Kentucky, Tennessee, and Vermont. These new courts needed judges and support staff such as attorneys, marshals, and clerks. As a result, during his last six months in office, Adams made more than two hundred nominations, with sixteen judgeships (the "midnight appointments") approved by the Senate during his final two weeks as president.

An even more important opportunity arose in December 1800, when the third chief justice of the United States, Federalist Oliver Ellsworth, resigned so that Adams—not Jefferson—could name his replacement. Adams offered the post to John Jay, who had served as the first chief justice before leaving to take what was in those days a more prestigious job—the governorship of New York. When Jay refused, Adams turned to his secretary of state, John Marshall, an ardent Federalist. The Senate confirmed Marshall in January 1801, while he continued as secretary of state.

In addition, the Federalist Congress passed the Organic Act authorizing Adams to appoint forty-two justices of the peace for the District of Columbia. It was this seemingly innocuous law that set the stage for the drama of *Marbury v. Madison.* In the confusion of the Adams administration's last days in office, Marshall, the outgoing secretary of state, failed to deliver some of these commissions. When the new administration came into office, James Madison, the new secretary of state, acting under orders from Jefferson, refused to deliver at least five commissions.[1] Some years later, Jefferson explained the situation this way: "I found the commissions on the table of the Department of State, on my entrance into office, and I forbade their delivery. Whatever is in the Executive offices is certainly deemed to be in the hands of the President, and in this case, was actually in my hands, because when I countermanded them, there was as yet no Secretary of State."[2]

As a result, in 1801 William Marbury and three others who were denied their commissions went *directly* to the Supreme Court (that is, they invoked the Court's original jurisdiction rather than beginning the case in a lower court) and asked it to issue a writ of mandamus ordering Madison to deliver the commissions. Marbury thought he could take his case directly to the Court because Section 13 of the 1789 Judiciary Act gave the Court the power to issue writs of mandamus to anyone holding federal office:

James Madison

Thomas Jefferson

1. Historical accounts differ, but it seems that Jefferson decreased the number of Adams's appointments to justice of the peace positions to thirty from forty-two. Twenty-five of the thirty appointees received their commissions, but five—including William Marbury—did not. See Francis N. Stites, *John Marshall* (Boston: Little, Brown, 1981), 84.

2. Quoted in Charles Warren, *The Supreme Court in United States History,* vol. 1 (Boston: Little, Brown, 1922), 244.

The Supreme Court . . . shall have power to issue . . . writs of mandamus, in cases warranted by the principles and usages of law, to any courts appointed, or persons holding office, under the authority of the United States.

In this volatile political climate, Marshall, now serving as chief justice, was perhaps in the most tenuous position of all. He had been a supporter of the Federalist Party, which now looked to him to "scold" the Jefferson administration. Marshall, however, wanted to avoid a confrontation between the Jefferson administration and the Supreme Court, which not only seemed imminent, but also could end in disaster for the struggling nation. Note the year in which the Court handed down *Marbury*. The case was not decided until two years after Marbury filed suit because Congress and the Jefferson administration had abolished the 1802 term of the Court.

The following of the court was delivered by THE CHIEF JUSTICE.

Opinion of the Court.

The peculiar delicacy of this case, the novelty of some of its circumstances, and the real difficulty attending the points which occur in it, require a complete exposition of the principles, on which the opinion to be given by the court, is founded. . . .

In the order in which the court has viewed this subject, the following questions have been considered and decided.

1st. Has the applicant a right to the commission he demands?

2dly. If he has a right, and that right has been violated, do the laws of his country afford him a remedy?

3dly. If they do afford him a remedy, is it a *mandamus* issuing from this court?

The first object of enquiry is,

1st. Has the applicant a right to the commission he demands? . . .

In order to determine whether he is entitled to this commission, it becomes necessary to enquire whether he has been appointed to the office. For if he has been appointed, the law continues him in office for five years, and he is entitled to the possession of those evidences of office, which, being completed, became his property. . . .

It is . . . decidedly the opinion of the court, that when a commission has been signed by the President, the appointment is made; and that the commission is complete, when the seal of the United States has been affixed to it by the secretary of state. . . .

Mr. Marbury, then, since his commission was signed by the President, and sealed by the secretary of state, was appointed; and as the law creating the office, gave the officer a right to hold for five years, independent of the executive, the appointment was not revocable; but vested in the officer legal rights, which are protected by the laws of his country.

To withhold his commission, therefore, is an act deemed by the court not warranted by law, but violative of a vested legal right.

This brings us to the second enquiry; which is,

2dly. If he has a right, and that right has been violated, do the laws of his country afford him a remedy?

The very essence of civil liberty certainly consists in the right of every individual to claim the protection of the laws, whenever he receives an injury. One of the first duties of government is to afford that protection. . . .

The government of the United States has been emphatically termed a government of laws, and not of men. It will certainly cease to deserve this high appellation, if the laws furnish no remedy for the violation of a vested legal right. . . .

It is then the opinion of the court,

1st. That by signing the commission of Mr. Marbury, the president of the United States appointed him a justice of peace, for the county of Washington in the district of Columbia; and that the seal of the United States, affixed thereto by the secretary of state, is conclusive testimony of the verity of the signature, and of the completion of the appointment; and that the appointment conferred on him a legal right to the office for the space of five years.

2dly. That, having this legal title to the office, he has a consequent right to the commission; a refusal to deliver which, is a plain violation of that right, for which the laws of his country afford him a remedy.

It remains to be enquired whether,

3dly. He is entitled to the remedy for which he applies. . . .

The act to establish the judicial courts of the United States authorizes the supreme court "to issue writs of mandamus, in cases warranted by the principles and usages of law, to any courts appointed, or persons holding office, under the authority of the United States."

The secretary of state, being a person holding an office under the authority of the United States, is precisely within the letter of the description; and if this court is not authorized to issue a writ of mandamus to such an officer, it must be because the law is unconstitutional, and therefore absolutely incapable of conferring the authority, and assigning the duties which its words purport to confer and assign.

The constitution vests the whole judicial power of the United States in one supreme court, and such inferior courts as congress shall, from time to time, ordain and establish. This power is expressly extended to all cases arising under the laws of the United States; and consequently, in some form, may be exercised over the present case; because the right claimed is given by a law of the United States.

In the distribution of this power it is declared that "the supreme court shall have original jurisdiction in all cases affecting ambassadors, other public ministers and consuls, and those in which a state shall be a party. In all other cases, the supreme court shall have appellate jurisdiction."

It has been insisted, at the bar, that as the original grant of jurisdiction, to the supreme and inferior courts, is general, and the clause, assigning original jurisdiction to the supreme court, contains no negative or restrictive words; the power remains to the legislature, to assign original jurisdiction to that court in other cases than those specified in the article which has been recited; provided those cases belong to the judicial power of the United States.

If it had been intended to leave it in the discretion of the legislature to apportion the judicial power between the supreme and inferior courts according to the will of that body, it would certainly have been useless to have proceeded further than to have defined the judicial power, and the tribunals in which it should be vested. The subsequent part of the section is mere surplussage, is entirely without meaning, if such is to be the construction. If congress remains at liberty to give this court appellate jurisdiction, where the constitution has declared their jurisdiction shall be original; and original jurisdiction where the constitution has declared it shall be appellate; the distribution of jurisdiction, made in the constitution, is form without substance.

Affirmative words are often, in their operation, negative of other objects than those affirmed; and in this case, a neg-ative or exclusive sense must be given to them or they have no operation at all.

It cannot be presumed that any clause in the constitution is intended to be without effect; and therefore such a construction is inadmissible, unless the words require it.

If the solicitude of the convention, respecting our peace with foreign powers, induced a provision that the supreme court should take original jurisdiction in cases which might be supposed to affect them; yet the clause would have proceeded no further than to provide for such cases, if no further restriction on the powers of congress had been intended. That they should have appellate jurisdiction in all other cases, with such exceptions as congress might make, is no restriction; unless the words be deemed exclusive of original jurisdiction.

When an instrument organizing fundamentally a judicial system, divides it into one supreme, and so many inferior courts as the legislature may ordain and establish; then enumerates its powers, and proceeds so far to distribute them, as to define the jurisdiction of the supreme court by declaring the cases in which it shall take original jurisdiction, and that in others it shall take appellate jurisdiction; the plain import of the words seems to be, that in one class of cases its jurisdiction is original, and not appellate; in the other it is appellate, and not original. If any other construction would render the clause inoperative, that is an additional reason for rejecting such other construction, and for adhering to their obvious meaning.

To enable this court then to issue a mandamus, it must be shewn to be an exercise of appellate jurisdiction, or to be necessary to enable them to exercise appellate jurisdiction.

It has been stated at the bar that the appellate jurisdiction may be exercised in a variety of forms, and that if it be the will of the legislature that a mandamus should be used for that purpose, that will must be obeyed. This is true, yet the jurisdiction must be appellate, not original.

It is the essential criterion of appellate jurisdiction, that it revises and corrects the proceedings in a cause already instituted, and does not create that cause. Although, therefore, a mandamus may be directed to courts, yet to issue such a writ to an officer for the delivery of a paper, is in effect the same as to sustain an original action for that paper, and therefore seems not to belong to appellate, but to original jurisdiction. Neither is it necessary in such a case as this, to enable the court to exercise its appellate jurisdiction.

The authority, therefore, given to the supreme court, by the act establishing the judicial courts of the United States, to issue writs of mandamus to public officers, appears not to be warranted by the constitution; and it becomes necessary to enquire whether a jurisdiction, so conferred, can be exercised.

The question, whether an act, repugnant to the constitution, can become the law of the land, is a question deeply interesting to the United States; but, happily, not of an intricacy proportioned to its interest. It seems only necessary to recognise certain principles, supposed to have been long and well established, to decide it.

That the people have an original right to establish, for their future government, such principles as, in their opinion, shall most conduce to their own happiness, is the basis, on which the whole American fabric has been erected. The exercise of this original right is a very great exertion; nor can it, nor ought it to be frequently repeated. The principles, therefore, so established, are deemed fundamental. And as the authority, from which they proceed, is supreme, and can seldom act, they are designed to be permanent.

This original and supreme will organizes the government, and assigns, to different departments, their respective powers. It may either stop here; or establish certain limits not to be transcended by those departments.

The government of the United States is of the latter description. The powers of the legislature are defined, and limited; and that those limits may not be mistaken, or forgotten, the constitution is written. To what purpose are powers limited, and to what purpose is that limitation committed to writing, if these limits may, at any time, be passed by those intended to be restrained? The distinction, between a government with limited and unlimited powers, is abolished, if those limits do not confine the persons on whom they are imposed, and if acts prohibited and acts allowed, are of equal obligation. It is a proposition too plain to be contested, that the constitution controls any legislative act repugnant to it; or, that the legislature may alter the constitution by an ordinary act.

Between these alternatives there is no middle ground. The constitution is either a superior, paramount law, unchangeable by ordinary means, or it is on a level with ordinary legislative acts, and like other acts, is alterable when the legislature shall please to alter it.

If the former part of the alternative be true, then a leg-

islative act contrary to the constitution is not law: if the latter part be true, then written constitutions are absurd attempts, on the part of the people, to limit a power, in its own nature illimitable.

Certainly all those who have framed written constitutions contemplate them as forming the fundamental and paramount law of the nation, and consequently the theory of every such government must be, that an act of the legislature, repugnant to the constitution, is void.

This theory is essentially attached to a written constitution, and is consequently to be considered, by this court, as one of the fundamental principles of our society. It is not therefore to be lost sight of in the further consideration of this subject.

If an act of the legislature, repugnant to the constitution, is void, does it, notwithstanding its invalidity, bind the courts, and oblige them to give it effect? Or, in other words, though it be not law, does it constitute a rule as operative as if it was a law? This would be to overthrow in fact what was established in theory; and would seem, at first view, an absurdity too gross to be insisted on. It shall, however, receive a more attentive consideration.

It is emphatically the province and duty of the judicial department to say what the law is. Those who apply the rule to particular cases, must of necessity expound and interpret that rule. If two laws conflict with each other, the courts must decide on the operation of each.

So if a law be in opposition to the constitution; if both the law and the constitution apply to a particular case, so that the court must either decide that case conformably to the law, disregarding the constitution; or conformably to the constitution, disregarding the law; the court must determine which of these conflicting rules governs the case. This is of the very essence of judicial duty.

If then the courts are to regard the constitution; and the constitution is superior to any ordinary act of the legislature; the constitution, and not such ordinary act, must govern the case to which they both apply.

Those then who controvert the principle that the constitution is to be considered, in court, as a paramount law, are reduced to the necessity of maintaining that courts must close their eyes on the constitution, and see only the law.

This doctrine would subvert the very foundation of all written constitutions. It would declare that an act, which, according to the principles and theory of our government, is entirely void; is yet, in practice, completely obligatory. It would declare, that if the legislature shall do what is expressly forbidden, such act, notwithstanding the express prohibition, is in reality effectual. It would be giving to the legislature a practical and real omnipotence, with the same breath which professes to restrict their powers within narrow limits. It is prescribing limits, and declaring that those limits may be passed at pleasure.

That it thus reduces to nothing what we have deemed the greatest improvement on political institutions—a written constitution—would of itself be sufficient, in America, where written constitutions have been viewed with so much reverence, for rejecting the construction. But the peculiar expressions of the constitution of the United States furnish additional arguments in favour of its rejection.

The judicial power of the United States is extended to all cases arising under the constitution.

Could it be the intention of those who gave this power, to say that, in using it, the constitution should not be looked into? That a case arising under the constitution should be decided without examining the instrument under which it arises?

This is too extravagant to be maintained.

In some cases then, the constitution must be looked into by the judges. And if they can open it at all, what part of it are they forbidden to read, or to obey?

There are many other parts of the constitution which serve to illustrate this subject.

It is declared that "no tax or duty shall be laid on articles exported from any state." Suppose a duty on the export of cotton, of tobacco, or of flour; and a suit instituted to recover it. Ought judgment to be rendered in such a case? ought the judges to close their eyes on the constitution, and only see the law.

The constitution declares that "no bill of attainder or *ex post facto* law shall be passed."

If, however, such a bill should be passed and a person should be prosecuted under it; must the court condemn to death those victims whom the constitution endeavours to preserve?

"No person," says the constitution, "shall be convicted of treason unless on the testimony of two witnesses to the same overt act, or on confession in open court."

Here the language of the constitution is addressed especially to the courts. It prescribes, directly for them, a rule of evidence not to be departed from. If the legislature should change that rule, and declare *one* witness, or a confession *out* of court, sufficient for conviction, must the constitutional principle yield to the legislative act?

From these, and many other selections which might be made, it is apparent, that the Framers of the constitution contemplated that instrument, as a rule for the government of *courts*, as well as of the legislature.

Why otherwise does it direct the judges to take an oath to support it? This oath certainly applies, in an especial manner, to their conduct in their official character. How immoral to impose it on them, if they were to be used as the instruments, and the knowing instruments, for violating what they swear to support!

The oath of office, too, imposed by the legislature, is completely demonstrative of the legislative opinion on this subject. It is in these words, "I do solemnly swear that I will administer justice without respect to persons, and do equal right to the poor and to the rich; and that I will faithfully and impartially discharge all the duties incumbent on me as according to the best of my abilities and understanding, agreeably to *the constitution*, and laws of the United States."

Why does a judge swear to discharge his duties agreeably to the constitution of the United States, if that constitution forms no rule for his government? if it is closed upon him, and cannot be inspected by him?

If such be the real state of things, this is worse than solemn mockery. To prescribe, or to take this oath, becomes equally a crime.

It is also not entirely worthy of observation, that in declaring what shall be the *supreme law* of the land, the *constitution* itself is first mentioned; and not the laws of the United States generally, but those only which shall be made in *pursuance* of the constitution, have that rank.

Thus, the particular phraseology of the constitution of the United States confirms and strengthens the principle, supposed to be essential to all written constitutions, that a law repugnant to the constitution is void; and that *courts*, as well as other departments, are bound by that instrument.

The rule must be discharged.

Many scholars consider Marshall's opinion in *Marbury* stunning, even brilliant. Think about the way the chief justice dealt with a delicate political situation. By ruling against Marbury, he avoided a potentially devastating clash with the new president; but, by exerting the power of judicial review, he sent a clear signal to Jefferson that the Court had a major role to play in the American government.

The decision helped to fix Marshall's reputation as perhaps the greatest justice in Supreme Court history. More relevant to our concerns, *Marbury* fully established the Court's authority to review and strike down government actions that were incompatible with the Constitution.[3] In Marshall's view, such authority, while not explicit in the Constitution, was clearly intended by the Framers of that document. Was he correct? His opinion makes a plausible argument, and current justices continue to invoke the logic of *Marbury*. Consider the Court's decision in *City of Boerne v. Flores* (1997) *(see pages 135–140)*. At issue was the Religious Freedom Restoration Act of 1993 (RFRA), which Congress passed in response to *Employment Division v. Smith* (1990) *(pages 126–133)*. RFRA directed the Court to adopt a particular standard of law in constitutional cases involving the Free Exercise Clause of the First Amendment—a standard the Court had rejected in *Smith*.

In striking down Congress's effort at constitutional interpretation, the Court did not hesitate to cite *Marbury:*

Our national experience teaches that the Constitution is preserved best when each part of the government respects both the Constitution and the proper actions and determinations of the other branches. When the Court has interpreted the Constitution, it has acted within the province of the Judicial Branch, which embraces the duty to say what the law is. *Marbury v. Madison.* When the political branches of the Government act against the background of a judicial interpretation of the Constitution already issued, it must be understood that in later cases and controversies the Court will treat its precedents with the respect due them under settled principles, including

stare decisis, and contrary expectations must be disappointed. RFRA was designed to control cases and controversies, such as the one before us; but as the provisions of the federal statute here invoked are beyond congressional authority, it is this Court's precedent, not RFRA, which must control.

It is not only current U.S. Supreme Court justices who continue to cite *Marbury* with approval. Many countries have written judicial review into their constitutions, refusing to leave its establishment to chance *(see Box 2-1).*

Even so, some judges and scholars have pointed out problems with *Marbury*. Table 2-1 summarizes the arguments over judicial review, many of which will resurface in the pages to come.[4] These controversies are important because they place judicial review into a theoretical context for debate. But the questions may never be resolved: as one side finds support for its position, the other side always does too.

Let us consider instead several issues arising from the way the Court actually has exercised the power of judicial review: the number of times it has invoked the power to strike laws and the significance of those decisions. As Lawrence Baum suggests, investigation of these issues can help us achieve a better understanding of judicial review and place it in a realistic context.[5] First, how often has the Court overturned a federal, state, or local law or ordinance? Figure 1-6 *(page 36)* depicts those numbers over time. The data seem to indicate that the Court has made frequent use of the power, striking down close to 1,500 government acts since 1790. However, as Baum notes, those acts are but a "minute fraction" of the laws enacted at various levels of government. Between the 1790s and 1990s, for example, Congress passed more than sixty thousand laws, with the Court striking far less than 1 percent of them.

3. In *Marbury* the Court addressed only the power to review acts of the federal government. Could the Court exert judicial review over the states? According to Section 25 of the 1789 Judiciary Act, it could. Congress expanded the Court's appellate jurisdiction to cover appeals from a state's highest court if that court upheld a state law against challenges of unconstitutionality or denied some claim based on the U.S. Constitution, federal laws, or treaties. In *Martin v. Hunter's Lessee* (1816) and *Cohens v. Virginia* (1821), the justices asserted their power to review state court decisions by upholding Section 25 of the Judiciary Act.

4. Some critics attack specific aspects of the ruling. Jefferson argued that once Marshall ruled that the Court did not have jurisdiction, he should have dismissed it. Another criticism is that Section 13 of the 1789 Judiciary Act—which *Marbury* held unconstitutional—did not "even remotely suggest an expansion of the Supreme Court's original jurisdiction." If this is so, then Marshall "had nothing to declare unconstitutional!" A counterargument is that Section 13 was seen as expanding the Court's original jurisdiction or else why did Marbury bring his suit directly to the Court? And why did his attorney specifically note that the act was constitutional?

5. Lawrence Baum, *The Supreme Court,* 7th ed. (Washington, D.C.: CQ Press, 2001), 194–202.

BOX 2-1 JUDICIAL REVIEW IN GLOBAL PERSPECTIVE

JUDICIAL AUTHORITY to invalidate acts of coordinate branches is not unique to the United States, although it is fair to say that the prestige of the U.S. Supreme Court has provided a model and incentive for other countries. By the middle of the nineteenth century, the Judicial Committee of the British Privy Council was functioning as a kind of constitutional arbiter for colonial governments within the British Empire—but not for the United Kingdom itself. Then Canada in the late nineteenth century and Australia in the first years of the twentieth created their own systems of constitutional review.

In the nineteenth century Argentina also modeled its Corte Suprema on that of the United States and even instructed its judges to pay special attention to precedents of the American tribunal. In the twentieth century Austria, Ireland, India, and the Philippines adopted judicial review, and variations of this power can be found in Norway, Switzerland, much of Latin America, and some countries in Africa.

After World War II the three defeated Axis powers—Italy, Japan, and West Germany—all institutionalized judicial review in their new constitutions. This development was due in part to a revulsion against their recent experiences with unchecked political power and in part to the influence of American occupying authorities. Japan, where the constitutional document was largely drafted by Americans, follows the decentralized model of the United States: the power of constitutional review is diffused throughout the entire judicial system.[1] Any court of general jurisdiction can declare a legislative or executive act invalid.

Germany and Italy, and later Belgium, Portugal, and Spain, followed a centralized model first adopted in the Austrian constitution of 1920. Each country has a single constitutional court (although some sit in divisions or senates) that has a judicial monopoly on reviewing acts of government for their compatibility with their constitutions. The most a lower court judge can do when a constitutional issue is raised is to refer the problem to the specialized constitutional court. *(See Box 1-2, page 21.)*

After the Berlin Wall collapsed in 1989 and the Soviet Union disintegrated soon after, many East European republics looked to judges' interpreting a constitutional text with a bill of rights to protect their new-found liberties. Most opted for centralized systems of constitutional review, establishing ordinary tribunals and a separate constitutional court. They made this choice despite familiarity with Chief Justice John Marshall's argument for a decentralized court system in *Marbury*; namely, all judges may face the problem of a conflict between a statute or executive order, on the one hand, and the terms of a constitutional document on the other. If judges cannot give preference to the constitutional provision over ordinary legislation or an executive act, they violate their oath to support the constitution.

The experience of these tribunals has been quite varied. The German Constitutional Court, for example, is largely regarded as a success story. In its first thirty-eight years, that tribunal invalidated 292 Bund (national) and 130 Land (state) laws, provoking frequent complaints that it "judicializes" politics.[2] The Court, however, has survived these attacks and has gone on to create a new and politically significant jurisprudence in the fields of federalism and civil liberties. The Russian Constitutional Court stands (or teeters) in stark contrast. It too began to make extensive use of judicial review to strike down government acts but quickly paid a steep price: In 1993 President Boris Yeltsin suspended the Court's operations; it did not resume its activities until nearly two years later.

1. Walter F. Murphy and Joseph Tanenhaus, eds. *Comparative Constitutional Law* (New York: St. Martin's Press, 1977), chaps. 1–6; C. Neal Tate and Torbjörn Vallinder, eds. *The Global Expansion of Judicial Power: The Judicialization of Politics* (New York: New York University Press, 1995).

2. Donald P. Kommers, *The Constitutional Jurisprudence of the Federal Republic of Germany*, 2d ed. (Durham: Duke University Press, 1997), 52.

SOURCE: Adapted from C. Herman Pritchett, Walter F. Murphy, and Lee Epstein, *Courts, Judges and Politics* (New York: McGraw-Hill, 2000), chap. 6.

TABLE 2-1 Major Controversies over Judicial Review

Controversy	Supporting Judicial Review	Opposing Judicial Review
Framers' Intent: Did the Framers intend the federal courts to exercise judicial review?	The Framers had knowledge of judicial review. Although Marshall often is credited with its first full enunciation, there is evidence that the concept was adopted in England in the 1600s. Morever, between 1776 and 1787, eight of the thirteen colonies incorporated judicial review into their constitutions, and by 1789 various state courts had struck down as unconstitutional eight acts passed by their legislatures. The Framers left judicial review out of the Constitution because they did not want to heighten controversy over Article III review, not because they opposed the practice. The Framers implicitly accepted judicial review. Historians have established that more than half of the delegates to the Constitutional Convention approved of judicial review. And, in *The Federalist Papers*, Hamilton adamantly defended the concept, arguing that one branch of government must safeguard the Constitution and that the courts would be in the best position to undertake that important responsibility.	Even though some states adopted judicial review, their courts rarely exercised the power. When they did, the public outrage that followed provides some indication that the practice was not widely accepted. The participants at the Constitutional Convention rejected the proposed Council of Revision, which would have enabled Supreme Court justices and the president to veto legislative acts.
Judicial Restraint: Should courts (composed of unelected members) defer to the elected institutions of government?	The government needs an umpire who will act neutrally and fairly in interpreting the constitutional strictures.	Unelected judges should defer to the wishes of elected officials, who represent the best interests of the people and who can be removed from office when they do not.
Democratic Checks: Are there sufficient checks on courts to prevent them from using judicial review in a way repugnant to the best interests of the people?	Acting in different combinations, Congress, the president, and the states can, for example, ratify a constitutional amendment to overturn a decision, change the size of the Court, or remove the Court's appellate jurisdiction. While Congress does not often take direct action against the Court, the mere fact that the legislature has weapons to use against the judiciary may influence the justices. In other words, if the justices care about the ultimate state of the law, they might seek to accommodate the wishes of Congress rather than face the wrath of the legislators, which could lead to the reversal of a ruling. It is the existence of congressional threat—not its actual advocation—that may affect how the Court rules in a given case. Some scholars suggest that this dynamic explains why the justices rarely strike down congressional acts.	The problem with these checks, in the eyes of some analysts, is that they are very rarely invoked: only four admendments have explicitly overturned Court decisions; the Court's size has not been changed since 1869; and only once has Congress removed the Court's appellate jurisdiction.

(table continues)

TABLE 2-1 *(continued)*

Controversy	Supporting Judicial Review	Opposing Judicial Review
Role of Courts in a Democratic Society: Do courts need the power of judicial review to protect minority interests?	The Court must have the power of judicial review if it is to fulfill its most important constitutional assignment: protection of minority rights. By their very nature—the fact that they are elected—legislatures and executives reflect the interests of the majority. Those interests may take action that is blatantly unconstitutional. So that the majority cannot tyrannize a minority, it is necessary for the one branch of government that lacks any electoral connection to have the power of judicial review.	This position conflicts with the idea of the Court as a body that defers to the elected branches. Courts have not always used judicial review in this manner: some of the acts they strike down are those that harmed a "privileged class," not disadvantaged minorities. For example, in *City of Richmond v. J. A. Croson Co.* (1989) and *Adarand Constructors v. Peña* (1995), the justices struck down affirmative action programs designed to help minority interests.

SOURCE: We adopt this framework from David Adamany, "The Supreme Court," in *The American Courts: A Critical Assessment*, ed. John B. Gates and Charles A. Johnson (Washington, D.C.: CQ Press, 1991).

Second, how significant are the laws the Court strikes down? Using *Scott v. Sandford* (1857) as an illustration, some argue that the Court often strikes significant legislation. Undoubtedly, that opinion had major consequences: by ruling that Congress could not prohibit slavery in the territories and by striking down the Missouri Compromise, even though the law had already been repealed, the Court fueled the growing divisions between the North and South, providing a major impetus for the Civil War. The decision also tarnished the prestige of the Court and the reputation of Chief Justice Roger B. Taney.

Some other Court opinions striking down government acts have been almost as important as *Scott*, for example, those nullifying state abortion and segregation laws, the federal child labor acts, and many pieces of New Deal legislation. But many others were minor. Consider *Monongahela Navigation Co. v. United States* (1893), in which the Court struck down, on Fifth Amendment grounds, a law concerning the amount of money to be paid to the United States by companies for the "purchase or condemnation of a certain lock and dam in the Monongahela River."

Despite the ambiguous record, we can reach two conclusions about the Court's use of judicial review. One is that "while judicial review allows the Court to play a major role in policy making, it certainly has not made the Court the dominant national policy maker."[6] The other is that the Court's *use* of judicial review may not be what is significant. Rather, like the president's ability to veto congressional legislation, its power may be the threat of its invocation. In either case, it has provided federal courts with their most significant political weapon.

CONSTRAINTS ON JUDICIAL POWER

Given all the attention paid to judicial review, it is easy to forget that the power of courts to exercise it and courts' judicial authority, more generally, has substantial limits. Article III—or the Court's interpretation of it—places three major constraints on the ability of federal tribunals to hear and decide cases: the court must have authority to hear a case (jurisdiction); the case must be appropriate for judicial resolution (justiciability); and the appropriate party must bring the case (standing). Following is a review of the doctrine surrounding these constraints. As you read, consider not only the Court's interpretation of its own limits but also the justifications it offers. Note in particular how fluid these can be: some Courts tend towards loose constructions of the rules, while others are anxious to enforce them. What factors might explain these different tendencies? Or, to put it

6. Ibid., 206.

another way, to what extent do these constraints limit the Court's authority?

Jurisdiction

According to Chief Justice Salmon P. Chase, "Without jurisdiction the court cannot proceed at all in any cause. Jurisdiction is power to declare the law, and when it ceases to exist, the only function remaining to the court is that of announcing the fact and dismissing the cause."[7] In other words, a court cannot hear a case unless it has the authority—the jurisdiction—to do so.

Article III, Section 2, defines the jurisdiction of U.S. federal courts. Lower courts have the authority to hear disputes involving particular parties and subject matter. The U.S. Supreme Court's jurisdiction is divided into original and appellate: the former are classes of cases that originate in the Court; the latter are those it hears after a lower court.

To what extent does jurisdiction constrain the federal courts? *Marbury v. Madison* provides some answers, although contradictory, to this question. Chief Justice Marshall informed Congress that it could not alter the original jurisdiction of the Court. Having reached this conclusion, perhaps Marshall should have dismissed the case on the grounds that the Court lacked authority to hear it, but that is not what he did.

The issue of appellate jurisdiction is a bit more complex. Article III explicitly states that for those cases over which the Court does not have original jurisdiction, it "shall have appellate Jurisdiction . . . with such Exceptions, and under such Regulations as the Congress shall make." In other words, the Exceptions Clause seems to give Congress authority to alter the Court's appellate jurisdiction.

Has the Supreme Court allowed Congress to do so? In *Martin v. Hunter's Lessee* (1816) the Supreme Court allowed Congress to *expand* its appellate jurisdiction *(see footnote 3)* the question the Court addresses in *Ex parte McCardle* is a bit different. Here the justices must determine if Congress can use its power under the Exceptions Clause to *remove* the Court's appellate jurisdiction over a particular category of cases.

7. *Ex parte McCardle* (1869).

Ex parte McCardle

7 WALL. (74 U.S.) 506 (1869)
www.law.cornell.edu/supct/cases/name.htm
Vote: 8 (Chase, Clifford, Davis, Field, Grier, Miller, Nelson, Swayne)

0

Opinion of the Court: Chase

After the Civil War the Radical Republican Congress imposed a series of restrictions on the South.[8] Known as the Reconstruction laws, they in effect placed the region under military rule. Journalist William McCardle opposed these measures and wrote editorials urging resistance to them. He was arrested for publishing allegedly "incendiary and libelous articles" and held for a trial before a military tribunal, established under Reconstruction.

Because he was a civilian, not a member of any militia, McCardle alleged that he was being illegally held. He petitioned for a writ of habeas corpus—an order issued to determine if a person held in custody is being unlawfully detained or imprisoned—under an 1867 act, which enabled federal judges "to grant habeas corpus to persons detained in violation" of the U.S. Constitution. When this effort failed, McCardle appealed to the U.S. Supreme Court.

In early March 1868 *McCardle* "was very thoroughly and ably [presented] upon the merits" to the U.S. Supreme Court. It was clear to most observers that "no Justice was still making up his mind": the Court's sympathies, as was widely known, lay with McCardle.[9] But before the justices issued their decision, Congress, on March 27, 1868, repealed the 1867 Habeas Corpus Act and removed the Supreme Court's authority to hear appeals emanating from it. This action was meant to punish the Court or, at the very least, to send it a strong message. In 1866, two years before *McCardle*, the Court had

8. For more information on *McCardle*, see Thomas G. Walker and Lee Epstein, "The Role of the Supreme Court in American Society: Playing the Reconstruction Game," in *Contemplating Courts*, ed. Lee Epstein (Washington, D.C.: CQ Press, 1995), 315–346.

9. Charles Fairman, *Reconstruction and Reunion*, vol. 7 of *History of the Supreme Court of the United States* (New York: Macmillan, 1971), 456.

invalidated President Lincoln's use of military tribunals in certain areas.[10] Congress did not want to see the Court take similar action in this dispute. Congress was so adamant on this issue that after President Andrew Johnson vetoed the 1868 repealer act, the legislature overrode the veto.

The Court responded by redocketing the case for oral arguments in March 1869. During the arguments and in its briefs, the government made its position clear: "When the jurisdiction of a court to determine a case or a class of cases depends upon a statute and that statute is repealed, the jurisdiction ceases absolutely." In short, the government contended that the Court no longer had authority to hear the case and should dismiss it.

THE CHIEF JUSTICE delivered the opinion of the Court.

It is unnecessary to consider whether, if Congress had made no exceptions and no regulations, this court might not have exercised general appellate jurisdiction under rules prescribed by itself. From among the earliest Acts of the first Congress, at its first session, was the Act of September 24th, 1789, to establish the judicial courts of the United States. That Act provided for the organization of this court, and prescribed regulations for the exercise of its jurisdiction. . . .

The exception to appellate jurisdiction in the case before us . . . is not an inference from the affirmation of other appellate jurisdiction. It is made in terms. The provision of the Act of 1867, affirming the appellate jurisdiction of this court in cases of habeas corpus, is expressly repealed. It is hardly possible to imagine a plainer instance of positive exception.

We are not at liberty to inquire into the motives of the Legislature. We can only examine into its power under the Constitution; and the power to make exceptions to the appellate jurisdiction of this court is given by express words.

What, then, is the effect of the repealing Act upon the case before us? We cannot doubt as to this. Without jurisdiction the court cannot proceed at all in any cause. Jurisdiction is power to declare the law, and when it ceases to exist, the only function remaining to the court is that of announcing the fact and dismissing the cause. And this is not less clear upon authority than upon principle. . . .

10. That action came in *Ex parte Milligan* (1866).

It is quite clear, therefore, that this . . . court cannot proceed to pronounce judgment in this case, for it has no longer jurisdiction of the appeal; and judicial duty is not less fitly performed by declining ungranted jurisdiction than in exercising firmly that which the Constitution and the laws confer. . . .

The appeal of the petitioner in this case must be dismissed for want of jurisdiction.

As we can see, the Court acceded and declined to hear the case. *McCardle* suggests that Congress has the authority to remove the Court's appellate jurisdiction as it deems necessary. Since *McCardle*, however, Congress has only considered, but not enacted, legislation—at least legislation aimed directly at the Court—to limit the Court's appellate jurisdiction. Table 2-2 lists some of the proposals members of Congress have offered. As noted, many involve controversial issue areas—abortion, prayer in school, busing—leading to the conclusion that modern Congresses are no different from the one that passed the 1868 repealer act: Congress would like to use the Exceptions Clause as a political tool, as a way to restrain the Court, but has yet to do so successfully.

In spite of *McCardle*, there are several reasons to believe that the Court might not uphold proposals of the kind depicted in Table 2-2. One is that *McCardle* was an odd case. According to many scholars, the Court had no choice but to acquiesce to Congress if it wanted to retain its legitimacy in post–Civil War America. The pressures of the day, rather than the Constitution or the beliefs of the justices, may have led to the decision.

Another reason is that a case a few years after *McCardle* cast some doubt on the precedent it seemed to set. In *United States v. Klein* (1872) the Court considered an 1870 law in which Congress sought to impinge on the president's authority to issue executive amnesties. In particular, it required those who wished to recover property taken by the government during the Civil War to prove their loyalty, even if they had received a presidential pardon. Moreover, the law withdrew the U.S. Supreme Court's (and a lower appellate court's) jurisdiction to hear such cases. Although the justices acknowledged that the Ex-

TABLE 2-2 A Sample of Congressional Proposals Aimed at Limiting the U.S. Supreme Court's Appellate Jurisdiction

Issue	Supreme Court Decision Provoking Proposal	Proposal
Criminal confessions	*Miranda v. Arizona* (1966) in which the Court required police to read those under arrest a series of rights.	1968 proposal that would have removed the Court's jurisdiction to hear state cases involving the admissibility of confessions.
School busing	*Swann v. Charlotte-Mecklenburg Board of Education* (1971) in which the Court permitted district courts to fashion their own school desegregation plans, which may include the busing of students to other schools.	During the 1970s and 1980s, many proposals offered to curb the Court's authority to hear busing cases and to limit the authority of courts to order busing.
School prayer	*Engel v. Vitale* (1962) and *Abington School District v. Schempp* (1963), which eliminated voluntary and mandatory prayer in school.	Several proposals, with a major effort coming in 1979, that would have eliminated the Court's as well as all other federal courts' ability to hear any cases involving voluntary school prayer.
Abortion	*Roe v. Wade* (1973) in which the Supreme Court struck down state laws criminalizing abortion. *Roe* legalized abortion during the first two trimesters of pregnancy.	During the 1970s and 1980s, several proposals to remove the Court's authority to hear abortion cases.

ceptions Clause gave Congress the right to remove their appellate jurisdiction "in a particular class of cases," it could not do so only as "a means to an end." That is, in previous cases, the Court had stated that the president had the power to grant pardons. Therefore, Congress was using the Exceptions Clause to skirt those decisions. If the Court allowed this, it would then permit Congress to "prescribe rules of decision to the Judicial Department . . . in cases pending before it," in violation of constitutional mandates requiring the separation of powers.

Still, *Klein* did not settle the issue. Compare, for example, the views of two twentieth-century justices. In 1948 Justice Felix Frankfurter wrote, "Congress need not give this Court any appellate power; it may withdraw appellate jurisdiction once conferred and it may do so even while a case is *sub judice*" [before a judge].[11] Thirteen years later, Justice William O. Douglas remarked, "There is a serious question whether the *McCardle* case could command a majority view today."[12]

Whether the Court would allow Congress to use the Exceptions Clause remains an open question until such litigation occurs. Until then, Chief Justice Chase perhaps summed up the situation best when he noted after

McCardle had been decided that use of the Exceptions Clause was "unusual and hardly to be justified except upon some imperious public exigency."[13]

Justiciability

According to Article III, the judicial power of the federal courts is restricted to "cases" and "controversies." Taken together, these words mean that a litigation must be justiciable—appropriate or suitable for a federal tribunal to hear or to solve. As Chief Justice Earl Warren asserted, cases and controversies

are two complementary but somewhat different limitations. In part those words limit the business of federal courts to questions presented in an adversary context and in a form historically viewed as capable of resolution through the judicial process. And in part those words define the role assigned to the judiciary in a tripartite allocation of power to assure that the federal courts will not intrude into areas committed to the other branches of government. Justiciability is the term of art employed to give expression to this dual limitation placed upon federal courts by the case-and-controversy doctrine.[14]

Although Warren also suggested that "justiciability is itself a concept of uncertain meaning and scope," he elu-

11. *National Mutual Insurance Co. v. Tidewater Transfer Co.* (1949).
12. *Glidden Co. v. Zdanok* (1962).

13. *Ex parte Yerger* (1869).
14. *Flast v. Cohen* (1968).

cidated several types of cases or characteristics of litigation that would render it nonjusticiable. In this section, we treat five: advisory opinions, collusion, mootness, ripeness, and political questions. In the following section we deal with another concept related to justiciability—standing to sue.

Advisory Opinions. A few states and some foreign countries require judges of the highest court to advise the executive or legislature, when so requested, as to their views on the constitutionality of a proposed policy. Since the time of Chief Justice Jay, however, federal judges in the United States have refused to issue advisory opinions. They do not render advice in hypothetical suits because if litigation is abstract, it possesses no real controversy. The language of the Constitution does not prohibit advisory opinions as opinions, but the Framers rejected a proposal that would have permitted the other branches of government to request judicial rulings "upon important questions of law, and upon solemn occasions." Madison was critical of this proposal on the grounds that the judiciary should have jurisdiction only over "cases of a Judiciary Nature."

The Supreme Court agreed with Madison. In July 1793 Secretary of State Thomas Jefferson asked the justices if they would be willing to address questions concerning the appropriate role America should play in the ongoing British-French war. Jefferson wrote that President Washington "would be much relieved if he found himself free to refer questions [involving the war] to the opinions of the judges of the Supreme Court in the United States, whose knowledge . . . would secure us against errors dangerous to the peace of the United States."[15] Less than a month later, in a written response sent directly to the president, the justices denied Jefferson's request:

We have considered [the] letter written by your direction to us by the Secretary of State [regarding] the lines of separation drawn by the Constitution between the three departments of government. These being in certain respects checks upon each

other, and our being judges of a court in the last resort, are considerations which afford strong arguments against the propriety of our extra-judicially deciding the questions alluded to, especially as the power given by the Constitution to the President, of calling on the heads of departments for opinions, seems to have been *purposely* as well as expressly united to the *executive* departments.

With these words, the justices sounded the death knell for advisory opinions: they would violate the separation of powers principle embedded in the Constitution. The subject has resurfaced only a few times in U.S. history; in the 1930s, for example, President Franklin Roosevelt considered a proposal that would require the Court to issue advisory opinions on the constitutionality of federal laws. But Roosevelt quickly gave up on the idea at least in part because of its dubious constitutionality.

Nevertheless, scholars still debate the Court's 1793 letter to Washington. Some agree with the justices' logic, but others assert that more institutional concerns were at work; perhaps the Court was concerned about being thrust into disputes prematurely. Whatever the reason, all subsequent Courts have followed that 1793 precedent: requests for advisory opinions to the U.S. Supreme Court present nonjusticiable disputes.

But this does not mean that justices have not found other ways of offering advice.[16] For example, they have sometimes offered political leaders informal suggestions in private conversations or correspondence.[17] Furthermore, justices of the Supreme Court have often given advice in an institutional but indirect manner. The Judiciary Act of 1925, which granted the Court wide discretion in controlling its docket, was largely drafted by Justice Willis Van Devanter. Chief Justice William Howard Taft and several associate justices openly lobbied for its passage, "patrolling the halls of Congress," as Taft put it. In 1937, when the Senate was considering President Roosevelt's Court-packing plan, opponents arranged for Chief Justice Charles Evans Hughes to send a letter to Sen. Burton K. Wheeler, advising him that increasing the

15. For the full text of Jefferson's request and the justices' response, see Henry M. Hart Jr. and Albert M. Sacks, *The Legal Process: Basic Problems in the Making and Application of Law,* prepared for publication from the 1958 tentative edition by and containing an introductory essay by William N. Eskridge Jr. and Philip P. Frickey (Westbury, N.Y.: Foundation Press, 1994), 630.

16. We adopt some of the material to follow from C. Herman Pritchett, Walter F. Murphy, and Lee Epstein, *Courts, Judges, and Politics* (New York: McGraw-Hill, 2000), chap. 6.

17. See, for example, Stewart Jay, *Most Humble Servants: The Advisory Role of Early Judges* (New Haven: Yale University Press, 1997).

number of justices would impede rather than facilitate the Court's work and that the justices' sitting in separate panels to hear cases—a procedure that increasing the number of justices was supposed to allow—would probably violate the constitutional command that there be "one Supreme Court." Like recent chief justices, William H. Rehnquist has sent an annual report on the state of the judiciary to Congress explaining not only what kind of legislation he deems good for the courts but also the likely impact of proposed legislation on the federal judicial system.

Finally, judges have occasionally used their opinions to provide advice to decision makers. In *Regents of the University of California v. Bakke* (1978), for instance, the Court held that a state medical school's version of affirmative action had deprived a white applicant of equal protection of the laws by rejecting him in favor of minority applicants whom the school ranked lower on all the relevant academic criteria. But, in his opinion, Justice Lewis F. Powell Jr. proffered the advice that the kind of affirmative action program operated by Harvard University would be constitutionally acceptable.

Collusive Suits. A second corollary of justiciability is collusion. The Court will not decide cases in which the litigants (1) want the same outcome, (2) evince no real adversity between them, or (3) are merely testing the law. Why the Court deems collusive suits nonjusticiable is well illustrated in *Muskrat v. United States* (1911). At issue here were several federal laws involving land distribution and appropriations to Native Americans. To determine whether these laws were constitutional, Congress enacted a statute authorizing David Muskrat and other Native Americans to challenge the land distribution law in court. This legislation also ordered the courts to give priority to Muskrat's suit and allowed the attorney general to defend his claim. Furthermore, Congress agreed to pay Muskrat's legal fees if his suit was successful. When the dispute reached the U.S. Supreme Court, it was dismissed. Justice William Day wrote,

[T]here is neither more nor less in this [litigation] than an attempt to provide for a judicial determination, final in this court, of the constitutional validity of an act of Congress. Is such a determination within the judicial power conferred by the Constitution, as the same has been interpreted and defined in the authoritative decisions to which we have referred? We think it is not. That judicial power, as we have seen, is the right to determine actual controversies arising between adverse litigants, duly instituted in courts of proper jurisdiction. The right to declare a law unconstitutional arises because an act of Congress relied upon by one or the other of such parties in determining their rights is in conflict with the fundamental law. The exercise of this, the most important and delicate duty of this court, is not given to it as a body with revisory power over the action of Congress, but because the rights of the litigants in justiciable controversies require the court to choose between the fundamental law and a law purporting to be enacted within constitutional authority, but in fact beyond the power delegated to the legislative branch of the Government. This attempt to obtain a judicial declaration of the validity of the act of Congress is not presented in a "case" or "controversy," to which, under the Constitution of the United States, the judicial power alone extends. It is true the United States is made a defendant to this action, but it has no interest adverse to the claimants. The object is not to assert a property right as against the Government, or to demand compensation for alleged wrongs because of action upon its part. The whole purpose of the law is to determine the constitutional validity of this class of legislation, in a suit not arising between parties concerning a property right necessarily involved in the decision in question, but in a proceeding against the Government in its sovereign capacity, and concerning which the only judgment required is to settle the doubtful character of the legislation in question.

However, the Court has not always followed the *Muskrat* precedent. Several landmark decisions were the result of collusive suits, including *Pollock v. Farmers' Loan and Trust Co.* (1895), in which the Court declared the federal income tax unconstitutional. The litigants in this dispute, a bank and a stockholder in the bank, both wanted the same outcome—the demise of the tax. *Carter v. Carter Coal Co.* (1936) is another example. Here the Court agreed to resolve a dispute over a major piece of New Deal legislation despite the fact that the litigants, a company president and the company, which included the president's father, both wanted the same outcome—the eradication of the legislation.

Why did the justices resolve these disputes? "The Court's decision to hear or dismiss such a test case," Joan Biskupic and Elder Witt claim, "usually turns on whether it presents an actual conflict of legal rights susceptible to judicial resolution."[18] In other words, the Court might overlook some element of collusion if the suit presents a real controversy or the potential for one. Others scholars are more skeptical. The temptation to set "good" public policy (or strike down "bad" public policy) is sometimes too strong for the justices to follow their own rules.

Mootness. In general, the Court will not decide cases in which the controversy is no longer live by the time it reaches the Court's doorstep. *DeFunis v. Odegaard* (1974) provides an example. Rejected for admission to the University of Washington Law School, Marco DeFunis Jr. brought suit against the school, alleging that it had engaged in reverse discrimination because it had denied him a place, but accepted statistically less qualified minority students. In 1971 a trial court found merit in his claim and ordered that the university admit him. While DeFunis was in his second year of law school, the state's high court reversed the trial judge's ruling. He then appealed to the U.S. Supreme Court. By that time, DeFunis had registered for his final quarter in school. In a *per curiam* opinion, the Court refused to rule on the merits of DeFunis's claim, asserting that it was moot.

Because [DeFunis] will complete his law school studies at the end of the term for which he has now registered regardless of any decision this Court might reach on the merits of this litigation, we conclude that the Court cannot, consistently with the limitations of Art. III of the Constitution, consider the substantive constitutional issues tendered by the parties.

Still, the rules governing mootness are a bit fuzzier than the *DeFunis* opinion characterized them. A well-known case is *Roe v. Wade* (1973) *(see pages 423–431)*, in which the Court legalized abortions performed during the first two trimesters of pregnancy. Norma McCorvey, also known as Roe, was pregnant when she filed suit in 1970. When the Court handed down the decision in 1973, she had long since given birth and put her baby up for adoption. But the justices did not declare this case moot.

Why not? What made *Roe* different from *DeFunis?* The justices provided two legal justifications. First, DeFunis brought the litigation in his own behalf, and *Roe* was

a class action—a lawsuit brought by one or more persons who represent themselves and all others similarly situated. Second, DeFunis had been admitted to law school, and he would "never again be required to run the gauntlet." Roe could become pregnant again; that is, pregnancy is a situation capable of repetition or recurrence. Are these reasonable points? Or is it possible, as some suspect, that the Court developed them to avoid particular legal issues? In either case, it is clear that mootness may be a rather slippery concept, open to interpretation by different justices and Courts.

Ripeness. Related to the concepts of advisory opinions and mootness is that of ripeness. Under existing Court interpretation a case is nonjusticiable if the controversy is premature—has insufficiently gelled—for review. *International Longshoreman's Union v. Boyd* (1954) provides an illustration. In 1952 Congress passed a law mandating that all aliens seeking admission into the United States from Alaska be "examined" as if they were entering from a foreign country. Believing that the law might affect seasonal American laborers working in Alaska temporarily, a union challenged the law. Writing for the Court, Justice Frankfurter dismissed the suit. In his view,

Appellants in effect asked [the Court] to rule that a statute the sanctions of which had not been set in motion against individuals on whose behalf relief was sought, because an occasion for doing so had not arisen, would not be applied to them if in the future such a contingency should arise. That is not a lawsuit to enforce a right; it is an endeavor to obtain a court's assurance that a statute does not govern hypothetical situations that may or may not make the challenged statute applicable. Determination of the . . . constitutionality of the legislation in advance of its immediate adverse effect in the context of a concrete case involves too remote and abstract an inquiry for the proper exercise of the judicial function.

Political Questions. Another type of nonjusticiable suit involves what is deemed a political question. Chief Justice Marshall stated in *Marbury v. Madison:*

The province of the court is, solely, to decide on the rights of individuals, not to inquire how the executive, or executive officers, perform duties in which they have a discretion. Questions in their nature political, or which are, by the constitution and laws, submitted to the executive, can never be made in this court.

18. Joan Biskupic and Elder Witt, *Guide to the U.S. Supreme Court,* 3d. ed. (Washington, D.C.: Congressional Quarterly, 1997), 300.

In other words, there is a class of questions that may be constitutional in nature but that the Court will not address because they are better solved by other branches of government.

But what exactly constitutes a political question? In *Luther v. Borden* (1849) the Court provided a partial answer. *Luther* involved a dispute between the existing government of Rhode Island and a group, led by Thomas Dorr, that was trying to institute a new government and a constitution (at the time Rhode Island had no constitution but operated under its old royal charter). Believing that the Dorrites' activities amounted to insurrection, the government sought to suppress the rebels through arrests made, in some instances, by police who entered homes without search warrants. Martin Luther, one of the Dorrites who had been arrested, sued state officials for trespass. He argued that the royal charter denied citizens a republican form of government, as mandated by the Guarantee Clause of Article IV: "The United States shall guarantee to every State in this Union a Republican Form of Government, and shall protect each of them against Invasion; and on Application of the Legislature, or the Executive (when the Legislature cannot be convened) against domestic Violence."

The Supreme Court, however, refused to go along with Luther. Writing for the majority, Chief Justice Taney held that the Court should avoid deciding any question arising out of the Guarantee Clause because such questions are inherently "political." He based the opinion largely on the words of Article IV, which he believed governed relations between the states and the federal government, not governments and courts. In other words, because the clause omits mention of the Court, it is enforceable only by the president or Congress.

For the next hundred years or so, the Court maintained Taney's position: any case involving the Guarantee Clause constituted a nonjusticiable dispute. In the 1940s an issue came before the Court that presented an opportunity to rethink *Luther*. The issue was reapportionment, the way the states draw legislative districts. Under the U.S. Constitution, each state is allotted a certain number of seats in the House of Representatives based on the population of the state. Once that number

has been determined, it is up to the state to map out the congressional districts. Article I specifies:

Representatives ... shall be apportioned among the several States which may be included within this Union, according to their respective Numbers. ... The actual Enumeration shall be made within three Years after the first Meeting of the Congress of the United States, and within every subsequent Term of ten Years, in such Manner as they shall by Law direct. The Number of Representatives shall not exceed one for every thirty Thousand, but each State shall have at Least one Representative.

In other words, Article I makes clear that the decennial census determines the number of representatives each state receives. But no guidelines exist as to how those representatives are to be allocated or apportioned within a given state.

As population shifts began occurring in the states early in the twentieth century, some legislatures redrew the congressional district lines. For most, the new maps meant creating greater parity for urban centers as citizens moved out of rural areas. Others, however, ignored these shifts and refused to reapportion seats. Over time, the results of their failure to draw new lines became readily apparent. It was possible for two districts within the same state, with large differences in populations, each to elect one member to the House.

The Court rejected initial attempts to force states to reapportion, which were based on the Article IV claim that failure to realign legislative districts deprived some voters of their right to a republican form of government. In *Colegrove v. Green* (1946) the Court invoked the logic of *Luther v. Borden* to hold that the question of legislative reapportionment within states was left open by the Constitution. If the Court intervened in this matter, it would be acting in a way "hostile to a democratic system." Put in different terms, reapportionment constituted a "political thicket" into which "courts ought not enter."

As a result of the Court's decision in *Colegrove*, disparities in voting power continued to grow. Naturally, many citizens and organizations wanted to force legislatures to reapportion, but under *Colegrove* they could not do so using the Guarantee Clause. They looked instead to another section of the Constitution, the Fourteenth Amendment's Equal Protection Clause, which says that no state shall "deny to any person within its jurisdiction the equal protection of the laws." From this clause, they made the argument, in *Baker v. Carr* (1962), that the failure to reapportion led to unequal treatment of voters.

A lower federal district court dismissed their suit on the grounds that *Colegrove* and other cases held reapportionment to constitute a political question on which it could not rule, but the Supreme Court disagreed. In a landmark opinion for the majority, Justice William J. Brennan Jr. first set out a definition of a political question:

Prominent on the surface of any case held to involve a political question is found a textually demonstrable constitutional commitment of the issue to a coordinate political department; or a lack of judicially discoverable and manageable standards for resolving it; or the impossibility of deciding without an initial policy determination of a kind clearly for nonjudicial discretion; or the impossibility of a court's undertaking independent resolution without expressing lack of the respect due coordinate branches of government; or an unusual need for unquestioning adherence to a political decision already made; or the potentiality of embarrassment from multifarious pronouncements by various departments on one question.

Based on this definition, he offered illustrations of the kinds of questions that would and would not meet the criteria. Cases grounded in the Guarantee Clause, like *Luther,* for example, met the criteria of a political question:

Clearly, several factors were thought by the Court in Luther to make the question there "political": the commitment to the other branches of the decision as to which is the lawful state government; the unambiguous action by the President, in recognizing the charter government as the lawful authority; the need for finality in the executive's decision; and the lack of criteria by which a court could determine which form of government was republican.

In Brennan's opinion, *Baker* did not implicate the Guarantee Clause; instead, it rested on a Fourteenth Amendment claim. That claim was justiciable because it did not meet the definition of a political question.

Baker is a significant decision for a number of reasons. One is that it opened the window for judicial resolution of reapportionment cases, a subject we consider in Chapter 13. Another and more relevant reason is that it estab-

lished a clear doctrinal base for determining political questions. In fact, over the years, the Court has used it to dismiss a range of substantive disputes; as recently as 1993, in *Nixon v. United States,* the Court relied heavily on *Baker v. Carr* to rule that the procedures used by Congress to handle impeachments are not subject to judicial review.

Standing to Sue

Another constraint on federal judicial power is standing: if the party bringing the litigation is not the appropriate party, the courts will not resolve the dispute. As Justice Brennan noted in *Baker,* Article III requires that litigants demonstrate "such a personal stake in the outcome of the controversy as to assure that concrete adverseness which sharpens the presentation of issues upon which the Court so largely depends for illumination of difficult constitutional questions."

In most private disputes, the litigants have no difficulty demonstrating a personal stake or injury. The more interesting constitutional questions have arisen in suits that involve parties wishing to challenge some government action on the grounds that they are taxpayers. Does the fact that one pays taxes provide a sufficiently personal stake in litigation to meet the requirement for standing?

The Court first addressed this question in *Frothingham v. Mellon* (1923). At issue was the Sheppard-Towner Maternity Act, in which Congress provided federal maternity aid to the states to fund programs designed to reduce infant mortality rates. Although many progressive groups had lobbied for the law, other organizations viewed it as an unconstitutional intrusion into the family and into the rights of states. They decided to challenge it and enlisted one among their ranks, Harriet Frothingham, to serve as a plaintiff. She was not a participant in the program, but a taxpayer who did not want her tax dollars spent on it. Her attorneys argued that her status as a taxpayer gave her sufficient grounds to bring suit.

The Court did not agree, holding that Frothingham lacked standing to bring the litigation. Justice George Sutherland wrote for the majority:

If one taxpayer may champion and litigate such a cause, then every other taxpayer may do the same, not only in respect of the statute here under review but also in respect of every other appropriation act and statute whose administration requires the outlay of public money, and whose validity may be questioned. The bare suggestion of such a result, with its attendant inconveniences, goes far to sustain the conclusion which we have reached, that a suit of this character cannot be maintained.

He also outlined an approach to standing:

The party . . . must be able to show not only that the statute is invalid but that he has sustained or is immediately in danger of sustaining some direct injury as the result of its enforcement, and not merely that he suffers in some indefinite way in common with people generally.

For the next forty years, *Frothingham* served as a major bar to taxpayer suits. Unless litigants could demonstrate that a government program injured them or threatened to do so—beyond the mere expenditure of tax dollars—they could not bring suit. In *Flast v. Cohen* (1968), however, the Court substantially relaxed that rule. *Flast* involved seven taxpayers who sought to challenge federal expenditures made under the Elementary and Secondary Education Act of 1965. Under this law, states could apply to the federal government for grants to assist in the education of children from low-income families. They could, for example, obtain funds for the acquisition of textbooks, school library materials, and so forth. The taxpayers alleged that some of the funds disbursed under this act were used to finance "instruction in reading, arithmetic, and other subjects and for guidance in religious and sectarian schools." Such expenditures, they argued, violated the First Amendment's prohibition on religious establishment ("Congress shall make no law respecting an establishment of religion").

A three-judge district court dismissed their complaint. It reasoned that because the plaintiffs had suffered no real injury and because their only claim of standard rested "solely on their status as federal taxpayers," they failed to meet the criteria established in *Frothingham.*

Writing for the Court, Chief Justice Warren disagreed, completely revamping the *Frothingham* standard. To determine whether a taxpayer has the requisite "personal stake" to bring suit, Warren wrote:

[I]t is both appropriate and necessary to look to the substantive issues for another purpose, namely, to determine whether there is a logical nexus between the status asserted and the claim sought to be adjudicated. . . .

The nexus demanded of federal taxpayers has two aspects to it. First, the taxpayer must establish a logical link between that status and the type of legislative enactment attacked. Thus, a taxpayer will be a proper party to allege the unconstitutionality only of exercises of congressional power under the taxing and spending clause of Art. I, §8, of the Constitution. It will not be sufficient to allege an incidental expenditure of tax funds in the administration of an essentially regulatory statute. . . . Secondly, the taxpayer must establish a nexus between that status and the precise nature of the constitutional infringement alleged. Under this requirement, the taxpayer must show that the challenged enactment exceeds specific constitutional limitations imposed upon the exercise of the congressional taxing and spending power and not simply that the enactment is generally beyond the powers delegated to Congress by Art. I, §8. When both nexuses are established, the litigant will have shown a taxpayer's stake in the outcome of the controversy and will be a proper and appropriate party to invoke a federal court's jurisdiction.

Applying this standard to the dispute at hand, Warren found that the *Flast* taxpayers had standing. "Their constitutional challenge is made to an exercise by Congress of its power under Art. I, §8, to spend for the general welfare, and the challenged program involves a substantial expenditure of federal tax funds. In addition, appellants have alleged that the challenged expenditures violate the Establishment and Free Exercise Clauses of the First Amendment."

Would Harriet Frothingham have met this new, more relaxed standard? To this question, Warren said no:

The allegations of the taxpayer in *Frothingham v. Mellon* were quite different from those made in this case, and the result in *Frothingham* is consistent with the test of taxpayer standing announced today. The taxpayer in *Frothingham* attacked a federal spending program and she, therefore, established the first nexus required. However, she lacked standing because her constitutional attack was not based on an allegation that Congress, in enacting the Maternity Act of 1921, had breached a specific limitation upon its taxing and spending power. . . . In essence, Mrs. Frothingham was attempting to assert the States' interest in their legislative prerogatives and not a federal taxpayer's interest in being free of taxing and spending in contravention of specific constitutional limitations imposed upon Congress' taxing and spending power.

In the end, *Flast* did not overrule *Frothingham;* in fact, as Warren states, the Court was careful to indicate that had the 1968 ruling been applied to *Frothingham,* the plaintiff still would have been unable to attain standing. But *Flast* substantially revised the 1923 precedent. If taxpayers could indicate a logical link between their status and the legislation, and one between their status and a specific constitutional infringement, then they might have standing.

Flast symbolized what was at that time a general trend toward lowering barriers to access to federal courts. Twenty-two years earlier, Congress had passed the Administrative Procedure Act of 1946, which, among other things, provided that any person "suffering legal wrong because of agency action, or adversely affected or aggrieved within the meaning of a relevant statute, is entitled to judicial review thereof." Congress had been reacting to pressure from the American Bar Association and business organizations concerned about regulation by federal administrative agencies; but other groups have been able to use this statute. *Association of Data Processing Service Organizations v. Camp* (1970) gave this provision a broad interpretation by specifically rejecting the old standing test of a "recognized legal interest."

But the days of easing standing requirements have apparently come to an end. During the last two decades, a majority of the justices have favored restoring strict standing requirements and limiting access to federal courts. They have, for example, read *Flast* rather narrowly, restricting its reach to precisely the kind of suit at issue there—a challenge to use of federal funds allegedly in violation of the First Amendment's ban against establishment of religion. Such a reading has led some scholars to suggest that current doctrine on standing now resembles *Frothingham* rather than *Flast.*

Those who hold that view may be overstating the case, but it is true that the doctrine on standing is open to interpretation. Various opinions filed in *Raines v. Byrd* (1997) support this point. This case involved the Line Item Veto Act of 1996, which allowed the president to cancel certain tax and spending benefits after they were signed into law. As a threshold matter, however, the justices had to decide whether the six members of Congress who had brought the suit had standing to challenge the law.

Writing for the majority, Chief Justice Rehnquist concluded that they did not: "[T]hese individual members of Congress do not have a sufficient 'personal stake' in this dispute and have not alleged a sufficiently concrete injury to have established Article III standing."

In a dissenting opinion, Justice Stevens took issue with this conclusion:

The Line Item Veto Act purports to establish a procedure for the creation of laws that are truncated versions of bills that have been passed by the Congress and presented to the President for signature. If the procedure were valid, it would deny every Senator and every Representative any opportunity to vote for or against the truncated measure that survives the exercise of the President's cancellation authority. Because the opportunity to cast such votes is a right guaranteed by the text of the Constitution, I think it clear that the persons who are deprived of that right by the Act have standing to challenge its constitutionality. Moreover, because the impairment of that constitutional right has an immediate impact on their official powers, in my judgment they need not wait until after the President has exercised his cancellation authority to bring suit. Finally, the same reason that the respondents have standing provides a sufficient basis for concluding that the statute is unconstitutional.

That these justices could reach such different conclusions underscores the notion that standing—like other constraints on judicial power (justiciability and jurisdiction)—may be more fluid than they appear or the Court sometimes lets on. Article III may place certain limits on the power of the federal judiciary. However, its language is sufficiently vague, allowing for a good deal of judicial latitude.

In the final analysis, then, we are left with many questions centering on judicial power and constraints on its exercise. We shall ask just one: To what extent are the limitations discussed in this chapter real or open to interpretation? Consider this as you read the many cases to come.

READINGS

Berger, Raoul. "Standing to Sue in Public Actions." *Yale Law Journal* 78 (1969): 816–840.

Bickel, Alexander M. *The Least Dangerous Branch.* New York: Bobbs-Merrill, 1962.

Canon, Bradley C. "Defining the Dimensions of Judicial Activism." *Judicature* 66 (1983): 237.

Casper, Jonathan D. "The Supreme Court and National Policy Making." *American Political Science Review* 70 (1976): 50–63.

Choper, Jesse H. *Judicial Review and the National Political Process.* Chicago: University of Chicago Press, 1980.

Clinton, Robert Lowry. *Marbury v. Madison and Judicial Review.* Lawrence: University Press of Kansas, 1989.

Cover, Robert M. "The Origins of Judicial Activism in the Protection of Minorities." *Yale Law Journal* 91 (1982): 1287.

Dahl, Robert. "Decision Making in a Democracy: The Supreme Court as a National Policy-Maker." *Journal of Public Law* 6 (1957): 279–295.

Ely, John Hart. *Democracy and Distrust.* Cambridge: Harvard University Press, 1980.

Fisher, Louis. *Constitutional Dialogues.* Princeton: Princeton University Press, 1988.

Franck, Thomas M. *Political Questions/Judicial Answers: Does the Rule of Law Apply to Foreign Affairs?* Princeton: Princeton University Press, 1992.

Funston, Richard. *A Vital National Seminar.* Palo Alto, Calif.: Mayfield, 1978.

Gettleman, Marvin E. *The Dorr Rebellion.* New York: Random House, 1973.

Grofman, Bernard, ed. *Political Gerrymandering and the Courts.* New York: Agathon Press, 1990.

Gunther, Gerald. "The Subtle Vices of the Passive Virtues—A Comment on Principle and Expediency in Judicial Review." *Columbia Law Review* 64 (1964): 1–25.

Henkin, Louis. "Is There a 'Political Question' Doctrine?" *Yale Law Journal* 85 (1976): 597.

Lasser, William. *The Limits of Judicial Power.* Chapel Hill: University of North Carolina Press, 1988.

Murphy, Walter F. *Congress and the Court.* Chicago: University of Chicago Press, 1962.

Orren, Karen. "Standing to Sue: Interest Group Conflict in the Federal Courts." *American Political Science Review* 70 (1976): 723–741.

Radcliffe, James E. *The Case-or-Controversy Provision.* University Park: Pennsylvania State University Press, 1978.

Rathjen, Gregory J., and Harold J. Spaeth. "Access to the Federal Courts: An Analysis of Burger Court Policy Making." *American Journal of Political Science* 23 (1979): 360–382.

Rowland, C. K., and Bridgett Todd. "Where You Stand Depends on Who Sits: Platform Promises and Judicial Gatekeeping in the Federal District Courts." *Journal of Politics* 53 (1991): 175–185.

Schuckman, John S. "The Political Background of the Political Question Doctrine: The Judges and the Dorr War." *American Journal of Legal History* 16 (1972): 111.

Strum, Philippa. *The Supreme Court and Political Questions.* Tuscaloosa: University of Alabama Press, 1974.

Sunstein, Cass R. *One Case at a Time: Judicial Minimalism on the Supreme Court.* Cambridge: Harvard University Press, 1999.

Tate, C. Neal, and Torbjörn Vallinder, eds. *The Global Expansion of Judicial Power: The Judicialization of Politics.* New York: New York University Press, 1995.

Wolfe, Christopher. *Judicial Activism.* Pacific Grove, Calif.: Brooks/Cole, 1991.

———. *The Rise of Modern Judicial Review.* New York: Basic Books, 1986.

CHAPTER 3
INCORPORATION OF THE BILL OF RIGHTS

T HE FIRST AMENDMENT to the U.S. Constitution contains a clear prohibition: "Congress shall make no law . . . abridging the freedom of speech." The wording specifically and exclusively limits the powers of Congress, reflecting the fact that the Bill of Rights was added to the Constitution because of fear that the *federal* government might become too powerful and encroach upon individual rights. Does the language of the First Amendment mean that state legislatures *may* enact laws curtailing their citizens' free speech? For more than a hundred years it did. The U.S. Supreme Court, following historical interpretations and emphasizing the intention of the Framers of the Constitution, refused to nationalize the Bill of Rights by making its protections binding on the state governments. The states were free to recognize those freedoms they deemed important and to develop their own guarantees against state violations of those rights.

Because of a process known as selective incorporation, however, this interpretation is no longer valid. As the nation entered the twentieth century, the Supreme Court slowly began to inform state governments that they too must abide by most guarantees contained in the first eight amendments of the federal Constitution. Today, we take for granted that the states in which we live may not infringe on our right to exercise our religion freely, that no officer of the state may enter our homes without a warrant, and so forth. But the process by which we obtained these rights was long, and the sup-

porters of incorporation lost many disputes along the way. The process caused acrimonious debates among Supreme Court justices. In fact, the question of whether states must honor the guarantees contained in the Bill of Rights is almost as old as the nation and has been debated by modern Courts as well.

MUST STATES ABIDE BY THE BILL OF RIGHTS? INITIAL RESPONSES

In drafting the original version of the Constitution of 1787, as we noted in the Part I opening essay, the delegates to the convention did not include a bill of rights, believing that such a list was unnecessary.[1] When some delegates clamored for a specification of rights, however, James Madison submitted to the First Congress a list of seventeen articles (amendments), mostly aimed at safeguarding personal freedoms against tyranny by the federal government. In a speech to the House, he suggested that "in revising the Constitution, we may throw into that section, which interdicts the abuse of certain powers of the State legislatures, some other provisions of equal, if not greater importance than those already made." To that end, Madison's proposed fourteenth amendment said "no State shall violate the equal right of conscience, freedom of the press, or trial by jury in criminal cases."[2]

1. Before the Framers adjourned, "It was moved and seconded to appoint a Committee to prepare a Bill of Rights." The motion, however, was defeated.

2. James Madison, Speech before the House of Representatives, June 7, 1789.

This article failed to garner congressional approval, so the states never considered it.

Although scholars now agree that Madison viewed this amendment as the most significant among the seventeen he proposed, Congress's refusal to adopt it may have meant that the Founders never intended for the Bill of Rights to be applied to the states or local governments. Chief Justice John Marshall's opinion in *Barron v. Baltimore* (1833), the first case in which the U.S. Supreme Court considered nationalizing the Bill of Rights, supports this conclusion. While reading *Barron*, note the relative ease with which Marshall reached the conclusion that historical circumstances could not possibly have implied that states were bound by the federal Bill of Rights.

Barron v. Baltimore

7 PET. (32 U.S.) 243 (1833)
www.law.cornell.edu/supct/cases/name.htm
Vote: 6 (Duvall, Johnson, Marshall, McLean, Story,
    Thompson)
    0
Opinion of the Court: Marshall
Not participating: Baldwin

The story of this case begins in Baltimore, a city undergoing major economic changes in the early 1800s.[3] Because of its busy harbor, Baltimore was becoming a major hub of economic activity in the United States. Such growth necessitated constant construction and excavation. While entrepreneurs erected new buildings, the city began to repair its badly worn streets.

Most of Baltimore's residents welcomed the activity, but a group of wharf owners saw problems. They noticed that the city's street construction altered the flow of streams coming into Baltimore Harbor. This redirection of water, the owners argued in a letter to the city, led to the accumulation of sand and earth near their wharves, causing the surrounding water to become too shallow for large ships. Because their livelihood depended on accom-

3. For an interesting account of this case, see Fred Friendly and Martha J. H. Elliot, *The Constitution: That Delicate Balance* (New York: Random House, 1984).

modating these ships, which unloaded goods on the wharves for storage in nearby warehouses, the owners wanted the city to dredge the sand and dirt at its expense.

Baltimore officials paid no heed to the wharf owners, and within five years city construction had ruined John Barron and John Craig's business. In 1822 they brought city representatives to county court in Maryland, asking for $20,000 in damages. The court ordered the city to pay them $4,500. When a state appellate court reversed the county court's decision, a determined Barron appealed to the U.S. Supreme Court.

Barron's lawyer tried to discuss the specific issue of the wharf, but the justices asked him to confine his argument to constitutional issues. The attorney responded by arguing that the Fifth Amendment of the U.S. Constitution, which guarantees that "private property cannot be taken for public use, without just compensation" should apply to states, and not just the federal government. Baltimore's attorney, Roger Brooke Taney, a future chief justice, must have thought otherwise, but the Court never gave him a chance to speak. As soon as he got up to argue the city's case, the Court cut him off, apparently having made up its mind.

Writing for a unanimous Court, in one of his last major opinions, Chief Justice Marshall, who previously had shown a propensity to enlarge the powers of national government, sent a clear message to the states on the question of nationalizing the Bill of Rights.

MR. CHIEF JUSTICE MARSHALL delivered the opinion of the Court.

The constitution was ordained and established by the people of the United States for themselves, for their own government, and not for the government of the individual states. Each state established a constitution for itself, and, in that constitution, provided such limitations and restrictions on the powers of its particular government as its judgment dictated. The people of the United States framed such a government for the United States as they supposed best adapted to their situation, and best calculated to promote their interests. The powers they conferred on this government were to be exercised by itself; and the limitations on

Conditions in Baltimore Harbor, depicted in 1830 by William J. Bennett, led to the 1833 Supreme Court decision in *Barron v. Baltimore.* Chief Justice Marshall's majority opinion in *Barron* explained why state and local governments were not constrained by the federal Bill of Rights.

power, if expressed in general terms, are naturally, and, we think, necessarily applicable to the government created by the instrument. They are limitations of power granted in the instrument itself; not of distinct governments, framed by different persons and for different purposes.

If these propositions be correct, the fifth amendment must be understood as restraining the power of the general government, not as applicable to the states. In their several constitutions they have imposed such restrictions on their respective governments as their own wisdom suggested; such as they deemed most proper for themselves. It is a subject on which they judge exclusively, and with which others interfere no farther than they are supposed to have a common interest. . . .

Had the people of the several states, or any of them, required changes in their constitutions; had they required additional safeguards to liberty from the apprehended encroachments of their particular governments: the remedy was in their own hands, and would have been applied by themselves. A convention would have been assembled by the discontented state, and the required improvements would have been made by itself. The unwieldy and cumbrous machinery of procuring a recommendation from two-thirds of congress, and the assent of three-fourths of their

sister states, could never have occurred to any human being as a mode of doing that which might be effected by the state itself. Had the framers of these amendments intended them to be limitations on the powers of the state governments, they would have imitated the framers of the original constitution, and have expressed that intention. Had congress engaged in the extraordinary occupation of improving the constitutions of the several states by affording the people additional protection from the exercise of power by their own governments in matters which concerned themselves alone, they would have declared this purpose in plain and intelligible language.

But it is universally understood, it is a part of the history of the day, that the great revolution which established the constitution of the United States, was not effected without immense opposition. Serious fears were extensively entertained that those powers which the patriot statesmen, who then watched over the interests of our country, deemed essential to union, and to the attainment of those invaluable objects for which union was sought, might be exercised in a manner dangerous to liberty. In almost every convention by which the constitution was adopted, amendments to guard against the abuse of power were recommended. These amendments demanded security against the apprehended encroachments of the general government not against those of the local governments.

In compliance with a sentiment thus generally expressed, to quiet fears thus extensively entertained, amendments were proposed by the required majority in congress, and adopted by the states. These amendments contain no expression indicating an intention to apply them to the state governments. This court cannot so apply them.

We are of opinion that the provision in the fifth amendment to the constitution, declaring that private property shall not be taken for public use without just compensation, is intended solely as a limitation on the exercise of power by the government of the United States, and is not applicable to the legislation of the states. We are therefore of opinion that there is no repugnancy between the several acts of the general assembly of Maryland, given in evidence by the defendants at the trial of this cause, in the court of that state, and the constitution of the United States. This court, therefore, has no jurisdiction of the cause; and it is dismissed.

INCORPORATION THROUGH THE FOURTEENTH AMENDMENT: EARLY INTERPRETATIONS

Marshall quipped that the Court did not have "much difficulty" in addressing the question at issue in *Barron*, but the question of the applicability of the Bill of Rights to state and local governments would not disappear with similar ease. In the years immediately preceding the Civil War, several Court decisions clearly showed the nature of a polity without universal application of national rights. Among the most significant of these was *Scott v. Sandford* (1857), in which the justices ruled that the Constitution did not grant U.S. citizenship to blacks.

Not surprisingly, the debate over the applicability of the Bill of Rights heated up after ratification of the Fourteenth Amendment in 1868. This amendment was ratified three years after the Civil War, and the goals of its framers seemed clear: to secure the Union and to ensure equality for blacks. Some lawyers saw additional opportunities under the Fourteenth Amendment. They viewed one of its provisions, the Privileges or Immunities Clause, as a vehicle by which to nationalize the Bill of Rights. The wording of this clause makes such an inter-

pretation possible: "No State shall make or enforce any law which shall abridge the privileges or immunities of citizens of the United States." Asserting that the privileges and immunities of U.S. citizenship included all those rights stipulated in the federal Bill of Rights, these attorneys argued that this provision of the Fourteenth Amendment "incorporated" the constitutional guarantees and obliged the states to conform to them.

The Supreme Court had its first opportunity to scrutinize this claim in the *Slaughterhouse Cases* (1873). This litigation grew out of the industrial revolution—an economic diversification that touched the whole country. Although this revolution changed the United States for the better in many ways, it also had negative effects. In Louisiana, for example, the state legislature claimed that the Mississippi River had become polluted because New Orleans butchers dumped garbage into it. To remedy this problem (or, as some have suggested, to use it as an excuse to form a monopolistic enterprise), the legislature created the Crescent City Live Stock Landing & Slaughter House Company to receive and slaughter all city livestock for twenty-five years.

Because they were forced to use its facilities, and to pay top dollar for the privilege, the butchers despised the new corporation. They formed their own organization, the Butchers' Benevolent Association, and hired John A. Campbell, a former U.S. Supreme Court justice, to sue the corporation for depriving them of their right to pursue their business, a basic guarantee, they argued, granted by the Fourteenth Amendment's Privileges or Immunities Clause. After a state district court and the Louisiana Supreme Court ruled in favor of the corporation, the butchers' association appealed to the U.S. Supreme Court.

Writing for a slim, five-person majority, Justice Samuel F. Miller affirmed the judgment of the Louisiana court. As he put it:

Was it the purpose of the fourteenth amendment, by the simple declaration that no State should make or enforce any law which shall abridge the privileges and immunities of *citizens of the United States,* to transfer the security and protection of all the civil rights which we have mentioned, from the States to the Federal government? And where it is declared that Congress shall have the power to enforce that article, was it intended to bring within the power of Congress the entire domain of civil rights heretofore belonging exclusively to the States?

All this and more must follow, if the proposition of the plaintiffs . . . be sound. For not only are these rights subject to the control of Congress whenever in its discretion any of them are supposed to be abridged by State legislation, but that body may also pass laws in advance, limiting and restricting the exercise of legislative power by the States, in their most ordinary and usual functions, as in its judgment it may think proper on all such subjects. And still further, such a construction followed by the reversal of the judgments of the Supreme Court of Louisiana in these cases, would constitute this court a perpetual censor upon all legislation of the States, on the civil rights of their own citizens, with authority to nullify such as it did not approve as consistent with those rights, as they existed at the time of the adoption of this amendment. The argument we admit is not always the most conclusive which is drawn from the consequences urged against the adoption of a particular construction of an instrument. But when, as in the case before us, these consequences are so serious, so far-reaching and pervading, so great a departure from the structure and spirit of our institutions; when the effect is to fetter and degrade the State governments by subjecting them to the control of Congress, in the exercise of powers heretofore universally conceded to them of the most ordinary and fundamental character; when in fact it radically changes the whole theory of the relations of the State and Federal governments to each other and of both these governments to the people; the argument has a force that is irresistible, in the absence of language which expresses such a purpose too clearly to admit of doubt.

We are convinced that no such results were intended by the Congress which proposed these amendments, nor by the legislatures of the States which ratified them.

Justice Miller's majority opinion had at least two major effects on the development of the law. First, its severely limited interpretation rendered the Privileges or Immunities Clause of the Fourteenth Amendment almost useless, a condition that has changed little since then.[4] Second, and more relevant to our understanding of incorporation, the Court made clear that it would not use this clause as a vehicle by which to nationalize the Bill of Rights.

With the *Slaughterhouse Cases* sounding the death

knell for incorporation via the Privileges or Immunities Clause, attorneys turned to yet another section of the Fourteenth Amendment, the Due Process Clause, which says, "Nor shall any State deprive any person of life, liberty, or property, without due process of law." The advocates of nationalizing the Bill of Rights hoped to convince the Court that the words *due process of law* incorporated or absorbed those rights protected by the first eight amendments. If this argument proved successful, the Due Process Clause would prohibit the states from violating any of the liberties protected under the federal Bill of Rights. But would the justices be willing to use this section as a mechanism for incorporation?

In its first opportunity to evaluate this claim, *Hurtado v. California* (1884), the Court rejected that interpretation of the Due Process Clause. While reading the opinions in *Hurtado*, consider two questions. First, did the Court completely shut the door on the use of the clause to incorporate the Bill of Rights? Second, how did Justice John Marshall Harlan's lone dissent differ from the views of the Court's majority?

Hurtado v. California

110 U.S. 516 (1884)
laws.findlaw.com/US/110/516.html
Vote: 7 (Blatchford, Bradley, Gray, Matthews, Miller, Waite, Woods)
    1 (Harlan)
Opinion of the Court: Matthews
Dissenting opinion: Harlan
Not participating: Field

Joseph Hurtado and his wife, Susie, lived in Sacramento, California, where they were friendly with Jose Antonio Estuardo, an immigrant from Chile. The friendship disintegrated, however, when Hurtado learned of Estuardo's affair with Susie. Hurtado asked his former crony to leave the city, but Estuardo continued to court Susie until Hurtado sent her to live with her parents. This arrangement proved only temporary; when Susie returned to Sacramento, Estuardo again pursued her. Faced with this continuing threat, Hurtado assaulted Estuardo in a bar,

---

4. But see the Court's opinion in *Saenz v. Roe* (pages 711–715) in which the majority relies on the "previously dormant" Privileges or Immunities Clause to address the question of whether states can deny welfare assistance to residents who had lived in their jurisdictions for less than one year.

and the police arrested him on battery charges. After his trial was postponed, Hurtado shot and killed his wife's lover.[5] The state charged Hurtado with murder, an offense punishable by death.

At the time, many states provided for grand jury hearings before a defendant went to trial. Typically, a grand jury listens exclusively to the prosecutor's side of a case and decides whether enough evidence exists to bring a defendant to trial. The California Constitution of 1879, however, specified that prosecutors could initiate trials from an *information* (a document issued by the prosecutor, officially charging an individual with criminal violations), reviewed by a judge in lieu of a grand jury. Using such a document, the state brought Hurtado to trial for murder. He was found guilty and sentenced to death. The California Supreme Court affirmed the sentence, and a date was set for his execution. Hurtado's counsel objected on the grounds that the state had denied the condemned man his right to a grand jury hearing and to due process of law. Because these guarantees applied to federal proceedings under the Fifth Amendment, he argued that they also should apply to the states under the Fourteenth Amendment's Due Process and Privileges or Immunities Clauses. The state responded that since *Barron v. Baltimore* it was settled law that the states were not constitutionally obliged to observe the provisions of the federal Bill of Rights. After Hurtado lost this point in the California Supreme Court, he sought a writ of error to the U.S. Supreme Court, urging the justices to incorporate the Fifth Amendment right to a grand jury hearing into the Due Process Clause of the Fourteenth Amendment and make it binding on the states.

MR. JUSTICE MATTHEWS delivered the opinion of the Court.

It is claimed on behalf of the prisoner that the conviction and sentence are void, on the ground that they are repugnant to that clause of the Fourteenth Article of Amendment of the Constitution of the United States which is in these words:

5. For more details on this case, see Richard C. Cortner, *The Supreme Court and the Second Bill of Rights* (Madison: University of Wisconsin Press, 1981).

"Nor shall any State deprive any person of life, liberty, or property without due process of law."

The proposition of law we are asked to affirm is that an indictment or presentment by a grand jury, as known to the common law of England, is essential to that "due process of law," when applied to prosecutions for felonies, which is secured and guaranteed by this provision of the Constitution of the United States, and which accordingly it is forbidden to the States respectively to dispense with in the administration of criminal law.

The question is one of grave and serious import, affecting both private and public rights and interests of great magnitude, and involves a consideration of what additional restrictions upon the legislative policy of the States has been imposed by the Fourteenth Amendment to the Constitution of the United States. . . .

We are to construe this phrase in the Fourteenth Amendment by the *usus loquendi* [common usage of ordinary speech] of the Constitution itself. The same words are contained in the Fifth Amendment. That article makes specific and express provision for perpetuating the institution of the grand jury, so far as relates to prosecution for the more aggravated crimes under the laws of the United States. . . .

According to a recognized canon of interpretation, especially applicable to formal and solemn instruments of constitutional law, we are forbidden to assume, without clear reason to the contrary, that any part of this most important amendment is superfluous. The natural and obvious inference is, that in the sense of the Constitution, "due process of law" was not meant or intended to include, *en vi termini* [by the force of the term], the institution and procedure of a grand jury in any case. The conclusion is equally irresistible, that when the same phrase was employed in the Fourteenth Amendment to restrain the action of the States, it was used in the same sense and with no greater extent; and that if in the adoption of that amendment it had been part of its purpose to perpetuate the institution of the grand jury in all the States, it would have embodied, as did the Fifth Amendment, express declarations to that effect. Due process of law in the latter refers to that law of the land which derives its authority from the legislative powers conferred upon Congress by the Constitution of the United States, exercised within the limits therein prescribed, and interpreted according to the principles of the common law. In the Fourteenth Amendment, by parity of reason, it refers to that law of the land in each State, which derives its authority from the inherent and reserved powers of the State, exerted within the limits of those fundamental principles of liberty and justice which lie at the base of all our civil and political institutions, and the greatest security for which resides in the right of the people to make their own laws, and alter them at their pleasure. . . .

But it is not to be supposed that these legislative powers are absolute and despotic, and that the amendment prescribing due process of law is too vague and indefinite to operate as a practical restraint. It is not every act, legislative in form, that is law. Law is something more than mere will exerted as an act of power. It must be not a special rule for a particular person or a particular case, but . . . "the general law, a law which hears before it condemns, which proceeds upon inquiry, and renders judgment only after trial," so "that every citizen shall hold his life, liberty, property and immunities under the protection of the general rules which govern society," and thus excluding, as not due process of law, acts of attainder, bills of pains and penalties, acts of confiscation, acts reversing judgments, and acts directly transferring one man's estate to another, legislative judgments and decrees, and other similar special, partial and arbitrary exertions of power under the forms of legislation. Arbitrary power, enforcing its edicts to the injury of the persons and property of its subjects, is not law, whether manifested as the decree of a personal monarch or of an impersonal multitude. And the limitations imposed by our constitutional law upon the action of the governments, both State and national, are essential to the preservation of public and private rights, notwithstanding the representative character of our political institutions. The enforcement of these limitations by judicial process is the device of self-governing communities to protect the rights of individuals and minorities, as well against the power of numbers, as against the violence of public agents transcending the limits of lawful authority, even when acting in the name and wielding the force of the government. . . .

It follows that any legal proceeding enforced by public authority, whether sanctioned by age and custom, or newly devised in the discretion of the legislative power, in furtherance of the general public good, which regards and preserves these principles of liberty and justice, must be held to be due process of law. . . .

Tried by these principles, we are unable to say that the

substitution for a presentment or indictment by a grand jury of the proceeding by information, after examination and commitment by a magistrate, certifying to the probable guilt of the defendant, with the right on his part to the aid of counsel, and to the cross-examination of the witnesses produced for the prosecution, is not due process of law. It is . . . an ancient proceeding at common law, which might include every case of an offence of less grade than a felony, except misprision of treason; and in every circumstance of its administration, as authorized by the statute of California, it carefully considers and guards the substantial interest of the prisoner. It is merely a preliminary proceeding, and can result in no final judgment, except as the consequence of a regular judicial trial, conducted precisely as in cases of indictments. . . .

For these reasons, finding no error therein, the judgment of the Supreme Court of California is

Affirmed.

MR. JUSTICE HARLAN, dissenting.

My brethren concede that there are principles of liberty and justice lying at the foundation of our civil and political institutions which no State can violate consistently with that due process of law required by the Fourteenth Amendment in proceedings involving life, liberty, or property. Some of these principles are enumerated in the opinion of the court. But, for reasons which do not impress my mind as satisfactory, they exclude from that enumeration the exemption from prosecution, by information, for a public offence involving life. By what authority is that exclusion made? . . .

[I]t is said that the framers of the Constitution did not suppose that due process of law necessarily required for a capital offence the institution and procedure of a grand jury, else they would not in the same amendment prohibiting the deprivation of life, liberty, or property, without due process of law, have made specific and express provision for a grand jury where the crime is capital or otherwise infamous; therefore, it is argued, the requirement by the Fourteenth Amendment of due process of law in all proceedings involving life, liberty, and property, without specific reference to grand juries in any case whatever, was not intended as a restriction upon the power which it is claimed the States previously had, so far as the express restrictions of the national Constitution are concerned, to dispense altogether with grand juries.

This line of argument, it seems to me, would lead to results which are inconsistent with the vital principles of republican government. If the presence in the Fifth Amendment of a specific provision for grand juries in capital cases, alongside the provision for due process of law in proceedings involving life, liberty, or property, is held to prove that "due process of law" did not, in the judgment of the framers of the Constitution, necessarily require a grand jury in capital cases, inexorable logic would require it to be, likewise, held that the right not to be put twice in jeopardy of life and limb for the same offence, nor compelled in a criminal case to testify against one's self—rights and immunities also specifically recognized in the Fifth Amendment—were not protected by that due process of law required by the settled usages and proceedings existing under the common and statute law of England at the settlement of this country. More than that, other amendments of the Constitution proposed at the same time, expressly recognize the right of persons to just compensation for private property taken for public use; their right, when accused of crime, to be informed of the nature and cause of the accusation against them, and to a speedy and public trial, by an impartial jury of the State and district wherein the crime was committed; to be confronted by the witnesses against them; and to have compulsory process for obtaining witnesses in their favor. . . . If the argument of my brethren be sound, those rights—although universally recognized at the establishment of our institutions as secured by that due process of law which for centuries had been the foundation of Anglo-Saxon liberty—were not deemed by our fathers as essential in the due process of law prescribed by our Constitution; because,—such seems to be the argument,—had they been regarded as involved in due process of law they would not have been specifically and expressly provided for, but left to the protection given by the general clause forbidding the deprivation of life, liberty, or property without due process of law. Further, the reasoning of the opinion indubitably leads to the conclusion that but for the specific provisions made in the Constitution for the security of the personal rights enumerated, the general inhibition against deprivation of life, liberty, and property without due process of law would not have prevented Congress from enacting a statute in derogation of each of them. . . .

It seems to me that too much stress is put upon the fact that the framers of the Constitution made express provision for the security of those rights which at common law were protected by the requirement of due process of law, and, in addition, declared, generally, that no person shall "be deprived of life, liberty or property without due process of law." The rights, for the security of which these express provisions were made, were of a character so essential to the safety of the people that it was deemed wise to avoid the possibility that Congress, in regulating the processes of law, would impair or destroy them. Hence, their specific enumeration in the earlier amendments of the Constitution, in connection with the general requirement of due process of law, the latter itself being broad enough to cover every right of life, liberty or property secured by the settled usages and modes of proceeding existing under the common and statute law of England at the time our government was founded. . . .

[D]ue process of law protects the fundamental principles of liberty and justice, adjudges, in effect, that an immunity or right, recognized at the common law to be essential to personal security, jealously guarded by our national Constitution against violation by any tribunal or body exercising authority under the general government, and expressly or impliedly recognized, *when the Fourteenth Amendment was adopted*, in the Bill of Rights or Constitution of every State in the Union, is, yet, not a fundamental principle in governments established, as those of the States of the Union are, to secure to the citizen liberty and justice, and, therefore, is not involved in that due process of law required in proceedings conducted under the sanction of a State. My sense of duty constrains me to dissent from this interpretation of the supreme law of the land.

Although it failed to adopt Hurtado's claims, the Court did not completely preclude the possibility of incorporation. The majority reasoned that because due process is explicitly part of the Fifth Amendment, it could not be the equivalent of the entire Bill of Rights. In other words, the Due Process Clause could not be used to apply the entire Bill of Rights to the states. But, as Richard C. Cortner points out, the Court ruled that the Due Process Clause "did protect against state encroachment those 'fundamental principles of liberty and justice which lie at the base of all our civil and political institutions.'"[6] For the legal community and citizens of the United States, however, the Court left a critical question unresolved: Did "fundamental principles" include those guarantees contained under the Bill of Rights?

Chicago, Burlington & Quincy Railroad v. Chicago (1897), one of the most important cases to come to the Court after *Hurtado,* involved an economic issue rather than criminal procedure. This case, like *Barron* and the *Slaughterhouse Cases,* grew out of a controversy caused by industrialization. As Chicago began to expand, it acquired, under the principle of eminent domain, large pieces of property belonging to railroad companies and private citizens. Based on local ordinances, the city offered property owners what it considered just compensation for the land. If the owners considered the offers unacceptable, they could challenge the city in county court, and many did so. In this particular county court, an interesting pattern emerged: individual property owners received almost $13,000 for their lands, while the railroad companies were given $1.

Viewing this apparent inequity as a violation of the Fifth Amendment's guarantee that private property shall not "be taken for public use, without just compensation," one railroad company took its case to the Illinois Supreme Court. When the judges affirmed the county court's decision, the company appealed to the U.S. Supreme Court, asking the justices to interpret the Fifth Amendment the same way John Barron had sixty-four years before: that the Just Compensation (or Takings) Clause should apply to states. The railroads, however, had a weapon that did not exist in Barron's day—the Fourteenth Amendment's Due Process Clause. And this Court did what the justices under John Marshall had refused to do: it ruled that the states must abide by the Fifth Amendment's commands regarding public use of private property. Writing for the majority, Justice Harlan had an opportunity to see the logic of his dissent in *Hurtado* become the basis for the opinion of the Court:

In determining what is due process of law regard must be had to substance, not to form. . . . If compensation for private property taken for public use is an essential element of due

process of law as ordained by the Fourteenth Amendment, then the final judgment of a state court . . . is to be decreed the act of the State within the meaning of that amendment.

Harlan added that just compensation indeed constituted "a vital principle of republican institutions" without which "almost all other rights would become worthless." As a consequence, a state violated the Due Process Clause of the Fourteenth Amendment when it did not provide just payment for seized private property.

The Court finally had incorporated, via the Fourteenth Amendment, a clause contained in the Bill of Rights. But it failed to bridge the apparent contradictions between *Hurtado* and *Chicago Railroad,* leaving open the question of which would provide controlling precedent in this area. In other words, why was the Court willing to incorporate the Fifth Amendment's guarantee of just compensation, but not the grand jury provision?

The next incorporation case, *Maxwell v. Dow* (1900), did little to shed light on this puzzling question. At issue were the antics of Charles L. "Gunplay" Maxwell, who robbed a Utah bank in 1898. Under the state's newly adopted constitution, an individual charged with a noncapital offense, such as armed robbery, could be tried by a jury of eight persons instead of the traditional twelve, and no provision was made for a defendant's right to a grand jury hearing. After an eight-person jury found him guilty and he was sentenced to eighteen years in prison, Maxwell hired an experienced criminal lawyer, J. W. N. Whitecotton, to represent him in the state supreme court. Whitecotton argued that the state's denial of grand jury proceedings and its jury trial system deprived Maxwell of his federal Fifth and Sixth Amendment rights, which should be incorporated under the Fourteenth Amendment's Due Process and Privileges or Immunities Clauses. Utah's highest court rejected this claim, and Maxwell filed for a writ of error with the U.S. Supreme Court, asking the justices specifically to rectify contradictions of interpretation between *Hurtado* and *Chicago Railroad.* The Court, 8–1, refused to do so and, in fact, virtually ignored the entire incorporation argument. Writing for the majority, Justice Rufus W. Peckham noted, "Trial by jury has never been affirmed to be a necessary requisite of due process of law."

6. Ibid., 21.

The three major cases following the *Slaughterhouse* decision—*Hurtado, Chicago Railroad,* and *Maxwell*—provided no clear answers to a legal community seeking direction on incorporation. If anything, more questions than answers remained because of the apparent contradictions among these decisions.

A STANDARD EMERGES

As legal scholars debated incorporation, the Court took a case that allowed the justices to impose some order on what had become a very confusing area of constitution interpretation. In *Twining v. New Jersey* (1908) the Court moved one cautious step closer to enunciating the doctrine of selective incorporation.

The case involved state fraud charges against Albert Twining and other officers of a bank trust. At his trial in state court, Twining refused to take the stand, invoking his guarantee against self-incrimination. The judge allowed him to do this, but in his charge to the jury he made reference to Twining's refusal to testify, insinuating that it implied guilt. If the federal Fifth Amendment provision against self-incrimination were applicable to the states, such comments clearly would be impermissible. Twining's attorney appealed to the state's high court, alleging that the judge's words denied Twining due process of law. But the New Jersey Supreme Court upheld the judge's right to highlight in his instructions to the jury a defendant's refusal to testify. Twining appealed to the U.S. Supreme Court, asking it to incorporate the Fifth Amendment protection against self-incrimination.

By an 8–1 vote (with only Justice Harlan dissenting) the Court rejected Twining's claim that the Fourteenth Amendment's Due Process Clause prohibited a state from denying a criminal defendant the right against compulsory self-incrimination. In Justice William H. Moody's words, "We think that the exemption from self-incrimination in the courts of the States is not secured by any part of the Federal Constitution." By so concluding, the Court affirmed the ruling against Twining by the Supreme Court of New Jersey.

The importance of this case, however, is not that the justices ruled against Twining, but that the Court for the first time articulated a position that opened the door for the future application of some rights to the states. In his majority opinion, Moody declared:

It is possible that some of the personal rights safeguarded by the first eight Amendments against National action may also be safeguarded against state action, because a denial of them would be a denial of due process of law. If this is so, it is not because those rights are enumerated in the first eight Amendments, but because they are of such a nature that they are included in the conception of due process of law. Few phrases of the law are so elusive of exact apprehension as this. Doubtless the difficulties of ascertaining its connotation have been increased in American jurisprudence, where it has been embodied in constitutions and put to new uses as a limit on legislative power. This court has always declined to give a comprehensive definition of it, and has preferred that its full meaning should be gradually ascertained by the process of inclusion and exclusion in the course of the decisions of cases as they arise. There are certain general principles well settled, however, which narrow the field of discussion and may serve as helps to correct conclusions. . . .

But . . . we prefer to rest our decision on broader grounds, and inquire whether the exemption from self-incrimination is of such a nature that it must be included in the conception of due process. Is it a fundamental principle of liberty and justice which inheres in the very idea of free government and is the inalienable right of a citizen of such a government? If it is, and if it is of a nature that pertains to process of law, this court has declared it to be essential to due process of law.

The Court's words in *Twining* established three important principles. First, some provisions of the Bill of Rights might be protected against state abridgment through the Due Process Clause of the Fourteenth Amendment. Second, the liberties included in due process of law attain such status not because they are enumerated in the first eight amendments, but because they are "fundamental and inalienable" rights. Third, the Court will not incorporate the entire Bill of Rights, but will consider rights individually when necessary as cases come before it. In this way, the Court moved cautiously toward an endorsement of selective incorporation. The justices would consider making the provisions of the Bill of Rights binding on the states on a case-by-case, right-by-right basis.

In the final analysis, the opinion in *Twining* is narrow in its approach to incorporation. The Court refused to make the entire Bill of Rights applicable to the states and denied that the specific right at issue—the exemption from compulsory self-incrimination—should be protected against state action. Still, *Twining* is an important decision because it created the *possibility* of incorporation by future Courts, if they could identify rights deemed fundamental and inalienable.

In *Twining*, Justice Moody provided several examples of fundamental and inalienable rights: a court must have jurisdiction to hear a case, it must provide adequate notice of trial dates and charges, and it must grant a trial for those accused of committing a crime. Beyond these, Moody did not specify what other guarantees might fall under this rubric; nor did he provide an adequate definition of what the Court meant by "fundamental and inalienable."

This gap put the burden on lawyers litigating claims of civil rights, civil liberties, and criminal justice to bring cases testing the boundaries of *Twining*. These lawyers had a vested interest in securing federal guarantees for their clients for whom such rights remained inapplicable in state courts. They recognized that cases involving free speech, religion, and search and seizure, which they were losing in state trial courts, could be won if the Court agreed that these and other rights were fundamental. It is not surprising, therefore, that one of the cases assessing the boundaries of *Twining* involved a free speech claim brought to the Court's attention by the American Civil Liberties Union.

The issues in *Gitlow v. New York* (1925) arose during the early 1900s when the United States was gripped by a fear of communist subversion. To combat the "red menace," several states, including New York, created commissions to investigate subversive organizations. The New York commission in 1919 raided one such group, arrested several Socialist Party leaders, and seized their materials, including the *Left Wing Manifesto*, a journal edited by Benjamin Gitlow, a leader in the Left Wing Section of the party. The journal called for mass action to overthrow the capitalist system in the United States.

Gitlow was prosecuted in a New York trial court for violating the state's criminal anarchy law. Under the leadership of Clarence Darrow, Gitlow's defense attorneys alleged that the statute violated the First Amendment's guarantee of free speech, a fundamental right deserving incorporation under the Due Process Clause.

In a 7–2 decision the Supreme Court affirmed Gitlow's conviction, but it also adopted Darrow's argument and incorporated the Free Speech and Press Clauses. As Justice Edward T. Sanford wrote for the majority,

For present purposes we may and do assume that freedom of speech and of the press . . . are among the fundamental personal rights and "liberties" protected by the due process clause of the Fourteenth Amendment from impairment by the states. . . . Reasonably limited . . . this freedom is an inestimable privilege in a free government.

The Court went no further: once again it refused to provide a more general principle by which to identify fundamental rights.

Nevertheless, *Gitlow* is an important case because it represents the Court's first solid steps to give meaning to the selective incorporation doctrine. In *Twining* the Court had declared that incorporation of some rights was possible; in *Gitlow* the justices made particular provisions of the Bill of Rights binding on the states. *Gitlow* was a portent of decisions to come, but it took the Court another twelve years to provide the next indication of what it meant by "fundamental rights." *Palko v. Connecticut* (1937), a case involving the Fifth Amendment's prohibition against double jeopardy, was the vehicle. While reading *Palko*, consider the signals it sent to lawyers across the nation. How did it help them to determine which rights were fundamental?

Palko v. Connecticut

302 U.S. 319 (1937)
laws.findlaw.com/US/302/319.html
Vote: 8 (Black, Brandeis, Cardozo, Hughes, McReynolds,
        Roberts, Stone, Sutherland)
        1 (Butler)
Opinion of the Court: Cardozo

The story of Frank Palka (whose name was misspelled as *Palko* in Court documents) begins in Connecticut, where he robbed a store and shot and killed two police officers. Arrested in Buffalo, New York, Palka confessed to the killings. At his trial for first-degree murder, the Connecticut judge refused to admit the confession, and, in the absence of such evidence, the jury found him guilty only of second-degree murder, for which Palka received a mandatory life sentence. State prosecutors appealed to the Connecticut Supreme Court of Errors, which reversed the trial judge's exclusion of Palka's confession and ordered a new trial. Palka's attorney objected, claiming that a new trial violated the Fifth Amendment's prohibition of double jeopardy. Nevertheless, Palka was tried and convicted again, but this time of first-degree murder, and sentenced to death. When his appeal to the Connecticut high court failed, Palka turned to the U.S. Supreme Court, asking it to incorporate double jeopardy.

MR. JUSTICE CARDOZO delivered the opinion of the Court.

The argument for appellant is that whatever is forbidden by the Fifth Amendment is forbidden by the Fourteenth also. The Fifth Amendment, which is not directed to the states, but solely to the federal government, creates immunity from double jeopardy. No person shall be "subject for the same offense to be twice put in jeopardy of life or limb." The Fourteenth Amendment ordains, "nor shall any State deprive any person of life, liberty, or property, without due process of law." To retry a defendant, though under one indictment and only one, subjects him, it is said, to double jeopardy in violation of the Fifth Amendment, if the prosecution is one on behalf of the United States. From this the consequence is said to follow that there is a denial of life or liberty without due process of law, if the prosecution is one on behalf of the People of a State. . . .

We have said that in appellant's view the Fourteenth Amendment is to be taken as embodying the prohibitions of the Fifth. His thesis is even broader. Whatever would be a violation of the original bill of rights (Amendments I to VIII) if done by the federal government is now equally unlawful by force of the Fourteenth Amendment if done by a state. There is no such general rule.

The Fifth Amendment provides, among other things, that no person shall be held to answer for a capital or otherwise infamous crime unless on presentment or indictment of a grand jury. This court has held that, in prosecutions by a state, presentment or indictment by a grand jury may give way to information at the instance of a public officer. The Fifth Amendment provides also that no person shall be compelled in any criminal case to be a witness against himself. This court has said that, in prosecutions by a state, the exemption will fail if the state elects to end it. The Sixth Amendment calls for a jury trial in criminal cases and the Seventh for a jury trial in civil cases at common law where the value in controversy shall exceed twenty dollars. This court has ruled that consistently with those amendments trial by jury may be modified by a state or abolished altogether. . . .

On the other hand, the due process clause of the Fourteenth Amendment may make it unlawful for a state to abridge by its statutes the freedom of speech which the First Amendment safeguards against encroachment by the Congress, or the like freedom of the press, or the free exercise of religion, or the right of peaceable assembly, without which speech would be unduly trammeled, or the right of one accused of crime to the benefit of counsel. In these and other situations immunities that are valid as against the federal government by force of the specific pledges of particular amendments have been found to be implicit in the concept of ordered liberty, and thus, through the Fourteenth Amendment, become valid as against the states.

The line of division may seem to be wavering and broken if there is a hasty catalogue of the cases on the one side and the other. Reflection and analysis will induce a different view. There emerges the perception of a rationalizing principle which gives to discrete instances a proper order and coherence. The right to trial by jury and the immunity from prosecution except as the result of an indictment may have value and importance. Even so, they are not of the very essence of a scheme of ordered liberty. To abolish them is not to violate a "principle of justice so rooted in the traditions and conscience of our people as to be ranked as fundamental." Few would be so narrow or provincial as to maintain that a fair and enlightened system of justice would be impossible without them. What is true of jury trials and indictments is true also, as the cases show, of the immunity from compulsory self-incrimination. This too might be lost, and justice still be done. Indeed, today as in the past there are students of our penal system who look upon the immu-

BOX 3-1 AFTERMATH . . . FRANK PALKA

ON THE EVENING of September 30, 1935, Frank Palka allegedly shot and killed two police officers in Bridgeport, Connecticut, after he had smashed a window of a music store and stolen a radio. Palka, a twenty-three-year-old aircraft riveter, had previously been in legal trouble for juvenile delinquency and statutory rape. He was found guilty of first-degree murder after an earlier trial had found him guilty of murder in the second degree. Palka's attorneys appealed to the U.S. Supreme Court, claiming that the second trial violated Palka's Fifth Amendment right against double jeopardy.

The Court in 1937 ruled against Palka, holding that the Double Jeopardy Clause was not binding on the states, but only on the federal government. However, in his opinion for the Court, Justice Benjamin Cardozo modified the standards of the selective incorporation doctrine making it easier for specific provisions of the Bill of Rights to be made applicable to the states. This doctrinal shift was a significant one for the expansion of civil liberties, but it did not help Frank Palka. On April 12, 1938, he was put to death in the Connecticut electric chair. Thirty-one years later, in *Benton v. Maryland*, the Supreme Court reversed its position and made the Double Jeopardy Clause binding on the states though the Due Process Clause of the Fourteenth Amendment.

Frank Palka as photographed with his mother in 1935.

SOURCE: Richard Polenberg, "Cardozo and the Criminal Law: Palko v. Connecticut Reconsidered," *Journal of Supreme Court History*, 1996 (Vol. 2), 92–105.

---

nity as a mischief rather than a benefit, and who would limit its scope, or destroy it altogether. No doubt there would remain the need to give protection against torture, physical or mental. Justice, however, would not perish if the accused were subject to a duty to respond to orderly inquiry. The exclusion of these immunities and privileges from the privileges and immunities protected against the action of the states has not been arbitrary or casual. It has been dictated by a study and appreciation of the meaning, the essential implications, of liberty itself.

We reach a different plane of social and moral values when we pass to the privileges and immunities that have been taken over from the earlier articles of the federal bill of rights and brought within the Fourteenth Amendment by a process of absorption. These in their origin were effective against the federal government alone. If the Fourteenth

Amendment has absorbed them, the process of absorption has had its source in the belief that neither liberty nor justice would exist if they were sacrificed. This is true, for illustration, of freedom of thought, and speech. Of that freedom one may say that it is the matrix, the indispensable condition, of nearly every other form of freedom. With rare aberrations a pervasive recognition of that truth can be traced in our history, political and legal. So it has come about that the domain of liberty, withdrawn by the Fourteenth Amendment from encroachment by the states, has been enlarged by latter-day judgments to include liberty of the mind as well as liberty of action. The extension became, indeed, a logical imperative when once it was recognized, as long ago it was, that liberty is something more than exemption from physical restraint, and that even in the field of substantive rights and duties the legislative judgment, if oppressive and arbitrary, may be overridden by the courts. Fundamental too in the concept of due process, and so in that of liberty, is the thought that condemnation shall be rendered only after trial. The hearing, moreover, must be a real one, not a sham or a pretense. . . .

Our survey of the cases serves, we think, to justify the statement that the dividing line between them, if not unfaltering throughout its course, has been true for the most part to a unifying principle. On which side of the line the case made out by the appellant has appropriate location must be the next inquiry and the final one. Is that kind of double jeopardy to which the statute has subjected him a hardship so acute and shocking that our polity will not endure it? Does it violate those "fundamental principles of liberty and justice which lie at the base of all our civil and political institutions"? The answer surely must be "no." What the answer would have to be if the state were permitted after a trial free from error to try the accused over again or to bring another case against him, we have no occasion to consider. We deal with the statute before us and no other. The state is not attempting to wear the accused out by a multitude of cases with accumulated trials. It asks no more than this, that the case against him shall go on until there shall be a trial free from the corrosion of substantial legal error. This is not cruelty at all, nor even vexation in any immoderate degree. If the trial had been infected with error adverse to the accused, there might have been review at his instance, and as often as necessary to purge the vicious taint. A reciprocal privilege, subject at all times to the discretion of the presiding judge, has now been granted to the state. There is here no seismic innovation. The edifice of justice stands, its symmetry, to many, greater than before. . . .

The judgment is

Affirmed.

In 1937 the Court did not consider the protection against double jeopardy a fundamental right, and this ruling set the groundwork for Palka's execution *(see Box 3-1)*. But did the Court provide attorneys with any further guidance as to what this elusive term included? To some extent it did. It defined fundamental rights as those without which liberty and justice could not exist, rights that were implicit in the concept of ordered liberty. But the process by which the Court planned to make known

exactly which rights fall into that category remained unchanged from *Twining* and *Gitlow.* The majority of justices adopted the doctrine of selective incorporation, from which they would determine fundamental rights on a case-by-case basis.

INCORPORATION IN THE AFTERMATH OF *PALKO*

What happened after *Palko?* As Table 3-1 shows, the Court continued to incorporate the various guarantees contained in the Bill of Rights. At first, the Court limited itself to those rights contained in the First Amendment, but in the 1960s it began to incorporate guarantees the Constitution affords to the rights of the criminally accused.

Selective incorporation of these guarantees came as a part of the Warren Court's revolution in defendants' rights. For example, under the Warren Court, indigents were guaranteed the right to counsel in certain kinds of cases, and police were required to read suspected offenders a set of statements known as Miranda warnings. In the coming chapters we shall have more to say about the Warren Court and its liberalizing decisions in this area and others involving rights and liberties. Here, we point out that the impact of the Warren Court revolution would have been less far reaching had it not incorporated these guarantees. Only indigents involved in federal—not state—crimes would be given attorneys; only federal agents—not state or local police officers—would be forced to read Miranda warnings, and so on. Because the majority of prosecutions originate in states (federal prosecutions are a small percentage of the total nationwide), these decisions would have affected few defendants. Instead, with incorporation, all levels of government must abide by the selected constitutional guarantees.

A second development after *Palko* is that justices continued to advocate different solutions to this long-standing problem. Most remained loyal to the selective incorporation doctrine. For example, in *Adamson v. California* (1947), an appeal asking the Court to apply the Fifth Amendment Self-Incrimination Clause to the states, Justice Stanley F. Reed, for the majority, stated, "*Palko* held that such provisions of the Bill of Rights as were 'implicit

TABLE 3-1 Cases Incorporating Provisions of the Bill of Rights into the Due Process Clause of the Fourteenth Amendment

Constitutional Provision	Case	Year
First Amendment		
Freedom of speech and press	*Gitlow v. New York*	1925
Freedom of assembly	*DeJonge v. Oregon*	1937
Freedom of petition	*Hague v. CIO*	1939
Free exercise of religion	*Cantwell v. Connecticut*	1940
Establishment of religion	*Everson v. Board of Education*	1947
Fourth Amendment		
Unreasonable search and seizure	*Wolf v. Colorado*	1949
Exclusionary rule	*Mapp v. Ohio*	1961
Fifth Amendment		
Payment of compensation for the taking of private property	*Chicago, Burlington and Quincy R. Co. v. Chicago*	1897
Self-incrimination	*Malloy v. Hogan*	1964
Double jeopardy	*Benton v. Maryland*	1969
When jeopardy attaches	*Crist v. Bretz*	1978
Sixth Amendment		
Public trial	*In re Oliver*	1948
Due notice	*Cole v. Arkansas*	1948
Right to counsel (felonies)	*Gideon v. Wainwright*	1963
Confrontation and cross-examination of adverse witnesses	*Pointer v. Texas*	1965
Speedy trial	*Klopfer v. North Carolina*	1967
Compulsory process to obtain witnesses	*Washington v. Texas*	1967
Jury trial	*Duncan v. Louisiana*	1968
Right to counsel (misdemeanor when jail is possible)	*Argersinger v. Hamlin*	1972
Eighth Amendment		
Cruel and unusual punishment	*Louisiana ex rel. Francis v. Resweber*	1947
Ninth Amendment		
Privacy[a]	*Griswold v. Connecticut*	1965

NOTE: Provisions the Court has not incorporated: Second Amendment right to keep and bear arms; Third Amendment right against quartering soldiers; Fifth Amendment right to a grand jury hearing; Seventh Amendment right to a jury trial in civil cases; and Eighth Amendment right against excessive bail and fines.

a. The word *privacy* does not appear in the Ninth Amendment (nor anywhere in the text of the Constitution). In *Griswold* several members of the Court viewed the Ninth Amendment as guaranteeing (and incorporating) that right.

in the concept of ordered liberty' became secure from state interference by the [Due Process] clause. But it held nothing more." In applying *Palko,* the Court declined to incorporate self-incrimination.

Other justices expressed different views. Some offered a more cramped version of incorporation, and others a more expansive perspective. Justices John Marshall Harlan (II)[7] and Potter Stewart represent the more restricted position. They endorsed an approach that, according to observers, is close to *Twining.* They viewed the term "due process of law" as requiring only that criminal trials "be fundamentally fair." Their solution, as Harlan writes, involves

a much more discriminating process of adjudication than does "incorporation.". . . It entails a "gradual process of judicial inclusion and exclusion," seeking, with due recognition of constitutional tolerance for state experimentation and disparity, to ascertain those immutable principles of justice which inhere in the very idea . . . of free government which no member of the Union may disregard.[8]

The more expansive approach was argued by justices such as Frank Murphy, Hugo Black, and William Douglas. They supported, as did the first John Marshall Harlan, complete incorporation of the Bill of Rights. Black's dissent in *Adamson,* joined by Douglas, states their view:

If the choice must be between the selective process of the *Palko* decision, applying some of the Bill of Rights to the States, or the *Twining* rule, applying none of them, I would choose the *Palko* selective process. But, rather than accept either of these choices, I would follow what I believe was the original purpose of the Fourteenth Amendment—to extend to all the people of the nation the complete protection of the Bill of Rights.

These two developments after *Palko*—the Warren Court's use of selective incorporation and the support for distinct approaches to incorporation—are well illustrated in *Duncan v. Louisiana* (1968).[9] As you read the case,

consider how the various opinions encapsulate a historical range of perspectives on the incorporation of the Bill of Rights.

Duncan v. Louisiana

391 U.S. 145 (1968)
laws.findlaw.com/US/391/145.html
Vote: 7 (Black, Brennan, Douglas, Fortas, Marshall, Warren, White)
    2 (Harlan, Stewart)
Opinion of the Court: White
Concurring opinions: Black, Fortas
Dissenting opinion: Harlan

In October 1966 Gary Duncan, a nineteen-year-old black man, was driving down a highway when he spotted two of his younger cousins on the side of the road with four white youths. Duncan apparently became alarmed because his cousins had recently transferred to a formerly all-white school where "racial incidents" had occurred. He pulled over and asked his cousins to get into his car. What happened next is in dispute. The white youths asserted that Duncan slapped one of them, Herman M. Landry Jr., before getting back into his car; Duncan and his cousins maintained that he "touched" Landry rather than slapped him.

Just after Duncan pulled away, P. E. Lathum, the principal of a private school formed in response to the desegregation of the area's public schools, called the police. He had observed the encounter and alleged that Duncan had hit Landry. The police questioned Duncan, but let him go in the belief that he had not committed an offense. But, just a few days later, they arrested Duncan on the charge of cruelty to juveniles.[10]

Believing that their son's arrest was racially motivated, Duncan's parents contacted Richard Sobol, an attorney for the Lawyers Constitutional Defense Committee, a civil rights organization with offices in New Orleans. Sobol agreed to represent Duncan after he became convinced that "Duncan's case was part of a pattern of

---

7. Two justices had the name John Marshall Harlan. To distinguish them, scholars and other writers call the elder one John Marshall Harlan (I). He served on the Court from 1877 to 1911. His grandson, identified as John Marshall Harlan (II), served from 1955 to 1971. Harlan (I) took quite liberal positions on issues such as incorporation and civil rights, often in dissent. Harlan (II) was conservative, frequently dissenting from liberal Warren Court rulings.

8. Justice Harlan, dissenting in *Duncan v. Louisiana* (1968).

9. For oral arguments in this case, navigate to: *oyez.nwu.edu.*

10. We adopt this paragraph and those that follow from Cortner, *The Supreme Court,* 248–251.

anti–civil rights intimidation and harassment" in the area.

Sobol filed a motion with a state trial court judge to dismiss the charge against Duncan. He asserted that Louisiana law permitted a cruelty to juveniles conviction only against an individual having supervision over the juveniles, which did not apply to Duncan. The prosecuting attorney reported to Landry's family that they would not be able to win the case.

Rather than see Duncan set free, Landry's mother asked the police to rearrest him on charges of simple battery, a misdemeanor punishable in Louisiana by a maximum of two years in jail and a $300 fine. Sobol went back to court, this time to request that Duncan be tried by a jury. The judge refused, citing the Louisiana Constitution, which grants jury trials only in cases involving punishments of hard labor or death.

The state supreme court also rejected Sobol's request, and he appealed to the U.S. Supreme Court. His argument was simple: the Due Process Clause of the Fourteenth Amendment should be used to apply the Sixth Amendment's jury trial guarantee to all state prosecutions where a sentence of two or more years could be imposed. The state countered with a reference to *Maxwell v. Dow*, in which the Court held that trial by jury has "never been affirmed to be a necessary requisite of due process of law."

MR. JUSTICE WHITE delivered the opinion of the Court.

The test for determining whether a right extended by the Fifth and Sixth Amendments with respect to federal criminal proceedings is also protected against state action by the Fourteenth Amendment has been phrased in a variety of ways in the opinions of this Court. The question has been asked whether a right is among those "'fundamental principles of liberty and justice which lie at the base of all our civil and political institutions,'" . . . whether it is "basic in our system of jurisprudence," . . . and whether it is "a fundamental right, essential to a fair trial.". . . The claim before us is that the right to trial by jury guaranteed by the Sixth Amendment meets these tests. The position of Louisiana, on the other hand, is that the Constitution im-

poses upon the States no duty to give a jury trial in any criminal case, regardless of the seriousness of the crime or the size of the punishment which may be imposed. Because we believe that trial by jury in criminal cases is fundamental to the American scheme of justice, we hold that the Fourteenth Amendment guarantees a right of jury trial in all criminal cases which—were they to be tried in a federal court—would come within the Sixth Amendment's guarantee. Since we consider the appeal before us to be such a case, we hold that the Constitution was violated when appellant's demand for jury trial was refused.

The history of trial by jury in criminal cases has been frequently told. It is sufficient for present purposes to say that by the time our Constitution was written, jury trial in criminal cases had been in existence in England for several centuries and carried impressive credentials traced by many to Magna Carta. Its preservation and proper operation as a protection against arbitrary rule were among the major objectives of the revolutionary settlement which was expressed in the Declaration and Bill of Rights of 1689. . . .

Jury trial came to America with English colonists, and received strong support from them. Royal interference with the jury trial was deeply resented. . . . The Declaration of Independence stated solemn objections to the King's making "Judges dependent on his Will alone, for the tenure of their offices, and the amount and payment of their salaries," to his "depriving us in many cases, of the benefits of Trial by Jury," and to his "transporting us beyond Seas to be tried for pretended offenses." The Constitution itself, in Art. III, §2, commanded:

"The Trial of all Crimes, except in Cases of Impeachment, shall be by Jury; and such Trial shall be held in the State where the said Crimes shall have been committed."

Objections to the Constitution because of the absence of a bill of rights were met by the immediate submission and adoption of the Bill of Rights. Included was the Sixth Amendment which, among other things, provided:

"In all criminal prosecutions, the accused shall enjoy the right to a speedy and public trial, by an impartial jury of the State and district wherein the crime shall have been committed."

The constitutions adopted by the original States guaranteed jury trial. Also, the constitution of every State entering the Union thereafter in one form or another protected the right to jury trial in criminal cases.

Even such skeletal history is impressive support for considering the right to jury trial in criminal cases to be fundamental to our system of justice. . . .

We are aware of prior cases in this Court in which the prevailing opinion contains statements contrary to our holding today that the right to jury trial in serious criminal cases is a fundamental right and hence must be recognized by the States as part of their obligation to extend due process of law to all persons within their jurisdiction. Louisiana relies especially on *Maxwell v. Dow* (1900); *Palko v. Connecticut* (1937); and *Snyder v. Massachusetts* (1934). None of these cases, however, dealt with a State which had purported to dispense entirely with a jury trial in serious criminal cases. *Maxwell* held that no provision of the Bill of Rights applied to the States—a position long since repudiated—and that the Due Process Clause of the Fourteenth Amendment did not prevent a State from trying a defendant for a noncapital offense with fewer than 12 men on the jury. It did not deal with a case in which no jury at all had been provided. In neither *Palko* nor *Snyder* was jury trial actually at issue, although both cases contain important dicta asserting that the right to jury trial is not essential to ordered liberty and may be dispensed with by the States regardless of the Sixth and Fourteenth Amendments. These observations, though weighty and respectable, are nevertheless dicta, unsupported by holdings in this Court that a State may refuse a defendant's demand for a jury trial when he is charged with a serious crime. . . . Respectfully, we reject the prior dicta regarding jury trial in criminal cases.

The guarantees of jury trial in the Federal and State Constitutions reflect a profound judgment about the way in which law should be enforced and justice administered. A right to jury trial is granted to criminal defendants in order to prevent oppression by the Government. Those who wrote our constitutions knew from history and experience that it was necessary to protect against unfounded criminal charges brought to eliminate enemies and against judges too responsive to the voice of higher authority. The framers of the constitutions strove to create an independent judiciary but insisted upon further protection against arbitrary action. Providing an accused with the right to be tried by a jury of his peers gave him an inestimable safeguard against the corrupt or overzealous prosecutor and against the compliant, biased, or eccentric judge. If the defendant preferred the common-sense judgment of a jury to the more tutored but perhaps less sympathetic reaction of the single judge, he was to have it. Beyond this, the jury trial provisions in the Federal and State Constitutions reflect a fundamental decision about the exercise of official power—a reluctance to entrust plenary powers over the life and liberty of the citizen to one judge or to a group of judges. Fear of unchecked power, so typical of our State and Federal Governments in other respects, found expression in the criminal law in this insistence upon community participation in the determination of guilt or innocence. The deep commitment of the Nation to the right of jury trial in serious criminal cases as a defense against arbitrary law enforcement qualifies for protection under the Due Process Clause of the Fourteenth Amendment, and must therefore be respected by the States. . . .

The judgment below is reversed and the case is remanded for proceedings not inconsistent with this opinion.

Reversed and remanded.

MR. JUSTICE BLACK, with whom MR. JUSTICE DOUGLAS joins, concurring.

The Court today holds that the right to trial by jury guaranteed defendants in criminal cases in federal courts by Art. III of the United States Constitution and by the Sixth Amendment is also guaranteed by the Fourteenth Amendment to defendants tried in state courts. With this holding I agree for reasons given by the Court. I also agree because of reasons given in my dissent in *Adamson v. California*. In that dissent, I took the position, contrary to the holding in *Twining v. New Jersey*, that the Fourteenth Amendment made all of the provisions of the Bill of Rights applicable to the States. This Court in *Palko v. Connecticut*, decided in 1937, . . . explain[ed] that certain Bill of Rights' provisions were made applicable to the States by bringing them "within the Fourteenth Amendment by a process of absorption." Thus *Twining v. New Jersey* refused to hold that any one of the Bill of Rights' provisions was made applicable to the States by the Fourteenth Amendment, but *Palko*, which must be read as overruling *Twining* on this point, concluded that the Bill of Rights Amendments that are "implicit in the concept of ordered liberty" are "absorbed" by the Fourteenth as protections against state invasion. In this situation I said in *Adamson v. California* that, while "I would . . . extend to all the people of the nation the complete protection of the Bill of Rights," that "if the choice must be between the selective process of the *Palko* decision applying some of the Bill of Rights to the States, or the *Twining* rule applying none of them, I would choose the *Palko* selective process." . . . And I am very happy to support this selective process through which our Court has since the *Adamson* case held most of the specific Bill of Rights' protections applicable to the States to the same extent they are applicable to the Federal Government. Among these are the right to trial by jury decided today, the right against compelled self-incrimination, the right to counsel, the right to compulsory process for witnesses, the right to confront witnesses, the right to a speedy and public trial, and the right to be free from unreasonable searches and seizures.

All of these holdings making Bill of Rights' provisions applicable as such to the States mark, of course, a departure from the *Twining* doctrine holding that none of those provisions were enforceable as such against the States. The dissent in this case, however, makes a spirited and forceful defense of that now discredited doctrine. . . .

While I do not wish at this time to discuss at length my disagreement with Brother HARLAN's forthright and frank restatement of the now discredited *Twining* doctrine, I do want to point out what appears to me to be the basic difference between us. His view, as was indeed the view of *Twining,* is that "due process is an evolving concept" and therefore that it entails a "gradual process of judicial inclusion and exclusion" to ascertain those "immutable principles . . . of free government which no member of the Union may disregard." Thus the Due Process Clause is treated as prescribing no specific and clearly ascertainable constitutional command that judges must obey in interpreting the Constitution, but rather as leaving judges free to decide at any particular time whether a particular rule or judicial formulation embodies an "immutable principle of free government" or is "implicit in the concept of ordered liberty," or whether certain conduct "shocks the judge's conscience" or runs counter to some other similar, undefined and undefinable standard. Thus due process, according to my Brother HARLAN, is to be a phrase with no permanent meaning, but one which is found to shift from time to time in accordance with judges' predilections and understandings of what is best for the country. If due process means this, the Fourteenth Amendment, in my opinion, might as well have been written that "no person shall be deprived of life, liberty or property except by laws that the judges of the United States

Supreme Court shall find to be consistent with the immutable principles of free government." It is impossible for me to believe that such unconfined power is given to judges in our Constitution that is a written one in order to limit governmental power.

Another tenet of the *Twining* doctrine as restated by my Brother HARLAN is that "due process of law requires only fundamental fairness." But the "fundamental fairness" test is one on a par with that of shocking the conscience of the Court. Each of such tests depends entirely on the particular judge's idea of ethics and morals instead of requiring him to depend on the boundaries fixed by the written words of the Constitution. Nothing in the history of the phrase "due process of law" suggests that constitutional controls are to depend on any particular judge's sense of values. . . . [Rather] the Due Process Clause gives all Americans, whoever they are and wherever they happen to be, the right to be tried by independent and unprejudiced courts using established procedures and applying valid pre-existing laws. There is not one word of legal history that justifies making the term "due process of law" mean a guarantee of a trial free from laws and conduct which the courts deem at the time to be "arbitrary," "unreasonable," "unfair," or "contrary to civilized standards." The due process of law standard for a trial is one in accordance with the Bill of Rights and laws passed pursuant to constitutional power, guaranteeing to all alike a trial under the general law of the land.

Finally I want to add that I am not bothered by the argument that applying the Bill of Rights to the States, "according to the same standards that protect those personal rights against federal encroachment," interferes with our concept of federalism in that it may prevent States from trying novel social and economic experiments. I have never believed that under the guise of federalism the States should be able to experiment with the protections afforded our citizens through the Bill of Rights. . . . It seems to me totally inconsistent to advocate, on the one hand, the power of this Court to strike down any state law or practice which it finds "unreasonable" or "unfair" and, on the other hand, urge that the States be given maximum power to develop their own laws and procedures. Yet the due process approach of my Brother HARLAN . . . does just that since in effect it restricts the States to practices which a majority of this Court is willing to approve on a case-by-case basis. . . .

In closing I want to emphasize that I believe as strongly

as ever that the Fourteenth Amendment was intended to make the Bill of Rights applicable to the States. I have been willing to support the selective incorporation doctrine, however, as an alternative, although perhaps less historically supportable than complete incorporation. The selective incorporation process, if used properly, does limit the Supreme Court in the Fourteenth Amendment field to specific Bill of Rights' protections only and keeps judges from roaming at will in their own notions of what policies outside the Bill of Rights are desirable and what are not. And, most importantly for me, the selective incorporation process has the virtue of having already worked to make most of the Bill of Rights' protections applicable to the States.

MR. JUSTICE FORTAS, concurring.

I join the judgments and opinions of the Court in these cases because I agree that the Due Process Clause of the Fourteenth Amendment requires that the States accord the right to jury trial in prosecutions for offenses that are not petty. . . . I believe, as my Brother WHITE's opinion for the Court . . . persuasively argues, that the right to jury trial in major prosecutions, state as well as federal, is so fundamental to the protection of justice and liberty that "due process of law" cannot be accorded without it.

It is the progression of history, and especially the deepening realization of the substance and procedures that justice and the demands of human dignity require, which has caused this Court to invest the command of "due process of law" with increasingly greater substance. . . . This Court has not been alone in its progressive recognition of the content of the great phrase which my Brother WHITE describes as "spacious language" and Learned Hand called a "majestic generality." The Congress, state courts, and state legislatures have moved forward with the advancing conception of human rights in according procedural as well as substantive rights to individuals accused of conflict with the criminal laws.

But although I agree with the decision of the Court, I cannot agree with the implication that the tail must go with the hide: that when we hold, influenced by the Sixth Amendment, that "due process" requires that the States accord the right of jury trial for all but petty offenses, we automatically import all of the ancillary rules which have been

or may hereafter be developed incidental to the right to jury trial in the federal courts. I see no reason whatever, for example, to assume that our decision today should require us to impose federal requirements such as unanimous verdicts or a jury of 12 upon the States. We may well conclude that these and other features of federal jury practice are by no means fundamental—that they are not essential to due process of law—and that they are not obligatory on the States.

I would make these points clear today. Neither logic nor history nor the intent of the draftsmen of the Fourteenth Amendment can possibly be said to require that the Sixth Amendment or its jury trial provision be applied to the States together with the total gloss that this Court's decisions have supplied. The draftsmen of the Fourteenth Amendment intended what they said, not more or less: that no State shall deprive any person of life, liberty, or property without due process of law. It is ultimately the duty of this Court to interpret, to ascribe specific meaning to this phrase. There is no reason whatever for us to conclude that, in so doing, we are bound slavishly to follow not only the Sixth Amendment but all of its bag and baggage, however securely or insecurely affixed they may be by law and precedent to federal proceedings. To take this course, in my judgment, would be not only unnecessary but mischievous because it would inflict a serious blow upon the principle of federalism. The Due Process Clause commands us to apply its great standard to state court proceedings to assure basic fairness. It does not command us rigidly and arbitrarily to impose the exact pattern of federal proceedings upon the 50 States. On the contrary, the Constitution's command, in my view, is that in our insistence upon state observance of due process, we should, so far as possible, allow the greatest latitude for state differences. It requires, within the limits of the lofty basic standards that it prescribes for the States as well as the Federal Government, maximum opportunity for diversity and minimal imposition of uniformity of method and detail upon the States. Our Constitution sets up a federal union, not a monolith.

This Court has heretofore held that various provisions of the Bill of Rights such as the freedom of speech and religion guarantees of the First Amendment, the prohibition of unreasonable searches and seizures in the Fourth Amendment, the privilege against self-incrimination of the Fifth Amendment, and the right to counsel and to confrontation under the Sixth Amendment "are all to be enforced against the States under the Fourteenth Amendment according to the same standards that protect those personal rights against federal encroachment." I need not quarrel with the specific conclusion in those specific instances. But unless one adheres slavishly to the incorporation theory, body and substance, the same conclusion need not be superimposed upon the jury trial right. I respectfully but urgently suggest that it should not be. Jury trial is more than a principle of justice applicable to individual cases. It is a system of administration of the business of the State. While we may believe (and I do believe) that the right of jury trial is fundamental, it does not follow that the particulars of according that right must be uniform. We should be ready to welcome state variations which do not impair—indeed, which may advance—the theory and purpose of trial by jury.

MR. JUSTICE HARLAN, whom MR. JUSTICE STEWART joins, dissenting.

The States have always borne primary responsibility for operating the machinery of criminal justice within their borders, and adapting it to their particular circumstances. In exercising this responsibility, each State is compelled to conform its procedures to the requirements of the Federal Constitution. The Due Process Clause of the Fourteenth Amendment requires that those procedures be fundamentally fair in all respects. It does not, in my view, impose or encourage nationwide uniformity for its own sake; it does not command adherence to forms that happen to be old; and it does not impose on the States the rules that may be in force in the federal courts except where such rules are also found to be essential to basic fairness.

The Court's approach to this case is an uneasy and illogical compromise among the views of various Justices on how the Due Process Clause should be interpreted. The Court does not say that those who framed the Fourteenth Amendment intended to make the Sixth Amendment applicable to the States. And the Court concedes that it finds nothing unfair about the procedure by which the present appellant was tried. Nevertheless, the Court reverses his conviction: it holds, for some reason not apparent to me, that the Due Process Clause incorporates the particular clause of the Sixth Amendment that requires trial by jury in federal criminal cases—including, as I read its opinion, the sometimes

trivial accompanying baggage of judicial interpretation in federal contexts. I have raised my voice many times before against the Court's continuing undiscriminating insistence upon fastening on the States federal notions of criminal justice, and I must do so again in this instance. With all respect, the Court's approach and its reading of history are altogether topsy-turvy. . . .

. . . In my view, often expressed elsewhere, the first section of the Fourteenth Amendment was meant neither to incorporate, nor to be limited to, the specific guarantees of the first eight Amendments. The overwhelming historical evidence . . . demonstrates, to me conclusively, that the Congressmen and state legislators who wrote, debated, and ratified the Fourteenth Amendment did not think they were "incorporating" the Bill of Rights and the very breadth and generality of the Amendment's provisions suggest that its authors did not suppose that the Nation would always be limited to mid-19th century conceptions of "liberty" and "due process of law" but that the increasing experience and evolving conscience of the American people would add new "intermediate premises." In short, neither history, nor sense, supports using the Fourteenth Amendment to put the States in a constitutional straitjacket with respect to their own development in the administration of criminal or civil law.

Although I therefore fundamentally disagree with the total incorporation view of the Fourteenth Amendment, it seems to me that such a position does at least have the virtue, lacking in the Court's selective incorporation approach, of internal consistency: we look to the Bill of Rights, word for word, clause for clause, precedent for precedent because, it is said, the men who wrote the Amendment wanted it that way. For those who do not accept this "history," a different source of "intermediate premises" must be found. The Bill of Rights is not necessarily irrelevant to the search for guidance in interpreting the Fourteenth Amendment, but the reason for and the nature of its relevance must be articulated.

Apart from the approach taken by the absolute incorporationists, I can see only one method of analysis that has any internal logic. That is to start with the words "liberty" and "due process of law" and attempt to define them in a way that accords with American traditions and our system of government. This approach, involving a much more discriminating process of adjudication than does "incorporation," is, albeit difficult, the one that was followed throughout the 19th and most of the present century. It entails a "gradual process of judicial inclusion and exclusion," seeking, with due recognition of constitutional tolerance for state experimentation and disparity, to ascertain those "immutable principles . . . of free government which no member of the Union may disregard." Due process was not restricted to rules fixed in the past, for that "would be to deny every quality of the law but its age, and to render it incapable of progress or improvement." Nor did it impose nationwide uniformity in details, for

"[t]he Fourteenth Amendment does not profess to secure to all persons in the United States the benefit of the same laws and the same remedies. Great diversities in these respects may exist in two States separated only by an imaginary line. On one side of this line there may be a right of trial by jury, and on the other side no such right. Each State prescribes its own modes of judicial proceeding."

Through this gradual process, this Court sought to define "liberty" by isolating freedoms that Americans of the past and of the present considered more important than any suggested countervailing public objective. The Court also, by interpretation of the phrase "due process of law," enforced the Constitution's guarantee that no State may imprison an individual except by fair and impartial procedures.

The relationship of the Bill of Rights to this "gradual process" seems to me to be twofold. In the first place it has long been clear that the Due Process Clause imposes some restrictions on state action that parallel Bill of Rights restrictions on federal action. Second, and more important than this accidental overlap, is the fact that the Bill of Rights is evidence, at various points, of the content Americans find in the term "liberty" and of American standards of fundamental fairness. . . .

Today's Court still remains unwilling to accept the total incorporationists' view of the history of the Fourteenth Amendment. This, if accepted, would afford a cogent reason for applying the Sixth Amendment to the States. The Court is also, apparently, unwilling to face the task of determining whether denial of trial by jury in the situation before us, or in other situations, is fundamentally unfair. Consequently, the Court has compromised on the ease of the incorporationist position, without its internal logic. It has simply assumed that the question before us is whether the

Jury Trial Clause of the Sixth Amendment should be incorporated into the Fourteenth, jot-for-jot and case-for-case, or ignored. Then the Court merely declares that the clause in question is "in" rather than "out."

The Court has justified neither its starting place nor its conclusion. If the problem is to discover and articulate the rules of fundamental fairness in criminal proceedings, there is no reason to assume that the whole body of rules developed in this Court constituting Sixth Amendment jury trial must be regarded as a unit. The requirement of trial by jury in federal criminal cases has given rise to numerous subsidiary questions respecting the exact scope and content of the right. It surely cannot be that every answer the Court has given, or will give, to such a question is attributable to the Founders; or even that every rule announced carries equal conviction of this Court; still less can it be that every such subprinciple is equally fundamental to ordered liberty. . . .

Even if I could agree that the question before us is whether Sixth Amendment jury trial is totally "in" or totally "out," I can find in the Court's opinion no real reasons for concluding that it should be "in." The basis for differentiating among clauses in the Bill of Rights cannot be that only some clauses are in the Bill of Rights, or that only some are old and much praised, or that only some have played an important role in the development of federal law. These things are true of all. The Court says that some clauses are more "fundamental" than others, but it turns out to be using this word in a sense that would have astonished Mr. Justice Cardozo and which, in addition, is of no help. The word does not mean "analytically critical to procedural fairness" for no real analysis of the role of the jury in making procedures fair is even attempted. Instead, the word turns out to mean "old," "much praised," and "found in the Bill of Rights." The definition of "fundamental" thus turns out to be circular. . . .

The argument that jury trial is not a requisite of due process is quite simple. The central proposition of *Palko,* a proposition to which I would adhere, is that "due process of law" requires only that criminal trials be fundamentally fair. As stated above, apart from the theory that it was historically intended as a mere shorthand for the Bill of Rights, I do not see what else "due process of law" can intelligibly be thought to mean. If due process of law requires only fundamental fairness, then the inquiry in each case must be whether a state trial process was a fair one. The Court has held, properly I think, that in an adversary process it is a requisite of fairness, for which there is no adequate substitute, that a criminal defendant be afforded a right to counsel and to cross-examine opposing witnesses. But it simply has not been demonstrated, nor, I think, can it be demonstrated, that trial by jury is the only fair means of resolving issues of fact. . . .

. . . [T]here is a wide range of views on the desirability of trial by jury, and on the ways to make it most effective when it is used; there is also considerable variation from State to State in local conditions such as the size of the criminal caseload, the ease or difficulty of summoning jurors, and other trial conditions bearing on fairness. We have before us, therefore, an almost perfect example of a situation in which the celebrated dictum of Mr. Justice Brandeis should be invoked. It is, he said,

"one of the happy incidents of the federal system that a single courageous State may, if its citizens choose, serve as a laboratory. . . ."

This Court, other courts, and the political process are available to correct any experiments in criminal procedure that prove fundamentally unfair to defendants. That is not what is being done today: instead, and quite without reason, the Court has chosen to impose upon every State one means of trying criminal cases; it is a good means, but it is not the only fair means, and it is not demonstrably better than the alternatives States might devise.

I would affirm the judgment of the Supreme Court of Louisiana.

As *Duncan* illustrates, the Court continued to abide by the compromise position of selective incorporation, applying only those rights about which the justices believed "that neither liberty nor justice would exist if they were sacrificed." But, *in practice,* the total incorporation approach favored by the first John Marshall Harlan and

Hugo Black has predominated. As depicted in Table 3-1, between 1897 and 1969 the Court incorporated almost every guarantee contained in the Bill of Rights, in several cases reversing earlier precedents denying the incorporation of specific provisions. In fact, the Court has done what Harlan advocated in his lone dissent in *Hurtado:* it has applied virtually all guarantees contained in the first eight amendments to the states. The last right incorporated, ironically, was double jeopardy.

The theory of selective incorporation, in concept, emerged the victor; but, for all practical purposes and with only a few exceptions, total nationalization has prevailed. As a result, present reading of the Constitution now ensures that the basic civil liberties of citizens of the United States are uniformly protected against infringement by any government entity—federal, state, or local.

READINGS

Berger, Raoul. *Government by Judiciary.* Cambridge: Harvard University Press, 1977.

Cortner, Richard C. *The Supreme Court and the Second Bill of Rights.* Madison: University of Wisconsin Press, 1981.

Fairman, Charles. "Does the Fourteenth Amendment Incorporate the Bill of Rights?" *Stanford Law Review* 2 (1949): 5.

Frankfurter, Felix. "Memorandum on 'Incorporation' of the Bill of Rights into the Due Process Clause of the Fourteenth Amendment." *Harvard Law Review* 78 (1965): 746–783.

Green, John R. "The Bill of Rights, the Fourteenth Amendment, and the Supreme Court." *Michigan Law Review* 46 (1948): 869.

Henkin, Louis. "Selective Incorporation in the Fourteenth Amendment." *Yale Law Journal* 73 (1963): 74–88.

Levy, Leonard. *Introduction to the Fourteenth Amendment and the Bill of Rights: The Incorporation Theory.* New York: Da Capo, 1970.

Tribe, Laurence H. "Does the Privileges or Immunities Revival Portend the Future—Or Reveal the Structure of the Present?" *Harvard Law Review* 113 (1999): 110–198.

Walker, Frank H. "Constitutional Law—Was It Intended That the Fourteenth Amendment Incorporate the Bill of Rights?" *North Carolina Law Review* 42 (1964): 925–936.

PART II
CIVIL LIBERTIES

APPROACHING CIVIL LIBERTIES

THE NEXT SIX CHAPTERS explore Supreme Court interpretation of guarantees contained in the First and Second Amendments and those that have been seen as relating to the right of privacy. These constitutional provisions allow Americans to live their lives as they please, to worship in whatever manner they wish, to hold and express political and social views of their own conviction, to place demands upon the government, to print and read what satisfies them, and to keep government out of those areas of human life that are considered private and personal. Yet in contemporary society few freedoms are absolute. To maintain order, the government must regulate in ways that may restrict some of these liberties. The history of the Supreme Court is a chronicle of how it has played its role as an interpreter of these fundamental rights and an umpire between the often contradictory values of freedom and order.

As a student approaching civil liberties, perhaps for the first time, you might be wondering why we devote so much space in Chapter 4 (Religion) and Chapters 5 through 7 (Expression) to the following few phrases:

Congress shall make no law respecting an establishment of religion, or prohibiting the free exercise thereof; or abridging the freedom of speech, or of the press; or the right of the people peaceably to assemble, and to petition the Government for a redress of grievances.

After all, the guarantees contained in the First Amendment seem specific enough—or do they? Suppose we read about a religion that required its members to ingest LSD before religious services, or about students who were so fed up with university policies they burned down the administration building in protest, or about a radio station that regularly allowed its announcers to use profanity. Taking the words of the First Amendment, "Congress shall make no law," to heart, we might conclude that its language—the guarantees of freedom of religion, speech, and press—protects these activities. Is that conclusion correct? Is society obliged to condone practices and forms of expression such as those in our examples? What these and the subsequent case examples illustrate is that a gap sometimes exists between the words of the First Amendment and reality. Although the language of the amendment may seem explicit, its meaning can be elusive and therefore difficult to apply to actual circumstances.

In contrast, the constitutional problems presented by the Second Amendment center on what exactly the amendment covers. Some argue that it creates only a narrow right—a right of the states to maintain "a well regulated militia"; others suggest that it creates a broader right that enables citizens to "keep and bear" guns. In Chapter 8, we sort through these competing approaches, as well as the Court's statements on the subject.

Supreme Court formulation and interpretation of a right to privacy, as we shall see in Chapter 9, present even more difficulties, primarily because the Constitution contains no explicit mention of such a guarantee. Even though most justices agree that it exists, they have disagreed over various questions, including from what provision of the Constitution the right to privacy arises and how far it extends.

It is the gap between what the Constitution says (or

does not say) and the kinds of questions litigants ask the Court to address that explains why we devote so much space to civil liberties. Because the meaning of those rights is less than crystal clear, the institution charged with interpreting and applying them—the Supreme Court of the United States—has approached its task in a somewhat erratic way. Throughout the Court's history, different justices have brought different modes of interpretation to the guarantees of religion, expression, and the press, and to the right to privacy, which in turn have significantly affected the way citizens enjoy those rights.

Figure II-1 provides one way of looking at how differently the Court has treated First Amendment and priva-

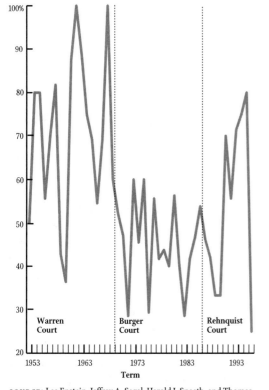

FIGURE II-1 Supreme Court Support for First Amendment and Privacy Claims, 1953–1996

SOURCE: Lee Epstein, Jeffrey A. Segal, Harold J. Spaeth, and Thomas G. Walker, *The Supreme Court Compendium: Data, Decisions, and Developments*, 2d ed. (Washington, D.C.: Congressional Quarterly, 1996), Table 3-8. Updated with the U.S. Supreme Court Judicial Data Base.

NOTE: The percentages after 1994 are based on very few cases and should be interpreted with caution.

cy claims over a period of more than four decades. The Court led by Earl Warren was generally supportive of such claims, ruling in favor of the party alleging some abridgment of his or her rights in more than two-thirds of the cases. The Court under Chief Justice Warren Burger moved in the opposite direction, with its support of the individual rights position well below that of its predecessor. It may be too soon to reach any conclusions about the Rehnquist Court, but, based on the data displayed in Figure II-1, it seems that the present justices will not be any less supportive of First Amendment and privacy rights than those who sat on the Burger Court.

Figure II-1 helps to reinforce the point that the amendments are open to interpretation, that the words of the Constitution alone do not necessarily provide a sufficient guidepost for the justices as they go about resolving cases. Even so, the data raise many questions. Why do the Burger and Rehnquist Courts evince patterns of decision making distinctly different from the Warren Court? Is it merely because recent Courts have had more conservative members? Or have the cases and the precedent governing their resolution changed? Perhaps the more recent justices have invoked different modes of analysis to resolve these disputes. Might it also be that the Court has responded to the public or to the other institutions of government? Another possibility is that the Warren Court was far more supportive of First Amendment and privacy claims than its predecessors, and the Burger and Rehnquist Courts, in turn, rebalanced the scales. Finding the answers to these questions will require careful study of the cases to come.

One of the more interesting trends regarding these personal rights cases is how they have—until recently—increased in number over time. As Figure II-2 shows, in the six years immediately prior to Earl Warren's appointment as chief justice, slightly more than 6 percent of the Court's rulings dealt with religion, expression, and privacy issues. During the Warren era, the number increased to 8.8 percent. The figure reached 10.3 percent and 8.5 percent during the Burger and Rehnquist years, respectively.

Why the proportion of the Court's docket devoted to these cases has grown is an interesting question. One an-

FIGURE II-2 Percentage of Agenda Space Allocated to Religion, Expression, and Privacy Cases, 1946–1998

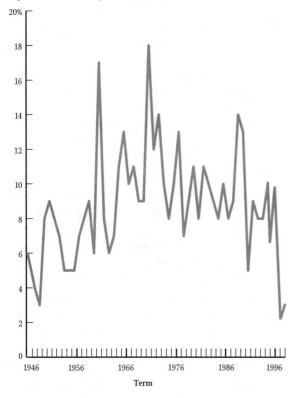

Term

SOURCE: Lee Epstein, Jeffrey A. Segal, Harold J. Spaeth, and Thomas G. Walker, *The Supreme Court Compendium: Data, Decisions, and Developments*, 2d ed. (Washington, D.C.: Congressional Quarterly, 1996), Table 2-9. Updated with the U.S. Supreme Court Judicial Database.

swer is that the justices themselves contributed to the growth with two decisions in the late 1930s, *Palko v. Connecticut* (1937) and *United States v. Carolene Products* (1938).[1] In *Palko*, as we saw in Chapter 3, a majority of the justices adopted the doctrine of selective incorporation, which would eventually lead the Court to apply most of the Bill of Rights to the states. This step, in turn, provided the Court with jurisdiction over a range of personal liberty disputes that it had previously denied itself.

Carolene Products, on its face, seems a less dramatic

step than *Palko.* In fact, at issue in this dispute was an economic, not civil liberties, regulation: a 1923 law prohibited the interstate shipment of milk blended with oil or fat. After Justice Harlan Fiske Stone, who wrote for the Court in the case, asserted that the justices would generally uphold such laws, he inserted a footnote, Footnote 4:

There may be narrower scope for operation of the presumption of constitutionality when legislation appears on its face to be within a specific prohibition of the Constitution, such as those of the first ten amendments, which are deemed equally specific when held to be embraced within the Fourteenth.

It is unnecessary to consider now whether legislation which restricts those political processes which can ordinarily be expected to bring about repeal of undesirable legislation, is to be subjected to more exacting judicial scrutiny under the general prohibitions of the Fourteenth Amendment than are most other types of legislation.

Nor need we enquire whether similar considerations enter into the review of statutes directed at particular religious, or national, or racial minorities; whether prejudice against discrete and insular minorities may be a special condition, which tends seriously to curtail the operation of those political processes ordinarily to be relied upon to protect minorities, and which may call for a correspondingly more searching judicial inquiry.[2]

With these words, Justice Stone advanced a doctrine that has become known as "preferred freedoms."[3] Under it, the Court presumes that *most* laws are constitutional; it is up to the challenger, not the government, to undermine that presumption. The presumption, however, shifts if the law in question abridges individual rights or liberties. For those, it is the government's responsibility to show that the law in question is narrowly tailored to achieve a compelling governmental interest. By articulating the preferred freedoms doctrine, which eventually made its way into the text of a majority opinion,[4] the Court signaled its willingness to give closer scrutiny to civil liberties (and rights) disputes and to remove itself from those involving economic issues.[5]

1. See Richard L. Pacelle, *The Transformation of the Supreme Court's Agenda* (Boulder: Westview Press, 1991); Jeffrey A. Segal and Harold J. Spaeth, *The Supreme Court and the Attitudinal Model* (New York: Cambridge University Press, 1993).

2. We have omitted the cases cited in the note. For the full version, navigate to: *supct.law.cornell.edu/supct/cases/name.htm.*
3. See Chapter 5 for more details.
4. *Murdock v. Pennsylvania* (1942).
5. *Erie Railroad v. Tompkins* (1938), decided the same day as *Carolene Products,* reinforced the message that the Court was interested in closing

FIGURE II-3 Percentage of Agenda Space Allocated to Rights and Liberties Cases by the U.S. Supreme Court, the Canadian Supreme Court, and Britain's Appellate Committee of the House of Lords

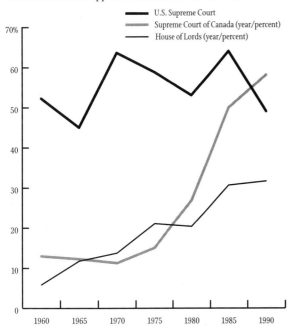

SOURCES: United States: U.S. Supreme Court Judicial Database, with orally argued citation as the unit of analysis. The data depicted cover all civil rights and liberties cases, not just those involving First Amendment and privacy disputes. Canada and Britain: We thank Charles R. Epp for providing these data.

NOTE: Data for the U.S. Supreme Court are by term; data for Canada and Britain are by year.

Another explanation for the increasing number of cases is that actors outside of the Court—most notably, lawyers and organized interests such as the American Civil Liberties Union and the NAACP—who had adequate, if not substantial, sources of financial support, generated something of a "rights revolution." As Charles R. Epp notes:

The rights revolution in the United States . . . developed within a broader political economy of litigation. The growth of a sup-

port structure for legal mobilization—consisting of rights-advocacy organizations, a diverse and organizationally sophisticated legal profession, a broad array of financing sources, and federal right-advocacy efforts—propelled new rights issues onto the Supreme Court's agenda. Although judicial policies [*Palko* and Footnote Four, for example] contributed to the development of that support structure, changes in the support structure have typically resulted from forces that are broader than the Court's policies alone.[6]

Lending credence to this explanation, which (like *Carolene Products*) extends not only to First Amendment but also to other rights and liberties cases, is that the number of cases has increased in other nations experiencing growth in their "support structure." Figure III-3 makes this clear. Just as these disputes have come to dominate the U.S. Supreme Court's docket, so are they now prominent on those of Britain's House of Lords and, especially, Canada's Supreme Court.

Whatever the cause of the growth, it is true that civil liberties cases represent some of the most significant issues in American constitutional law. Disputes involving aid to religious institutions, prayer in schools, the rights of protesters, censorship of the press, libel, obscenity, and reproductive rights all fall into this category. The Court's response to these issues determines the extent to which the government can constitutionally impose regulations that impinge on personal freedom.

Each decade brings to the Court new questions regarding these fundamental freedoms, as well as novel approaches to more traditional issues. In the coming pages, we examine the major controversies that the justices have been asked to settle. In some areas they have been successful in developing coherent and settled doctrine. In others the Court has repeatedly returned to the same conflicts between personal freedoms and government authority without reaching conclusions that stand the test of time. This is not surprising. As you read the coming chapters you will discover that these issues are not easy to resolve; rather, they present perplexing conflicts among values that go to the very core of what it means to be an American citizen.

the door on ordinary economic disputes, which had been "staples" on its agenda for many years. In this case, the Court held that the federal courts were not free to make their own common law to resolve diversity cases—those between citizens of different states. As the Court put it, "There is no general federal common law." See Pacelle, *Transformation of the Supreme Court's Agenda.*

6. *The Rights Revolution* (University of Chicago Press, 1998), 69.

CHAPTER 4
RELIGION: EXERCISE AND ESTABLISHMENT

O N MY ARRIVAL in the United States," wrote Alexis de Tocqueville in the 1830s, "the religious aspect of the country was the first thing that struck my attention; and the longer I stayed there, the more I perceived the great political consequences resulting from this new state of things. In France I had almost always seen the spirit of religion and the spirit of freedom marching in opposite directions. But in America I found they were intimately united and that they reigned in common over the same country."[1] Writing in the 1990s, political commentator Garry Wills asserted, "We may not realize that we live in the most religious nation in the developed world. But nine out of ten Americans say that they have never doubted the existence of God, and internationally, Americans rank second (behind only Malta) when rating the importance of God in their lives. So why is it surprising when the decisions we make in the voting booth reflect our basic religious values?"[2]

Two of the most astute observers of American politics, writing 155 years apart, reached similar conclusions: religion plays an important role in the lives of most Americans. In a nation where 60 percent to 75 percent of the population belongs to one of the more than 340,000 churches, temples, mosques, and synagogues, it is not surprising to find chaplains reading invocations before legislative sessions or cities putting up Christmas displays.[3]

Indeed, as Tocqueville observed, Americans have always been a religious people. We all learned in elementary school that the first settlers came to America to escape religious persecution in Europe and to practice their religion freely in a new land. What we often forget, however, is that as the colonies developed during the seventeenth century, they too became intolerant toward "minority" religions: many passed anti-Catholic laws or imposed ecclesiastical views on their citizens. Prior to the adoption of the Constitution, only two states (Maryland and Rhode Island) provided full religious freedoms—the remaining eleven had some restrictive laws. Six states had established state religions. Puritanism was the official faith of the Massachusetts Bay Colony, for instance, while Virginia established itself under the Church of England.

More tolerant attitudes toward religious liberty developed with time. After independence was declared, some states adopted constitutions that contained guarantees of religious freedom. For example, North Carolina's 1776 constitution proclaimed, "All men have a natural and unalienable right to worship Almighty God according to the dictates of their own consciences." But other constitutions continued to favor some religions over others. While Delaware's said that "[t]here shall be no establishment of any religious sect in this State in preference to another," it required all state officers to "profess faith in God the Father, and in Jesus Christ His Only Son."

1. Alexis de Tocqueville, *Democracy in America*, vol. 1 (New York: Vintage Books, 1954), 319.

2. Garry Wills, *Under God* (New York: Simon and Schuster, 1990), book jacket.

3. For excellent reviews of the role religion plays in American political

culture, see Kenneth D. Wald, *Religion and Politics in the United States,* 3d ed. (Washington, D.C.: CQ Press, 1997); and Wills, *Under God.*

It would be fair to say that when the Framers gathered in Philadelphia, they—like modern-day Americans—held divergent views about the relationship between religion and the state. Even so, the subject of religion arose only occasionally during the course of the debates. After one particularly difficult session, Benjamin Franklin moved that the delegates pray "for the assistance of Heaven, and its blessings on our deliberations." With virtual unanimity, the delegates attacked Franklin, arguing that a prayer session might offend some members and that it would require them to pay a minister "to officiate in [the] service."[4] In the end, the Founders mentioned religion only once in the Constitution. Article VI provides that all government officials must take an oath to "support this Constitution; but no religious Test shall ever be required as a Qualification to any Office or public Trust under the United States."

Opponents of the new Constitution objected to its lack of any guarantees of religious liberty. New York Anti-Federalists, for example, condemned the document for "not securing the rights of conscience in matters of religion, of granting the liberty of worshipping God agreeable to the mode thereby dictated."[5] Many states proposed amendments to the Constitution that centered on religious liberty. When James Madison drew up what would become the Bill of Rights, he included a section on religion: "The Civil Rights of none shall be abridged on account of religious belief or worship, nor shall any national religion be established, nor shall the full and equal rights of conscience be in any manner, or on any pretext, infringed." After several rounds of changes, the Framers adopted two provisions to protect religious liberty: the Establishment Clause and the Free Exercise Clause. Together they became the first two guarantees contained in the First Amendment of the Constitution: "Congress shall make no law respecting an establishment of religion, or prohibiting the free exercise thereof."

How has the Court interpreted these two clauses? Are their meanings the same today as when the Framers wrote them? In this chapter, we examine these and other questions, and we begin with a basic question that has implications for both clauses: What is religion?

DEFINING RELIGION

Suppose some prisoners form a religion holding that God requires them to eat filet mignon and drink Cabernet Sauvignon every day. Members of this new religion ask prison officials to serve them these things, but the officials, believing that the religion is nothing more than a ploy to get expensive meat and wine, refuse the request. The prisoners file a lawsuit to force the prison to comply. They claim that the government is depriving them of their right to freely exercise their religion.

This dispute may strike you as easy to resolve; after all, it seems clear that the prisoners formed this religion only to obtain steak and wine. But how would you distinguish their "religion" from others that also seek to obtain benefits for their members at society's expense? For example, if an Orthodox Jew is fired from her job because she refuses to work on Saturdays, may the state deny her unemployment benefits? Is she using her religion to take money from the state? You would probably answer no to both questions because you perceive a difference between the religion of the prisoners and the religion of the unemployed worker. But what is that difference? How do we distinguish a genuine religion from a sham?

These questions are critical to our discussion because if a religion is not genuine or bona fide, it is not entitled to protection under the religion clauses of the First Amendment. But the cases that come before the Supreme Court are never as obvious as our gourmet prisoners' lawsuit, and, in fact, the Court has had a good deal of difficulty in defining religion in terms of the First Amendment. Its first attempt came in 1879 in *Reynolds v. United States*. In the next section, which deals with the free exercise of religion, we discuss this case in some detail. Here, it is enough to say that it involved the Mormon church, whose adherents at the time of this dispute lived mostly in the Utah territory. Apparently, because the church was relatively new (it had formed in 1830) and its practices, particularly polygamy, were unfamiliar, if not distasteful, to the Court, the justices felt the need to

4. Quoted in *A History of the American Constitution* by Daniel A. Farber and Suzanna Sherry (St. Paul, Minn.: West Publishing, 1990), 122–123.

5. Address of the Albany Antifederal Committee, April 26, 1788, excerpted in ibid., 181.

consider whether it was a religion at all. Writing for the Court, Chief Justice Morrison R. Waite suggested the following:

The word "religion" is not defined in the Constitution. We must go elsewhere, therefore, to ascertain its meaning, and nowhere more appropriately, we think, than to the history of the times in the midst of which the provision was adopted.

Using this approach, Waite did not declare that the Mormons were not a religion; but he did say that the government could outlaw one of its teachings—the practice of polygamy—because there was no support for it at the time of the founding of our nation.

In fact, at the time the Mormon religion was founded, its adherents were persecuted and even attacked by hostile mobs. Many Mormons moved to the West because other states would not tolerate their presence. For example, in 1838 Missouri called out the militia because, as the state governor wrote, "The Mormons must be treated as enemies, and must be exterminated."[6] As *Reynolds* indicates, government efforts to undermine the religion did not stop after the Mormons settled in Utah. In addition to the antipolygamy law, Congress in 1887 passed an act that allowed the government to "disenfranchise Mormon voters, remove corporate status from the Mormon church, and confiscate all church property."[7] About thirteen hundred Mormons were arrested.

A decade or so after the decision in *Reynolds*, the Court had an opportunity to reconsider it when a Mormon challenged a law that disqualified individuals from voting if they refused to take an oath "abjuring bigamy or polygamy." But in *Davis v. Beason* (1890), the Court only reinforced *Reynolds*, this time with a statement about beliefs in God and "morals":

The term "religion" has reference to one's views of his relations to his Creator, and to the obligations they impose of reverence for his being and character, and of obedience to his will. . . . With man's relations to his Maker and the obligations he may think they impose, and the manner in which an expression shall be made by him of his belief on those subjects, no interference can be permitted, provided always the laws of society,

designed to secure its peace and prosperity, and the morals of its people, are not interfered with.

These are narrow approaches to religion; *Reynolds* suggests that religious practices that are new or were unknown to the Framers can be regulated by the government. When we consider that during the eighteenth century there were only a few dozen major religions or sects compared with more than 250 today—to say nothing of the hundreds of small "fringe" groups—we can see why this ruling was so underinclusive.[8] *Davis* binds religion to a belief in God, a belief that some religions do not hold or about which some "religious" individuals are skeptical. It also permits regulation of religious practices if those practices interfere with the "morals" of the people. In short, through the nineteenth century, courts defined religion, as legal scholar Laurence Tribe has written, in terms of "theistic notions respecting divinity, morality, and worship. In order to be considered legitimate, religions had to be viewed as 'civilized' by Western standards."[9]

Fortunately for adherents of nonmainstream religions, *Reynolds* and *Davis* were not the Court's last words on the subject. Since the 1940s two types of cases have provided the Court with opportunities to reconsider Chief Justice Waite's approach. The first centers on religions that appear to be shams and is well exemplified by *United States v. Ballard* (1944). Guy Ballard and his wife asserted that Saint Germain had chosen him as a "divine messenger." According to Ballard, to carry out the saint's wishes, he founded the "I Am" religion in California. As the spiritual leader of I Am, Ballard claimed supernatural healing powers and told his followers that he needed money to continue his work. Ballard used the postal service to collect these funds, making a good deal of money along the way.

Asserting that the I Am sect was not a religion, the federal government accused Ballard of using the mails to defraud people. When the case reached the Supreme Court, it addressed the question of what a jury could consider in determining whether to convict Ballard. The

6. Quoted in *American Constitutional Law* by Laurence Tribe (Mineola, N.Y.: Foundation Press, 1988), 1271.
7. Ibid.

8. These figures were quoted in ibid., 1179.
9. Ibid.

trial court judge had told the jury that it could not take into account the truth of Ballard's views (for example, whether Saint Germain had chosen Ballard as a messenger); rather, it could consider only the sincerity with which Ballard held his views. The Supreme Court agreed with this approach. Writing for the majority, Justice William O. Douglas asserted:

Men may believe what they cannot prove. They may not be put to the proof of their religious doctrines or beliefs. Religious experiences which are as real as life to some may be incomprehensible to others. Yet the fact that they may be beyond the ken of mortals does not mean that they can be made suspect before the law. Many take their gospel from the New Testament. But it would hardly be supposed that they could be tried before a jury charged with the duty of determining whether those teachings contained false representations. The miracles of the New Testament, the Divinity of Christ, life after death, the power of prayer are deep in the religious convictions of many. If one could be sent to jail because a jury in a hostile environment found those teachings false, little indeed would be left of religious freedom.

As for the Ballards, Douglas had this to say:

The religious views espoused by [Ballard] might seem incredible, if not preposterous, to most people. But if those doctrines are subject to trial before a jury charged with finding their truth or falsity, then the same can be done with the religious beliefs of any sect. When the triers of fact undertake that task, they enter a forbidden domain.

Under the *Ballard* approach, the proper test of a constitutionally protected religious belief is not the truth of its doctrine, but the sincerity with which it is held. For our gourmet prisoners, then, we would ask if they sincerely held their religious views, rather than if those views were factually accurate.

The second category of cases in which the Court has considered what religion is involves conscientious objector exemptions from the military. In the Universal Military Training and Service Act of 1940, Congress provided exemptions from military combat to individuals "who, by reason of religious training and belief, [are] conscientiously opposed to participation in war in any form." The law defined religious training and belief as "an individual's belief in a relation to a Supreme Being involving duties superior to those arising by any human relation but [not including] essentially political, sociological, or

philosophical views or a merely personal moral code."

Using Congress's definition, members of some organized religions, such as the Quakers, would qualify for exemptions. But what about those who are not members of a traditional, organized religion or those who do not necessarily frame their religious views with reference to a supreme being? Could they obtain religious exemptions from military service?

As the Vietnam War raged on in the 1960s, several cases presented the Court with an opportunity to answer these questions. In *United States v. Seeger* (1965) the justices considered whether individuals who were not members of an organized religion could obtain a military exemption on religious grounds. The appellee, Seeger, asserted that although he opposed participation in the war on the basis of his religious belief, that "he preferred to leave the question as to his belief in a Supreme Being open 'rather than answer yes or no.'" Did his declared "skepticism or disbelief in the existence of God" disqualify him from a religious exemption? Writing for the Court, Justice Tom C. Clark said it did not, for

Congress, in using the expression "Supreme Being" rather than the designation "God," was merely clarifying the meaning of religious training and belief so as to embrace all religions and to exclude essentially political, sociological, or philosophical views.

Clark then provided a standard to govern future litigation, a standard that again stressed the sincerity of the beliefs held:

[T]he test of belief "in relation to a Supreme Being" is whether a given belief that is sincere and meaningful occupies a place in the life of its possessor parallel to . . . the orthodox belief in God.

In response to the Court's ruling in *Seeger,* Congress removed from the 1940 law the words "in relation to a Supreme Being." But more litigation ensued. In *Welsh v. United States* (1970) the Court considered another section of the law, which excluded from exemption coverage individuals whose views were "essentially political, sociological, or philosophical." In a judgment for the Court,[10] Justice Black wrote:

10. A judgment represents the view of a plurality, not a majority, of the Court's members. Unlike a majority opinion (or "opinion of the Court"), a judgment lacks precedential value.

We certainly do not think that [the law's] exclusion of those persons with "essentially political, sociological, or philosophical views or a merely personal moral code" should be read to exclude those who hold strong beliefs about our domestic and foreign affairs or even those whose conscientious objection to participation in all wars is founded to a substantial extent upon considerations of public policy. The two groups of registrants that obviously do fall within these exclusions from the exemption are those whose beliefs are not deeply held and those whose objection to war does not rest at all upon moral, ethical, or religious principle but instead rests solely upon considerations of policy, pragmatism, or expediency. In applying [the law's] exclusion of those whose views are "essentially political, sociological, or philosophical" or of those who have "a merely personal moral code," it should be remembered that these exclusions are definitional and do not therefore restrict the category of persons who are conscientious objectors by "religious training and belief."

In other words, the Court expanded its ruling in *Seeger:* even if a draftee's objection to the war was not based strictly on traditional religious grounds, he could obtain a religious exemption if his moral and ethical beliefs were sincerely held—as sincerely held as traditionally defined religious beliefs. For if those views are so strong, they take on a religious character falling within the protection of the law.

In the conscientious objector cases, the Court moved away from the strictly theistic view of religion it had expressed in *Reynolds.* To be considered "religious," that is, to come under the protection of the Free Exercise Clause, one's religion need not be based in a belief in God. Rather, the Court's inquiries have focused on the sincerity (but not the truth) with which someone (or one's religion) holds a particular view.

The cases and narrative to come provide many opportunities to think about what elements define religion. As you read them, ask yourself whether the Court still evinces a bias toward established, major religions or has it significantly changed its approach in response to the expanding diversity of religions in contemporary America? You may also want to consider the competing charge that the Court has gone too far, that it extends First Amendment coverage to religions that are undeserving. How, for example, would the Court treat our prisoners' religion? Under the case law we have just reviewed, would the Court rule in their favor or in the favor of the prison officials?

FREE EXERCISE OF RELIGION

Instead of the prisoners and their demands, let us imagine a religious sect whose members handle poisonous snakes in the belief that such activity demonstrates their faith in God. Should government prohibit such activity because it is dangerous? Or would a law banning such behavior violate the First Amendment's Free Exercise Clause, which proclaims that there can be "no law . . . prohibiting the free exercise" of religion?

A literal approach to the Free Exercise Clause would suggest the latter; that is, religious denominations can pursue any exercise of their religion they desire. Yet it seems clear that the majority of Americans did not think the free exercise of religion meant any such thing at the time the clause was framed. While we do not know specifically what the Framers intended by the words "free exercise" (congressional debates over religious guarantees tended to focus on the Establishment Clause rather than the Free Exercise Clause), writings and documents of the day point to a universally accepted limit.[11] As Thomas Jefferson set it out in an 1802 letter to the Danbury Baptist Association: "[I believe] that religion is a matter which lies solely between man and his God; that he owes account to none other for his faith or his worship; that the legislative powers of the Government reach actions only, and not opinion."[12] In other words, the free exercise of religion is not limitless, as a literal reading of the amendment would suggest. Rather, at least under Jefferson's interpretation, governments can regulate "actions."

The Belief-Action Distinction and the Valid Secular Policy Test

Like Jefferson, the Court has never taken a literal approach to the Free Exercise Clause. Rather, in its first major decision in this area, it seized on his words to pro-

11. For an interesting view, see Michael W. McConnell, "Free Exercise as the Framers Understood It," in *The Bill of Rights,* ed. Eugene W. Hickok Jr. (Charlottesville: University of Virginia Press, 1991).

12. Letter to the Danbury Baptist Association, 1802, quoted in *Reynolds v. United States* (1879).

claim that some religious activities lie beyond First Amendment protections. As we mentioned, that case was *Reynolds v. United States,* which involved the Mormon practice of polygamy. Mormons believed that males "had the duty . . . to practice polygamy" and that failure to do so would result in "damnation in the life to come." Word of this practice found its way to the U.S. Congress, which was charged with governing the Utah territory, where many Mormons lived. In 1874 Congress outlawed polygamy. After Mormon follower George Reynolds took his second wife, he was charged with violating the law. In his defense, Reynolds argued that he was following the dictates of his faith, a right reserved to him under the Free Exercise Clause.

The U.S. Supreme Court disagreed. In a unanimous opinion, the justices rejected an absolutist interpretation of the clause and instead sought to draw a distinction between the behavior it did and did not protect. Chief Justice Waite's opinion for the Court asserted, "Congress was deprived of all legislative power over mere opinion, but was left free to reach actions which were in violation of social duties or subversive of the good order." This distinction between opinions (or beliefs) and actions (or practices) became, as we shall see, the centerpiece for several future religion cases.

Some have argued that the belief-action distinction was simply a way for the Court to uphold a government prohibition of an almost universally condemned practice advocated by a particularly unpopular church.[13] This view receives support from the Court's failure to use the distinction in its next major Free Exercise Clause case, *Pierce v. Society of Sisters* (1925). In 1922 Oregon had passed a compulsory public school education act, requiring children between the ages of eight and sixteen to attend public school. A diverse body of interests supported this measure for equally diverse reasons: progressives hailed it as a necessary step for the assimilation of immigrants, while the Ku Klux Klan backed it because it was viewed as anti-Catholic. Indeed, the ultimate effect of the Oregon law was to force closure of the state's privately run schools, many of which were Roman Catholic. The Society of Sisters, organized in 1880 to provide secular and religious instruction to children, faced dissolution because it derived more than $30,000 of its annual income from its school.

Rather than shut its doors, the society chose to sue the state, arguing that the law impinged on its free exercise rights. The sisters received support from organizations representing the spectrum of religions in the United States. Jews, Lutherans, Episcopalians, and Seventh-Day Adventists also had a vested interest in the case's outcome because most ran private schools. In addition, they wanted to show their unity of distaste for the Klan-backed law, believing it repressed "pluralism in education."[14]

In a unanimous opinion, the Court held for the Society of Sisters, but virtually ignored the *Reynolds* belief-action distinction. Instead, the Court rested its ruling on the view that the sisters (as opposed to the Mormons) engaged in a "useful and meritorious" undertaking. In the eyes of the justices:

The inevitable practical result of enforcing the act . . . would be the destruction of appellees' primary schools. . . . Appellees are engaged in a kind of undertaking not inherently harmful but long regarded as useful and meritorious. Certainly, there is nothing in the present record to indicate that they have failed to discharge their obligations to patrons, students, or the state.

The Court did not return to the belief-action dichotomy until 1940. That year the Court for the first time specifically applied the Free Exercise Clause to state action, in this instance, taken against the Jehovah's Witnesses *(see Box 4-1).* The Jehovah's Witnesses denomination actively promotes its religion and vigorously proselytizes to gain converts to the faith. Church members regularly distribute religious pamphlets and solicit money, activities regulated by laws in many states. In *Cantwell v. Connecticut,* among other cases, the Witnesses asked the Court to strike down such regulation as infringements upon their right to practice their religion freely.

13. John Brigham, *Civil Liberties and American Democracy* (Washington, D.C.: CQ Press, 1984), 77.

14. For more details on this case, see Clement E. Vose, *Constitutional Change* (Lexington, Mass.: Lexington Books, 1972).

BOX 4-1   THE JEHOVAH'S WITNESSES

THE JEHOVAH'S WITNESSES began in the 1870s in Pittsburgh, Pennsylvania. Starting as a Bible study class directed by Charles Taze Russell, the sect became a powerful grassroots movement. By the late 1930s, under the leadership of Joseph Franklin Rutherford, the Witnesses were preaching all over the United States and in several foreign countries.

Members see themselves as evangelical ministers with the mission to preach about Jehovah's struggle with Satan. They denounce organized religion, particularly Catholicism. In the past, their views made them very unpopular, and they were often in trouble with the law. Because they preached on street corners and distributed their literature door-to-door, the Witnesses could be prosecuted for violating city ordinances.

The Supreme Court decided the following cases:

Lovell v. City of Griffin (1938). May a town prohibit the distribution of pamphlets unless a permit has been obtained? No. The Court struck down the prohibition on First Amendment prior restraint grounds.

Cantwell v. Connecticut (1940). May a state prohibit the solicitation of money for any cause without first obtaining a license from a public official? No. The Court asserted that the law, as implemented, violated the Free Exercise Clause.

Jones v. Opelika (1942). May a town place a tax on those selling any goods door-to-door? Yes. The Court upheld the tax on the grounds that it covered commercial activity, which fell beyond First Amendment protection.

Murdock v. Pennsylvania (1943). May a city place a tax on those selling any goods door-to-door? No. The Court overruled *Jones v. Opelika* and held that the ordinance violated religious liberty guarantees.

Martin v. Struthers (1943). May a city prohibit all forms of door-to-door solicitation? No. The Court held that the ordinance violated First Amendment free speech guarantees.

Cantwell v. Connecticut

310 U.S. 296 (1940)
laws.findlaw.com/US/310/296.html
Vote: 9 (Black, Douglas, Frankfurter, Hughes, McReynolds, Murphy, Reed, Roberts, Stone)
        0
Opinion of the Court: Roberts

Newton Cantwell and his sons, Jesse and Russell, members of the Jehovah's Witnesses sect, were playing records and distributing pamphlets to citizens walking the streets in New Haven, Connecticut, in an area that was predominately Catholic. Two passersby took offense at the anti-Catholic messages in the material and complained. The next day, police arrested the Cantwells for violating a state law prohibiting individuals "from soliciting money for any cause" without a license. The law required those who wanted to solicit to obtain a "certificate of approval" from the state's secretary of the Public Wel-

Russell Cantwell raising funds for the Jehovah's Witnesses in Brooklyn in 1991. He, his brother Jesse, and his father Newton Cantwell were convicted for soliciting without a license; the Supreme Court overturned the convictions in 1940.

fare Council. The state charged this official with determining whether "the cause is a religious one" or one of a "bona fide object of charity." If the official found neither, he was authorized to withhold the necessary certificate.

Although this law was neutral—that is, it applied to all those engaging in solicitation—the Witnesses challenged it as a restriction on their free exercise rights. Hayden Covington, their attorney and a member of the American Civil Liberties Union (ACLU), argued that the law "deprived the Cantwells of their right of freedom to worship Almighty God."

MR. JUSTICE ROBERTS delivered the opinion of the Court.

The First Amendment declares that Congress shall make no law respecting an establishment of religion or prohibiting the free exercise thereof. The Fourteenth Amendment has rendered the legislatures of the states as incompetent as Congress to enact such laws. The constitutional inhibition of legislation on the subject of religion has a double aspect. On the one hand, it forestalls compulsion by law of the acceptance of any creed or the practice of any form of worship. Freedom of conscience and freedom to adhere to such religious organization or form of worship as the individual may choose cannot be restricted by law. On the other hand, it safeguards the free exercise of the chosen form of religion. Thus the Amendment embraces two concepts—freedom to believe and freedom to act. The first is absolute but, in the nature of things, the second cannot be. Conduct remains subject to regulation for the protection of society. The freedom to act must have appropriate definition to preserve the enforcement of that protection. In every case the power to regulate must be so exercised as not, in attaining a permissible end, unduly to infringe the protected freedom. No one would contest the proposition that a state may not, by statute, wholly deny the right to preach or to disseminate religious views. Plainly such a previous and absolute restraint would violate the terms of the guarantee. It is equally clear that a state may by general and non-discriminatory legislation regulate the times, the places, and the manner of soliciting upon its streets, and of holding meetings thereon; and may in other respects safeguard the peace, good order and comfort of the community, without unconstitutionally invading the liberties protected by the Fourteenth Amendment. The appellants are right in their insistence that the Act in question is not such a regulation. If a certificate is procured, solicitation is permitted without restraint but, in the absence of a certificate, solicitation is altogether prohibited.

The appellants urge that to require them to obtain a certificate as a condition of soliciting support for their views amounts to a prior restraint on the exercise of their religion within the meaning of the Constitution. The State insists that the Act, as construed by the Supreme Court of Connecticut, imposes no previous restraint upon the dissemination of religious views or teaching but merely safeguards against the perpetration of frauds under the cloak of religion. Conceding that this is so, the question remains whether the method adopted by Connecticut to that end transgresses the liberty safeguarded by the Constitution.

The general regulation, in the public interest, of solicitation, which does not involve any religious test and does not unreasonably obstruct or delay the collection of funds, is not open to any constitutional objection, even though the collection be for a religious purpose. Such regulation would not constitute a prohibited previous restraint on the free exercise of religion or interpose an inadmissible obstacle to its exercise.

It will be noted, however, that the Act requires an application to the secretary of the public welfare council of the State; that he is empowered to determine whether the cause is a religious one, and that the issue of a certificate depends upon his affirmative action. If he finds that the cause is not that of religion, to solicit for it becomes a crime. He is not to issue a certificate as a matter of course. His decision to issue or refuse it involves appraisal of facts, the exercise of judgment, and the formation of an opinion. He is authorized to withhold his approval if he determines that the cause is not a religious one. Such a censorship of religion as the means of determining its right to survive is a denial of liberty protected by the First Amendment and included in the liberty which is within the protection of the Fourteenth. . . .

Nothing we have said is intended even remotely to imply that, under the cloak of religion, persons may, with impunity, commit frauds upon the public. Certainly penal laws are available to punish such conduct. Even the exercise of religion may be at some slight inconvenience in order that the state may protect its citizens from injury. Without doubt a state may protect its citizens from fraudulent solicitation by requiring a stranger in the community, before permitting him publicly to solicit funds for any purpose, to establish his identity and his authority to act for the cause which he purports to represent. The state is likewise free to regulate the time and manner of solicitation generally, in the interest of public safety, peace, comfort, or convenience. But to condition the solicitation of aid for the perpetuation of religious views or systems upon a license, the grant of which rests in the exercise of a determination by state authority as to what is a religious cause, is to lay a forbidden burden upon the exercise of liberty protected by the Constitution. . . .

The judgment affirming the convictions . . . is reversed and the cause is remanded for further proceedings not inconsistent with this opinion. So ordered.

Reversed and remanded.

In this opinion, Justice Owen Roberts returned to the belief-action dichotomy, but treated it in a slightly different manner. He claimed that although the Free Exercise Clause covered belief and action, "The first is absolute but, in the nature of things, the second cannot be." How then would the Court distinguish protected action from illegal action? Under the principles articulated in *Cantwell*, which some analysts refer to as the "valid secular policy" test, the Court looks at the particular legislation or policy adopted by the government. If the policy serves a legitimate nonreligious government goal, not directed at any particular religion, the Court will uphold it, even if the legislation has the effect of conflicting with religious practices. In *Cantwell* the Court said that the state could regulate the collection of funds, even if those funds were for a religious purpose, because it has a valid interest in protecting its citizens from fraudulent solicitation. If Connecticut's law had not empowered a government official to determine whether a cause is religious or not, the Court probably would have upheld it as a legitimate secular policy.

Had the Court upheld the law, the Jehovah's Witnesses would have found it more difficult to carry out the dictates of their religion. By the same token, all other would-be solicitors—charitable organizations and the like—

would be similarly affected. In other words, the religious and the nonreligious would be subject to the regulations. Looking at *Cantwell* this way reveals an important underpinning of the logic of the valid secular policy test: neutrality. If the government has a valid secular reason for its policy, then in the eyes of the justices, religions should not be exempt from its coverage simply because they are religions. Exempting them would be to give religion an elevated position in society. One could argue that there is a difference between making it more difficult for a religion to carry out its mandate and a charity to collect funds. But, by adopting the valid secular policy test, the Court suggested that the effect on the Jehovah's Witnesses amounts to only an incidental intrusion on religion that comes about as the government pursues a legitimate interest.

Application of the Valid Secular Policy Test

How has this test worked? In particular, what constitutes a valid secular policy, a legitimate state interest? In *Cantwell*, Justice Roberts provided some clues as to what these concepts might encompass: the prevention of fraud, the regulation of the time and manner of solicitation, and actions involving the interest of "public safety, peace, comfort or convenience." Shortly after *Cantwell*, the Court added to Roberts's list when it reviewed cases involving mandatory flag salutes and child labor laws.

At issue in the first flag salute case, *Minersville School District v. Gobitis* (1940), were the recitation of the Pledge of Allegiance and the hand gesture or salute that accompanied it. For most individuals, particularly school children, the pledge and salute are noncontroversial routines that illustrate their loyalty to the basic tenets of American society. Such is not the case for the Jehovah's Witnesses, who exalt religious laws over all others. They claim that the salute and the pledge violate a teaching from Exodus:

Thou shalt not make unto thee any graven image, or any likeness of anything that is in heaven above, or that is in earth beneath, or that is in the water under the earth; thou shalt not bow down thyself to them, nor serve them.

Accordingly, Jehovah's Witnesses do not want their children to recite the pledge or salute the flag. The prob-

Walter Gobitas sued the Minersville, Pennsylvania, school district after his children, William and Lillian, were expelled for refusing to salute the flag because of their Jehovah's Witnesses faith.

lem, at the time of this case, was that schools made the pledge and salute to the flag mandatory for all public school children. Flag salute laws became particularly pervasive after World War I as a show of patriotism. Before the war only five states required flag salutes; by 1935 that figure had risen to eighteen, with many local school boards compelling the salute in absence of state legislation.[15]

Beginning in the mid-1930s, the Witnesses actively campaigned to do away with the salutes. The campaign began in Nazi Germany, where Jehovah's Witnesses refused to salute Hitler with raised palms and were punished by imprisonment in concentration camps. Joseph Rutherford, who was the Witnesses' leader in the United States, spoke out against the American flag salute, which, at that time, was regularly done with a straight, extended arm, resembling the Nazi-Fascist salute. He asserted that Witnesses "do not 'Heil Hitler' nor any other creature."

After Rutherford's speech, some members of the Jehovah's Witnesses asked their children not to salute the flag. Among these was Walter Gobitas,[16] whose two children—twelve-year-old Lillian and her younger brother William—attended a Pennsylvania public school with a mandatory flag salute policy. When they refused to salute the flag, they were expelled. Represented by attorneys from the Witnesses, including Hayden Covington, Gobitas brought suit against the school board, arguing that the expulsion violated his children's free speech and free exercise of religion rights. In Chapter 5 we explore the free speech component of Gobitas's claim. For now, we note that the Supreme Court rejected these arguments. Writing for the Court, Justice Felix Frankfurter asserted that:

[T]he ultimate foundation of a free society is the binding tie of cohesive sentiment. . . . The flag is the symbol of our national unity, transcending all internal differences. . . . To stigmatize legislative judgment in providing for this universal gesture of

15. We derive this account from Peter Irons, *The Courage of Their Convictions* (New York: Free Press, 1988), 17–24.

16. The family name, Gobitas, was misspelled in the records.

respect for the symbol of our national life . . . would amount to no less than the pronouncement of pedagogical and psychological dogma in a field where courts possess . . . no controlling competence.

To put it in terms of the valid secular policy test, Frankfurter was claiming that the state had a legitimate secular reason for requiring flag salutes: to foster patriotism. That the law affected the religious practice of the Jehovah's Witnesses did not, in Frankfurter's view, detract from its constitutionality. Besides, Frankfurter believed that the Court should not interfere with local policies because that "would in effect make [the Court] the school board for the country."

There were extraordinary repercussions from the Court's decision in *Gobitis*. After the ruling many states either retained or passed laws requiring flag salutes and pledges for all public school children and threatening to expel anyone who did not comply. What was startling was the violence against Jehovah's Witnesses. "Within two weeks of the Court's decision," two federal officials later wrote, "hundreds of attacks upon the Witnesses were reported to the Department of Justice."[17] Viewing their refusal to salute the flag as unpatriotic—especially as the country fought in World War II—mobs throughout the United States stoned, kidnapped, beat, and even castrated Jehovah's Witnesses.

These episodes of violence prompted many newspapers and major organizations, such as the American Bar Association, to condemn the Court's ruling. Three years later in *West Virginia Board of Education v. Barnette* (1943), after the initial intensity of the war years had subsided and the criticisms of the flag salute case had made their mark, the justices overruled *Gobitis*. However, as shown in Chapter 5, the *Barnette* decision was primarily based on freedom of speech grounds rather than on religious exercise.

The justices' response to the issues raised in *Prince v. Massachusetts* (1944) provides a second example of the valid secular policy test, this time applied in the area of child welfare. *Prince* involved a Massachusetts law prohibiting minors (girls under eighteen and boys under

twelve) from selling "upon the streets or in other public places, any newspaper, magazines, periodicals, or other articles of merchandise." It further specified that any parent or guardian allowing minors to perform such activity would be engaging in criminal behavior. Sarah Prince, a Jehovah's Witness, allowed her nine-year-old niece, Betty Simmons, for whom Prince was the legal guardian, to help her distribute religious pamphlets. Prince knew she was violating the law—she had been warned by school authorities—but she continued and was arrested.

At the trial court level, there was some doubt as to whether the child actually had sold materials, but when the case reached the Supreme Court, it dealt exclusively with this question: Did the state law violate First Amendment principles? A divided Court held that it did not. Writing for a five-person majority, Justice Wiley Rutledge asserted:

The State's authority over children's activities is broader than over like actions of adults. This is peculiarly true of public activities and in matters of employment. A democratic society rests . . . upon the healthy, well-rounded growth of young people into full maturity as citizens. . . . It may secure this against impeding restraints and dangers, within a broad range of selection. Among evils most appropriate for such action are the crippling effects of child employment . . . and the possible harms arising from other activities subject to all the diverse influences of the street. It is too late now to doubt that legislation appropriately designed to reach such evils is within the state's police power, whether against the parent's claim to control of the child or one that religious scruples dictate contrary action.

Clearly, legislatures can regulate religious practices of potential harm to children as well as those of questionable morality and safety. Such laws, in the eyes of the justices, present a reasonable use of state police power, which is the ability of states to regulate in the best interests of their citizens. In other words, child labor laws represent a valid secular policy and, when in opposition to a free exercise claim, the free exercise claim falls.

The Sherbert-Yoder *Compelling Interest Test*

Cantwell, *Gobitis*, and *Prince* have several traits in common: they were brought by a minority religion; they were decided during the 1940s, a period when the Court

17. Irons, *Courage of Their Convictions*, 22–23.

was neither particularly conservative nor liberal in ideological outlook; and they often involved free exercise arguments combined with other constitutional claims, such as freedom of expression. By the same token, the Court's approaches to the cases were relatively consistent. Religious beliefs were not questioned, but when a person's religious actions were at issue, the Court invoked the valid secular policy test to resolve the disputes. These approaches occasionally led the justices to strike down state policies (*Cantwell*), as well as to uphold them (*Gobitis, Prince*).

In the 1960s, however, major changes began to occur in the direction of precedent governing free exercise claims and in the kinds of cases the Court decided. The first signs came in *Braunfeld v. Brown*, which was one of several cases the Court heard in 1961 involving "blue" or Sunday closing laws. At issue in *Braunfeld* was Pennsylvania's blue law, which allowed only certain kinds of stores to remain open on Sunday. Abraham Braunfeld, an Orthodox Jew, owned a retail clothing and home furnishing store in Philadelphia. Because such stores were not among those permitted to remain open on Sunday, Braunfeld wanted the Court to issue a permanent injunction against the law. His religious principles dictated that he could not work on Saturday, the Jewish Sabbath, but he needed to be open six days a week for economic reasons. He challenged the law as a violation of, among other things, his right to exercise his religion.

In a judgment, Chief Justice Earl Warren upheld the constitutionality of blue laws and restated the belief-action dichotomy:

Certain aspects of religious exercise cannot, in any way, be restricted or burdened by either federal or state legislation. Compulsion by law of the acceptance of any creed or the practice of any form of worship is strictly forbidden. The freedom to hold religious beliefs and opinions is absolute. . . .

However, the freedom to act, even where the action is in accord with one's religious convictions, is not totally free from legislative restrictions. . . . [L]egislative power over mere opinion is forbidden but it may reach people's action when they are found to be in violation of important social duties or subversive of good order, even when the actions are demanded by one's religion.

But, according to many observers, Warren's opinion veered significantly from established precedent. Consider the following passage:

Of course, to hold unassailable all legislation regulating conduct which imposes solely an indirect burden on the observance of religion would be a gross oversimplification. If the purpose or effect of a law is to impede the observance of one or all religions or is to discriminate invidiously between religions, that law is constitutionally invalid even though the burden may be characterized as being only indirect. But if the State regulates conduct by enacting a general law within its power, the purpose and effect of which is to advance the State's secular goals, the statute is valid despite its indirect burden on religious observance *unless the State may accomplish its purpose by means which do not impose such a burden* (emphasis added).

In some ways, this statement merely restates the logic of *Cantwell* and the valid secular policy test. But note the italicized phrase: it represents an important addition to the test because it suggests that the state must show that its legislation achieves an important secular end that it cannot achieve with less restrictive legislation, that is, legislation that would place less of a burden on religious freedom.

Sunday closing laws, Warren reasoned, met both these standards. According to the chief justice, in passing blue laws, the state intended to set up a day of "rest, repose, recreation and tranquillity—a day which all members of the family and community have the opportunity to spend and enjoy together." In other words, the Sunday closing laws reflect a valid secular purpose. They also are the least restrictive way of accomplishing that purpose. Even though the laws indirectly burden members of some religions (for example, Orthodox Jews), Warren reasoned that the states had adopted a relatively unburdensome way of accomplishing their goal of creating a uniform "weekly respite from all labor."

Other members of the Court took issue with Warren's analysis, which, as a judgment, represented the views of only a plurality of the justices. Especially memorable were dissents by William Brennan and Potter Stewart. Brennan thought the Court had taken a misguided approach to the issue: "I would approach this case differently, from the point of view of the individuals whose liberty is—concededly—curtailed by these enactments. For the values of the First Amendment . . . look primarily towards the preservation of personal liberty, rather than towards the fulfillment of collective goals." In a one-paragraph dissent, Stewart put the issue even more starkly:

Pennsylvania has passed a law which compels an Orthodox Jew to choose between his religious faith and his economic survival. That is a cruel choice. It is a choice which I think no State can constitutionally demand. For me this is not something that can be swept under the rug and forgotten in the interest of enforced Sunday togetherness. I think the impact of this law upon the appellants grossly violates their constitutional right to free exercise of their religion.

The divided opinion over *Braunfeld* created something of a quandary for legal scholars: Was the Court—through its adoption of a least restrictive means approach—signaling a change in the way it would resolve free exercise disputes? Or was *Braunfeld* an aberration? Consider these questions as you read *Sherbert v. Verner*, decided just two years later.

Sherbert v. Verner

374 U.S. 398 (1963)
laws.findlaw.com/US/374/398.html
Vote: 7 (Black, Brennan, Clark, Douglas, Goldberg, Stewart, Warren)
2 (Harlan, White)
Opinion of the Court: Brennan
Concurring opinions: Douglas, Stewart
Dissenting opinion: Harlan

Adell Sherbert was spool tender in a Spartanburg, South Carolina, textile mill, a job she had held for thirty-five years. Sherbert worked Monday though Friday from 7 A.M. to 3 P.M. She had the option of working Saturdays, but chose not to. Sherbert was a member of the Seventh-Day Adventist church, which held that no work be performed between sundown on Friday and sundown on Saturday. In other words, Saturday was her church's Sabbath.

On June 5, 1959, Sherbert's employer informed her

that starting the next day work on Saturdays would no longer be voluntary: to retain her job she would need to report to the mill every Saturday. Sherbert continued to work Monday through Friday but, in accord with her religious beliefs, failed to show up on six successive Saturdays. Her employer fired her July 27.

Between June 5 and July 27, Sherbert had tried to find a job at three other textile mills, but they too operated on Saturdays. Sherbert filed for state unemployment benefits. Under South Carolina law, a claimant who is eligible for benefits must be "able to work . . . and available for work"; a claimant is ineligible for benefits if he or she has "failed, without good cause . . . to accept available suitable work when offered him by the employment office or the employer." The benefits examiner in charge of Sherbert's claim turned her down on the grounds that she failed, without good cause, to accept "suitable work when offered" it by her employer. In other words, her religious preference was an insufficient justification for her refusal of a job.

Sherbert and her lawyers filed suit in a state court, which ruled in favor of the employment office, as did the state supreme court. Sherbert's attorneys asked the U.S. Supreme Court to review the case, raising several claims emanating from the Court's previous rulings on the free exercise of religion. First, after reviewing the belief-action distinction of *Reynolds* and *Cantwell*, the lawyers tried to show that the state's denial actually impinged on the forbidden territory of beliefs. They illustrated the fine line that separates beliefs from actions: the South Carolina law

conditions [Sherbert's] eligibility for benefits . . . upon being willing to accept work on Saturday and disqualified her for her refusal to accept a job involving work on Saturday. In effect this requires her to repudiate her religious belief by professing a willingness to do something in conflict with the tenets of her church. This is not mere regulation of conduct. It invades the sphere of belief and intellect.

In essence, the attorneys were adopting a page out of Stewart's dissent in *Braunfeld:* the state was using economic coercion to force Sherbert to give up a religious belief.

Second, Sherbert's attorneys tried to use *Braunfeld,* a

precedent seemingly adverse to their client's interests, by flipping *Braunfeld* so that it worked for her.

The right to observe the Sabbath by abstaining from labor is of the essence. Take away that right or stifle it, and there is no freedom of religion so far as a Saturday Sabbatarian is concerned. Most Sunday-observing Christians probably feel as strongly with respect to their right similarly to refrain from labor in observance of Sunday as the Lord's Day.

The state had an easier task, or so it seemed. It could rely on *Braunfeld* to show that South Carolina, just like Pennsylvania, had not criminalized religious beliefs. Moreover, it offered—as did Pennsylvania in *Braunfeld*—a secular and, in its view, "legitimate governmental purposes for the law." According to the state, it sought to encourage "stable employment" and to discourage fraudulent behavior in those seeking unemployment benefits. Finally, while the state admitted that its denial of benefits financially burdened Sherbert, it argued that the burden was no more direct or greater than the economic hardship Braunfeld had alleged.

So the question for the Court to settle was the following: May a state deny unemployment benefits to persons whose religious beliefs preclude working on Saturdays?

MR. JUSTICE BRENNAN delivered the opinion of the Court.

The door of the Free Exercise Clause stands tightly closed against any governmental regulation of religious beliefs as such, *Cantwell v. Connecticut.* . . . On the other hand, the Court has rejected challenges under the Free Exercise Clause to governmental regulation of certain overt acts prompted by religious beliefs or principles, for "even when the action is in accord with one's religious convictions, [it] is not totally free from legislative restrictions." *Braunfeld v. Brown.* The conduct or actions so regulated have invariably posed some substantial threat to public safety, peace or order. See, e.g., *Reynolds v. United States; Prince v. Massachusetts.* . . .

Plainly enough, appellant's conscientious objection to Saturday work constitutes no conduct prompted by religious principles of a kind within the reach of state legislation. If, therefore, the decision of the South Carolina Supreme Court is to withstand appellant's constitutional

challenge, it must be either because her disqualification as a beneficiary represents no infringement by the State of her constitutional rights of free exercise, or because any incidental burden on the free exercise of appellant's religion may be justified by a "compelling state interest in the regulation of a subject within the State's constitutional power to regulate. . . ."

We turn first to the question whether the disqualification for benefits imposes any burden on the free exercise of appellant's religion. We think it is clear that it does. In a sense the consequences of such a disqualification to religious principles and practices may be only an indirect result of welfare legislation within the State's general competence to enact; it is true that no criminal sanctions directly compel appellant to work a six-day week. But this is only the beginning, not the end, of our inquiry. For "if the purpose or effect of a law is to impede the observance of one or all religions or is to discriminate invidiously between religions, that law is constitutionally invalid even though the burden may be characterized as being only indirect." *Braunfeld v. Brown.* Here not only is it apparent that appellant's declared ineligibility for benefits derives solely from the practice of her religion, but the pressure upon her to forego that practice is unmistakable. The ruling forces her to choose between following the precepts of her religion and forfeiting benefits, on the one hand, and abandoning one of the precepts of her religion in order to accept work, on the other hand. Governmental imposition of such a choice puts the same kind of burden upon the free exercise of religion as would a fine imposed against appellant for her Saturday worship.

Nor may the South Carolina court's construction of the statute be saved from constitutional infirmity on the ground that unemployment compensation benefits are not appellant's "right" but merely a "privilege." It is too late in the day to doubt that the liberties of religion and expression may be infringed by the denial of or placing of conditions upon a benefit or privilege. . . .

We must next consider whether some compelling state interest enforced in the eligibility provisions of the South Carolina statute justifies the substantial infringement of appellant's First Amendment right. It is basic that no showing merely of a rational relationship to some colorable state interest would suffice; in this highly sensitive constitutional area, "[o]nly the gravest abuses, endangering paramount interests, give occasion for permissible limitation.". . . No such abuse or danger has been advanced in the present case. The appellees suggest no more than a possibility that the filing of fraudulent claims by unscrupulous claimants feigning religious objections to Saturday work might not only dilute the unemployment compensation fund but also hinder the scheduling by employers of necessary Saturday work. But that possibility is not apposite here because no such objection appears to have been made before the South Carolina Supreme Court, and we are unwilling to assess the importance of an asserted state interest without the views of the state court. Nor, if the contention had been made below, would the record appear to sustain it; there is no proof whatever to warrant such fears of malingering or deceit as those which the respondents now advance. Even if consideration of such evidence is not foreclosed by the prohibition against judicial inquiry into the truth or falsity of religious beliefs, *United States v. Ballard*, . . . it is highly doubtful whether such evidence would be sufficient to warrant a substantial infringement of religious liberties. For even if the possibility of spurious claims did threaten to dilute the fund and disrupt the scheduling of work, it would plainly be incumbent upon the appellees to demonstrate that no alternative forms of regulation would combat such abuses without infringing First Amendment rights. . . .

In these respects, then, the state interest asserted in the present case is wholly dissimilar to the interests which were found to justify the less direct burden upon religious practices in *Braunfeld v. Brown*. The Court recognized that the Sunday closing law which that decision sustained undoubtedly served "to make the practice of [the Orthodox Jewish merchants'] . . . religious beliefs more expensive." But the statute was nevertheless saved by a countervailing factor which finds no equivalent in the instant case—a strong state interest in providing one uniform day of rest for all workers. That secular objective could be achieved, the Court found, only by declaring Sunday to be that day of rest. Requiring exemptions for Sabbatarians, while theoretically possible, appeared to present an administrative problem of such magnitude, or to afford the exempted class so great a competitive advantage, that such a requirement would have rendered the entire statutory scheme unworkable. In the present case no such justifications underlie the determination of the state court that appellant's religion makes her ineligible to receive benefits. . . .

The judgment of the South Carolina Supreme Court is reversed and the case is remanded for further proceedings not inconsistent with this opinion.

It is so ordered.

MR. JUSTICE DOUGLAS, concurring.

The case we have for decision seems to me to be of small dimensions, though profoundly important. The question is whether the South Carolina law which denies unemployment compensation to a Seventh-day Adventist who, because of her religion, has declined to work on her Sabbath, is a law "prohibiting the free exercise" of religion as those words are used in the First Amendment. It seems obvious to me that this law does run afoul of that clause. . . .

Some have thought that a majority of a community can, through state action, compel a minority to observe their particular religious scruples so long as the majority's rule can be said to perform some valid secular function. That was the essence of the Court's decision in the Sunday Blue Law Cases . . . a ruling from which I then dissented and still dissent.

That ruling of the Court travels part of the distance that South Carolina asks us to go now. She asks us to hold that when it comes to a day of rest a Sabbatarian must conform with the scruples of the majority in order to obtain unemployment benefits.

The result turns not on the degree of injury, which may indeed be nonexistent by ordinary standards. The harm is the interference with the individual's scruples or conscience—an important area of privacy which the First Amendment fences off from government. The interference here is as plain as it is in Soviet Russia, where a churchgoer is given a second-class citizenship, resulting in harm though perhaps not in measurable damages.

This case is resolvable not in terms of what an individual can demand of government, but solely in terms of what government may not do to an individual in violation of his religious scruples. The fact that government cannot exact from me a surrender of one iota of my religious scruples does not, of course, mean that I can demand of government a sum of money, the better to exercise them. For the Free Exercise Clause is written in terms of what the government cannot do to the individual, not in terms of what the individual can exact from the government.

Those considerations, however, are not relevant here. If

appellant is otherwise qualified for unemployment benefits, payments will be made to her not as a Seventh-day Adventist, but as an unemployed worker.

MR. JUSTICE STEWART, concurring in the result.

My . . . difference with the Court's opinion is that I cannot agree that today's decision can stand consistently with *Braunfeld v. Brown*. The Court says that there was a "less direct burden upon religious practices" in that case than in this. With all respect, I think the Court is mistaken, simply as a matter of fact. The *Braunfeld* case involved a state criminal statute. The undisputed effect of that statute, as pointed out by MR. JUSTICE BRENNAN in his dissenting opinion in that case, was that "'Plaintiff, Abraham Braunfeld, will be unable to continue in his business if he may not stay open on Sunday and he will thereby lose his capital investment.' In other words, the issue in this case—and we do not understand either appellees or the Court to contend otherwise— is whether a State may put an individual to a choice between his business and his religion."

The impact upon the appellant's religious freedom in the present case is considerably less onerous. We deal here not with a criminal statute, but with the particularized administration of South Carolina's Unemployment Compensation Act. Even upon the unlikely assumption that the appellant could not find suitable non-Saturday employment, the appellant at the worst would be denied a maximum of 22 weeks of compensation payments. I agree with the Court that the possibility of that denial is enough to infringe upon the appellant's constitutional right to the free exercise of her religion. But it is clear to me that in order to reach this conclusion the Court must explicitly reject the reasoning of *Braunfeld v. Brown*. I think the *Braunfeld* case was wrongly decided and should be overruled, and accordingly I concur in the result reached by the Court in the case before us.

MR. JUSTICE HARLAN, whom MR. JUSTICE WHITE joins, dissenting.

Today's decision is disturbing both in its rejection of existing precedent and in its implications for the future. The significance of the decision can best be understood after an examination of the state law applied in this case.

South Carolina's Unemployment Compensation Law was enacted in 1936 in response to the grave social and economic problems that arose during the depression of that period. . . . [T]he purpose of the legislature was to tide people over, and to avoid social and economic chaos, during periods when *work was unavailable*. But at the same time there was clearly no intent to provide relief for those who for purely personal reasons were or became *unavailable for work*. In accordance with this design, the legislature provided that "an unemployed insured worker shall be eligible to receive benefits with respect to any week *only* if the Commission finds that . . . [h]e is able to work and is available for work. . . ." (Emphasis added.)

The South Carolina Supreme Court has uniformly applied this law in conformity with its clearly expressed purpose. It has consistently held that one is not "available for work" if his unemployment has resulted not from the inability of industry to provide a job but rather from personal circumstances, no matter how compelling. . . .

. . . What the Court is holding is that if the State chooses to condition unemployment compensation on the applicant's availability for work, it is constitutionally compelled to *carve out an exception*—and to provide benefits—for those whose unavailability is due to their religious convictions. Such a holding has particular significance in two respects.

First, despite the Court's protestations to the contrary, the decision necessarily overrules *Braunfeld v. Brown*, which held that it did not offend the "Free Exercise" Clause of the Constitution for a State to forbid a Sabbatarian to do business on Sunday. The secular purpose of the statute before us today is even clearer than that involved in *Braunfeld*. And just as in *Braunfeld*—where exceptions to the Sunday closing laws for Sabbatarians would have been inconsistent with the purpose to achieve a uniform day of rest and would have required case-by-case inquiry into religious beliefs—so here, an exception to the rules of eligibility based on religious convictions would necessitate judicial examination of those convictions and would be at odds with the limited purpose of the statute to smooth out the economy during periods of industrial instability. Finally, the indirect financial burden of the present law is far less than that involved in *Braunfeld*. Forcing a store owner to close his business on Sunday may well have the effect of depriving him of a satisfactory livelihood if his religious convictions require him to close on Saturday as well. Here we are dealing only with temporary benefits, amounting to a fraction of regular weekly wages and running for not more than 22 weeks.

Clearly, any differences between this case and *Braunfeld* cut against the present appellant.

Second, the implications of the present decision are far more troublesome than its apparently narrow dimensions would indicate at first glance. The meaning of today's holding, as already noted, is that the State must furnish unemployment benefits to one who is unavailable for work if the unavailability stems from the exercise of religious convictions. The State, in other words, must *single out* for financial assistance those whose behavior is religiously motivated, even though it denies such assistance to others whose identical behavior (in this case, inability to work on Saturdays) is not religiously motivated.

It has been suggested that such singling out of religious conduct for special treatment may violate the constitutional limitations on state action. My own view, however, is that at least under the circumstances of this case it would be a permissible accommodation of religion for the State, if it chose to do so, to create an exception to its eligibility requirements for persons like the appellant. The constitutional obligation of "neutrality" . . . is not so narrow a channel that the slightest deviation from an absolutely straight course leads to condemnation. There are too many instances in which no such course can be charted, too many areas in which the pervasive activities of the State justify some special provision for religion to prevent it from being submerged by an all-embracing secularism. The State violates its obligation of neutrality when, for example, it mandates a daily religious exercise in its public schools, with all the attendant pressures on the school children that such an exercise entails. . . . But there is, I believe, enough flexibility in the Constitution to permit a legislative judgment accommodating an unemployment compensation law to the exercise of religious beliefs such as appellant's.

For very much the same reasons, however, I cannot subscribe to the conclusion that the State is constitutionally compelled to carve out an exception to its general rule of eligibility in the present case. Those situations in which the Constitution may require special treatment on account of religion are, in my view, few and far between, and this view is amply supported by the course of constitutional litigation in this area. . . . Such compulsion in the present case is particularly inappropriate in light of the indirect, remote, and insubstantial effect of the decision below on the exercise of appellant's religion and in light of the direct financial assistance to religion that today's decision requires.

For these reasons I respectfully dissent from the opinion and judgment of the Court.

Does Brennan's majority opinion represent a significant break from past free exercise claims? Some analysts suggest that it does. Although Brennan affirmed the belief-action dichotomy, he agreed with Sherbert's attorney that the lines were blurred. Accordingly, he made it far more difficult for states to regulate "action." No longer would a secular legislative purpose suffice; rather, under *Sherbert,* when the government enacts a law that burdens free exercise of religion, it must show that it is protecting an important, compelling government interest and in the least restrictive manner possible. *Sherbert* also represented a step away from previous free exercise cases in which the Court insisted on neutrality, for here the Court was striking down a law that was neutral in application on the grounds that it burdened the free exercise of religion with a less-than-compelling interest. Other analysts argue that *Sherbert* represented a logical step from *Braunfeld.* It was in *Braunfeld* that Warren first articulated the least restrictive manner standard on which Brennan relied to strike the South Carolina law.

Either way, the standard articulated in *Sherbert* was much more favorable to religious exercise claims, and much less sympathetic to government efforts to regulate religious practices.

How would the Court use this new standard? Many analysts believed that the compelling interest–least restrictive means approach would almost always result in a victory for the free exercise claimant. Governments would have to demonstrate that policies burdening religion are of sufficient magnitude to override the free exercise interest and that the policy is cast in the least restrictive possible manner. As indicated by *Sherbert,* this is a very difficult task.

Although the Warren Court ushered in the change in free exercise standards in *Braunfeld* and *Sherbert,* it was up to the justices of the Court led by Chief Justice Warren Burger to apply those standards because the Warren Court heard very few free exercise cases after *Sherbert.*

The opportunity for the Burger Court to put its stamp on this area of the law arose early in the new chief justice's tenure. The case was *Wisconsin v. Yoder* (1972).[18] As you read the excerpt from *Yoder*, consider how the Burger Court dealt with the standard it inherited from its predecessor. Do you detect any differences in approach? Or does Burger's opinion parallel Warren's in *Braunfeld* and Brennan's in *Sherbert?*

Wisconsin v. Yoder

406 U.S. 205 (1972)
laws.findlaw.com/US/406/205.html
Vote: 6 (Blackmun, Brennan, Burger, Marshall, Stewart, White)
    1 (Douglas)
Opinion of the Court: Burger
Concurring opinions: Stewart, White
Dissenting in part: Douglas
Not participating: Powell, Rehnquist

Like many states, Wisconsin had a compulsory education law, mandating that children attend public or private schools until the age of sixteen. This law violated the norms of the Amish, who were among the first religious groups to arrive in the United States. As a simple people, who eschew technology, including automobiles and electricity, the Amish do not permit their children to attend school after the eighth grade, believing that they will be adversely exposed "to worldly influences in terms of attitudes, goals, and values contrary to their beliefs." Instead, they prefer to educate their older children at home.

For several decades prior to the 1970s, the Amish had many skirmishes with education officials over this issue. After one particularly nasty incident in Iowa, "a group of ministers, bankers, lawyers, and professors formed a group called the National Committee for Amish Religious Freedom (NCARF)" to provide legal defense for the Amish. NCARF's leaders included the general counsel of the American Jewish Committee, the dean of Boston University Law School, and the executive director of the Commission on Religious Liberty of the National Council of Churches.

18. To hear oral arguments in this case, navigate to: *oyez.nwu.edu.*

Among the suits for which NCARF provided legal assistance was a controversy emanating from New Glarus, Wisconsin, where the school district administrator brought a complaint against Amish families for not sending their older children to school. When the parents were fined $5 by the county court, they claimed that the compulsory attendance law violated their First and Fourteenth Amendment rights.

At the heart of this case, attorney William Ball argued, were two fundamental issues. First, he claimed that the Amish did not want their children to be uneducated or ignorant. In fact, the teenagers pursued rigorous home study after their public school education. Second, because education was continuing at home, the state could demonstrate no compelling reason to require the children to attend public school. Amicus curiae briefs, representing the full spectrum of religious beliefs in the United States, supported Ball's view. In contrast, the attorney general of Wisconsin compared this case to *Prince v. Massachusetts,* in which the Court upheld child labor regulations. He claimed that the two laws were similar because both were enacted out of a legitimate "concern for the welfare" of children.

MR. CHIEF JUSTICE BURGER delivered the opinion of the Court.

On petition of the State of Wisconsin, we granted the writ of certiorari in this case to review a decision of the Wisconsin Supreme Court holding that respondents' convictions for violating the State's compulsory school-attendance law were invalid under the Free Exercise Clause of the First Amendment to the United States Constitution made applicable to the States by the Fourteenth Amendment. For the reasons hereafter stated we affirm the judgment of the Supreme Court of Wisconsin. . . .

Amish objection to formal education beyond the eighth grade is firmly grounded in . . . central religious concepts. They object to the high school, and higher education generally, because the values they teach are in marked variance with Amish values and the Amish way of life; they view secondary school education as an impermissible exposure of their children to a "worldly" influence in conflict with their beliefs. The high school tends to emphasize intellectual and scientific accomplishments, self-distinction, competitiveness, worldly success, and social life with other students. Amish society emphasizes informal learning-through-doing; a life of "goodness," rather than a life of intellect; wisdom, rather than technical knowledge; community welfare, rather than competition; and separation from, rather than integration with, contemporary worldly society.

Formal high school education beyond the eighth grade is contrary to Amish beliefs, not only because it places Amish children in an environment hostile to Amish beliefs with increasing emphasis on competition in class work and sports and with pressure to conform to the styles, manners, and ways of the peer group, but also because it takes them away from their community, physically and emotionally, during the crucial and formative adolescent period of life. During this period, the children must acquire Amish attitudes favoring manual work and self-reliance and the specific skills needed to perform the adult role of an Amish farmer or housewife. . . .

The Amish do not object to elementary education through the first eight grades as a general proposition because they agree that their children must have basic skills in the "three R's" in order to read the Bible, to be good farmers and citizens, and to be able to deal with non-Amish people when necessary in the course of daily affairs. They view such a basic education as acceptable because it does not significantly expose their children to worldly values or interfere with their development in the Amish community during the crucial adolescent period. While Amish accept compulsory elementary education generally, wherever possible they have established their own elementary schools in many respects like the small local schools of the past. In the Amish belief higher learning tends to develop values they reject as influences that alienate man from God. . . .

There is no doubt as to the power of a State, having a high responsibility for education of its citizens, to impose reasonable regulations for the control and duration of basic education. . . . [But] a State's interest in universal education, however highly we rank it, is not totally free from a balancing process when it impinges on fundamental rights and interests, such as those specifically protected by the Free Exercise Clause of the First Amendment, and the traditional interest of parents with respect to the religious upbringing of their children so long as they . . . "prepare them for additional obligations."

It follows that in order for Wisconsin to compel school attendance beyond the eighth grade against a claim that such attendance interferes with the practice of a legitimate religious belief, it must appear either that the State does not deny the free exercise of religious belief by its requirement, or that there is a state interest of sufficient magnitude to override the interest claiming protection under the Free Exercise Clause. . . .

The essence of all that has been said and written on the subject is that only those interests of the highest order and those not otherwise served can overbalance legitimate claims of free exercise of religion. We can accept it as settled, therefore, that, however strong the State's interest in universal compulsory education, it is by no means absolute to the exclusion or subordination of all other interests. *E.g., Sherbert v. Verner* (1963). . . .

We come then to the quality of the claims of the respondents concerning the alleged encroachment of Wisconsin's compulsory school-attendance statute on their rights and the rights of their children to the free exercise of the religious beliefs they and their forebears have adhered to for almost three centuries. In evaluating those claims we must be careful to determine whether the Amish religion and their mode of life are, as they claim, inseparable and interdependent. A way of life, however virtuous and admirable, may not be interposed as a barrier to reasonable state regulation of education if it is based on purely secular considerations: to have the protection of the Religion Clauses, the claims must be rooted in religious belief. . . .

Giving no weight to . . . secular considerations . . . we see that the record in this case abundantly supports the claim that the traditional way of life of the Amish is not merely a matter of personal preference, but one of deep religious conviction, shared by an organized group, and intimately related to daily living. . . .

. . . The conclusion is inescapable that secondary schooling, by exposing Amish children to worldly influences in terms of attitudes, goals, and values contrary to beliefs, and by substantially interfering with the religious development of the Amish child and his integration into the way of life of the Amish faith community at the crucial adolescent stage of development, contravenes the basic religious tenets and practice of the Amish faith, both as to the parent and the child. . . .

In sum . . . the State's requirement of compulsory formal education after the eighth grade would gravely endanger if not destroy the free exercise of respondents' religious beliefs.

Neither the findings of the trial court nor the Amish claims as to the nature of their faith are challenged in this Court by the State of Wisconsin. Its position is that the State's interest in universal compulsory formal secondary education to age 16 is so great that it is paramount to the undisputed claims of respondents that their mode of preparing their youth for Amish life, after the traditional elementary education, is an essential part of their religious belief and practice. Nor does the State undertake to meet the claim that the Amish mode of life and education is inseparable from and a part of the basic tenets of their religion—indeed, as much a part of their religious belief and practices as baptism, the confessional, or a sabbath may be for others.

Wisconsin concedes that under the Religion Clauses religious beliefs are absolutely free from the State's control, but it argues that "actions," even though religiously grounded, are outside the protection of the First Amendment. But our decisions have rejected the idea that religiously grounded conduct is always outside the protection of the Free Exercise Clause. . . . This case, therefore, does not become easier because respondents were convicted for their "actions" in refusing to send their children to the public high school; in this context belief and action cannot be neatly confined in logic-tight compartments. . . .

Nor can this case be disposed of on the grounds that Wisconsin's requirement for school attendance to age 16 applies uniformly to all citizens of the State and does not, on its face, discriminate against religions or a particular religion, or that it is motivated by legitimate secular concerns. A regulation neutral on its face may, in its application, nonetheless offend the constitutional requirement for governmental neutrality if it unduly burdens free exercise of religion. *Sherbert v. Verner*. . . .

We turn, then, to the State's broader contention that its interest in its system of compulsory education is so compelling that even the established religious practices of the Amish must give way. Where fundamental claims of religious freedom are at stake, however, we cannot accept such a sweeping claim; despite its admitted validity in the generality of cases, we must searchingly examine the interests that the State seeks to promote by its requirement for compulsory education to age 16, and the impediment to those

objectives that would flow from recognizing the claimed Amish exemption. . . .

The State advances two primary arguments in support of its system of compulsory education. It notes . . . that some degree of education is necessary to prepare citizens to participate effectively and intelligently in our open political system if we are to preserve freedom and independence. Further, education prepares individuals to be self-reliant and self-sufficient. We accept these propositions.

However, the evidence adduced by the Amish in this case is persuasively to the effect that an additional one or two years of formal high school for Amish children in place of their long-established program of informal vocational education would do little to serve those interests. . . . It is one thing to say that compulsory education for a year or two beyond the eighth grade may be necessary when its goal is the preparation of the child for life in modern society as the majority live, but it is quite another if the goal of education be viewed as the preparation of the child for life in the separated agrarian community that is the keystone of the Amish faith. . . .

The State attacks respondents' position as one fostering "ignorance" from which the child must be protected by the State. No one can question the State's duty to protect children from ignorance but this argument does not square with the facts disclosed in the record. Whatever their idiosyncrasies as seen by the majority, this record strongly shows that the Amish community has been a highly successful social unit within our society, even if apart from the conventional "mainstream." Its members are productive and very law-abiding members of society. . . .

Insofar as the State's claim rests on the view that a brief additional period of formal education is imperative to enable the Amish to participate effectively and intelligently in our democratic process, it must fall. The Amish alternative to formal secondary school education has enabled them to function effectively in their day-to-day life under self-imposed limitations on relations with the world, and to survive and prosper in contemporary society as a separate, sharply identifiable and highly self-sufficient community for more than 200 years in this country. In itself this is strong evidence that they are capable of fulfilling the social and political responsibilities of citizenship without compelled attendance beyond the eighth grade at the price of jeopardizing their free exercise of religious belief. When

Thomas Jefferson emphasized the need for education as a bulwark of a free people against tyranny, there is nothing to indicate he had in mind compulsory education through any fixed age beyond a basic education. Indeed, the Amish communities singularly parallel and reflect many of the virtues of Jefferson's ideal of the "sturdy yeoman" who would form the basis of what he considered as the ideal of a democratic society. Even their idiosyncratic separateness exemplifies the diversity we profess to admire and encourage. . . .

Finally, the State, on authority of *Prince v. Massachusetts,* argues that a decision exempting Amish children from the State's requirement fails to recognize the substantive right of the Amish child to a secondary education, and fails to give due regard to the power of the State as *parens patriae* to extend the benefit of secondary education to children regardless of the wishes of their parents. Taken at its broadest sweep, the Court's language in *Prince* might be read to give support to the State's position. However, the Court was not confronted in *Prince* with a situation comparable to that of the Amish as revealed in this record; this is shown by the Court's severe characterization of the evils that it thought the legislature could legitimately associate with child labor, even when performed in the company of an adult. . . .

This case, of course, is not one in which any harm to the physical or mental health of the child or to the public safety, peace, order, or welfare has been demonstrated or may be properly inferred. The record is to the contrary, and any reliance on that theory would find no support in the evidence. . . .

For the reasons stated we hold, with the Supreme Court of Wisconsin, that the First and Fourteenth Amendments prevent the State from compelling respondents to cause their children to attend formal high school to age 16. Our disposition of this case, however, in no way alters our recognition of the obvious fact that courts are not school boards or legislatures, and are ill-equipped to determine the "necessity" of discrete aspects of a State's program of compulsory education. This should suggest that courts must move with great circumspection in performing the sensitive and delicate task of weighing a State's legitimate social concern when faced with religious claims for exemption from generally applicable educational requirements. . . .

Affirmed.

MR. JUSTICE WHITE, with whom MR. JUSTICE BRENNAN and MR. JUSTICE STEWART join, concurring.

Cases such as this one inevitably call for a delicate balancing of important but conflicting interests. I join the opinion and judgment of the Court because I cannot say that the State's interest in requiring two more years of compulsory education in the ninth and tenth grades outweighs the importance of the concededly sincere Amish religious practice to the survival of that sect.

This would be a very different case for me if respondents' claim were that their religion forbade their children from attending any school at any time and from complying in any way with the educational standards set by the State. Since the Amish children are permitted to acquire the basic tools of literacy to survive in modern society by attending grades one through eight, and since the deviation from the State's compulsory education law is relatively slight, I conclude that respondents' claim must prevail. . . .

. . . *Pierce v. Society of Sisters* (1925) lends no support to the contention that parents may replace state educational requirements with their own idiosyncratic views of what knowledge a child needs to be a productive and happy member of society. . . . A State has a legitimate interest not only in seeking to develop the latent talents of its children, but also in seeking to prepare them for the lifestyle that they may later choose, or at least to provide them with an option other than the life they have led in the past. In the circumstances of this case, although the question is close, I am unable to say that the State has demonstrated that Amish children who leave school in the eighth grade will be intellectually stultified or unable to acquire new academic skills later. The statutory minimum school attendance age set by the State is, after all, only 16.

. . . I join the Court because the sincerity of the Amish religious policy here is uncontested, because the potentially adverse impact of the state requirement is great, and because the State's valid interest in education has already been largely satisfied by the eight years the children have already spent in school.

MR. JUSTICE DOUGLAS, dissenting in part.

I agree with the Court that the religious scruples of the Amish are opposed to the education of their children beyond the grade schools, yet I disagree with the Court's conclusion that the matter is within the dispensation of parents alone. The Court's analysis assumes that the only interests at stake in the case are those of the Amish parents on the one hand, and those of the State on the other. The difficulty with this approach is that, despite the Court's claim, the parents are seeking to vindicate not only their own free exercise claims, but also those of their high-school-age children. . . .

. . . [I]t is essential to reach the question to decide the case . . . because no analysis of religious-liberty claims can take place in a vacuum. If the parents in this case are allowed religious exemption, the inevitable effect is to impose the parent's notions of religious duty upon their children. Where the child is mature enough to express potential conflicting desires, it would be an invasion of the child's rights to permit such an imposition without canvassing his views. . . . As the child has no other effective forum, it is in this litigation that his rights should be considered. And, if an Amish child desires to attend high school, and is mature enough to have that desire respected, the State may well be able to override the parents' religiously motivated objections.

What are we to make of Chief Justice Burger's first major statement on the free exercise of religion? He cited *Sherbert* with approval and invoked its approach to find that the state's interest was not sufficiently compelling to outweigh the free exercise claim. That Burger found for the religious claimants lends support to those analysts who argue that the *Sherbert* standard would almost always lead to such a conclusion. But some scholars allege that Burger grounded his opinion on respect for the history and the practices of the Amish rather than the logic of *Sherbert*. If Burger had followed such a course, he would not be the first nor probably the last to do so. Remember Chief Justice Waite's opinion in *Reynolds*? Did it not rest as much on the Court's perception of the Mormons as a strange and bizarre sect as it did on legal factors?

Whatever Burger's motivation, it looked as if the Court would continue to apply the compelling interest standard to free exercise claims. Less than a decade after *Yoder*, the justices decided *Thomas v. Review Board of Indi-*

ana Employment Security Division (1981), the facts of which bore a marked resemblance to *Sherbert*. Thomas was a Jehovah's Witness who worked in a steel mill. When the owners closed the mill down, they transferred Thomas to another plant. Because his new job required him to make tanks for use by the military, Thomas quit on religious grounds and filed for unemployment benefits, which the state denied. Writing for the Court, Chief Justice Burger acknowledged the parallels between *Sherbert* and this dispute: "Here, as in *Sherbert*, the employee was put to a choice between fidelity to his religious beliefs or cessation of work; the coercive impact on Thomas is indistinguishable from *Sherbert*." Accordingly, he said, "Unless we are prepared to overrule *Sherbert*, Thomas can not be denied the benefits due him."

Two years after *Thomas*, in *Bob Jones University v. United States* (1983), the Supreme Court examined yet another free exercise question: May the government punish a sectarian institution for its religiously divined racist policy? Bob Jones University was not affiliated with any denomination, but described itself as "dedicated to the teaching and propagation of . . . fundamentalist Christian beliefs." These beliefs included, among others, a strong prohibition against interracial dating and marriage. To enforce this particular tenet, the school excluded African Americans until 1971, when it began to accept applications from married blacks only. Litigation forced the school to begin admitting unmarried blacks in 1976, but only if they adhered to a strict set of rules; for example, interracial dating or marriage would lead to expulsion. The school continued to deny admission to individuals in interracial marriages. The Internal Revenue Service (IRS) revoked Bob Jones's tax-exempt status on the grounds that the school's policies were racist. The university challenged the decision, saying that the IRS action punished the practice of religious beliefs. Therefore, one of the issues before the Court was whether the government's interest in prohibiting race discrimination was sufficiently compelling to abridge free exercise guarantees.

Writing for the Court, Chief Justice Burger applied the compelling interest–least restrictive means standard of *Sherbert* to rule against Bob Jones:

The governmental interest at stake here is compelling. . . . [T]he government has a fundamental, overriding interest in eradicating racial discrimination in education—discrimination that prevailed . . . for the first 165 years of this Nation's constitutional history. That governmental interest substantially outweighs whatever burden denial of tax benefits places on petitioners' exercise of their religious beliefs. The interests asserted by petitioners cannot be accommodated with that compelling governmental interest, and no "less restrictive means" are available to achieve the governmental interest.

Burger also noted that this policy—unlike the one at issue in *Yoder*—would not prevent Bob Jones from practicing its religion. Seen in this way, the IRS policy was more akin to Sunday closing laws. In *Braunfeld*, Chief Justice Warren acknowledged that while blue laws would place an economic burden on some Orthodox Jews, they would not stop them from practicing their religion. Here Burger wrote: "Denial of tax benefits will inevitably have a substantial impact on the operation of private religious schools, but will not prevent these schools from observing their religious tenets."

Bob Jones is interesting for a number of reasons, not the least of which is that it demonstrates the Court's use of the compelling interest standard to uphold a government policy that allegedly infringes on the free exercise of religion. The eradication of racism, in the eyes of the justices, is an important government objective.

The Demise of Sherbert/Yoder *and the Adoption of the* Smith *Test*

Despite the Burger Court's application of the compelling interest standard in *Bob Jones*, there were signs in the early to mid-1980s that some of the justices wanted to rethink that standard or at least make it easier for the state to respond to free exercise challenges. *United States v. Lee*—decided in 1982, a year before *Bob Jones*—was the first of these signs.

Lee, a member of the Amish faith, owned a farm and a carpentry shop. In violation of federal law, he refused to withhold Social Security taxes or pay the employers' share of those taxes, arguing that the payment of taxes and the receipt of Social Security benefits violated his religious tenets. To support his argument, Lee's attorneys pointed out that Congress had provided a Social Security tax exemption to self-employed Amish. And, while Lee did not fall under that specific exemption—he employed others—the very existence of the exemption demonstrated Congress's sensitivity toward the Amish.

In a short opinion for the Court, Chief Justice Burger disagreed. To be sure, Burger conceded, "compulsory participation" in the Social Security system interferes with the free exercise rights of the Amish. But the government was able to justify that burden on religion by showing that compulsory participation is "essential to accomplish an overriding governmental interest" in the maintenance of the Social Security system in the United States. As Burger put it: "To maintain an organized society that guarantees religious freedom to a great variety of faiths requires that some religious practices yield to the common good."

Why do some scholars cite *Lee* as a first cut into the compelling interest standard of *Sherbert*? What they see is a discrepancy between *Lee* and *Yoder*. Why was Burger willing to exempt the Amish from mandatory education laws but unwilling to exempt them from compulsory participation in the Social Security system? In *Lee* Burger tried to address this question when he wrote: "It would be difficult to accommodate the comprehensive Social Security system with myriad exceptions flowing from a wide variety of religious beliefs." But this point caused observers to suggest that the Burger Court was willing to override an important government interest if only a few groups would be affected or if the impact of the religious exemption would be fairly negligible, as was the case in *Yoder*.

Goldman v. Weinberger (1986), one of the last major free exercise cases of the Burger Court era, did little to quell these and other suspicions about the direction of Court doctrine. S. Simcha Goldman was an Orthodox Jew, an ordained rabbi, and a captain in the Air Force. He was stationed at March Air Force Base in Riverside, California, as a clinical psychologist in the base hospital. From the time Goldman began his service at the base, he wore a yarmulke (skull cap) while in and out of uniform. Goldman did so because his religion requires its adherents to keep their heads covered at all times.

After a superior told him that the yarmulke violated

Air Force Dress Code Regulation (AFR) 35-10, a 190-page regulation that describes in minute detail all of the various items of apparel that constitute the air force uniform, Goldman brought suit against the secretary of defense, arguing that the regulation violated his First Amendment free exercise rights. A U.S. district court agreed, but a panel of judges on the Court of Appeals for the District of Columbia reversed.

With the court of appeals' rejection, Goldman brought the case to the Supreme Court. There, his attorneys argued that Goldman's conduct was of a nonintrusive nature that "interferes with no one else, does not harm the public health, and imposes no burden on accommodation." They were attempting to show that Goldman's behavior was markedly different from activities the Court had struck down in *Reynolds* and *Prince*. They also maintained that the Air Force lacked any overriding government interest that would justify this intrusion into Goldman's religious practice.

The government's response was that "there can be no serious doubt that uniform dress and appearance standards serve the military interest in maintaining discipline, morale, and esprit de corps" and that enforcement of the dress code "is a necessary means to the undeniably critical ends of molding soldiers into an effective fighting force." The government also urged the justices to consider what might happen if they allowed Goldman to wear his yarmulke: other religions could request exemptions to wear turbans, dreadlocks, kum kums (red dots on foreheads), and so forth.

Writing for the majority, Justice William Rehnquist agreed with the government and ruled against Goldman. He wrote:

Petitioner argues that AFR 35-10, as applied to him, prohibits religiously motivated conduct and should therefore be analyzed under the standard enunciated in *Sherbert v. Verner* (1963). . . . But we have repeatedly held that "the military is, by necessity, a specialized society separate from civilian society." . . . "[T]he military must insist upon a respect for duty and a discipline without counterpart in civilian life" . . . in order to prepare for and perform its vital role. . . .

Our review of military regulations challenged on First Amendment grounds is far more deferential than constitutional review of similar laws or regulations designed for civilian society. The military need not encourage debate or tolerate protest to the extent that such tolerance is required of the civilian state by the First Amendment; to accomplish its mission the military must foster instinctive obedience, unity, commitment, and esprit de corps. . . . The essence of military service "is the subordination of the desires and interests of the individual to the needs of the service.". . .

These aspects of military life do not, of course, render entirely nugatory in the military context the guarantees of the First Amendment. . . . But "within the military community there is simply not the same [individual] autonomy as there is in the larger civilian community.". . . In the context of the present case, when evaluating whether military needs justify a particular restriction on religiously motivated conduct, courts must give great deference to the professional judgment of military authorities concerning the relative importance of a particular military interest. . . . Not only are courts "'ill-equipped to determine the impact upon discipline that any particular intrusion upon military authority might have,'" . . . but the military authorities have been charged by the Executive and Legislative Branches with carrying out our Nation's military policy. "[J]udicial deference . . . is at its apogee when legislative action under the congressional authority to raise and support armies and make rules and regulations for their governance is challenged."

The Court's decision in *Goldman* fueled debate in political and academic circles. Taking up an invitation issued by Justice Brennan in a dissenting opinion—"The Court and the military have refused these servicemen their constitutional rights; we must hope that Congress will correct this wrong"—members of Congress introduced legislation to overturn the ruling. The bill allowed members of the armed forces "to wear an item of religious apparel while in uniform" so long as the item is "neat and conservative" and does not "interfere with the performance" of military duties. Congress passed the law in September 1987, and *Goldman* was effectively overturned.

Academic and legal debate centered on the rationale the Court invoked to resolve *Goldman*. Was *Goldman* a substantial break from the *Sherbert* standard? Clearly, the four dissenters saw it that way. Justice Sandra Day O'Connor's opinion is particularly interesting. After noting that Court cases in this area adopted slightly different versions of a similar standard, she set out the "two consistent themes" running through precedent from *Sherbert* to *Lee*. First, the government "must show that an unusually important interest is at stake, whether or not that interest is denominated 'compelling.'" Second, "the government must show that granting the requested exemption will do substantial harm to that interest, whether by showing that the means adopted is the 'least restrictive' or 'essential.'" O'Connor saw no reason to jettison this two-pronged standard—as she thought the majority had done in *Goldman*—simply because the military was involved.

In contrast, some scholars (along with a few members of the Court) did not think *Goldman* represented a significant shift in Court opinion. They argued that *Goldman* was an exceptional case: it involved the interests of the armed forces, interests to which the justices traditionally defer. Accordingly, they asserted that the Court would return to the compelling interest–least restrictive means standard, mentioned in the dissents, in future cases.

Just months after the *Goldman* decision was handed down, significant changes occurred on the Court. Warren Burger stepped down as chief justice. President Reagan promoted Justice Rehnquist to replace Burger and appointed Antonin Scalia to take Rehnquist's former seat. These changes prompted increased speculation that some alteration in the Court's free exercise jurisprudence might be forthcoming.

In the first year or so of the Rehnquist Court, it appeared that those scholars who argued that *Goldman* was an anomalous ruling were correct. In *Hobbie v. Unemployment Appeals Commission of Florida* (1987) the Court returned to the compelling interest standard. The facts of *Hobbie* were similar to those of *Sherbert* and *Thomas*: a Seventh-Day Adventist was fired from her job for refusing to work certain hours, and the state denied her claim for unemployment benefits. The state claimed Hobbie had failed to meet the standard that she became "unemployed through no fault of her own." The only significant difference between *Hobbie* and *Sherbert/Thomas* was that Hobbie had converted to the Seventh-Day Adventist church after working at the company for two and a half years.

This distinction, however, was trivial to the majority:

We see no meaningful distinction among the situations of Sherbert, Thomas, and Hobbie. We again affirm, as we stated in *Thomas:* "Where the state conditions receipt of an important benefit upon the conduct proscribed by a religious faith, or where it denies such a benefit because of conduct mandated by a religious belief, thereby putting substantial pressure on an adherent to modify his behavior and to violate his beliefs, a burden upon religion exists."

In writing for a majority of eight, Justice Brennan used the logic of *Sherbert* and similar cases to find for Hobbie: "Both *Sherbert* and *Thomas* held that such infringements [on the free exercise of religion] must be subjected to strict scrutiny and could be justified only by proof by the State of a compelling interest."

Hobbie seemed to indicate the willingness of most of the justices to return to the *Sherbert* standard. Whether they feared congressional retaliation (the justices knew that Congress was considering legislation to overturn *Goldman*) or because they never had really abandoned *Sherbert* is open to speculation. What is clear, however, is that Chief Justice Rehnquist was unhappy with the *Sherbert* standard. He had written the Court's opinion in *Goldman*, in which he abstained from applying *Sherbert*, and he dissented in *Thomas*. Rehnquist stated:

Where . . . the State has enacted a general statute, the purpose and effect of which is to advance the State's secular goals, the Free Exercise Clause does not in my view require the State to conform that statute to the dictates of religious conscience of any group. As Justice Harlan recognized in his dissent in *Sherbert:* "Those situations in which the Constitution may require special treatment on account of religion are . . . few and far between."

Applying this logic to *Hobbie*, Rehnquist voted in favor of Florida: the state had not discriminated against Hobbie because she was a Seventh-Day Adventist.

The new chief justice may not have prevailed in *Hobbie*, but in a series of subsequent decisions his position appeared to be gaining support inside the Court. In *O'Lone v. Shabazz* (1987) a Rehnquist-led five-justice majority held that for security and other relevant reasons prison officials could restrict certain prisoners from attending Muslim religious services. In 1988 another five-justice majority in *Lyng v. Northwest Indian Cemetery Protective Association* upheld a United States Forest Service plan to construct roadways through federal lands that were used by Native American tribes for religious rituals. While the tribes argued that the roads "could have devastating effects on traditional Indian religious practices" and therefore constituted a major intrusion into the free exercise of their religion, the Court rejected their First Amendment claims. *Lyng* was followed by *Hernandez v. Commissioner* (1989), disallowing certain payments to the Church of Scientology as tax deductible contributions, and *Swaggart Ministries v. California Board of Equalization* (1990), upholding a state tax on the sale of religious articles.

These decisions indicated an increasing tendency for the Court to support government programs when challenged by free exercise claims. It became clear that the *Sherbert/Yoder* compelling interest standard was losing support and that a significant change was likely. That change occurred in 1990, when the justices handed down their ruling in *Employment Division v. Smith*.[19] In *Smith* the Court seemed to turn its back on nearly three decades of free exercise cases from *Braunfeld* and *Sherbert/Yoder* through *Hobbie*. How did the majority justify its position? Do you find its logic compelling? Keep these questions in mind as you read the facts and excerpts that follow.

Employment Division, Department of Human Resources of Oregon v. Smith

494 U.S. 872 (1990)
laws.findlaw.com/US/494/872.html
Vote: 6 (Kennedy, O'Connor, Rehnquist, Scalia, Stevens, White)
    3 (Blackmun, Brennan, Marshall)
Opinion of the Court: Scalia
Concurring opinion: O'Connor
Dissenting opinion: Blackmun

This case centers on the use of peyote, which is a controlled substance under Oregon law. In other words, it is

19. To hear oral arguments in this case, navigate to: *oyez.nwu.edu*.

illegal to possess the drug unless it is prescribed by a doctor. Peyote is a hallucinogen produced by certain cactus plants found in the southwestern United States and northern Mexico. Unlike other hallucinogenic drugs, such as LSD, peyote has never been widely used or problematic. One reason is that peyote is taken by eating the buds of certain cactus plants, which are unpleasant to the taste and can induce nausea and vomiting. However, one group uses peyote on a regular basis, and they are members of a bona fide religion—the Native American church. To them peyote is a sacramental substance, necessary for religious rituals.

The spiritual nature of the church's use of peyote has been acknowledged by various governments. Although states, including Oregon, have laws criminalizing the general use of peyote, twenty-three states (those with large Native American populations) and the federal government exempt the religious use of peyote from such laws. The federal government even provides licenses to grow peyote for sacramental purposes.

The dispute at issue in *Smith* arose when two members of the Native American church, Alfred Smith and Galen Black, were fired from their jobs as counselors at a private drug and alcohol abuse clinic for ingesting peyote at a religious ceremony. Smith and Black applied for unemployment benefits but were turned down by the state, which found them ineligible because they had been fired for "misconduct"; under state law, workers discharged for that reason cannot obtain benefits.

Smith and Black brought suit in state court arguing that under the U.S. Supreme Court's precedents of *Sherbert* and *Thomas* (they later added *Hobbie*, which had yet to be handed down by the Court), the state could not deny them benefits. The issue for them was not that the state had criminalized peyote—they had not been charged with committing a criminal offense. Rather, they pointed to the Supreme Court's previous rulings, which indicated that states may not deny unemployment benefits because of an individual's unwillingness to give up an activity mandated by religion. The state argued that it could deny the benefits—regardless of Smith and Black's free exercise claim—because the use of peyote was prohibited by a general criminal statute, which was not aimed at inhibiting religion. Oregon also noted that—like all other government entities—it has a compelling interest in regulating drug use and that the state's law represented the least intrusive means of achieving that interest.

The Oregon Supreme Court thought otherwise, however, and relied on *Sherbert* and *Thomas* to find in favor of Smith and Black. The state appealed to the U.S. Supreme Court, which heard arguments in the case in 1987. But, because the Oregon Supreme Court had not determined whether peyote use at religious ceremonies violated the state's criminal laws, the justices remanded the case back to Oregon for a decision.

That court ruled that the state law's prohibition against the use of peyote did not exempt the sacramental use of peyote, but it also said that the prohibition violated the Free Exercise Clause. The state brought its case back to the Supreme Court, where both sides assumed that the Court would use the *Sherbert* standard to resolve the dispute.

JUSTICE SCALIA delivered the opinion of the Court.

The free exercise of religion means, first and foremost, the right to believe and profess whatever religious doctrine one desires. Thus, the First Amendment obviously excludes all "governmental regulation of religious *beliefs* as such.". . .

But the "exercise of religion" often involves not only belief and profession but the performance of (or abstention from) physical acts: assembling with others for a worship service, participating in sacramental use of bread and wine, proselytizing, abstaining from certain foods or certain modes of transportation. It would be true, we think (though no case of ours has involved the point), that a state would be "prohibiting the free exercise [of religion]" if it sought to ban such acts or abstentions only when they are engaged in for religious reasons, or only because of the religious belief that they display. It would doubtless be unconstitutional, for example, to ban the casting of "statues that are to be used for worship purposes," or to prohibit bowing down before a golden calf.

Respondents in the present case, however, seek to carry the meaning of "prohibiting the free exercise [of religion]" one large step further. They contend that their religious mo-

tivation for using peyote places them beyond the reach of a criminal law that is not specifically directed at their religious practice, and that is concededly constitutional as applied to those who use the drug for other reasons. They assert, in other words, that "prohibiting the free exercise [of religion]" includes requiring any individual to observe a generally applicable law that requires (or forbids) the performance of an act that his religious belief forbids (or requires). As a textual matter, we do not think the words must be given that meaning. . . .

. . . We have never held that an individual's religious beliefs excuse him from compliance with an otherwise valid law prohibiting conduct that the State is free to regulate. On the contrary, the record of more than a century of our free exercise jurisprudence contradicts that proposition. . . . We first had occasion to assert that principle in *Reynolds v. United States* (1879), where we rejected the claim that criminal laws against polygamy could not be constitutionally applied to those whose religion commanded the practice. . . .

Subsequent decisions have consistently held that the right of free exercise does not relieve an individual of the obligation to comply with a "valid and neutral law of general applicability on the ground that the law proscribes (or prescribes) conduct that his religion prescribes (or proscribes)." *United States v. Lee* (1982). . . . In *Prince v. Massachusetts* (1944) we held that a mother could be prosecuted under the child labor laws for using her children to dispense literature in the streets, her religious motivation notwithstanding. We found no constitutional infirmity in "excluding [these children] from doing there what no other children may do." In *Braunfeld v. Brown* (1961) (plurality opinion) we upheld Sunday-closing laws against the claim that they burdened the religious practices of persons whose religions compelled them to refrain from work on other days. . . .

The only decisions in which we have held that the First Amendment bars application of a neutral, generally applicable law to religiously motivated action have involved not the Free Exercise Clause alone, but the Free Exercise Clause in conjunction with other constitutional protections, such as freedom of speech and of the press, see *Cantwell v. Connecticut*, . . . *Pierce v. Society of Sisters*, . . . *Wisconsin v. Yoder*. . . .

The present case does not present such a hybrid situation, but a free exercise claim unconnected with any communicative activity or parental right. Respondents urge us to hold, quite simply, that when otherwise prohibitable conduct is accompanied by religious convictions, not only the convictions but the conduct itself must be free from governmental regulation. We have never held that, and decline to do so now. There being no contention that Oregon's drug law represents an attempt to regulate religious beliefs, the communication of religious beliefs, or the raising of one's children in those beliefs, the rule to which we have adhered ever since *Reynolds* plainly controls. "Our cases do not at their farthest reach support the proposition that a stance of conscientious opposition relieves an objector from any colliding duty fixed by a democratic government.". . .

Respondents argue that even though exemption from generally applicable criminal laws need not automatically be extended to religiously motivated actors, at least the claim for a religious exemption must be evaluated under the balancing test set forth in *Sherbert v. Verner* (1963). Under the *Sherbert* test, governmental actions that substantially burden a religious practice must be justified by a compelling governmental interest. . . . Applying that test we have, on three occasions, invalidated state unemployment compensation rules that conditioned the availability of benefits upon an applicant's willingness to work under conditions forbidden by his religion. See *Sherbert v. Verner; Thomas v. Review Bd. of Indiana Employment Security Div.* (1981); *Hobbie v. Unemployment Appeals Comm'n of Florida* (1987). We have never invalidated any governmental action on the basis of the *Sherbert* test except the denial of unemployment compensation. Although we have sometimes purported to apply the *Sherbert* test in contexts other than that, we have always found the test satisfied. . . . In recent years we have abstained from applying the *Sherbert* test (outside the unemployment compensation field) at all. . . . In *Goldman v. Weinberger* (1986) we rejected application of the *Sherbert* test to military dress regulations that forbade the wearing of yarmulkes. . . .

Even if we were inclined to breathe into *Sherbert* some life beyond the unemployment compensation field, we would not apply it to require exemptions from a generally applicable criminal law. The *Sherbert* test, it must be recalled, was developed in a context that lent itself to individualized governmental assessment of the reasons for the relevant conduct. . . .

Whether or not the decisions are that limited, they at least have nothing to do with an across-the-board criminal prohibition on a particular form of conduct. Although, as noted earlier, we have sometimes used the *Sherbert* test to analyze free exercise challenges to such laws . . . we have never applied the test to invalidate one. We conclude today that the sounder approach, and the approach in accord with the vast majority of our precedents, is to hold the test inapplicable to such challenges. The government's ability to enforce generally applicable prohibitions of socially harmful conduct, like its ability to carry out other aspects of public policy, "cannot depend on measuring the effects of a governmental action on a religious objector's spiritual development.". . . To make an individual's obligation to obey such a law contingent upon the law's coincidence with his religious beliefs, except where the State's interest is "compelling"—permitting him, by virtue of his beliefs, "to become a law unto himself," *Reynolds v. United States*—contradicts both constitutional tradition and common sense.

The "compelling government interest" requirement seems benign, because it is familiar from other fields. But using it as the standard that must be met before the government may accord different treatment on the basis of race . . . or before the government may regulate the content of speech . . . is not remotely comparable to using it for the purpose asserted here. What it produces in those other fields—equality of treatment and an unrestricted flow of contending speech—are constitutional norms; what it would produce here—a private right to ignore generally applicable laws—is a constitutional anomaly.

Nor is it possible to limit the impact of respondents' proposal by requiring a "compelling state interest" only when the conduct prohibited is "central" to the individual's religion. . . . It is no more appropriate for judges to determine the "centrality" of religious beliefs before applying a "compelling interest" test in the free exercise field, than it would be for them to determine the "importance" of ideas before applying the "compelling interest" test in the free speech field. What principle of law or logic can be brought to bear to contradict a believer's assertion that a particular act is "central" to his personal faith? Judging the centrality of different religious practices is akin to the unacceptable "business of evaluating the relative merits of differing religious claims.". . . Repeatedly and in many different contexts, we have warned that courts must not presume to determine the place of a particular belief in a religion or the plausibility of a religious claim. . . .

If the "compelling interest" test is to be applied at all,

then, it must be applied across the board, to all actions thought to be religiously commanded. Moreover, if "compelling interest" really means what it says (and watering it down here would subvert its rigor in the other fields where it is applied), many laws will not meet the test. Any society adopting such a system would be courting anarchy, but that danger increases in direct proportion to the society's diversity of religious beliefs, and its determination to coerce or suppress none of them. Precisely because "we are a cosmopolitan nation made up of people of almost every conceivable religious preference," *Braunfeld v. Brown,* and precisely because we value and protect that religious divergence, we cannot afford the luxury of deeming presumptively invalid, as applied to the religious objector, every regulation of conduct that does not protect an interest of the highest order. The rule respondents favor would open the prospect of constitutionally required religious exemptions from civic obligations of almost every conceivable kind—ranging from compulsory military service . . . to the payment of taxes . . . to health and safety regulation such as manslaughter and child neglect laws . . . compulsory vaccination laws . . . drug laws . . . and traffic laws . . . to social welfare legislation such as minimum wage laws . . . child labor laws . . . animal cruelty laws . . . environmental protection laws . . . and laws providing for equality of opportunity for the races. . . . The First Amendment's protection of religious liberty does not require this.

Values that are protected against government interference through enshrinement in the Bill of Rights are not thereby banished from the political process. Just as a society that believes in the negative protection accorded to the press by the First Amendment is likely to enact laws that affirmatively foster the dissemination of the printed word, so also a society that believes in the negative protection accorded to religious belief can be expected to be solicitous of that value in its legislation as well. It is therefore not surprising that a number of States have made an exception to their drug laws for sacramental peyote use. . . . But to say that a nondiscriminatory religious-practice exemption is permitted, or even that it is desirable, is not to say that it is constitutionally required, and that the appropriate occasions for its creation can be discerned by the courts. It may fairly be said that leaving accommodation to the political process will place at a relative disadvantage those religious practices that are not widely engaged in; but that unavoidable conse-

quence of democratic government must be preferred to a system in which each conscience is a law unto itself or in which judges weigh the social importance of all laws against the centrality of all religious beliefs.

Because respondents' ingestion of peyote was prohibited under Oregon law, and because that prohibition is constitutional, Oregon may, consistent with the Free Exercise Clause, deny respondents unemployment compensation when their dismissal results from use of the drug. The decision of the Oregon Supreme Court is accordingly reversed.

It is so ordered.

JUSTICE O'CONNOR, with whom JUSTICE BRENNAN, JUSTICE MARSHALL, and JUSTICE BLACKMUN join as to Parts I and II, concurring in the judgment.*

Although I agree with the result the Court reaches in this case, I cannot join its opinion. In my view, today's holding dramatically departs from well-settled First Amendment jurisprudence, appears unnecessary to resolve the question presented, and is incompatible with our Nation's fundamental commitment to individual religious liberty.

[Part I omitted]

II

The Court today extracts from our long history of free exercise precedents the single categorical rule that "if prohibiting the exercise of religion . . . is . . . merely the incidental effect of a generally applicable and otherwise valid provision, the First Amendment has not been offended." Indeed, the Court holds that where the law is a generally applicable criminal prohibition, our usual free exercise jurisprudence does not even apply. To reach this sweeping result, however, the Court must not only give a strained reading of the First Amendment but must also disregard our consistent application of free exercise doctrine to cases involving generally applicable regulations that burden religious conduct.

The Free Exercise Clause of the First Amendment commands that "Congress shall make no law . . . prohibiting the free exercise [of religion]." In *Cantwell v. Connecticut* (1940) we held that this prohibition applies to the States by incor-

*Although JUSTICE BRENNAN, JUSTICE MARSHALL, and JUSTICE BLACKMUN join as to Parts I and II of this opinion, they do not concur in the judgment.

poration into the Fourteenth Amendment and that it categorically forbids government regulation of religious beliefs. As the Court recognizes, however, the "free exercise" of religion often, if not invariably, requires the performance of (or abstention from) certain acts. . . . Because the First Amendment does not distinguish between religious belief and religious conduct, conduct motivated by sincere religious belief, like the belief itself, must be at least presumptively protected by the Free Exercise Clause.

The Court today, however, interprets the Clause to permit the government to prohibit, without justification, conduct mandated by an individual's religious beliefs, so long as that prohibition is generally applicable. But a law that prohibits certain conduct—conduct that happens to be an act of worship for someone—manifestly does prohibit that person's free exercise of his religion. A person who is barred from engaging in religiously motivated conduct is barred from freely exercising his religion. Moreover, that person is barred from freely exercising his religion regardless of whether the law prohibits the conduct only when engaged in for religious reasons, only by members of that religion, or by all persons. It is difficult to deny that a law that prohibits religiously motivated conduct, even if the law is generally applicable, does not at least implicate First Amendment concerns.

The Court responds that generally applicable laws are "one large step" removed from laws aimed at specific religious practices. The First Amendment, however, does not distinguish between laws that are generally applicable and laws that target particular religious practices. Indeed, few States would be so naive as to enact a law directly prohibiting or burdening a religious practice as such. Our free exercise cases have all concerned generally applicable laws that had the effect of significantly burdening a religious practice. If the First Amendment is to have any vitality, it ought not be construed to cover only the extreme and hypothetical situation in which a State directly targets a religious practice. . . .

To say that a person's right to free exercise has been burdened, of course, does not mean that he has an absolute right to engage in the conduct. Under our established First Amendment jurisprudence, we have recognized that the freedom to act, unlike the freedom to believe, cannot be absolute. See, e.g., *Cantwell; Reynolds v. United States* (1879). Instead, we have respected both the First Amendment's ex-

press textual mandate and the governmental interest in regulation of conduct by requiring the government to justify any substantial burden on religiously motivated conduct by a compelling state interest and by means narrowly tailored to achieve that interest. . . .

The Court attempts to support its narrow reading of the Clause by claiming that "[w]e have never held that an individual's religious beliefs excuse him from compliance with an otherwise valid law prohibiting conduct that the State is free to regulate." But as the Court later notes, as it must, in cases such as *Cantwell* and *Yoder* we have in fact interpreted the Free Exercise Clause to forbid application of a generally applicable prohibition to religiously motivated conduct. . . . Indeed, in *Yoder* we expressly rejected the interpretation the Court now adopts. . . .

The Court endeavors to escape from our decisions in *Cantwell* and *Yoder* by labeling them "hybrid" decisions, but there is no denying that both cases expressly relied on the Free Exercise Clause . . . and that we have consistently regarded those cases as part of the mainstream of our free exercise jurisprudence. Moreover, in each of the other cases cited by the Court to support its categorical rule, we rejected the particular constitutional claims before us only after carefully weighing the competing interests. See *Prince v. Massachusetts . . . Braunfeld v. Brown. . . .* That we rejected the free exercise claims in those cases hardly calls into question the applicability of First Amendment doctrine in the first place. Indeed, it is surely unusual to judge the vitality of a constitutional doctrine by looking to the win-loss record of the plaintiffs who happen to come before us.

Respondents, of course, do not contend that their conduct is automatically immune from all governmental regulation simply because it is motivated by their sincere religious beliefs. The Court's rejection of that argument might therefore be regarded as merely harmless dictum. Rather, respondents invoke our traditional compelling interest test to argue that the Free Exercise Clause requires the State to grant them a limited exemption from its general criminal prohibition against the possession of peyote. The Court today, however, denies them even the opportunity to make that argument, concluding that "the sounder approach, and the approach in accord with the vast majority of our precedents, is to hold the [compelling interest] test inapplicable to" challenges to general criminal prohibitions.

In my view, however, the essence of a free exercise claim

is relief from a burden imposed by government on religious practices or beliefs, whether the burden is imposed directly through laws that prohibit or compel specific religious practices, or indirectly through laws that, in effect, make abandonment of one's own religion or conformity to the religious beliefs of others the price of an equal place in the civil community. . . . A State that makes criminal an individual's religiously motivated conduct burdens that individual's free exercise of religion in the severest manner possible, for it "results in the choice to the individual of either abandoning his religious principle or facing criminal prosecution.". . . I would have thought it beyond argument that such laws implicate free exercise concerns.

Indeed, we have never distinguished between cases in which a State conditions receipt of a benefit on conduct prohibited by religious beliefs and cases in which a State affirmatively prohibits such conduct. The *Sherbert* compelling interest test applies in both kinds of cases. . . . I would reaffirm that principle today: a neutral criminal law prohibiting conduct that a State may legitimately regulate is, if anything, more burdensome than a neutral civil statute placing legitimate conditions on the award of a state benefit.

Legislatures, of course, have always been "left free to reach actions which were in violation of social duties or subversive of good order." . . . Yet because of the close relationship between conduct and religious belief, "[i]n every case the power to regulate must be so exercised as not, in attaining a permissible end, unduly to infringe the protected freedom.". . . Once it has been shown that a government regulation or criminal prohibition burdens the free exercise of religion, we have consistently asked the Government to demonstrate that unbending application of its regulation to the religious objector "is essential to accomplish an overriding governmental interest," or represents "the least restrictive means of achieving some compelling state interest.". . . To me, the sounder approach—the approach more consistent with our role as judges to decide each case on its individual merits—is to apply this test in each case to determine whether the burden on the specific plaintiffs before us is constitutionally significant and whether the particular criminal interest asserted by the State before us is compelling. Even if, as an empirical matter, a government's criminal laws might usually serve a compelling interest in health, safety, or public order, the First Amendment at least requires a case-by-case determination of the question, sensi-

tive to the facts of each particular claim. . . . Given the range of conduct that a State might legitimately make criminal, we cannot assume, merely because a law carries criminal sanctions and is generally applicable, that the First Amendment never requires the State to grant a limited exemption for religiously motivated conduct. . . .

The Court today gives no convincing reason to depart from settled First Amendment jurisprudence. There is nothing talismanic about neutral laws of general applicability or general criminal prohibitions, for laws neutral toward religion can coerce a person to violate his religious conscience or intrude upon his religious duties just as effectively as laws aimed at religion. Although the Court suggests that the compelling interest test, as applied to generally applicable laws, would result in a "constitutional anomaly," the First Amendment unequivocally makes freedom of religion, like freedom from race discrimination and freedom of speech, a "constitutional nor[m]," not an "anomaly.". . . The Court's parade of horribles not only fails as a reason for discarding the compelling interest test, it instead demonstrates just the opposite: that courts have been quite capable of applying our free exercise jurisprudence to strike sensible balances between religious liberty and competing state interests.

Finally, the Court today suggests that the disfavoring of minority religions is an "unavoidable consequence" under our system of government and that accommodation of such religions must be left to the political process. In my view, however, the First Amendment was enacted precisely to protect the rights of those whose religious practices are not shared by the majority and may be viewed with hostility. The history of our free exercise doctrine amply demonstrates the harsh impact majoritarian rule has had on unpopular or emerging religious groups such as the Jehovah's Witnesses and the Amish. . . .

III

The Court's holding today not only misreads settled First Amendment precedent; it appears to be unnecessary to this case. I would reach the same result applying our established free exercise jurisprudence.

There is no dispute that Oregon's criminal prohibition of peyote places a severe burden on the ability of respondents to freely exercise their religion. Peyote is a sacrament of the Native American Church and is regarded as vital to respondents' ability to practice their religion. . . .

There is also no dispute that Oregon has a significant interest in enforcing laws that control the possession and use of controlled substances by its citizens. . . .

Thus, the critical question in this case is whether exempting respondents from the State's general criminal prohibition "will unduly interfere with fulfillment of the governmental interest.". . . Although the question is close, I would conclude that uniform application of Oregon's criminal prohibition is "essential to accomplish," . . . its overriding interest in preventing the physical harm caused by the use of a . . . controlled substance. Oregon's criminal prohibition represents that State's judgment that the possession and use of controlled substances, even by only one person, is inherently harmful and dangerous. Because the health effects caused by the use of controlled substances exist regardless of the motivation of the user, the use of such substances, even for religious purposes, violates the very purpose of the laws that prohibit them. . . . Moreover, in view of the societal interest in preventing trafficking in controlled substances, uniform application of the criminal prohibition at issue is essential to the effectiveness of Oregon's stated interest in preventing any possession of peyote. . . .

I would therefore adhere to our established free exercise jurisprudence and hold that the State in this case has a compelling interest in regulating peyote use by its citizens and that accommodating respondents' religiously motivated conduct "will unduly interfere with fulfillment of the governmental interest.". . . Accordingly, I concur in the judgment of the Court.

JUSTICE BLACKMUN, with whom JUSTICE BRENNAN and JUSTICE MARSHALL join, dissenting.

This Court over the years painstakingly has developed a consistent and exacting standard to test the constitutionality of a state statute that burdens the free exercise of religion. Such a statute may stand only if the law in general, and the State's refusal to allow a religious exemption in particular, are justified by a compelling interest that cannot be served by less restrictive means.

Until today, I thought this was a settled and inviolate principle of this Court's First Amendment jurisprudence. The majority, however, perfunctorily dismisses it as a "constitutional anomaly." As carefully detailed in JUSTICE O'CONNOR's concurring opinion, the majority is able to arrive at this view only by mischaracterizing this Court's precedents. The Court discards leading free exercise cases such as *Cantwell v. Connecticut* (1940) and *Wisconsin v. Yoder* (1972) as "hybrid." The Court views traditional free exercise analysis as somehow inapplicable to criminal prohibitions (as opposed to conditions on the receipt of benefits), and to state laws of general applicability (as opposed, presumably, to laws that expressly single out religious practices). The Court cites cases in which, due to various exceptional circumstances, we found strict scrutiny inapposite, to hint that the Court has repudiated that standard altogether. In short, it effectuates a wholesale overturning of settled law concerning the Religion Clauses of our Constitution. One hopes that the Court is aware of the consequences, and that its result is not a product of overreaction to the serious problems the country's drug crisis has generated.

This distorted view of our precedents leads the majority to conclude that strict scrutiny of a state law burdening the free exercise of religion is a "luxury" that a well-ordered society cannot afford, and that the repression of minority religions is an "unavoidable consequence of democratic government." I do not believe the Founders thought their dearly bought freedom from religious persecution a "luxury," but an essential element of liberty—and they could not have thought religious intolerance "unavoidable," for they drafted the Religion Clauses precisely in order to avoid that intolerance.

For these reasons, I agree with JUSTICE O'CONNOR's analysis of the applicable free exercise doctrine, and I join parts I and II of her opinion. As she points out, "the critical question in this case is whether exempting respondents from the State's general criminal prohibition 'will unduly interfere with fulfillment of the governmental interest.'" I do disagree, however, with her specific answer to that question.

In weighing respondents' clear interest in the free exercise of their religion against Oregon's asserted interest in enforcing its drug laws, it is important to articulate in precise terms the state interest involved. It is not the State's broad interest in fighting the critical "war on drugs" that must be weighed against respondents' claim, but the State's narrow interest in refusing to make an exception for the religious, ceremonial use of peyote. . . .

The State's interest in enforcing its prohibition, in order to be sufficiently compelling to outweigh a free exercise claim, cannot be merely abstract or symbolic. The State cannot plausibly assert that unbending application of a criminal prohibition is essential to fulfill any compelling interest, if it does not, in fact, attempt to enforce that prohibition. In this case, the State actually has not evinced any concrete interest in enforcing its drug laws against religious users of peyote. Oregon has never sought to prosecute respondents, and does not claim that it has made significant enforcement efforts against other religious users of peyote. The State's asserted interest thus amounts only to the symbolic preservation of an unenforced prohibition. But a government interest in "symbolism, even symbolism for so worthy a cause as the abolition of unlawful drugs," cannot suffice to abrogate the constitutional rights of individuals. . . .

Similarly, this Court's prior decisions have not allowed a government to rely on mere speculation about potential harms, but have demanded evidentiary support for a refusal to allow a religious exception. . . . In this case, the State's justification for refusing to recognize an exception to its criminal laws for religious peyote use is entirely speculative. . . .

I dissent.

Smith represents a change in the standards governing free exercise disputes. For the first time since it was articulated, the Court explicitly rejected the *Sherbert* test. To be sure, the justices had failed to apply it in cases such as *Goldman* and *Lyng*, but here the Court was eradicating the *Sherbert/Yoder* lineage of cases and returning to the kind of analysis it used in *Reynolds v. United States*. As Scalia wrote:

To make an individual's obligation to obey . . . a law contingent upon the law's coincidence with his religious beliefs, except where the State's interest is "compelling"—permitting him, by virtue of his beliefs, "to become a law unto himself," *Reynolds v. United States*—contradicts both constitutional tradition and common sense.

In place of the *Sherbert* test, the Court now held that the Free Exercise Clause does not relieve an individual from the obligation to comply with a valid and neutral law of general applicability on the ground that the law commands behavior inconsistent with a person's religious teachings. The articulation of this new standard meant, as one scholar put it, that the Court had "brought free exercise jurisprudence full circle by reaffirming the

. . . doctrine of *Reynolds*," and rejecting the compelling interest approach of *Sherbert*.[20]

As you might expect, *Smith* generated enormous controversy. The opinions written by Justices O'Connor and Blackmun made clear their displeasure with the majority's break from precedent, asserting that the Court should stick with the compelling interest–least restrictive means approach of *Sherbert* and *Yoder*. Members of Congress also voiced their disapproval. Soon after the justices handed down *Smith*, interest groups began to lobby Congress to overturn the decision. As Sen. Edward M. Kennedy, D-Mass., put it, these interests feared that, under the new standard "dry communities could ban the use of wine in communion services, Government meat inspectors could require changes in the preparation of kosher food and school boards could force children to attend sex education classes [contrary to their religious beliefs]."[21] Led by politicians as varied in ideological approach as Kennedy and Orrin Hatch, R-Utah, Congress began debating legislative options to counteract the Supreme Court's newly articulated position on religious liberty.

Before Congress could arrive at a legislative response to *Smith*, the Supreme Court heard another free exercise case. In *Church of the Lukumi Babalu Aye v. City of Hialeah* (1993) the justices considered whether ordinances prohibiting animal slaughter for religious purposes violate the Free Exercise Clause. The particular targets of this law were adherents of the Santeria religion, a faith that has a mixture of African, Caribbean, and Roman Catholic roots. Central to this religion is animal sacrifice. Practitioners sacrifice chickens, pigeons, doves, ducks, guinea pigs, goats, sheep, and turtles at various events, including the initiation of new priests, weddings, births, and deaths, and as cures for the ailing. The animals, which are killed by cutting the carotid arteries in the neck, are cooked and eaten after some of the rituals. Santerians may sacrifice as many as thirty animals during a given ritual.

20. Frederick Mark Gedicks, "Religion," in *The Oxford Companion to the Supreme Court*, ed. Kermit L. Hall (New York: Oxford University Press, 1992), 725.
21. Quoted by Adam Clymer in "Congress Moves to Ease Curb on Religious Acts," *New York Times*, May 10, 1993, A9.

Santeria priest Rigoberto Zamora cooks lamb and goat he sacrificed in a religious ritual the previous day. Zamora and other members of his church celebrated the Supreme Court's decision striking down city attempts to prohibit animal sacrifices in religious worship.

Members of the Hialeah, Florida, community—who apparently were less than enthusiastic about the practice of animal sacrifice—enacted six ordinances limiting animal sacrifice, which was defined as "to unnecessarily kill, torment, or mutilate an animal in a public or private ritual or ceremony not for the primary purpose of food consumption."

The Supreme Court struck down the Hialeah ordinances by a 9–0 vote. Although the justices were no more in agreement over the appropriate standard to use than they were in *Smith,* they unanimously concluded that the city had violated the Free Exercise Clause. In spite of the fact that the ordinances were generally worded, there was no doubt that the laws were passed to prohibit the practices of a particular religious group, the Santerians. As such, the statutes would fall under either the *Sherbert/Yoder* or *Smith* tests. As Justice Blackmun put it in a concurring opinion, "Because the respondent [Hialeah] here does single out religion in this way, the present case is an easy one to decide."

That the Court unanimously had supported a religious practice over state regulation did not stop Congress from continuing to ways to blunt the impact of the

Smith decision. In spite of the Court's finding for the Santerians, the majority opinion liberally cited *Smith* as the governing standard in religious liberty cases. Almost no one viewed *Lukumi Babalu* as a retreat from the *Smith* test. As a consequence, in November 1993 Congress passed the Religious Freedom Restoration Act (RFRA). The law's most important provision, which applied to both state and federal governments, reads as follows:

Government shall not substantially burden a person's exercise of religion even if the burden results from a rule of general applicability [unless the government can show that the burden] (1) is in furtherance of a compelling governmental interest; and (2) is the least restrictive means of furthering that compelling governmental interest.

The language should sound familiar: the statute codified the compelling interest–least restrictive means test used in *Sherbert* and *Yoder.* It explicitly rejected the general applicability approach ushered in by *Smith.* Congress was extending more protection to religious exercise rights than the Court was offering through its interpretation of the First Amendment.

Although RFRA was praised by most religious groups, it troubled state and local officials. Did the act mean that a city would violate federal civil rights laws if it enforced an antinoise ordinance against a religious group that used sound trucks to spread its message, or arrested for disorderly conduct a group of religious zealots who paraded down streets blocking traffic, or failed to make religious accommodations for jail inmates? What did the statute mean when it prohibited a government from imposing a substantial burden on a person's religious exercise? What standards would be used to determine a compelling government interest and the least restrictive means?

It did not take long for the statute to be challenged. A dispute arose between a local Catholic church and the city of Boerne, Texas.[22] The city had denied the church permission to tear down its existing building and erect a new structure. The Catholic archdiocese claimed that under RFRA the city was without power to block construction. Did Congress act constitutionally when it passed a statute substituting its own preferred Free Exercise test for the one handed down by the Court in *Smith?*

P. F. Flores, on behalf of the church, sued in federal court, claiming that constructing a new church was a form of religious exercise that was protected against government interference by Religious Freedom Restoration Act. The city countered by arguing that the statute was unconstitutional. The district court agreed with the city, striking down the law. But the court of appeals reversed, concluding that the law was a proper exercise of federal legislative power.

On appeal to the Supreme Court, the city argued that the statute impermissibly interfered with the powers of local governments and violated the separation of powers doctrine that leaves to the judiciary, not the legislature, the authority to decide what the proper standards should be in balancing individual rights with government authority. The church responded that Congress acted within its power to protect religious liberty against government encroachment in much the same manner as it had when it passed the various civil rights statutes.

City of Boerne v. Flores

521 U.S. 507 (1997)
supct.law.cornell.edu/supct/html/95-2074.ZS.html
*Vote: 6 (Ginsburg, Kennedy, Rehnquist, Scalia, Stevens,
        Thomas)*
    3 (Breyer, O'Connor, Souter)
Opinion of the Court: Kennedy
Concurring opinions: Scalia, Stevens
Dissenting opinions: Breyer, O'Connor, Souter

In 1991 St. Peter the Apostle Church received permission from the archbishop of San Antonio to demolish its current structure, which it had outgrown, and to build a new seven-hundred-seat church, more than tripling its capacity. When the local parish applied for the necessary building permits, however, city officials rejected the project on the grounds that the existing church was covered by the city's historical preservation program. Archbishop

Father Tony Cummins in front of St. Peter the Apostle Catholic Church in Boerne, Texas. In 1997 the church lost its battle to replace the structure, which the city had declared a historic landmark.

22. To hear oral arguments and the announcement of the decision in this case, navigate to: *oyez.nwu.edu.*

JUSTICE KENNEDY delivered the opinion of the Court.

A decision by local zoning authorities to deny a church a building permit was challenged under the Religious Freedom Restoration Act of 1993 (RFRA). The case calls into question the authority of Congress to enact RFRA. We conclude the statute exceeds Congress' power. . . .

Congress enacted RFRA in direct response to the Court's decision in *Employment Div., Dept. of Human Resources of Ore. v. Smith* (1990). . . . In evaluating the claim, we declined to apply the balancing test set forth in *Sherbert v. Verner* (1963), under which we would have asked whether Oregon's prohibition substantially burdened a religious practice and, if it did, whether the burden was justified by a compelling government interest. . . .

The application of the *Sherbert* test, the *Smith* decision explained, would have produced an anomaly in the law, a constitutional right to ignore neutral laws of general applicability. The anomaly would have been accentuated, the Court reasoned, by the difficulty of determining whether a particular practice was central to an individual's religion. We explained, moreover, that it "is not within the judicial ken to question the centrality of particular beliefs or practices to a faith, or the validity of particular litigants' interpretations of those creeds.". . .

Four Members of the Court disagreed. They argued the law placed a substantial burden on the Native American Church members so that it could be upheld only if the law served a compelling state interest and was narrowly tailored to achieve that end. JUSTICE O'CONNOR concluded Oregon had satisfied the test, while Justice Blackmun, joined by Justice Brennan and Justice Marshall, could see no compelling interest justifying the law's application to the members.

These points of constitutional interpretation were debated by Members of Congress in hearings and floor debates. Many criticized the Court's reasoning, and this disagreement resulted in the passage of RFRA. Congress announced:

"(1) [T]he framers of the Constitution, recognizing free exercise of religion as an unalienable right, secured its protection in the First Amendment to the Constitution;

"(2) laws 'neutral' toward religion may burden religious exercise as surely as laws intended to interfere with religious exercise;

"(3) governments should not substantially burden religious exercise without compelling justification;

"(4) in *Employment Division v. Smith* (1990), the Supreme Court virtually eliminated the requirement that the government justify burdens on religious exercise imposed by laws neutral toward religion; and

"(5) the compelling interest test as set forth in prior Federal court rulings is a workable test for striking sensible balances between religious liberty and competing prior governmental interests."

The Act's stated purposes are:

"(1) to restore the compelling interest test as set forth in *Sherbert v. Verner* (1963) and *Wisconsin v. Yoder* (1972) and to guarantee its application in all cases where free exercise of religion is substantially burdened; and

"(2) to provide a claim or defense to persons whose religious exercise is substantially burdened by government."

RFRA prohibits "[g]overnment" from "substantially burden[ing]" a person's exercise of religion even if the burden results from a rule of general applicability unless the government can demonstrate the burden "(1) is in furtherance of a compelling governmental interest; and (2) is the least restrictive means of furthering that compelling governmental interest." The Act's mandate applies to any "branch, department, agency, instrumentality, and official (or other person acting under color of law) of the United States," as well as to any "State, or . . . subdivision of a State.". . .

Under our Constitution, the Federal Government is one of enumerated powers. *McCulloch v. Maryland* (1819). The judicial authority to determine the constitutionality of laws, in cases and controversies, is based on the premise that the "powers of the legislature are defined and limited; and that those limits may not be mistaken, or forgotten, the constitution is written." *Marbury v. Madison* (1803).

Congress relied on its Fourteenth Amendment enforcement power in enacting the most far reaching and substantial of RFRA's provisions, those which impose its requirements on the States. The Fourteenth Amendment provides, in relevant part:

"Section 1. . . . No State shall make or enforce any law which shall abridge the privileges or immunities of citizens of the United States; nor shall any State deprive any person of life, liberty, or property, without due process of law; nor deny to any person within its jurisdiction the equal protection of the laws.

"Section 5. The Congress shall have power to enforce, by appropriate legislation, the provisions of this article."

The parties disagree over whether RFRA is a proper exercise of Congress' §5 power "to enforce" by "appropriate legislation" the constitutional guarantee that no State shall deprive any person of "life, liberty, or property, without due process of law" nor deny any person "equal protection of the laws.". . .

Legislation which deters or remedies constitutional violations can fall within the sweep of Congress' enforcement power even if in the process it prohibits conduct which is not itself unconstitutional and intrudes into "legislative spheres of autonomy previously reserved to the States." *Fitzpatrick v. Bitzer* (1976). . . .

It is also true, however, that "[a]s broad as the congressional enforcement power is, it is not unlimited." *Oregon v. Mitchell* [1970]. . . .

Congress' power under §5 . . . extends only to "enforc[ing]" the provisions of the Fourteenth Amendment. The Court has described this power as "remedial," *South Carolina v. Katzenbach* [1966]. The design of the Amendment and the text of §5 are inconsistent with the suggestion that Congress has the power to decree the substance of the Fourteenth Amendment's restrictions on the States. Legislation which alters the meaning of the Free Exercise Clause cannot be said to be enforcing the Clause. Congress does not enforce a constitutional right by changing what the right is. It has been given the power "to enforce," not the power to determine what constitutes a constitutional violation. Were it not so, what Congress would be enforcing would no longer be, in any meaningful sense, the "provisions of [the Fourteenth Amendment]."

While the line between measures that remedy or prevent unconstitutional actions and measures that make a substantive change in the governing law is not easy to discern, and Congress must have wide latitude in determining where it lies, the distinction exists and must be observed. There must be a congruence and proportionality between the injury to be prevented or remedied and the means adopted to that end. Lacking such a connection, legislation may become substantive in operation and effect. . . .

The design of the Fourteenth Amendment has proved significant also in maintaining the traditional separation of powers between Congress and the Judiciary. The first eight Amendments to the Constitution set forth self-executing prohibitions on governmental action, and this Court has had primary authority to interpret those prohibitions. . . . As enacted, the Fourteenth Amendment confers substantive rights against the States which, like the provisions of the Bill of Rights, are self-executing. The power to interpret the Constitution in a case or controversy remains in the Judiciary.

The remedial and preventive nature of Congress' enforcement power, and the limitation inherent in the power, were confirmed in our earliest cases on the Fourteenth Amendment. In the *Civil Rights Cases* (1883), the Court invalidated sections of the Civil Rights Act of 1875 which prescribed criminal penalties for denying to any person "the full enjoyment of" public accommodations and conveyances, on the grounds that it exceeded Congress' power by seeking to regulate private conduct. The Enforcement Clause, the Court said, did not authorize Congress to pass "general legislation upon the rights of the citizen, but corrective legislation; that is, such as may be necessary and proper for counteracting such laws as the States may adopt or enforce, and which, by the amendment, they are prohibited from making or enforcing. . . ." . . .

Any suggestion that Congress has a substantive, nonremedial power under the Fourteenth Amendment is not supported by our case law. . . .

If Congress could define its own powers by altering the Fourteenth Amendment's meaning, no longer would the Constitution be "superior paramount law, unchangeable by ordinary means." It would be "on a level with ordinary legislative acts, and, like other acts, . . . alterable when the legislature shall please to alter it." *Marbury v. Madison.* Under this approach, it is difficult to conceive of a principle that would limit congressional power. Shifting legislative majorities could change the Constitution and effectively circumvent the difficult and detailed amendment process contained in Article V.

We now turn to consider whether RFRA can be considered enforcement legislation under §5 of the Fourteenth Amendment.

Respondent contends that RFRA is a proper exercise of Congress' remedial or preventive power. The Act, it is said, is a reasonable means of protecting the free exercise of religion as defined by *Smith*. . . . If Congress can prohibit laws with discriminatory effects in order to prevent racial discrimination in violation of the Equal Protection Clause, then it can do the same, respondent argues, to promote religious liberty.

While preventive rules are sometimes appropriate remedial measures, there must be a congruence between the means used and the ends to be achieved. The appropriateness of remedial measures must be considered in light of the evil presented. Strong measures appropriate to address one harm may be an unwarranted response to another, lesser one.

A comparison between RFRA and the Voting Rights Act is instructive. In contrast to the record which confronted Congress and the judiciary in the voting rights cases, RFRA's legislative record lacks examples of modern instances of generally applicable laws passed because of religious bigotry. The history of persecution in this country detailed in the hearings mentions no episodes occurring in the past 40 years. . . .

Regardless of the state of the legislative record, RFRA cannot be considered remedial, preventive legislation, if those terms are to have any meaning. RFRA is so out of proportion to a supposed remedial or preventive object that it cannot be understood as responsive to, or designed to prevent, unconstitutional behavior. It appears, instead, to attempt a substantive change in constitutional protections. Preventive measures prohibiting certain types of laws may be appropriate when there is reason to believe that many of the laws affected by the congressional enactment have a significant likelihood of being unconstitutional. Remedial legislation under §5 "should be adapted to the mischief and wrong which the [Fourteenth] [A]mendment was intended to provide against." *Civil Rights Cases.*

RFRA is not so confined. Sweeping coverage ensures its intrusion at every level of government, displacing laws and prohibiting official actions of almost every description and regardless of subject matter. RFRA's restrictions apply to every agency and official of the Federal, State, and local Governments. RFRA applies to all federal and state law, statutory or otherwise, whether adopted before or after its enactment. RFRA has no termination date or termination mechanism. Any law is subject to challenge at any time by any individual who alleges a substantial burden on his or her free exercise of religion. . . .

The stringent test RFRA demands of state laws reflects a lack of proportionality or congruence between the means adopted and the legitimate end to be achieved. If an objector can show a substantial burden on his free exercise, the State must demonstrate a compelling governmental interest and show that the law is the least restrictive means of furthering its interest. Claims that a law substantially burdens someone's exercise of religion will often be difficult to contest. Requiring a State to demonstrate a compelling interest and show that it has adopted the least restrictive means of achieving that interest is the most demanding test known to constitutional law. . . . This is a considerable congressional intrusion into the States' traditional prerogatives and general authority to regulate for the health and welfare of their citizens.

. . . It is a reality of the modern regulatory state that numerous state laws, such as the zoning regulations at issue here, impose a substantial burden on a large class of individuals. When the exercise of religion has been burdened in an incidental way by a law of general application, it does not follow that the persons affected have been burdened any more than other citizens, let alone burdened because of their religious beliefs. In addition, the Act imposes in every case a least restrictive means requirement—a requirement that was not used in the pre-*Smith* jurisprudence RFRA purported to codify—which also indicates that the legislation is broader than is appropriate if the goal is to prevent and remedy constitutional violations.

When Congress acts within its sphere of power and responsibilities, it has not just the right but the duty to make its own informed judgment on the meaning and force of the Constitution. This has been clear from the early days of the Republic. . . . Were it otherwise, we would not afford Congress the presumption of validity its enactments now enjoy.

Our national experience teaches that the Constitution is preserved best when each part of the government respects both the Constitution and the proper actions and determinations of the other branches. When the Court has interpreted the Constitution, it has acted within the province of the Judicial Branch, which embraces the duty to say what the law is. *Marbury v. Madison.* When the political branches of the Government act against the background of a judicial interpretation of the Constitution already issued, it must be understood that in later cases and controversies the Court will treat its precedents with the respect due them under settled principles, including stare decisis, and contrary expectations must be disappointed. RFRA was designed to control cases and controversies, such as the one before us; but as the provisions of the federal statute here invoked are beyond congressional authority, it is this Court's precedent, not RFRA, which must control.

It is for Congress in the first instance to "determin[e] whether and what legislation is needed to secure the guarantees of the Fourteenth Amendment," and its conclusions are entitled to much deference. Congress' discretion is not unlimited, however, and the courts retain the power, as they have since *Marbury v. Madison,* to determine if Congress has exceeded its authority under the Constitution. Broad as the power of Congress is under the Enforcement Clause of the Fourteenth Amendment, RFRA contradicts vital principles necessary to maintain separation of powers and the federal balance. The judgment of the Court of Appeals sustaining the Act's constitutionality is reversed.

It is so ordered.

JUSTICE STEVENS, concurring.

In my opinion, the Religious Freedom Restoration Act of 1993 (RFRA) is a "law respecting an establishment of religion" that violates the First Amendment to the Constitution.

If the historic landmark on the hill in Boerne happened to be a museum or an art gallery owned by an atheist, it would not be eligible for an exemption from the city ordinances that forbid an enlargement of the structure. Because the landmark is owned by the Catholic Church, it is claimed that RFRA gives its owner a federal statutory entitlement to an exemption from a generally applicable, neutral civil law. Whether the Church would actually prevail under the statute or not, the statute has provided the Church with a legal weapon that no atheist or agnostic can obtain. This governmental preference for religion, as opposed to irreligion, is forbidden by the First Amendment. *Wallace v. Jaffree* (1985).

JUSTICE SCALIA, with whom JUSTICE STEVENS joins, concurring in part.

We held in *Smith* that the Constitution's Free Exercise Clause "does not relieve an individual of the obligation to comply with a 'valid and neutral law of general applicability on the ground that the law proscribes (or prescribes) con-

duct that his religion prescribes (or proscribes).'" The material that the dissent claims is at odds with *Smith* either has little to say about the issue or is in fact more consistent with *Smith* than with the dissent's interpretation of the Free Exercise Clause. . . .

. . . The dissent's approach has, of course, great popular attraction. Who can possibly be against the abstract proposition that government should not, even in its general, nondiscriminatory laws, place unreasonable burdens upon religious practice? Unfortunately, however, that abstract proposition must ultimately be reduced to concrete cases. The issue presented by *Smith* is, quite simply, whether the people, through their elected representatives, or rather this Court, shall control the outcome of those concrete cases. For example, shall it be the determination of this Court, or rather of the people, whether (as the dissent apparently believes) church construction will be exempt from zoning laws? The historical evidence put forward by the dissent does nothing to undermine the conclusion we reached in *Smith:* It shall be the people.

JUSTICE O'CONNOR, with whom JUSTICE BREYER joins . . . dissenting.*

I dissent from the Court's disposition of this case. I agree with the Court that the issue before us is whether the Religious Freedom Restoration Act (RFRA) is a proper exercise of Congress' power to enforce §5 of the Fourteenth Amendment. But as a yardstick for measuring the constitutionality of RFRA, the Court uses its holding in *Employment Div., Dept. of Human Resources of Ore. v. Smith* (1990), the decision that prompted Congress to enact RFRA as a means of more rigorously enforcing the Free Exercise Clause. I remain of the view that *Smith* was wrongly decided, and I would use this case to reexamine the Court's holding there. Therefore, I would direct the parties to brief the question whether *Smith* represents the correct understanding of the Free Exercise Clause and set the case for reargument. If the Court were to correct the misinterpretation of the Free Exercise Clause set forth in *Smith,* it would simultaneously put our First Amendment jurisprudence back on course and allay the legitimate concerns of a majority in Congress who be-

*Authors' note: Justice Breyer joins this dissent with the reservation that he does not agree with all of the points made in the second paragraph of the material excerpted here.

lieved that *Smith* improperly restricted religious liberty. We would then be in a position to review RFRA in light of a proper interpretation of the Free Exercise Clause.

I agree with much of the reasoning . . . of the Court's opinion. Indeed, if I agreed with the Court's standard in *Smith*, I would join the opinion. As the Court's careful and thorough historical analysis shows, Congress lacks the "power to decree the *substance* of the Fourteenth Amendment's restrictions on the States." (Emphasis added.) Rather, its power under §5 of the Fourteenth Amendment extends only to enforcing the Amendment's provisions. In short, Congress lacks the ability independently to define or expand the scope of constitutional rights by statute. Accordingly, whether Congress has exceeded its §5 powers turns on whether there is a "congruence and proportionality between the injury to be prevented or remedied and the means adopted to that end." This recognition does not, of course, in any way diminish Congress' obligation to draw its own conclusions regarding the Constitution's meaning. Congress, no less than this Court, is called upon to consider the requirements of the Constitution and to act in accordance with its dictates. But when it enacts legislation in furtherance of its delegated powers, Congress must make its judgments consistent with this Court's exposition of the Constitution and with the limits placed on its legislative authority by provisions such as the Fourteenth Amendment. . . .

Stare decisis concerns should not prevent us from revisiting our holding in *Smith*. "'[S]tare decisis is a principle of policy and not a mechanical formula of adherence to the latest decision, however recent and questionable, when such adherence involves collision with a prior doctrine more embracing in its scope, intrinsically sounder, and verified by experience.'" *Adarand Constructors, Inc. v. Peña* (1995). This principle is particularly true in constitutional cases, where—as this case so plainly illustrates—"correction through legislative action is practically impossible." *Seminole Tribe of Fla. v. Florida* (1996). . . .

Accordingly, I believe that we should reexamine our holding in *Smith*, and do so in this very case. In its place, I would return to a rule that requires government to justify any substantial burden on religiously motivated conduct by a compelling state interest and to impose that burden only by means narrowly tailored to achieve that interest. . . .

The historical evidence casts doubt on the Court's cur-

rent interpretation of the Free Exercise Clause. The record instead reveals that its drafters and ratifiers more likely viewed the Free Exercise Clause as a guarantee that government may not unnecessarily hinder believers from freely practicing their religion, a position consistent with our pre-*Smith* jurisprudence. . . .

The Religion Clauses of the Constitution represent a profound commitment to religious liberty. Our Nation's Founders conceived of a Republic receptive to voluntary religious expression, not of a secular society in which religious expression is tolerated only when it does not conflict with a generally applicable law. . . . [T]he Free Exercise Clause is properly understood as an affirmative guarantee of the right to participate in religious activities without impermissible governmental interference, even where a believer's conduct is in tension with a law of general application. Certainly, it is in no way anomalous to accord heightened protection to a right identified in the text of the First Amendment. For example, it has long been the Court's position that freedom of speech—a right enumerated only a few words after the right to free exercise—has special constitutional status. Given the centrality of freedom of speech and religion to the American concept of personal liberty, it is altogether reasonable to conclude that both should be treated with the highest degree of respect.

Although it may provide a bright line, the rule the Court declared in *Smith* does not faithfully serve the purpose of the Constitution. Accordingly, I believe that it is essential for the Court to reconsider its holding in *Smith*—and to do so in this very case. I would therefore direct the parties to brief this issue and set the case for reargument.

I respectfully dissent from the Court's disposition of this case.

JUSTICE SOUTER, dissenting.

To decide whether the Fourteenth Amendment gives Congress sufficient power to enact the Religious Freedom Restoration Act, the Court measures the legislation against the free exercise standard of *Employment Div., Dept. of Human Resources of Ore. v. Smith* (1990). For the reasons stated in my opinion in *Church of Lukumi Babalu Aye, Inc. v. Hialeah* (1993) (opinion concurring in part and concurring in judgment), I have serious doubts about the precedential value of the *Smith* rule and its entitlement to adherence. These doubts are intensified today by the historical arguments go-

TABLE 4-1 Free Exercise Approaches Advocated by the Justices in *Smith*, *Lukumi Babalu,* and *City of Boerne*

Smith (1990)	*Lukumi Babalu* (1993)	*City of Boerne* (1997)
Blackmun ⟶ (*Sherbert/Yoder* standard)	Blackmun ⟶ (*Sherbert/Yoder* standard)	Breyer (*Sherbert/Yoder* standard)
Brennan ⟶ (*Sherbert/Yoder* standard)	Souter ⟶ (Reconsider *Smith*)	Souter (Reconsider *Smith*)
Kennedy ⟶ (*Smith* rule)	Kennedy ⟶ (*Smith* rule)	Kennedy (*Smith* rule)
Marshall ⟶ (*Sherbert/Yoder* standard)	Thomas ⟶ (*Smith* rule)	Thomas (*Smith* rule)
O'Connor ⟶ (*Sherbert/Yoder* standard)	O'Connor ⟶ (*Sherbert/Yoder* standard)	O'Connor (*Sherbert/Yoder* standard)
Rehnquist ⟶ (*Smith* rule)	Rehnquist ⟶ (*Smith* rule)	Rehnquist (*Smith* rule)
Scalia ⟶ (*Smith* rule)	Scalia ⟶ (*Smith* rule)	Scalia (*Smith* rule)
Stevens ⟶ (*Smith* rule)	Stevens ⟶ (*Smith* rule)	Stevens (*Smith* rule)
White ⟶ (*Smith* rule)	White ⟶ (*Smith* rule)	Ginsburg (*Smith* rule)

ing to the original understanding of the Free Exercise Clause presented in JUSTICE O'CONNOR'S opinion, which raises very substantial issues about the soundness of the *Smith* rule. But without briefing and argument on the merits of that rule (which this Court has never had in any case, including *Smith* itself), I am not now prepared to join JUSTICE O'CONNOR in rejecting it or the majority in assuming it to be correct.

What does the future hold for Free Exercise Clause cases? As Table 4-1 indicates, as the Court entered the year 2000 the justices were badly split over the appropriate standard to use in religious exercise disputes. The justices supporting the rule of law developed in *Smith* remain in control, but a significant minority has expressed

a desire to reconsider *Smith*. Given the continuing divisions among the justices over the appropriate standard to impose and the intense congressional opposition to the prevailing *Smith* test, the Court's free exercise jurisprudence is quite unstable.

Religious freedom cases are often controversial, especially when the justices rule against a religious exercise claim. Several such rulings have been reversed by later Courts. Still others have been nullified by actions of Congress or the state legislatures. Table 4-2 lists a number of rulings in which the Court rejected free exercise claims against government regulation and the subsequent fate of those decisions. As you can see, a significant portion of these decisions have not stood the test of time.

TABLE 4-2 Aftermath of Select Court Cases Rejecting Free Exercise Claims

Issue	Case	Status
Polygamy	*Reynolds v. United States* (1879)	Invoked as justification for *Smith* rule; remains good law
Exemption from oath "abjuring" polygamy as a condition to vote	*Davis v. Beason* (1890)	Remains good law
Exemption from naturalization pledge to "take up arms" on behalf of the U.S.	*United States v. Schwimmer* (1929)	Overruled by Court in *Girouard v. United States* (1946)
Exemption from naturalization pledge to "take up arms" on behalf of the U.S.	*United States v. MacIntosh* (1931)	Overturned by Court in *Girouard v. United States* (1946)
Exemption from compulsory classes in military science	*Hamilton v. Regents of the University of California* (1934)	Remains good law
Exemption from compulsory flag salute	*Minersville School District v. Gobitis* (1940)	Overruled by Court in *West Virginia Board of Education v. Barnette* (1943)
Exemption from license requirement for parade	*Cox v. New Hampshire* (1941)	Remains good law
Exemption from paying license taxes on book selling	*Jones v. Opelika I* (1942)	Overruled by Court in *Jones v. Opelika II* (1943)
Solicitation of religious materials by minors	*Prince v. Massachusetts* (1944)	Remains good law
Keeping stores open on Sunday	*Sunday Closing Laws* (1961)	Many states have revised blue laws to allow stores to open on Sundays
Solicitations/sales on fairgrounds	*Heffron v. International Society* (1981)	Remains good law
Exemption from Social Security taxes	*United States v. Lee* (1982)	Law changed by Congress in 1988
Racial discrimination	*Bob Jones University v. United States* (1983)	Remains good law
Exemption from minimum wage laws	*Tony and Susan Alamo Foundation v. Secretary of Labor* (1985)	Remains good law
Wearing yarmulke in military	*Goldman v. Weinberger* (1986)	Reversed by Congress in 1987
Exemption from receiving Social Security number	*Bowen v. Roy* (1986)	Remains good law
Attendance at religious services in prison	*O'Lone v. Shabazz* (1987)	Remains good law
Use of national parks for religious purposes against U.S. claims for road construction	*Lyng v. Northwest Indian Cemetery Protective Association* (1988)	Remains good law
Tax deduction for church contributions	*Hernandez v. Commissioner of Internal Revenue Service* (1989)	Remains good law
Exemption from state sales tax on religious material	*Swaggart v. Board of Equalization* (1990)	Remains good law
Attainment of unemployment benefits for loss of job due to ingestion of controlled drugs	*Employment Division v. Smith* (1990)	Reversed by Congress in 1993; statute declared unconstitutional in *City of Boerne v. Flores* (1997)
Church exemption from historic building preservation laws	*City of Boerne v. Flores* (1997)	Congressional response threatened

SOURCE: Adapted from Henry J. Abraham and Barbara A. Perry, *Freedom and the Court*, 6th ed. (New York: Oxford University Press, 1994), 244–249.

BOX 4-2 AFTERMATH . . . PROTECTING RELIGIOUS LIBERTY

WHEN THE SUPREME COURT issued its ruling in *City of Boerne v. Flores,* congressional reaction was swift and critical. Sponsors of the Religious Freedom Restoration Act of 1993 (RFRA), which the Court struck down, vowed to pass new legislation with the goal of restoring the *Sher-bert/Yoder* "compelling interest" test as the standard governments must meet to justify restrictions on religious exercise.

Although congressional criticism was quick, legislative action was slow to develop, and new legislation did not reach the floor of the House until 1999. That bill, the Religious Liberty Protection Act, was supported by a large and diverse coalition of religious interests. The House passed the proposal by an overwhelming 306–118 vote. As the bill moved to the Senate, however, serious questions about the impact of the proposed legislation were raised. Would prisoners, in the name of their religions, be able to demand unreasonable concessions from corrections departments? Would small business owners, invoking their religious principles, be protected if they denied employment to gays and lesbians? Would landlords, motivated by religious beliefs, be able to refuse renting apartments to interracial couples or unmarried couples? Would local governments be unable to use zoning laws to curb the building activities of churches that might have an adverse impact on the surrounding community? With these questions unanswered, supporters of the bill began to desert its cause. As a result, the legislation languished in the Senate, and the odds of passage, without significant amendment, became remote.

But what of St. Peter the Apostle Church and the City of Boerne? The parties reached a compromise two months after the Supreme Court's 1997 ruling. The city approved a church plan to preserve 80 percent of the church building, while significantly expanding its seating. The compromise allowed the church to serve its growing congregation and the city to preserve a building with historic importance.

SOURCES: *Houston Chronicle,* November 3, 1996, August 14, 1997; *Washington Post,* February 10, 1997; *USA Today,* June 26, 1997; *New York Times,* August 14, 1997; *Kansas City Star,* August 26, 1999; *New Orleans Times-Picayune,* October 23, 1999; and *Los Angeles Times,* August 1, 1999.

RELIGIOUS ESTABLISHMENT

In an 1802 letter to the Danbury Baptist Association, Thomas Jefferson proclaimed that the First Amendment built "a wall of separation between Church and State." But what sort of wall did Jefferson conceive? Was it to be flimsy, connoting, as some suggest, that commingling between church and state is constitutional so long as government does not establish a national religion? Or was it to be a solid wall that bars all cooperative interactions between church and state? Or something in between?

Underlying the cases involving the Religious Establishment Clause is that question: What is the nature of the wall that separates church from state? To answer it, many Court opinions, as we shall see, look to the intent of the Framers, a highly elusive concept, particularly in this area of the law. As the nation's Founders were of many minds, it is possible to find evidence supporting the following interpretations of the Establishment Clause:

1. The Religious Establishment Clause erects a solid wall of separation between church and state, prohibiting most, if not all, forms of public aid for or support of religion.

2. The Religious Establishment Clause may erect a wall of separation between church and state, but that wall of separation only forbids the state to prefer one religion over another. Nondiscriminatory support or aid for all religions is constitutionally permissible.

3. The Religious Establishment Clause simply prohibits the establishment of an official national religion.

In a detailed analysis of the intent of the Framers, Michael J. Malbin found that the *majority* of the Founders ascribed to views 2 or 3 (accommodationist positions), but not view 1 (a separationist position), which erects the highest wall.[23] However, two of the most influential figures during the nation's founding, Thomas Jefferson and James Madison, are described by some scholars as leaning toward view 1, believing that government

23. Michael J. Malbin, *Religion and Politics: The Intentions of the Authors of the First Amendment* (Washington, D.C.: American Enterprise Institute, 1978).

BOX 4-3   WHAT DID MADISON, JEFFERSON, AND THE OTHER FOUNDERS WANT?

FOR MANY YEARS, legal scholars have sought to throw light on Thomas Jefferson's, James Madison's, and other Founders' views on the relationship between church and state. Why they have devoted so much time to this enterprise is not difficult to explain. From its first major decision on religious liberty, *Reynolds v. United States,* through its more recent cases, the Supreme Court has used the intent of the Founders—particularly Madison and Jefferson—as a guide to resolving religious establishment disputes. And, if anything, the search for original intent has escalated over the past two decades when members of the Reagan administration and Chief Justice Rehnquist, among others, argued that the Court's (and scholars') previous interpretations of that intent were historically incorrect. Here we summarize the positions of both sides and the major sources of support they use to justify them.

	Wall of Separation	Nonpreferential Treatment
Position	Jefferson and Madison advocated a wall of separation between church and state that prohibited most, if not all, forms of public aid or support of religion.	Jefferson, Madison, and the majority of the Founders merely argued that the state could not establish a national religion or give preference to one religion over another.
Notable Adherents	Constitutional law scholar Leonard W. Levy, Justice Hugo Black, political commentator Garry Wills	Constitutional law scholar Walter Berns, Chief Justice William Rehnquist, former attorney general Edwin Meese
Support (Examples)	1. In 1779 the Virginia legislature considered a bill that would have used tax dollars to support churches. At that time, Jefferson introduced a "Bill for Religious Freedom," which said that "no man shall be compelled to frequent or support any religious worship, place, or ministry whatsoever." Neither bill received majority support. Debate resumed in 1784, when Patrick Henry introduced the General Assessment Bill, which would have used tax dollars to support the "Christian religion." Jefferson was in Paris at the time this bill was introduced, but when Madison wrote him of this new attempt to use public monies Jefferson responded: "What we have to do is devoutly to pray for [Henry's] death" (Alley, 10). Madison took less drastic, but not less effective measures. Through clever political maneuvers, Madison rid the Virginia legislature of Henry (he became governor) and got the legislature to postpone the vote on the bill for one year. In the meantime, Madison distributed a pamphlet called "Memorial and Remonstrance Against Religious Assessments." It was a *tour de force* on the need for separation of church and state so that both could remain strong. Madison's arguments were so persuasive that the Assessment Bill died without consideration, while Jefferson's proposal was passed.	1. Madison may have pushed for Virginia's Bill for Religious Freedom, but he did not advocate its incorporation into the U.S. Constitution. Indeed, he thought a Bill of Rights completely unnecessary. But, being an astute politician, Madison realized that the Constitution might not be ratified without a Bill of Rights. So he took on the task of drafting one. Madison's original version of the Establishment Clause said only that Congress shall not establish "any national religion." This, as Rehnquist wrote in *Wallace v. Jaffree,* "obviously does not conform to the 'wall of separation' between church and State idea which latter-day commentators have ascribed to him." Rather, his language and his comments during congressional debate over the amendment in 1789 make it clear that he thought it prohibited Congress from establishing a national religion and from giving preference to particular religions. There is simply no evidence that Madison attempted to get Congress to enact anything resembling Virginia's Bill for Religious Freedom. Whatever he and Jefferson did in Virginia is irrelevant to understanding his intent for the Bill of Rights.
	2. In 1802 Jefferson wrote a letter to the Danbury Baptist Association asserting that the religious Establishment Clause built a "wall of separation" between church and state.	2. Jefferson was in France when Congress passed the Bill of Rights. His letter to the Danbury Baptist Association, as Rehnquist claims, was "a short note of courtesy, written fourteen years after the Amendments were passed by Congress." It is not

(continued)

(Box 4-3 continued)

	Wall of Separation	Nonpreferential Treatment
	As president, Jefferson refused to proclaim Thanksgiving Day on religious establishment grounds.	an "ideal source" for understanding the intent of the Framers. Jefferson's two predecessors, Washington and Adams, issued Thanksgiving Day proclamations.
	3. Madison, as Wills presents it, devoted much of his life to campaigning for separation of church and state. A partial list (Wills, 374) includes: 1774: Madison, denouncing the jailing of Baptist preachers in Virginia, concluded that "ecclesiastical establishments tend to great ignorance and corruption." 1776: At Virginia's revolutionary convention, Madison tried to amend George Mason's preamble to the new Virginia constitution, in order to remove all "emoluments or privileges" from religion. He failed at that, but substituted "free exercise of religion" for "fullest toleration in the exercise of religion." His first important legislative act, undertaken when he was only twenty-five, struck a blow for religious freedom. 1785: Madison published his major statement on religious freedom, "Memorial and Remonstrance against Religious Assessments." 1789: Drafting what will become the First Amendment, Madison proposed not only disestablishment at a national level but that "no *state* shall violate the equal rights of conscience." Although disestablishment at the federal level was all he could accomplish in his lifetime, he regularly referred to the First Amendment as opposing "establishments," reflecting his original intent.	3. To understand the intent of the Framers, one also ought to look at the actions of early Congresses: 1789: On the same day Madison introduced his Amendments, the House enacted the Northwest Ordinance, which gave federal land grants to sectarian schools. 1789: The day after the House passed the version of the Religious Establishment Clause that was ratified by the states, it proposed a resolution asking President Washington to issue a Thanksgiving Day proclamation. 1789: Washington issued the proclamation: "I do recommend and assign Thursday . . . to be devoted by the people of these States to the service of that great and glorious Being, who is the beneficent author of all the good that was, that is, or that will be; that we may then all unite in rendering unto Him our sincere and humble thanks." 1789–1823: Congress provided public land grants to the Society of the United Brethren for "propagating the Gospel among the Heathen." Early 1800s: Congress approved treaties with Native American tribes requiring financial support of tribes' religious education programs, churches, and clergy.
The Bottom Line	"If Madison is any guide, our churches are not, even now, too separated from political support." "Though he is called the father of the Constitution, [Madison] has an even better claim as the father of disestablishment." (Wills, 373, 380) An establishment of religion in America at the time of the framing of the Bill of Rights meant government aid and sponsorship of religion, principally by impartial tax support of the institutions of religion, the churches. (Levy, 161)	"It is impossible to build sound constitutional doctrine upon a mistaken understanding of constitutional history, but unfortunately the Establishment Clause has been expressly freighted with Jefferson's misleading metaphor for nearly 40 years." (Rehnquist) "Probably at the time of the adoption of the Constitution . . . the general if not universal sentiment in America was that Christianity ought to receive encouragement from the State so far as was not incompatible with . . . the freedom of religious worship. An attempt to level all religions, and to make it a matter of state policy to hold all in utter indifference, would have created universal disapprobation." (Story, 630–632)

WORKS CITED: Robert S. Alley, *The Supreme Court on Church and State* (New York: Oxford University Press, 1988); Leonard W. Levy, *Constitutional Opinions* (New York: Oxford University Press, 1986); William H. Rehnquist, dissenting opinion in *Wallace v. Jaffree*, 472 U.S. 38 (1985); Joseph Story, *Commentaries on the Constitution of the United States*, vol. 2, 5th ed., (1891); Garry Wills, *Under God* (New York: Simon and Schuster, 1990).

NOTE: Material in the "Strict Separation" column draws heavily on Levy, *Constitutional Opinions*, and Levy, *The Establishment Clause* (New York: Macmillan, 1986); material in the "Nonpreferential" column comes largely from Rehnquist's dissent in *Wallace v. Jaffree* (1985).

should have very little to do with religion. Because the Framers did not speak with a single voice on the matter, the Court has frequently come to very different conclusions regarding their intent in proposing the Establishment Clause. Generally speaking, the decisions of the Court have fluctuated between some version of views 1 and 2. But the Court's treatment of the conflicts between church and state have been neither clear nor consistent.

In the remainder of this chapter, we review the Court's attempts to develop a workable understanding of the meaning of the Establishment Clause and then turn our attention to some of the major controversies surrounding the elusive wall of separation.

The Search for an Establishment Clause Standard

The Supreme Court began its search for the meaning of the Establishment Clause in 1899, and more than a century later the justices are still having difficulty developing a coherent and consistent jurisprudence. As one scholar explained, "From a lawyer's point of view, the Establishment Clause is the most frustrating part of First Amendment law. The cases are an impossible tangle of divergent doctrines and seemingly conflicting results."[24]

Initial Attempts. Bradfield v. Roberts (1899) was the Court's first Establishment Clause dispute. It involved a $30,000 appropriation to a hospital in Washington, D.C., for the construction of facilities to be used to treat indigent patients. The appropriation was challenged because the hospital was operated by Roman Catholic nuns. The justices, however, unanimously rejected the challenge, finding little relevance in the fact that Catholic nuns administered the hospital. It was the purpose of the facility that mattered to the Court; and in this case the justices found the hospital to have a secular, not religious, purpose.

Bradfield was important because it demonstrated from the start the Court's willingness to allow some public money to go to religious institutions, especially if the aid was intended to advance a clear secular purpose. Although the Court did not offer a comprehensive legal standard by which to adjudicate future claims, the secu-

lar purpose requirement first articulated in *Bradfield* has remained a core principle in Establishment Clause jurisprudence.

Almost fifty years elapsed between *Bradfield* and the next important religious establishment case, *Everson v. Board of Education* (1947). While reading the Court's decision in *Everson,* consider these questions: Did the Court establish any legal standards by which to determine whether state practices violate the Establishment Clause? What view of the Establishment Clause did it adopt?

Everson v. Board of Education

330 U.S. 1 (1947)
laws.findlaw.com/US/330/1.html
Vote: 5 (Black, Douglas, Murphy, Reed, Vinson)
    4 (Burton, Frankfurter, Jackson, Rutledge)
Opinion of the Court: Black
Dissenting opinions: Jackson, Rutledge

In 1941 New Jersey passed a law authorizing local school boards that provided "any transportation for public school children to and from school" also to supply transportation to children living in the district who attended nonprofit private schools. At the time New Jersey enacted this legislation, at least fifteen other states had similar laws.

Ewing Township decided to use tax dollars to reimburse parents for transportation costs incurred in sending their children to school. Because the township had no public high schools of its own, the reimbursement policy covered transportation expenses to parents sending their children to three neighboring public high schools. It also covered four private schools, all of which were affiliated with the Roman Catholic church and provided regular religious instruction along with normal secular subjects. The average payment to parents sending their children to public or Catholic schools was $40 per student.

Arch Everson, a taxpayer living in the district, challenged the reimbursements to parents sending their children to religious schools. He argued that this money supported religion in violation of the Establishment Clause of the First Amendment.

---

24. Daniel A. Farber, *The First Amendment* (New York: Foundation Press, 1998), 263.

MR. JUSTICE BLACK delivered the opinion of the Court.

The New Jersey statute is challenged as a "law respecting an establishment of religion." The First Amendment ... commands that a state "shall make no law respecting an establishment of religion, or prohibiting the free exercise thereof." These words of the First Amendment reflected in the minds of early Americans a vivid mental picture of conditions and practices which they fervently wished to stamp out in order to preserve liberty for themselves and for their posterity. Doubtless their goal has not been entirely reached; but so far has the Nation moved toward it that the expression "law respecting an establishment of religion," probably does not so vividly remind present-day Americans of the evils, fears, and political problems that caused that expression to be written into our Bill of Rights. Whether this New Jersey law is one respecting the "establishment of religion" requires an understanding of the meaning of that language, particularly with respect to the imposition of taxes. Once again, therefore, it is not inappropriate briefly to review the background and environment of the period in which that constitutional language was fashioned and adopted.

A large proportion of the early settlers of this country came here from Europe to escape the bondage of laws which compelled them to support and attend government favored churches. The centuries immediately before and contemporaneous with the colonization of America had been filled with turmoil, civil strife, and persecutions, generated in large part by established sects determined to maintain their absolute political and religious supremacy. With the power of government supporting them, at various times and places, Catholics had persecuted Protestants, Protestants had persecuted Catholics, Protestant sects had persecuted other Protestant sects, Catholics of one shade of belief had persecuted Catholics of another shade of belief, and all of these had from time to time persecuted Jews. In efforts to force loyalty to whatever religious group happened to be on top and in league with the government of a particular time and place, men and women had been fined, cast in jail, cruelly tortured, and killed. . . .

These practices of the old world were transplanted to and began to thrive in the soil of the new America. The very charters granted by the English Crown to the individuals and companies designated to make the laws which would control the destinies of the colonials authorized these individuals and companies to erect religious establishments which all, whether believers or non-believers, would be required to support and attend. An exercise of this authority was accompanied by a repetition of many of the old world practices and persecutions. Catholics found themselves hounded and proscribed because of their faith; Quakers who followed their conscience went to jail; Baptists were peculiarly obnoxious to certain dominant Protestant sects; men and women of varied faiths who happened to be in a minority in a particular locality were persecuted because they steadfastly persisted in worshipping God only as their own consciences dictated. And all of these dissenters were compelled to pay tithes and taxes to support government-sponsored churches whose ministers preached inflammatory sermons designed to strengthen and consolidate the established faith by generating a burning hatred against dissenters.

These practices became so commonplace as to shock the freedom-loving colonials into a feeling of abhorrence. The imposition of taxes to pay ministers' salaries and to build and maintain churches and church property aroused their indignation. It was these feelings which found expression in the First Amendment. No one locality and no one group throughout the Colonies can rightly be given entire credit for having aroused the sentiment that culminated in an adoption of the Bill of Rights' provisions embracing religious liberty. But Virginia, where the established church had achieved a dominant influence in political affairs and where many excesses attracted wide public attention, provided a great stimulus and able leadership for the movement. The people there, as elsewhere, reached the conviction that individual religious liberty could be achieved best under a government which was stripped of all power to tax, to support, or otherwise to assist any or all religions, or to interfere with the beliefs of any religious individual or group.

The movement toward this end reached its dramatic climax in Virginia in 1785–86 when the Virginia legislative body was about to renew Virginia's tax levy for the support of the established church. Thomas Jefferson and James Madison led the fight against this tax. Madison wrote his great Memorial and Remonstrance against the law. In it, he eloquently argued that a true religion did not need the support of law; that no person, either believer or non-believer, should be taxed to support a religious institution of any kind; that the best interest of a society required that the minds of men always be wholly free; and that cruel persecutions were the inevitable result of government-established religions. . . .

The meaning and scope of the First Amendment, preventing establishment of religion or prohibiting the free exercise thereof, in the light of its history and the evils it was designed forever to suppress, have been several times elaborated by the decisions of this Court prior to the application of the First Amendment to the states by the Fourteenth. The broad meaning given the Amendment by these earlier cases has been accepted by this Court in its decisions concerning an individual's religious freedom rendered since the Fourteenth Amendment was interpreted to make the prohibitions of the First applicable to state action abridging religious freedom. There is every reason to give the same application and broad interpretation to the "establishment of religion" clause. . . .

The "establishment of religion" clause of the First Amendment means at least this: Neither a state nor the Federal Government can set up a church. Neither can pass laws which aid one religion, aid all religions, or prefer one religion over another. Neither can force nor influence a person to go to or to remain away from church against his will or force him to profess a belief or disbelief in any religion. No person can be punished for entertaining or professing religious beliefs or disbeliefs, for church attendance or nonattendance. No tax in any amount, large or small, can be levied to support any religious activities or institutions, whatever they may be called, or whatever form they may adopt to teach or practice religion. Neither a state nor the Federal Government can, openly or secretly, participate in the affairs of any religious organizations or groups and vice versa. In the words of Jefferson, the clause against establishment of religion by law was intended to erect "a wall of separation between Church and State."

We must consider the New Jersey statute in accordance with the foregoing limitations imposed by the First Amendment. But we must not strike that state statute down if it is within the state's constitutional power even though it approaches the verge of that power. New Jersey cannot consistently with the "establishment of religion" clause of the First Amendment contribute tax-raised funds to the support of an institution which teaches the tenets and faith of any church. On the other hand, other language of the amendment commands that New Jersey cannot hamper its citizens in the free exercise of their own religion. Consequently, it cannot exclude individual Catholics, Lutherans, Mohammedans, Baptists, Jews, Methodists, Non-believers, Presbyterians, or the members of any other faith, *because of their faith, or lack of it,* from receiving the benefits of public welfare legislation. While we do not mean to intimate that a state could not provide transportation only to children attending public schools, we must be careful, in protecting the citizens of New Jersey against state-established churches, to be sure that we do not inadvertently prohibit New Jersey from extending its general State law benefits to all its citizens without regard to their religious belief.

Measured by these standards, we cannot say that the First Amendment prohibits New Jersey from spending tax-raised funds to pay the bus fares of parochial school pupils as a part of a general program under which it pays the fares of pupils attending public and other schools. It is undoubtedly true that children are helped to get to church schools. There is even a possibility that some of the children might not be sent to the church schools if the parents were compelled to pay their children's bus fares out of their own pockets when transportation to a public school would have been paid for by the State. The same possibility exists where the state requires a local transit company to provide reduced fares to school children including those attending parochial schools, or where a municipally owned transportation system undertakes to carry all school children free of charge. Moreover, state-paid policemen, detailed to protect children going to and from church schools from the very real hazards of traffic, would serve much the same purpose and accomplish much the same result as state provisions intended to guarantee free transportation of a kind which the state deems to be best for the school children's welfare. And parents might refuse to risk their children to the serious danger of traffic accidents going to and from parochial schools, the approaches to which were not protected by policemen. Similarly, parents might be reluctant to permit their children to attend schools which the state had cut off from such general government services as ordinary police and fire protection, connections for sewage disposal, public highways and sidewalks. Of course, cutting off church schools from these services, so separate and so indisputably marked off from the religious function, would make it far more difficult for the schools to operate. But such is obviously not the purpose of the First Amendment. That Amendment requires the state to be a neutral in its relations with groups of religious believers and non-believers; it does not require the state to be their adversary. State power is no more to be used so as to handicap religions, than it is to favor them.

This Court has said that parents may, in the discharge of their duty under state compulsory education laws, send their children to a religious rather than a public school if the school meets the secular educational requirements which the state has power to impose. It appears that these parochial schools meet New Jersey's requirements. The State contributes no money to the schools. It does not support them. Its legislation, as applied, does no more than provide a general program to help parents get their children, regardless of their religion, safely and expeditiously to and from accredited schools.

The First Amendment has erected a wall between church and state. That wall must be kept high and impregnable. We could not approve the slightest breach. New Jersey has not breached it here.

Affirmed.

MR. JUSTICE JACKSON, dissenting.

I find myself, contrary to first impressions, unable to join in this decision. I have a sympathy, though it is not ideological, with Catholic citizens who are compelled by law to pay taxes for public schools, and also feel constrained by conscience and discipline to support other schools for their own children. Such relief to them as this case involves is not in itself a serious burden to taxpayers and I had assumed it to be as little serious in principle. Study of this case convinces me otherwise. . . .

If we are to decide this case on the facts before us, our question is simply this: Is it constitutional to tax this complainant to pay the cost of carrying pupils to Church schools of one specified denomination?

Whether the taxpayer constitutionally can be made to contribute aid to parents of students because of their attendance at parochial schools depends upon the nature of those schools and their relation to the Church. . . .

I should be surprised if any Catholic would deny that the parochial school is a vital, if not the most vital, part of the Roman Catholic Church. If put to the choice, that venerable institution, I should expect, would forego its whole service for mature persons before it would give up education of the young, and it would be a wise choice. Its growth and cohesion, discipline and loyalty, spring from its schools. Catholic education is the rock on which the whole structure rests, and to render tax aid to its Church school is indistinguishable to me from rendering the same aid to the Church itself. . . .

The Court, however, compares this to other subsidies and loans to individuals and says, "Nor does it follow that a law has a private rather than a public purpose because it provides that tax-raised funds will be paid to reimburse individuals on account of money spent by them in a way which furthers a public program. . . ." Of course, the state may pay out tax-raised funds to relieve pauperism, but it may not under our Constitution do so to induce or reward piety. It may spend funds to secure old age against want, but it may not spend funds to secure religion against skepticism. It may compensate individuals for loss of employment, but it cannot compensate them for adherence to a creed.

It seems to me that the basic fallacy in the Court's reasoning, which accounts for its failure to apply the principles it avows, is in ignoring the essentially religious test by which beneficiaries of this expenditure are selected. A policeman protects a Catholic, of course—but not because he is a Catholic; it is because he is a man and a member of our society. The fireman protects the Church school—but not because it is a Church school; it is because it is property, part of the assets of our society. Neither the fireman nor the policeman has to ask before he renders aid "Is this man or building identified with the Catholic Church?" But before these school authorities draw a check to reimburse for a student's fare they must ask just that question, and if the school is a Catholic one they may render aid because it is such, while if it is of any other faith or is run for profit, the help must be withheld. To consider the converse of the Court's reasoning will best disclose its fallacy. That there is no parallel between police and fire protection and this plan of reimbursement is apparent from the incongruity of the limitation of this Act if applied to police and fire service. Could we sustain an Act that said the police shall protect pupils on the way to or from public schools and Catholic schools but not while going to and coming from other schools, and firemen shall extinguish a blaze in public or

Catholic school buildings but shall not put out a blaze in Protestant Church schools or private schools operated for profit? That is the true analogy to the case we have before us and I should think it pretty plain that such a scheme would not be valid.

The Court's holding is that this taxpayer has no grievance because the state has decided to make the reimbursement a public purpose and therefore we are bound to regard it as such. I agree that this Court has left, and always should leave to each state, great latitude in deciding for itself, in the light of its own conditions, what shall be public purposes in its scheme of things. It may socialize utilities and economic enterprises and make taxpayers' business out of what conventionally had been private business. It may make public business of individual welfare, health, education, entertainment or security. But it cannot make public business of religious worship or instruction, or of attendance at religious institutions of any character.

MR. JUSTICE FRANKFURTER joins in this opinion.

MR. JUSTICE RUTLEDGE, with whom MR. JUSTICE FRANKFURTER, MR. JUSTICE JACKSON, and MR. JUSTICE BURTON agree, dissenting.

"Congress shall make no law respecting an establishment of religion, or prohibiting the free exercise thereof. . . ." U.S. Const., Amend. I. . . .

"We, the General Assembly, do enact, That no man shall be compelled to frequent or support any religious worship, place, or ministry whatsoever, nor shall be enforced, restrained, molested, or burthened in his body or goods, nor shall otherwise suffer, on account of his religious opinions or belief. . . ."*

I cannot believe that the great author of those words, or the men who made them law, could have joined in this decision. Neither so high nor so impregnable today as yesterday is the wall raised between church and state by Virginia's great statute of religious freedom and the First Amendment, now made applicable to all the states by the Fourteenth. . . .

Not simply an established church, but any law respecting an establishment of religion is forbidden. The Amendment was broadly but not loosely phrased. It is the compact

and exact summation of its author's views formed during his long struggle for religious freedom. . . .

The Amendment's purpose was not to strike merely at the official establishment of a single sect, creed or religion, outlawing only a formal relation such as had prevailed in England and some of the colonies. Necessarily it was to uproot all such relationships. But the object was broader than separating church and state in this narrow sense. It was to create a complete and permanent separation of the spheres of religious activity and civil authority by comprehensively forbidding every form of public aid or support for religion. In proof the Amendment's wording and history unite with this Court's consistent utterances whenever attention has been fixed directly upon the question. . . .

No provision of the Constitution is more closely tied to or given content by its generating history than the religious clause of the First Amendment. It is at once the refined product and the terse summation of that history. The history includes not only Madison's authorship and the proceedings before the First Congress, but also the long and intensive struggle for religious freedom in America, more especially in Virginia, of which the Amendment was the direct culmination. In the documents of the times, particularly of Madison, who was leader in the Virginia struggle before he became the Amendment's sponsor, but also in the writings of Jefferson and others and in the issues which engendered them is to be found irrefutable confirmation of the Amendment's sweeping content. . . .

As the Remonstrance discloses throughout, Madison opposed every form and degree of official relation between religion and civil authority. For him religion was a wholly private matter beyond the scope of civil power either to restrain or to support. Denial or abridgment of religious freedom was a violation of rights both of conscience and of natural equality. State aid was no less obnoxious or destructive to freedom and to religion itself than other forms of state interference. "Establishment" and "free exercise" were correlative and coextensive ideas, representing only different facets of the single great and fundamental freedom. The Remonstrance, following the Virginia statute's example, referred to the history of religious conflicts and the effects of all sorts of establishments, current and historical, to suppress religion's free exercise. With Jefferson, Madison believed that to tolerate any fragment of establishment would be by so much to perpetuate restraint upon that freedom.

* "A Bill for Establishing Religious Freedom," enacted by the General Assembly of Virginia, January 19, 1786.

Hence he sought to tear out the institution not partially but root and branch, and to bar its return forever. . . .

Does New Jersey's action furnish support for religion by use of the taxing power? Certainly it does, if the test remains undiluted as Jefferson and Madison made it, that money taken by taxation from one is not to be used or given to support another's religious training or belief, or indeed one's own. Today as then the furnishing of "contributions of money for the propagation of opinions which he disbelieves" is the forbidden exaction; and the prohibition is absolute for whatever measure brings that consequence and whatever amount may be sought or given to that end.

The funds used here were raised by taxation. The Court does not dispute, nor could it, that their use does in fact give aid and encouragement to religious instruction. It only concludes that this aid is not "support" in law. But Madison and Jefferson were concerned with aid and support in fact, not as a legal conclusion "entangled in precedents." Here parents pay money to send their children to parochial schools and funds raised by taxation are used to reimburse them. This not only helps the children to get to school and the parents to send them. It aids them in a substantial way to get the very thing which they are sent to the particular school to secure, namely, religious training and teaching. . . .

New Jersey's action therefore exactly fits the type of exaction and the kind of evil at which Madison and Jefferson struck. Under the test they framed it cannot be said that the cost of transportation is no part of the cost of education or of the religious instruction given. That it is a substantial and a necessary element is shown most plainly by the continuing and increasing demand for the state to assume it. Nor is there pretense that it relates only to the secular instruction given in religious schools or that any attempt is or could be made toward allocating proportional shares as between the secular and the religious instruction. It is precisely because the instruction is religious and relates to a particular faith, whether one or another, that parents send their children to religious schools. . . . And the very purpose of the state's contribution is to defray the cost of conveying the pupil to the place where he will receive not simply secular, but also and primarily religious, teaching and guidance.

Indeed the view is sincerely avowed by many of various faiths, that the basic purpose of all education is or should be religious, that the secular cannot be and should not be separated from the religious phase and emphasis. Hence, the inadequacy of public or secular education and the necessity for sending the child to a school where religion is taught. But whatever may be the philosophy or its justification, there is undeniably an admixture of religious with secular teaching in all such institutions. . . .

Yet this very admixture is what was disestablished when the First Amendment forbade "an establishment of religion." Commingling the religious with the secular teaching does not divest the whole of its religious permeation and emphasis or make them of minor part, if proportion were material. Indeed, on any other view, the constitutional prohibition always could be brought to naught by adding a modicum of the secular. . . .

No one conscious of religious values can be unsympathetic toward the burden which our constitutional separation puts on parents who desire religious instruction mixed with secular for their children. They pay taxes for others' children's education, at the same time the added cost of instruction for their own. Nor can one happily see benefits denied to children which others receive, because in conscience they or their parents for them desire a different kind of training others do not demand.

But if those feelings should prevail, there would be an end to our historic constitutional policy and command. No more unjust or discriminatory in fact is it to deny attendants at religious schools the cost of their transportation than it is to deny them tuitions, sustenance for their teachers, or any other educational expense which others receive at public cost. Hardship in fact there is which none can blink. But, for assuring to those who undergo it the greater, the most comprehensive freedom, it is one written by design and firm intent into our basic law. . . .

Two great drives are constantly in motion to abridge, in the name of education, the complete division of religion and civil authority which our forefathers made. One is to introduce religious education and observances into the public schools. The other, to obtain public funds for the aid and support of various private religious schools. In my opinion both avenues were closed by the Constitution. Neither should be opened by this Court. The matter is not one of quantity, to be measured by the amount of money expended. Now as in Madison's day it is one of principle, to keep separate the separate spheres as the First Amendment drew them; to prevent the first experiment upon our liberties; and to keep the question from becoming entangled in corrosive precedents. We should not be less strict to keep strong and untarnished the one side of the shield of religious freedom than we have been of the other.

The judgment should be reversed.

The Court's decision in *Everson* is notable for a number of reasons. First, it applied the Establishment Clause to the states, an important step because the Court had not received many cases in this area. With incorporation, the Court now opened the gates to challenges to state and local practices on establishment grounds. After nearly 150 years of dormancy, the Establishment Clause would become, on average, an annual issue for the justices.

Second, even though Black's opinion for the majority ruled in favor of the state's funding program, it etched into law an interpretation of Madison's and Jefferson's philosophies that supports a clear division between government and religion. Black even quoted Jefferson's comment that the clause was intended to build "a wall of separation between Church and State," thereby "constitutionalizing" the phrase. Although Black's opinion does not lay down a concrete legal standard, it stresses several fundamental ideas, most notably that the aid was secular in purpose (it was going to parents for a nonreligious expense); that the beneficiaries of the aid were children (not churches); and that the state was neutral with respect to religious believers and nonbelievers (all school children were eligible for aid). As we shall see, these themes recur in later Court opinions and foreshadow aspects of a legal standard the Court eventually formulates.

Third, *Everson* provides the first indication of the sensitive and salient nature of religious establishment questions. After the Court issued its ruling, Roman Catholic bishops in the United States mounted a public attack on it. Even though the decision supported reimbursements for costs incurred in sending children to Catholic schools, the bishops lambasted the justices for fundamentally misconstruing Jefferson's position on church and state. They argued that the Founders supported the view that "the First Amendment means only that the Federal government may not prefer one religion over another."[25]

Finally, and perhaps most important, *Everson* indi-

cates the divisive and complex nature of religious establishment questions. On the one hand, all the justices—the majority and dissenters alike—agreed with Black's portrayal of the intent of the Framers. In other words, the entire Court believed that Jefferson and Madison preferred strict separation of church and state. On the other hand—and this is the crux of the matter—the justices applied that historical framework to reach wholly disparate conclusions about the reimbursement plan. The majority, as Frank Sorauf put it, "succeeded . . . in combining the strictest separationist rhetoric with an accommodationist outcome."[26] That is, Black's opinion, while adopting Jefferson's metaphor, found in favor of the township. The dissenters also advocated the same general approach but thought it led to a disposition against the township. Indeed, they took Black to task for heading in one direction and landing in another.

That the adoption of a similar historical vision of religious establishment could lead to such disparate outcomes is a problem that continued to confound this area of the law at least through the Warren Court (and, as we shall see, crops up today). As Table 4-3 illustrates, between 1947 and 1968 the Court decided seven major cases involving the Establishment Clause. Three led to an accommodationist outcome (upholding a government policy challenged as a violation of the Establishment Clause), and four to a separationist outcome (striking down a government policy as a violation of the Establishment Clause). Many of these cases will be discussed in detail later, but here we simply underscore several points.

First, although the Court continued to adhere to Black's (and Rutledge's) historical account of the separation between church and state, it was willing to uphold some kinds of support for religion, as it had in *Everson*, while ruling others unconstitutional. But, as Table 4-3 shows, a pattern began to emerge from the Court's rulings. The justices seemed more willing to tolerate some public support of private education, such as transporting children to school (*Everson*) and loaning secular subject textbooks (*Board of Education v. Allen*, 1968) than it was to permit the entry of religion into public education, such as prayer in school (*Abington School District v.*

---

25. Quoted in *Bill of Rights Reader* by Milton R. Konvitz (Ithaca, N.Y.: Cornell University Press, 1973), 31.

26. Frank Sorauf, *The Wall of Separation* (Princeton: Princeton University Press, 1976), 20.

TABLE 4-3 Major Religious Establishment Cases from *Everson* Through the Warren Court

Case	Issue	Vote (Outcome)	Rationale
Everson v. Board of Education (1947)	Reimbursement for transportation costs incurred by parents sending their children to private schools	5–4 (accommodationist)	Secular purpose; child benefits; neutral
Illinois ex rel. McCollum v. Board of Education (1948)	Time-release program in which religious instructors come to public school weekly and provide religious training	8–1 (separationist)	State provides "invaluable aid" to religion
Zorach v. Clauson (1952)	Time-release program in which students are released an hour or so early each week to obtain religious instruction off school premises	6–3 (accommodationist)	State and religion need not be "hostile, suspicious, and even unfriendly"
Engel v. Vitale (1962)	Prayer, recited by public school children each morning, written by state's board of regents	8–1 (separationist)	Government cannot be in the prayer-writing business
School District of Abington Township v. Schempp (1963)	Reading of the Lord's Prayer and verses from the Bible in public schools	8–1 (separationist)	Public school prayer does not have (1) a secular legislative purpose or (2) a primary purpose that neither advances nor inhibits religion
Board of Education v. Allen (1968)	Public school loans of secular textbooks to students attending private schools	6–3 (accommodationist)	Primary purpose of the law furthers education, not religion
Epperson v. Arkansas (1968)	Barring the teaching of evolutionary theory in public schools	9–0 (separationist)	Not neutral; nonsecular purpose

Schempp, 1963) and the teaching of creationism (*Epperson v. Arkansas,* 1968).

A second point highlighted in Table 4-3 is this: after *Everson,* the Court began to formulate a test, flowing from Jefferson's metaphor and Black's decision in *Everson,* to determine whether government actions violated the Establishment Clause. During the Warren Court era, that test received its fullest articulation in *Abington Township.* (Near the end of this chapter, we examine in some detail the Court's important decisions involving prayer in school.) Writing for the majority, Justice Tom C. Clark explained that standard:

The test may be stated as follows: What are the purpose and primary effect of the enactment? If either is the advancement or inhibition of religion then the enactment exceeds the scope of legislative power as circumscribed by the Constitution. That is to say that to withstand the strictures of the Establishment Clause there must be a secular legislative purpose and a primary effect that neither advances nor inhibits religion.

With these words, Clark accomplished what Black had failed to do in *Everson:* provide attorneys and lower court judges with a benchmark for future litigation and decisions.

Early on, some analysts argued that this standard would always lead to separationist outcomes. These scholars thought it would be difficult for government attorneys to show that their policies met the two-pronged standard reached in *Abington:* that the policy has a secular legislative purpose and that its primary effect neither advances nor inhibits religion. But, as Table 4-3 shows, those commentators were wrong. In *Allen,* for example, the Court considered a New York State requirement that public schools lend, upon request, secular books to private school students in the seventh to twelfth grades. Attorneys for the American Civil Liberties Union argued that the requirement violated the Establishment Clause, but the Court disagreed. Writing for a six-person majority, Justice Byron White asserted:

The express purpose [of the law] was stated by the New York legislature to be furtherance of the educational opportunities available to the young. Appellants have shown us nothing about the necessary effects of the statute that is contrary to this stated purpose. The law merely makes available to all children the benefits of a general program to lend school books free of charge. Perhaps free books make it more likely that some children choose to attend a sectarian school, but that was true of the state-paid bus fare in *Everson* and does not alone demonstrate an unconstitutional degree of support for a religious institution.

In other words, White used the *Abington* "purpose" prong to reach an accommodationist outcome. Three justices—Douglas, Fortas, and Black, the author of *Everson*—dissented. Both Black and Douglas differentiated between the kind of aid at issue in *Everson* (reimbursement for transportation costs) and in *Allen* (book loans). As Douglas put it:

Whatever may be said of *Everson,* there is nothing ideological about a bus. . . . [But] the textbook goes to the very heart of education in a parochial school. It is the chief, although not solitary, instrumentality for propagating a particular religious creed or faith. How can we possibly approve such state aid to a religion?

The third point about the Warren Court's handling of religious establishment cases is that, although the justices generally adopted Jefferson's "wall of separation" metaphor and agreed on the test for adjudicating Establishment Clause cases, they continued to split on case outcomes. Note the votes depicted in Table 4-3: with the exception of cases centering on prayer and teaching religious principles in schools, from *Everson* through *Allen,* the justices were divided over the resolution of cases.

***The* Lemon Test.** By the time Warren Burger became

chief justice in 1969, observers were predicting that the Court would change its approach to adjudicating Establishment Clause cases. Even though the justices generally coalesced around the *Everson* historical understanding and the *Abington* standard, they were divided over how to apply those approaches to particular disputes. What is more, organized interest groups reacted to perceived inconsistencies in the Court's handling of these cases and were pressing the justices to formulate more coherent standards. Separationist groups such as the American Civil Liberties Union and Americans United for Separation of Church and State wanted the Court to reach outcomes in line with a strict separation of church and state, while accommodationist interests were asking the Court to move in precisely the opposite direction *(see Box 4-4).* These competing groups were unrelenting in sponsoring and supporting cases brought to the Supreme Court.

In addition, observers expected that Burger would be more inclined than Chief Justice Warren to rule with the government in many areas of the law. Analysts predicted that Burger would push for wholesale changes in the Court's approaches to cases involving rights, liberties, and justice. Most of this speculation centered on criminal law because one of the primary reasons President Nixon appointed Burger was to turn back the Warren Court's liberal rulings in this area. But, as it turned out, the new chief justice had a strong interest in taking a leadership role in religion cases. In fact, Burger was so determined to exert influence over this area of the law that during his tenure on the Court (1969–1985 terms), he wrote 69 percent (eighteen of twenty-six) of the Court's majority opinions dealing with religion, a much higher percentage than his overall rate of 20 percent in all formally decided cases.[27]

What was Burger's "understanding" of the Establishment Clause? How did he seek to change the law? Was he successful? We address these questions by considering Burger's first two religious establishment cases, *Walz v. Tax Commission of the City of New York* (1970) and *Lemon v. Kurtzman* (1971).

Walz involved the property tax exemptions enjoyed

27. Joseph F. Kobylka, "Leadership in the Supreme Court: Chief Justice Burger and Establishment Clause Litigation," *Western Political Quarterly* 42 (December 1989): 545.

BOX 4-4 CLASHING INTERESTS: SEPARATIONIST VERSUS ACCOMMODATIONIST INTEREST GROUPS IN RELIGIOUS ESTABLISHMENT LITIGATION

As THE SUPREME COURT devoted more attention to issues involving religion, interest groups increased their level of participation in Establishment Clause litigation. These groups represent two points of view: the separationist groups want a strict separation of church and state, and the accommodationist groups support greater intermingling between political and religious institutions. Below we provide information about the major groups belonging to these competing coalitions.

Examples of Separationist Groups

Group	Founding	Purpose
American Civil Liberties Union	1920	Formed to defend rights and liberties generally, with religious establishment litigation representing just one of its concerns.
American Jewish Congress	1918	Dedicated to protecting civil rights and liberties of all Americans, particularly Jewish Americans, whom it views as adversely affected by intermingling between church and state.
Americans United for Separation of Church and State	1947	Formed in response to *Everson* to revitalize the principle of separation between church and state.
PEARL (the New York Committee for Public Education and Religious Liberty)	1968	A coalition representing several other separationist groups. Formed in the aftermath of *Allen* to oppose the expansion of government funding of religious schools.

Examples of Accommodationist Groups

Group	Founding	Purpose
U.S. Catholic Conference	1968	Formed to speak for the American Catholic bishops on matters of social and educational policy. Litigates to bring about greater accommodation between church and state.
Christian Legal Society	1976	Dedicated to supporting state accommodation of religious beliefs.
COLPA (National Jewish Commission on Law and Public Affairs)	1965	Formed to represent the interests of Orthodox American Jews, whose interests are often divergent from those of other Jewish groups. Litigates to combat separatism.

SOURCES: Lee Epstein, "Interest Group Litigation During the Rehnquist Court Era," *Journal of Law and Politics* 4 (1993): 639–717; Frank J. Sorauf, *The Wall of Separation* (Princeton: Princeton University Press, 1976); and Leo Pfeffer, *Religion, State, and the Burger Court* (Buffalo, N.Y.: Prometheus Books, 1984).

BOX 4-5 WARREN EARL BURGER (1969–1986)

WARREN BURGER was born September 17, 1907, in St. Paul, Minnesota, the fourth of seven children. His Swiss-German-Austrian grandparents had come to the Middle West before the Civil War. Financially unable to attend college full time, Burger spent the years following his 1925 graduation from high school attending college and law school evening classes—two years at the University of Minnesota and four at St. Paul College of Law, now William Mitchell College of Law. To support himself, Burger worked full time as an accountant for a life insurance company.

He graduated magna cum laude from law school in 1931 and joined a respected law firm in Minnesota, where he practiced until 1953. He also taught part time at Mitchell from 1931 to 1948.

Burger married Elvera Stromberg, November 8, 1933. They had one son and one daughter.

As a boy, Burger developed a deep interest in art and was an accomplished sculptor. As chief justice, he served as chairman of the board of the National Gallery of Art. He was an antiques buff and a connoisseur of fine wines. He also served as chancellor of the Smithsonian Institution.

Soon after beginning his law career in Minnesota, Burger became involved in Republican state politics. In 1938 he helped in Harold E. Stassen's successful campaign for governor of Minnesota.

During Stassen's unsuccessful bid for the Republican presidential nomination ten years later, Burger met a man who was to figure prominently in his future—Herbert Brownell, then campaign manager for GOP presidential nominee Thomas E. Dewey. Brownell, who became attorney general during the Eisenhower administration, brought Burger to Washington in 1953 to serve as assistant attorney general in charge of the Justice Department's Civil Division.

Burger's stint as assistant attorney general from 1953 to 1956 was not without controversy. His decision to defend the government's action in the dismissal of John F. Peters, a part-time federal employee, on grounds of disloyalty—after Solicitor General Simon E. Sobeloff had refused to do so on grounds of conscience—won Burger the enmity of many liberals.

But Burger's overall record as assistant attorney general apparently met with President Dwight D. Eisenhower's approval, and in 1956 Burger was appointed to the U.S. Court of Appeals for the District of Columbia circuit. As an appeals court judge, Burger developed a reputation as a conservative, especially in criminal justice cases.

Off the bench, Burger became increasingly outspoken in his support of major administrative reform of the judicial system—a cause he continued to advocate as chief justice. During Burger's years as chief justice, Congress approved a number of measures to modernize the operations of the federal judiciary.

President Richard Nixon's appointment of Burger as chief justice on May 21, 1969, caught most observers by surprise. Despite Burger's years of service in the Justice Department and the court of appeals, he was little known outside the legal community. But Nixon apparently was impressed by Burger's consistent argument as an appeals judge that the Constitution should be read narrowly—a belief Nixon shared. Burger was confirmed by the Senate, 74–3, June 9, 1969.

Burger served for seventeen years as chief justice, retiring in 1986 to devote full time to the chairmanship of the commission that planned the Constitution's bicentennial celebration in 1987. He continued to speak and write about judicial administration and reform of the legal system until his death in Washington on June 25, 1995. A few months before he died, Burger published a book entitled *It Is So Ordered: A Constitution Unfolds.*

SOURCE: Adapted from Joan Biskupic and Elder Witt, *Guide to the U.S. Supreme Court,* 3d ed. (Washington, D.C.: Congressional Quarterly, 1997), 951–952.

by religious institutions. Frederick Walz bought a small, useless lot on Staten Island, New York, for the sole purpose of challenging the state's tax laws, which gave religious organizations exemptions from property taxes. Walz contended that the tax exemptions resulted in property owners making involuntary contributions to churches in violation of the Establishment Clause. After losing in the lower courts, Walz and his ACLU attorneys appealed to the U.S. Supreme Court, arguing that "The First Amendment's objective was to create a complete and permanent separation of the sphere of religious activity and civil authority by comprehensively . . . forbidding any form of . . . support for religion." New York pointed to the fact that all fifty states had property tax exemptions for religious organizations and that religious groups carry out charitable functions of interest to the state.

Writing for a seven-person majority (only Justice Douglas dissented), Chief Justice Burger found in favor of the state. The outcome was not surprising; after all, had the Court ruled the other way, the tax status of every religious institution in the United States would have been dramatically altered. The startling aspect of *Walz* was that Burger, in his first writing on the Establishment Clause, sought to usher in a major change. The opinion started traditionally enough, with an examination of the "purpose" prong of *Abington*:

The legislative purpose of property tax exemptions is neither the advancement nor the inhibition of religion; it is neither sponsorship nor hostility. New York, in common with the other States, has determined that certain entities that exist in a harmonious relationship to the community at large, and that foster its "moral or mental improvement," should not be inhibited in their activities by property taxation or the hazard of loss of those properties for nonpayment of taxes.

But, instead of exploring whether the effect of the legislation inhibited or advanced religion, as the *Abington* standard specified, Burger suggested the following:

Determining that the legislative purpose of tax exemption is not aimed at establishing, sponsoring, or supporting religion does not end the inquiry, however. We must also be sure that the end result—the effect—is not *an excessive government entanglement* with religion. [Emphasis added.]

He went on to hold that property tax exemptions did not create an excessive entanglement with religion: to the contrary, even though tax exemptions to churches "necessarily operate to afford an indirect economic benefit," involvement with religion would be far greater if the exemptions did not exist. State officials might occasionally want to examine church records, or they might need to speak with clergy about expenditures, and so forth. As Burger concluded, the tax exemption "restricts the fiscal relationship between church and state, and tends to complement and reinforce the desired separation insulating each from the other."

In the end, *Walz* probably raised more questions about Burger and the fate of Establishment Clause litigation than it answered. Did Burger seek to redesign the *Abington* standard—through adoption of an "excessive entanglement" criteria—as a way to bring down the wall of separation between church and state? Would excessive entanglement now become a part of the Court's analytic toolbag for examining establishment claims? Or would the majority of the justices favor a return to a strict reading of *Abington*? Consider these questions as you read *Lemon v. Kurtzman* and its companion case, *Earley v. DiCenso*.[28]

Lemon v. Kurtzman
Earley v. DiCenso

403 U.S. 602 (1971)
laws.findlaw.com/US/403/602.html
Vote in Lemon: 8 (Black, Blackmun, Brennan, Burger, Douglas, Harlan, Stewart, White)
0
Opinion of the Court: Burger
Concurring opinions: Brennan, White
Not participating: Marshall
Vote in DiCenso: 8 (Black, Blackmun, Brennan, Burger, Douglas, Harlan, Marshall, Stewart)
1 (White)
Opinion of the Court: Burger
Concurring opinion: Douglas
Dissenting opinion: White

28. To hear oral arguments in this case, navigate to: *oyez.nwu.edu.*

Lemon v. Kurtzman (The Pennsylvania Program). With the assistance of numerous organized interests, including the Pennsylvania Civil Liberties Union, the American Jewish Congress, the NAACP, and the Pennsylvania Educational Association, Alton Lemon brought suit against David Kurtzman, state superintendent of schools. Lemon wanted the trial court to declare unconstitutional a Pennsylvania law that authorized Kurtzman to "purchase" secular educational services for nonpublic schools. Under this law, the superintendent would use state taxes levied on cigarettes to reimburse nonpublic schools for expenses incurred for teachers' salaries, textbooks, and instructional materials. The state authorized such funding with certain restrictions: it would pay for secular expenses only, that is, secular books and teachers' salaries for the same courses taught in public schools. To receive payments, schools had to keep separate records, identifying secular and nonsecular expenses.

The act took effect in July 1968. Up to the time the Supreme Court heard the case, Pennsylvania had spent about $5 million annually. It reimbursed expenses at 1,181 nonpublic elementary and secondary schools, which accounted for about a half million students, around 20 percent of the school population. About 96 percent of the nonpublic school students attended religious schools, primarily Roman Catholic.

Earley v. DiCenso (The Rhode Island Program). In this case, the American Jewish Congress (AJC) challenged the Rhode Island Salary Supplement Act. Aimed at improving the quality of private education, this law supplemented the salaries of teachers of secular subjects in private elementary schools up to 15 percent of their current salaries with the restrictions that payments could be made only to those who agreed in writing not to teach religious subjects and salaries could not exceed the maximum salaries paid to public school instructors. The AJC challenged this law as a violation of the Establishment Clause, in part because 95 percent of the schools falling under the terms of the act were affiliated with the Roman Catholic church. Moreover, all of the 250 teachers who had applied for salary supplements worked at Catholic schools. And, as evidence submitted at trial indicated, about two-thirds of them were Roman Catholic nuns.

MR. CHIEF JUSTICE BURGER delivered the opinion of the Court.

These two appeals raise questions as to Pennsylvania and Rhode Island statutes providing state aid to church-related elementary and secondary schools. Both statutes are challenged as violative of the Establishment and Free Exercise Clauses of the First Amendment and the Due Process Clause of the Fourteenth Amendment. . . .

In *Everson v. Board of Education* (1947), this Court upheld a state statute that reimbursed the parents of parochial school children for bus transportation expenses. There MR. JUSTICE BLACK, writing for the majority, suggested that the decision carried to "the verge" of forbidden territory under the Religion Clauses. Candor compels acknowledgment, moreover, that we can only dimly perceive the lines of demarcation in this extraordinarily sensitive area of constitutional law.

The language of the Religion Clauses of the First Amendment is at best opaque, particularly when compared with other portions of the Amendment. Its authors did not simply prohibit the establishment of a state church or a state religion, an area history shows they regarded as very important and fraught with great dangers. Instead they commanded that there should be "no law respecting an establishment of religion." A law may be one "respecting" the forbidden objective while falling short of its total realization. A law "respecting" the proscribed result, that is, the establishment of religion, is not always easily identifiable as one violative of the Clause. A given law might not establish a state religion but nevertheless be one "respecting" that end in the sense of being a step that could lead to such establishment and hence offend the First Amendment.

In the absence of precisely stated constitutional prohibitions, we must draw lines with reference to the three main evils against which the Establishment Clause was intended to afford protection: "sponsorship, financial support, and active involvement of the sovereign in religious activity." *Walz v. Tax Commission* (1970).

Every analysis in this area must begin with consideration of the cumulative criteria developed by the Court over many years. Three such tests may be gleaned from our cases. First, the statute must have a secular legislative purpose; second, its principal or primary effect must be one that neither advances nor inhibits religion; finally, the statute must not foster "an excessive government entanglement with religion."

Inquiry into the legislative purposes of the Pennsylvania and Rhode Island statutes affords no basis for a conclusion that the legislative intent was to advance religion. On the contrary, the statutes themselves clearly state that they are intended to enhance the quality of the secular education in all schools covered by the compulsory attendance laws. There is no reason to believe the legislatures meant anything else. A State always has a legitimate concern for maintaining minimum standards in all schools it allows to operate. As in [*Board of Education v.*] *Allen,* [1968] we find nothing here that undermines the stated legislative intent; it must therefore be accorded appropriate deference.

In *Allen* the Court acknowledged that secular and religious teachings were not necessarily so intertwined that secular textbooks furnished to students by the State were in fact instrumental in the teaching of religion. The legislatures of Rhode Island and Pennsylvania have concluded that secular and religious education are identifiable and separable. In the abstract we have no quarrel with this conclusion.

The two legislatures, however, have also recognized that church-related elementary and secondary schools have a significant religious mission and that a substantial portion of their activities is religiously oriented. They have therefore sought to create statutory restrictions designed to guarantee the separation between secular and religious educational functions and to ensure that State financial aid supports only the former. All these provisions are precautions taken in candid recognition that these programs approached, even if they did not intrude upon, the forbidden areas under the Religion Clauses. We need not decide whether these legislative precautions restrict the principal or primary effect of the programs to the point where they do not offend the Religion Clauses, for we conclude that the cumulative impact of the entire relationship arising under the statutes in each State involves excessive entanglement between government and religion.

In *Walz v. Tax Commission,* the Court upheld state tax exemptions for real property owned by religious organizations and used for religious worship. That holding, however, tended to confine rather than enlarge the area of permissible state involvement with religious institutions by calling for close scrutiny of the degree of entanglement involved in the relationship. The objective is to prevent, as far as possible, the intrusion of either into the precincts of the other. . . .

In order to determine whether the government entanglement with religion is excessive, we must examine the character and purposes of the institutions that are benefited, the nature of the aid that the State provides, and the resulting relationship between the government and the religious authority. . . . Here we find that both statutes foster an impermissible degree of entanglement.

Rhode Island program. The District Court made extensive findings on the grave potential for excessive entanglement that inheres in the religious character and purpose of the Roman Catholic elementary schools of Rhode Island, to date the sole beneficiaries of the Rhode Island Salary Supplement Act.

The church schools involved in the program are located close to parish churches. This understandably permits convenient access for religious exercises since instruction in faith and morals is part of the total educational process. The school buildings contain identifying religious symbols such as crosses on the exterior and crucifixes, and religious paintings and statues either in the classrooms or hallways. Although only approximately 30 minutes a day are devoted to direct religious instruction, there are religiously oriented extracurricular activities. Approximately two-thirds of the teachers in these schools are nuns of various religious orders. Their dedicated efforts provide an atmosphere in which religious instruction and religious vocations are natural and proper parts of life in such schools. Indeed, as the District Court found, the role of teaching nuns in enhancing the religious atmosphere has led the parochial school authorities to attempt to maintain a one-to-one ratio between nuns and lay teachers in all schools rather than to permit some to be staffed almost entirely by lay teachers.

On the basis of these findings the District Court concluded that the parochial schools constituted "an integral part of the religious mission of the Catholic Church." The various characteristics of the schools make them "a powerful vehicle for transmitting the Catholic faith to the next generation." This process of inculcating religious doctrine is, of course, enhanced by the impressionable age of the pupils, in primary schools particularly. In short, parochial schools involve substantial religious activity and purpose. . . .

The dangers and corresponding entanglements are enhanced by the particular form of aid that the Rhode Island

Act provides. Our decisions from *Everson* to *Allen* have permitted the States to provide church-related schools with secular, neutral, or nonideological services, facilities, or materials. Bus transportation, school lunches, public health services, and secular textbooks supplied in common to all students were not thought to offend the Establishment Clause. We note that the dissenters in *Allen* seemed chiefly concerned with the pragmatic difficulties involved in ensuring the truly secular content of the textbooks provided at state expense. . . .

In our view the record shows these dangers are present to a substantial degree. The Rhode Island Roman Catholic elementary schools are under the general supervision of the Bishop of Providence and his appointed representative, the Diocesan Superintendent of Schools. In most cases, each individual parish, however, assumes the ultimate financial responsibility for the school, with the parish priest authorizing the allocation of parish funds. With only two exceptions, school principals are nuns appointed either by the Superintendent or the Mother Provincial of the order whose members staff the school. By 1969 lay teachers constituted more than a third of all teachers in the parochial elementary schools, and their number is growing. They are first interviewed by the superintendent's office and then by the school principal. The contracts are signed by the parish priest, and he retains some discretion in negotiating salary levels. Religious authority necessarily pervades the school system.

The schools are governed by the standards set forth in a "Handbook of School Regulations," which has the force of synodal law in the diocese. It emphasizes the role and importance of the teacher in parochial schools: "The prime factor for the success or the failure of the school is the spirit and personality, as well as the professional competency, of the teacher. . . ." The Handbook also states that: "Religious formation is not confined to formal courses; nor is it restricted to a single subject area." Finally, the Handbook advises teachers to stimulate interest in religious vocations and missionary work. Given the mission of the church school, these instructions are consistent and logical.

Several teachers testified, however, that they did not inject religion into their secular classes. And the District Court found that religious values did not necessarily affect the content of the secular instruction. But what has been recounted suggests the potential if not actual hazards of this

form of state aid. The teacher is employed by a religious organization, subject to the direction and discipline of religious authorities, and works in a system dedicated to rearing children in a particular faith. These controls are not lessened by the fact that most of the lay teachers are of the Catholic faith. Inevitably some of a teacher's responsibilities hover on the border between secular and religious orientation. . . .

We do not assume, however, that parochial school teachers will be unsuccessful in their attempts to segregate their religious beliefs from their secular educational responsibilities. But the potential for impermissible fostering of religion is present. The Rhode Island Legislature has not, and could not, provide state aid on the basis of a mere assumption that secular teachers under religious discipline can avoid conflicts. The State must be certain, given the Religion Clauses, that subsidized teachers do not inculcate religion—indeed the State here has undertaken to do so. To ensure that no trespass occurs, the State has therefore carefully conditioned its aid with pervasive restrictions. An eligible recipient must teach only those courses that are offered in the public schools and use only those texts and materials that are found in the public schools. In addition the teacher must not engage in teaching any course in religion.

A comprehensive, discriminating, and continuing state surveillance will inevitably be required to ensure that these restrictions are obeyed and the First Amendment otherwise respected. Unlike a book, a teacher cannot be inspected once so as to determine the extent and intent of his or her personal beliefs and subjective acceptance of the limitations imposed by the First Amendment. These prophylactic contacts will involve excessive and enduring entanglement between state and church. . . .

Pennsylvania program. The Pennsylvania statute also provides state aid to church-related schools for teachers' salaries. The complaint describes an educational system that is very similar to the one existing in Rhode Island. According to the allegations, the church-related elementary and secondary schools are controlled by religious organizations, have the purpose of propagating and promoting a particular religious faith, and conduct their operations to fulfill that purpose. . . .

As we noted earlier, the very restrictions and surveillance necessary to ensure that teachers play a strictly non-ideological role give rise to entanglements between church and state. The Pennsylvania statute, like that of Rhode Island, fosters this kind of relationship. Reimbursement is not only limited to courses offered in the public schools and materials approved by state officials, but the statute excludes "any subject matter expressing religious teaching, or the morals or forms of worship of any sect." In addition, schools seeking reimbursements must maintain accounting procedures that require the State to establish the cost of the secular as distinguished from the religious instruction.

The Pennsylvania statute, moreover, has the further defect of providing state financial aid directly to the church-related schools. This factor distinguishes both *Everson* and *Allen*, for in both those cases the Court was careful to point out that state aid was provided to the student and his parents—not to the church-related school. . . . The history of government grants of a continuing cash subsidy indicates that such programs have almost always been accompanied by varying measures of control and surveillance. The government cash grants before us now provide no basis for predicting that comprehensive measures of surveillance and controls will not follow. In particular the government's post-audit power to inspect and evaluate a church-related school's financial records and to determine which expenditures are religious and which are secular creates an intimate and continuing relationship between church and state. . . .

The sole question is whether state aid to these schools can be squared with the dictates of the Religion Clauses. Under our system the choice has been made that government is to be entirely excluded from the area of religious instruction and churches excluded from the affairs of government. The Constitution decrees that religion must be a private matter for the individual, the family, and the institutions of private choice, and that while some involvement and entanglements are inevitable, lines must be drawn.

The judgment of the Rhode Island District Court . . . is affirmed. The judgment of the Pennsylvania District Court . . . is reversed, and the case is remanded for further proceedings consistent with this opinion.

MR. JUSTICE DOUGLAS, whom MR. JUSTICE BLACK joins, concurring.

We said in unequivocal words in *Everson v. Board of Education* [1947], "No tax in any amount, large or small, can be levied to support any religious activities or institutions, whatever they may be called, or whatever form they may adopt to teach or practice religion." We reiterated the same idea in *Zorach v. Clauson* [1952] and in *McGowan v. Maryland* [1961] and in *Torcaso v. Watkins* [1961]. We repeated the same idea in *McCollum v. Board of Education* [1948] and added that a State's tax-supported public schools could not be used "for the dissemination of religious doctrines" nor could a State provide the church "pupils for their religious classes through use of the State's compulsory public school machinery."

Yet in spite of this long and consistent history there are those who have the courage to announce that a State may nonetheless finance the *secular* part of a sectarian school's educational program. That, however, makes a grave constitutional decision turn merely on cost accounting and bookkeeping entries. A history class, a literature class, or a science class in a parochial school is not a separate institute; it is part of the organic whole which the State subsidizes. The funds are used in these cases to pay or help pay the salaries of teachers in parochial schools; and the presence of teachers is critical to the essential purpose of the parochial school, viz., to advance the religious endeavors of the particular church. It matters not that the teacher receiving taxpayers' money only teaches religion a fraction of the time. Nor does it matter that he or she teaches no religion. The school is an organism living on one budget. What the taxpayers give for salaries of those who teach only the humanities or science without any trace of proselytizing enables the school to use all of its own funds for religious training. . . .

In my view, the taxpayers' forced contribution to the parochial schools in the present cases violates the First Amendment.

The same day the Court handed down *Lemon,* it also decided *Tilton v. Richardson,* involving the constitutionality of the Higher Education Facilities Act. Passed by Congress in 1963, the law provided building grants to colleges and universities so long as the funded facility would not be "used for sectarian instruction or a place for religious worship" for twenty years. A group of taxpayers from Connecticut brought suit against the secretary of the Health, Education and Welfare Department and four church-run colleges, claiming that federal aid to these religious institutions violated the Establishment Clause.

BOX 4-6   THE ROOTS OF THE *LEMON* TEST

Test	*Everson* (1947)	*Abington* (1963)	*Walz* (1970)	*Lemon* (1971)
Secular Purpose	The state ⟶ has a legitimate, general interest in helping "parents get their children, regardless of their religion, safely and expeditiously to and from accredited schools."	"What [is] ⟶ the purpose ... of the enactment? If [it] is the advancement or inhibition of religion then the enactment exceeds the scope of legislative power.... That is to say that to withstand the strictures of the Establishment Clause there must be secular legislative purpose."	"The ⟶ legislative purpose of a property tax exemption is neither the advancement nor the inhibition of religion."	"The statute must have a secular legislative pupose."
Primary Effect	Governments ⟶ cannot "pass laws which aid one religion, aid all religions, or prefer one religion over another."	"What [is] ... the primary effect of the enactment? If [it] is the advancement or inhibition of religion then the enactment exceeds the scope of legislative power.... That is to say that to withstand the strictures of the Establishment Clause there must be a ... primary effect that neither advances nor inhibits religion."	⟶	The statute's "principal or primary effect must be one that neither advances nor inhibits religion."
Excessive Entanglement			"We ⟶ must ... be sure that the end result—the effect—is not an excessive government entanglement with religion."	"The statute must not foster an excessive government entanglement with religion."

The schools countered that this point was irrelevant as they had used government funding exclusively for secular purposes; for example, Sacred Heart College had built a library, and Fairfield University, a science building.

A three-judge federal district court upheld the validity of the funding program. The challengers appealed to the Supreme Court, asking the following question: Does federal aid to religious universities for secular purposes violate the Establishment Clause? Writing for a five-person majority, Burger held that it did not. As he noted, the

stated legislative purpose "expresses a legitimate secular objective to assist the nation's colleges and universities entirely appropriate for governmental action"; that its "provisions ... will not advance religion"; and that there are sufficiently "significant differences between religious aspects of church-related institutions of higher learning and parochial elementary and secondary schools" to nullify complaints of excessive entanglement. The Court, however, struck down the act's twenty-year provision.

What is the significance of *Lemon, DiCenso,* and

Tilton? The cases cleared up some of the confusion created by *Walz* over legal standards governing Establishment Clause cases. It now seemed that the justices planned to adhere to a tripartite test, referred to as the *Lemon* test. First, to be constitutional the statute must have a *secular legislative purpose;* second, its principal or primary effect must be one that *neither advances nor inhibits religion;* and third, the statute must not foster an *excessive government entanglement* with religion.

None of these prongs is new. As Box 4-6 illustrates, they had their genesis in early Supreme Court cases. In addition, because the *Lemon* test finds its roots in earlier Court decisions that were based on the belief that Madison and Jefferson envisioned a strict wall of separation between church and state, it seemed that the Court was not only following precedent but also reinforcing the historical understanding from which the precedent flowed. By adhering to history and precedent the Court reached a seperationist outcome in *Lemon* that it had not reached in *Everson* or *Allen,* the two major cases on aid to public schools.

If you are surprised that Chief Justice Burger, who, at least in *Walz,* seemed to want to lower the wall of separation, wrote these 1971 opinions, you are not alone. Members of separatist groups were surprised and overjoyed. After handing down major rulings upholding aid to religious schools, the Court finally had defined the constitutional line that government aid programs could not cross.

The enunciation of a legal standard by which to judge religious establishment claims raises some questions: Would the justices of the Burger Court and their successors continue to apply the *Lemon* test? Would it stand the test of time? *Lemon* is still good law, although many commentators would argue that its days are numbered. The three-pronged standard may continue to dominate Court adjudication of Establishment Clause claims, but this does not mean that the Court always applies *Lemon,* nor does it mean that when *Lemon* is applied the Court reaches consistent decisions.

The current justices are not united behind *Lemon* as the most appropriate standard to use in Establishment Clause cases, nor do they all subscribe to its historical underpinnings. As we shall see, some justices have been openly critical of *Lemon.* Alternative approaches have been offered. Three of the most prominent of these competing tests are described in Table 4-4 and compared to the *Lemon* test.

In spite of the criticism it has received, the *Lemon* test hangs on because a majority of justices have yet to coalesce behind any of the alternative standards. In the pages to come we review the Supreme Court's response to a number of recurring Establishment Clause questions. The justices' various views will become clear in the debates over which of the competing tests of the Establishment Clause should be adopted to guide the Court's decisionmaking.

Recurring Establishment Clause Issues

Certain areas of Establishment Clause law have generated disputes that repeatedly have found their way to the Supreme Court's door. In this section we examine five of them: aid to religious schools, the use of public facilities and funds for religious purposes, religious instruction in public schools, religious holiday displays, and school prayer.

Aid to Religious Schools. Questions concerning "parochiaid"—aid to religious schools—are among the most enduring of those raised in religious establishment litigation. Since *Everson,* when the Court signaled that some government aid programs to nonpublic schools is constitutionally permissible, state legislatures have responded by developing creative assistance programs. Each time the Court ruled in favor of such policies, states were encouraged to develop even more comprehensive programs. When the Court found fault with some of these programs, states returned to the drawing board to devise policies that would pass constitutional muster.

Complicating this process has been a Supreme Court that has had a great deal of difficulty developing a consistent and coherent interpretation of the Establishment Clause for parochiaid cases. Table 4-5 lists the major school assistance decisions beginning with *Everson* and continuing into the Rehnquist Court years. The list quickly reveals the confusion and inconsistencies that have plagued this area of litigation. However, certain patterns do emerge.

First, since 1971 the Court has regularly used the

TABLE 4-4 Religious Establishment Standards Advocated by Members of the Supreme Court

Standard	Definition	Chief Supporters	Occasional Adherents
Lemon (1971)	"Every analysis in this area must begin with consideration of the cumulative criteria developed by the Court over many years. Three such tests may be gleaned from our cases. First, the statute must have a secular legislative purpose; second, its principal or primary effect must be one that neither advances not inhibits religion; finally, the statute must not foster an excessive government entanglement with religion." (Burger, majority opinion in *Lemon v. Kurtzman*)	Powell, Stewart	Burger, *Stevens, O'Connor,* Douglas, Marshall, Blackmun
Nonpreferentialism (1983)	"The Framers intended the Establishment Clause to prohibit the designation of any church as a 'national' one. The Clause was also designed to stop the Federal Government from asserting a preference for one religious denomination or sect over others." (Rehnquist, dissenting in *Wallace v. Jaffree*)	*Rehnquist*	*Scalia, Thomas,* White, Burger
Endorsement Approach to *Lemon* (1984)	"The Establishment Clause prohibits government from making adherence to a religion relevant in any person's standing in the political community. Government can run afoul of that prohibition in two principal ways. One is excessive entanglement with religious institutions.... The second and more direct infringement is government endorsed or disapproval of religion. Under this view, *Lemon*'s inquiry as to the purpose and effect of a statute requires courts to examine whether government's purpose is to endorse religion and whether the statute actually conveys a message of endorsement." (O'Connor, concurring in *Lynch v. Donnelly* and in *Wallace v. Jaffree*)	*O'Connor*	Blackmun, *Stevens, Souter,* White
Coercion	"Our cases disclose two limiting principles: government may not coerce anyone to support or participate in any religion or its exercise; and it may not, in the guise of avoiding hostility or callous indifference, give direct benefits to a religion in such a degree that it in fact 'establishes a religion or religious faith, or tends to do so.'" (Kennedy, concurring and dissenting in *County of Allegheny v. American Civil Liberties Union*)	*Kennedy*	*Scalia, Thomas, Rehnquist,* White

NOTE: Justices in italic are members of the current Court. Ginsburg and Breyer are not included because as of 2000 neither had yet written an opinion declaring a clear preference for one of the competing Establishment Clause tests. Also keep in mind that justices adhering to a particular approach do not always agree on its application in a given case. For example, Justices Scalia and Kennedy, who generally agree with the "coercion" standard, have vehemently disagreed over the kinds of coercion the Court should consider.

Lemon test to decide these issues, but applying *Lemon* has not resulted in consistently accommodationist or separationist outcomes. In fact, the results are almost equally divided. Second, the Court has been more sympathetic to programs that allocate benefits such as transportation support and textbook loans directly to the child, or the child's parents, rather than to the religious school. But the Court has shown had little sympathy for state appropriations supporting teachers' salaries. Third, the justices are more likely to approve aid to colleges and universities than assistance for similar programs aimed at primary and secondary schools. The Court seemingly has taken the position that greater vigilance is necessary when dealing with younger, more impressionable students. Fourth, federal aid programs are more likely to be permitted than programs sponsored by state and local governments.

In spite of these patterns, inconsistencies abound. As further evidence of the Court's inability to achieve a stable consensus on an Establishment Clause jurisprudence, note in Table 4-5 how many important rulings have been decided by 5–4 margins, especially over the past two

TABLE 4-5 Aid to Religious Schools: Supreme Court Cases, 1947–2000

Case	Outcome (Opinion Type)[a]	Aid Upheld	Aid Struck	Standard Used
Everson v. Bd. of Ed. (1947)	accommodation (majority, 5–4)	transportation reimbursements		neutrality, child benefit, secular purpose
Bd. of Ed. v. Allen (1968)	accommodation (majority, 6–3)	textbook loans		*Abington*
Lemon v. Kurtzman (1971)	separation (majority, 8–0)		reimbursements for teacher salaries, textbooks, instructional materials	*Lemon*
Early v. DiCenso (1971)	separation (majority, 8–1)		teacher salary supplements	*Lemon*
Tilton v. Richardson (1971)	accommodation (judgment, 5–4)	funds for secular buildings (colleges and universities)		*Lemon*
Levitt v. CPEARL (1973)	separation (majority, 8–1)		reimbursements for administering and grading tests and examinations required by state	*Lemon*
CPEARL v. Nyquist (1973)	separation (majority, 6–3)		grants for maintenance and building repair, tax benefits, tuition reimbursements	*Lemon*
Meek v. Pittenger (1975)	mixed (majority/ judgment, 6–3)	textbook loans	counseling, testing, speech therapy; loans of "instructional materials and equipment"	*Lemon*
Roemer v. Maryland Public Works Bd. (1976)	accommodation (judgment, 5–4)	general-purpose funds to colleges and universities for secular purposes		*Lemon*
Wolman v. Walter (1977)	mixed (majority/ judgment, 6–3)	diagnostic, health, therapeutic, and testing services; textbooks	instructional materials, equipment; field trips	*Lemon*
New York v. Cathedral Academy (1977)	separation (majority, 6–3)		direct reimbursement for record keeping and testing	*Lemon*
CPEARL v. Regan (1980)	accommodation (majority, 5–4)	reimbursements for meeting state requirements for regents examinations, "pupil attendance reporting" and so forth		*Lemon*

(table continues)

TABLE 4-5 *(continued)*

Case	Outcome (Opinion Type)[a]	Aid Upheld	Aid Struck	Standard Used
Mueller v. Allen (1983)	accommodation (majority, 5–4)	tax deductions for tuition, textbooks, transportation		*Lemon*
Grand Rapids School Dist. v. Ball (1985)	separation (majority, 7–2 and 5–4)		Community Education Program offering courses (chess, home economics, languages) at end of school day; employing private school teachers and using public and private school facilities Shared Time Program offering secular classes to private school children in private school facilities (leased by the state) during regular school hours and taught by public school teachers	*Lemon*
Aguilar v. Felton (1985)	separation (majority, 5–4)		teacher/counselor salaries and supplies/materials for remedial instruction to private school students in private school facilities	*Lemon*
Witters v. Washington Serv. for the Blind (1986)	accommodation (majority, 9–0)	disabled student at Christian college cannot be denied state vocational rehabilitation assistance		*Lemon*
Zobrest v. Catalina Foothills School Dist. (1993)	accommodation (majority, 5–4)	disabled student at Roman Catholic high school can be furnished with a state-funded sign-language interpreter		neutrality; child benefit
Bd. of Ed. of Kiryas Joel Village School Dist. v. Grumet (1994)	separation (majority, 6–3)		school district created to accommodate handicapped children of particular sect	neutrality
Agostini v. Felton (1997)	accommodation (majority, 5–4)	special education classes taught in parochial schools; overruled *Aguilar v. Felton, Grand Rapids School District v. Ball* (in part)		accommodationist interpretation of *Lemon*
Mitchell v. Helms (2000)	accommodation (judgment, 6–3)	library services and materials, computer hardware and software, curricular materials. *Meek v. Pittenger, Wolman v. Walter* overruled		*Agostini,* neutrality

a. A judgment represents the views of a plurality, not a majority, of the Court's members. Unlike a majority opinion, a judgment lacks precedential value.

decades. The change of a single vote may cause radically different outcomes.

On occasion the Court's position on specific government aid programs has changed, sometimes quite markedly. Consider, for example, *Aguilar v. Felton* (1985), a decision that many think is the high-water mark for the Court's separationist rulings. A 5–4 Court applied the *Lemon* test to strike down a New York program that allowed state-supported remedial instruction of students in private schools. Twelve years later, in *Agostini v. Felton* (1997), the justices reconsidered the issue.[29] As you read the opinions in *Agostini*, ask yourself if the justices have come any closer to bringing greater coherence to their Establishment Clause jurisprudence.

Agostini v. Felton

521 U.S. 203 (1997)
http://supct.law.cornell.edu/supct/html/96-552.ZS.html
Vote: 5 (Kennedy, O'Connor, Rehnquist, Scalia, Thomas)
    4 (Breyer, Ginsburg, Souter, Stevens)
Opinion of the Court: O'Connor
Dissenting opinions: Ginsburg, Souter

Aguilar v. Felton tested the constitutionality of New York City's provision of educational assistance under Title I of the Elementary and Secondary Education Act of 1965. Congress passed Title I to fund services for students at risk of academic failure—regardless of whether they attended public or private schools. Eligible under the program were all students who lived in low income areas and were failing or at risk of failing at school. Local school systems received federal money to implement remedial education, guidance, and counseling programs for these students. New York received its first Title I funds in 1966. About 10 percent of the eligible students attended private, mostly religious, schools, and initially the city transported these students to public schools for the funded services. When this system proved unworkable, the city allowed public school employees to go to the private schools, with strict instructions to maintain

29. To hear oral arguments and the announcement of the Court's opinion in this case, navigate to: *oyez.nwu.edu*.

the secular purposes of the programs. In *Aguilar* the Court found this program in violation of the Establishment Clause. Crucial to the Court's decision was that the public school teachers provided the services inside the religious school buildings. At the same time, in *School District of Grand Rapids v. Ball* (1985) the Court struck down a similar "shared time" program in Michigan.

In response to *Aguilar,* New York revised its program by leasing more than one hundred vans to transport public school teachers to the private schools. The teachers would then use the vans, which were parked in public areas near the private schools, as a place to provide services for the eligible students. Between 1986 and 1993, New York estimated that it spent more than $100 million to operate these mobile instructional units.

In 1995 parents of private school students and the City of New York went into federal court requesting that they be released from complying with the *Aguilar* decision. They argued that compliance was unreasonably expensive. They also claimed that the Supreme Court's Establishment Clause jurisprudence had so significantly changed since 1985 as to make *Aguilar* no longer good law. As evidence, they cited the more accommodationist decisions the Supreme Court was handing down. They also pointed to *Board of Education of Kiryas Joel Village School District v. Grumet* (1994), in which five justices had called for the reconsideration or overruling of *Aguilar.* In fact, by 1997 Justice Stevens was the sole remaining member of the five-justice *Aguilar* majority. The district judge refused the request, noting, "There may be good reason to conclude that *Aguilar*'s demise is imminent, but it has not yet occurred." The court of appeals affirmed.

JUSTICE O'CONNOR delivered the opinion of the Court.

In *Aguilar v. Felton* (1985), this Court held that the Establishment Clause of the First Amendment barred the city of New York from sending public school teachers into parochial schools to provide remedial education to disadvantaged children pursuant to a congressionally mandated program. . . . We agree with petitioners that *Aguilar* is not consistent with our subsequent Establishment Clause decisions. . . .

Petitioners point to three changes in the factual and

legal landscape that they believe justify their claim for relief. . . . They first contend that the exorbitant costs of complying with the District Court's injunction constitute a significant factual development warranting modification of the injunction. Petitioners also argue that there have been two significant legal developments since *Aguilar* was decided: a majority of Justices have expressed their views that *Aguilar* should be reconsidered or overruled; and *Aguilar* has in any event been undermined by subsequent Establishment Clause decisions. . . .

We agree with respondents that petitioners have failed to establish the significant change in factual conditions. . . . Both petitioners and this Court were, at the time *Aguilar* was decided, aware that additional costs would be incurred if Title I services could not be provided in parochial school classrooms. That these predictions of additional costs turned out to be accurate does not constitute a change in factual conditions warranting relief. . . .

We also agree with respondents that the statements made by five Justices in [*Board of Education of*] *Kiryas Joel* [*v. Grumet*, 1994] do not, in themselves, furnish a basis for concluding that our Establishment Clause jurisprudence has changed. . . .

In light of these conclusions, petitioners' ability to satisfy the [requirements for relief] hinges on whether our later Establishment Clause cases have so undermined *Aguilar* that it is no longer good law. We now turn to that inquiry.

In order to evaluate whether *Aguilar* has been eroded by our subsequent Establishment Clause cases, it is necessary to understand the rationale upon which *Aguilar,* as well as its companion case, *School Dist. of Grand Rapids v. Ball* (1985), rested.

In *Ball*, the Court evaluated two programs implemented by the School District of Grand Rapids, Michigan. The district's Shared Time program, the one most analogous to Title I, provided remedial and "enrichment" classes, at public expense, to students attending nonpublic schools. The classes were taught during regular school hours by publicly employed teachers, using materials purchased with public funds, on the premises of nonpublic schools. The Shared Time courses were in subjects designed to supplement the "core curriculum" of the nonpublic schools. Of the 41 nonpublic schools eligible for the program, 40 were "'pervasively sectarian'" in character—that is, "the purpos[e] of [those] schools [was] to advance their particular religions."

The Court conducted its analysis by applying the three part test set forth in *Lemon v. Kurtzman* (1971):

"First, the statute must have a secular legislative purpose; second, its principal or primary effect must be one that neither advances nor inhibits religion; finally, the statute must not foster an excessive government entanglement with religion."

The Court acknowledged that the Shared Time program served a purely secular purpose, thereby satisfying the first part of the so called *Lemon* test. Nevertheless, it ultimately concluded that the program had the impermissible effect of advancing religion.

The Court found that the program violated the Establishment Clause's prohibition against "government financed or government sponsored indoctrination into the beliefs of a particular religious faith" in at least three ways. First, drawing upon the analysis in *Meek v. Pittenger* (1975), the Court observed that "the teachers participating in the programs may become involved in intentionally or inadvertently inculcating particular religious tenets or beliefs.". . .

The presence of public teachers on parochial school grounds had a second, related impermissible effect: It created a "graphic symbol of the 'concert or union or dependency' of church and state," especially when perceived by "children in their formative years." The Court feared that this perception of a symbolic union between church and state would "convey[] a message of government endorsement . . . of religion" and thereby violate a "core purpose" of the Establishment Clause.

Third, the Court found that the Shared Time program impermissibly financed religious indoctrination by subsidizing "the primary religious mission of the institutions affected.". . .

The New York City Title I program challenged in *Aguilar* closely resembled the Shared Time program struck down in *Ball*, but the Court found fault with an aspect of the Title I program not present in *Ball*: The Board had "adopted a system for monitoring the religious content of publicly funded Title I classes in the religious schools." Even though this monitoring system might prevent the Title I program from being used to inculcate religion, the Court concluded, as it had in *Lemon* and *Meek*, that the level of monitoring necessary to be "certain" that the program had an exclusively secular effect would "inevitably resul[t] in the excessive entanglement of church and state," thereby running afoul of *Lemon*'s third prong. . . .

Distilled to essentials, the Court's conclusion that the Shared Time program in *Ball* had the impermissible effect of advancing religion rested on three assumptions: (i) any public employee who works on the premises of a religious school is presumed to inculcate religion in her work; (ii) the presence of public employees on private school premises creates a symbolic union between church and state; and (iii) any and all public aid that directly aids the educational function of religious schools impermissibly finances religious indoctrination, even if the aid reaches such schools as a consequence of private decisionmaking. Additionally, in *Aguilar* there was a fourth assumption: that New York City's Title I program necessitated an excessive government entanglement with religion because public employees who teach on the premises of religious schools must be closely monitored to ensure that they do not inculcate religion.

Our more recent cases have undermined the assumptions upon which *Ball* and *Aguilar* relied. To be sure, the general principles we use to evaluate whether government aid violates the Establishment Clause have not changed since *Aguilar* was decided. For example, we continue to ask whether the government acted with the purpose of advancing or inhibiting religion, and the nature of that inquiry has remained largely unchanged. Likewise, we continue to explore whether the aid has the "effect" of advancing or inhibiting religion. What has changed since we decided *Ball* and *Aguilar* is our understanding of the criteria used to assess whether aid to religion has an impermissible effect.

As we have repeatedly recognized, government inculcation of religious beliefs has the impermissible effect of advancing religion. Our cases subsequent to *Aguilar* have, however, modified in two significant respects the approach we use to assess indoctrination. First, we have abandoned the presumption erected in *Meek* and *Ball* that the placement of public employees on parochial school grounds inevitably results in the impermissible effect of state sponsored indoctrination or constitutes a symbolic union between government and religion. In *Zobrest v. Catalina Foothills School Dist.* (1993), we . . . expressly disavow[ed] the notion that "the Establishment Clause [laid] down [an] absolute bar to the placing of a public employee in a sectarian school.". . .

Second, we have departed from the rule relied on in *Ball* that all government aid that directly aids the educational function of religious schools is invalid. In *Witters v. Washing-*

ton Dept. of Servs. for Blind (1986), we held that the Establishment Clause did not bar a State from issuing a vocational tuition grant to a blind person who wished to use the grant to attend a Christian college and become a pastor, missionary, or youth director. Even though the grant recipient clearly would use the money to obtain religious education, we observed that the tuition grants were "'made available generally without regard to the sectarian nonsectarian, or public nonpublic nature of the institution benefited.'". . . *Zobrest* and *Witters* make clear that, under current law, the Shared Time program in *Ball* and New York City's Title I program in *Aguilar* will not, as a matter of law, be deemed to have the effect of advancing religion through indoctrination. Indeed, each of the premises upon which we relied in *Ball* to reach a contrary conclusion is no longer valid. First, there is no reason to presume that, simply because she enters a parochial school classroom, a full time public employee such as a Title I teacher will depart from her assigned duties and instructions and embark on religious indoctrination, any more than there was a reason in *Zobrest* to think an interpreter would inculcate religion by altering her translation of classroom lectures. Certainly, no evidence has ever shown that any New York City Title I instructor teaching on parochial school premises attempted to inculcate religion in students. Thus, both our precedent and our experience require us to reject respondents' remarkable argument that we must presume Title I instructors to be "uncontrollable and sometimes very unprofessional."

. . . *Zobrest* also repudiates *Ball*'s assumption that the presence of Title I teachers in parochial school classrooms will, without more, create the impression of a "symbolic union" between church and state. . . . We do not see any perceptible (let alone dispositive) difference in the degree of symbolic union between a student receiving remedial instruction in a classroom on his sectarian school's campus and one receiving instruction in a van parked just at the school's curbside. To draw this line based solely on the location of the public employee is neither "sensible" nor "sound," and the Court in *Zobrest* rejected it.

Nor under current law can we conclude that a program placing full time public employees on parochial campuses to provide Title I instruction would impermissibly finance religious indoctrination. . . . Moreover, as in *Zobrest*, Title I services are by law supplemental to the regular curricula. These services do not, therefore, "reliev[e] sectarian schools of costs they otherwise would have borne in educating their students.". . .

What is most fatal to the argument that New York City's Title I program directly subsidizes religion is that it applies with equal force when those services are provided off campus, and *Aguilar* implied that providing the services off campus is entirely consistent with the Establishment Clause. . . . Because the incentive is the same either way, we find no logical basis upon which to conclude that Title I services are an impermissible subsidy of religion when offered on campus, but not when offered off campus. Accordingly, contrary to our conclusion in *Aguilar,* placing full time employees on parochial school campuses does not as a matter of law have the impermissible effect of advancing religion through indoctrination. . . .

. . . Title I services are allocated on the basis of criteria that neither favor nor disfavor religion. The services are available to all children who meet the Act's eligibility requirements, no matter what their religious beliefs or where they go to school. The Board's program does not, therefore, give aid recipients any incentive to modify their religious beliefs or practices in order to obtain those services.

We turn now to *Aguilar's* conclusion that New York City's Title I program resulted in an excessive entanglement between church and state. Whether a government aid program results in such an entanglement has consistently been an aspect of our Establishment Clause analysis. We have considered entanglement both in the course of assessing whether an aid program has an impermissible effect of advancing religion, and as a factor separate and apart from "effect," *Lemon v. Kurtzman.* . . .

Not all entanglements, of course, have the effect of advancing or inhibiting religion. Interaction between church and state is inevitable, and we have always tolerated some level of involvement between the two. Entanglement must be "excessive" before it runs afoul of the Establishment Clause.

The pre-*Aguilar* Title I program does not result in an "excessive" entanglement that advances or inhibits religion. As discussed previously, the Court's finding of "excessive" entanglement in *Aguilar* rested on three grounds: (i) the program would require "pervasive monitoring by public authorities" to ensure that Title I employees did not inculcate religion; (ii) the program required "administrative cooperation" between the Board and parochial schools; and (iii) the

program might increase the dangers of "political divisiveness." Under our current understanding of the Establishment Clause, the last two considerations are insufficient by themselves to create an "excessive" entanglement. They are present no matter where Title I services are offered, and no court has held that Title I services cannot be offered off campus. Further, the assumption underlying the first consideration has been undermined. In *Aguilar,* the Court presumed that full time public employees on parochial school grounds would be tempted to inculcate religion, despite the ethical standards they were required to uphold. Because of this risk *pervasive* monitoring would be required. But after *Zobrest* we no longer presume that public employees will inculcate religion simply because they happen to be in a sectarian environment. Since we have abandoned the assumption that properly instructed public employees will fail to discharge their duties faithfully, we must also discard the assumption that *pervasive* monitoring of Title I teachers is required. There is no suggestion in the record before us that unannounced monthly visits of public supervisors are insufficient to prevent or to detect inculcation of religion by public employees. Moreover, we have not found excessive entanglement in cases in which States imposed far more onerous burdens on religious institutions than the monitoring system at issue here.

To summarize, New York City's Title I program does not run afoul of any of three primary criteria we currently use to evaluate whether government aid has the effect of advancing religion: it does not result in governmental indoctrination; define its recipients by reference to religion; or create an excessive entanglement. We therefore hold that a federally funded program providing supplemental, remedial instruction to disadvantaged children on a neutral basis is not invalid under the Establishment Clause when such instruction is given on the premises of sectarian schools by government employees pursuant to a program containing safeguards such as those present here. The same considerations that justify this holding require us to conclude that this carefully constrained program also cannot reasonably be viewed as an endorsement of religion. Accordingly, we must acknowledge that *Aguilar,* as well as the portion of *Ball* addressing Grand Rapids' Shared Time program, are no longer good law.

The doctrine of *stare decisis* does not preclude us from recognizing the change in our law and overruling *Aguilar* and those portions of *Ball* inconsistent with our more recent decisions. As we have often noted, *"[s]tare decisis* is not an inexorable command," but instead reflects a policy judgment that "in most matters it is more important that the applicable rule of law be settled than that it be settled right." That policy is at its weakest when we interpret the Constitution because our interpretation can be altered only by constitutional amendment or by overruling our prior decisions. Thus, we have held in several cases that *stare decisis* does not prevent us from overruling a previous decision where there has been a significant change in or subsequent development of our constitutional law. As discussed above, our Establishment Clause jurisprudence has changed significantly since we decided *Ball* and *Aguilar,* so our decision to overturn those cases rests on far more than "a present doctrinal disposition to come out differently from the Court of [1985]." We therefore overrule *Ball* and *Aguilar* to the extent those decisions are inconsistent with our current understanding of the Establishment Clause. . . .

For these reasons, we reverse the judgment of the Court of Appeals and remand to the District Court with instructions to vacate its September 26, 1985, order.

It is so ordered.

JUSTICE SOUTER, with whom JUSTICE STEVENS and JUSTICE GINSBURG join, and with whom JUSTICE BREYER joins as to Part II, dissenting.

I.

In both *Aguilar* and *Ball,* we held that supplemental instruction by public school teachers on the premises of religious schools during regular school hours violated the Establishment Clause. . . .

. . . I believe *Aguilar* was a correct and sensible decision, and my only reservation about its opinion is that the emphasis on the excessive entanglement produced by monitoring religious instructional content obscured those facts that independently called for the application of two central tenets of Establishment Clause jurisprudence. The State is forbidden to subsidize religion directly and is just as surely forbidden to act in any way that could reasonably be viewed as religious endorsement.

. . . [T]he flat ban on subsidization antedates the Bill of Rights and has been an unwavering rule in Establishment Clause cases, qualified only by the conclusion two Terms ago that state exactions from college students are not the sort of public revenues subject to the ban. See *Rosenberger v. Rector and Visitors of Univ. of Va.* (1995). The rule expresses the hard lesson learned over and over again in the American past and in the experiences of the countries from which we have come, that religions supported by governments are compromised just as surely as the religious freedom of dissenters is burdened when the government supports religion. . . . The human tendency, of course, is to forget the hard lessons, and to overlook the history of governmental partnership with religion when a cause is worthy, and bureaucrats have programs. That tendency to forget is the reason for having the Establishment Clause (along with the Constitution's other structural and libertarian guarantees), in the hope of stopping the corrosion before it starts. . . .

What was true of the Title I scheme as struck down in *Aguilar* will be just as true when New York reverts to the old practices with the Court's approval after today. . . . If a State may constitutionally enter the schools to teach in the manner in question, it must in constitutional principle be free to assume, or assume payment for, the entire cost of instruction provided in any ostensibly secular subject in any religious school. . . .

In sum, if a line is to be drawn short of barring all state aid to religious schools for teaching standard subjects, the *Aguilar-Ball* line was a sensible one capable of principled adherence. It is no less sound, and no less necessary, today.

II.

The Court today ignores this doctrine and claims that recent cases rejected the elemental assumptions underlying *Aguilar* and much of *Ball.* But the Court errs. Its holding that *Aguilar* and the portion of *Ball* addressing the Shared Time program are "no longer good law," rests on mistaken reading. . . .

In *Zobrest* the Court did indeed recognize that the Establishment Clause lays down no absolute bar to placing public employees in a sectarian school, but the rejection of such a *per se* rule was hinged expressly on the nature of the employee's job, sign language interpretation (or signing) and the circumscribed role of the signer. On this point (and without reference to the facts that the benefited student had received the same aid before enrolling in the religious school and the employee was to be assigned to the student not to the school) the Court explained itself this way: "[T]he task of a sign language interpreter seems to us quite different from that of a teacher or guidance counselor. . . . Nothing in this record suggests that a sign language interpreter would do more than accurately interpret whatever material is presented to the class as a whole. In fact, ethical guidelines require interpreters to 'transmit everything that is said in exactly the same way it was intended.'" The signer could thus be seen as more like a hearing aid than a teacher, and the signing could not be understood as an opportunity to inject religious content in what was supposed to be secular instruction. *Zobrest* accordingly holds only that in these limited circumstances where a public employee simply translates for one student the material presented to the class for the benefit of all students, the employee's presence in the sectarian school does not violate the Establishment Clause.

The Court, however, ignores the careful distinction drawn in *Zobrest* and insists that a full time public employee such as a Title I teacher is just like the signer, asserting that "there is no reason to presume that, simply because she enters a parochial school classroom, . . . [this] teacher will depart from her assigned duties and instructions and embark on religious indoctrination. . . ." Whatever may be the merits of this position (and I find it short on merit), it does not enjoy the authority of *Zobrest*. The Court may disagree with *Ball's* assertion that a publicly employed teacher working in a sectarian school is apt to reinforce the pervasive inculcation of religious beliefs, but its disagreement is fresh law. . . .

Finally, instead of aid that comes to the religious school indirectly in the sense that its distribution results from private decisionmaking, a public educational agency distributes Title I aid in the form of programs and services directly to the religious schools. In *Zobrest* and *Witters*, it was fair to say that individual students were themselves applicants for individual benefits on a scale that could not amount to a systemic supplement. But under Title I, a local educational agency (which in New York City is the Board of Education) may receive federal funding by proposing programs approved to serve individual students who meet the criteria of need, which it then uses to provide such programs at the religious schools; students eligible for such programs may not apply directly for Title I funds. The aid, accordingly, is not even formally aid to the individual students (and even formally individual aid must be seen as aid to a school system when so many individuals receive it that it becomes a significant feature of the system).

In sum, nothing since *Ball* and *Aguilar* and before this case has eroded the distinction between "direct and substantial" and "indirect and incidental." That principled line is being breached only here and now. . . .

III.

Finally, there is the issue of precedent. *Stare decisis* is no barrier in the Court's eyes because it reads *Aguilar* and *Ball* for exaggerated propositions that *Witters* and *Zobrest* are supposed to have limited to the point of abandoned doctrine. The Court's dispensation from *stare decisis* is, accordingly, no more convincing than its reading of those cases. Since *Aguilar* came down, no case has held that there need be no concern about a risk that publicly paid school teachers may further religious doctrine; no case has repudiated the distinction between direct and substantial aid and aid that is indirect and incidental; no case has held that fusing public and private faculties in one religious school does not create an impermissible union or carry an impermissible endorsement; and no case has held that direct subsidization of religious education is constitutional or that the assumption of a portion of a religious school's teaching responsibility is not direct subsidization. . . .

. . . [T]he object of Title I is worthy without doubt, and the cost of compliance is high. In the short run there is much that is genuinely unfortunate about the administration of the scheme under *Aguilar's* rule. But constitutional lines have to be drawn, and on one side of every one of them is an otherwise sympathetic case that provokes impatience with the Constitution and with the line. But constitutional lines are the price of constitutional government.

For those who expected the Court finally to resolve the issue of aid to religious schools, *Agostini* was a disappointment. Once again, the Court split 5–4. *Lemon* was cited as the prevailing standard for deciding Establishment Clause cases, but Justice O'Connor acknowledged that the Court's use of that standard had evolved over the years. Compared with the past, the justices were now using a more accommodationist view of what constitutes an impermissible advancement of religion, and they were no longer categorically opposed to funding that directly supports the educational function of private schools.

Agostini's more accommodationist posture toward

parochial school aid, combined with the overruling of *Aguilar v. Felton* and *Grand Rapids School District v. Ball*, sent a strong signal. The justices may have had differences over the most appropriate test to use, but the Court's majority was generally sympathetic to government aid for religious schools. That position was solidified when the justices announced their decision three years later in *Mitchell v. Helms* (2000).

In *Mitchell* the Court responded to a legal challenge to Chapter 2 of the Education Consolidation and Improvement Act of 1981, a law allowing federal aid to public and private schools for educational materials, library holdings, and computer resources. The case focused on the program's distribution of federal funds in Jefferson Parish, Louisiana. Thirty percent of the allocated funds supported programs in accredited private schools; the remaining aid went to local public schools. Of the forty-six private schools benefiting from the aid, thirty-four were Roman Catholic, seven were otherwise religiously affiliated, and five were not affiliated with any church. The federal funds went first to state and local school officials who then reallocated the support on the basis of the number of students served by the various schools. Public school authorities purchased the educational materials and equipment, which were then loaned to the individual schools.

The continuing divisions among the justices prevented them from arriving at a majority opinion deciding the case. Six of the justices, however, concluded that Chapter 2 was a constitutionally valid program. In the process of reaching that decision, the Court overruled two important precedents that had invalidated earlier aid programs, *Meek v. Pittenger* (1975) and *Wolman v. Walter* (1977).

In the plurality opinion Justice Thomas, joined by Kennedy, Rehnquist, and Scalia, concluded that *Mitchell* was controlled by the modified interpretation of the *Lemon* test established in *Agostini v. Felton*. The main question was whether the government aid in question advanced religion. According to the plurality opinion, such advancement occurs (1) if any religious indoctrination is attributable to the government aid; (2) if the aid program defines its recipients with reference to religion; or (3) if

the aid creates an excessive government entanglement with religion. Of particular relevance is the program's neutrality. If the aid is allocated on the basis of secular criteria that neither favor nor disfavor religion and is made available to both religious and public schools on a nondiscriminatory basis, then the program is neutral in nature and is likely to be constitutionally valid.

The plurality rejected two major arguments advanced by the law's challengers: first, that it is always constitutionally impermissible to give aid directly to the religious schools and, second, that aid that can be diverted to religious use is always unconstitutional. Taking this approach, the plurality had little difficulty deciding that the challenged program was neutral and there was no evidence of religious indoctrination attributable to the government.

Justices O'Connor and Breyer concurred in the Court's conclusions, but thought that the plurality opinion was much too broad. They specifically questioned the wisdom of placing so much emphasis on neutrality and ignoring other factors that had been important in developing the Court's Establishment Clause jurisprudence.

The three dissenters, Justices Souter, Stevens, and Ginsburg, decried the Court's willingness to approve aid given directly to sectarian institutions. They claimed that under the approach endorsed by the plurality, almost any aid program for religious schools would be permissible. While the dissenters' position is arguable, it is reasonably clear that the decisions in *Agostini* and *Mitchell*, combined with the four separationist precedents overruled by them, clear away many legal barriers to government programs that aid religious schools. The Court's decisions will undoubtedly encourage those who favor expanded public support for private schools, including government-funded vouchers for students to attend non-public schools.

The Religious Use of Public School Facilities and Funds. These cases involve two questions: Do religious groups have the same right to use public school buildings as other groups? Is a campus religious group entitled to a share of student activity funds to support its activities?

Litigation involving the use of public facilities for religious purposes predated *Lemon v. Kurtzman*. In fact, the

Court delved into this subject in 1948 in *Illinois ex rel. Mc-Collum v. Board of Education,* just one year after it decided *Everson. McCollum* centered on so-called released-time programs, which began in the early 1900s. At that time, Catholics and Jews, who were immigrating to the United States in record numbers, expressed their displeasure with the overtly Protestant nature of America's public school systems. In response to their pressure, school boards devised various programs to meet the religious needs of these children.

The *McCollum* decision involved such a program in Champaign, Illinois. The public schools arranged to have religious instructors from local churches and synagogues conduct weekly classes during school hours in school buildings. The religious instructors had to be approved by the school superintendent, but they did not receive any compensation for their efforts. For those students whose parents consented, attendance at the religion classes was mandatory. Students whose parents did not want their children to participate were not released from school, but took secular courses or went to study hall. Although such programs generally received support from the public, critics attacked their constitutionality because the public schools organized and provided space for the religious instruction, as well as enforced the attendance requirements.

The Supreme Court, 8–1, had little trouble ruling that these on-site programs presented too much intermingling between church and state. Writing for the majority, Justice Black relied heavily on his *Everson* opinion:

Here not only are the State's tax-supported public school buildings used for the dissemination of religious doctrine. The state also affords sectarian groups an invaluable aid in that it helps to provide pupils for their religious classes. . . . This is not separation of church and state.

But Black's opinion did not end the matter. Because *McCollum* proscribed a widespread, popular practice, the Court's decision generated a backlash. School boards and state legislatures were pressured to adopt released-time programs that would conform to *McCollum.* In response, school boards revised their programs, hoping to avoid constitution problems.

The Court confronted one of the new released-time programs in *Zorach v. Clauson* (1952), a challenge to a New York City plan that allowed students, upon written consent from their parents, to be released from school to attend classes at religious centers off the school grounds. Nonparticipating students remained in school. For those receiving religious instruction, attendance at the classes was mandatory, and the religious centers reported attendance to the school authorities.

Writing for the majority, Justice Douglas, who normally advocated strong separatist positions, concluded that the new program corrected the fundamental defect of the old one; no longer would religious instruction occur on public school premises. But Douglas went further. He noted that the prohibition against religious establishment "does not say that in every and all respects there shall be separation of Church and State." If it did, according to Douglas, state and religion would be "hostile, suspicious, and even unfriendly" toward each other. This state of affairs would be out of line with the spirit of the First Amendment and the desires of the American people. For, as Douglas wrote in one of the most often-quoted passages in this area of the law,

We are a religious people whose institutions presuppose a Supreme Being. We guarantee the freedom to worship as one chooses. We make room for as wide a variety of beliefs and creeds as the spiritual needs of man deem. . . . When the state encourages religious instruction or cooperates with religious authorities by adjusting the schedule of public events to sectarian needs, it follows the best of our traditions. For it then respects the religious nature of our people and accommodates the public service to their spiritual needs. To hold that it may not would be to find callous indifference to religious groups. That would be preferring those who believe in no religion over those who do believe.

This logic troubled Justice Black, who, along with Frankfurter and Jackson, dissented. He believed that the Court had yielded to the public pressure resulting from *McCollum.* Black wrote:

I am aware that our *McCollum* decision has been subjected to a most searching examination throughout the country. Probably few opinions from this Court in recent years have attracted more attention. . . . Our insistence on a "wall of separation between Church and State which must be kept high and impregnable" has seemed to some a correct exposition . . . to which we should strictly adhere. With equal conviction and sincerity, others have thought the *McCollum* decision fundamentally wrong and have pledged continuous warfare against it.

As the author of *McCollum*, Black could find "no significant difference between the invalid Illinois program and that of New York sustained here." In his view, the *McCollum* program was unconstitutional not simply because it took place on school grounds, but because it gave "invaluable aid to religion," a characteristic of all released-time programs, as well.

With *Zorach* the Court closed the released-time issue. So long as instruction takes place off school premises, it is constitutionally permissible. But, by the 1980s, the Court was confronted with yet another set of questions in this area: May public schools deny religious groups use of their facilities for meetings or other programs? This new generation of suits was different from the early released-time cases. Now public schools were denying religious groups access to their buildings, rather than seeking to facilitate the teaching of religion on or off their premises. Keep in mind that when these cases came up the Court had a standard of law, the *Lemon* test, which it did not have at the time of *McCollum* and *Zorach*. How would the Court resolve this new kind of access case?

In the first of these cases, *Widmar v. Vincent* (1981), the Court provided a few answers. This dispute arose at a public institution, the University of Missouri in Kansas City, where students had organized a religious group called Cornerstone. From 1973 through 1977 Cornerstone held meetings in university facilities. In 1977 university officials, citing a 1972 school policy, denied the participants access, saying that their presence would violate the Establishment Clause because, the officials argued, during their meetings the students prayed, sang hymns, and discussed religious experiences.

Cornerstone members challenged the ruling as a violation of their right to free exercise of religion and to free speech. The school countered that it could regulate religious exercise and free speech if it had a compelling reason to do so and that the prevention of religious establishment was such a reason. If the university adopted an equal access policy, which would have permitted the group to continue to use school facilities, it would cross the line between church and state. The Supreme Court

disagreed. Writing for the majority, Justice Powell applied the *Lemon* rule to find in favor of the students. He said that equal access policies have the secular purpose of encouraging the exchange of ideas. Further, he asserted that if the university retained its closed access policy, it would risk excessive entanglement with religion, as it would have to determine whether groups were engaging in religious speech or worship. Finally, Powell claimed that equal access policies do not have the primary effect of advancing religion; rather they encourage "all forms of discourse."

Widmar dealt exclusively with colleges and universities, asserting that equal access policies at these institutions would not violate the Establishment Clause. In 1984, with passage of the Equal Access Act, Congress built on *Widmar*. The act required all public secondary schools with "limited open forum" policies to give equal access to "any students who wish to conduct a meeting within that limited open forum," regardless of the "religious, political, philosophical, or content of the speech at such meetings." A limited open forum is in effect if a school permits "one or more noncurriculum related student groups to meet in school premises during noninstructional times."

Some observers speculated that the Court would strike down the Equal Access Act as a violation of the Religious Establishment Clause because the justices might be reluctant to apply a university policy to less mature secondary school students. In *Board of Education of Westside Community School v. Mergens* (1990), however, a divided Court voted to uphold the law. In a plurality opinion (fully endorsed by only four members of the Court) Justice O'Connor held that the law did not have the primary effect of advancing religion. In her argument, O'Connor adopted the logic of the endorsement test, which itself built on *Lemon (see Table 4-4)*: religion was not advanced because the speech endorsing religion was private, not governmental. Private endorsements of religion, such as those that might occur during a group meeting, she asserted, were protected by the Free Speech and Free Exercise Clauses of the First Amendment, but government endorsements violated the Establishment Clause.

Justices Kennedy and Scalia agreed that the act was

constitutional, but they took issue with O'Connor's endorsement approach. They advocated a standard emphasizing the relative "coercive" nature of government policies. Justice Kennedy wrote:

I should think it inevitable that a public high school "endorses" a religious club, in a commonsense use of the term, if the club happens to be one of many activities that the school permits students to choose in order to further the development of their intellect and character in an extracurricular setting. But no constitutional violation occurs if the school's action is based upon a recognition of the fact that membership in a religious club is one of many permissible ways for a student to further his or her own personal enrichment. The inquiry with respect to coercion must be whether the government imposes pressure upon a student to participate in a religious activity. This inquiry, of course, must be undertaken with sensitivity to the special circumstances that exist in a secondary school where the line between voluntary and coerced participation may be difficult to draw. No such coercion . . . has been shown to exist as a necessary result of this statute.

Mergens indicates the Court's willingness to uphold government policies that allow religious groups equal access to school facilities. It also shows the Court's division over the appropriate standard by which to adjudicate religious establishment cases. That is why observers anxiously awaited the decision in *Lamb's Chapel v. Center Moriches Union Free School District* (1993). Some thought that by 1993 the justices would coalesce around a particular test, but the Court's decision revealed only continued division.

Lamb's Chapel concerned the policies of Long Island's Center Moriches School District with respect to the use of school property by outside groups and/or its use for purposes other than education. Consistent with state law, the school board issued rules allowing use of school property only for social, civic, or recreational purposes or by political organizations. Its rules prohibited use by groups for religious purposes.

Lamb's Chapel, an evangelical church located in the Center Moriches community, twice asked the school board for permission to show a six-part film series in school buildings. The series contained lectures by a psychologist on "the undermining influences of the media [which] could only be counterbalanced by returning to traditional, Christian family values instilled at an early age." Believing that the films were church related, the school district denied both requests.

Lamb's Chapel took the school district to court, asserting that the denial violated the church's First Amendment guarantees of free speech and religious liberty. It presented evidence that district officials had permitted other religious groups to use school facilities, including a New Age religious group known as the Mind Center, the Southern Harmonize Gospel Singers, and the Hampton Council of Churches. The school district countered that it could deny use of its property to a "radical" church "for the purpose of proselytizing," which might lead to violence. Just as the University of Missouri had said in *Widmar*, the school district claimed that it had a compelling interest in restricting the church's First Amendment rights: use of its property for religious purposes would violate the Religious Establishment Clause.

After the lower courts rejected its claims, the church appealed to the U.S. Supreme Court, and the justices unanimously struck down the school board's policy. Writing for the Court, Justice White found that the school board's denial of permission to show the films violated the free speech provisions of the First Amendment. Refusing access based on the religious content of the films constituted government regulation of speech "in ways that favor some viewpoints or ideas at the expense of others."

White next rejected the school board's defense that its policies were required by the Establishment Clause. Using a combination of the *Lemon* test and O'Connor's endorsement approach, he explained:

We have no more trouble than did the *Widmar* Court in disposing of the claimed defense on the ground that the posited fears of an Establishment Clause violation are unfounded. The showing of this film series would not have been during school hours, would not have been sponsored by the school, and would have been open to the public, not just to church members. The District property had repeatedly been used by a wide variety of private organizations. Under these circumstances, as in *Widmar*, there would have been no realistic danger that the community would think that the District was endorsing religion or any particular creed, and any benefit to religion or to the Church would have been no more than incidental. As in

Widmar, permitting District property to be used to exhibit the film series involved in this case would not have been an establishment of religion under the three-part test articulated in *Lemon v. Kurtzman* (1971). The challenged governmental action has a secular purpose, does not have the principal or primary effect of advancing or inhibiting religion, and does not foster an excessive entanglement with religion.

Although the vote was unanimous, disagreements over the appropriate standard to use continued to divide the justices, and their rhetoric became more extreme. Consider this portion of Justice Scalia's concurring opinion in which he attacks the majority's use of the *Lemon* test:

Like some ghoul in a late-night horror movie that repeatedly sits up in its grave and shuffles abroad, after being repeatedly killed and buried, *Lemon* stalks our Establishment Clause jurisprudence once again, frightening the little children and school attorneys of Center Moriches Union Free School District. . . . Over the years, however, no fewer than five of the currently sitting Justices [Kennedy, O'Connor, Rehnquist, Scalia, and White] have, in their own opinions, personally driven pencils through the creature's heart (the author of today's opinion repeatedly), and a sixth [Thomas] has joined an opinion doing so.

Given the disagreements among the justices in this area, Court observers eagerly awaited the next public access case. It came two years later in *Rosenberger v. University of Virginia* (1995). Rosenberger presented a different twist to the access issue. Here the question was not access to public buildings, but instead access to public funding programs for student activities. In this dispute, Ronald Rosenberger, a member of a recognized organization of Christian students at the University of Virginia, objected to a denial of student activity funds to support the printing of the group's newsletter, *A Christian Perspective*. Other student groups received funding to support their publications, but the University's rules prohibited support for religious activities.

A closely divided Supreme Court ruled in favor of Rosenberger. Relying on decisions such as *Lamb's Chapel*, Justice Kennedy, writing for the Court, found the university's policies to be an unconstitutional form of "viewpoint discrimination." He explained that "it does not violate the Establishment Clause for a public university to

Ronald Rosenberger, right, cofounder of the religious newspaper *Wide Awake*, holds a copy outside the Supreme Court after oral arguments. At left is cofounder Robert Prince.

grant access to its facilities on a religion-neutral basis to a wide spectrum of student groups." Ruling otherwise, according to Kennedy, would require the university to scrutinize all student speech to ensure that it did not contain excessively religious content. Four justices dissented from this view, condemning the majority for approving for the first time direct government expenditures to support core religious activities.

Clearly, the *Rosenberger* decision did little to settle the disagreements within the Court over the governing standard to use in this line of Establishment Clause cases. Although many thought that the Court might use *Rosen-*

berger to overrule *Lemon,* that did not occur. In fact, the majority opinion largely avoided any direct mention of *Lemon,* although the opinion certainly rested on precedents based on that decision. The justices seem to have left this battle for another day.

The Court continued to take an accommodationist position on access issues, expanding its policy to include access to funding sources. As predicted, the newly appointed Ruth Bader Ginsburg and Stephen Breyer joined their more separationist colleagues, David Souter and John Paul Stevens. The 5–4 vote in *Rosenberger* indicates that the Court's position on these cases is fragile and that it has not finished its work in this area.

Teaching Religious Principles in Public Schools. Some public schools have sought to disseminate tenets held by particular religions by slanting the curriculum to favor religious views about secular subjects. The best-known and most enduring example is the way teachers address the origin of human life. Did humankind evolve, as scientists suggest (evolutionary theory), or did it come about as a result of some divine intervention, as various religions argue (creationism)?

This debate received an unusual amount of attention in 1925 when the American Civil Liberties Union—represented in court by Clarence Darrow—sponsored a legal challenge to a Tennessee law that made it a crime to teach evolutionary principles or any theory denigrating the biblical version of the creation. That case, popularized by the Scopes monkey trial, never made it to the Supreme Court *(see Box 4-7),* but two similar challenges did.

The first was *Epperson v. Arkansas,* a 1968 case in which the Court considered the constitutionality of a 1928 state law that was an adaptation of Tennessee's 1925 law. The Arkansas law made it a crime for any state university or public school instructor "to teach the theory or doctrine that mankind ascended or descended from a lower order of animals" or to "adopt or use . . . a textbook that teaches" evolutionary theory. The history of the law's adoption makes it clear that its purpose was to further religious beliefs about the beginning of life. For example, an advertisement placed in an Arkansas newspaper to drum up support for the act said: "The Bible or atheism, which? All atheists favor evolution. . . . Shall conscientious church members be forced to pay taxes to support teachers to teach evolution which will undermine the faith of their children?"

Epperson began in the mid-1960s when the school system in Little Rock, Arkansas, decided to adopt a biology book that contained a chapter on evolutionary theory. Susan Epperson, a biology teacher in a Little Rock high school, wanted to use the new book but was afraid—in light of the 1928 law—that she could face criminal prosecution if she did so. She asked the Arkansas courts to nullify the law, and, when the Arkansas Supreme Court turned down her request, she appealed her case to the U.S. Supreme Court.

Writing for a unanimous Court, Justice Fortas reversed the state supreme court's ruling. Relying heavily on *Everson* (the *Lemon* test had yet to be established), Fortas said, "The First Amendment mandates governmental neutrality between religion and religion, between religion and nonreligion." Under this standard the outcome was clear to the justices:

Arkansas' law cannot be defended as an act of religious neutrality. Arkansas did not seek to excise from the curricula of its schools . . . all discussion of the origin of man. The law's effort was confined to an attempt to blot out a particular theory because of its supposed conflict with the Biblical account, literally read. Plainly, the law is contrary to the mandate of the First . . . Amendment.

Despite the Court's clear statement about the constitutional violation posed by anti-evolutionary laws, some states devised other ways to teach creationism. In *Edwards v. Aguillard* (1987) the Court reviewed one of these attempts.[30] This case was decided after the *Lemon* test had been established and during the chief justiceship of William Rehnquist, who—along with Antonin Scalia—sought greater accommodation between church and state. As you read this case, consider the difference between the Court's opinion and the dissent filed by Scalia and joined by Rehnquist.

---

30. To hear oral arguments in this case, navigate to: *oyez.nwu.edu.*

BOX 4-7   THE SCOPES MONKEY TRIAL

"THE LAW IS A ASS," observed Charles Dickens's character, Mr. Bumble, in *Oliver Twist*. In 1925 many Americans, watching with amazement the circus-like proceedings of the dramatic Scopes trial in Tennessee, found themselves echoing the same sentiments. "Isn't it difficult to realize that a trial of this kind is possible in the twentieth century in the United States of America?" demanded the lawyer for the defense, the famed Clarence Darrow. In truth, the case appeared a vestigial survival from an earlier day when people were prosecuted for witchcraft or for offenses like imagining the king's death. Headlined in the press as the Great Monkey Trial, it pitted the Biblical version of creation against the teachings of Charles Darwin, and did so in a courtroom atmosphere more closely resembling that of a revival meeting than a hall of justice.

The defendant, John T. Scopes, was a twenty-four-year-old high school teacher in Dayton, Tennessee, who was prosecuted for teaching evolution in violation of a state statute that prohibited the teaching in any public school of "any theory that denies the story of the divine creation of man as taught in the Bible, and to teach instead that man has descended from a lower order of animals." Conducted in the heat of July, the trial was a parody of all that a legal proceeding should be. Dayton was ready for what it hoped would be the Waterloo of science. "One was hard put . . . ," an observer wrote, "to know whether Dayton was holding a camp meeting, a Chautauqua, a street fair, a carnival or a belated Fourth of July celebration. Literally, it was drunk on religious excitement."

The courtroom itself was decked with a large banner, exhorting everyone to "Read your Bible daily." Darrow finally got it removed by demanding equal space for a banner urging, "Read your Evolution." The stars of the trial were the lawyers: Clarence Darrow, perhaps the best known criminal lawyer in American history (Lincoln Steffens had called him "the attorney for the damned") representing Scopes and, indirectly, Darwin and evolution, and, against him, William Jennings Bryan, the Great Commoner, orator of the famed "Cross of Gold" speech in 1896, three-time candidate for President, and Secretary of State under Woodrow Wilson,

who had volunteered to direct the prosecution. Aging and sanctimonious, Bryan was the leading Fundamentalist of the day. "I am more interested in the Rock of Ages than in the age of rocks," he proclaimed.

At the trial's beginning, Darrow said later, "the judge . . . with great solemnity and all the dignity possible announced that Brother Twitchell would invoke the Divine blessing. This was new to me. I had practiced law for more that forty years, and had never before heard God called in to referee a court trial." Darrow's objection to the blessing was overruled, and each day's session began with a prayer by a different preacher. The high point of the trial saw Darrow put Bryan himself on the stand as an expert on "religion." The *New York Times* described this as the most amazing court scene in history, and out-of-state reporters and observers like the iconoclast H. L. Mencken had a field day conveying the incongruous proceedings to the nation. Bryan stuck doggedly to his insistence on the literal truth of the Bible, refusing, in Darrow's phrase, "to choose between his crude beliefs and the common intelligence of modern times."

In the end, the local population felt it won a righteous victory when the jury found Scopes guilty. But the judge imposed only a $100 fine, and, on appeal, the Tennessee Supreme Court reversed the decision on a technicality: the court, rather than the jury, had set the fine. The case itself was more dramatic than significant—unless it deserved remembrance as an example of the law at its worst. "I think," said Darrow during the trial, "this case will be remembered because it is the first case of this sort since we stopped trying people in America for witchcraft." On another plane, Darrow's withering examination during the trial went far to discredit Fundamentalist dogma. Though anti-evolution laws remained on the books in what Mencken referred to as "the Bible Belt" of the South, they were never again enforced. And in 1968, the U.S. Supreme Court finally struck down an Arkansas anti-evolution law, though admitting that by then "the statute is presently more of a curiosity than a vital fact of life."

SOURCE: Bernard Schwartz, *The Law in America* (New York: McGraw-Hill, 1974), 224. Reprinted by permission of the author.

Don Aguillard, assistant principal at Acadiana High School in Scott, Louisiana, filed suit against the state's creation science law in 1981. Six years later, in *Edwards v. Aguillard,* the Supreme Court found that law to be in violation of the Establishment Clause.

Edwards v. Aguillard

482 U.S. 578 (1987)
laws.findlaw.com/US/482/578.html
Vote: 7 (Blackmun, Brennan, Marshall, O'Connor, Powell,
    Stevens, White)
    2 (Rehnquist, Scalia)
Opinion of the Court: Brennan
Concurring opinions: Powell, White
Dissenting opinion: Scalia

After *Epperson,* organized interests—particularly religious groups—lobbied state legislatures to pass new laws. Louisiana enacted the Balanced Treatment for Creation-Science and Evolution-Science in Public School Instruction Act in 1981. This law differed from the one struck down in *Epperson* because it did not outlaw the teaching of evolution. Rather, it prohibited schools from teaching evolutionary principles unless theories of creationism also were taught.

The state and various organizations offered two major lines of argument in support of this legislation. One is that evolutionary theory is a religious tenet, and the reli-

gion is secular humanism. If evolution is taught then so should creationism, which has its origin in a literal reading of Genesis. In other words, public school teachers must give equal time to the two primary "religious" views of the origin of humankind. The second argument states that creationism is a science just like evolutionary theory and, therefore, deserves equal treatment in public school curricula.

Represented by the ACLU, Assistant Principal Don Aguillard and several teachers, parents, and religious groups challenged the act as a violation of the Establishment Clause. Attorneys and *amici* attacked the argument that creationism is a science. As *amicus curiae* National Academy of Sciences put it: "The explanatory power of a scientific hypothesis or theory is, in effect, the medium of exchange by which the value of a scientific theory is determined in the market place of ideas that constitutes the scientific community. Creationists do not compete in the marketplace, and creation-science does not offer scientific value." From this base, attorneys found it easy to reject notions of academic freedom and fairness, at least as it pertained to this debate. What the legislature had done, in the eyes of the ACLU, was to give equal time to a particular religion's view of the origins of humankind, which, the ACLU argued, violated the Establishment Clause.

JUSTICE BRENNAN delivered the opinion of the Court.

The Establishment Clause forbids the enactment of any law "respecting an establishment of religion." The Court has applied a three-pronged test to determine whether legislation comports with the Establishment Clause. First, the legislature must have adopted the law with a secular purpose. Second, the statute's principal or primary effect must be one that neither advances nor inhibits religion. Third, the statute must not result in an excessive entanglement of government with religion. State action violates the Establishment Clause if it fails to satisfy any of these prongs.

In this case, the Court must determine whether the Establishment Clause was violated in the special context of the public elementary and secondary school system. States and local school boards are generally afforded considerable discretion in operating public schools. . . .

The Court has been particularly vigilant in monitoring compliance with the Establishment Clause in elementary and secondary schools. Families entrust public schools with the education of their children, but condition their trust on the understanding that the classroom will not purposely be used to advance religious views that may conflict with the private beliefs of the student and his or her family. Students in such institutions are impressionable and their attendance is involuntary. The State exerts great authority and coercive power through mandatory attendance requirements, and because of the students' emulation of teachers as role models and the children's susceptibility to peer pressure. . . .

Therefore, in employing the three-pronged *Lemon* test, we must do so mindful of the particular concerns that arise in the context of public elementary and secondary schools. We now turn to the evaluation of the Act under the *Lemon* test.

Lemon's first prong focuses on the purpose that animated adoption of the Act. . . . If the law was enacted for the purpose of endorsing religion, "no consideration of the second or third criteria [of *Lemon*] is necessary." In this case, the petitioners have identified no clear secular purpose for the Louisiana Act.

True, the Act's stated purpose is to protect academic freedom. This phrase might, in common parlance, be understood as referring to enhancing the freedom of teachers to teach what they will. The Court of Appeals, however, correctly concluded that the Act was not designed to further that goal. We find no merit in the State's argument that the "legislature may not [have] use[d] the terms 'academic freedom' in the correct legal sense. They might have [had] in mind, instead, a basic concept of fairness; teaching all of the evidence." Even if "academic freedom" is read to mean "teaching all of the evidence" with respect to the origin of human beings, the Act does not further this purpose. The goal of providing a more comprehensive science curriculum is not furthered either by outlawing the teaching of evolution or by requiring the teaching of creation science.

While the Court is normally deferential to a State's articulation of a secular purpose, it is required that the statement of such purpose be sincere and not a sham. . . .

It is clear from the legislative history that the purpose of the legislative sponsor, Senator Bill Keith, was to narrow the science curriculum. During the legislative hearings, Senator Keith stated: "My preference would be that neither [creationism nor evolution] be taught." Such a ban on teaching does not promote—indeed, it undermines—the provision of a comprehensive scientific education.

It is equally clear that requiring schools to teach creation science with evolution does not advance academic freedom. The Act does not grant teachers a flexibility that they did not already possess to supplant the present science curriculum with the presentation of theories, besides evolution, about the origin of life. Indeed, the Court of Appeals found that no law prohibited Louisiana public schoolteachers from teaching any scientific theory. As the president of the Louisiana Science Teachers Association testified, "[a]ny scientific concept that's based on established fact can be included in our curriculum already, and no legislation allowing this is necessary." The Act provides Louisiana schoolteachers with no new authority. Thus the stated purpose is not furthered by it. . . .

Furthermore, the goal of basic "fairness" is hardly furthered by the Act's discriminatory preference for the teaching of creation science and against the teaching of evolution. While requiring that curriculum guides be developed for creation science, the Act says nothing of comparable guides for evolution. Similarly, research services are supplied for creation science but not for evolution. Only "creation scientists" can serve on the panel that supplies the resource services. The Act forbids school boards to discriminate against anyone who "chooses to be a creation-scientist" or to teach "creationism," but fails to protect those who choose to teach evolution or any other non-creation science theory, or who refuse to teach creation science.

If the Louisiana legislature's purpose was solely to maximize the comprehensiveness and effectiveness of science instruction, it would have encouraged the teaching of all scientific theories about the origins of humankind. But under the Act's requirements, teachers who were once free to teach any and all facets of this subject are now unable to do so. Moreover, the Act fails even to ensure that creation science will be taught, but instead requires the teaching of this theory only when the theory of evolution is taught. Thus we agree with the Court of Appeals' conclusion that the Act does not serve to protect academic freedom, but has the distinctly different purpose of discrediting "evolution by counterbalancing its teaching at every turn with the teaching of creation science.". . .

[W]e need not be blind in this case to the legislature's preeminent religious purpose in enacting this statute. There is a historic and contemporaneous link between the teachings of certain religious denominations and the teaching of evolution. It was this link that concerned the Court in *Epperson v. Arkansas* (1968), which also involved a facial challenge to a statute regulating the teaching of evolution. In that case, the Court reviewed an Arkansas statute that made it unlawful for an instructor to teach evolution or to use a textbook that referred to this scientific theory. Although the Arkansas anti-evolution law did not explicitly state its predominant religious purpose, the Court could not ignore that "[t]he statute was a product of the upsurge of 'fundamentalist' religious fervor" that has long viewed this particular scientific theory as contradicting the literal interpretation of the Bible. After reviewing the history of anti-evolution statutes, the Court determined that "there can be no doubt that the motivation for the [Arkansas] law was the same [as other anti-evolution statutes]: to suppress the teaching of a theory which, it was thought, 'denied' the divine creation of man." The Court found that there can be no legitimate state interest in protecting particular religions from scientific views "distasteful to them" and concluded "that the First Amendment does not permit the State to require that teaching and learning must be tailored to the principles or prohibitions of any religious sect or dogma."

These same historic and contemporaneous antagonisms between the teachings of certain religious denominations and the teaching of evolution are present in this case. The preeminent purpose of the Louisiana legislature was clearly to advance the religious viewpoint that a supernatural being created humankind. The term "creation science" was defined as embracing this particular religious doctrine by those responsible for the passage of the Creationism Act. Senator Keith's leading expert on creation science, Edward Boudreaux, testified at the legislative hearings that the theory of creation science included belief in the existence of a supernatural creator. Senator Keith also cited testimony from other experts to support the creation science view that "a creator [was] responsible for the universe and everything in it." The legislative history therefore reveals that the term "creation science," as contemplated by the legislature that adopted this Act, embodies the religious belief that a supernatural creator was responsible for the creation of humankind.

Furthermore, it is not happenstance that the legislature required the teaching of a theory that coincided with this religious view. The legislative history documents that the Act's primary purpose was to change the science curriculum of public schools in order to provide persuasive advantage to a particular religious doctrine that rejects the factual basis of evolution in its entirety. The sponsor of the Creationism Act, Senator Keith, explained during the legislative hearings that his disdain for the theory of evolution resulted from the support that evolution supplied to views contrary to his own religious beliefs. . . . The legislation therefore sought to alter the science curriculum to reflect endorsement of a religious view that is antagonistic to the theory of evolution.

In this case, the purpose of the Creationism Act was to restructure the science curriculum to conform with a particular religious viewpoint. Out of many possible science subjects taught in the public schools, the legislature chose to affect the teaching of the one scientific theory that historically has been opposed by certain religious sects. As in *Epperson*, the legislature passed the Act to give preference to those religious groups which have as one of their tenets the creation of humankind by a divine creator. The "overriding fact" that confronted the Court in *Epperson* was "that Arkansas' law selects from the body of knowledge a particular segment which it proscribes for the sole reason that it is deemed to conflict with . . . a particular interpretation of the Book of Genesis by a particular religious group." Similarly, the Creationism Act is designed *either* to promote the theory of creation science which embodies a particular religious tenet by requiring that creation science is taught whenever evolution is taught *or* to prohibit the teaching of a scientific theory disfavored by certain religious sects by forbidding the teaching of evolution when creation science is not also taught. The Establishment Clause, however, "forbids alike the preference of a religious doctrine or the prohibition of theory which is deemed antagonistic to a particular dogma." Because the primary purpose of the Creationism Act is to advance a particular religious belief, the Act endorses religion in violation of the First Amendment.

We do not imply that a legislature could never require that scientific critiques of prevailing scientific theories be taught. . . . But because the primary purpose of the Creationism Act is to endorse a particular religious doctrine, the Act furthers religion in violation of the Establishment Clause. . . .

The Louisiana Creationism Act advances a religious doctrine by requiring either the banishment of the theory of evolution from public school classrooms or the presentation of a religious viewpoint that rejects evolution in its entirety. The Act violates the Establishment Clause of the First Amendment because it seeks to employ the symbolic and financial support of government to achieve a religious purpose. The judgment of the Court of Appeals therefore is

Affirmed.

JUSTICE SCALIA, with whom THE CHIEF JUSTICE joins, dissenting.

Even if I agreed with the questionable premise that legislation can be invalidated under the Establishment Clause on the basis of its motivation alone, without regard to its effects, I would still find no justification for today's decision. The Louisiana legislators who passed the "Balanced Treatment for Creation-Science and Evolution-Science Act" (Balanced Treatment Act), each of whom had sworn to support the Constitution, were well aware of the potential Establishment Clause problems and considered that aspect of the legislation with great care. After seven hearings and several months of study, resulting in substantial revision of the original proposal, they approved the Act overwhelmingly and specifically articulated the secular purpose they meant it to serve. Although the record contains abundant evidence of the sincerity of that purpose (the only issue pertinent to this case), the Court today holds, essentially on the basis of "its visceral knowledge regarding what must have motivated the legislators," that the members of the Louisiana Legislature knowingly violated their oaths and then lied about it. I dissent. Had requirements of the Balanced Treatment Act that are not apparent on its face been clarified by an interpretation of the Louisiana Supreme Court, or by the manner of its implementation, the Act might well be found unconstitutional; but the question of its constitutionality cannot rightly be disposed of on the gallop, by impugning the motives of its supporters. . . .

It is important to stress that the purpose forbidden by *Lemon* is the purpose to "advance religion.". . . Our cases in no way imply that the Establishment Clause forbids legislators merely to act upon their religious convictions. We surely would not strike down a law providing money to feed the hungry or shelter the homeless if it could be demonstrated

that, but for the religious beliefs of the legislators, the funds would not have been approved. Notwithstanding the majority's implication to the contrary, we do not presume that the sole purpose of a law is to advance religion merely because it was supported strongly by organized religions or by adherents of particular faiths. . . . To do so would deprive religious men and women of their right to participate in the political process. Today's religious activism may give us the Balanced Treatment Act, but yesterday's resulted in the abolition of slavery, and tomorrow's may bring relief for famine victims. . . .

With the foregoing in mind, I now turn to the purposes underlying adoption of the Balanced Treatment Act.

We have relatively little information upon which to judge the motives of those who supported the Act. About the only direct evidence is the statute itself and transcripts of the seven committee hearings at which it was considered. . . . Nevertheless, there is ample evidence that the majority is wrong in holding that the Balanced Treatment Act is without secular purpose.

At the outset, it is important to note that the Balanced Treatment Act did not fly through the Louisiana Legislature on wings of fundamentalist religious fervor—which would be unlikely, in any event, since only a small minority of the State's citizens belong to fundamentalist religious denominations. The Act had its genesis (so to speak) in legislation introduced by Senator Bill Keith in June 1980. . . .

Before summarizing the testimony of Senator Keith and his supporters, I wish to make clear that I by no means intend to endorse its accuracy. But my views (and the views of this Court) about creation science and evolution are (or should be) beside the point. Our task is not to judge the debate about teaching the origins of life, but to ascertain what the members of the Louisiana Legislature believed. The vast majority of them voted to approve a bill which explicitly stated a secular purpose; what is crucial is not their *wisdom* in believing that purpose would be achieved by the bill, but their *sincerity* in believing it would be.

Most of the testimony in support of Senator Keith's bill came from the Senator himself and from scientists and educators he presented, many of whom enjoyed academic credentials that may have been regarded as quite impressive by members of the Louisiana Legislature. . . .

Senator Keith and his witnesses testified essentially as set forth in the following numbered paragraphs:

(1) There are two and only two scientific explanations for the beginning of life—evolution and creation science. . . .

(2) The body of scientific evidence supporting creation science is as strong as that supporting evolution. . . .

(3) Creation science is educationally valuable. Students exposed to it better understand the current state of scientific evidence about the origin of life. . . .

(4) Although creation science is educationally valuable and strictly scientific, it is now being censored from or misrepresented in the public schools. Evolution, in turn, is misrepresented as an absolute truth. . . .

(5) The censorship of creation science has at least two harmful effects. First, it deprives students of knowledge of one of the two scientific explanations for the origin of life and leads them to believe that evolution is proven fact; thus, their education suffers and they are wrongly taught that science has proved their religious beliefs false. Second, it violates the Establishment Clause. The United States Supreme Court has held that secular humanism is a religion. . . .

We have no way of knowing, of course, how many legislators believed the testimony of Senator Keith and his witnesses. But in the absence of evidence to the contrary, we have to assume that many of them did. Given that assumption, the Court today plainly errs in holding that the Louisiana Legislature passed the Balanced Treatment Act for exclusively religious purposes. . . .

I have to this point assumed the validity of the *Lemon* "purpose" test. In fact, however, I think the pessimistic evaluation that THE CHIEF JUSTICE made of the totality of *Lemon* is particularly applicable to the "purpose" prong: it is "a constitutional theory [that] has no basis in the history of the amendment it seeks to interpret, is difficult to apply and yields unprincipled results. . . ."

Our cases interpreting and applying the purpose test have made such a maze of the Establishment Clause that even the most conscientious governmental officials can only guess what motives will be held unconstitutional. We have said essentially the following: Government may not act with the purpose of advancing religion, except when forced to do so by the Free Exercise Clause (which is now and then); or when eliminating existing governmental hostility to religion (which exists sometimes); or even when merely accommodating governmentally uninhibited religious practices, ex-

cept that at some point (it is unclear where) intentional accommodation results in the fostering of religion, which is of course unconstitutional.

But the difficulty of knowing what vitiating purpose one is looking for is as nothing compared with the difficulty of knowing how or where to find it. For while it is possible to discern the objective "purpose" of a statute (i.e., the public good at which its provisions appear to be directed), or even the formal motivation for a statute where that is explicitly set forth (as it was, to no avail, here), discerning the subjective motivation of those enacting the statute is, to be honest, almost always an impossible task. The number of possible motivations, to begin with, is not binary, or indeed even finite. In the present case, for example, a particular legislator need not have voted for the Act either because he wanted to foster religion or because he wanted to improve education. He may have thought the bill would provide jobs for his district, or may have wanted to make amends with a faction of his party he had alienated on another vote, or he may have been a close friend of the bill's sponsor, or he may have been repaying a favor he owed the Majority Leader, or he may have hoped the Governor would appreciate his vote and make a fundraising appearance for him, or he may have been pressured to vote for a bill he disliked by a wealthy contributor . . . or, of course, he may have had (and very likely did have) a combination of some of the above and many other motivations. To look for *the sole purpose* of even a single legislator is probably to look for something that does not exist.

Putting that problem aside, however, where ought we to look for the individual legislator's purpose? We cannot of course assume that every member present (if, as is unlikely, we know who or even how many they were) agreed with the motivation expressed in a particular legislator's pre-enactment floor or committee statement. Quite obviously, "[w]hat motivates one legislator to make a speech about a statute is not necessarily what motivates scores of others to enact it.". . . Can we assume, then, that they all agree with the motivation expressed in the staff-prepared committee reports they might have read—even though we are unwilling to assume that they agreed with the motivation expressed in the very statute that they voted for? Should we consider post-enactment floor statements? Or post-enactment testimony from legislators, obtained expressly for the lawsuit? Should we consider media reports on the realities of the legislative bargaining? All of these sources, of course, are eminently manipulable. . . .

Given the many hazards involved in assessing the subjective intent of governmental decisionmakers, the first prong of *Lemon* is defensible, I think, only if the text of the Establishment Clause demands it. That is surely not the case. The Clause states that "Congress shall make no law respecting an establishment of religion." One could argue, I suppose, that any time Congress acts with the *intent* of advancing religion, it has enacted a "law respecting an establishment of religion"; but far from being an unavoidable reading, it is quite an unnatural one. . . . It is, in short, far from an inevitable reading of the Establishment Clause that it forbids all governmental action intended to advance religion; and if not inevitable, any reading with such untoward consequences must be wrong.

In the past we have attempted to justify our embarrassing Establishment Clause jurisprudence on the ground that it "sacrifices clarity and predictability for flexibility.". . . One commentator has aptly characterized this as "a euphemism . . . for . . . the absence of any principled rationale." I think it time that we sacrifice some "flexibility" for "clarity and predictability." Abandoning *Lemon's* purpose test—a test which exacerbates the tension between the Free Exercise and Establishment Clauses, has no basis in the language or history of the Amendment, and, as today's decision shows, has wonderfully flexible consequences—would be a good place to start.

Writing for the Court, Brennan had little trouble applying *Lemon* to rule against the state. The majority found that the law lacked a secular purpose; rather, its purpose was to "endorse a particular religious view." But Justice Scalia's dissent is a sign of things to come. Not only did Scalia adopt the state's argument that there is "ample uncontradicted testimony" to indicate that "creation science is a body of scientific knowledge rather than a revealed belief," but also he criticizes the purpose prong of *Lemon* as "indefensible" and as a main contributor to the Court's "embarrassing Establishment Clause jurisprudence." This may have been Scalia's first attack on *Lemon* but, as we know from *Lamb's Chapel*, it would not be his last. Since *Edwards v. Aguillard*, Scalia has become more adamant in his view that *Lemon* should be

discarded in favor of a standard that would bring more "clarity and predictability" to this area of the law.

Government Endorsement of Religion: Holiday Displays. In *Epperson* Justice Fortas wrote, "The First Amendment mandates governmental neutrality between religion and religion, between religion and nonreligion." His statement provides a theoretical way to think about the relationship between church and state, but as citizens we are confronted with daily reminders that the United States does not follow Fortas's words. For example, all the U.S. currency in your pocket carries the words: "In God We Trust." Does that motto represent government endorsement of religion over nonreligion? What about the national Christmas tree? It stands on the grounds of the White House, the home of the head of our secular nation. Yet the tree is a symbol associated with Christianity. Its annual appearance seems to violate Fortas's principle because it represents government endorsement of one religion over another. In fact, the presence (and general acceptance) of religious mottoes and symbols supports Justice Douglas's classic statement, "We are a religious people whose institutions presuppose a Supreme Being."

That Americans "are a religious people," the majority of whom accept "In God We Trust" on currency or even a national Christmas tree, however, should not be taken to mean that all symbolic endorsements of religion are legally acceptable. The problem is separating the permissible from the impermissible, and this issue has not been easy for the Court to resolve, as its cases dealing with holiday displays indicate.

When private store owners place religious symbols in their windows, no constitutional questions arise. But when governments pay to put up such symbols or allow their property to be used for the placement of religious displays, questions arise concerning the separation of church and state.

The Court first considered these questions in 1984 in *Lynch v. Donnelly,* which involved the constitutionality of a state-sponsored Christmas display of a crèche (nativity scene). For more than forty years, the city of Pawtucket, Rhode Island, and its Retail Merchants Association erected a Christmas display in a park owned by a nonprofit organization. The display included a Santa Claus house, reindeer, a Christmas tree, a clown, colored lights, a Season's Greetings banner, and a crèche with the Christ child, Mary, and Joseph, angels, animals, and so forth. In 1973 the city spent $1,365 for a new crèche, and it cost $20 to set it up and take it down each year. Believing that these annual expenditures for the crèche constituted a violation of the Establishment Clause, the state Civil Liberties Union brought suit against the city. City officials and area business people countered that the Christmas display had a secular purpose: to attract customers to the city's downtown shopping area.

Writing for a five-person majority, Chief Justice Burger found that the display was not an impermissible breach of the Establishment Clause. In one of his more strongly worded accommodationist opinions, he pointed to many examples indicating "an unbroken history of official acknowledgment by all three branches of government of the role of religion in American life": executive orders proclaiming Christmas and Thanksgiving as national holidays, "In God We Trust" on currency, publicly supported art galleries full of religious paintings. This examination led him to conclude that

the crèche is identified with one religious faith. . . . [But] to forbid the use of this one passive symbol—the crèche—at the very time people are taking note of the season with Christmas hymns and carols in public schools and other public places, and while the Congress and legislatures open session with prayers by paid chaplains, would be a stilted overreaction contrary to our history and to our holdings. If the presence of the crèche violates the Establishment Clause, a host of other forms of taking official note of Christmas, and our religious heritage, are equally offensive to the Constitution.

In short, Burger implied that Christmas was so much a part of our heritage that it came close to representing a national, nonsectarian celebration, rather than a religious holiday.

Burger's opinion is interesting because, although he applied *Lemon* to find that there was a secular purpose for the crèche, he also said, "We have repeatedly emphasized our unwillingness to be confined to any single test." This modifying statement did not go unnoticed; it was, after all, the first time a majority opinion hinted at the possible demise of *Lemon*.

In dissent, Brennan (joined by Marshall, Blackmun, and Stevens) wrote, "The Court's less-than-vigorous application of the *Lemon* test suggests that its commitment to those standards may only be superficial." He then went on to assert that applying a more vigorous version of *Lemon* to the case leads to the conclusion that the crèche's inclusion in the display "does not reflect a clearly secular purpose."

The dissenters wanted the Court to apply *Lemon* strictly, but O'Connor, in a concurring opinion, suggested a new way to frame the three-pronged standard. She proposed to focus *Lemon*'s purpose prong on "whether the government's actual purpose is to endorse or disapprove religions" and the effect prong on "whether, irrespective of government's actual purpose, the practice under review in fact conveys a message of endorsement or disapproval." Invocation of this endorsement standard led her to conclude that the city did not "intend to convey any message of endorsement of Christianity or disapproval of non-Christian religions." She based this conclusion mainly on the fact that the crèche was a small part of a larger holiday display. "Celebration of public holidays," O'Connor reasoned, "which have cultural significance even if they also have religious aspects, is a legitimate secular purpose."

Justice Blackmun invoked this endorsement standard to resolve *County of Allegheny v. ACLU* (1989), the next major "display" case. *County of Allegheny* involved the constitutionality of two holiday displays erected every year in downtown Pittsburgh, Pennsylvania. The first is a crèche that belongs to a Roman Catholic group, the Holy Name Society. Beginning with the Christmas season of 1981, the city allowed the society to place the crèche on the grand staircase of the county courthouse, which is, by all accounts, the "main," "most beautiful," and "most public" part of the courthouse. The second challenged display was a Hanukkah menorah located outside of the City-County Building, where the mayor and other city officials have their offices. For much of its history, the city erected only a Christmas tree outside this building, but, beginning in the 1980s, it began to include the menorah. By 1986 the entire display included a forty-five-foot Christmas tree complete with lights and ornaments

As part of its holiday decorations, Allegheny County, Pennsylvania, erected on public property a nativity scene and a combined Christmas tree and menorah display. In *County of Allegheny v. ACLU* (1989) the Supreme Court ruled that the crèche violated the separation of church and state principle, but that the combined exhibit did not.

and an eighteen-foot Hanukkah menorah, owned by a Jewish group, but stored and erected by the city.

Do these displays violate the Establishment Clause? This question gave the Court a good deal of trouble: a majority of justices could not agree over the appropriate standard by which to answer it. In the end, the Court issued a judgment written by Justice Blackmun.

Blackmun began by outlining the approach he would take to the case:

Our . . . decisions [subsequent to *Lemon*] further have refined the definition of governmental action that unconstitutionally advances religion. In recent years, we have paid particularly close attention to whether the challenged governmental practice either has the purpose or effect of "endorsing" religion, a concern that has long had a place in our Establishment Clause jurisprudence.

Applying these principles to the case at hand, Blackmun set out the Court's task: to determine whether the display of the crèche and the menorah, in their respective "particular physical settings," has the effect of endorsing or disapproving religious beliefs. In the end, he found that "the display of the crèche in the County Courthouse has this unconstitutional effect." His reason was that this crèche, unlike the one at issue in *Lynch*, did not contain

"objects of attention" (such as Santa's house and his reindeer) that were separate from the crèche and had their specific visual story to tell. Rather the crèche at issue here "stands alone: it is the single element of the display on the Grand Staircase." In Blackmun's mind, "by permitting the 'display of the crèche in this particular physical setting,' the county sends an unmistakable message that it supports and promotes the Christian praise to God."

The display of the menorah in front of the City-County Building, however, did not—in Blackmun's view—have this unconstitutional effect. Blackmun offered several reasons why. One is that the "the menorah here stands next to a Christmas tree and a sign saluting liberty. . . . The necessary result of placing a menorah next to a Christmas tree is to create an 'overall holiday setting' that represents both Christmas and Chanukah—two holidays, not one." Accordingly, Blackmun found that "it is not 'sufficiently likely' that residents of Pittsburgh will perceive the combined display of the tree, the sign, and the menorah as an 'endorsement' or 'disapproval . . . of their individual religious choices.'"

Throughout this chapter, we have noted that scholars criticize the Court for reaching inconsistent, puzzling, and even amusing decisions. *County of Allegheny* provides ammunition for these critics. Because Blackmun's judgment centers on the kinds of objects, in juxtaposition to one another, that holiday displays may or may not contain, it has been the source of some ridicule. As a 1993 newspaper article put it:

Pity the public school principal in December. Between Hanukkah, Christmas and Kwanzaa, this long last month lays a minefield of grand proportions for educators trying to acknowledge the holidays without bridging the separation of church and state. Every decoration is fraught with peril. Every lesson and every song must pass the "does not promote religion" test. Red and green cookies? Maybe. "A Christmas Carol?" Maybe. "Silent Night?" Definitely not.[31]

County of Allegheny also sends mixed signals about the appropriate legal standards to adjudicate religious establishment claims. Blackmun's judgment adopted O'Connor's endorsement standard from her concurrence in *Lynch.* But this standard does not end reliance on *Lemon;* it merely gives another way to apply parts of it *(see Table 4-4).* In an opinion concurring in judgment in part and dissenting in part, Justice Kennedy (joined by Rehnquist, White, and Scalia) attacked the endorsement standard as "an unwelcome addition to our tangled Establishment Clause jurisprudence." In its (and *Lemon's*) place, he would adopt a "coercion" standard. Under this approach, the justices would prohibit government activities only if they "coerce anyone to support or participate in any religion" or if they "give direct benefits to religion in such a degree" that it in fact "established a religion . . . or tends to do so." Applying this standard to holiday displays, Kennedy found the crèche and the menorah permissible under the Establishment Clause because neither fosters even subtle coercion.

Since *County of Allegheny,* has the Court provided any indication as to which of these approaches may move to the forefront? The answer is no. In its most recent decision in this area, *Capitol Square Review Board v. Pinette* (1995), the justices held that Ohio violated the free speech rights of the Ku Klux Klan when it denied the KKK the right to erect a cross—during the Christmas season—in a state-owned park in Columbus. However,

the justices could not agree on an appropriate standard of review. O'Connor (joined by Souter and Breyer) continued to press her endorsement standard; Scalia (joined by Rehnquist, Thomas, and Kennedy) rejected O'Connor's approach and seemed to advocate a rule that would hold all religious expression in public places, such as state-owned parks, permissible under the Establishment Clause; and, finally, the dissenters, Stevens and Ginsburg, took a somewhat different tack. They argued that a passerby would not know that the cross was the KKK's private expression and, instead, would "identify the state either as the messenger, or, at the very least, as the one who has endorsed the [private religious] message."

Prayer in School. Throughout this section, we have seen the Court change the standards by which it adjudicates religious establishment claims, reason through cases in seemingly inconsistent ways, divide over the resolution of major issues, and cause public consternation and debate. The subject of prayer magnifies all of these observations. Moreover, prayer is a topic that has occupied part of the Court's agenda since the 1960s. It therefore provides us with an excellent vehicle by which to reexamine and summarize what we have learned about how the Court has approached establishment questions.

Throughout most of the nation's history, almost all public schools engaged in religious practices of some kind: they may have held devotional services, distributed Bibles, or taught about religion. Particularly prevalent was prayer in school. As Table 4-6 indicates, in the 1960s the Bible was read regularly in most public schools in the South and East; in other schools, students recited state-

TABLE 4-6 Incidence of Bible Reading in Public School by Region, 1960 and 1966

Region	Percentage of Schools Reporting Bible Reading	
	1960	1966
East	67.6	4.3
Midwest	18.3	5.2
South	76.8	49.5
West	11.0	2.3

SOURCE: Frank J. Sorauf, *The Wall of Separation* (Princeton: Princeton University Press, 1976), 297.

31. Kimberly J. McLarin, "Holiday Dilemma at Schools: Is That a Legal Decoration?" *New York Times,* December 16, 1993, 1, 15.

written prayers. Separationist groups believed that these practices violated the Establishment Clause and set out to persuade the Court to eradicate them. Their initial suit, *Engel v. Vitale* (1962), challenged a New York requirement that teachers each morning lead public school children in reciting a prayer written by the state's board of regents: "Almighty God, we acknowledge our dependence upon Thee, and we beg Thy blessings upon us, our parents, our teachers and our country." New York representatives argued that this prayer was innocuous and purposefully drafted so that it would not favor one religion over another. They also argued that recitation was voluntary: students who did not want to participate could remain silent or leave the room. The New York Civil Liberties Union, representing parents from a Long Island school district, claimed the religious neutrality of the prayer and the voluntary aspect were irrelevant. What mattered was that the state had written it and, therefore, it violated the Establishment Clause.

Writing for the Court, Justice Black adopted the separationist argument:

We think the constitutional prohibition against laws respecting the establishment of religion must at least mean that in this country it is no part of the business of government to compose official prayers for any group of the American people to recite as a part of a religious program carried out by the government.

Only Justice Stewart dissented from the Court's opinion. After citing many examples of congressional approval of religion, including the legislation adding the words "In God We Trust" on currency, he quoted Justice Douglas's statement, written a decade before in the released-time case: "We are a religious people whose institutions presuppose a Supreme Being." What New York "has done has been to recognize and to follow the deeply entrenched and highly cherished spiritual traditions of our Nation," he said.

Despite the majority's strong words, the decision was not a complete victory for separationists. The Court failed to enunciate a strict legal definition of establishment (it announced no standard), and it dealt with only one aspect of prayer in school—state-written prayers—and not the more widespread practice of Bible readings. Moreover, *Engel* generated a tremendous public back-

lash. Less than 20 percent of the public supported the Court's decision. Church leaders condemned it, and Congress considered constitutional amendments to overturn it. Most of the justices described themselves as "surprised and pained" by the negative reaction. Chief Justice Warren later wrote: "I vividly remember one bold newspaper headline, 'Court outlaws God.' Many religious leaders in this same spirit condemned the Court." Justice Clark defended the Court's opinion in a public address: "Here was a state-written prayer circulated by the school district to state-employed teachers with instructions to have their pupils recite it. [The Constitution] provides that both state and Federal governments shall take no part respecting the establishment of religion. . . . 'No' means 'No.' That was all the Court decided."[32]

With all this uproar, it is no wonder that separationist groups were concerned when the Court agreed to hear arguments in *School District of Abington Township v. Schempp*,[33] and its companion case, *Murray v. Curlett*, appeals involving the more prevalent practice of Bible readings in public schools. Would the justices cave in to public pressure and reverse their stance in *Engel*?

School District of Abington Township v. Schempp

374 U.S. 203 (1963)
laws.findlaw.com/US/374/203.html
Vote: 8 (Black, Brennan, Clark, Douglas, Goldberg, Harlan, Warren, White)
     1 (Stewart)
Opinion of the Court: Clark
Concurring opinions: Brennan, Douglas, Goldberg
Dissenting opinion: Stewart

Successful in persuading the Court to strike down the recitation of state-written prayers in school, separationist groups came back to challenge more common occurrences—readings from the Bible and the recitation of the Lord's Prayer—at the beginning of each day. Although

32. Quotes from the justices come from Bernard Schwartz, *Super Chief* (New York: New York University Press, 1983), 441–442.
33. To hear oral arguments in this case, navigate to: *oyez.nwu.edu.*

these practices were most prevalent in the South, separationists decided to avoid litigating in that region, fearing a negative outcome. Instead, they found a Pennsylvania family that was willing to serve as plaintiffs.

The Schempps were not atheists; in fact, they were members of a Unitarian church, where they regularly attended services. But they did not want their children, Roger and Donna, to engage in Bible reading at their public school. To them "specific religious doctrines purveyed by a literal reading of the Bible" were not in accord with their particular religious beliefs. Pennsylvania law, however, mandated that "at least ten verses from the Holy Bible shall be read, without comment, at the opening of each public school on each school day." Following the law, Roger and Donna's school, Abington High, held opening exercises each morning while the students were in their homerooms. The required number of Bible verses were read over the school's public address system, and the reading was followed by a recitation of the Lord's Prayer, during which students stood and repeated the prayer in unison. Those students whose parents did not want them to participate could, under the Pennsylvania law, leave the room.

Edward Schempp decided to challenge the practice. The reasons he gave were that teachers and classmates would label Donna and Roger as "oddballs," or "atheists," a term with "very bad" connotations to Schempp; Roger and Donna would miss hearing morning announcements that were read after the religious readings; and other students, seeing Donna and Roger in the halls, would think they were being punished for "bad conduct."

Separationist groups presented Schempp's reasons to the trial court. They also brought in religious leaders and other religious experts to support the claim that Bible readings inherently favored some religions over others and violated principles of religious establishment. Attorneys for the school board, on the other hand, sought to frame the case in moral rather than religious terms. They also found their own expert witnesses to testify that the Bible was nonsectarian. By the time the case reached the Supreme Court, it was quite clear that they were asking the justices to overrule *Engel.*

MR. JUSTICE CLARK delivered the opinion of the Court.

[T]his Court has rejected unequivocally the contention that the Establishment Clause forbids only governmental preference of one religion over another. Almost 20 years ago in *Everson* the Court said that "[n]either a state nor the Federal Government can set up a church. Neither can pass laws which aid one religion, aid all religions, or prefer one religion over another.". . .

. . . In short, the Court held that the Amendment

"requires the state to be a neutral in its relations with groups of religious believers and non-believers; it does not require the state to be their adversary. State power is no more to be used so as to handicap religions than it is to favor them."

. . . The wholesome "neutrality" of which this Court's cases speak . . . stems from a recognition of the teachings of history that powerful sects or groups might bring about a fusion of governmental and religious functions or a concert or dependency of one upon the other to the end that official support of the State or Federal Government would be placed behind the tenets of one or of all orthodoxies. This the Establishment Clause prohibits. And a further reason for neutrality is found in the Free Exercise Clause, which recognizes the value of religious training, teaching and observance and, more particularly, the right of every person to freely choose his own course with reference thereto, free of any compulsion from the state. This the Free Exercise Clause guarantees. Thus, as we have seen, the two clauses may overlap. As we have indicated, the Establishment Clause has been directly considered by this Court eight times in the past score of years and, with only one Justice dissenting on the point, it has consistently held that the clause withdrew all legislative power respecting religious belief or the expression thereof. The test may be stated as follows: what are the purpose and the primary effect of the enactment? If either is the advancement or inhibition of religion then the enactment exceeds the scope of legislative power as circumscribed by the Constitution. That is to say that to withstand the strictures of the Establishment Clause there must be a secular legislative purpose and a primary effect that neither advances nor inhibits religion. *Everson v. Board of Education.* . . . The Free Exercise Clause, likewise considered many times here, withdraws from legislative power, state and federal, the exertion of any restraint on the free exercise of religion. Its purpose is to secure religious liberty in the individual by prohibiting any invasions thereof by civil authority. Hence it is necessary in a free exercise case for one to show the coercive effect of the enactment as it operates against him in the practice of his religion. The distinction between the two clauses is apparent—a violation of the Free Exercise Clause is predicated on coercion while the Establishment Clause violation need not be so attended.

Applying the Establishment Clause principles to the cases at bar we find that the States are requiring the selection and reading at the opening of the school day of verses from the Holy Bible and the recitation of the Lord's Prayer by the students in unison. These exercises are prescribed as part of the curricular activities of students who are required by law to attend school. They are held in the school buildings under the supervision and with the participation of teachers employed in those schools. None of these factors, other than compulsory school attendance, was present in the program upheld in *Zorach v. Clauson.* The trial court in [*Schempp*] has found that such an opening exercise is a religious ceremony and was intended by the State to be so. We agree with the trial court's finding as to the religious character of the exercises. Given that finding, the exercises and the law requiring them are in violation of the Establishment Clause. . . .

The conclusion follows that . . . the [law] require[s] religious exercises and such exercises are being conducted in direct violation of the rights of the appellees and petitioners. Nor are these required exercises mitigated by the fact that individual students may absent themselves upon parental request, for that fact furnishes no defense to a claim of unconstitutionality under the Establishment Clause. Further, it is no defense to urge that the religious practices here may be relatively minor encroachments on the First Amendment. The breach of neutrality that is today a trickling stream may all too soon become a raging torrent and, in the words of Madison, "it is proper to take alarm at the first experiment on our liberties."

It is insisted that unless these religious exercises are permitted a "religion of secularism" is established in the schools. We agree of course that the State may not establish a "religion of secularism" in the sense of affirmatively opposing or showing hostility to religion, thus "preferring those who believe in no religion over those who do believe." . . . We do not agree, however, that this decision in

any sense has that effect. In addition, it might well be said that one's education is not complete without a study of comparative religion or the history of religion and its relationship to the advancement of civilization. It certainly may be said that the Bible is worthy of study for its literary and historic qualities. Nothing we have said here indicates that such study of the Bible or of religion, when presented objectively as part of a secular program of education, may not be effected consistently with the First Amendment. But the exercises here do not fall into those categories. They are religious exercises, required by the States in violation of the command of the First Amendment that the Government maintain strict neutrality, neither aiding nor opposing religion.

Finally, we cannot accept that the concept of neutrality, which does not permit a State to require a religious exercise even with the consent of the majority of those affected, collides with the majority's right to free exercise of religion. While the Free Exercise Clause clearly prohibits the use of state action to deny the rights of free exercise to anyone, it has never meant that a majority could use the machinery of the State to practice its beliefs. . . .

The place of religion in our society is an exalted one, achieved through a long tradition of reliance on the home, the church and the inviolable citadel of the individual heart and mind. We have come to recognize through bitter experience that it is not within the power of government to invade that citadel, whether its purpose or effect be to aid or oppose, to advance or retard. In the relationship between man and religion, the State is firmly committed to a position of neutrality. Though the application of that rule requires interpretation of a delicate sort, the rule itself is clearly and concisely stated in the words of the First Amendment. Applying that rule to the facts of these cases, we affirm the judgment in [*Schempp*]. In [*Murray*] the judgment is reversed and the cause remanded to the Maryland Court of Appeals for further proceedings consistent with this opinion.

It is so ordered.

MR. JUSTICE DOUGLAS, concurring.

These regimes violate the Establishment Clause in two different ways. In each case, the State is conducting a religious exercise; and, as the Court holds, that cannot be done without violating the "neutrality" required of the State by the balance of power between individual, church and state that has been struck by the First Amendment. But the Establishment Clause is not limited to precluding the State itself from conducting religious exercises. It also forbids the State to employ its facilities or funds in a way that gives any church, or all churches, greater strength in our society than it would have by relying on its members alone. Thus, the present regimes must fall under that clause for the additional reason that public funds, though small in amount, are being used to promote a religious exercise. Through the mechanism of the State, all of the people are being required to finance a religious exercise that only some of the people want and that violates the sensibilities of others.

MR. JUSTICE BRENNAN, concurring.

I join fully in the opinion and the judgment of the Court. I see no escape from the conclusion that the exercises called in question in these two cases violate the constitutional mandate. The reasons we gave only last Term in *Engel v. Vitale* for finding in the New York Regents' prayer an impermissible establishment of religion compel the same judgment of the practices at bar. The involvement of the secular with the religious is no less intimate here; and it is constitutionally irrelevant that the State has not composed the material for the inspirational exercises presently involved. It should be unnecessary to observe that our holding does not declare that the First Amendment manifests hostility to the practice or teaching of religion, but only applies prohibitions incorporated in the Bill of Rights in recognition of historic needs shared by Church and State alike. While it is my view that not every involvement of religion in public life is unconstitutional, I consider the exercises at bar a form of involvement which clearly violates the Establishment Clause.

MR. JUSTICE GOLDBERG, with whom MR. JUSTICE HARLAN joins, concurring.

The practices here involved do not fall within any sensible or acceptable concept of compelled or permitted accommodation, and involve the state so significantly and directly in the realm of the sectarian as to give rise to those very divisive influences and inhibitions of freedom which both religion clauses of the First Amendment preclude. The state has ordained and has utilized its facilities to en-

gage in unmistakably religious exercises—the devotional reading and recitation of the Holy Bible—in a manner having substantial and significant import and impact. That it has selected, rather than written, a particular devotional liturgy seems to me without constitutional import. The pervasive religiosity and direct governmental involvement inhering in the prescription of prayer and Bible reading in the public schools, during and as part of the curricular day, involving young impressionable children whose school attendance is statutorily compelled, and utilizing the prestige, power, and influence of school administration, staff, and authority, cannot realistically be termed simply accommodation, and must fall within the interdiction of the First Amendment.

MR. JUSTICE STEWART, dissenting.

I think the records in the two cases before us are so fundamentally deficient as to make impossible an informed or responsible determination of the constitutional issues presented. Specifically, I cannot agree that on these records we can say that the Establishment Clause has necessarily been violated. But I think there exist serious questions under both that provision and the Free Exercise Clause . . . which require the remand of these cases for the taking of additional evidence. . . .

. . . For there is involved in these cases a substantial free exercise claim on the part of those who affirmatively desire to have their children's school day open with the reading of passages from the Bible. . . .

It might . . . be argued that parents who want their children exposed to religious influences can adequately fulfill that wish off school property and outside school time. With all its surface persuasiveness, however, this argument seriously misconceives the basic constitutional justification for permitting the exercises at issue in these cases. For a compulsory state educational system so structures a child's life that if religious exercises are held to be an impermissible activity in schools, religion is placed at an artificial and state-created disadvantage. Viewed in this light, permission of such exercises for those who want them is necessary if the schools are truly to be neutral in the matter of religion. And a refusal to permit religious exercises thus is seen, not as the realization of state neutrality, but rather as the establishment of a religion of secularism, or at the least, as government support of the beliefs of those who think that religious exercises should be conducted only in private. . . .

. . . [I]t is important to stress that, strictly speaking, what is at issue here is a privilege rather than a right. In other words, the question presented is not whether exercises such as those at issue here are constitutionally compelled, but rather whether they are constitutionally invalid. And that issue, in my view, turns on the question of coercion.

It is clear that the dangers of coercion involved in the holding of religious exercises in a schoolroom differ qualitatively from those presented by the use of similar exercises or affirmations in ceremonies attended by adults. Even as to children, however, the duty laid upon government in connection with religious exercises in the public schools is that of refraining from so structuring the school environment as to put any kind of pressure on a child to participate in those exercises; it is not that of providing an atmosphere in which children are kept scrupulously insulated from any awareness that some of their fellows may want to open the school day with prayer, or of the fact that there exist in our pluralistic society differences of religious belief. . . .

Viewed in this light, it seems to me clear that the records in both of the cases before us are wholly inadequate to support an informed or responsible decision. Both cases involve provisions which explicitly permit any student who wishes, to be excused from participation in the exercises. There is no evidence . . . as to whether there would exist any coercion of any kind upon a student who did not want to participate. . . . In the *Schempp* case the record shows no more than a subjective prophecy by a parent of what he thought would happen if a request were made to be excused from participation in the exercises under the amended statute. No such request was ever made, and there is no evidence whatever as to what might or would actually happen, nor of what administrative arrangements the school actually might or could make to free from pressure of any kind those who do not want to participate in the exercises. . . .

What our Constitution indispensably protects is the freedom of each of us, be he Jew or Agnostic, Christian or Atheist, Buddhist or Freethinker, to believe or disbelieve, to worship or not worship, to pray or keep silent, according to his own conscience, uncoerced and unrestrained by government. It is conceivable that these school boards, or even all school boards, might eventually find it impossible to administer a system of religious exercises during school hours

in such a way as to meet this constitutional standard—in such a way as completely to free from any kind of official coercion those who do not affirmatively want to participate. But I think we must not assume that school boards so lack the qualities of inventiveness and good will as to make impossible the achievement of that goal.

I would remand both cases for further hearings.

These two cases, following on the heels of *Engel v. Vitale*, set firmly in American jurisprudence the principle that state-sponsored prayers in public schools violate the Establishment Clause. In addition, these decisions set out a standard of law, a two-pronged test that served as the forerunner of *Lemon*. But take note of Justice Stewart's dissent: his coercion approach provided fodder for justices of the Rehnquist Court—particularly Anthony Kennedy—who would later attempt to etch some version of it into law. In 1963 it represented the position of one justice.

However, if the justices thought that *Abington* would quell the prayer-in-school controversy they had ignited in *Engel*, they could not have been more wrong. Opinion polls taken after *Abington* indicated that only 24 percent of the public supported the Court's decision. That number remained relatively stable; support has never surpassed the 50 percent mark.[34] Given the public antipathy for *Engel* and *Abington*, it is not surprising to find widespread noncompliance with the Court's decisions. Note the 1966 data in Table 4-6 showing that almost half of the schools in the South continued to allow Bible readings, despite the Court's decision in *Abington*.

The American public's support for prayer in school and the determination of many local school systems to maintain voluntary prayer programs have run contrary to the general trend among nations of the world (*see Box 4-9*). While other countries and their constitutional courts have grappled with the school prayer problem, the overwhelming majority have eliminated prayer programs from public education.

In the United States, in spite of the Court's rulings in *Engel*, *Abington*, and *Murray*, the school prayer issue was

34. Harold W. Stanley and Richard G. Niemi, *Vital Statistics on American Politics*, 6th ed. (Washington, D.C.: Congressional Quarterly, 1998).

BOX 4-8 AFTERMATH . . . MADALYN MURRAY O'HAIR

IN 1963 the U.S. Supreme Court, in *School District of Abington Township v. Schempp* and its companion case, *Murray v. Curlett*, declared Bible reading and the recitation of the Lord's Prayer in public schools to be unconstitutional. *Murray v. Curlett* was a lawsuit brought by Madalyn Murray on behalf of her son William, then a fourteen-year-old student in Baltimore. Madalyn Murray O'Hair, as she became known after her marriage to Richard O'Hair, was no stranger to controversy or the courts. Dubbed by *Life* magazine in 1964 "the most hated woman in America," O'Hair initiated several lawsuits based on First Amendment claims, including legal actions to have the words "In God We Trust" removed from U.S. currency and to prohibit astronauts from praying in space. She described the Bible as "nauseating, historically inaccurate and replete with the ravings of madmen." O'Hair, an abrasive, profane woman, attempted to defect to the Soviet Union in 1960 and later became associated with Larry Flynt, the publisher of *Hustler* magazine. But she is probably best known as the founder of American Atheists, Inc., a national organization devoted to advancing the interests of atheists, headquartered in Austin, Texas.

On August 28, 1995, O'Hair, age seventy-six and in declining health, mysteriously vanished, along with her second son, Jon Murray, and her granddaughter Robin. Nothing appeared missing from their house—clothes were in the closet and food was on the table. Many thought that O'Hair and her family were fleeing from her organization's declining membership and troubled financial condition. Speculation was fueled by evidence that more than $500,000 of American Atheist funds, most of it in gold coins, was missing and allegations that O'Hair had hidden organization funds in New Zealand bank accounts.

Law enforcement authorities, however, were convinced that O'Hair and the others were victims of foul play. The chief suspects were David Waters, Gary Karr, and Danny Fry. Waters was a former American Atheist employee. He had pleaded guilty to stealing $54,000 from the organization and had a grudge against O'Hair. Karr and Fry were associates of Waters, and all three had criminal records. Prosecutors believed that the three suspects kidnapped O'Hair and her family and held them hostage for a month in San Antonio while extorting $500,000 from them. The authorities think the hostages were then killed and dismembered in a North Austin storage unit before their remains were buried.

Fry was removed from the suspect list when DNA tests revealed that a body discovered on the banks of the Trinity River in Texas five weeks after Madalyn O'Hair's disappearance was his. The head and hands had been severed in an obvious attempt to block identification. Waters and Karr remain under investigation, but, because the O'Hair family bodies have never been found, murder charges are difficult to prove. In 2000 Karr was convicted on four counts of extorting money from O'Hair, but for lack of evidence he was acquitted on charges of kidnapping the family. Waters is serving a sixty-year sentence for probation and firearms violations.

Another twist to the O'Hair story involves William Murray. After being treated for alcoholism, Murray publicly rejected atheism in May 1980 and became a Southern Baptist. Later as a Christian activist, he chaired Religious Coalition USA, a conservative religious organization that supports, among other things, the reintroduction of prayer in the public schools. As might be expected, Murray and his mother had been estranged for many years.

SOURCES: *Arizona Republic*, May 15, 2000; *Atlanta Journal-Constitution*, June 3, 2000; *Houston Chronicle*, December 29, 1996, March 3, 2000; *Washington Post*, March 28, 1999, August 16–17, 1999; *Buffalo News*, April 25, 1999; *San Diego Union-Tribune*, October 22, 1999; *New York Times*, December 8, 1999.

far from settled. Responding to public opposition to these decisions, over the years members of Congress have introduced close to 150 constitutional amendments to return prayer to the nation's classrooms. None was successful. The last significant attempt to secure congressional passage occurred in 1984 when the Senate voted on the following amendment proposed by President Ronald Reagan:

Nothing in this Constitution shall be construed to prohibit individual or group prayer in public schools or other public institutions. No person shall be required by the United States or any state to participate in prayer.

Fifty-six senators voted to recommend Reagan's proposed amendment, but this number fell short of the two-thirds majority required to refer an amendment proposal to the states for ratification.

Once the proposal was defeated, all eyes turned to the Burger Court, which had given signs of being sympathetic to the use of prayer in public places. This signal occurred in *Marsh v. Chambers* (1983), in which the Court found nothing unconstitutional about the Nebraska legislature hiring a Presbyterian minister to say a public prayer before each daily session. Chief Justice Burger's opinion for the Court rested primarily on original intent, as demonstrated by the long tradition of American legislatures, starting with the first Congress, of beginning their sessions with a prayer. The Court largely ignored the precedents set in the school prayer cases and did not apply the *Lemon* test, which quite probably would have led to a different result.

For the Reagan administration, Burger's opinion was cause for optimism. The chief justice had invoked originalism, an approach to adjudication Reagan and his colleagues advocated. The decision provided some indica-

---

BOX 4-9   SCHOOL PRAYER IN GLOBAL PERSPECTIVE

IN WHAT MAY BE the only existing inventory of international practices regarding state-sanctioned school prayer, the American Civil Liberties Union concluded that "the major countries of the world, including Western Europe, Central America, and Asia, have rejected state-sponsored prayer in their public school systems." Indeed, only eleven of the seventy-two countries included in the study continue to permit the sort of state-sanctioned prayer that the U.S. Supreme Court rejected in *Engel v. Vitale* (1962)—and many of the eleven (including Finland, Greece, Libya, Nepal, Pakistan, Romania, Saudi Arabia, and Thailand) are countries that have state religions or are religiously homogeneous. Yet, according to the study, even nations that meet those criteria, such as Italy and Israel, have "steered a careful course around imposing prayer in the schools."

On the other hand, some religiously diverse countries—Great Britain and Sweden, for example—permit government-sponsored prayer or some form of voluntary prayer, even in the face of court challenges. In the *School Prayer Case* (1979) the Federal Constitutional Court of Germany took the position that voluntary prayer in public schools was constitutionally permissible so long as schools "guarantee the dissenting pupil the right to decide freely and without compulsion whether to participate in the prayer." The court justified its position in the following terms:

[Germany's constitutional document] grants not only freedom of belief but also the external freedom publicly to acknowledge one's belief. In this sense Articles 4 (1) and 4 (2) [guaranteeing freedom of religion and the right to practice religion free from harassment] guarantee a sphere in which to express these convictions actively. If the state permits school prayer in interdenominational state schools, then it does nothing more than exercise its right to establish a school system so that pupils who wish to do so may acknowledge their religious beliefs, even if only in the limited form of a universal and transdenominational appeal to God. . . .

To be sure, the state must balance this affirmative freedom to worship as expressed by permitting school prayer with the negative freedom of confession of other parents and pupils opposed to school prayer. Basically [schools] may achieve this balance by guaranteeing that participation be voluntary for pupils and teachers.

This decision stands in marked contrast to *School District of Abington Township v. Schempp* (1963). There, Edward Schempp's attorney impressed on the justices the ridicule his children would face when they left the room to avoid religious readings. For this and other reasons, the Supreme Court ruled that even voluntary prayer violated the U.S. Constitution.

The German justices also were sensitive to the problem Schempp had raised: "Admittedly," the Constitutional Court wrote, "whenever the class prays, [the failure to participate] will have the effect of distinguishing the pupil in question from the praying pupils—especially if only one pupil professes other beliefs." Nonetheless, the court concluded that "one cannot assume that abstaining from school prayer will generally or even in a substantial number of cases force a dissenting pupil into an unbearable position as an outsider."

SOURCES: http://www.aclu.org/news/n051595A.html; Donald Kommers, *The Constitutional Jurisprudence of the Federal Republic of Germany* (Durham, N.C.: Duke University Press, 1997).

Ishmael Jaffree of Mobile, Alabama, shown with his family, challenged the constitutionality of an Alabama law that required prayer and moments of silence in public schools. In *Wallace v. Jaffree* (1985) the Supreme Court said the law was in conflict with the Establishment Clause.

tion that the Court might be ready to reconsider prayer in school. Accordingly, when the Court agreed to hear *Wallace v. Jaffree* (1985), there was speculation that the justices might be on the verge of overruling precedents such as *Engel* and *Abington.*

Wallace v. Jaffree involved a challenge to an Alabama law, authorizing, among other things, a daily period of silence in all public schools "for meditation or voluntary prayer." Ishmael Jaffree, a lawyer for the Legal Services Administration, objected when the provisions of the law were implemented in his son's kindergarten class. When his protests were not acted upon by local school officials, Jaffree filed suit.

Jaffree and other opponents of the Alabama law argued that it was unconstitutional because it lacked a sec-

ular purpose as required by *Lemon,* and because its legislative sponsors clearly viewed it as a way to return prayer to school. The state countered that the law does not in any way offend the Constitution because it does not affirm religious belief or coerce participation in any prayer. The Reagan administration supported this position. In an amicus curiae brief, the solicitor general argued that the law was "perfectly neutral with respect religious practices. It neither favors one religion over another nor conveys endorsement of religion."

Despite public opinion and political pressure, the Court did not overturn *Engel* or *Abington.* To the contrary, by invoking the *Lemon* test to strike down the Alabama law, the Court reaffirmed its commitment to those decisions and to the standards of law on which they were based—the forerunners of *Lemon.* Specifically, the Court found that the Alabama law's primary purpose was not secular. In fact, the law, according to the Court, had no secular purpose at all.

Still, while the majority opinion invoked *Lemon,* the justices were not unanimous in their support for the three-pronged test. Powell expressed concern over some justices' criticism of the test, and O'Connor continued to press for her endorsement approach to *Lemon.* In dissent, Burger lamented that the majority's "extended treatment" of the *Lemon* test "suggests a naïve preoccupation with an easy, bright-line approach for addressing constitutional issues." But it was Rehnquist's dissenting opinion that raised the most eyebrows because it questioned the Court's entire approach to Establishment Clause cases beginning with *Everson.* He said the Court was wrong to "concede" Jefferson's metaphor of a "wall of separation" or to etch into law such a strict separation. In other words, he asserted that for the four decades since *Everson,* the Court had operated under a misguided understanding of what the Framers meant by religious establishment. The truth, according to Rehnquist, was that the Founders, particularly Madison, intended something more in line with the nonpreferential position that the Establishment Clause simply "forbade the establishment of a national religion and forbade preference among religious sects or denominations. . . . [I]t did not prohibit the federal government from providing nondiscriminatory aid to religion." Justice White, who admitted that he had "been out of step" with the Court's rulings in this area, was happy to "appreciate" Rehnquist's reexamination of history.

Whether Rehnquist was correct or had misinterpreted history is a question that is probably unresolvable. What is true, however, is that *Wallace* was the Burger Court's last major religious establishment case; a year after the opinion was handed down, the chief justice retired. As we noted at the beginning of this section, Burger had sought to influence this area of the law, first by establishing the *Lemon* test and, then, after realizing that *Lemon* might lead to a stronger wall of separation than he envisioned, through the adoption of a Framers' intent approach (used in *Marsh*) or of a softened version of *Lemon*.

As chief justice, Rehnquist has continued Burger's efforts to lead the Court toward a more accommodationist position. It is no secret that Rehnquist would like to see the Court overrule *Lemon*. The problem he faces is that his colleagues do not agree on a standard of law by which to adjudicate these cases.

In 1992 the Rehnquist Court faced its first major school prayer case, *Lee v. Weisman*.[35] Some observers thought the Court would overturn *Lemon*, a position advocated by President Bush's solicitor general. Did the Court take this step? Note, too, how fractured the Court was. How did the dissenters and concurrers' positions differ from that proposed by the majority? Pay special attention to Justice Souter's concurring opinion, which was his first independent statement in a religious establishment case.

Lee v. Weisman

505 U.S. 577 (1992)
laws.findlaw.com/US/505/577.html
Vote: 5 (Blackmun, Kennedy, O'Connor, Souter, Stevens)
      4 (Rehnquist, Scalia, Thomas, White)
Opinion of the Court: Kennedy
Concurring opinions: Blackmun, Souter
Dissenting opinion: Scalia

35. To hear oral arguments in this case, navigate to: *oyez.nwu.edu*.

Each June the Nathan Bishop Middle School, a public school in Providence, Rhode Island, holds formal graduation exercises on school grounds. Attendance is voluntary. For years, it has been the practice of the school district to allow principals to invite local clergy to give invocations and benedictions at the middle and high school graduation exercises. Typically, what happens is this: school principals contact members of the clergy and ask them to give an invocation/benediction; if the clergy agree, principals give them a copy of a pamphlet entitled "Guidelines for Civic Occasions." Prepared by the National Conference of Christians and Jews, the guidelines stress "inclusiveness and sensitivity" in writing nonsectarian prayers.

For the June 1989 graduation, Principal Robert E. Lee followed this procedure. He invited Rabbi Leslie Gutterman to give the invocation and benediction and gave him a copy of the guidelines. Lee also advised Rabbi Gutterman that any prayers should be nonsectarian.

At the graduation the rabbi gave the following invocation:

Daniel Weisman and his daughter, Deborah, challenged the practice of having a member of the clergy deliver invocation and benediction prayers at public junior high school graduation exercises in Providence, Rhode Island. The Supreme Court ruled in their favor in *Lee v. Weisman*.

God of the Free, Hope of the Brave:

For the legacy of America where diversity is celebrated and the rights of minorities are protected, we thank You. May these young men and women grow up to enrich it.

For the liberty of America, we thank You. May these new graduates grow up to guard it.

For the political process of America in which all its citizens may participate, for its court system where all may seek justice, we thank You. May those we honor this morning always turn to it in trust.

For the destiny of America, we thank You. May the graduates of Nathan Bishop Middle School so live that they might help to share it.

May our aspirations for our country and for these young people, who are our hope for the future, be richly fulfilled.

Amen.

In his benediction, the rabbi said:

O God, we are grateful to You for having endowed us with the capacity for learning which we have celebrated on this joyous commencement.

Happy families give thanks for seeing their children achieve an important milestone. Send Your blessings upon the teachers and administrators who helped prepare them.

The graduates now need strength and guidance for the future. Help them to understand that we are not complete with academic knowledge alone. We must each strive to fulfill what You require from all of us: To do justly, to love mercy, to walk humbly.

We give thanks to You, Lord, for keeping us alive, sustaining us, and allowing us to reach this special, happy occasion.

Amen.

Daniel Weisman, whose daughter, Deborah, was in the graduating class, challenged as a violation of the First Amendment the school's allowing invocations and benedictions at graduation exercises. He asked a federal trial court to issue an order to Lee and other Providence officials prohibiting them from continuing this practice. The trial court found for Weisman, and a federal appellate court affirmed. As a result, Lee and the school board appealed to the U.S. Supreme Court. Joined by the Bush administration's solicitor general as an amicus curiae, they argued, as one justice later put it, "that these short prayers . . . are of profound meaning to many students and parents throughout this country who consider that due respect and acknowledgment for divine guidance and for the deepest spiritual aspirations of our people

ought to be expressed at an event as important in life as a graduation." The school board and the solicitor general also asked the Supreme Court to reconsider the *Lemon* test, which the district court had used to find against Principal Lee.

JUSTICE KENNEDY delivered the opinion of the Court.

These dominant facts mark and control the confines of our decision: State officials direct the performance of a formal religious exercise at promotional and graduation ceremonies for secondary schools. Even for those students who object to the religious exercise, their attendance and participation in the state-sponsored religious activity are in a fair and real sense obligatory, though the school district does not require attendance as a condition for receipt of the diploma.

This case does not require us to revisit the difficult questions dividing us in recent cases, questions of the definition and full scope of the principles governing the extent of permitted accommodation by the State for the religious beliefs and practices of many of its citizens. See *Allegheny County v. Greater Pittsburgh ACLU* (1989); *Wallace v. Jaffree* (1985); *Lynch v. Donnelly* (1984). For without reference to those principles in other contexts, the controlling precedents as they relate to prayer and religious exercise in primary and secondary public schools compel the holding here that the policy of the city of Providence is an unconstitutional one. We can decide the case without reconsidering the general constitutional framework by which public schools' efforts to accommodate religion are measured. Thus we do not accept the invitation of petitioners and amicus the United States to reconsider our decision in *Lemon v. Kurtzman.* The government involvement with religious activity in this case is pervasive, to the point of creating a state-sponsored and state-directed religious exercise in a public school. Conducting this formal religious observance conflicts with settled rules pertaining to prayer exercises for students, and that suffices to determine the question before us.

The principle that government may accommodate the free exercise of religion does not supersede the fundamental limitations imposed by the Establishment Clause. It is beyond dispute that, at a minimum, the Constitution guarantees that government may not coerce anyone to support or participate in religion or its exercise, or otherwise act in a way which "establishes a [state] religion or religious faith, or tends to do so."... The State's involvement in the school prayers challenged today violates these central principles.

That involvement is as troubling as it is undenied. A school official, the principal, decided that an invocation and a benediction should be given; this is a choice attributable to the State, and from a constitutional perspective it is as if a state statute decreed that the prayers must occur. The principal chose the religious participant, here a rabbi, and that choice is also attributable to the State. The reason for the choice of a rabbi is not disclosed by the record, but the potential for divisiveness over the choice of a particular member of the clergy to conduct the ceremony is apparent.

Divisiveness, of course, can attend any state decision respecting religions, and neither its existence nor its potential necessarily invalidates the State's attempts to accommodate religion in all cases. The potential for divisiveness is of particular relevance here, though, because it centers around an overt religious exercise in a secondary school environment where, as we discuss below, subtle coercive pressures exist and where the student had no real alternative which would have allowed her to avoid the fact or appearance of participation.

The State's role did not end with the decision to include a prayer and with the choice of clergyman. Principal Lee provided Rabbi Gutterman with a copy of the "Guidelines for Civic Occasions" and advised him that his prayers should be nonsectarian. Through these means, the principal directed and controlled the content of the prayer. Even if the only sanction for ignoring the instructions were that the rabbi would not be invited back, we think no religious representative who valued his or her continued reputation and effectiveness in the community would incur the State's displeasure in this regard. It is a cornerstone principle of our Establishment Clause jurisprudence that it is "no part of the business of government to compose official prayers for any group of the American people to recite as a part of a religious program carried on by government," *Engel v. Vitale* (1962), and that is what the school officials attempted to do.

Petitioners argue, and we find nothing in the case to refute it, that the directions for the content of the prayers were a good-faith attempt by the school to ensure that the sectarianism which is so often the flashpoint for religious animosity be removed from the graduation ceremony. The concern is understandable, as a prayer which uses ideas or images identified with a particular religion may foster a different sort of sectarian rivalry than an invocation or benediction in terms more neutral. The school's explanation, however, does not resolve the dilemma caused by its participation. The question is not the good faith of the school in attempting to make the prayer acceptable to most persons, but the legitimacy of its undertaking that enterprise at all when the object is to produce a prayer to be used in a formal religious exercise which students, for all practical purposes, are obliged to attend.

We are asked to recognize the existence of a practice of nonsectarian prayer, prayer within the embrace of what is known as the Judeo-Christian tradition, prayer which is more acceptable than one which, for example, makes explicit references to the God of Israel, or to Jesus Christ, or to a patron saint. There may be some support, as an empirical observation, to the statement of the Court of Appeals for the Sixth Circuit, picked up by Judge Campbell's dissent in the Court of Appeals in this case, that there has emerged in this country a civic religion, one which is tolerated when sectarian exercises are not. If common ground can be defined which permits once conflicting faiths to express the shared conviction that there is an ethic and a morality which transcend human invention, the sense of community and purpose sought by all decent societies might be advanced. But though the First Amendment does not allow the government to stifle prayers which aspire to these ends, neither does it permit the government to undertake that task for itself. . . .

These concerns have particular application in the case of school officials, whose effort to monitor prayer will be perceived by the students as inducing a participation they might otherwise reject. Though the efforts of the school officials in this case to find common ground appear to have been a good-faith attempt to recognize the common aspects of religions and not the divisive ones, our precedents do not permit school officials to assist in composing prayers as an incident to a formal exercise for their students. *Engel v. Vitale.* And these same precedents caution us to measure the idea of a civic religion against the central meaning of the Religion Clauses of the First Amendment, which is that all creeds must be tolerated and none favored. The suggestion that government may establish an official or civic religion as a means of avoiding the establishment of a religion with more specific creeds strikes us as a contradiction that cannot be accepted.

The degree of school involvement here made it clear that the graduation prayers bore the imprint of the State and thus put school-age children who objected in an untenable position. We turn our attention now to consider the position of the students, both those who desired the prayer and she who did not. . . .

As we have observed before, there are heightened concerns with protecting freedom of conscience from subtle coercive pressure in the elementary and secondary public schools. . . . Our decisions in *Engel v. Vitale* and *Abington School District* recognize, among other things, that prayer exercises in public schools carry a particular risk of indirect coercion. The concern may not be limited to the context of schools, but it is most pronounced there. . . . What to most believers may seem nothing more than a reasonable request that the nonbeliever respect their religious practices, in a school context may appear to the nonbeliever or dissenter to be an attempt to employ the machinery of the State to enforce a religious orthodoxy.

We need not look beyond the circumstances of this case to see the phenomenon at work. The undeniable fact is that the school district's supervision and control of a high school graduation ceremony places public pressure, as well as peer pressure, on attending students to stand as a group or, at least, maintain respectful silence during the Invocation and Benediction. This pressure, though subtle and indirect, can be as real as any overt compulsion. Of course, in our culture standing or remaining silent can signify adherence to a view or simple respect for the views of others. And no doubt some persons who have no desire to join a prayer have little objection to standing as a sign of respect for those who do. But for the dissenter of high school age, who has a reasonable perception that she is being forced by the State to pray in a manner her conscience will not allow, the injury is no less real. There can be no doubt that for many, if not most, of the students at the graduation, the act of standing or remaining silent was an expression of participation in the rabbi's prayer. That was the very point of the religious exercise. It is of little comfort to a dissenter, then, to be told that for her the act of standing or remaining in silence signifies mere respect, rather than participation. What matters is that, given our social conventions, a reasonable dissenter in this milieu could believe that the group exercise signified her own participation or approval of it.

Finding no violation under these circumstances would place objectors in the dilemma of participating, with all that implies, or protesting. We do not address whether that choice is acceptable if the affected citizens are mature adults, but we think the State may not, consistent with the Establishment Clause, place primary and secondary school children in this position. Research in psychology supports the common assumption that adolescents are often susceptible to pressure from their peers towards conformity, and that the influence is strongest in matters of social convention. Brittain, Adolescent Choices and Parent-Peer Cross-Pressures, 28 Am. Sociological Rev. 385 (June 1963); Clasen & Brown, The Multidimensionality of Peer Pressure in Adolescence, 14 J. of Youth and Adolescence 451 (Dec. 1985). . . . To recognize that the choice imposed by the State constitutes an unacceptable constraint only acknowledges that the government may no more use social pressure to enforce orthodoxy than it may use more direct means. . . .

There was a stipulation in the District Court that attendance at graduation and promotional ceremonies is voluntary. Petitioners and the United States, as amicus, made this a center point of the case, arguing that the option of not attending the graduation excuses any inducement or coercion in the ceremony itself. The argument lacks all persuasion. Law reaches past formalism. And to say a teenage student has a real choice not to attend her high school graduation is formalistic in the extreme. True, Deborah could elect not to attend commencement without renouncing her diploma; but we shall not allow the case to turn on this point. Everyone knows that, in our society and in our culture, high school graduation is one of life's most significant occasions. A school rule which excuses attendance is beside the point. Attendance may not be required by official decree, yet it is apparent that a student is not free to absent herself from the graduation exercise in any real sense of the term "voluntary," for absence would require forfeiture of those intangible benefits which have motivated the student through youth and all her high school years. Graduation is a time for family and those closest to the student to celebrate success and express mutual wishes of gratitude and respect, all to the end of impressing upon the young person the role that it is his or her right and duty to assume in the community and all of its diverse parts.

The importance of the event is the point the school district and the United States rely upon to argue that a formal prayer ought to be permitted, but it becomes one of the principal reasons why their argument must fail. Their contention, one of considerable force were it not for the constitutional constraints applied to state action, is that the prayers are an essential part of these ceremonies because for many persons an occasion of this significance lacks meaning if there is no recognition, however brief, that human achievements cannot be understood apart from their spiritual essence. We think the Government's position that this interest suffices to force students to choose between compliance or forfeiture demonstrates fundamental inconsistency in its argumentation. It fails to acknowledge that what for many of Deborah's classmates and their parents was a spiritual imperative was for Daniel and Deborah Weisman religious conformance compelled by the State. While in some societies the wishes of the majority might prevail, the Establishment Clause of the First Amendment is addressed to this contingency and rejects the balance urged upon us. The Constitution forbids the State to exact religious conformity from a student as the price of attending her own high school graduation. This is the calculus the Constitution commands. . . .

We do not hold that every state action implicating religion is invalid if one or a few citizens find it offensive. People may take offense at all manner of religious as well as nonreligious messages, but offense alone does not in every case show a violation. We know too that sometimes to endure social isolation or even anger may be the price of conscience or nonconformity. But, by any reading of our cases, the conformity required of the student in this case was too high an exaction to withstand the test of the Establishment Clause. The prayer exercises in this case are especially improper because the State has in every practical sense compelled attendance and participation in an explicit religious exercise at an event of singular importance to every student, one the objecting student had no real alternative to avoid. . . .

. . . No holding by this Court suggests that a school can persuade or compel a student to participate in a religious exercise. That is being done here, and it is forbidden by the Establishment Clause of the First Amendment.

For the reasons we have stated, the judgment of the Court of Appeals is

Affirmed.

JUSTICE BLACKMUN, with whom JUSTICE STEVENS and JUSTICE O'CONNOR join, concurring.

In 1971, Chief Justice Burger reviewed the Court's past decisions and found: "Three . . . tests may be gleaned from our cases." *Lemon v. Kurtzman*. . . . After *Lemon*, the Court continued to rely on these basic principles in resolving Establishment Clause disputes.

Application of these principles to the facts of this case is straightforward. There can be "no doubt" that the "invocation of God's blessings" delivered at Nathan Bishop Middle School "is a religious activity.". . . The question then is whether the government has "placed its official stamp of approval" on the prayer. As the Court ably demonstrates, when the government "compose[s] official prayers," selects the member of the clergy to deliver the prayer, has the prayer delivered at a public school event that is planned, supervised, and given by school officials, and pressures students to attend and participate in the prayer, there can be no doubt that the government is advancing and promoting religion. As our prior decisions teach us, it is this that the Constitution prohibits.

I join the Court's opinion today because I find nothing in it inconsistent with the essential precepts of the Establishment Clause developed in our precedents. The Court holds that the graduation prayer is unconstitutional because the State "in effect required participation in a religious exercise." Although our precedents make clear that proof of government coercion is not necessary to prove an Establishment Clause violation, it is sufficient. Government pressure to participate in a religious activity is an obvious indication that the government is endorsing or promoting religion.

But it is not enough that the government restrain from compelling religious practices: it must not engage in them either. . . . The Court repeatedly has recognized that a violation of the Establishment Clause is not predicated on coercion. . . . The Establishment Clause proscribes public schools from "conveying or attempting to convey a message that religion or a particular religious belief is favored or preferred," *County of Allegheny v. ACLU* (1989), even if the schools do not actually "impose pressure upon a student to participate in a religious activity.". . .

It is these understandings . . . that underlie our Establishment Clause jurisprudence. We have believed that religious freedom cannot exist in the absence of a free democratic government, and that such a government cannot endure when there is fusion between religion and the political regime. We have believed that religious freedom cannot thrive in the absence of a vibrant religious community and that such a community cannot prosper when it is bound to the secular. And we have believed that these were the animating principles behind the adoption of the Establishment Clause. To that end, our cases have prohibited government endorsement of religion, its sponsorship, and active involvement in religion, whether or not citizens were coerced to conform.

I remain convinced that our jurisprudence is not misguided, and that it requires the decision reached by the Court today. Accordingly, I join the Court in affirming the judgment of the Court of Appeals.

JUSTICE SOUTER, with whom JUSTICE STEVENS and JUSTICE O'CONNOR join, concurring.

I join the whole of the Court's opinion, and fully agree that prayers at public school graduation ceremonies indirectly coerce religious observance. I write separately nonetheless on two issues of Establishment Clause analysis that underlie my independent resolution of this case: whether the Clause applies to governmental practices that do not favor one religion or denomination over others, and whether state coercion of religious conformity, over and above state endorsement of religious exercise or belief, is a necessary element of an Establishment Clause violation.

Forty-five years ago, this Court announced a basic principle of constitutional law from which it has not strayed: the Establishment Clause forbids not only state practices that "aid one religion . . . or prefer one religion over another," but also those that "aid all religions." *Everson v. Board of Education of Ewing* (1947). Today we reaffirm that principle, holding that the Establishment Clause forbids state-sponsored prayers in public school settings no matter how nondenominational the prayers may be. In barring the State from sponsoring generically theistic prayers where it could not sponsor sectarian ones, we hold true to a line of precedent from which there is no adequate historical case to depart. . . .

Some have challenged this precedent by reading the Establishment Clause to permit "nonpreferential" state pro-

motion of religion. The challengers argue that, as originally understood by the Framers, "the Establishment Clause did not require government neutrality between religion and irreligion, nor did it prohibit the Federal Government from providing nondiscriminatory aid to religion." *Wallace* (REHNQUIST, J., dissenting). While a case has been made for this position, it is not so convincing as to warrant reconsideration of our settled law; indeed, I find in the history of the Clause's textual development a more powerful argument supporting the Court's jurisprudence following *Everson.* . . .

What we . . . know of the Framers' experience underscores the observation of one prominent commentator, that confining the Establishment Clause to a prohibition on preferential aid "requires a premise that the Framers were extraordinarily bad drafters—that they believed one thing but adopted language that said something substantially different, and that they did so after repeatedly attending to the choice of language.". . . We must presume, since there is no conclusive evidence to the contrary, that the Framers embraced the significance of their textual judgment. Thus, on balance, history neither contradicts nor warrants reconsideration of the settled principle that the Establishment Clause forbids support for religion in general no less than support for one religion or some. . . .

Petitioners rest most of their argument on a theory that, whether or not the Establishment Clause permits extensive nonsectarian support for religion, it does not forbid the state to sponsor affirmations of religious belief that coerce neither support for religion nor participation in religious observance. I appreciate the force of some of the arguments supporting a "coercion" analysis of the Clause. See generally *Allegheny County* (opinion of KENNEDY, J.). But we could not adopt that reading without abandoning our settled law, a course that, in my view, the text of the Clause would not readily permit. Nor does the extratextual evidence of original meaning stand so unequivocally at odds with the textual premise inherent in existing precedent that we should fundamentally reconsider our course.

Over the years, this Court has declared the invalidity of many noncoercive state laws and practices conveying a message of religious endorsement. For example, in *Allegheny County* we forbade the prominent display of a nativity scene on public property; without contesting the dissent's observation that the crèche coerced no one into accepting or supporting whatever message it proclaimed, five Members of the Court found its display unconstitutional as a state endorsement of Christianity. Likewise, in *Wallace v. Jaffree* (1985), we struck down a state law requiring a moment of silence in public classrooms not because the statute coerced students to participate in prayer (for it did not), but because the manner of its enactment "conveyed a message of state approval of prayer activities in the public schools.". . .

Our precedents may not always have drawn perfectly straight lines. They simply cannot, however, support the position that a showing of coercion is necessary to a successful Establishment Clause claim. . . .

Petitioners argue from the political setting in which the Establishment Clause was framed, and from the Framers' own political practices following ratification, that government may constitutionally endorse religion so long as it does not coerce religious conformity. The setting and the practices warrant canvassing, but while they yield some evidence for petitioners' argument, they do not reveal the degree of consensus in early constitutional thought that would raise a threat to *stare decisis* by challenging the presumption that the Establishment Clause adds something to the Free Exercise Clause that follows it. . . .

Petitioners contend that because the early Presidents included religious messages in their inaugural and Thanksgiving Day addresses, the Framers could not have meant the Establishment Clause to forbid noncoercive state endorsement of religion. The argument ignores the fact, however, that Americans today find such proclamations less controversial than did the founding generation, whose published thoughts on the matter belie petitioners' claim. President Jefferson, for example, steadfastly refused to issue Thanksgiving proclamations of any kind, in part because he thought they violated the Religion Clauses. . . .

. . . While we may be unable to know for certain what the Framers meant by the Clause, we do know that, around the time of its ratification, a respectable body of opinion supported a considerably broader reading than petitioners urge upon us. This consistency with the textual considerations is enough to preclude fundamentally reexamining our settled law, and I am accordingly left with the task of considering whether the state practice at issue here violates our traditional understanding of the Clause's proscriptions.

While the Establishment Clause's concept of neutrality is not self-revealing, our recent cases have invested it with

specific content: the state may not favor or endorse either religion generally over nonreligion or one religion over others. . . . This principle against favoritism and endorsement has become the foundation of Establishment Clause jurisprudence, ensuring that religious belief is irrelevant to every citizen's standing in the political community. . . . Our aspiration to religious liberty, embodied in the First Amendment, permits no other standard.

JUSTICE SCALIA, with whom the CHIEF JUSTICE, JUSTICE WHITE, and JUSTICE THOMAS join, dissenting.

Three Terms ago, I joined an opinion recognizing that the Establishment Clause must be construed in light of the "[g]overnment policies of accommodation, acknowledgment, and support for religion [that] are an accepted part of our political and cultural heritage." That opinion affirmed that "the meaning of the Clause is to be determined by reference to historical practices and understandings." It said that "[a] test for implementing the protections of the Establishment Clause that, if applied with consistency, would invalidate long-standing traditions cannot be a proper reading of the Clause." *Allegheny County v. Greater Pittsburgh ACLU* (1989) (KENNEDY, J., concurring in judgment in part and dissenting in part).

These views of course prevent me from joining today's opinion, which is conspicuously bereft of any reference to history. In holding that the Establishment Clause prohibits invocations and benedictions at public-school graduation ceremonies, the Court—with nary a mention that it is doing so—lays waste a tradition that is as old as public-school graduation ceremonies themselves, and that is a component of an even more long-standing American tradition of nonsectarian prayer to God at public celebrations generally. As its instrument of destruction, the bulldozer of its social engineering, the Court invents a boundless, and boundlessly manipulable, test of psychological coercion. . . . Today's opinion shows more forcefully than volumes of argumentation why our Nation's protection, that fortress which is our Constitution, cannot possibly rest upon the changeable philosophical predilections of the Justices of this Court, but must have deep foundations in the historic practices of our people. . . .

The history and tradition of our Nation are replete with

Youth group members from the Santa Fe and Bayou Drive Baptist churches conduct a prayer circle under the Santa Fe High School scoreboard. A student's prayer delivered over the loudspeaker prior to the kickoff of a high school football game became the subject of a Supreme Court case.

public ceremonies featuring prayers of thanksgiving and petition. . . . Most recently, President Bush, continuing the tradition established by President Washington, asked those attending his inauguration to bow their heads, and made a prayer his first official act as President. . . .

The Court presumably would separate graduation invocations and benedictions from other instances of public "preservation and transmission of religious beliefs" on the ground that they involve "psychological coercion." I find it a sufficient embarrassment that our Establishment Clause jurisprudence regarding holiday displays . . . has come to "requir[e] scrutiny more commonly associated with interior decorators than with the judiciary.". . . But interior decorating is a rock-hard science compared to psychology practiced by amateurs. A few citations of "[r]esearch in psychology" that have no particular bearing upon the precise issue here cannot disguise the fact that the Court has gone beyond the realm where judges know what they are doing. The Court's argument that state officials have "coerced" students to take part in the invocation and benediction at graduation ceremonies is, not to put too fine a point on it, incoherent. . . .

The deeper flaw in the Court's opinion does not lie in its wrong answer to the question whether there was state-induced "peer-pressure" coercion; it lies, rather, in the Court's making violation of the Establishment Clause hinge on such a precious question. . . .

. . . [W]hile I have no quarrel with the Court's general proposition that the Establishment Clause "guarantees that government may not coerce anyone to support or participate in religion or its exercise," I see no warrant for expanding the concept of coercion beyond acts backed by threat of penalty—a brand of coercion that, happily, is readily discernible to those of us who have made a career of reading the disciples of Blackstone rather than of Freud. The Framers were indeed opposed to coercion of religious worship by the National Government; but, as their own sponsorship of nonsectarian prayer in public events demonstrates, they understood that "speech is not coercive; the listener may do as he likes.". . .

Our Religion Clause jurisprudence has become bedeviled (so to speak) by reliance on formulaic abstractions that are not derived from, but positively conflict with, our long-accepted constitutional traditions. Foremost among these has been the so-called *Lemon* test, see *Lemon v. Kurtzman* (1971), which has received well-earned criticism from many members of this Court. . . . The Court today demonstrates the irrelevance of *Lemon* by essentially ignoring it, and the interment of that case may be the one happy byproduct of the Court's otherwise lamentable decision. Unfortunately, however, the Court has replaced *Lemon* with its psycho-coercion test, which suffers the double disability of having no roots whatever in our people's historic practice, and being as infinitely expandable as the reasons for psychotherapy itself.

Another happy aspect of the case is that it is only a jurisprudential disaster and not a practical one. Given the odd basis for the Court's decision, invocations and benedictions will be able to be given at public-school graduations next June, as they have for the past century and a half, so long as school authorities make clear that anyone who abstains from screaming in protest does not necessarily participate in the prayers. All that is seemingly needed is an announcement, or perhaps a written insertion at the beginning of the graduation Program, to the effect that, while all are asked to rise for the invocation and benediction, none is compelled to join in them, nor will be assumed, by rising, to have done so. That obvious fact recited, the graduates and their parents may proceed to thank God, as Americans have always done, for the blessings He has generously bestowed on them and on their country. . . .

For the foregoing reasons, I dissent.

Justice Kennedy may not have applied *Lemon* to resolve *Weisman*, but neither did he overturn it. To the contrary, he specifically declined to revisit *Lemon* on the grounds that the Court's previous cases on prayer in school established clear precedent for this case. Returning to the coercion standard he advocated in *County of Allegheny*, Kennedy noted that *Engel* and *Abington* recognized that "prayer exercises in public schools carry a particular risk of indirect coercion." It was this coercion, however subtle, at which Kennedy took offense. The concurrers, on the other hand, complained that coercion was insufficient: Stevens, Blackmun, and O'Connor continued to advocate an endorsement approach to *Lemon*. Souter, joined by Stevens and O'Connor, explicitly rejected Kennedy's coercion standard and Rehnquist's nonpreferentialism in favor of the endorsement approach. Souter also stressed that the Court should not abandon precedent governing religious establishment cases, yet he had very little to say about *Lemon* in particular.

Most interesting of all may be Scalia's dissent because it indicates that justices can agree over a standard of law but disagree vehemently over its application. Scalia endorsed the coercion standard in *County of Allegheny*, but here took issue with the way Kennedy applied it, arguing that the majority opinion was ahistorical and too grounded in psychology. Joined by Rehnquist, White, and Thomas, Scalia lambasted the Court for engaging in amateur psychology and for paying more attention to Freud than to the Framers. About the only thing the dissenters found redeemable in *Weisman* was that the majority opinion seemed to "inter" *Lemon*. But they were wrong: *Lemon* reemerged as a guiding standard the very next year in *Lamb's Chapel*. Scalia and his colleagues also lost on the holding in *Weisman:* the Court once again rejected prayer in school.

It took eight years for the school prayer issue to find its way to the Supreme Court once again. In *Santa Fe Independent School District v. Doe* (2000) the justices faced a tradition of long standing in many communities: public prayer at high school football games. At issue was the policy of a Texas public school district that allowed student-led invocations to be delivered on the public address system during pre-game ceremonies. To ensure continuing support for this practice, the school district required an annual vote of students, by secret ballot, on whether they wanted public prayers at the games. If the vote favored the invocations, a second election took place to select a single student who would deliver the prayers at all home games for that season. The school required that the prayers be consistent with the district's policy goals: to solemnize the event, to promote sportsmanship and safety, and to establish the appropriate environment for competition. Otherwise the content of the message was left to the discretion of the student delivering it.

Two families, one Mormon and the other Catholic, challenged the district's policy. Local sentiment strongly supported the pre-game prayers, and as a consequence the lower courts allowed the individuals filing the challenge to proceed anonymously to protect them from intimidation and harassment.

The school district defended its policy on several grounds. First, it argued that because the invocations were controlled by the students and not by the district administration, the prayers constituted private expression, not government-mandated expression. Second, the two-stage election system ensured that the prayers would not be said without the support of the majority of the students. Third, the school district only permitted the process to take place—it was not in any way involved in the writing or presentation of the prayers. Finally, the prayers were said at a completely voluntary, extracurricular event. Attendance was not required, nor was participation in the recitation of the prayers. There was no coercion to participate.

Based on precedents such as *Weisman* and *Lemon*, a six-justice majority struck down the district's prayer practices as violations of the Establishment Clause. In an uncommon expression of unity, all six members of the majority subscribed to a single opinion written by Justice Stevens. No concurring opinions were issued. The majority found the district policy unconstitutional on several grounds. First, the practice constituted an endorsement of religion. The invocations were authorized by a government policy and took place on government property at a government-sponsored, school-related event. The school district clearly invited and encouraged the religious activity. The prayers sent a constitutionally impermissible message that nonadherents are "outsiders, not full members of the political community, and an accompanying message to adherents that they are insiders, favored members of the political community."

Second, the policy contained an element of coercion. Although generally voluntary, for some students (players, cheerleaders, and band members) attendance was not optional. In addition, in many communities high school football games are important social events with strong peer pressure to attend. The majority found it constitutionally unacceptable to force students to forgo attending such school-sponsored events to avoid conforming with a state-sponsored religious practice.

Finally, the majority found the district's policy to be in direct violation of the *Lemon* test's requirement that government policies have a secular purpose. In spite of the district's arguments to the contrary, the Court concluded that the primary purpose of the prayers was religious.

Chief Justice Rehnquist, joined by Justices Scalia and Thomas, dissented. They objected not only to the outcome, but also to the tone of the Court's opinion, which, Rehnquist said, "bristles with hostility to all things religious in public life." According to the minority, the country's traditions allow voluntary religious expressions by private individuals at public events such as football games.

The *Santa Fe* decision is the most recent in a long line of decisions in which the justices have found various forms of school prayer constitutionally impermissible. In an area of the law that is characterized by inconsistencies, the school prayer decisions stand out as remarkably stable. Although justices have squabbled over the most appropriate test to apply, the outcomes have never been in serious doubt—prayer in public schools is unconstitutional.

What can we conclude about the Court's handling of Establishment Clause litigation in general? At the very least, we can say that this area of the law is unstable, with the justices badly divided and professing very different approaches to resolve the cases. As we have observed, each time the Court seems on the verge of eliminating *Lemon*, that test reappears, as Justice Scalia put it in *Lamb's Chapel*, "like some ghoul in a late-night horror movie." Whether the Court kills off *Lemon* once and for all seems to hinge on the justices' ability to agree on a replacement and on the application of that replacement, which—as *Lee v. Weisman* illustrates—they have been unable to do.

At its most extreme, religion litigation is an area rife with contradictions and unprincipled decisions. As Justice Thomas noted in *Rosenberger v. University of Virginia*, "our Establishment Clause jurisprudence is in hopeless disarray," a view shared by many Court scholars.

Will the Court seek to resolve the law's inconsistencies in the religious establishment area? What standard or test will it invoke to do so? Will *Lemon* survive or be modified, overruled, or simply ignored? Will the Court adopt any of the competing standards, such as coercion, endorsement, or nonpreferentialism, or will a new standard emerge? Now that you have read about many of the significant cases of the past, you probably realize that there are no easy answers.

READINGS

Alley, Robert S. *The Supreme Court on Church and State.* New York: Oxford University Press, 1988.

Carter, Stephen L. *The Culture of Disbelief.* New York: Basic Books, 1993.

Choper, Jesse H. *Securing Religious Liberty: Principles for Judicial Interpretation of the Religion Clauses.* Chicago: University of Chicago Press, 1995.

Currey, Thomas J. *The First Amendment Freedoms: Church and State in America to the Passage of the First Amendment.* New York: Oxford University Press, 1986.

Dolbeare, Kenneth M., and Phillip E. Hammond. *The School Prayer Decision.* Chicago: University of Chicago Press, 1971.

Howe, Mark Dewolfe. *The Garden and the Wilderness: Religion and Government in American Constitutional History.* Chicago: University of Chicago Press, 1965.

Ivers, Gregg. *Redefining the First Freedom.* New Brunswick, N.J.: Transaction Publishers, 1993.

Levy, Leonard W. *The Establishment Clause.* 2d ed. Chapel Hill: University of North Carolina Press, 1994.

Malbin, Michael J. *Religion and Politics.* Washington, D.C.: American Enterprise Institute, 1978.

Manwaring, David B. *Render Unto Caesar: The Flag Salute Controversy.* Chicago: University of Chicago Press, 1962.

Monsma, Stephen V. *When Sacred and Secular Mix.* Lanham, Md.: Rowman and Littlefield, 1996.

Morgan, Richard E. *The Supreme Court and Religion.* New York: Free Press, 1972.

Noonan, John T., Jr. *The Lustre of Our Country: The American Experience of Religious Freedom.* Berkeley: University of California Press, 1998.

Peters, Shawn Francis. *Judging Jehovah's Witnesses: Religious Persecution and the Dawn of the Rights Revolution.* Lawrence: University Press of Kansas, 2000.

Pfeffer, Leo. *Religion, State, and the Burger Court.* Buffalo, N.Y.: Prometheus Books, 1985.

Sheffer, Martin S. *God versus Caesar: Belief, Worship, and Proselytizing Under the First Amendment.* Albany: State University of New York Press, 1999.

Smith, Steven D. *Foreordained Failure: The Quest for a Constitutional Principle of Religious Freedom.* New York: Oxford University Press, 1995.

Sorauf, Frank J. *The Wall of Separation.* Princeton: Princeton University Press, 1976.

Wills, Garry. *Under God.* New York: Simon and Schuster, 1990.

CHAPTER 5

FREEDOM OF SPEECH, ASSEMBLY, AND ASSOCIATION

A T ONE TIME or another, everyone has criticized someone in government. The president, the mayor, or some other public official has said or done something we thought was wrong. We may have been polite, simply noting our displeasure, or we may have used more colorful language to voice our criticism. Either way, we expressed our views. Speaking our minds is a privilege we enjoy in the United States, a privilege guaranteed by the First Amendment.

While the Bill of Rights was making its way through Congress and state legislatures, the First Amendment's freedom of expression provisions were hardly debated. The Framers had a fundamental commitment to speech and press freedoms, especially as they related to the public discussion of political and social issues. After all, vigorous public oratory had fueled the Revolution and helped shape the contours of the new government.

The First Amendment's language is very bold: "Congress shall make no law ... abridging the freedom of speech, or of the press; or the right of the people peaceably to assemble, and to petition the Government for a redress of grievances." These words seem to provide an impregnable shield against government actions that would restrict any of the four components of freedom of expression: speech, press, assembly, and petition. But to what extent *does* the Constitution protect these rights? May mischievous patrons stand up in a crowded movie theater and shout *fire* when they know there is no fire? May a publisher knowingly print lies about a member of

the community to destroy that person's reputation? May a political group attempt to spread its message by driving sound trucks through residential neighborhoods at all hours? May an antimilitary activist burn his draft registration card in protest?

Despite the clear wording of the First Amendment, the answer to each of these questions is no. The Supreme Court never has adhered to a literal interpretation of the expression guarantees; rather, it has ruled that certain expressions, whether communicated verbally, in print, or by actions, may be restricted because of their possible effect.

This chapter is the first of three dealing with the right of expression. Here we first examine the development of constitutional standards for freedom of expression and then the application of those standards to various kinds of expression. In the next two chapters we look at issues specific to the freedom of the press and discuss forms of expression that traditionally have been considered outside First Amendment protection.

THE DEVELOPMENT OF LEGAL STANDARDS: THE EMERGENCE OF LAW IN TIMES OF CRISIS

History teaches that governments tend to be more repressive in times of crisis. Emergencies may result from war, economic collapse, natural catastrophes, or internal rebellion. During such times a nation's survival may be at stake, the government may be unstable, and political dissent and opposition to the government are more likely to occur. The responses of political leaders are predictable: they will place a priority on national unity and take firm action against subversive groups and opposition criticism. Often these reactions take the form of policies that restrict the right of the people to speak, publish, and organize.

The United States is no exception to this rule. In times of peace and general prosperity there is little reason to restrict freedom of expression. The government and the nation are secure, and the people are relatively content. In times of crisis, however, the president and Congress may react harshly, contending that some forms of expression must be curtailed to protect national security. In response, political dissidents may challenge such laws, arguing that repressive government policies are unconstitutional—even in times of war or national emergency.

The justices of the Supreme Court ultimately must decide where constitutional protections end and the government's right to restrict expression begins. These questions have come to the Court during actual periods of crisis or in the months immediately after. At these times the Constitution has been most seriously tested, and the Court has been called upon to develop fundamental doctrines regarding freedom of expression.

To demonstrate this point, we have organized this section around times of crisis—the Revolution (1775–1781) and the Civil War (1861–1865), World War I (1917–1918), World War II (1941–1945) and resultant cold war, and the Vietnam War (1963–1975). As you read the cases associated with these times, you will be asked questions about the development of law and legal doctrine. Perhaps the most basic question is this: Had a crisis not existed, would the Court have decided this case the same way? This question should serve as a constant reminder that Supreme Court justices may be as vulnerable to public pressures and to waves of patriotism as the average citizen.

Early Crises: The Revolutionary and Civil Wars

Despite their support for freedom of expression, the Founders were vulnerable to the patriotic atmosphere that seems to permeate society following a major crisis.

Once in power, they also were concerned with staying in power. Not long after the Revolution, Congress passed one of the most restrictive laws in American history, the Sedition Act of 1798:

If any person shall write, print, utter or publish, or shall cause to procure to be written, printed, uttered or published, or shall knowingly and willingly assist or aid in writing, printing, uttering or publishing any false, scandalous and malicious writing or writings against the government of the United States, or either House of the Congress of the United States, or the President of the United States, with intent to defame the said government, or either House of the said Congress, or the said President, or to bring them, or either of them into contempt or disrepute; or to excite against them, or either or any of them, the hatred of the good people of the United States, done in pursuance of any such law, or of the powers in him vested by the Constitution of the United States, or to resist, oppose, or defeat any such law or act, or to aid, encourage or abet any hostile designs of any foreign nation against the United States, their people or government, then such person, being thereof convicted before any court of the United States having jurisdiction thereof, shall be punished by a fine not exceeding $2,000, and by imprisonment not exceeding two years.

The act expired in 1801, without any significant court challenges to its validity. But why did our Founding Fathers, who so dearly treasured liberty, pass such a repressive law? First, the Federalist Party controlled Congress. Although dominant in the nation's earliest years, the Federalists were beginning to lose ground to the rising Jeffersonians. Some argue that the Sedition Act was little more than a Federalist attempt to suppress opposition. Indeed, Thomas Jefferson, leader of the Anti-Federalist (Democratic-Republican) Party, vigorously attacked the law, claiming that it led to witch hunts. Second, it is undoubtedly true that the Framers held a view of free expression that was different from the present-day view. They had known only the British system, which often imposed laws that severely curtailed free expression.

For the next sixty years, the United States enjoyed relative tranquillity interrupted only by the War of 1812. Congress passed no major restrictive legislation, and the Supreme Court decided no major expression cases. In the 1860s, however, peaceful times came to a crashing halt as the nation divided over the issue of slavery. As

Government officers and clerks loading a police ambulance with literature seized at the Communist Party headquarters in Cambridge, Massachusetts, in 1919. Such raids against communist organizations were not uncommon during the Red Scare era.

civil war broke out, President Abraham Lincoln took a number of steps to suppress "treacherous" behavior, believing "that the nation must be able to protect itself in war against utterances which actually cause insubordination."[1] Still, the Supreme Court had no opportunity to rule on the constitutionality of the president's actions, at least on First Amendment grounds.

World War I

Patriotic passions were again released with the outbreak of war in Europe in 1914 and the Russian Revolution in 1917. The United States turned its attention away from domestic programs and toward defending the American system of government.

Today, the patriotic fervor unleashed by World War I is difficult to imagine. No American was immune, not even Supreme Court justices. Consider Chief Justice Edward D. White's response to an attorney who argued that the selective draft, enacted by Congress in 1917, lacked

public support: "I don't think your statement has anything to do with legal arguments and should not have been said in this Court. It is a very unpatriotic statement to make."[2] Members of Congress, too, were caught up in the patriotic fervor gripping the nation. They, like the Founders, felt it necessary to enact legislation to ensure that Americans presented a unified front to the world. The Espionage Act of 1917 prohibited any attempt to "interfere with the operation or success of the military or naval forces of the United States . . . to cause insubordination . . . in the military or naval forces . . . or willfully obstruct the recruiting or enlistment service of the United States." One year later, Congress passed the Sedition Act, which prohibited the uttering of, writing, or publishing of anything disloyal to the government, flag, or military forces of the United States.

Although the majority of Americans probably supported these laws, some groups and individuals thought they constituted intolerable infringements on civil liber-

1. Zechariah Chafee Jr., *Free Speech in the United States* (Cambridge: Harvard University Press, 1941), 266.

2. Quoted by John R. Schmidhauser in *Constitutional Law in American Politics* (Monterey, Calif.: Brooks/Cole, 1984), 325.

ties guarantees contained in the First Amendment. Dissenters, however, were not of one political voice: some, most notably the American Union Against Militarism (a predecessor of the American Civil Liberties Union), were blatantly pacifist; others, primarily leaders of the Progressive Movement, were pure civil libertarians, opposed to any government intrusion into free expression; and, finally, there were the radicals, individuals who hoped to see the United States undergo a socialist or communist revolution. Regardless of their motivation, these individuals and groups brought legal challenges to the repressive laws and pushed the Supreme Court into freedom of expression cases for the first time. The first of the World War I cases, *Schenck v. United States,* was decided by the Court in 1919, followed by three others the same year.

While reading *Schenck,* keep in mind the circumstances surrounding the Court's decision. The United States had just successfully completed a war effort in which more than 4 million Americans were in uniform and more than 1 million troops had been sent to fight in Europe. The number of Americans killed or seriously wounded exceeded 300,000. There had been tremendous national fervor and support for the war effort. In the face of this national unity, a socialist had engaged in active opposition to America's participation in the war. His appeal from an espionage conviction allowed the Supreme Court to make its first major doctrinal statement on freedom of expression. What did the Court decide? What standard did it develop to adjudicate future claims?

Schenck v. United States

249 U.S. 47 (1919)
laws.findlaw.com/US/249/47.html
Vote: 9 (Brandeis, Clarke, Day, Holmes, McKenna,
    McReynolds, Pitney, Van Devanter, White)
    0
Opinion of the Court: Holmes

In 1917 Charles Schenck, the general secretary of the Socialist Party of Philadelphia, printed fifteen thousand pamphlets urging resistance to the draft. He sent these leaflets, described by the government's case as "frank, bitter, passionate appeal[s] for resistance to the Selective Service Law," to men listed in a local newspaper as eligible for service. Federal authorities charged him with violating the Espionage Act; specifically, the United States alleged that Schenck attempted to obstruct recruitment and illegally used the mail to do so.

Henry J. Gibbons, Schenck's attorney, did not dispute the government's charges; rather, he argued that the Espionage Act violated the First Amendment's Free Speech Clause because it placed a chilling effect on expression. That is, the act prohibited speech or publication before the words are uttered, and not after, as, Gibbons argued, the Constitution mandated.

MR. JUSTICE HOLMES delivered the opinion of the Court.

The document in question upon its first printed side recited the first section of the Thirteenth Amendment, said that the idea embodied in it was violated by the Conscription Act and that a conscript is little better than a convict. In impassioned language it intimated that conscription was despotism in its worst form and a monstrous wrong against humanity in the interest of Wall Street's chosen few. It said "Do not submit to intimidation," but in form at least confined itself to peaceful measures such as a petition for the repeal of the act. The other and later printed side of the sheet was headed "Assert Your Rights." It stated reasons for alleging that any one violated the Constitution when he refused to recognize "your right to assert your opposition to the draft," and went on "If you do not assert and support your rights, you are helping to deny or disparage rights which it is the solemn duty of all citizens and residents of the United States to retain." It described the arguments on the other side as coming from cunning politicians and a mercenary capitalist press, and even silent consent to the conscription law as helping to support an infamous conspiracy. It denied the power to send our citizens away to foreign shores to shoot up the people of other lands, and added that words could not express the condemnation such cold-blooded ruthlessness deserves, &c., &c., winding up "You must do your share to maintain, support and uphold the rights of the people of this country." Of course the document would not have been sent unless it had been intended to have some effect, and we do not see what effect it could be expected to have upon persons subject to the draft except to influence them to obstruct the carrying of it out. The defendants do not deny that the jury might find against them on this point.

But it is said, suppose that that was the tendency of this circular, it is protected by the First Amendment to the Constitution. Two of the strongest expressions are said to be quoted respectively from well-known public men. It may well be that the prohibition of laws abridging the freedom of speech is not confined to previous constraints, although to prevent them may have been the main purpose. We admit that in many places and in ordinary times the defendants in saying all that was said in the circular would have been within their constitutional rights. But the character of every act depends upon the circumstances in which it is done. The most stringent protection of free speech would not protect a man in falsely shouting fire in a theatre and causing a panic. It does not even protect a man from an injunction against uttering words that may have all the effect of force. The question in every case is whether the words used are used in such circumstances and are of such a nature as to create a clear and present danger that they will bring about the substantive evils that Congress has a right to prevent. It is a question of proximity and degree. When a nation is at war many things that might be said in time of peace are such a hindrance to its effort that their utterance will not be endured so long as men fight and that no Court could regard them as protected by any constitutional right. It seems to be admitted that if an actual obstruction of the recruiting service were proved, liability for words that produced that effect might be enforced. The statute of 1917 in §4 punishes conspiracies to obstruct as well as actual obstruction. If the act, (speaking, or circulating a paper), its tendency and the intent with which it is done are the same, we perceive no ground for saying that success alone warrants making the act a crime. Indeed that case might be said to dispose of the present contention if the precedent covers all *media concludendi* [the steps of an argument]. But as the right to free speech was not referred to specifically, we have thought fit to add a few words.

It was not argued that a conspiracy to obstruct the draft was not within the words of the Act of 1917. The words are "obstruct the recruiting or enlistment service," and it might be suggested that they refer only to making it hard to get volunteers. Recruiting heretofore usually having been accomplished by getting volunteers the word is apt to call up that method only in our minds. But recruiting is gaining fresh supplies for the forces, as well by draft as otherwise. It is put as an alternative to enlistment or voluntary enrollment in this act. . . .

Judgments affirmed.

Many scholars assert that Holmes's opinion in *Schenck* represents not only his finest work but also a most important and substantial explication of free speech. Why? First, Holmes provided the Court with a mechanism for framing such cases and a standard by which to adjudicate future claims:

The question in every case is whether the words used are used in such circumstances and are of such a nature as to create a clear and present danger that they will bring about the substantive evils that Congress has a right to prevent.

Known as the clear and present danger test, the standard apparently reflected the other justices' views on free speech because the Court's decision in *Schenck* was unanimous.

Second, Holmes's opinion was a politically astute compromise. On the one hand, the clear and present danger test was a rather liberal interpretation of expression rights. On the other, the justices recognized that free speech rights were not absolute and found room within the clear and present danger test to uphold the conviction of an unpopular opponent of the war effort. By doing so, Holmes was able to write into law a test favorable to expression rights without arousing the ire of Congress.

One week after *Schenck*, Holmes applied his clear and present danger standard to two other challenges to the Espionage Act. In *Frohwerk v. United States* a newspaper editor and an editorial writer for the *Missouri Staats Zeitung* urged the Court to overturn their convictions for publishing a series of articles accusing the United States of pursuing an imperialistic policy toward Germany. In *Frohwerk*'s companion case, *Debs v. United States*, Eugene V. Debs, a leader of the Socialist Party in the United States, had been convicted for a speech he delivered in Canton, Ohio. Extolling the virtues of socialism and praising the Bolshevik Revolution, Debs said:

The Socialist has a great idea. An expanding philosophy. It is spreading over the face of the earth. It is as useless to resist it as it is to resist the rising sunrise. . . . What a privilege it is to serve it. I have regretted a thousand times I can do so little for the movement that has done so much for me. . . . Do not worry over the charge of treason to your masters, but be concerned about the treason that involves yourself. This year we are going to sweep into power . . . and we are going to destroy capitalistic institutions and recreate them.

Federal authorities arrested Debs, charging him with attempting to incite insubordination, a violation of the Espionage Act. They cited as "evidence" not only his words, but the timing of his speech, just after Congress passed the Selective Service Act. Writing for the Court in both cases, Justice Holmes relied on the clear and present danger test to uphold the Debs and Frohwerk convictions. In fact, his only new statement of any significance was "that the First Amendment while prohibiting legislation against free speech as such cannot have been, and obviously was not intended to give immunity for every possible use of language."

Such an assertion again underscores the Court's unwillingness to read literally and absolutely First Amendment guarantees. Moreover, because Holmes wrote for the majority in both cases, the future vitality of the clear and present danger test seemed assured; the Court apparently agreed that it provided a reasonable vehicle for judging First Amendment claims.

But, just eight months after the *Debs* and *Frohwerk* decisions, a majority of justices banished this test to a legal exile that would last for almost two decades. The first hint of their disaffection came in *Abrams v. United States*, the last of the 1919 quartet. In reading the *Abrams* decision, notice how Justice John H. Clarke's majority opinion moves away from the clear and present danger language and instead emphasizes the defendants' intentions and the tendency of the expression to cause illegal actions. Holmes's dissent, on the other hand, uses the clear and present danger philosophy to defend the right of political expression.

Abrams v. United States

250 U.S. 616 (1919)
laws.findlaw.com/US/250/616.html
Vote: 7 *(Clarke, Day, McKenna, McReynolds, Pitney,*
*   Van Devanter, White)*
*   2 (Brandeis, Holmes)*
Opinion of the Court: Clarke
Dissenting opinion: Holmes

In October 1918, just weeks before the end of World War I, Jacob Abrams and four others were convicted of violating the Espionage Act. The defendants, well-educated Russian immigrants, all professed revolutionary, anarchist, or socialist political views. The conspirators had published and distributed leaflets, written in English and Yiddish, criticizing President Wilson's decision to send U.S. troops into Russia and calling for a general strike to protest that policy. The leaflets were written in language characteristic of the rhetoric of the Russian Revolution: "Workers of the World! Awake! Rise! Put down your enemy and mine!" and "Yes! friends, there is only one enemy of the workers of the world and that is CAPITALISM." They described the government of the United States as a "hypocritical," "cowardly," and "capitalistic" enemy. The protesters branded Wilson a "Kaiser." The government charged Abrams and the others with intent to "cripple or hinder the United States in the prosecution of the war." The trial court sentenced the defendants to prison terms of fifteen to twenty years.

MR. JUSTICE CLARKE delivered the opinion of the Court.

It was admitted on the trial that the defendants had united to print and distribute the described circulars and that five thousand of them had been printed and distributed about the 22d day of August, 1918. The group had a meeting place in New York City, in rooms rented by defendant Abrams, under an assumed name, and there the subject of printing the circulars was discussed about two weeks before the defendants were arrested. The defendant Abrams, although not a printer, on July 27, 1918, purchased the printing outfit with which the circulars were printed

Samuel Lipman, Hyman Lychowsky, Mollie Steimer, and Jacob Abrams, World War I–era anarchists and revolutionaries, were found guilty of attempting to hinder the war effort. The Supreme Court upheld the convictions in *Abrams v. New York.*

and installed it in a basement room where the work was done at night. The circulars were distributed, some by throwing them from a window of a building where one of the defendants was employed and others secretly, in New York City.

The defendants pleaded "not guilty," and the case of the Government consisted in showing the facts we have stated, and in introducing in evidence copies of the two printed circulars attached to the indictment, a sheet entitled "Revolutionists Unite for Action," written by the defendant Lipman, and found on him when he was arrested, and another paper, found at the headquarters of the group, and for which Abrams assumed responsibility. . . .

The claim chiefly elaborated upon by the defendants in the oral argument and in their brief is that there is no substantial evidence in the record to support the judgment upon the verdict of guilty and that the motion of the defendants for an instructed verdict in their favor was erroneously denied. A question of law is thus presented, which calls for an examination of the record, not for the purpose of weighing conflicting testimony, but only to determine whether there was some evidence, competent and substantial, before the jury, fairly tending to sustain the verdict. . . .

It will not do to say, as is now argued, that the only intent of these defendants was to prevent injury to the Russian cause. Men must be held to have intended, and to be accountable for, the effects which their acts were likely to produce. Even if their primary purpose and intent was to aid the cause of the Russian Revolution, the plan of action which they adopted necessarily involved, before it could be realized, defeat of the war program of the United States, for the obvious effect of this appeal, if it should become effective, as they hoped it might, would be to persuade persons of character such as those whom they regarded themselves as addressing, not to aid government loans and not to work in ammunition factories, where their work would produce "bullets, bayonets, cannon" and other munitions of war, the use of which would cause the "murder" of Germans and Russians. . . .

This is not an attempt to bring about a change of administration by candid discussion, for no matter what may have incited the outbreak on the part of the defendant anarchists, the manifest purpose of such a publication was to create an attempt to defeat the war plans of the Government of the United States, by bringing upon the country the paralysis of a general strike, thereby arresting the production of all munitions and other things essential to the conduct of the war. . . .

That the interpretation we have put upon these articles, circulated in the greatest port of our land, from which great numbers of soldiers were at the time taking ship daily, and in which great quantities of war supplies of every kind were at the time being manufactured for transportation overseas, is not only the fair interpretation of them, but that it is the meaning which their authors consciously intended should be conveyed by them to others is further shown by the additional writings found in the meeting place of the defendant group and on the person of one of them. . . .

Thus was again avowed the purpose to throw the country into a state of revolution if possible and to thereby frustrate the military program of the Government. . . .

. . . [T]he immediate occasion for this particular outbreak of lawlessness, on the part of the defendant alien anarchists, may have been resentment caused by our Government sending troops into Russia as a strategic operation against the Germans on the eastern battle front, yet the plain purpose of their propaganda was to excite, at the supreme crisis of the war, disaffection, sedition, riots, and, as they hoped, revolution, in this country for the purpose of embarrassing and if possible defeating the military plans of the Government in Europe. A technical distinction may perhaps be taken between disloyal and abusive language applied to the *form* of our government or language intended to bring the *form* of our government into contempt and disrepute, and language of like character and intended to produce like results directed against the President and Congress, the agencies through which that form of government must function in time of war. But it is not necessary to a decision of this case to consider whether such distinction is vital or merely formal, for the language of these circulars was obviously intended to provoke and to encourage resistance to the United States in the war, as the third count runs, and, the defendants, in terms, plainly urged and advocated a resort to a general strike of workers in ammunition factories for the purpose of curtailing the production of ordnance and munitions necessary and essential to the prosecution of the war as is charged in the fourth count. Thus it is clear not only that some evidence but that much persuasive evidence was before the jury tending to prove that the defendants were guilty as charged in both the third and fourth counts of the indictment and under the long established rule of law hereinbefore stated the judgment of the District Court must be

Affirmed.

MR. JUSTICE HOLMES, dissenting.

I never have seen any reason to doubt that the questions of law that alone were before this Court in the cases of *Schenck, Frohwerk* and *Debs* were rightly decided. I do not doubt for a moment that by the same reasoning that would justify punishing persuasion to murder, the United States constitutionally may punish speech that produces or is intended to produce a clear and imminent danger that it will bring about forthwith certain substantive evils that the United States constitutionally may seek to prevent. The power undoubtedly is greater in time of war than in time of peace because war opens dangers that do not exist at other times.

But as against dangers peculiar to war, as against others, the principle of the right to free speech is always the same.

It is only the present danger of immediate evil or an intent to bring it about that warrants Congress in setting a limit to the expression of opinion where private rights are not concerned. Congress certainly cannot forbid all effort to change the mind of the country. Now nobody can suppose that the surreptitious publishing of a silly leaflet by an unknown man, without more, would present any immediate danger that its opinions would hinder the success of the government arms or have any appreciable tendency to do so. Publishing those opinions for the very purpose of obstructing however, might indicate a greater danger and at any rate would have the quality of an attempt. So I assume that the second leaflet if published for the purposes alleged in the fourth count might be punishable. But it seems pretty clear to me that nothing less than that would bring these papers within the scope of this law. An actual intent in the sense that I have explained is necessary to constitute an attempt, where a further act of the same individual is required to complete the substantive crime. . . . It is necessary where the success of the attempt depends upon others because if that intent is not present the actor's aim may be accomplished without bringing about the evils sought to be checked. An intent to prevent interference with the revolution in Russia might have been satisfied without any hindrance to carrying on the war in which we were engaged.

I do not see how anyone can find the intent required by the statute in any of the defendants' words. . . .

In this case sentences of twenty years imprisonment have been imposed for the publishing of two leaflets that I believe the defendants had as much right to publish as the Government has to publish the Constitution of the United States now vainly invoked by them. Even if I am technically wrong and enough can be squeezed from these poor and puny anonymities to turn the color of legal litmus paper; I will add, even if what I think the necessary intent were shown; the most nominal punishment seems to me all that possibly could be inflicted, unless the defendants are to be made to suffer not for what the indictment alleges but for the creed that they avow—a creed that I believe to be the creed of ignorance and immaturity when honestly held, as I see no reason to doubt that it was held here, but which, although made the subject of examination at the trial, no one has a right even to consider in dealing with the charges before the Court.

Persecution for the expression of opinions seems to me perfectly logical. If you have no doubt of your premises or your power and want a certain result with all your heart you naturally express your wishes in law and sweep away all opposition. To allow opposition by speech seems to indicate that you think the speech impotent, as when a man says that he has squared the circle, or that you do not care whole-heartedly for the result, or that you doubt either your power or your premises. But when men have realized that time has upset many fighting faiths, they may come to believe even more than they believe the very foundations of their own conduct that the ultimate good desired is better reached by free trade in ideas—that the best test of truth is the power of the thought to get itself accepted in the competition of the market, and that truth is the only ground upon which their wishes safely can be carried out. That at any rate is the theory of our Constitution. It is an experiment, as all life is an experiment. Every year if not every day we have to wager our salvation upon some prophecy based upon imperfect knowledge. While that experiment is part of our system I think that we should be eternally vigilant against attempts to check the expression of opinions that we loathe and believe to be fraught with death, unless they so imminently threaten immediate interference with the lawful and pressing purposes of the law that an immediate check is required to save the country. I wholly disagree with the argument of the Government that the First Amendment left the common law as to seditious libel in force. History seems to me against the notion. I had conceived that the United States through many years had shown its repentance for the Sedition Act of 1798, by repaying fines that it imposed. Only the emergency that makes it immediately dangerous to leave the correction of evil counsels to time warrants making any exception to the sweeping command, "Congress shall make no law . . . abridging the freedom of speech." Of course I am speaking only of expressions of opinion and exhortations, which were all that were uttered here, but I regret that I cannot put into more impressive words my belief that in their conviction upon this indictment the defendants were deprived of their rights under the Constitution of the United States.

MR. JUSTICE BRANDEIS concurs with the foregoing opinion.

It was evident to Holmes that the *Abrams* decision marked a turning away from the clear and present danger standard. In his dissent he tried to refine the test to show how the *Schenck* rationale could work in a variety of contexts. Many view this dissent as one of Holmes's finest, earning him the sobriquet "the Great Dissenter." *(See Box 5-1.)*

But Holmes failed to convince his colleagues in *Abrams*. Instead, Clarke's majority opinion used a standard known as the bad tendency test, an approach derived from English common law. It asks, "Do the words have a *tendency* to bring about something evil?" rather than "Do the words bring about an immediate substantive evil?" Why the majority shifted constitutional standards is a mystery. We cannot say that the clear and present danger test produced results markedly different from the bad tendency standard. After all, Holmes had used the clear and present danger test in *Schenck, Debs,* and *Frohwerk* to uphold convictions, not overturn them.

Regardless of their motivation, by the early 1920s it was obvious that a majority of justices rejected the clear and present danger standard in favor of more stringent constitutional interpretations, such as the bad tendency test. Two cases, *Gitlow v. New York* (1925) and *Whitney v. California* (1927), exemplify this shift, but with a slightly different twist. *Gitlow* and *Whitney* involved state prosecutions, not Espionage Act violations. Just as the federal government wanted to foster patriotism during wartime, the states also felt the need to promulgate their own versions of nationalism. The result was passage of so-called state criminal syndicalism laws, which made it a crime to advocate, teach, aid, or abet in any activity designed to bring about the overthrow of the government by force or violence. The actual effect of such laws was to outlaw any association with views "abhorrent" to the interests of the United States, such as communism and socialism. Would the Court be willing to tolerate state intrusions into free speech? That was the question with which the justices grappled in *Gitlow* and *Whitney*.

BOX 5-1 OLIVER WENDELL HOLMES JR. (1902–1932)

OLIVER WENDELL HOLMES JR. was born March 8, 1841, in Boston. He was named after his father, a professor of anatomy at Harvard Medical School as well as a poet, essayist, and novelist in the New England literary circle that included Longfellow, Emerson, Lowell, and Whittier. Dr. Holmes's wife, Amelia Lee Jackson Holmes, was the third daughter of Justice Charles Jackson of the Supreme Judicial Court of Massachusetts. Young Holmes attended a private Latin school in Cambridge and received his undergraduate education at Harvard, graduating as class poet in 1861 as had his father thirty-two years before him.

Commissioned a second lieutenant in the Massachusetts Twentieth Volunteers, known as the Harvard Regiment, Holmes was wounded three times in battle. Serving three years, he was mustered out a captain in recognition of his bravery and gallant service. After the Civil War, Holmes returned to Harvard to study law despite his father's conviction that "a lawyer can't be a great man."

He was admitted to the Massachusetts bar in 1867 and practiced in Boston for fifteen years, beginning with the firm of Chandler, Shattuck, and Thayer and later forming his own partnership with Shattuck. In 1872 Holmes married Fanny Bowdich Dixwell, the daughter of his former schoolmaster and a friend since childhood. They were married fifty-seven years.

During his legal career Holmes taught constitutional law at his alma mater, edited the *American Law Review,* and lectured on common law at the Lowell Institute. His twelve lectures were compiled in a book called *The Common Law* and published shortly before his fortieth birthday. The London *Spectator* heralded Holmes's treatise as the most original work of legal speculation in decades. *The Common Law* was translated into German, Italian, and French.

IN 1882 THE GOVERNOR of Massachusetts appointed Holmes— then a full professor at the Harvard Law School in a chair established by Boston lawyer Louis D. Brandeis— an associate justice of the Massachusetts Supreme Court.

Holmes served on the state court for twenty years, the last three as chief justice, and wrote more than 1,000 opinions, many of them involving labor disputes. Holmes's progressive labor views, criticized by railroad and corporate interests, were considered favorably by President Theodore Roosevelt during his search in 1902 for someone to fill the "Massachusetts seat" on the U.S. Supreme Court, vacated by Bostonian Horace Gray. Convinced of Holmes's compatibility with the administration's national policies, Roosevelt nominated him associate justice December 2 and he was confirmed without objection two days later.

Holmes's twenty-nine years of service on the Supreme Court spanned the tenures of Chief Justices Fuller, White, Taft, and Hughes and the administrations of Presidents Roosevelt, Taft, Wilson, Harding, Coolidge, and Hoover.

For twenty-five years he never missed a session and daily walked the two and a half miles from his home to the Court. Like Justice Brandeis, Holmes voluntarily paid an income tax despite the majority's ruling that exempted federal judges. Unlike the idealistic and often moralistic Brandeis, with whom he is frequently compared, Holmes was pragmatic, approaching each case on its own set of facts without a preconceived notion of the proper result.

Although a lifelong Republican, on the Court Holmes did not fulfill Roosevelt's expectations as a loyal party man. His dissent shortly after his appointment from the Court's decision to break up the railroad trust of the Northern Securities Company surprised the nation and angered the president.

At the suggestion of Chief Justice Hughes and his colleagues on the bench, Holmes retired on January 12, 1932, at the age of ninety. A widower since 1929, he continued to spend his winters in Washington, D.C., and his summers in Beverly Farms, Massachusetts. He died at his Washington home March 6, 1935, two days before his ninety-fourth birthday.

SOURCE: Adapted from Joan Biskupic and Elder Witt, *Guide to the U.S. Supreme Court,* 3d ed. (Washington, D.C.: Congressional Quarterly, 1997), 911–912.

Gitlow v. New York

268 U.S. 652 (1925)
laws.findlaw.com/US/268/652.html
Vote: 7 (Butler, Reynolds, Sanford, Stone, Sutherland, Taft,
      Van Devanter)
      2 (Brandeis, Holmes)
Opinion of the Court: Sanford
Dissenting opinion: Holmes

The issues in *Gitlow v. New York* arose during the early part of the twentieth century when fear of communist subversion gripped the United States. To combat the so-called red menace, several states, including New York, created commissions to investigate subversive organizations. In 1919 and 1920 the New York Commission conducted raids on socialist and communist leaders and seized their materials. Among those arrested was Benjamin Gitlow, a socialist charged with distributing a pamphlet called the *Left Wing Manifesto.* The *Manifesto* called for mass action to overthrow the capitalist system in the United States. Gitlow was prosecuted in a New York trial court for violating the state's criminal anarchy law. Under the leadership of Clarence Darrow, Gitlow's defense attorneys alleged that the statute violated the First Amendment's guarantee of freedom of expression. The defense was unsuccessful, and Gitlow appealed.

William Foster, left, and Benjamin Gitlow, presidential and vice presidential candidates for the Workers (Communist) Party, at Madison Square Garden in 1928. Gitlow's publication of a "Left Wing Manifesto" led to his arrest and conviction under New York's criminal anarchy act. The Supreme Court upheld the conviction, but ruled that states were bound by the freedom of speech provision of the First Amendment.

MR. JUSTICE SANFORD delivered the opinion of the Court.

Benjamin Gitlow was indicted in the Supreme Court of New York, with three others, for the statutory crime of criminal anarchy. He was separately tried, convicted, and sentenced to imprisonment. . . .

The sole contention here is, essentially, that as there was no evidence of any concrete result flowing from the publication of the Manifesto or of circumstances showing the likelihood of such result, the statute as construed and applied by the trial court penalizes the mere utterance, as such, of "doctrine" having no quality of incitement, without regard either to the circumstances of its utterance or to the likelihood of unlawful sequences; and that, as the exercise of the right of free expression with relation to government is only

punishable "in circumstances involving likelihood of substantive evil," the statute contravenes the due process clause of the Fourteenth Amendment. The argument in support of this contention rests primarily upon the following propositions: 1st, That the "liberty" protected by the Fourteenth Amendment includes the liberty of speech and of the press; and 2d, That while liberty of expression "is not absolute," it may be restrained "only in circumstances where its exercise bears a causal relation with some substantive evil, consummated, attempted or likely," and as the statute "takes no account of circumstances," it unduly restrains this liberty and is therefore unconstitutional.

The precise question presented, and the only question which we can consider under this writ of error, then is, whether the statute, as construed and applied in this case by the State courts, deprived the defendant of his liberty of expression in violation of the due process clause of the Fourteenth Amendment.

The statute does not penalize the utterance or publication of abstract "doctrine" or academic discussion having no quality of incitement to any concrete action. It is not aimed against mere historical or philosophical essays. It does not restrain the advocacy of changes in the form of government by constitutional and lawful means. What it prohibits is language advocating, advising or teaching the overthrow of organized government by unlawful means. These words imply urging to action. Advocacy is defined in the Century Dictionary as: "1. The act of pleading for, supporting, or recommending; active espousal." It is not the abstract "doctrine" of overthrowing organized government by unlawful means which is denounced by the statute, but the advocacy of action for the accomplishment of that purpose. . . .

The Manifesto, plainly, is neither the statement of abstract doctrine nor, as suggested by counsel, mere prediction that industrial disturbances and revolutionary mass strikes will result spontaneously in an inevitable process of evolution in the economic system. It advocates and urges in fervent language mass action which shall progressively foment industrial disturbances and through political mass strikes and revolutionary mass action overthrow and destroy organized parliamentary government. It concludes with a call to action in these words:

"The proletariat revolution and the Communist reconstruction of society—*the struggle for these*—is now indispensable. . . . The Communist International calls the proletariat of the world to the final struggle!"

This is not the expression of philosophical abstraction, the mere prediction of future events; it is the language of direct incitement.

The means advocated for bringing about the destruction of organized parliamentary government, namely, mass industrial revolts usurping the functions of municipal government, political mass strikes directed against the parliamentary state, and revolutionary mass action for its final destruction, necessarily imply the use of force and violence, and in their essential nature are inherently unlawful in a constitutional government of law and order. That the jury were warranted in finding that the Manifesto advocated not merely the abstract doctrine of overthrowing organized government by force, violence and unlawful means, but action to that end, is clear.

For present purposes we may and do assume that freedom of speech and of the press—which are protected by the First Amendment from abridgment by Congress—are among the fundamental personal rights and "liberties" protected by the due process clause of the Fourteenth Amendment from impairment by the States. . . . It is a fundamental principle, long established, that the freedom of speech and of the press which is secured by the Constitution, does not confer an absolute right to speak or publish, without responsibility, whatever one may choose, or an unrestricted and unbridled license that gives immunity for every possible use of language and prevents the punishment of those who abuse this freedom. Reasonably limited . . . this freedom is an inestimable privilege in a free government; without such limitation, it might become the scourge of the republic.

That a State in the exercise of its police power may punish those who abuse this freedom by utterances inimical to the public welfare, tending to corrupt public morals, incite to crime, or disturb the public peace, is not open to question.

And, for yet more imperative reasons, a State may punish utterances endangering the foundations of organized government and threatening its overthrow by unlawful means. These imperil its own existence as a constitutional State. Freedom of speech and press . . . does not protect disturbances to the public peace or the attempt to subvert the government. It does not protect publications or teachings which tend to subvert or imperil the government or to impede or hinder it in the performance of its governmental duties. It does not protect publications prompting the overthrow of government by force; the punishment of those who publish articles which tend to destroy organized society being essential to the security of freedom and the stability of the State. And a State may penalize utterances which openly advocate the overthrow of the representative and constitutional form of government of the United States and the several States, by violence or other unlawful means. In short this freedom does not deprive a State of the primary and essential right of self preservation; which, so long as human governments endure, they cannot be denied.

By enacting the present statute the State has determined, through its legislative body, that utterances advocating the overthrow of organized government by force, violence and unlawful means, are so inimical to the general welfare and involve such danger of substantive evil that they may be penalized in the exercise of its police power. That determination must be given great weight. Every presumption is to be indulged in favor of the validity of the statute. And the case is to be considered "in the light of the principle that the State is primarily the judge of regulations required in the interest of public safety and welfare"; and that its police "statutes may only be declared unconstitutional where they are arbitrary or unreasonable attempts to exercise authority vested in the State in the public interest." That utterances inciting to the overthrow of organized government by unlawful means, present a sufficient danger of substantive evil to bring their punishment within the range of legislative discretion, is clear. Such utterances, by their very nature, involve danger to the public peace and to the security of the State. They threaten breaches of the peace and ultimate revolution. And the immediate danger is none the less real and substantial, because the effect of a given utterance cannot be accurately foreseen. The State cannot reasonably be required to measure the danger from every such utterance in the nice balance of a jeweler's scale. A single revolutionary spark may kindle a fire that, smouldering for a time, may burst into a sweeping and destructive conflagration. It cannot be said that the State is acting arbitrarily or unreasonably when in the exercise of its judgment as to the measures necessary to protect the public peace and safety, it seeks to extinguish the spark without waiting until it has enkindled the flame or blazed into the conflagration. It cannot reasonably be required to defer the adoption of measures for its own peace and safety until the revolutionary utterances lead to actual disturbances of the public peace or imminent and immediate danger of its own destruction; but it may, in the exercise of its judgment, suppress the threatened danger in its incipiency.

We cannot hold that the present statute is an arbitrary or unreasonable exercise of the police power of the State unwarrantably infringing the freedom of speech or press; and we must and do sustain its constitutionality.

This being so it may be applied to every utterance—not too trivial to be beneath the notice of the law—which is of such a character and used with such intent and purpose as to bring it within the prohibition of the statute. In other words, when the legislative body has determined generally, in the constitutional exercise of its discretion, that utterances of a certain kind involve such danger of substantive evil that they may be punished, the question whether any specific utterance coming within the prohibited class is likely, in and of itself, to bring about the substantive evil, is not open to consideration. It is sufficient that the statute itself be constitutional and that the use of the language comes within its prohibition.

It is clear that the question in such cases is entirely different from that involved in those cases where the statute merely prohibits certain acts involving the danger of substantive evil, without any reference to language itself, and it is sought to apply its provisions to language used by the defendant for the purpose of bringing about the prohibited results. There, if it be contended that the statute cannot be applied to the language used by the defendant because of its protection by the freedom of speech or press, it must necessarily be found, as an original question, without any previous determination by the legislative body, whether the specific language used involved such likelihood of bringing about the substantive evil as to deprive it of the constitutional protection. In such case it has been held that the general provisions of the statute may be constitutionally applied to the specific utterance of the defendant if its natural tendency and probable effect was to bring about the substantive evil which the legislative body might prevent. And the general statement in the Schenck Case, that the "question in every case is whether the words used are used in such circumstances and are of such a nature as to create a clear and present danger that they will bring about the substantive evils,"—upon which great reliance is placed in the defendant's argument—was manifestly intended, as shown by the context, to apply only in cases of this class, and has no application to those like the present, where the legislative body itself has previously determined the danger of substantive evil arising from utterances of a specified character.

The defendant's brief does not separately discuss any of the rulings of the trial court. It is only necessary to say that, applying the general rules already stated, we find that none of them involved any invasion of the constitutional rights of the defendant. It was not necessary, within the meaning of the statute, that the defendant should have advocated "some definite or immediate act or acts" of force, violence or unlawfulness. It was sufficient if such acts were advocated in general terms; and it was not essential that their immediate execution should have been advocated. Nor was it necessary that the language should have been "reasonably and ordinarily calculated to incite certain persons" to acts of force, violence or unlawfulness. The advocacy need not be addressed to specific persons. . . .

And finding, for the reasons stated, that the statute is not in itself unconstitutional, and that it has not been applied in the present case in derogation of any constitutional right, the judgment of the Court of Appeals is

Affirmed.

MR. JUSTICE HOLMES, dissenting.

MR. JUSTICE BRANDEIS and I are of opinion that this judgment should be reversed. The general principle of free speech, it seems to me, must be taken to be included in the Fourteenth Amendment, in view of the scope that has been given to the word "liberty" as there used, although perhaps it may be accepted with a somewhat larger latitude of interpretation than is allowed to Congress by the sweeping language that governs or ought to govern the laws of the United States. If I am right, then I think that the criterion sanctioned by the full Court in *Schenck v. United States* applies. "The question in every case is whether the words used are used in such circumstances and are of such a nature as to create a clear and present danger that they will bring about the substantive evils that [the State] has a right to prevent." It is true that in my opinion this criterion was departed from in *Abrams v. United States,* but the convictions that I expressed in that case are too deep for it to be possible for me as yet to believe that it and *Schaefer v. United States* [1920] have settled the law. If what I think the correct test is applied, it is manifest that there was no present danger of an attempt to overthrow the government by force on the part of the admittedly small minority who shared the defendant's views. It is said that this manifesto was more than a theory, that it was an incitement. Every idea is an incitement. It offers itself for belief and if believed it is acted on unless some other belief outweighs it or some failure of energy stifles the movement at its birth. The only difference between the expression of an opinion and an incitement in the narrower sense is the speaker's enthusiasm for the result. Eloquence may set fire to reason. But whatever may be thought of the redundant discourse

before us it had no chance of starting a present conflagration. If in the long run the beliefs expressed in proletarian dictatorship are destined to be accepted by the dominant forces of the community, the only meaning of free speech is that they should be given their chance and have their way.

If the publication of this document had been laid as an attempt to induce an uprising against government at once and not at some indefinite time in the future it would have presented a different question. The object would have been one with which the law might deal, subject to the doubt whether there was any danger that the publication could produce any result, or in other words, whether it was not futile and too remote from possible consequences. But the indictment alleges the publication and nothing more.

Gitlow's effect on the development of civil liberties law is somewhat mixed. Perhaps its most enduring contribution is the statement that for "present purposes we may and do assume that freedom of speech and of the press—which are protected by the First Amendment from abridgment by Congress—are among the fundamental personal rights and 'liberties' protected by the due process clause of the Fourteenth Amendment from impairment by the States." This sweeping incorporation vastly expanded constitutional guarantees for freedom of expression. The prohibition against infringing on the freedoms of speech and press now applied to state and local governments as well as the federal government.

However, *Gitlow* also limited personal freedom by moving farther away from the clear and present danger approach and embracing the bad tendency test. Look carefully at Justice Edward Sanford's majority opinion. He emphasizes that the possible danger resulting from speech need not be immediate to justify regulation: "A single revolutionary spark may kindle a fire that, smouldering for a time, may burst into a sweeping and destructive conflagration." The effect of the speech cannot be immediately foreseen. In addition, the Court held that great deference should be given to the legislature's determination of what dangers warrant regulation and that "every presumption is to be indulged in favor of the validity of the statute."

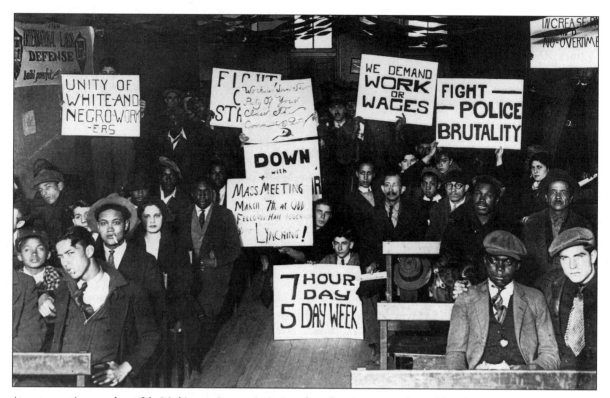

At a 1930 meeting, members of the Washington Communist Society plan a demonstration in front of the White House. The protest activities of such organizations frequently led to arrests and charges of First Amendment violations.

In dissent, Holmes continued to press his clear and present danger standard, arguing that Gitlow's actions posed no obvious and immediate danger. He challenges the majority's view that speech can be regulated for evil effects that might occur sometime in the future by arguing that "every idea is an incitement." For Holmes, whatever danger Gitlow's message might pose, it was too inconsequential and too remote to justify government repression of expression rights.

Whitney v. California involved Charlotte Whitney, a well-known California heiress and a niece of Stephen J. Field, a former Supreme Court justice. She was an active member of the Oakland branch of the Socialist Party and voted for delegates sent by the chapter to a national party meeting held in 1919 in Chicago. At that convention the party ejected its more radical members, including the Oakland delegates, who in turn formed the Communist

Labor Party of the United States. Local party chapters from California then held a state meeting in Oakland, where they created the Communist Labor Party of California.

Although Whitney had opposed the radical platform "urging a revolutionary class struggle" offered at the national convention, she nevertheless served as one of her chapter's delegates to the local meeting and, in fact, became chair of the credentials committee. Based on her association with this group and its predecessor, California authorities charged Whitney with violating the state's syndicalism law. She was found guilty of organizing and associating with a party dedicated to overthrowing the U.S. government.

On appeal to the Supreme Court, her attorneys from the newly formed American Civil Liberties Union *(see Box 5-2)* argued that the California act violated the Free

BOX 5-2 THE AMERICAN CIVIL LIBERTIES UNION

BY ALMOST ALL MEASURES, the American Civil Liberties Union (ACLU) is the largest and most complex organization dedicated to public interest litigation in the United States. Beyond its national organization, the ACLU maintains fifty state and local affiliates and, via its foundation, runs several specialized projects.

Given its current form, the humble origins of the ACLU may come as quite a surprise: the ACLU "was ... very much a phenomenon of the Progressive-Populist era with its concern over government abuse." Indeed, the ACLU's roots lie in a small organization called the Henry Street Group, which was started by several leaders of the Progressive Movement to combat growing militarism. One year later, this group united with another to become the American Union Against Militarism (AUAM).

Between 1915 and 1917 the AUAM tried to lobby against any legislation designed to stimulate the U.S. "war machine." But in 1917, when Germany announced "its intention to resume unrestricted warfare," the AUAM turned its attention to the draft. The organization sought to defend those who had conscientious objections to serving in the military. This goal was handled primarily by an agency within the AUAM, the Bureau of Conscientious Objectors (BCO).

Under the leadership of the young, charismatic Roger Baldwin, the BCO eventually dominated the AUAM. Baldwin's BCO doubled the size of AUAM's membership and spent more than 50 percent of its funds. Clearly, Baldwin was an effective leader, but the old-line Progressive leaders of the AUAM disliked Baldwin's strategy of providing direct assistance to conscientious objectors and threatened to resign. To save the AUAM and to show solidarity with its "greater" agenda, Baldwin changed the name of the BCO to the Civil Liberties Bureau (CLB). This last-ditch effort failed, however, and in 1917 the new National CLB split from its parent organization, which expired shortly thereafter.

Between 1917 and 1919, the NCLB continued to defend conscientious objectors. Unfortunately, it could not prevent Baldwin's imprisonment for draft violations in 1918. Ironically, during Baldwin's jail term the seed for what is now known as the American Civil Liberties Union was planted. In prison, Baldwin became acquainted with the activities of a radical labor union, the Industrial Workers of the World, an organization that made no secret of its use of violence and sabotage to achieve its policy needs.

This name alteration and reorganization forever changed the NCLB. After 1920 the newly formed ACLU would never be a single-purpose organization; by 1925 it was involved with labor, pacifists, and the "Red Scare" caused by the Palmer raids.

Defending the right of free speech eventually became the ACLU's major trademark as the organization moved into the 1930s, 1940s, and 1950s. But while cultivating such expertise, ACLU leaders realized they had to "nationalize" the growing group. Such steps included fuller recognition of the growing chain of ACLU affiliates throughout the United States and provision of more information to its membership, which increased by almost 5,000 annually.

Fortunately for the organization, its efforts to build and regroup during the 1950s were quite timely: the 1960s turned out to be critical years for the union. Not only was the decade significant in the development of law governing civil rights and liberties, but the ACLU itself seemed to embody the goals of the nation. The union's stance against the Vietnam War, President Richard Nixon, and racism, and its defense of draft dodgers and student protesters proved to be highly popular. Between 1966 and 1973, the ACLU's membership skyrocketed from 77,200 to 222,000, and its litigation activities exploded.

To deal with its increasing caseload and to focus its energies on specific areas of the law, the ACLU established the ACLU Foundation in 1967. This foundation, in turn, established special national projects, including the National Prison, Women's Rights, and Reproductive Freedom projects. Today, the union has about 250,000 members and affiliates in every state. The organization currently operates on a $12 million budget.

The ACLU has used these financial and personnel resources to build an increasingly vast and active organization. Currently, the union and its affiliates employ 225 persons and 5 to 10 student interns per year. Staff attorneys account for 38 of its 125 national employees and 35 of the 100 affiliated workers. At the state and local levels, ACLU organizations use volunteer attorneys for 65 percent of their legal work.

SOURCE: Adapted from Karen O'Connor and Lee Epstein, *Public Interest Law Groups* (Westport, Conn.: Greenwood Press, 1989).

Speech Clause of the First Amendment. But the justices upheld her conviction. They treated her claim just as they had Gitlow's, relying on the bad tendency test. The majority asserted in *Whitney,*

That the freedom of speech which is secured by the Constitution does not confer an absolute right to speak . . . whatever one may choose . . . and that a State in the exercise of its police power may punish those who abuse this freedom by utterances inimical to the public welfare, tending to incite crime, disturb the public peace, or endanger the foundations of organized government and threaten its overthrow by unlawful means, is not open to question.

The Court's ruling allowed the punishment of mere membership in a subversive organization without requiring proof of any concrete criminal actions to overthrow the government by illegal means.

Brandeis and Holmes filed a concurrence in *Whitney.* They favored a return to the clear and present danger standard, but with this modification: that the evil take the form of behavior. Justice Brandeis wrote, "No danger flowing from speech can be deemed clear and present, unless the incidence of evil apprehended is so imminent that it may befall before there is opportunity for full discussions." What is even more curious (and a matter of some scholarly interest) is why the duo concurred rather than dissented. It seems clear that Whitney's behavior did not meet the standard they articulated, making the question all the more intriguing. One reasonable hypothesis is that Brandeis wanted to demonstrate that the clear and present danger test was not necessarily a vehicle created to overturn convictions, but merely a more equitable way to adjudge First Amendment claims.

Regardless of the philosophical debates triggered by the series of cases from *Schenck* to *Whitney,* one fact remains clear: the justices seemed swept away by the wave of nationalism and patriotism in the aftermath of World War I. With but one exception, they acceded to the wishes of Congress and the states, which centered around the complementary goals of promoting nationalism and suppressing radicalism.[3]

3. The exception was *Fiske v. Kansas* (1927), decided the same day as *Whitney.* The justices concluded that there was insufficient evidence to sustain Fisk's conviction, and the Court for the first time overturned a conviction under a state syndicalism law.

The 1930s and 1940s: A Return to Clear and Present Danger

As the anxieties of World War I and its aftermath faded, the debate over seditious speech was argued in calmer voices. As part of this general trend, the Supreme Court began to reevaluate its decisions from *Schenck* to *Whitney.*

The Court's greater willingness to consider the message of civil liberties advocates was first signaled in *Stromberg v. California* (1931). Yetta Stromberg, a nineteen-year-old member of the Young Communist League, served as a counselor at a summer camp for children ages ten to fifteen. She regularly introduced her campers to Marxist theory. In addition, she would raise a red banner and lead the children in reciting a workers' pledge of allegiance. She was convicted of violating a state statute make it a crime to raise publicly a red flag or banner as a symbol of opposition to organized government or in support of anarchy. The Supreme Court reversed the conviction, holding that the California statute was excessively broad, applying not only to those who advocated violent overthrow of the government, but also those who supported political change by orderly and peaceful means. Such vagueness and ambiguity do not comport with the demands of the First Amendment.

Stromberg was followed six years later by *DeJonge v. Oregon* (1937). As a member of the Communist Party in Portland, Oregon, Dirk DeJonge distributed handbills throughout the city, calling for a meeting of all members and other interested parties. The purpose of the gathering was to protest police raids of members' houses. DeJonge held the meeting on July 27, 1934, and between 160 and 200 people attended, only a small percentage of whom belonged to the party. Although the members tried to sell copies of the party's newspaper, the *Daily Worker,* the agenda of the meeting was quite general, with all proceeding in an orderly fashion until the police raided it. They arrested DeJonge for violating Oregon's criminal syndicalism law, which prohibited the organization of the Communist Party.

The Supreme Court overturned DeJonge's conviction on this charge. The justices unanimously held that the state violated the First Amendment. The meeting was peaceful and orderly. DeJonge had not engaged in any "forcible subversion." According to the majority opinion by Chief Justice Charles Evans Hughes, written in language closely resembling the clear and present danger test, "peaceful assembly for lawful discussion cannot be made a crime."

Even more dramatic was a seemingly insignificant bit of writing—a footnote contained in Justice Harlan F. Stone's opinion in *United States v. Carolene Products* (1938). This case dealt with a federal ban on the shipment of a certain kind of milk—an economic, not a First Amendment, issue. Stone's fourth footnote in this opinion includes the following:

There may be narrower scope for operation of the presumption of constitutionality when legislation appears on its face to be within a specific prohibition of the Constitution, such as those of the first ten Amendments, which are deemed equally specific when held to be embraced by the Fourteenth Amendment. . . .

It is unnecessary to consider now whether legislation which restricts those political processes which can ordinarily be expected to bring about repeal of undesirable legislation, is to be subjected to more exacting judicial scrutiny under the general prohibitions of the Fourteenth Amendment than are most other types of legislation. . . .

Nor need we enquire whether similar considerations enter into the review of statutes directed at particular religious, or national, or racial minorities; whether prejudice against discrete and insular minorities may be a special condition, which tends seriously to curtail the operation of those political processes ordinarily to be relied upon to protect minorities, and which may call for a correspondingly more searching judicial inquiry.

What appeared to be an obscure footnote in a relatively insignificant case took on tremendous importance for civil liberties claims, especially those based on First Amendment expression rights. As Alpheus Mason and Grier Stephenson explain, each of the footnote's three paragraphs contained powerful ideas regarding the status of constitutional rights.[4] The first paragraph holds that whenever a government regulation appears on its face to be in conflict with the Bill of Rights, the usual pre-

sumption that laws are constitutional should be reduced or waived altogether. The second paragraph hints that the judiciary has a special responsibility to defend those rights essential to the effective functioning of the political process, a class of liberties that clearly includes freedom of expression rights. And finally, the third paragraph suggests a special role for the Court in protecting the rights of minorities and unpopular groups. The standard expressed in Footnote Four has become known as the preferred freedoms doctrine. This doctrine has special significance for First Amendment claims because it means that the judiciary will proceed with a special scrutiny when faced with laws that restrict freedom of expression, especially as those laws may relate to the articulation of unpopular political views. Put another way, "Laws restricting fundamental rights . . . would be regarded as suspect and potentially dangerous to the functioning of democracy."[5]

The importance of Justice Stone's footnote goes beyond its obvious declaration of a new standard for evaluating First Amendment claims. In *Carolene Products* Stone announces a modification in the fundamental role of the Court. He declares that the Court will assume a special responsibility for protecting civil rights and civil liberties and be particularly vigilant in guarding the rights of minorities and the politically unpopular. Although the groundwork for his position had been laid by earlier justices *(see Box 5-3)*, Stone's statement marked a major change in course for an institution that had, for its entire history, been tilted toward settling private economic disputes and wrestling with questions of government power. From this point forward the civil liberties docket began to grow, and the Court rapidly began to evolve into an institution with a primary focus on civil liberties issues.[6]

But would the majority of the justices adopt Stone's preferred freedoms approach to First Amendment claims? Moreover, how would such an approach square with the clear and present danger standard to which

---

4. Alpheus Thomas Mason and Donald Grier Stephenson Jr., *American Constitutional Law,* 10th ed. (Englewood Cliffs, N.J.: Prentice-Hall, 1993), 279.

5. Stanley I. Kutler, ed., *The Supreme Court and the Constitution* (New York: W.W. Norton, 1984), 429.

6. Richard L. Pacelle, *The Transformation of the Supreme Court's Agenda: From the New Deal to the Reagan Administration* (Boulder: Westview Press, 1991).

BOX 5-3   THE PREFERRED FREEDOMS DOCTRINE

JUSTICE HARLAN FISKE STONE's famous Footnote Four in *United States v. Carolene Products* (1938) gave birth to the preferred freedoms doctrine. This doctrine holds that some constitutional rights, particularly those protected by the First Amendment, are so fundamental to a free society that they deserve an especially high degree of judicial protection.

Stone's position built on theories advanced by earlier justices. Oliver Wendell Holmes Jr., for example, contended in several cases that government regulation of the economy required only a rational basis to establish its constitutionality, but that regulation of speech could take place only if a "clear and present danger" could be shown. Justice Benjamin Cardozo argued in *Palko v. Connecticut* (1937) that certain rights are so fundamental as to be indispensable for our system of liberty. Stone expanded these arguments to enlarge the role of the judiciary as a protector of freedom and to carve out a special responsibility for the protection of minority rights.

The preferred freedoms doctrine became more prominent in the years immediately after *Carolene Products*. Several judges who wanted expanded protection for First Amendment rights based their argument on the doctrine. In *Murdock v. Pennsylvania* (1943), Justice William O. Douglas declared, "The Freedom of press, freedom of speech, freedom of religion are in a preferred position." Justice Hugo Black frequently stated that the rights contained in the First Amendment are the very heart of our government.

In contemporary times, the preferred freedoms doctrine is rarely applied in its original form, but its spirit lives on in subsequently adopted rules of judicial interpretation. The Court today often distinguishes between fundamental rights and other liberties, designating certain rights as deserving "strict scrutiny." Government may restrict such rights only if there is a compelling reason to do so. These doctrines directly flow from Stone's assertion in 1938 that the rights most central to our system of liberty deserve special status and protection.

SOURCE: C. Herman Pritchett, "Preferred Freedoms Doctrine," in *The Oxford Companion to the Supreme Court of the United States*, ed. Kermit L. Hall (New York: Oxford University Press, 1992), 663–664.

most of them seemed to want to return? Attorneys, states, and civil libertarians had to wait only a year until the Court addressed these questions in *Schneider v. State of New Jersey (Town of Irvington)* (1939). This case involved not a radical leader of the Communist Party, but a member of the Jehovah's Witnesses. In accordance with her religious tenets, Clara Schneider distributed literature from house to house, leaving residents her card. Town authorities arrested her because she had failed to obtain a solicitation permit, an action Schneider claimed violated her religion, but which the city required to keep the streets uncluttered. Although this case, and three others decided with it, involved elements of religion, the Court was more interested in Schneider's claim that the permit ordinance violated her free speech guarantees. In an 8–1 decision, it struck down the municipal regulation as an unconstitutional burden on free speech. Justice Owen Roberts stated:

We are of the opinion that the purpose to keep the streets clean [is] insufficient to justify an ordinance which prohibits a person rightfully on a public street from handing literature to one willing to receive it. Any burden imposed upon the city authorities in cleaning . . . the streets . . . results from the constitutional protection of the freedom of speech.

Six years later in *Thomas v. Collins* (1945) the Court moved even closer to embracing the preferred freedoms approach. The case arose when R. J. Thomas, president of the United Automobile, Aircraft and Agricultural Workers (UAW) and vice president of the Congress of Industrial Organizations (CIO), arrived in Houston, Texas, to deliver a speech to a group of workers the CIO wanted to organize. Six hours before Thomas was to speak, Texas authorities served him with a restraining order, prohibiting him from making his scheduled address. Believing that the order constituted a violation of his free speech guarantees, Thomas delivered his speech anyway to an audience of three hundred people. The meeting was described as "peaceful and orderly," but authorities arrested Thomas. He was sentenced to three days in jail and a $100 fine. On appeal to the U.S. Supreme Court, Thomas's claim of a free speech infringement received reinforcement from several civil liberties organizations including the National Federation for Constitutional Liberties, which argued, "The activities of labor organizations involve the exercise of peaceful assembly, freedom of speech and freedom of the press."

In a 6–3 opinion, the Supreme Court agreed, ruling against the state, and, most significant, the Court used a preferred freedoms approach to reach that conclusion. Justice Wiley Rutledge, writing for the majority, asserted:

[This] case confronts us again with the duty our system places on this Court to say where the individual's freedom ends and the State's power begins. Choice of that border, now as always delicate, is perhaps more so where the usual presumptive supporting legislation is balanced *by the preferred place given in our scheme to the great, the indispensable democratic freedoms secured by the First Amendment.* . . . For [this] reason any attempt to restrict those liberties must be justified by clear public interest, threatened not . . . remotely, but by *a clear and present danger* [emphasis added].

Constitutional experts claim that this decision represented another major breakthrough in the area of freedom of speech, but why? First, it reinforces the majority view in *Schneider* that the Preferred Freedoms doctrine provides an appropriate solution to First Amendment problems. Second, Rutledge's language—"Any attempt to restrict the liberties of speech and assembly must be justified . . . by a clear and present danger"—indicates that the Court, instead of abandoning Holmes's standard, had combined the clear and present danger standard with the preferred freedoms framework. The preferred freedoms "concept was never a repudiation of the notion of clear and present danger, but was seen as giving its purposes a firmer base and texture—incorporating it much as Einsteinian physics incorporates Newtonian."[7]

Aftermath of World War II: Cold War Politics and the Court

As *Thomas* indicates, by the mid-1940s it seemed as if the Court had finally settled on an approach to solve First Amendment problems. Stone's preferred freedoms doctrine had gained acceptance among the justices, even though it served as a vehicle by which to overturn many

laws restricting speech. Compare it to the bad tendency test of the *Gitlow* era, a test under which many restrictions on free speech could pass muster. In three decades the Court had altered its position dramatically.

Like the bad tendency test, however, the preferred freedoms doctrine was short-lived. In the early 1950s the Court turned to a modified version of the conservative bad tendency test—the clear and probable danger standard. Between 1950 and 1956 the application of this stricter standard led the Court to uphold the vast majority of free speech convictions. What caused this sudden change in direction? Three factors may explain it.

First, several changes in Court personnel occurred between 1945 and 1952. Chief Justice Frederick M. Vinson replaced Stone, the author of Footnote Four. Two relatively conservative justices, Tom C. Clark and Sherman Minton, took the place of two liberals, Frank Murphy and Wiley Rutledge. As we have seen in other areas of the law, such changes can have a substantial impact on Court outcomes.

Second, by 1949 it became evident that some of the justices were not satisfied with the preferred freedoms framework. Keep in mind that several had dissented in *Thomas,* but at the time they offered no alternative standard. This situation changed dramatically in 1949 with *Kovacs v. Cooper,* which involved a challenge to a local ordinance prohibiting the use of sound and amplifying devices on city streets. Writing for the majority, Justice Stanley F. Reed argued that the law withstood the preferred freedoms test and was, therefore, constitutional. In a long concurring opinion Justice Frankfurter agreed with the outcome in *Kovacs,* but not with Reed's reasoning. Calling preferred freedoms a "mischievous phrase," Frankfurter articulated a new standard by which to review First Amendment claims:

So long as a legislature does not prescribe what ideas may be . . . expressed and what may not be, nor discriminate among those who would make inroads upon the public peace, it is not for us to supervise the limits the legislature may impose.

Often called the ad hoc balancing test, it urges the justices to balance, on a case-by-case basis, the individual free speech claim versus the government's reason for regulating the behavior. But, in Frankfurter's judgment,

7. Malcolm M. Feeley and Samuel Krislov, *Constitutional Law* (Boston: Little, Brown, 1985), 427.

During the anticommunist hysteria of post–World War II America, the House Un-American Activities Committee investigated alleged communist influence in the movie industry. Jack L. Warner, vice president of Warner Brothers, took the witness chair in 1947. Committee members include future president Richard Nixon (second from right).

these competing claims were not of equal merit; the latter should be taken more seriously as legislators had already determined that the law in question met a compelling government interest.

A third reason for the Court's dramatic turnaround in the 1950s was the change in its external environment. After World War II the United States entered into a cold war with the Soviet Union. This period was characterized by an intense fear of communism, not unlike the time following the First World War. Some politicians, led by Sen. Joseph McCarthy, R-Wis. (1947–1957), fed the fear by alleging that Communist Party sympathizers had infiltrated the upper echelon of government. Others asserted that the Communist Party of the United States was growing in strength and numbers and spreading its message through motion pictures and plays.

Reflecting this fear of communism, Congress enacted legislation designed to suppress communist and other forms of subversive activity in the United States. For example, a section of the Labor-Management Relations Act of 1947 required union leaders to file affidavits proclaiming nonaffiliation with the Communist Party before they could attain National Labor Relations Board recognition

of their unions. Congress passed this law in recognition of Marxist-Leninist theory, which assumes that it will be the "workers" who lead the "Revolution." In *American Communications Association v. Douds* (1950) union leaders mounted a First Amendment challenge to the law. Because this was one of the earliest of the cold war cases, many eagerly awaited the Court's decision: Would the justices, now under the leadership of Chief Justice Vinson, use the preferred freedoms approach or would they adopt Frankfurter's ad hoc balancing test?

Apparently not immune to the pressures of the day, the Court adopted the latter. Writing for the Court, Vinson rejected the clear and present danger standard—the heart of the preferred freedoms approach—noting, "It is the considerations that gave birth to the phrase clear and present danger, not the phrase itself, that are vital in our decisions of questions involving . . . the First Amendment." In his view, the ad hoc balancing approach fully encapsulated that genesis: because Congress has determined that communism constitutes harmful conduct carried on by people, it may regulate it in the public interest.

Vinson's standard is akin to the bad tendency test of

the 1920s. Both operate under the assumption that the First Amendment protects the public good, as defined by legislatures, rather than individual expression. In fact, just one year after *Douds,* in *Dennis v. United States,* the Court adopted the clear and probable danger test. At issue in *Dennis* was the Smith Act. Enacted in 1940, this statute prohibited anyone from knowingly or willfully advocating or teaching the overthrow of any government of the United States by force, from organizing any society to teach, advocate, or encourage the overthrow of the United States by force, or from becoming a member of any such society. By covering so many kinds of activities, the law provided authorities with a significant weapon to stop the spread of communism in the United States.

While reading *Dennis,* keep in mind the environment in which the justices operated. Remember that tremendous political pressures influenced the Court just as they did many other sectors of American life. If *Dennis* came before the Court today, would the justices reach the same conclusion?

Dennis v. United States

341 U.S. 494 (1951)
laws.findlaw.com/US/341/494.html
Vote: 6 (*Burton, Frankfurter, Jackson, Minton, Reed, Vinson*)
      2 (*Black, Douglas*)
Opinion announcing the judgment of the Court: Vinson
Concurring opinions: Frankfurter, Jackson
Dissenting opinions: Black, Douglas
Not participating: Clark

On July 20, 1948, twelve leaders of the National Board of the Communist Party were indicted for conspiring to teach and advocate the overthrow of the government by force and violence and to organize the Communist Party for that purpose. Such actions were in violation of the Smith Act. The trial was a protracted affair, lasting nine months and generating sixteen thousand pages of evidence. A great deal of the testimony on both sides involved Marxist-Leninist theory and the inner workings of the Communist Party. The prosecutor's case read like a spy novel, full of international conspiracies, secret pass-

Eleven leaders of the American Communist Party, including Eugene Dennis, second from left, were sentenced to prison in 1949 for conspiring to teach and advocate the overthrow of the U.S. government, a violation of the Smith Act. In *Dennis v. United States* (1951) the Court upheld the law on the grounds that the threat of communism was grave enough to justify restricting free speech.

words and code books, aliases, and plots to overthrow the U.S. government. The defense was a bit more philosophical as it attempted to demonstrate that the leaders of this particular branch of the party wanted "to work for the improvement of conditions under capitalism and not for chaos and depression."

Not sympathetic to this line of reasoning, the trial court sentenced each defendant to five years in prison and a $10,000 fine. After their convictions were sustained by the court of appeals, Dennis and the others appealed to the U.S. Supreme Court, requesting it to overturn their convictions and strike down the Smith Act as an unconstitutional infringement on free speech. They said, "The statute and the convictions which are here for review cannot be validated without at the same time destroying the constitutional foundations of American democracy."

MR. CHIEF JUSTICE VINSON announced the judgment of the Court.

The obvious purpose of the statute is to protect existing Government, not from change by peaceable, lawful and constitutional means, but from change by violence, revolution and terrorism. That it is within the *power* of the Congress to protect the Government of the United States from armed rebellion is a proposition which requires little discussion. Whatever theoretical merit there may be to the argument that there is a "right" to rebellion against dictatorial governments is without force where the existing structure of the government provides for peaceful and orderly change. We reject any principle of governmental helplessness in the face of preparation for revolution, which principle, carried to its logical conclusion, must lead to anarchy. No one could conceive that it is not within the power of Congress to prohibit acts intended to overthrow the Government by force and violence. The question with which we are concerned here is not whether Congress has such *power*, but whether the *means* which it has employed conflict with the First and Fifth Amendments to the Constitution. . . .

The very language of the Smith Act negates the interpretation which petitioners would have us impose on that Act. It is directed at advocacy, not discussion. Thus, the trial judge properly charged the jury that they could not convict if they found that petitioners did "no more than pursue peaceful studies and discussions or teaching and advocacy in the realm of ideas." He further charged that it was not unlawful "to conduct in an American college and university a course explaining the philosophical theories set forth in the books which have been placed in evidence." Such a charge is in strict accord with the statutory language, and illustrates the meaning to be placed on those words. Congress did not intend to eradicate the free discussion of political theories, to destroy the traditional rights of Americans to discuss and evaluate ideas without fear of governmental sanction. Rather Congress was concerned with the very kind of activity in which the evidence showed these petitioners engaged.

But although the statute is not directed at the hypothetical cases which petitioners have conjured, its application in this case has resulted in convictions for the teaching and advocacy of the overthrow of the Government by force and violence, which, even though coupled with the intent to accomplish that overthrow, contains an element of speech. For this reason, we must pay special heed to the demands of the First Amendment marking out the boundaries of speech.

We pointed out in [*American Communications Association v.*] *Douds* [1950] that the basis of the First Amendment is the hypothesis that speech can rebut speech, propaganda will answer propaganda, free debate of ideas will result in the wisest governmental policies. It is for this reason that this Court has recognized the inherent value of free discourse. An analysis of the leading cases in this Court which have involved direct limitations on speech, however, will demonstrate that both the majority of the Court and the dissenters in particular cases have recognized that this is not an unlimited, unqualified right, but that the societal value of speech must, on occasion, be subordinated to other values and considerations.

No important case involving free speech was decided by this Court prior to *Schenck v. United States*. Indeed, the summary treatment accorded an argument based upon an individual's claim that the First Amendment protected certain utterances indicates that the Court at earlier dates placed no unique emphasis upon that right. It was not until the classic dictum of Justice Holmes in the *Schenck* case that speech *per se* received that emphasis in a majority opinion. . . . Writing for a unanimous Court, Justice Holmes stated that the "question in every case is whether the words used are used in such circumstances and are of such a nature as to create a clear and present danger that they will bring about the substantive evils that Congress has a right to prevent." But the force of even this expression is considerably weakened by the reference at the end of the opinion to *Goldman v. United States*, 1918, a prosecution under the same statute. Said Justice Holmes, "Indeed *Goldman* might be said to dispose of the present contention if the precedent covers all *media concludendi* [the steps of an argument]. But as the right to free speech was not referred to specially, we have thought fit to add a few words." The fact is inescapable, too, that the phrase bore no connotation that the danger was to be any threat to the safety of the Republic. The charge was causing and attempting to cause insubordination in the military forces and obstruct recruiting. The objectionable document denounced conscription and its most inciting sentence was, "You must do your share to maintain, support and uphold the rights of the people of this country." Fifteen thousand copies were printed and some circulated. This insubstantial gesture toward insubordination in 1917 during war was held to be a clear and present danger of bringing about the evil of military insubordination.

In several later cases involving convictions under the Criminal Espionage Act, the nub of the evidence the Court held sufficient to meet the "clear and present danger" test enunciated in *Schenck* was as follows: *Frohwerk v. United States*—publication of twelve newspaper articles attacking the war; *Debs v. United States*—one speech attacking United States' participation in the war; *Abrams v. United States*—circulation of copies of two different socialist circulars attacking the war. . . .

The rule we deduce from these cases is that where an offense is specified by a statute in nonspeech or nonpress terms, a conviction relying upon speech or press as evidence of violation may be sustained only when the speech or publication created a "clear and present danger" of attempting or accomplishing the prohibited crime, *e.g.*, interference with enlistment. The dissents, we repeat, in emphasizing the value of speech, were addressed to the argument of the sufficiency of the evidence.

The next important case before the Court in which free speech was the crux of the conflict was *Gitlow v. People of State of New York*. There New York had made it a crime to advocate "the necessity or propriety of overthrowing . . . organized government by force. . . ." The evidence of violation of the statute was that the defendant had published a Manifesto attacking the Government and capitalism. The convictions were sustained. The majority refused to apply the "clear and present danger" test to the specific utterance. . . .

Although no case subsequent to . . . *Gitlow* has expressly overruled the majority . . . there is little doubt that subsequent opinions have inclined toward the Holmes-Brandeis rationale. . . . But . . . neither Justice Holmes nor Justice Brandeis ever envisioned that a shorthand phrase should be crystallized into a rigid rule to be applied inflexibly without regard to the circumstances of each case. Speech is not an absolute, above and beyond control by the legislature when its judgment, subject to review here, is that certain kinds of speech are so undesirable as to warrant criminal sanction. Nothing is more certain in modern society than the principle that there are no absolutes, that a name, a phrase, a standard has meaning only when associated with the considerations which gave birth to the nomenclature. To those who would paralyze our Government in the face of impending threat by encasing it in a semantic straitjacket we must reply that all concepts are relative.

In this case we are squarely presented with the application of the "clear and present danger" test, and must decide what that phrase imports. We first note that many of the cases in which this Court has reversed convictions by use of this or similar tests have been based on the fact that the interest which the State was attempting to protect was itself too insubstantial to warrant restriction of speech. Overthrow of the Government by force and violence is certainly a substantial enough interest for the Government to limit speech. Indeed, this is the ultimate value of any society, for if a society cannot protect its very structure from armed internal attack, it must follow that no subordinate value can be protected. If, then, this interest may be protected, the literal problem which is presented is what has been meant by the use of the phrase "clear and present danger" of the utterances bringing about the evil within the power of Congress to punish.

Obviously, the words cannot mean that before the Government may act, it must wait until the *putsch* is about to be executed, the plans have been laid and the signal is awaited. If Government is aware that a group aiming at its overthrow is attempting to indoctrinate its members and to commit them to a course whereby they will strike when the leaders feel the circumstances permit, action by the Government is required. The argument that there is no need for Government to concern itself, for Government is strong, it possesses ample powers to put down a rebellion, it may defeat the revolution with ease needs no answer. For that is not the question. Certainly an attempt to overthrow the Government by force, even though doomed from the outset because of inadequate numbers or power of the revolutionists, is a sufficient evil for Congress to prevent. The damage which such attempts create both physically and politically to a nation makes it impossible to measure the validity in terms of the probability of success, or the immediacy of a successful attempt. In the instant case the trial judge charged the jury that they could not convict unless they found that petitioners intended to overthrow the Government "as speedily as circumstances would permit." This does not mean, and could not properly mean, that they would not strike until there was certainty of success. What was meant was that the revolutionists would strike when they thought the time was ripe. We must therefore reject the contention that success or probability of success is the criterion.

The situation with which Justices Holmes and Brandeis were concerned in *Gitlow* was a comparatively isolated event, bearing little relation in their minds to any substantial threat to the safety of the community. They were not confronted with any situation comparable to the instant one—the development of an apparatus designed and dedicated to the overthrow of the Government, in the context of world crisis after crisis.

Chief Judge Learned Hand, writing for the majority below, interpreted the phrase as follows: "In each case [courts] must ask whether the gravity of the 'evil,' discounted by its improbability, justifies such invasion of free speech as is necessary to avoid the danger." We adopt this statement of the rule. As articulated by Chief Judge Hand, it is as succinct and inclusive as any other we might devise at this time. It takes into consideration those factors which we deem relevant, and relates their significances. More we cannot expect from words. . . .

We hold that the Smith Act, do[es] not inherently, or as construed or applied in the instant case, violate the First Amendment and other provisions of the Bill of Rights. . . . Petitioners intended to overthrow the Government of the United States as speedily as the circumstances would permit. Their conspiracy to organize the Communist Party and to teach and advocate the overthrow of the Government of the United States by force and violence created a "clear and present danger" of an attempt to overthrow the Government by force and violence. They were properly and constitutionally convicted for violation of the Smith Act. The judgments of conviction are affirmed.

Affirmed.

MR. JUSTICE FRANKFURTER, concurring in affirmance of the judgment.

Primary responsibility for adjusting the interests which compete in the situation before us of necessity belongs to the Congress. The nature of the power to be exercised by this Court has been delineated in decisions not charged with the emotional appeal of situations such as that now before us. We are to set aside the judgment of those whose

duty it is to legislate only if there is no reasonable basis for it. . . .

It is not for us to decide how we would adjust the clash of interests which this case presents were the primary responsibility for reconciling it ours. Congress has determined that the danger created by advocacy of overthrow justifies the ensuing restriction on freedom of speech. The determination was made after due deliberation, and the seriousness of the congressional purpose is attested by the volume of legislation passed to effectuate the same ends.

Can we then say that the judgment Congress exercised was denied it by the Constitution? Can we establish a constitutional doctrine which forbids the elected representatives of the people to make this choice? Can we hold that the First Amendment deprives Congress of what it deemed necessary for the Government's protection?

To make validity of legislation depend on judicial reading of events still in the womb of time—a forecast, that is, of the outcome of forces at best appreciated only with knowledge of the topmost secrets of nations—is to charge the judiciary with duties beyond its equipment.

MR. JUSTICE BLACK, dissenting.

[M]y basic disagreement with the Court is not as to how we should explain or reconcile what was said in prior decisions but springs from a fundamental difference in constitutional approach. Consequently, it would serve no useful purpose to state my position at length.

At the outset I want to emphasize what the crime involved in this case is, and what it is not. These petitioners were not charged with an attempt to overthrow the Government. They were not charged with overt acts of any kind designed to overthrow the Government. They were not even charged with saying anything or writing anything designed to overthrow the Government. The charge was that they agreed to assemble and to talk and publish certain ideas at a later date: The indictment is that they conspired to organize the Communist Party and to use speech or newspapers and other publications in the future to teach and advocate the forcible overthrow of the Government. No matter how it is worded, this is a virulent form of prior censorship of speech and press, which I believe the First Amendment forbids. I would hold §3 of the Smith Act authorizing this prior restraint unconstitutional on its face and as applied.

But let us assume, contrary to all constitutional ideas of fair criminal procedure, that petitioners although not indicted for the crime of actual advocacy, may be punished for it. Even on this radical assumption, the other opinions in this case show that the only way to affirm these convictions is to repudiate directly or indirectly the established "clear and present danger" rule. This the Court does in a way which greatly restricts the protections afforded by the First Amendment. The opinions for affirmance indicate that the chief reason for jettisoning the rule is the expressed fear that advocacy of Communist doctrine endangers the safety of the Republic. Undoubtedly, a governmental policy of unfettered communication of ideas does entail dangers. To the Founders of this Nation, however, the benefits derived from free expression were worth the risk. They embodied this philosophy in the First Amendment's command that "Congress shall make no law . . . abridging the freedom of speech, or of the press. . . ." I have always believed that the First Amendment is the keystone of our Government, that the freedoms it guarantees provide the best insurance against destruction of all freedom. At least as to speech in the realm of public matters, I believe that the "clear and present danger" test does not "mark the furthermost constitutional boundaries of protected expression" but does "no more than recognize a minimum compulsion of the Bill of Rights." *Bridges v. California* [1941].

So long as this Court exercises the power of judicial review of legislation, I cannot agree that the First Amendment permits us to sustain laws suppressing freedom of speech and press on the basis of Congress' or our own notions of mere "reasonableness." Such a doctrine waters down the First Amendment so that it amounts to little more than an admonition to Congress. The Amendment as so construed is not likely to protect any but those "safe" or orthodox views which rarely need its protection. . . .

Public opinion being what it now is, few will protest the conviction of these Communist petitioners. There is hope, however, that in calmer times, when present pressures, passions and fears subside, this or some later Court will restore the First Amendment liberties to the high preferred place where they belong in a free society.

MR. JUSTICE DOUGLAS, dissenting.

Free speech has occupied an exalted position because of the high service it has given our society. Its protection is es-

sential to the very existence of a democracy. The airing of ideas releases pressures which otherwise might become destructive. When ideas compete in the market for acceptance, full and free discussion exposes the false and they gain few adherents. Full and free discussion even of ideas we hate encourages the testing of our own prejudices and preconceptions. Full and free discussion keeps a society from becoming stagnant and unprepared for the stresses and strains that work to tear all civilizations apart.

Full and free discussion has indeed been the first article of our faith. We have founded our political system on it. It has been the safeguard of every religious, political, philosophical, economic, and racial group amongst us. We have counted on it to keep us from embracing what is cheap and false; we have trusted the common sense of our people to choose the doctrine true to our genius and to reject the rest. This has been the one single outstanding tenet that has made our institutions the symbol of freedom and equality. We have deemed it more costly to liberty to suppress a despised minority than to let them vent their spleen. We have above all else feared the political censor. We have wanted a land where our people can be exposed to all the diverse creeds and cultures of the world.

There comes a time when even speech loses its constitutional immunity. Speech innocuous one year may at another time fan such destructive flames that it must be halted in the interests of the safety of the Republic. That is the meaning of the clear and present danger test. When conditions are so critical that there will be no time to avoid the evil that the speech threatens, it is time to call a halt. Otherwise, free speech which is the strength of the Nation will be the cause of its destruction.

Yet free speech is the rule, not the exception. The restraint to be constitutional must be based on more than fear, on more than passionate opposition against the speech, on more than a revolted dislike for its contents. There must be some immediate injury to society that is likely if speech is allowed. . . .

Free speech—the glory of our system of government—should not be sacrificed on anything less than plain and objective proof of danger that the evil advocated is imminent. On this record no one can say that petitioners and their converts are in such a strategic position as to have even the slightest chance of achieving their aims.

The First Amendment provides that "Congress shall

BOX 5-4   AFTERMATH . . .
EUGENE DENNIS

EUGENE DENNIS was the most prominent of the twelve members of the Communist Party charged in 1949 with violating the Smith Act, criminal accusations that ultimately resulted in the Supreme Court's decision in *Dennis v. United States* (1951).

Born Francis X. Waldron, Dennis became involved Communist Party activities in his early twenties. In 1931, faced with the prospect of being indicted on charges of inciting a riot, he changed his name to Tim Ryan and fled to Russia with his wife Peggy and their two-year-old son. He returned to the United States in 1935, leaving his son in the Soviet Union to be raised as a Russian communist. Assuming the name Eugene Dennis, he quickly moved up in the hierarchy of the American Communist Party. During World War II Dennis cooperated with the Russian KGB on intelligence activities and helped infiltrate the United States Office of Strategic Services. Following the war, he was chosen to be general secretary of the party.

Dennis's legal problems began to mount in 1947 when he was sentenced to a year in prison for contempt of Congress stemming from his refusal to answer questions about his background. In 1949 he was put on trial for violating the Smith Act. When the Supreme Court upheld his conviction, he and his fellow defendants planned to jump bail and go underground. His plan miscarried, and Dennis went to prison in July 1951. After being released in 1955, Dennis resumed his activities with the party. Stricken with cancer, he gave up his leadership position in 1959 and died two years later.

Dennis's son, known as Timur Timofeev, became a Soviet citizen and directed the World Labor Movement in Moscow. Peggy Dennis continued her work with leftist causes after her husband's death. She died in 1993 and was buried next to her husband in the German Waldheim Cemetery in Chicago in a section reserved for communist leaders.

SOURCES: *San Francisco Chronicle*, September 28, 1993; *New York Times*, October 12, 1993; Bernard K. Johnpoll and Harvey Klehr, *Biographical Dictionary of the American Left* (New York: Greenwood Press, 1986); and John Earl Haynes and Harvey Klehr, *Venona* (New Haven: Yale University Press, 1999).

make no law . . . abridging the freedom of speech." The Constitution provides no exception. This does not mean, however, that the Nation need hold its hand until it is in such weakened condition that there is no time to protect itself from incitement to revolution. Seditious conduct can always be punished. But the command of the First Amendment is so clear that we should not allow Congress to call a halt to free speech except in the extreme case of peril from the speech itself. The First Amendment makes confidence in the common sense of our people and in their maturity of judgment the great postulate of our democracy. Its philosophy is that violence is rarely, if ever, stopped by denying civil liberties to those advocating resort to force. The First Amendment reflects the philosophy of Jefferson "that it is time enough for the rightful purposes of civil government, for its officers to interfere when principles break out into overt acts against peace and good order." The political censor has no place in our public debates. Unless and until extreme and necessitous circumstances are shown our aim should be to keep speech unfettered and to allow the processes of law to be invoked only when the provocateurs among us move from speech to action.

Vishinsky wrote in 1938 in *The Law of the Soviet State,* "In our state, naturally, there is and can be no place for freedom of speech, press, and so on for the foes of socialism."

Our concern should be that we accept no such standard for the United States. Our faith should be that our people will never give support to these advocates of revolution, so long as we remain loyal to the purposes for which our Nation was founded.

Scholars consider *Dennis* a significant case for several reasons. First, a plurality of the Court accepted Vinson's clear and probable danger test: "In each case courts must ask whether the gravity of the 'evil,' discounted by its improbability, justifies such invasion of free speech as is necessary to avoid the danger." But is this a reasonable interpretation of the test emanating from *Schenck;* that is, would Holmes have agreed with this language? Or does it more closely resemble the bad tendency standard, with which Holmes disagreed?

The second reason why scholars think *Dennis* is a significant case is what the dissenters, Justices Black and Douglas, had to say. Both take a strong stand in favor of

First Amendment protection of political speech, even speech that represents unpopular views. As Douglas argued, the First Amendment prohibits Congress from abridging the freedom of speech and it "provides no exception." This argument is often referred to as the "absolute freedoms" test. As we shall see, this pair of civil libertarians remained in relative isolation during the early 1950s, but the Warren Court of the late 1950s and 1960s adopted many of their views.

A third reason *Dennis* is significant is precedent: between 1951 and 1956 the justices used Vinson's clear and probable danger standard to uphold a number of loyalty programs.[8] Moreover, *Dennis* served as a benchmark in other areas of the law in which the federal government asked the Court for sweeping powers to investigate the Communist Party, other subversive groups, and their alleged adherents.

In sum, once again we see the Supreme Court responding to perceived threats to national security. As was the case during the 1920s, when the justices moved from a clear and present danger test to a bad tendency standard, in the 1950s they moved from a preferred freedoms approach to a revisionist interpretation of the Holmes standard, clear and probable danger, which itself "marked a return to the 'bad tendency' views of the post–World War I period."[9]

Free Speech During the Warren Court Era

In 1957 the Court decided *Yates v. United States*, a case that closely resembled *Dennis*. Federal authorities alleged that fourteen second-tier leaders of the Communist Party, including Oleta O'Connor Yates, engaged in subversive activities forbidden by the Smith Act. Specifically, they belonged to the party, organized party units in California, helped publish the *Daily Worker*, and conducted courses to recruit and indoctrinate potential members. At their trial, the judge explained the Smith Act to the jurors, but he did not tell them that it prohibited only the advocacy of unlawful activity, not the teaching of abstract doctrines. The jury found the defendants guilty,

and the court sentenced them to five years in prison and a $10,000 fine. On appeal, Yates's attorneys seized on this discrepancy in the judge's charge. They stated, "Lawful activities and associations not shown to be unlawful cannot by addition or multiplication be cemented into illegality." The government argued that *Dennis* should control the Court's decision.

A majority rejected the government's position. Justice John Marshall Harlan wrote:

> The legislative history of the Smith Act and related bills shows beyond all question that Congress was aware of the distinction between advocacy or teaching of abstract doctrine and the advocacy or teaching of action, and that it did not intend to disregard it. The statute was aimed at the advocacy and teaching of concrete action for the forcible overthrow of the Government, and not of principles divorced from action.
>
> The government's reliance on this Court's decision is misplaced. It is true that at one point in the . . . opinion it is stated that the Smith Act "is directed at advocacy, not discussion," but it is clear that the reference was *to advocacy of action, not ideas* [emphasis added].

With the decision in *Yates*, despite some protestation to the contrary, the Court altered its position: by distinguishing between the advocacy of abstract doctrines (protected) and the advocacy of unlawful action (unprotected), the Court substantially modified the *Dennis* standard. And although *Yates* did not advocate the preferred freedoms or absolutist approach favored by Black, it certainly liberalized free speech doctrine, making Smith Act prosecutions far more difficult.

Why did the Court alter its view? Some scholars point to changes in Court personnel. Dramatic alterations occurred between *Dennis* and *Yates:* the more liberal Earl Warren replaced Fred Vinson as chief justice; Harlan, grandson and namesake of another "great dissenter," stepped in for Robert H. Jackson; and President Eisenhower appointed William J. Brennan Jr. to Sherman Minton's vacant seat.

Although fear of communist infiltration among Americans was beginning to decline, 1957 was far from the end of the cold war era, and *Yates* was not the last of the Court's cases on subversive activities. Moreover, the decision in *Yates* did not mean an end to Court approval of legislation making such activities a crime. For exam-

---

8. See, for example, *Adler v. Board of Education* (1952), in which the Court upheld a New York law (the so-called Feinberg Act) disqualifying from teaching positions persons affiliated with subversive groups.

9. Kutler, *Supreme Court,* 429.

ple, in *Scales v. United States* (1961) the Court upheld the membership clause of the Smith Act. That same year, it also sustained a clause of the Subversive Activities Control Act of 1950, mandating that all organizations affiliated with the Communist Party register with the attorney general. Nonetheless, by 1957 the hysteria had substantially subsided. One indication was the rapid decline of Senator McCarthy's influence. As his accusations grew "ever more wild . . . and arrogant," focusing on all sorts of government officials, including senators and President Eisenhower, his "conduct became too destructive for all but his closest associates to tolerate."[10] In 1954 the Senate censured him by a 67–22 vote: the man who symbolized the communist witch hunt had lost his power. He died May 2, 1957, the same year as the *Yates* decision.

Once the Red Scare was over, the Supreme Court began taking positions defending freedom of expression and association against the repressive legislation passed during the McCarthy era. It handed down a series of decisions upholding the constitutional rights of communists and other so-called subversives. For example, in *Communist Party v. United States* (1963) and *Albertson v. Subversive Activities Control Board* (1965) the justices repudiated federal laws requiring communist organizations to register with the government. In *Elfbrandt v. Russell* (1966) and *Whitehill v. Elkins* (1967) loyalty oath requirements directed at subversives were found constitutionally defective. The Court also struck down laws and enforcement actions barring communists from holding office in labor unions (*United States v. Brown*, 1965), prohibiting communists from working in defense plants (*United States v. Robel*, 1967), and stripping passports from Communist Party leaders (*Aptheker v. Secretary of State*, 1964). Clearly, these decisions and others handed down during more tranquil years would have been unheard of during the anticommunist hysteria.

By the end of the 1960s the Court had turned away from many of its cold war rulings. It struck down as being in violation of the freedom to speak, publish, or associate much of the federal and state anticommunist legislation still on the books. With its decision in *Branden-*

burg v. Ohio (1969), one of the Warren Court's last major rulings, the justices finally closed the door on the repressive McCarthy era. Ironically, the *Brandenburg* decision had nothing to do with the Communist Party or other groups dedicated to violent overthrow of the U.S. government. Instead, the dispute involved a group with a much different purpose, the racist Ku Klux Klan. As you read the Court's decision in *Brandenburg,* notice how the justices treat the right to speak and organize even when the group's message and purpose are repugnant to American values.[11] Note also how the Court uses this Ku Klux Klan prosecution to overrule *Whitney v. California,* one of the more repressive precedents from an earlier time.

Brandenburg v. Ohio

395 U.S. 444 (1969)
laws.findlaw.com/US/395/444.html
Vote: 8 (*Black, Brennan, Douglas, Harlan, Marshall, Stewart, Warren, White*)
    0

Per curiam opinion
Concurring opinions: Black, Douglas

Clarence Brandenburg was the leader of an Ohio affiliate of the Ku Klux Klan, an organization dedicated to white supremacy. To obtain publicity for the KKK's goals, he invited a Cincinnati reporter and camera crew to attend a rally. Subsequently, local and national television stations aired some of the events that occurred at this gathering. One film showed twelve hooded figures, some of whom carried firearms, gathered around a large wooden cross, which they burned. In another film, Brandenburg delivered a speech to the group in which he said, "Personally I believe the nigger should be returned to Africa, the Jew returned to Israel." Based on these films, Ohio authorities arrested Brandenburg for violating the Ohio Criminal Syndicalism law, passed in 1919 to prevent the spread of unpatriotic views. Similar to many other state laws of the sort upheld in *Gitlow,* the Ohio act

---

10. Arthur M. Schlesinger Jr., *The Almanac of American History* (New York: Putnam, 1983), 541.

11. To hear oral arguments in this case, navigate to: *oyez.nwu.edu.*

A Ku Klux Klan demonstration in Washington, D.C., in 1926. In 1969 the Supreme Court struck down an Ohio law that punished the advocacy of criminal activities.

prohibited "advocat[ing] . . . the duty, necessity, or propriety of crime, sabotage, violence, or unlawful methods of terrorism as a means of accomplishing industrial or political reform" and voluntarily assembling with any group of persons formed to teach or advocate the doctrines of criminal syndicalism.

PER CURIAM.

The appellant, a leader of a Ku Klux Klan group, was convicted under the Ohio Criminal Syndicalism statute.

The . . . statute was enacted in 1919. From 1917 to 1920, identical or quite similar laws were adopted by 20 States and two territories. In 1927, this Court sustained the constitutionality of California's Criminal Syndicalism Act, the text of which is quite similar to that of the laws of Ohio. *Whitney*

v. California (1927). The Court upheld the statute on the ground that, without more, "advocating" violent means to effect political and economic change involves such danger to the security of the State that the State may outlaw it. But *Whitney* has been thoroughly discredited by later decisions. See *Dennis v. United States* (1951). These later decisions have fashioned the principle that the constitutional guarantees of free speech and free press do not permit a State to forbid or proscribe advocacy of the use of force or of law violation except where such advocacy is directed to inciting or producing imminent lawless action and is likely to incite or produce such action. As we said in *Noto v. United States* (1961), "the mere abstract teaching . . . of the moral propriety or even moral necessity for a resort to force and violence, is not the same as preparing a group for violent action and steeling it to such action." A statute which fails to draw this distinction impermissibly intrudes upon the freedoms guaranteed by the First and Fourteenth Amendments. It sweeps within its condemnation speech which our Constitution has immunized from governmental control.

Measured by this test, Ohio's Criminal Syndicalism Act cannot be sustained. The Act punishes persons who "advocate or teach the duty, necessity, or propriety" of violence "as a means of accomplishing industrial or political reform"; or who publish or circulate or display any book or paper containing such advocacy; or who "justify" the commission of violent acts "with intent to exemplify, spread or advocate the propriety of the doctrines of criminal syndicalism"; or who "voluntarily assemble" with a group formed "to teach or advocate the doctrines of criminal syndicalism." Neither the indictment nor the judge's trial judge's instructions to the jury in any way refined the statute's bald definition of the crime in terms of mere advocacy not distinguished from incitement to imminent lawless action.

Accordingly, we are here confronted with a statute which, by its own words and as applied, purports to punish mere advocacy and to forbid, on pain of criminal punishment, assembly with others merely to advocate the described type of action. Such a statute falls within the condemnation of the First and Fourteenth Amendments. The contrary teaching of *Whitney v. California* cannot be supported, and that decision is therefore overruled.

Reversed.

The Court in *Brandenberg* claimed that "the constitutional guarantees of free speech and free press do not permit a State to forbid or proscribe advocacy of the use of force or of law violation except where such advocacy is directed to inciting or producing imminent lawless action and is likely to incite or produce such action." Measured by this test, the Ohio law could not be sustained. By so ruling, the justices closed the door on the long series of repressive expression rulings. Indeed, as if to underscore the point, *Whitney v. California* was explicitly overruled by *Brandenburg.*

Vietnam, the Civil Rights Movement, and Beyond

As the nation's fear of communist infiltration ebbed, a new international crisis was brewing in Vietnam. Although our involvement in that conflict dated back to the Truman administration, it grew significantly in 1964 when President Lyndon Johnson announced that the North Vietnamese had attacked U.S. ships in the Gulf of Tonkin. Johnson launched a massive military buildup: by 1968, 541,000 U.S. troops had been sent to Vietnam. Initially, many Americans approved of Johnson's pursuit of the war, but by the late 1960s, approval had turned to criticism. A peace movement, centered on college campuses, arose throughout the country.

In addition, another cause was gathering strength. The civil rights movement, which in the 1950s was isolated in the South, by the 1960s had taken hold in all major urban centers. Because of these two social currents, and the resistance to them, the decade was marked by domestic upheaval and turmoil. Although Congress did not respond with any legislation like the Smith Act, these protest movements generated many free expression cases. Some involved the constitutionality of mass demonstrations, the chief weapon of the civil rights and peace movements. Others involved the issues of political expression associated with that decade—flag desecration, draft card burning, and so forth.

The freedom of expression cases flowing from the Vietnam War and civil rights protests presented the Court with a host of novel constitutional claims. The character of the Court was also undergoing change. In 1969 Warren Burger, a conservative Nixon appointee, replaced the retiring Earl Warren as chief justice. Burger would soon be followed by three additional Nixon appointees—William H. Rehnquist, Harry A. Blackmun, and Lewis F. Powell Jr. With these appointments the Court began to take on a more conservative posture. This trend continued without interruption for the next twenty-three years as Republican presidents Ford, Reagan, and Bush filled vacancies with an eye to moving the Court to the right. It was not until the mid-1990s with Bill Clinton's appointment of Justices Ruth Bader Ginsburg and Stephen Breyer that a Democratic president had an opportunity to fill Court vacancies.

As the Court confronted new disputes over expression rights, the justices had at their disposal a half-century of doctrinal development. The internal security cases beginning with *Schenck* and continuing into the 1960s

TABLE 5-1 Summary of Legal Standards Governing Free Speech

Standard	Major Proponents	Court Usage: Example
Clear and Present Danger test "Whether the words are used in such circumstances and are of such a nature as to create a clear and present danger that they will bring about substantive evils that Congress has a right to prevent."	Holmes, Brandeis	*Schenck v. United States*, 1919
Bad Tendency test Do the words have a tendency to bring about something evil?	Clarke, Sanford	*Abrams v. United States*, 1919
Preferred Freedoms "There may be a narrower scope for operation of the presumption of constitutionality when legislation appears on its face to be within a specific prohibition of the Constitution, such as those of the first ten Amendments."	Douglas, Stone, Rutledge	*United States v. Carolene Products*, 1938; *Thomas v. Collins*, 1945
Absolutism "The First Amendment, its prohibition in terms absolute, was designed to preclude courts as well as legislatures from weighing values of speech against silence."	Black, Douglas	Never adopted. See Black's dissent in *Dennis v. United States*, 1951; Douglas's dissent in *Roth v. United States*, 1957
Ad Hoc Balancing "So long as a legislature does not prescribe what ideas may be . . . expressed and what may not be, nor discriminate among those who would make inroads upon the public peace, it is not for us to supervise the limits the legislature may impose."	Frankfurter	Frankfurter's concurrence in *Kovacs v. Cooper*, 1949
Clear and Probable Danger "Whether the gravity of the 'evil,' discounted by its improbability, justifies such an invasion of free speech as is necessary to avoid danger."	Vinson	*Dennis v. United States*, 1951

had given birth to six major tests of how the First Amendment should be interpreted and applied *(see Table 5-1)*. In the years that followed, the justices created no significant additions to this list of competing approaches to First Amendment interpretation, but continued to debate their relative merits as applied to various expressive forms and contexts. Just as the justices before them, modern members of the Court have had to struggle with the perennial conflict between the need for an ordered society and the desire for individual liberty.

The United States is not alone in facing conflicts between the principle of free expression and the exercise of that right in a manner the government views as undesirable. Box 5-5 provides examples of the way expression rights have been incorporated into the constitutions of several nations. Many of these countries have adopted democratic regimes quite recently following a history of more authoritarian rule. Like the United States before them, these nations must develop ways to apply constitutional principles to actual disputes. It is the application of abstract doctrine to real situations that will ultimately determine the level of openness and freedom that will be enjoyed by the citizens of those nations.

BOX 5-5 FREEDOM OF EXPRESSION IN GLOBAL PERSPECTIVE

As the following quotations from constitutional documents indicate, the United States is not the only country to guarantee its citizens freedom of expression. Many others protect the right as well.

Austria—Basic Law on the General Rights of Nationals (1867)

"Everyone has the right, within the limits of the law, to freely express his opinion by word of mouth and in writing, print, or pictorial representation."

Belgium—Constitution (1970)

"Freedom of worship, public practice of the latter, as well as freedom to demonstrate one's opinions on all matters, are guaranteed, except for the repression of offenses committed when using this freedom."

Bulgaria—Constitution (1991)

"Everyone is entitled to express an opinion or to publicize it through words, written or oral, sound, or image, or in any other way."

Congo—Constitution (1992)

"Every citizen shall have the right to freely express and diffuse his opinion by speech, by writing, and by image."

Ireland—Constitution (1937)

"The State guarantees the right of the citizens to express freely their convictions and opinions."

Germany—Basic Law (1949)

"Every person shall have the right freely to express and disseminate his opinions in speech, writing, and pictures and to inform himself without hindrance from generally accessible sources."

Italy—Constitution (1948)

"All shall have the right to express their thoughts freely by speech, in writing, and by all other means of communication."

Japan—Constitution (1947)

"Freedom of assembly and association as well as speech, press, and all other forms of expression are guaranteed."

New Zealand—Bill of Rights Act (1990)

"Everyone has the right to freedom of expression, including the freedom to seek, receive, and impart information and opinions of any kind in any form."

Russia—Constitution (1993)

"Everyone shall have the right to freedom of thought and speech."

The presence of a right in the Constitution, however, does not guarantee that citizens can exercise it. For example, the former Soviet Union—by all accounts, a highly repressive society—guaranteed its citizens the "freedom of speech, of the press, and of assembly, meetings, street processions, and demonstrations," but the rights were without meaning.

Moreover, courts do not always interpret the words of constitutional documents in literal or absolute fashions. Consider, for example, the Canadian Charter of Rights and Freedoms, which reads: "Everyone has the following fundamental freedoms: freedom of thought, belief, opinion, and expression, including freedom of the press and other media of communication." These words would seem to work to the advantage of James Keegstra, a high school teacher who promoted anti-Semitism in his classroom. Keegstra described Jews to his students as "subversive," "money-loving," and "child killers."

But the Canadian Supreme Court did not rule in Keegstra's favor once when he was found guilty of violating the criminal code by "unlawfully promoting hatred against an identifiable group." Rather, in a 1990 decision, the Court held:

[G]iven the unparalleled vigour with which hate propaganda repudiates and undermines democratic values, and in particular its condemnation of the view that all citizens need be treated with equal respect and dignity so as to make participation in the political process meaningful, [we are] unable to see the protection of such expression as integral to the democratic ideal.

How did the Court hurdle the Charter's freedom of expression provision? It did so, in part, by pointing to another provision—a provision unlike any in the U.S. Constitution: "This Charter shall be interpreted in a manner consistent with the preservation and enhancement of the multicultural heritage of Canadians."

Similar provisions are not unusual in newer constitutional documents, as South Africa's illustrates. After guaranteeing "everyone" the right to freedom of expression, the Constitution specifically states that this right does not extend to "advocacy of hatred that is based on race, ethnicity, gender or religion, and that constitutes incitement to cause harm." Such provisions, at least on their face, seem to give courts great latitude in punishing those who engage in "hate speech," even though, as we have seen in the United States, they are not necessarily required to do so.

source: Links to constitutional documents are available at: *www.urich.edu/~jpjones/confinder/const.htm.*

REGULATING EXPRESSION: CONTENT AND CONTEXTS

Justice Holmes noted in *Schenck* that the legitimacy of expression often depends upon the nature of the words and the conditions under which they are uttered. The major tests of the First Amendment, developed in the national security cases, provide broad guidelines for determining the boundaries of constitutional protection. Yet even if the justices could agree on a controlling philosophy of what the First Amendment means, they would still have to wrestle with the task of applying that doctrine to specific cases. In the remaining portions of this chapter, we present some of the recurring expression issues that the justices have confronted and the rules of law they developed as a response.

Guiding Principles

Before we turn our attention to specific types of expression, we set forth some of the principles the Court has deemed relevant in deciding freedom of expression issues. Keep in mind that these principles are flexible and may be applied in slightly different ways depending upon the nature of the expression and the forum in which it occurs.

When the Framers drafted the First Amendment they had specific purposes in mind. The goal was to create a society in which expression would thrive and the government could not use its power to keep individuals from expressing themselves by speaking, publishing, or associating with others of similar opinion. The Supreme Court has accepted the duty to interpret the First Amendment with these purposes in mind. Over the years the justices have referred to the goal of creating a free marketplace of ideas and a society in which a robust exchange of views occurs without government censorship.

Although the vibrant exchange of thoughts and opinions might be the goal, the justices never have concluded that the First Amendment absolutely protects all forms of speech. Instead, the Court's decisions have acknowledged that freedom of expression carries certain limitations with it. These limitations are responses to the need for an ordered society that functions well. In general, the Court has recognized that freedom of expression must be balanced against the need to safeguard the rights of others and the right of the government to carry out its legitimate functions in a reasonable fashion.

The First Amendment does not explicitly differentiate, but the Framers approached freedom of expression with a definite hierarchy in mind. Of primary concern was the need to protect political and social speech. Other forms of expression, such as those intended for entertainment or commercial gain, ranked lower in the hierarchy. Still others, like libel and obscenity, were viewed as illegitimate and occupied a position outside the scope of First Amendment protections. As we shall see in this section and the next two chapters, the Court has often approached freedom of expression disputes with this hierarchy in mind. It is especially vigilant in protecting political and social communication, but allows greater deference to government in regulating other forms.

Under what conditions, then, may the government regulate expression? In general, government may encroach on speech rights if the expression itself or its consequences involve matters of legitimate government concern. Justice Holmes may have defined it best when he referred to "substantive evils that Congress has a right to prevent." The Court has applied this admittedly vague standard by designating certain conditions that justify government's authority to intervene. Although not exhaustive, the following list includes the major categories of conditions that may trigger valid government regulation of expression.

Violence. The government has authority to protect citizens from personal injury. If expression takes a violent form or incites others to violence the government may regulate it.

Property Damage. The government has the right to protect private and public property from being destroyed or damaged. Antiwar protesters, for example, who express themselves by setting fire to a National Guard armory have gone beyond their First Amendment protections and can be arrested for their conduct.

Criminal Speech. Some forms of expression are crimes by their very nature. For example, the Constitution does not protect those who might give military secrets to the enemy in time of war or engage in conspiracies to violate valid criminal laws.

Encroaching on the Rights of Others. Freedom of expression does not provide a license to infringe on the rights of others. If animal rights protesters block an entrance to a zoo or pro-life groups prevent access to an abortion clinic, the government may intervene. In both cases, the protesters have curtailed the right of the public to move about without interference.

Burdens on Government Functions. Regulation is permissible if expression places a burden on a legitimate government function. If, for example, environmentalists opposed to the construction of a Corps of Engineers dam lie down in front of bulldozers, the government may arrest them.

Trespass. The freedom of expression does not include the right to speak anywhere one wishes. A campaign worker, for example, does not have the right to come into your home without permission to promote the candidate's cause. Similarly, some public facilities are not legitimate places for groups of demonstrators to congregate. The government may, for example, prohibit antiwar protesters from demonstrating inside a defense facility.

Forms of Expression Outside First Amendment Scope. Certain classes of expression have always been considered unprotected by the Constitution. Chief among these are obscenity and libel. As we shall see in Chapter 7, if expression meets the Court's rather strict definitions of libel or obscenity, the First Amendment imposes no barrier to government regulation.

These various aspects of legitimate government concern have given rise to the Court's time, place, and manner doctrine. By this standard the Court acknowledges that government has the general authority to impose reasonable time, place, and manner restrictions on the freedom of expression. Therefore, the Court would certainly uphold the arrest of demonstrators who gathered in the middle of an expressway or of political zealots who promoted their candidate by driving a sound truck through a residential area at 2:00 A.M.

Although the Court has been sympathetic to the government's need to regulate expression under certain carefully defined conditions, the justices also have been careful to place restraints on the government to prevent abuse. The Court has constructed certain generally accepted criteria to hold the government's power within acceptable bounds. Some of the more frequently invoked standards follow:

Legitimate Purpose. Any government restriction on freedom of expression must have a clearly defined, legitimate government purpose. A law that makes inciting to riot a crime, for example, would rest on the legitimate government purpose of curtailing violence. A law prohibiting criticism of the president, motivated by an interest in keeping incumbents in power, would clearly fail this test.

Narrow Construction/Overbreadth. Any regulation of expression must be narrowly tailored to meet the government's objectives. If a legislature, concerned with protests that cause violence, passed a law prohibiting all public demonstrations, the statue would fail the narrow construction requirement. This regulatory scheme would be overbroad, going far beyond what is necessary to deal with the legislature's legitimate concern by restricting constitutionally protected expression along with unprotected speech.

Vagueness. Legislatures must draft laws restricting freedom of expression with sufficient precision to give fair notice as to what is being regulated. If normally intelligent people have to guess what a statute means and come to different conclusions about what is prohibited by it, the statute is unconstitutionally vague.

Chilling Effect. A law intended to regulate certain forms of illegitimate expression cannot be written so as to make people fearful of engaging in legitimate activity. Often such a "chilling effect" stems from statutes that are vague or overbroad. Assume that a state legislature, concerned about sexual activities that occur in certain nightclubs, passes a statute making it illegal to serve alcoholic beverages in any establishment that features nude entertainment. In response to that law, museum officials may be fearful of sponsoring a gathering at which patrons would sip wine while viewing an exhibit of paintings that include some nude figures. Here a statute designed to curb obscenity creates a chilling effect on the exercise of legitimate activities.

Prior Restraint. Government may prosecute individuals who violate legitimate restrictions on expression, but, absent extraordinary circumstances, may not intervene before the fact. For example, the government may not constitutionally require a speaker to submit for review a copy of the speech before its delivery to make sure that nothing in it may incite the audience to riot.

Content Discrimination. Laws regulating expression should be content neutral. For example, a local ordinance enforced in a way that allowed Democrats to conduct a public rally but prohibited Republicans from engaging in the same activity would violate this principle.

As you read the cases and commentary in the rest of this chapter and the two that follow, keep these principles in mind. You will observe many examples of the justices debating whether the expression in question merits regulation and whether the methods of regulation are proper. You will witness the flexibility of these standards as the Court adjusts them to different contexts. Finally, you will see how individual justices differ in the way they apply these standards based on their own ideologies and preferences.

Symbolic Speech

The First Amendment specifically protects the freedoms of speech and press, two forms of expression with which the Framers were thoroughly familiar. In the days of the Revolution, political protest customarily took the form of eloquent addresses, sharply worded editorials, and fiery publications. Verbal expression and published communication were the methods of political debate, and the Framers unambiguously sought to protect them from government encroachment by drafting and ratifying the First Amendment.

But what if someone wishes to communicate a message by means other than spoken words or print? If a point is made by action rather than by verbal expression, does the First Amendment still grant immunity from government regulation? These questions deal with symbolic speech and whether expressive conduct qualifies as speech under the meaning of the First Amendment.

Most of the symbolic speech cases have occurred in the modern period, but the debate over expressive conduct began much earlier. Recall the discussion of *Stromberg v. California.* In that 1931 case, a camp counselor was convicted not because of anything she said, but because of an expressive act that was in conflict with California law. In reversing her conviction on First Amendment grounds, the Supreme Court acknowledged that at least some forms of symbolic speech merit constitutional protection.

In the years that followed, the Court had to decide whether the same principles applied to various forms of picketing in labor disputes. Some states sought to hinder the development and success of labor unions by passing laws prohibiting workers from carrying placards and walking picket lines to protest alleged unfair labor practices. The most significant case of this era was *Thornhill v. Alabama* (1940). Byron Thornhill had been arrested for violating an Alabama law that made picketing a crime. Supporters of the antipicketing statutes argued that picketing was conduct and not speech, but the Supreme Court reversed the conviction on First Amendment grounds. For the Court, Justice Murphy concluded, "In the circumstances of our times the dissemination of information concerning the facts of a labor dispute must be regarded as within that area of free discussion that is guaranteed by the Constitution."

Decisions such as these established the principle that symbolic actions can qualify as speech and be accorded First Amendment protection. This principle does not mean, however, that the First Amendment shields from government regulation *any* act committed to express an idea or opinion. No one, for example, would seriously claim that assassination is a protected form of expressing political opposition. Perhaps even more than verbal expression, symbolic speech presents especially difficult questions of drawing constitutional boundaries.

The turbulence of the late 1960s brought a number of difficult symbolic expression issues before the Court. The first of these cases was *United States v. O'Brien* (1968), in which the defendants had expressed their opposition to the war in Southeast Asia by publicly and illegally burning their draft cards.[12] The case presents a difficult clash of values. The Warren Court had demonstrated a growing tolerance for First Amendment expression claims, but would this trend continue? Or would the fact that

12. To hear oral arguments in this case, navigate to: *oyez.nwu.edu.*

On March 31, 1966, David O'Brien and three other antiwar protesters demonstrated their opposition to U.S. military action in Vietnam by burning their draft cards on the steps of the South Boston courthouse. Their convictions for violating the Selective Service Act were affirmed in *United States v. O'Brien*.

thousands of American troops were engaged in combat abroad influence the Court?

United States v. O'Brien

391 U.S. 367 (1968)
laws.findlaw.com/US/391/367.html
Vote: 7 (Black, Brennan, Fortas, Harlan, Stewart, Warren, White)
　1 (Douglas)
Opinion of the Court: Warren
Concurring opinion: Harlan
Dissenting opinion: Douglas
Not participating: Marshall

On March 31, 1966, David O'Brien and three others burned their draft cards on the steps of a South Boston courthouse. A sizable, hostile crowd gathered. FBI agents took the four into the courthouse to protect them and to question them. The agents told O'Brien that he had vio-

lated a 1965 amendment to the Selective Service Act, making it illegal to "destroy or mutilate" draft cards. O'Brien replied that he understood, but had burned his card anyway because he was "a pacifist and as such [could not] kill."

After a federal court ruled that O'Brien had acted within the bounds of the Constitution, the United States asked the Supreme Court to hear the case. In his petition for certiorari, Solicitor General Thurgood Marshall argued that O'Brien's actions thwarted a valid function of government—to draft men into the armed forces—because his purpose was "to influence others to adopt his anti-war beliefs."[13] The government also tried to negate the chief argument made by O'Brien's ACLU attorney that his action constituted symbolic speech of the kind upheld by the Court in *Stromberg*. To this, the government replied, "Terming [O'Brien's] conduct 'symbolic speech' does not transform it into activity entitled to the

13. After Marshall's elevation to the Supreme Court, Erwin Griswold took over the litigation, writing the major brief.

same kind of constitutional protection given to words and other modes of expression."

MR. CHIEF JUSTICE WARREN delivered the opinion of the Court.

O'Brien . . . argues that the 1965 Amendment is unconstitutional in its application to him, and is unconstitutional as enacted because what he calls the "purpose" of Congress was "to suppress freedom of speech." We consider these arguments separately.

O'Brien first argues that the 1965 Amendment is unconstitutional as applied to him because his act of burning his registration certificate was protected "symbolic speech" within the First Amendment. His argument is that the freedom of expression which the First Amendment guarantees includes all modes of "communication of ideas by conduct," and that his conduct is within this definition because he did it in "demonstration against the war and against the draft."

We cannot accept the view that an apparently limitless variety of conduct can be labeled "speech" whenever the person engaging in the conduct intends thereby to express an idea. However, even on the assumption that the alleged communicative element in O'Brien's conduct is sufficient to bring into play the First Amendment, it does not necessarily follow that the destruction of a registration certificate is constitutionally protected activity. This Court has held that when "speech" and "nonspeech" elements are combined in the same course of conduct, a sufficiently important governmental interest in regulating the nonspeech element can justify incidental limitations on First Amendment freedoms. To characterize the quality of the governmental interest which must appear, the Court has employed a variety of descriptive terms: compelling; substantial; subordinating; paramount; cogent; strong. Whatever imprecision inheres in these terms, we think it clear that a government regulation is sufficiently justified if it is within the constitutional power of the Government; if it furthers an important or substantial governmental interest; if the governmental interest is unrelated to the suppression of free expression; and if the incidental restriction on alleged First Amendment freedoms is no greater than is essential to the furtherance of that interest. We find that the 1965 Amendment to §12(b)(3) of the Universal Military Training and Service Act meets all

of these requirements, and consequently that O'Brien can be constitutionally convicted for violating it.

The constitutional power of Congress to raise and support armies and to make all laws necessary and proper to that end is broad and sweeping. The power of Congress to classify and conscript manpower for military service is "beyond question." Pursuant to this power, Congress may establish a system of registration for individuals liable for training and service, and may require such individuals within reason to cooperate in the registration system. The issuance of certificates indicating the registration and eligibility classification of individuals is a legitimate and substantial administrative aid in the functioning of this system. And legislation to insure the continuing availability of issued certificates serves a legitimate and substantial purpose in the system's administration.

O'Brien's argument to the contrary is necessarily premised upon his unrealistic characterization of Selective Service certificates. He essentially adopts the position that such certificates are so many pieces of paper designed to notify registrants of their registration or classification, to be retained or tossed in the wastebasket according to the convenience or taste of the registrant. Once the registrant has received notification, according to this view, there is no reason for him to retain the certificates. O'Brien notes that most of the information on a registration certificate serves no notification purpose at all; the registrant hardly needs to be told his address and physical characteristics. We agree that the registration certificate contains much information of which the registrant needs no notification. This circumstance, however, does not lead to the conclusion that the certificate serves no purpose, but that, like the classification certificate, it serves purposes in addition to initial notification. Many of these purposes would be defeated by the certificates' destruction or mutilation. Among these are:

1. The registration certificate serves as proof that the individual described thereon has registered for the draft. The classification certificate shows the eligibility classification of a named but undescribed individual. Voluntarily displaying the two certificates is an easy and painless way for a young man to dispel a question as to whether he might be delinquent in his Selective Service obligations. . . . Additionally, in a time of national crisis, reasonable availability to each registrant of the two small cards assures a rapid and uncom-

plicated means for determining his fitness for immediate induction, no matter how distant in our mobile society he may be from his local board.

2. The information supplied on the certificates facilitates communication between registrants and local boards, simplifying the system and benefiting all concerned. To begin with, each certificate bears the address of the registrant's local board, an item unlikely to be committed to memory. Further, each card bears the registrant's Selective Service number, and a registrant who has his number readily available so that he can communicate it to his local board can make simpler the board's task in locating his file. Finally, a registrant's inquiry, particularly through a local board other than his own, concerning his eligibility status is frequently answerable simply on the basis of his classification certificate; whereas, if the certificate were not reasonably available and the registrants were uncertain of his classification, the task of answering his questions would be considerably complicated.

3. Both certificates carry continual reminders that the registrant must notify his local board of any change of address, and other specified changes in his status. The smooth functioning of the system requires that local boards be continually aware of the status and whereabouts of registrants, and the destruction of certificates deprives the system of a potentially useful notice device.

4. The regulatory scheme involving Selective Service certificates includes clearly valid prohibitions against the alteration, forgery, or similar deceptive misuse of certificates. The destruction or mutilation of certificates obviously increases the difficulty of detecting and tracing abuses such as these. Further, a mutilated certificate might itself be used for deceptive purposes.

The many functions performed by Selective Service certificates establish beyond doubt that Congress has a legitimate and substantial interest in preventing their wanton and unrestrained destruction and assuring their continuing availability by punishing people who knowingly and willfully destroy or mutilate them. And we are unpersuaded that the pre-existence of the non-possession regulations in any way negates this interest. . . .

We think it apparent that the continuing availability to each registrant of his Selective Service certificates substantially furthers the smooth and proper functioning of the system that Congress has established to raise armies. We think

it also apparent that the Nation has a vital interest in having a system for raising armies that functions with maximum efficiency and is capable of easily and quickly responding to continually changing circumstances. For these reasons, the Government has a substantial interest in assuring the continuing availability of issued Selective Service certificates.

It is equally clear that the 1965 Amendment specifically protects this substantial government interest. We perceive no alternative means that would more precisely and narrowly assure the continuing availability of issued Selective Service certificates than a law which prohibits their willful mutilation or destruction. The 1965 Amendment prohibits such conduct and does nothing more. In other words, both the governmental interest and the operation of the 1965 Amendment are limited to the noncommunicative aspect of O'Brien's conduct. The governmental interest and the scope of the 1965 Amendment are limited to preventing harm to the smooth and efficient functioning of the Selective Service System. When O'Brien deliberately rendered unavailable his registration certificate, he willfully frustrated this governmental interest. For this noncommunicative impact of his conduct, and for nothing else, he was convicted.

The case at bar is therefore unlike one where the alleged governmental interest in regulating conduct arises in some measure because the communication allegedly integral to the conduct is itself thought to be harmful. In *Stromberg v. People of State of California* (1931), for example, this Court struck down a statutory phrase which punished people who expressed their "opposition to organized government" by displaying "any flag, badge, banner, or device." Since the statute there was aimed at suppressing communication it could not be sustained as a regulation of noncommunicative conduct.

In conclusion, we find that because of the Government's substantial interest in assuring the continuing availability of issued Selective Service certificates, because amended §462(b) is an appropriately narrow means of protecting this interest and condemns only the independent noncommunicative impact of conduct within its reach, and because the noncommunicative impact of O'Brien's act of burning his registration certificate frustrated the Government's interest, a sufficient governmental interest has been shown to justify O'Brien's conviction.

O'Brien finally argues that the 1965 Amendment is unconstitutional as enacted because what he calls the "purpose" of Congress was "to suppress freedom of speech." We reject this argument because under settled principles the purpose of Congress, as O'Brien uses that term, is not a basis for declaring this legislation unconstitutional.

Warren's opinion explicitly rejects the idea that conduct used to express an idea automatically merits First Amendment protection. The Court held that whenever "speech" and "nonspeech" elements are combined, a sufficiently important government interest in regulating the nonspeech element can justify limitations on First Amendment rights. As applied in this case, the Court found that O'Brien's conduct (burning the draft card) placed a burden on a legitimate government activity (the power to raise and support armies). The government had a substantial interest in exercising its military authority, and the draft registration system was a reasonable means of achieving that end. Consequently, the government had the constitutional power to prosecute individuals who violated the Selective Service laws even if the acts in question communicated a message of political protest.

One year later the Court heard another symbolic speech case stemming from protests against the Vietnam War, *Tinker v. Des Moines* (1969).[14] This appeal came from public school students who had been suspended for engaging in a peaceful but prohibited protest during the school day. As you read the excerpt of this case, ask yourself how the nature and impact of the symbolic expression in *Tinker* compare with O'Brien's draft card burning. Notice also how the justices differ on the question of First Amendment rights in the public schools.

Tinker v. Des Moines

393 U.S. 503 (1969)
laws.findlaw.com/US/393/503.html
Vote: 7 *(Brennan, Douglas, Fortas, Marshall, Stewart, Warren, White)*
    2 *(Black, Harlan)*
Opinion of the Court: Fortas
Concurring opinions: Stewart, White
Dissenting opinions: Black, Harlan

14. To hear oral arguments in this case, navigate to: *oyez.nwu.edu.*

In December 1965 a group of adults and secondary school students in Des Moines, Iowa, devised two strategies to demonstrate their opposition to the Vietnam War: they would fast on December 16 and New Year's Day, and they would wear black armbands every day in between. Principals of the students' schools learned of the plan and agreed to suspend any students wearing armbands. Despite the warning, the parents of five children, including John and Mary Beth Tinker, allowed them to wear black armbands to school. All five were suspended. ACLU attorneys representing the students argued that the armbands constituted legitimate symbolic speech and, because the principals suppressed such expression, they engaged in illegal prior restraint.

MR. JUSTICE FORTAS delivered the opinion of the Court.

The District Court recognized that the wearing of an armband for the purpose of expressing certain views is the type of symbolic act that is within the Free Speech Clause of the First Amendment. As we shall discuss, the wearing of armbands in the circumstances of this case was entirely divorced from actually or potentially disruptive conduct by those participating in it. It was closely akin to "pure speech" which, we have repeatedly held, is entitled to comprehensive protection under the First Amendment.

First Amendment rights, applied in light of the special characteristics of the school environment, are available to teachers and students. It can hardly be argued that either students or teachers shed their constitutional rights to freedom of speech or expression at the schoolhouse gate. This has been the unmistakable holding of this Court for almost 50 years. . . .

In *West Virginia State Board of Education v. Barnette*, this Court held that under the First Amendment, the student in public school may not be compelled to salute the flag. . . . On the other hand, the Court has repeatedly emphasized the need for affirming the comprehensive authority of the States and of school officials, consistent with fundamental constitutional safeguards, to prescribe and control conduct in the schools. Our problem lies in the area where students in the exercise of First Amendment rights collide with the rules of the school authorities.

The problem posed by the present case does not relate to

Mary Beth Tinker and her brother John display the black armbands that got them suspended from school in 1965. The two were protesting the Vietnam War. In *Tinker v. Des Moines* (1969) the Supreme Court held that the suspensions violated the Tinkers' right to freedom of expression.

regulation of the length of skirts or the type of clothing, to hair style, or deportment. It does not concern aggressive, disruptive action or even group demonstrations. Our problem involves direct, primary First Amendment rights akin to "pure speech."

The school officials banned and sought to punish petitioners for a silent, passive expression of opinion, unaccompanied by any disorder or disturbance on the part of petitioners. There is here no evidence whatever of petitioners' interference, actual or nascent, with the schools' work or of collision with the rights of other students to be secure and to be let alone. Accordingly, this case does not concern speech or action that intrudes upon the work of the schools or the rights of other students.

Only a few of the 18,000 students in the school system wore the black armbands. Only five students were suspended for wearing them. There is no indication that the work of the schools or any class was disrupted. Outside the classrooms, a few students made hostile remarks to the children wearing armbands, but there were no threats or acts of violence on school premises.

. . . [I]n our system, undifferentiated fear or apprehension of disturbance is not enough to overcome the right to freedom of expression. Any departure from absolute regimentation may cause trouble. Any variation from the majority's opinion may inspire fear. Any word spoken, in class, in the lunchroom, or on the campus, that deviates from the views of another person may start an argument or cause a disturbance. But our Constitution says we must take this risk, and our history says that it is this sort of hazardous freedom—this kind of openness—that is the basis of our national strength and of the independence and vigor of Americans who grow up and live in this relatively permissive, often disputatious, society.

In order for the State in the person of school officials to justify prohibition of a particular expression of opinion, it must be able to show that its action was caused by something more than a mere desire to avoid the discomfort and unpleasantness that always accompany an unpopular viewpoint. Certainly where there is no finding and no showing that engaging in the forbidden conduct would "materially and substantially interfere with the requirements of appropriate discipline in the operation of the school," the prohibition cannot be sustained.

In the present case, the District Court made no such finding, and our independent examination of the record fails to yield evidence that the school authorities had reason to anticipate that the wearing of the armbands would substantially interfere with the work of the school or impinge upon the rights of other students. . . .

It is also relevant that the school authorities did not purport to prohibit the wearing of all symbols of political or controversial significance. The record shows that students in some of the schools wore buttons relating to national political campaigns, and some even wore the Iron Cross, traditionally a symbol of Nazism. The order prohibiting the wearing of armbands did not extend to these. Instead, a particular symbol—black armbands worn to exhibit opposition to this Nation's involvement in Vietnam—was singled out for prohibition. Clearly, the prohibition of expression of one particular opinion, at least without evidence that it is necessary to avoid material and substantial interference with schoolwork or discipline, is not constitutionally permissible.

In our system, state-operated schools may not be enclaves of totalitarianism. School officials do not possess absolute authority over their students. Students in school as well as out of school are "persons" under our Constitution. They are possessed of fundamental rights which the State must respect, just as they themselves must respect their obligations to the State. In our system, students may not be regarded as closed-circuit recipients of only that which the State chooses to communicate. They may not be confined to the expression of those sentiments that are officially approved. In the absence of a specific showing of constitutionally valid reasons to regulate their speech, students are entitled to freedom of expression of their views. . . .

The principal use to which the schools are dedicated is to accommodate students during prescribed hours for the purpose of certain types of activities. Among those activities is personal intercommunication among the students. This is not only an inevitable part of the process of attending school; it is also an important part of the educational process. A student's rights, therefore, do not embrace merely the classroom hours. When he is in the cafeteria, or on the playing field, or on the campus during the authorized hours, he may express his opinions, even on controversial subjects like the conflict in Vietnam, if he does so without "materially and substantially interfer[ing] with the require-

ments of appropriate discipline in the operation of the school" and without colliding with the rights of others. But conduct by the student, in class or out of it, which for any reason—whether it stems from time, place, or type of behavior—materially disrupts classwork or involves substantial disorder or invasion of the rights of others is, of course, not immunized by the constitutional guarantee of freedom of speech.

Under our Constitution, free speech is not a right that is given only to be so circumscribed that it exists in principle but not in fact. Freedom of expression would not truly exist if the right could be exercised only in an area that a benevolent government has provided as a safe haven for crackpots. The Constitution says that Congress (and the States) may not abridge the right to free speech. This provision means what it says. We properly read it to permit reasonable regulation of speech-connected activities in carefully restricted circumstances. But we do not confine the permissible exercise of First Amendment rights to a telephone booth or the four corners of a pamphlet, or to supervised and ordained discussion in a school classroom.

If a regulation were adopted by school officials forbidding discussion of the Vietnam conflict, or the expression by any student of opposition to it anywhere on school property except as part of a prescribed classroom exercise, it would be obvious that the regulation would violate the constitutional rights of students, at least if it could not be justified by a showing that the students' activities would materially and substantially disrupt the work and discipline of the school. . . .

As we have discussed, the record does not demonstrate any facts which might reasonably have led school authorities to forecast substantial disruption of or material interference with school activities, and no disturbances or disorders on the school premises in fact occurred. These petitioners merely went about their ordained rounds in school. Their deviation consisted only in wearing on their sleeve a band of black cloth, not more than two inches wide. They wore it to exhibit their disapproval of the Vietnam hostilities and their advocacy of a truce, to make their views known, and, by their example, to influence others to adopt them. They neither interrupted school activities nor sought to intrude in the school affairs or the lives of others. They caused discussion outside of the classrooms, but no interference with work and no disorder. In the circumstances, our Constitution does not permit officials of the State to deny their form of expression.

Reversed and remanded.

MR. JUSTICE BLACK, dissenting.

As I read the Court's opinion it relies upon the following grounds for holding unconstitutional the judgment of the Des Moines school officials and the two courts below. First, the Court concludes that the wearing of armbands is "symbolic speech" which is "akin to 'pure speech'" and therefore protected by the First and Fourteenth Amendments. Secondly, the Court decides that the public schools are an appropriate place to exercise "symbolic speech" as long as normal school functions are not "unreasonably" disrupted. Finally, the Court arrogates to itself, rather than to the State's elected officials charged with running the schools, the decision as to which school disciplinary regulations are "reasonable."

Assuming that the Court is correct in holding that the conduct of wearing armbands for the purpose of conveying political ideas is protected by the First Amendment, the crucial remaining questions are whether students and teachers may use the schools at their whim as a platform for the exercise of free speech—"symbolic" or "pure"—and whether the courts will allocate to themselves the function of deciding how the pupils' school day will be spent. While I have always believed that under the First and Fourteenth Amendments neither the State nor the Federal Government has any authority to regulate or censor the content of speech, I have never believed that any person has a right to give speeches or engage in demonstrations where he pleases and when he pleases. This Court has already rejected such a notion. In *Cox v. Louisiana* (1965), for example, the Court clearly stated that the rights of free speech and assembly "do not mean that everyone with opinions or beliefs to express may address a group at any public place and at any time."

While the record does not show that any of these armband students shouted, used profane language, or were violent in any manner, detailed testimony by some of them shows their armbands caused comments, warnings by other students, the poking of fun at them, and a warning by an older football player that other, nonprotesting students had better let them alone. There is also evidence that a teacher of mathematics had his lesson period practically "wrecked" chiefly by disputes with Mary Beth Tinker, who wore her armband for her "demonstration.". . .

I deny . . . that it has been the "unmistakable holding of this Court for almost 50 years" that "students" and "teachers" take with them into the "schoolhouse gate" constitutional rights to "freedom of speech or expression." Even *Meyer* [*v. Nebraska,* 1923] did not hold that. It makes no reference to "symbolic speech" at all; what it did was to strike down as "unreasonable" and therefore unconstitutional a Nebraska law barring the teaching of the German language before the children reached the eighth grade. One can well agree with Mr. Justice Holmes and Mr. Justice Sutherland, as I do, that such a law was no more unreasonable than it would be to bar the teaching of Latin and Greek to pupils who have not reached the eighth grade. In fact, I think the majority's reason for invalidating the Nebraska law was that it did not like it or in legal jargon that it "shocked the Court's conscience," "offended its sense of justice," or was "contrary to fundamental concepts of the English-speaking world," as the Court has sometimes said. The truth is that a teacher of kindergarten, grammar school, or high school pupils no more carries into a school with him a complete right to freedom of speech and expression than an anti-Catholic or anti-Semite carries with him a complete freedom of speech and religion into a Catholic church or Jewish synagogue. Nor does a person carry with him into the United States Senate or House, or into the Supreme Court, or any other court, a complete constitutional right to go into those places contrary to their rules and speak his mind on any subject he pleases. It is a myth to say that any person has a constitutional right to say what he pleases, where he pleases, and when he pleases. Our Court has decided precisely the opposite. . . .

Change has been said to be truly the law of life but sometimes the old and the tried and true are worth holding. The schools of this Nation have undoubtedly contributed to giving us tranquility and to making us a more law-abiding people. Uncontrolled and uncontrollable liberty is an enemy to domestic peace. We cannot close our eyes to the fact that some of the country's greatest problems are crimes committed by the youth, too many of school age. School discipline, like parental discipline, is an integral and important part of training our children to be good citizens—to be better citizens. Here a very small number of students have crisply and summarily refused to obey a school order designed to give pupils who want to learn the opportunity to do so. One does not need to be a prophet or the son of a prophet to know that after the Court's holding today some students in Iowa schools and indeed in all schools will be ready, able, and willing to defy their teachers on practically all orders. This is the more unfortunate for the schools since groups of students all over the land are already running loose, conducting break-ins, sit-ins, lie-ins, and smash-ins. Many of these student groups, as is all too familiar to all who read the newspapers and watch the television news programs, have already engaged in rioting, property seizures, and destruction. They have picketed schools to force students not to cross their picket lines and have too often violently attacked earnest but frightened students who wanted an education that the pickets did not want them to get. Students engaged in such activities are apparently confident that they know far more about how to operate public school systems than do their parents, teachers, and elected school officials. It is no answer to say that the particular students here have not yet reached such high points in their demands to attend class in order to exercise their political pressures. Turned loose with lawsuits for damages and injunctions against their teachers as they are here, it is nothing but wishful thinking to imagine that young, immature students will not soon believe it is their right to control the schools rather than the right of the States that collect the taxes to hire the teachers for the benefit of the pupils. This case, therefore, wholly without constitutional reasons in my judgment, subjects all the public schools in the country to the whims and caprices of their loudest-mouthed, but maybe not their brightest, students. I, for one, am not fully persuaded that school pupils are wise enough, even with this Court's expert help from Washington, to run the 23,390 public school systems in our 50 States. I wish, therefore, wholly to disclaim any purpose on my part to hold that the Federal Constitution compels the teachers, parents, and elected school officials to surrender control of the American public school system to public school students. I dissent.

The Court ruled in favor of the Tinkers, declaring that students and teachers do not "shed their constitutional rights to freedom of speech or expression at the schoolhouse gate." Important to the Court was that the protest was peaceful: there was no violence, no property damage, and no significant disruption of the school day. On this count, *Tinker* differed from *O'Brien*, in which the justices found that the burning of Selective Service documents placed a burden on a legitimate government function. In dissent, Justice Black took issue with the majority, arguing that the freedom of speech does not extend equally to every place and circumstance. School administrators, he said, should be allowed to impose reasonable regulations to ensure conditions conducive to learning.

Among all symbolic expression issues none has given the Court greater difficulty than flag desecration. As a national symbol, the American flag evokes intense emotional feelings, especially among those who, like members of the Supreme Court, have long histories of public service. Even those justices most committed to freedom of expression have indicated their discomfort in extending First Amendment protection to someone who destroys the flag as a method of political expression.

During the civil rights and Vietnam War protest years, the Court heard two cases involving mistreatment of the flag. In the first, *Street v. New York* (1969), the justices heard the appeal of a civil rights protestor who had verbally insulted the flag and set it on fire. The justices held that the pure speech elements of the protest were protected under the First Amendment, but, due to a 4–4 deadlock, they were unable to resolve whether the burning of the flag enjoyed a similar constitutional privilege. In the second case, *Spence v. Washington* (1974), the Court again took up the physical desecration issue. Here an antiwar protestor displayed an American flag with a large peace symbol taped to both sides. The justices ruled that the protestor's actions constituted symbolic speech constitutionally immune from government regulation.

As the war in Vietnam abated, so did the protest cases. *Spence* had given constitutional protection to one fairly mild version of flag desecration, but would the justices come to the same conclusion with respect to more extreme forms of abusing the flag? That question was not answered until 1989 when the Court heard *Texas v. Johnson.*[15]

---

15. To hear oral arguments in this case, navigate to: *oyez.nwu.edu.*

Gregory Johnson, who has a record of flag burning, holds the American flag while another protester sets it alight. In 1989 the Supreme Court ruled that the conviction of Johnson for burning a flag during a demonstration in Dallas violated his First Amendment expression rights.

Texas v. Johnson

491 U.S. 397 (1989)
laws.findlaw.com/US/491/397.html
Vote: 5 (Blackmun, Brennan, Kennedy, Marshall, Scalia)
    4 (O'Connor, Rehnquist, Stevens, White)
Opinion of the Court: Brennan
Concurring opinion: Kennedy
Dissenting opinions: Rehnquist, Stevens

In the summer of 1984 the Republican Party held its national convention in Dallas, Texas, and overwhelming-ly supported President Ronald Reagan's reelection bid. While the party was meeting, a group of demonstrators marched through the city to protest the Reagan administration's policies. One of the demonstrators gave an American flag to Gregory Lee Johnson, who also was marching. When the march ended, Johnson "unfurled the flag, doused it with kerosene and set it on fire." As it burned, the protestors chanted, "America, the red, white, and blue, we spit on you." Authorities arrested Johnson, charging him with violating the Texas flag desecration law. He was convicted and sentenced to a one-year prison term and a $2,000 fine. A state court of appeals affirmed. However, the Texas Court of Criminal Appeals reversed that holding.

JUSTICE BRENNAN delivered the opinion of the Court.

Johnson was convicted of flag desecration for burning the flag rather than for uttering insulting words. This fact somewhat complicates our consideration of his conviction under the First Amendment. We must first determine whether Johnson's burning of the flag constituted expressive conduct, permitting him to invoke the First Amendment in challenging his conviction. If his conduct was expressive, we next decide whether the State's regulation is related to the suppression of free expression. If the State's regulation is not related to expression, then the less stringent standard we announced in *United States v. O'Brien* for regulations of noncommunicative conduct controls. If it is, then we are outside of *O'Brien's* test, and we must ask whether this interest justifies Johnson's conviction under a more demanding standard. A third possibility is that the State's asserted interest is simply not implicated on these facts, and in that event the interest drops out of the picture.

The First Amendment literally forbids the abridgement only of "speech," but we have long recognized that its protection does not end at the spoken or written word. While we have rejected "the view that an apparently limitless variety of conduct can be labeled 'speech' whenever the person engaging in the conduct intends thereby to express an idea," we have acknowledged that conduct may be "sufficiently imbued with elements of communication to fall within the scope of the First and Fourteenth Amendments."

In deciding whether particular conduct possesses sufficient communicative elements to bring the First Amendment into play, we have asked whether "[a]n intent to convey a particularized message was present, and [whether] the likelihood was great that the message would be understood by those who viewed it." Hence, we have recognized the expressive nature of students' wearing of black armbands to protest American military involvement in Vietnam. . . .

Especially pertinent to this case are our decisions recognizing the communicative nature of conduct relating to flags. Attaching a peace sign to the flag, saluting the flag, and displaying a red flag, we have held, all may find shelter under the First Amendment. That we have had little difficulty identifying an expressive element in conduct relating to flags should not be surprising. The very purpose of a national flag is to serve as a symbol of our country; it is, one might say, "the one visible manifestation of two hundred years of nationhood.". . .

We have not automatically concluded, however, that any action taken with respect to our flag is expressive. Instead, in characterizing such action for First Amendment purposes, we have considered the context in which it occurred. . . .

Johnson burned an American flag as part—indeed, as the culmination—of a political demonstration that coincided with the convening of the Republican Party and its renomination of Ronald Reagan for President. In these circumstances, Johnson's burning of the flag was conduct "sufficiently imbued with elements of communication" to implicate the First Amendment.

The Government generally has a freer hand in restricting expressive conduct than it has in restricting the written or spoken word. . . . "A law *directed at* communicative nature of conduct must, like a law directed at speech itself, be justified by the substantial showing of need that the First Amendment requires." It is, in short, not simply the verbal or nonverbal nature of the expression, but the governmental interest at stake, that helps to determine whether a restriction on that expression is valid.

Thus, although we have recognized that where "'speech' and 'nonspeech' elements are combined in the same course of conduct, a sufficiently important governmental interest in regulating the nonspeech element can justify incidental limitations on First Amendment freedoms," we have limited the applicability of *O'Brien*'s relatively lenient standard to those cases in which "the governmental interest is unrelated to the suppression of free expression." In stating,

moreover, that *O'Brien*'s test "in the last analysis is little, if any, different from the standard applied to time, place, or manner restrictions," we have highlighted the requirement that the governmental interest in question be unconnected to expression in order to come under *O'Brien*'s less demanding rule.

In order to decide whether *O'Brien*'s test applies here, therefore, we must decide whether Texas has asserted an interest in support of Johnson's conviction that is unrelated to the suppression of expression. If we find that an interest asserted by the State is simply not implicated on the facts before us, we need not ask whether *O'Brien*'s test applies. The State offers two separate interests to justify this conviction: preventing breaches of the peace, and preserving the flag as a symbol of nationhood and national unity. We hold that the first interest is not implicated on this record and that the second is related to the suppression of expression.

Texas claims that its interest in preventing breaches of the peace justifies Johnson's conviction for flag desecration. However, no disturbance of the peace actually occurred or threatened to occur because of Johnson's burning of the flag. . . .

The State's position, therefore, amounts to a claim that an audience that takes serious offense at particular expression is necessarily likely to disturb the peace and that the expression may be prohibited on this basis. Our precedents do not countenance such a presumption. On the contrary, they recognize that a principal "function of free speech under our system of government is to invite dispute. It may indeed best serve its high purpose when it induces a condition of unrest, creates dissatisfaction with conditions as they are, or even stirs people to anger.". . .

Nor does Johnson's expressive conduct fall within that small class of "fighting words" that are "likely to provoke the average person to retaliation, and thereby cause a breach of the peace." No reasonable onlooker would have regarded Johnson's generalized expression of dissatisfaction with the policies of the Federal Government as a direct personal insult or an invitation to exchange fisticuffs.

We thus conclude that the State's interest in maintaining order is not implicated on these facts. The State need not worry that our holding will disable it from preserving the peace. We do not suggest that the First Amendment forbids a State to prevent "imminent lawless action.". . .

The State also asserts an interest in preserving the flag as a symbol of nationhood and national unity. In *Spence* [*v. Washington*, 1974], we acknowledged that the Government's interest in preserving the flag's special symbolic value "is directly related to expression in the context of activity" such as affixing a peace symbol to a flag. We are equally persuaded that this interest is related to expression in the case of Johnson's burning of the flag. The State, apparently, is concerned that such conduct will lead people to believe either that the flag does not stand for nationhood and national unity, but instead reflects other, less positive concepts, or that the concepts reflected in the flag do not in fact exist, that is, we do not enjoy unity as a Nation. These concerns blossom only when a person's treatment of the flag communicates some message, and thus are related "to the suppression of free expression" within the meaning of *O'Brien*. We are thus outside of *O'Brien*'s test altogether.

It remains to consider whether the State's interest in preserving the flag as a symbol of nationhood and national unity justifies Johnson's conviction. . . .

Johnson's political expression was restricted because of the content of the message he conveyed. We must therefore subject the State's asserted interest in preserving the special symbolic character of the flag to "the most exacting scrutiny."

Texas argues that its interest in preserving the flag as a symbol of nationhood and national unity survives this close analysis. Quoting extensively from the writings of this Court chronicling the flag's historic and symbolic role in our society, the State emphasizes the "'special place'" reserved for the flag in our Nation. The State's argument is not that it has an interest simply in maintaining the flag as a symbol of *something*, no matter what it symbolizes; indeed, if that were the State's position, it would be difficult to see how that interest is endangered by highly symbolic conduct such as Johnson's. Rather, the State's claim is that it has an interest in preserving the flag as a symbol of *nationhood* and *national unity*, a symbol with a determinate range of meanings. According to Texas, if one physically treats the flag in a way that would tend to cast doubt on either the idea that nationhood and national unity are the flag's referents or that national unity actually exists, the message conveyed thereby is a harmful one and therefore may be prohibited.

If there is a bedrock principle underlying the First Amendment, it is that the Government may not prohibit the expression of an idea simply because society finds the idea itself offensive or disagreeable.

We have not recognized an exception to this principle even where our flag has been involved. In *Street v. New York* we held that a State may not criminally punish a person for uttering words critical of the flag. . . .

In short, nothing in our precedents suggests that a State may foster its own view of the flag by prohibiting expressive conduct relating to it. To bring its argument outside our precedents, Texas attempts to convince us that even if its interest in preserving the flag's symbolic role does not allow it to prohibit words or some expressive conduct critical of the flag, it does permit it to forbid the outright destruction of the flag. The State's argument cannot depend here on the distinction between written or spoken words and nonverbal conduct. That distinction, we have shown, is of no moment where the nonverbal conduct is expressive, as it is here, and where the regulation of that conduct is related to expression, as it is here. . . .

Texas' focus on the precise nature of Johnson's expression, moreover, misses the point of our prior decisions: their enduring lesson, that the Government may not prohibit expression simply because it disagrees with its message, is not dependent on the particular mode in which one chooses to express an idea. If we were to hold that a State may forbid flag-burning wherever it is likely to endanger the flag's symbolic role, but allow it wherever burning a flag promotes that role—as where, for example, a person ceremoniously burns a dirty flag—we would be saying that when it comes to impairing the flag's physical integrity, the flag itself may be used as a symbol—as a substitute for the written or spoken word or a "short cut from mind to mind"—only in one direction. We would be permitting a State to "prescribe what shall be orthodox" by saying that one may burn the flag to convey one's attitude toward it and its referents only if one does not endanger the flag's representation of nationhood and national unity. . . .

There is, moreover, no indication—either in the text of the Constitution or in our cases interpreting it—that a separate juridical category exists for the American flag alone. Indeed, we would not be surprised to learn that the persons who framed our Constitution and wrote the Amendment that we now construe were not known for their reverence for the Union Jack. The First Amendment does not guarantee that other concepts virtually sacred to our Nation as a whole—such as the principle that discrimination on the basis of race is odious and destructive—will go unquestioned in the marketplace of ideas. We decline, therefore, to create for the flag an exception to the joust of principles protected by the First Amendment. . . .

The way to preserve the flag's special role is not to punish those who feel differently about these matters. It is to persuade them that they are wrong. . . . And, precisely because it is our flag that is involved, one's response to the flag-burner may exploit the uniquely persuasive power of the flag itself. We can imagine no more appropriate response to burning a flag than waving one's own, no better way to counter a flag-burner's message than by saluting the flag that burns, no surer means of preserving the dignity even of the flag that burned than by—as one witness here did—according its remains a respectful burial. We do not consecrate the flag by punishing its desecration, for in doing so we dilute the freedom that this cherished emblem represents.

Johnson was convicted for engaging in expressive conduct. The State's interest in preventing breaches of the peace does not support his conviction because Johnson's conduct did not threaten to disturb the peace. Nor does the State's interest in preserving the flag as a symbol of nationhood and national unity justify his criminal conviction for engaging in political expression. The judgment of the Texas Court of Criminal Appeals is therefore

Affirmed.

JUSTICE KENNEDY, concurring.

I write not to qualify the words JUSTICE BRENNAN chooses so well, for he says with power all that is necessary to explain our ruling. I join his opinion without reservation, but with a keen sense that this case, like others before us from time to time, exacts its personal toll. . . .

The hard fact is that sometimes we must make decisions we do not like. We make them because they are right, right in the sense that the law and the Constitution, as we see them, compel the result. And so great is our commitment to the process that, except in the rare case, we do not pause to express distaste for the result, perhaps for fear of undermining a valued principle that dictates the decision. This is one of those rare cases. . . .

. . . I do not believe the Constitution gives us the right to

rule as the dissenting members of the Court urge, however painful this judgment is to announce. Though symbols often are what we ourselves make of them, the flag is constant in expressing beliefs Americans share, beliefs in law and peace and that freedom which sustains the human spirit. The case here today forces recognition of the costs to which those beliefs commit us. It is poignant but fundamental that the flag protects those who hold it in contempt.

For all the record shows, this respondent was not a philosopher and perhaps did not even possess the ability to comprehend how repellent his statements must be to the Republic itself. But whether or not he could appreciate the enormity of the offense he gave, the fact remains that his acts were speech, in both the technical and the fundamental meaning of the Constitution. So I agree with the Court that he must go free.

CHIEF JUSTICE REHNQUIST, with whom JUSTICE WHITE and JUSTICE O'CONNOR join, dissenting.

In holding this Texas statute unconstitutional, the Court ignores Justice Holmes' familiar aphorism that "a page of history is worth a volume of logic." *New York Trust Co. v. Eisner* (1921). For more than 200 years, the American flag has occupied a unique position as the symbol of our Nation, a uniqueness that justifies a governmental prohibition against flag burning in the way respondent Johnson did here. . . .

The American flag . . . has come to be the visible symbol embodying our Nation. It does not represent the views of any particular political party, and it does not represent any particular political philosophy. The flag is not simply another "idea" or "point of view" competing for recognition in the marketplace of ideas. Millions and millions of Americans regard it with an almost mystical reverence regardless of what sort of social, political, or philosophical beliefs they may have. I cannot agree that the First Amendment invalidates the Act of Congress, and the laws of 48 of the 50 States, which make criminal the public burning of the flag. . . .

. . . [T]he public burning of the American flag by Johnson was no essential part of any exposition of ideas, and at the same time it had a tendency to incite a breach of the peace. Johnson was free to make any verbal denunciation of the flag that he wished; indeed, he was free to burn the flag in private. He could publicly burn other symbols of the

Government or effigies of political leaders. He did lead a march through the streets of Dallas, and conducted a rally in front of the Dallas City Hall. He engaged in a "die-in" to protest nuclear weapons. He shouted out various slogans during the march, including: "Reagan, Mondale which will it be? Either one means World War III"; "Ronald Reagan, killer of the hour, Perfect example of U.S. power"; and "red, white and blue, we spit on you, you stand for plunder, you will go under." For none of these acts was he arrested or prosecuted; it was only when he proceeded to burn publicly an American flag stolen from its rightful owner that he violated the Texas statute. . . .

. . . The Texas statute deprived Johnson of only one rather inarticulate symbolic form of protest—a form of protest that was profoundly offensive to many—and left him with a full panoply of other symbols and every conceivable form of verbal expression to express his deep disapproval of national policy. Thus, in no way can it be said that Texas is punishing him because his hearers—or any other group of people—were profoundly opposed to the message that he sought to convey. Such opposition is no proper basis for restricting speech or expression under the First Amendment. It was Johnson's use of this particular symbol, and not the idea that he sought to convey by it or by his many other expressions, for which he was punished. . . .

. . . Uncritical extension of constitutional protection to the burning of the flag risks the frustration of the very purpose for which organized governments are instituted. The Court decides that the American flag is just another symbol, about which not only must opinions pro and con be tolerated, but for which the most minimal public respect may not be enjoined. The government may conscript men into the Armed Forces where they must fight and perhaps die for the flag, but the government may not prohibit the public burning of the banner under which they fight. I would uphold the Texas statute as applied in this case.

JUSTICE STEVENS, dissenting.

As the Court analyzes this case, it presents the question whether the State of Texas, or indeed the Federal Government, has the power to prohibit the public desecration of the American flag. The question is unique. In my judgment, rules that apply to a host of other symbols, such as state flag, armbands, or various privately promoted emblems of

political or commercial identity, are not necessarily controlling. Even if flagburning could be considered just another species of symbolic speech under the logical application of the rules that the Court has developed in its interpretation of the First Amendment in other contexts, this case has an intangible dimension that makes those rules inapplicable. . . .

The value of the flag as a symbol cannot be measured. Even so, I have no doubt that the interest in preserving that value for the future is both significant and legitimate. Conceivably, that value will be enhanced by the Court's conclusion that our national commitment to free expression is so strong that even the United States, as ultimate guarantor of that freedom, is without power to prohibit the desecration of its unique symbol. But I am unpersuaded. The creation of a federal right to post bulletin boards and graffiti on the Washington Monument might enlarge the market for free expression, but at a cost I would not pay. Similarly, in my considered judgment, sanctioning the public desecration of the flag will tarnish its value—both for those who cherish the ideas for which it waves and for those who desire to don the robes of martyrdom by burning it. That tarnish is not justified by the trivial burden on free expression occasioned by requiring that an available, alternative mode of expression—including uttering words critical of the flag, see *Street v. New York* (1969)—be employed. . . .

I respectfully dissent.

The Court's decision in *Johnson* is intriguing for a number of reasons. Note, for example, the rather odd alignments: two of the more conservative members of the Rehnquist Court, Antonin Scalia and Anthony M. Kennedy, voted with the majority; John Paul Stevens, usually found with the liberal wing of the Court, dissented.

Perhaps most important was the tremendous—and to some, surprising—uproar created by the Court's ruling. President George Bush immediately condemned it, and public opinion polls indicated that Americans generally favored a constitutional amendment overturning *Johnson*. But, after some politicking by civil liberties groups, senators, and representatives, Congress did not propose an amendment. Instead, it passed the Flag Protection Act of 1989, which penalized by a one-year jail

BOX 5-6 AFTERMATH . . .
GREGORY LEE JOHNSON

SHORTLY AFTER the Supreme Court decided that Gregory Lee Johnson's burning of the American flag during the 1984 Republican National Convention was political expression protected by the First Amendment, Congress responded. The legislature passed the Flag Protection Act of 1989.

On October 30, two days after the new law took effect, a small group of demonstrators gathered on the steps of the Capitol in Washington to protest. Because the press had been informed that the protesters would burn flags, reporters, police, and curious passersby crowded the area. Suddenly four men separated themselves from the crowd and began to set fire to American flags.

Police reacted quickly—too quickly for one of the protesters. Gregory Lee Johnson was stopped before he could ignite his flag. Authorities arrested and prosecuted the other three demonstrators, but ignored Johnson.

Represented by William Kunstler, an attorney well known for defending radical causes, the three protestors argued that the new flag desecration law was just as constitutionally flawed as the Texas statute struck down earlier. When the justices issued their opinion in *United States v. Eichman*, the protesters prevailed, defeating the government's case presented by Solicitor General Kenneth Starr. (Starr later gained notoriety as the independent counsel who investigated President Clinton.)

In the end, it was Shawn Eichman's name, not Johnson's, that was attached to the Supreme Court's decision. Johnson, who had hoped to win another place in legal history, sharply criticized police and prosecutors, claiming that his failure to be prosecuted with the others was a "gross miscarriage of justice."

SOURCES: *Washington Post*, October 31, 1989, November 1, 1989; and *New York Times*, April 11, 1990.

sentence and a $1,000 fine anyone who "knowingly mutilates, defaces, physically defiles, burns, maintains on the floor or ground, or tramples upon any flag of the United States."

Because the federal act differed from the Texas law at issue in *Johnson*—it banned flag desecration regardless of the motivation of the burner, whereas the Texas law did so only if a jury found the activity to be offensive—some thought it would meet approval in the Supreme Court. Others saw this difference as relatively insignificant, and they were correct. In *United States v. Eichman* (1990) the Court, using the same reasoning expressed in *Johnson* and by the same vote, struck down this law as a violation of the First Amendment *(See Box 5-6)*.

Public Forums and the Preservation of Order

Preserving public order and protecting citizens from injury caused by violence are among the essential duties of government. The Preamble to the Constitution includes insuring "domestic Tranquility" among the six basic purposes for which the new government was formed. In some instances free expression can threaten order, especially when the expression takes place in a public forum or when it takes the form of a mass demonstration. If order breaks down, results may include bodily injury, property destruction, and the inability of the public to move freely. The government may not be able to carry out its duties. In any of these situations a conflict arises between the nation's commitment to freedom of expression and the government's duty to maintain order. At what point is government constitutionally justified in repressing expression to stop or prevent violence?

To deal with such expression, the justices have promulgated legal criteria distinct from those they use to adjudicate pure speech cases. The Court began to develop these standards in 1942 with *Chaplinsky v. New Hampshire*. As you read Justice Murphy's opinion in *Chaplinsky*, try to ascertain the legal standard he articulates and remember it as we look at the later Court decisions in these areas. Did Murphy's approach continue to permeate Court decisions of the civil rights and Vietnam War movements, or did the Court revise it to fit changing times?

Chaplinsky v. New Hampshire

315 U.S. 568 (1942)
laws.findlaw.com/US/315/568.html
Vote: 9 (Black, Byrnes, Douglas, Frankfurter, Jackson, Murphy,
   Reed, Roberts, Stone)
   0
Opinion of the Court: Murphy

On April 6, 1940, Jehovah's Witness member Walter Chaplinsky was selling biblical pamphlets and literature, including *Watchtower* and *Consolation,* on a public street in New Hampshire. While he was announcing the sale of his pamphlets, a crowd began to gather. After one person tried to attack Chaplinsky, the rest joined in. When the police arrived and handcuffed a very agitated Chaplinsky, he demanded to know why they had arrested him and not the mob. An officer replied, "Shut up, you damn bastard," and Chaplinsky in turn called the officer a "damned fascist" and "a God damned racketeer." For those words, the state charged him with breaking a law prohibiting the use of "any offensive, derisive, or annoying word to any other person who is lawfully in the street."

On appeal to the Supreme Court, Chaplinsky's attorneys asked it to overturn the state statute on free speech grounds, arguing that "the fact that speech is likely to cause violence is no grounds for suppressing it." The state countered that the law constituted a valid exercise of its police powers.

MR. JUSTICE MURPHY delivered the opinion of the Court.

Allowing the broadest scope to the language and purpose of the Fourteenth Amendment, it is well understood that the right of free speech is not absolute at all times and under all circumstances. There are certain well-defined and narrowly limited classes of speech, the prevention and punishment of which have never been thought to raise any Constitutional problem. These include the lewd and obscene, the profane, the libelous, and the insulting or "fighting" words—those which by their very utterance inflict injury or tend to incite an immediate breach of the peace. It has been well observed that such utterances are no essential part of any exposition of ideas, and are of such slight social value as a step to truth that any benefit that may be derived from them is clearly outweighed by the social interest in order and morality. . . .

The state statute here challenged comes to us authoritatively construed by the highest court of New Hampshire. It has two provisions—the first relates to words or names addressed to another in a public place; the second refers to noises and exclamations. The court said: "the two provisions are distinct. One may stand separately from the other. Assuming, without holding, that the second were unconstitutional, the first could stand if constitutional." We accept that construction of severability and limit our consideration to the first provision of the statute.

On the authority of its earlier decisions, the state court declared that the state's purpose was to preserve the public peace, no words being "forbidden except such as have a direct tendency to cause acts of violence by the persons to whom, individually, the remark is addressed." It was further said: "The word 'offensive' is not to be defined in terms of what a particular addressee thinks. . . . The test is what men of common intelligence would understand would be words likely to cause an average addressee to fight. . . . The English language has a number of words and expressions which by general consent are 'fighting words' when said without a disarming smile. . . . Such words, as ordinary men know, are likely to cause a fight. So are threatening, profane or obscene revilings. Derisive and annoying words can be taken as coming within the purview of the statute as heretofore interpreted only when they have this characteristic of plainly tending to excite the addressee to a breach of the peace. . . . The statute, as construed, does no more than prohibit the face-to-face words plainly likely to cause a breach of the peace by the addressee, words whose speaking constitutes a breach of the peace by the speaker—including 'classical fighting words,' words in current use less 'classical' but equally likely to cause violence, and other disorderly words, including profanity, obscenity and threats."

We are unable to say that the limited scope of the statute as thus construed contravenes the Constitutional right of free expression. It is a statute narrowly drawn and limited to define and punish specific conduct lying within the domain of state power, the use in a public place of words likely to cause a breach of the peace. . . .

Nor can we say that the application of the statute to the facts disclosed by the record substantially or unreasonably impinges upon the privilege of free speech. Argument is unnecessary to demonstrate that the appellations "damned racketeer" and "damned Fascist" are epithets likely to provoke the average person to retaliation, and thereby cause a breach of the peace.

Affirmed.

In unanimously affirming Chaplinsky's conviction, the Court agreed with Murphy's enunciation of the so-called fighting words doctrine: that the government may regulate words "which by their very utterance inflict injury or tend to incite an immediate breach of peace."

Not all public forum cases involve individuals shouting words that may prompt a violent response from the person to whom they are directed. Sometimes a small group or even a single individual uses public property as a place of political protest. Occasionally, such expression occurs quite silently, such as in *Cohen v. California* (1971).[16] Here the justices examined the use of a county courthouse as a forum for expression where the message is communicated in a way that many may find offensive.

Cohen v. California

403 U.S. 15 (1971)
laws.findlaw.com/US/403/15.html
Vote: 5 (Brennan, Douglas, Harlan, Marshall, Stewart)
        4 (Black, Blackmun, Burger, White)
Opinion of the Court: Harlan
Dissenting opinion: Blackmun

In April 1968, at the height of the protest against the Vietnam War, Paul Cohen visited some friends in Los Angeles, his hometown. While they were discussing their opposition to the war, someone scrawled on Cohen's jacket the words *Fuck the Draft* and *Stop the War*. The following morning, Cohen wore his jacket in the corridors of a Los Angeles county courthouse, knowing it bore these messages.

16. To hear oral arguments in this case, navigate to: *oyez.nwu.edu.*

Although Cohen took off the jacket before entering the courtroom, a police sergeant had observed it in the corridor. The officer asked the judge to cite Cohen for contempt of court. The judge refused, but the officer arrested Cohen, charging him with "willfully and unlawfully and maliciously disturbing the peace and quiet by engaging in tumultuous and offensive conduct."

Given the nature of Cohen's alleged offense, this case could have ended where it started, in a California trial court. No violence occurred, nor were large groups of people or spectators involved. But that was not to be. By the time of Cohen's trial in September, his cause had attracted the attention of the ACLU. Its Southern California affiliate decided that Cohen's case presented a significant issue—that the message on his jacket represented a form of protected, albeit symbolic, expression—and it offered to finance Cohen's case.

Affirming Cohen's municipal court conviction, the California Court of Appeals found that it was "reasonably foreseeable that such conduct might cause others to rise up to commit a violent act." The California Supreme Court declined to review that decision, but Cohen's ACLU lawyers successfully petitioned the U.S. Supreme Court to consider the First Amendment issues at stake.[17]

MR. JUSTICE HARLAN delivered the opinion of the Court.

In order to lay hands on the precise issue which this case involves, it is useful first to canvass various matters which this record does *not* present.

The conviction quite clearly rests upon the asserted offensiveness of the *words* Cohen used to convey his message to the public. The only "conduct" which the State sought to punish is the fact of communication. Thus, we deal here with a conviction resting solely upon "speech," *Stromberg v.*

17. In addition to its significant constitutional ramifications, *Cohen* also provides a unique opportunity to view intra-organizational politics. As Richard Cortner reports, the Southern California affiliate of the ACLU always felt the "key issue . . . and the one that arguments before the Court should focus on was the free expression issue." At the Supreme Court level, however, the ACLU's Northern California affiliate "urged the Court not to decide the case on the freedom of expression issue." The Southern California affiliate refused to give its consent to the filing of the brief, but the justices granted permission. See Richard C. Cortner, *The Supreme Court and Civil Liberties Policy* (Palo Alto, Calif.: Mayfield, 1975), 128–129.

California (1931), not upon any separately identifiable conduct which allegedly was intended by Cohen to be perceived by others as expressive of particular views but which, on its face, does not necessarily convey any message and hence arguably could be regulated without effectively repressing Cohen's ability to express himself. Further, the State certainly lacks power to punish Cohen for the underlying content of the message the inscription conveyed. At least so long as there is no showing of an intent to incite disobedience to or disruption of the draft, Cohen could not, consistently with the First and Fourteenth Amendments, be punished for asserting the evident position on the inutility or immorality of the draft his jacket reflected. *Yates v. United States.*

Appellant's conviction, then, rests squarely upon his exercise of the "freedom of speech" protected from arbitrary governmental interference by the Constitution and can be justified, if at all, only as a valid regulation of the manner in which he exercised that freedom, not as a permissible prohibition on the substantive message it conveys. This does not end the inquiry, of course, for the First and Fourteenth Amendments have never been thought to give absolute protection to every individual to speak whenever or wherever he pleases or to use any form of address in any circumstances that he chooses. In this vein, too, however, we think it important to note that several issues typically associated with such problems are not presented here.

In the first place, Cohen was tried under a statute applicable throughout the entire State. Any attempt to support this conviction on the ground that the statute seeks to preserve an appropriately decorous atmosphere in the courthouse where Cohen was arrested must fail in the absence of any language in the statute that would have put appellant on notice that certain kinds of otherwise permissible speech or conduct would nevertheless, under California law, not be tolerated in certain places. No fair reading of the phrase "offensive conduct" can be said sufficiently to inform the ordinary person that distinctions between certain locations are thereby created.

In the second place, as it comes to us, this case cannot be said to fall within those relatively few categories of instances where prior decisions have established the power of government to deal more comprehensively with certain forms of individual expression simply upon a showing that such a form was employed. This is not, for example, an obscenity case. Whatever else may be necessary to give rise to the States' broader power to prohibit obscene expression, such expression must be, in some significant way, erotic. It cannot plausibly be maintained that this vulgar allusion to the Selective Service System would conjure up such psychic stimulation in anyone likely to be confronted with Cohen's crudely defaced jacket.

This Court has also held that the States are free to ban the simple use, without a demonstration of additional justifying circumstances, of so-called "fighting words," those personally abusive epithets which, when addressed to the ordinary citizens, are, as a matter of common knowledge, inherently likely to provoke violent reaction. *Chaplinsky v. New Hampshire* (1942). While the four-letter word displayed by Cohen in relation to the draft is not uncommonly employed in a personally provocative fashion, in this instance it was clearly not "directed to the person of the hearer." *Cantwell v. Connecticut* (1940). No individual actually or likely to be present could reasonably have regarded the words on appellant's jacket as a direct personal insult. Nor do we have here an instance of the exercise of the State's police power to prevent a speaker from intentionally provoking a given group to hostile reaction. *Feiner v. New York* (1951); *Terminiello v. Chicago* (1949). There is, as noted above, no showing that anyone who saw Cohen was in fact violently aroused or that appellant intended such a result.

Finally, in arguments before this Court much has been made of the claim that Cohen's distasteful mode of expression was thrust upon unwilling or unsuspecting viewers, and that the State might therefore legitimately act as it did in order to protect the sensitive from otherwise unavoidable exposure to appellant's crude form of protest. Of course, the mere presumed presence of unwitting listeners or viewers does not serve automatically to justify curtailing all speech capable of giving offense. While this Court has recognized that government may properly act in many situations to prohibit intrusion into the privacy of the home of unwelcome views and ideas which cannot be totally banned from the public dialogue, we have at the same time consistently stressed that "we are often 'captives' outside the sanctuary of the home and subject to objectionable speech." The ability of government, consonant with the Constitution, to shut off discourse solely to protect others from hearing it is, in other words, dependent upon a showing that substantial privacy interests are being invaded in an essentially intolerable manner. Any broader view of this authority would effectively empower a majority to silence dissidents simply as a matter of personal predilections.

In this regard, persons confronted with Cohen's jacket were in a quite different posture than, say, those subjected to the raucous emissions of sound trucks blaring outside their residences. Those in the Los Angeles courthouse could effectively avoid further bombardment of their sensibilities simply by averting their eyes. And, while it may be that one has a more substantial claim to a recognizable privacy interest when walking through a courthouse corridor than, for example, strolling through Central Park, surely it is nothing like the interest in being free from unwanted expression in the confines of one's own home. Given the subtlety and complexity of the factors involved, if Cohen's "speech" was otherwise entitled to constitutional protection, we do not think the fact that some unwilling "listeners" in a public building may have been briefly exposed to it can serve to justify this breach of the peace conviction where, as here, there was no evidence that persons powerless to avoid appellant's conduct did in fact object to it, and where that portion of the statute upon which Cohen's conviction rests evinces no concern, either on its face or as construed by the California courts, with the special plight of the captive auditor, but, instead, indiscriminately sweeps within its prohibitions all "offensive conduct" that disturbs "any neighborhood or person."

Against this background, the issue flushed by this case stands out in bold relief. It is whether California can excise, as "offensive conduct," one particular scurrilous epithet from the public discourse, either upon the theory of the court below that its use is inherently likely to cause violent reaction or upon a more general assertion that the States, acting as guardians of public morality, may properly remove this offensive word from the public vocabulary.

The rationale of the California court is plainly untenable. At most it reflects an "undifferentiated fear or apprehension of disturbance which is not enough to overcome the right to freedom of expression." We have been shown no evidence that substantial numbers of citizens are standing ready to strike out physically at whoever may assault their sensibilities with execrations like that uttered by Cohen. There may be some persons about with such lawless and violent proclivities, but that is an insufficient base upon which to erect, consistently with constitutional values, a governmental power to force persons who wish to ventilate

their dissident views into avoiding particular forms of expression. The argument amounts to little more than the self-defeating proposition that to avoid physical censorship of one who has not sought to provoke such a response by a hypothetical coterie of the violent and lawless, the States may more appropriately effectuate that censorship themselves.

Admittedly, it is not so obvious that the First and Fourteenth Amendments must be taken to disable the States from punishing public utterance of this unseemly expletive in order to maintain what they regard as a suitable level of discourse within the body politic. We think, however, that examination and reflection will reveal the shortcomings of a contrary viewpoint.

At the outset, we cannot overemphasize that, in our judgment, most situations where the State has a justifiable interest in regulating speech will fall within one or more of the various established exceptions, discussed above but not applicable here, to the usual rule that governmental bodies may not prescribe the form or content of individual expression. Equally important to our conclusion is the constitutional backdrop against which our decision must be made. The constitutional right of free expression is powerful medicine in a society as diverse and populous as ours. It is designed and intended to remove governmental restraints from the arena of public discussion, putting the decision as to what views shall be voiced largely into the hands of each of us, in the hope that use of such freedom will ultimately produce a more capable citizenry and more perfect polity and in the belief that no other approach would comport with the premise of individual dignity and choice upon which our political system rests.

To many, the immediate consequence of this freedom may often appear to be only verbal tumult, discord, and even offensive utterance. These are, however, within established limits, in truth necessary side effects of the broader enduring values which the process of open debate permits us to achieve. That the air may at times seem filled with verbal cacophony is, in this sense not a sign of weakness but of strength. We cannot lose sight of the fact that, in what otherwise might seem a trifling and annoying instance of individual distasteful abuse of a privilege, these fundamental societal values are truly implicated. . . .

Against this perception of the constitutional policies involved, we discern certain more particularized considerations that peculiarly call for reversal of this conviction. First, the principle contended for by the State seems inherently boundless. How is one to distinguish this from any other offensive word? Surely the State has no right to cleanse public debate to the point where it is grammatically palatable to the most squeamish among us. Yet no readily ascertainable general principle exists for stopping short of that result were we to affirm the judgment below. For, while the particular four-letter word being litigated here is perhaps more distasteful than most others of its genre, it is nevertheless often true that one man's vulgarity is another's lyric. Indeed, we think it is largely because governmental officials cannot make principled distinctions in this area that the Constitution leaves matters of taste and style so largely to the individual.

Additionally, we cannot overlook the fact, because it is well illustrated by the episode involved here, that much linguistic expression serves a dual communicative function: it conveys not only ideas capable of relatively precise, detached explication, but otherwise inexpressible emotions as well. In fact, words are often chosen as much for their emotive as their cognitive force. We cannot sanction the view that the Constitution, while solicitous of the cognitive content of individual speech has little or no regard for that emotive function which practically speaking, may often be the more important element of the overall message sought to be communicated. . . .

Finally, and in the same vein, we cannot indulge the facile assumption that one can forbid particular words without also running a substantial risk of suppressing ideas in the process. Indeed, governments might soon seize upon the censorship of particular words as a convenient guise for banning the expression of unpopular views. We have been able, as noted above, to discern little social benefit that might result from running the risk of opening the door to such grave results.

It is, in sum, our judgment that, absent a more particularized and compelling reason for its actions, the State may not, consistently with the First and Fourteenth Amendments, make the simple public display here involved of this single four-letter expletive a criminal offense. Because that is the only arguably sustainable rationale for the conviction here at issue, the judgment below must be reversed.

Reversed.

MR. JUSTICE BLACKMUN, with whom THE CHIEF JUSTICE and MR. JUSTICE BLACK join, dissenting.

Cohen's absurd and immature antic, in my view, was mainly conduct and little speech. The California Court of Appeal appears so to have described it, and I cannot characterize it otherwise. Further, the case appears to me to be well within the sphere of *Chaplinsky v. New Hampshire* (1942), where Justice Murphy, a known champion of First Amendment freedoms, wrote for a unanimous bench. As a consequence, this Court's agonizing over First Amendment values seems misplaced and unnecessary.

Whether you agree with Justice Harlan that "one man's vulgarity is another man's lyric" or with Justice Blackmun that the case presents only an "absurd and immature antic," the Court clearly extended First Amendment protection to words used in a public place that many may find offensive and unacceptable. This ruling, however, does not mean that offensive words are constitutionally protected in every context. In *Cohen* there was no evidence of disruption, violence, or other matters of legitimate concern to the state. In different situations, regulation might be permissible. For example, the lower courts of several states have struggled with laws that prohibit use of obscene or offensive language on bumper stickers. States that have enacted these laws claim that such bumper stickers divert drivers' attention away from the proper operation of their vehicles, posing a risk to public safety. Civil libertarians, however, argue that banning these bumper stickers runs contrary to the teachings of *Cohen* and related cases. This issue illustrates the often difficult choices judges must make in balancing legitimate state concerns with individual expression.

Chaplinsky and *Cohen* involved individuals who expressed themselves in a way that caused local officials to be concerned about a breakdown in order. Public safety interests become even more acute when the expression takes the form of a mass demonstration rather than individual speech. In addition to the hostility the group's message may provoke, the presence of significant numbers of people raises the potential danger of personal injury and property damage. Large crowds may interfere with the free movement of individuals along streets, side-

Mass demonstrations were an important element in the civil rights movement during the 1960s. A huge crowd attended a 1963 demonstration in front of the Washington Monument.

walks, or other public areas. A demonstration that occurs near a government facility may place a burden on legitimate government activity. For these reasons, local police tend to watch such gatherings with great care. If the police, believing that a breakdown in order is about to occur, move to end the demonstration, the protesters may feel that their First Amendment rights are being violated. This scenario was replayed time after time during the civil rights and antiwar protest era. Numerous disputes worked their way to the Supreme Court giving the justices an opportunity to develop coherent rules of constitutional law governing public demonstrations. Comparing the Court's response to two cases, *Edwards v. South Carolina* (1963) and *Adderley v. Florida* (1966), pro-

vides insight into the way the justices responded to these disputes.

Edwards v. South Carolina involved an appeal by 187 African American high school and college students who were arrested for breach of peace during a 1961 civil rights protest. These students had joined with others to march from a Baptist church to the state capitol building "to submit a protest to the citizens of South Carolina to show their feelings and dissatisfaction with the present condition of discriminatory actions against Negroes." The students peacefully marched to the capitol grounds where they were met by about thirty law enforcement officials, who informed them that as long as they stayed peaceful they could remain in the public area. For the next hour the group marched in an orderly fashion carrying signs with messages such as "I am proud to be a Negro." A crowd of onlookers, numbering two hundred to three hundred watched the activities. There were no signs of imminent violence. The police then informed the students that they had five more minutes to protest, after which they should disperse or face arrest. Large numbers of students refused to go, holding hands and singing "We shall not be moved." Police arrested the students who refused to comply with the order.

The Supreme Court, 8–1, reversed the students' convictions. Important to the justices were the following points. First, the protesters had come to the seat of the government to present their views. There is little better place to exercise the First Amendment right "to petition the Government for a redress of grievances." Second, the students did not engage in violence, and there was no meaningful threat of violence from the crowd. Third, no damage was done to public or private property. Fourth, the students stayed in a designated public area, placing no burden on the administration of lawful government activities or the free movement of the public. Based on these facts, the Court said it was contrary to the First Amendment for the police to order the students to stop their protest and to arrest the students who did not comply.

Adderley v. Florida, also based on a civil rights demonstration, presents a different situation. Approximately two hundred Florida A&M students marched from the university to the county jail to protest an earlier arrest of several schoolmates. The group assembled outside the jailhouse entrance and engaged in singing, clapping, and dancing to express their opposition to the county's segregation policies. A deputy sheriff asked them to move back, claiming that they were blocking entry to the building. They partially complied by moving away from the door, but not pulling back as far as the deputy requested. In their new location the students blocked a driveway used for deliveries and the transportation of inmates. The sheriff then told the protesters that because they were trespassing on jail property they would be arrested if they did not disperse within ten minutes. Some of the students left, but most remained. After a second

warning, the sheriff arrested 107 students for trespass. Following a jury trial, Harriett Louise Adderley and thirty-one other persons were convicted of "trespass with a malicious and mischievous intent."

Although no violence had occurred, a five-justice majority found sufficient justification for the arrests. Unlike the state capitol grounds in *Edwards,* a jail is not an appropriate place for a mass public protest. A jail is a government facility dedicated to securing prisoners. Security interests must be given high priority, and these interests are incompatible with a gathering of protesters. "The State, no less than a private owner of property," Justice Black explained, "has power to preserve the property under its control for the use to which it is lawfully dedicated." In addition, blocking the driveway and the jailhouse entry placed a burden on the execution of government business and restricted the access of people who had business at the jail.

Cases such as *Edwards* and *Adderley* are typical public forum disputes. Each involved large numbers of people collectively expressing their political opinions by assembling in a public place. Although the 1960s may have been the heyday for such activity, disputes over government regulation of public gatherings have not disappeared and are likely to continue.

What new public forum issues will arise in the twenty-first century, and what direction will the Court take? One way to address these questions is to consider several cases decided by the Rehnquist Court. Table 5-2 provides the facts of those disputes, their outcome, and a synopsis of the Court's reasoning. As you can see, the Court continues to face questions of how far the government may go in restricting the manner and place of protests. We also see that civil rights, religion, and foreign policy protests still dominate First Amendment litigation. But the 1990s cases include a new protest issue: abortion. These cases usually involve a clash between pro-life advocates who protest at women's clinics and pro-choice groups that want the courts to curtail the demonstrations. The demonstrators see the issue as freedom of speech; their opponents see it as needing to guarantee free access to legal abortion services without undue interference.

TABLE 5-2 Public Forum Cases Decided by the Rehnquist Court

Case	Facts	Outcome
Board of Airport Commissioners of the City of Los Angeles v. Jews for Jesus (1987)	Challenge to a resolution of a board of airport commissioners banning all "First Amendment activities" within the terminal.	Regardless of whether an airport is a public or nonpublic forum, the resolution is overly broad and, therefore, violative of the First Amendment.
Boos v. Barry (1988)	Challenge to a District of Columbia ordinance prohibiting the display of any sign within 500 feet of a foreign embassy that brings that foreign government into public disrepute, and prohibiting the congregation of three or more persons within 500 feet of an embassy.	The sign-display provision is an unconstitutional, content-based restriction on political expression. The congregation provision is a constitutional manner and place restriction.
Frisby v. Schultz (1988)	Challenge to a city ordinance prohibiting picketing before a particular residence of an individual.	Ordinance serves a legitimate governmental interest. It does not violate the First Amendment.
Ward v. Rock Against Racism (1989)	Challenge to a city regulation requiring bands playing in a city park to use a band shell.	Government may impose reasonable restrictions on speech in public forums. This regulation was reasonable and tailored to meet a significant governmental objective. It does not violate the First Amendment.
United States v. Kokinda (1990)	Challenge to a postal service regulation prohibiting the solicitation of contributions on sidewalks outside a post office.	Sidewalk outside a post office is not a traditional public forum. The regulation does not violate the First Amendment.
International Society for Krishna Consciousness v. Lee (1992)	Challenge to a New York Port Authority regulation forbidding the repetitive solicitation of money or distribution of literature in airport terminals.	An airport terminal is not a public forum. Repetitive, face-to-face solicitation may be disruptive, impede the normal flow of the public, and be fraudulent. The regulation is reasonable. However, the ban on the distribution of literature violates the First Amendment.
Forsyth County, Georgia v. Nationalist Movement (1992)	Challenge to a county ordinance allowing an official to fix the cost of a parade permit based on the estimated cost of providing sufficient security to maintain public order during the gathering.	The ordinance is unconstitutional because it gives excessive discretion to the official and allows the fee to be fixed on the content of the message and the projected public response to it.
Bray v. Alexandria Women's Health Clinic (1993)	An abortion clinic and its supporters sued to enjoin anti-abortion protesters from demonstrating at clinics in the Washington, D.C., area, claiming that such protests are in violation of the Civil Rights Act of 1871 because they reflect an "animus" against women and restrict freedom of interstate travel.	The protests were not directed at women as a class, but were intended to protect victims of abortion, stop its practice, and reverse its legalization. Although many women travel interstate to obtain abortion services, the right to interstate travel was not the focus of the protesters' activity.
National Organization for Women v. Scheidler (1994)	Pro-choice groups sued anti-abortion groups claiming they were in violation of the Racketeer Influenced and Corrupt Organizations Act (RICO) by conspiring to engage in protests designed to shut down abortion clinics and persuade women not to have abortions.	Although the RICO law primarily targets organized crime motivated by hopes of financial gain, the statute is not restricted to crimes having economic motives. RICO laws may be applied to organized criminal activity inspired by noneconomic goals.
Madsen v. Women's Health Center, Inc. (1994)	Anti-abortion groups challenged a state court injunction prohibiting them from protesting within 36 feet of an abortion clinic, restricting noise levels during times abortion surgeries were being conducted, prohibiting protesters from physically approaching clinic clients within 300 feet of the facility, and prohibiting protests within 300 feet of the residences of clinic workers.	The injunction against protests within 36 feet of clinic is generally upheld, as are the noise level restrictions. Banning protest activity within 300 feet of clinic or private residences, however, is unconstitutional.
Schenck v. Pro-Choice Network of Western New York (1997)	Injunction issued to protect access rights of abortion clinic patients by 1) creating a fixed 15-foot buffer zone around clinic entrances and driveways, and 2) creating a floating 15-foot buffer zone around all individuals and vehicles entering and leaving the clinic.	Floating buffer zone violates First Amendment as excessively regulating the speech rights of the protesters, but fixed buffer zone is a valid restriction to protect access rights of clinic patients.

The decision in *Hill v. Colorado* (2000) illustrates both the issue and the Court's reaction to it. As you read the facts and opinions in this case, compare it to the Court's decisions on the antiwar and civil rights protest disputes. Is the Court applying the same standards it did in the earlier disputes? Or does the abortion controversy involve interests and concerns that distinguish it from the civil rights and antiwar protests? Finally, to what extent do you think the justices' views on abortion rights influenced their individual votes in this freedom of expression case?

Hill v. Colorado

530 U.S. — (2000)
supct.law.cornell.edu/supct/html/98-1856.ZS.html
Vote: 6 (Breyer, Ginsburg, O'Connor, Rehnquist, Souter, Stevens
   3 (Kennedy, Scalia, Thomas)
Opinion of the Court: Stevens
Concurring Opinion: Souter
Dissenting Opinions: Kennedy, Scalia

In 1993 the Colorado legislature, concerned about protest activity occurring at abortion clinics, enacted a law placing restrictions on protesters within a radius of one hundred feet of the entrance to any "health care facility." Within that zone, the law prohibited any person from approaching within eight feet of any other person, without that person's consent, for the purpose of distributing literature, displaying a sign, or engaging in oral protest, education, or counseling. A violation of the law was a misdemeanor punishable by a fine of $50–$750 and/or up to six months imprisonment.

Shortly after the statute was passed, Leila Jeanne Hill, Audrey Himmelmann, and Everitt W. Simpson Jr. filed suit claiming that the law on its face violates the First and Fourteenth Amendments. The challengers described themselves as sidewalk counselors who urge women seeking abortions to reconsider their decisions. Their activities at abortion clinics include verbal communication with women and their escorts, the displaying of anti-abortion signs, and the distribution of anti-abortion literature. The law, they claimed, prohibits constitutionally protected peaceful communication and protest on sidewalks and similar areas that are traditional public forums. In addition, the challenge asserted that the law is a content-based regulation of expression and that the statute's consent provision constitutes an impermissible prior restraint. Supporters of the law argued that the legislation protects women from harassment. They also claimed that anti-abortion protests often became an impediment to women who wish to exercise their constitutional right to terminate a pregnancy. Colorado state courts upheld the law.

JUSTICE STEVENS delivered the opinion of the Court.

Before confronting the question whether the Colorado statute reflects an acceptable balance between the constitutionally protected rights of law-abiding speakers and the interests of unwilling listeners, it is appropriate to examine the competing interests at stake. A brief review of both sides of the dispute reveals that each has legitimate and important concerns.

The First Amendment interests of petitioners are clear and undisputed. As a preface to their legal challenge, petitioners emphasize three propositions. First, they accurately explain that the areas protected by the statute encompass all the public ways within 100 feet of every entrance to every health care facility everywhere in the State of Colorado. There is no disagreement on this point, even though the legislative history makes it clear that its enactment was primarily motivated by activities in the vicinity of abortion clinics. Second, they correctly state that their leafletting, sign displays, and oral communications are protected by the First Amendment. The fact that the messages conveyed by those communications may be offensive to their recipients does not deprive them of constitutional protection. Third, the public sidewalks, streets, and ways affected by the statute are "quintessential" public forums for free speech. Finally, although there is debate about the magnitude of the statutory impediment to their ability to communicate effectively with persons in the regulated zones, that ability, particularly the ability to distribute leaflets, is unquestionably lessened by this statute.

On the other hand, petitioners do not challenge the legitimacy of the state interests that the statute is intended to serve. It is a traditional exercise of the States' "police powers to protect the health and safety of their citizens." *Medtronic, Inc. v. Lohr* (1996). That interest may justify a special focus on unimpeded access to health care facilities and the avoidance of potential trauma to patients associated with confrontational protests. See *Madsen v. Women's Health Center, Inc.* (1994); *NLRB v. Baptist Hospital, Inc.* (1979). . . .

It is also important when conducting this interest analysis to recognize the significant difference between state restrictions on a speaker's right to address a willing audience and those that protect listeners from unwanted communication. This statute deals only with the latter.

The right to free speech, of course, includes the right to attempt to persuade others to change their views, and may not be curtailed simply because the speaker's message may be offensive to his audience. But the protection afforded to offensive messages does not always embrace offensive speech that is so intrusive that the unwilling audience cannot avoid it. . . .

We have . . . recognized that the "right to persuade" . . . is protected by the First Amendment, *Thornhill v. Alabama* (1940), as well as by federal statutes. Yet we have continued to maintain that "no one has a right to press even 'good' ideas on an unwilling recipient." None of our decisions has minimized the enduring importance of "the right to be free" from persistent "importunity, following and dogging" after an offer to communicate has been declined. While the freedom to communicate is substantial, "the right of every person 'to be let alone' must be placed in the scales with the right of others to communicate." It is that right, as well as the right of "passage without obstruction," that the Colorado statute legitimately seeks to protect. The restrictions imposed by the Colorado statute only apply to communications that interfere with these rights rather than those that involve willing listeners. . . .

All four of the state court opinions upholding the validity of this statute concluded that it is a content-neutral time, place, and manner regulation. Moreover, they all found support for their analysis in *Ward v. Rock Against Racism* (1989). It is therefore appropriate to comment on the "content neutrality" of the statute. As we explained in *Ward*:

"The principal inquiry in determining content neutrality, in speech cases generally and in time, place, or manner cases in particular, is whether the government has adopted a regulation of speech because of disagreement with the message it conveys."

The Colorado statute passes that test for three independent reasons. First, it is not a "regulation of speech." Rather, it is a regulation of the places where some speech may occur. Second, it was not adopted "because of disagreement with the message it conveys." This conclusion is supported not just by the Colorado courts' interpretation of legislative history, but more importantly by the State Supreme Court's unequivocal holding that the statute's "restrictions apply equally to all demonstrators, regardless of viewpoint, and the statutory language makes no reference to the content of the speech." Third, the State's interests in protecting access and privacy, and providing the police with clear guidelines, are unrelated to the content of the demonstrators' speech. As we have repeatedly explained, government regulation of expressive activity is "content neutral" if it is justified without reference to the content of regulated speech. . . .

The Colorado statute's regulation of the location of protests, education, and counseling . . . places no restrictions on—and clearly does not prohibit—either a particular viewpoint or any subject matter that may be discussed by a speaker. Rather, it simply establishes a minor place restriction on an extremely broad category of communications with unwilling listeners. Instead of drawing distinctions based on the subject that the approaching speaker may wish to address, the statute applies equally to used car salesmen, animal rights activists, fundraisers, environmentalists, and missionaries. Each can attempt to educate unwilling listeners on any subject, but without consent may not approach within eight feet to do so. . . .

. . . [T]he statute's restriction seeks to protect those who enter a health care facility from the harassment, the nuisance, the persistent importuning, the following, the dogging, and the implied threat of physical touching that can accompany an unwelcome approach within eight feet of a patient by a person wishing to argue vociferously face-to-face and perhaps thrust an undesired handbill upon her. The statutory phrases, "oral protest, education, or counseling," distinguish speech activities likely to have those consequences from speech activities . . . that are most unlikely to have those consequences. . . .

Similarly, the contention that a statute is "viewpoint based" simply because its enactment was motivated by the conduct of the partisans on one side of a debate is without support. . . . *Frisby v. Schultz* (1988). . . .

We also agree with the state courts' conclusion that [the

statute] is a valid time, place, and manner regulation under the test applied in *Ward* because it is "narrowly tailored." We already have noted that the statute serves governmental interests that are significant and legitimate and that the restrictions are content neutral. We are likewise persuaded that the statute is "narrowly tailored" to serve those interests and that it leaves open ample alternative channels for communication. As we have emphasized on more than one occasion, when a content-neutral regulation does not entirely foreclose any means of communication, it may satisfy the tailoring requirement even though it is not the least restrictive or least intrusive means of serving the statutory goal.

The three types of communication regulated . . . are the display of signs, leafletting, and oral speech. The 8-foot separation between the speaker and the audience should not have any adverse impact on the readers' ability to read signs displayed by demonstrators. In fact, the separation might actually aid the pedestrians' ability to see the signs by preventing others from surrounding them and impeding their view. Furthermore, the statute places no limitations on the number, size, text, or images of the placards. And, as with all of the restrictions, the 8-foot zone does not affect demonstrators with signs who remain in place.

With respect to oral statements, the distance certainly can make it more difficult for a speaker to be heard, particularly if the level of background noise is high and other speakers are competing for the pedestrian's attention. Notably, the statute places no limitation on the number of speakers or the noise level, including the use of amplification equipment, although we have upheld such restrictions in past cases. . . . Unlike the 15-foot zone in *Schenck* [*v. Pro-Choice Network of Western New York*, 1997], this 8-foot zone allows the speaker to communicate at a "normal conversational distance." Additionally, the statute allows the speaker to remain in one place, and other individuals can pass within eight feet of the protester without causing the protester to violate the statute. Finally, here there is a "knowing" requirement that protects speakers "who thought they were keeping pace with the targeted individual" at the proscribed distance from inadvertently violating the statute. . . .

The burden on the ability to distribute handbills is more serious because it seems possible that an 8-foot interval could hinder the ability of a leafletter to deliver handbills to some unwilling recipients. The statute does not, however, prevent a leafletter from simply standing near the path of oncoming pedestrians and proffering his or her material, which the pedestrians can easily accept. And, as in all leafletting situations, pedestrians continue to be free to decline the tender. . . .

Finally, in determining whether a statute is narrowly tailored, we have noted that "[w]e must, of course, take account of the place to which the regulations apply in determining whether these restrictions burden more speech than necessary." *Madsen.* . . .

Persons who are attempting to enter health care facilities—for any purpose—are often in particularly vulnerable physical and emotional conditions. The State of Colorado has responded to its substantial and legitimate interest in protecting these persons from unwanted encounters, confrontations, and even assaults by enacting an exceedingly modest restriction on the speakers' ability to approach. . . .

This restriction is thus reasonable and narrowly tailored. . . .

Finally, petitioners argue that [the statute's] consent requirement is invalid because it imposes an unconstitutional "prior restraint" on speech. We rejected this argument previously in *Schenck* and *Madsen*. . . . Under this statute, absolutely no channel of communication is foreclosed. No speaker is silenced. And no message is prohibited. Petitioners are simply wrong when they assert that "[t]he statute compels speakers to obtain consent to speak and it authorizes private citizens to deny petitioners' requests to engage in expressive activities." To the contrary, this statute does not provide for a "heckler's veto" but rather allows every speaker to engage freely in any expressive activity communicating all messages and viewpoints subject only to the narrow place requirement imbedded within the "approach" restriction.

Furthermore, our concerns about "prior restraints" relate to restrictions imposed by official censorship. The regulations in this case, however, only apply if the pedestrian does not consent to the approach. Private citizens have always retained the power to decide for themselves what they wish to read, and within limits, what oral messages they want to consider. This statute simply empowers private citizens entering a health care facility with the ability to prevent a speaker, who is within eight feet and advancing, from communicating a message they do not wish to hear. Further, the statute does not authorize the pedestrian to affect any other activity at any other location or relating to any other person. These restrictions thus do not constitute an unlawful prior restraint.

The judgment of the Colorado Supreme Court is affirmed.

It is so ordered.

JUSTICE SOUTER, with whom JUSTICE O'CONNOR, JUSTICE GINSBURG, and JUSTICE BREYER join, concurring.

[The law] simply does not forbid the statement of any position on any subject. It does not declare any view as unfit for expression within the 100-foot zone or beyond it. What it forbids, and all it forbids, is approaching another person closer than eight feet (absent permission) to deliver the message. Anyone (let him be called protester, counselor, or educator) may take a stationary position within the regulated area and address any message to any person within sight or hearing. The stationary protester may be quiet and ingratiating, or loud and offensive; the law does not touch him.

JUSTICE SCALIA, with whom JUSTICE THOMAS joins, dissenting.

The Court today concludes that a regulation requiring speakers on the public thoroughfares bordering medical facilities to speak from a distance of eight feet is "not a 'regulation of speech,'" but "a regulation of the places where some speech may occur," and that a regulation directed to only certain categories of speech (protest, education, and counseling) is not "content-based." For these reasons, it says, the regulation is immune from the exacting scrutiny we apply to content-based suppression of speech in the public forum. The Court then determines that the regulation survives the less rigorous scrutiny afforded content-neutral time, place, and manner restrictions because it is narrowly tailored to serve a government interest—protection of citizens' "right to be let alone.". . .

None of these remarkable conclusions should come as a surprise. What is before us, after all, is a speech regulation directed against the opponents of abortion, and it therefore enjoys the benefit of the "ad hoc nullification machine" that the Court has set in motion to push aside whatever doctrines of constitutional law stand in the way of that highly favored practice. Having deprived abortion opponents of the political right to persuade the electorate that abortion should be restricted by law, the Court today continues and expands its assault upon their individual right to persuade women contemplating abortion that what they are doing is wrong. Because, like the rest of our abortion jurisprudence, today's decision is in stark contradiction of the constitutional principles we apply in all other contexts, I dissent.

. . . Whatever may be said about the restrictions on the other types of expressive activity, the regulation as it applies to oral communications is obviously and undeniably content-based. A speaker wishing to approach another for the purpose of communicating *any* message except one of protest, education, or counseling may do so without first securing the other's consent. Whether a speaker must obtain permission before approaching within eight feet—and whether he will be sent to prison for failing to do so—depends entirely on *what he intends to say* when he gets there. I have no doubt that this regulation would be deemed content-based *in an instant* if the case before us involved anti-war protesters, or union members seeking to "educate" the public about the reasons for their strike. "[I]t is," we would say, "the content of the speech that determines whether it is within or without the statute's blunt prohibition," *Carey v. Brown* (1980). But the jurisprudence of this Court has a way of changing when abortion is involved. . . .

. . . [I]t blinks reality to regard this statute, in its application to oral communications, as anything other than a content-based restriction upon speech in the public forum. As such, it must survive that stringent mode of constitutional analysis our cases refer to as "strict scrutiny," which requires that the restriction be narrowly tailored to serve a compelling state interest. . . . Suffice it to say that if protecting people from unwelcome communications (the governmental interest the Court posits) is a compelling state interest, the First Amendment is a dead letter. And if . . . forbidding peaceful, nonthreatening, but uninvited speech from a distance closer than eight feet is a "narrowly tailored" means of preventing the obstruction of entrance to medical facilities (the governmental interest the State asserts) narrow tailoring must refer not to the standards of Versace, but to those of Omar the tentmaker. . . .

[T]he 8-foot buffer zone attaches to *every* person on the public way or sidewalk within 100 feet of the entrance of a medical facility, regardless of whether that person is seeking to enter or exit the facility. In fact, the State acknowledged at oral argument that the buffer zone would attach to any person within 100 feet of the entrance door of a skyscraper in which a single doctor occupied an office on the 18th floor. And even with respect to those who *are* seeking to enter or exit the facilities, the statute does not protect them only from speech that is so intimidating or threatening as to impede access. Rather, it covers *all* unconsented-to approaches for the purpose of oral protest, education, or counseling (including those made for the purpose of the most peaceful appeals) and, perhaps even more significantly, *every* approach made for the purposes of leafletting or handbilling, which we have never considered, standing alone, obstructive or unduly intrusive. The sweep of this prohibition is breathtaking. . . .

Those whose concern is for the physical safety and security of clinic patients, workers, and doctors should take no comfort from today's decision. Individuals or groups intent on bullying or frightening women out of an abortion, or doctors out of performing that procedure, will not be deterred by Colorado's statute; bullhorns and screaming from eight feet away will serve their purposes well. But those who would accomplish their moral and religious objectives by peaceful and civil means, by trying to persuade individual women of the rightness of their cause, will be deterred; and that is not a good thing in a democracy. This Court once recognized, as the Framers surely did, that the freedom to speak and persuade is inseparable from, and antecedent to, the survival of self-government. The Court today rotates that essential safety valve on our democracy one-half turn to the right, and no one who seeks safe access to health care facilities in Colorado or elsewhere should feel that her security has by this decision been enhanced. . . .

Does the deck seem stacked? You bet. As I have suggested throughout this opinion, today's decision is not an isolated distortion of our traditional constitutional principles, but is one of many aggressively proabortion novelties announced by the Court in recent years. Today's distortions, however, are particularly blatant. Restrictive views of the First Amendment that have been in dissent since the 1930's suddenly find themselves in the majority. "Uninhibited, robust, and wide open" debate is replaced by the power of the state to protect an unheard-of "right to be let alone" on the public streets. I dissent.

JUSTICE KENNEDY, dissenting.

The Court's holding contradicts more than a half century of well-established First Amendment principles. For the first time, the Court approves a law which bars a private citizen from passing a message, in a peaceful manner and on a profound moral issue, to a fellow citizen on a public sidewalk. If from this time forward the Court repeats its grave errors of analysis, we shall have no longer the proud tradition of free and open discourse in a public forum. In my view, JUSTICE SCALIA's First Amendment analysis is correct and mandates outright reversal. . . .

. . . The law imposes content-based restrictions on speech by reason of the terms it uses, the categories it employs, and the conditions for its enforcement. It is content based, too, by its predictable and intended operation. Whether particular messages violate the statute is determined by their substance. The law is a prime example of a statute inviting screening and censoring of individual speech; and it is serious error to hold otherwise. . . .

The statute is content based for an additional reason: It restricts speech on particular topics. Of course, the enactment restricts "oral protest, education, or counseling" on any subject; but a statute of broad application is not content neutral if its terms control the substance of a speaker's message. If oral protest, education, or counseling on every subject within an 8-foot zone present a danger to the public, the statute should apply to every building entrance in the State. It does not. It applies only to a special class of locations: entrances to buildings with health care facilities. We would close our eyes to reality were we to deny that "oral protest, education, or counseling" outside the entrances to medical facilities concern a narrow range of topics—indeed, one topic in particular. By confining the law's application to the specific locations where the prohibited discourse occurs, the State has made a content-based determination. The Court ought to so acknowledge. Clever content-based restrictions are no less offensive than censoring on the basis of content. If, just a few decades ago, a State with a history of enforcing racial discrimination had enacted a statute like this one, regulating "oral protest, education, or counseling" within 100 feet of the entrance to any lunch counter, our predecessors would not have hesitated to hold it was content based or viewpoint based. It should be a profound disappointment to defenders of the First

Amendment that the Court today refuses to apply the same structural analysis when the speech involved is less palatable to it. . . .

There runs through our First Amendment theory a concept of immediacy, the idea that thoughts and pleas and petitions must not be lost with the passage of time. In a fleeting existence we have but little time to find truth through discourse. No better illustration of the immediacy of speech, of the urgency of persuasion, of the preciousness of time, is presented than in this case. Here the citizens who claim First Amendment protection seek it for speech which, if it is to be effective, must take place at the very time and place a grievous moral wrong, in their view, is about to occur. The Court tears away from the protesters the guarantees of the First Amendment when they most need it. So committed is the Court to its course that it denies these protesters, in the face of what they consider to be one of life's gravest moral crises, even the opportunity to try to offer a fellow citizen a little pamphlet, a handheld paper seeking to reach a higher law.

I dissent.

Hate Speech

The cases we have discussed so far demonstrate a great diversity in the content and method of communication. Individuals in some of these cases have used conventional forms of protest, such as speeches, parades, and published documents; others have used unconventional methods that are offensive to many, such as Paul Cohen's crude jacket or Gregory Johnson's burning of the American flag. Their expressions have included a wide array of philosophies and causes—communism, socialism, civil rights, religious beliefs, and opposition to war or abortion. In spite of this diversity, these cases share some common elements. Each case has involved an individual or group communicating a political or social message, usually expressing dissatisfaction with certain government policies. This speech is the traditional form of political expression that the Framers sought to protect when they approved the First Amendment.

Since the mid-1970s another form of communication, which differs markedly from the traditional, has come before the Court. Expression based on hatred goes well beyond offending the standards of appropriateness or good taste. It arises from hostile, discriminatory, and prejudicial attitudes toward another person's innate characteristics: sex, race, ethnicity, religion, or sexual orientation. When directed at a member of a targeted group, such expression is demeaning and hurtful. Hate speech tends to be devoid of traditional commentary on political issues or on the need for changes in public policy. Instead, its central theme is hostility toward individuals belonging to the target group. May hate speech be banned, or does the First Amendment protect it? If regulation is permissible, under what conditions? And what standard should control?

One of the first modern cases involving these issues was *National Socialist Party v. Skokie* (1977). The National Socialist Party was a minor political party with no hope of gaining electoral victories. Because such parties understand they have no chance of winning elections, they often set their sights a bit lower. They see public activities, such as marches and demonstrations, as public education, a way to communicate their messages. *Skokie* concerned the party's desire to exercise its First Amendment right to assemble. More specifically, the party wanted to "educate" the public by marching in Skokie, Illinois, a suburb of Chicago.

Such marches are commonplace in America; almost daily a political organization or other group stages a demonstration or protest somewhere. But this proposed march was anything but commonplace. The National Socialist Party is an American version of the Nazi Party, which came into power under Adolf Hitler in Germany. A large number of Jews, including survivors of Hitler's concentration camps and their families, live in Skokie. Together the two groups formed a potentially explosive combination. In fact, as soon as the town heard of the Nazis' plan to march in full regalia, it passed a variety of ordinances aimed specifically at stopping it. Believing that these measures abridged their First Amendment rights, party leaders turned to the ACLU for legal assistance. Many ACLU members objected to the organization's agreeing to represent Nazi interests, but the ACLU participated because Skokie's prohibitions were what the organization was founded to fight—abridgments of the

First Amendment.[18] Skokie residents saw the matter in a different light: the presence of Nazi uniforms in their town constituted fighting words. Therefore, Skokie argued that it could legitimately regulate such speech to prevent a riot.

A state circuit court agreed with the town and entered an injunction prohibiting the Nazis from marching in Skokie. The ACLU asked the Illinois Supreme Court for a stay and for an expedited appeal. When both requests were denied, the matter came before the U.S. Supreme Court.

In a short *per curiam* opinion, five members of the Court reversed the Illinois Supreme Court's denial of the stay. The Court said:

> The outstanding injunction will deprive [the Nazis] of rights protected by the First Amendment. . . . If a State seeks to impose a restraint of this kind, it must provide strict procedural safeguards . . . including immediate appellate review. . . . Absent such review, the State must instead allow a stay. The order of the Illinois Supreme Court constituted a denial of that right.

The Court refused to uphold ordinances regulating speech before it occurred, claiming that such laws amounted to censorship. In the Court's eyes, governments can deal with such expression only after it occurs, an opportunity the Town of Skokie never had, as the party chose instead to march in Chicago.

In the *Skokie* case, and in *Brandenburg* before it, the justices struck down government regulation of racially based hate speech. In both cases, however, the Court's decision rested on defects in the way the government attempted to block the unacceptable expression. In *Brandenburg* the Court found constitutional problems with Ohio's Criminal Syndicalism Act upon which the prosecution of a Ku Klux Klan leader was based. In *Skokie* the Court found that the local government was unconstitutionally attempting to repress speech before it occurred, a form of prior restraint. In neither case did the Court directly confront the question of whether the First Amendment allows government to punish expression based on hatred.

In response to an increase in hate speech incidents, many state and local governments, as well as colleges and universities, passed ordinances in the 1990s making hate speech punishable. Even though most Americans consider hate-based expression reprehensible, there is a deep division of opinion over whether it can be constitutionally banned. Individuals concerned with minority rights and elimination of bigotry have argued that laws making hate speech illegal are both necessary and constitutionally permissible. Free speech advocates, however, contend that such laws run in direct contradiction to the First Amendment. Often this issue has divided groups that have been traditional allies in the attempt to expand personal rights and liberties *(see Box 5-7)*. The issue first found its way to the Supreme Court in the case of *R. A. V. v. City of St. Paul, Minnesota* (1992).[19]

R.A.V. v. City of St. Paul, Minnesota

505 U.S. 377 (1992)
laws.findlaw.com/US/505/377.html
Vote: 9 (*Blackmun, Kennedy, O'Connor, Rehnquist, Scalia, Souter, Stevens, Thomas, White*)

0

Opinion of the Court: Scalia
Concurring opinions: Blackmun, Stevens, White

The city of St. Paul alleges that between 1:00 A.M. and 3:00 A.M. on June 21, 1990, Robert A. Viktora, a seventeen-year-old high school dropout, and several other teenagers "assembled a crudely made cross by taping together broken chair legs" and then burned the cross inside the fenced backyard of a black family across the street from Viktora's house.[20] St. Paul could have prosecuted him under several criminal laws—for example, arson, which carries a maximum penalty of five years in prison and a $10,000 fine. Instead, it charged him with violating two laws, including the St. Paul Bias-Motivated Crime Ordinance. This law stated:

---

18. Many ACLU members also agreed with the town: almost half resigned in protest of its decision to defend Nazis. For an interesting account of this episode, see Aryeh Neier, *Defending My Enemy* (New York: Dutton, 1979).

19. To hear oral arguments in this case, navigate to: *oyez.nwu.edu.*
20. Because of his age at the time, Viktora was identified in court proceedings only by his initials.

BOX 5-7 HATE SPEECH AND THE CIVIL LIBERTIES COMMUNITY

REGULATING HATE SPEECH is an issue that divides the civil liberties community. Groups that historically have worked together to advance civil liberties and civil rights have found themselves in the uncomfortable position of fighting against each other over the hate speech controversy. Listed below are short excerpts from amicus curiae briefs submitted by traditionally liberal groups in the case of *R.A.V. v. City of St. Paul* (1992). Notice how the briefs emphasize different values. Those in favor of striking down the St. Paul ordinance stress the primacy of the First Amendment. Supporters of the law focus on the significance of equality considerations.

IN SUPPORT OF R.A.V.:

[T]he antibias ordinance cannot be defended on the ground that the State has a compelling interest in banning messages of racial and religious bigotry and intolerance. Although these messages are inconsistent with the Nation's highest aspirations, the Court has repeatedly held that the First Amendment does not permit a State to prohibit the communication of ideas simply because they are offensive or at odds with national policies.

—*Center for Individual Rights*

It is quite clear from the Court's First Amendment jurisprudence that government cannot criminalize such speech simply because it arouses anger, alarm and resentment.

—*Association of American Publishers and the Freedom to Read Foundation*

This society has rested its faith on the proposition that "the remedy [for speech] is more speech, not enforced silence." [Justice Brandeis concurring in *Whitney v. California*] Accordingly, our constitutional tradition demands that even a message of racial supremacy is entitled to be heard so long as it remains in the realm of advocacy. Those who articulated this faith in public debate were not naive about the power of words or symbols. To the contrary, they believed that pernicious ideas were more dangerous when suppressed than when exposed.

—*American Civil Liberties Union, Minnesota Civil Liberties Union, and the American Jewish Congress*

IN SUPPORT OF THE ST. PAUL ORDINANCE:

Crossburnings, of which defendant R.A.V. is accused, should be recognized as a terrorist hate practice of intimidation and harassment, which, contrary to the purposes of the Fourteenth Amendment, works to institutionalize the civil inequality of protected groups.... [T]he statute in question does not violate the First Amendment because social inequality, including through expressive conduct, is a harm for which states are entitled leeway in regulation.

—*National Black Women's Health Project*

When used in a personally threatening or assaultive manner, these symbols [burning cross and Nazi swastika] are part of the marketplace of ideas of which our society is justifiably tolerant; however, when used as a form of a bias-motivated personal attack, they cease to symbolize ideas and become violent tools that inflict injury. This Court has consistently recognized that this type of "expression" should not be afforded First Amendment protection.

—*Anti-Defamation League of B'nai B'rith*

Cross burning is an especially invidious act. A burning cross is an insult and a threat; it carries with it the historical baggage of past terrorism and physical attacks. When a cross burning is targeted against an individual and his family, it is more than just expression; it is a form of violence itself—symbolic violence.

—*Asian American Legal Defense and Education Fund, the Asian Law Caucus, the Asian Pacific American Legal Center, and the National Asian Pacific American Bar Association*

In his brief, [R.A.V.] intones principles of freedom of speech with which, in the abstract, no one will disagree. But the State of Minnesota was not indulging in theory when it charged [him] with a violation of the ordinance in controversy. It was dealing with what can only fairly be described as an act of terrorism. This conduct cannot rationally be viewed as protected by the First Amendment.

—*National Association for the Advancement of Colored People and the Clarendon Foundation*

Russell and Laura Jones and their children. The Jones family awoke in the middle of the night to find a cross burning in their yard. The incident led to the Supreme Court's decision in *R.A.V. v. City of St. Paul.*

Whoever places on public or private property a symbol, object, appellation, characterization or graffiti, including, but not limited to, a burning cross or Nazi swastika, which one knows or has reasonable grounds to know arouses anger, alarm, or resentment in others on the basis of race, color, creed, religion, or gender commits disorderly conduct and shall be guilty of a misdemeanor.

Before Viktora's trial, his attorney asked the judge to dismiss the charge, arguing that the ordinance violated the First Amendment because it was "substantially overbroad and impermissibly content-based." The trial court judge granted the motion, and the city appealed to the Minnesota Supreme Court.

The Minnesota high court reversed the trial court's decision, holding that the ordinance did not violate freedom of expression guarantees contained in the First Amendment. The court found that the ordinance prohibits conduct equivalent to "fighting words," unprotected expression under the First Amendment. It also ruled that the ordinance was not impermissibly content based because it was "a narrowly tailored means toward accomplishing the compelling governmental interest in protecting the community against bias-motivated threats to public safety and order."

JUSTICE SCALIA delivered the opinion of the Court.

In construing the St. Paul ordinance, we are bound by the construction given to it by the Minnesota court. Accordingly, we accept the Minnesota Supreme Court's authoritative statement that the ordinance reaches only those expressions that constitute "fighting words" within the meaning of *Chaplinsky* [*v. New Hampshire*, 1942]. Petitioner . . . urge[s] us to modify the scope of the *Chaplinsky* formulation, thereby invalidating the ordinance as "substantially overbroad." We find it unnecessary to consider this issue. Assuming, *arguendo*, that all of the expression reached by the ordinance is proscribable under the "fighting words" doctrine, we nonetheless conclude that the ordinance is facially unconstitutional in that it prohibits otherwise permitted speech solely on the basis of the subjects the speech addresses.

The First Amendment generally prevents government from proscribing speech, *Cantwell v. Connecticut* (1940), or even expressive conduct, see *Texas v. Johnson* (1989), because of disapproval of the ideas expressed. Content-based regulations are presumptively invalid. *Simon & Schuster, Inc. v. Members of N.Y. State Crime Victims Bd.* (1991). From 1791 to the present, however, our society, like other free but civilized societies, has permitted restrictions upon the content of speech in a few limited areas, which are "of such slight social value as a step to truth that any benefit that may be derived from them is clearly outweighed by the social interest in order and morality." *Chaplinsky.* We have recognized that "the freedom of speech" referred to by the First Amendment does not include a freedom to disregard these traditional limitations. See, *e.g., Roth v. United States* (1957) (obscenity); *Beauharnais v. Illinois* (1952) (defamation); *Chaplinsky v. New Hampshire* ("fighting words"). Our decisions since the

1960's have narrowed the scope of the traditional categorical exceptions for defamation and for obscenity, but a limited categorical approach has remained an important part of our First Amendment jurisprudence.

We have sometimes said that these categories of expression are "not within the area of constitutionally protected speech" or that the "protection of the First Amendment does not extend" to them. Such statements must be taken in context, however, and are no more literally true than is the occasionally repeated shorthand characterizing obscenity "as not being speech at all." What they mean is that these areas of speech can, consistently with the First Amendment, be regulated *because of their constitutionally proscribable content* (obscenity, defamation, etc.)—not that they are categories of speech entirely invisible to the Constitution, so that they may be made the vehicles for content discrimination unrelated to their distinctively proscribable content. Thus, the government may proscribe libel; but it may not make the further content discrimination of proscribing *only* libel critical of the government. We recently acknowledged this distinction in [*New York v.*] *Ferber* [1982], where, in upholding New York's child pornography law, we expressly recognized that there was no "question here of censoring a particular literary theme. . . ."

Our cases surely do not establish the proposition that the First Amendment imposes no obstacle whatsoever to regulation of particular instances of such proscribable expression, so that the government "may regulate [them] freely." That would mean that a city council could enact an ordinance prohibiting only those legally obscene works that contain criticism of the city government or, indeed, that do not include endorsement of the city government. Such a simplistic, all-or-nothing-at-all approach to First Amendment protection is at odds with common sense and with our jurisprudence as well. It is not true that "fighting words" have at most a "*de minimis*" expressive content, or that their content is *in all* respects "worthless and undeserving of constitutional protection"; sometimes they are quite expressive indeed. We have not said that they constitute "*no* part of the expression of ideas," but only that they constitute "no *essential* part of any exposition of ideas."

The proposition that a particular instance of speech can be proscribable on the basis of one feature (*e.g.,* obscenity) but not on the basis of another (*e.g.,* opposition to the city government) is commonplace, and has found application in many contexts. We have long held, for example, that non-verbal expressive activity can be banned because of the action it entails, but not because of the ideas it expresses—so that burning a flag in violation of an ordinance against outdoor fires could be punishable, whereas burning a flag in violation of an ordinance against dishonoring the flag is not. . . .

In other words, the exclusion of "fighting words" from the scope of the First Amendment simply means that, for purposes of that Amendment, the unprotected features of the words are, despite their verbal character, essentially a "nonspeech" element of communication. Fighting words are thus analogous to a noisy sound truck: Each is, as Justice Frankfurter recognized, a "mode of speech"; both can be used to convey an idea; but neither has, in and of itself, a claim upon the First Amendment. As with the sound truck, however, so also with fighting words: The government may not regulate use based on hostility—or favoritism—towards the underlying message expressed. . . .

Even the prohibition against content discrimination that we assert the First Amendment requires is not absolute. It applies differently in the context of proscribable speech than in the area of fully protected speech. The rationale of the general prohibition, after all, is that content discrimination "rais[es] the specter that the Government may effectively drive certain ideas or viewpoints from the marketplace." *Simon & Schuster.* But content discrimination among various instances of a class of proscribable speech often does not pose this threat.

When the basis for the content discrimination consists entirely of the very reason the entire class of speech at issue is proscribable, no significant danger of idea or viewpoint discrimination exists. Such a reason, having been adjudged neutral enough to support exclusion of the entire class of speech from First Amendment protection, is also neutral enough to form the basis of distinction within the class. To illustrate: A State might choose to prohibit only that obscenity which is the most patently offensive *in its prurience*—i.e., that which involves the most lascivious displays of sexual activity. But it may not prohibit, for example, only that obscenity which includes offensive *political* messages. . . .

Another valid basis for according differential treatment to even a content-defined subclass of proscribable speech is that the subclass happens to be associated with particular "secondary effects" of the speech, so that the regulation is "*justified* without reference to the content of the . . . speech." A State could, for example, permit all obscene live performances except those involving minors. Moreover, since words can in some circumstances violate laws directed not against speech but against conduct (a law against treason, for example, is violated by telling the enemy the nation's defense secrets), a particular content-based subcategory of a proscribable class of speech can be swept up incidentally within the reach of a statute directed at conduct rather than speech. Thus, for example, sexually derogatory "fighting words," among other words, may produce a violation of Title VII's general prohibition against sexual discrimination in employment practices. Where the government does not target conduct on the basis of its expressive content, acts are not shielded from regulation merely because they express a discriminatory idea or philosophy. . . .

Applying these principles to the St. Paul ordinance, we conclude that, even as narrowly construed by the Minnesota Supreme Court, the ordinance is facially unconstitutional. Although the phrase in the ordinance, "arouses anger, alarm or resentment in others," has been limited by the Minnesota Supreme Court's construction to reach only those symbols or displays that amount to "fighting words," the remaining, unmodified terms make clear that the ordinance applies only to "fighting words" that insult, or provoke violence, "on the basis of race, color, creed, religion or gender." Displays containing abusive invective, no matter how vicious or severe, are permissible unless they are addressed to one of the specified disfavored topics. Those who wish to use "fighting words" in connection with other ideas—to express hostility, for example, on the basis of political affiliation, union membership, or homosexuality— are not covered. The First Amendment does not permit St. Paul to impose special prohibitions on those speakers who express views on disfavored subjects.

In its practical operation, moreover, the ordinance goes even beyond mere content discrimination, to actual viewpoint discrimination. Displays containing some words— odious racial epithets, for example—would be prohibited to proponents of all views. But "fighting words" that do not themselves invoke race, color, creed, religion, or gender— aspersions upon a person's mother, for example—would seemingly be usable *ad libitum* in the placards of those arguing *in favor* of racial, color, etc. tolerance and equality, but could not be used by that speaker's opponents. One could hold up a sign saying, for example, that all "anti-Catholic bigots" are misbegotten; but not that all "papists" are, for that would insult and provoke violence "on the basis of religion." St. Paul has no such authority to license one side of a debate to fight freestyle, while requiring the other to follow Marquis of Queensbury Rules.

What we have here, it must be emphasized, is not a prohibition of fighting words that are directed at certain persons or groups (which would be *facially* valid if it met the requirements of the Equal Protection Clause); but rather, a prohibition of fighting words that contain (as the Minnesota Supreme Court repeatedly emphasized) messages of "bias-motivated" hatred and in particular, as applied to this case, messages "based on virulent notions of racial supremacy." One must wholeheartedly agree with the Minnesota Supreme Court that "[i]t is the responsibility, even the obligation, of diverse communities to confront such notions in whatever form they appear," but the manner of that confrontation cannot consist of selective limitations upon speech. St. Paul's brief asserts that a general "fighting words" law would not meet the city's needs because only a content-specific measure can communicate to minority groups that the "group hatred" aspect of such speech "is not condoned by the majority." The point of the First Amendment is that majority preferences must be expressed in some fashion other than silencing speech on the basis of its content. . . .

The content-based discrimination reflected in the St. Paul ordinance comes within neither any of the specific exceptions to the First Amendment prohibition we discussed earlier, nor within a more general exception for content discrimination that does not threaten censorship of ideas. It assuredly does not fall within the exception for content discrimination based on the very reasons why the particular class of speech at issue (here, fighting words) is proscribable. . . . [T]he reason why fighting words are categorically excluded from the protection of the First Amendment is not that their content communicates any particular idea, but that their content embodies a particularly intolerable (and socially unnecessary) *mode* of expressing *whatever* idea the speaker wishes to convey. St. Paul has not singled out an especially offensive mode of expression—it has not, for example, selected for prohibition only those fighting words that communicate ideas in a threatening (as opposed to a merely obnoxious) manner. Rather, it has proscribed fighting words of whatever manner that communicate messages of racial, gender, or religious intolerance. Selectivity of this sort creates the possibility that the city is seeking to handicap the expression of particular ideas. That possibility would alone be enough to render the ordinance presumptively invalid, but St. Paul's comments and concessions in this case elevate the possibility to a certainty. . . .

Finally, St. Paul . . . defend[s] the conclusion of the Minnesota Supreme Court that, even if the ordinance regulates expression based on hostility towards its protected ideological content, this discrimination is nonetheless justified because it is narrowly tailored to serve compelling state interests. Specifically, they assert that the ordinance helps to ensure the basic human rights of members of groups that have historically been subjected to discrimination, including the right of such group members to live in peace where they wish. We do not doubt that these interests are compelling, and that the ordinance can be said to promote them. But the "danger of censorship" presented by a facially content-based statute requires that that weapon be employed only where it is "*necessary* to serve the asserted [compelling] interest.". . . The dispositive question in this case, therefore, is whether content discrimination is reasonably necessary to achieve St. Paul's compelling interests; it plainly is not. An ordinance not limited to the favored topics, for example, would have precisely the same beneficial effect. In fact the only interest distinctively served by the content limitation is that of displaying the city council's special hostility towards the particular biases thus singled out. That is precisely what the First Amendment forbids. The politicians of St. Paul are entitled to express that hostility—but not through the means of imposing unique limitations upon speakers who (however benightedly) disagree.

Let there be no mistake about our belief that burning a cross in someone's front yard is reprehensible. But St. Paul has sufficient means at its disposal to prevent such behavior without adding the First Amendment to the fire.

The judgment of the Minnesota Supreme Court is reversed, and the case is remanded for proceedings not inconsistent with this opinion.

It is so ordered.

JUSTICE WHITE, with whom JUSTICE BLACKMUN, JUSTICE O'CONNOR, and . . . JUSTICE STEVENS join . . . concurring in the judgment.

Although I disagree with the Court's analysis, I do agree with its conclusion: The St. Paul ordinance is unconstitutional. However, I would decide the case on overbreadth grounds. . . .

In the First Amendment context, "[c]riminal statutes must be scrutinized with particular care; those that make unlawful a substantial amount of constitutionally protected conduct may be held facially invalid even if they also have legitimate application." The St. Paul antibias ordinance is such a law. Although the ordinance reaches conduct that is unprotected, it also makes criminal expressive conduct that causes only hurt feelings, offense, or resentment, and is protected by the First Amendment. The ordinance is therefore fatally overbroad and invalid on its face.

The Supreme Court unanimously declared the St. Paul hate speech ordinance to be unconstitutional. The justices found the law defective because it singled out a particular kind of hate speech. The ordinance, therefore, violated the principle that laws regulating expression must not discriminate on the basis of content. The concurring justices also found the law unacceptable, but preferred to strike it down for being unconstitutionally vague and overbroad.

It would be incorrect, however, to generalize from *R.A.V.* that the Court will strike down any law that imposes a penalty for hateful expression. In 1993, for example, the justices considered a Wisconsin statute that allowed judges to impose more severe sentences on defendants whose crimes were motivated by prejudicial attitudes based on race, religion, sexual orientation, national origin, and so forth. The Wisconsin law was similar to those enacted by many state and local governments in an attempt to reduce the incidence of hate crimes. Forty-nine states submitted a joint brief urging the Court to uphold Wisconsin's law. The federal government also submitted arguments in support of the constitutionality of the hate crimes provision. As you read the Court's unanimous decision in *Wisconsin v. Mitchell,* compare it to *R.A.V.* Are the two decisions compatible?

Wisconsin v. Mitchell

508 U.S. 476 (1993)
laws.findlaw.com/US/508/476.html
Vote: 9 (Blackmun, Kennedy, O'Connor, Rehnquist, Scalia,
*   Souter, Stevens, Thomas, White)*
    0
Opinion of the Court: Rehnquist

In October 1989 Todd Mitchell and several other young black men were discussing the scene in the film *Mississippi Burning* in which a white man beats a black boy. During the conversation, Mitchell asked his companions, "Do you all feel hyped up to move on some white people?"

A little later Mitchell and his friends spotted a young white boy across the street. As the boy neared, Mitchell said, "You all want to fuck somebody up? There goes a white boy; go get him." The group then attacked the boy, beating him and stealing his sneakers. They left him unconscious, a state in which he remained for four days.

A jury found Mitchell guilty of aggravated battery, an offense that usually carries a maximum sentence of two years in prison. But, under Wisconsin's penalty-enhancement law, that maximum could reach seven years should the jury find that the convicted person had intentionally selected his victim because of his race, religion, color, disability, sexual orientation, national origin, or ancestry. In other words, the state law enhanced the punishment for so-called hate crimes. In Mitchell's case, the jury in fact found that he had intentionally chosen his victim on the basis of race, and he was sentenced to four years in prison.

Mitchell asked the Wisconsin courts to overturn his conviction on the ground that the state penalty-enhancement law violated freedom of expression guarantees contained in the First Amendment. Based in some measure on *R. A. V. v. St. Paul*, the Wisconsin Supreme Court ruled in favor of Mitchell, striking down the state law on constitutional grounds.

CHIEF JUSTICE REHNQUIST delivered the opinion of the Court.

Respondent Todd Mitchell's sentence for aggravated battery was enhanced because he intentionally selected his victim on account of the victim's race. The question presented in this case is whether this penalty enhancement is prohibited by the First and Fourteenth Amendments. We hold that it is not. . . .

We granted certiorari because of the importance of the question presented and the existence of a conflict of authority among state high courts on the constitutionality of statutes similar to Wisconsin's penalty-enhancement provision.* We reverse. . . .

The State argues that the statute does not punish bigoted thought, as the Supreme Court of Wisconsin said, but instead punishes only conduct. While this argument is literally correct, it does not dispose of Mitchell's First Amendment challenge. To be sure, our cases reject the "view that apparently limitless variety of conduct can be labeled 'speech' whenever the person engaging in the conduct intends thereby to express an idea." Thus, a physical assault is not by any stretch of the imagination expressive conduct protected by the First Amendment.

But the fact remains that under the Wisconsin statute the same criminal conduct may be more heavily punished if the victim is selected because of his race or other protected status than if no such motive obtained. Thus, although the statute punishes criminal conduct, it enhances the maximum penalty for conduct motivated by a discriminatory point of view more severely than the same conduct engaged in for some other reason or for no reason at all. Because the only reason for the enhancement is the defendant's discrim-

---

*Several states have enacted penalty-enhancement provisions similar to the Wisconsin statute at issue in this case. Proposed federal legislation to the same effect passed the House of Representatives in 1992, but failed to pass the Senate (1992). The state high courts are divided over the constitutionality of penalty-enhancing statutes and analogous statutes covering bias-motivated offenses. According to *amici*, bias-motivated violence is on the rise throughout the United States. . . . In 1990, Congress enacted the Hate Crimes Statistics Act, directing the Attorney General to compile data "about crimes that manifest evidence of prejudice based on race, religion, sexual orientation, or ethnicity." Pursuant to the Act, the Federal Bureau of Investigation reported in January 1993, that 4,558 bias-motivated offenses were committed in 1991, including 1,614 incidents of intimidation, 1,301 incidents of vandalism, 796 simple assaults, 773 aggravated assaults, and 12 murders.

inatory motive for selecting his victim, Mitchell argues (and the Wisconsin Supreme Court held) that the statute violates the First Amendment by punishing offenders' bigoted beliefs.

Traditionally, sentencing judges have considered a wide variety of factors in addition to evidence bearing on guilt in determining what sentence to impose on a convicted defendant. The defendant's motive for committing the offense is one important factor. Thus, in many States the commission of a murder, or other capital offense, for pecuniary gain is a separate aggravating circumstance under the capital-sentencing statute.

But it is equally true that a defendant's abstract beliefs, however obnoxious to most people, may not be taken into consideration by a sentencing judge. In *Dawson* [v. *Delaware*, 1992], the State introduced evidence at a capital sentencing hearing that the defendant was a member of a white supremacist prison gang. Because "the evidence proved nothing more than [the defendant's] abstract beliefs," we held that its admission violated the defendant's First Amendment rights. In so holding, however, we emphasized that "the Constitution does not erect a *per se* barrier to the admission of evidence concerning one's beliefs and associations at sentencing simply because those beliefs and associations are protected by the First Amendment." Thus, in *Barclay v. Florida* (1983) (plurality opinion), we allowed the sentencing judge to take into account the defendant's racial animus towards his victim. The evidence in that case showed that the defendant's membership in the Black Liberation Army and desire to provoke a "race war" were related to the murder of a white man for which he was convicted. Because "the elements of racial hatred in [the] murder" were relevant to several aggravating factors, we held that the trial judge permissibly took this evidence into account in sentencing the defendant to death.

Mitchell suggests that *Dawson* and *Barclay* are inapposite because they did not involve application of a penalty-enhancement provision. But in *Barclay* we held that it was permissible for the sentencing court to consider the defendant's racial animus in determining whether he should be sentenced to death, surely the most severe "enhancement" of all. And the fact that the Wisconsin Legislature has decided, as a general matter, that bias-motivated offenses warrant greater maximum penalties across the board does not alter the result here. For the primary respon-

sibility for fixing criminal penalties lies with the legislature. . . .

Nothing in our decision last Term in *R. A. V.* compels a different result here. That case involved a First Amendment challenge to a municipal ordinance prohibiting the use of "'fighting words' that insult, or provoke violence, 'on the basis of race, color, creed, religion or gender.'" Because the ordinance only proscribed a class of "fighting words" deemed particularly offensive by the city—*i.e.*, those "that contain . . . messages of 'bias-motivated' hatred," we held that it violated the rule against content-based discrimination. But whereas the ordinance struck down in *R. A. V.* was explicitly directed at expression, *i.e.*, "speech" or "messages," the statute in this case is aimed at conduct unprotected by the First Amendment.

Moreover, the Wisconsin statute singles out for enhancement bias-inspired conduct because this conduct is thought to inflict greater individual and societal harm. For example, according to the State and its *amici*, bias-motivated crimes are more likely to provoke retaliatory crimes, inflict distinct emotional harms on their victims, and incite community unrest. The State's desire to redress these perceived harms provides an adequate explanation for its penalty-enhancement provision over and above mere disagreement with offenders' beliefs or biases. . . .

Finally, there remains to be considered Mitchell's argument that the Wisconsin statute is unconstitutionally overbroad because of its "chilling effect" on free speech. Mitchell argues (and the Wisconsin Supreme Court agreed) that the statute is "overbroad" because evidence of the defendant's prior speech or associations may be used to prove that the defendant intentionally selected his victim on account of the victim's protected status. Consequently, the argument goes, the statute impermissibly chills free expression with respect to such matters by those concerned about the possibility of enhanced sentences if they should in the future commit a criminal offense covered by the statute. We find no merit in this contention.

The sort of chill envisioned here is far more attenuated and unlikely than that contemplated in traditional "overbreadth" cases. We must conjure up a vision of a Wisconsin citizen suppressing his unpopular bigoted opinions for fear that if he later commits an offense covered by the statute, these opinions will be offered at trial to establish that he selected his victim on account of the victim's protected status, thus qualifying him for penalty-enhancement. To stay within the realm of rationality, we must surely put to one side minor misdemeanor offenses covered by the statute, such as negligent operation of a motor vehicle; for it is difficult, if not impossible, to conceive of a situation where such offenses would be racially motivated. We are left, then, with the prospect of a citizen suppressing his bigoted beliefs for fear that evidence of such beliefs will be introduced against him at trial if he commits a more serious offense against person or property. This is simply too speculative a hypothesis to support Mitchell's overbreadth claim.

The First Amendment, moreover, does not prohibit the evidentiary use of speech to establish the elements of a crime or to prove motive or intent. Evidence of a defendant's previous declarations or statements is commonly admitted in criminal trials subject to evidentiary rules dealing with relevancy, reliability, and the like. Nearly half a century ago, in *Haupt v. United States* (1947), we rejected a contention similar to that advanced by Mitchell here. Haupt was tried for the offense of treason, which, as defined by the Constitution (Art. III, §3), may depend very much on proof of motive. To prove that the acts in question were committed out of "adherence to the enemy" rather than "parental solicitude," the Government introduced evidence of conversations that had taken place long prior to the indictment, some of which consisted of statements showing Haupt's sympathy with Germany and Hitler and hostility towards the United States. We rejected Haupt's argument that this evidence was improperly admitted. While "[s]uch testimony is to be scrutinized with care to be certain the statements are not expressions of mere lawful and permissible difference of opinion with our own government or quite proper appreciation of the land of birth," we held that "these statements . . . clearly were admissible on the question of intent and adherence to the enemy."

For the foregoing reasons, we hold that Mitchell's First Amendment rights were not violated by the application of the Wisconsin penalty-enhancement provision in sentencing him. The judgment of the Supreme Court of Wisconsin is therefore reversed, and the case is remanded for further proceedings not inconsistent with this opinion.

It is so ordered.

Although the votes were unanimous in *R.A.V.* and *Mitchell,* the justices did not settle the hate speech issue,

perhaps because the two rulings reached different conclusions: *Mitchell* supported government regulation, while *R.A.V.* did not. Supporters of broad First Amendment protection and those who favor restricting discriminatory expression both can find encouragement in the Court's opinions. As a result, the battle over hateful and harassing expression continues on college campuses, in the workplace, and in legislatures, and the Court certainly has not seen its last dispute in this area.

The Right Not To Speak

So far we have discussed the constitutionality of government attempts to restrict or prohibit certain kinds of expression. While curtailing expression is the most common form of government regulation, there are situations in which the government requires us to speak or write. For example, we may be ordered to appear as a witness before a court, grand jury, or legislative investigating committee. The government compels us to provide information when we file our tax returns. We may be required to take an oath when we become citizens, provide court testimony, take public office, or apply for a gun permit. Americans generally consider these regulations to be reasonable requirements relevant to legitimate government functions. But what if an individual does not want to comply with a government regulation that requires expression? Other than the Fifth Amendment's protection against the government compelling self-incriminating testimony, is there any restraint on the government's authority to coerce expression? To put it another way, does the First Amendment's guarantee of freedom of speech carry with it the freedom not to speak?

To understand this issue we need once again to turn our attention to the flag salute cases discussed in Chapter 4. As you recall, in 1940 the Court in *Minersville School District v. Gobitis* upheld flag salute regulations against claims that the school system was violating the children's right to free exercise of religion. Just three years later, in *West Virginia Board of Education v. Barnette,* the Court again considered the constitutionality of the compulsory flag salute laws, and once again the case was brought by Jehovah's Witnesses. By this time, however, some conditions had changed. First, due to American victories on the battlefield, the feverishly patriotic mood so strong at the beginning of World War II had moderated somewhat. Second, the Court had undergone some personnel changes that strengthened its civil libertarian wing. Third, the *Gobitis* decision had been roundly criticized in legal circles. These circumstances encouraged the Witnesses to be more optimistic about their chances of winning. But there was one additional factor that distinguished *Gobitis* from *Barnette*. Hayden Covington and the other lawyers supporting the challenge made a significant strategy decision to base the attack not so much on freedom of religion, but instead on the freedom of speech. As you read Justice Jackson's majority opinion in *Barnette*, notice how he weaves religion and expression rights into his explanation for striking down the flag salute laws.

West Virginia Board of Education v. Barnette

319 U.S. 624 (1943)
laws.findlaw.com/US/319/624.html
Vote: 6 (Black, Douglas, Jackson, Murphy, Rutledge, Stone)
     3 (Frankfurter, Reed, Roberts)
Opinion of the Court: Jackson
Concurring opinions: Black and Douglas (joint), Murphy
Dissenting opinions: Frankfurter, Reed and Roberts (joint)

Following the *Gobitis* decision, the West Virginia legislature amended its laws to require that all public schools teach courses to increase students' knowledge of the American system of government and foster patriotism. In support of this policy, the state board of education required that the American flag be saluted and the Pledge of Allegiance be recited each day. Students who refused to participate could be charged with insubordination and expelled. Not attending school because of such an expulsion was grounds for the child being declared delinquent. Parents of delinquent children were subject to fines and jail penalties of up to thirty days. In some cases officials threatened noncomplying students with reform school.

The Jehovah's Witnesses challenged these regulations in the name of the Barnette family, church members who had been harassed by the school system for failure to

participate in the flag salute ritual. One of the Barnette children had, in fact, been expelled.

Despite the Supreme Court's decision in *Gobitis*, a three-judge district court sympathized with the Barnette family's plight. According to the well-respected circuit court judge, John J. Parker: "The salute to the United States' flag is an expression of the homage of the soul. To force it upon one who has conscientious scruples against giving it is petty tyranny unworthy of the spirit of the Republic, and forbidden, we think, by the United States Constitution." After the decision, the West Virginia School Board appealed to the U.S. Supreme Court.

MR. JUSTICE JACKSON delivered the opinion of the Court.

As the present Chief Justice said in dissent in the *Gobitis* case, the State may "require teaching by instruction and study of all in our history and in the structure and organization of our government, including the guaranties of civil liberty which tend to inspire patriotism and love of country." Here, however, we are dealing with a compulsion of students to declare a belief. They are not merely made acquainted with the flag salute so that they may be informed as to what it is or even what it means. The issue here is whether this slow and easily neglected route to aroused loyalties constitutionally may be short-cut by substituting a compulsory salute and slogan. . . .

There is no doubt that, in connection with the pledges, the flag salute is a form of utterance. Symbolism is a primitive but effective way of communicating ideas. The use of an emblem or flag to symbolize some system, idea, institution, or personality, is a short cut from mind to mind. Causes and nations, political parties, lodges and ecclesiastical groups seek to knit the loyalty of their following to a flag or banner, a color or design. The State announces rank, function, and authority through crowns and maces, uniforms and black robes; the church speaks through the Cross, the Crucifix, the altar and shrine, and clerical raiment. Symbols of State often convey political ideas just as religious symbols come to convey theological ones. Associated with many of these symbols are appropriate gestures of acceptance or respect: a salute, a bowed or bared head, a bended knee. A person gets from a symbol the meaning he puts into it, and what is one man's comfort and inspiration is another's jest and scorn.

Over a decade ago Chief Justice Hughes led this Court in holding that the display of a red flag as a symbol of opposition by peaceful and legal means to organized government was protected by the free speech guaranties of the Constitution. *Stromberg v. California* [1931]. Here it is the State that employs a flag as a symbol of adherence to government as presently organized. It requires the individual to communicate by word and sign his acceptance of the political ideas it thus bespeaks. Objection to this form of communication when coerced is an old one, well known to the framers of the Bill of Rights.

It is also to be noted that the compulsory flag salute and pledge requires affirmation of a belief and an attitude of mind. It is not clear whether the regulation contemplates that pupils forego any contrary convictions of their own and become unwilling converts to the prescribed ceremony or whether it will be acceptable if they simulate assent by words without belief and by a gesture barren of meaning. It is now a commonplace that censorship or suppression of expression of opinion is tolerated by our Constitution only when the expression presents a clear and present danger of action of a kind the State is empowered to prevent and punish. It would seem that involuntary affirmation could be commanded only on even more immediate and urgent grounds than silence. But here the power of compulsion is invoked without any allegation that remaining passive during a flag salute ritual creates a clear and present danger that would justify an effort even to muffle expression. To sustain the compulsory flag salute we are required to say that a Bill of Rights which guards the individual's right to speak his own mind, left it open to public authorities to compel him to utter what is not in his mind.

Whether the First Amendment to the Constitution will permit officials to order observance of ritual of this nature does not depend upon whether as a voluntary exercise we would think it to be good, bad or merely innocuous. Any credo of nationalism is likely to include what some disapprove or to omit what others think essential, and to give off different overtones as it takes on different accents or interpretations. If official power exists to coerce acceptance of any patriotic creed, what it shall contain cannot be decided by courts, but must be largely discretionary with the ordaining authority, whose power to prescribe would no doubt include power to amend. Hence validity of the asserted power to force an American citizen publicly to profess

any statement of belief or to engage in any ceremony of assent to one presents questions of power that must be considered independently of any idea we may have as to the utility of the ceremony in question.

Nor does the issue as we see it turn on one's possession of particular religious views or the sincerity with which they are held. While religion supplies appellees' motive for enduring the discomforts of making the issue in this case, many citizens who do not share these religious views hold such a compulsory rite to infringe constitutional liberty of the individual. It is not necessary to inquire whether nonconformist beliefs will exempt from the duty to salute unless we first find power to make the salute a legal duty.

The *Gobitis* decision, however, *assumed* as did the argument in that case and in this, that power exists in the State to impose the flag salute discipline upon school children in general. The Court only examined and rejected a claim based on religious beliefs of immunity from an unquestioned general rule. The question which underlies the flag salute controversy is whether such a ceremony so touching matters of opinion and political attitude may be imposed upon the individual by official authority under powers committed to any political organization under our Constitution. We examine rather than assume existence of this power and, against this broader definition of issues in this case, re-examine specific grounds assigned for the *Gobitis* decision.

1. It was said that the flag-salute controversy confronted the Court with "the problem which Lincoln cast in memorable dilemma: 'Must a government of necessity be too *strong* for the liberties of its people, or too *weak* to maintain its own existence?'" and that the answer must be in favor of strength. *Minersville School District v. Gobitis.*

We think these issues may be examined free of pressure or restraint growing out of such considerations.

It may be doubted whether Mr. Lincoln would have thought that the strength of government to maintain itself would be impressively vindicated by our confirming power of the state to expel a handful of children from school. Such oversimplification, so handy in political debate, often lacks the precision necessary to postulates of judicial reasoning. If validly applied to this problem, the utterance cited would resolve every issue of power in favor of those in authority and would require us to override every liberty thought to weaken or delay execution of their policies.

Government of limited power need not be anemic government. Assurance that rights are secure tends to diminish fear and jealousy of strong government, and by making us feel safe to live under it makes for its better support. Without promise of a limiting Bill of Rights it is doubtful if our Constitution could have mustered enough strength to enable its ratification. To enforce those rights today is not to choose weak government over strong government. It is only to adhere as a means of strength to individual freedom of mind in preference to officially disciplined uniformity for which history indicates a disappointing and disastrous end.

The subject now before us exemplifies this principle. Free public education, if faithful to the ideal of secular instruction and political neutrality, will not be partisan or enemy of any class, creed, party, or faction. If it is to impose any ideological discipline, however, each party or denomination must seek to control, or failing that, to weaken the influence of the educational system. Observance of the limitations of the Constitution will not weaken government in the field appropriate for its exercise.

2. It was also considered in the *Gobitis* case that functions of educational officers in states, counties and school districts were such that to interfere with their authority "would in effect make us the school board for the country."

The Fourteenth Amendment, as now applied to the States, protects the citizen against the State itself and all of its creatures—Boards of Education not excepted. These have, of course, important, delicate, and highly discretionary functions, but none that they may not perform within the limits of the Bill of Rights. That they are educating the young for citizenship is reason for scrupulous protection of Constitutional freedoms of the individual, if we are not to strangle the free mind at its source and teach youth to discount important principles of our government as mere platitudes.

Such Boards are numerous and their territorial jurisdiction often small. But small and local authority may feel less sense of responsibility to the Constitution, and agencies of publicity may be less vigilant in calling it to account. The action of Congress in making flag observance voluntary and respecting the conscience of the objector in a matter so vital as raising the Army contrasts sharply with these local regulations in matters relatively trivial to the welfare of the nation. There are village tyrants as well as village Hampdens, but none who acts under color of law is beyond reach of the Constitution.

3. The *Gobitis* opinion reasoned that this is a field "where courts possess no marked and certainly no controlling competence," that it is committed to the legislatures as well as the courts to guard cherished liberties and that it is constitutionally appropriate to "fight out the wise use of legislative authority in the forum of public opinion and before legislative assemblies rather than to transfer such a contest to the judicial arena," since all the "effective means of inducing political changes are left free."

The very purpose of a Bill of Rights was to withdraw certain subjects from the vicissitudes of political controversy, to place them beyond the reach of majorities and officials and to establish them as legal principles to be applied by the courts. One's right to life, liberty, and property, to free speech, a free press, freedom of worship and assembly, and other fundamental rights may not be submitted to vote; they depend on the outcome of no elections.

In weighing arguments of the parties it is important to distinguish between the due process clause of the Fourteenth Amendment as an instrument for transmitting the principles of the First Amendment and those cases in which it is applied for its own sake. The test of legislation which collides with the Fourteenth Amendment, because it also collides with the principles of the First, is much more definite than the test when only the Fourteenth is involved. Much of the vagueness of the due process clause disappears when the specific prohibitions of the First become its standard. The right of a State to regulate, for example, a public utility may well include, so far as the due process test is concerned, power to impose all of the restrictions which a legislature may have a "rational basis" for adopting. But freedoms of speech and of press, of assembly, and of worship may not be infringed on such slender grounds. They are susceptible of restriction only to prevent grave and immediate danger to interests which the state may lawfully protect. It is important to note that while it is the Fourteenth Amendment which bears directly upon the State it is the more specific limiting principles of the First Amendment that finally govern this case. . . .

4. Lastly, and this is the very heart of the *Gobitis* opinion, it reasons that "National unity is the basis of national security," that the authorities have "the right to select appropriate means for its attainment," and hence reaches the con-

clusion that such compulsory measures toward "national unity" are constitutional. Upon the verity of this assumption depends our answer in this case.

National unity as an end which officials may foster by persuasion and example is not in question. The problem is whether under our Constitution compulsion as here employed is a permissible means for its achievement.

Struggles to coerce uniformity of sentiment in support of some end thought essential to their time and country have been waged by many good as well as by evil men. Nationalism is a relatively recent phenomenon but at other times and places the ends have been racial or territorial security, support of a dynasty or regime, and particular plans for saving souls. As first and moderate methods to attain unity have failed, those bent on its accomplishment must resort to an ever-increasing severity. . . . Those who begin coercive elimination of dissent soon find themselves exterminating dissenters. Compulsory unification of opinion achieves only the unanimity of the graveyard.

It seems trite but necessary to say that the First Amendment to our Constitution was designed to avoid these ends by avoiding these beginnings. There is no mysticism in the American concept of the State or of the nature or origin of its authority. We set up government by consent of the governed, and the Bill of Rights denies those in power any legal opportunity to coerce that consent. Authority here is to be controlled by public opinion, not public opinion by authority.

The case is made difficult not because the principles of its decision are obscure but because the flag involved is our own. Nevertheless, we apply the limitations of the Constitution with no fear that freedom to be intellectually and spiritually diverse or even contrary will disintegrate the social organization. To believe that patriotism will not flourish if patriotic ceremonies are voluntary and spontaneous instead of a compulsory routine is to make an unflattering estimate of the appeal of our institutions to free minds. We can have intellectual individualism and the rich cultural diversity that we owe to exceptional minds only at the price of occasional eccentricity and abnormal attitudes. When they are so harmless to others or to the State as those we deal with here, the price is not too great. But freedom to differ is not limited to things that do not matter much. That would be a mere shadow of freedom. The test of its substance is the right to differ as to things that touch the heart of the existing order.

If there is any fixed star in our constitutional constellation, it is that no official, high or petty, can prescribe what shall be orthodox in politics, nationalism, religion, or other matters of opinion or force citizens to confess by word or act their faith therein. If there are any circumstances which permit an exception, they do not now occur to us.

We think the action of the local authorities in compelling the flag salute and pledge transcends constitutional limitations on their power and invades the sphere of intellect and spirit which it is the purpose of the First Amendment to our Constitution to reserve from all official control.

The decision of this Court in *Minersville School District v. Gobitis* and the holdings of those few per curiam decisions which preceded and foreshadowed it are overruled, and the judgment enjoining enforcement of the West Virginia Regulation is affirmed.

Affirmed.

MR. JUSTICE FRANKFURTER, dissenting.

One who belongs to the most vilified and persecuted minority in history is not likely to be insensible to the freedoms guaranteed by our Constitution. Were my purely personal attitude relevant I should wholeheartedly associate myself with the general libertarian views in the Court's opinion, representing as they do the thought and action of a lifetime. But as judges we are neither Jew nor Gentile, neither Catholic nor agnostic. We owe equal attachment to the Constitution and are equally bound by our judicial obligations whether we derive our citizenship from the earliest or latest immigrants to these shores. As a member of this Court I am not justified in writing my private notions of policy into the Constitution, no matter how deeply I may cherish them or how mischievous I may deem their disregard. The duty of a judge who must decide which of two claims before the Court shall prevail, that of a State to enact and enforce laws within its general competence or that of an individual to refuse obedience because of the demands of his conscience, is not that of the ordinary person. It can never be emphasized too much that one's own opinion about the wisdom or evil of a law should be excluded altogether when one is doing one's duty on the bench. . . . [I]t would require more daring than I possess to deny that reasonable legislators could have taken the action which is before us for review. Most unwillingly, therefore, I must differ from my brethren with regard to legislation like this. I cannot bring my mind to believe that the "liberty" secured by the Due Process Clause gives this Court authority to deny to the State of West Virginia the attainment of that which we all recognize as a legitimate legislative end, namely, the promotion of good citizenship, by employment of the means here chosen.

In striking down the West Virginia compulsory flag salute law, the Court ruled that the individual has at least a qualified right to be free of government coercion to express views he or she disavows. This decision does not go so far as to hold that an individual's First Amendment right can be used to avoid obligations such as testifying in a court case or providing information on a tax return, but it precludes certain forms of coerced expression.

For another example of this principle, consider the plight of George and Maxine Maynard of Lebanon, New Hampshire. Like the Gobitas and Barnette families, the Maynards were Jehovah's Witnesses. Their entanglement with the law stemmed from a statute mandating that the state slogan appear on all vehicle license plates. The Maynards considered the slogan "Live Free or Die" to be repugnant to their moral, religious, and political beliefs. To disassociate himself from the slogan, George Maynard cut a portion of the slogan from the plates on his cars and covered the remaining words with tape, but did not conceal the identifying letters or numbers. In November 1974 local authorities arrested Maynard for obscuring a license plate, a misdemeanor under New Hampshire law. He explained his objections to the slogan, but the court found him guilty. The judge imposed a $25.00 fine, but agreed to suspend it if Maynard would comply with the law. The next month authorities arrested Maynard again for the same offense. The court found him guilty and sentenced him to six months in jail and a $50.00 fine. The judge again showed leniency by permitting Maynard to avoid jail if he would pay the two fines. Maynard announced that as a matter of conscience, he would pay no fines. The judge ordered him to serve a fifteen-day jail sentence, which he did. The Maynards then sued, challenging the constitutionality of the law. They won, and the state appealed.

The case of *Wooley v. Maynard* (1977) presented the justices with a classic conflict between individual and state interests. The Maynards argued that their First Amendment rights protected them from state compulsion. George Maynard filed a statement saying, "I refuse to be coerced by the State into advertising a slogan which I find morally, ethically, religiously, and politically abhorrent." The state responded by contending that its interest in promoting an appreciation of history, individualism, and state pride outweighed the narrow interests of the Maynards.

Speaking for the Court, Chief Justice Burger ruled in favor of the Maynards. He explained:

We begin with the proposition that the right of freedom of thought protected by the First Amendment against state action includes both the right to speak freely and the right to refrain from speaking at all. A system which secures the right to proselytize religious, political, and ideological causes must also guarantee the concomitant right to decline to foster such concepts. The right to speak and the right to refrain from speaking are complementary components of the broader concept of "individual freedom of mind."

The justices concluded that the countervailing interests of the state were insufficiently compelling to outweigh the First Amendment liberties at stake. The state slogan was not ideologically neutral, but proclaimed an official view of history, state pride, and individualism. While the state may have an interest in promoting these beliefs, such an interest cannot outweigh an individual's First Amendment right to avoid becoming an unwilling spokesperson for that message.

In a more recent case, *Board of Regents of the University of Wisconsin System v. Southworth* (2000), a group of students at the University of Wisconsin-Madison claimed that the university's funding policies violated their constitutional right not to speak. Like many colleges, the University of Wisconsin assesses a student activity fee in addition to tuition charges. Significant portions of these fees are used to fund student organizations. The complaining students objected to their funds being spent to subsidize groups whose purposes they opposed, specifically, gay, socialist, labor, women's, and other liberal causes. They argued that the mandatory fees compelled them to financially support messages they found offensive.

A unanimous Supreme Court rejected this claim. The justices held that the university was pursuing a legitimate educational policy of encouraging a free and open exchange of ideas among students. A mandatory fee is a reasonable way to promote this goal. The Court emphasized that the Constitution requires that such programs be administered in a viewpoint neutral fashion. The Wisconsin program satisfied this requirement and was therefore constitutionally acceptable.

Money as Political Speech

For more than three decades national elections have regularly placed the issue of campaign finance reform on the political agenda. Many see the high cost of political campaigns as a threat to the integrity of the electoral process. Candidates spend enormous amounts of time raising funds. No sooner is a candidate elected than the quest for money to fund the next campaign begins. Fund raising diverts the attention of public officials from the primary demands of their offices. The need for large sums of money, fueled by the high cost of today's media campaigns, disqualifies or discourages many people who do not have access to sufficient funds to mount a viable campaign, while candidates with large fortunes have a distinct advantage. Members of the public may perceive successful candidates with large campaign chests as buying the election. Moreover, many fear that special interest groups that make significant campaign contributions have access to officeholders that other citizens do not enjoy.

In the Federal Election Campaign Act of 1974, Congress took bold moves to improve the system, placing strict limits on campaign contributions and expenditures, imposing strong recordkeeping and disclosure rules, and implementing federal financing of presidential campaigns. But did the legislation square with the First Amendment? Could Congress constitutionally limit the amount of money donated or spent to promote a political cause? Are campaign funds the same as speech itself? The Supreme Court addressed these questions in *Buckley v. Valeo* (1976).[21]

21. To hear oral arguments in this case, navigate to: *oyez.nwu.edu.*

Buckley v. Valeo

424 U.S. 1 (1976)
laws.findlaw.com/US/424/1.html
Vote on statutory limits on campaign spending:
        7 (*Blackmun, Brennan, Burger, Marshall, Powell, Rehnquist, Stuart*)
        1 (*White*)
Vote on statutory limits on campaign contributions:
        6 (*Brennan, Marshall, Powell, Rehnquist, Stewart, White*)
        2 (*Blackmun, Burger*)
Opinion for the Court: Per curiam
Opinions concurring in part and dissenting in part: (*Blackmun, Burger, Marshall, Rehnquist, White*)
Not participating: Stevens

In 1974 Congress amended the Federal Election Campaign Act of 1971 to impose significantly greater federal regulation of federal election campaigns. The legislation had five major components. First, it limited individual contributions to political candidates to $1,000 per election and contributions by political committees to $5,000 per election. It placed a $25,000 annual limit on total campaign contributions by any individual. Second, the law placed a $1,000 limit on individual and group expenditures on behalf of any candidate and limited the amount any candidate could spend in an election campaign. The law also placed a limit on a candidate's campaign expenditures from personal or family resources. Third, the legislation required candidates to keep records of every campaign contribution over $10 and to disclose contributions and expenditures quarterly. Fourth, the act created a Federal Election Commission to administer and enforce the law. Fifth, the statute created a system of public financing of presidential elections.

Sen. James Buckley of New York and a coalition of legislators, candidates, contributors, parties, and political groups sued to have the act declared unconstitutional on several grounds. In the excerpt that appears below, the Court answers the question of whether the campaign contribution and expenditure limitations violate the First Amendment right to freedom of expression.

PER CURIAM.

The constitutional power of Congress to regulate federal elections is well established and is not questioned by any of the parties in this case. Thus, the critical constitutional questions presented here go not to the basic power of Congress to legislate in this area, but to whether the specific legislation that Congress has enacted interferes with First Amendment freedoms. . . .

A. General Principles

The Act's contribution and expenditure limitations operate in an area of the most fundamental First Amendment activities. Discussion of public issues and debate on the qualifications of candidates are integral to the operation of the system of government established by our Constitution. The First Amendment affords the broadest protection to such political expression in order "to assure [the] unfettered interchange of ideas for the bringing about of political and social changes desired by the people." *Roth v. United States* (1957). Although First Amendment protections are not confined to "the exposition of ideas," *Winters v. New York* (1948), "there is practically universal agreement that a major purpose of that Amendment was to protect the free discussion of governmental affairs, . . . of course includ[ing] discussions of candidates. . . ." *Mills v. Alabama* (1966). This no more than reflects our "profound national commitment to the principle that debate on public issues should be uninhibited, robust, and wide-open," *New York Times Co. v. Sullivan* (1964). . . .

It is with these principles in mind that we consider the primary contentions of the parties with respect to the Act's limitations upon the giving and spending of money in political campaigns. . . .

B. Contribution Limitations

1. The $1,000 Limitation on Contributions by Individuals and Groups to Candidates and Authorized Campaign Committees

Section 608(b) provides, with certain limited exceptions, that "no person shall make contributions to any candidate with respect to any election for Federal office which, in the aggregate, exceed $1,000.". . .

It is unnecessary to look beyond the Act's primary purpose—to limit the actuality and appearance of corruption resulting from large individual financial contributions—in order to find a constitutionally sufficient justification for the $1,000 contribution limitation. Under a system of private financing of elections, a candidate lacking immense personal or family wealth must depend on financial contributions from others to provide the resources necessary to conduct a successful campaign. The increasing importance of the communications media and sophisticated mass-mailing and polling operations to effective campaigning make the raising of large sums of money an ever more essential ingredient of an effective candidacy. To the extent that large contributions are given to secure a political *quid pro quo* from current and potential office holders, the integrity of our system of representative democracy is undermined. Although the scope of such pernicious practices can never be reliably ascertained, the deeply disturbing examples surfacing after the 1972 election demonstrate that the problem is not an illusory one. . . .

The Act's $1,000 contribution limitation focuses precisely on the problem of large campaign contributions—the narrow aspect of political association where the actuality and potential for corruption have been identified—while leaving persons free to engage in independent political expression, to associate actively through volunteering their services, and to assist to a limited but nonetheless substantial extent in supporting candidates and committees with financial resources. Significantly, the Act's contribution limitations in themselves do not undermine to any material degree the potential for robust and effective discussion of candidates and campaign issues by individual citizens, associations, the institutional press, candidates, and political parties.

We find that, under the rigorous standard of review established by our prior decisions, the weighty interests served by restricting the size of financial contributions to political candidates are sufficient to justify the limited effect upon First Amendment freedoms caused by the $1,000 contribution ceiling. . . .

2. The $5,000 Limitation on Contributions by Political Committees

Section 608(b)(2) permits certain committees, designated as "political committees," to contribute up to $5,000 to any candidate with respect to any election for federal office. In order to qualify for the higher contribution ceiling, a group must have been registered with the [Federal Election] Commission as a political committee . . . for not less than six months, have received contributions from more than 50 persons, and, except for state political party organizations, have contributed to five or more candidates for federal office. Appellants argue that these qualifications unconstitutionally discriminate against ad hoc organizations in favor of established interest groups and impermissibly burden free association. The argument is without merit. Rather than undermining freedom of association, the basic provision enhances the opportunity of bona fide groups to participate in the election process, and the registration, contribution, and candidate conditions serve the permissible purpose of preventing individuals from evading the applicable contribution limitations by labeling themselves committees.

3. Limitations on Volunteers' Incidental Expenses [Omitted]

4. The $25,000 Limitation on Total Contributions During any Calendar Year

In addition to the $1,000 limitation on the nonexempt contributions that an individual may make to a particular candidate for any single election, the Act contains an overall $25,000 limitation on total contributions by an individual during any calendar year. . . . The overall $25,000 ceiling does impose an ultimate restriction upon the number of candidates and committees with which an individual may associate himself by means of financial support. But this quite modest restraint upon protected political activity serves to prevent evasion of the $1,000 contribution limitation by a person who might otherwise contribute massive amounts of money to a particular candidate through the use of unearmarked contributions to political committees likely to contribute to that candidate, or huge contributions to the candidate's political party. The limited, additional restriction on associational freedom imposed by the overall ceiling is thus no more than a corollary of the basic individual contribution limitation that we have found to be constitutionally valid.

C. Expenditure Limitations

The Act's expenditure ceilings impose direct and substantial restraints on the quantity of political speech. . . .

1. The $1,000 Limitation on Expenditures "Relative to a Clearly Identified Candidate"

Section 608(e)(1) provides that "[n]o person may make any expenditure . . . relative to a clearly identified candidate during a calendar year which, when added to all other expenditures made by such person during the year advocating the election or defeat of such candidate, exceeds $1,000.". . .

. . . [T]he constitutionality of 608(e)(1) turns on whether the governmental interests advanced in its support satisfy the exacting scrutiny applicable to limitations on core First Amendment rights of political expression.

We find that the governmental interest in preventing corruption and the appearance of corruption is inadequate to justify 608(e)(1)'s ceiling on independent expenditures. First, assuming, *arguendo,* that large independent expenditures pose the same dangers of actual or apparent *quid pro quo* arrangements as do large contributions, 608(e)(1) does not provide an answer that sufficiently relates to the elimination of those dangers. . . .

Second, quite apart from the shortcomings of 608(e) in preventing any abuses generated by large independent expenditures, the independent advocacy restricted by the provision does not presently appear to pose dangers of real or apparent corruption comparable to those identified with large campaign contributions. . . .

While the independent expenditure ceiling thus fails to serve any substantial governmental interest in stemming the reality or appearance of corruption in the electoral process, it heavily burdens core First Amendment expression. For the First Amendment right to "'speak one's mind . . . on all public institutions'" includes the right to engage in "'vigorous advocacy' no less than 'abstract discussion.'" *New York Times Co. v. Sullivan.* Advocacy of the election or defeat of candidates for federal office is no less entitled to protection under the First Amendment than the discussion of political policy generally or advocacy of the passage or defeat of legislation. . . .

For the reasons stated, we conclude that 608(e)(1)'s independent expenditure limitation is unconstitutional under the First Amendment.

2. Limitation on Expenditures by Candidates from Personal or Family Resources

The Act also sets limits on expenditures by a candidate "from his personal funds, or the personal funds of his immediate family, in connection with his campaigns during any calendar year." These ceilings vary from $50,000 for Presidential or Vice Presidential candidates to $35,000 for senatorial candidates, and $25,000 for most candidates for the House of Representatives.

The ceiling on personal expenditures by candidates on their own behalf, like the limitations on independent expenditures contained in 608(e)(1), imposes a substantial restraint on the ability of persons to engage in protected First Amendment expression. The candidate, no less than any other person, has a First Amendment right to engage in the discussion of public issues and vigorously and tirelessly to advocate his own election and the election of other candidates. Indeed, it is of particular importance that candidates have the unfettered opportunity to make their views known so that the electorate may intelligently evaluate the candidates' personal qualities and their positions on vital public issues before choosing among them on election day. Mr. Justice Brandeis' observation that in our country "public discussion is a political duty," *Whitney v. California* (1927) (concurring opinion), applies with special force to candidates for public office. Section 608(a)'s ceiling on personal expenditures by a candidate in furtherance of his own candidacy thus clearly and directly interferes with constitutionally protected freedoms.

The primary governmental interest served by the Act—the prevention of actual and apparent corruption of the political process—does not support the limitation on the candidate's expenditure of his own personal funds. . . .

3. Limitations on Campaign Expenditures

Section 608(c) places limitations on overall campaign expenditures by candidates seeking nomination for election and election to federal office. . . .

No governmental interest that has been suggested is sufficient to justify the restriction on the quantity of political expression imposed by 608(c)'s campaign expenditure limitations. The major evil associated with rapidly increasing campaign expenditures is the danger of candidate dependence on large contributions. The interest in alleviating the corrupting influence of large contributions is served by the Act's contribution limitations and disclosure provisions rather than by 608(c)'s campaign expenditure ceilings. . . .

The interest in equalizing the financial resources of candidates competing for federal office is no more convincing a justification for restricting the scope of federal election campaigns. Given the limitation on the size of outside contributions, the financial resources available to a candidate's campaign, like the number of volunteers recruited, will normally vary with the size and intensity of the candidate's support. There is nothing invidious, improper, or unhealthy in

permitting such funds to be spent to carry the candidate's message to the electorate. . . .

. . . The First Amendment denies government the power to determine that spending to promote one's political views is wasteful, excessive, or unwise. In the free society ordained by our Constitution it is not the government, but the people—individually as citizens and candidates and collectively as associations and political committees—who must retain control over the quantity and range of debate on public issues in a political campaign.

For these reasons we hold that 608(c) is constitutionally invalid.

In sum, the provisions of the Act that impose a $1,000 limitation on contributions to a single candidate, 608(b)(1), a $5,000 limitation on contributions by a political committee to a single candidate, 608(b)(2), and a $25,000 limitation on total contributions by an individual during any calendar year, 608(b)(3), are constitutionally valid. These limitations, along with the disclosure provisions, constitute the Act's primary weapons against the reality or appearance of improper influence stemming from the dependence of candidates on large campaign contributions. The contribution ceilings thus serve the basic governmental interest in safeguarding the integrity of the electoral process without directly impinging upon the rights of individual citizens and candidates to engage in political debate and discussion. By contrast, the First Amendment requires the invalidation of the Act's independent expenditure ceiling, 608(e)(1), its limitation on a candidate's expenditures from his own personal funds, 608(a), and its ceilings on overall campaign expenditures, 608(c). These provisions place substantial and direct restrictions on the ability of candidates, citizens, and associations to engage in protected political expression, restrictions that the First Amendment cannot tolerate.

MR. CHIEF JUSTICE BURGER, concurring in part and dissenting in part.

I agree fully with that part of the Court's opinion that holds unconstitutional the limitations the Act puts on campaign expenditures which "place substantial and direct restrictions on the ability of candidates, citizens, and associations to engage in protected political expression, restrictions that the First Amendment cannot tolerate." Yet when it approves similarly stringent limitations on contributions, the Court ignores the reasons it finds so persuasive in the context of expenditures. For me contributions and expenditures are two sides of the same First Amendment coin.

By limiting campaign contributions, the Act restricts the amount of money that will be spent on political activity—and does so directly. Appellees argue, as the Court notes, that these limits will "act as a brake on the skyrocketing cost of political campaigns." In treating campaign expenditure limitations, the Court says that the "First Amendment denies government the power to determine that spending to promote one's political views is wasteful, excessive, or unwise." Limiting contributions, as a practical matter, will limit expenditures and will put an effective ceiling on the amount of political activity and debate that the Government will permit to take place. The argument that the ceiling is not, after all, very low as matters now stand gives little comfort for the future, since the Court elsewhere notes the rapid inflation in the cost of political campaigning. . . .

The Court's attempt to distinguish the communication inherent in political contributions from the speech aspects of political expenditures simply "will not wash." We do little but engage in word games unless we recognize that people—candidates and contributors—spend money on political activity because they wish to communicate ideas, and their constitutional interest in doing so is precisely the same whether they or someone else utters the words.

MR. JUSTICE WHITE, concurring in part and dissenting in part.

[M]oney is not always equivalent to or used for speech, even in the context of political campaigns. I accept the reality that communicating with potential voters is the heart of an election campaign and that widespread communication has become very expensive. There are, however, many expensive campaign activities that are not themselves communicative or remotely related to speech. . . .

It is also important to restore and maintain public confidence in federal elections. It is critical to obviate or dispel the impression that federal elections are purely and simply a function of money, that federal offices are bought and sold or that political races are reserved for those who have the facility—and the stomach—for doing whatever it takes to bring together those interests, groups, and individuals that can raise or contribute large fortunes in order to prevail at the polls.

The ceiling on candidate expenditures represents the considered judgment of Congress that elections are to be decided among candidates none of whom has overpowering advantage by reason of a huge campaign war chest. At least so long as the ceiling placed upon the candidates is not plainly too low, elections are not to turn on the difference in the amounts of money that candidates have to spend. This seems an acceptable purpose and the means chosen a commonsense way to achieve it. The Court nevertheless holds that a candidate has a constitutional right to spend unlimited amounts of money, mostly that of other people, in order to be elected. The holding perhaps is not that federal candidates have the constitutional right to purchase their election, but many will so interpret the Court's conclusion in this case. I cannot join the Court in this respect.

I also disagree with the Court's judgment that 608(a), which limits the amount of money that a candidate or his family may spend on his campaign, violates the Constitution. Although it is true that this provision does not promote any interest in preventing the corruption of candidates, the provision does, nevertheless, serve salutary purposes related to the integrity of federal campaigns. By limiting the importance of personal wealth, 608(a) helps to assure that only individuals with a modicum of support from others will be viable candidates. This in turn would tend to discourage any notion that the outcome of elections is primarily a function of money. Similarly, 608(a) tends to equalize access to the political arena, encouraging the less wealthy, unable to bankroll their own campaigns, to run for political office.

As with the campaign expenditure limits, Congress was entitled to determine that personal wealth ought to play a less important role in political campaigns than it has in the past. Nothing in the First Amendment stands in the way of that determination.

For these reasons I respectfully dissent.

In addition to ruling on the campaign contribution and spending limits, the Court upheld the recordkeeping and disclosure requirements and the creation of the Federal Election Commission, although it struck down the way the FEC commissioners were selected. It also approved the federal financing of presidential election campaigns and allowed the voluntary acceptance of spending limits as a prerequisite for a candidate to receive federal funds.

The Court's decision in *Buckley* gave a constitutional stamp of approval to extensive regulation of federal election campaigns, including placing limitations on campaign contributions to political candidates by individuals and political groups. The justices have generally remained wedded to the *Buckley* principle. In *Nixon v. Shrink Missouri Government PAC* (2000), for example, the Court approved a Missouri law that placed similar restrictions on contributions to candidates for state office. Three justices (Kennedy, Scalia, and Thomas) dissented from that ruling, with Thomas condemning the Court for adopting the "fallacies of our flawed decision in *Buckley v. Valeo*" and approving Missouri's "sweeping repression of political speech." In spite of this opposition, the constitutionality of reasonable campaign contribution limits seems firmly established.

However, *Buckley*'s declaration that no limitations may constitutionally be imposed on individual or group independent campaign expenditures, known as soft money, places a significant restriction on future regulation. Those who argue that meaningful reform of U.S. elections cannot take place without the regulation of independent campaign expenditures face a large obstacle in the *Buckley* decision. So far, the Court has not backed down from the First Amendment position it took in *Buckley*. In *Colorado Republican Federal Campaign Committee v. Federal Election Commission* (1996), for example, the justices ruled that the FEC had no constitutional authority to regulate an independent expenditure for political advertising that was not coordinated with any candidate.

The Court's position rests on the linkage between money and speech. Are campaign expenditure limitations equal to limitations on political speech? As long as the answer to that question is in the affirmative, the prospects for legislative passage and judicial approval of more comprehensive election regulation remain in doubt.

Commercial Speech

As consumers of all sorts of goods and services, we are constantly bombarded with commercial speech—advertisements. Open a newspaper, turn on a television or radio, or log on to the Internet and you are bound to find hundreds of ads aimed at communicating all kinds of messages. Although we see ads every day, we probably do not think about them in terms of the First Amendment. Does the First Amendment apply to this form of expression? If so, does it deserve the same constitutional protection as more traditional, equally commonplace, forms of speech?

Historically, courts have viewed commercial expression as more closely related to commerce than to speech. Government has an interest in regulating fraudulent or deceptive messages that may be found in advertisements. In addition, the subject matter of commercial expression is substantially different from the political and social speech at the heart of First Amendment protections. For these reasons, the courts have allowed more extensive government regulation of commercial expression than of other forms of speech. This principle was articulated in *Valentine v. Chrestensen* (1942) in which the Court upheld a law banning the distribution of handbills that advertised commercial goods and services. The Court concluded that the First Amendment does not protect "purely commercial advertising."

In the mid-1970s, however, the justices handed down four decisions that indicated a reconsideration of the constitutional status of commercial expression. The cases involved the advertising of abortion services, pharmaceutical prices, legal fees, and real estate.

The first of these decisions was *Bigelow v. Virginia* (1975). The dispute began when Jeffrey C. Bigelow, the managing editor of the *Virginia Weekly,* a Charlottesville newspaper focusing on the University of Virginia community, approved for publication the advertisement reproduced on the next page. It ran on February 8, 1971, two years before the Supreme Court's decision in *Roe v. Wade,* which legalized abortions nationwide. Three months later, Virginia charged Bigelow with violating an 1878 state law, which said "if any person, by publication, lecture, advertisement . . . encourage or prompt the procuring of abortion . . . he shall be guilty of a misdemeanor." Bigelow was the first individual ever accused of violating the law, despite its duration.

UNWANTED PREGNANCY
LET US HELP YOU
Abortions are now legal in New York.
There are no residency requirements.
FOR IMMEDIATE PLACEMENT IN
ACCREDITED HOSPITALS AND
CLINICS AT LOW COST
Contact
WOMEN'S PAVILION
515 Madison Avenue
New York, N.Y. 10022
or call anytime
(212) 371-6670 or (212) 371-6650
AVAILABLE 7 DAYS A WEEK

STRICTLY CONFIDENTIAL. We
will make all arrangements for you
and help you with information and
counseling.

Throughout his trial and appeals, Bigelow's attorneys argued that the First Amendment protected commercial speech and as a consequence Virginia's law was unconstitutional. Several judicial bodies, including the Supreme Court of Virginia, rejected this line of reasoning, concluding that the Free Speech Clause does not apply to paid commercial advertisements.

The Supreme Court, however, reversed, finding that the lower courts interpreted *Valentine v. Chrestensen* much too broadly. For a majority of seven, Justice Blackmun explained, "The fact that the particular advertisement . . . had commercial aspects . . . did not negate all First Amendment guarantees. . . . The existence of 'commercial activity, in itself, is no justification for narrowing the protection of expression secured by the First Amendment.'" Bigelow was advertising a legal service. There was no evidence that the advertisement was deceptive or fraudulent. The ad provided information about a service that existed in another state. If the state were able to restrict advertisements about such activities, it would violate the spirit of the First Amendment, which favors the widespread dissemination of information and opinion.

Although the justices ruled that Virginia could not apply its law to Bigelow's advertisement, it failed to provide a comprehensive response to the issue of First Amendment protection of commercial speech. Blackmun noted that the First Amendment protected commercial expression to "some degree," but the justices refused to decide "the precise extent to which the First Amendment permits regulation of advertising that is related to activities the State may legitimately regulate or even prohibit." Although *Bigelow* extended First Amendment protection to commercial speech, it also implied that certain ads, under certain circumstances, may be subject to state limitations. Commercial speech does not equal political speech in the eyes of the Constitution.

It did not take long for the Court to address some of the questions left unanswered in *Bigelow*. Its first opportunity came the very next year in *Virginia State Board of Pharmacy v. Virginia Citizens Consumer Council, Inc.* (1976). This litigation centered on a constitutional challenge to a Virginia regulation making it unlawful for a pharmacy to advertise the prices of its prescription medications. A pharmacist who violated the rule risked being cited for unprofessional conduct and possible monetary fines or license suspension. The state justified its regulation as protecting the public from deceptive advertising and maintaining the professionalism of the state's pharmacists. Further, it argued that advertising prices is pure commercial expression that (unlike Bigelow's advertisement) carries no political or social information. Such advertising, the state claimed, deserves no First Amendment protection and is fully subject to state regulation. In response, the Consumer Council claimed that drug pricing information is socially relevant and the public has the right to a free flow of information without state interference.

The Court struck down the Virginia regulation as inconsistent with the First Amendment. Again speaking for the Court Justice Blackmun explained that the purely economic content of the advertisement does not disqualify it from First Amendment protection. The public has the right to receive truthful information about lawful products and services. Likewise, the pharmacist has the right to communicate that information. The state could achieve its legitimate goals of promoting professionalism and protecting the public from misleading advertising by methods less severe than banning commercial expression altogether.

Taken together, the decisions in *Bigelow* and *Virginia State Board of Pharmacy* indicated that the Court was expanding constitutional protections for commercial speech. Only Justice Rehnquist voted to uphold the state restrictions in both cases. Yet certain factors made unclear how far the Court would go. First, Blackmun's opinion in the pharmacy decision said only that advertising is not "wholly outside" First Amendment protections. He acknowledged that "some forms of commercial speech regulation are surely permissible." Second, the justices who concurred in the pharmacy case also expressed some uneasiness. Justice Stewart's concurring opinion, for example, emphasized that the Court's opinion should not be interpreted as removing the distinction between product and price advertising on one hand and ideological expression on the other. Chief Justice Burger cautioned against applying the Court's decision to other professions. After all, he explained, today's pharmacists deal primarily in standardized products. They are not like physicians and lawyers whose services are not standardized and whose fees, therefore, cannot be directly compared.

Burger may have written his concurring opinion with one eye on the Court's docket. The very next year the justices considered *Bates v. State Bar of Arizona* (1977), a challenge to a law prohibiting lawyers from advertising the prices for their services.[22] Does the Court back away from its trend of expanding protections for commercial expression? Or does it continue along the road it started in *Bigelow?*

22. To hear oral arguments in this case, navigate to: *oyez.nwu.edu.*

Bates v. State Bar of Arizona

433 U.S. 350 (1977)
laws.findlaw.com/US/433/350.html
Vote: 5 (Blackmun, Brennan, Marshall, Stevens, White)
        4 (Burger, Powell, Rehnquist, Stewart)
Opinion of the Court: Blackmun
Opinions dissenting in part and concurring in part: Burger, Powell, Rehnquist

John Bates and Van O'Steen graduated from the Arizona State University College of Law in 1972 and took jobs at a state legal aid society. After two years, they developed what was then a unique idea—to open a legal clinic to provide "legal services at modest fees to persons of moderate income who did not qualify for government aid." In March 1974 they opened their clinic in Phoenix, Arizona, but two years later they were barely surviving. The pair decided to take a risky step: they placed an ad in an Arizona newspaper *(see next page).*

Why was their ad risky? Today, attorney advertisements are commonplace. From the 1910s through the 1970s, however, most state bar associations explicitly prohibited such activity. Arizona's rules contained this provision: "A lawyer shall not . . . display advertisement in the city or telephone directories or by other means of commercial publicity." So, upon seeing Bates and O'Steen's ad, the president of the state bar association initiated proceedings against them. They were found guilty and given the rather mild sentence of a one-week suspension from legal practice. Nonetheless, with the help of the ACLU, they decided to appeal the judgment, claiming that the ban constituted a violation of their First Amendment guarantee, under the Court's decision in *Virginia Pharmacy.*[23]

As the case moved up the judicial ladder, the debate over attorney advertisement became heated. The Arizona State Bar, backed by amicus curiae briefs from professional groups such as the American Bar Association, the American Dental Association, and the American

23. They also claimed that the prohibition violated the Sherman Anti-Trust Act, legislation the Court applied to the legal profession in *Goldfarb v. Virginia State Bar* (1975).

Optometric Association, expressed its disdain for professional advertising through a number of legal and nonlegal arguments. The state bar, like the pharmacy board in *Virginia Pharmacy,* claimed that ads would have a negative effect on the profession, which was already held in low esteem by the public; that ads would be inherently misleading because legal skills vary from attorney to attorney; and that ads would have an adverse effect on the administration of justice by "stirring up" litigation. Bates and O'Steen argued that the First Amendment guaranteed them the right to place advertisements in newspapers. Their position also received legal reinforcement from several consumer groups and, significantly, from the solicitor general, who argued orally as an amicus curiae.

MR. JUSTICE BLACKMUN delivered the opinion of the Court.

Last Term, in *Virginia Pharmacy Board v. Virginia Consumer Council* (1976), the Court considered the validity under the First Amendment of a Virginia statute declaring that a pharmacist was guilty of "unprofessional conduct" if he advertised prescription drug prices. . . . [W]e held that commercial speech of that kind was entitled to the protection of the First Amendment. . . .

The issue presently before us is a narrow one. First, we need not address the peculiar problems associated with advertising claims relating to the *quality* of legal services. Such claims probably are not susceptible of precise measurement or verification and, under some circumstances, might well be deceptive or misleading to the public, or even false. Appellee does not suggest, nor do we perceive, that appellants' advertisement contained claims, extravagant or otherwise, as to the quality of services. Accordingly, we leave that issue for another day. Second, we also need not resolve the problems associated with in-person solicitation of clients—at the hospital room or the accident site, or in any other situation that breeds undue influence—by attorneys or their agents or "runners." Activity of that kind might well pose dangers of overreaching and misrepresentation not encountered in newspaper announcement advertising. Hence, this issue also is not before us. Third, we note that appellee's criticism of advertising by attorneys does not apply with much force to some of the basic factual content of advertising: information as to the attorney's name, address, and telephone number, office hours, and the like. The American Bar Association itself has a provision in its current Code of Professional Responsibility that would allow the disclosure of such information, and more, in the classified section of the telephone directory. We recognize, however, that an advertising diet limited to such spartan fare would provide scant nourishment.

The heart of the dispute before us today is whether lawyers also may constitutionally advertise the *prices* at which certain routine services will be performed. Numerous justifications are proffered for the restriction of such price advertising. We consider each in turn:

1. *The Adverse Effect on Professionalism.* Appellee places particular emphasis on the adverse effects that it feels price advertising will have on the legal profession. The key to professionalism, it is argued, is the sense of pride that involvement in the discipline generates. It is claimed that price advertising will bring about commercialization, which will undermine the attorney's sense of dignity and self-worth. The hustle of the marketplace will adversely affect the profession's service orientation, and irreparably damage the delicate balance between the lawyer's need to earn and his obligation selflessly to serve. Advertising is also said to erode the client's trust in his attorney: Once the client perceives that the lawyer is motivated by profit, his confidence that the attorney is acting out of a commitment to the client's welfare is jeopardized. And advertising is said to tarnish the dignified public image of the profession.

We recognize, of course, and commend the spirit of public service with which the profession of law is practiced and to which it is dedicated. The present Members of this Court, licensed attorneys all, could not feel otherwise. And we would have reason to pause if we felt that our decision today would undercut that spirit. But we find the postulated connection between advertising and the erosion of true professionalism to be severely strained. At its core, the argument presumes that attorneys must conceal from themselves and from their clients the real-life fact that lawyers earn their livelihood at the bar. We suspect that few attorneys engage in such self-deception. And rare is the client, moreover, even one of the modest means, who enlists the aid of an attorney with the expectation that his services will be rendered free of charge. In fact, the American Bar Association advises that an attorney should reach "a clear agreement with his client as to the basis of the fee charges to be made," and that this is to be done "[a]s soon as feasible after a lawyer has been employed." If the commercial basis of the relationship is to be promptly disclosed on ethical grounds, once the client is in the office, it seems inconsistent to condemn the candid revelation of the same information before he arrives at that office.

Moreover, the assertion that advertising will diminish the attorney's reputation in the community is open to question. Bankers and engineers advertise, and yet these professions are not regarded as undignified. In fact, it has been suggested that the failure of lawyers to advertise creates public disillusionment with the profession. The absence of advertising may be seen to reflect the profession's failure to reach out and serve the community: Studies reveal that many persons do not obtain counsel even when they perceive a need because of the feared price of services or because of an inability to locate a competent attorney. Indeed, cynicism with regard to the profession may be created by the fact that it long has publicly eschewed advertising, while condoning the actions of the attorney who structures his social or civic associations so as to provide contacts with potential clients.

It appears that the ban on advertising originated as a rule of etiquette and not as a rule of ethics. Early lawyers in Great Britain viewed the law as a form of public service, rather than as a means of earning a living, and they looked down on "trade" as unseemly. Eventually, the attitude toward advertising fostered by this view evolved into an aspect of the ethics of the profession. But habit and tradition are not in themselves an adequate answer to a constitutional challenge. In this day, we do not belittle the person who earns his living by the strength of his arm or the force of his mind. Since the belief that lawyers are somehow "above" trade has become an anachronism, the historical foundation for the advertising restraint has crumbled.

2. *The Inherently Misleading Nature of Attorney Advertising.* It is argued that advertising of legal services inevitably will be misleading (a) because such services are so individualized with regard to content and quality as to prevent informed comparison on the basis of an advertisement, (b) because the consumer of legal services is unable to determine in advance just what services he needs, and

(c) because advertising by attorneys will highlight irrelevant factors and fail to show the relevant factor of skill.

We are not persuaded that restrained professional advertising by lawyers inevitably will be misleading. Although many services performed by attorneys are indeed unique, it is doubtful that any attorney would or could advertise fixed prices for services of that type. The only services that lend themselves to advertising are the routine ones: the uncontested divorce, the simple adoption, the uncontested personal bankruptcy, the change of name, and the like—the very services advertised by appellants. Although the precise service demanded in each task may vary slightly, and although legal services are not fungible, these facts do not make advertising misleading so long as the attorney does the necessary work at the advertised price. The argument that legal services are so unique that fixed rates cannot meaningfully be established is refuted by the record in this case: The appellee, State Bar, itself sponsors a Legal Services Program in which the participating attorneys agree to perform services like those advertised by the appellants at standardized rates. . . .

The second component of the argument—that advertising ignores the diagnostic role—fares little better. It is unlikely that many people go to an attorney merely to ascertain if they have a clean bill of legal health. Rather, attorneys are likely to be employed to perform specific tasks. Although the client may not know the detail involved in performing the task, he no doubt is able to identify the service he desires at the level of generality to which advertising lends itself.

The third component is not without merit: Advertising does not provide a complete foundation on which to select an attorney. But it seems peculiar to deny the consumer, on the ground that the information is incomplete, at least some of the relevant information needed to reach an informed decision. The alternative—the prohibition of advertising—serves only to restrict the information that flows to consumers. Moreover, the argument assumes that the public is not sophisticated enough to realize the limitations of advertising, and that the public is better kept in ignorance than trusted with correct but incomplete information. We suspect the argument rests on an underestimation of the public. In any event, we view as dubious any justification that is based on the benefits of public ignorance. See *Virginia Pharmacy Board v. Virginia Consumer Council.* Al-

though, of course, the bar retains the power to correct omissions that have the effect of presenting an inaccurate picture, the preferred remedy is more disclosure, rather than less. If the naivete of the public will cause advertising by attorneys to be misleading, then it is the bar's role to assure that the populace is sufficiently informed as to enable it to place advertising in its proper perspective.

3. *The Adverse Effect on the Administration of Justice.* Advertising is said to have the undesirable effect of stirring up litigation. The judicial machinery is designed to serve those who feel sufficiently aggrieved to bring forward their claims. Advertising, it is argued, serves to encourage the assertion of legal rights in the courts, thereby undesirably unsettling societal repose. There is even a suggestion of barratry.

But advertising by attorneys is not an unmitigated source of harm to the administration of justice. It may offer great benefits. Although advertising might increase the use of the judicial machinery, we cannot accept the notion that it is always better for a person to suffer a wrong silently than to redress it by legal action. As the bar acknowledges, "the middle 70% of our population is not being reached or served adequately by the legal profession." Among the reasons for this underutilization is fear of the cost, and an inability to locate a suitable lawyer. Advertising can help to solve this acknowledged problem: Advertising is the traditional mechanism in a free-market economy for a supplier to inform a potential purchaser of the availability and terms of exchange. The disciplinary rule at issue likely has served to burden access to legal services, particularly for the not-quite-poor and the unknowledgeable. A rule allowing restrained advertising would be in accord with the bar's obligation to "facilitate the process of intelligent selection of lawyers, and to assist in making legal services fully available."

4. *The Undesirable Economic Effects of Advertising.* It is claimed that advertising will increase the overhead costs of the profession, and that these costs then will be passed along to consumers in the form of increased fees. Moreover, it is claimed that the additional cost of practice will create a substantial entry barrier, deterring or preventing young attorneys from penetrating the market and entrenching the position of the bar's established members.

These two arguments seem dubious at best. Neither distinguishes lawyers from others, and neither appears relevant to the First Amendment. The ban on advertising serves to increase the difficulty of discovering the lowest cost seller of acceptable ability. As a result, to this extent attorneys are isolated from competition, and the incentive to price competitively is reduced. Although it is true that the effect of advertising on the price of services has not been demonstrated, there is revealing evidence with regard to products: where consumers have the benefit of price advertising, retail prices often are dramatically lower than they would be without advertising. It is entirely possible that advertising will serve to reduce, not advance, the cost of legal services to the consumer.

The entry-barrier argument is equally unpersuasive. In the absence of advertising, an attorney must rely on his contacts with the community to generate a flow of business. In view of the time necessary to develop such contacts, the ban in fact serves to perpetuate the market position of established attorneys. Consideration of entry-barrier problems would urge that advertising be allowed so as to aid the new competitor in penetrating the market.

5. *The Adverse Effect of Advertising on the Quality of Service.* It is argued that the attorney may advertise a given "package" of service at a set price, and will be inclined to provide, by indiscriminate use, the standard package regardless of whether it fits the client's needs.

Restraints on advertising, however, are an ineffective way of deterring shoddy work. An attorney who is inclined to cut quality will do so regardless of the rule on advertising. And the advertisement of a standardized fee does not necessarily mean that the services offered are undesirably standardized. Indeed, the assertion that an attorney who advertises a standard fee will cut quality is substantially undermined by the fixed-fee schedule of appellee's own prepaid Legal Services Program. Even if advertising leads to the creation of "legal clinics" like that of appellants'—clinics that emphasize standardized procedures for routine problems—it is possible that such clinics will improve service by reducing the likelihood of error.

6. *The Difficulties of Enforcement.* Finally, it is argued that the wholesale restriction is justified by the problems of enforcement if any other course is taken. Because the public lacks sophistication in legal matters, it may be particularly susceptible to misleading or deceptive advertising by lawyers. After-the-fact action by the consumer lured by such advertising may not provide a realistic restraint because of the inability of the layman to assess whether the service he has received meets professional standards. Thus, the vigilance of a regulatory agency will be required. But because of the numerous purveyors of services, the overseeing of advertising will be burdensome.

It is at least somewhat incongruous for the opponents of advertising to extol the virtues and altruism of the legal profession at one point, and, at another, to assert that its members will seize the opportunity to mislead and distort. We suspect that, with advertising, most lawyers will behave as they always have: They will abide by their solemn oaths to uphold the integrity and honor of their profession and of the legal system. For every attorney who overreaches through advertising, there will be thousands of others who will be candid and honest and straightforward. And, of course, it will be in the latter's interest, as in other cases of misconduct at the bar, to assist in weeding out those few who abuse their trust.

In sum, we are not persuaded that any of the proffered justifications rise to the level of an acceptable reason for the suppression of all advertising by attorneys. . . .

In holding that advertising by attorneys may not be subjected to blanket suppression, and that the advertisement at issue is protected, we, of course, do not hold that advertising by attorneys may not be regulated in any way. We mention some of the clearly permissible limitations on advertising not foreclosed by our holding.

Advertising that is false, deceptive, or misleading of course is subject to restraint. Since the advertiser knows his product and has a commercial interest in its dissemination, we have little worry that regulation to assure truthfulness will discourage protected speech. And any concern that strict requirements for truthfulness will undesirably inhibit spontaneity seems inapplicable because commercial speech generally is calculated. Indeed, the public and private benefits from commercial speech derive from confidence in its accuracy and reliability. Thus, the leeway for untruthful or misleading expression that has been allowed in other contexts has little force in the commercial arena. In fact, because the public lacks sophistication concerning legal services, misstatements that might be overlooked or deemed unimportant in other advertising may be found quite inappropriate in legal advertising. For example, advertising claims as to the quality of services—a matter we do not address today—are not susceptible of measurement or verification; accordingly, such claims may be so likely to be misleading as to warrant restriction. Similar objections might justify restraints on in-person solicitation. We do not foreclose the possibility that some limited supplementation, by way of warning or disclaimer or the like, might be required of even an advertisement of the kind ruled upon today so as to assure that the consumer is not misled. In sum, we recognize that many of the problems in defining the boundary between deceptive and nondeceptive advertising remain to be resolved, and we expect that the bar will have a special role to play in assuring that advertising by attorneys flows both freely and cleanly.

As with other varieties of speech, it follows as well that there may be reasonable restrictions on the time, place, and manner of advertising. Advertising concerning transactions that are themselves illegal obviously may be suppressed. And the special problems of advertising on the electronic broadcast media will warrant special consideration.

The constitutional issue in this case is only whether the State may prevent the publication in a newspaper of appellants' truthful advertisement concerning the availability and terms of routine legal services. We rule simply that the flow of such information may not be restrained, and we therefore hold the present application of the disciplinary rule against appellants to be violative of the First Amendment.

The judgment of the Supreme Court of Arizona is therefore affirmed in part and reversed in part.

It is so ordered.

MR. JUSTICE REHNQUIST, dissenting in part.

I continue to believe that the First Amendment speech provision, long regarded by this Court as a sanctuary for expressions of public importance or intellectual interest, is demeaned by invocation to protect advertisements of goods and services. I would hold quite simply that the appellants' advertisement, however truthful or reasonable it may be, is not the sort of expression that the Amendment was adopted to protect.

. . . [T]he Court's opinion offers very little guidance as to the extent or nature of permissible state regulation of professions such as law and medicine. . . . [O]nce the Court took the first step down the "slippery slope" in *Virginia*

Pharmacy Board, the possibility of understandable and workable differentiations between protected speech and unprotected speech in the field of advertising largely evaporated. Once the exception of commercial speech from the protection of the First Amendment which had been established by *Valentine v. Chrestensen* was abandoned, the shift to case-by-case adjudication of First Amendment claims of advertisers was a predictable consequence.

. . . The *Valentine* distinction was constitutionally sound and practically workable, and I am still unwilling to take even one step down the "slippery slope" away from it.

In *Bates* the Court provided one of its clearest statements on the issue of advertising. While refuting the bar association's arguments, Blackmun also listed the conditions under which attorneys may or may not advertise; for example, he stressed that Bates and O'Steen's ad mentioned only simple legal services, which any attorney could perform. Many have surmised from this distinction that bar associations probably could limit advertisements for complex legal work.

In the years following *Bates,* the judiciary has wrestled with questions of how much regulation of legal advertising is constitutionally permissible and under what circumstances.[24] Many lawyers and law firms have taken advantage of the ruling to advertise their services and fees, but the state bar associations have insisted that the advertisements be truthful and not demean the profession. Despite widespread advertising of legal services, studies have shown that a majority of the nation's attorneys oppose advertising and feel that it detracts from the dignity of the profession.[25]

The final important commercial advertising case of the mid-1970s was *Linmark Associates v. Township of Willingboro* (1977). Here, the Court dealt with posted signs, not printed ads; but more important, it addressed a form of suppressed expression that appeared to have not economic, but social and political ends. *Linmark* arose in March 1974, when the town of Willingboro, New Jersey,

24. See, for example, *Ohralik v. Ohio State Bar* (1978) and *In re Primus* (1978).

25. Lauren Bowen, "Do Court Decisions Matter?" in *Contemplating Courts,* ed. Lee Epstein (Washington, D.C.: CQ Press, 1995), 376–389.

passed an ordinance outlawing the posting of For Sale signs on most property. Enacted at the urging of property owners, the statute attempted to halt certain economic and social trends within the town. Located near Fort Dix, McGuire Air Force Base, and several major corporations, the town was a natural for suburban development. By the 1960s the white population of the town had increased 350 percent. But, as suburban growth stabilized during the 1970s, so did Willingboro's. By the early 1970s the town's white population had declined by 5 percent, and the black population had grown from 11.7 percent in the 1960s to 18.2 percent. To stop what some called panic selling by whites and to maintain property values steadily dropping in the face of white flight, the town passed the ordinance banning For Sale signs.

A real estate agency that wanted to erect a For Sale sign challenged the ordinance as a violation of its free expression guarantees. Backed by an amicus curiae brief from the ACLU, the agency argued that For Sale signs were not distinguishable from advertisements for drugs, abortions, or attorney services. The town countered with two sets of arguments. First, the law was limited, restricting one method of communication and leaving ample alternative channels available. Second, it claimed that the statute sought to achieve a legitimate and, in fact, vital government objective—to promote racial integration. This last argument attracted the attention of the NAACP Legal Defense Fund, which filed a supporting amicus curiae brief. By the time this case appeared before the Court, the stage was set for high drama: *Linmark* was one of only a handful of occasions when two powerful allies, the ACLU and the LDF, opposed each other.

Writing for a unanimous Court, Justice Thurgood Marshall, a former LDF attorney, agreed with the ACLU and struck down the town's ordinance. He acknowledged that although it had important objectives, in the final analysis the ordinance was no different from the law at issue in *Virginia Pharmacy*: it prevented "residents from obtaining certain information" without providing sufficient justification. As Marshall asserted, "If dissemination of this information can be restricted, then every locality in the country can suppress any facts that reflect poorly on it, so long as a plausible claim can be made

that disclosure would cause recipients of the information to act 'irrationally.'"

The years between 1975 and 1977 were important for commercial speech. The Court's decisions in *Bigelow, Virginia Pharmacy, Bates,* and *Linmark Associates* signaled a major change by significantly elevating the degree of constitutional protection enjoyed by commercial expression. In the years that followed, the justices continued in that policy direction, although never elevating commercial advertising to the same level as enjoyed by political and social speech. For example, the Court struck down laws prohibiting the erection of advertising billboards (*Metromedia, Inc. v. San Diego,* 1981); banning the advertising of contraceptives by mail (*Bolger v. Youngs Drug Products Corporation,* 1983); and blocking a public utility from sending, along with monthly bills, statements that expressed the company's position on issues of public policy (*Consolidated Edison Company of New York, Inc. v. Public Service Commission of New York,* 1980). For the most part, the Court's decisions in the commercial expression cases were by substantial majorities, with only Justice Rehnquist consistently supporting the position of government regulators.

Because the Court acknowledged that advertising merits a lower level of protection than political or social speech, there was some confusion over the appropriate test to use in commercial expression cases. The justices remedied this situation in *Central Hudson Gas and Electric Corporation v. Public Service Commission of New York* (1980), a dispute over an energy conservation law prohibiting utility companies from advertising to promote the sale of their products.

Central Hudson Gas and Electric Corporation v. Public Service Commission of New York

447 U.S. 557 (1980)
laws.findlaw.com/US/447/557.html
Vote: 8 (Blackmun, Brennan, Burger, Marshall, Powell, Stevens, Stewart, White)
    1 (Rehnquist)
Opinion of the Court: Powell
Concurring opinions: Blackmun, Brennan, Stevens
Dissenting opinion: Rehnquist

Facing an energy shortage during the winter of 1973 and 1974, the New York Public Service Commission ordered state public utility companies to stop all advertising that promoted the use of electricity. Three years later, when the shortage had eased, the commission requested public comments on a proposal to continue the ban on promotional advertising. Central Hudson Gas and Electric Corporation opposed the ban on First Amendment grounds. Declaring all advertising promoting the use of electricity to be contrary to the national policy of conserving energy, the commission extended the ban. Central Hudson challenged the regulation in state court. The New York Court of Appeals, upholding lower court rulings, concluded that government interests outweighed the limited constitutional value of the commercial speech at issue. Central Hudson appealed to the Supreme Court.

MR. JUSTICE POWELL delivered the opinion of the Court.

This case presents the question whether a regulation of the Public Service Commission of the State of New York violates the First and Fourteenth Amendments because it completely bans promotional advertising by an electrical utility. . . .

The Commission's order restricts only commercial speech, that is, expression related solely to the economic interests of the speaker and its audience. The First Amendment, as applied to the States through the Fourteenth Amendment, protects commercial speech from unwarranted governmental regulation. Commercial expression not only serves the economic interest of the speaker, but also assists consumers and furthers the societal interest in the fullest possible dissemination of information. In applying the First Amendment to this area, we have rejected the "highly paternalistic" view that government has complete power to suppress or regulate commercial speech. . . . Even when advertising communicates only an incomplete version of the relevant facts, the First Amendment presumes that some accurate information is better than no information at all.

Nevertheless, our decisions have recognized "the 'commonsense' distinction between speech proposing a commercial transaction, which occurs in an area traditionally subject to government regulation, and other varieties of speech." The Constitution therefore accords a lesser protection to commercial speech than to other constitutionally guaranteed expression. The protection available for particular commercial expression turns on the nature both of the expression and of the governmental interests served by its regulation.

The First Amendment's concern for commercial speech is based on the informational function of advertising. Consequently, there can be no constitutional objection to the suppression of commercial messages that do not accurately inform the public about lawful activity. The government may ban forms of communication more likely to deceive the public than to inform it, or commercial speech related to illegal activity. . . .

In commercial speech cases, . . . a four-part analysis has developed. At the outset, we must determine whether the expression is protected by the First Amendment. For commercial speech to come within that provision, it at least must concern lawful activity and not be misleading. Next, we ask whether the asserted governmental interest is substantial. If both inquiries yield positive answers, we must determine whether the regulation directly advances the governmental interest asserted, and whether it is not more extensive than is necessary to serve that interest.

We now apply this four-step analysis for commercial speech to the Commission's arguments in support of its ban on promotional advertising.

The Commission does not claim that the expression at issue either is inaccurate or relates to unlawful activity. . . .

The Commission offers two state interests as justifications for the ban on promotional advertising. The first concerns energy conservation. Any increase in demand for electricity—during peak or off-peak periods—means greater consumption of energy. The Commission argues, and the New York court agreed, that the State's interest in conserving energy is sufficient to support suppression of advertising designed to increase consumption of electricity. In view of our country's dependence on energy resources beyond our control, no one can doubt the importance of energy conservation. Plainly, therefore, the state interest asserted is substantial.

The Commission also argues that promotional advertising will aggravate inequities caused by the failure to base the utilities' rates on marginal cost. . . . The State's concern that rates be fair and efficient represents a clear and substantial governmental interest.

Next, we focus on the relationship between the State's interests and the advertising ban. Under this criterion, the Commission's laudable concern over the equity and efficiency of appellant's rates does not provide a constitutionally adequate reason for restricting protected speech. The link between the advertising prohibition and appellant's rate structure is, at most, tenuous. The impact of promotional advertising on the equity of appellant's rates is highly speculative. Advertising to increase off-peak usage would have to increase peak usage, while other factors that directly affect the fairness and efficiency of appellant's rates remained constant. Such conditional and remote eventualities simply cannot justify silencing appellant's promotional advertising.

In contrast, the State's interest in energy conservation is directly advanced by the Commission order at issue here. There is an immediate connection between advertising and demand for electricity. Central Hudson would not contest the advertising ban unless it believed that promotion would increase its sales. Thus, we find a direct link between the state interest in conservation and the Commission's order.

We come finally to the critical inquiry in this case: whether the Commission's complete suppression of speech ordinarily protected by the First Amendment is no more extensive than necessary to further the State's interest in energy conservation. The Commission's order reaches all promotional advertising, regardless of the impact of the touted service on overall energy use. But the energy conservation rationale, as important as it is, cannot justify suppressing information about electric devices or services that would cause no net increase in total energy use. In addition, no showing has been made that a more limited restriction on the content of promotional advertising would not serve adequately the State's interests. . . .

The Commission's order prevents appellant from promoting electric services that would reduce energy use by diverting demand from less efficient sources, or that would consume roughly the same amount of energy as do alternative sources. In neither situation would the utility's advertising endanger conservation or mislead the public. To the extent that the Commission's order suppresses speech that in no way impairs the State's interest in energy conservation, the Commission's order violates the First and Fourteenth Amendments, and must be invalidated.

The Commission also has not demonstrated that its interest in conservation cannot be protected adequately by more limited regulation of appellant's commercial expression. To further its policy of conservation, the Commission could attempt to restrict the format and content of Central Hudson's advertising. It might, for example, require that the advertisements include information about the relative efficiency and expense of the offered service, both under current conditions and for the foreseeable future. In the absence of a showing that more limited speech regulation would be ineffective, we cannot approve the complete suppression of Central Hudson's advertising. . . .

Accordingly, the judgment of the New York Court of Appeals is

Reversed.

MR. JUSTICE REHNQUIST, dissenting.

The Court's analysis, in my view, is wrong in several respects. Initially, I disagree with the Court's conclusion that the speech of a state-created monopoly, which is the subject of a comprehensive regulatory scheme, is entitled to protection under the First Amendment. I also think that the Court errs here in failing to recognize that the state law is most accurately viewed as an economic regulation, and that the speech involved (if it falls within the scope of the First Amendment at all) occupies a significantly more subordinate position in the hierarchy of First Amendment values than the Court gives it today. Finally, the Court, in reaching its decision, improperly substitutes its own judgment for that of the State in deciding how a proper ban on promotional advertising should be drafted. With regard to this latter point, the Court adopts as its final part of a four-part test a "no more extensive than necessary" analysis that will unduly impair a state legislature's ability to adopt legislation reasonably designed to promote interests that have always been rightly thought to be of great importance to the State.

The *Central Hudson* decision provided a welcome explanation of how the Court approached commercial expression cases. If the commercial expression concerns a lawful activity and is not misleading, it merits First Amendment protection. The state may still regulate that expression, however, if the regulation serves a substantial government interest, directly advances that interest, and is no more extensive than necessary to achieve it.

The Court has applied the *Central Hudson* test in subsequent cases. In *City of Cincinnati v. Discovery Network* (1993) the justices struck down the enforcement of a city ordinance ordering the removal of newsracks used for the distribution of free magazines and advertisements. In *44 Liquormart, Inc. v. Rhode Island* (1996) the justices by unanimous vote declared unconstitutional a state law that prohibited advertising alcoholic beverage prices. Although the justices did not agree as to rationale, *44 Liquormart* is especially significant because the justices voided the regulation in spite of the Twenty-first Amendment, which gives the states strong authority to control alcoholic beverages. Decisions such as these indicate that governments have difficult standards to meet when they attempt to regulate nondeceptive commercial speech that concerns a lawful product or service.

Freedom of Association

Essential to the exercise of political and social expression is the ability to join with likeminded individuals to advance mutual goals. The Supreme Court has long recognized that the right of association is implicit in the First Amendment's freedoms of speech, press, assembly, and petition.[26]

Protecting the right of individuals to form groups for political or social purposes often means extending constitutional guarantees to organizations that that hold unpopular or even dangerous views. For example, in the 1960s the justices struck down government attempts to regulate the Communist Party by requiring membership registration (*Albertson v. Subversive Activities Control Board*, 1965), by penalizing individuals for party membership (*United States v. Robel*, 1967), or by removing from party members privileges other citizens enjoy (*Aptheker v. Secretary of State*, 1964).

Similarly, the Court intervened when southern states opposed to the goals of civil rights groups took actions to restrict the associational rights of their members. In *NAACP v. Alabama* (1958) the justices unanimously invalidated an Alabama requirement that civil rights groups

submit their membership rolls to state authorities; and in *NAACP v. Button* (1963) the Court blocked an action by the state of Virginia designed to cripple the use of litigation by civil rights organizations.

In more recent times, conflicts have arisen between groups asserting First Amendment association rights and states enforcing legislation to reduce discrimination. Most frequently at issue are the policies of private organizations that restrict membership or services based on characteristics such as race, sex, sexual orientation, or religion. Country clubs, businessmen's clubs, fraternal organizations, and civic groups often have such membership restrictions. Do the members of private organizations have the constitutional right to impose whatever membership qualifications they desire? Or may the state, concerned that the exclusion of people could deprive them of opportunities for business and professional networking and advancement, enforce anti-discrimination statutes that make such membership restrictions unlawful?

The justices addressed this question in *Roberts v. United States Jaycees* (1984). The Jaycees, established in 1920 as the Junior Chamber of Commerce, is a private, civic organization that helps young men participate in the affairs of their community. This dispute centered on the policy of the Jaycees to restrict regular membership to men between the ages of eighteen and thirty-five. The Minnesota Department of Human Rights claimed that the exclusion of women by the organization violated a state law prohibiting sex-based discrimination in public accommodations. The United States Jaycees argued that applying the Minnesota anti-discrimination law to its membership policies was a violation of the First Amendment freedom of association.

In a 7–0 decision, the Supreme Court ruled against the Jaycees. The justices acknowledged that freedom of association is a necessary component of the First Amendment, but that the right is neither absolute nor does it apply equally to all private organizations. The greatest degree of protection goes to small, intimate relationships, such as marriage and family, and to those organizations expressing sincerely held political or ideological messages. Large groups with nonideological or com-

26. In addition, the Court has invoked the relevance of association rights to the protection intimate human relationships (marriage, family, childbearing). We discuss these issues at length in Chapter 9.

mercial purposes and nonselective membership policies are less deserving. The Jaycees, according to Court, is a large, national organization, with no firm ideological views and membership selectivity based only on age and sex. As such, the group merited a level of First Amendment protection inferior to the state's interest in reducing arbitrary discrimination.

The Court in *Roberts* not only considered the nature of the organization itself, but also the relationship between the expressive activities of the group and the effect of the government regulation. Two important questions must be asked: Is the group an expressive organization that attempts to communicate its viewpoints either publicly or privately? And, does the state regulation significantly burden the expression of those viewpoints?

The scheme adopted in the Jaycees' case subsequently was applied in two similar disputes. First, in *Board of Directors of Rotary International v. Rotary Club of Duarte* (1987) the Court approved the enforcement of California's anti-discrimination laws against Rotary Club chapters that excluded women as regular members. And in *New York State Club Association v. City of New York* (1988) the justices upheld a New York ordinance that applied anti-discrimination regulations to organizations having more than four hundred members, providing regular meal service, and receiving payment from nonmembers for services or facilities for the furtherance of business interests. These decisions emphasized factors such as the size of the group, the commercial activities of the group, and the low level of selectivity exercised in conferring membership. Both decisions concluded that the application of the nondiscrimination law would not significantly burden the group's expressive activities.

Roberts, Rotary, and *New York State Club Association* were unanimous rulings, creating the impression that the law was relatively settled: freedom of association rights must give way to state interests in combating discrimination. This impression was weakened in 1995, however, when the justices decided *Hurley v. Irish-American Gay, Lesbian and Bisexual Group of Boston.* This dispute arose when a private association organizing a St. Patrick's Day parade in Boston rejected the application of a gay rights group to march in the celebration. The gay

rights group sued, claiming that its exclusion from the parade violated the Massachusetts anti-discrimination statute. The Supreme Court unanimously ruled in favor of the parade organizers. The justices held that the First Amendment is violated by a state law requiring private sponsors of a parade to include among the marchers a group imparting a message that the organizers do not wish to convey. The Court applied the principles set in *Roberts,* but came to quite a different result. Here the forced inclusion of the gay rights group was found to place a significant burden on the expression rights of the parade organizers.

This decision set the stage for the next major freedom of association dispute, *Boy Scouts of America v. Dale* (2000), a challenge to the dismissal of a scout leader on sexual orientation grounds. Would the Court find the facts in this case similar to the exclusion of women in *Roberts, Rotary,* and *New York State Club Association,* or would the justices conclude that the Boy Scouts' membership policies were protected by the First Amendment's freedom of association?

Boy Scouts of America v. Dale

530 U.S. — (2000)
supct.law.cornell.edu/supct/html/99-699.ZS.html
Vote: 5 (Kennedy, O'Connor, Rehnquist, Scalia, Thomas)
    4 (Breyer, Ginsburg, Souter, Stevens)
Opinion of the Court: Rehnquist
Dissenting opinions: Souter, Stevens

James Dale began his involvement in the Boy Scout organization in 1978, when, at the age of eight, he joined Cub Scout Pack 142 in Monmouth, New Jersey. He became a Boy Scout in 1981 and remained an active scout until he turned eighteen. Dale was an exemplary member of the organization, being admitted to the prestigious Order of the Arrow and achieving the rank of Eagle Scout, scouting's highest honor. In 1989 he became an adult member of the organization and was an assistant scoutmaster.

Around the same time, Dale left home to attend Rutgers University. At college, Dale first acknowledged to

The Boy Scouts revoked the adult membership of James Dale because of his admitted homosexuality. In *Boy Scouts of America v. Dale*, the Court determined that the organization had the right to exclude him.

himself and to others that he was gay. He joined and later became co-president of Rutgers University Gay/Lesbian Alliance. After attending a seminar devoted to gay/lesbian health issues in 1990, he was interviewed and photographed for a newspaper story. He discussed the need for gay teenagers to have appropriate role models.

Shortly after the publication of the newspaper article, Dale received a letter from the Monmouth Council revoking his adult membership in the Boy Scouts. When he requested a reason for this action, the Council informed him that the Scouts "specifically forbid membership to homosexuals." In 1992 Dale filed a complaint against the Boy Scouts claiming that the revocation of his membership violated a New Jersey law prohibiting discrimination based on sexual orientation in public accommodations. The Boy Scouts countered that as a private,

nonprofit organization it had the right under the freedom of association guarantees of the First Amendment to deny membership to individuals whose views are not consistent with the group's values. The New Jersey Supreme Court ruled in favor of Dale, and the Boy Scouts asked for review by the U.S. Supreme Court.

CHIEF JUSTICE REHNQUIST delivered the opinion of the Court.

In *Roberts v. United States Jaycees* (1984), we observed that "implicit in the right to engage in activities protected by the First Amendment" is "a corresponding right to associate with others in pursuit of a wide variety of political, social, economic, educational, religious, and cultural ends." This right is crucial in preventing the majority from imposing its views on groups that would rather express other, perhaps unpopular, ideas. Government actions that may unconstitutionally burden this freedom may take many forms, one of which is "intrusion into the internal structure or affairs of an association" like a "regulation that forces the group to accept members it does not desire." Forcing a group to accept certain members may impair the ability of the group to express those views, and only those views, that it intends to express. Thus, "[f]reedom of association . . . plainly presupposes a freedom not to associate."

The forced inclusion of an unwanted person in a group infringes the group's freedom of expressive association if the presence of that person affects in a significant way the group's ability to advocate public or private viewpoints. *New York State Club Assn., Inc. v. City of New York* (1988). But the freedom of expressive association, like many freedoms, is not absolute. We have held that the freedom could be overridden "by regulations adopted to serve compelling state interests, unrelated to the suppression of ideas, that cannot be achieved through means significantly less restrictive of associational freedoms." *Roberts.*

To determine whether a group is protected by the First Amendment's expressive associational right, we must determine whether the group engages in "expressive association." The First Amendment's protection of expressive association is not reserved for advocacy groups. But to come within its ambit, a group must engage in some form of expression, whether it be public or private. . . .

. . . [T]he general mission of the Boy Scouts is clear:

"[T]o instill values in young people." The Boy Scouts seeks to instill these values by having its adult leaders spend time with the youth members, instructing and engaging them in activities like camping, archery, and fishing. During the time spent with the youth members, the scoutmasters and assistant scoutmasters inculcate them with the Boy Scouts' values—both expressly and by example. It seems indisputable that an association that seeks to transmit such a system of values engages in expressive activity.

Given that the Boy Scouts engages in expressive activity, we must determine whether the forced inclusion of Dale as an assistant scoutmaster would significantly affect the Boy Scouts' ability to advocate public or private viewpoints. This inquiry necessarily requires us first to explore, to a limited extent, the nature of the Boy Scouts' view of homosexuality.

The values the Boy Scouts seeks to instill are "based on" those listed in the Scout Oath and Law. The Boy Scouts explains that the Scout Oath and Law provide "a positive moral code for living; they are a list of 'do's' rather than 'don'ts.'" The Boy Scouts asserts that homosexual conduct is inconsistent with the values embodied in the Scout Oath and Law, particularly with the values represented by the terms "morally straight" and "clean."

Obviously, the Scout Oath and Law do not expressly mention sexuality or sexual orientation. And the terms "morally straight" and "clean" are by no means self-defining. Different people would attribute to those terms very different meanings. For example, some people may believe that engaging in homosexual conduct is not at odds with being "morally straight" and "clean." And others may believe that engaging in homosexual conduct is contrary to being "morally straight" and "clean." The Boy Scouts says it falls within the latter category.

The New Jersey Supreme Court analyzed the Boy Scouts' beliefs and found that the "exclusion of members solely on the basis of their sexual orientation is inconsistent with Boy Scouts' commitment to a diverse and 'representative' membership . . . [and] contradicts Boy Scouts' overarching objective to reach 'all eligible youth.'" The court concluded that the exclusion of members like Dale "appears antithetical to the organization's goals and philosophy." But our cases reject this sort of inquiry; it is not the role of the courts to reject a group's expressed values because they disagree with those values or find them internally inconsistent.

The Boy Scouts asserts that it "teach[es] that homosexual conduct is not morally straight," and that it does "not want to promote homosexual conduct as a legitimate form of behavior." We accept the Boy Scouts' assertion. We need not inquire further to determine the nature of the Boy Scouts' expression with respect to homosexuality. But because the record before us contains written evidence of the Boy Scouts' viewpoint, we look to it as instructive, if only on the question of the sincerity of the professed beliefs.

A 1978 position statement to the Boy Scouts' Executive Committee . . . expresses the Boy Scouts' "official position" with regard to "homosexuality and Scouting":

". . . The Boy Scouts of America is a private, membership organization and leadership therein is a privilege and not a right. We do not believe that homosexuality and leadership in Scouting are appropriate. We will continue to select only those who in our judgment meet our standards and qualifications for leadership."

Thus, at least as of 1978—the year James Dale entered Scouting—the official position of the Boy Scouts was that avowed homosexuals were not to be Scout leaders.

A position statement promulgated by the Boy Scouts in 1991 (after Dale's membership was revoked but before this litigation was filed) also supports its current view:

"We believe that homosexual conduct is inconsistent with the requirement in the Scout Oath that a Scout be morally straight and in the Scout Law that a Scout be clean in word and deed, and that homosexuals do not provide a desirable role model for Scouts."

This position statement was redrafted numerous times but its core message remained consistent. . . .

. . . We cannot doubt that the Boy Scouts sincerely holds this view.

We must then determine whether Dale's presence as an assistant scoutmaster would significantly burden the Boy Scouts' desire to not "promote homosexual conduct as a legitimate form of behavior." As we give deference to an association's assertions regarding the nature of its expression, we must also give deference to an association's view of what would impair its expression. That is not to say that an expressive association can erect a shield against antidiscrimination laws simply by asserting that mere acceptance of a member from a particular group would impair its message. But here Dale, by his own admission, is one of a group of gay Scouts who have "become leaders in their community and are open and honest about their sexual orientation." Dale was the copresident of a gay and lesbian organization at college and remains a gay rights activist. Dale's presence in the Boy Scouts would, at the very least, force the organization to send a message, both to the youth members and the world, that the Boy Scouts accepts homosexual conduct as a legitimate form of behavior. . . .

The New Jersey Supreme Court determined that the Boy Scouts' ability to disseminate its message was not significantly affected by the forced inclusion of Dale as an assistant scoutmaster. . . .

We disagree with the New Jersey Supreme Court's conclusion. . . .

First, associations do not have to associate for the "purpose" of disseminating a certain message in order to be entitled to the protections of the First Amendment. An association must merely engage in expressive activity that could be impaired in order to be entitled to protection. . . .

Second, even if the Boy Scouts discourages Scout leaders from disseminating views on sexual issues—a fact that the Boy Scouts disputes with contrary evidence—the First Amendment protects the Boy Scouts' method of expression. If the Boy Scouts wishes Scout leaders to avoid questions of sexuality and teach only by example, this fact does not negate the sincerity of its belief discussed above.

Third, the First Amendment simply does not require that every member of a group agree on every issue in order for the group's policy to be "expressive association." The Boy Scouts takes an official position with respect to homosexual conduct, and that is sufficient for First Amendment purposes. . . . The fact that the organization does not trumpet its views from the housetops, or that it tolerates dissent within its ranks, does not mean that its views receive no First Amendment protection.

Having determined that the Boy Scouts is an expressive association and that the forced inclusion of Dale would significantly affect its expression, we inquire whether the application of New Jersey's public accommodations law to require that the Boy Scouts accept Dale as an assistant scoutmaster runs afoul of the Scouts' freedom of expressive association. We conclude that it does. . . .

. . . The state interests embodied in New Jersey's public accommodations law do not justify such a severe intrusion on the Boy Scouts' rights to freedom of expressive association. That being the case, we hold that the First Amendment prohibits the State from imposing such a requirement through the application of its public accommodations law. . . .

We are not, as we must not be, guided by our views of whether the Boy Scouts' teachings with respect to homosexual conduct are right or wrong; public or judicial disapproval of a tenet of an organization's expression does not justify the State's effort to compel the organization to accept members where such acceptance would derogate from the organization's expressive message. . . .

The judgment of the New Jersey Supreme Court is reversed, and the cause remanded for further proceedings not inconsistent with this opinion.

It is so ordered.

JUSTICE STEVENS, with whom JUSTICE SOUTER, JUSTICE GINSBURG, and JUSTICE BREYER join, dissenting.

The majority holds that New Jersey's law violates BSA's right to associate and its right to free speech. But that law does not "impos[e] any serious burdens" on BSA's "collective effort on behalf of [its] shared goals," *Roberts v. United States Jaycees* (1984), nor does it force BSA to communicate any message that it does not wish to endorse. New Jersey's law, therefore, abridges no constitutional right of the Boy Scouts. . . .

In this case, Boy Scouts of America contends that it teaches the young boys who are Scouts that homosexuality is immoral. Consequently, it argues, it would violate its right to associate to force it to admit homosexuals as members, as doing so would be at odds with its own shared goals and values. This contention, quite plainly, requires us to look at what, exactly, are the values that BSA actually teaches.

BSA's mission statement reads as follows: "It is the mission of the Boy Scouts of America to serve others by helping to instill values in young people and, in other ways, to prepare them to make ethical choices over their lifetime in achieving their full potential." . . . BSA describes itself as having a "representative membership," which it defines as "boy membership [that] reflects proportionately the characteristics of the boy population of its service area." In particular, the group emphasizes that "[n]either the charter nor the bylaws of the Boy Scouts of America permits the exclusion of any boy. . . . To meet these responsibilities we have made a commitment that our membership shall be representative of *all* the population in every community, district, and council.". . .

To bolster its claim that its shared goals include teaching that homosexuality is wrong, BSA directs our attention to two terms appearing in the Scout Oath and Law. The first is the phrase "morally straight," which appears in the Oath ("On my honor I will do my best . . . To keep myself . . . morally straight"); the second term is the word "clean," which appears in a list of 12 characteristics together comprising the Scout Law. . . .

It is plain as the light of day that neither one of these principles—"morally straight" and "clean"—says the slightest thing about homosexuality. Indeed, neither term in the Boy Scouts' Law and Oath expresses any position whatsoever on sexual matters.

BSA's published guidance on that topic underscores this point. Scouts, for example, are directed to receive their sex education at home or in school, but not from the organization: "Your parents or guardian or a sex education teacher should give you the facts about sex that you must know." To be sure, Scouts are not forbidden from asking their Scoutmaster about issues of a sexual nature, but Scoutmasters are, literally, the last person Scouts are encouraged to ask: "If you have questions about growing up, about relationships, sex, or making good decisions, ask. Talk with your parents, religious leaders, teachers, or Scoutmaster." Moreover, Scoutmasters are specifically directed to steer curious adolescents to other sources of information. . . .

In light of BSA's self-proclaimed ecumenism, furthermore, it is even more difficult to discern any shared goals or common moral stance on homosexuality. . . .

BSA's claim finds no support in our cases. We have recognized "a right to associate for the purpose of engaging in those activities protected by the First Amendment—speech, assembly, petition for the redress of grievances, and the exercise of religion." *Roberts.* And we have acknowledged that "when the State interferes with individuals' selection of those with whom they wish to join in a common endeavor, freedom of association . . . may be implicated." But "[t]he right to associate for expressive purposes is not . . . absolute"; rather, "the nature and degree of constitutional protection afforded freedom of association may vary depending on the extent to which . . . the constitutionally protected liberty is at stake in a given case." Indeed, the right to associate

does not mean "that in every setting in which individuals exercise some discrimination in choosing associates, their selective process of inclusion and exclusion is protected by the Constitution." *New York State Club Assn., Inc. v. City of New York* (1988). For example, we have routinely and easily rejected assertions of this right by expressive organizations with discriminatory membership policies, such as private schools, law firms, and labor organizations. In fact, until today, we have never once found a claimed right to associate in the selection of members to prevail in the face of a State's antidiscrimination law. To the contrary, we have squarely held that a State's antidiscrimination law does not violate a group's right to associate simply because the law conflicts with that group's exclusionary membership policy. . . .

. . . [T]he majority insists that we must "give deference to an association's assertions regarding the nature of its expression" and "we must also give deference to an association's view of what would impair its expression." . . .

This is an astounding view of the law. I am unaware of any previous instance in which our analysis of the scope of a constitutional right was determined by looking at what a litigant asserts in his or her brief and inquiring no further. . . . But the majority insists that our inquiry must be "limited" because "it is not the role of the courts to reject a group's expressed values because they disagree with those values or find them internally inconsistent."

But nothing in our cases calls for this Court to do any such thing. An organization can adopt the message of its choice, and it is not this Court's place to disagree with it. But we must inquire whether the group is, in fact, expressing a message (whatever it may be) and whether that message (if one is expressed) is significantly affected by a State's antidiscrimination law. More critically, that inquiry requires our *independent* analysis, rather than deference to a group's litigating posture. . . .

There is, of course, a valid concern that a court's independent review may run the risk of paying too little heed to an organization's sincerely held views. But unless one is prepared to turn the right to associate into a free pass out of antidiscrimination laws, an independent inquiry is a necessity. . . .

In this case, no such concern is warranted. It is entirely clear that BSA in fact expresses no clear, unequivocal message burdened by New Jersey's law. . . .

. . . . Over the years, BSA has generously welcomed over

87 million young Americans into its ranks. In 1992 over one million adults were active BSA members. The notion that an organization of that size and enormous prestige implicitly endorses the views that each of those adults may express in a non-Scouting context is simply mind boggling. . . .

Unfavorable opinions about homosexuals "have ancient roots." *Bowers v. Hardwick* (1986). . . .

That such prejudices are still prevalent and that they have caused serious and tangible harm to countless members of the class New Jersey seeks to protect are established matters of fact that neither the Boy Scouts nor the Court disputes. That harm can only be aggravated by the creation of a constitutional shield for a policy that is itself the product of a habitual way of thinking about strangers. As Justice Brandeis so wisely advised, "we must be ever on our guard, lest we erect our prejudices into legal principles."

If we would guide by the light of reason, we must let our minds be bold. I respectfully dissent.

Also in 2000 the Supreme Court handed down a second important freedom of association ruling. At issue in *California Democratic Party v. Jones* was California's blanket primary law, a statute that extended participation in party primary elections to all registered voters regardless of their political party affiliation. The justices struck down the law, holding that the statute forced political parties to associate with those who do not share their beliefs. *(See pages 763–766.)*

Emerging Issues: Regulation of the Internet

The development of the Internet and other forms of electronic expression has created an entirely new method of communication. What began in 1969 as a military project has grown into a vast international network of interconnected computers. Internet communication is instantaneous and interactive. Unlike radio, the electronic media can carry text, graphics, and sound. Unlike a television station, the Internet does not reside in a single location, but is a network of communicators not confined by state or national boundaries. Unlike the broadcast media, which is restricted by the number of frequencies available, the number of people who can communicate via the Internet may be infinite. And unlike many other forms of expression, electronic speech does not require

large expenditures for participation. These factors make electronic communication potentially the most effective and participatory method of expression yet devised. The Internet carries the promise of creating a truly robust, free marketplace of ideas.

But electronic expression also carries certain dangers. Readily available computers allow children access to materials that might be inappropriate for them. The potential for fraud and deception is perhaps even greater in electronic communication than in more traditional forms of expression. The ability to collect and catalogue huge amounts of data allows for invasions of privacy. Open access to the Internet means that there is no supervising authority to ensure the veracity of posted messages. Harassment based on sex, race, ethnicity, or sexual orientation can easily occur in an electronic world. Groups with political or social messages repugnant to the majority have an equal voice with mainstream organizations in spite of small numbers and minimal funds.

There is little doubt that confronting the Internet will provide significant challenges to government regulators at all levels. Congress has considered several pieces of legislation that respond to potential misuses of the Internet. The Clinton administration imposed administrative regulations to prohibit the publishing of certain encryption information in electronic form. The states also have been active in drafting legislation to limit Internet abuses. Initially, states passed laws banning individuals from sending indecent material on the Internet and barring the use of pseudonyms and anonymous communications. Although designed to curb undesirable activity, these laws may restrict legitimate and protected expression.

An indication of how the Court will respond to these questions came in the 1997 decision in *Reno v. American Civil Liberties Union*, a decision we discuss in length in Chapter 7. The justices struck down the first major federal regulation of the Internet, the Communications Decency Act of 1996, and in doing so indicated a willingness to extend significant First Amendment protection to electronic communications.

Reno v. ACLU certainly will not be the last decision on the regulation of the Internet. Federal and state governments continue to consider laws designed to place restrictions on electronic communications that may involve libel, fraud, obscenity, or other behaviors of legitimate government concern. But can such statutes be drafted and enforced in ways that do not violate the First Amendment? For legislators and judges alike the task will be difficult because the Internet is a form of communication unlike the others with which government has previously dealt.

READINGS

Bosmajian, Haig. *The Freedom Not To Speak.* New York: New York University Press, 1999.

Chafee, Zechariah, Jr. *Free Speech in the United States.* Cambridge: Harvard University Press, 1941.

Cleary, Edward J. *Beyond the Burning Cross: The First Amendment and the Landmark R.A.V. Case.* New York: Random House, 1994.

Cox, Archibald. *Freedom of Expression.* Cambridge: Harvard University Press, 1981.

Easton, Susan. *The Case for the Right to Silence,* 2d ed. Brookfield, Vt.: Ashgate Publishing Company, 1998.

Farber, Daniel A. *The First Amendment.* New York: Foundation Press, 1998.

Fish, Stanley. *There's No Such Thing as Free Speech, and It's a Good Thing, Too.* New York: Oxford University Press, 1994.

Goldstein, Robert Justin. *Burning The Flag: The Great 1989–1990 American Flag Desecration Controversy.* Kent, Ohio: Kent State University Press, 1996.

Graber, Mark A. *Transforming Free Speech.* Berkeley: University of California Press, 1991.

Heumann, Milton, Thomas Church, with David Redlawsk, eds. *Hate Speech on Campus: Cases, Case Studies and Commentary.* Boston: Northeastern University Press, 1997.

Ingelhart, Louis Edward, ed. *Press and Speech Freedoms In America, 1619–1995: A Chronology.* Westport, Conn.: Greenwood Press, 1997.

Johnson, John W. *The Struggle for Student Rights: Tinker v. Des Moines and the 1960s.* Lawrence: University Press of Kansas, 1997.

Levy, Leonard W. *Legacy of Suppression.* Cambridge: Harvard University Press, 1960.

MacKinnon, Catherine A. *Only Words.* Cambridge: Harvard University Press, 1993.

Rabban, David M. *Free Speech in Its Forgotten Years.* New York: Cambridge University Press, 1997.

Smolla, Rodney A. *Free Speech in an Open Society.* New York: Knopf, 1992.

Strum, Philippa. *When The Nazis Came To Skokie: Freedom For Speech We Hate.* Lawrence: University Press of Kansas, 1999.

Sunstein, Cass A. *Democracy and the Problem of Free Speech.* New York: Free Press, 1993.

Van Alstyne, William W. *Interpretations of the First Amendment.* Durham: Duke University Press, 1984.

Walker, Samuel. *Hate Speech: The History of an American Controversy.* Lincoln: University of Nebraska Press, 1994.

Washburn, Patrick S. *A Question of Sedition.* New York: Oxford University Press, 1986.

Wolfson, Nicholas. *Hate Speech, Sex Speech, Free Speech.* Westport, Conn.: Praeger Publishers, 1997.

CHAPTER 6
FREEDOM OF THE PRESS

FREEDOM OF THE PRESS is perhaps the most visible manifestation of Americans exercising their expression rights. Each day the print and broadcast media blanket the nation with news, commentaries, and entertainment from varied perspectives. Newsstands and bookstores flourish by offering periodicals and books devoted to every imaginable interest. Interactive media, such as talk radio, op-ed pages, and letters to the editor, allow citizens to become participants in the press rather than just consumers. The result is a robust exchange of information and opinion.

Much of what appears in the press is critical of government and government policies. Unlike the case in some other countries, those who criticize officials in the United States can do so without government censorship or fear of retaliation. They enjoy protection provided by the First Amendment's stipulation that "Congress shall make no law . . . abridging the freedom . . . of the press."

This constitutional provision reflects the Framers' strong commitment to the rights of the press. They saw the right to publish freely not only as important for its own sake, but also as a significant protection against the government denying other political and personal liberties. The press is the watchdog that sounds a warning when other rights are threatened. The Founders believed, for example, that the rights of speech and religion would be meaningless without a free press. Thomas Jefferson was so certain of this precept that in 1816 he proclaimed, "When the press is free, and every man is able to read, all is safe."

As British colonists, the Framers were well schooled in the values of a free press. But history also taught them that this right could not be taken for granted. England had controlled the press from the fifteenth through seventeenth centuries, and the government's repressive measures had become common law. Following the introduction of printing into England in the 1400s, Britain developed a licensing system under which nothing could be printed without prior approval from the government.[1] When these licensing laws expired in 1695, the right to publish materials free from censorship became recognized under common law. This led William Blackstone, the English jurist, to write: "The liberty of the press consists in laying no previous restraint upon publications and not in freedom from censure for criminal matter when published."[2]

Blackstone's words, while not fully embraced by the U.S. Supreme Court, convey a significant message about freedom of the press, which was understood by the Framers of the Constitution. They recognized that for a society to remain free, it must allow for the emergence of divergent views and opinions, which can be formed only through the open exchange of ideas. Without a free and uncensored press, government takes away a major mechanism (indeed, *the* major one during the eighteenth and nineteenth centuries) by which to accomplish that objec-

1. See Thomas I. Emerson, *The System of Freedom of Expression* (New York: Vintage Books, 1970), 504.
2. *Blackstone's Commentaries on the Laws of England*, vol. 4 (London, 1765–1769), 151–152.

tive, and the people know only what the government wants them to know. Under such circumstances, the press becomes an extension of government, not an independent observer, a check, or even a reliable source of information.

Why is this state of affairs so dangerous? Consider one of the most heinous regimes in the history of the world—Nazi Germany. How the Nazis came to power and carried out their deeds is still being debated, but certainly their ability to control the press and to use it as a propaganda tool is part of the explanation. The danger of government control of the press also can be seen closer to home. The Watergate scandal involved political manipulation and illegal behavior at the highest levels of government and led to the resignation of President Richard Nixon in 1974. We should remember that it was the press that first discovered the wrongdoing and brought it to light. If we allowed government to censor—to place prior restraints on—the press, the Watergate story would never have been published.

In the first part of this chapter, we examine the development of doctrine dealing with prior restraints. Does the Court today permit any censorship of the press, or is the press free to publish all the news it sees fit to print? But prior restraints are not the only limits government has tried to place on the press. In the second part of the chapter, we explore a less obvious constraint—government control of press content. Rather than question whether the government can completely prohibit the publication of certain items, these cases ask the Court to determine whether the government has any say in regulating the content of the items the press chooses to print. We conclude the chapter with a discussion of the special privileges claimed by the media. Reporters argue that they should enjoy a unique set of guarantees to perform their jobs. How has the Court reacted to these claims?

Taken together, these issues—prior restraint, government control of press content, and the special rights of reporters—form the heart of freedom of the press questions. But the Court's decisions also distinguish the type of "press" in question. In general, the justices have treated printed matter (newspapers, magazines, and books)

differently from the broadcast media (radio and television). Why? How have those differences manifested themselves? Are they justified?

PRIOR RESTRAINT

No concept is more important to understanding freedom of the press than prior restraint, which occurs when the government reviews material to determine whether publication will be allowed. It is government censorship and antithetical to freedom of the press. If the First Amendment means anything, it means that no government has the authority to decide what may be published. The government may punish press activity that violates legitimate criminal laws, but such government sanctions may take place only *after* publication, not before.

Establishing a Standard

The principle that prior restraint runs contrary to the Constitution was established in the formative case *Near v. Minnesota* (1931). The justices took a strong stance against censorship, but does their decision imply that the government may never block the publication of material it considers inappropriate or harmful? Are there exceptions to the constitutional prohibition against prior restraint? Consider these questions as you read Chief Justice Charles Evans Hughes's opinion in *Near*.

Near v. Minnesota

283 U.S. 697 (1931)
laws.findlaw.com/US/283/697.html
Vote: 5 (Brandeis, Holmes, Hughes, Roberts, Stone)
      4 (Butler, McReynolds, Sutherland, Van Devanter)
Opinion of the Court: Hughes
Dissenting opinion: Butler

A 1925 Minnesota law provided for "the abatement, as a public nuisance, of a 'malicious, scandalous, and defamatory newspaper, magazine, or other periodical.'" In the fall of 1927, a county attorney asked a state judge to issue a restraining order banning publication of the *Saturday Press*. In the attorney's view, the newspaper, partly owned by Jay Near, was the epitome of a mali-

The only known photograph of *Saturday Press* editor Jay Near appeared April 19, 1936, in the *Minneapolis Tribune*. Near's successful appeal to the Supreme Court in 1931 marked the first time the Court enforced the First Amendment's guarantee of freedom of the press to strike a state law that imposed a prior restraint on a newspaper.

cious, scandalous, and defamatory publication.[3] The *Saturday Press* committed itself to exposing corruption, bribery, gambling, and prostitution in Minneapolis, which Near often connected to Jews. It attacked specific city officials for being in league with gangsters and chided the established press for refusing to uncover the corruption. These attacks were colored by Near's racist, anti-Semitic attitudes. In one issue, Near wrote:

I simply state a fact when I say that ninety per cent of the crimes committed against society in this city are committed by Jew gangsters. . . . It is Jew, Jew, Jew, as long as one cares to comb over the records. I am launching no attack against the Jewish people AS A RACE. I am merely calling attention to a FACT. And if people of that race and faith wish to rid themselves of the odium and stigma THE RODENTS OF THEIR OWN RACE HAVE BROUGHT UPON THEM, they need only to step to the front and help the decent citizens of Minneapolis rid the city of these criminal Jews.

In a piece attacking establishment journalism, Near proclaimed: "Journalism today isn't prostituted so much as it is disgustingly flabby. I'd rather be a louse in the cotton shirt of a nigger than be a journalistic prostitute."

3. For an in-depth account of this case, see Fred W. Friendly, *Minnesota Rag* (New York: Random House, 1981). The quotes in this and the next paragraph come from this account.

Based on the paper's past record, a judge issued a temporary restraining order prohibiting the sale of printed and future editions. Believing that this action violated his rights, Near contacted the ACLU, which agreed to take his case. But he grew uncomfortable with the organization and instead obtained assistance from the publisher of the *Chicago Tribune*. Together, they challenged the Minnesota law as a violation of the First Amendment freedom of press guarantee, arguing that the law was tantamount to censorship. In their view, states could not place gag orders restraining newspapers from publishing in the future; newspapers could be punished only after publication through libel or defamation proceedings. The state's attorney thought otherwise, arguing that freedom of the press does not give publishers an unrestricted right to print anything and everything; instead, they must act responsibly.

MR. CHIEF JUSTICE HUGHES delivered the opinion of the Court.

[The Minnesota] statute, for the suppression as a public nuisance of a newspaper or periodical, is unusual, if not unique, and raises questions of grave importance transcending the local interests involved in the particular action. It is no longer open to doubt that the liberty of the press and of speech is within the liberty safeguarded by the due process clause of the Fourteenth Amendment from invasion by state action. It was found impossible to conclude that this essential personal liberty of the citizen was left unprotected by the general guaranty of fundamental rights of person and property. *Gitlow v. New York, Whitney v. California, Fiske v. Kansas.* In maintaining this guaranty, the authority of the state to enact laws to promote the health, safety, morals, and general welfare of its people is necessarily admitted. The limits of this sovereign power must always be determined with appropriate regard to the particular subject of its exercise. . . .

It is thus important to note precisely the purpose and effect of the statute as the state court has construed it.

First. The statute is not aimed at the redress of individual or private wrongs. Remedies for libel remain available and unaffected. . . . It is aimed at the distribution of scandalous matter as "detrimental to public morals and to the general welfare," tending "to disturb the peace of the community" and "to provoke assaults and the commission of crime." In order to obtain an injunction to suppress the future publication of the newspaper or periodical, it is not necessary to prove the falsity of the charges that have been made in the publication condemned. In the present action there was no allegation that the matter published was not true. It is alleged, and the statute requires the allegation that the publication was "malicious." But, as in prosecutions for libel, there is no requirement of proof by the state of malice in fact as distinguished from malice inferred from the mere publication of the defamatory matter. The judgment in this case proceeded upon the mere proof of publication. The statute permits the defense, not of the truth alone, but only that the truth was published with good motives and for justifiable ends. It is apparent that under the statute the publication is to be regarded as defamatory if it injures reputation, and that it is scandalous if it circulates charges of reprehensible conduct, whether criminal or otherwise, and the publication is thus deemed to invite public reprobation and to constitute a public scandal. . . .

Second. The statute is directed not simply at the circulation of scandalous and defamatory statements with regard to private citizens, but at the continued publication by newspapers and periodicals of charges against public officers of corruption, malfeasance in office, or serious neglect of duty. Such charges by their very nature create a public scandal. They are scandalous and defamatory within the meaning of the statute, which has its normal operation in relation to publications dealing prominently and chiefly with the alleged derelictions of public officers.

Third. The object of the statute is not punishment, in the ordinary sense, but suppression of the offending newspaper or periodical. The reason for the enactment, as the state court has said, is that prosecutions to enforce penal statutes for libel do not result in "efficient repression or suppression of the evils of scandal." Describing the business of publication as a public nuisance does not obscure the substance of the proceeding which the statute authorizes. It is the continued publication of scandalous and defamatory matter that constitutes the business and the declared nuisance. In the case of public officers, it is the reiteration of charges of official misconduct, and the fact that the newspaper or periodical is principally devoted to that purpose, that exposes it to suppression. . . .

This suppression is accomplished by enjoining publication, and that restraint is the object and effect of the statute.

Fourth. The statute not only operates to suppress the offending newspaper or periodical, but to put the publisher under an effective censorship. When a newspaper or periodical is found to be "malicious, scandalous and defamatory," and is suppressed as such, resumption of publication is punishable as a contempt of court by fine or imprisonment. Thus, where a newspaper or periodical has been suppressed because of the circulation of charges against public officers of official misconduct, it would seem to be clear that the renewal of the publication of such charges would constitute a contempt, and that the judgment would lay a permanent restraint upon the publisher, to escape which he must satisfy the court as to the character of a new publication. Whether he would be permitted again to publish matter deemed to be derogatory to the same or other public officers would depend upon the court's ruling. . . .

If we cut through mere details of procedure, the operation and effect of the statute in substance is that public authorities may bring the owner or publisher of a newspaper or periodical before a judge upon a charge of conducting a business of publishing scandalous and defamatory matter—in particular that the matter consists of charges against public officers of official dereliction—and, unless the owner or publisher is able and disposed to bring competent evidence to satisfy the judge that the charges are true and are published with good motives and for justifiable ends, his newspaper or periodical is suppressed and further publication is made punishable as a contempt. This is of the essence of censorship.

The question is whether a statute authorizing such proceedings in restraint of publication is consistent with the conception of the liberty of the press as historically conceived and guaranteed. In determining the extent of the constitutional protection, it has been generally, if not universally, considered that it is the chief purpose of the guaranty to prevent previous restraints upon publication. The struggle in England, directed against the legislative power of the licenser, resulted in renunciation of the censorship of the press. The liberty deemed to be established was thus described by Blackstone: "The liberty of the press is indeed essential to the nature of a free state; but this consists in laying no *previous* restraints upon publications, and not in freedom from censure for criminal matter when published.

Every freeman has an undoubted right to lay what sentiments he pleases before the public; to forbid this, is to destroy the freedom of the press; but if he publishes what is improper, mischievous or illegal, he must take the consequence of his own temerity." The distinction was early pointed out between the extent of the freedom with respect to censorship under our constitutional system and that enjoyed in England. Here, as Madison said, "the great and essential rights of the people are secured against legislative as well as against executive ambition. They are secured, not by laws paramount to prerogative, but by constitutions paramount to laws. This security of the freedom of the press requires that it should be exempt not only from previous restraint by the Executive, as in Great Britain, but from legislative restraint also.". . .

The criticism upon Blackstone's statement has not been because immunity from previous restraint upon publication has not been regarded as deserving of special emphasis, but chiefly because that immunity cannot be deemed to exhaust the conception of the liberty guaranteed by State and Federal Constitutions. The point of criticism has been "that the mere exemption from previous restraints cannot be all that is secured by the constitutional provisions," and that "the liberty of the press might be rendered a mockery and a delusion, and the phrase itself a by-word, if, while every man was at liberty to publish what he pleased, the public authorities might nevertheless punish him for harmless publications." But it is recognized that punishment for the abuse of the liberty accorded to the press is essential to the protection of the public, and that the common-law rules that subject the libeler to responsibility for the public offense, as well as for the private injury, are not abolished by the protection extended in our Constitutions. The law of criminal libel rests upon that secure foundation. There is also the conceded authority of courts to punish for contempt when publications directly tend to prevent the proper discharge of judicial functions. In the present case, we have no occasion to inquire as to the permissible scope of subsequent punishment. For whatever wrong the appellant has committed or may commit, by his publications, the state appropriately affords both public and private redress by its libel laws. As has been noted, the statute in question does not deal with punishments; it provides for no punishment, except in case of contempt for violation of the court's order, but for suppression and injunction—that is, for restraint upon publication.

The objection has also been made that the principle as to immunity from previous restraint is stated too broadly, if every such restraint is deemed to be prohibited. That is undoubtedly true; the protection even as to previous restraint is not absolutely unlimited. But the limitation has been recognized only in exceptional cases. "When a nation is at war many things that might be said in time of peace are such a hindrance to its effort that their utterance will not be endured so long as men fight and that no Court could regard them as protected by any constitutional right." No one would question but that a government might prevent actual obstruction to its recruiting service or the publication of the sailing dates of transports or the number and location of troops. On similar grounds, the primary requirements of decency may be enforced against obscene publications. The security of the community life may be protected against incitements to acts of violence and the overthrow by force of orderly government. The constitutional guaranty of free speech does not "protect a man from an injunction against uttering words that may have all the effect of force." These limitations are not applicable here. Nor are we now concerned with questions as to the extent of authority to prevent publications in order to protect private rights according to the principles governing the exercise of the jurisdiction of courts of equity.

The exceptional nature of its limitations places in a strong light the general conception that liberty of the press, historically considered and taken up by the Federal Constitution, has meant, principally although not exclusively, immunity from previous restraints or censorship. The conception of the liberty of the press in this country had broadened with the exigencies of the colonial period and with the efforts to secure freedom from oppressive administration. That liberty was especially cherished for the immunity it afforded from previous restraint of the publication of censure of public officers and charges of official misconduct. . . .

The fact that for approximately one hundred and fifty years there has been almost an entire absence of attempts to impose previous restraints upon publications relating to the malfeasance of public officers is significant of the deep-seated conviction that such restraints would violate constitutional right. Public officers, whose character and conduct remains open to debate and free discussion in the press, find their remedies for false accusations in actions under libel laws providing for redress and punishment, and not in proceedings to restrain the publication of newspapers and periodicals. The general principle that the constitutional guaranty of the liberty of the press gives immunity from previous restraints has been approved in many decisions under the provisions of state constitutions.

The importance of this immunity has not lessened. While reckless assaults upon public men, and efforts to bring obloquy upon those who are endeavoring faithfully to discharge official duties, exert a baleful influence and deserve the severest condemnation in public opinion, it cannot be said that this abuse is greater, and it is believed to be less, than that which characterized the period in which our institutions took shape. Meanwhile, the administration of government has become more complex, the opportunities for malfeasance and corruption have multiplied, crime has grown to most serious proportions, and the danger of its protection by unfaithful officials and of the impairment of the fundamental security of life and property by criminal alliances and official neglect, emphasizes the primary need of a vigilant and courageous press, especially in great cities. The fact that the liberty of the press may be abused by miscreant purveyors of scandal does not make any the less necessary the immunity of the press from previous restraint in dealing with official misconduct. Subsequent punishment for such abuses as may exist is the appropriate remedy, consistent with constitutional privilege.

In attempted justification of the statute, it is said that it deals not with publication per se, but with the "business" of publishing defamation. If, however, the publisher has a constitutional right to publish, without previous restraint, an edition of his newspaper charging official derelictions, it cannot be denied that he may publish subsequent editions for the same purpose. He does not lose his right by exercising it. If his right exists, it may be exercised in publishing nine editions, as in this case, as well as in one edition. If previous restraint is permissible, it may be imposed at once; indeed, the wrong may be as serious in one publication as in several. Characterizing the publication as a business, and the business as a nuisance, does not permit an invasion of the constitutional immunity against restraint. Similarly, it does not matter that the newspaper or periodical is found to be "largely" or "chiefly" devoted to the publication of such derelictions. If the publisher has a right, without previous restraint, to publish them, his right cannot be deemed to be dependent upon his publishing something else, more or less, with the matter to which objection is made.

Nor can it be said that the constitutional freedom from previous restraint is lost because charges are made of derelictions which constitute crimes. With the multiplying provisions of penal codes, and of municipal charters and ordinances carrying penal sanctions, the conduct of public officers is very largely within the purview of criminal statutes. The freedom of the press from previous restraint has never been regarded as limited to such animadversions as lay outside the range of penal enactments. Historically, there is no such limitation; it is inconsistent with the reason which underlies the privilege, as the privilege so limited would be of slight value for the purposes for which it came to be established.

The statute in question cannot be justified by reason of the fact that the publisher is permitted to show, before injunction issues, that the matter published is true and is published with good motives and for justifiable ends. If such a statute, authorizing suppression and injunction on such a basis, is constitutionally valid, it would be equally permissible for the Legislature to provide that at any time the publisher of any newspaper could be brought before a court, or even an administrative officer (as the constitutional protection may not be regarded as resting on mere procedural details), and required to produce proof of the truth of his publication, or of what he intended to publish and of his motives, or stand enjoined. If this can be done, the Legislature may provide machinery for determining in the complete exercise of its discretion what are justifiable ends and restrain publication accordingly. And it would be but a step to a complete system of censorship. The recognition of authority to impose previous restraint upon publication in order to protect the community against the circulation of charges of misconduct, and especially of official misconduct, necessarily would carry with it the admission of the authority of the censor against which the constitutional barrier was erected. The preliminary freedom, by virtue of the very reason for its existence, does not depend, as this court has said, on proof of truth.

Equally unavailing is the insistence that the statute is designed to prevent the circulation of scandal which tends to disturb the public peace and to provoke assaults and the commission of crime. Charges of reprehensible conduct, and in particular of official malfeasance, unquestionably create a public scandal, but the theory of the constitutional guaranty is that even a more serious public evil would be caused by authority to prevent publication. . . . There is nothing new in the fact that charges of reprehensible conduct may create resentment and the disposition to resort to violent means of redress, but this well-understood tendency did not alter the determination to protect the press against censorship and restraint upon publication. As was said in *New Yorker Staats-Zeitung v. Nolan,* "If the township may prevent the circulation of a newspaper for no reason other than that some of its inhabitants may violently disagree with it, and resent its circulation by resorting to physical violence, there is no limit to what may be prohibited." The danger of violent reactions becomes greater with effective organization of defiant groups resenting exposure, and, if this consideration warranted legislative interference with the initial freedom of publication, the constitutional protection would be reduced to a mere form of words.

For these reasons we hold the statute, so far as it authorized the proceedings in this action . . . , to be an infringement of the liberty of the press guaranteed by the Fourteenth Amendment. We should add that this decision rests upon the operation and effect of the statute, without regard to the question of the truth of the charges contained in the particular periodical. The fact that the public officers named in this case, and those associated with the charges of official dereliction, may be deemed to be impeccable, cannot affect the conclusion that the statute imposes an unconstitutional restraint upon publication.

Judgment reversed.

Chief Justice Hughes's opinion appears to take a definitive position against prior censorship. He wrote, "The statute not only seeks to suppress the offending newspaper . . . but to put the publisher under an effective censorship." But he acknowledged that the protection against "previous restraint is not absolutely unlimited." There may be exceptional circumstances under which government restraint is necessary. Hughes cited three vital interests that may justify government censorship: the protection of national security, the regulation of obscenity, and the prohibition of expression that would incite acts of violence. In the preceding chapter we discussed the Court's rulings on expression and violence, and we will be examining the question of obscenity in

Chapter 7. Here, we turn our attention to the national security exception and then to an exception that Hughes did not consider: the authority of educators to control the content of student publications.

Prior Restraint and National Security

In *Near,* Hughes explained that the government may legitimately prohibit the publication of certain material in times of war that it might not constitutionally regulate in times of peace. To see the Court's logic, suppose that during World War II a major newspaper received classified information about the coming Allied invasion of Normandy and announced that it would publish that information so the American people would be fully informed about the war effort. The military would understandably be concerned because publication would give the enemy advance knowledge of the military operation. Could the government take action to prohibit publication, or would it be confined only to pursuing criminal charges against the paper for illegal dissemination of classified documents after publication? According to *Near,* the courts would likely rule in favor of the government.

Fortunately, the United States rarely has faced a situation in which the press threatened to publish material that would seriously jeopardize vital national security interests. However, the national security issue has come before the Court, with *New York Times v. United States* (1971) providing the most important example.[4] In this case, the government attempted to stop the *New York Times* and the *Washington Post* from publishing classified documents pertaining to the Vietnam War.

New York Times v. United States

403 U.S. 713 (1971)
laws.findlaw.com/US/403/713.html
Vote: 6 (Black, Brennan, Douglas, Marshall, Stewart, White)
  3 (Blackmun, Burger, Harlan)
Per curiam opinion
Concurring opinions: Black, Brennan, Douglas, Marshall,
  Stewart, White
Dissenting opinions: Blackmun, Burger, Harlan

---

4. For oral arguments in this case, navigate to: *oyez.nwu.edu.*

In June 1971 two prominent newspapers, the *New York Times* and the *Washington Post*, began publishing articles based on two government documents: a 1965 Defense Department depiction of the Gulf of Tonkin incident and the 1968 "History of U.S. Decision-Making Process on Viet Nam Policy," a seven-thousand-page, forty-seven-volume study undertaken by the Pentagon. Known as the "Pentagon Papers," the documents constituted a history of U.S. involvement in the war in Indochina, a subject of acute interest in the early 1970s.

After the newspapers published several installments, the U.S. government brought a motion in federal district court asking the court to order the papers to refrain from publishing any more installments. The government argued that the articles would cause "irreparable injury" to the country's national security. To support this assertion, the government said that the entire 1968 study was top secret, a classification "applied only to that information or material the defense aspect of which is paramount, and the unauthorized disclosure of which could result in exceptionally grave damage to the Nation." The newspapers disagreed, arguing that the material was largely of historical, not current, interest, and that nothing in the documents related to a time period after 1968. As such, the government's attempt to enjoin publication amounted to nothing less than prior restraint.

Because the issues in this case were so important and the public controversy so intense, the judicial system responded to the dispute in a very unusual manner. The government had asked the district court to prohibit publication on June 15, 1971, and, because the lower courts handled the case in an expedited fashion, only nine days later the issue was before the Supreme Court. By then the justices had completed their work for the term and were about to go into their summer recess. To accommodate the case, the Court extended its session and heard arguments on June 26. Four days later, the Court issued a short "per curiam" opinion announcing that the majority rejected the government's demands. Then each of the justices submitted an opinion expressing his view. Six supported the newspapers, and three sided with the government.

Signaling a victory for the *Washington Post* and *New York Times,* the chief of presses at the *Post* holds the first edition of the paper announcing the Court's decision in *New York Times v. United States,* also known as the Pentagon Papers case, June 30, 1971.

PER CURIAM.

We granted certiorari in these cases in which the United States seeks to enjoin the New York Times and the Washington Post from publishing the contents of a classified study entitled "History of U.S. Decision-Making Process on Viet Nam Policy."

"Any system of prior restraints of expression comes to this Court bearing a heavy presumption against its constitutional validity." The Government "thus carries a heavy burden of showing justification for the imposition of such a restraint." The District Court for the Southern District of New York in the *New York Times* case held that the Government had not met that burden. We agree.

. . . The order of the Court of Appeals for the Second Circuit is reversed, and the case is remanded with directions to enter a judgment affirming the judgment of the District Court for the Southern District of New York. The stays entered . . . by the Court are vacated. The judgments shall issue forthwith.

MR. JUSTICE BLACK, with whom MR. JUSTICE DOUGLAS joins, concurring.

I adhere to the view that the Government's case against the Washington Post should have been dismissed and that the injunction against the New York Times should have been vacated without oral argument when the cases were first presented to this Court. I believe that every moment's continuance of the injunctions against these newspapers amounts to a flagrant, indefensible, and continuing violation of the First Amendment. . . . In my view it is unfortunate that some of my Brethren are apparently willing to hold that the publication of news may sometimes be enjoined. Such a holding would make a shambles of the First Amendment.

Our Government was launched in 1789 with the adoption of the Constitution. The Bill of Rights, including the First Amendment, followed in 1791. Now, for the first time in the 182 years since the founding of the Republic, the federal courts are asked to hold that the First Amendment does not mean what it says, but rather means that the Government can halt the publication of current news of vital importance to the people of this country.

In seeking injunctions against these newspapers and in its presentation to the Court, the Executive Branch seems to have forgotten the essential purpose and history of the First Amendment. When the Constitution was adopted, many people strongly opposed it because the document contained no Bill of Rights to safeguard certain basic freedoms. They especially feared that the new powers granted to a central government might be interpreted to permit the government to curtail freedom of religion, press, assembly, and speech. In response to an overwhelming public clamor, James Madison offered a series of amendments to satisfy citizens that these great liberties would remain safe and beyond the power of government to abridge. Madison proposed what later became the First Amendment in three parts, two of which are set out below, and one of which proclaimed: "The people shall not be deprived or abridged of their right to speak, to write, or to publish their sentiments; *and the freedom of the press, as one of the great bulwarks of liberty, shall be inviolable.*" The amendments were offered to curtail and restrict the general powers granted in the Executive, Legislative, and Judicial Branches two years before in the original Constitution. The Bill of Rights changed the original Constitution into a new charter under which no branch of government could abridge the people's freedoms of press, speech, religion, and assembly. Yet the Solicitor General argues and some members of the Court appear to agree that the general powers of the Government adopted in the original Constitution should be interpreted to limit and restrict the specific and emphatic guarantees of the Bill of Rights adopted later. I can imagine no greater perversion of history. Madison and the other Framers of the First Amendment, able men that they were, wrote in language they earnestly believed could never be misunderstood: "Congress shall make no law . . . abridging the freedom . . . of the press. . . ." Both the history and language of the First Amendment support the view that the press must be left free to publish news, whatever the source, without censorship, injunctions, or prior restraints.

In the First Amendment the Founding Fathers gave the free press the protection it must have to fulfill its essential role in our democracy. The press was to serve the governed, not the governors. The Government's power to censor the press was abolished so that the press would remain forever free to censure the Government. The press was protected so that it could bare the secrets of government and inform the people. Only a free and unrestrained press can effectively expose deception in government. And paramount among the responsibilities of a free press is the duty to prevent any part of the government from deceiving the people and sending them off to distant lands to die of foreign fevers and foreign shot and shell. In my view, far from deserving condemnation for their courageous reporting, the New York Times, the Washington Post, and other newspapers should be commended for serving the purpose that the Founding Fathers saw so clearly. In revealing the workings of government that led to the Vietnam war, the newspapers nobly did precisely that which the Founders hoped and trusted they would do.

The Government's case here is based on premises entirely different from those that guided the Framers of the First Amendment. . . .

[T]he Government argues in its brief that in spite of the First Amendment, "[t]he authority of the Executive Department to protect the nation against publication of information whose disclosure would endanger the national security stems from two interrelated sources: the constitutional power of the President over the conduct of foreign affairs and his authority as Commander-in-Chief."

In other words, we are asked to hold that despite the

First Amendment's emphatic command, the Executive Branch, the Congress, and the Judiciary can make laws enjoining publication of current news and abridging freedom of the press in the name of "national security." The Government does not even attempt to rely on any act of Congress. Instead, it makes the bold and dangerously far-reaching contention that the courts should take it upon themselves to "make" a law abridging freedom of the press in the name of equity, presidential power and national security, even when the representatives of the people in Congress have adhered to the command of the First Amendment and refused to make such a law. To find that the President has "inherent power" to halt the publication of news by resort to the courts would wipe out the First Amendment and destroy the fundamental liberty and security of the very people the Government hopes to make "secure." No one can read the history of the adoption of the First Amendment without being convinced beyond any doubt that it was injunctions like those sought here that Madison and his collaborators intended to outlaw in this Nation for all time.

The word "security" is a broad, vague generality whose contours should not be invoked to abrogate the fundamental law embodied in the First Amendment. The guarding of military and diplomatic secrets at the expense of informed representative government provides no real security for our Republic. The Framers of the First Amendment, fully aware of both the need to defend a new nation and the abuses of the English and Colonial Governments, sought to give this new society strength and security by providing that freedom of speech, press, religion, and assembly should not be abridged.

MR. JUSTICE DOUGLAS, with whom MR. JUSTICE BLACK joins, concurring.

While I join the opinion of the Court I believe it necessary to express my views more fully.

It should be noted at the outset that the First Amendment provides that "Congress shall make no law . . . abridging the freedom of speech, or of the press." That leaves, in my view, no room for governmental restraint on the press. . . .

The dominant purpose of the First Amendment was to prohibit the widespread practice of governmental suppression of embarrassing information. It is common knowledge that the First Amendment was adopted against the widespread use of the common law of seditious libel to punish the dissemination of material that is embarrassing to the powers-that-be. The present cases will, I think, go down in history as the most dramatic illustration of that principle. A debate of large proportions goes on in the Nation over our posture in Vietnam. That debate antedated the disclosure of the contents of the present documents. The latter are highly relevant to the debate in progress.

Secrecy in government is fundamentally anti-democratic, perpetuating bureaucratic errors. Open debate and discussion of public issues are vital to our national health. On public questions there should be "uninhibited, robust, and wide-open" debate.

MR. JUSTICE BRENNAN, concurring.

I write separately in these cases only to emphasize what should be apparent, that our judgments in the present cases may not be taken to indicate the propriety, in the future, of issuing temporary stays and restraining orders to block the publication of material sought to be suppressed by the Government. So far as I can determine, never before has the United States sought to enjoin a newspaper from publishing information in its possession. The relative novelty of the questions presented, the necessary haste with which decisions were reached, the magnitude of the interests asserted, and the fact that all the parties have concentrated their arguments upon the question whether permanent restraints were proper may have justified at least some of the restraints heretofore imposed in these cases. Certainly it is difficult to fault the several courts below for seeking to assure that the issues here involved were preserved for ultimate review by this Court. But even if it be assumed that some of the interim restraints were proper in the two cases before us, that assumption has no bearing upon the propriety of similar judicial action in the future. To begin with, there has now been ample time for reflection and judgment; whatever values there may be in the preservation of novel questions for appellate review may not support any restraints in the future. More important, the First Amendment stands as an absolute bar to the imposition of judicial restraints in circumstances of the kind presented by these cases. . . .

The entire thrust of the Government's claim throughout

these cases has been that publication of the material sought to be enjoined "could," or "might," or "may" prejudice the national interest in various ways. But the First Amendment tolerates absolutely no prior judicial restraints of the press predicated upon surmise or conjecture that untoward consequences may result. Our cases, it is true, have indicated that there is a single, extremely narrow class of cases in which the First Amendment's ban on prior judicial restraint may be overridden. Our cases have thus far indicated that such cases may arise only when the Nation "is at war," during which times "[n]o one would question but that a government might prevent actual obstruction to its recruiting service or the publication of the sailing dates of transports or the number and location of troops." Even if the present world situation were assumed to be tantamount to a time of war, or if the power of presently available armaments would justify even in peacetime the suppression of information that would set in motion a nuclear holocaust, in neither of these actions has the Government presented or even alleged that publication of items from or based upon the material at issue would cause the happening of an event of that nature. "[T]he chief purpose of [the First Amendment's] guaranty [is] to prevent previous restraints upon publication." Thus, only governmental allegation and proof that publication must inevitably, directly, and immediately cause the occurrence of an event kindred to imperiling the safety of a transport already at sea can support even the issuance of an interim restraining order. In no event may mere conclusions be sufficient: for if the Executive Branch seeks judicial aid in preventing publication, it must inevitably submit the basis upon which that aid is sought to scrutiny by the judiciary. And therefore, every restraint issued in this case, whatever its form, has violated the First Amendment—and not less so because that restraint was justified as necessary to afford the courts an opportunity to examine the claim more thoroughly. Unless and until the Government has clearly made out its case, the First Amendment commands that no injunction may issue.

MR. JUSTICE STEWART, with whom MR. JUSTICE WHITE joins, concurring.

In the governmental structure created by our Constitution, the Executive is endowed with enormous power in the two related areas of national defense and international relations. This power, largely unchecked by the Legislative and Judicial branches, has been pressed to the very hilt since the advent of the nuclear missile age. For better or for worse, the simple fact is that a President of the United States possesses vastly greater constitutional independence in these two vital areas of power than does, say, a prime minister of a country with a parliamentary form of government.

In the absence of the governmental checks and balances present in other areas of our national life, the only effective restraint upon executive policy and power in the areas of national defense and international affairs may lie in an enlightened citizenry—in an informed and critical public opinion which alone can here protect the values of democratic government. For this reason, it is perhaps here that a press that is alert, aware, and free most vitally serves the basic purpose of the First Amendment. For without an informed and free press there cannot be an enlightened people.

Yet it is elementary that the successful conduct of international diplomacy and the maintenance of an effective national defense require both confidentiality and secrecy. Other nations can hardly deal with this Nation in an atmosphere of mutual trust unless they can be assured that their confidences will be kept. And within our own executive departments, the development of considered and intelligent international policies would be impossible if those charged with their formulation could not communicate with each other freely, frankly, and in confidence. In the area of basic national defense the frequent need for absolute secrecy is, of course, self-evident.

I think there can be but one answer to this dilemma, if dilemma it be. The responsibility must be where the power is. If the Constitution gives the Executive a large degree of unshared power in the conduct of foreign affairs and the maintenance of our national defense, then under the Constitution the Executive must have the largely unshared duty to determine and preserve the degree of internal security necessary to exercise that power successfully. It is an awesome responsibility, requiring judgment and wisdom of a high order. I should suppose that moral, political, and practical considerations would dictate that a very first principle of that wisdom would be an insistence upon avoiding secrecy for its own sake. For when everything is classified, then nothing is classified, and the system becomes one to be disregarded by the cynical or the careless, and to be manipulated by those intent on self-protection or self-promotion. I should suppose, in short, that the hallmark of a truly effective internal security system would be the maximum possible disclosure, recognizing that secrecy can best be preserved only when credibility is truly maintained. But be that as it may, it is clear to me that it is the constitutional duty of the Executive—as a matter of sovereign prerogative and not as a matter of law as the courts know law—through the promulgation and enforcement of executive regulations, to protect the confidentiality necessary to carry out its responsibilities in the fields of international relations and national defense.

This is not to say that Congress and the courts have no role to play. Undoubtedly Congress has the power to enact specific and appropriate criminal laws to protect government property and preserve government secrets. Congress has passed such laws, and several of them are of very colorable relevance to the apparent circumstances of these cases. And if a criminal prosecution is instituted, it will be the responsibility of the courts to decide the applicability of the criminal law under which the charge is brought. Moreover, if Congress should pass a specific law authorizing civil proceedings in this field, the courts would likewise have the duty to decide the constitutionality of such a law as well as its applicability to the facts proved.

But in the cases before us we are asked neither to construe specific regulations nor to apply specific laws. We are asked, instead, to perform a function that the Constitution gave to the Executive, not the Judiciary. We are asked, quite simply, to prevent the publication by two newspapers of material that the Executive Branch insists should not, in the national interest, be published. I am convinced that the Executive is correct with respect to some of the documents involved. But I cannot say that disclosure of any of them will surely result in direct, immediate, and irreparable damage to our Nation or its people. That being so, there can under the First Amendment be but one judicial resolution of the issues before us. I join the judgments of the Court.

MR. JUSTICE WHITE, with whom MR. JUSTICE STEWART joins, concurring.

I concur in today's judgments, but only because of the concededly extraordinary protection against prior restraints enjoyed by the press under our constitutional system. I do not say that in no circumstances would the First Amendment permit an injunction against publishing information about government plans or operations. Nor, after examining the materials the Government characterizes as the most sensitive and destructive, can I deny that revelation of these documents will do substantial damage to public interests. Indeed, I am confident that their disclosure will have that result. But I nevertheless agree that the United States has not satisfied the very heavy burden that it must meet to warrant an injunction against publication in these cases, at least in the absence of express and appropriately limited congressional authorization for prior restraints in circumstances such as these.

The Government's position is simply stated: The responsibility of the Executive for the conduct of the foreign affairs and for the security of the nation is so basic that the President is entitled to an injunction against publication of a newspaper story whenever he can convince a court that the information to be revealed threatens "grave and irreparable" injury to the public interest; and the injunction should issue whether or not the material to be published is classified, whether or not publication would be lawful under relevant criminal statutes enacted by Congress, and regardless of the circumstances by which the newspaper came into possession of the information.

At least in the absence of legislation by Congress, based on its own investigations and findings, I am quite unable to agree that the inherent powers of the Executive and the courts reach so far as to authorize remedies having such sweeping potential for inhibiting publications by the press. Much of the difficulty inheres in the "grave and irreparable danger" standard suggested by the United States. If the United States were to have judgment under such a standard in these cases, our decision would be of little guidance to other courts in other cases, for the material at issue here would not be available from the Court's opinion or from public records, nor would it be published by the press. Indeed, even today where we hold that the United States has not met its burden, the material remains sealed in court records and it is properly not discussed in today's opinions. Moreover, because the material poses substantial dangers to national interests and because of the hazards of criminal sanctions, a responsible press may choose never to publish the more sensitive materials. To sustain the Government in these cases would start the courts down a long and hazardous road that I am not willing to travel, at least without congressional guidance and direction.

It is not easy to reject the proposition urged by the

United States and to deny relief on its good-faith claims in these cases that publication will work serious damage to the country. But that discomfiture is considerably dispelled by the infrequency of prior-restraint cases. Normally, publication will occur and the damage be done before the Government has either opportunity or grounds for suppression. So here, publication has already begun and a substantial part of the threatened damage has already occurred. The fact of a massive breakdown in security is known, access to the documents by many unauthorized people is undeniable, and the efficacy of equitable relief against these or other newspapers to avert anticipated damage is doubtful at best.

MR. JUSTICE MARSHALL, concurring.

The Government contends that the only issue in these cases is whether, in a suit by the United States, "the First Amendment bars a court from prohibiting a newspaper from publishing material whose disclosure would pose a 'grave and immediate danger to the security of the United States.'" With all due respect, I believe the ultimate issue in this case is even more basic than the one posed by the Solicitor General. The issue is whether this Court or the Congress has the power to make law.

In these cases there is no problem concerning the President's power to classify information as "secret" or "top secret." Congress has specifically recognized Presidential authority . . . to classify documents and information. Nor is there any issue here regarding the President's power as Chief Executive and Commander in Chief to protect national security by disciplining employees who disclose information and by taking precautions to prevent leaks.

The problem here is whether in these particular cases the Executive Branch has authority to invoke the equity jurisdiction of the courts to protect what it believes to be the national interest. The Government argues that in addition to the inherent power of any government to protect itself, the President's power to conduct foreign affairs and his position as Commander in Chief give him authority to impose censorship on the press to protect his ability to deal effectively with foreign nations and to conduct the military affairs of the country. Of course, it is beyond cavil that the President has broad powers by virtue of his primary responsibility for the conduct of our foreign affairs and his position as Commander in Chief. And in some situations it may be that under whatever inherent powers the Government

may have, as well as the implicit authority derived from the President's mandate to conduct foreign affairs and to act as Commander in Chief, there is a basis for the invocation of the equity jurisdiction of this Court as an aid to prevent the publication of material damaging to "national security," however that term may be defined.

It would, however, be utterly inconsistent with the concept of separation of powers for this Court to use its power of contempt to prevent behavior that Congress has specifically declined to prohibit. There would be a similar damage to the basic concept of these co-equal branches of Government if when the Executive Branch has adequate authority granted by Congress to protect "national security" it can choose instead to invoke the contempt power of a court to enjoin the threatened conduct. The Constitution provides that Congress shall make laws, the President execute laws, and courts interpret laws. It did not provide for government by injunction in which the courts and the Executive Branch can "make law" without regard to the action of Congress. It may be more convenient for the Executive Branch if it need only convince a judge to prohibit conduct rather than ask the Congress to pass a law, and it may be more convenient to enforce a contempt order than to seek a criminal conviction in a jury trial. Moreover, it may be considered politically wise to get a court to share the responsibility for arresting those who the Executive Branch has probable cause to believe are violating the law. But convenience and political considerations of the moment do not justify a basic departure from the principles of our system of government.

MR. CHIEF JUSTICE BURGER, dissenting.

So clear are the constitutional limitations on prior restraint against expression, that from the time of *Near v. Minnesota* we have had little occasion to be concerned with cases involving prior restraints against news reporting on matters of public interest. There is, therefore, little variation among the members of the Court in terms of resistance to prior restraints against publication. Adherence to this basic constitutional principle, however, does not make these cases simple ones. In these cases, the imperative of a free and unfettered press comes into collision with another imperative, the effective functioning of a complex modern government and specifically the effective exercise of certain constitutional powers of the Executive. Only those who view the First Amendment as an absolute in all circumstances—a view I respect, but reject—can find such cases as these to be simple or easy.

These cases are not simple for another and more immediate reason. We do not know the facts of the cases. No District Judge knew all the facts. No Court of Appeals Judge knew all the facts. No member of this Court knows all the facts.

Why are we in this posture, in which only those judges to whom the First Amendment is absolute and permits of no restraint in any circumstances or for any reason, are really in a position to act?

I suggest we are in this posture because these cases have been conducted in unseemly haste. . . . The prompt settling of these cases reflects our universal abhorrence of prior restraint. But prompt judicial action does not mean unjudicial haste.

Here, moreover, the frenetic haste is due in large part to the manner in which the Times proceeded from the date it obtained the purloined documents. It seems reasonably clear now that the haste precluded reasonable and deliberate judicial treatment of these cases and was not warranted. The precipitate action of this Court aborting trials not yet completed is not the kind of judicial conduct that ought to attend the disposition of a great issue.

MR. JUSTICE HARLAN, with whom THE CHIEF JUSTICE and MR. JUSTICE BLACKMUN join, dissenting.

With all respect, I consider that the Court has been almost irresponsibly feverish in dealing with these cases.

Both the Court of Appeals for the Second Circuit and the Court of Appeals for the District of Columbia Circuit rendered judgment on June 23. The New York Times' petition for certiorari, its motion for accelerated consideration thereof, and its application for interim relief were filed in this Court on June 24 at about 11 A.M. The application of the United States for interim relief in the Post case was also filed here on June 24 at about 7:15 P.M. This Court's order setting a hearing before us on June 26 at 11 A.M., a course which I joined only to avoid the possibility of an even more peremptory action by the Court, was issued less than 24 hours before. The record in the Post case was filed with the Clerk shortly before 1 P.M. on June 25; the record in the Times case did not arrive until 7 or 8 o'clock that same night. The briefs of the parties were received less than two hours before argument on June 26.

This frenzied train of events took place in the name of the presumption against prior restraints created by the First Amendment. Due regard for the extraordinarily important and difficult questions involved in these litigations should have led the Court to shun such a precipitate timetable. In order to decide the merits of these cases properly, some or all of the following questions should have been faced:

1. Whether the Attorney General is authorized to bring these suits in the name of the United States.

2. Whether the First Amendment permits the federal courts to enjoin publication of stories which would present a serious threat to national security.

3. Whether the threat to publish highly secret documents is of itself a sufficient implication of national security to justify an injunction on the theory that regardless of the contents of the documents harm enough results simply from the demonstration of such a breach of secrecy.

4. Whether the unauthorized disclosure of any of these particular documents would seriously impair the national security.

5. What weight should be given to the opinion of high officers in the Executive Branch of the Government with respect to questions 3 and 4.

6. Whether the newspapers are entitled to retain and use the documents notwithstanding the seemingly uncontested facts that the documents, or the originals of which they are duplicates, were purloined from the Government's possession and that the newspapers received them with knowledge that they had been feloniously acquired.

7. Whether the threatened harm to the national security or the Government's possessory interest in the documents justifies the issuance of an injunction against publication in light of—

a. The strong First Amendment policy against prior restraints on publication;

b. The doctrine against enjoining conduct in violation of criminal statutes; and

c. The extent to which the materials at issue have apparently already been otherwise disseminated.

These are difficult questions of fact, of law, and of judgment; the potential consequences of erroneous decision are enormous. The time which has been available to us, to the lower courts, and to the parties has been wholly inadequate for giving these cases the kind of consideration they deserve. It is a reflection on the stability of the judicial process that these great issues—as important as any that have arisen during my time on the Court—should have been decided under the pressures engendered by the torrent of publicity that has attended these litigations from their inception.

Forced as I am to reach the merits of these cases, I dissent from the opinion and judgments of the Court. Within the severe limitations imposed by the time constraints under which I have been required to operate, I can only state my reasons in telescoped form, even though in different circumstances I would have felt constrained to deal with the cases in the fuller sweep indicated above.

It is a sufficient basis for affirming the Court of Appeals for the Second Circuit in the Times litigation to observe that its order must rest on the conclusion that because of the time elements the Government had not been given an adequate opportunity to present its case to the District Court. At the least this conclusion was not an abuse of discretion.

In the Post litigation the Government had more time to prepare; this was apparently the basis for the refusal of the Court of Appeals for the District of Columbia Circuit on rehearing to conform its judgment to that of the Second Circuit. But I think there is another and more fundamental reason why this judgment cannot stand—a reason which also furnishes an additional ground for not reinstating the judgment of the District Court in the Times litigation, set aside by the Court of Appeals. It is plain to me that the scope of the judicial function in passing upon the activities of the Executive Branch of the Government in the field of foreign affairs is very narrowly restricted. This view is, I think, dictated by the concept of separation of powers upon which our constitutional system rests.

In a speech on the floor of the House of Representatives, Chief Justice John Marshall, then a member of that body, stated:

"The President is the sole organ of the nation in its external relations, and its sole representative with foreign nations."

From that time, shortly after the founding of the Nation, to this, there has been no substantial challenge to this description of the scope of executive power.

From this constitutional primacy in the field of foreign affairs, it seems to me that certain conclusions necessarily follow. Some of these were stated concisely by President Washington, declining the request of the House of Representatives for the papers leading up to the negotiation of the Jay Treaty:

"The nature of foreign negotiations requires caution, and their success must often depend on secrecy; and even when brought to a conclusion, a full disclosure of all the measures, demands, or eventual concessions which may have been proposed or contemplated would be extremely impolitic; for this might have a pernicious influence on future negotiations, or produce immediate inconveniences, perhaps danger and mischief, in relation to other powers."

The power to evaluate the "pernicious influence" of premature disclosure is not, however, lodged in the Executive alone. I agree that, in performance of its duty to protect the values of the First Amendment against political pressures, the judiciary must review the initial Executive determination to the point of satisfying itself that the subject matter of the dispute does lie within the proper compass of the President's foreign relations power. . . .

But in my judgment the judiciary may not properly go beyond these . . . inquiries and redetermine for itself the probable impact of disclosure on the national security.

Even if there is some room for the judiciary to override the executive determination, it is plain that the scope of review must be exceedingly narrow. I can see no indication in the opinions of either the District Court or the Court of Appeals in the Post litigation that the conclusions of the Executive were given even the deference owing to an administrative agency, much less that owing to a co-equal branch of the Government operating within the field of its constitutional prerogative.

Accordingly, I would vacate the judgment of the Court of Appeals for the District of Columbia Circuit on this ground and remand the case for further proceedings in the District Court.

MR. JUSTICE BLACKMUN, dissenting.

The First Amendment . . . is only one part of an entire Constitution. Article II of the great document vests in the Executive Branch primary power over the conduct of foreign affairs, and places in that branch the responsibility for the Nation's safety. Each provision of the Constitution is important, and I cannot subscribe to a doctrine of unlimited absolutism for the First Amendment at the cost of downgrading other provisions. First Amendment absolutism has never commanded a majority of this Court. See, for example, *Near v. Minnesota*. What is needed here is a weighing, upon properly developed standards, of the broad right of the press to print and of the very narrow right of the Government to prevent. Such standards are not yet developed.

From start to finish, it took the federal judiciary only two weeks to decide this major constitutional dispute, but legal scholars continue to debate *New York Times*. Some suggest that it was the Court's, or at least the individual justices', strongest statement to date on freedom of the press, that the justices virtually eradicated Hughes's national security exception to prior restraint. These observers say that the justices were telling the government that there are few—if any—compelling reasons to justify government censorship of the press. Others disagree, noting that while the result may have been clear, the individual opinions were not a resounding defense of the free press guarantee because the justices were divided in their views. Compare, for example, White's opinion with Black's; one could hardly imagine greater divergence of thought while still voting for the same outcome.

Since *New York Times* the Court has not had another important case dealing with prior restraints and national security concerns. But in 1991, during the war with Iraq, the U.S. government placed many constraints on the media. Most reporting had to be cleared by a designated representative of the military. Although there were no serious legal challenges to these restrictions, how do you think the Rehnquist Court would have ruled if one had occurred?

Prior Restraint and the Student Press

Chief Justice Hughes's opinion in *Near*, as we have noted, articulated three possible exceptions to the general rule against government censorship of the press: protecting national security, regulating obscenity, and prohibiting expression that would incite acts of violence. The 1988 case of *Hazelwood School District v. Kuhlmeier* asked the Court to consider another exception: allowing school administrators to impose certain standards on public school newspapers.[5] As you read Justice White's

5. For oral arguments in this case, navigate to: *oyez.nwu.edu*.

opinion, ask yourself these questions. What importance do the justices place on the fact that the newspaper was run by students? Does the case have any implications beyond the student press? Is the decision an isolated exception, or does it significantly dilute the prior restraint doctrine that the justices have supported since *Near*?

Hazelwood School District v. Kuhlmeier

484 U.S. 260 (1988)
laws.findlaw.com/US/484/260.html
Vote: 5 (O'Connor, Rehnquist, Scalia, Stevens, White)
   3 (Blackmun, Brennan, Marshall)
Opinion of the Court: White
Dissenting opinion: Brennan

In May 1983 the editors of the *Spectrum*, Hazelwood East High School's newspaper, planned to publish articles on divorce and teenage pregnancy *(see Box 6-1)*. Principal Robert E. Reynolds decided to excise two pages because, in his view, "The students and families in the articles were described in such a way that the readers could tell who they were. When it became clear that [they] were going to tread on the right to privacy of students and their parents, I stepped in to stop the process."[6]

The *Spectrum* staff objected to the principal's decision. Believing it amounted to the same kind of prior censorship that the Court had condemned in *Near*, the student editors hired a lawyer and challenged it in court. A federal district court ruled for the principal, holding that no First Amendment violation had occurred. The court of appeals, however, reversed. In its view, the *Spectrum* was a public forum *(see page 327)* because it "was intended to be operated as a conduit for student viewpoint." Its status as a public forum, therefore, prevented the principal from censoring its contents except when, according to the Supreme Court's ruling in *Tinker v. Des Moines* (1969) *(see pages 247–251)*, "necessary to avoid material and substantial interference with school work or discipline . . . or the rights of others." The court could find no such evidence in the record.

6. Mark A. Uhlig, "From Hazelwood to the High Court," *New York Times Magazine*, September 13, 1987, 102.

BOX 6-1 CENSORED HIGH SCHOOL NEWSPAPER ARTICLE

The uncorrected page proof of part of one of the two stories censored from the May 13, 1983, issue of the Hazelwood East High School *Spectrum*. Student editors took their objections all the way to the Supreme Court.

Divorce's impact on kids may have lifelong effect

by Shari Gordon

In the United States one marriage ends for every two that begin. The North County percentage of divorce is three marriages end out of four marriages that start.

There are more than two central characters in the painful drama of divorce. Children of divorced parents, literally million os them, are torn by the end of their parents' marriage.

"In the beginning I thought I caused the problem, but now I realize it wasn't me."

What causes divorce? According to Mr. Ken Kerkhoff, social studies teacher some of the causes are:
- Poor dating habits that lead to marriage.
- Not enough variables in common.
- Lack f communication.
- Lack of desire or effort to make the relationship work.

Figures aren't the whole story. The fact is that divorce has a psychological and sociological change on the child.

One junior commented on how the divorce occurred, "My dad dian't make any money, so my mother divorced him."

"My father was an alcoholic and he always came home drunk and my mom really couldn't stand it any longer," said another junior.

Diana Herbert, freshman, said "My dad wasn't spending enough time with my mom, my sister and I. He was always out of town or out late playing cards with the guys. My parents always argued about everything."

"In the beginning I thought I caused the problem, but now I realize it wasn't me," added Diana.

"I was only five when my parents got divorced," said Susan Kiefer, junior. "I didn't quite understand what the divorce really meant until about the age of seven. I understood that divorce meant my mother and father wouldn't be together again."

"It stinks!" exclaimed Jill Viola, junior. "They can, afterwards, remarry and start their lives over again, but their kids will always be caught in between."

Out of the 25 students interviewe 17 f them have parents that have remarried.

The feelings of divorce affects the kids for the rest of their lives, according to Mr. Kerckhoff. The effects of divorce on the kids lead to the following:
- Higher not of absenteeism in school.
- Higher rate of trouble with school, officials and police.
- Higher rate of depression and insecurity.
- Run a higher risk of divorce themselves.

All of these are the latest findings in research on single parent homes.

JUSTICE WHITE delivered the opinion of the Court.

This case concerns the extent to which educators may exercise editorial control over the contents of a high school newspaper produced as part of the school's journalism curriculum. . . .

Students in the public schools do not "shed their constitutional rights to freedom of speech or expression at the schoolhouse gate." They cannot be punished merely for expressing their personal views on the school premises—whether "in the cafeteria, or on the playing field, or on the campus during the authorized hours"—unless school authorities have reason to believe that such expression will "substantially interfere with the work of the school or impinge upon the rights of other students."

We have nonetheless recognized that the First Amendment rights of students in the public schools "are not automatically coextensive with the rights of adults in other settings" and must be "applied in light of the special characteristics of the school environment." A school need not tolerate student speech that is inconsistent with its "basic educational mission," even though the government could not censor similar speech outside the school. Accordingly, we held in [Bethel School District No. 403 v.] Fraser [1986] that a student could be disciplined for having delivered a speech that was "sexually explicit" but not legally obscene at an official school assembly, because the school was entitled to "disassociate itself" from the speech in a manner that would demonstrate to others that such vulgarity is "wholly inconsistent with the 'fundamental values' of public school education." We thus recognized that "[t]he determination of what manner of speech in the classroom or in school assembly is inappropriate properly rests with the school board," rather than with the federal courts. It is in this context that respondents' First Amendment claims must be considered.

We deal first with the question whether Spectrum may appropriately be characterized as a forum for public expression. The public schools do not possess all of the attributes of streets, parks, and other traditional public forums that "time out of mind, have been used for purposes of assembly, communicating thoughts between citizens, and discussing public questions." Hence, school facilities may be deemed to be public forums only if school authorities have "by policy or by practice" opened those facilities "for indiscriminate use by the general public," or by some segment of the public, such as student organizations. If the facilities have instead been reserved for other intended purposes, "communicative or otherwise," then no public forum has been created, and school officials may impose reasonable restrictions on the speech of students, teachers, and other members of the school community. . . .

The evidence relied upon by the Court of Appeals in finding Spectrum to be a public forum, is equivocal, at best. For example, Board Policy 348.51, which stated in part that "[s]chool sponsored student publications will not restrict free expression or diverse viewpoints within the rules of responsible journalism," also stated that such publications were "developed within the adopted curriculum and its educational implications." One might reasonably infer from the full text of Policy 348.51 that school officials retained ultimate control over what constituted "responsible journalism" in a school-sponsored newspaper. Although the Statement of Policy published in the September 14, 1982, issue of Spectrum declared that "Spectrum, as a student-press publication, accepts all rights implied by the First Amendment," this statement, understood in the context of the paper's role in the school's curriculum, suggests, at most, that the administration will not interfere with the students' exercise of those First Amendment rights that attend the publication of a school-sponsored newspaper. It does not reflect an intent to expand those rights by converting a curricular newspaper into a public forum. . . . In sum, the evidence relied upon by the Court of Appeals fails to demonstrate the "clear intent to create a public forum" that existed in cases in which we found public forums to have been created. School officials did not evince either "by policy or by practice," any intent to open the pages of Spectrum to "indiscriminate use" by its student reporters and editors, or by the student body generally. Instead, they "reserve[d] the forum for its intended purpos[e]" as a supervised learning experience for journalism students. Accordingly, school officials were entitled to regulate the contents of Spectrum in any reasonable manner. It is this standard, rather than our decision in Tinker, that governs this case.

The question whether the First Amendment requires a school to tolerate particular student speech—the question that we addressed in Tinker [v. Des Moines, 1969]—is different from the question whether the First Amendment requires a school affirmatively to promote particular student speech. The former question addresses educators' ability to silence a student's personal expression that happens to occur on the school premises. The latter question concerns educators' authority over school-sponsored publications, theatrical productions, and other expressive activities that students, parents, and members of the public might reasonably perceive to bear the imprimatur of the school. These activities may fairly be characterized as part of the school curriculum, whether or not they occur in a traditional classroom setting, so long as they are supervised by faculty members and designed to impart particular knowledge or skills to student participants and audiences.

Educators are entitled to exercise greater control over this second form of student expression to assure that participants learn whatever lessons the activity is designed to teach, that readers or listeners are not exposed to material that may be inappropriate for their level of maturity, and that the views of the individual speakers are not erroneously attributed to the school. Hence, a school may in its capacity as publisher of a school newspaper or producer of a school play "disassociate itself" not only from speech that would "substantially interfere with [its] work . . . or impinge upon the rights of other students," but also from speech that is, for example, ungrammatical, poorly written, inadequately researched, biased or prejudiced, vulgar or profane, or unsuitable for immature audiences. A school must be able to set high standards for the student speech that is disseminated under its auspices—standards that may be higher than those demanded by some newspaper publishers or theatrical producers in the "real" world—and may refuse to disseminate student speech that does not meet those standards. In addition, a school must be able to take into account the emotional maturity of the intended audience in determining whether to disseminate student speech on potentially sensitive topics, which might range from the existence of Santa Claus in an elementary school setting to the particulars of teenage sexual activity in a high school setting. A school must also retain the authority to refuse to sponsor student speech that might reasonably be perceived to advocate drug or alcohol use, irresponsible sex, or conduct otherwise inconsistent with "the shared values of a civilized social order" or to associate the school with any position other than neutrality on matters of political controversy. Otherwise, the schools would be unduly constrained from fulfilling their role as "a principal instrument in awakening the child to cultural values, in preparing him for later

professional training, and in helping him to adjust normally to his environment."

Accordingly, we conclude that the standard articulated in *Tinker* for determining when a school may punish student expression need not also be the standard for determining when a school may refuse to lend its name and resources to the dissemination of student expression. Instead, we hold that educators do not offend the First Amendment by exercising editorial control over the style and content of student speech in school-sponsored expressive activities so long as their actions are reasonably related to legitimate pedagogical concerns.

This standard is consistent with our oft-expressed view that the education of the Nation's youth is primarily the responsibility of parents, teachers, and state and local school officials, and not of federal judges. It is only when the decision to censor a school-sponsored publication, theatrical production, or other vehicle of student expression has no valid educational purpose that the First Amendment is so "directly and sharply implicate[d]" as to require judicial intervention to protect students' constitutional rights.

We also conclude that Principal Reynolds acted reasonably in requiring the deletion from the May 13 issue of Spectrum of the pregnancy article, the divorce article, and the remaining articles that were to appear on the same pages of the newspaper.

The initial paragraph of the pregnancy article declared that "[a]ll names have been changed to keep the identity of these girls a secret." The principal concluded that the students' anonymity was not adequately protected, however, given the other identifying information in the article and the small number of pregnant students at the school. Indeed, a teacher at the school credibly testified that she could positively identify at least one of the girls and possibly all three. It is likely that many students at Hazelwood East would have been at least as successful in identifying the girls. Reynolds therefore could reasonably have feared that the article violated whatever pledge of anonymity had been given to the pregnant students. In addition, he could reasonably have been concerned that the article was not sufficiently sensitive to the privacy interests of the students' boyfriends and parents, who were discussed in the article but who were given no opportunity to consent to its publication or to offer a response. The article did not contain graphic accounts of sexual activity. The girls did comment in the article, however, concerning their sexual histories and their use or nonuse of birth control. It was not unreasonable for the principal to have concluded that such frank talk was inappropriate in a school-sponsored publication distributed to 14-year-old freshmen and presumably taken home to be read by students' even younger brothers and sisters.

The student who was quoted by name in the version of the divorce article seen by Principal Reynolds made comments sharply critical of her father. The principal could reasonably have concluded that an individual publicly identified as an inattentive parent—indeed, as one who chose "playing cards with the guys" over home and family—was entitled to an opportunity to defend himself as a matter of journalistic fairness. These concerns were shared by both of Spectrum's faculty advisers for the 1982–1983 school year, who testified that they would not have allowed the article to be printed without deletion of the student's name. . . .

In sum, we cannot reject as unreasonable Principal Reynolds' conclusion that neither the pregnancy article nor the divorce article was suitable for publication in Spectrum. Reynolds could reasonably have concluded that the students who had written and edited these articles had not sufficiently mastered those portions of the Journalism II curriculum that pertained to the treatment of controversial issues and personal attacks, the need to protect the privacy of individuals whose most intimate concerns are to be revealed in the newspaper, and "the legal, moral, and ethical restrictions imposed upon journalists within a school community" that includes adolescent subjects and readers. Finally, we conclude that the principal's decision to delete two pages of Spectrum, rather than to delete only the offending articles or to require that they be modified, was reasonable under the circumstances as he understood them. Accordingly, no violation of First Amendment rights occurred.

The judgment of the Court of Appeals for the Eighth Circuit is therefore

Reversed.

JUSTICE BRENNAN, with whom JUSTICE MARSHALL and JUSTICE BLACKMUN join, dissenting.

When the young men and women of Hazelwood East High School registered for Journalism II, they expected a civics lesson. Spectrum, the newspaper they were to publish, "was not just a class exercise in which students learned to prepare papers and hone writing skills, it was a . . . forum established to give students an opportunity to express their views while gaining an appreciation of their rights and responsibilities under the First Amendment to the United States Constitution. . . ." [T]he student journalists published a Statement of Policy—tacitly approved each year by school authorities—announcing their expectation that "*Spectrum*, as a student-press publication, accepts all rights implied by the First Amendment. . . . Only speech that 'materially and substantially interferes with the requirements of appropriate discipline' can be found unacceptable and therefore prohibited." The school board itself affirmatively guaranteed the students of Journalism II an atmosphere conducive to fostering such an appreciation and exercising the full panoply of rights associated with a free student press. "School sponsored student publications," it vowed, "will not restrict free expression or diverse viewpoints within the rules of responsible journalism."

This case arose when the Hazelwood East administration breached its own promise, dashing its students' expectations. The school principal, without prior consultation or explanation, excised six articles—comprising two full pages—of the May 13, 1983, issue of Spectrum. He did so not because any of the articles would "materially and substantially interfere with the requirements of appropriate discipline," but simply because he considered two of the six "inappropriate, personal, sensitive, and unsuitable" for student consumption.

In my view the principal broke more than just a promise. He violated the First Amendment's prohibitions against censorship of any student expression that neither disrupts classwork nor invades the rights of others, and against any censorship that is not narrowly tailored to serve its purpose. . . .

The Court opens its analysis in this case by purporting to reaffirm *Tinker*'s time-tested proposition that public school students "do not 'shed their constitutional rights to freedom of speech or expression at the schoolhouse gate.'" That is an ironic introduction to an opinion that denudes high school students of much of the First Amendment protection that *Tinker* itself prescribed. . . . The young men and women of Hazelwood East expected a civics lesson, but not the one the Court teaches them today.

I dissent.

While deciding whether *Hazelwood* fits compatibly with *Near*, keep this caveat in mind: the Court generally has recognized more limits on the First Amendment rights of students and juveniles than of adults. White sought to make this point clear in his opinion, but does he do so effectively? For example, how did he distinguish this case from *Tinker v. Des Moines?*

We will revisit the prior restraint controversy in the next chapter when we take up the issue of government regulation of indecent and obscene expression. For now, let us turn to a related topic: government control of the content of messages from the press.

GOVERNMENT CONTROL OF PRESS CONTENT

Prior restraints of the media may constitute the most obvious way a government can control what its citizens see, hear, and read, but it is not the only way. Beyond preventing dissemination, governments can try to control the content of the message. This practice may be less overt, but it is no less dangerous. To see why, we only have to consider again the example of the Nazi government in Germany. By controlling the press, the Nazi regime was able to disseminate the message that it wanted to get across to the public.

But why, in America, a country founded on democratic ideals, would questions of government control of the media ever come up? After all, such practices contradict values Americans hold dear. The answer is that the government may have a good reason for seeking to control the media, such as the protection of the best interests of its citizens and of the democratic process. In the cases we review next involving regulations on what the media must *exclude* and *include,* that defense was offered by states and the United States. Does the argument convince you that government should be allowed to place controls on the freedom of the fourth estate? Does the Court go along with this rationale?

Regulating the Press by Prohibiting Content

To begin to answer these questions, let us consider the case of *Cox Broadcasting Corporation v. Cohn* (1975). At issue was a Georgia statute making it a crime for "any

news media" to publish or broadcast "the name or identity of any female who may have been raped or upon whom an assault with intent to commit rape may have been made." The law was passed with the best of intentions. The victims of such brutal crimes have already suffered a great deal and to publicize their names would only add to their anguish. Because rape, unlike other crimes, often carries with it an unfortunate and undeserved stigma, the privacy of the victim should be protected.

The circumstances of *Cox Broadcasting* illustrate the point. The case began with events that took place in August 1971, when seventeen-year-old Cynthia Cohn attended a party with a large number of other high school students. A great deal of drinking took place. At the party six teenage boys raped Cohn, and, at some point during the rape, she died from suffocation. The six boys were indicted for rape and murder.

Eight months later, five of the six boys pleaded guilty to the rape charge after the murder accusation was dropped. The sixth boy pleaded not guilty. While covering this crime, a reporter for a television station owned by Cox Broadcasting found the name of the victim written in the indictments. Because indictments are public documents, the reporter violated no law by inspecting them, but, in a news broadcast later that day, the reporter included Cynthia Cohn's name in his story. Martin Cohn, Cynthia's father, filed suit against Cox Broadcasting claiming that the news reports containing the name of his daughter violated his right to privacy. His case was bolstered by the fact that Georgia law makes such reports unlawful. Cox Broadcasting claimed that the reports were protected under the First Amendment. The issue is straightforward: May a state constitutionally prohibit the press from reporting the names of rape victims?

With only Justice Rehnquist dissenting, the Court held that a state may not, consistent with the First and Fourteenth Amendments, impose sanctions on the accurate publication of the name of a rape victim obtained from judicial records that are open to public inspection. Furthermore, the Court ruled that the publication of accurate reports of judicial proceedings merits special constitutional protection. The commission of crimes and the manner in which the judiciary handles criminal prosecutions are legitimate matters of public concern and, therefore, subjects the press is entitled to cover.

In *Cox Broadcasting* the Court developed a general principle of law: it would be loath to allow states to prohibit publication, in a truthful way, of public information. Indeed, since 1975 it has clung to this general principle. The next year, in *Nebraska Press Association v. Stuart* (1976), for example, the Court refused to allow a trial court judge to place a gag order on the press coverage of pretrial proceedings, even though the order was designed to protect the defendant from prejudicial publicity. Three years later, in *Smith v. Daily Mail Publishing Co.* (1979), it struck down a law prohibiting the publication of the identity of juvenile offenders.

In addition to these outright prohibitions of content, governments have attempted to discourage certain kinds of publications. The law at issue in *Simon & Schuster, Inc. v. Members of the New York State Crime Victims Board* (1991) provides a good example. It had its origins in 1977, when a serial killer popularly known as the Son of Sam terrorized New York City. After a long investigation, police arrested David Berkowitz for the murders. To stop individuals like Berkowitz from profiting from their crimes by making book or movie deals, the state of New York passed a statute that became known as the Son of Sam law. The law required any entity contracting with an accused or convicted person for a depiction of the crime to submit a copy of the contract to the state crime victims board. The law also stipulated that any and all income from such projects be deposited with the board to be held in escrow for five years. The board would use the money to pay any civil damage claims filed by the victims of the crimes. If no civil claims were pending at the end of the five-year period, the board would turn the remaining funds over to the party who had deposited it.

Once again, the state may have been attempting to achieve a commendable goal, but did the law violate the constitutional right to freedom of the press? By an 8–0 vote—Justice Thomas did not participate—the Court said that it did. Justice O'Connor's majority opinion was to the point:

A statute is presumptively inconsistent with the First Amendment if it imposes a financial burden on speakers because of the content of their speech. . . .

This is a notion so engrained in our First Amendment jurisprudence that last Term we found it so "obvious" as to not require explanation. *Leathers* [*v. Medlock*, 1991]. It is but one manifestation of a far broader principle: "Regulations which permit the Government to discriminate on the basis of the content of the message cannot be tolerated under the First Amendment." In the context of financial regulation, it bears repeating . . . that the Government's ability to impose content-based burdens on speech raises the specter that the Government may effectively drive certain ideas or viewpoints from the marketplace. . . .

The Son of Sam law is such a content-based statute. It singles out income derived from expressive activity for a burden the State places on no other income, and it is directed only at works with a specified content.

"To justify such differential treatment," O'Connor said, "the State must show that its regulation is necessary to serve a compelling state interest and is narrowly drawn to achieve that end." But, in this case, she asserted that New York had not made such a showing: "The State's interest in compensating victims from the fruits of crime is a compelling one, but the Son of Sam law is not narrowly tailored to advance that objective. As a result, the statute is inconsistent with the First Amendment."

Simon & Schuster reinforces the lesson of *Cox Broadcasting:* the Court generally is unwilling to support laws that prohibit the press from publishing otherwise legitimate information or attempting to accomplish the same goal by the imposition of financial penalties.

Regulating the Press by Mandating Content

Another way governments try to control the press is to *require* that it disseminate certain information. Totalitarian regimes have used this method to convert the press into a propaganda arm of the government. In the United States, government regulations requiring the press to carry specific information or publish particular stories have been motivated, some suggest, by more worthy purposes. *Miami Herald v. Tornillo* (1974) is an appropriate example. This suit challenged a Florida law that under certain circumstances compelled newspapers to

BOX 6-2 FREE PRESS IN GLOBAL PERSPECTIVE

SINCE 1972 Freedom House has evaluated levels of political rights and civil liberties in nations throughout the world. The following reports some results from its 1999 survey on press freedom practices.[1] The countries were evaluated on four criteria: (1) laws and regulations that influence media content; (2) political pressures and controls on media content; (3) economic influences over media content; and (4) repressive actions such as the killing of journalists, physical violence, censorship, self-censorship, and arrests. Countries were rated on a scale from 0 to 100, with 0 representing the greatest degree of press freedom.

SAMPLE OF COUNTRIES WITH A FREE PRESS

Chile. Journalists still practice self-censorship almost ten years after military censorship ended. The print and broadcast media are largely independent of government control. Although the state is the majority owner of one major newspaper, it remains editorially independent. The national television network is state-owned but not under direct government control. It does not receive government subsidies. Chile's overall rating was 27 on a scale of 0 to 30.

Germany. There is no official censorship, but Nazi propaganda and other hate speech are illegal. A 1997 bill to regulate standards for child protection on the Internet defines which online activities should be subject to licensing and other regulatory requirements. Newspapers and broadcasting networks, public and private, reflect a wide range of views. A constitutional amendment was introduced to restore broad police surveillance powers. Journalists, among other professionals, however, would be exempt from bugging. Germany's overall rating was 13.

Israel. Israeli, Palestinian, and foreign media must practice self-censorship according to a "voluntary" agreement last revised in 1996. The defense emergency regulations dating back to 1945 allow the government to ban publications and restrict distribution summarily. The law authorizes the government and the military to censor any material reported from Israel or the occupied territories regarded as sensitive on national security grounds. Israel's overall rating was 28.

Japan. Press clubs associated with government ministries and police tie journalists closely to officials. Five mainstream daily newspapers and some television stations belong to these groups. There are two separate radio and television broadcasting systems: NHK is a public entity running three nationwide radio networks. There are two nationwide television networks financed by subscription fees. About 6,900 private radio and TV stations are financed by advertising revenues. The ruling Liberal Democratic Party revealed a plan to establish a twenty-four-hour system to monitor radio, newspapers, and TV for incorrect or biased reports about the party. Although this plan could limit certain types of political coverage, there was scant mention of it in the mainstream press. Constraints already at work within the press suggest that little uproar is likely. Japan's overall rating was 19.

South Africa. The daily and weekly black press edit mainly for a black audience. Former president Nelson Mandela has accused black papers of not writing from a favorable black viewpoint and accused white-owned newspapers of racial bias. The country's human rights commission has said it will investigate, with subpoena power, this charge of racism in the media. The government has been pressed to write a law to help journalists secure government information. South Africa's overall rating was 28.

United States. National Public Radio and the public broadcasting system are partly funded by the federal government, but increasingly supported by private grants. There is no editorial control by government over NPR or Public Broadcasting. The Supreme Court in 1997 declared unconstitutional Congress's banning of pornographic material on the Internet. Congress in 1998 tried again to write a law to ban pornography on the Internet, which was also struck down. Newspapers perceive commercial threats from electronic competitors sapping audiences and advertising, and are pressured by readers who oppose "politically correct" coverage of topics such as race and gender, on the one hand, or are turned off by sensationalism and reduced credibility of the press, on the other. Television's network news divisions suffered continuing reduced viewership, pressed by cable TV news and other media. The United States' overall rating was 13.

SAMPLE OF COUNTRIES WITH A PARTLY FREE PRESS

India. State-run Doordarshan television still controls the world's largest terrestrial network. It delivers news and

---

1. Full survey results, as well as the accompanying report, are available at: *www.freedomhouse.org/pfs99*.

views to 80 percent of the population of nearly 1 billion. All India Radio operates almost all radio stations. Reports on both systems generally favor the government, either by omission of negative information or emphasis on officials or their policies. The government retains its monopoly on news programs. Certain information is either not reported or is given in biased form. There is a robust print press in many languages. Journalists covering controversial stories, however, face possible violence. In 1998, one newspaper office was attacked by armed men. India's overall rating was 37.

Mexico. The murder of four journalists and death threats to others made this one of the most dangerous countries for reporting. Immigration officials have also held up visas of foreign journalists and harassed those in the country with visa checks. The ruling party dominates television, especially during elections. Two private systems do not generally oppose the government's positions. Independent radio and TV station owners do not permit full freedom to their staffs for fear of losing broadcast licenses, which can be withdrawn without prior notice. Newspapers, while mostly private and nominally independent, depend on the government for advertising revenues. Defamation laws are used to harass journalists. Mexico's overall rating was 54.

Russia. Seemingly vigorous and diverse journalism belies serious editorial controls on virtually all broadcast and print media. Constitutional guarantees of press freedom are negated by financial and political pressures on journalists to conform to the wishes of owners or political operatives who control the particular print or broadcast medium. The nation's critical financial situation and the political instability tied to Boris Yeltsin's declining health add to the pressures on journalists to reflect the patron's political position. Libel cases have become a common form of intimidation by public officials. There were 353 incidents in which journalists and media sources were accused by authorities of "abuse of their journalistic privileges." Penalties are usually financial. The courts have ruled that journalists and editors are guilty of disseminating false information even if they use such disclaimers as "it is said," or "according to unverified information." Only a few newspapers have the financial ability to be independent. To add to the fears and resulting self-censoring of journalists, four were murdered in 1998. Russia's overall rating was 59.

Uganda. The government owns and controls the largest radio and television system and the largest newspaper. There are two private radio stations and one private TV channel. These provide broadly opposing views. More than two dozen daily and weekly newspapers are highly critical of officials. Old censorship laws are still used to restrict journalists. An editor of an independent paper was arrested, and the office of the newspaper was searched and documents confiscated. He was charged with promoting ill will. Uganda's overall rating was 40.

SAMPLE OF COUNTRIES WITHOUT A FREE PRESS

China. Between show trials of human rights activists, usually without defense lawyers, several small weekly newspapers provide avant-garde coverage of news that the Communist dailies and government sources do not reveal. The small papers write about local corruption, faulty public services, and investigative news that does not implicate top Communist policy makers. Just how far editors can go is left uncertain, providing for self-censorship. The government withdrew visas of Hong Kong journalists wanting to cover a visit by President Clinton, arrested a CBS correspondent and seized her videos, deported a Japanese journalist after he traveled to Tibet, and ordered a German reporter to leave China. There is a special office in Shanghai's police department to monitor "harmful information" on the Internet, which 1.2 million Chinese use. Voice of Tibet radio was jammed by the authorities. China's overall rating was 81.

Cuba. Total control of all domestic news media continues, with the occasional crackdown on foreign journalists and the acceptance after many years of permanent news bureaus, first of CNN and then the Associated Press. During the Pope's visit, several foreign journalists were denied visas and two BBC reporters were threatened with imprisonment for writing stories that "tarnish the image of Cuba." Eight journalists from independent press agencies were detained to keep them from covering a trial. The faint, occasional relaxation of press controls was followed by crackdowns, thereby continuing to intimidate the few domestic journalists attempting to press for a further opening. Cuba's overall rating was 94.

Libya. Media are strictly controlled by Col. Muammar Gaddafi. Journalists know it is dangerous to publish news contrary to the government view. Foreign news entering the country is censored. A daily newspaper was banned indefinitely for articles that "attack fraternal Arab States and friendly countries." The staff was suspended. Libya's overall rating was 92.

publish articles by candidates for political office. The goal of the legislation was to ensure that full and fair information was available to the voters. The *Miami Herald* refused to comply, arguing that the government had no constitutional authority to order the newspaper to publish anything.

In a 9–0 decision the justices agreed; indeed, they were no more sympathetic to the government trying to compel the press to publish stories than they were to the government prohibiting the press from disseminating certain information. As Chief Justice Burger put it for the Court:

A responsible press is an undoubtedly desirable goal, but press responsibility is not mandated by the Constitution and like many other virtues it cannot be legislated.

Appellee's argument that the Florida statute does not amount to a restriction of appellant's right to speak because "the statute in question here has not prevented the *Miami Herald* from saying anything it wished" begs the core question. Compelling editors or publishers to publish that which "'reason' tells them should not be published" is what is at issue in this case. The Florida statute operates as a command in the same sense as a statute or regulation forbidding appellant to publish specified matter. Governmental restraint on publishing need not fall into familiar or traditional patterns to be subject to constitutional limitations on governmental powers. The Florida statute exacts a penalty on the basis of the content of a newspaper. The first phase of the penalty resulting from the compelled printing of a reply is exacted in terms of the cost in printing and composing time and materials and in taking up space that could be devoted to other material the newspaper may have preferred to print. . . .

Faced with the penalties that would accrue to any newspaper that published news or commentary arguably within the reach of the right-of-access statute, editors might well conclude that the safe course is to avoid controversy. Therefore, under the operation of the Florida statute, political and electoral coverage would be blunted or reduced. Government-enforced right of access inescapably "dampens the vigor and limits the variety of public debate.". . .

Even if a newspaper would face no additional costs to comply with a compulsory access law and would not be forced to forgo publication of news or opinion by the inclusion of a reply, the Florida statute fails to clear the barriers of the First Amendment because of its intrusion into the function of editors. A newspaper is more than a passive receptacle or conduit for news, comment, and advertising. The choice of material to go into a newspaper, and the decisions made as to limitations on the size and content of the paper, and treatment of public issues and public officials—whether fair or unfair—constitute the exercise of editorial control and judgment. It has yet to be demonstrated how governmental regulation of this crucial process can be exercised consistent with First Amendment guarantees of a free press as they have evolved to this time.

Once again, we see that the Court has little tolerance for content-based regulations of the printed media. Indeed, over time, *Tornillo* has come to stand for the principle that governments in the United States should keep their "hands off" newspapers.[7]

The same cannot be said of governments elsewhere. Box 6-2 offers data from Freedom House's 1999 press freedom survey.[8] Overall, only 36 percent of the 186 nations in the survey were found to have a truly free press—that is, a press free from serious legal, economic, and political influences on press content; 28 percent were found to be partly free; and the balance, 36 percent, were deemed not free. To put it another way, only 20 percent of the world's population (1.2 billion people) live in a nation with a press that is free from governmental or other intrusion.

Regulating the Broadcast Media

Tornillo and most of the cases we have examined so far involve the print media. But over time, as Table 6-1 shows, Americans have come to rely more heavily on broadcast media at least for political information. Should the radio and television industry enjoy the same degree of protection as newspapers? The Court addressed this general question in the 1969 case of *Red Lion Broadcasting v. FCC.*[9]

This question was of great interest to Congress, which regulates the broadcast industry through its power over interstate commerce. The legislature establishes general

7. See, for example, C. Edwin Baker, "Turner Broadcasting: Content-Based Regulation of Persons and Presses," *Supreme Court Review* (1994): 58–59.

8. Freedom House, an "advocate for democracy and human rights worldwide," has, since 1972, evaluated levels of political rights and civil liberties in nations throughout the world. For more information, navigate to: *www.freedomhouse.org.*

9. For oral arguments in this case, navigate to: *oyez.nwu.edu.*

TABLE 6-1 Where Do Americans Learn About Elections?

Primary Source for Election News	April 1996	Setpember 1996	January 2000
Television	81%	75%	75%
Network	39	29	24
Local	34	31	25
Cable	23	25	31
Newspapers	48	44	31
Radio	21	14	12
Magazines	6	5	3
Internet	2	2	6

SOURCE: The Pew Research Center for the People & the Press (www.people-press.org/janoorpt.2.htm).

regulatory policy for the broadcast industry, and the Federal Communications Commission (FCC), which Congress created, implements those policies and carries out the day-to-day regulatory activity. The regulation is comprehensive. The federal government issues licenses to broadcast, requires that certain public interest programming be included, and prohibits certain kinds of language on the air. Radio and television stations must adhere to strict codes of operation and conform to regulations that are designed to promote the public interest. A station that does not conform to these rules may lose its license to broadcast, essentially putting the operation out of business.

Although the degree of regulation imposed by Congress has varied over the years, the federal government has always maintained that the electronic media may be regulated in ways that would not be allowed for the print media. The broadcast industry is different because, unlike the print media, radio and television stations operate by using the public airways. As the public airways can accommodate only a limited number of stations, the government must regulate the broadcast industry to ensure that it can operate effectively and for the public good. Does this argument have merit?

As you read *Red Lion Broadcasting,* in which the Court addressed this and more specific questions related to FCC policy, keep in mind that the justices had to answer

them without help from the Framers who naturally had no way to anticipate modern technology. Also, compare *Red Lion* to the *Tornillo* decision. Are the two compatible?

Red Lion Broadcasting v. FCC

395 U.S. 367 (1969)
laws.findlaw.com/US/395/367.html
Vote: 7 (Black, Brennan, Harlan, Marshall, Stewart, Warren, White)

0

Opinion of the Court: White
Not participating: Douglas

Virtually since its creation in 1934, the FCC has required radio and television broadcasters to discuss public issues on their stations, and to provide each side of those issues fair coverage. This policy is widely known as the fairness doctrine.

Red Lion arose when Pennsylvania radio station WGCB, owned by the Red Lion Broadcasting Company, aired a program entitled the "Christian Crusade." During the show, Rev. Billy James Hargis attacked the book *Goldwater—Extremist on the Right* and its author, Fred J. Cook. Hargis asserted, among other things, that Cook "was fired [from a reporting job] after he made a false charge on television against an unnamed official of New York City government," that "after losing his job, Cook went to work for [a] left-wing publication," and that he wrote this book to "smear and destroy Barry Goldwater." Believing he had been personally attacked, Cook asked WGCB to allow him to respond on the air, asserting that the fairness doctrine mandated the right to reply. When WGCB refused, Cook took his case to the FCC, which ruled that Red Lion had failed to meet its obligation under the fairness doctrine and ordered the station to give Cook the air time. Rather than obeying the order, Red Lion challenged it on First Amendment grounds. Its attorneys argued that the media have a right to print and broadcast whatever they wish, free from any undue government influence.

MR. JUSTICE WHITE delivered the opinion of the Court.

The broadcasters challenge the fairness doctrine and its specific manifestations in the personal attack and political editorial rules on conventional First Amendment grounds, alleging that the rules abridge their freedom of speech and press. Their contention is that the First Amendment protects their desire to use their allotted frequencies continuously to broadcast whatever they choose and to exclude whomever they choose from ever using that frequency. No man may be prevented from saying or publishing what he thinks, or from refusing in his speech or other utterances to give equal weight to the views of his opponents. This right, they say, applies equally to broadcasters.

Although broadcasting is clearly a medium affected by a First Amendment interest, differences in the characteristics of new media justify differences in the First Amendment standards applied to them. . . .

Where there are substantially more individuals who want to broadcast than there are frequencies to allocate, it is idle to posit an unabridgeable First Amendment right to broadcast comparable to the right of every individual to speak, write, or publish. If 100 persons want broadcast licenses but there are only 10 frequencies to allocate, all of them may have the same "right" to a license; but if there is to be any effective communication by radio, only a few can be licensed and the rest must be barred from the airwaves. It would be strange if the First Amendment, aimed at protecting and furthering communications, prevented the Government from making radio communication possible by requiring licenses to broadcast and by limiting the number of licenses so as not to overcrowd the spectrum.

This has been the consistent view of the Court. Congress unquestionably has the power to grant and deny licenses and to eliminate existing stations. No one has a First Amendment right to a license or to monopolize a radio frequency; to deny a station license because "the public interest" requires it "is not a denial of free speech."

By the same token, as far as the First Amendment is concerned those who are licensed stand no better than those to whom licenses are refused. A license permits broadcasting, but the licensee has no constitutional right to be the one who holds the license or to monopolize a radio frequency to the exclusion of his fellow citizens. There is nothing in the First Amendment which prevents the Government from requiring a licensee to share his frequency with others and to conduct himself as a proxy or fiduciary with obligations to present those views and voices which are representative of his community and which would otherwise, by necessity, be barred from the airwaves.

This is not to say that the First Amendment is irrelevant to public broadcasting. On the contrary, it has a major role to play as the Congress itself recognized in §326 [of the Communications Act], which forbids FCC interference with "the right of free speech by means of radio communication." Because of the scarcity of radio frequencies, the Government is permitted to put restraints on licensees in favor of others whose views should be expressed on this unique medium. But the people as a whole retain their interest in free speech by radio and their collective right to have the medium function consistently with the ends and purposes of the First Amendment. It is the right of the viewers and listeners, not the right of the broadcasters, which is paramount. It is the purpose of the First Amendment to preserve an uninhibited marketplace of ideas in which truth will ultimately prevail, rather than to countenance monopolization of that market, whether it be by the Government itself or a private licensee. It is the right of the public to receive suitable access to social, political, esthetic, moral, and other ideas and experiences which is crucial here. That right may not constitutionally be abridged either by Congress or by the FCC. . . .

. . . [But it is not] inconsistent with the First Amendment goal of producing an informed public capable of conducting its own affairs to require a broadcaster to permit answers to personal attacks occurring in the course of discussing controversial issues, or to require that the political opponents of those endorsed by the station be given a chance to communicate with the public. Otherwise, station owners and a few networks would have unfettered power to make time available only to the highest bidders, to communicate only their own views on public issues, people and candidates, and to permit on the air only those with whom they agreed. There is no sanctuary in the First Amendment for unlimited private censorship operating in a medium not open to all. . . .

It is strenuously argued, however, that if political editorials or personal attacks will trigger an obligation in broadcasters to afford the opportunity for expression to speakers who need not pay for time and whose views are unpalatable to the licensees, then broadcasters will be irresistibly forced to self-censorship and their coverage of controversial public issues will be eliminated or at least rendered wholly ineffective. Such a result would indeed be a serious matter, for should licensees actually eliminate their coverage of controversial issues, the purposes of the doctrine would be stifled.

At this point, however, as the Federal Communications Commission has indicated, that possibility is at best speculative. The communications industry, and in particular the networks, have taken pains to present controversial issues in the past, and even now they do not assert that they intend to abandon their efforts in this regard. It would be better if the FCC's encouragement were never necessary to induce the broadcasters to meet their responsibility. And if experience with the administration of those doctrines indicates that they have the net effect of reducing rather than enhancing the volume and quality of coverage, there will be time enough to reconsider the constitutional implications. The fairness doctrine in the past has had no such overall effect.

That this will occur now seems unlikely, however, since if present licensees should suddenly prove timorous, the Commission is not powerless to insist that they give adequate and fair attention to public issues. It does not violate the First Amendment to treat licensees given the privilege of using scarce radio frequencies as proxies for the entire community, obligated to give suitable time and attention to matters of great public concern. To condition the granting or renewal of licenses on a willingness to present representative community views on controversial issues is consistent with the ends and purposes of those constitutional provisions forbidding the abridgment of freedom of speech and freedom of the press. Congress need not stand idly by and permit those with licenses to ignore the problems which beset the people or to exclude from the airwaves anything but their own views of fundamental questions. . . .

We need not and do not now ratify every past and future decision by the FCC with regard to programming. There is no question here of the Commission's refusal to permit the broadcaster to carry a particular program or to publish his own views; of a discriminatory refusal to require the licensee to broadcast certain views which have been denied access to the airwaves; of government censorship of a particular program contrary to §26; or of the official government view dominating public broadcasting. Such questions

would raise more serious First Amendment issues. But we do hold that the Congress and the Commission do not violate the First Amendment when they require a radio or television station to give reply time to answer personal attacks and political editorials.

Affirmed.

The degree to which the government regulates the broadcast media increases and decreases as political tides change. The fairness doctrine, for example, was repealed in 1987. Yet *Red Lion* remains good law. It establishes that, while the First Amendment applies to electronic media, the amendment is no barrier to reasonable government control and that Congress may treat broadcasting differently from the print media. In other words, for the reasons it gave in *Red Lion,* the Court holds regulations aimed at the electronic media to a less rigorous standard of First Amendment scrutiny than it does those geared at the print media.[10] To see this point, we need only compare the right-to-reply requirement at issue in *Tornillo* with the fairness doctrine. With but one exception, the regulations were identical: the first was geared to newspapers, and the second to the broadcast media. The Court unanimously struck down the right-to-reply requirement, but unanimously upheld the fairness doctrine.

Federal Communications Commission v. Pacifica Foundation (1978) provides another interesting example of how the Court treats the electronic and print media differently. This dispute began when a radio station owned by the Pacifica Foundation one afternoon broadcast a recorded monologue by humorist George Carlin, entitled "Filthy Words." In it Carlin uses a litany of words and phrases that, although not obscene, are considered indecent and offensive by many. In response to this broadcast, a man wrote a letter of complaint to the FCC, claiming that he heard the monologue while driving with his young son. After an investigation, the FCC issued an order declaring the broadcast to have been in violation of a

10. This is the interpretation that commentators and the Court have adopted; see, for example, our discussion of *Turner Broadcasting v. FCC* (1994). It is interesting to note, however, that neither *Tornillo* nor *Red Lion Broadcasting* made reference to standards or levels of scrutiny. For more on this point, see Baker, "Turner Broadcasting."

federal statute that prohibits the transmission of indecent language on the public airways. Pacifica appealed
and was initially successful. But the Supreme Court reversed. In a 5–4 vote the justices held that of all forms of
communication, broadcasting has the most limited First
Amendment protection. The electronic media, the majority held, differ from the print media because they have
a pervasive presence that can invade the privacy of the
home and because they are uniquely available to children. Clearly, the regulation of indecent language upheld
here would never be sustained by the Court if it were applied to the print media.

Nor would the Court uphold other laws aimed at the
regulation of content. Consider, for example, the Children's Television Act. Enacted in 1990 and reinforced
with new regulations in 1996, the law requires that TV
stations wishing to renew their licenses demonstrate how
they were serving the "educational and informational"
needs of children aged two to sixteen. The law (coupled
with FCC regulations) also contains sections on what
broadcasters are to include and to exclude: they are required to televise a minimum of three hours of core educational programs for children and to limit commercials
on children's programs to twelve minutes per hour on
weekdays and ten and a half minutes per hour on week-
ends. Although the Supreme Court has not ruled on the
constitutionality of these regulations, there seems to be
little doubt—if it relied on *Red Lion, Pacifica Foundation,*
and other cases—that it would uphold them. This takes
us back to the difference between the government's (including the Court's) treatment of the print and broadcast
media. Can you imagine the Court permitting Congress
to dictate to the *New York Times* the number of articles
that it needed to publish on matters of interest to children?

We might raise the same questions about revelations,
in early 2000, that the White House Office of National
Drug Control Policy was working with television networks to get antidrug messages into their programs.
While some members of Congress acknowledged the
"good intentions" behind the program—to underscore,
especially to teenagers, the dangers of drugs—they wondered whether government had gone too far. Alan Levitt,

director of the White House's antidrug media campaign
has called these "allegations of attacks on the First
Amendment, Big Brother" plainly "unfair." "Nothing,"
Levitt said, "could be further from the truth." Based on
existing case law, would the Supreme Court agree? Or
did government go too far in its attempt, however noble,
to prod the media into televising certain messages?

New Media and Government Control of Content

If our discussion so far has indicated anything, it is
that the Court treats the broadcast media differently
from the printed press. But this traditional dichotomy
may become obsolete as more and more Americans rely
on newer forms of communication *(see Table 6-1)* and the
justices attempt to consider the extent to which government can regulate them.

Indeed, the justices have already begun to confront
the issue as it pertains to cable television. In *Turner
Broadcasting System, Inc. v. FCC* (1994) the Court examined the "must-carry" provisions of the Cable Television
Act of 1992, which require most cable television systems
(those with more than three hundred subscribers and
twelve channels) to devote up to one-third of their channels to local and public outlets. Believing that the law interfered with their ability to make decisions about what
should appear on their systems, cable operators challenged it as a violation of expression guarantees.

In *Turner* all of the justices agreed that the First
Amendment protects the cable industry and held that
cable television systems merit a higher level of First
Amendment protection than does conventionally broadcast television and radio programming but a lower level
than the printed media. Why? The Court provided the
following explanation:

[The government contends] that regulation of cable television
should be analyzed under the same First Amendment standard
that applies to regulation of broadcast television. It is true that
our cases have permitted more intrusive regulation of broadcast speakers than of speakers in other media. But the rationale
for applying a less rigorous standard of First Amendment
scrutiny to broadcast regulation, whatever its validity in the
cases elaborating it, does not apply in the context of cable regulation.

The justification for our distinct approach to broadcast regulation rests upon the unique physical limitations of the broadcast medium. As a general matter, there are more would-be broadcasters than frequencies available in the electromagnetic spectrum. And if two broadcasters were to attempt to transmit over the same frequency in the same locale, they would interfere with one another's signals, so that neither could be heard at all. . . . In addition, the inherent physical limitation on the number of speakers who may use the broadcast medium has been thought to require some adjustment in traditional First Amendment analysis to permit the Government to place limited content restraints, and impose certain affirmative obligations, on broadcast licensees. . . .

. . . The broadcast cases are inapposite in the present context because cable television does not suffer from the inherent limitations that characterize the broadcast medium. Indeed, given the rapid advances in fiber optics and digital compression technology, soon there may be no practical limitation on the number of speakers who may use the cable medium. Nor is there any danger of physical interference between two cable speakers attempting to share the same channel.

But the justices did not fully define the extent of that protection. Nor did they deal squarely with the regulations at issue. While four (O'Connor, Scalia, Thomas, and Ginsburg) wanted to declare them unconstitutional, five agreed to send the case back to the three-judge court that had upheld the law in the first instance. The majority wanted more evidence of the government's claim that the law was necessary to protect local broadcasters and that it did not interfere with the First Amendment rights of cable companies.

Finally, in 1996 the justices resolved the issue. In *Turner Broadcasting*'s second appearance before the Court, a slim majority upheld the law. In its view the United States had met the requirement of showing that the law furthered an important government interest without unnecessarily burdening speech.

Central to the Court's decision in *Turner* was its belief that the "must carry" provision was content neutral and, therefore, had to pass only an intermediate level standard. This premise suggests that cable operators, in terms of constitutional protection, fall somewhere between the broadcast and print media, at least when government regulations are deemed content neutral.

The Court reached a very different conclusion about the Internet, the fastest growing form of global communication. In considering the constitutionality of the Communications Decency Act of 1996 (CDA), which prohibited on-line communication to minors (under age eigh-teen) that is "indecent" or "obscene," the justices differentiated cyberspace from the broadcast media:

We [have] observed that "[e]ach medium of expression . . . may present its own problems." Thus, some of our cases have recognized special justifications for regulation of the broadcast media that are not applicable to other speakers, see *Red Lion Broadcasting Co. v. FCC* (1969). In these cases, the Court relied on the history of extensive government regulation of the broadcast medium; the scarcity of available frequencies at its inception; and its "invasive" nature.

These factors are not present in cyberspace. Neither before nor after the enactment of the CDA have the vast democratic fora of the Internet been subject to the type of government supervision and regulation that has attended the broadcast industry. Moreover, the Internet is not as "invasive" as radio or television. The District Court specifically found that "[c]ommunications over the Internet do not 'invade' an individual's home or appear on one's computer screen unbidden. Users seldom encounter content 'by accident.'". . .

Finally, unlike the conditions that prevailed when Congress first authorized regulation of the broadcast spectrum, the Internet can hardly be considered a "scarce" expressive commodity. It provides relatively unlimited, low cost capacity for communications of all kinds. The Government estimates that "[a]s many as 40 million people use the Internet today, and that figure is expected to grow to 200 million by 1999." This dynamic, multifaceted category of communication includes not only traditional print and news services, but also audio, video, and still images, as well as interactive, real time dialogue. Through the use of chat rooms, any person with a phone line can become a town crier with a voice that resonates farther than it could from any soapbox. Through the use of Web pages, mail exploders, and newsgroups, the same individual can become a pamphleteer. As the District Court found, "The content on the Internet is as diverse as human thought." We agree with its conclusion that our cases provide no basis for qualifying the level of First Amendment scrutiny that should be applied to this medium.

Do you agree with the Court's logic? In your opinion, is the Internet more akin to the printed press, as the justices seem to think, than to the broadcast media? Whatever your belief, the answer supplied by the Court indicates that the federal government will have a more difficult time regulating the Internet, than, say, cable television. *(See pages 373–377 for a longer excerpt of* Reno v. ACLU.*)*

THE MEDIA AND SPECIAL RIGHTS

Challenging restraints on First Amendment rights is not the only battle the media have fought. For many years, the media asked courts for "special rights" not normally accorded average citizens, but which the press considered necessary to provide "full and robust" coverage of local, national, and world events. In this section, we discuss two of those—reporters' privilege and the right of access. While reading about them, ask yourself whether, in fact, the media should enjoy a special legal status. Also consider the extent to which the Court's rulings on these issues are consistent with those centering on government control of press content.

Reporters' Privilege

As far back as 1840 reporters asserted the need for unusual legal privileges. That year the Senate held a secret meeting to debate a proposed treaty to end the Mexican-American War. John Nugent, a reporter for the *New York Herald*, managed to obtain a copy of the proposed draft and mailed it to his editor. The Senate subpoenaed Nugent, and, when he refused to reveal his source of information, it held him in contempt. Nugent was later sent to prison for protecting his source.[11]

Although from time to time others faced the same fate as Nugent, during the 1960s and 1970s there was a marked increase in the claims of reporters' privilege. Some credit this increase to the trial of the Chicago Seven in which the government charged individuals with starting a riot in the streets outside of the Democratic Party's 1968 convention. The United States served subpoenas on the major networks, newspapers, and magazines to obtain any information they had on the disturbances. Others suggest that it was the Nixon administration's disdain for the press that led to the increase, and

still others argue that the rise in investigative reporting ushered in by Watergate led reporters to assert their right to protect sources absolutely and unconditionally.

Whatever the cause, the debate over reporters' privilege reached its climax in 1972 when the Supreme Court agreed to hear several cases involving such claims. The cases presented somewhat different issues, but the points of view were clear on both sides. The government asserted that reporters were entitled to no special rights and privileges: if ordinary citizens were forced to testify upon subpoena, then so should the media. The media responded that there were, in fact, certain privileged relationships. Doctors, for example, cannot be forced to reveal information about their patients. Reporters also argued that if they were forced to answer questions about their sources, those sources would dry up, which would have a chilling effect on their ability to do their jobs and would violate their free press guarantee.

Branzburg v. Hayes

408 U.S. 665 (1972)
laws.findlaw.com/US/408/665.html
Vote: 5 (Blackmun, Burger, Powell, Rehnquist, White)
    4 (Brennan, Douglas, Marshall, Stewart)
Opinion of the Court: White
Concurring opinion: Powell
Dissenting opinions: Douglas, Stewart

This case involved two articles written by Paul M. Branzburg, a reporter for the Louisville, Kentucky, *Courier-Journal.*[12] In the first article, Branzburg detailed his observations of two individuals, "synthesizing hashish from Marijuana, an activity which they asserted earned them about $5,000 in three weeks." The article contained this statement:

"I don't know why I am letting you do this story," [one of the individuals] said quietly. "To make the narcs mad I guess. That's the main reason." However, [the two individuals] *asked for and received a promise that their names would be changed* (emphasis added).

11. This paragraph and the next draw heavily on Mark Neubauer, "The Newsmen's Privilege after Branzburg," *UCLA Law Review* 24 (1976): 160–192.

12. For oral arguments in this case, navigate to: *oyez.nwu.edu.*

The second piece contained interviews Branzburg conducted with drug users in Frankfort, Kentucky.

Branzburg was subpoenaed by a grand jury. He appeared but refused to answer the following questions:

1. Who was the person or persons you observed in possession of Marijuana, about which you wrote an article?

2. Who was the person or persons you observed compounding Marijuana, producing same to a compound known as hashish?

MR. JUSTICE WHITE delivered the opinion of the Court.

The issue in these cases is whether requiring newsmen to appear and testify before state or federal grand juries abridges the freedom of speech and press guaranteed by the First Amendment. We hold that it does not. . . .

Petitioner . . . Branzburg . . . press[es] First Amendment claims that may be simply put: that to gather news it is often necessary to agree either not to identify the source of information published or to publish only part of the facts revealed, or both; that if the reporter is nevertheless forced to reveal these confidences to a grand jury, the source so identified and other confidential sources of other reporters will be measurably deterred from furnishing publishable information, all to the detriment of the free flow of information protected by the First Amendment. Although the newsmen in these cases do not claim an absolute privilege against official interrogation in all circumstances, they assert that the reporter should not be forced either to appear or to testify before a grand jury or at trial until and unless sufficient grounds are shown for believing that the reporter possesses information relevant to a crime the grand jury is investigating, that the information the reporter has is unavailable from other sources, and that the need for the information is sufficiently compelling to override the claimed invasion of First Amendment interests occasioned by the disclosure. Principally relied upon are prior cases emphasizing the importance of the First Amendment guarantees to individual development and to our system of representative government, decisions requiring that official action with adverse impact on First Amendment rights be justified by a public interest that is "compelling" or "paramount," and those precedents establishing the principle that justifiable governmental goals may not be achieved by unduly broad means having an unnecessary impact on protected rights of speech, press, or association. The heart of the claim is that the burden on news gathering resulting from compelling reporters to disclose confidential information outweighs any public interest in obtaining the information.

We do not question the significance of free speech, press, or assembly to the country's welfare. Nor is it suggested that news gathering does not qualify for First Amendment protection; without some protection for seeking out the news, freedom of the press could be eviscerated. But these cases involve no intrusions upon speech or assembly, no prior restraint or restriction on what the press may publish, and no express or implied command that the press publish what it prefers to withhold. No exaction or tax for the privilege of publishing, and no penalty, civil or criminal, related to the content of published material is at issue here. The use of confidential sources by the press is not forbidden or restricted; reporters remain free to seek news from any source by means within the law. No attempt is made to require the press to publish its sources of information or indiscriminately to disclose them on request.

The sole issue before us is the obligation of reporters to respond to grand jury subpoenas as other citizens do and to answer questions relevant to an investigation into the commission of crime. Citizens generally are not constitutionally immune from grand jury subpoenas; and neither the First Amendment nor any other constitutional provision protects the average citizen from disclosing to a grand jury information that he has received in confidence. The claim is, however, that reporters are exempt from these obligations because if forced to respond to subpoenas and identify their sources or disclose other confidences, their informants will refuse or be reluctant to furnish newsworthy information in the future. This asserted burden on news gathering is said to make compelled testimony from newsmen constitutionally suspect and to require a privileged position for them.

It is clear that the First Amendment does not invalidate every incidental burdening of the press that may result from the enforcement of civil or criminal statutes of general applicability. Under prior cases, otherwise valid laws serving substantial public interests may be enforced against the press as against others, despite the possible burden that may be imposed. The Court has emphasized that "[t]he publisher of a newspaper has no special immunity from the application of general laws. He has no special privilege to invade the rights and liberties of others.". . .

A number of States have provided newsmen a statutory privilege of varying breadth, but the majority have not done so, and none has been provided by federal statute. Until now the only testimonial privilege for unofficial witnesses that is rooted in the Federal Constitution is the Fifth Amendment privilege against compelled self-incrimination. We are asked to create another by interpreting the First Amendment to grant newsmen a testimonial privilege that other citizens do not enjoy. This we decline to do. Fair and effective law enforcement aimed at providing security for the person and property of the individual is a fundamental function of government, and the grand jury plays an important, constitutionally mandated role in this process. On the records now before us, we perceive no basis for holding that the public interest in law enforcement and in ensuring effective grand jury proceedings is insufficient to override the consequential, but uncertain, burden on news gathering that is said to result from insisting that reporters, like other citizens, respond to relevant questions put to them in the course of a valid grand jury investigation or criminal trial.

This conclusion itself involves no restraint on what newspapers may publish or on the type or quality of information reporters may seek to acquire, nor does it threaten the vast bulk of confidential relationships between reporters and their sources. Grand juries address themselves to the issues of whether crimes have been committed and who committed them. Only where news sources themselves are implicated in crime or possess information relevant to the grand jury's task need they or the reporter be concerned about grand jury subpoenas. Nothing before us indicates that a large number or percentage of all confidential news sources falls into either category and would in any way be deterred by our holding that the Constitution does not, as it never has, exempt the newsman from performing the citizen's normal duty of appearing and furnishing information relevant to the grand jury's task.

The preference for anonymity of those confidential informants involved in actual criminal conduct is presumably a product of their desire to escape criminal prosecution, and this preference, while understandable, is hardly deserving of constitutional protection. It would be frivolous to assert—and no one does in these cases—that the First Amendment, in the interest of securing news or otherwise, confers a li-

cense on either the reporter or his news sources to violate valid criminal laws. Although stealing documents or private wiretapping could provide newsworthy information, neither reporter nor source is immune from conviction for such conduct, whatever the impact on the flow of news. Neither is immune, on First Amendment grounds, from testifying against the other, before the grand jury or at a criminal trial. The Amendment does not reach so far as to override the interest of the public in ensuring that neither reporter nor source is invading the rights of other citizens through reprehensible conduct forbidden to all other persons. . . .

Thus, we cannot seriously entertain the notion that the First Amendment protects a newsman's agreement to conceal the criminal conduct of his source, or evidence thereof, on the theory that it is better to write about crime than to do something about it. Insofar as any reporter in these cases undertook not to reveal or testify about the crime he witnessed, his claim of privilege under the First Amendment presents no substantial question. The crimes of news sources are no less reprehensible and threatening to the public interest when witnessed by a reporter than when they are not. . . .

The argument that the flow of news will be diminished by compelling reporters to aid the grand jury in a criminal investigation is not irrational, nor are the records before us silent on the matter. But we remain unclear how often and to what extent informers are actually deterred from furnishing information when newsmen are forced to testify before a grand jury. The available data indicate that some newsmen rely a great deal on confidential sources and that some informants are particularly sensitive to the threat of exposure and may be silenced if it is held by this Court that, ordinarily, newsmen must testify pursuant to subpoenas, but the evidence fails to demonstrate that there would be a significant constriction of the flow of news to the public if this Court reaffirms the prior common-law and constitutional rule regarding the testimonial obligations of newsmen. Estimates of the inhibiting effect of such subpoenas on the willingness of informants to make disclosures to newsmen are widely divergent and to a great extent speculative. It would be difficult to canvass the views of the informants themselves: surveys of reporters on this topic are chiefly opinions of predicted informant behavior and must be viewed in the light of the professional self-interest of the interviewees. Reliance by the press on confidential informants does not mean that all such sources will in fact dry up because of the later possible appearance of the newsman before a grand jury. The reporter may never be called and if he objects to testifying, the prosecution may not insist. Also, the relationship of many informants to the press is a symbiotic one which is unlikely to be greatly inhibited by the threat of subpoena: quite often, such informants are members of a minority political or cultural group that relies heavily on the media to propagate its views, publicize its aims, and magnify its exposure to the public. . . .

Accepting the fact, however, that an undetermined number of informants not themselves implicated in crime will nevertheless, for whatever reason, refuse to talk to newsmen if they fear identification by a reporter in an official investigation, we cannot accept the argument that the public interest in possible future news about crime from undisclosed, unverified sources must take precedence over the public interest in pursuing and prosecuting those crimes reported to the press by informants and in thus deterring the commission of such crimes in the future.

We note first that the privilege claimed is that of the reporter, not the informant, and that if the authorities independently identify the informant, neither his own reluctance to testify nor the objection of the newsman would shield him from grand jury inquiry, whatever the impact on the flow of news or on his future usefulness as a secret source of information. More important, it is obvious that agreements to conceal information relevant to commission of crime have very little to recommend them from the standpoint of public policy. . . . It is apparent . . . from our history and that of England, that concealment of crime and agreements to do so are not looked upon with favor. Such conduct deserves no encomium, and we decline now to afford it First Amendment protection by denigrating the duty of a citizen, whether reporter or informer, to respond to grand jury subpoena and answer relevant questions put to him.

We are admonished that refusal to provide a First Amendment reporter's privilege will undermine the freedom of the press to collect and disseminate news. But this is not the lesson history teaches us. . . . [T]he common law recognized no such privilege, and the constitutional argument was not even asserted until 1958. From the beginning of our country the press has operated without constitutional protection for press informants, and the press has flourished. The existing constitutional rules have not been a serious obstacle to either the development or retention of confidential news sources by the press.

It is said that currently press subpoenas have multiplied, that mutual distrust and tension between press and officialdom have increased, that reporting styles have changed, and that there is now more need for confidential sources, particularly where the press seeks news about minority cultural and political groups or dissident organizations suspicious of the law and public officials. These developments, even if true, are treacherous grounds for a far-reaching interpretation of the First Amendment fastening a nationwide rule on courts, grand juries, and prosecuting officials everywhere. The obligation to testify in response to grand jury subpoenas will not threaten these sources not involved with criminal conduct and without information relevant to grand jury investigations, and we cannot hold that the Constitution places the sources in these two categories either above the law or beyond its reach. . . .

At the federal level, Congress has freedom to determine whether a statutory newsman's privilege is necessary and desirable and to fashion standards and rules as narrow or broad as deemed necessary to deal with the evil discerned and, equally important, to refashion those rules as experience from time to time may dictate. There is also merit in leaving state legislatures free, within First Amendment limits, to fashion their own standards in light of the conditions and problems with respect to the relations between law enforcement officials and press in their own areas. It goes without saying, of course, that we are powerless to bar state courts from responding in their own way and construing their own constitutions so as to recognize a newsman's privilege, either qualified or absolute. . . .

The decision . . . in *Branzburg v. Hayes* . . . must be affirmed. Here, petitioner refused to answer questions that directly related to criminal conduct that he had observed and written about. The Kentucky Court of Appeals noted that marijuana is defined as a narcotic drug by statute and that unlicensed possession or compounding of it is a felony punishable by both fine and imprisonment. It held that petitioner "saw the commission of the statutory felonies of unlawful possession of marijuana and the unlawful conversion of it into hashish.". . . [I]f what the petitioner wrote was true, he had direct information to provide the grand jury concerning the commission of serious crimes.

Affirmed.

MR. JUSTICE DOUGLAS, dissenting.

Today's decision will impede the wide-open and robust dissemination of ideas and counterthought which a free press both fosters and protects and which is essential to the success of intelligent self-government. Forcing a reporter before a grand jury will have two retarding effects upon the ear and the pen of the press. Fear of exposure will cause dissidents to communicate less openly to trusted reporters. And, fear of accountability will cause editors and critics to write with more restrained pens. . . .

A reporter is no better than his source of information. Unless he has a privilege to withhold the identity of his source, he will be the victim of governmental intrigue or aggression. If he can be summoned to testify in secret before a grand jury, his sources will dry up and the attempted exposure, the effort to enlighten the public, will be ended. If what the Court sanctions today becomes settled law, then the reporter's main function in American society will be to pass on to the public the press releases which the various departments of government issue. . . .

Today's decision is more than a clog upon news gathering. It is a signal to publishers and editors that they should exercise caution in how they use whatever information they can obtain. Without immunity they may be summoned to account for their criticism. Entrenched officers have been quick to crash their powers down upon unfriendly commentators.

The intrusion of government into this domain is symptomatic of the disease of this society. As the years pass the power of government becomes more and more pervasive. It is a power to suffocate both people and causes. Those in power, whatever their politics, want only to perpetuate it. Now that the fences of the law and the tradition that has protected the press are broken down, the people are the victims. The First Amendment, as I read it, was designed precisely to prevent that tragedy.

MR. JUSTICE STEWART, with whom MR. JUSTICE BRENNAN and MR. JUSTICE MARSHALL join, dissenting.

The Court's crabbed view of the First Amendment reflects a disturbing insensitivity to the critical role of an independent press in our society. The question whether a reporter has a constitutional right to a confidential relationship with his source is of first impression here, but the principles that should guide our decision are as basic as any to be found in the Constitution. . . . [T]he Court . . . holds that a newsman has no First Amendment right to protect his sources when called before a grand jury. The Court thus invites state and federal authorities to undermine the historic independence of the press by attempting to annex the journalistic profession as an investigative arm of government. Not only will this decision impair performance of the press' constitutionally protected functions, but it will, I am convinced, in the long run harm rather than help the administration of justice. . . .

Accordingly, when a reporter is asked to appear before a grand jury and reveal confidences, I would hold that the government must (1) show that there is probable cause to believe that the newsman has information that is clearly relevant to a specific probable violation of law; (2) demonstrate that the information sought cannot be obtained by alternative means less destructive of First Amendment rights; and (3) demonstrate a compelling and overriding interest in the information.

In *Branzburg* the majority emphatically denied the existence of reporters' privilege. The dissenters were distraught: Justice Stewart, who in his youth had worked as a reporter for a Cincinnati newspaper and also edited the *Yale Daily News* while in college, condemned the "Court's crabbed view of the First Amendment." Some legal scholars later criticized the Court for invoking contradictory premises about the role of the press. In *Branzburg* the majority refused to recognize the reporters' privilege even against arguments that its absence would hamper the ability of the press to cover events of public concern because it would deter informants from speaking with reporters. But, recall that in *Tornillo*, the Court struck down the right-to-reply regulation at least in part because it would "blunt or reduce" political coverage.[13]

The reaction of the media was even more vehement, with an outpouring of condemnation of *Branzburg* and calls for federal and state statutes that would shield reporters from revealing their sources. As a result of this

13. For more on this point, see William P. Marshall and Susan Gilles, "The Supreme Court, the First Amendment, and Bad Journalism," *Supreme Court Review* (1994): 169–208.

pressure, some twenty-six states (but not Congress) enacted reporters' privilege laws allowing reporters to refuse to divulge information about certain news-gathering activities. But because these laws often limit protections to specific circumstances, they may not be particularly effective. Kentucky already had a shield law on the books at the time of Branzburg's grand jury proceedings. Unfortunately for the reporter, it covered only sources of information and not personal observation. Journalists still face the threat of imprisonment if they refuse to answer questions pertaining to their stories—as Branzburg himself learned only a few months after the Supreme Court handed down the decision in his case.

What is more, reporters have not fared particularly well in asserting the need for other sorts of privileges. *Zurcher v. Stanford Daily* (1978), in which student journalists pressed for special treatment under the Fourth Amendment, illustrates the point. In April 1971 the *Daily*, a Stanford University student newspaper, published a special edition devoted to an incident at the university's hospital. A group of demonstrators had seized the hospital's administrative offices and barricaded the doors. When police forced their way in, a riot broke out, resulting in injuries to the officers. They could not identify their assailants, but one claimed to have seen a photographer in the building. In fact, the *Daily* published several pictures of the incident, none of which fully revealed the identity of the demonstrators. But, because it was reasonable to think that the photographer had more pictures, the day after the special edition, police obtained a warrant to search the *Daily's* office for the pictures. They found none.

The *Daily* initiated a civil action against all those involved in issuing and executing the warrant. Its lawyers rejected the argument that the case involved only Fourth Amendment issues and argued that the First Amendment, together with the Fourth Amendment, forbade such searches. The attorneys suggested that searches of newspapers were not necessarily unconstitutional, but that they should be based on a subpoena rather than a warrant. This distinction, in their view, would eliminate "police scrutiny [of] unrelated material, which may be highly confidential and sensitive, retained in the

BOX 6-3   AFTERMATH . . .
PAUL BRANZBURG

BETWEEN 1969 AND 1971 Paul M. Branzburg, an investigative reporter for the *Louisville Courier-Journal*, wrote a series of articles on illegal drug activities in central Kentucky. He was subpoenaed by two different grand juries and asked to provide information about his sources. When he refused to answer, contempt citations were issued. He appealed to the United States Supreme Court, which ruled on June 29, 1972, that the First Amendment confers no special privilege on reporters who do not answer grand jury questions.

In the aftermath of the Supreme Court ruling, Kentucky prosecutors again sought information from Branzburg concerning the drug users and dealers he had observed while researching his stories. Branzburg, who by this time had moved to Michigan to do investigative reporting for the *Detroit Free Press*, again declined to answer questions. On September 1, 1972, Branzburg was found in contempt of the Jefferson County court and was sentenced to six months in prison. When Branzburg refused to return to Kentucky voluntarily, state officials requested that Michigan authorities extradite him. Michigan's governor, William G. Milliken, denied the request, and Branzburg never served the six-month sentence.

SOURCES: *Louisville Courier-Journal*, June 30, 1972; Contemporary Authors On Line, Gale Group, 2000.

newspaper's files." The government responded that the warrant had been properly obtained and executed and that newspapers were undeserving of special Fourth Amendment protection.

Writing for a divided Court, Justice White agreed with the government. He relied on the intent of the Framers, noting that they "did not forbid warrants where the press was involved." He also suggested there was no reason to believe that those authorizing search warrants could not "guard against searches of the type, scope, and intrusiveness that would actually interfere with the timely publication of a newspaper." The Court dismissed the *Stanford Daily's* claim, and here the alignments were almost identical to those in *Branzburg*. White reiterated the *Branzburg* position that the press is not above the law, and Stewart reasserted his dissenting view in no uncertain terms: "It seems to me self-evident that police searches of newspapers burden the freedom of the press."[14]

The Right of Access

Several months after *Zurcher* the Court decided *Houchins v. KQED* (1978), which raised another claim of privilege asserted by the press. Of concern in *Houchins* was the right of reporters to have access to inmates in a county jail, which ordinarily would be denied to other individuals. Although this case is different from *Zurcher*, it poses a similar question: Should the justices accord the press rights and privileges beyond those enjoyed by average citizens?

A divided Court once again ruled against the press, holding that it should not. As Chief Justice Burger explained in his plurality opinion:

The media are not a substitute for or an adjunct of the government, and like the courts, are "ill equipped" to deal with the problems of prison administration. We must not confuse the role of the media with that of government; each has special, crucial functions, each complementing—and sometimes conflicting with—the other.

14. Congress responded to these decisions by passing the Privacy Protection Act, which prohibits government officials from conducting search and seizures of materials related to the journalism enterprise unless authorities believe that the writer has committed a crime or some life-threatening situation exists.

Burger also said that the Court would be no more amenable to special access claims than it was to newsmen's privilege; indeed, relying on past decisions such as *Branzburg*, Burger called the media's arguments "flawed." He held that the First Amendment did not mandate "a right of access to government information or sources of information within the government's control." This was strong language, which could be understood to limit press access to a wide range of state and federal proceedings.

In cases following *Houchins*, however, the Court has not gone so far as Burger's words suggested. In *Richmond Newspapers v. Virginia* (1980) *(see Chapter 10)*, for example, it overruled a trial court judge who had denied the press access to a highly publicized murder trial. Burger wrote, "The right to attend criminal trials is implicit within the guarantees of the First Amendment," and, if such access were denied, "important aspects of freedom of speech and of the press could be eviscerated."

This holding again raises the question of consistency. Based on your reading of the materials in this chapter, do you think the Court has taken a consistent position on the First Amendment guarantee of a free press? We leave this, as well as the other questions we have raised throughout, for you to answer. What is indisputable, however, is that the Court has played an important role in establishing the parameters of journalistic practice in the United States.

READINGS

Anderson, David A. "The Origins of the Press Clause." *UCLA Law Review* 30 (1983): 456–541.

Bollinger, Lee C. *Images of a Free Press.* Chicago: University of Chicago Press, 1991.

Carter, T. Barton. *The First Amendment and the Fifth Estate: Regulation of Electronic Mass Media.* Westbury, N.Y.: Foundation Press, 1993.

Daly, John Charles. *The Press and the Courts.* Washington, D.C.: American Enterprise Institute, 1978.

Flink, Stanley E. *Sentinel Under Siege: The Triumphs and Troubles of America's Free Press.* Boulder: Westview Press, 1998.

Friendly, Fred. *Minnesota Rag.* New York: Random House, 1981.

Garry, Patrick M. *Scrambling for Protection: The New Media and the First Amendment.* Pittsburgh: University of Pittsburgh Press, 1994.

Ingelhart, Louis Edward. *Press and Speech Freedoms in the World, from Antiquity until 1998.* Westport, Conn.: Greenwood, 1998.

Kelly, Sean. *Access Denied: The Politics of Press Censorship*. Beverly Hills, Calif.: Sage Publications, 1978.

Lahav, Pnina. *Press Law in Modern Democracies*. New York: Longman, 1984.

Levy, Leonard W., ed. *Freedom of Press from Zenger to Jefferson*. Durham, N.C.: Carolina Academic Press, 1996.

———. *Emergence of a Free Press*. New York: Oxford University Press, 1985.

Lichtenberg, Judith. *Democracy and the Mass Media*. New York: Cambridge University Press, 1990.

Marshall, William P., and Susan Gilles, "The Supreme Court, the First Amendment, and Bad Journalism." *Supreme Court Review* (1994): 169–208.

McCoy, Ralph E. *Freedom of the Press: An Annotated Bibliography, Second Supplement, 1978–1992*. Carbondale: Southern Illinois University Press, 1994.

Neubauer, Mark. "The Newsmen's Privilege after *Branzburg*." *UCLA Law Review* 24 (1976): 160–192.

Orme, William A., ed. *A Culture of Collusion: An Inside Look at the Mexican Press*. Coral Gables: University of Miami's North/South Center Press, 1996.

Powe, Lucas A., Jr. *The Fourth Estate and the Constitution*. Berkeley: University of California Press, 1991.

Reeves, Richard. *What the People Know: Freedom and the Press*. Cambridge: Harvard University Press, 1999.

Rudenstine, David. *The Day the Presses Stopped: A History of the Pentagon Papers Case*. Berkeley: University of California Press, 1996.

Sharma, B. R. *Freedom of Press under the Indian Constitution*. Columbia, Mo.: South Asia Books, 1993.

Shapiro, Martin. *The Pentagon Papers and the Courts*. San Francisco: Chandler, 1972.

Smith, Jeffrey Alan. *War and Press Freedom: The Problem of Prerogative Power*. Oxford University Press, 1999.

"Symposium: The Day the Presses Stopped: A History of the Pentagon Papers Case." *Cardozo Law Review* 19 (1998): 1295.

CHAPTER 7
THE BOUNDARIES OF FREE EXPRESSION: OBSCENITY AND LIBEL

ONE OF THE Supreme Court's consistent teachings is that the First Amendment is not absolute. This lesson began in 1919 when Justice Holmes noted in that the First Amendment would not protect a person who falsely yelled "fire" in a crowded theater, and it continues today. Put simply, some varieties of expression are illegitimate and may be punished. Many examples come to mind. One may not communicate military secrets to the enemy or make terrorist threats. One may not provide fraudulent information in commercial transactions or engage in discussions that amount to criminal conspiracies. One may not lie under oath or exchange insider information in securities transactions. And one may not yell "fire" in a crowded theater. In each of these cases the expression falls outside the boundaries of First Amendment protection.

This chapter explores the limits of First Amendment protection by examining obscenity and libel, two types of expression that have presented the justices with perplexing constitutional questions. There is almost universal agreement that the Framers considered neither to be legitimate expression and did not intend the First Amendment to protect them from government regulation. Accepting this proposition, however, does not settle the matter because other questions remain. How do we define obscenity and libel? What distinguishes obscene and libelous expression from protected speech and press? What standards of evidence should be imposed?

How can government regulate obscenity and libel without imposing a "chilling effect" on protected expression?

OBSCENITY

According to Justice Harlan (II), "The subject of obscenity has produced a variety of views among the members of the Court unmatched in any other course of constitutional interpretation."[1] An even more candid statement came from Justice Brennan, the member of the Court most associated with the subject *(see Box 7-1)*. Discussing service on the Court, Brennan noted, "It takes a while before you can become even calm about approaching a job like this. Which is not to say you do not make mistakes. In my case, there has been the obscenity area."[2]

What is it about obscenity that has produced such extraordinary statements? After all, the Court uniformly has held that obscenity is not entitled to First Amendment protection. The problem is determining what makes a work obscene. In other words, how should we define the term? The answer is important because how we differentiate protected expression from unprotected expression has broad implications for what we see, read, and hear. Consider the movie industry: in the not-so-distant past, strict definitions of obscenity required an actor to keep one foot on the floor when performing a

1. *Interstate Circuit v. Dallas* (1968).
2. Nat Hentoff, "Profiles—The Constitutionalists," *New Yorker*, March 12, 1990, 54.

BOX 7-1   WILLIAM JOSEPH BRENNAN JR. (1956–1990)

WILLIAM J. BRENNAN JR. was born April 25, 1906, in Newark, New Jersey. He was the second of eight children of Irish parents who immigrated to the United States in 1890. Brennan displayed impressive academic abilities early in life. He was an outstanding student in high school, an honors student at the University of Pennsylvania's Wharton School of Finance, and in the top 10 percent of his Harvard Law School class in 1931.

Brennan married Marjorie Leonard, May 5, 1928, and they had two sons and one daughter. (Marjorie Brennan died in 1982, and Brennan married Mary Fowler, March 9, 1983.) After law school Brennan returned to Newark, where he joined a prominent law firm. Following passage of the Wagner Labor Act in 1935, Brennan began to specialize in labor law.

With the outbreak of World War II, Brennan entered the Army, serving as a manpower troubleshooter on the staff of the undersecretary of war, Robert B. Patterson. At the conclusion of the war, Brennan returned to his old law firm. But as his practice swelled, Brennan, a dedicated family man, began to resent the demands it placed on his time.

A DESIRE TO TEMPER the pace of his work was one of the reasons Brennan accepted an appointment to the newly created New Jersey Superior Court in 1949. Brennan had been a leader in the movement to establish the court as part of a large program of judicial reform. It came as no surprise when Republican governor Alfred E. Driscoll named Brennan, a registered but inactive Democrat, to the court.

During his tenure on the superior court, Brennan's use of pretrial procedures to speed up the disposition of cases brought him to the attention of New Jersey Supreme Court justice Arthur T. Vanderbilt. It was reportedly at Vanderbilt's suggestion that Brennan was moved first in 1950 to the appellate division of the superior court and then in 1952 to the state supreme court.

Late in 1956, when President Eisenhower was looking for a justice to replace Sherman Minton, Vanderbilt and others strongly recommended Brennan for the post, and Eisenhower gave him a recess appointment in October. There was some criticism that Eisenhower was currying favor with voters by nominating a Roman Catholic Democrat to the bench so close to the election, but Brennan's established integrity and nonpolitical background minimized the impact of the charges. He was confirmed by the Senate March 19, 1957. Brennan retired from the Court July 20, 1990. He died July 24, 1997.

SOURCE: Adapted from Joan Biskupic and Elder Witt, *Guide to the U.S. Supreme Court*, 3d ed. (Washington, D.C.: Congressional Quarterly, 1997), 944.

---

bedroom scene. Imagine the number of contemporary movies the courts would ban under such a standard! But, today, the issues are no less salient: groups throughout the country try to bar certain books from public schools, to prohibit the sale of particular records to minors, to stop libraries from subscribing to certain magazines, and to ban the transmission of some material on the Internet—all on obscenity grounds.

Given the importance of the task, one might think the Court has set definitive policy in this area. Perhaps that is now the case, but for more than four decades the Court grappled with the issue, particularly with fashioning a definition of obscenity. Why did this issue cause such problems? Has the Court come up with a reasonable solution? Or does the Court still face difficulty, floundering among competing schools of thought?

Obscenity in Perspective: Origins

The adjudication of obscenity claims is a relatively modern phenomenon. Before the 1950s the Court generally avoided the issue by adopting the British definition of obscenity:

whether the tendency of the matter charged as obscenity is to deprave and corrupt those whose minds are open to such immoral influences and into whose hands a publication of this sort might fall.

This definition, first promulgated in the 1868 case of *Regina v. Hicklin,* contained three aspects that made it particularly difficult to overcome. First, the *Hicklin* test required the material to meet a stringent level of acceptability—whether the material could be seen by a child. If the material could not meet this aspect of the test, then it was declared obscene. Second, the *Hicklin* test did not require that the publication be considered as a whole. Instead, a work could be declared obscene based upon one of its parts. Third, the *Hicklin* test did not direct the courts to consider the social value of the work; rather, it only provided that the impact of the offensive sections be examined. As a result, the *Hicklin* standard left a wide range of expression unprotected.

The U.S. Supreme Court not only adopted the *Hicklin* standard, but also strengthened it. In *Ex parte Jackson* (1878) the Court upheld the Comstock Act, which made it a crime to send obscene materials, including information on abortion and birth control, through the U.S. mail. The justices applied the *Hicklin* test and extended its coverage to include materials discussing reproduction.

While the Supreme Court clung to *Hicklin,* some U.S. lower courts were attempting to liberalize it or even reject it. Among the better-known examples is *United States v. One Book Entitled "Ulysses" by James Joyce* (1934), in which Judge Augustus Hand argued that the proper standard should be whether the author *intended* to produce obscene materials. The diverse rulings from the lower courts, coupled with the Supreme Court's silence on the issue, began to have an effect. By the 1950s the pornography business was flourishing in this country, with little restriction on who could buy or view such material. This situation led to a backlash, with irate citizens clamoring for tighter controls. Others, particularly attorneys with the American Civil Liberties Union (ACLU), pressured courts to move in precisely the opposite direction—to rule that the First Amendment covers all materials, including those previously adjudged obscene. By the late 1950s these different interests were sending the same message to the justices: the time had come to deal with the issue.

In *Butler v. Michigan* (1957) the Court responded by declaring unconstitutional a state statute that defined obscenity along *Hicklin* test lines. The law made it a crime to distribute material "found to have a potentially deleterious influence on youth." The justices struck down the statute, finding fault with the child standard. It is incompatible with the First Amendment, the justices said, to reduce the reading material available to adults to that which is fit for children. To do so, according to Justice Frankfurter's opinion, is "to burn the house to roast the pig."

Although the *Butler* decision mortally wounded the *Hicklin* test, the justices failed to provide an alternative. Later that year, however, the Court took its first stab at creating a contemporary American obscenity standard. The case was *Roth v. United States,* decided with a companion case, *Alberts v. California.* While reading *Roth,* consider the critical issue of standards: Justice Brennan continued to find fault with *Hicklin,* but what did he propose as a replacement?[3]

Roth v. United States

354 U.S. 476 (1957)
laws.findlaw.com/US/354/476.html
Vote: 6 (Brennan, Burton, Clark, Frankfurter, Warren,
       Whittaker)
    3 (Black, Douglas, Harlan)
Opinion of the Court: Brennan
Concurring opinion: Warren
Dissenting opinions: Douglas, Harlan[4]

3. For oral arguments in this case, navigate to: *oyez.nwu.edu.*
4. Harlan dissented in *Roth,* but concurred in the companion case, *Alberts v. California.*

In 1955 the U.S. government obtained a twenty-six-count indictment against Samuel Roth for violating a federal obscenity law. The government alleged that Roth had sent "obscene, indecent, and filthy matter" through the mail. Among those materials was a circular advertising *Photo and Body, Good Times,* and *American Aphrodite Number Thirteen.*

At Roth's trial the judge instructed the jury with this definition of obscenity: the material "must be calculated to debauch the minds and morals of those into whose hands it may fall and that the test in each case is the effect of the book, picture or publication considered as a whole, not upon any particular class, but upon all those whom it is likely to reach. In other words, you determine its impact upon the average person in the community." The jury found Roth guilty on four of the counts, and the judge sentenced him to the maximum punishment of five years in prison and a $5,000 fine.

MR. JUSTICE BRENNAN delivered the opinion of the Court.

In *Roth,* the primary constitutional question is whether the federal obscenity statute violates the provision of the First Amendment that "Congress shall make no law . . . abridging the freedom of speech, or of the press. . . ."

The dispositive question is whether obscenity is utterance within the area of protected speech and press. Although this is the first time the question has been squarely presented to this Court, either under the First Amendment or under the Fourteenth Amendment, expressions found in numerous opinions indicate that this Court has always assumed that obscenity is not protected by the freedom of speech and press.

The guaranties of freedom of expression in effect in 10 of the 14 States which by 1792 had ratified the Constitution, gave no absolute protection for every utterance. Thirteen of the 14 States provided for the prosecution of libel, and all of those States made either blasphemy or profanity, or both, statutory crimes. As early as 1712, Massachusetts made it criminal to publish "any filthy, obscene, or profane song, pamphlet, libel or mock sermon" in imitation or mimicking of religious services. Thus, profanity and obscenity were related offenses.

In light of this history, it is apparent that the unconditional phrasing of the First Amendment was not intended to protect every utterance. This phrasing did not prevent this Court from concluding that libelous utterances are not within the area of constitutionally protected speech. At the time of the adoption of the First Amendment, obscenity law was not as fully developed as libel law, but there is sufficiently contemporaneous evidence to show that obscenity, too, was outside the protection intended for speech and press.

The protection given speech and press was fashioned to assure unfettered interchange of ideas for the bringing about of political and social changes desired by the people. . . .

All ideas having even the slightest redeeming social importance—unorthodox ideas, controversial ideas, even ideas hateful to the prevailing climate of opinion—have the full protection of the guaranties, unless excludable because they encroach upon the limited area of more important interests. But implicit in the history of the First Amendment is the rejection of obscenity as utterly without redeeming social importance. This rejection for that reason is mirrored in the universal judgment that obscenity should be restrained, reflected in the international agreement of over 50 nations, in the obscenity laws of all of the 48 States, and in the 20 obscenity laws enacted by the Congress from 1842 to 1956. This is the same judgment expressed by this Court in *Chaplinsky v. New Hampshire.* . . . We hold that obscenity is not within the area of constitutionally protected speech or press.

It is strenuously urged that these obscenity statutes offend the constitutional guaranties because they punish incitation to impure sexual *thoughts,* not shown to be related to any overt antisocial conduct which is or may be incited in the persons stimulated to such *thoughts.* In *Roth,* the trial judge instructed the jury: "The words 'obscene, lewd and lascivious' as used in the law, signify that form of immorality which has relation to sexual impurity and has a tendency to excite lustful *thoughts.*" It is insisted that the constitutional guaranties are violated because convictions may be had without proof either that obscene material will perceptibly create a clear and present danger of antisocial conduct, or will probably induce its recipients to such conduct. . . .

However, sex and obscenity are not synonymous. Obscene material is material which deals with sex in a manner appealing to prurient interest. The portrayal of sex, *e.g.*, in art, literature and scientific works, is not itself sufficient reason to deny material the constitutional protection of freedom of speech and press. Sex, a great and mysterious motive force in human life, has indisputably been a subject of absorbing interest to mankind through the ages; it is one of the vital problems of human interest and public concern. . . .

The fundamental freedoms of speech and press have contributed greatly to the development and well-being of our free society and are indispensable to its continued growth. Ceaseless vigilance is the watchword to prevent their erosion by Congress or by the States. The door barring federal and state intrusion into this area cannot be left ajar; it must be kept tightly closed and opened only the slightest crack necessary to prevent encroachment upon more important interests. It is therefore vital that the standards for judging obscenity safeguard the protection of freedom of speech and press for material which does not treat sex in a manner appealing to prurient interest.

The early leading standard of obscenity allowed material to be judged merely by the effect of an isolated excerpt upon particularly susceptible persons. *Regina v. Hicklin.* Some American courts adopted this standard but later decisions have rejected it and substituted this test: whether to the average person, applying contemporary community standards, the dominant theme of the material taken as a whole appeals to prurient interest. The *Hicklin* test, judging obscenity by the effect of isolated passages upon the most susceptible persons, might well encompass material legitimately treating with sex, and so it must be rejected as unconstitutionally restrictive of the freedoms of speech and press. On the other hand, the substituted standard provides safeguards adequate to withstand the charge of constitutional infirmity.

Both trial courts below sufficiently followed the proper standard. Both courts used the proper definition of obscenity. . . . [I]n *Roth,* the trial judge instructed the jury as follows:

". . . The test is not whether it would arouse sexual desires or sexual impure thoughts in those comprising a particular segment of the community, the young, the immature or the highly prudish or would leave another segment, the scientific or highly educated or the so-called worldly-wise and sophisticated indifferent and unmoved. . . .

"The test in each case is the effect of the book, picture or publication considered as a whole, not upon any particular class, but upon all those whom it is likely to reach. In other words, you determine its impact upon the average person in the community. The books, pictures and circulars must be judged as a whole, in their entire context, and you are not to consider detached or separate portions in reaching a conclusion. You judge the circulars, pictures and publications which have been put in evidence by present-day standards of the community. You may ask yourselves does it offend the common conscience of the community by present-day standards.

"In this case, ladies and gentlemen of the jury, you and you alone are the exclusive judges of what the common conscience of the community is, and in determining that conscience you are to consider the community as a whole, young and old, educated and uneducated, the religious and the irreligious—men, women and children.". . .

In summary, then, we hold that these statutes, applied according to the proper standard for judging obscenity, do not offend constitutional safeguards against convictions based upon protected material, or fail to give men in acting adequate notice of what is prohibited.

The judgment [is] affirmed.

MR. CHIEF JUSTICE WARREN, concurring in the result.

I agree with the result reached by the Court in these cases, but, because we are operating in a field of expression and because broad language used here may eventually be applied to the arts and sciences and freedom of communication generally, I would limit our decision to the facts before us and to the validity of the statutes in question as applied. . . .

The line dividing the salacious or pornographic from literature or science is not straight and unwavering. Present laws depend largely upon the effect that the materials may have upon those who receive them. It is manifest that the same object may have a different impact, varying according to the part of the community it reached. But there is more to these cases. It is not the book that is on trial; it is a person. The conduct of the defendant is the central issue, not the obscenity of a book or picture. The nature of the materials is, of course, relevant as an attribute of the defendant's conduct, but the materials are thus placed in context from which they draw color and character. A wholly different result might be reached in a different setting.

MR. JUSTICE HARLAN, concurring in [part and dissenting in part].

In final analysis, the problem presented by these cases is how far, and on what terms, the state and federal governments have power to punish individuals for disseminating books considered to be undesirable because of their nature or supposed deleterious effect upon human conduct. Proceeding from the premise that "no issue is presented in either case, concerning the obscenity of the material involved," the Court finds the "dispositive question" to be "whether obscenity is utterance within the area of protected speech and press," and then holds that "obscenity" is not so protected because it is "utterly without redeeming social importance." This sweeping formula appears to me to beg the very question before us. The Court seems to assume that "obscenity" is a peculiar *genus* of "speech and press," which is as distinct, recognizable, and classifiable as poison ivy is among other plants. On this basis the *constitutional* question before us simply becomes, as the Court says, whether "obscenity," as an abstraction, is protected by the First and Fourteenth amendments, and the question whether a *particular* book may be suppressed becomes a mere matter of classification, of "fact," to be entrusted to a fact-finder and insulated from independent constitutional judgment. But surely the problem cannot be solved in such a generalized fashion. Every communication has an individuality and "value" of its own. The suppression of a particular writing or other tangible form of expression is, therefore, an *individual* matter, and in the nature of things every such suppression raises an individual constitutional problem, in which a reviewing court must determine for *itself* whether the attacked expression is suppressible within constitutional standards. Since those standards do not readily lend themselves to generalized definitions, the constitutional problem in the last analysis becomes one of particularized judgments which appellate courts must make for themselves.

MR. JUSTICE DOUGLAS, with whom MR. JUSTICE BLACK CONCURS, dissenting.

When we sustain these convictions, we make the legality of a publication turn on the purity of thought which a book or tract instills in the mind of the reader. I do not think we can approve that standard and be faithful to the command of the First Amendment, which by its terms is a restraint on Congress and which by the Fourteenth is a restraint on the states. . . .

I do not think that the problem can be resolved by the Court's statement that "obscenity is not expression protected by the First Amendment." With the exception of *Beauharnais v. Illinois,* none of our cases has resolved problems of free speech and free press by placing any form of expression beyond the pale of the absolute prohibition of the First Amendment. . . . I reject too the implication that problems of freedom of speech and of the press are to be resolved by weighing against the values of free expression, the judgment of the Court that a particular form of that expression has "no redeeming social importance." The First Amendment, its prohibition in terms absolute, was designed to preclude courts as well as legislatures from weighing the values of speech against silence. The First Amendment puts free speech in the preferred position. . . .

I would give the broad sweep of the First Amendment full support. I have the same confidence in the ability of our people to reject noxious literature as I have in their capacity to sort out the true from the false in theology, economics, politics, or any other field.

At first glance, Brennan's opinion seems to forge a compromise between competing views. He appeased pro-decency forces by rejecting the view that nothing is obscene, but he also set a new standard of obscenity—"whether to the average person, applying contemporary community standards, the dominant theme of the material taken as a whole appeals to prurient interests"—that was less restrictive than the *Hicklin* standard. *Roth* imposed an "average person" test, replacing *Hicklin's* child standard with that of an adult. Moreover, the "contemporary community standards" criterion recognized the evolving nature of society's views of sexual morality. The "dominant theme of the material taken as a whole" approach rejected *Hicklin's* notion that a work can be declared obscene based on the content of a single part. Finally, the "prurient interests" element ensured that only material with sexual content could fall under the obscenity rubric.

The Court may have thought this a workable standard, but experience with it raised several questions. What did the Court mean by "contemporary community standards"? Was it referring to the nation, a state, or a town? The values of citizens living in a rural area may be somewhat different from those living in a big city. Also, what is the meaning of the phrase "dominant theme"? How much social value need a book or movie have to offset portions of the work that might appeal to prurient interests? And how could police and prosecutors enforce this standard?

For nearly two decades after *Roth*, the Court tried to fill these gaps. As you read the cases and narrative, consider not only the answers the Court gave, but also the difficulty it had in reaching them. *Roth* created divisions among the justices, and the Court remained divided as it tried to refine Brennan's test.

Contemporary Community Standards. A major question emerging from *Roth* was whether the new standard left it to states and localities to differentiate obscenity based on their own norms, or whether they had to base their distinctions on those found nationwide. In other words, would Tulsa, Oklahoma, have to follow the same standard as New York City? In *Jacobellis v. Ohio* (1964) the Court attempted to address this issue. Ohio charged Nico Jacobellis, the manager of a movie theater, with showing an obscene film called *Les Amants* (The Lovers). The movie depicts the love affair of an archaeologist and a woman who leaves her husband and child, and it contains one "explicit love scene" near the end.

Brennan again wrote in *Jacobellis*, and his judgment for the Court is noteworthy in several regards. First, Brennan refined the *Roth* test, stating that contemporary community standards were those of the nation, not of a local community. In doing so, he not only held the film to be protected speech but also substantially liberalized *Roth*. It is bound to be the case that communities seeking to ban obscenity have stricter standards than those of the country at large. But, under Brennan's refinement, Tulsa would indeed be required to invoke the same obscenity standards as New York. Second, Brennan's opinion gave the legal community some insight into the inner workings of the Court. He noted that the justices had viewed the film and not found it obscene. Would the justices now be watching every movie coming to their doorstep? According to Brennan's private papers, that is precisely

what they did, going so far as to have movie days. Third, we begin to see the intractable problem of obscenity take its toll. Brennan's may have been the judgment of the Court, but the other eight justices also filed opinions. Dissenting, Chief Justice Warren argued that "contemporary community standards" referred to a local community standard. But among the best known is Justice Potter Stewart's concurrence: he was becoming so disgruntled with the issue that he almost gave up, penning the line, "I shall not today attempt further to define [hard-core pornography]. . . . But I know it when I see it."

Dominant Theme. The *Roth* test places emphasis on the "dominant theme of the material taken as a whole," rather than a small piece of the work. In *Jacobellis* Brennan provided insight into what he meant by that phrase. He suggested that only work "utterly without redeeming social value," perhaps hard-core pornography, would represent unprotected expression.

Even with that admonition, prosecutors were uncertain about what Brennan was attempting to do. Could they seek to ban books and movies that were generally obscene, but had some element of artistry or social value? Or were they limited to banning those works totally devoid of merit? The Court tried to address these questions in *Memoirs v. Massachusetts* (1966). The state urged the Court to find obscene *Memoirs of a Woman of Pleasure*, popularly known as *Fanny Hill*, written by John Cleland in 1749. *Memoirs* is an erotic novel that traces the escapades of a London prostitute. The highest state court in Massachusetts held that a book need not be "unqualifiedly worthless before it could be deemed obscene"; that is, just because *Memoirs* contained some nonerotic passages did not mean that it had redeeming value. Once again, the Court was divided: no majority could agree on a rationale. In his judgment for the Court, Brennan argued for an expansion of the parameters of *Roth*. If a work had a "modicum of social value," it could not be adjudged obscene. Only two other justices agreed with Brennan's argument. Three other justices concurred with the result but for varying reasons, and the remaining three justices each issues separate dissenting opinions.

By 1966 a divided Court had radically altered *Roth*,

BOX 7-2 *ROTH, JACOBELLIS,*
AND *MEMOIRS* COMPARED

ROTH: "Whether to the average person applying contemporary community standards, the dominant theme of the material, taken as a whole, appeals to prurient interests."

ROTH and *JACOBELLIS:* "Whether to the average person applying" standards of "the society at large," the material is "utterly without redeeming social importance."

ROTH, JACOBELLIS, and *MEMOIRS:* "Whether to the average person applying standards of the society at large, the material is utterly without redeeming social importance," possessing not "a modicum of social value."

as shown in Box 7-2, which compares the test in 1957 to that articulated in 1966. Would anything be defined as obscene under the *Roth-Jacobellis-Memoirs* standards? Which of the various standards articulated by the justices should prosecutors and lower court judges apply? We might think that hard-core pornography would fall outside of it, but could not a clever movie maker, author, or publisher circumvent it? If a short passage of some merit appears in the middle of an erotic book or pornographic movie, does the product have redeeming value?

Enforcing Roth. The Court's decisions had the effect of eliminating most works from the obscene category. Prosecutors remained uncertain about what the Court was doing with the obscenity issue. In fact, the only bright spot for them was the Court's decision in *Ginzburg v. United States* (1966), in which Court ruled that anyone who deliberately portrays material for sale in an "erotically arousing" way could be convicted of selling obscene materials. By doing so, they acknowledged that courts and juries could use the manner in which the seller of the material advertised it to determine if the material was obscene even if the Court, reviewing the material without reference to the manner in which it was advertised, would find the material to not be obscene.

But *Ginzburg* was the exception, not the rule. The majority of the obscenity convictions that made it to the Court during the late 1960s were reversed, often with only short, *per curiam* decisions. The justices simply announced the judgment of the Court without giving any detailed rationale behind their decision, but sometimes revealing the depth of their disagreement. For example, in *Redrup v. New York* (1967) the Court reversed Robert Redrup's pandering conviction under a New York state law. In its *per curiam* opinion the Court stated:

Two members of this Court have consistently adhered to the view that a State is utterly without power to suppress, control, or punish the distribution of any writings or pictures upon the ground of their "obscenity." A third has held to the opinion that a State's power in this area is narrowly limited to a distinct and clearly identifiable class of material. Others have subscribed to a not dissimilar standard, holding that a State may not constitutionally inhibit the distribution of literary material as obscene unless "(a) the dominant theme of the material taken as a whole appeals to a prurient interest in sex; (b) the material is patently offensive because it affronts contemporary community standards relating to the description or representation of sexual matters; and (c) the material is utterly without redeeming social value," emphasizing that the "three elements must coalesce," and that no such material can "be proscribed unless it is found to be utterly without redeeming social value." Another justice has not viewed the "social value" element as an independent factor in the judgment of obscenity.

Whichever of these constitutional views is brought to bear upon the cases before us, it is clear the judgments cannot stand.

The only point of agreement in *Redrup* was that under various tests the material at issue was not obscene. Otherwise, the opinion smacked of resignation; apparently, some of the justices had given up on the issue, and the rest were fractionalized. In fact, by 1967 the members of the Court had adopted so many different views of obscenity that state prosecutors and legislators had no firm guidelines *(see Box 7-3)*. Should they adopt the principles set forth in *Roth* when many of the justices now rejected that standard? If not, what could they substitute for it?

The justices' inability to define obscenity in turn crippled enforcement efforts. If *Redrup* did not meet *Ginzburg's* pandering standard, what would? Apparently, very little. After 1967 the Court summarily reversed

BOX 7-3 WHAT IS OBSCENE?

Justice	Case	Standard
Brennan	*Roth v. United States*, 1957 (as modified by *Jacobellis v. Ohio*, 1964, and *Memoirs v. Massachusetts*, 1966)	"[W]hether to the average person, applying contemporary community standards, the dominant theme of the material taken as a whole appeals to the prurient interest." Contemporary community standards mean national standards. The material must be utterly without redeeming social value.
Warren	*Jacobellis*	"For all the sound and fury that the *Roth* test has generated, it has not been proved unsound, and I believe that we should try to live with it—at least until a more satisfactory definition is evolved. . . . It is my belief that when the Court said in *Roth* that obscenity is to be defined by reference to 'community standards' it meant community standards—not a national standard. . . ."
Harlan	*Jacobellis*	"[T]he states are constitutionally permitted greater latitude in determining what is bannable on the score of obscenity than is so with the Federal Government. . . . I would not prohibit [the states] from banning any material which, taken as a whole, has been reasonably found in state judicial proceedings to treat sex in a fundamentally offensive manner, under rationally established criteria for judging such material."
Douglas, Black	*Roth, Jacobellis, Memoirs*	"[I]f the First Amendment guarantee of freedom of speech and press is to mean anything in this field, it must allow protests even against the moral code that the standard of the day sets for the community." "[T]he First Amendment leaves no power in government to regulate expression of ideas."
Stewart	*Jacobellis*	"Under the First and Fourteenth Amendments criminal laws in this area are constitutionally limited to hard-core pornography. I shall not today attempt further to define [hard-core pornography]. . . . But I know it when I see it."
Clark	*Memoirs*	"I [believe that today's decision] rejects the basic holding of *Roth*. . . . I understand [the obscenity test] to include only two constitutional requirements: (1) the [material] must be judged as a whole, not by its parts; and (2) it must be judged in terms of its appeal to the prurient interest of the average person, applying contemporary community standards. . . . [S]ocial importance does not constitute a separate and distinct constitutional test. Such evidence must be considered together with evidence that the material in question appeals to the prurient interest and is patently offensive."

NOTE: Warren joined Brennan's *Memoirs* opinion; therefore, he also adopted the utterly without redeeming social value standard.

thirty-two cases by citing *Redrup*.[5] This move led many scholars to suggest that by the end of the 1960s obscenity prosecutions were almost impossible to obtain. In other words, after *Redrup*, it appeared that the Court was protecting almost any kind of expression. The country was approaching the "end of obscenity."

The Political Environment and the "Nixon" Court

As the Court puzzled over obscenity, Congress took matters into its own hands. In July 1968 it created the Federal Commission on Obscenity and Pornography "to investigate the effect of pornography on social behavior, to determine the need for new laws and to report on the constitutionality of such laws." Composed mainly of Lyndon Johnson appointees—most of whom had liberal viewpoints—the commission issued its first report in 1970. Its conclusion seemed to parallel that of the Court: "federal, state, and local legislation prohibiting the sale, exhibition, or distribution of sexual material to consenting adults should be repealed."[6]

By the time the commission handed in its report, however, the nation had a new president, Richard Nixon, who firmly and emphatically rejected these conclusions. During his presidential campaign Nixon had criticized the liberal Warren Court's rulings on obscenity as well as other areas of the law and had vowed to work for their reversal. His chance came with the appointment of four new justices to the Court. But the question remained whether the so-called Nixon Court, led by the new chief justice, Warren Burger, could handle the issue any better than its predecessor.

Miller v. California (1973), the Burger Court's first major obscenity case, provides an answer. Here justices turned their attention to revamping the definition of obscenity and, therefore, the whole approach to the topic.[7]

5. Joseph F. Kobylka, *The Politics of Obscenity* (Westport, Conn.: Greenwood Press, 1991), 6.

6. President's Commission on Obscenity and Pornography, *Report* (New York: Bantam Books, 1970), 57.

7. For oral arguments in this case, navigate to: *oyez.nwu.edu.*

Miller v. California

413 U.S. 15 (1973)
laws.findlaw.com/US/413/15.html
Vote: 5 (Blackmun, Burger, Powell, Rehnquist, White)
    4 (Brennan, Douglas, Marshall, Stewart)
Opinion of the Court: Burger
Dissenting opinions: Douglas, Brennan

Marvin Miller, a vendor of so-called adult material, conducted a mass-mail campaign to drum up sales for his books. The pamphlets were fairly explicit, containing pictures of men and women engaging in various sexual activities, often with their genitals prominently displayed.

Had Miller sent the brochures to interested individuals only, he might not have been caught. But because he did a mass mailing, some pamphlets ended up in the hands of people who did not want them. Miller was arrested when the manager of a restaurant and his mother opened one of the envelopes and complained to the police.

MR. CHIEF JUSTICE BURGER delivered the opinion of the Court.

This is one of a group of "obscenity-pornography" cases being reviewed by the Court in a re-examination of standards enunciated in earlier cases involving what Mr. Justice Harlan called "the intractable obscenity problem.". . . .

This case involves the application of a State's criminal obscenity statute to a situation in which sexually explicit materials have been thrust by aggressive sales action upon unwilling recipients who had in no way indicated any desire to receive such materials. This Court has recognized that the States have a legitimate interest in prohibiting dissemination or exhibition of obscene material when the mode of dissemination carries with it a significant danger of offending the sensibilities of unwilling recipients or of exposure to juveniles. It is in this context that we are called on to define the standards which must be used to identify obscene material that a State may regulate without infringing on the First Amendment as applicable to the States through the Fourteenth Amendment. . . .

[O]bscene material is unprotected by the First Amendment. We acknowledge, however, the inherent dangers of undertaking to regulate any form of expression. State statutes designed to regulate obscene materials must be carefully limited. As a result, we now confine the permissible scope of such regulation to works which depict or describe sexual conduct. That conduct must be specifically defined by the applicable state law, as written or authoritatively construed. A state offense must also be limited to works which, taken as a whole, appeal to the prurient interest in sex, which portray sexual conduct in a patently offensive way, and which, taken as a whole, do not have serious literary, artistic, political, or scientific value.

The basic guidelines for the trier of fact must be: (a) whether "the average person, applying contemporary community standards" would find that the work, taken as a whole, appeals to the prurient interest; (b) whether the work depicts or describes, in a patently offensive way, sexual conduct specifically defined by the applicable state law; and (c) whether the work, taken as a whole, lacks serious literary, artistic, political, or scientific value. We do not adopt as a constitutional standard the *"utterly* without redeeming social value" test of *Memoirs v. Massachusetts;* that concept has never commanded the adherence of more than three Justices at one time. If a state law that regulates obscene material is thus limited, as written or construed, the First Amendment values applicable to the States through the Fourteenth Amendment are adequately protected by the ultimate power of appellate courts to conduct an independent review of constitutional claims when necessary.

We emphasize that it is not our function to propose regulatory schemes for the States. That must await their concrete legislative efforts. It is possible, however, to give a few plain examples of what a state statute could define for regulation under part (b) of the standard announced in this opinion.

(a) Patently offensive representations or descriptions of ultimate sexual acts, normal or perverted, actual or simulated.

(b) Patently offensive representation or descriptions of masturbation, excretory functions, and lewd exhibition of the genitals.

Sex and nudity may not be exploited without limit by films or pictures exhibited or sold in places of public accommodation any more than live sex and nudity can be exhibited or sold without limit in such public places. At a minimum, prurient, patently offensive depiction or description of sexual conduct must have serious literary, artistic, political, or scientific value to merit First Amendment protection. . . .

Under the holdings announced today, no one will be subject to prosecution for the sale or exposure of obscene materials unless these materials depict or describe patently offensive "hard core" sexual conduct specifically defined by the regulating state law, as written or construed. We are satisfied that these specific prerequisites will provide fair notice to a dealer in such materials that his public and commercial activities may bring prosecution. If the inability to define regulated materials with ultimate, god-like precision altogether removes the power of the States or the Congress to regulate, then "hard core" pornography may be exposed without limit to the juvenile, the passerby, and the consenting adult alike. . . .

It is certainly true that the absence, since *Roth,* of a single majority view of this Court as to proper standards for testing obscenity has placed a strain on both state and federal courts. But today, for the first time since *Roth* was decided in 1957, a majority of this Court has agreed on concrete guidelines to isolate "hard core" pornography from expression protected by the First Amendment. Now we . . . attempt to provide positive guidance to federal and state courts alike.

This may not be an easy road, free from difficulty. But no amount of "fatigue" should lead us to adopt a convenient "institutional" rationale—an absolutist, "anything goes" view of the First Amendment—because it will lighten our burdens. "Such an abnegation of judicial supervision in this field would be inconsistent with our duty to uphold the constitutional guarantees." Nor should we remedy "tension between state and federal courts" by arbitrarily depriving the States of a power reserved to them under the Constitution, a power which they have enjoyed and exercised continuously from before the adoption of the First Amendment to this day. "Our duty admits of no 'substitute for facing up to the tough individual problems of constitutional judgment involved in every obscenity case.'"

Under a National Constitution, fundamental First Amendment limitations on the powers of the States do not vary from community to community, but this does not mean that there are, or should or can be, fixed, uniform national standards of precisely what appeals to the "prurient interest" or is "patently offensive." These are essentially questions of fact, and our Nation is simply too big and too diverse for this Court to reasonably expect that such standards could be articulated for all 50 States in a single formulation, even assuming the prerequisite consensus exists. When triers of fact are asked to decide whether "the average person, applying contemporary community standards" would consider certain materials "prurient," it would be unrealistic to require that the answer be based on some abstract formulation. The adversary system, with lay jurors as the usual ultimate fact-finders in criminal prosecutions, has historically permitted triers of fact to draw on the standards of their community, guided always by limiting instructions on the law. To require a State to structure obscenity proceedings around evidence of a *national* "community standard" would be an exercise in futility.

. . . [T]his case was tried on the theory that the California obscenity statute sought to incorporate the tripartite test of *Memoirs.* This, a "national" standard of First Amendment protection enumerated by a plurality of this Court, was correctly regarded at the time of trial as limiting state prosecution under the controlling case law. The jury, however, was explicitly instructed that, in determining whether the "dominant theme of the material as a whole . . . appeals to the prurient interest" and in determining whether the material "goes substantially beyond customary limits of candor and affronts contemporary community standards of decency," it was to apply "contemporary community standards of the State of California.". . .

We conclude that neither the State's alleged failure to offer evidence of "national standards," nor the trial court's charge that the jury consider state community standards, were constitutional errors. Nothing in the First Amendment requires that a jury must consider hypothetical and unascertainable "national standards" when attempting to determine whether certain materials are obscene as a matter of fact. . . . It is neither realistic nor constitutionally sound to read the First Amendment as requiring that the people of Maine or Mississippi accept public depiction of conduct found tolerable in Las Vegas or New York City. People in different States vary in their tastes and attitudes, and this diversity is not to be strangled by the absolutism of imposed uniformity. . . . We hold that the requirement that the jury evaluate the materials with reference to "contempo-

rary standards of the State of California" serves this protective purpose and is constitutionally adequate.

The dissenting Justices sound the alarm of repression. But, in our view, to equate the free and robust exchange of ideas and political debate with commercial exploitation of obscene material demeans the grand conception of the First Amendment and its high purposes in the historic struggle for freedom. It is a "misuse of the great guarantees of free speech and free press. . . ." The First Amendment protects works which, taken as a whole, have serious literary, artistic, political, or scientific value, regardless of whether the government or a majority of the people approve of the ideas these works represent. . . . But the public portrayal of hardcore sexual conduct for its own sake, and for the ensuing commercial gain, is a different matter. . . .

In sum, we (a) reaffirm the *Roth* holding that obscene material is not protected by the First Amendment; (b) hold that such material can be regulated by the States, subject to the specific safeguards enunciated above, without a showing that the material is *"utterly* without redeeming social value"; and (c) hold that obscenity is to be determined by applying "contemporary community standards," not "national standards.". . .

Vacated and remanded.

MR. JUSTICE DOUGLAS, dissenting.

Today we leave open the way for California to send a man to prison for distributing brochures that advertise books and a movie under freshly written standards defining obscenity which until today's decision were never the part of any law. . . .

Today the Court retreats from the earlier formulations of the constitutional test and undertakes to make new definitions. This effort, like the earlier ones, is earnest and well intentioned. The difficulty is that we do not deal with constitutional terms, since "obscenity" is not mentioned in the Constitution or Bill of Rights. And the First Amendment makes no such exception from "the press" which it undertakes to protect nor, as I have said on other occasions, is an exception necessarily implied for there was no recognized exception to the free press at the time the Bill of Rights was adopted which treated "obscene" publications differently from other types of papers, magazines, and books. So there are no constitutional guidelines for deciding what is and what is not "obscene." The Court is at large because we deal with tastes and standards of literature. What shocks me may be sustenance for my neighbor. What causes one person to boil up in rage over one pamphlet or movie may reflect only his neurosis, not shared by others. We deal here with a regime of censorship which, if adopted, should be done by constitutional amendment after full debate by the people. . . .

We deal with highly emotional, not rational, questions. To many the Song of Solomon is obscene. I do not think we, the judges, were ever given the constitutional power to make definitions of obscenity. If it is to be defined, let the people debate and decide by a constitutional amendment what they want to ban as obscene and what standards they want the legislatures and the courts to apply. Perhaps the people will decide that the path towards a mature, integrated society requires that all ideas competing for acceptance must have no censor. Perhaps they will decide otherwise. Whatever the choice, the courts will have some guidelines. Now we have none except our own predilections.

MR. JUSTICE BRENNAN, with whom MR. JUSTICE STEWART and MR. JUSTICE MARSHALL join, dissenting.[8]

In the case before us, appellant was convicted of distributing obscene matter in violation of California Penal Code §311.2, on the basis of evidence that he had caused to be mailed unsolicited brochures advertising various books and a movie. I need not now decide whether a statute might be drawn to impose, within the requirements of the First Amendment, criminal penalties for the precise conduct at issue here. For it is clear that . . . the statute under which the prosecution was brought is unconstitutionally overbroad, and therefore invalid on its face.

The same day, the Court also handed down a decision in *Paris Adult Theatre I v. Slaton,* which involved a 1970 complaint filed by Atlanta, Georgia, against the Paris Adult Theatre. The complaint asserted that the theater was showing obscene films. During the trial, the judge

8. [Authors' note: Brennan filed a more pointed dissent in *Paris Adult Theatre I v. Slaton,* decided on the same day as *Miller.* See excerpt, this page.]

viewed two of the offending films, which depicted simulated fellatio, cunnilingus, and group sexual intercourse. The judge ruled in favor of the theater, mainly because the owners did not admit anyone under age twenty-one. After the Georgia Supreme Court reversed, the owners appealed to the U.S. Supreme Court. The justices, however, affirmed the ruling, refusing to extend the theater First Amendment protection, even though only consenting adults would be exposed to the films.

Some have suggested that *Miller* and *Paris Adult Theatre I* did not substantially alter *Roth* et al., but we see significant changes. In Table 7-1 we compare the *Roth* test and its expansions with the new *Miller* standard. Although the Court retained three important elements of the *Roth* test—the adult standard, the work taken as a whole, and the restriction of obscenity to sexually oriented materials—two major changes stand out. First, the *Miller* test specifically gives the states the authority to define what is obscene. The Court, therefore, emphasized local values rather than the national standard suggested in *Jacobellis.* Second, the Court did away with the notion that a work merited protection as long as it did not meet the "utterly without redeeming social value" criterion. Instead, the justices held that to receive First Amendment protection, sexually oriented materials had to have serious literary, artistic, political, or scientific value. As a consequence, the new *Miller* test permitted much greater regulation of sexually explicit materials than did the *Roth* standard.

In addition to the significant change in obscenity law ushered in by *Miller* and its companion case, *Paris Adult Theatre I,* liberals from the Warren Court era also noted the change in approach. Justice Brennan wrote in his dissenting opinion in *Paris Adult Theatre I:*

Our experience since *Roth* requires us not only to abandon the effort to pick out obscene materials on a case-by-case basis, but also to reconsider a fundamental postulate of *Roth:* that there exists a definable class of sexually oriented expression that may be totally suppressed by the Federal and State Governments. Assuming that such a class of expression does in fact exist, I am forced to conclude that the concept of "obscenity" cannot be defined with sufficient specificity and clarity to provide fair notice to persons who create and distribute sexually oriented ma-

TABLE 7-1 *Roth-Jacobellis-Memoirs* and *Miller* Compared

	Roth-Jacobellis-Memoirs (The Warren Court)	*Miller* (The Burger Court)
Relevant audience:	Average person	Average person
Scope of consideration:	Work taken as a whole	Work taken as a whole
Standard:	Sexual material found patently offensive by the national standards of society at large	Sexual conduct found patently offensive by contemporary community standards as specifically defined by applicable state law
Value of the work:	Utterly without redeeming social importance	Lacks serious literary, artistic, political, or scientific value

terials, to prevent substantial erosion of protected speech as a byproduct of the attempt to suppress unprotected speech, and to avoid very costly institutional harms. Given these inevitable side effects of state efforts to suppress what is assumed to be *unprotected* speech, we must scrutinize with care the state interest that is asserted to justify the suppression. For in the absence of some very substantial interest in suppressing such speech, we can hardly condone the ill effects that seem to flow inevitably from the effort. . . .

In short, while I cannot say that the interests of the State—apart from the question of juveniles and unconsenting adults—are trivial or nonexistent, I am compelled to conclude that these interests cannot justify the substantial damage to constitutional rights and to this Nation's judicial machinery that inevitably results from state efforts to bar the distribution even of unprotected material to consenting adults. . . . I would hold, therefore, that at least in the absence of distribution to juveniles or obtrusive exposure to unconsenting adults, the First and Fourteenth Amendments prohibit the State and Federal Governments from attempting wholly to suppress sexually oriented materials on the basis of their allegedly "obscene" contents.

Brennan's opinion, which was joined by Justices Marshall and Stewart, is remarkable for three reasons. First, after almost two decades of leading the Court in attempts to define obscenity, the author of *Roth* finally decided that it could not be done. Second, the three liberals argued that efforts to regulate "obscene" material inevitably led to unacceptable restrictions on protected expression. Third, Brennan and the others concluded that,

except for protecting juveniles and unconsenting adults, state and federal authorities should be banned from regulating sexually oriented expression altogether.

It would be difficult to imagine two more different positions than those taken by the majority and the dissenters in these obscenity cases, but they are alike in this respect: both sides wanted to extricate the Court from the obscenity business. Brennan and the other dissenters advocated an almost total end to government regulation of obscenity, while the *Miller* majority wanted to put an end to federal obscenity cases by shifting authority to the states.

The Warren Court's message to prosecutors had been that obscenity convictions would not stand, but the Nixon justices signaled encouragement. Law enforcement officials, state legislators, and prosecutors now recognized that they could enforce obscenity laws with some hope of obtaining solid convictions.

Miller *in Action*

The most significant change *Miller* produced was the shift from a national to a local focus on obscenity. As a result, towns felt relatively free to enact laws that fit their community values. As anticipated, the number of cases coming before the Court decreased, but *Miller* did not free the justices entirely. Indeed, between 1974 and 1988, the Court decided more than thirty cases involving many different issues. Three examples follow:

1. Could a city prohibit the performance of the play *Hair* on the basis of reports that it was obscene? (Maybe. Refusal to rent an auditorium for the production of a show that some think obscene constitutes prior restraint, and the city could prohibit the performance only if it took proper procedural steps. See *Southeastern Promotions, Ltd. v. Conrad*, 1975.)

2. Could a city ban the showing of movies containing nudity, but which are not necessarily obscene, at drive-in theaters? (No. Such statutes violate the First Amendment rights of film exhibitors. See *Erznoznik v. City of Jacksonville*, 1975.)

3. Does a community have free reign to define obscenity in a more stringent way than that specified in *Miller*? (Not necessarily. Local juries do not have "unbridled discretion" to determine what is obscene; they are to follow the *Miller* standard. See *Jenkins v. Georgia*, 1974.)

That this Court answered these and other questions in diverse ways lends some credence to the view that its "path on obscenity material proved almost as serpentine as that of its predecessor."[9] The observation is true to the extent that *Miller* did not end the Court's involvement with the issue, but the way the Burger Court treated the subject was very different from the Warren Court's treatment. Between 1957 and 1969—the heyday of the *Roth* test—the justices supported First Amendment claims in 88 percent of their obscenity decisions; that number dropped to 32 percent after *Miller*.[10] The Court did not side with government in every obscenity case it heard, but, as those percentages indicate, the shift in jurisprudence from *Roth* to *Miller* was significant.

The evolution of the Court's philosophy can best be seen, not through aggregated statistics, but in its handling of one issue, child pornography. We do not suggest that the case, *New York v. Ferber* (1982), is typical of obscenity cases; on the contrary, the justices have treated child pornography differently from other forms of obscenity. But it indicates the Court's increased willingness to leave the issue to state authorities and thereby to encourage prosecutions.[11]

9. Melvin I. Urofsky, *A March of Liberty* (New York: Knopf, 1988), 913.
10. Data are from Harold J. Spaeth's U.S. Supreme Court Judicial Data Base. The post-*Miller* data run through the 1998 term.
11. For oral arguments in this case, navigate to: *oyez.nwu.edu*.

New York v. Ferber

458 U.S. 747 (1982)
laws.findlaw.com/US/458/747.html
Vote: 9 (Blackmun, Brennan, Burger, Marshall, O'Connor,
       Powell, Rehnquist, Stevens, White)
       0

Opinion of the Court: White
Concurring opinions: Brennan, O'Connor, Stevens

New York and nineteen other states prohibited the "dissemination of material depicting children [under the age of sixteen] engaged in sexual conduct regardless of whether the material is obscene." Bookstore owner Paul Ferber was charged with violating this law when he sold two movies to an undercover police officer. The films were "devoted almost exclusively to depicting two young boys masturbating." In his defense, Ferber argued that the law "works serious and substantial violation of the First Amendment by measures and means unnecessary to accomplish its legislative objectives." State attorneys acknowledged the potential ramifications of closing an entire area to constitutional protection, but they suggested that the state had a compelling and overriding interest "in protecting children from sexual abuse."

JUSTICE WHITE delivered the opinion of the Court.

At issue in this case is the constitutionality of a New York criminal statute which prohibits persons from knowingly promoting sexual performances by children under the age of 16 by distributing material which depicts such performances.

In recent years, the exploitative use of children in the production of pornography has become a serious national problem. The Federal Government and 47 States have sought to combat the problem with statutes specifically directed at the production of child pornography. At least half of such statutes do not require that the materials produced be legally obscene. Thirty-five States and the United States Congress have also passed legislation prohibiting the distribution of such materials; 20 States prohibit the distribution of material depicting children engaged in sexual conduct without requiring that the material be legally obscene.

New York is one of the 20. In 1977, the New York Legislature enacted Article 263 of its Penal Law. Section 263.05 criminalizes as a class C felony the use of a child in a sexual performance:

"A person is guilty of the use of a child in a sexual performance if knowing the character and content thereof he employs, authorizes or induces a child less than sixteen years of age to engage in a sexual performance or being a parent, legal guardian or custodian of such child, he consents to the participation by such child in a sexual performance.". . .

In *Chaplinsky v. New Hampshire* (1942), the Court laid the foundation for the excision of obscenity from the realm of constitutionally protected expression:

"There are certain well-defined and narrowly limited classes of speech, the prevention and punishment of which have never been thought to raise any Constitutional problem. These include the lewd and obscene. . . . It has been well observed that such utterances are no essential part of any exposition of ideas, and are of such slight social value as a step to truth that any benefit that may be derived from them is clearly outweighed by the social interest in order and morality."

Embracing this judgment, the Court squarely held in *Roth v. United States* (1957) that "obscenity is not within the area of constitutionally protected speech or press." The Court recognized that "rejection of obscenity as utterly without redeeming social importance" was implicit in the history of the First Amendment: The original States provided for the prosecution of libel, blasphemy, and profanity, and the "universal judgment that obscenity should be restrained [is] reflected in the international agreement of over 50 nations, in the obscenity laws of all of the 48 states, and in the 20 obscenity laws enacted by Congress from 1842 to 1956."

Roth was followed by 15 years during which this Court struggled with "the intractable obscenity problem." Despite considerable vacillation over the proper definition of obscenity, a majority of the Members of the Court remained firm in the position that "the States have a legitimate interest in prohibiting dissemination or exhibition of obscene material when the mode of dissemination carries with it a significant danger of offending the sensibilities of unwilling recipients or of exposure to juveniles."

Throughout this period, we recognized "the inherent dangers of undertaking to regulate any form of expression." Consequently, our difficulty was not only to assure that statutes designed to regulate obscene materials sufficiently defined what was prohibited, but also to devise substantial

limits on what fell within the permissible scope of regulation. In *Miller v. California* a majority of the Court agreed that a "state offense must also be limited to works which, taken as a whole, appeal to the prurient interest in sex, which portray sexual conduct in a patently offensive way, and which, taken as a whole, do not have serious literary, artistic, political, or scientific value." Over the past decade, we have adhered to the guidelines expressed in *Miller*, which subsequently has been followed in the regulatory schemes of most States.

The *Miller* standard, like its predecessors, was an accommodation between the State's interests in protecting the "sensibilities of unwilling recipients" from exposure to pornographic material and the dangers of censorship inherent in unabashedly content-based laws. Like obscenity statutes, laws directed at the dissemination of child pornography run the risk of suppressing protected expression by allowing the hand of the censor to become unduly heavy. For the following reasons, however, we are persuaded that the States are entitled to greater leeway in the regulation of pornographic depictions of children.

First. It is evident beyond the need for elaboration that a State's interest in "safeguarding the physical and psychological well-being of a minor" is "compelling.". . .

The prevention of sexual exploitation and abuse of children constitutes a government objective of surpassing importance. The legislative findings accompanying passage of the New York laws reflect this concern:

"[T]here has been a proliferation of exploitation of children as subjects in sexual performances. The care of children is a sacred trust and should not be abused by those who seek to profit through a commercial network based upon the exploitation of children. The public policy of the state demands the protection of children from exploitation through sexual performances."

We shall not second-guess this legislative judgment. Respondent has not intimated that we do so. Suffice it to say that virtually all of the States and the United States have passed legislation proscribing the production of or otherwise combating "child pornography." The legislative judgment, as well as the judgment found in the relevant literature, is that the use of children as subjects of pornographic materials is harmful to the physiological, emotional, and mental health of the child. That judgment, we think, easily passes muster under the First Amendment.

Second. The distribution of photographs and films depicting sexual activity by juveniles is intrinsically related to the sexual abuse of children in at least two ways. First, the materials produced are a permanent record of the children's participation and the harm to the child is exacerbated by their circulation. Second, the distribution network for child pornography must be closed if the production of material which requires the sexual exploitation of children is to be effectively controlled. Indeed, there is no serious contention that the legislature was unjustified in believing that it is difficult, if not impossible, to halt the exploitation of children by pursuing only those who produce the photographs and movies. While the production of pornographic materials is a low-profile, clandestine industry, the need to market the resulting products requires a visible apparatus of distribution. The most expeditious if not the only practical method of law enforcement may be to dry up the market for this material by imposing severe criminal penalties on persons selling, advertising, or otherwise promoting the product. Thirty-five States and Congress have concluded that restraints on the distribution of pornographic materials are required in order to effectively combat the problem, and there is a body of literature and testimony to support these legislative conclusions.

Respondent does not contend that the State is unjustified in pursuing those who distribute child pornography. Rather, he argues that it is enough for the State to prohibit the distribution of materials that are legally obscene under the *Miller* test. While some States may find that this approach properly accommodates its interests, it does not follow that the First Amendment prohibits a State from going further. The *Miller* standard, like all general definitions of what may be banned as obscene, does not reflect the State's particular and more compelling interest in prosecuting those who promote the sexual exploitation of children. Thus, the question under the *Miller* test of whether a work, taken as a whole, appeals to the prurient interest of the average person bears no connection to the issue of whether a child has been physically or psychologically harmed in the production of the work. Similarly, a sexually explicit depiction need not be "patently offensive" in order to have required the sexual exploitation of a child for its production. In addition, a work which, taken on the whole, contains serious literary, artistic, political, or scientific value may nev-

ertheless embody the hardest core of child pornography. "It is irrelevant to the child [who has been abused] whether or not the material . . . has a literary, artistic, political, or social value." We therefore cannot conclude that the *Miller* standard is a satisfactory solution to the child pornography problem.

Third. The advertising and selling of child pornography provide an economic motive for and are thus an integral part of the production of such materials, an activity illegal throughout the Nation. "It rarely has been suggested that the constitutional freedom for speech and press extends its immunity to speech or writing used as an integral part of conduct in violation of a valid criminal statute." We note that were the statutes outlawing the employment of children in these films and photographs fully effective, and the constitutionality of these laws has not been questioned, the First Amendment implications would be no greater than that presented by laws against distribution: enforceable production laws would leave no child pornography to be marketed.

Fourth. The value of permitting live performances and photographic reproductions of children engaged in lewd sexual conduct is exceedingly modest, if not *de minimis.* We consider it unlikely that visual depictions of children performing sexual acts or lewdly exhibiting their genitals would often constitute an important and necessary part of a literary performance or scientific or educational work. As a state judge in this case observed, if it were necessary for literary or artistic value, a person over the statutory age who perhaps looked younger could be utilized. Simulation outside of the prohibition of the statute could provide another alternative. Nor is there any question here of censoring a particular literary theme or portrayal of sexual activity. The First Amendment interest is limited to that of rendering the portrayal somewhat more "realistic" by utilizing or photographing children.

Fifth. Recognizing and classifying child pornography as a category of material outside the protection of the First Amendment is not incompatible with our earlier decisions. . . .

There are, of course, limits on the category of child pornography which, like obscenity, is unprotected by the First Amendment. As with all legislation in this sensitive area, the conduct to be prohibited must be adequately defined by the applicable state law, as written or authoritatively construed. Here the nature of the harm to be combated requires that the state offense be limited to works that *visually* depict sexual conduct by children below a specified age. The category of "sexual conduct" proscribed must also be suitably limited and described.

The test for child pornography is separate from the obscenity standard enunciated in *Miller,* but may be compared to it for the purpose of clarity. The *Miller* formulation is adjusted in the following respects: A trier of fact need not find that the material appeals to the prurient interest of the average person; it is not required that sexual conduct portrayed be done so in a patently offensive manner; and the material at issue need not be considered as a whole. We note that the distribution of descriptions or other depictions of sexual conduct, not otherwise obscene, which do not involve live performance or photographic or other visual reproduction of live performances, retains First Amendment protection. As with obscenity laws, criminal responsibility may not be imposed without some element of scienter on the part of the defendant.

Reversed and remanded.

JUSTICE BRENNAN, with whom JUSTICE MARSHALL joins, concurring in the judgment.

I agree with much of what is said in the Court's opinion. As I made clear in the opinion I delivered for the Court in *Ginsberg v. New York* (1968), the State has a special interest in protecting the well-being of its youth. This special and compelling interest, and the particular vulnerability of children, afford the State the leeway to regulate pornographic material, the promotion of which is harmful to children, even though the State does not have such leeway when it seeks only to protect consenting adults from exposure to such material. . . .

But, in my view, application of §263.15 or any similar statute to depictions of children that, in themselves, do have serious literary, artistic, scientific, or medical value would violate the First Amendment. As the Court recognizes, the limited classes of speech the suppression of which does not raise serious First Amendment concerns have two attributes. They are of exceedingly "slight social value," and the State has a compelling interest in their regulation. The First Amendment value of depictions of children that are, in

themselves, serious contributions to art, literature, or science is, by definition, simply not *"de minimis."* At the same time, the State's interest in suppression of such materials is likely to be far less compelling. For the Court's assumption of harm to the child resulting from the "permanent record" and "circulation" of the child's "participation," lacks much of its force where the depiction is a serious contribution to art or science. The production of materials of serious value is not the "low profile, clandestine industry" that, according to the Court, produces purely pornographic materials. In short, it is inconceivable how a depiction of a child that is itself a serious contribution to the world of art or literature or science can be deemed "material outside the protection of the First Amendment."

I, of course, adhere to my view that, in the absence of exposure, or particular harm, to juveniles or unconsenting adults, the State lacks power to suppress sexually oriented materials. See, *e.g., Paris Adult Theatre I v. Slaton* (1973) (BRENNAN, J., dissenting). With this understanding, I concur in the Court's judgment in this case.

Child pornography hit a nerve with the justices: even the most liberal agreed with the *Ferber* resolution. But does *Ferber* tell us much about the future of obscenity litigation? One way to address that question is to consider a Rehnquist Court foray into the area, *Barnes v. Glen Theatre, Inc.* (1991). The Kitty Kat Lounge and Glen Theatre, Inc., sued to have the Indiana public indecency statute declared unconstitutional as an infringement on the First Amendment. The law bans total nudity in public places. The businesses involved in this case wanted to show totally nude dancers, but, because this would be illegal under the public nudity statute, the dancers were required to wear pasties and G-strings. According to the businesses and some of their female entertainers, the public nudity law infringed on the right to engage in expressive conduct. The case did not present a question of obscenity, but rather whether the state could prohibit public nudity—obscene or not.

A fractured Court upheld the Indiana public nudity law in a judgment announced by Chief Justice Rehnquist. Although acknowledging that "nude dancing may involve only the barest minimum of protected expression,"

Rehnquist argued that the Indiana law was not directed at expressive conduct. Instead, the law controlled public nudity generally, whether it occurred in the streets, on the beaches, or in any other public area—including nightclubs. The majority concluded that the state had a legitimate interest in regulating public nudity. The fact that the law applied to nude dancers whose conduct may have expressive content is not controlling. Citing *United States v. O'Brien* (the draft card burning case discussed in Chapter 5), Rehnquist's plurality opinion argued that in pursuing a substantial government interest the state may regulate conduct even if it results in an incidental limitation on some expressive activity. Regulating public nudity is just such a substantial government interest. The application of the law does not prohibit the dancers from expressing themselves, but only blunts how graphic those dances may be.

Reframing the Obscenity Debate

Clearly, the efforts by the Burger and Rehnquist Courts to finish with the obscenity battle have not been a complete success. The questions of what constitutes obscenity and to what degree the dissemination of sexually explicit materials merits constitutional protection have proven stubbornly persistent. So again we ask: Will the Supreme Court continue to rely on *Miller*, or will the justices need to reformulate obscenity standards to settle future disputes? These questions have taken on added significance in light of attempts by some feminist scholars to refocus the obscenity debate.

As we now know, since *Roth* the justices have viewed obscenity as largely a First Amendment question, but some feminist scholars have sought to frame the question in different terms.[12] The issue of obscenity, they argue, should not focus on the rights of the author, producer, or distributor. Instead, society should look at the negative impact pornographic materials have on women.

Sexually explicit material does not merit First Amendment protection if it objectifies and demeans women. It is discriminatory on the basis of sex. According to this argument, the courts should view obscenity as a sexual equality issue, not a freedom of expression question. Adopting this view would allow government to regulate sexually oriented materials as part of an effort to bring about greater equality between the sexes. Support for this position has divided the liberal community, which traditionally has fought to defeat conservative efforts to restrict freedom of expression.

In *American Booksellers Association, Inc. v. Hudnut* (1986), the only case presented to the Court involving the issue of obscenity as a sexual equality issue, the justices summarily affirmed the Seventh Circuit Court of Appeal's ruling that an Indianapolis ordinance that, in accord with a model statute offered by feminists scholars, defined pornography as "the graphic sexually explicit subordination of women" was unconstitutional. The Seventh Circuit Court of Appeals reasoned as follows:

The Indianapolis ordinance does not refer to the prurient interest, the offensiveness, or to the standards of the community. It demands attention to particular depictions, not to the work judged as a whole. It is irrelevant under the ordinance whether the work has literary, artistic, political, or scientific value. . . .

We do not try to balance the arguments for and against an ordinance such as this. The ordinance discriminates on the ground of the content of speech. Speech treating women in the approved way—in sexual encounters "premised on equality"—is lawful no matter how sexually explicit. Speech treating women in the disapproved way—as submissive in matters sexual or as enjoying humiliation—is unlawful no matter how significant the literary, artistic, or political qualities of the work taken as a whole. The state may not ordain preferred viewpoints in this way. The Constitution forbids the state to declare on perspective right and silence opponents.

Because it did not issue an opinion on the merits in this dispute, we can say that at least for now the Supreme Court continues to treat obscenity as a First Amendment issue, not a matter of sexual equality. In contrast, in 1992 the Supreme Court of Canada essentially adopted the approached urged by feminists' groups there and in the United States (*see Box 7-4*).

12. See, for example, Catharine MacKinnon, *Only Words* (Cambridge: Harvard University Press, 1993). Not all feminists subscribe to MacKinnon's position, as Nadine Strossen makes clear in her *Defending Pornography: Free Speech, Sex, and the Fight for Women's Rights* (New York: New York University Press, 2000). See also Pamela Church Gibson and Roma Gibson, eds., *Dirty Looks: Women, Pornography, Power* (London: British Film Institute, 1993).

BOX 7-4   OBSCENITY AND FEMINISM

THE LIBERAL COMMUNITY traditionally has supported the position that the First Amendment provides broad protection for those who produce and distribute sexually explicit materials. Some members of the feminist movement have attacked that solidly pro-expression position. They argue that because of pornography's negative impact on women, government should be allowed to regulate it. To advance that end, Andrea Dworkin and Catherine MacKinnon, two feminist legal scholars, drafted a Model Antipornography Civil Rights Ordinance, which contains the following definition of pornography:

1. "Pornography" means the graphic sexually explicit subordination of women through pictures and/or words, including by electronic or other data retrieval systems, that also includes one or more of the following:

Women are presented dehumanized as sexual objects, things, or commodities. Women are presented as sexual objects who enjoy humiliation or pain; or as sexual objects experiencing sexual pleasure in rape, incest, or other sexual assault; or as sexual objects tied up, cut up, mutilated, bruised, or physically hurt. Women are presented in postures or positions of sexual submission, servility, or display. Women's body parts—including but not limited to vaginas, breasts, or buttocks—are exhibited such that women are reduced to those parts. Women are presented being penetrated by objects or animals. Women are presented in scenarios of degradation, humiliation, injury, or torture, shown as filthy or inferior, bleeding, bruised, or hurt in a context that makes these conditions sexual.

2. The use of men, children, or transsexuals in the place of women is also pornography for purposes of this law.[1]

The Supreme Court has ruled on only one case involving the issue of obscenity as a sexual equality issue. In *American Booksellers Association, Inc. v. Hudnut* (1986), the Court summarily affirmed the Seventh Circuit Court of Appeal's ruling that an Indianapolis ordinance, which, in accord with the model statute, defined pornography as "the graphic sexually explicit subordination of women," was unconstitutional. But, in the [*R. v.*] *Butler* case of 1992, at the urging of a women's rights organization, which was working with MacKinnon, the Supreme Court of Canada adopted the Dworkin-MacKinnon "equality" approach to define pornography. In the eyes of the Court, "The message of obscenity which degrades and dehumanizes is analagous to that of hate propaganda."

Free speech advocates have been quite critical of the Canadian approach, claiming that it has been used by officials there to confiscate gay, lesbian, and feminist books—including work by Dworkin herself.

In what follows, MacKinnon responds to this and other charges in a discussion with Floyd Abrams, a prominent advocate of the traditional freedom of expression position. *New York Times* columnist Anthony Lewis moderated the conversation.

Lewis: Am I right in thinking that coercion as you would define it in the law you drafted with Andrea Dworkin—that is, graphic, sexually explicit materials that subordinate women through pictures and words—disallows voluntarily engaging in a pornographic film since it says that a written consent shall not be proof that there was no coercion?

MacKinnon: No, you're not. If you can force a woman to have sex with a dog, you can force her to sign a contract. The mere fact of a contract being signed doesn't in itself negate a finding of coercion. The coercion itself would have to be proven under our ordinance.

Abrams: Look, your statute provides in part that graphic, sexually explicit subordination of women in which women are pre-

sented as sexual objects for domination, conquest, violation, exploitation, possession or use, etc., can give rise to a private cause of action. The Court of Appeals in holding the statute unconstitutional—a decision affirmed by the Supreme Court—indicated that books like Joyce's "Ulysses," Homer's "Iliad," poems by Yeats, novels by D. H. Lawrence and the like could all be subject to a finding of violation of the statute that you have drafted.

MacKinnon: And that's just simply false.

Abrams: Well, I don't think it *is* false.

MacKinnon: Those materials are not even sexually explicit. They don't even get in the door.

Lewis: Why don't you just repeat your definition of pornography?

MacKinnon: Professor Abrams just quoted the definition. Andrea Dworkin's and my approach to pornography is to define it in terms of what it does, not in terms of what it says, not by whether somebody doesn't like it. None of that has anything to do with our definition. Our definition, and our legal caus-

es of action, all have to do with what it does to the women in it, to the children in it and to the other people who can prove that as a direct result of these materials they were assaulted or made second-class citizens on the basis of sex.

Abrams: You mean because people will think less of women on account of how they're portrayed?

MacKinnon: No, because people will *do* things to them like not hiring them, like sexualizing them and not taking them seriously as students, the entire array of violent and nonviolent civil subordination, when they can prove it comes from pornography.

Abrams: That is why your legislation is so frontal an attack on the First Amendment. When the Court of Appeals said that the impact of your statute is such that it could apply to everything from hard-core films to the collected works of James Joyce, D. H. Lawrence and John Cleland, it was entirely correct. It is correct because what you have

1. This code originally appeared in their *Pornography and Civil rights: A New Day for Women's Equality* (Minneapolis: Organizing Against Pornography, 1988), 138–142. It is now available at: *www.igc.org/Womensnet/dworkin/OrdinanceCanada.html.*

(box continues)

(Box 7-4 continued)

drafted as a definition of actionable pornography is "graphic sexual explicit subordination of women, in which women are presented as sexual objects for domination." Lots of great art as well as cheap and vile productions have depicted women in just that way—"The Rape of the Sabine Women," for example. And my point is not that your definition is vague, but that it is clear. It includes any art, whether it is good or bad, art or nonart, that you have concluded may do harm. That's an unacceptable basis and it should be.

MacKinnon: O.K., there are several things wrong with this. No. 1, those materials are not sexually explicit. The court was told exactly what sexually explicit means in law and in ordinary use, and it should have known better. No. 2, these materials have never yet been shown in any study to have produced any of the effects that pornography produces. So no one could prove that women are subordinated as a result of them. This statute does not cover those materials, period. It is false as a matter of statutory construction. The statute could potentially cover something like a film in which somebody was actually killed but claims are made that it has artistic value—an artistic snuff film—or in which someone is raped but the film has interesting camera angles. That does raise a conflict between existing law and our statute. The examples you cite do not.

Lewis: Professor MacKinnon, we do have a concrete example of what your view of the law might result in. The Canadian Supreme Court adopted your view. Since then, there has been an intensification of gay and lesbian books' being intercepted at the border. That seems to be the result of a country actually adopting your standard.

MacKinnon: That's disinformation. Canada customs has singled out those materials for years, and customs laws were not involved in the case I was part of in Canada. What happened was, the Supreme Court of Canada rejected its morality-based standard for obscenity and held that when pornography hurts equality it can be stopped. Customs has not reviewed its standards since. I think that if Canada customs is still stopping materials because they are gay or lesbian, on a moral ground not a harm ground, they have lost their constitutional authority to do

it under this ruling. If the materials hurt women or men or their equality, they can still stop them. But Andrea Dworkin and I do not favor addressing pornography through criminal law, especially obscenity law, so in that way Canada has not adopted our approach.

Lewis: Professor MacKinnon, there's an assumption explicitly stated in your book that pornography as you define it results in antisocial, abusive activity by the customers.

MacKinnon: There's overwhelming documentation of it.

Lewis: But it is a fact that in countries in which pornography is lawful and there are no legal restraints whatever on sexually explicit materials the incidence of sexual crimes is much lower than in this country.

MacKinnon: Actually, that isn't true. It's urban legend.

Lewis: In Denmark, in Germany, in Japan—

MacKinnon: In Denmark, data on reported rape after liberalization is inconclusive. It did not drop, though. Also, the definitions and categories of sexual offenses were changed at the same time that pornography was decriminalized. Also, reporting may well have dropped. If your government supports pornography, reporting sexual abuse seems totally pointless to women. So, too, Germany and Sweden. Once pornography is legitimized throughout society, you get an explosion in sexual abuse, but women don't report it anymore because they know that nothing will be done about it. Feminists and sex educators in Denmark are beginning to say that selling 12-year-old children on street corners is not what they mean by sexual liberation. What's happened in Japan and other places is that much of sexual abuse is just part of the way women are normally treated. If you're still essentially chattel, what is it to rape you? In Sweden there aren't any rape-crisis centers. All there is is battered-women shelters. So the battered-women's movement has been pushing the government to look at the reality of rape there, which is massive.

Abrams: But those countries that are harshest on what you would call pornography are also harshest on women. In China promulgation of pornography leads to capital punishment. In Iran it leads to the harshest and most outrageous physical torture.

These are not good countries for women to live in. If you look at countries like Sweden and Japan and Holland and Germany, which have allowed more rather than less free expression in this area of sexually explicit speech, you'll find that these are the countries in which sexual abuse of women is not particularly prevalent. It's one thing for you to advocate a statute such as you have proposed in Sweden, but I daresay it has not been seriously suggested that Swedish women as a group have been victimized by their free-press and free-speech laws.

MacKinnon: Swedish women have seriously supported our law, against the legalized victimization of pornography. But it's hard to know what the reality is. It's wrong to base how much rape there is on reported rape. It's also very hard to know how much pornography is actually available. You could look at the United States laws and get the impression that pornography was being taken seriously as a problem in this country.

Abrams: But when you cite, for example, the Balkans as a place where there's been a vast amount of rape and infer that it has something to do with the existence of sexually explicit materials, you don't tell us that in 1913 there was an orgy of rapes at a time when such material didn't exist at all. It puts into question the validity of the whole thesis.

MacKinnon: It is not an exclusive thesis. There are lots of ways of sexualizing subordination—religion, veiling, clitoridectomies. Pornography is one way, and some of the abuses it is connected to we can do something about. In countries where women have recently got more voice, like the United States and Sweden, women are becoming more able to identify the sources of our subordination. The United States is a mass culture, media-saturated and capitalistic. In asking how women are subordinated in the United States, it would be wrong to eliminate the capitalistic mass media of the pornography industry. At other times and places, the ways in which women are subordinated are different. But now, the United States is exporting this form of subordination to the rest of the world.

SOURCE: "The First Amendment, Under Fire From the Left," *New York Times Magazine*, March 13, 1994, 57ff.

Enforcing Obscenity Statutes

While the major pornography controversies have involved questions of defining what is obscene, simultaneous legal battles have been fought over methods of enforcing anti-obscenity statutes. If material is legally obscene, what weapons does government have to combat it? How can the government enforce such restrictions without unduly impinging on legitimate expression?

Distribution. A major strategy in controlling obscenity is to attack its distribution channels. The federal effort in the past has relied on three types of laws. The first prohibits the importation of pornography. Customs officials may intercept shipments of obscene films and publications produced abroad and intended for U.S. distribution. The second prohibits the interstate shipment of obscene materials and allows federal officials to take legal action against individuals who commercially transport materials across state lines. The third prohibits use of the U.S. mail to distribute obscene goods and brings federal postal officials into the fight against obscenity. If a book, magazine, or film meets the legal definition of obscenity, the federal government may use any of these laws to block its distribution.

State authorities regulate local activities such as pornographic book stores and adult movie theaters. Under the *Miller* test, states and localities have broad authority to define what is patently offensive and to enforce laws against selling obscene materials or commercially showing obscene films. Individuals who knowingly sell or otherwise distribute legally obscene materials may be prosecuted under state criminal laws or be subject to other state legal action.[13]

Prior Restraint. In Chapter 6 you read that Chief Justice Hughes in *Near v. Minnesota* (1931) ruled that prior restraint generally was incompatible with First Amendment freedoms. But he also said that there were certain exceptions to this principle, one of which pertained to publications "that threatened public decency." This cited exception has encouraged governments to impose certain forms of prior censorship as part of their battle against obscenity, which often provoke legal challenge.

13. *Smith v. California* (1959).

The first battle over this type of regulation occurred in *Kingsley Books v. Brown* (1957). The dispute began when New York State charged Kingsley Books with selling obscene materials, compiled as *Nights of Horror.* Under New York law, the state could request a temporary injunction blocking the sale of such materials after publication, but before a trial judge determined whether the material was legally obscene. The statute further required that the determination be made promptly. New York obtained an injunction against Kingsley Books, and the company appealed, arguing that the law amounted to prior restraint. The Supreme Court upheld the statute. Writing for a majority of five, Justice Frankfurter declared,

[O]ver a long stretch of this Court's history, it has been accepted as a postulate that "the primary requirement of decency may be enforced against obscene publication. . . ." Unlike *Near* [the law here] is concerned solely with obscenity and, as authoritatively construed, it studiously withholds restraint upon matters not already published and not yet found to be offensive.

This ruling constituted the Court's first application of the prior restraint doctrine in the field of obscenity. The majority seemed to agree with Chief Justice Hughes that public decency considerations provided an exception to the constitutional prohibition against prior restraint. However, the majority also made clear that prior censorship would be tolerated only if proper safeguards (temporary injunctions imposed only after publication and speedy judicial determinations) were included.

Similar questions regarding prior restraint have been raised with respect to motion pictures, although films have proven to be a more difficult issue for the Court than printed material. In *Mutual Film Corporation v. Industrial Commission* (1915), its earliest ruling on motion pictures, the Court even ruled that movies were undeserving of First Amendment protection because they were "business pure and simple." The justices, therefore, allowed the states to censor films that might corrupt the morals of their citizens.

The Court abandoned its position that motion pictures were qualitatively unlike printed matter with its decision in *Burstyn v. Wilson* (1953). Although acknowledging that films might possess a greater potential for harm than books, newspapers, or magazines, the justices held that movies deserved a degree of First Amendment protection that precluded unbridled censorship. The Court did not, however, disallow all community control over the showing of motion pictures.

As the film industry produced more movies with content that many found morally objectionable, cities and states developed comprehensive regulatory measures. One of the most controversial was the requirement that movie distributors submit their films to local authorities prior to showing them to the public. The authorities would review each film for possible obscenity violations and then decide whether to issue a license allowing it to be shown. These laws appeared to be flagrant examples of prior restraint, but, because they were imposed to combat obscenity and promote public decency, there was reason to believe that the Court might approve them.

In two decisions, *Times Film Corporation v. Chicago* (1961) and *Freedman v. Maryland* (1965), the justices settled the issue of prior submission of films. Consistent with the public decency exception articulated by Chief Justice Hughes, the Court held that nothing in the Constitution necessarily prohibited state or local governments from requiring film exhibitors to submit films before showing them commercially. However, the Court demanded that such plans meet exacting procedural safeguards. The government must initiate any procedures to determine whether the film is obscene, and the government must also bear the burden of proof. Only a judicial body, not an administrative agency, has the authority to declare a work obscene. Furthermore, prior to a judicial determination, any restraint against the showing of the film must be temporary. Finally, if a temporary restraint is imposed, the state must have procedures for a prompt judicial resolution of the obscenity question.

The *Times Film* and *Freedman* decisions pleased neither local governments nor the film industry. State and local governments were satisfied that the Court upheld their authority to impose prior submission laws, but did not like the cumbersome procedural safeguards the justices demanded. The film industry did not like any prior restraint, but was comforted by the fact that the Court

was not granting unfettered regulatory authority to the states. In response, three years after *Freedman*, the Motion Picture Association of America and the International Film Importers and Distributors of America devised a system for rating and labeling movies. The industry informs the public of the "general suitability" of a film by assigning it one of the following ratings:

G: suitable for all audiences
PG: parental guidance suggested
PG-13: parental guidance strongly suggested for children under 13
R: restricted to those 17 or older unless accompanied by a guardian
NC-17: no one under 17 admitted[14]

This system of voluntary ratings has been successful. Although the Court has stuck with its *Times Film* and *Freedman* decisions, state and local governments deferred to the ratings system and ceased their prior submission programs. The film industry is more comfortable with self-regulation rather than with the scrutiny of state and local censorship boards. The system has worked so well that the recording industry, pressured by criticism from various parent groups about explicit lyrics, developed a voluntary labeling system to avoid government regulation. In 1996 the television industry followed suit *(see Box 7–5)*.

Zoning. To combat the effects of adult theaters, nightclubs, and bookstores, local governments frequently rely on their zoning powers. The Court examined the question of zoning restrictions on such establishments in *Young v. American Mini Theatres, Inc.* (1976). At issue were amendments to Detroit's "anti–Skid Row" ordinance, which targeted theaters exhibiting sexually explicit films. The law prohibited the location of an "adult" theater within five hundred feet of a residential area or within one thousand feet of two or more similar theaters or bars, pool halls, dance halls, pawn shops, or other specified establishments. The goal of the legislation was to avoid a concentration of businesses considered undesirable. American Mini Theatres was in the adult entertainment business. The company had converted a corner gas

14. Originally, NC-17 was the X-rating.

BOX 7-5 INDUSTRY WARNING LABELS

In a move designed to head off government regulation, in May 1990 the recording industry introduced a uniform, voluntary warning label to go on recordings that have explicit lyrics.

Whether to apply the label, which reads "Parental Advisory—Explicit Lyrics," was at the discretion of record companies and individual artists. The system was intended to alert consumers to recordings that could be deemed objectionable because of explicit lyrics dealing with sex, violence, suicide, and substance abuse.

In December 1996 the television industry, under heavy public pressure, also adopted a ratings system. The following six categories are now in use:

Y: Material suitable for children of all ages. Show contains little or no violence, strong language, or sexual content.

Y-7: Material suitable for children seven and older.

TV-G: Material suitable for all audiences.

TV-PG: Parental guidance is suggested. Program may contain infrequent coarse language, limited violence, some suggestive sexual dialogue and situations.

TV-14: Material may be inappropriate for children under fourteen. Program may contain sophisticated themes, strong language, and sexual content.

TV-M: For mature audiences only. Program may contain profane language, graphic violence, and explicit sexual content.

station into a mini-theater called the Pussy Cat, at which it hoped to show sexually explicit films. The city denied the company's request for a license to operate on the grounds that the theater's location was in violation of the anti–Skid Row amendments. The company challenged the denial on First Amendment grounds. The Supreme Court upheld the denial by a 5–4 vote, but did not issue an opinion endorsed by a majority of the justices.

Zoning was revisited in *City of Renton v. Playtime Theatres, Inc.* (1986). In this case Renton, Washington, passed a zoning ordinance similar to the Detroit law upheld in *American Mini Theatres.* The city prohibited adult theaters within a thousand feet of any residential area, church, school, or park. In a majority opinion written by Justice Rehnquist, the Court upheld the ordinance in spite of arguments by the theater company that it constituted content-based discrimination. Because the ordinance did not prohibit adult theaters, but only regulated their placement, the Court treated the law as a "time, place or manner" restriction. Over the dissents of Justices Brennan and Marshall, the majority found that the law was not aimed at the content of the expression, but designed to control the secondary effects of such establishments on the surrounding community. Taken together, the rulings in *American Mini Theatres* and *Playtime Theatres* strongly reinforced the authority of local governments to use their zoning powers to regulate for public decency.

Racketeering Statutes. As part of a strategy to combat obscenity, some jurisdictions have employed RICO (Racketeer Influenced and Corrupt Organizations) laws. RICO statutes are commonly used to prosecute organized crime and apply when a party engages in a demonstrable pattern of repeated criminal violations. RICO laws impose severe penalties, including seizures of property that may have been acquired with the profits from criminal acts. But are RICO laws appropriate for use in obscenity cases? Or are they so harsh that they place an unconstitutional burden on freedom of expression? The Rehnquist Court provided answers to these questions in *Fort Wayne Books, Inc. v. Indiana* (1989).

To bolster its enforcement efforts, Indiana amended its state RICO law to include obscenity violations. The law allowed the state to seize all allegedly obscene materials and to padlock adult book stores prior to any judicial determination of whether the books, films, and other materials were obscene. The penalties were steep: violators could spend substantial time in prison, be forced to pay large fines, and forfeit all property, real and personal, used in or derived from the criminal activity. Normally, obscenity violations were misdemeanors; but prosecuted under the RICO statute, they became felonies.

In March 1984 Indiana attempted to apply its RICO statute to a number of bookstores, including Fort Wayne Books, Inc. The bookstores had long histories of obscenity violations, which established the pattern of criminal behavior required under the RICO laws. Prosecutors asked the local court to allow police to seize all property contained in the stores and to authorize the sheriff to padlock the buildings. The judge agreed, even though the material at issue had yet to be judged obscene. The bookstores countered that the judge's order amounted to a prior restraint, that it had a "chilling effect" on First Amendment rights by making booksellers so fearful of prosecution that they would significantly reduce the range of materials offered for sale. They also argued that the use of RICO laws against obscenity was draconian.

The Supreme Court, through an opinion by Justice White, generally upheld the authority of the state to use RICO laws to combat obscenity. The Court concluded that the "deterrence of the sale of obscene materials is a legitimate end of state anti-obscenity laws," and that there was no constitutional bar to enhancing obscenity penalties through the use of a RICO statute. It also rejected the bookstores' chilling effect argument, holding that, "The mere assertion of some possible self-censorship resulting from a statute is not enough to render an anti-obscenity law unconstitutional under our precedents." The justices ruled in favor of the bookstores on the prior restraint question, holding that the *pretrial* seizure of the bookstores and their contents was constitutionally improper.

Government Funding. A final way that the government has gone about dealing with the obscenity "problem" is by withholding funds for material it deems obscene. In 1965 Congress established the National Endowment for the Arts (NEA) as part of a general policy of supporting the arts through federal grants. Historically, the funding provided by the NEA has provided numerous performers, artists, and authors with desperately needed money, without which, their works of art could not have been produced. In recent years, some of the NEA's funding de-

cisions have come under intense public scrutiny because they were thought to support work that many in the public and Congress believed to be obscene. In response to the public outcry over these decisions, Congress in 1990 revised the NEA funding law to require the head of the agency to take into consideration "general standards of decency and respect for the diverse beliefs and values of the American public." This change by Congress caused an outcry among fund recipients and liberals both in Congress and the public. In the only Supreme Court case to thus far challenge the provision, *National Endowment for the Arts v. Finley* (1998), the Court took up the issue of whether the government could set standards for public support that take into consideration factors that would be illegitimate in a regulatory statute. Writing for the majority in an 8–1 decision, Justice O'Connor reasoned that Congress has a "wide latitude to set spending priorities" and that the admonition to take decency and respect into account did not silence speakers by censoring their ideas.

Emerging Issues in the Obscenity Debate: The Internet

The decisions in *Kingsley, Freedman, City of Renton, Fort Wayne Books,* and *National Endowment for the Arts* are representative of the Court's rulings on laws dealing with the dissemination of the traditional forms of obscene material—books, magazines, and movies. When it comes to obscene material in those forms, the justices generally have been sympathetic to government attempts to combat it, and are willing to provide state and local authorities the necessary constitutional leeway to deal with it as they see fit.

But what about the newest vehicle for the spread of obscenity, the Internet? It is probably the case that very few people would quarrel with the observation that the Internet provides easy access to materials, whether legally obscene or not, that many would consider inappropriate for children.[15] A search on as simple and childlike word as "dollhouse" could yield scores of URLs to pornographic sites. Accordingly, many groups have pressured Congress and the states to pass laws designed to regulate

15. Recent polls indicate that obscenity on the Internet is a concern of more than 80 percent of Americans.

expression on the Internet, and they have responded with legislation ranging from laws designed to curtail the electronic dissemination of sexually oriented material that is inappropriate for children to those that bar the use of pseudonyms and anonymous communications. Opponents of these laws contend that, however well intentioned, they restrict legitimate and protected expression. Laws against the use of pseudonyms, for example, might have prohibited Samuel Clemens from making his stories available on the Internet or prevented Madison, Hamilton, and Jay from publishing the *Federalist Papers* electronically because their essays were written under the pen name Publius.

The passage of each state or federal law restricting expression on the Internet has been met by immediate legal challenges. Newly formed organizations devoted to keeping the Internet free of regulation have joined with traditional civil liberties groups, such as the ACLU, to attack these regulations as violations of the First Amendment.

Initial lower court decisions overwhelmingly supported freedom of expression claims against these laws, but how would the U.S. Supreme Court respond? Would the Court simply adjust its current standards to fit the Internet or write new standards? The first indication of how the justices would address these questions came in its *1997* decision in *Reno v. American Civil Liberties Union.*[16] The case involved a challenge to the first major federal regulation of the Internet, the Communications Decency Act of 1996.

Reno v. American Civil Liberties Union

521 U. S. 844 (1997)
laws.findlaw.com/us/000/96-511.html
Vote: 7 (Breyer, Ginsburg, Kennedy, Scalia, Souter, Stevens,
    Thomas)
    2 (O'Connor, Rehnquist)
Opinion of the Court: Stevens
Opinion concurring in the judgment in part and dissenting in part: O'Connor

16. For oral arguments in this case, navigate to: *oyez.nwu.edu.*

Passed in 1996 by large majorities in both houses of Congress and signed into law by President Clinton, the Communications Decency Act—part of a larger legislative package regulating the telecommunications industry—sought to control children's access to sexually explicit material transmitted electronically, especially via the Internet. As soon as the law was passed, a coalition of about fifty organizations and businesses, led by the ACLU, filed suit, asserting that it violated the First Amendment.

Specifically, the lawsuit challenged two provisions of the act, known as the indecent transmission provision and the patently offensive display provision. The indecent transmission section prohibited on-line communication to minors (under the age of eighteen) that is indecent or obscene, "regardless of whether the user of such service placed the call or initiated the communication." The patently offensive display provision prohibited the transmission of messages that depict or describe, "in terms patently offensive as measured by community standards, sexual or excretory activities or organs"—in a manner that "is available to a person under the age of eighteen." Violators of these provisions could be fined or imprisoned for two years, or both. The law recognized as a legitimate defense "good faith, reasonable, effective, and appropriate actions" to restrict access by minors to the prohibited communications.

Those attacking the law argued that it was not narrowly tailored to accomplish the goal of protecting minors because it also restricted adult access to sexually explicit communications. Moreover, they charged that terms such as *indecent* and *patently offensive* were unconstitutionally vague. The government responded that the law was no more vague than the obscenity standard established in *Miller* v. *California* (1973).

A three-judge district court, although divided over the rationale, held that the law was unconstitutionally vague. Attorney General Janet Reno, representing the United States, appealed to the Supreme Court.

JUSTICE STEVENS delivered the opinion of the Court.

In *Southeastern Promotions, Ltd.* v. *Conrad* (1975), we observed that "each medium of expression . . . may present its own problems." Thus, some of our cases have recognized special justifications for regulation of the broadcast media that are not applicable to other speakers. In these cases, the Court relied on the history of extensive government regulation of the broadcast medium; the scarcity of available frequencies at its inception; and its "invasive" nature.

Those factors are not present in cyberspace. Neither before nor after the enactment of the CDA [Communications Decency Act] have the vast democratic fora of the Internet been subject to the type of government supervision and regulation that has attended the broadcast industry. Moreover, the Internet is not as "invasive" as radio or television. The District Court specifically found that "communications over the Internet do not 'invade' an individual's home or appear on one's computer screen unbidden. Users seldom encounter content 'by accident.'" It also found that "almost all sexually explicit images are preceded by warnings as to the content," and cited testimony that "'odds are slim' that a user would come across a sexually explicit sight by accident.". . .

[U]nlike the conditions that prevailed when Congress first authorized regulation of the broadcast spectrum, the Internet can hardly be considered a "scarce" expressive commodity. It provides relatively unlimited, low-cost capacity for communication of all kinds. The Government estimates that "as many as 40 million people use the Internet today, and that figure is expected to grow to 200 million by 1999." This dynamic, multifaceted category of communication includes not only traditional print and news services, but also audio, video, and still images, as well as interactive, real-time dialogue. Through the use of chat rooms, any person with a phone line can become a town crier with a voice that resonates farther than it could from any soapbox. Through the use of Web pages, mail exploders, and newsgroups, the same individual can become a pamphleteer. As the District Court found, "the content on the Internet is as diverse as human thought." We agree with its conclusion that our cases provide no basis for qualifying the level of First Amendment scrutiny that should be applied to this medium.

. . . [T]he many ambiguities [of the CDA] concerning the scope of its coverage render it problematic for purposes of the First Amendment. For instance, each of the two parts of the CDA uses a different linguistic form. The first uses the word "indecent," while the second speaks of material that "in context, depicts or describes, in terms patently offensive as measured by contemporary community standards, sexual or excretory activities or organs." Given the absence of a definition of either term, this difference in language will provoke uncertainty among speakers about how the two standards relate to each other and just what they mean. Could a speaker confidently assume that a serious discussion about birth control practices, homosexuality . . . or the consequences of prison rape would not violate the CDA? This uncertainty undermines the likelihood that the CDA has been carefully tailored to the congressional goal of protecting minors from potentially harmful materials.

The vagueness of the CDA is a matter of special concern for two reasons. First, the CDA is a content-based regulation of speech. The vagueness of such a regulation raises special First Amendment concerns because of its obvious chilling effect on free speech. Second, the CDA is a criminal statute. In addition to the opprobrium and stigma of a criminal conviction, the CDA threatens violators with penalties including up to two years in prison for each act of violation. The severity of criminal sanctions may well cause speakers to remain silent rather than communicate even arguably unlawful words, ideas, and images. . . .

The Government argues that the statute is no more vague than the obscenity standard this Court established in *Miller v. California* (1973). But that is not so. In *Miller*, this Court reviewed a criminal conviction against a commercial vendor who mailed brochures containing pictures of sexually explicit activities to individuals who had not requested such materials. Having struggled for some time to establish a definition of obscenity, we set forth in *Miller* the test for obscenity that controls to this day:

"(a) whether the average person, applying contemporary community standards would find that the work, taken as a whole, appeals to the prurient interest; (b) whether the work depicts or describes, in a patently offensive way, sexual conduct specifically defined by the applicable state law; and (c) whether the work, taken as a whole, lacks serious literary, artistic, political, or scientific value."

Because the CDA's "patently offensive" standard (and, we assume *arguendo*, its synonymous "indecent" standard) is one part of the three-prong *Miller* test, the Government reasons, it cannot be unconstitutionally vague.

The Government's assertion is incorrect as a matter of fact. The second prong of the *Miller* test—the purportedly analogous standard—contains a critical requirement that is omitted from the CDA: that the proscribed material be "specifically defined by the applicable state law." This requirement reduces the vagueness inherent in the open-ended term "patently offensive" as used in the CDA. Moreover, the *Miller* definition is limited to "sexual conduct," whereas the CDA extends also to include (1) "excretory activities" as well as (2) "organs" of both a sexual and excretory nature.

The Government's reasoning is also flawed. Just because a definition including three limitations is not vague, it does not follow that one of those limitations, standing by itself, is not vague. Each of *Miller*'s additional two prongs—(1) that, taken as a whole, the material appeal to the "prurient" interest, and (2) that it "lack serious literary, artistic, political, or scientific value"—critically limits the uncertain sweep of the obscenity definition. The second requirement is particularly important because, unlike the "patently offensive" and "prurient interest" criteria, it is not judged by contemporary community standards. This "societal value" requirement, absent in the CDA, allows appellate courts to impose some limitations and regularity on the definition by setting, as a matter of law, a national floor for socially redeeming value. The Government's contention that courts will be able to give such legal limitations to the CDA's standards is belied by *Miller*'s own rationale for having juries determine whether material is "patently offensive" according to community standards: that such questions are essentially ones of *fact*.

In contrast to *Miller* and our other previous cases, the CDA thus presents a greater threat of censoring speech that, in fact, falls outside the statute's scope. Given the vague contours of the coverage of the statute, it unquestionably silences some speakers whose messages would be entitled to constitutional protection. That danger provides further reason for insisting that the statute not be overly broad. The CDA's burden on protected speech cannot be justified if it could be avoided by a more carefully drafted statute.

We are persuaded that the CDA lacks the precision that the First Amendment requires when a statute regulates the content of speech. In order to deny minors access to potentially harmful speech, the CDA effectively suppresses a large amount of speech that adults have a constitutional right to receive and to address to one another. That burden on adult speech is unacceptable if less restrictive alternatives would be at least as effective in achieving the legitimate purpose that the statute was enacted to serve.

In evaluating the free speech rights of adults, we have made it perfectly clear that "sexual expression which is indecent but not obscene is protected by the First Amendment." Indeed, [we have] admonished that "the fact that society may find speech offensive is not a sufficient reason for suppressing it."

It is true that we have repeatedly recognized the governmental interest in protecting children from harmful materials. See *Ginsberg*. But that interest does not justify an unnecessarily broad suppression of speech addressed to adults. As we have explained, the Government may not "reduce the adult population . . . to . . . only what is fit for children.". . .

In arguing that the CDA does not so diminish adult communication, the Government relies on the incorrect factual premise that prohibiting a transmission whenever it is known that one of its recipients is a minor would not interfere with adult-to-adult communication. The findings of the District Court make clear that this premise is untenable.

Given the size of the potential audience for most messages, in the absence of a viable age verification process, the sender must be charged with knowing that one or more minors will likely view it. Knowledge that, for instance, one or more members of a 100-person chat group will be minor—and therefore that it would be a crime to send the group an indecent message—would surely burden communication among adults.

The District Court found that at the time of trial existing technology did not include any effective method for a sender to prevent minors from obtaining access to its communications on the Internet without also denying access to adults. The Court found no effective way to determine the age of a user who is accessing material through e-mail, mail exploders, newsgroups, or chat rooms. As a practical matter, the Court also found that it would be prohibitively expensive for noncommercial—as well as some commercial—speakers who have Web sites to verify that their users are adults. These limitations must inevitably curtail a significant amount of adult communication on the Internet. By contrast, the District Court found that "despite its limitations, currently available *user-based* software suggests that a reasonably effective method by which *parents* can prevent their children from accessing sexually explicit and other material which *parents* may believe is inappropriate for their children will soon be widely available" (emphases added).

The breadth of the CDA's coverage is wholly unprecedented. Unlike the regulations upheld in *Ginsberg* and

Pacifica, the scope of the CDA is not limited to commercial speech or commercial entities. Its open-ended prohibitions embrace all nonprofit entities and individuals posting indecent messages or displaying them on their own computers in the presence of minors. The general, undefined terms "indecent" and "patently offensive" cover large amounts of nonpornographic material with serious educational or other value. Moreover, the "community standards" criterion as applied to the Internet means that any communication available to a nationwide audience will be judged by the standards of the community most likely to be offended by the message. The regulated subject matter . . . may also extend to discussions about prison rape or safe sexual practices, artistic images that include nude subjects, and arguably the card catalogue of the Carnegie Library. . . .

In this Court, though not in the District Court, the Government asserts that—in addition to its interest in protecting children—its "equally significant" interest in fostering the growth of the Internet provides an independent basis for upholding the constitutionality of the CDA. The Government apparently assumes that the unregulated availability of "indecent" and "patently offensive" material on the Internet is driving countless citizens away from the medium because of the risk of exposing themselves or their children to harmful material.

We find this argument singularly unpersuasive. The dramatic expansion of this new marketplace of ideas contradicts the factual basis of this contention. The record demonstrates that the growth of the Internet has been and continues to be phenomenal. As a matter of constitutional tradition, in the absence of evidence to the contrary, we presume that governmental regulation of the content of speech is more likely to interfere with the free exchange of ideas than to encourage it. The interest in encouraging freedom of expression in a democratic society outweighs any theoretical but unproven benefit of censorship.

For the foregoing reasons, the judgment of the district court is affirmed.

It is so ordered.

JUSTICE O'CONNOR, with whom THE CHIEF JUSTICE joins, concurring in the judgment in part and dissenting in part.

I write separately to explain why I view the Communications Decency Act of 1996 (CDA) as little more than an attempt by Congress to create "adult zones" on the Internet. Our precedent indicates that the creation of such zones can be constitutionally sound. Despite the soundness of its purpose, however, portions of the CDA are unconstitutional because they stray from the blueprint our prior cases have developed for constructing a "zoning law" that passes constitutional muster. . . .

Our cases make clear that a "zoning" law is valid only if adults are still able to obtain the regulated speech. If they cannot, the law does more than simply keep children away from speech they have no right to obtain—it interferes with the rights of adults to obtain constitutionally protected speech and effectively "reduces the adult population . . . to reading only what is fit for children.". . .

The electronic world is fundamentally different. Because it is no more than the interconnection of electronic pathways, cyberspace allows speakers and listeners to mask their identities. Cyberspace undeniably reflects some form of geography; chat rooms and Web sites, for example, exist at fixed "locations" on the Internet. Since users can transmit and receive messages on the Internet without revealing anything about their identities or ages, however, it is not currently possible to exclude persons from accessing certain messages on the basis of their identity.

Cyberspace differs from the physical world in another basic way: Cyberspace is malleable. Thus, it is possible to construct barriers in cyberspace and use them to screen for identity, making cyberspace more like the physical world and, consequently, more amenable to zoning laws. This transformation of cyberspace is already underway. . . .

Despite this progress, the transformation of cyberspace is not complete. Although gateway technology has been available on the World Wide Web for some time. it is not available to *all* Web speakers, and is just now becoming technologically feasible for chat rooms and USENET newsgroups. Gateway technology is not ubiquitous in cyberspace, and because without it "there is no means of age verification," cyberspace still remains largely unzoned—and unzoneable. . . .

Although the prospects for the eventual zoning of the Internet appear promising, I agree with the Court that we must evaluate the constitutionality of the CDA as it applies to the Internet as it exists today. Given the present state of cyberspace, I agree with the Court that the "display" provision cannot pass muster. Until gateway technology is available throughout cyberspace, and it is not in 1997, a speaker cannot be reasonably assured that the speech he displays will reach only adults because it is impossible to confine speech to an "adult zone." Thus, the only way for a speaker to avoid liability under the CDA is to refrain completely from using indecent speech. But this forced silence impinges on the First Amendment right of adults to make and obtain this speech and, for all intents and purposes, "reduces the adult population [on the Internet] to reading only what is fit for children." As a result, the "display" provision cannot withstand scrutiny.

The "indecency transmission" and "specific person" provisions present a closer issue, for they are not unconstitutional in all of their applications. ... [T]he "indecency transmission" provision makes it a crime to transmit knowingly an indecent message to a person the sender knows is under 18 years of age. The "specific person" provision proscribes the same conduct, although it does not as explicitly require the sender to know that the intended recipient of his indecent message is a minor. Appellant urges the Court to construe the provision to impose such a knowledge requirement, and I would do so.

So construed, both provisions are constitutional as applied to a conversation involving only an adult and one or more minors—e.g.. when an adult speaker sends an e-mail knowing the addressee is a minor, or when an adult and minor converse by themselves or with other minors in a chat room. ...

Thus, the constitutionality of the CDA as a zoning law hinges on the extent to which it substantially interferes with the First Amendment rights of adults. Because the rights of adults are infringed only by the "display" provision and by the "indecency transmission" and the "specific person" provisions as applied to communications involving more than one adult, I would invalidate the CDA only to that extent. Insofar as the "indecency transmission" and "specific person" provisions prohibit the use of indecent speech in communications between an adult and one or more minors, however, they can and should be sustained. The Court reaches a contrary conclusion, and from that holding that I respectfully dissent.

The Supreme Court thus agreed with the district court—the CDA was constitutionally defective. It did, however, "save" the CDA in one respect:

Appellees do not challenge the application of the statute to obscene speech, which, they acknowledge, can be banned totally because it enjoys no First Amendment protection. See *Miller*. As set forth by the statute, the restriction of "obscene" material enjoys a textual manifestation separate from that for "indecent" material, which we have held unconstitutional. Therefore, we will sever the term "or indecent" from the statute. ... In no other respect, however, can [the law] be saved by such a textual surgery.

Will *Reno* put an end to the government's efforts to regulate material on the Internet? Justice Stevens was clear that Congress cannot limit adults to seeing material that is only "fit for children." But supporters of the CDA are equally adamant that some regulation is needed. As Sen. Christopher Bond, R-Mo., put it: [This ruling] "is an unfortunate blow to those of us who want to protect our children from sexual predators using the Internet. ... I believe Congress will try again, and that we'll get it right next time."[17]

Bond was correct about Congress trying again. In 1998 it passed the Child OnLine Protection Act (often called CDA II), which makes it illegal to distribute "any communication for commercial purposes that is available to any minor and that includes any material that is harmful to minors."[18] A federal district court has already struck down CDA II on much the same grounds as the Supreme Court used in *Reno*.[19] The debate, however, continued. It became an issue in the 2000 presidential campaign, with several candidates complaining about the lack of regulation of pornography on the Internet. Moreover, states continue to pass laws, mini-CDAs really, that ban the communication of indecent material to minors. In light of *Reno*, lower courts have been loathe to uphold

---

17. Quoted in the *St. Louis Post Dispatch*, June 27, 1997, A16.

18. The act defines material that is "harmful to minors" as "any communication, picture, image, graphic image file, article, recording, writing, or other matter of any kind that is obscene or that (A) the average person, applying contemporary community standards, would find, taking the material as a whole and with respect to minors, is designed to appeal to, or is designed to pander to, the prurient interest; (B) depicts, describes, or represents, in a manner patently offensive with respect to minors, an actual or simulated sexual act or sexual contact, an actual or simulated normal or perverted sexual act, or a lewd exhibition of the genitals or post-pubescent female breast; and (C) taken as a whole, lacks serious literary, artistic, political, or scientific value for minors."

19. See *American Civil Liberties Union v. Janet Reno*, No. 98-5591 (E.D. Pa. 1998), available at *www.paed.uscourts.gov/opinions/99D0078P.html*.

such laws, but it may be only a matter of time before they develop regulations that would pass constitutional muster. The question is how to frame the legislation, given the rationale in *Reno*.

Reno is noteworthy not only because it provided some indication of the Court's current thinking on obscenity, but also because it presented the first opportunity for the justices to consider the legal status of the Internet—a medium that has grown by leaps and bounds over the last decade.

Like the Internet itself, the impact of the decision is likely to go well beyond the borders of the United States. Although Supreme Court decisions lack the force of law in other nations, it is such a well-respected body that its ruling may affect the actions that other democratic countries take. As the representative of an international Internet civil liberties group put it, the Court has sent "a clear signal about what is and is not an appropriate government involvement in this medium—in a democracy anyway."[20]

Nevertheless, other nations are beginning to take serious steps to regulate the flow of pornography on the Internet. Germany, for example, has been especially "aggressive," with the federal government keeping lists of and cracking down on illegal sites.[21] The European Union may pass legislation that would give law enforcement officials the authority to shut down pornographic sites. In addition, the members of the Association of Southeast Asian Nations (Brunei, Indonesia, Malaysia, Philippines, Singapore, Thailand, and Vietnam) have agreed to block access to Internet sites that are counter to "Asian values." This last step may reflect more than an attempt to protect citizens against obscenity; it may represent a fear of an "'Americanized' Internet culture, as anathemic to traditional Asian mores."[22] Japan, a leading source of Internet child pornography, has banned the distribution and sale of on-line child pornography of any kind. But the Internet transcends national boundaries—243 million people in more than 140 countries are now on line.[23] Therefore, the effectiveness of any one of these steps will depend not just on the efforts of one nation but on a far-reaching worldwide effort—with specific regulations, at least in some nations, subject to judicial review. Inevitably, some will fail to satisfy various constitutional requirements, just as was the case with the CDA.

In the meantime, the number of pornographic sites on the Internet continues to increase—one expert estimates that there are between 30,000 and 60,000 sex-oriented Web sites.[24] This situation has caused some parents and libraries to take matters into their own hands though the use of "filtering" software, that is, software developed to block pornographic sites. But these too are generating law suits. In a Florida suit, the plaintiff wanted the judge to "order that software filters be used on all school computers wired to the Internet and that proper procedures for Internet use be instituted so that children do not have access to pornography and are protected from pedophiles during school." On the other side, some complain that filters are ineffective at screening out many pornographic sites but too effective in preventing students access to information on important health issues.

How the Court will rule as these matters make their way up the judicial ladder is hard to say. What is certain is that we have not heard the last word from the Court or Congress on the dissemination of obscenity via the Internet.

LIBEL

On any given day in America, we can buy a newspaper, navigate to a Web site, or turn on the television and find information on the activities of public officials, well-known figures, and even private citizens who, for various reasons, have made news. Sometimes the reports imply criticism—for instance, a newspaper article about a public official accused of wrongdoing. In other cases, the re-

20. Quoted by Pamela Mendels in "Court's Ruling Expected to Have Global Impact," originally posted at: *http://search.nytimes.com/web/docsroot/library/cyber/week/1207decency.html*.

21. Edmund L. Andrews, "German Court Overturns Pornography Ruling Against Compuserve," *New York Times*, November 18, 1999, 4.

22. See Lewis S. Malakoff, "Are You My Mommy, or My Big Brother? Comparing Internet Censorship in Singapore and the United States," *Pacific Rim Law & Policy Journal* 8 (1999): 423.

23. Data on Internet use are available at: *www.euromktg.com/globstats*.

24. Frederick S. Lane III, *Obscene Profits: The Entrepreneurs of Pornography in the Cyber Age* (New York: Routledge, 2000).

ports are blatantly false. To see this phenomenon we need go no farther than a supermarket checkout and read the tabloid headlines about the alleged doings of celebrities.

As we know from our readings on freedom of the press, individuals or even governments generally cannot prohibit the media from disseminating such information—true or false. But once the story is published or televised, do the subjects of the stories have any recourse? Under U.S. law they do: they can bring a *libel* action against the offender. If individuals believe that falsehoods in a published or televised story resulted in the defamation of their character, they can ask a court to hold the media responsible for their actions. They have this recourse because, like obscenity, libelous statements remain outside the reach of the First Amendment.

Public Officials and Libel

The lack of First Amendment protection does not mean that libel is a simple area of law. In fact, the Supreme Court has had a difficult time developing standards for its application. One reason for the Court's problem is that, before 1964, libel was an undeveloped area of law.

Recall that in 1798 the Federalist Congress enacted the Sedition Act, which outlawed seditious libel, defined as criticism of the government and of government officials. Under this act, the government could bring criminal charges against those who made "false, scandalous, and malicious" statements that brought the United States or its representatives into "contempt or disrepute." Because President Jefferson later pardoned all those who had been convicted under it, the Supreme Court never had an opportunity to rule on the law's constitutionality. For most of the nation's history, it was unclear whether seditious libel was protected or unprotected speech. Some scholars argued that the purpose of the First Amendment was to "abolish seditious libel," while others contended the contrary.[25]

25. See Zechariah Chafee Jr., *Free Speech in the United States* (Cambridge: Harvard University Press, 1941); and Leonard W. Levy, *Legacy of Suppression* (Cambridge: Harvard University Press, 1960). See also Levy's revised and enlarged edition, *Emergence of a Free Press* (New York: Oxford University Press, 1985).

What is clear is that, until the Court decided a landmark case in 1964, its position was that the states were free to determine their own standards for the more typical version of libel—civil actions brought by individuals against other individuals, for example, those running a newspaper. Some variation existed among state laws, but most allowed defamed individuals to seek two kinds of damages: compensatory, which provide money for actual financial loss (an individual loses his or her job because of the story), and punitive, which punish the offender. To collect such monies, all the plaintiff generally had to demonstrate was that the story was false—truth is always a defense against claims of libel—and damaging.

These criteria might sound like simple standards for plaintiffs to meet, but the simplicity further compounded the Court's problems. Many newspapers, television stations, and other media argued that the traditional standard had a chilling effect on their First Amendment guarantee of a free press. They feared printing anything critical of government or public officials, in particular, because if the story contained even the smallest factual error, they could face a costly lawsuit. They felt constrained in their reporting of news. In *New York Times v. Sullivan* the Court radically departed from its former position.[26] What standard did the Court articulate? How did it alter existing libel law?

New York Times v. Sullivan

376 U.S. 254 (1964)
laws.findlaw.com/US/376/254.html
Vote: 9 (Black, Brennan, Clark, Douglas, Goldberg, Harlan, Stewart, Warren, White)
    0

Opinion of the Court: Brennan
Concurring opinions: Black, Goldberg

The March 29, 1960, edition of the *New York Times* ran an advertisement to publicize the struggle for civil rights and to raise money for the cause. L. B. Sullivan, an elected commissioner of the city of Montgomery, Alaba-

26. For oral arguments in this case, navigate to: *oyez.nwu.edu.*

"The growing movement of peaceful mass demonstrations by Negroes is something new in the South, something understandable.... Let Congress heed their rising voices, for they will be heard."

—New York Times editorial
Saturday, March 19, 1960

Heed Their Rising Voices

AS the whole world knows by now, thousands of Southern Negro students are engaged in widespread non-violent demonstrations in positive affirmation of the right to live in human dignity as guaranteed by the U. S. Constitution and the Bill of Rights. In their efforts to uphold these guarantees, they are being met by an unprecedented wave of terror by those who would deny and negate that document which the whole world looks upon as setting the pattern for modern freedom...

In Orangeburg, South Carolina, when 400 students peacefully sought to buy doughnuts and coffee at lunch counters in the business district, they were forcibly ejected, tear-gassed, soaked to the skin in freezing weather with fire hoses, arrested en masse and herded into an open barbed-wire stockade to stand for hours in the bitter cold.

In Montgomery, Alabama, after students sang "My Country, 'Tis of Thee" on the State Capitol steps, their leaders were expelled from school, and truckloads of police armed with shotguns and tear-gas ringed the Alabama State College Campus. When the entire student body protested to state authorities by refusing to re-register, their dining hall was padlocked in an attempt to starve them into submission.

In Tallahassee, Atlanta, Nashville, Savannah, Greensboro, Memphis, Richmond, Charlotte, and a host of other cities in the South, young American teenagers, in face of the entire weight of official state apparatus and police power, have boldly stepped forth as protagonists of democracy. Their courage and amazing restraint have inspired millions and given a new dignity to the cause of freedom.

Small wonder that the Southern violators of the Constitution fear this new, non-violent brand of freedom fighter... even as they fear the upswelling right-to-vote movement. Small wonder that they are determined to destroy the one man who, more than any other, symbolizes the new spirit now sweeping the South—the Rev. Dr. Martin Luther King, Jr., world-famous leader of the Montgomery Bus Protest. For it is his doctrine of non-violence which has inspired and guided the students in their widening wave of sit-ins; and it is this same Dr. King who founded and is president of the Southern Christian Leadership Conference—the organization which is spearheading the surging right-to-vote movement. Under Dr. King's direction the Leadership Conference conducts Student Workshops and Seminars in the philosophy and techniques of non-violent resistance.

Again and again the Southern violators have answered Dr. King's peaceful protests with intimidation and violence. They have bombed his home almost killing his wife and child. They have assaulted his person. They have arrested him seven times—for "speeding," "loitering" and similar "offenses." And now they have charged him with "perjury"—a *felony* under which they could imprison him for *ten years*. Obviously, their real purpose is to remove him physically as the leader to whom the students and millions of others—look for guidance and support, and thereby to intimidate *all* leaders who may rise in the South. Their strategy is to behead this affirmative movement, and thus to demoralize Negro Americans and weaken their will to struggle. The defense of Martin Luther King, spiritual leader of the student sit-in movement, clearly, therefore, is an integral part of the total struggle for freedom in the South.

Decent-minded Americans cannot help but applaud the creative daring of the students and the quiet heroism of Dr. King. But this is one of those moments in the stormy history of Freedom when men and women of good will must do more than applaud the rising-to-glory of others. The America whose good name hangs in the balance before a watchful world, the America whose heritage of Liberty these Southern Upholders of the Constitution are defending, is *our* America as well as theirs...

We must heed their rising voices—yes—but we must add our own.

We must extend ourselves above and beyond moral support and render the material help so urgently needed by those who are taking the risks, facing jail, and <u>even death</u> in a glorious re-affirmation of our Constitution and its Bill of Rights.

We urge you to join hands with our fellow Americans in the South by supporting, with your dollars, this combined appeal for all three needs—the defense of Martin Luther King—the support of the embattled students—and the struggle for the right-to-vote.

Your Help Is Urgently Needed . . . NOW!!

Stella Adler	Dr. Alan Knight Chalmers	Anthony Franciosa	John Killens	L. Joseph Overton	Maureen Stapleton
Raymond Pace Alexander	Richard Coe	Lorraine Hansbury	Eartha Kitt	Clarence Pickett	Frank Silvera
Harry Van Arsdale	Nat King Cole	Rev. Donald Harrington	Rabbi Edward Klein	Shad Polier	Hope Stevens
Harry Belafonte	Cheryl Crawford	Nat Hentoff	Hope Lange	Sidney Poitier	George Tabor
Julie Belafonte	Dorothy Dandridge	James Hicks	John Lewis	A. Philip Randolph	Rev. Gardner C.
Dr. Algernon Black	Ossie Davis	Mary Hinkson	Viveca Lindfors	John Raitt	Taylor
Marc Blitzstein	Sammy Davis, Jr.	Van Heflin	Carl Murphy	Elmer Rice	Norman Thomas
William Branch	Ruby Dee	Langston Hughes	Don Murray	Jackie Robinson	Kenneth Tynan
Marlon Brando	Dr. Philip Elliott	Morris Iushevitz	John Murray	Mrs. Eleanor Roosevelt	Charles White
Mrs. Ralph Bunche	Dr. Harry Emerson	Mahalia Jackson	A. J. Muste	Bayard Rustin	Shelley Winters
Diahann Carroll	Fosdick	Mordecai Johnson	Frederick O'Neal	Robert Ryan	Max Youngstein

We in the south who are struggling daily for dignity and freedom warmly endorse this appeal

Rev. Ralph D. Abernathy (Montgomery, Ala.)	Rev. Matthew D. McCollom (Orangeburg, S.C.)	Rev. Walter L. Hamilton (Norfolk, Va.)	Rev. A. L. Davis (New Orleans, La.)
Rev. Fred L. Shuttlesworth (Birmingham, Ala.)	Rev. William Holmes Borders (Atlanta, Ga.)	I. S. Levy (Columbia, S.C.) Rev. Martin Luther King, Sr. (Atlanta, Ga.)	Mrs. Katie E. Whickham (New Orleans, La.)
Rev. Kelley Miller Smith (Nashville, Tenn.)	Rev. Douglas Moore (Durham, N.C.)	Rev. Henry C. Bunton (Memphis, Tenn.)	Rev. W. H. Hall (Hattiesburg, Miss.)
Rev. W. A. Dennis (Chattanooga, Tenn.)		Rev. S.S. Seay, Sr. (Montgomery, Ala.)	Rev. J. E. Lowery (Mobile, Ala.)
Rev. C. K. Steele (Tallahassee, Fla.)	Rev. Wyatt Tee Walker (Petersburg, Va.)	Rev. Samuel W. Williams (Atlanta, Ga.)	Rev. T. J. Jemison (Baton Rouge, La.)

Please mail this coupon TODAY!

Committee To Defend Martin Luther King
and
The Struggle For Freedom in The South
312 West 125th Street, New York 27, N.Y.
UNiversity 6-1700

I am enclosing my contribution of $_____
for the work of the Committee.

Name _____
Address _____
City _____ Zone _____ State _____

☐ I want to help ☐ Please send further information

Please make checks payable to:
Committee to Defend Martin Luther King

COMMITTEE TO DEFEND MARTIN LUTHER KING AND THE STRUGGLE FOR FREEDOM IN THE SOUTH

312 West 125th Street, New York 27, N.Y. UNiversity 6-1700

Chairmen: A. Philip Randolph, Dr. Gardner C. Taylor; *Chairmen of Cultural Division:* Harry Belafonte, Sidney Poitier; *Treasurer:* Nat King Cole; *Executive Director:* Bayard Rustin; *Chairman of Church Division:* Father George B. Ford, Rev. Harry Emerson Fosdick, Rev. Thomas Kilgore, Jr., Rabbi Edward E. Klein; *Chairman of Labor Division:* Morris Iushevitz

L. B. Sullivan, second from right, poses with his attorneys after winning his libel suit against the *New York Times*. The Supreme Court overturned the decision in 1964. Justice Brennan's opinion stated that public officials are held to a higher standard than private citizens when proving libel.

ma, took offense at the ad. It did not mention his name, but it gave an account of a racial incident that had occurred in Montgomery. The ad suggested that the police, of whom Sullivan was in charge, had participated in wrongdoing.

Sullivan brought a libel action against the paper, alleging that the ad contained falsehoods, which, in fact, it did. For example, it claimed that demonstrating students sang "My Country, 'Tis of Thee," when they actually sang the "Star-Spangled Banner." In his charge to the jury, the judge said that the ad was "libelous per se," meaning that because it contained lies, it was unprotected speech, and, that if the jury found that the statements were made "of and concerning" Sullivan, it could hold the *Times* liable. Taking these words to heart, the jury awarded Sullivan $500,000 in damages.

The Supreme Court of Alabama affirmed this judgment. It specified that words are libelous per se when they "tend to injure a person labeled by them in his reputation, profession, trade or business, or charge him with an indictable offense, or tend to bring the individual into public contempt." This definition was fairly typical. The

New York Times challenged the decision, arguing that the libel standard "presumes malice and falsity. . . . Such a rule of liability works an abridgment of the free press." Its attorneys added, "It is implicit in this Court's decisions that speech which is critical of governmental action may not be repressed upon the ground that it diminishes the reputation of those officers whose conduct it deplores."

MR. JUSTICE BRENNAN delivered the opinion of the Court.

We are required in this case to determine for the first time the extent to which the constitutional protections for speech and press limit a State's power to award damages in a libel action brought by a public official against critics of his official conduct. . . .

Because of the importance of the constitutional issues involved, we granted the separate petitions for certiorari of the individual petitioners and of the *Times*. We reverse the judgment. We hold that the rule of law applied by the Alabama courts is constitutionally deficient for failure to provide the safeguards for freedom of speech and of the press that are required by the First and Fourteenth Amendments in a libel action brought by a public official against critics of his official conduct. We further hold that under the proper safeguards the evidence presented in this case is constitutionally insufficient to support the judgment for respondent.

We may dispose at the outset of [t]he . . . contention . . . that the constitutional guarantees of freedom of speech and of the press are inapplicable here, at least so far as the *Times* is concerned, because the allegedly libelous statements were published as part of a paid, "commercial" advertisement. . . .

The publication here was not a "commercial" advertisement in the sense in which the word was used in [*Valentine v.*] *Chrestensen* [1942]. It communicated information, expressed opinion, recited grievances, protested claimed abuses, and sought financial support on behalf of a movement whose existence and objectives are matters of the highest public interest and concern. That the *Times* was paid for publishing the advertisement is as immaterial in this connection as is the fact that newspapers and books are sold. Any other conclusion would discourage newspapers from carrying "editorial advertisements" of this type, and so might shut off an important outlet for the promulgation of information and ideas by persons who do not themselves have access to publishing facilities—who wish to exercise their freedom of speech even though they are not members of the press. The effect would be to shackle the First Amendment in its attempt to secure "the widest possible dissemination of information from diverse and antagonistic sources." To avoid placing such a handicap upon the freedoms of expression, we hold that if the allegedly libelous statements would otherwise be constitutionally protected from the present judgment, they do not forfeit that protection because they were published in the form of a paid advertisement.

Under Alabama law as applied in this case, a publication is "libelous per se" if the words "tend to injure a person . . . in his reputation" or to "bring [him] into public contempt"; the trial court stated that the standard was met if the words are such as to "injure him in his public office, or impute misconduct to him in his office, or want of official integrity, or want of fidelity to a public trust. . . ." The jury must find that the words were published "of and concerning" the plaintiff, but where the plaintiff is a public official his place

in the governmental hierarchy is sufficient evidence to support a finding that his reputation has been affected by statements that reflect upon the agency of which he is in charge. Once "libel per se" has been established, the defendant has no defense as to stated facts unless he can persuade the jury that they were true in all their particulars. His privilege of "fair comment" for expressions of opinion depends on the truth of the facts upon which the comment is based. Unless he can discharge the burden of proving truth, general damages are presumed, and may be awarded without proof of pecuniary injury. A showing of actual malice is apparently a prerequisite to recovery of punitive damages, and the defendant may in any event forestall a punitive award by a retraction meeting the statutory requirements. Good motives and belief in truth do not negate an inference of malice, but are relevant only in mitigation of punitive damages if the jury chooses to accord them weight.

The question before us is whether this rule of liability, as applied to an action brought by a public official against critics of his official conduct, abridges the freedom of speech and of the press that is guaranteed by the First and Fourteenth Amendments.

Respondent relies heavily, as did the Alabama courts, on statements of this Court to the effect that the Constitution does not protect libelous publications. Those statements do not foreclose our inquiry here. None of the cases sustained the use of libel laws to impose sanctions upon expression critical of the official conduct of public officials. . . . In deciding the question now, we are compelled by neither precedent nor policy to give any more weight to the epithet "libel" than we have to other "mere labels" of state law. Like insurrection, contempt, advocacy of unlawful acts, breach of the peace, obscenity, solicitation of legal business, and the various other formulae for the repression of expression that have been challenged in this Court, libel can claim no talismanic immunity from constitutional limitations. It must be measured by standards that satisfy the First Amendment. . . .

[W]e consider this case against the background of a profound national commitment to the principle that debate on public issues should be uninhibited, robust, and wide open, and that it may well include vehement, caustic, and sometimes unpleasantly sharp attacks on government and public officials. The present advertisement, as an expression of grievance and protest on one of the major public issues of our time, would seem clearly to qualify for the constitutional protection. The question is whether it forfeits that protection by the falsity of some of its factual statements and by its alleged defamation of respondent.

Authoritative interpretations of the First Amendment guarantees have consistently refused to recognize an exception for any test of truth—whether administered by judges, juries, or administrative officials—and especially one that puts the burden of proving truth on the speaker. The constitutional protection does not turn upon "the truth, popularity, or social utility of the ideas and beliefs which are offered.". . . That erroneous statement is inevitable in free debate, and that it must be protected if the freedoms of expression are to have the "breathing space" that they "need . . . to survive," was . . . recognized by the Court of Appeals for the District of Columbia Circuit in *Sweeney v. Patterson* [1942]. . . .

Injury to official reputation error affords no more warrant for repressing speech that would otherwise be free than does factual error. Where judicial officers are involved, this Court has held that concern for the dignity and reputation of the courts does not justify the punishment as criminal contempt of criticism of the judge or his decision. This is true even though the utterance contains "half-truths" and "misinformation." Such repression can be justified, if at all, only by a clear and present danger of the obstruction of justice. If judges are to be treated as "men of fortitude, able to thrive in a hardy climate," surely the same must be true of other government officials, such as elected city commissioners. Criticism of their official conduct does not lose its constitutional protection merely because it is effective criticism and hence diminishes their official reputations.

If neither factual error nor defamatory content suffices to remove the constitutional shield from criticism of official conduct, the combination of the two elements is no less inadequate. This is the lesson to be drawn from the great controversy over the Sedition Act of 1798, which first crystallized a national awareness of the central meaning of the First Amendment. That statute made it a crime, punishable by a $5,000 fine and five years in prison, "if any person shall write, print, utter or publish . . . any false, scandalous and malicious writing or writings against the government of the United States, or either House of the Congress . . . or the President . . . , with intent to defame . . . or to bring them, or either of them, into contempt or disrepute; or to excite

against them, or either or any of them, the hatred of the good people of the United States.". . .

Although the Sedition Act was never tested in this Court, the attack upon its validity has carried the day in the court of history. Fines levied in its prosecution were repaid by Act of Congress on the ground that it was unconstitutional. Calhoun, reporting to the Senate on February 4, 1836, assumed that its invalidity was a matter "which no one now doubts." Jefferson, as President, pardoned those who had been convicted and sentenced under the Act and remitted their fines, stating: "I discharged every person under punishment or prosecution under the sedition law, because I considered, and now consider, that law to be a nullity, as absolute and as palpable as if Congress had ordered us to fall down and worship a golden image." The invalidity of the Act has also been assumed by Justices of this Court. These views reflect a broad consensus that the Act, because of the restraint it imposed upon criticism of government and public officials, was inconsistent with the First Amendment.

There is no force in respondent's argument that the constitutional limitations implicit in the history of the Sedition Act apply only to Congress and not to the States. It is true that the First Amendment was originally addressed only to action by the Federal Government, and that Jefferson, for one, while denying the power of Congress "to controul the freedom of the press," recognized such a power in the States. But this distinction was eliminated with the adoption of the Fourteenth Amendment and the application to the States of the First Amendment's restrictions.

What a State may not constitutionally bring about by means of a criminal statute is likewise beyond the reach of its civil law of libel. The fear of damage awards under a rule such as that invoked by the Alabama courts here may be markedly more inhibiting than the fear of prosecution under a criminal statute. Alabama, for example, has a criminal libel law which subjects to prosecution "any person who speaks, writes, or prints of and concerning another any accusation falsely and maliciously importing the commission by such person of a felony, or any other indictable offense involving moral turpitude," and which allows as punishment upon conviction a fine not exceeding $500 and a prison sentence of six months. Presumably a person charged with violation of this statute enjoys ordinary criminal-law safeguards such as the requirements of an indictment and of proof beyond a reasonable doubt. These safeguards are not available to the defendant in a civil action. The judgment awarded in this case—without the need for any proof of actual pecuniary loss—was one thousand times greater than the maximum fine provided by the Alabama criminal statute, and one hundred times greater than that provided by the Sedition Act. And since there is no double-jeopardy limitation applicable to civil lawsuits, this is not the only judgment that may be awarded against petitioners for the same publication. Whether or not a newspaper can survive a succession of such judgments, the pall of fear and timidity imposed upon those who would give voice to public criticism is an atmosphere in which the First Amendment freedoms cannot survive. Plainly the Alabama law of civil libel is "a form of regulation that creates hazards to protected freedoms markedly greater than those that attend reliance upon the criminal law."

The state rule of law is not saved by its allowance of the defense of truth. A defense for erroneous statements honestly made is no less essential here than was the requirement of proof of guilty knowledge which we held indispensable to a valid conviction of a bookseller for possessing obscene writings for sale. . . . A rule compelling the critic of official conduct to guarantee the truth of all his factual assertions—and to do so on pain of libel judgments virtually unlimited in amount—leads to a comparable "self-censorship." Allowance of the defense of truth, with the burden of proving it on the defendant, does not mean that only false speech will be deterred. Even courts accepting this defense as an adequate safeguard have recognized the difficulties of adducing legal proofs that the alleged libel was true in all its factual particulars. Under such a rule, would-be critics of official conduct may be deterred from voicing their criticism, even though it is believed to be true and even though it is in fact true, because of doubt whether it can be proved in court or fear of the expense of having to do so. They tend to make only statements which "steer far wider of the unlawful zone." The rule thus dampens the vigor and limits the variety of public debate. It is inconsistent with the First and Fourteenth Amendments.

The constitutional guarantees require, we think, a federal rule that prohibits a public official from recovering damages for a defamatory falsehood relating to his official conduct unless he proves that the statement was made with "actual malice"—that is, with knowledge that it was false or

with reckless disregard of whether it was false or not. . . .

. . . [A] privilege for criticism of official conduct is appropriately analogous to the protection accorded a public official when he is sued for libel by a private citizen. . . . The reason for the official privilege is said to be that the threat of damage suits would otherwise "inhibit the fearless, vigorous, and effective administration of policies of government" and "dampen the ardor of all but the most resolute, or the most irresponsible, in the unflinching discharge of their duties." Analogous considerations support the privilege for the citizen-critic of government. It is as much his duty to criticize as it is the official's duty to administer. As Madison said, "the censorial power is in the people over the Government, and not in the Government over the people." It would give public servants an unjustified preference over the public they serve, if critics of official conduct did not have a fair equivalent of the immunity granted to the officials themselves.

We conclude that such a privilege is required by the First and Fourteenth Amendments.

We hold today that the Constitution delimits a State's power to award damages for libel in actions brought by public officials against critics of their official conduct. Since this is such an action, the rule requiring proof of actual malice is applicable. While Alabama law apparently requires proof of actual malice for an award of punitive damages, where general damages are concerned malice is "presumed." Such a presumption is inconsistent with the federal rule. . . . Since the trial judge did not instruct the jury to differentiate between general and punitive damages, it may be that the verdict was wholly an award of one or the other. But it is impossible to know, in view of the general verdict returned. Because of this uncertainty, the judgment must be reversed and the case remanded.

Since respondent may seek a new trial, we deem that considerations of effective judicial administration require us to review the evidence in the present record to determine whether it could constitutionally support a judgment for respondent. This Court's duty is not limited to the elaboration of constitutional principles; we must also in proper cases review the evidence to make certain that those principles have been constitutionally applied. This is such a case, particularly since the question is one of alleged trespass across "the line between speech unconditionally guaranteed and speech which may legitimately be regulated." In cases where that line must be drawn, the rule is that we "examine for ourselves the statements in issue and the circumstances under which they were made to see . . . whether they are of a character which the principles of the First Amendment, as adopted by the Due Process Clause of the Fourteenth Amendment, protect." We must "make an independent examination of the whole record," so as to assure ourselves that the judgment does not constitute a forbidden intrusion on the field of free expression.

Applying these standards, we consider that the proof presented to show actual malice lacks the convincing clarity which the constitutional standard demands, and hence that it would not constitutionally sustain the judgment for respondent under the proper rule of law. The case of the individual petitioners requires little discussion. Even assuming that they could constitutionally be found to have authorized the use of their names on the advertisement, there was no evidence whatever that they were aware of any erroneous statements or were in any way reckless in that regard. The judgment against them is thus without constitutional support.

As to the *Times*, we similarly conclude that the facts do not support a finding of actual malice. The statement by the *Times'* Secretary that . . . he thought the advertisement was "substantially correct" affords no constitutional warrant for the Alabama Supreme Court's conclusion that it was a "cavalier ignoring of the falsity of the advertisement from which, the jury could not have but been impressed with the bad faith of the *Times*, and its maliciousness inferable therefrom." The statement does not indicate malice at the time of the publication; even if the advertisement was not "substantially correct"—although respondent's own proofs tend to show that it was—that opinion was at least a reasonable one, and there was no evidence to impeach the witness' good faith in holding it. . . .

We also think the evidence was constitutionally defective in another respect: it was incapable of supporting the jury's finding that the allegedly libelous statements were made "of and concerning" respondent. Respondent relies on the words of the advertisement and the testimony of six witnesses to establish a connection between it and himself. . . . There was no reference to respondent in the advertisement, either by name or official position. A number of the allegedly libelous statements—the charges that the dining hall was padlocked and that Dr. King's home was bombed,

his person assaulted, and a perjury prosecution instituted against him—did not even concern the police; despite the ingenuity of the arguments which would attach this significance to the word "They," it is plain that these statements could not reasonably be read as accusing respondent of personal involvement in the acts in question. . . .

The judgment of the Supreme Court of Alabama is reversed and the case is remanded to that court for further proceedings not inconsistent with this opinion.

Reversed and remanded.

MR. JUSTICE BLACK, with whom MR. JUSTICE DOUGLAS joins, concurring.

I concur in reversing this half-million-dollar judgment against the New York Times Company and the four individual defendants. In reversing the Court holds that "the Constitution delimits a State's power to award damages for libel in actions brought by public officials against critics of their official conduct." I base my vote to reverse on the belief that the First and Fourteenth Amendments not merely "delimit" a State's power to award damages to "public officials against critics of their official conduct" but completely prohibit a State from exercising such a power. The Court goes on to hold that a State can subject such critics to damages if "actual malice" can be proved against them. "Malice," even as defined by the Court, is an elusive, abstract concept, hard to prove and hard to disprove. The requirement that malice be proved provides at best an evanescent protection for the right critically to discuss public affairs and certainly does not measure up to the sturdy safeguard embodied in the First Amendment. Unlike the Court, therefore, I vote to reverse exclusively on the ground that the Times and the individual defendants had an absolute, unconditional constitutional right to publish in the Times advertisement their criticisms of the Montgomery agencies and officials.

Many consider Brennan's opinion a *tour de force* on the subject of libel. By holding the Sedition Act of 1798 unconstitutional, however belatedly, Brennan said that the First Amendment protects seditious libel, that the government may not criminally punish individuals who speak out against government, in a true or false manner. But more important was the part of the opinion that dealt with civil actions. The concurrers argued that the

BOX 7-6   LIBEL IN GLOBAL PERSPECTIVE

ACCORDING to some scholars, the U.S. Supreme Court has adopted rules that, compared with practices elsewhere, make it difficult for plaintiffs (the persons alleging libel) to prevail in lawsuits—especially if they are public officials and figures. For example, in the United States it is up to the plaintiff to prove that allegedly libelous statements are false, but, under British law, it is the defendant who must prove that the statements are true.

Moreover, in most countries plaintiffs do not have to meet the kind of "actual malice" standard that the Court adopted in *New York Times v. Sullivan*. The Canadian Supreme Court, in fact, explicitly declined to adopt this standard, saying in *Hill v. Church of Scientology* that democracies need to take reputation as seriously as freedom of expression. Germany's Constitutional Court has expressed similar sentiments, suggesting in several cases that no matter how important speech about politics is, it may be unwise to elevate it to the detriment of other societal interests, such as truth and human dignity. This attitude may reflect differences in American and German political experiences: Germany paid a steep price for tolerating unbridled political communication and does not want to make the same mistake again.

The sweep of U.S. protection has some interesting implications. First and most obvious, the likelihood of recovering damages in libel suits—even those involving public officials and figures—is far greater in other nations than in the United States. According to the media in some countries, this has a chilling effect on the press. In Ireland, for example, where libel law heavily favors plaintiffs and large awards are far from infrequent, the newspapers say they must exercise care in publishing controversial material and in encouraging aggressive reporting. In response, scholars and courts have suggested that societies must protect values such as reputation, dignity, and truth, in addition to a free press.

A second implication is less obvious: as more and more allegedly libelous material appears on the Internet, variation in nations' practices may encourage "country shopping" among plaintiffs. We have more to say on this point on page 401.

SOURCES: Charles Tingley, "Reputation, Freedom of Expression and the Tort of Defamation in the United States and Canada: A Deceptive Polarity," *Alberta Law Review* 37 (1999): 620; Sarah Frazier, "Liberty of Expression in Ireland and the Need for a Constitutional Law of Defamation," *Vanderbilt Journal of Transnational Law* 32 (1999): 391; and Vicki C. Jackson and Mark Tushnet, *Comparative Constitutional Law* (New York: Foundation Press, 1999).

press had an absolute and unconditional right to criticize government officials and that states could not permit civil actions in such cases. Brennan and the majority did not go that far, but they radically altered the standards that public officials acting in a public capacity had to meet before they could prove libel and receive damages. Calling previous rules of falsehood and defamation "constitutionally deficient," Brennan asserted that if plaintiffs were public officials, they had to demonstrate that the statement was false, damaging, and "made with 'actual malice'—that is, with knowledge that it was false or with reckless disregard of whether it was false or not." In his view, such an exacting standard—now called the *New York Times* test—was necessary because of a "profound national commitment to the principle that debate on public issues should be uninhibited, robust, and wide-open." It is interesting to note that although other demo-

cratic countries might agree with this sentiment, at least some have not made it as difficult for public officials to sue for libel as the U.S. Supreme Court did in *Sullivan* (see Box 7-6).

Expanding the New York Times *Test*

Brennan's opinion in *New York Times v. Sullivan* significantly altered the course of libel law, making it more difficult for public officials to bring actions against the media. But the decision raised further questions, for example, who is considered a public official? In footnote 23 Brennan wrote, "We have no occasion here to determine how far down into lower ranks of government employees the 'public official' designation would extend." When an appropriate case presented itself, the Court would have to draw some distinctions. How it did so would have significant ramifications because, under the *New York Times* test, only public officials had to prove actual malice; other plaintiffs were bound only to the traditional standards that the statements were false and damaging. Equally difficult were other questions raised by the decision: Did this new standard apply only to public officials engaged in their official duty? How could a public official prove actual malice? What did that term encompass?

In 1967 the Court decided two cases, *Curtis Publishing Company v. Butts* and *Associated Press v. Walker*, in hopes of clarifying its *New York Times* ruling. At issue in *Curtis* was a *Saturday Evening Post* article entitled "The Story of a College Football Fix." The author asserted that Wally Butts, the athletic director at the University of Georgia, had given Paul Bryant, the football coach at the University of Alabama, "the plays, defensive patterns, and all the significant secrets Georgia's football team possessed." According to the article, Butts was attempting to fix a 1962 game between the two schools. The author claimed he had obtained this information from an Atlanta insurance salesman, who accidentally overheard the conversation between Butts and Bryant. Butts initiated a libel suit against the publishing company, arguing that the article was false and damaging.[27] And, although the Court had yet to hand down the *New York Times* decision, Butts's suit also alleged that actual malice had occurred because the *Saturday Evening Post* "had departed greatly from the standards of good investigation and reporting." Evidence introduced at the trial showed that the *Saturday Evening Post* had done little to verify the insurance salesman's story. The magazine's attorneys "were aware of the progress" of the *New York Times* case, but offered only a defense of truth. A jury awarded Butts $3,060,000 in damages, but the judge reduced the award to $460,000. The *Post* asked for a new trial on *New York Times* grounds—that Butts was a public figure and should have to prove actual malice. The judge refused, asserting that Butts was not a public official and, even if he were, there was sufficient evidence to conclude that the magazine had acted with "reckless disregard for the truth."

27. Up to this point, Butts had been a respected figure in coaching ranks and had been negotiating for a coaching position with a professional team. After the *Saturday Evening Post* published the story, he resigned from the University of Georgia for "health" reasons.

Associated Press v. Walker concerned a 1962 AP story, an eyewitness account of the riots at the University of Mississippi over the government-ordered admission of James Meredith, a black student. According to the story, retired army general Edwin Walker "took command of the violent crowd and . . . led a charge against federal marshals," who were in Mississippi to oversee the desegregation process. It also alleged that Walker gave the segregationists instructions on how to combat the effects of tear gas. Walker sued the Associated Press for $2 million in compensatory and punitive damages, arguing that the article was false and damaging. The jury awarded $500,000 in compensatory damages and $300,000 in punitive damages, but the judge set aside the latter on the ground that Walker, while not a public official, was a public figure—his views on integration were well known and, as such, he had to prove actual malice under the *New York Times* standard.

The justices were unable to agree upon an opinion, but a majority (although for different reasons, which we review below) ruled in favor of Butts's claim and against Walker's. Seven justices (Brennan, Clark, Fortas, Harlan, Stewart, Warren, and White) agreed that Walker and Butts were public figures. Beyond that there were substantial differences among them. Five (Black, Brennan, Douglas, Warren, and White) ruled that the *New York Times* standard applies to public figures. In other words, even though Walker and Butts were not officials of the government, they would have to meet the *New York Times* test to win their suits because they were individuals in the public eye. The remaining four argued that a lesser standard of "highly unreasonable conduct constituting extreme departure from standards of investigating and reporting" should apply to public figures. Five justices (Clark, Fortas, Harlan, Stewart, and Warren) ruled in favor of Butts, upholding the lower court's decision, on the ground that Butts had demonstrated that the magazine had abandoned professional standards (Harlan, joined by Clark, Fortas, and Stewart) or exhibited a reckless disregard for the truth (Warren). The other four justices would have held against Butts. Brennan (joined by White) agreed with Warren that the *New York Times* standard could be met by evidence presented, but argued that new trial was needed because the jury was not properly instructed in this regard. Black (joined by Douglas) argued for complete reversal. All nine justices rejected Walker's claim. They said that Walker had failed to prove press improprieties, but they invoked different standards of such improprieties. Harlan (joined Clark, Fortas, and Stewart) argued that Walker had not met the "unreasonable conduct" standard; Black, Brennan, Douglas, Warren, and White asserted that he had not met the *New York Times* standard.[28]

Amid all this disagreement, one principle emerged: those in the public eye would have to meet the *New York Times* test to win their libel cases. But this was not the only shift in the rapidly changing interpretations of press freedoms. Another came in *Time, Inc. v. Hill* (1967). This case involved not public figures, but private individuals who became the victims of false media reports. In 1952, three escaped convicts held the Hill family hostage for nineteen hours, an incident that received national press attention and was later depicted in a novel and a play entitled *The Desperate Hours.* As the story evolved from news-to-novel-to-play it became more fictionalized. The most significant departure from reality concerned the play's description of violence against the Hills. In fact, the convicts had treated the Hills relatively well, and no violence had taken place. *Life* magazine, owned by Time, Inc., published a pictorial essay on the play's opening, but failed to point out that the play was not an accurate representation of what had occurred. The Hill family successfully sued for invasion of privacy, receiving a judgment of $30,000 on the basis of a New York law that allowed compensation for the victims of stories containing "substantial falsification."

Time appealed this decision, asking the Supreme Court to apply the *New York Times* test. It argued that the opening of the play was a newsworthy event and the press should be given latitude in covering matters of public interest. The Hills countered that they were private individuals and that they should only have to show that Time invaded their privacy by publishing false infor-

mation about them. The Court, in an opinion written by Justice Brennan, extended the *New York Times* test to press coverage of such matters of public interest. Although the Hills were private individuals, the First Amendment must provide sufficient protection so that the press can responsibly cover newsworthy events without an unreasonable fear of damage awards. Consequently, the Hills would have to prove not only that the story's description of them was false, but also that it was published with knowledge of the falsity or reckless disregard for the truth.

If *Butts* and *Walker* helped clarify some aspects of *New York Times,* they also focused attention on this question: For purposes of libel law, how far does the "public figure" definition stretch? The *Hill* case further complicated matters by taking a standard of proof for libel actions and applying it to invasion of privacy claims and by expanding the coverage of that standard of proof to matters of public interest. Did the Court totally blur the distinction between public figures and private citizens? What constituted a matter of public interest? In the 1971 case of *Rosenbloom v. Metromedia,* the Court attempted to provide some answers.

At issue in *Rosenbloom* were the actions of a Philadelphia police captain who, in an attempt to enforce his city's obscenity laws, purchased magazines from more than twenty city newsstands. Concluding that the magazines were obscene, he directed officers to arrest the vendors. As police were carrying out the order, they happened upon George Rosenbloom, who was delivering adult magazines to one of the stands. They arrested him and obtained a warrant to search his home and warehouse. The search led to the seizure of a high volume of allegedly obscene material, and the police captain reported this point to several radio stations and newspapers. In response, a Metromedia-owned station, WIP, broadcast a series of reports identifying Rosenbloom and indicating that the police had searched both his home and warehouse and had seized approximately 4,000 volumes of allegedly obscene material. However, in at least two of the broadcasts, the station failed to qualify the seized material as "reportedly" or "allegedly" obscene. In a later broadcast the station referred to a

28. Black and Douglas claimed that they did so only to obtain a majority, otherwise they would haved adhered to their view that the First Amendment protects the press from all libel claims.

lawsuit in which Rosenbloom was the plaintiff as an action by a "smut distributor" to force local officials to "lay off the smut literature racket." Rosenbloom initiated a libel action against the station, arguing that his books were not obscene, that, in fact, a jury had acquitted him on those charges. WIP offered a defense of truth, but the jury found for Rosenbloom, awarding him $750,000 in damages.

The Court reversed the decision of the lower court, but could not agree on a rationale for doing so.[29] Writing for a plurality of three justices, Justice Brennan argued that the primary emphasis of the *New York Times* test "derives not so much from whether the plaintiff is a 'public official,' 'public figure,'" or "'private individual' as it derives from the question whether the allegedly defamatory publication concerns a matter of public or general interest." In writing these words, Brennan claimed that the *New York Times* test applied to all stories of public interest regardless of the public status of the individual.

The Court Retrenches

The reaction to *Rosenbloom* was mixed. The media were delighted: it would now be extremely difficult for any individual mentioned in a story of public interest to prove libel. Others were quick to criticize: Justice Marshall, usually an ally of Brennan's, thought the opinion went way too far, that Rosenbloom was "just one of the millions of Americans who live their lives in obscurity"; others argued that it put a heavy burden on lower court judges to determine what is in the public's interest.

Just three years later, the Court largely abandoned the *Rosenbloom* framework. While reading *Gertz v. Welch* (1974), consider the following: With what did the Court replace the *Rosenbloom* standard? Did it substantially alter the entire *New York Times* test or just that portion at issue in *Rosenbloom*? Note too the views of Justices Brennan and White. Although they both dissented, they articulated very different positions. What were their preferred positions?

29. Justice Douglas did not participate in this case.

Gertz v. Welch

418 U.S. 323 (1974)
laws.findlaw.com/US/418/323.html
Vote: 5 (Blackmun, Marshall, Powell, Rehnquist, Stewart)
      4 (Brennan, Burger, Douglas, White)
Opinion of the Court: Powell
Concurring opinion: Blackmun
Dissenting opinions: Brennan, Burger, Douglas, White

After a jury convicted a police officer for murder, the victim's family retained Elmer Gertz, a Chicago attorney, to bring a civil action against the officer. Robert Welch published a story in *American Opinion*, an outlet for the views of the John Birch Society, a far-right, anticommunist group. The story suggested that Gertz was a "Communist-fronter," engaged in a plot to disgrace and frame the police. Gertz sued Welch for libel. He argued that the story was false and damaging to his career.

MR. JUSTICE POWELL delivered the opinion of the Court.

This Court has struggled for nearly a decade to define the proper accommodation between the law of defamation and the freedoms of speech and press protected by the First Amendment. With this decision we return to that effort. We granted certiorari to reconsider the extent of a publisher's constitutional privilege against liability for defamation of a private citizen. . . .

The principal issue in this case is whether a newspaper or broadcaster that publishes defamatory falsehoods about an individual who is neither a public official nor a public figure may claim a constitutional privilege against liability for the injury inflicted by those statements. The Court considered this question on the rather different set of facts presented in *Rosenbloom v. Metromedia, Inc.* . . .

This Court affirmed the decision below, but no majority could agree on a controlling rationale. The eight Justices who participated in *Rosenbloom* announced their views in five separate opinions, none of which commanded more than three votes. The several statements not only reveal disagreement about the appropriate result in that case, they also reflect divergent traditions of thought about the general problem of reconciling the law of defamation with the First Amendment. One approach has been to extend the *New York Times* test to an expanding variety of situations. Another has been to vary the level of constitutional privilege for defamatory falsehood with the status of the person defamed. And a third view would grant to the press and broadcast media absolute immunity from liability for defamation. . . .

We begin with the common ground. Under the First Amendment there is no such thing as a false idea. However pernicious an opinion may seem, we depend for its correction not on the conscience of judges and juries but on the competition of other ideas. But there is no constitutional value in false statements of fact. Neither the intentional lie nor the careless error materially advances society's interest in "uninhibited, robust, and wide-open" debate on public issues. *New York Times Co. v. Sullivan.* They belong to that category of utterances which "are no essential part of any exposition of ideas, and are of such slight social value as a step to truth that any benefit that may be derived from them is clearly outweighed by the social interest in order and morality." *Chaplinsky v. New Hampshire* (1942).

. . . The First Amendment requires that we protect some falsehood in order to protect speech that matters.

The need to avoid self-censorship by the news media is, however, not the only societal value at issue. If it were, this Court would have embraced long ago the view that publishers and broadcasters enjoy an unconditional and indefeasible immunity from liability for defamation. Such a rule would, indeed, obviate the fear that the prospect of civil liability for injurious falsehood might dissuade a timorous press from the effective exercise of First Amendment freedoms. Yet absolute protection for the communications media requires a total sacrifice of the competing value served by the law of defamation.

The legitimate state interest underlying the law of libel is the compensation of individuals for the harm inflicted on them by defamatory falsehood. We would not lightly require the State to abandon this purpose, . . . the individual's right to the protection of his own good name. . . .

Some tension necessarily exists between the need for a vigorous and uninhibited press and the legitimate interest in redressing wrongful injury. . . . In our continuing effort to define the proper accommodation between these competing concerns, we have been especially anxious to assure

to the freedoms of speech and press that "breathing space" essential to their fruitful exercise. To that end this Court has extended a measure of strategic protection to defamatory falsehood.

The *New York Times* standard defines the level of constitutional protection appropriate to the context of defamation of a public person. Those who, by reason of the notoriety of their achievements or the vigor and success with which they seek the public's attention, are properly classed as public figures and those who hold governmental office may recover for injury to reputation only on clear and convincing proof that the defamatory falsehood was made with knowledge of its falsity or with reckless disregard for the truth. This standard administers an extremely powerful antidote to the inducement to media self-censorship of the common-law rule of strict liability for libel and slander. And it exacts a correspondingly high price from the victims of defamatory falsehood. Plainly many deserving plaintiffs, including some intentionally subjected to injury, will be unable to surmount the barrier of the *New York Times* test. Despite this substantial abridgment of the state law right to compensation for wrongful hurt to one's reputation, the Court has concluded that the protection of the *New York Times* privilege should be available to publishers and broadcasters of defamatory falsehood concerning public officials and public figures. *New York Times Co. v. Sullivan; Curtis Publishing Co. v. Butts.* We think that these decisions are correct, but we do not find their holdings justified solely by reference to the interest of the press and broadcast media in immunity from liability. Rather, we believe that the *New York Times* rule states an accommodation between this concern and the limited state interest present in the context of libel actions brought by public persons. For the reasons stated below, we conclude that the state interest in compensating injury to the reputation of private individuals requires that a different rule should obtain with respect to them.

Theoretically, of course, the balance between the needs of the press and the individual's claim to compensation for wrongful injury might be struck on a case-by-case basis. As Mr. Justice Harlan hypothesized, "it might seem, purely as an abstract matter, that the most utilitarian approach would be to scrutinize carefully every jury verdict in every libel case, in order to ascertain whether the final judgment leaves fully protected whatever First Amendment values transcend the legitimate state interest in protecting the particular plaintiff who prevailed." But this approach would lead to unpredictable results and uncertain expectations, and it could render our duty to supervise the lower courts unmanageable. Because an *ad hoc* resolution of the competing interests at stake in each particular case is not feasible, we must lay down broad rules of general application. Such rules necessarily treat alike various cases involving differences as well as similarities. Thus it is often true that not all of the considerations which justify adoption of a given rule will obtain in each particular case decided under its authority.

With that caveat we have no difficulty in distinguishing among defamation plaintiffs. The first remedy of any victim of defamation is self-help—using available opportunities to contradict the lie or correct the error and thereby to minimize its adverse impact on reputation. Public officials and public figures usually enjoy significantly greater access to the channels of effective communication and hence have a more realistic opportunity to counteract false statements than private individuals normally enjoy. Private individuals are therefore more vulnerable to injury, and the state interest in protecting them is correspondingly greater.

More important than the likelihood that private individuals will lack effective opportunities for rebuttal, there is a compelling normative consideration underlying the distinction between public and private defamation plaintiffs. An individual who decides to seek governmental office must accept certain necessary consequences of that involvement in public affairs. He runs the risk of closer public scrutiny than might otherwise be the case. And society's interest in the officers of government is not strictly limited to the formal discharge of official duties. . . .

Those classed as public figures stand in a similar position. Hypothetically, it may be possible for someone to become a public figure through no purposeful action of his own, but the instances of truly involuntary public figures must be exceedingly rare. For the most part those who attain this status have assumed roles of especial prominence in the affairs of society. Some occupy positions of such persuasive power and influence that they are deemed public figures for all purposes. More commonly, those classed as public figures have thrust themselves to the forefront of particular public controversies in order to influence the resolution of the issues involved. In either event, they invite attention and comment.

Even if the foregoing generalities do not obtain in every

instance, the communications media are entitled to act on the assumption that public officials and public figures have voluntarily exposed themselves to increased risk of injury from defamatory falsehood concerning them. No such assumption is justified with respect to a private individual. He has not accepted public office or assumed an "influential role in ordering society." He has relinquished no part of his interest in the protection of his own good name, and consequently he has a more compelling call on the courts for redress of injury inflicted by defamatory falsehood. Thus, private individuals are not only more vulnerable to injury than public officials and public figures; they are also more deserving of recovery.

For these reasons we conclude that the States should retain substantial latitude in their efforts to enforce a legal remedy for defamatory falsehood injurious to the reputation of a private individual. The extension of the *New York Times* test proposed by the *Rosenbloom* plurality would abridge this legitimate state interest to a degree that we find unacceptable. And it would occasion the additional difficulty of forcing state and federal judges to decide on an *ad hoc* basis which publications address issues of "general or public interest" and which do not—to determine, in the words of MR. JUSTICE MARSHALL, "what information is relevant to self-government." *Rosenbloom v. Metromedia, Inc.* We doubt the wisdom of committing this task to the conscience of judges. Nor does the Constitution require us to draw so thin a line between the drastic alternatives of the *New York Times* privilege and the common law of strict liability for defamatory error. The "public or general interest" test for determining the applicability of the *New York Times* standard to private defamation actions inadequately serves both of the competing values at stake. On the one hand, a private individual whose reputation is injured by defamatory falsehood that does concern an issue of public or general interest has no recourse unless he can meet the rigorous requirements of *New York Times*. This is true despite the factors that distinguish the state interest in compensating private individuals from the analogous interest involved in the context of public persons. On the other hand, a publisher or broadcaster of a defamatory error which a court deems unrelated to an issue of public or general interest may be held liable in damages even if it took every reasonable precaution to ensure the accuracy of its assertions. And liability may far exceed compensation for any actual injury to the plaintiff, for the jury may be permitted to presume damages without proof of loss and even to award punitive damages.

We hold that, so long as they do not impose liability without fault, the States may define for themselves the appropriate standard of liability for a publisher or broadcaster of defamatory falsehood injurious to a private individual. This approach provides a more equitable boundary between the competing concerns involved here. It recognizes the strength of the legitimate state interest in compensating private individuals for wrongful injury to reputation, yet shields the press and broadcast media from the rigors of strict liability for defamation. At least this conclusion obtains where, as here, the substance of the defamatory statement "makes substantial danger to reputation apparent." This phrase places in perspective the conclusion we announce today. Our inquiry would involve considerations somewhat different from those discussed above if a State purported to condition civil liability on a factual misstatement whose content did not warn a reasonably prudent editor or broadcaster of its defamatory potential. *Time, Inc. v. Hill.* Such a case is not now before us, and we intimate no view as to its proper resolution.

Our accommodation of the competing values at stake in defamation suits by private individuals allows the States to impose liability on the publisher or broadcaster of defamatory falsehood on a less demanding showing than that required by *New York Times.* This conclusion is not based on a belief that the considerations which prompted the adoption of the *New York Times* privilege for defamation of public officials and its extension to public figures are wholly inapplicable to the context of private individuals. Rather, we endorse this approach in recognition of the strong and legitimate state interest in compensating private individuals for injury to reputation. But this countervailing state interest extends no further than compensation for actual injury. . . . [W]e hold that the States may not permit recovery of presumed or punitive damages, at least when liability is not based on a showing of knowledge of falsity or reckless disregard for the truth. . . .

Notwithstanding our refusal to extend the *New York Times* privilege to defamation of private individuals, respondent contends that we should affirm the judgment below on the ground that petitioner is either a public official or a public figure. There is little basis for the former assertion. Several years prior to the present incident, petitioner had served briefly on housing committees appointed by the mayor of Chicago, but at the time of publication he had never held any remunerative governmental position. Respondent admits this but argues that petitioner's appearance at the coroner's inquest rendered him a "de facto public official." Our cases recognized no such concept. Respondent's suggestion would sweep all lawyers under the *New York Times* rule as officers of the court and distort the plain meaning of the "public official" category beyond all recognition. We decline to follow it.

Respondent's characterization of petitioner as a public figure . . . may rest on either of two alternative bases. In some instances an individual may achieve such pervasive fame or notoriety that he becomes a public figure for all purposes and in all contexts. More commonly, an individual voluntarily injects himself or is drawn into a particular public controversy and thereby becomes a public figure for a limited range of issues. In either case such persons assume special prominence in the resolution of public questions.

Petitioner has long been active in community and professional affairs. He has served as an officer of local civic groups and of various professional organizations, and he has published several books and articles on legal subjects. Although petitioner was consequently well known in some circles, he had achieved no general fame or notoriety in the community. None of the prospective jurors called at the trial had ever heard of petitioner prior to this litigation, and respondent offered no proof that this response was atypical of the local population. We would not lightly assume that a citizen's participation in community and professional affairs rendered him a public figure for all purposes. Absent clear evidence of general fame or notoriety in the community, and pervasive involvement in the affairs of society, an individual should not be deemed a public personality for all aspects of his life. It is preferable to reduce the public-figure question to a more meaningful context by looking to the nature and extent of an individual's participation in the particular controversy giving rise to the defamation.

In this context it is plain that petitioner was not a public figure. He played a minimal role at the coroner's inquest, and his participation related solely to his representation of a private client. He took no part in the criminal prosecution of Officer Nuccio. Moreover, he never discussed either the criminal or civil litigation with the press and was never quoted as having done so. He plainly did not thrust himself into the vortex of this public issue, nor did he engage the public's attention in an attempt to influence its outcome. We are persuaded that the trial court did not err in refusing to characterize petitioner as a public figure for the purpose of this litigation.

We therefore conclude that the *New York Times* standard is inapplicable to this case and that the trial court erred in entering judgment for respondent. Because the jury was allowed to impose liability without fault and was permitted to presume damages without proof of injury, a new trial is necessary. We reverse and remand for further proceedings in accordance with this opinion.

It is so ordered.

Reversed and remanded.

MR. JUSTICE BRENNAN, dissenting.

I agree with the conclusion . . . that, at the time of publication of respondent's article, petitioner could not properly have been viewed as either a "public official" or "public figure"; instead, respondent's article, dealing with an alleged conspiracy to discredit local police forces, concerned petitioner's purported involvement in "an event of 'public or general interest.'" *Rosenbloom v. Metromedia, Inc.* (1971). I cannot agree, however, that free and robust debate—so essential to the proper functioning of our system of government—is permitted adequate "breathing space," when, as the Court holds, the States may impose all but strict liability for defamation if the defamed party is a private person and "the substance of the defamatory statement 'makes substantial danger to reputation apparent.'" I adhere to my view expressed in *Rosenbloom v. Metromedia, Inc.* that we strike the proper accommodation between avoidance of media self-censorship and protection of individual reputations only when we require States to apply the *New York Times Co. v. Sullivan* knowing-or-reckless-falsity standard in civil libel actions concerning media reports of the involvement of private individuals in events of public or general interest.

MR. JUSTICE WHITE, dissenting.

For some 200 years—from the very founding of the Nation—the law of defamation and right of the ordinary citizen to recover for false publication injurious to his reputation have been almost exclusively the business of state courts and legislatures. Under typical state defamation law, the defamed private citizen had to prove only a false publication that would subject him to hatred, contempt, or ridicule. Given such publication, general damage to reputation was presumed, while punitive damages required proof of additional facts. The law governing the defamation of private citizens remained untouched by the First Amendment, because, until relatively recently, the consistent view of the Court was that libelous words constitute a class of speech wholly unprotected by the First Amendment, subject only to limited exceptions carved out since 1964.

But now, using that Amendment as the chosen instrument, the Court, in a few printed pages, has federalized major aspects of libel law by declaring unconstitutional in important respects the prevailing defamation law in all or most of the 50 States. That result is accomplished by requiring the plaintiff in each and every defamation action to prove not only the defendant's culpability beyond his act of publishing defamatory material but also actual damage to reputation resulting from the publication. Moreover, punitive damages may not be recovered by showing malice in the traditional sense of ill will; knowing falsehood or reckless disregard of the truth will not be required.

I assume these sweeping changes will be popular with the press, but this is not the road to salvation for a court of law. As I see it, there are wholly insufficient grounds for scuttling the libel laws of the States in such wholesale fashion, to say nothing of deprecating the reputation interest of ordinary citizens and rendering them powerless to protect themselves. I do not suggest that the decision is illegitimate or beyond the bounds of judicial review, but it is an ill-considered exercise of the power entrusted to this Court. . . .

The impact of today's decision on the traditional law of libel is immediately obvious and indisputable. No longer will the plaintiff be able to rest his case with proof of a libel defamatory on its face or proof of a slander historically actionable *per se.* In addition, he must prove some further degree of culpable conduct on the part of the publisher, such as intentional or reckless falsehood or negligence. And if he succeeds in this respect, he faces still another obstacle: recovery for loss of reputation will be conditioned upon "competent" proof of actual injury to his standing in the community. This will be true regardless of the nature of the defamation and even though it is one of those particularly reprehensible statements that have traditionally made slanderous words actionable without proof of fault by the publisher or of the damaging impact of his publication. The Court rejects the judgment of experience that some publications are so inherently capable of injury, and actual injury so difficult to prove, that the risk of falsehood should be borne by the publisher, not the victim. Plainly, with the additional burden on the plaintiff of proving negligence or other fault, it will be exceedingly difficult, perhaps impossible, for him to vindicate his reputation interest by securing a judgment for nominal damages, the practical effect of such a judgment being a judicial declaration that the publication was indeed false. Under the new rule, the plaintiff can lose not because the statement is true, but because it was not negligently made. . . .

These are radical changes in the law and severe invasions of the prerogatives of the States. They should at least be shown to be required by the First Amendment or necessitated by our present circumstances. Neither has been demonstrated.

Two years later, in *Time, Inc. v. Firestone*, the Court dealt with a similar issue. In 1961 Mary Alice Sullivan married Russell Firestone, heir to the tire fortune. Three years later she filed for separation, and he countered with a plea for a divorce. The trial was a protracted, well-publicized affair, owing to the notoriety of the Firestones and the details of their relationship. In granting the divorce, the trial judge noted that each of the parties had accused the other of outrageous extramarital affairs but that he found the testimony to be unreliable. After the divorce was final, *Time* magazine ran the following story in its "Milestones" section:

DIVORCED. By Russell A. Firestone Jr., 41, heir to the tire fortune: Mary Alice Sullivan Firestone, 32, his third wife; a onetime Palm Beach schoolteacher; on grounds of extreme cruelty and adultery; after six years of marriage, one son; in West Palm Beach, Fla. The 17-month intermittent trial produced enough testimony of extramarital adventures on both sides, said the judge, "to make Dr. Freud's hair curl."

Because the magazine reported as true material the judge explicitly discounted as unreliable, Ms. Firestone requested a printed retraction. When *Time* refused, she sued on the ground that the story was "false, malicious, and defamatory." *Time* argued that she was a public figure and, therefore, had to prove "actual malice."

Relying on its ruling in *Gertz*, the Supreme Court disagreed. As it suggested,

[Ms. Firestone] did not assume any role of especial prominence in the affairs of society, other than perhaps Palm Beach society, and did not thrust herself to the forefront of any particular public controversy in order to influence the resolution of the issues involved in it.

Although White, in his *Gertz* dissent, did not think the Court went far enough in protecting private citizens, most observers suggest that the combination of *Gertz* and *Firestone* excised *Rosenbloom* to the point of virtually overruling it. Under *Gertz* and *Firestone*, the focus moved back to the individual's status and away from the nature of the story or event. In the eyes of the majority, both Gertz and Firestone were essentially private figures who came into public view only because of the defamation itself. Under these circumstances, the *New York Times* test is not applicable; in other words, private citizens need not prove actual malice to win a libel case.

Why did the majority reject the *Rosenbloom* approach? For one thing, it led to a situation in which trial court judges had to determine "on an ad hoc basis which publications address issues of 'general or public interest' and which do not." Further, the Court reasoned that while public figures and officials often have access to the media, which would enable them to repudiate articles, private citizens do not enjoy this privilege, and, therefore, they deserve more legal leeway than those in the public eye.

Have *Gertz* and *Firestone* made it easier for plaintiffs to prove libel? Certainly they eased the burden carried by private citizens, but, because the *New York Times* test remains, it can be quite difficult for public officials and public figures to meet the legal standards. Some have gone even further, suggesting that the *Times* test makes it virtually impossible for public figures to win libel judgments against the press, even when stories contain falsehoods.

Libel and the Rehnquist Court

The Court's treatment of claims raised in *Gertz* and *Firestone* led many commentators to suggest that it would further narrow the scope of *New York Times*. Indeed, when the justices agreed to hear arguments in *Hus-*

tler Magazine v. Falwell, some looked for a decision that would run counter to, if not overrule, *New York Times.*[30] Did the Court do so?

Hustler Magazine v. Falwell

485 U.S. 46 (1988)
laws.findlaw.com/US/485/46.html
Vote: 8 (Blackmun, Brennan, Marshall, O'Connor, Rehnquist, Scalia, Stevens, White)
        0
Opinion of the Court: Rehnquist
Concurring opinion: White
Not participating: Kennedy

In the March 1984 issue of *Hustler* magazine, publisher Larry Flynt printed a parody of an advertisement for Campari Liqueur. The advertisement mimicked a Campari promotional campaign based on interviews with various celebrities in which they described their "first time." While these interviews were laced with sexual double entendres, it became clear by the end of the ads that the celebrities were actually referring to the first time they tasted Campari. The *Hustler* magazine advertisement used the same format and layout as the real Campari ads. It was entitled, "Jerry Falwell talks about his first time." Falwell was a nationally prominent Protestant minister, a leading political conservative, and the head of the now-defunct Moral Majority organization. In the interview portion of the advertisement, Falwell discussed his "first time"—an incestuous sexual encounter with his mother in an outhouse while both were intoxicated from drinking Campari. The advertisement portrayed Falwell as drunk, immoral, and hypocritical. At the bottom of the ad the following words appeared in small print: "Ad parody—not to be taken seriously." The magazine's table of contents listed the item as "Fiction: Ad and Personality Parody."

Shortly after the issue was available for public purchase, Falwell sued the magazine and its publisher for libel, invasion of privacy, and intentional infliction of

30. For oral arguments in this case, navigate to: *oyez.nwu.edu.*

Thomas Nast's 1871 cartoon depicting "Boss" Tweed and his cronies was typical of the artist's hard-hitting depictions of public figures. In *Hustler Magazine v. Falwell,* Chief Justice Rehnquist refers directly to Nast's work as well as to several other examples of satirical political cartoons and caricatures.

emotional distress. The trial judge dismissed the privacy claim before sending the case to the jury. The jury decided in favor of the magazine on the libel issue, concluding that the advertisement could not reasonably be understood as describing actual facts about Falwell or actual events in which he participated. However, the jury awarded Falwell $150,000 on the claim that the publisher of *Hustler* intentionally inflicted emotional distress.

At the Supreme Court level, there was no question as to whether Falwell was a public figure—he clearly was and, as such, had to prove malicious intent. Rather, the issue was whether Falwell could even bring a suit against a cartoon that did not purport to be factually accurate.

CHIEF JUSTICE REHNQUIST delivered the opinion of the Court.

Petitioner Hustler Magazine, Inc., is a magazine of nationwide circulation. Respondent Jerry Falwell, a nationally known minister who has been active as a commentator on politics and public affairs, sued petitioner and its publisher, petitioner Larry Flynt, to recover damages for invasion of privacy, libel, and intentional infliction of emotional distress. The District Court directed a verdict against respondent on the privacy claim, and submitted the other two claims to a jury. The jury found for petitioners on the defamation claim, but found for respondent on the claim for intentional infliction of emotional distress and awarded damages. We now consider whether this award is consistent with the First and Fourteenth Amendments of the United States Constitution. . . .

This case presents us with a novel question involving First Amendment limitations upon a State's authority to protect its citizens from the intentional infliction of emotional distress. We must decide whether a public figure may recover damages for emotional harm caused by the publication of an ad parody offensive to him, and doubtless gross and repugnant in the eyes of most. Respondent would have us find that a State's interest in protecting public figures from emotional distress is sufficient to deny First Amendment protection to speech that is patently offensive and is intended to inflict emotional injury, even when that speech could not reasonably have been interpreted as stating actual facts about the public figure involved. This we decline to do.

At the heart of the First Amendment is the recognition of the fundamental importance of the free flow of ideas and opinions on matters of public interest and concern. . . . We have therefore been particularly vigilant to ensure that individual expressions of ideas remain free from governmentally imposed sanctions. The First Amendment recognizes no such thing as a "false" idea. . . .

The sort of robust political debate encouraged by the First Amendment is bound to produce speech that is critical of those who hold public office or those public figures who are "intimately involved in the resolution of important public questions or, by reason of their fame, shape events in areas of concern to society at large." Such criticism, inevitably,

will not always be reasoned or moderate; public figures as well as public officials will be subject to "vehement, caustic, and sometimes unpleasantly sharp attacks.". . .

Of course, this does not mean that any speech about a public figure is immune from sanction in the form of damages. Since *New York Times v. Sullivan*, we have consistently ruled that a public figure may hold a speaker liable for the damage to reputation caused by publication of a defamatory falsehood, but only if the statement was made "with knowledge that it was false or with reckless disregard of whether it was false or not." False statements of fact are particularly valueless; they interfere with the truth-seeking function of the marketplace of ideas, and they cause damage to an individual's reputation that cannot easily be repaired by counterspeech, however persuasive or effective. But even though falsehoods have little value in and of themselves, they are "nevertheless inevitable in free debate," and a rule that would impose strict liability on a publisher for false factual assertions would have an undoubted "chilling" effect on speech relating to public figures that does have constitutional value. "Freedoms of expression require 'breathing space.'" This breathing space is provided by a constitutional rule that allows public figures to recover for libel or defamation only when they can prove *both* that the statement was false and that the statement was made with the requisite level of culpability.

Respondent argues, however, that a different standard should apply in this case because here the State seeks to prevent not reputational damage, but the severe emotional distress suffered by the person who is the subject of an offensive publication. In respondent's view, and in the view of the Court of Appeals, so long as the utterance was intended to inflict emotional distress, was outrageous, and did in fact inflict serious emotional distress, it is of no constitutional import whether the statement was a fact or an opinion, or whether it was true or false. It is the intent to cause injury that is the gravamen of the tort, and the State's interest in preventing emotional harm simply outweighs whatever interest a speaker may have in speech of this type.

Generally speaking the law does not regard the intent to inflict emotional distress as one which should receive much solicitude, and it is quite understandable that most if not all jurisdictions have chosen to make it civilly culpable where the conduct in question is sufficiently "outrageous." But in the world of debate about public affairs, many things done with motives that are less than admirable are protected by the First Amendment. In *Garrison v. Louisiana* (1964) we held that even when a speaker or writer is motivated by hatred or ill-will his expression was protected by the First Amendment:

"Debate on public issues will not be uninhibited if the speaker must run the risk that it will be proved in court that he spoke out of hatred; even if he did speak out of hatred, utterances honestly believed contribute to the free interchange of ideas and the ascertainment of truth."

Thus while such a bad motive may be deemed controlling for purposes of tort liability in other areas of the law, we think the First Amendment prohibits such a result in the area of public debate about public figures.

Were we to hold otherwise, there can be little doubt that political cartoonists and satirists would be subjected to damages awards without any showing that their work falsely defamed its subject. Webster's defines a caricature as "the deliberately distorted picturing or imitating of a person, literary style, etc. by exaggerating features or mannerisms for satirical effect." The appeal of the political cartoon or caricature is often based on exploration of unfortunate physical traits or politically embarrassing events—an exploration often calculated to injure the feelings of the subject of the portrayal. The art of the cartoonist is often not reasoned or evenhanded, but slashing and one-sided. One cartoonist expressed the nature of the art in these words:

"The political cartoon is a weapon of attack, of scorn and ridicule and satire; it is least effective when it tries to pat some politician on the back. It is usually as welcome as a bee sting and is always controversial in some quarters."

Several famous examples of this type of intentionally injurious speech were drawn by Thomas Nast, probably the greatest American cartoonist to date, who was associated for many years during the post–Civil War era with *Harper's Weekly*. In the pages of that publication Nast conducted a graphic vendetta against William M. "Boss" Tweed and his corrupt associates in New York City's "Tweed Ring." It has been described by one historian of the subject as "a sustained attack which in its passion and effectiveness stands alone in the history of American graphic art." Another writer explains that the success of the Nast cartoon was achieved "because of the emotional impact of its presentation. It continuously goes beyond the bounds of good taste and conventional manners."

Despite their sometimes caustic nature, from the early

cartoon portraying George Washington as an ass down to the present day, graphic depictions and satirical cartoons have played a prominent role in public and political debate. Nast's castigation of the Tweed Ring, Walt McDougall's characterization of presidential candidate James G. Blaine's banquet with the millionaires at Delmonico's as "The Royal Feast of Belshazzar," and numerous other efforts have undoubtedly had an effect on the course and outcome of contemporaneous debate. Lincoln's tall, gangling posture, Teddy Roosevelt's glasses and teeth, and Franklin D. Roosevelt's jutting jaw and cigarette holder have been memorialized by political cartoons with an effect that could not have been obtained by the photographer or the portrait artist. From the viewpoint of history it is clear that our political discourse would have been considerably poorer without them.

Respondent contends, however, that the caricature in question here was so "outrageous" as to distinguish it from more traditional political cartoons. There is no doubt that the caricature of respondent and his mother published in *Hustler* is at best a distant cousin of the political cartoons described above, and a rather poor relation at that. If it were possible by laying down a principled standard to separate the one from the other, public discourse would probably suffer little or no harm. But we doubt that there is any such standard, and we are quite sure that the pejorative description "outrageous" does not supply one. "Outrageousness" in the area of political and social discourse has an inherent subjectiveness about it which would allow a jury to impose liability on the basis of the jurors' tastes or views, or perhaps on the basis of their dislike of a particular expression. An "outrageousness" standard thus runs afoul of our long-standing refusal to allow damages to be awarded because the speech in question may have an adverse emotional impact on the audience. . . .

Admittedly. . . First Amendment principles, like other principles, are subject to limitations. We recognized that speech that is "'vulgar,' 'offensive,' and 'shocking'" is "not entitled to absolute constitutional protection under all circumstances." In *Chaplinsky v. New Hampshire* (1942), we held that a state could lawfully punish an individual for the use of insulting "'fighting' words—those which by their very utterance inflict injury or tend to incite an immediate breach of the peace." These limitations are but recognition . . . that this Court has "long recognized that not all speech is of equal First Amendment importance." But the sort of expression involved in this case does not seem to us to be governed by any exception to the general First Amendment principles stated above.

We conclude that public figures and public officials may not recover for the tort of intentional infliction of emotional distress by reason of publications such as the one here at issue without showing in addition that the publication contains a false statement of fact which was made with "actual malice," *i.e.*, with knowledge that the statement was false or with reckless disregard as to whether or not it was true. This is not merely a "blind application" of the *New York Times* standard; it reflects our considered judgment that such a standard is necessary to give adequate "breathing space" to the freedoms protected by the First Amendment.

Here it is clear that respondent Falwell is a "public figure" for purposes of First Amendment law. The jury found against respondent on his libel claim when it decided that the *Hustler* ad parody could not "reasonably be understood as describing actual facts about [respondent] or actual events in which [he] participated." The Court of Appeals interpreted the jury's finding to be that the ad parody "was not reasonably believable," and in accordance with our custom we accept this finding. Respondent is thus relegated to his claim for damages awarded by the jury for the intentional infliction of emotional distress by "outrageous" conduct. But for reasons heretofore stated this claim cannot, consistently with the First Amendment, form a basis for the award of damages when the conduct in question is the publication of a caricature such as the ad parody involved here. The judgment of the Court of Appeals is accordingly

Reversed.

The opinion surprised some Court observers: after all, it was written by Chief Justice Rehnquist, who is not particularly well known for supporting free press claims, and it was unanimous, a rarity in libel law. The media applauded the opinion, while Falwell fumed that "the Supreme Court has given the green light to Larry Flynt and his ilk to print what they wish about any public figure at any time with no fear of reprisal."[31] A green light it may be, but one through which Flynt went at considerable cost (*see Box 7-7*).

31. Quoted in "Court 8–0, Extends Right to Criticize Those in Public Eye," by Stuart Taylor Jr., *New York Times*, February 25, 1988, 1, 14.

The *Hustler Magazine* decision, then, not only failed to reverse *New York Times* but actually reinforced it. In *Hustler Magazine* the Court continued the trend set by *New York Times* to extend First Amendment protections to the press when it covers public officials and public figures. To sue successfully for damages, well-known persons must prove actual malice as well as falsity. But what kinds of actions on the part of the press might qualify as proof of reckless disregard for the truth? How much leeway should the press be given in the interpretation and presentation of factual material? In *Masson v. New Yorker Magazine, Inc.* (1991) the justices faced these questions.

At issue in *Masson* was an article by Janet Malcolm about Jeffrey Masson that appeared in the *New Yorker* magazine and later provided the basis for a book. Masson was a prominent psychoanalyst who, at the time, had been the Projects Director of the Sigmund Freud Archives outside of London. He was dismissed from this position after he became disillusioned with Freudian psychology and advanced his own psychoanalytic theories. The article—written in Malcolm's journalistic style, which was to use long block quotes—discussed Masson's relationship with the Freud Archives and portrayed Masson in an extremely unflattering light. A reviewer for the *Boston Globe* described it this way:

Masson the promising psychoanalytic scholar emerges gradually, as a grandiose egotist—mean-spirited, self-serving, full of braggadocio, impossibly arrogant and, in the end, a self-destructive fool. But it is not Janet Malcolm who calls him such: his own words reveal this psychological profile.

Masson brought a libel suit against Malcolm, the *New Yorker*, and the publisher of the book in federal district court in California. He based his case on quotations attributed to him that he claimed were fabrications. During pretrial discovery the printed quotations were compared to the more than forty hours of taped interviews. In a number of instances the quotations were substantially correct; however, in at least five cases it appeared that the long quotations published in the magazine had little or no relation to the taped conversations, although they dealt with some subjects the two had discussed. Malcolm explained that not all of the interviews were taped and that some of the quotations were based on her memory from the nontaped sessions.

BOX 7-7   AFTERMATH . . . LARRY FLYNT

HUSTLER MAGAZINE V. FALWELL (1988) was just one skirmish in a long series of legal battles fought by magazine publisher Larry Flynt. After introducing *Hustler* in 1974, Flynt frequently found himself in court defending against obscenity charges, usually stemming from the magazine's portrayal of women, sexual activities, and violence. Flynt claims he has spent almost $50 million in legal fees over a thirty-year period. He has always unabashedly promoted his cause. Prior to the Supreme Court's decision in the *Falwell* case, Flynt sent complementary *Hustler* magazine subscriptions to each of the nine justices.

Larry Flynt holding the ad parody that was the cause of a libel suit brought by Jerry Falwell against *Hustler* magazine.

Flynt has continued to engage in controversial activities. In 1988 accusations were made that he had paid $1 million to a hit man to kill *Playboy* founder Hugh Hefner, singer Frank Sinatra, publisher Walter Annenberg, and *Penthouse* publisher Bob Guccione. While nothing came of those charges, Flynt or individuals closely associated with him have been rumored to have been involved in a number of murder plots.

In 1996 Flynt's daughter Tonya publicly accused him of sexually molesting her from the age of ten until she was eighteen. Flynt denied the charges, claiming that his estranged daughter had "serious mental problems" and was a "habitual liar." That same year, Oliver Stone produced a feature film on Flynt's life, *The People v. Larry Flynt.* The movie was a commercial and critical success but was attacked by feminists and antipornography organizations for portraying Flynt as a champion of the First Amendment rather than as a dangerous purveyor of obscenity.

In 1998 Flynt, a fiercely partisan Democrat, entered the controversy surrounding the impeachment of President Clinton by offering up to $1 million for information about members of Congress who had engaged in illicit sexual activities. Flynt's threat to release the information he gathered is said to have prompted the resignation of incoming Republican Speaker of the House Robert Livingston, who publicly admitted to an extramarital affair.

Flynt, who operates his business from California, uses a gold-plated wheel chair, a consequence of being shot by a sniper in 1978 while standing trial in Georgia. Flynt publishes more than twenty magazines, but *Hustler,* with a circulation in excess of 500,000, remains the centerpiece of his publishing empire. As to his legal battles, Flynt has said, "If the law protects a scumbag like me, then it protects all of us."

SOURCES: *Louisville Courier-Journal,* October 28, 1988; *New Orleans Times-Picayune,* May 25, 1996; *USA Today,* May 24, 1996; and *Washington Post,* March 20, 1979, February 10, 1997, December 19, 1998, and January 11, 1999.

At trial, the parties agreed that Masson was a public figure and, therefore, had to prove that the falsehoods contained in the article were printed with actual malice. At issue in the Supreme Court was whether the intentional distortion of the quoted material established actual malice. In a 7–2 decision, the Court rejected the argument that alterations other than the correction of grammar or syntax prove actual malice by themselves. Instead, the Court held that to prove actual malice in such a context, the plaintiff would have to show that the delib-

erate alteration of the words had resulted in a material change in the meaning conveyed by the statement. Writing for the majority, Justice Kennedy reasoned as follows:

We reject the idea that any alteration beyond correction of grammar or syntax by itself proves falsity in the sense relevant to determining actual malice under the First Amendment. An interviewer who writes from notes often will engage in the task of attempting a reconstruction of the speaker's statement. That author would, we may assume, act with knowledge that at times she has attributed to her subject words other than those actually used. Under petitioner's proposed standard, an author in this situation would lack First Amendment protection if she reported as quotations the substance of a subject's derogatory statements about himself.

Even if a journalist has tape recorded the spoken statement of a public figure, the full and exact statement will be reported in only rare circumstances. The existence of both a speaker and a reporter; the translation between two media, speech and the printed word; the addition of punctuation; and the practical necessity to edit and make intelligible a speaker's perhaps rambling comments, all make it misleading to suggest that a quotation will be reconstructed with complete accuracy. The use or absence of punctuation may distort a speaker's meaning, for example, where that meaning turns upon a speaker's emphasis of a particular word. In other cases, if a speaker makes an obvious misstatement, for example by unconscious substitution of one name for another, a journalist might alter the speaker's words but preserve his intended meaning. And conversely, an exact quotation out of context can distort meaning, although the speaker did use each reported word. . . .

Deliberate or reckless falsification that comprises actual malice turns upon words and punctuation only because words and punctuation express meaning. Meaning is the life of language. And, for the reasons we have given, quotations may be a devastating instrument for conveying false meaning. In the case under consideration, readers of *In the Freud Archives* may have found Malcolm's portrait of petitioner especially damning because so much of it appeared to be a self-portrait, told by petitioner in his own words. And if the alterations of petitioner's words gave a different meaning to the statements, bearing upon their defamatory character, then the device of quotations might well be critical in finding the words actionable. . . .

The Court found that there was sufficient evidence that Malcolm may have offended this standard to compel the Court to reverse the lower court's summary judgment for the magazine and order a jury trial on Masson's lawsuit. The first trial after the Court decision ended with jurors finding that some of the quotes were libelous but deadlocking on the amount of damages to be paid. The case was then retried, with a verdict clearing Malcolm. While the jury found that some of the quotes were false, it concluded that Masson had not shown that Malcolm had acted deliberately or recklessly. In 1996 a U.S. Court of Appeals upheld the verdict, thereby bringing to a close Masson's twelve-year court battle against Malcolm.

Libel and the Internet

The *Masson* case reveals that even though the Court has steadfastly adhered to the *New York Times* test for public figures, the justices have spent more than three decades fleshing out its details. It may take just as many to resolve the new problems cropping up as a result of the rapid expansion of the Internet.

Suppose Student X enters an on-line discussion on a university network about professors and writes falsely that "Professor John Smith is a fraud. He says he has a Ph.D. but really doesn't."[32] Even this very simple example raises extremely complex questions. Let us deal with one: Would the *New York Times* test apply? The answer, you may think, is obviously no because Smith is not a public figure. But one of the Court's most important ways of differentiating public from private figures is that public figures have access to the media and can easily refute charges against them. Could Professor Smith not do the

Janet Malcolm's less-than-flattering article about psychoanalyst Jeffrey Masson was the impetus for a battle that eventually reached the Supreme Court.

32. We adapt the material in this section from the Cyberspace Law Institute at: *http://www.cli.org.*

A Supreme Court ruling allowed Jeffrey M. Masson to reinstate his $10 million lawsuit against Janet Malcolm. He eventually lost his suit.

same? He can tell his side of the story through the Internet. Moreover, because his university system could probably determine all the users who had read Student X's comment, the professor could target his response, a luxury not afforded to public officials. Does this mean that all Internet users should be treated as public figures for purposes of libel suits?

The Supreme Court has yet to address this question and the many others relating to libel on the Internet—such as, whom can Professor Smith sue? Student X, the university (as the carrier of the message), or both? Suppose the allegedly libelous statement was not uttered during an on-line discussion but was a part of a Web site linked to Student X's site? Would Student X still be held responsible?[33] As litigation percolates up from the lower

courts, it is only a matter of time before the Court jumps into the fray. How do you suppose it will rule? Will it apply precedent from its libel cases or will it develop an entirely new body of cyberspace libel law?

Further complicating matters is that countries treat traditional libel claims in very different ways (see *Box 7-6*). This, coupled with the fact that the Internet transcends national boundaries, may lead litigants to engage in forum shopping—country shopping, that is—to find the national jurisdiction with libel standards most favorable to their interests. In anticipation of this eventuality, some communities have said that litigants alleging Internet libel must bring suit in the country where the material was published. The effectiveness of this policy—as well as others being developed—naturally depends on the extent to which nations around the world adopt it.

33. See Brenda Sandburg, "The Great Linkin' Debate: Finding Defamation in Cyberspace," *American Lawyer Media—The Recorder*, February 8, 2000, 4.

READINGS

Adler, Renata. *Reckless Disregard.* New York: Vintage Books, 1986.

Baird, Robert M., and Stuart E. Rosenbaum, eds. *Pornography: Private Right or Public Menace?* Amherst, N.Y.: Prometheus Books, 1998.

Barendt, Eric M., Laurence Lustgarten, Kenneth Norrie, and Hugh Stephenson, eds. *Libel and the Media: The Chilling Effect.* New York: Oxford University Press, 1997.

Berger, Ronald. *Feminism and Pornography.* New York: Praeger, 1991.

Caputi, Mary. *Voluptuous Yearnings: A Feminist Theory of the Obscene.* Lanham, Md.: Rowman & Littlefield, 1997.

Cossman, Brenda, Shannon Bell, Becki Ross, and Lise Gotell. *Bad Attitudes on Trial: Pornography, Feminism, and the Butler Decision.* Toronto: University of Toronto Press, 1997.

Cottrell, Jill. *Law of Defamation in Commonwealth Africa.* Brookfield, Vt.: Ashgate Publishing Company, 1998.

Downs, Donald Alexander. *The New Politics of Pornography.* Chicago: University of Chicago Press, 1989.

Forer, Lois G. *A Chilling Effect.* New York: Norton, 1987.

Gertz, Elmer. *Gertz v. Robert Welch, Inc.: The Story of a Landmark Libel Case.* Carbondale: Southern Illinois University Press, 1992.

Gibson, Pamela Church, and Roma Gibson, eds., *Dirty Looks: Women, Pornography, Power.* London: British Film Institute, 1993.

Gillmor, Donald M. *Power, Publicity, and the Abuse of Libel Law.* New York: Oxford University Press, 1992.

Goldschmidt, Paul W. *Pornography and Democratization: Legislating Obscenity in Post-Communist Russia.* Boulder: Westview Press, 1999.

Gubar, Susan. *For Adult Use Only: The Dilemmas of Violent Pornography.* Bloomington: Indiana University Press, 1989.

Hadley, Michael. "The *Gertz* Doctrine and Internet Defamation." *Virginia Law Review* 84 (1998): 477.

Hixson, Richard F. *Pornography and the Justices: The Supreme Court and the Intractable Obscenity Problem.* Carbondale: Southern Illinois University Press, 1996.

Hopkins, W. Wat. *Actual Malice.* New York: Praeger, 1989.

Itzin, Catherine, ed. *Pornography: Women, Violence, and Civil Liberties.* Oxford: Oxford University Press, 1993.

Kane, Peter E. *Errors, Lies, and Libel.* Carbondale: Southern Illinois University Press, 1992.

Kirby, James. *Fumble: Bear Bryant, Wally Butts, and the Great College Football Scandal.* San Diego: Harcourt Brace Jovanovich, 1986.

Kobylka, Joseph F. *The Politics of Obscenity: Group Litigation in a Time of Legal Change.* New York: Greenwood Press, 1991.

Lewis, Anthony. *Make No Law: The Sullivan Case and the First Amendment.* New York: Random House, 1991.

MacKinnon, Catharine. *Only Words.* Cambridge: Harvard University Press, 1993.

Randall, Richard S. *Freedom and Taboo.* Berkeley: University of California Press, 1989.

Rembar, Charles. *The End of Obscenity.* New York: Bantam Books, 1968.

Saunders, Kevin W. *Violence as Obscenity: Limiting the Media's First Amendment Protection.* Durham: Duke University Press, 1996.

Smolla, Rodney A. *Jerry Falwell v. Larry Flynt: The First Amendment on Trial.* Champaign: University of Illinois Press, 1990.

Strossen, Nadine. *Defending Pornography: Free Speech, Sex, and the Fight for Women's Rights.* New York: New York University Press, 2000.

Zimring, Franklin E., and Gordon J. Hawkins. *Pornography in a Free Society.* Cambridge: Cambridge University Press, 1991.

CHAPTER 8
THE RIGHT TO KEEP AND BEAR ARMS

Prominently displayed in the literature distributed by the National Rifle Association (NRA) and similar groups are statements invoking the Second Amendment. Advocates of gun ownership rights assert that the Second Amendment protects the fundamental right for individuals to keep and bear arms. But does the amendment actually guarantee that right?

The Second Amendment states in full, "A well regulated Militia, being necessary to the security of a free State, the right of the people to keep and bear arms shall not be infringed." The wording of this amendment makes it somewhat of an oddity compared to the other provisions of the Bill of Rights; it comes with its own preamble. As written, the amendment ties the right to keep and bear arms directly to the purpose of maintaining a well regulated militia.

This situation gives rise to two distinctly different interpretations of the Second Amendment. The first, advocated by pro-gun interests, emphasizes the second half of the amendment and concludes that there is a constitutional *individual* right to keep and bear arms. A second interpretation, often expressed by those who favor government restrictions on private gun ownership, emphasizes the first half of the amendment. According to this view, the amendment guarantees only a *collective* right of the states to arm their militias; there is no *individual* right, unless it is in conjunction with a state militia, to own firearms.

The U.S. Supreme Court *seems* to favor the collective right interpretation. We emphasize "seems" because the Court has issued very few interpretations of the Second Amendment, and the rulings it has handed down are rather old and, at least to some in the legal community, not altogether clear. Perhaps that is why few constitutional law texts discuss the Second Amendment.

We think the subject is worthy of treatment for at least two reasons. First, the split over gun control versus gun ownership is a political issue with important consequences for society. Second, lawyers and historians have taken a new look at the meaning of the Second Amendment and have drawn some surprising conclusions. On the basis of this new evidence, many scholars believe that the NRA may have a stronger legal argument than previously thought. Or, as Justice Thomas put it in a footnote to his concurring opinion in *Printz v. United States* (1997), "Marshaling an impressive array of historical evidence, a growing body of scholarly commentary indicates that the 'right to keep and bear arms' is, as the amendment's text suggests, a personal right."

In this chapter we consider these arguments, as well as the few court cases that have interpreted the Second Amendment. But be forewarned: unlike other legal areas we have considered, there are no clear answers on the right to keep and bear arms, and there is unlikely to be a resolution of the debate until the Supreme Court hands down a definitive interpretation. Until then, it will be up to you to sort through the competing claims to determine which side you believe has the better case.

THE SUPREME COURT AND THE SECOND AMENDMENT

As we noted, the U.S. Supreme Court has issued very few decisions dealing directly with the Second Amendment—perhaps less than a half dozen over the last two hundred years.[1] Of these, *United States v. Miller* (1939) is particularly worthy of consideration because scholars and practitioners believe it to be the justices' most authoritative interpretation of the amendment. As you read *Miller*, ask yourself what the Court claimed to be the "obvious purpose" of the amendment and whether you agree with its answer.

United States v. Miller

307 U.S. 174 (1939)

laws.findlaw.com/US/307/174.html

Vote: 8 (Black, Butler, Frankfurter, Hughes, McReynolds, Reed, Roberts, Stone)

  0

Opinion of the Court: McReynolds

Not participating: Douglas

Jack Miller and Frank Layton were indicted for transporting in interstate commerce (from Oklahoma to Arkansas) an unregistered "shotgun having a barrel of less than eighteen inches in length," that is, a sawed-off shotgun. The indictment charged them with violating the National Firearms Act of 1934, which among other things, required them to register the gun. After a federal district court held that the relevant section of the Firearms Act violated the Second Amendment, the case went to the U.S. Supreme Court on direct appeal.

MR. JUSTICE MCREYNOLDS delivered the opinion of the Court.

In the absence of any evidence tending to show that possession or use of a "shotgun having a barrel of less than eighteen inches in length" at this time has some reasonable

---

1. For example, *United States v. Cruikshank* (1876), *Presser v. Illinois* (1886), *Miller v. Texas* (1894), *United States v. Miller* (1939), and *Lewis v. United States* (1980).

relationship to the preservation or efficiency of a well regulated militia, we cannot say that the Second Amendment guarantees the right to keep and bear such an instrument. Certainly it is not within judicial notice that this weapon is any part of the ordinary military equipment or that its use could contribute to the common defense.

The Constitution as originally adopted granted to the Congress power—"To provide for calling forth the Militia to execute the Laws of the Union, suppress Insurrections and repel Invasions; To provide for organizing, arming, and disciplining, the Militia, and for governing such Part of them as may be employed in the Service of the United States, reserving to the States respectively, the Appointment of the Officers, and the Authority of training the Militia according to the discipline prescribed by Congress." U.S.C.A. Const. art. 1, 8. With obvious purpose to assure the continuation and render possible the effectiveness of such forces the declaration and guarantee of the Second Amendment were made. It must be interpreted and applied with that end in view.

The Militia which the States were expected to maintain and train is set in contrast with Troops which they were forbidden to keep without the consent of Congress. The sentiment of the time strongly disfavored standing armies; the common view was that adequate defense of country and laws could be secured through the Militia—civilians primarily, soldiers on occasion.

The signification attributed to the term Militia appears from the debates in the Convention, the history and legislation of Colonies and States, and the writings of approved commentators. These show plainly enough that the Militia comprised all males physically capable of acting in concert for the common defense. "A body of citizens enrolled for military discipline." And further, that ordinarily when called for service these men were expected to appear bearing arms supplied by themselves and of the kind in common use at the time.

Blackstone's Commentaries, Vol. 2, Ch. 13, p. 409, points out "that king Alfred first settled a national militia in this kingdom" and traces the subsequent development and use of such forces.

Adam Smith's Wealth of Nations, Book V. Ch. 1, contains an extended account of the Militia. It is there said: "Men of republican principles have been jealous of a standing army as dangerous to liberty." "In a militia, the character of the labourer, artificer, or tradesman, predominates over that of the soldier: in a standing army, that of the soldier predominates over every other character; and in this distinction seems to consist the essential difference between those two different species of military force."

"The American Colonies In The 17th Century," Osgood, Vol. 1, ch. XIII, affirms in reference to the early system of defense in New England—

"In all the colonies, as in England, the militia system was based on the principle of the assize of arms. This implied the general obligation of all adult male inhabitants to possess arms, and, with certain exceptions, to cooperate in the work of defence." "The possession of arms also implied the possession of ammunition, and the authorities paid quite as much attention to the latter as to the former." "A year later (1632) it was ordered that any single man who had not furnished himself with arms might be put out to service, and this became a permanent part of the legislation of the colony (Massachusetts)."

Also "Clauses intended to insure the possession of arms and ammunition by all who were subject to military service appear in all the important enactments concerning military affairs. Fines were the penalty for delinquency, whether of towns or individuals. According to the usage of the times, the infantry of Massachusetts consisted of pikemen and musketeers. The law, as enacted in 1649 and thereafter, provided that each of the former should be armed with a pike, corselet, head-piece, sword, and knapsack. The musketeer should carry a 'good fixed musket,' not under bastard musket bore, not less than three feet, nine inches, nor more than four feet three inches in length, a priming wire, scourer, and mould, a sword, rest, bandoleers, one pound of powder, twenty bullets, and two fathoms of match. The law also required that two-thirds of each company should be musketeers."

The General Court of Massachusetts, January Session 1784, provided for the organization and government of the Militia. It directed that the Train Band should "contain all able bodied men, from sixteen to forty years of age, and the Alarm List, all other men under sixty years of age. . . ." Also, "That every non-commissioned officer and private soldier of the said militia not under the controul of parents, masters or guardians, and being of sufficient ability therefor in the judgment of the Selectmen of the town in which he shall dwell, shall equip himself, and be constantly provided with a good fire arm, &c."

By an Act passed April 4, 1786, the New York Legislature directed: "That every able-bodied Male Person, being a Citizen of this State, or of any of the United States, and residing in this State, (except such Persons as are herein after excepted) and who are of the Age of Sixteen, and under the Age of Forty-five Years, shall, by the Captain or commanding Officer of the Beat in which such Citizens shall reside, within four Months after the passing of this Act, be enrolled in the Company of such Beat. . . . That every Citizen so enrolled and notified, shall, within three Months thereafter, provide himself, at his own Expense, with a good Musket or Firelock, a sufficient Bayonet and Belt, a Pouch with a Box therein to contain not less than Twenty-four Cartridges suited to the Bore of his Musket or Firelock, each Cartridge containing a proper Quantity of Powder and Ball, two spare Flints, a Blanket and Knapsack; . . ."

The General Assembly of Virginia, October, 1785 declared: "The defense and safety of the commonwealth depend upon having its citizens properly armed and taught the knowledge of military duty."

It further provided for organization and control of the Militia and directed that "All free male persons between the ages of eighteen and fifty years," with certain exceptions, "shall be inrolled or formed into companies." "There shall be a private muster of every company once in two months."

Also that "Every officer and soldier shall appear at his respective muster-field on the day appointed, by eleven o'clock in the forenoon, armed, equipped, and accoutred, as follows: . . . every non-commissioned officer and private with a good, clean musket carrying an ounce ball, and three feet eight inches long in the barrel, with a good bayonet and iron ramrod well fitted thereto, a cartridge box properly made, to contain and secure twenty cartridges fitted to his musket, a good knapsack and canteen, and moreover, each non-commissioned officer and private shall have at every muster one pound of good powder, and four pounds of lead, including twenty blind cartridges; and each serjeant shall have a pair of moulds fit to cast balls for their respective companies, to be purchased by the commanding officer out of the monies arising on delinquencies. Provided, That the militia of the counties westward of the Blue Ridge, and the counties below adjoining thereto, shall not be obliged to be armed with muskets, but may have good rifles with proper accoutrements, in lieu thereof. And every of the said officers, non-commissioned officers, and privates, shall constantly keep the aforesaid arms, accoutrements, and ammunition, ready to be produced whenever called for by his commanding officer. If any private shall make it appear to the satisfaction of the court hereafter to be appointed for trying delinquencies under this act that he is so poor that he cannot purchase the arms herein required, such court shall cause them to be purchased out of the money arising from delinquents."

Most if not all of the States have adopted provisions touching the right to keep and bear arms. Differences in the language employed in these have naturally led to somewhat variant conclusions concerning the scope of the right guaranteed. But none of them seem to afford any material support for the challenged ruling of the court below.

. . . We are unable to accept the conclusion of the court below and the challenged judgment must be reversed. The cause will be remanded for further proceedings.

Reversed and remanded.

To the justices, the purpose of the Second Amendment was plain: "to assure the continuation and render possible the effectiveness" of state militias. "It must be interpreted and applied with that end in view," according to a unanimous Court.

Given these words, it is not surprising that, at least through the 1980s, scholars and lawyers seemed to agree about the reach of the Second Amendment: "the Amendment guarantees a collective not an individual right to bear arms."[2] In other words, the amendment protects the right to keep and bear arms only as that right pertains to state militias; it does not grant *individuals* the right to own guns. Therefore, the amendment does not stand as an obstacle to government attempts to regulate firearms.

Although individual justices have taken issue with this interpretation, the Court's decisions have not veered from it.[3] For example, in the course of interpreting a sec-

tion of the Omnibus Crime Control Act of 1968, which prohibits convicted felons from possessing guns, the Court noted:

These legislative restrictions on the use of firearms are neither based upon constitutionally suspect criteria, nor do they trench upon any constitutionally protected liberties. See *United States v. Miller* (1939) (the Second Amendment guarantees no right to keep and bear a firearm that does not have "some reasonable relationship to the preservation or efficiency of a well regulated militia").[4]

Many other courts have followed suit. In *Burton v. Sills* (1968), the New Jersey Supreme Court decision that the U.S. Supreme Court declined to hear for want of a substantial federal question, the state court held, "It is sufficient here to suggest that under *Miller*, Congress, though admittedly governed by the second amendment, may regulate interstate firearms so long as the regulation does not impair the maintenance of the active, organized militias of the states." Lower federal appellate courts have, with rare exceptions, concurred. Against Second Amendment challenges, federal judges have upheld various laws mandating gun registration and those barring citizens from possessing handguns and machine guns, among others. In so doing, they too have relied on the logic of *Miller*. As the U.S. Court of Appeals for the Eighth Circuit put it in *United States v. Hale* (1992): "We cannot conclude that the Second Amendment protects the individual possession of military weapons. The rule emerging from *Miller* is that, absent a showing that the possession of a certain weapon has 'some reasonable relationship to the preservation or efficiency of a well-regulated militia,' the Second Amendment does not guarantee the right to possess the weapon."

THE STATES AND THE SECOND AMENDMENT

In addition to understanding how the Supreme Court has ruled on Second Amendment claims, it is important to be aware of what the Court has *not* done. The Second Amendment is one of the few provisions of the Bill of Rights that has not been incorporated and made applica-

---

2. This quotation comes from Edward S. Corwin's, *The Constitution and What it Means Today,* as revised by Harold W. Chase and Craig R. Ducat (Princeton: Princeton University Press, 1978), 341. Similar interpretations of *Miller* abound.

3. This is not to suggest that the Court has upheld every law regulating firearms; in fact, it has not. See, for example, *Printz v. United States* (1997), striking down the Brady Handgun Violence Prevention Act of 1993 for intruding too heavily on the rights of states. The point is that the Court has not struck down gun control legislation on *Second Amendment* grounds.

4. *Lewis v. United States* (1980).

ble to the states *(see Chapter 3)*. Indeed, in *United States v. Cruikshank* (1875) the Court explicitly refused to do so, noting, "This is one of the amendments that has no other effect than to restrict the powers of the national government." This statement is consistent with the Court's position that the Second Amendment does not confer any fundamental personal right. Recall that under the doctrine established in *Palko v. Connecticut* (1937) and subsequent cases, only those Bill of Rights provisions that constitute fundamental rights are binding on the states through the Due Process Clause of the Fourteenth Amendment.

Because the Second Amendment is not applicable to them, the states have exercised a great deal of latitude in protecting or restricting gun ownership. At the state level, the trend has been to broaden legal protection of gun ownership. Forty-four states now have constitutional provisions that in one form or another protect the right to keep and bear arms. About a third of these provisions have been enacted or strengthened since 1970. For example, the citizens of Wisconsin added a section to their constitution in 1998 that states: "The people have the right to keep and bear arms for security, defense, hunting, recreation, or any other lawful purpose."[5] In addition, several state legislatures have recently passed statutes that expand the right to obtain concealed weapon permits.

Although the trend has been for the states to expand gun ownership rights, state and local governments are also free to exercise their regulatory powers to restrict the ownership and use of firearms. Because the Supreme Court has not made the Second Amendment binding on the states, there is no federal constitutional protection to prohibit a state from restricting or even eliminating the freedom to own and use guns.

RETHINKING THE SECOND AMENDMENT

Given the Supreme Court's reluctance to reconsider the legal policy set in *Miller* and the near unanimity among lower courts on the meaning of the Second

Amendment, you might think that no further discussion is necessary. But, as we noted at the beginning of the chapter, the Second Amendment has become an area of intense scholarly debate.

This debate has occurred primarily at the insistence of a growing number of legal analysts who argue that the Supreme Court got it wrong in *Miller*. According to these analysts, courts should begin interpreting the Second Amendment as establishing an individual right to keep and bear arms—a right that, like those of religion, speech, and others contained in the Constitution, Congress cannot abridge.[6]

How do legal scholars justify this conclusion? For starters, they point to the text of the Second Amendment, which they say could not be clearer: "the right of the *people* to keep and bear arms, shall not be infringed." What of the first clause: "A well regulated Militia, being necessary to the security of a free State"? To many adopting an individual rights vision of the Second Amendment, this is little more than a preamble to its real purpose: to protect gun ownership. After all, those advocating this position argue, if the Framers had meant otherwise, why did they not cast the Second Amendment as follows: "Congress shall have no power to prohibit state-organized and directed militias"? Proponents of this view also suggest that the Framers intended to provide all citizens with a right to keep and bear arms, for to the Framers the words "militia" and "citizens" were interchangeable: "the militia was the people and the people were the militia."[7] What the Framers intended was therefore to give all citizens an opportunity to protect themselves against potential oppression by the federal government. Finally, individual rights advocates suggest that *Miller* either was wrong or did not mean what subse-

---

5. For more on state guarantees, see Robert Dowlut, "Federal and State Constitutional Guarantees to Arms," *University of Dayton Law Review* 15 (1989): 1–89.

6. The articles typically credited with renewing interest in the Second Amendment are Don Kates, "Handgun Prohibition and the Original Meaning of the Second Amendment," *Michigan Law Review* 82 (1983): 204–273; and Sanford Levinson, "The Embarrassing Second Amendment," *Yale Law Journal* 99 (1989): 637–659. Since their publication, a staggering number of essays have appeared. Many are available on the Internet at *www.2ndlawlib.org/journals*.

7. Levinson, "The Embarrassing Second Amendment," 645. See also Nelson Lund, "The Past and Future of the Individual's Right to Arms," *Georgia Law Review* 31 (1996): 1–76; and William Van Alstyne "The Second Amendment and the Personal Right to Arms," *Duke Law Journal* 43 (1994): 1236–55.

quent justices and judges have suggested. What the Court said, according to the individual rights scholars, was that guns that could be useful to a militia enjoy constitutional protection. Under this interpretation, as law professor Sanford Levinson notes, "It is difficult to read *Miller* as rendering the Second Amendment meaningless as a control on Congress." He goes on to suggest:

Ironically, *Miller* can be read to support some of the most extreme anti-gun control arguments, e.g., that the individual citizen has a right to keep and bear bazookas, rocket launchers, and other armaments that are clearly relevant to modern warfare, including, of course, assault weapons. Arguments about the constitutional legitimacy of a prohibition by Congress of private ownership of handguns or, what is much more likely, assault rifles, might turn on the usefulness of such guns in military settings.[8]

Because so many scholars now find the individual rights argument persuasive, some have labeled it the "standard model" for Second Amendment interpretation.[9] Surely, this is a misnomer, given the weight of legal precedent and the intense debates it has engendered.[10] Indeed, scholars taking the more traditional collective rights position accuse the individual rights advocates of writing words out of the Constitution—those in the first clause of the Second Amendment. Although the amendment speaks of "people," it starts with "A well regulated Militia." These words do not amount to a casual "prefatory" phrase, as some expounders of the individual rights position claim, but an important qualification to the right itself.

Other "collective theorists" argue that those advocating an individual view need a history lesson. It is not the case, they claim, that the Framers viewed "militia" as the same as an "armed citizenry"; rather, they defined militia in much the same way as do we, as an organized military force. The Second Amendment then was not written to give all citizens the right to bear arms but as a response to the concerns of state rights' advocates who did not want the federal government to be able to disarm state militias. Or, as Chief Justice Burger put it: "The real purpose of the Second Amendment was to ensure that 'state armies'—the 'militia'—would be maintained for the defense of the state."[11]

Still others in the collective camp suggest that the individual right scholars and groups such as the NRA are distorting judicial decisions to suit their purposes. Erwin Griswold, the former dean of Harvard Law School, said, "To assert that the Constitution is a barrier to reasonable gun laws, in the face of the unanimous judgment of the federal courts to the contrary, exceeds the limits of principled advocacy. It is time for the NRA and its followers in Congress to stop trying to twist the Second Amendment from a reasoned (if antiquated) empowerment for a militia into a bulletproof personal right for anyone to wield deadly weaponry beyond legislative control."[12]

Despite such arguments and significant legal precedent, evidence exists that the individual rights approach is beginning to have some influence. Consider, for example, the case of *United States v. Emerson* (1999), a dispute heard in the United States District Court for the Northern District of Texas. Sacha Emerson filed for a divorce from Timothy Emerson and obtained a restraining order that prohibited him from approaching her or their daughter. Under federal law, the restraining order makes it a criminal violation for such individuals to possess a firearm. Emerson allegedly threatened to kill a man with whom his wife had been having an affair and was indicted. But Sam R. Cummings, the district court judge hearing the case, dismissed the indictment, holding that the Second Amendment prohibited the government from denying gun ownership to people under restraining orders. In so doing, he made extensive use of some of the arguments made by individual rights advocates. Cummings began with a textual analysis of the Second Amendment:

8. Levinson, "The Embarrassing Second Amendment," 654–655.

9. See Glenn Harlan Reynolds, "A Critical Guide to the Second Amendment," *Tennessee Law Review* 62 (1995): 461–511.

10. For various critiques of the so-called standard model, see, for example, Saul Cornell, "Commonplace or Anachronism: The Standard Model, the Second Amendment, and the Problem of History in Contemporary Constitutional Theory," *Constitutional Commentary* 16 (1999): 221; Michael A. Bellesiles, "Gun Laws in Early America: The Regulation of Firearms Ownership, 1607–1794," *Law and History Review* 16 (1998): 567; and Gary Wills, "To Keep and Bear Arms," *New York Review of Books*, September 21, 1995.

11. "The Meaning, and Distortion, of the Second Amendment," *Keene Sentinel*, November 26, 1991.

12. Quoted in the *Washington Post*, November 4, 1990.

BOX 8-1   THE RIGHT TO KEEP AND BEAR ARMS IN
GLOBAL PERSPECTIVE

In a 1988 speech before the American Bar Association, Justice Lewis F. Powell Jr. noted that roughly 60 percent of the 40,000 murders in the United States in 1986 and 1987 were committed with guns, while during the same period in Wales and England there were 662 homicides, and only 8 percent involved firearms. Such data led Powell to conclude that "with respect to handguns . . . it is not easy to understand why the Second Amendment, or the notion of liberty, should be viewed as creating a right to own and carry a weapon that contributes so directly to the shocking number of murders in our society."

Groups in favor of gun control legislation often make this type of pragmatic argument in their appeals to Congress and, increasingly, in the courts. Indeed, as the table below indicates, there seems to be a positive relationship between guns in the possession of citizens and homicide rates.

Country	Homicide with Firearm Rate per 100,000 (N)	Number of Guns in Possession Rate per 100,000 (N)	Country	Homicide with Firearm Rate per 100,000 (N)	Number of Guns in Possession Rate per 100,000 (N)
Japan	.06 (74)	414 (517,675)	Canada	.67 (193)	24,138 (7 m)
Britain	.14 (74)	3,307 (1.7 m)	Switzerland	1.4 (96)	42,857 (3 m)
Australia	.36 (64)	19,444 (3.5 m)	France	2.32 (1,324)	22.6% of all households
New Zealand	.49 (18)	29,412 (1 m)	United States	6.4 (16,704)	85,385 (222 m)

In making global comparisons, however, groups that favor more stringent legislation may be falling prey to a chicken-and-egg problem, for we do not have a clear answer to the question of whether firearm ownership is a response to high homicide rates or the cause of them. Surely, these groups think the latter but, just as surely, a case could be made for the former.

SOURCES: www.cfc-ccaf.gc.ca/research/publications/reports/1990-95/reports/siter_rpt_en.html; Lewis Powell, "Capital Punishment," remarks delivered to the Criminal Justice Section of the American Bar Association, August 7, 1988; Sanford Levinson, "The Embarrassing Second Amendment," *Yale Law Journal* 99 (1989): 637–659.

Only if the Second Amendment guarantees Emerson a personal right to bear arms can he claim a constitutional violation. . . . Emerson claims that he has a personal right to bear arms which the Act infringes, while at oral argument . . . the Government claimed it is "well settled" that the Second Amendment creates a right held by the States and does not protect an individual right to bear arms. . . .

A textual analysis of the Second Amendment supports an individual right to bear arms. A distinguishing characteristic of the Second Amendment is the inclusion of an opening clause or preamble, which sets out its purpose. No similar clause is found in any other amendment. Sanford Levinson, The Embarrassing Second Amendment, 99 YALE L.J. 637, 644 (1989). While [some scholars] seize upon this first clause to the exclusion of the second, both clauses should be read *in pari*

materia [on the same subject], to give effect and harmonize both clauses rather than construe them as being mutually exclusive.

The amendment reads "[a] well regulated Militia, being necessary to the security of a free State, the right of the people to keep and bear Arms, shall not be infringed." Within the amendment are two distinct clauses, the first subordinate and the second independent. If the amendment consisted solely of its independent clause, "the right of the people to keep and bear Arms, shall not be infringed," then there would be no question whether the right is individual in nature.

Collective rights theorists argue that addition of the subordinate clause qualifies the rest of the amendment by placing a limitation on the people's right to bear arms. However, if the amendment truly meant what collective rights advocates propose, then the text would read "[a] well regulated Militia, being necessary to the security of a free State, the right of the *States* to keep and bear Arms, shall not be infringed." However, that is not what the framers of the amendment drafted. The plain language of the amendment, without attenuate inferences therefrom, shows that the function of the subordinate clause was not to qualify the right, but instead to show why it must be protected. The right exists independent of the existence of the militia. If this right were not protected, the existence of the militia, and consequently the security of the state, would be jeopardized. . . .

Thus, a textual analysis of the Second Amendment clearly declares a substantive right to bear arms recognized in the people of the United States.

Cummings also considered existing precedent, especially *Miller*. Once again, he echoed the sentiments expressed by Levinson and other individual rights advocates:

It is difficult to interpret *Miller* as rendering the Second Amendment meaningless as a control on Congress. Ironically, one can read *Miller* as supporting some of the most extreme anti–gun control arguments; for example, that the individual citizen has a right to keep and bear bazookas, rocket launchers, and other armaments that are clearly used for modern warfare, including, of course, assault weapons. Under *Miller*, arguments about the constitutional legitimacy of a prohibition by Congress of private ownership of handguns or, what is much more likely, assault rifles, thus might turn on the usefulness of such guns in military settings. Sanford Levinson, The Embarrassing Second Amendment, 99 YALE L.J. 637, 654–55 (1989).

Miller did not answer the crucial question of whether the Second Amendment embodies an individual or collective right to bear arms. Although its holding has been used to justify many previous lower federal court rulings circumscribing Second Amendment rights, the Court in *Miller* simply chose a very narrow way to rule on the issue of gun possession under the Second Amendment, and left for another day further questions of Second Amendment construction. See *Printz v. United States* (1997) (Thomas, J., concurring).

The United States has appealed Judge Cummings's decision to the U.S. Court of Appeals for the Fifth Circuit. Supporting it, as amici curiae, are gun control organizations, police associations, and various law professors and historians. The National Rifle Association, among others, has filed a brief on the other side that makes extensive use of the individual rights literature.

TABLE 8-1 Public Opinion on Gun Control Proposals

	Favor	Oppose
Raise the minimum age for handgun possession to 21 years	82%	17%
Hold parents legally responsible if their children commit crimes with the parents' guns	57	39
Require safety locks or trigger guards to be included with all new handgun purchases	85	14
Ban the importing of high-capacity ammunition clips	68	29
Impose a mandatory prison sentence on felons who commit crimes with guns	89	9
Impose a lifetime ban on gun ownership for any juvenile convicted of a felony	77	21
Require mandatory background checks before people—including gun dealers— could buy guns at gun shows	87	12
Require registration of all firearms	79	20

SOURCE: Gallup Organization, with data available at: *www.gallup.com/poll/releases/pr990713.asp*. The poll was conducted in June 1999.
NOTES: The poll asked the following: "Please tell me whether you would generally favor or oppose each of the following proposals which some people have made to reduce the amount of gun violence."
Percentages do not equal 100 because respondents with mixed or no opinion were excluded.

What will the U.S. Supreme Court do if this case or a similar one reaches it? Will it adhere to *Miller* or perhaps even strengthen it, or will it find some validity in the individual rights vision of the Second Amendment? These are questions on which we can only speculate; but regardless of which way the Court ultimately rules, its decision is bound to have a major impact on American society. In the wake of shootings at schools and other acts of violence, several interest groups have attempted to pressure Congress to enact stricter gun control legislation. In support of their position they invoke comparative data, which tends to show a positive relationship between gun ownership and homicide rates *(see Box 8-1)*, along with public opinion polls demonstrating that Americans favor a range of proposals to regulate the use of guns *(see Table 8-1)*.

Working just as hard are those organizations, such as the NRA, that view most—if not all—restrictions as infringing on the constitutional rights of Americans. Obviously, a Court decision supporting the individual rights position could bring tremendous validation for their claims, while one reinforcing *Miller* could spell disaster for their arguments about the real meaning of the Second Amendment.

READINGS

Amar, Akhil Reed. "The Bill of Rights as a Constitution." *Yale Law Journal* 100 (1991): 1131–75.

Barnett, Randy E., and Don B. Kates. "Under Fire: The New Consensus on the Second Amendment." *Emory Law Journal* 45 (1996): 1140–1259.

Bellesiles, Michael A. "Gun Laws in Early America: The Regulation of Firearms Ownership, 1607–1794." *Law and History Review* 16 (1998): 567.

Cornell, Saul. "Commonplace or Anachronism: The Standard Model, the Second Amendment, and the Problem of History in Contemporary Constitutional Theory." *Constitutional Commentary* 16 (1999): 221.

Cornell, Saul. *Whose Right to Bear Arms Did the Second Amendment Protect?* New York: St. Martin's, 2000.

Cottrol, Robert, and Raymond Diamond. "The Second Amendment: Toward an Afro-Americanist Reconsideration." *Georgetown Law Journal* 80 (1991): 309–361.

Davidson, Osha Gray. *Under Fire: The NRA and the Battle for Gun Control.* Iowa City: University of Iowa Press, 1998.

Dowlut, Robert. "Federal and State Constitutional Guarantees to Arms." *University of Dayton Law Review* 15 (1989): 1–89.

Halbrook, Stephen P. "The Right of the People or the Power of the State: Bearing Arms, Arming Militias, and the Second Amendment." *Valaparaiso University Law Review* 26 (1991): 131–207.

Herz, Andrew D. "Gun Crazy: Constitutional False Consciousness and Dereliction of Dialogic Responsibility." *Boston University Law Review* 75 (1995): 57.

Kates, Don B. "Handgun Prohibition and the Original Meaning of the Second Amendment." *Michigan Law Review* 82 (1983): 204–273.

Levinson, Sanford. "The Embarrassing Second Amendment." *Yale Law Journal* 99 (1989): 637–659.

Lott, John R. *More Guns, Less Crime: Understanding Crime and Gun-Control Laws.* Chicago: University of Chicago Press, 1998.

Malcolm, Joyce Lee. *To Keep and Bear Arms: The Origins of an Anglo-American Right.* Cambridge: Harvard University Press, 1996.

Reynolds, Glenn Harlan. "A Critical Guide to the Second Amendment." *Tennessee Law Review* 62 (1995): 461–512.

Shalhope, Robert E. "The Ideological Origins of the Second Amendment." *Journal of American History* 6 (1982): 599–614.

Van Alstyne, William. "The Second Amendment and the Personal Right to Arms." *Duke Law Journal* 43 (1994): 1236–55.

Volokh, Eugene. "The Commonplace Second Amendment." *New York University Law Review* 73 (1998): 793–821.

———. "The Amazing Vanishing Second Amendment." *New York University Law Review* 73 (1998): 831–840.

Wills, Gary. "To Keep and Bear Arms." *New York Review of Books*, September 21, 1995.

CHAPTER 9

THE RIGHT TO PRIVACY

SUPPOSE THE SEMESTER is drawing to a close and final examinations are only a week away. Two roommates plan to spend the week studying in their dorm room. For many, studying is a solitary activity carried on behind closed doors. Assume the roommates went to their room, closed the door, and placed a Do Not Disturb sign outside. They would expect others to leave them alone and respect their privacy.

But is that expectation reasonable? The answer seems obvious: people have a right to be let alone. To many Americans, privacy is a basic and fundamental part of civil liberties and rights. But the issue is far more complicated than that, primarily because the Constitution makes no explicit mention of this right. The word *privacy* appears neither in the text of the charter nor in the Bill of Rights. This omission has led to questions about this presumed guarantee that the Supreme Court has had difficulty answering.

Do Americans have a constitutional right to privacy and, if so, where does this right originate? Justices of recent Courts have responded affirmatively to the first part of the query, but offered different answers to the second. As we shall see, some assert that the right emanates from several specific constitutional guarantees, most notably,

1. The First Amendment's right of association

2. The Third Amendment's prohibition against quartering soldiers

3. The Fourth Amendment's Search and Seizure Clause

4. The Fifth Amendment guarantees against self-incrimination

5. The Ninth Amendment

Other justices argue they need look only at the Ninth Amendment, which says that the "enumeration in the Constitution, of certain rights, shall not be construed to deny or disparage others retained by the people." Finally, some find that the Fourteenth Amendment's Due Process Clause prohibits government intrusion in ways that infringe upon liberties of citizens.

Another question concerns the areas the right covers. Today, many Americans equate the right to privacy with reproductive freedom, and, indeed, the Court has used privacy as a basis for legalizing birth control and abortion. But, suppose the two studious roommates, in the privacy of their room, decide to use some cocaine. Because possession of this drug is illegal, does someone have the right to use it—engage in criminal activity—in private? Or does the government have the right to invade that privacy? In short, where do we draw the line? To what extent should the state limit the right to privacy so that it may act in the best interests of its citizens?

In the end, we are left with many questions concerning the amorphous right to privacy. But, while reading this chapter, also consider these: Have approaches to privacy and the rights encompassed in privacy, such as abortion, changed substantially over the years? If so, why? Have alterations in the membership of the Court generated changes in the reach of the right to privacy? Or has the Court responded to pressure from the larger political environment?

THE RIGHT TO PRIVACY: FOUNDATIONS

In today's legal and political context, the right to privacy has become almost synonymous with reproductive freedom. The reason may be that the case in which the Court first articulated a constitutional right to privacy, *Griswold v. Connecticut* (1965), involved birth control, and *Roe v. Wade* (1973), a decision that depended on *Griswold*, legalized abortion.

Prior to these decisions, the Court had contemplated privacy in somewhat different contexts. Following the common law dictates that "a man's home is his castle" and all "have the right to be left alone," Louis Brandeis, a future Supreme Court justice, coauthored an 1890 *Harvard Law Review* article, asserting that privacy rights should be applied to civil law cases of libel.[1] The article had enormous long-term influence in no small part because it created a new legal "wrong"—the invasion of privacy.

After Brandeis joined the Court, he continued his quest to see a right to privacy etched into law. Among his best-known attempts was a dissent in *Olmstead v. United States* (1928), which involved the ability of federal agents to wiretap telephones without warrants. The majority of the justices ruled that neither the Fifth Amendment's protection against self-incrimination nor the Fourth Amendment's search and seizure provision protected individuals against wiretaps. Brandeis dissented, saying that the Fourth and Fifth Amendments prohibited such activity:

The makers of our Constitution undertook to secure conditions favorable to the pursuit of happiness. They recognized the significance of man's spiritual nature, of his feelings and of his intellect. They knew that only a part of the pain, pleasure and satisfactions of life are to be found in material things. They sought to protect Americans in their beliefs, their thoughts, their emotions and their sensations. They conferred, as against the Government, the right to be let alone—the most comprehensive of rights and the right most valued by civilized men. To protect that right, every unjustifiable intrusion by the Government upon the privacy of the individual, whatever the means employed, must be deemed a violation of the Fourth Amendment. And the use, as evidence in a criminal proceeding, of facts ascertained by such intrusion must be deemed a violation of the Fifth.

However persuasive Brandeis's words might appear, they stood for nearly thirty years as the only serious mention of a right to privacy. Court after Court ignored this dissent.

Justices of earlier eras, however, had paid attention to a concept that would later become associated with privacy—the concept of liberty. The word *liberty* appears in the Due Process Clauses of the Fifth and Fourteenth Amendments. The Fifth Amendment states that Congress shall not deprive any person of "life, liberty, or property, without due process of law," and the Fourteenth Amendment uses the same wording to apply to the states. In the early 1900s, the Supreme Court created a doctrine called substantive due process to guide its interpretation of some government policies challenged as violations of the guarantees contained in the Due Process Clauses.

Under the doctrine of substantive due process, the Court stressed the word *liberty* in the Due Process Clauses to prevent governments from enacting certain kinds of laws, particularly those that regulated business practices. *Lochner v. New York* (1905) illustrates the point. In this case, the Court reviewed an 1897 New York law that prohibited employees of bakeries from working more than ten hours per day and sixty hours per week. Joseph Lochner, the owner of a New York bakery who was convicted of violating the law, challenged it on Fourteenth Amendment due process grounds. He argued that the Due Process Clause gives employers and employees the liberty to enter into contracts specifying the number of hours employees could work. By interfering with that contractual arrangement with no valid reason, the New York law, in his view, violated this guarantee. Five of the nine justices agreed. Writing for the majority, Justice Rufus W. Peckham noted:

---

1. Louis Brandeis and Samuel Warren, "The Right of Privacy," *Harvard Law Review* 4 (1890): 193. William L. Prosser notes that Brandeis and Warren wrote this piece in response to the yellow journalism of the day. See "Privacy," *California Law Review* 48 (1960): 383–423.

The statute necessarily interferes with the right of contract between the employer and employees, concerning the number of hours in which the latter may labor in the bakery of the employer. The general right to make a contract in relation to his business is part of the liberty of the individual protected by the 14th Amendment of the Federal Constitution. *Allgeyer v. Louisiana.* Under that provision no state can deprive any person of life, liberty, or property without due process of law. The right to purchase or to sell labor is part of the liberty protected by this amendment, unless there are circumstances which exclude the right. There are, however, certain powers, existing in the sovereignty of each state in the Union, somewhat vaguely termed police powers, the exact description and limitation of which have not been attempted by the courts. Those powers, broadly stated, and without, at present, any attempt at a more specific limitation, relate to the safety, health, morals, and general welfare of the public. Both property and liberty are held on such reasonable conditions as may be imposed by the governing power of the state in the exercise of those powers, and with such conditions the 14th Amendment was not designed to interfere.

The Court struck down the law on the ground that it was a "meddlesome" and "unreasonable interference with an employer's right of contract protected in the liberty guarantee of the 14th Amendment."

The Court also applied the doctrine of substantive due process to regulations outside of business. In *Meyer v. Nebraska* (1923) the justices considered a state law, enacted after World War I, that forbade schools to teach German and other foreign languages to students below the eighth grade. They invoked a substantive due process approach to strike down the law, reasoning that the word liberty in the Fourteenth Amendment protects more than the right to contract. It also covers "the right of the individual . . . to engage in any of the common occupations of life, to acquire useful knowledge, to marry, establish a home and bring up children, to worship God according to the dictates of his own conscience, and generally to enjoy those privileges long recognized at common law as essential to the orderly pursuit of happiness by free men." According to the Court, government cannot interfere with these liberties, "under the guise of protecting the public interest, by legislative action which is arbitrary or without reasonable relation to some purpose within the competency of the State to that effect."

Meyer and *Lochner* are examples of substantive due process in action: under this approach, the Court strikes down legislation interfering with liberty unless governments can demonstrate that they are seeking to achieve an end that is not "arbitrary," "capricious," or "unreasonable." To some analysts, this doctrine was the epitome of judicial activism because it allowed the Court to function as "super legislature," a censor on what governments can and cannot do.

Through the 1930s the Court used the doctrine of substantive due process to nullify many laws, particularly those—as in *Lochner*—that sought to regulate businesses. The members of the Court were laissez-faire–oriented justices who believed that the government should not interfere with the business of business. During the New Deal, however, substantive due process fell into disrepute because the public demanded government involvement to straighten out the economy. The Court changed its approach: the justices would allow states to adopt whatever economic policy they desired if the policy is reasonably related to a legitimate government interest. Known as the rational basis approach to the Fourteenth Amendment, it differs significantly from substantive due process because, under it, courts generally defer to governments and presume the validity of their policies.

Application of the rational basis test led the Court to uphold legislation such as minimum wage and maximum hour laws, which it had previously struck down on liberty grounds, even if the laws did not necessarily seem reasonable to the justices. In one case, in fact, the justices characterized a particular state's economic policy as "needless" and "wasteful." They upheld the law anyway, proclaiming, "The day is gone when this Court uses the Due Process Clause of the Fourteenth Amendment to strike down state laws, regulatory of business and industrial conditions, because they may be unwise, improvident, or out of harmony with a particular school of thought."[2] The majority added that if the people did not like the legislation their governments passed they should "resort to the polls, not to the courts." With this declara-

2. The case was *Williamson v. Lee Optical Company* (1955). The law at issue prohibited persons other than ophthalmologists and optometrists from fitting, adjusting, adapting, or applying lenses and frames.

tion, the Court seemed to strike the death knell for substantive due process. It would no longer substitute its "social and economic beliefs for the judgment of legislative bodies, who are elected to pass laws."[3]

What does the discredited doctrine of substantive due process have to do with the right to privacy? Justice Harlan (II) tied these two concepts together. Neither an activist nor a liberal, he took great offense at the Court's handling of a 1961 case, *Poe v. Ullman*. At issue in *Poe* was the constitutionality of an 1879 Connecticut law prohibiting the use of birth control, even by married couples. A physician challenged the act on behalf of two women who wanted to use contraceptives for health reasons.

The majority of the Court voted to dismiss the case on procedural grounds. Several other justices disagreed with this holding, but Harlan's dissent was memorable. He argued that the Fourteenth Amendment's Due Process Clause could be used to strike the law:

I consider that this Connecticut legislation . . . violates the Fourteenth Amendment. . . . [It] involves what, by common understanding throughout the English-speaking world, must be granted to be the fundamental aspect of "liberty," the privacy of the home in its most basic sense, and it is this which requires that the statute be subjected to "strict scrutiny."

In making this claim, Harlan sought to demonstrate that the concepts of liberty and privacy were constitutionally bound together, that the word *liberty*, as used in the Due Process Clauses, "embraced" a right to privacy. And, because that right was fundamental, laws that touched on liberty/privacy interests, such as the one at issue in *Poe*, must be subjected to "strict scrutiny," meaning that the Court should presume that laws infringing on liberty/privacy were unconstitutional unless the state could show that the policies were the least restrictive means to accomplish a compelling interest.

Harlan's opinion was extraordinary in two ways.[4]

3. *Ferguson v. Skrupa* (1963).

4. As was Douglas's, which read: "Though I believe that 'due process' as used in the Fourteenth Amendment includes all of the first eight Amendments, I do not think it is restricted . . . to them. The right 'to marry, establish a home and bring up children' was said in *Meyer v. State of Nebraska* to come within the 'liberty' of the person protected by the Due Process Clause of the Fourteenth Amendment . . . 'liberty' within the purview of the Fifth Amendment includes the right of 'privacy.' . . . This notion of privacy is not drawn from the blue. It emanates from the totality of the constitutional scheme under which we live."

First, some scholars have pointed out that it resurrected the long-dead (and discredited) doctrine of substantive due process, which the Court had buried in the 1930s. Now Harlan wanted to reinject some substance into the word *liberty*, but with a twist. In his view, rather than protecting economic rights, due process protects fundamental rights, those the Court believes to be important in the concept of ordered liberty. One of these fundamental liberties—privacy—provides the second novel aspect of Harlan's opinion. As we have indicated, he was not writing on a blank slate; Brandeis had talked about a right to privacy in the contexts of libel and search and seizure. In fact, Harlan cited—with approval—Brandeis's dissent in *Olmstead*. Still, Harlan's application of the doctrine to marital sexual relations was bold. As he wrote, "It is difficult to imagine what is more private or more intimate than a husband and wife's marital relations."

Harlan's assertion (and that by Douglas, another dissenter) of a constitutional right to privacy proved too much, too soon for the Court; the majority was not yet willing to adopt it. But just four years later in *Griswold v. Connecticut*, a dramatic change took place when the justices suddenly altered their views. More important is what they said about the right to privacy: the majority agreed that it existed, even if they disagreed over where it resided in the Constitution.[5]

Griswold v. Connecticut

381 U.S. 479 (1965)
laws.findlaw.com/US/381/479.html
Vote: 7 (Brennan, Clark, Douglas, Goldberg, Harlan, Warren, White)
    2 (Black, Stewart)
Opinion of the Court: Douglas
Concurring opinions: Goldberg, Harlan, White
Dissenting opinions: Black, Stewart

In *Poe v. Ullman* (1961) Dr. C. Lee Buxton, a physician acting on behalf of two women who wanted to use contraceptives for health reasons, challenged the constitu-

5. For oral arguments, navigate to: *oyez.nwu.edu.*

Estelle Griswold opened a birth control clinic in New Haven in violation of an 1879 Connecticut law prohibiting the use of contraceptives. She challenged the constitutionality of the statute, and in *Griswold v. Connecticut* (1965) the Supreme Court struck down the law and established a constitutionally protected right to privacy.

tionality of an 1879 Connecticut law prohibiting the use of birth control, even by married couples. The majority of the Court voted to dismiss the case on procedural grounds.

Griswold was virtually a carbon copy of *Poe*, with but a few differences designed to meet some of the shortcomings of the earlier case.[6] Estelle Griswold, the executive

6. For interesting accounts of *Griswold*, see Fred W. Friendly and Martha J. H. Elliot, *The Constitution—That Delicate Balance* (New York: Random House, 1984); and Bernard Schwartz, *The Unpublished Opinions of the Warren Court* (New York: Oxford University Press, 1985).

director of the Planned Parenthood League of Connecticut, and Buxton opened a birth control clinic in 1961 with the intent of being arrested for violating the same Connecticut law at issue in *Poe*. Three days later, Griswold was arrested for dispensing contraceptives to a married couple.

In the U.S. Supreme Court, Griswold's attorney, Yale Law School professor Thomas Emerson, challenged the Connecticut law on some of the same grounds set forth in the *Poe* dissent. Emerson took a substantive due process approach to the Fourteenth Amendment, arguing that the law infringed on individual liberty. He strengthened the privacy argument by asserting that it could be found in five amendments: the First, Third, Fourth, Ninth, and Fourteenth.

MR. JUSTICE DOUGLAS delivered the opinion of the Court.

[W]e are met with a wide range of questions that implicate the Due Process Clause of the Fourteenth Amendment. . . . We do not sit as a super-legislature to determine the wisdom, need, and propriety of laws that touch economic problems, business affairs, or social conditions. This law, however, operates directly on an intimate relation of husband and wife and their physician's role in one aspect of that relation.

The association of people is not mentioned in the Constitution nor in the Bill of Rights. The right to educate a child in a school of the parents' choice—whether public or private or parochial—is also not mentioned. Nor is the right to study any particular subject or any foreign language. Yet the First Amendment has been construed to include certain of those rights. . . .

Without those peripheral rights the specific rights would be less secure. . . .

. . . [Previous] cases suggest that specific guarantees in the Bill of Rights have penumbras, formed by emanations from those guarantees that help give them life and substance. Various guarantees create zones of privacy. The right of association contained in the penumbra of the First Amendment is one. . . . The Third Amendment in its prohibition against the quartering of soldiers "in any house" in time of peace without the consent of the owner is another facet of that privacy. The Fourth Amendment explicitly affirms the "right of the people to be secure in their persons, houses, papers, and effects, against unreasonable searches and seizures." The Fifth Amendment in its Self-Incrimination Clause enables the citizen to create a zone of privacy which government may not force him to surrender to his detriment. The Ninth Amendment provides: "The enumeration in the Constitution, of certain rights, shall not be construed to deny or disparage others retained by the people."

The Fourth and Fifth Amendments were described in *Boyd v. United States* as protection against all governmental invasions "of the sanctity of a man's home and the privacies of life. We recently referred to the Fourth Amendment as creating a "right to privacy, no less important than any other right carefully and particularly reserved to the people."

We have had many controversies over these penumbral rights of "privacy and repose." These cases bear witness that the right of privacy which presses for recognition here is a legitimate one.

The present case, then, concerns a relationship lying within the zone of privacy created by several fundamental constitutional guarantees. And it concerns a law which, in forbidding the *use* of contraceptives rather than regulating their manufacture or sale, seeks to achieve its goals by means having a maximum destructive impact upon that relationship. Such a law cannot stand in light of the familiar principle, so often applied by this Court, that a "governmental purpose to control or prevent activities constitutionally subject to state regulation may not be achieved by means which sweep unnecessarily broadly and thereby invade the area of protected freedoms." Would we allow the police to search the sacred precincts of marital bedrooms for telltale signs of the use of contraceptives? The very idea is repulsive to the notions of privacy surrounding the marriage relationship.

We deal with a right of privacy older than the Bill of Rights—older than our political parties, older than our school system. Marriage is a coming together for better or for worse, hopefully enduring, and intimate to the degree of being sacred. It is an association that promotes a way of life, not causes; harmony in living, not political faiths; bilateral loyalty, not commercial or social projects. Yet it is an association for as noble a purpose as any involved in our prior decisions.

Reversed.

MR. JUSTICE GOLDBERG, whom THE CHIEF JUSTICE and MR. JUSTICE BRENNAN join, concurring.

I agree with the Court that Connecticut's birth-control law unconstitutionally intrudes upon the right of marital privacy, and I join in its opinion and judgment. Although I have not accepted the view that "due process" as used in the Fourteenth Amendment includes all of the first eight Amendments, I do agree that the concept of liberty protects those personal rights that are fundamental, and is not confined to the specific terms of the Bill of Rights. My conclusion that the concept of liberty is not so restricted and that it embraces the right of marital privacy though that right is not mentioned explicitly in the Constitution is supported both by numerous decisions of this Court, referred to in the Court's opinion, and by the language and history of the Ninth Amendment. In reaching the conclusion that the right of marital privacy is protected, as being within the protected penumbra of specific guarantees of the Bill of Rights, the Court refers to the Ninth Amendment. . . .

The language and history of the Ninth Amendment reveal that the Framers of the Constitution believed that there are additional fundamental rights, protected from governmental infringement, which exist alongside those fundamental rights specifically mentioned in the first eight constitutional amendments.

The Ninth Amendment reads, "The enumeration in the Constitution, of certain rights, shall not be construed to deny or disparage others retained by the people." The Amendment is almost entirely the work of James Madison. It was introduced in Congress by him and passed the House and Senate with little or no debate and virtually no change in language. It was proffered to quiet expressed fears that a bill of specifically enumerated rights could not be sufficiently broad to cover all essential rights and that the specific mention of certain rights would be interpreted as a denial that others were protected. . . .

While this Court has had little occasion to interpret the Ninth Amendment, "it cannot be presumed that any clause in the constitution is intended to be without effect." The Ninth Amendment to the Constitution may be regarded by some as a recent discovery and may be forgotten by others, but since 1791 it has been a basic part of the Constitution which we are sworn to uphold. To hold that a right so basic and fundamental and so deep-rooted in our society as the right of privacy in marriage may be infringed because that right is not guaranteed in so many words by the first eight amendments to the Constitution is to ignore the Ninth Amendment and to give it no effect whatsoever. Moreover, a judicial construction that this fundamental right is not protected by the Constitution because it is not mentioned in explicit terms by one of the first eight amendments or elsewhere in the Constitution would violate the Ninth Amendment, which specifically states that "the enumeration in the Constitution, of certain rights shall not be *construed* to deny or disparage others retained by the people." (Emphasis added.) . . .

In sum, I believe that the right of privacy in the marital relation is fundamental and basic—a personal right "retained by the people" within the meaning of the Ninth Amendment. Connecticut cannot constitutionally abridge this fundamental right, which is protected by the Fourteenth Amendment from infringement by the States. I agree with the Court that petitioners' convictions must therefore be reversed.

MR. JUSTICE HARLAN, concurring in the judgment.

I fully agree with the judgment of reversal, but find myself unable to join the Court's opinion. . . .

In my view, the proper constitutional inquiry in this case is whether this Connecticut statute infringes the Due Process Clause of the Fourteenth Amendment because the enactment violates basic values "implicit in the concept of ordered liberty." For reasons stated at length in my dissenting opinion in *Poe v. Ullman,* I believe that it does. While the relevant inquiry may be aided by resort to one or more of the provisions of the Bill of Rights, it is not dependent on them or any of their radiations. The Due Process Clause of the Fourteenth Amendment stands, in my opinion, on its own bottom.

MR. JUSTICE BLACK, with whom MR. JUSTICE STEWART joins, dissenting.

The Court talks about a constitutional "right of privacy" as though there is some constitutional provision or provisions forbidding any law ever to be passed which might abridge the "privacy" of individuals. But there is not. There are, of course, guarantees in certain specific constitutional provisions which are designed in part to protect privacy at certain times and places with respect to certain activities. Such, for example, is the Fourth Amendment's guarantee against "unreasonable searches and seizures." But I think it belittles that Amendment to talk about it as though it protects nothing but "privacy." To treat it that way is to give it a niggardly interpretation, not the kind of liberal reading I think any Bill of Rights provision should be given. The average man would very likely not have his feelings soothed any more by having his property seized openly than by having it seized privately and by stealth. He simply wants his property left alone. And a person can be just as much, if not more, irritated, annoyed and injured by an unceremonious public arrest by a policeman as he is by a seizure in the privacy of his office or home.

One of the most effective ways of diluting or expanding a constitutionally guaranteed right is to substitute for the crucial word or words of a constitutional guarantee another word or words, more or less flexible and more or less restricted in meaning. This fact is well illustrated by the use of the term "right of privacy" as a comprehensive substitute for the Fourth Amendment's guarantee against "unreasonable searches and seizures." "Privacy" is a broad, abstract and ambiguous concept which can easily be shrunken in meaning but which can also, on the other hand, easily be interpreted as a constitutional ban against many things other than searches and seizures. I have expressed the view many times that First Amendment freedoms, for example, have suffered from a failure of the courts to stick to the simple language of the First Amendment in construing it, instead of invoking multitudes of words substituted for those the Framers used. . . . For these reasons I get nowhere in this case by talk about a constitutional "right of privacy" as an emanation from one or more constitutional provisions. I like my privacy as well as the next one, but I am nevertheless compelled to admit that government has a right to invade it unless prohibited by some specific constitutional provision. For these reasons I cannot agree with the Court's judgment and the reasons it gives for holding this Connecticut law unconstitutional.

This brings me to the arguments made by my Brothers HARLAN, WHITE and GOLDBERG for invalidating the Connecticut law. Brothers HARLAN and WHITE would invalidate it by reliance on the Due Process Clause of the Fourteenth Amendment, but Brother GOLDBERG, while agreeing with Brother HARLAN, relies also on the Ninth

Amendment. I have no doubt that the Connecticut law could be applied in such a way as to abridge freedom of speech and press and therefore violate the First and Fourteenth Amendments. My disagreement with the Court's opinion holding that there is such a violation here is a narrow one, relating to the application of the First Amendment to the facts and circumstances of this particular case. But my disagreement with Brothers HARLAN, WHITE and GOLDBERG is more basic. I think that if properly construed neither the Due Process Clause nor the Ninth Amendment, nor both together, could under any circumstances be a proper basis for invalidating the Connecticut law. I discuss the due process and Ninth Amendment arguments together because on analysis they turn out to be the same thing—merely using different words to claim for this Court and the federal judiciary power to invalidate any legislative act which the judges find irrational, unreasonable or offensive.

The due process argument which my Brothers HARLAN and WHITE adopt here is based, as their opinions indicate, on the premise that this Court is vested with power to invalidate all state laws that it considers to be arbitrary, capricious, unreasonable, or oppressive, or on this Court's belief that a particular state law under scrutiny has no "rational or justifying" purpose, or is offensive to a "sense of fairness and justice." If these formulas based on "natural justice," or others which mean the same thing, are to prevail, they require judges to determine what is or is not constitutional on the basis of their own appraisal of what laws are unwise or unnecessary. The power to make such decisions is of course that of a legislative body. Surely it has to be admitted that no provision of the Constitution specifically gives such blanket power to courts to exercise such a supervisory veto over the wisdom and value of legislative policies and to hold unconstitutional those laws which they believe unwise or dangerous. I readily admit that no legislative body, state or national, should pass laws that can justly be given any of the invidious labels invoked as constitutional excuses to strike down state laws. But perhaps it is not too much to say that no legislative body ever does pass laws without believing that they will accomplish a sane, rational, wise and justifiable purpose. While . . . our Court has constitutional power to strike down statutes, state or federal, that violate commands of the Federal Constitution, I do not believe that we are granted power by the Due Process Clause or any other

constitutional provision or provisions to measure constitutionality by our belief that legislation is arbitrary, capricious or unreasonable, or accomplishes no justifiable purpose, or is offensive to our own notions of "civilized standards of conduct." Such an appraisal of the wisdom of legislation is an attribute of the power to make laws, not of the power to interpret them. The use by federal courts of such a formula or doctrine or whatnot to veto federal or state laws simply takes away from Congress and States the power to make laws based on their own judgment of fairness and wisdom and transfers that power to this Court for ultimate determination—a power which was specifically denied to federal courts by the convention that framed the Constitution. . . .

My Brother GOLDBERG has adopted the recent discovery that the Ninth Amendment as well as the Due Process Clause can be used by this Court as authority to strike down all state legislation which this Court thinks violates "fundamental principles of liberty and justice," or is contrary to the "traditions and [collective] conscience of our people." He also states, without proof satisfactory to me, that in making decisions on this basis judges will not consider "their personal and private notions." One may ask how they can avoid considering them. Our Court certainly has no machinery with which to take a Gallup Poll. And the scientific miracles of this age have not yet produced a gadget which the Court can use to determine what traditions are rooted in the "[collective] conscience of our people." Moreover, one would certainly have to look far beyond the language of the Ninth Amendment to find that the Framers vested in this Court any such awesome veto powers over lawmaking, either by the States or by the Congress. Nor does anything in the history of the Amendment offer any support for such a shocking doctrine. The whole history of the adoption of the Constitution and Bill of Rights points the other way. . . . That Amendment was passed, not to broaden the powers of this Court or any other department of "the General Government," but, as every student of history knows, to assure the people that the Constitution in all its provisions was intended to limit the Federal Government to the powers granted expressly or by necessary implication. . . . [F]or a period of a century and a half no serious suggestion was ever made that the Ninth Amendment, enacted to protect state powers against federal invasion, could be used as a weapon of federal power to prevent state legislatures from passing laws they consider appropriate to govern local affairs. Use of any such broad, unbounded judicial authority would make of this Court's members a day-to-day constitutional convention. . . .

I realize that many good and able men have eloquently spoken and written, sometimes in rhapsodical strains, about the duty of this Court to keep the Constitution in tune with the times. The idea is that the Constitution must be changed from time to time and that this Court is charged with a duty to make those changes. For myself, I must with all deference reject that philosophy. The Constitution makers knew the need for change and provided for it. Amendments suggested by the people's elected representatives can be submitted to the people or their selected agents for ratification. That method of change was good for our Fathers, and being somewhat old-fashioned I must add it is good enough for me. And so, I cannot rely on the Due Process Clause or the Ninth Amendment or any mysterious and uncertain natural law concept as a reason for striking down this state law. The Due Process Clause with an "arbitrary and capricious" . . . formula was liberally used by this Court to strike down economic legislation in the early decades of this century, threatening, many people thought, the tranquility and stability of the Nation. See, e.g., *Lochner v. New York*. That formula, based on subjective considerations of "natural justice," is no less dangerous when used to enforce this Court's views about personal rights than those about economic rights. I had thought that we had laid that formula, as a means for striking down state legislation, to rest once and for all.

MR. JUSTICE STEWART, whom MR. JUSTICE BLACK joins, dissenting.

Since 1879 Connecticut has had on its books a law which forbids the use of contraceptives by anyone. I think this is an uncommonly silly law. As a practical matter, the law is obviously unenforceable, except in the oblique context of the present case. As a philosophical matter, I believe the use of contraceptives in the relationship of marriage should be left to personal and private choice, based upon each individual's moral, ethical, and religious beliefs. As a matter of social policy, I think professional counsel about methods of birth control should be available to all, so that each individual's choice can be meaningfully made. But we are not asked in this case to say whether we think this law is unwise,

or even asinine. We are asked to hold that it violates the United States Constitution. And that I cannot do.

In the course of its opinion the Court refers to no less than six Amendments to the Constitution: the First, the Third, the Fourth, the Fifth, the Ninth, and the Fourteenth. But the Court does not say which of these Amendments, if any, it thinks is infringed by this Connecticut law.

We *are* told that the Due Process Clause of the Fourteenth Amendment is not, as such, the "guide" in this case. With that much I agree. . . . [A]s the Court says, the day has long passed since the Due Process Clause was regarded as a proper instrument for determining "the wisdom, need, and propriety" of state laws. . . .

The Court also quotes the Ninth Amendment, and my Brother GOLDBERG's concurring opinion relies heavily upon it. But to say that the Ninth Amendment has anything to do with this case is to turn somersaults with history. The Ninth Amendment, like its companion the Tenth, which this Court held "states but a truism that all is retained which has not been surrendered," was framed by James Madison and adopted by the States simply to make clear that the adoption of the Bill of Rights did not alter the plan that the *Federal* Government was to be a government of express and limited powers, and that all rights and powers not delegated to it were retained by the people and the individual States. Until today no member of this Court has ever suggested that the Ninth Amendment meant anything else, and the idea that a federal court could ever use the Ninth Amendment to annul a law passed by the elected representatives of the people of the State of Connecticut would have caused James Madison no little wonder.

What provision of the Constitution, then, does make this state law invalid? The Court says it is the right of privacy "created by several fundamental constitutional guarantees." With all deference, I can find no such general right of privacy in the Bill of Rights, in any other part of the Constitution, or in any case ever before decided by this Court.

Griswold was a landmark decision because it created a constitutional right to privacy and deemed that right fundamental. Under *Griswold*, governments may place limits on the right to privacy only if those limits survive "strict" constitutional scrutiny, which means that the government must demonstrate that its restrictions are

TABLE 9-1 The *Griswold* Splits

Location of the Privacy Right	Justices
First, Third, Fourth, Fifth, and Ninth Amendments	Douglas, Clark
Ninth Amendment	Goldberg, Brennan, Warren
Fourteenth Amendment (Due Process Clause)	Harlan, White
No general right to privacy in the Constitution	Black, Stewart

necessary and narrowly tailored to serve a compelling government interest. However, the justices disagreed about where that right existed within the Constitution (*see Table 9-1*). Douglas's opinion for the Court asserted that specific guarantees in the Bill of Rights have penumbras, formed by emanations from First, Third, Fourth, Fifth, and Ninth Amendment guarantees "that help give them life and substance." In other words, Douglas claimed that even though the Constitution failed to mention privacy, clauses within the document created zones that gave rise to the right. In making this argument, Douglas avoided reliance on the Fourteenth Amendment's Due Process Clause. He apparently believed that grounding privacy in that clause would hark back to the days of *Lochner* and substantive due process, a doctrine he explicitly rejected.

Justice Goldberg, writing for Earl Warren and William Brennan, did not dispute Douglas's penumbra theory, but chose to emphasize the relevance of the Ninth Amendment. In Goldberg's view, that amendment could be read to contain a right to privacy. His logic was simple: the wording of the amendment, coupled with its history, suggested that it was "proffered to quiet expressed fears that a bill of specifically enumerated rights could not be sufficiently broad to cover all essential rights," including the right to privacy. Harlan reiterated his stance in *Poe* that the Due Process Clause of the Fourteenth Amendment prohibits such legislation. In holding to his *Poe* opinion, however, Harlan went one step be-

yond the Goldberg concurrers. He rejected Douglas's penumbra theory and asserted, "While the relevant inquiry may be aided by resort to one or more of the provisions of the Bill of Rights, it is not dependent on them or any of their radiations." Justice White also filed a concurring opinion lending support to Harlan's due process view of privacy.

The *Griswold* opinions make clear that the justices did not speak with one voice. Seven agreed, more or less, that a right to privacy existed, but they located that right in three distinct constitutional spheres. The other two—Black and Stewart—argued that the Constitution did not contain a general right to privacy, but they did more than that. They took their colleagues to task for, in their view, reverting back to the days of *Lochner* and substantive due process. Black and Stewart maintained that the people, not the courts, should pressure legislatures to change "unwise" laws.

Whether a right to privacy existed and where the right was located, however, were not the only questions raised by *Griswold*. Another issue concerned what this newly found right covered. Clearly, it protected "notions of privacy surrounding the marriage relationship," but beyond that observers could only speculate.

In this chapter we examine the other areas where the Court has applied *Griswold*. We look first at its role in the issue of abortion and then into extensions into other private activities. Keep the *Griswold* precedent in mind. To which interpretation of the right to privacy has the Court subscribed in the cases that follow? Has the Court's approach changed with its increasing conservatism? Or do the majority of justices continue to adopt its basic tenets?

REPRODUCTIVE FREEDOM AND THE RIGHT TO PRIVACY: ABORTION

While many of the issues flowing from *Griswold*—such as drug-testing and the right to die—are hotly debated, as we shall see in the next sections, those discussions are mild compared to the controversy stirred up by the Court's use of the right to privacy doctrine to legalize abortion in *Roe v. Wade* (1973). Since this decision, no other issue has come close to abortion on any political,

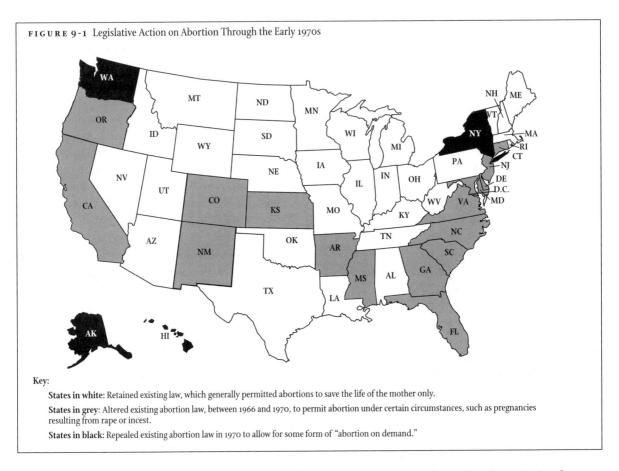

FIGURE 9-1 Legislative Action on Abortion Through the Early 1970s

Key:

States in white: Retained existing law, which generally permitted abortions to save the life of the mother only.

States in grey: Altered existing abortion law, between 1966 and 1970, to permit abortion under certain circumstances, such as pregnancies resulting from rape or incest.

States in black: Repealed existing abortion law in 1970 to allow for some form of "abortion on demand."

legal, or emotional scale. It has affected the outcome of many political races; occupied preeminent places on legislative, executive, and judicial agendas; and played a role in the nomination proceedings for Supreme Court and lower federal court judges.

What is particularly intriguing about the issue is that the Court generated the furor. Prior to the decision in *Roe,* abortion was not a significant political issue. As Figure 9-1 shows, many states had on their books laws enacted in the late 1800s that permitted abortion only to save the life of the mother. Other states had reformed their legislation in the 1960s to include legal abortion for pregnancies resulting from rape or incest or those in which there was a high likelihood of a deformed baby. The majority of states defined performing or obtaining an abortion, under all other circumstances, as criminal offenses. These conditions do not mean that states were

under no pressure to change their laws. During the 1960s a growing pro-choice movement, consisting of groups such as the ACLU and NARAL, which at that time stood for the National Association for Repeal of Abortion Laws, sought to convince states to legalize fully the procedure, that is, allow abortion on demand.

When only a handful of states even considered taking such action, attorneys and leaders of the pro-choice movement supplemented their legislative lobbying with litigation, initiating dozens of suits in federal and state courts. These cases challenged restrictive abortion laws on several grounds, including the First Amendment's freedoms of association and speech for doctors (and patients) and the Fourteenth Amendment's Equal Protection Clause (discrimination against women). But the most commonly invoked legal ground was *Griswold*'s right to privacy. Because it was unclear to attorneys which clause of the Constitution generated the right to privacy, in many cases, pro-choice lawyers covered their bases by arguing on all three specific grounds. Their larger point was clear: the right to privacy was broad enough to encompass the right to obtain an abortion. Moreover, because the right to privacy was "fundamental," logic would hold that the right to obtain an abortion was also fundamental, meaning that states could proscribe the procedure only with a compelling interest. Such an interest, pro-choice attorneys asserted, did not exist.

The result of this legal activity was an avalanche of litigation. Pro-choice groups had flooded the U.S. courts with lawsuits—some on behalf of doctors, some for women—challenging both major kinds of abortion laws: those that permitted abortion only to save the life of the mother and those that allowed abortion in cases of rape or incest or to save the life of the mother. They were hoping that the Supreme Court would hear at least one.

Their wish was granted when the Court agreed to hear arguments in December of 1971 in two cases, *Roe v. Wade*, a challenge to a Texas law, representing the most restrictive kinds of abortion laws, and *Doe v. Bolton*, a challenge to a Georgia law, representing the newer, less restrictive laws. Because the Court had problems resolving these cases, they were reargued at the beginning of the next term.

In the meantime, the justices handed down a decision that had some bearing on the debate. In 1972 the Court struck down a Massachusetts law that prohibited the sale of contraceptives to unmarried people. Writing for a six-person majority (with only Chief Justice Burger dissenting) in *Eisenstadt v. Baird* Justice Brennan asserted that the law violated the "rights of single people" under the Fourteenth Amendment's Equal Protection Clause. But, in dicta, he went much further:

If under *Griswold* the distribution of contraceptives to married persons cannot be prohibited, a ban on distribution to unmarried persons would be equally impermissible. It is true that in *Griswold* the right of privacy in question inhered in the marital relationship. Yet the marital couple is not an independent entity with a mind and heart of its own, but an association of two individuals each with separate intellectual and emotional makeup. If the right of privacy means anything, it is the right of the individual, married or single, to be free from unwarranted

governmental intrusion into matters so fundamentally affecting a person as the decision whether to bear or beget a child.

Whether Brennan wrote this with *Roe* and *Doe* in mind we do not know, but clearly *Eisenstadt* heartened pro-choice forces. Their optimism was not misplaced, for, on January 22, 1973, when the Court handed down its decisions in *Roe* and *Doe*, they had won. As you read *Roe*, pay particular attention to the Court's logic: On what grounds did it strike the Texas law?[7]

Roe v. Wade

410 U.S. 113 (1973)
laws.findlaw.com/US/410/113.html
Vote: 7 (Blackmun, Brennan, Burger, Douglas, Marshall, Powell, Stewart)
   2 (Rehnquist, White)
Opinion of the Court: Blackmun
Concurring opinions: Burger, Douglas, Stewart
Dissenting opinions: Rehnquist, White

In August 1969, twenty-one-year-old Norma McCorvey claimed to have been raped and was pregnant as a result of that rape.[8] Her doctor refused to perform an abortion, citing an 1857 Texas law, revised in 1879, that made it a crime to "procure an abortion" unless it was necessary to save the life of a mother. He provided her with the name of a lawyer who handled adoptions. The lawyer, in turn, sent her to two other attorneys, Linda Coffee and Sarah Weddington, whom he knew were interested in challenging the Texas law.

Coffee and Weddington went after the Texas law with a vengeance, challenging it on all possible grounds: privacy, women's rights, due process, and so forth. Their efforts paid off; a three-judge district court ruled in their

7. For oral arguments, navigate to: *oyez.nwu.edu.*

8. We draw this discussion from the papers of William J. Brennan Jr., Manuscript Division, Library of Congress; Lee Epstein and Joseph F. Kobylka, *The Supreme Court and Legal Change* (Chapel Hill: University of North Carolina Press, 1992); Lee Epstein and Jack Knight, *The Choices Justices Make* (Washington, D.C.: CQ Press, 1998); and Marion Faux, *Roe v. Wade* (New York: Macmillan, 1988). For other accounts, see Eva Rubin, *Abortion, Politics, and the Courts* (Westport, Conn.: Greenwood Press, 1987); and Richard C. Cortner, *The Supreme Court and Civil Liberties Policy* (Palo Alto, Calif: Mayfield, 1975).

favor, mostly on Ninth Amendment privacy grounds. But because the district court ruling did not overturn the state law, McCorvey, using the pseudonym Jane Roe, and her attorneys appealed to the U.S. Supreme Court.

Once the Court agreed to hear the case, pro-choice and pro-life forces mobilized. On the pro-choice side, the ACLU and other groups helped Weddington and Coffee, who had never appeared before the Court, prepare their briefs and arguments. These groups also lined up numerous amici, ranging from the American College of Obstetricians and Gynecologists to the Planned Parenthood Federation to the American Association of University Women. In general, the pro-choice side wanted to convince the Court that abortion was a fundamental right under the *Griswold* doctrine. Unless Texas could provide a compelling and narrowly drawn interest, the law should fall. It also presented a mass of data indicating that physical and mental health risks are associated with restrictive abortion laws.

The state countered with arguments concerning the rights of fetuses. In its brief, it devoted twenty-four pages, along with nine photographs of fetuses at various stages of development, to depict the "humanness" of the unborn and to support its argument that a state has a compelling interest in protecting human life. The state's position was supported by several pro-life organizations (including the National Right to Life Committee and the League for Infants, Fetuses, and the Elderly) and groups of doctors and nurses.

On December 13, 1971, the Supreme Court heard oral arguments, and three days later it met to decide the abortion cases. Only seven justices were present because President Nixon's newest appointees, Lewis F. Powell Jr. and William H. Rehnquist, had not participated in orals. Of the seven participating justices, a four-person majority (Brennan, Douglas, Marshall, and Stewart) thought the abortion laws should be stricken, although for somewhat different reasons. Moreover, they were unsure about the "time problem"—whether a woman could obtain an abortion any time during her pregnancy or over a more limited period, such as the first six months. White came down most definitively in favor of the pro-life position. Burger and Blackmun, who had joined the Court in

1969 and 1970, respectively, were less decisive; the chief justice leaned toward upholding laws prohibiting abortion, and Blackmun leaned toward the pro-choice camp. Although there was disagreement over the reason why the laws were unconstitutional and over the time frame for abortions, the result was clear: the pro-choice side would win by a 5–2 or 4–3 vote, depending on how Blackmun voted. Burger assigned the opinion to Blackmun, whom he had known since grade school *(see Box 9-1)*.

This (mis)assignment triggered a series of events. The first was an irate letter from Douglas to Burger, in which Douglas had two bones to pick: first, as the senior member of the majority, he should have assigned the opinion; second, Blackmun should not have received the assignment in any event because his docket sheet put him in the minority. Burger responded that he would not change the assignment. He said, "At the close of discussion of this case, I remarked to the Conference that there were, literally, not enough columns to mark up an accurate reflection of the voting. . . . I therefore marked down no votes and said this was a case that would have to stand or fall on the writing, when it was done. . . . This is still my view of how to handle . . . this sensitive case."

Still uncertain of how Blackmun would dispose of the case and of what rationale he would use, some of the justices began preparing opinions. Indeed, it took Douglas only a few weeks to circulate a memorandum to Brennan, who responded with some suggestions for revision and the admonition that Douglas hold onto the opinion until Blackmun circulated his.

It was a long wait. In mid-May 1972 Blackmun sent around his first draft in *Roe*—a draft that came to the "right" result in Brennan's and Douglas's minds but did so for the wrong (that is, narrowest possible) reason: that the restrictive Texas abortion law was void because it was vague, not because it interfered with any fundamental right. The four pro-choicers were disappointed and urged Blackmun to recast his draft. In so doing, they raised the opinion assignment issue again. Douglas wrote to Blackmun:

In *Roe v. Wade,* my notes confirm what Bill Brennan wrote yesterday in his memo to you—that abortion statutes were invalid

BOX 9-1   HARRY ANDREW BLACKMUN (1970–1994)

HARRY A. BLACKMUN was born November 12, 1908, in Nashville, Illinois. He spent most of his early life in the Minneapolis-St. Paul area, where his father was an official of the Twin Cities Savings and Loan Company. In grade school Blackmun began a friendship with Warren Burger, with whom he was later to serve on the Supreme Court.

Showing an early aptitude for mathematics, Blackmun attended Harvard University on a scholarship. He majored in mathematics and thought briefly of becoming a physician, but chose the law instead. He graduated Phi Beta Kappa from Harvard in 1929 and entered Harvard Law School, graduating in 1932. During his law school years, Blackmun

supported himself with a variety of odd jobs, including tutoring in math and driving the launch for the college crew team.

After law school, Blackmun returned to St. Paul, where he served for a year and a half as a law clerk to Judge John B. Sanborn, whom Blackmun was to succeed on the U.S. Circuit Court twenty-six years later. He left the clerkship in 1933 to enter private practice with a Minneapolis law firm, where he remained for sixteen years. During that time he also taught at the Mitchell College of Law in St. Paul, Chief Justice Burger's alma mater, and at the University of Minnesota Law School.

Blackmun married Dorothy E. Clark, June 21, 1941; the couple had three daughters.

In 1950 he accepted a post as "house counsel" for the world-famous Mayo Clinic in Rochester, Minnesota. There, Blackmun quickly developed a reputation among his colleagues as a serious man totally engrossed in his profession.

BLACKMUN'S reputation followed him to the bench of the Eighth Circuit Court of Appeals, to which he was appointed by President Dwight D. Eisenhower in 1959. As an appeals court judge, Blackmun became known for his scholarly and thorough opinions.

Blackmun's nomination to the Supreme Court was President Richard Nixon's third try to fill the seat vacated by Justice Abe Fortas's resignation. The Senate had refused to confirm Nixon's first two nominees—Clement F. Haynesworth Jr. of South Carolina and G. Harrold Carswell of Florida. Nixon remarked that he had concluded from the rejection of his first two nominees that the Senate "as it is presently constituted" would not confirm a southern nominee who was also a judicial conservative.

Nixon then turned to Blackmun, who was confirmed without opposition. During his first years on the Court, Blackmun was frequently linked with Burger as the "Minnesota Twins," who thought and voted alike, but, beginning with his authorship of the Court's 1973 ruling in *Roe v. Wade*, which legalized abortion, Blackmun moved in a steadily more liberal direction, leaving Burger behind in the Court's conservative wing.

Blackmun retired from the Court August 3, 1994. He died March 4, 1999.

SOURCE: Adapted from Joan Biskupic and Elder Witt, *Guide to the U.S. Supreme Court*, 3d ed. (Washington, D.C.: Congressional Quarterly, 1997), 952. Updated by the authors.

save as they required that an abortion be performed by a licensed physician within a limited time after conception.

That was the clear view of a majority of the seven who heard argument. My notes also indicate that the Chief had the opposed view, which made it puzzling as to why he made the assignment at all except that he indicated he might affirm on vagueness. My notes indicate that Byron was not firmly settled and that you might join the majority of four.

So I think we should meet what Bill Brennan calls the "core constitutional issue."

At the same time, Douglas and the others were ready to sign Blackmun's draft, believing that it represented the best they could do.

They were happier with Blackmun's effort in *Doe v. Bolton*, the Georgia abortion case, because it adopted much of Douglas's and Brennan's beliefs about the importance of privacy and women's rights. Where they thought Blackmun went astray was in exploring the state's interest in protecting life. In this version, he stressed the point that somewhere around quickening a woman's right to privacy is no longer "unlimited. It must be balanced against the state. We cannot automatically strike down . . . features of the Georgia statute simply because they restrict any right on the part of the woman to have an abortion at will." Despite the qualms Brennan and Douglas had over such a balancing approach, they planned to sign the opinion; it led Blackmun to the "right" result. Douglas went so far as to "congratulate" Blackmun on his "fine job" and expressed the hope that "we can agree to get the cases down this Term, so that we can spend our energies next Term on other matters."[9]

Just when it appeared that a five-person majority would coalesce around Blackmun's opinion, on May 31 Burger initiated efforts to have the case reargued. Ostensibly, his reason was that "These cases . . . are not as simple for me as they appear for the others." He also "complained that part of his problem . . . resulted from the poor quality of oral argument." Brennan, Douglas, Stewart, and Marshall disagreed. In their view, Burger pushed for reargument because he was displeased with Blackmun's opinion in *Doe* and thought his side would stand a better chance of victory next term when Powell and Rehnquist would participate in orals. Douglas later suggested that Burger believed the *Doe* opinion would prove embarrassing to President Nixon's reelection campaign and sought to minimize the damage. The same day Burger issued his memo, Blackmun also suggested that the cases be reargued. In a memo to conference, he wrote: "Although it would prove costly to me personally, in the light of energy and hours expended, I have now concluded, somewhat reluctantly, that reargument in both cases at an early date in the next term, would perhaps be advisable." Despite Brennan's and Douglas's attempts to thwart this action, after White and the two new appointees voted with Burger, on the last day of the 1971

term the Court ordered rearguments in both *Roe* and *Doe*.[10]

MR. JUSTICE BLACKMUN delivered the opinion of the Court.

We forthwith acknowledge our awareness of the sensitive and emotional nature of the abortion controversy, of the vigorous opposing views, even among physicians, and of the deep and seemingly absolute convictions that the subject inspires. One's philosophy, one's experiences, one's exposure to the raw edges of human existence, one's religious training, one's attitudes toward life and family and their values, and the moral standards one establishes and seeks to observe, are all likely to influence and to color one's thinking and conclusions about abortion.

In addition, population growth, pollution, poverty, and racial overtones tend to complicate and not to simplify the problem.

Our task, of course, is to resolve the issue by constitutional measurement, free of emotion and of predilection. We seek earnestly to do this, and, because we do, we have inquired into, and in this opinion place some emphasis upon, medical and medical-legal history and what that history reveals about man's attitudes toward the abortion procedure over the centuries. . . .

The principal thrust of appellant's attack on the Texas statutes is that they improperly invade a right, said to be possessed by the pregnant woman, to choose to terminate her pregnancy. Appellant would discover this right in the concept of personal "liberty" embodied in the Fourteenth Amendment's Due Process Clause in personal, marital, familial, and sexual privacy said to be protected by the Bill of Rights or its penumbras, see *Griswold v. Connecticut* (1965), or among those rights reserved to the people by the Ninth Amendment, *Griswold v. Connecticut*. . . .

It perhaps is not generally appreciated that the restrictive criminal abortion laws in effect in a majority of States

---

9. This memo was, in part, a response to Burger's (and Blackmun's) suggestion that the cases be reargued.

10. Both Brennan and Douglas wrote letters to Blackmun attempting to convince him that the cases should not be reargued. When they failed to convince Blackmun, Douglas warned Burger, saying, "If the vote of Conference is to reargue, then I will file a statement telling what is happening to us and the tragedy it entails." He also accused Burger, in a memo to conference, of trying "to bend the Court to his will" and imperiling "the integrity of the institution." Douglas never carried through on his threat to take the matter public, but the *Washington Post* carried a story about it.

today are of relatively recent vintage. Those laws, generally proscribing abortion or its attempt at any time during pregnancy except when necessary to preserve the pregnant woman's life, are not of ancient or even of common-law origin. Instead, they derive from statutory changes effected, for the most part, in the latter half of the 19th century. . . .

Three reasons have been advanced to explain historically the enactment of criminal abortion laws in the 19th century and to justify their continued existence.

It has been argued occasionally that these laws were the product of a Victorian social concern to discourage illicit sexual conduct. Texas, however, does not advance this justification in the present case, and it appears that no court or commentator has taken the argument seriously. . . .

A second reason is concerned with abortion as a medical procedure. When most criminal abortion laws were first enacted, the procedure was a hazardous one for the woman. This was particularly true prior to the development of antisepsis. . . . Thus, it has been argued that a State's real concern in enacting a criminal abortion law was to protect the pregnant woman, that is, to restrain her from submitting to a procedure that placed her life in serious jeopardy.

The modern medical techniques have altered this situation. . . . Consequently, any interest of the State in protecting the woman from an inherently hazardous procedure, except when it would be equally dangerous for her to forgo it, has largely disappeared. Of course, important state interests in the areas of health and medical standards do remain. The State has a legitimate interest in seeing to it that abortion, like any other medical procedure, is performed under circumstances that insure maximum safety for the patient. . . . Moreover, the risk to the woman increases as her pregnancy continues. Thus, the State retains a definite interest in protecting the woman's own health and safety when an abortion is proposed at a late stage of pregnancy.

The third reason is the State's interest—some phrase it in terms of duty—in protecting prenatal life. Some of the argument for this justification rests on the theory that a new human life is present from the moment of conception. The State's interest and general obligation to protect life then extends, it is argued, to prenatal life. Only when the life of the pregnant mother herself is at stake, balanced against the life she carries within her, should the interest of the embryo or fetus not prevail. Logically, of course, a legitimate state interest in this area need not stand or fall on acceptance of the belief that life begins at conception or at some other point prior to live birth. In assessing the State's interest, recognition may be given to the less rigid claim that as long as at least *potential* life is involved, the State may assert interests beyond the protection of the pregnant woman alone. . . .

It is with these interests, and the weight to be attached to them, that this case is concerned.

The Constitution does not explicitly mention any right of privacy. In a line of decisions, however, the Court has recognized that a right of personal privacy, or a guarantee of certain areas or zones of privacy, does exist under the Constitution. In varying contexts, the Court or individual Justices have, indeed, found at least the roots of that right in the First Amendment, in the Fourth and Fifth Amendments, in the penumbras of the Bill of Rights, in the Ninth Amendment, or in the concept of liberty guaranteed by the first section of the Fourteenth Amendment. These decisions make it clear that only personal rights that can be deemed "fundamental" or "implicit in the concept of ordered liberty" are included in this guarantee of personal privacy. They also make it clear that the right has some extension to activities relating to marriage, procreation, family relationships, and child rearing and education.

This right of privacy, whether it be founded in the Fourteenth Amendment's concept of personal liberty and restrictions upon state action, as we feel it is, or, as the District Court determined, in the Ninth Amendment's reservation of rights to the people, is broad enough to encompass a woman's decision whether or not to terminate her pregnancy. The detriment that the State would impose upon the pregnant woman by denying this choice altogether is apparent. Specific and direct harm medically diagnosable even in early pregnancy may be involved. Maternity, or additional offspring, may force upon the woman a distressful life and future. Psychological harm may be imminent. Mental and physical health may be taxed by child care. There is also the distress, for all concerned, associated with the unwanted child, and there is the problem of bringing a child into a family already unable, psychologically and otherwise, to care for it. In other cases, as in this one, the additional difficulties and continuing stigma of unwed motherhood may be involved. All these are factors the woman and her responsible physician necessarily will consider in consultation.

On the basis of elements such as these, appellant and

some *amici* argue that the woman's right is absolute and that she is entitled to terminate her pregnancy at whatever time, in whatever way, and for whatever reason she alone chooses. With this we do not agree. Appellant's arguments that Texas either has no valid interest at all in regulating the abortion decision, or no interest strong enough to support any limitation upon the woman's sole determination, are unpersuasive. The Court's decisions recognizing a right of privacy also acknowledge that some state regulation in areas protected by that right is appropriate. As noted above, a State may properly assert important interests in safeguarding health, in maintaining medical standards, and in protecting potential life. At some point in pregnancy, these respective interests become sufficiently compelling to sustain regulation of the factors that govern the abortion decision. The privacy right involved, therefore, cannot be said to be absolute. . . .

We, therefore, conclude that the right of personal privacy includes the abortion decision, but that this right is not unqualified and must be considered against important state interests in regulation. . . .

The District Court held that the appellee failed to meet his burden of demonstrating that the Texas statute's infringement upon Roe's rights was necessary to support a compelling state interest, and that, although the appellee presented "several compelling justifications for state presence in the area of abortions," the statutes outstripped these justifications and swept "far beyond any areas of compelling state interest." Appellant and appellee both contest that holding. Appellant, as has been indicated, claims an absolute right that bars any state imposition of criminal penalties in the area. Appellee argues that the State's determination to recognize and protect prenatal life from and after conception constitutes a compelling state interest. As noted above, we do not agree fully with either formulation.

A. The appellee and certain *amici* argue that the fetus is a "person" within the language and meaning of the Fourteenth Amendment. . . .

The Constitution does not define "person" in so many words. Section 1 of the Fourteenth Amendment contains three references to "person." The first, in defining "citizens," speaks of "persons born or naturalized in the United States." The word also appears both in the Due Process Clause and in the Equal Protection Clause. "Person" is used in other places in the Constitution: in the listing of qualifi-

cations for Representatives and Senators, Art. I, §2, cl. 2, and §3, cl. 3; in the Apportionment Clause, Art. I, §2, §3. . . . But in nearly all these instances, the use of the word is such that it has application only postnatally. None indicates, with any assurance, that it has any possible prenatal application.

All this, together with our observation that throughout the major portion of the 19th century prevailing legal abortion practices were far freer than they are today, persuades us that the word "person," as used in the Fourteenth Amendment, does not include the unborn. . . .

This conclusion, however, does not of itself fully answer the contentions raised by Texas, and we pass on to other considerations.

B. The pregnant woman cannot be isolated in her privacy. She carries an embryo and, later, a fetus, if one accepts the medical definitions of the developing young in the human uterus. The situation therefore is inherently different from marital intimacy, or bedroom possession of obscene material, or marriage, or procreation. . . . As we have intimated above, it is reasonable and appropriate for a State to decide that at some point in time another interest, that of health of the mother or that of potential human life, becomes significantly involved. The woman's privacy is no longer sole and any right of privacy she possesses must be measured accordingly.

Texas urges that, apart from the Fourteenth Amendment, life begins at conception and is present throughout pregnancy, and that, therefore, the State has a compelling interest in protecting that life from and after conception. We need not resolve the difficult question of when life begins. When those trained in the respective disciplines of medicine, philosophy, and theology are unable to arrive at any consensus, the judiciary, at this point in the development of man's knowledge, is not in a position to speculate as to the answer. . . .

In view of all this, we do not agree that, by adopting one theory of life, Texas may override the rights of the pregnant woman that are at stake. We repeat, however, that the State does have an important and legitimate interest in preserving and protecting the health of the pregnant woman, whether she be a resident of the State or a non-resident who seeks medical consultation and treatment there, and that it has still another important and legitimate interest in protecting the potentiality of human life. These interests are separate and distinct. Each grows in substantiality as the woman approaches term and, at a point during pregnancy, each becomes "compelling."

With respect to the State's important and legitimate interest in the health of the mother, the "compelling" point, in the light of present medical knowledge, is at approximately the end of the first trimester. This is so because of the now-established medical fact . . . that until the end of the first trimester mortality in abortion may be less than mortality in normal childbirth. It follows that, from and after this point, a State may regulate the abortion procedure to the extent that the regulation reasonably relates to the preservation and protection of maternal health. Examples of permissible state regulation in this area are requirements as to the qualifications of the person who is to perform the abortion; as to the licensure of that person; as to the facility in which the procedure is to be performed, that is, whether it must be a hospital or may be a clinic or some other place of less-than-hospital status; as to the licensing of the facility; and the like.

This means, on the other hand, that, for the period of pregnancy prior to this "compelling" point, the attending physician, in consultation with his patient, is free to determine, without regulation by the State, that, in his medical judgment, the patient's pregnancy should be terminated. If that decision is reached, the judgment may be effectuated by an abortion free of interference by the State.

With respect to the State's important and legitimate interest in potential life, the "compelling" point is at viability. This is so because the fetus then presumably has the capability of meaningful life outside the mother's womb. State regulation protective of fetal life after viability thus has both logical and biological justifications. If the State is interested in protecting fetal life after viability, it may go so far as to proscribe abortion during that period, except when it is necessary to preserve the life or health of the mother.

Measured against these standards, . . . the Texas [law] . . . , in restricting legal abortions to those "procured or attempted by medical advice for the purpose of saving the life of the mother," sweeps too broadly. The statute makes no distinction between abortions performed early in pregnancy and those performed later, and it limits to a single reason, "saving" the mother's life, the legal justification for the procedure. The statute, therefore, cannot survive the constitutional attack made upon it here. . . .

To summarize and to repeat:

1. A state criminal abortion statute of the current Texas type, that excepts from criminality only a *life-saving* procedure on behalf of the mother, without regard to pregnancy stage and without recognition of the other interests involved, is violative of the Due Process Clause of the Fourteenth Amendment.

(a) For the stage prior to approximately the end of the first trimester, the abortion decision and its effectuation must be left to the medical judgment of the pregnant woman's attending physician.

(b) For the stage subsequent to approximately the end of the first trimester, the State, in promoting its interest in the health of the mother, may, if it chooses, regulate the abortion procedure in ways that are reasonably related to maternal health.

(c) For the stage subsequent to viability, the State in promoting its interest in the potentiality of human life may, if it chooses, regulate, and even proscribe, abortion except where it is necessary, in appropriate medical judgment, for the preservation of the life or health of the mother. . . .

This holding, we feel, is consistent with the relative weights of the respective interests involved, with the lessons and examples of medical and legal history, with the lenity of the common law, and with the demands of the profound problems of the present day. The decision leaves the State free to place increasing restrictions on abortion as the period of pregnancy lengthens, so long as those restrictions are tailored to the recognized state interests. The decision vindicates the right of the physician to administer medical treatment according to his professional judgment up to the points where important state interests provide compelling justifications for intervention. Up to those points, the abortion decision in all its aspects is inherently, and primarily, a medical decision, and basic responsibility for it must rest with the physician. If an individual practitioner abuses the privilege of exercising proper medical judgment, the usual remedies, judicial and intra-professional, are available.[11]

Affirmed in part and reversed in part.

11. [Authors' note.] In *Doe*, decided the same day as *Roe*, the Court reviewed a challenge to the newer abortion laws, enacted by some states in the 1960s. While Texas permitted abortions only to save a mother's life, Georgia allowed them under the following circumstances: (1) when a "duly licensed Georgia physician" determines in "his best clinical judgment" that carrying the baby to term would injure the mother's life or health; (2) when a high likelihood existed that the fetus would be born with a serious defor-

MR. JUSTICE REHNQUIST, dissenting.

The Court's opinion brings to the decision of this troubling question both extensive historical fact and a wealth of legal scholarship. While the opinion thus commands my respect, I find myself nonetheless in fundamental disagreement with those parts of it that invalidate the Texas statute in question, and therefore dissent. . . .

. . . I have difficulty in concluding, as the Court does, that the right of "privacy" is involved in this case. Texas, by the statute here challenged, bars the performance of a medical abortion by a licensed physician on a plaintiff such as Roe. A transaction resulting in an operation such as this is not "private" in the ordinary usage of that word. Nor is the "privacy" that the Court finds here even a distant relative of the freedom from searches and seizures protected by the Fourth Amendment to the Constitution, which the Court has referred to as embodying a right to privacy. *Katz v. United States* (1967).

If the Court means by the term "privacy" no more than that the claim of a person to be free from unwanted state regulation of consensual transactions may be a form of "liberty" protected by the Fourteenth Amendment, there is no doubt that similar claims have been upheld in our earlier decisions on the basis of that liberty. I agree . . . that the "liberty," against deprivation of which without due process the Fourteenth Amendment protects, embraces more than the rights found in the Bill of Rights. But that liberty is not guaranteed absolutely against deprivation, only against deprivation without due process of law. The test traditionally applied in the area of social and economic legislation is whether or not a law such as that challenged has a rational relation to a valid state objective. . . . The Due Process Clause of the Fourteenth Amendment undoubtedly does place a limit, albeit a broad one, on legislative power to enact laws such as this. If the Texas statute were to prohibit an abortion even where the mother's life is in jeopardy, I have little doubt that such a statute would lack a rational relation to a valid state objective. . . . But the Court's sweeping invalidation of any restrictions on abortion during the first trimester is impossible to justify under that standard, and the conscious weighing of competing factors that the Court's opinion apparently substitutes for the established test is far more appropriate to a legislative judgment than to a judicial one.

The Court eschews the history of the Fourteenth Amendment in its reliance on the "compelling state interest" test. . . . But the Court adds a new wrinkle to this test by transposing it from the legal considerations associated with the Equal Protection Clause of the Fourteenth Amendment to this case arising under the Due Process Clause of the Fourteenth Amendment. Unless I misapprehend the consequences of this transplanting of the "compelling state interest test," the Court's opinion will accomplish the seemingly impossible feat of leaving this area of the law more confused than it found it.

While the Court's opinion quotes from the dissent of Mr. Justice Holmes in *Lochner v. New York* (1905), the result it reaches is more closely attuned to the majority opinion . . . in that case. As in *Lochner* and similar cases applying substantive due process standards to economic and social welfare legislation, the adoption of the compelling state interest standard will inevitably require this Court to examine the legislative policies and pass on the wisdom of these policies in the very process of deciding whether a particular state interest put forward may or may not be "compelling." The decision here to break pregnancy into three distinct terms and to outline the permissible restrictions the State may impose in each one, for example, partakes more of judicial legislation than it does of a determination of the intent of the drafters of the Fourteenth Amendment.

The fact that a majority of the States reflecting, after all, the majority sentiment in those States, have had restrictions on abortions for at least a century is a strong indication, it seems to me, that the asserted right to an abortion is not "so rooted in the traditions and conscience of our people as to be ranked as fundamental.". . . Even today, when society's views on abortion are changing, the very existence of the debate is evidence that the "right" to an abortion is not so universally accepted as the appellant would have us believe.

To reach its result, the Court necessarily has had to find within the scope of the Fourteenth Amendment a right that was apparently completely unknown to the drafters of the Amendment. As early as 1821, the first state law dealing di-

---

mity; and (3) when the pregnancy was the result of rape. The law contained other requirements, the most stringent of which was that two other doctors agree with the judgment of the one performing the abortion. Reiterating his opinion in *Roe*, Blackmun struck down the Georgia law as a violation of Fourteenth Amendment guarantees. Once again, six other members of the Court agreed with his conclusion.

rectly with abortion was enacted by the Connecticut Legislature. By the time of the adoption of the Fourteenth Amendment in 1868, there were at least 36 laws enacted by state or territorial legislatures limiting abortion. While many States have amended or updated their laws, 21 of the laws on the books in 1868 remain in effect today. Indeed, the Texas statute struck down today was, as the majority notes, first enacted in 1857 and "has remained substantially unchanged to the present time."

There apparently was no question concerning the validity of this provision or of any of the other state statutes when the Fourteenth Amendment was adopted. The only conclusion possible from this history is that the drafters did not intend to have the Fourteenth Amendment withdraw from the States the power to legislate with respect to this matter. . . .

For all of the foregoing reasons, I respectfully dissent.

MR. JUSTICE WHITE, with whom MR. JUSTICE REHNQUIST joins, dissenting.

The Court for the most part sustains this position: During the period prior to the time the fetus becomes viable, the Constitution of the United States values the convenience, whim, or caprice of the putative mother more than the life or potential life of the fetus; the Constitution, therefore, guarantees the right to an abortion as against any state law or policy seeking to protect the fetus from an abortion not prompted by more compelling reasons of the mother.

With all due respect, I dissent. I find nothing in the language or history of the Constitution to support the Court's judgment. The Court simply fashions and announces a new constitutional right for pregnant women and, with scarcely any reason or authority for its action, invests that right with sufficient substance to override most existing state abortion statutes. The upshot is that the people and the legislatures of the 50 States are constitutionally disentitled to weigh the relative importance of the continued existence and development of the fetus, on the one hand, against a spectrum of possible impacts on the mother, on the other hand. As an exercise of raw judicial power, the Court perhaps has authority to do what it does today; but in my view its judgment is an improvident and extravagant exercise of the power of judicial review that the Constitution extends to this Court.

The Court apparently values the convenience of the pregnant mother more than the continued existence and development of the life or potential life that she carries. Whether or not I might agree with that marshaling of values, I can in no event join the Court's judgment because I find no constitutional warrant for imposing such an order of priorities on the people and legislatures of the States. In a sensitive area such as this, involving as it does issues over which reasonable men may easily and heatedly differ, I cannot accept the Court's exercise of its clear power of choice by interposing a constitutional barrier to state efforts to protect human life and by investing mothers and doctors with the constitutionally protected right to exterminate it. This issue, for the most part, should be left with the people and to the political processes the people have devised to govern their affairs.

Chief Justice Burger had initiated the campaign to have *Roe* and *Doe* reargued in part because he believed that the new Nixon appointees would strengthen the pro-life side. This assumption, as we now know, turned out to be only half right. Justice Rehnquist dissented, but Justice Powell placed his feet firmly in the pro-choice camp. Moreover, the second time around, Justice Blackmun wrote an opinion that was far broader than his original draft.

Indeed, Blackmun's decisions in *Roe* and *Doe* were a *tour de force* on the subject of abortion. They provided a comprehensive history of government regulation of abortion and reviewed in some detail arguments for and against the procedure.[12] Most important was his conclusion: the right to privacy "is broad enough to encompass a woman's decision whether or not to terminate a pregnancy." Behind this assertion are several ideas. First, the Court, while not rejecting a Ninth Amendment theory of privacy, preferred to locate the right in the Fourteenth Amendment's Due Process Clause, an approach suggested by Justices Harlan and White in their concurring opinions in *Griswold* (see Table 9-1). Second, the Court found the abortion right fundamental and, therefore, would use a compelling state interest test to assess the

12. We omit the long history in our excerpt. For the full version, navigate to: *laws.findlaw.com/US/410/113.html.*

TABLE 9-2 The *Roe v. Wade* Trimester Framework

Stage of Pregnancy	Degree of Permissible State Regulation of the Decision to Terminate Pregnancy
Prior to the end of the first trimester (approximately months 1–3)	Almost none: "the abortion and its effectuation must be left to [the woman and] the medical judgment of the pregnant woman's attending physician."
The end of the first trimester through "viability" (approximately months 4–6)	Some: "the state, in promoting its interest in the health of the mother, may, if it chooses, regulate the abortion procedure in ways that are reasonably related to maternal health." But it may not prohibit abortions.
Subsequent to viability (approximately months 7–9)	High: "the state, in promoting its interest in the potentiality of human life, may, if it chooses, regulate, and even proscribe, abortion except where necessary, in appropriate medical judgment, for the preservation of the life or health of the mother."

constitutionality of restrictions on that right—but with something of a twist. For the reasons Blackmun gave in his opinion, the state's interests in protecting the woman's health and in protecting the "potentiality of human life" grow "in substantiality as the woman approaches term and, at a point during pregnancy . . . become compelling." This point led the majority to adopt the trimester scheme *(see Table 9-2)*. Under this scheme, the state's compelling interest arises at the point of viability. It may, however, regulate second trimester abortions in ways that "are reasonably related to the mother's health."

In their dissents, Justices White and Rehnquist lambasted the trimester scheme, as well as almost every other aspect of the opinion. They thought it relied on "raw judicial power" to reach an "extravagant" and "improvident" decision. Rehnquist found that the Court's use of a compelling state interest test to assess statutes under the Fourteenth Amendment's Due Process Clause represented a return to the discredited doctrine of substantive due process as expressed in *Lochner v. New York*, a complaint that echoed Black's dissent in *Griswold*. Rehnquist would have preferred that the Court adopt a "rational basis" approach to the abortion right as it had to regulations challenged on due process grounds after the fall of substantive due process. Under this approach, the Court would

have to decide only whether the government had acted reasonably to achieve a legitimate government objective. Using a rational basis approach, as you can imagine, the Court generally defers to the government and presumes the validity of the government's action. Had the Court adopted this approach to the abortion right, it would have upheld the Texas and Georgia restrictions. White, joined by Rehnquist, thought the Court had gone well beyond the scope of its powers and of the text and history of the Constitution to generate a policy statement that smacked of judicial activism. To White, it was up to the people and their elected officials to determine the fate of abortion, not the Court.

As Blackmun's opinion was nearly two years in the making, the other justices knew that, if nothing else, it would be a comprehensive statement. Outsiders, however, were shocked; few expected such an opinion from a Nixon appointee. But Blackmun's opinion was not the only surprise; Burger's decision to go along with the majority also startled many observers. Moreover, White and Stewart cast rather puzzling votes given their opinions in *Griswold*. Stewart had dissented in *Griswold*, asserting that the Constitution did not guarantee a general right to privacy. If he believed that, how could he agree to the creation of the right to obtain legal abortions, a right that rested on privacy? White, on the other hand, had been in the majority in *Griswold*. But, for him, apparently the right to privacy was not broad enough to cover abortion.

The factors that explain the justices' position in *Roe* and *Doe* are matters of speculation, for, as Justice Blackmun once noted, it is always hard to predict how a new justice will come down on the abortion issue. What is not a matter of speculation is that the responses to *Roe*—both positive and negative—were (and still are) among the strongest in the Court's history.

Reaction came from all quarters of American life. Some legal scholars applauded the *Roe* opinion, asserting that it indicated the Court's sensitivity to changing times. Others ripped it to shreds. They called the trimester scheme unworkable and said that, as medical technology advanced, viability would come earlier in pregnancy. Others attacked the decision's use of the Fourteenth Amendment, agreeing with Justice Rehnquist that it was a retreat to pre–New Deal days. Still others claimed it usurped the intention of *Griswold*. Legal scholar John Hart Ely wrote that a right to privacy against "governmental snooping" is legitimate, but a general freedom of "autonomy"—"to live one's life without governmental interference"—goes beyond the scope of *Griswold*.[13]

Roe also divided the political community. Some legislators were relieved that the Court, and not they, had handled a political hot potato. Others were outraged on moral grounds (believing that abortion is murder) and on constitutional grounds (this is a matter of public policy for legislators, not judges, to determine).

As Figure 9-2 shows, the public was split over its support for the Court's ruling. But divisions over the abortion right did not come about as a result of *Roe*. Since the first public opinion polls taken on abortion in the 1960s, citizens have been of many different minds on the subject. For example, today more than 80 percent of Americans believe that a pregnant woman should be able to obtain an abortion if the woman's own health is seriously endangered by the pregnancy, while only 40 percent say that a woman should be able to terminate a pregnancy because she "is not married and does not want to marry the man." In the final analysis, all *Roe* did, as political sci-

FIGURE 9-2 Percentage of Respondents Supporting *Roe v. Wade*, 1974–1993

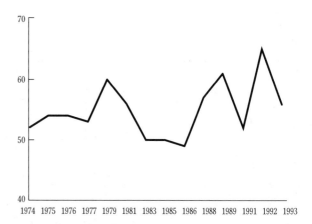

SOURCE: Lee Epstein, Jeffrey A. Segal, Harold J. Spaeth, and Thomas G. Walker, *The Supreme Court Compendium: Data, Decisions, and Developments*, 2d ed. (Washington, D.C.: Congressional Quarterly, 1996), Table 8-19.

NOTE: Since the decision in *Planned Parenthood of Southeastern Pennsylvania v. Casey* (1992), very few polls ask about support for *Roe*. Indeed, for many years now most surveys have framed questions in terms of whether the respondent supports abortion under particular circumstances, for example, if the woman "is not married and does not want to marry the man."

entists Charles Franklin and Liane Kosaki show, was to intensify basic divisions over abortion: if one was pro-choice before the decision, one became even more so; the same held true for those favoring the pro-life side.[14]

Although *Roe* may not have changed public opinion on abortion, it had the important effect of mobilizing the pro-life movement. Before 1973 groups opposed to legalized abortion had lobbied successfully against efforts to liberalize state laws. When *Roe* nullified these legislative victories, these groups vowed to see the decision overturned; in short, *Roe* and *Doe* fanned the fire, rather than quenched it. As for Norma McCorvey, whose unwanted pregnancy started the conflict, she has changed her mind about abortion (*see Box 9-2*).

The Aftermath of Roe: *Attempts to Limit the Decision*

Pro-life groups are dedicated to the eradication of *Roe v. Wade*, a goal that they can best accomplish in one of two ways: they can persuade Congress to propose an

13. John Hart Ely, "The Wages of Crying Wolf: A Comment on *Roe v. Wade*," *Yale Law Journal* 82 (1973): 920.

14. Charles H. Franklin and Liane C. Kosaki, "The Republican Schoolmaster: The Supreme Court, Public Opinion, and Abortion," *American Political Science Review* 83 (1989): 751–772.

BOX 9-2   AFTERMATH . . . NORMA MCCORVEY

THE LIFE OF NORMA MCCOR-VEY, the pregnant carnival worker who, as Jane Roe, challenged Texas' abortion laws in the Supreme Court, took several interesting turns after *Roe v. Wade* was handed down.

At first, McCorvey's personal life was relatively untouched by the decision. She did not have an abortion, but gave her baby up for adoption. She remained anonymous, continuing to lead a life that included poverty, homelessness, drug and alcohol addiction, petty crimes, and attempted suicide. Then, in the 1980s McCorvey went public and announced that she was the real "Jane Roe." She also confessed that she had lied at the time of her case when she claimed that her pregnancy was the result of rape.

McCorvey worked for several years in Dallas abortion clinics, using her wages to help support her drug habit. She also dabbled in New Age religions and the occult and entered a romantic relationship with a store clerk who had caught her shoplifting.

In 1995 Operation Rescue, the Christian-based anti-abortion activist group, moved its headquarters to Dallas, taking office space next door to the abortion clinic where McCorvey worked. Rev. Philip "Flip" Benham, an Operation Rescue leader, and other members of the group befriended McCorvey. Subsequently, she underwent a religious conversion, became an evangelical Christian, and joined Benham's

Norma McCorvey stands with nine-year-old Meredith Champion at an Operation Rescue rally in downtown Dallas in January 1997. McCorvey, the real "Jane Roe" of *Roe v. Wade* (1973), is now pro-life and works with the anti-abortion group.

nondenominational Hillcrest Church. Her 1995 baptism in a backyard swimming pool was nationally televised. McCorvey left the abortion clinic and began working for Operation Rescue, proclaiming, "I don't have to go to the death camps anymore, to earn six bucks an hour." McCorvey also founded an organization, Roe No More Ministry, that provides information to anti-abortion groups. She experienced a second religious conversion in 1998 when she became a Roman Catholic. In 2000 McCorvey signed her name to a lawsuit asking the federal courts to declare that women seeking abortions have the right to be told that they are carrying a human being and to be shown a sonogram of the fetus.

Looking back at her participation in *Roe v. Wade*, McCorvey now says that she feels exploited by the pro-choice movement. She claims she met her lawyers in the case only twice, the first time over pizza and beer, and that she did not even know what the word "abortion" meant. "All I simply did was sign," she says. "I never appeared in any court. I never testified in front of any jury or judge."

SOURCES: *St. Louis Post Dispatch*, June 12, 1998; *Chicago Sun-Times*, July 27, 1998; *Boston Globe*, October 19, 1998; *Omaha World-Herald*, October 29 and 30, 1998; *Los Angeles Times*, December 8, 1999; *Houston Chronicle*, January 13, 2000; and *Independent* (London), March 16, 2000.

amendment to the Constitution or persuade the Court to overrule its decision. In the immediate aftermath of *Roe*, neither of these options was viable. Despite the public's mixed view of abortion, during the 1970s only about one-third of Americans supported a constitutional amendment to proscribe it. The lack of support may explain why Congress, ever cognizant of the polls, did not pass any of the "human life" amendments it considered in the

1970s. And, given the 7–2 vote in *Roe*, wholesale changes in the Court's membership would be required before the Court would reconsider its stance on abortion.

Faced with this situation, pro-life groups determined that their best course of action was to seek limitations on the ways in which women could obtain and pay for abortions. They lobbied legislatures to enact restrictions on the right to an abortion. Two types of restrictions predominated—those that required consent of a woman's parents or husband and those that limited government funding for abortion services. These efforts were quite successful. During the 1970s, eighteen states required some form of consent, and thirty (along with the federal government) restricted funding. To put it another way, by 1978 only about fifteen states had not enacted laws requiring consent or restricting funding.

Consent. As pro-life forces persuaded states to enact these laws, pro-choice forces just as quickly challenged them in court. The first major post-*Roe* battle, *Planned Parenthood v. Danforth* (1976), involved consent, a subject the Court had not considered in *Roe*. The state of Missouri had passed legislation that required the written consent of a pregnant woman and her spouse or, for an unmarried minor, her parents, before an abortion could be performed.

While the Court found no constitutional violation in requiring a woman to give her own consent to the procedure, it struck down spousal and parental consent provisions as violative of the Constitution and inconsistent with *Roe*. However, Justice Blackmun's majority opinion gave the pro-life movement a little hope. It struck down Missouri's parental consent requirement, but it also stated: "We emphasize that our holding that parental consent is invalid does not suggest that every minor, regardless of age or maturity, may give effective consent for the termination of her pregnancy." With these words, Blackmun opened the door to the possibility of some form of required parental consent.

As illustrated in Table 9-3, pro-life forces took advantage of Blackmun's statement, persuading states to enact various parental and other consent requirements, many of which were tested by the Court. And, although the Court has continued to strike down laws forcing a woman to obtain the consent of or to notify her spouse/partner prior to obtaining an abortion, as shown in the table, it has generally allowed states to require parental consent or notification, especially if the law allowed a minor to bypass the parent and instead to seek the consent of a judge.

Funding. Consent laws were not the only way pro-life forces sought to restrict the abortion right in the wake of

Roe. They also sought to persuade states and the federal government to restrict government funding for abortions.[15] To pro-life organizations, this type of restriction was another step toward the eradication of *Roe*. Funding was inextricably bound to implementation: if women could not afford abortions and the government did not pay for them, then either doctors would not perform them or women would be deterred from having them. Pro-choice groups viewed these laws as backdoor attempts to gut *Roe*. From their perspective, *Roe* was a victory not just for doctors or even middle-class women, but for those women who could not afford to travel to other countries or states to obtain abortions. Logically, they assumed, once the Court established the right to choose, governments had an obligation to protect that right, even if meant funding for the poor through government health insurance programs.

Few governments, however, shared this pro-choice vision, at least in the immediate aftermath of *Roe*. In September 1976, after several years of prodding by pro-life forces, Congress passed the Hyde Amendment (named after its sponsor, Rep. Henry Hyde, R-Ill.). In its original form, it stated that no federal funds "shall be used to perform abortions except where the life of the mother would be endangered if the fetus were carried to full term." In 1977 and 1978 Congress altered the language to expand the circumstances under which funding could be obtained. Even so, under the Hyde Amendment federal funds paid for only about 10 percent of all abortion services for women.[16] Following the lead of the federal government, more than half the states passed legislation restricting the use of Medicaid funds for abortion procedures. The states were particularly easy targets for pro-life groups: all these organizations needed to do was to point out that funding limits constituted fiscally prudent measures. Before the limitations went into effect, 25 percent of all abortions were funded by state monies.

In response to these pro-life legislative victories, pro-

15. Material in the next two paragraphs draws heavily on Epstein and Kobylka, *The Supreme Court and Legal Change*, 220–221.

16. At one point, the Hyde Amendment provided Medicaid funding if two doctors certified that carrying a pregnancy to full term would result in "severe and long lasting physical health damages" or the pregnancy was the result of incest or rape.

TABLE 9-3 Cases Involving Consent to Abortions, 1976–present

Case	Consent Provision at Issue	Court Holding
Planned Parenthood v. Danforth (1976)	Written consent required of the (1) pregnant woman, (2) her spouse, or (3) her parents.	The Court struck spousal and parental requirements. It upheld the provision requiring the woman's consent.
Bellotti v. Baird II (1979)	Parental consent required prior to abortions performed on unmarried women under eighteen. If one or both parents refuse, the "abortion may be obtained by order of a judge . . . for good cause shown."	The Court struck the law, but claimed that it was not "persuaded as a general rule" that parental consent "unconstitutionally burdens a minor's right to seek an abortion."
H. L. v. Matheson (1981)	Doctors should "notify, if possible" a minor's parents prior to performing an abortion.	The Court upheld the law on the ground that "the Constitution does not compel a state to fine-tune its statutes as to encourage or facilitate abortions."
Akron v. Akron Center for Reproductive Health (1983)	Parental notification and consent required prior to abortions performed on unmarried minors under fifteen. Doctors must make "certain specified statements" to ensure that consent for all those seeking abortions is "truly informed." Requires a twenty-four-hour waiting period "between the time a woman signs a consent form and the time the abortion is performed."	The Court invalidated all three provisions.
Planned Parenthood v. Ashcroft (1983)	Parental or judicial consent required prior to abortions performed on unmarried minors.	The Court upheld the provision, asserting that judges may give their consent to abortions.
Hodgson v. Minnesota (1990)	Requirement that both parents be notified prior to the performance of an abortion (unless a court orders otherwise). Abortions cannot be performed on minors until forty-eight hours after both parents have been notified.	The Court upheld the two-parent requirement with an exemption option. It upheld the forty-eight-hour waiting period.
Ohio v. Akron Center for Reproductive Health (1990)	Requirement that one parent be notified prior to the performance of an abortion on an unmarried, unemancipated minor (unless a court authorizes it).	The Court upheld the law.
Planned Parenthood of Southeastern Pennsylvania v. Casey (1992)	Required three kinds of consent: (1) informed consent of the woman; (2) statement from woman indicating that she has notified her spouse; and (3) in the case of minors, informed consent of one parent.	The Court upheld informed consent, struck spousal notifications, and upheld parental consent.

TABLE 9-4 Cases Involving Funding Restrictions for Abortions

Case	Funding Restriction at Issue	Court Holding
Beal v. Doe (1977)	Pennsylvania law limiting Medicaid funding "to those abortions that are certified by physicians as medically necessary."	The Court upheld the restriction against constitutional claims that the law interfered with the fundamental right to obtain an abortion as articulated in *Roe* and that it discriminated on the basis of socioeconomic status and against those choosing abortion over childbirth.
Maher v. Roe (1977)	Connecticut Welfare Department regulation limiting state Medicaid "benefits for first trimester abortions ... that are 'medically necessary.'"	The Court upheld the restriction against various constitutional claims (see above).
Poelker v. Doe (1977)	St. Louis policy directive that barred city-owned hospitals from performing abortions.	The Court upheld the restriction against various constitutional claims (see above).
Harris v. McCrae (1980)	Federal government regulation (the Hyde Amendment) limiting Medicaid funding of abortions to those "where the life of the mother would be endangered if the fetus were carried to term."	The Court upheld the restrictions against claims that the law violated due process (impinges on a fundamental right), equal protection (discriminates against women, especially poor women), and First Amendment (burdens religious exercise and constitutes religious establishment) guarantees.

choice groups challenged the funding laws as violations of the fundamental right to obtain an abortion, as articulated in *Roe*. The courts again became battlefields, and the Supreme Court reentered the fray in 1977. As Table 9-4 shows, the Court decided three cases that year, *Maher v. Roe*, *Beal v. Doe*, and *Poelker v. Doe*—all of which involved state or local restrictions on abortion funding. The Court upheld all of these various restrictions. In the eyes of the justices, the regulations did not infringe significantly on abortion rights and, as Justice Powell wrote in *Maher*, "The State unquestionably has 'a strong and legitimate interest in encouraging normal childbirth.'" In short, the justices found that there is a right to abortion, but states have no obligation to fund it. It is worth emphasizing that these rulings did not prohibit states from funding abortions; rather, they held that, because the Constitution does not mandate such funding, states could enact restrictions.

As Table 9-4 indicates, pro-choice groups also failed in their challenge to the Hyde Amendment. Immediately

after the amendment was passed, a coalition of pro-choice advocates, including the ACLU and Planned Parenthood challenged its constitutionality. In bringing *Harris v. McCrae* (1980) they marshaled an array of legal arguments and sociological evidence suggesting that poor women might resort to self-abortion or other unsafe procedures if the Hyde Amendment remained law. In a 5–4 decision the Court rejected their arguments, asserting that it "cannot overturn duly enacted statutes simply because they may be unwise, improvident or out of harmony with a particular school of thought." More important, however, was its legal rationale:

[R]egardless of whether the freedom of a woman to choose to terminate her pregnancy for health reasons lies at the core or the periphery of the due process liberty recognized in [*Roe v.*] *Wade*, it simply does not follow that a woman's freedom of choice carries with it a constitutional entitlement to the financial resources to avail herself of the full range of protected choices. . . . [A]lthough government may not place obstacles in the path of a woman's exercise of her freedom of choice, it need not remove those not of its own creation. Indigency falls in the latter category.

Justice Marshall, a dissenter in the case along with Justice Blackmun, *Roe*'s author, summarized accurately the greatest fears of the pro-choice movement when he wrote:

The denial of Medicaid benefits to individuals who meet all the statutory criteria for eligibility, solely because the treatment that is medically necessary involves the exercise of the fundamental right to choose abortion, is a form of discrimination repugnant to the equal protection of the laws guaranteed by the Constitution. The Court's decision today marks a retreat from *Roe v. Wade* and represents a cruel blow to the most powerless members of our society.

Attempts to Overrule Roe: Akron, Webster, *and* Casey

As the nation entered the 1980s, pro-life forces had reason to feel optimistic. First they had achieved considerable success in the funding decisions. Second, the 1980 elections placed Ronald Reagan, the first presidential contender ever to support, unequivocally, the goals of the pro-life movement, into the White House. It was almost assured that Reagan's judicial appointees would be proponents of the pro-life position. And third, personnel changes on the Supreme Court, damaging to the pro-choice position, had already taken place. John Paul Stevens replaced William O. Douglas. Although Stevens appeared to lean to toward the pro-choice position, he could hardly embrace that view more enthusiastically than the man he replaced. After all, Douglas had written the opinion in *Griswold* and supported the pro-choice position in every subsequent case. Sandra Day O'Connor, Reagan's first appointment, replaced Potter Stewart, who had voted with the *Roe* majority. O'Connor's position on abortion was far from clear. Some pro-life groups alleged that O'Connor supported the pro-choice side because of votes she had cast in the Arizona state legislature. But during her confirmation proceedings, she refused to answer questions on abortion, saying only that it was "a practice in which I would not have engaged." But, she added, she was "over the hill" and "not going to be pregnant any more . . . so perhaps it's easy for me to speak."

Given the changing context, pro-life forces began mounting a more direct attack on *Roe*, still hoping to overturn it. The first major battle occurred in *Akron v. Akron Center for Reproductive Health* (1983). At issue was a 1978 ordinance passed by the city council of Akron, Ohio, that contained the following provisions:

1. Hospital requirement. All post–first trimester abortions must be performed in a hospital.

2. Consent for minors. If a minor is under the age of fifteen, she must obtain the informed written consent of a parent or a court before a physician can perform an abortion.

3. Informed consent. A woman's consent to abortion services must be informed. That is, a physician must tell her (1) the number of weeks she is pregnant; (2) that the "unborn child is a human life form from the moment of conception"; (3) about the "anatomical and physiological characteristics of the particular unborn child" at the gestational point of development at which time the abortion is to be performed; (4) that the "unborn child" may be viable if "more than 22 weeks have elapsed from the time of conception"; and (5) about public and private adoption agencies.

4. Twenty-four-hour waiting period. A physician cannot perform an abortion until twenty-four hours after the pregnant woman signs a consent form.

5. Disposal of remains. Doctors who perform abortion "shall insure that the remains of the unborn child are disposed of in a humane and sanitary manner."

Writing for himself and five others—Brennan, Blackmun, Burger, Marshall, and Stevens—Justice Powell struck down the Akron law. The first four provisions were seen as unnecessary and unconstitutional impediments placed in the way of a woman's rights to choose; and the fifth provision was struck down as unconstitutionally vague. Moreover, Powell firmly reiterated the Court's commitment to *Roe*:

[*Akron Center* comes] to us a decade after we held in *Roe v. Wade* (1973) that the right of privacy, grounded in the concept of personal liberty guaranteed by the Constitution, encompasses a woman's right to decide whether to terminate her pregnancy. Legislative responses to the Court's decision have required us on several occasions, and again today, to define the limits of a State's authority to regulate the performance of abortions. And arguments continue to be made, in these cases as well, that we erred in interpreting the Constitution. Nonetheless, the doctrine of *stare decisis,* while perhaps never entirely persuasive on a constitutional question, is a doctrine that demands respect in a society governed by the rule of law. We respect it today, and reaffirm *Roe v. Wade.*

Despite this resounding affirmation of *Roe,* the pro-choice side had lost a vote. The 7–2 *Roe* majority was now 6–3, with O'Connor writing a dissent in *Akron* that was signed by Rehnquist and White. O'Connor's opinion was a scathing critique of *Roe.* Citing medical advances, she wrote that at the time of *Roe,* "viability before 28 weeks was considered unusual," but newer studies indicated viability as early as twenty-five weeks. This proved, she said, that (1) because it is inherently tied to ever-changing medical technology, "the *Roe* framework . . . is clearly on a collision course with itself"; and (2) because lines separating viability from nonviability are fading, compelling state interests exist throughout pregnancy. O'Connor urged that the trimester framework be abandoned and replaced with one that "protects the woman from *unduly burdensome* interference with her freedom to decide whether to terminate her pregnancy" (our emphasis).[17] But what would O'Connor count as "unduly burdensome" regulation? Powell claimed that "the dissent would uphold virtually any abortion regulation under a rational-basis test," meaning that it would find constitutional any regulation that was reasonably related to a governmental interest. Such a standard, Powell noted, would gut *Roe.* O'Connor did not go that far. Rather, she suggested that if the law in question "unduly burdened" the fundamental right to seek an abortion, the Court should apply strict scrutiny; if the law does not "unduly burden" the abortion right, then the Court should apply a rational basis test.

Thus, as displayed in Box 9-3, by 1983 the justices had proposed three different approaches to restrictive abor-

tion laws. Although the majority of the justices continued to support *Roe's* strict scrutiny standard, O'Connor's dissent raised questions. Would she stick with her "undue burden" standard? If so, would she be able to persuade other justices to adopt it? And what exactly did she mean by an "undue burden?" Would she use it as a vehicle to overrule *Roe?*

These questions were on the minds of observers when the Court ruled in *Webster v. Reproductive Health Services* (1989), a case involving a Missouri law that, like the regulations at issue in *Akron,* sought to restrict the abortion right.[18] Moreover, in the years between *Akron* and *Webster,* additional personnel changes on the Court had weakened *Roe's* prospects for survival. William Rehnquist, a persistent *Roe* critic, replaced Warren Burger as chief justice. Joining the Court were Antonin Scalia, who took Rehnquist's associate justice position, and Anthony Kennedy, who replaced the retiring Lewis Powell. Scalia and Kennedy, both Reagan appointees, were seen as two probable anti-*Roe* votes. Was *Roe* doomed? Justice Blackmun, *Roe's* author, thought so. He wondered out loud: "Will *Roe v. Wade* go down the drain? I think there's a very distinct possibility that it will, this term. You can count the votes."[19]

The possibility that *Webster* would reverse *Roe* was not lost on pro-choice and pro-life forces, who filed seventy-eight amicus curiae briefs (the largest number ever submitted to the Court in a single case), representing more than five thousand different groups and interests. The Bush administration's solicitor general not only filed a brief supporting state regulation of abortions but also participated in oral argument, again requesting the Court to overrule *Roe.* Would the newly configured Rehnquist Court accept this invitation? Was the ruling as much of a landmark as many Court watchers expected?

The answer to both these questions is a qualified no. Only one justice, Scalia, explicitly wrote that *Roe* should

---

17. O'Connor's analysis paralleled the one that Reagan's solicitor general, Rex E. Lee, offered in an amicus curiae brief he filed on behalf of the United States in *Akron.* Lee's reading of *Roe's* progeny led him to conclude that from *Danforth* on, the justices had never really "applied" *Roe's* "sweeping" language regarding first-trimester abortions, but had made exceptions. He argued that the Court "has repeatedly adopted an 'unduly burdensome' analysis." That is, the Court had permitted state regulations of abortion as long as they did not "unduly burden" that decision.

18. In between *Akron* and *Webster,* the Court decided *Thornburgh v. American College of Obstetricians and Gynecologists* (1986). At issue in *Thornburgh* was a Pennsylvania law similar to the one that the Court had struck down in *Akron.* Reiterating its position in *Akron,* a five-person Court invalidated the law. After thirteen years of generally supporting the abortion right, Chief Justice Burger joined *Roe's* opponents and voted to uphold the law. Also dissenting were White, O'Connor, and Rehnquist.

19. "Justice Fears for *Roe* Ruling," *New York Times,* September 14, 1988.

BOX 9-3   PROPOSED APPROACHES TO RESTRICTIVE ABORTION LAWS

Approach	Exemplary opinions	Definition
Strict scrutiny	Blackmun in *Roe;* Powell in *Akron*	The right to abortion is fundamental. So laws restricting that right must be the least restrictive means available to achieve a compelling state interest. In the abortion context, a state's interest grows more compelling as the pregnancy passes from the first to second to third trimesters.
Undue burden	O'Connor in *Akron Center*	The right to decide whether to terminate a pregnancy is fundamental. So laws placing an undue burden on the women's decision to terminate her pregnancy may be subject to strict scrutiny; other kinds of laws need only be rationally related to a legitimate state interest (rational basis test).
Rational basis	Rehnquist in *Roe*	The right to abortion is no different from economic rights claimed under the Fourteenth Amendment Due Process Clause. So the law must be a reasonable measure designed to achieve a legitimate state interest.

be overruled. Chief Justice Rehnquist, in an opinion joined by White and Kennedy, came close to agreeing with Scalia when he wrote that *Roe* was a highly problematic decision:

Stare decisis is a cornerstone of our legal system, but it has less power in constitutional cases, where, save for constitutional amendments, this Court is the only body able to make needed changes. We have not refrained from reconsideration of a prior construction of the Constitution that has proved "unsound in principle and unworkable in practice.". . . We think the *Roe* trimester framework falls into that category.

In the first place, the rigid *Roe* framework is hardly consistent with the notion of a Constitution cast in general terms, as ours is, and usually speaking in general principles, as ours does. The key elements of the *Roe* framework—trimesters and viability—are not found in the text of the Constitution or in any place else one would expect to find a constitutional principle. Since the bounds of the inquiry are essentially indeterminate, the result has been a web of legal rules that have become increasingly intricate, resembling a code of regulations rather than a body of constitutional doctrine. . . .

In the second place, we do not see why the State's interest in protecting potential human life should come into existence only at the point of viability, and that there should therefore be

a rigid line allowing state regulation after viability but prohibiting it before viability.

Despite these harsh words, the three refused to take the ultimate step and overrule *Roe*. As Rehnquist wrote, "This case therefore affords us no occasion to revisit the holding of *Roe*, which was that the Texas statute unconstitutionally infringed the right to an abortion derived from the Due Process Clause, and we leave it undisturbed. To the extent indicated in our opinion, we would modify and narrow *Roe* and succeeding cases."

With O'Connor continuing to push her "unduly burdensome" approach and the four remaining justices (Blackmun, Brennan, Marshall, and Stevens) clinging to the 1973 precedent, it seemed that the Court was only one vote short of overturning *Roe*. Many commentators thought that Rehnquist, White, and Kennedy would have gone along with Scalia and overruled *Roe* had they been able to persuade O'Connor to join them. In the end, it was her advocacy of the "unduly burdensome" approach that kept *Roe* alive and kept *Webster* from being the landmark decision many had expected.

Even so, *Roe* seemed to be operating on borrowed

TABLE 9-5 Diminishing Support for *Roe v. Wade*

Roe v. Wade (1973)	*Akron v. Akron Center* (1983)	*Webster v. Reproductive Health Services* (1989)
Blackmun	Blackmun	Blackmun
Brennan	Brennan	Brennan
Burger	Burger	*Rehnquist*
Douglas	Stevens	Stevens
Marshall	Marshall	Marshall
Powell	Powell	*Kennedy*
Rehnquist	*Rehnquist*	*Scalia*
Stewart	*O'Connor*	*O'Connor*
White	*White*	*White*

KEY: Justices in boldface support *Roe*; justices in italics either voiced concerns about *Roe* or would overturn it.

time because President Bush eventually would have the opportunity to appoint justices who could tip the balance against the abortion decision. It was not long before this view was tested. By the time the Court agreed to hear arguments in another major abortion case, *Planned Parenthood of Southeastern Pennsylvania v. Casey* (1992), Bush had appointed two justices. David Souter and Clarence Thomas replaced the pro-choice justices Brennan and Marshall, respectively. These membership changes, as Table 9-5 indicates, seemed to confirm the greatest hope and fear of the pro-life and pro-choice movements: *Roe* would finally go. Or would it?[20]

Planned Parenthood of Southeastern Pennsylvania v. Casey

505 U.S. 833 (1992)
laws.findlaw.com/US/505/833.html
Opinion announcing the judgment of the Court and delivering the opinion of the Court: Kennedy, O'Connor, Souter
Concurring in part: Blackmun, Rehnquist, Scalia, Stevens, Thomas, White
Dissenting in part: Blackmun, Rehnquist, Scalia, Stevens, Thomas, White
Opinions concurring in part and dissenting in part: Blackmun, Rehnquist, Scalia, Stevens

After the Court's decision in *Webster v. Reproductive Health Services,* Pennsylvania revised its Abortion Control Act, which the Court had, by a 5–4 vote, struck down in *Thornburgh v. American College of Obstetricians and Gynecologists* (1986).[21] Given the membership changes on the Court and the *Webster* decision, the state thought the Court would now uphold the amended law, which contained the following provisions:

Informed consent/twenty-four-hour waiting period. At least twenty-four hours before a physician performs an abortion, physicians must inform women of "the nature of the procedure, the health risks of the abortion and of childbirth, and the 'probable gestational age of the unborn child.'" The physician also must provide women with a list of adoption agencies. Abortions may not be performed unless the woman "certifies in writing" that she has given her informed consent. Twenty-four hours must elapse between the time women give their consent and the abortion procedure is performed (§3205).

Spousal notice. Before performing an abortion on a married woman, a physician must receive a statement from her stating that she has notified her spouse that she "is about to undergo an abortion." Alternatively, the woman may "provide a statement certifying that her husband is not the man who impregnated her; that her husband could not be located; that the pregnancy is the result of spousal sexual assault which she has reported; or that the woman believes that notifying her husband will cause him or someone else to inflict bodily injury upon her" (§3209).

Parental consent. Unless she exercises a judicial bypass option, a woman under the age of eighteen must obtain the informed consent of one parent prior to obtaining an abortion (§3206).

Reporting and recordkeeping. All facilities performing abortions must file reports containing information about the procedure, including: the physician, the woman's age, the number of prior pregnancies or abortions she has had, "pre-existing medical conditions that would complicate the pregnancy," the weight and age of the aborted fetus, whether or not the woman was married, and, if relevant, the reason(s) the woman has failed to notify her spouse. If the abortion is performed in a facility funded by the state, the information becomes public (§3207).

Before these provisions went into effect, five women's clinics challenged their constitutionality. A federal district court generally agreed with the clinics, but the Court of Appeals for the Third Circuit reversed, using O'Connor's "undue burden" standard, which—based on its reading of *Webster*—was "the law of the land." In the appeals court's opinion, the provisions, with the exception of spousal consent, did not place an undue burden on the decision of whether to terminate a pregnancy. The court applied a rational basis test under which the three provisions easily passed constitutional muster. The spousal consent provision, in the court's view, placed an undue burden on the abortion decision by exposing women to spousal abuse and violence. It, therefore, applied the strict scrutiny test and concluded that the provision could not stand.

As a result of this mixed opinion, the state and the clinics appealed to the Supreme Court. In a move designed to intensify the debate over abortion before the 1992 elections, Planned Parenthood asked the justices to issue a nonambiguous decision: either affirm or overturn *Roe*. The state, joined by the Bush administration's solicitor general, Kenneth Starr, also asked the Court "to end the current uncertainty" surrounding the abortion issue and overrule *Roe*. The state and the federal government wanted the Court to adopt a rational basis approach to abortion and to use that standard to uphold all of Pennsylvania's laws. Given the membership changes on the Court, many observers predicted the Court would do precisely that.

JUSTICE O'CONNOR, JUSTICE KENNEDY, and JUSTICE SOUTER announced the judgment of the Court and delivered the opinion of the Court with respect to Parts I, II, III, V-A, V-C, and VI, an opinion with respect to Part V-E, in which JUSTICE STEVENS joins, and an opinion with respect to Parts IV, V-B, and V-D.

Liberty finds no refuge in a jurisprudence of doubt. Yet 19 years after our holding that the Constitution protects a woman's right to terminate her pregnancy in its early stages, *Roe v. Wade* (1973), that definition of liberty is still questioned. Joining the respondents as amicus curiae, the United States, as it has done in five other cases in the last decade, again asks us to overrule *Roe*.

. . . And at oral argument in this Court, the attorney for the parties challenging the statute took the position that none of the enactments can be upheld without overruling *Roe v. Wade*. We disagree with that analysis; but we acknowledge that our decisions after *Roe* cast doubt upon the meaning and reach of its holding. Further, the chief justice admits that he would overrule the central holding of *Roe* and adopt the rational relationship test as the sole criterion of constitutionality. State and federal courts as well as legislatures throughout the Union must have guidance as they seek to address this subject in conformance with the Constitution. Given these premises, we find it imperative to review once more the principles that define the rights of the woman and the legitimate authority of the State respecting the termination of pregnancies by abortion procedures.

After considering the fundamental constitutional questions resolved by *Roe*, principles of institutional integrity, and the rule of *stare decisis*, we are led to conclude this: the essential holding of *Roe v. Wade* should be retained and once again reaffirmed.

It must be stated at the outset and with clarity that *Roe's* essential holding, the holding we reaffirm, has three parts. First is a recognition of the right of the woman to choose to have an abortion before viability and to obtain it without undue interference from the State. Before viability, the State's interests are not strong enough to support a prohibition of abortion or the imposition of a substantial obstacle to the woman's effective right to elect the procedure. Second is a confirmation of the State's power to restrict abortions after fetal viability, if the law contains exceptions for pregnancies which endanger a woman's life or health. And third is the principle that the State has legitimate interests from the outset of the pregnancy in protecting the health of the woman and the life of the fetus that may become a child. These principles do not contradict one another; and we adhere to each.

II

. . . These considerations begin our analysis of the woman's interest in terminating her pregnancy but cannot end it, for this reason: though the abortion decision may originate within the zone of conscience and belief, it is more than a philosophic exercise. Abortion is a unique act. It is an act fraught with consequences for others: for the woman who must live with the implications of her decision; for the persons who perform and assist in the procedure; for the spouse, family, and society which must confront the knowledge that these procedures exist, procedures some deem nothing short of an act of violence against innocent human life; and, depending on one's beliefs, for the life or potential life that is aborted. Though abortion is conduct, it does not follow that the State is entitled to proscribe it in all instances. That is because the liberty of the woman is at stake in a sense unique to the human condition and so unique to the law. The mother who carries a child to full term is subject to anxieties, to physical constraints, to pain that only she must bear. That these sacrifices have from the beginning of the human race been endured by woman with a pride that ennobles her in the eyes of others and gives to the infant a bond of love cannot alone be grounds for the State to insist she make the sacrifice. Her suffering is too intimate and personal for the State to insist, without more, upon its own vision of the woman's role, however dominant that vision has been in the course of our history and our culture. The destiny of the woman must be shaped to a large extent on her own conception of her spiritual imperatives and her place in society. . . .

While we appreciate the weight of the arguments made on behalf of the State in the case before us, arguments which in their ultimate formulation conclude that *Roe* should be overruled, the reservations any of us may have in reaffirming the central holding of *Roe* are outweighed by the explication of individual liberty we have given combined with the force of stare decisis. We turn now to that doctrine.

III

A

. . . The sum of . . . precedential inquiry . . . shows *Roe's* underpinnings unweakened in any way affecting its central holding. While it has engendered disapproval, it has not been unworkable. An entire generation has come of age free to assume *Roe's* concept of liberty in defining the capacity of women to act in society, and to make reproductive decisions; no erosion of principle going to liberty or personal autonomy has left *Roe's* central holding a doctrinal rem-

nant; *Roe* portends no developments at odds with other precedent for the analysis of personal liberty; and no changes of fact have rendered viability more or less appropriate as the point at which the balance of interests tips. Within the bounds of normal *stare decisis* analysis, then, and subject to the considerations on which it customarily turns, the stronger argument is for affirming *Roe's* central holding, with whatever degree of personal reluctance any of us may have, not for overruling it.

B

In a less significant case, *stare decisis* analysis could, and would, stop at the point we have reached. . . .

C

. . . Our analysis would not be complete, however, without explaining why overruling *Roe's* central holding would not only reach an unjustifiable result under principles of *stare decisis,* but would seriously weaken the Court's capacity to exercise the judicial power and to function as the Supreme Court of a Nation dedicated to the rule of law. To understand why this would be so it is necessary to understand the source of this Court's authority, the conditions necessary for its preservation, and its relationship to the country's understanding of itself as a constitutional Republic.

The root of American governmental power is revealed most clearly in the instance of the power conferred by the Constitution upon the Judiciary of the United States and specifically upon this Court. As Americans of each succeeding generation are rightly told, the Court cannot buy support for its decisions by spending money and, except to a minor degree, it cannot independently coerce obedience to its decrees. The Court's power lies, rather, in its legitimacy, a product of substance and perception that shows itself in the people's acceptance of the Judiciary as fit to determine what the Nation's law means and to declare what it demands.

The underlying substance of this legitimacy is of course the warrant for the Court's decisions in the Constitution and the lesser sources of legal principle on which the Court draws. That substance is expressed in the Court's opinions, and our contemporary understanding is such that a decision without principled justification would be no judicial act at all. But even when justification is furnished by apposite legal principle, something more is required. Because not every conscientious claim of principled justification will be accepted as such, the justification claimed must be beyond dispute. The Court must take care to speak and act in ways that allow people to accept its decisions on the terms the Court claims for them, as grounded truly in principle, not as compromises with social and political pressures having, as such, no bearing on the principled choices that the Court is obliged to make. Thus, the Court's legitimacy depends on making legally principled decisions under circumstances in which their principled character is sufficiently plausible to be accepted by the Nation.

The need for principled action to be perceived as such is implicated to some degree whenever this, or any other appellate court, overrules a prior case. This is not to say, of course, that this Court cannot give a perfectly satisfactory explanation in most cases. People understand that some of the Constitution's language is hard to fathom and that the Court's Justices are sometimes able to perceive significant facts or to understand principles of law that eluded their predecessors and that justify departures from existing decisions. However upsetting it may be to those most directly affected when one judicially derived rule replaces another, the country can accept some correction of error without necessarily questioning the legitimacy of the Court.

In two circumstances, however, the Court would almost certainly fail to receive the benefit of the doubt in overruling prior cases. There is, first, a point beyond which frequent overruling would overtax the country's belief in the Court's good faith. Despite the variety of reasons that may inform and justify a decision to overrule, we cannot forget that such a decision is usually perceived (and perceived correctly) as, at the least, a statement that a prior decision was wrong. There is a limit to the amount of error that can plausibly be imputed to prior courts. If that limit should be exceeded, disturbance of prior rulings would be taken as evidence that justifiable reexamination of principle had given way to drives for particular results in the short term. The legitimacy of the Court would fade with the frequency of its vacillation.

That first circumstance can be described as hypothetical; the second is to the point here and now. Where, in the performance of its judicial duties, the Court decides a case in such a way as to resolve the sort of intensely divisive controversy reflected in *Roe* and those rare, comparable cases, its decision has a dimension that the resolution of the nor-

mal case does not carry. It is the dimension present whenever the Court's interpretation of the Constitution calls the contending sides of a national controversy to end their national division by accepting a common mandate rooted in the Constitution.

The Court is not asked to do this very often, having thus addressed the Nation only twice in our lifetime, in the decisions of *Brown* [*v. Board of Education*] and *Roe*. But when the Court does act in this way, its decision requires an equally rare precedential force to counter the inevitable efforts to overturn it and to thwart its implementation. Some of those efforts may be mere unprincipled emotional reactions; others may proceed from principles worthy of profound respect. But whatever the premises of opposition may be, only the most convincing justification under accepted standards of precedent could suffice to demonstrate that a later decision overruling the first was anything but a surrender to political pressure, and an unjustified repudiation of the principle on which the Court staked its authority in the first instance. So to overrule under fire in the absence of the most compelling reason to reexamine a watershed decision would subvert the Court's legitimacy beyond any serious question. . . .

The Court's duty in the present case is clear. In 1973, it confronted the already-divisive issue of governmental power to limit personal choice to undergo abortion, for which it provided a new resolution based on the due process guaranteed by the Fourteenth Amendment. Whether or not a new social consensus is developing on that issue, its divisiveness is no less today than in 1973, and pressure to overrule the decision, like pressure to retain it, has grown only more intense. A decision to overrule *Roe*'s essential holding under the existing circumstances would address error, if error there was, at the cost of both profound and unnecessary damage to the Court's legitimacy, and to the Nation's commitment to the rule of law. It is therefore imperative to adhere to the essence of *Roe*'s original decision, and we do so today.

IV

. . . The woman's right to terminate her pregnancy before viability is the most central principle of *Roe v. Wade*. It is a rule of law and a component of liberty we cannot renounce. . . .

Yet it must be remembered that *Roe v. Wade* speaks with

clarity in establishing not only the woman's liberty but also the State's "important and legitimate interest in potential life." That portion of the decision in *Roe* has been given too little acknowledgment and implementation by the Court in its subsequent cases. Those cases decided that any regulation touching upon the abortion decision must survive strict scrutiny, to be sustained only if drawn in narrow terms to further a compelling state interest. Not all of the cases decided under that formulation can be reconciled with the holding in *Roe* itself that the State has legitimate interests in the health of the woman and in protecting the potential life within her. In resolving this tension, we choose to rely upon *Roe*, as against the later cases.

Roe established a trimester framework to govern abortion regulations. Under this elaborate but rigid construct, almost no regulation at all is permitted during the first trimester of pregnancy; regulations designed to protect the woman's health, but not to further the State's interest in potential life, are permitted during the second trimester; and during the third trimester, when the fetus is viable, prohibitions are permitted provided the life or health of the mother is not at stake. Most of our cases since *Roe* have involved the application of rules derived from the trimester framework. See, *e.g., Thornburgh v. American College of Obstetricians and Gynecologists; Akron* [*v. Akron Center*]. . . .

We reject the trimester framework, which we do not consider to be part of the essential holding of *Roe*. . . . Measures aimed at ensuring that a woman's choice contemplates the consequences for the fetus do not necessarily interfere with the right recognized in *Roe*, although those measures have been found to be inconsistent with the rigid trimester framework announced in that case. A logical reading of the central holding in *Roe* itself, and a necessary reconciliation of the liberty of the woman and the interest of the State in promoting prenatal life, require, in our view, that we abandon the trimester framework as a rigid prohibition on all previability regulation aimed at the protection of fetal life. The trimester framework suffers from these basic flaws: in its formulation it misconceives the nature of the pregnant woman's interest; and in practice it undervalues the State's interest in potential life, as recognized in *Roe*.

As our jurisprudence relating to all liberties save perhaps abortion has recognized, not every law which makes a right more difficult to exercise is, *ipso facto*, an infringement of that right. An example clarifies the point. We have held

that not every ballot access limitation amounts to an infringement of the right to vote. Rather, the States are granted substantial flexibility in establishing the framework within which voters choose the candidates for whom they wish to vote.

The abortion right is similar. Numerous forms of state regulation might have the incidental effect of increasing the cost or decreasing the availability of medical care, whether for abortion or any other medical procedure. The fact that a law which serves a valid purpose, one not designed to strike at the right itself, has the incidental effect of making it more difficult or more expensive to procure an abortion cannot be enough to invalidate it. Only where state regulation imposes an undue burden on a woman's ability to make this decision does the power of the State reach into the heart of the liberty protected by the Due Process Clause. . . .

The concept of an undue burden has been utilized by the Court as well as individual members of the Court, including two of us, in ways that could be considered inconsistent. . . . Because we set forth a standard of general application to which we intend to adhere, it is important to clarify what is meant by an undue burden.

A finding of an undue burden is a shorthand for the conclusion that a state regulation has the purpose or effect of placing a substantial obstacle in the path of a woman seeking an abortion of a nonviable fetus. A statute with this purpose is invalid because the means chosen by the State to further the interest in potential life must be calculated to inform the woman's free choice, not hinder it. And a statute which, while furthering the interest in potential life or some other valid state interest, has the effect of placing a substantial obstacle in the path of a woman's choice cannot be considered a permissible means of serving its legitimate ends. To the extent that the opinions of the Court or of individual Justices use the undue burden standard in a manner that is inconsistent with this analysis, we set out what in our view should be the controlling standard. . . . Understood another way, we answer the question, left open in previous opinions discussing the undue burden formulation, whether a law designed to further the State's interest in fetal life which imposes an undue burden on the woman's decision before fetal viability could be constitutional. See, *e.g., Akron I* (O'CONNOR, J., dissenting). The answer is no.

Some guiding principles should emerge. What is at stake is the woman's right to make the ultimate decision, not a right to be insulated from all others in doing so. Regulations which do no more than create a structural mechanism by which the State, or the parent or guardian of a minor, may express profound respect for the life of the unborn are permitted, if they are not a substantial obstacle to the woman's exercise of the right to choose. Unless it has that effect on her right of choice, a state measure designed to persuade her to choose childbirth over abortion will be upheld if reasonably related to that goal. Regulations designed to foster the health of a woman seeking an abortion are valid if they do not constitute an undue burden.

Even when jurists reason from shared premises, some disagreement is inevitable. That is to be expected in the application of any legal standard which must accommodate life's complexity. We do not expect it to be otherwise with respect to the undue burden standard. We give this summary:

(a) To protect the central right recognized by *Roe v. Wade* while at the same time accommodating the State's profound interest in potential life, we will employ the undue burden analysis as explained in this opinion. An undue burden exists, and therefore a provision of law is invalid, if its purpose or effect is to place a substantial obstacle in the path of a woman seeking an abortion before the fetus attains viability.

(b) We reject the rigid trimester framework of *Roe v. Wade.* To promote the State's profound interest in potential life, throughout pregnancy the State may take measures to ensure that the woman's choice is informed, and measures designed to advance this interest will not be invalidated as long as their purpose is to persuade the woman to choose childbirth over abortion. These measures must not be an undue burden on the right.

(c) As with any medical procedure, the State may enact regulations to further the health or safety of a woman seeking an abortion. Unnecessary health regulations that have the purpose or effect of presenting a substantial obstacle to a woman seeking an abortion impose an undue burden on the right.

(d) Our adoption of the undue burden analysis does not disturb the central holding of *Roe v. Wade,* and we reaffirm that holding. Regardless of whether exceptions are made for particular circumstances, a State may not prohibit any woman from making the ultimate decision to terminate her pregnancy before viability.

(e) We also reaffirm *Roe's* holding that "subsequent to viability, the State in promoting its interest in the potentiality of human life may, if it chooses, regulate, and even proscribe, abortion except where it is necessary, in appropriate medical judgment, for the preservation of the life or health of the mother." *Roe v. Wade.*

These principles control our assessment of the Pennsylvania statute, and we now turn to the issue of the validity of its challenged provisions.

V

The Court of Appeals applied what it believed to be the undue burden standard and upheld each of the provisions except for the husband notification requirement. We agree generally with this conclusion, but refine the undue burden analysis in accordance with the principles articulated above. We now consider the separate statutory sections at issue.

[A omitted]

B [Informed Consent]

. . . Our prior decisions establish that as with any medical procedure, the State may require a woman to give her written informed consent to an abortion. . . . In this respect, the statute is unexceptional. Petitioners challenge the statute's definition of informed consent because it includes the provision of specific information by the doctors and the mandatory 24-hour waiting period. The conclusions reached by a majority of the Justices in separate opinions filed today and the undue burden standard adopted in this opinion require us to overrule in part some of the Court's past decisions, decisions driven by the trimester framework's prohibition of all previability regulation designed to further the State's interest in fetal life.

In *Akron I* (1983), we invalidated an ordinance which required that a woman seeking an abortion be provided by her physician with specific information "designed to influence the woman's informed choice between abortion or childbirth." As we later described the *Akron I* holding in *Thornburgh v. American College of Obstetricians and Gynecologists,* there were two purported flaws in the Akron ordinance: the information was designed to dissuade the woman from having an abortion and the ordinance imposed "a rigid requirement that a specific body of information be given in all cases, irrespective of the particular needs of the patient. . . ."

To the extent *Akron I* and *Thornburgh* find a constitutional violation when the government requires, as it does here, the giving of truthful, nonmisleading information about the nature of the procedure, the attendant health risks and those of childbirth, and the "probable gestational age" of the fetus, those cases go too far, are inconsistent with *Roe's* acknowledgment of an important interest in potential life, and are overruled. . . .

. . . Even the broadest reading of *Roe* . . . has not suggested that there is a constitutional right to abortion on demand. . . . Rather, the right protected by *Roe* is a right to decide to terminate a pregnancy free of undue interference by the State. Because the informed consent requirement facilitates the wise exercise of that right it cannot be classified as an interference with the right *Roe* protects. The informed consent requirement is not an undue burden on that right.

C [Spousal Notification]
. . . The limited research that has been conducted with respect to notifying one's husband about an abortion, although involving samples too small to be representative . . . [suggests that] [t]he vast majority of women notify their male partners of their decision to obtain an abortion. In many cases in which married women do not notify their husbands, the pregnancy is the result of an extramarital affair. Where the husband is the father, the primary reason women do not notify their husbands is that the husband and wife are experiencing marital difficulties, often accompanied by incidents of violence.

This information . . . reinforce[s] what common sense would suggest. In well-functioning marriages, spouses discuss important intimate decisions such as whether to bear a child. But there are millions of women in this country who are the victims of regular physical and psychological abuse at the hands of their husbands. Should these women become pregnant, they may have very good reasons for not wishing to inform their husbands of their decision to obtain an abortion. Many may have justifiable fears of physical abuse, but may be no less fearful of the consequences of reporting prior abuse to the Commonwealth of Pennsylvania. Many may have a reasonable fear that notifying their husbands will provoke further instances of child abuse. . . .

The spousal notification requirement is thus likely to prevent a significant number of women from obtaining an abortion. It does not merely make abortions a little more difficult or expensive to obtain; for many women, it will impose a substantial obstacle. We must not blind ourselves to the fact that the significant number of women who fear for their safety and the safety of their children are likely to be deterred from procuring an abortion as surely as if the Commonwealth had outlawed abortion in all cases. . . .

Section 3209 embodies a view of marriage consonant with the common-law status of married women but repugnant to our present understanding of marriage and of the nature of the rights secured by the Constitution. Women do not lose their constitutionally protected liberty when they marry. The Constitution protects all individuals, male or female, married or unmarried, from the abuse of governmental power, even where that power is employed for the supposed benefit of a member of the individual's family. These considerations confirm our conclusion that §3209 is invalid.

D [Parental Consent]
We next consider the parental consent provision. . . .
We have been over most of this ground before. Our cases establish, and we reaffirm today, that a State may require a minor seeking an abortion to obtain the consent of a parent or guardian, provided that there is an adequate judicial bypass procedure. . . .

E [Recordkeeping and Reporting]
. . . In [*Planned Parenthood v.*] *Danforth*, we held that recordkeeping and reporting provisions "that are reasonably directed to the preservation of maternal health and that properly respect a patient's confidentiality and privacy are permissible." We think that under this standard, all the provisions at issue here except that relating to spousal notice are constitutional. Although they do not relate to the State's interest in informing the woman's choice, they do relate to health. The collection of information with respect to actual patients is a vital element of medical research, and so it cannot be said that the requirements serve no purpose other than to make abortions more difficult. Nor do we find that the requirements impose a substantial obstacle to a woman's choice. At most they might increase the cost of some abortions by a slight amount. While at some point increased cost could become a substantial obstacle, there is no such showing on the record before us.

Subsection (12) of the reporting provision requires the reporting of, among other things, a married woman's "reason for failure to provide notice" to her husband. This provision in effect requires women, as a condition of obtaining an abortion, to provide the Commonwealth with the precise information we have already recognized that many women have pressing reasons not to reveal. Like the spousal notice requirement itself, this provision places an undue burden on a woman's choice, and must be invalidated for that reason.

VI

Our Constitution is a covenant running from the first generation of Americans to us and then to future generations. It is a coherent succession. Each generation must learn anew that the Constitution's written terms embody ideas and aspirations that must survive more ages than one. We accept our responsibility not to retreat from interpreting the full meaning of the covenant in light of all of our precedents. We invoke it once again to define the freedom guaranteed by the Constitution's own promise, the promise of liberty.

Affirmed in part, reversed in part, and remanded.

JUSTICE STEVENS, concurring in part and dissenting in part.

[I omitted]

II

My disagreement with the joint opinion begins with its understanding of the trimester framework established in *Roe*. Contrary to the suggestion of the joint opinion, it is not a "contradiction" to recognize that the State may have a legitimate interest in potential human life and, at the same time, to conclude that interest does not justify the regulation of abortion before viability (although other interests, such as maternal health, may). The fact that the State's interest is legitimate does not tell us when, if ever, that interest outweighs the pregnant woman's interest in personal liberty. . . .

In my opinion, the principles established in this long line of cases and the wisdom reflected in Justice Powell's opinion for the Court in *Akron* (and followed by the Court just six years ago in *Thornburgh*) should govern our decision today. Under these principles, §§3205(a)(2)(i)–(iii) of the Pennsylvania statute are unconstitutional. Those sections

require a physician or counselor to provide the woman with a range of materials clearly designed to persuade her to choose not to undergo the abortion. While the State is free . . . to produce and disseminate such material, the State may not inject such information into the woman's deliberations just as she is weighing such an important choice.

Under this same analysis, §§3205(a)(1)(i) and (iii) of the Pennsylvania statute are constitutional. Those sections, which require the physician to inform a woman of the nature and risks of the abortion procedure and the medical risks of carrying to term, are neutral requirements comparable to those imposed in other medical procedures. Those sections indicate no effort by the State to influence the woman's choice in any way. If anything, such requirements enhance, rather than skew, the woman's decisionmaking.

III

The 24-hour waiting period . . . raises even more serious concerns. Such a requirement arguably furthers the State's interests in two ways, neither of which is constitutionally permissible.

First, it may be argued that the 24-hour delay is justified by the mere fact that it is likely to reduce the number of abortions, thus furthering the State's interest in potential life. But such an argument would justify any form of coercion that placed an obstacle in the woman's path. The State cannot further its interests by simply wearing down the ability of the pregnant woman to exercise her constitutional right.

Second, it can more reasonably be argued that the 24-hour delay furthers the State's interest in ensuring that the woman's decision is informed and thoughtful. But there is no evidence that the mandated delay benefits women or that it is necessary to enable the physician to convey any relevant information to the patient. The mandatory delay thus appears to rest on outmoded and unacceptable assumptions about the decisionmaking capacity of women. While there are well-established and consistently maintained reasons for the State to view with skepticism the ability of minors to make decisions, none of those reasons applies to an adult woman's decisionmaking ability. Just as we have left behind the belief that a woman must consult her husband before undertaking serious matters, so we must reject the notion that a woman is less capable of deciding matters of gravity. . . .

IV

In my opinion, a correct application of the "undue burden" standard leads to the same conclusion concerning the constitutionality of these requirements. A state-imposed burden on the exercise of a constitutional right is measured both by its effects and by its character: A burden may be "undue" either because the burden is too severe or because it lacks a legitimate, rational justification.

The 24-hour delay requirement fails both parts of this test. The findings of the District Court establish the severity of the burden that the 24-hour delay imposes on many pregnant women. Yet even in those cases in which the delay is not especially onerous, it is, in my opinion, "undue" because there is no evidence that such a delay serves a useful and legitimate purpose. As indicated above, there is no legitimate reason to require a woman who has agonized over her decision to leave the clinic or hospital and return again another day. While a general requirement that a physician notify her patients about the risks of a proposed medical procedure is appropriate, a rigid requirement that all patients wait 24 hours or (what is true in practice) much longer to evaluate the significance of information that is either common knowledge or irrelevant is an irrational and, therefore, "undue" burden. . . .

Accordingly, while I disagree with Parts IV, V-B, and V-D of the joint opinion, I join the remainder of the Court's opinion.

JUSTICE BLACKMUN, concurring in part, concurring in the judgment in part, and dissenting in part.

I join parts I, II, III, V-A, V-C, and VI of the joint opinion of JUSTICES O'CONNOR, KENNEDY, and SOUTER.

Three years ago, in *Webster v. Reproductive Health Serv.*, four Members of this Court appeared poised to "cas[t] into darkness the hopes and visions of every woman in this country" who had come to believe that the Constitution guaranteed her the right to reproductive choice. All that remained between the promise of *Roe* and the darkness of the plurality was a single, flickering flame. . . . But now, just when so many expected the darkness to fall, the flame has grown bright.

I do not underestimate the significance of today's joint opinion. Yet I remain steadfast in my belief that the right to reproductive choice is entitled to the full protection afforded by this Court before *Webster*. And I fear for the darkness as four Justices anxiously await the single vote necessary to extinguish the light.

I

Make no mistake, the joint opinion of JUSTICES O'CONNOR, KENNEDY, and SOUTER is an act of personal courage and constitutional principle. In contrast to previous decisions in which JUSTICES O'CONNOR and KENNEDY postponed reconsideration of *Roe v. Wade* (1973), the authors of the joint opinion today join JUSTICE STEVENS and me in concluding that "the essential holding of *Roe* should be retained and once again reaffirmed." In brief, five Members of this Court today recognize that "the Constitution protects a woman's right to terminate her pregnancy in its early stages.". . .

In striking down the Pennsylvania statute's spousal notification requirement, the Court has established a framework for evaluating abortion regulations that responds to the social context of women facing issues of reproductive choice. In determining the burden imposed by the challenged regulation, the Court inquires whether the regulation's *"purpose* or *effect* is to place a substantial obstacle in the path of a woman seeking an abortion before the fetus attains viability.". . .

. . . [W]hile I believe that the joint opinion errs in failing to invalidate the other regulations, I am pleased that the joint opinion has not ruled out the possibility that these regulations may be shown to impose an unconstitutional burden. The joint opinion makes clear that its specific holdings are based on the insufficiency of the record before it. I am confident that in the future evidence will be produced to show that "in a large fraction of the cases in which [these regulations are] relevant, [they] will operate as a substantial obstacle to a woman's choice to undergo an abortion.". . .

II

. . . *Roe*'s requirement of strict scrutiny as implemented through a trimester framework should not be disturbed. No other approach has gained a majority, and no other is more protective of the woman's fundamental right. Lastly, no other approach properly accommodates the woman's constitutional right with the State's legitimate interests. . . .

Application of the strict scrutiny standard results in the invalidation of all the challenged provisions. Indeed, as this

Court has invalidated virtually identical provisions in prior cases, *stare decisis* requires that we again strike them down. . . .

III

At long last, THE CHIEF JUSTICE admits it. Gone are the contentions that the issue need not be (or has not been) considered. There, on the first page, for all to see, is what was expected: "We believe that *Roe* was wrongly decided, and that it can and should be overruled consistently with our traditional approach to *stare decisis* in constitutional cases." If there is much reason to applaud the advances made by the joint opinion today, there is far more to fear from the chief justice's opinion. . . .

IV

In one sense, the Court's approach is worlds apart from that of THE CHIEF JUSTICE and JUSTICE SCALIA. And yet, in another sense, the distance between the two approaches is short—the distance is but a single vote.

I am 83 years old. I cannot remain on this Court forever, and when I do step down, the confirmation process for my successor well may focus on the issue before us today. That, I regret, may be exactly where the choice between the two worlds will be made.

CHIEF JUSTICE REHNQUIST, with whom JUSTICE WHITE, JUSTICE SCALIA, and JUSTICE THOMAS join, concurring in the judgment in part and dissenting in part.

The joint opinion, following its newly-minted variation on *stare decisis,* retains the outer shell of *Roe v. Wade* (1973), but beats a wholesale retreat from the substance of that case. We believe that *Roe* was wrongly decided, and that it can and should be overruled consistently with our traditional approach to *stare decisis* in constitutional cases. We would adopt the approach of the plurality in *Webster v. Reproductive Health Services* (1989), and uphold the challenged provisions of the Pennsylvania statute in their entirety.

I

. . . We think . . . both in view of this history and of our decided cases dealing with substantive liberty under the Due Process Clause, that the Court was mistaken in *Roe*

when it classified a woman's decision to terminate her pregnancy as a "fundamental right" that could be abridged only in a manner which withstood "strict scrutiny.". . .

We believe that the sort of constitutionally imposed abortion code of the type illustrated by our decisions following *Roe* is inconsistent "with the notion of a Constitution cast in general terms, as ours is, and usually speaking in general principles, as ours does." *Webster v. Reproductive Health Services* (plurality opinion). The Court in *Roe* reached too far when it analogized the right to abort a fetus to the right . . . involved in . . . *Griswold*, and thereby deemed the right to abortion fundamental. . . .

II

. . . [T]he joint opinion . . . state[s] that when the Court "resolve[s] the sort of intensely divisive controversy reflected in *Roe* and those rare, comparable cases," its decision is exempt from reconsideration under established principles of *stare decisis* in constitutional cases. This is so, the joint opinion contends, because in those "intensely divisive" cases the Court has "call[ed] the contending sides of a national controversy to end their national division by accepting a common mandate rooted in the Constitution," and must therefore take special care not to be perceived as "surrender[ing] to political pressure" and continued opposition. This is a truly novel principle, one which is contrary to both the Court's historical practice and to the Court's traditional willingness to tolerate criticism of its opinions. Under this principle, when the Court has ruled on a divisive issue, it is apparently prevented from overruling that decision for the sole reason that it was incorrect, *unless opposition to the original decision has died away.*

The . . . difficulty with this principle lies in its assumption that cases which are "intensely divisive" can be readily distinguished from those that are not. The question of whether a particular issue is "intensely divisive" enough to qualify for special protection is entirely subjective and dependent on the individual assumptions of the members of this Court. In addition, because the Court's duty is to ignore public opinion and criticism on issues that come before it, its members are in perhaps the worst position to judge whether a decision divides the Nation deeply enough to justify such uncommon protection. Although many of the Court's decisions divide the populace to a large degree, we have not previously on that account shied away from apply-

THE RIGHT TO PRIVACY 451

ing normal rules of *stare decisis* when urged to reconsider earlier decisions. Over the past 21 years, for example, the Court has overruled in whole or in part 34 of its previous constitutional decisions. . . .

The end result of the joint opinion's paeans of praise for legitimacy is the enunciation of a brand new standard for evaluating state regulation of a woman's right to abortion— the "undue burden" standard. As indicated above, *Roe v. Wade* adopted a "fundamental right" standard under which state regulations could survive only if they met the requirement of "strict scrutiny." While we disagree with that standard, it at least had a recognized basis in constitutional law at the time *Roe* was decided. The same cannot be said for the "undue burden" standard, which is created largely out of whole cloth by the authors of the joint opinion. It is a standard which even today does not command the support of a majority of this Court. And it will not, we believe, result in the sort of "simple limitation," easily applied, which the joint opinion anticipates. In sum, it is a standard which is not built to last.

. . . Accordingly, we think that the correct analysis is that set forth by the plurality opinion in *Webster.* A woman's interest in having an abortion is a form of liberty protected by the Due Process Clause, but States may regulate abortion procedures in ways rationally related to a legitimate state interest. . . .

[III omitted]

IV

[Using this standard] we . . . would hold that each of the challenged provisions of the Pennsylvania statute is consistent with the Constitution. It bears emphasis that our conclusion in this regard does not carry with it any necessary approval of these regulations. Our task is, as always, to decide only whether the challenged provisions of a law comport with the United States Constitution. If, as we believe, these do, their wisdom as a matter of public policy is for the people of Pennsylvania to decide.

JUSTICE SCALIA, with whom THE CHIEF JUSTICE, JUSTICE WHITE, and JUSTICE THOMAS join, concurring in the judgment in part and dissenting in part.

My views on this matter are unchanged from those I set forth in my separate opinion . . . in *Webster v. Reproductive*

Health Services (1989) (SCALIA, J., concurring in part and concurring in judgment). . . . The States may, if they wish, permit abortion-on-demand, but the Constitution does not *require* them to do so. The permissibility of abortion, and the limitations upon it, are to be resolved like most important questions in our democracy: by citizens trying to persuade one another and then voting. . . .

Beyond that brief summary of the essence of my position, I will not swell the United States Reports with repetition of what I have said before; and applying the rational basis test, I would uphold the Pennsylvania statute in its entirety. I must, however, respond to a few of the more outrageous arguments in today's opinion, which it is beyond human nature to leave unanswered. I shall discuss each of them under a quotation from the Court's opinion to which they pertain. . . .

"Liberty finds no refuge in a jurisprudence of doubt."

One might have feared to encounter this august and sonorous phrase in an opinion defending the real *Roe v. Wade,* rather than the revised version fabricated today by the authors of the joint opinion. The shortcomings of *Roe* did not include lack of clarity: Virtually all regulation of abortion before the third trimester was invalid. But to come across this phrase in the joint opinion—which calls upon federal district judges to apply an "undue burden" standard as doubtful in application as it is unprincipled in origin—is really more than one should have to bear.

The joint opinion frankly concedes that the amorphous concept of "undue burden" has been inconsistently applied by the Members of this Court in the few brief years since that "test" was first explicitly propounded by JUSTICE O'CONNOR in her dissent in *Akron I.* Because the three Justices now wish to "set forth a standard of general application," the joint opinion announces that "it is important to clarify what is meant by an undue burden." I certainly agree with that, but I do not agree that the joint opinion succeeds in the announced endeavor. To the contrary, its efforts at clarification make clear only that the standard is inherently manipulable and will prove hopelessly unworkable in practice.

The joint opinion explains that a state regulation imposes an "undue burden" if it "has the purpose or effect of placing a substantial obstacle in the path of a woman seeking an abortion of a nonviable fetus." An obstacle is "substantial," we are told, if it is "calculated, [not] to inform the woman's free choice, [but to] hinder it." This latter statement cannot possibly mean what it says. *Any* regulation of abortion that is intended to advance what the joint opinion concedes is the State's "substantial" interest in protecting unborn life will be "calculated [to] hinder" a decision to have an abortion. It thus seems more accurate to say that the joint opinion would uphold abortion regulations only if they do not *unduly* hinder the woman's decision. That, of course, brings us right back to square one: Defining an "undue burden" as an "undue hindrance" (or a "substantial obstacle") hardly "clarifies" the test. Consciously or not, the joint opinion's verbal shell game will conceal raw judicial policy choices concerning what is "appropriate" abortion legislation. . . .

"While we appreciate the weight of the arguments . . . that *Roe* should be overruled, the reservations any of us may have in reaffirming the central holding of *Roe* are outweighed by the explication of individual liberty we have given combined with the force of *stare decisis*."

The Court's reliance upon *stare decisis* can best be described as contrived. It insists upon the necessity of adhering not to all of *Roe*, but only to what it calls the "central holding." . . .

I am certainly not in a good position to dispute that the Court *has saved* the "central holding" of *Roe*, since to do that effectively I would have to know what the Court has saved, which in turn would require me to understand (as I do not) what the "undue burden" test means. I must confess, however, that I have always thought, and I think a lot of other people have always thought, that the arbitrary trimester framework, which the Court today discards, was quite as central to *Roe* as the arbitrary viability test, which the Court today retains. It seems particularly ungrateful to carve the trimester framework out of the core of *Roe*, since its very rigidity (in sharp contrast to the utter indeterminability of the "undue burden" test) is probably the only reason the Court is able to say, in urging *stare decisis*, that *Roe* "has in no sense proven 'unworkable.'" I suppose the Court is entitled to call a "central holding" whatever it wants to call a "central holding"—which is, come to think of it, perhaps one of the difficulties with this modified version of *stare decisis*. I thought I might note, however, that the following portions of *Roe* have not been saved:

• Under *Roe*, requiring that a woman seeking an abortion be provided truthful information about abortion be-

fore giving informed written consent is unconstitutional, if the information is designed to influence her choice, *Thornburgh; Akron I.* Under the joint opinion's "undue burden" regime (as applied today, at least) such a requirement is constitutional.

• Under *Roe*, requiring that information be provided by a doctor, rather than by nonphysician counselors, is unconstitutional, *Akron I.* Under the "undue burden" regime (as applied today, at least) it is not.

• Under *Roe*, requiring a 24-hour waiting period between the time the woman gives her informed consent and the time of the abortion is unconstitutional, *Akron I.* Under the "undue burden" regime (as applied today, at least) it is not.

• Under *Roe*, requiring detailed reports that include demographic data about each woman who seeks an abortion and various information about each abortion is unconstitutional, *Thornburgh.* Under the "undue burden" regime (as applied today, at least) it generally is not. . . .

The Imperial Judiciary lives. . . .

We should get out of this area, where we have no right to be, and where we do neither ourselves nor the country any good by remaining.

What are we to make of *Casey?* On the one hand, reports of *Roe's* demise were exaggerated. The Court did not overrule *Roe:* to the contrary, it reaffirmed the "central holding" of the 1973 decision that a woman should have "some" freedom to terminate a pregnancy. On the other, the "joint opinion" gutted the core of *Roe.* The trimester framework was gone. Under *Casey*, states may now enact laws—regulating the entire pregnancy—that further their interest in potential life so long as those laws are rationally related to that end and do not put an undue burden on the right to terminate a pregnancy. Laws that do not meet this standard will be subject to strict scrutiny, such as the spousal notification provision at issue in *Casey.*

In general, this undue burden approach, which Justice O'Connor originally proposed in 1983 in her *Akron Center* dissent, could lead to very different outcomes in abortion cases. Justice Scalia's dissent indicates that many of the provisions at issue in *Casey* that the Court upheld under the undue burden standard would have been struck down under *Roe's* strict scrutiny approach. Yet, Justice Blackmun's opinion holds out hope that the undue burden standard could be applied, in the future, to strike down restrictive laws.

In the only major post-*Casey* case to date, *Stenberg v. Carhart* (2000), the Court fulfilled Blackmun's hope. Here the justices considered a Nebraska law banning "partial birth abortion"—a phrase often used to describe one of several different kinds of (controversial) procedures used to terminate pregnancies after four months. Specifically, the law stated, "No partial birth abortion shall be performed in this state, unless such procedure is necessary to save the life of the mother whose life is endangered by a physical disorder, physical illness, or physical injury, including a life-endangering physical condition caused by or arising from the pregnancy itself." The statute defines "partial birth abortion" as: "an abortion procedure in which the person performing the abortion partially delivers vaginally a living unborn child before killing the unborn child and completing the delivery." It further defines "partially delivers vaginally a living unborn child before killing the unborn child" to mean "deliberately and intentionally delivering into the vagina a living unborn child, or a substantial portion thereof, for the purpose of performing a procedure that the person performing such procedure knows will kill the unborn child and does kill the unborn child." Violators of the Nebraska law could receive a prison term of up to twenty years and a fine of up to $25,000. Moreover, the state would automatically revoke the licenses of doctors found guilty of performing partial birth abortions. About thirty other states have laws similar to Nebraska's.

Writing for a majority of five, Justice Breyer began his opinion with these words:

We understand the controversial nature of the problem. Millions of Americans believe that life begins at conception and consequently that an abortion is akin to causing the death of an innocent child; they recoil at the thought of a law that would permit it. Other millions fear that a law that forbids abortion would condemn many American women to lives that lack dignity, depriving them of equal liberty and leading those with least resources to undergo illegal abortions with the attendant risks of death and suffering. Taking account of these virtually irreconcilable points of view, aware that constitutional law

must govern a society whose different members sincerely hold directly opposing views, and considering the matter in light of the Constitution's guarantees of fundamental individual liberty, this Court, in the course of a generation, has determined and then redetermined that the Constitution offers basic protection to the woman's right to choose. *Roe v. Wade* (1973); *Planned Parenthood of Southeastern Pa. v. Casey* (1992). We shall not revisit those legal principles. Rather, we apply them to the circumstances of this case.

In applying *Roe* and *Casey*, Breyer found that Nebraska's law ran into two constitutional problems. First, it provided no exception for the preservation of the *health* of the mother. Such an omission, Breyer asserted, violated the language of *Roe*, which *Casey* reiterated: "'subsequent to viability, the State in promoting its interest in the potentiality of human life may, if it chooses, regulate, and even proscribe, abortion *except where it is necessary, in appropriate medical judgment, for the preservation of the life or health of the mother.*'" The Nebraska law, which covered both pre- and postviability, clearly did not meet this standard in Breyer's mind. Second, Breyer believed that the law failed *Casey's* undue burden test: It "'imposes an undue burden on a woman's ability'" to choose particular abortion procedures, thereby unduly burdening the right to choose abortion itself. In particular, "All those who perform abortion procedures using [this] method must fear prosecution, conviction, and imprisonment."

Four justices, Rehnquist, Scalia, Kennedy, and Thomas—in four dissenting opinions—disagreed. The chief justice was short and to the point: "I did not join the joint opinion in *Planned Parenthood of Southeastern Pa. v. Casey* (1992), and continue to believe that case is wrongly decided. Despite my disagreement with the opinion . . . the *Casey* joint opinion represents the holding of the Court in that case. I believe JUSTICE KENNEDY and JUSTICE THOMAS have correctly applied *Casey's* principles and join their dissenting opinions." Indeed, as Rehnquist suggests, both Kennedy and Thomas believed that application of the undue burden standard led to a conclusion different from that reached by the Court. As Kennedy put it:

For close to two decades after *Roe v. Wade* (1973), the Court gave but slight weight to the interests of the separate States when their legislatures sought to address persisting concerns raised by the existence of a woman's right to elect an abortion in defined circumstances. When the Court reaffirmed the essential holding of *Roe*, a central premise was that the States retain a critical and legitimate role in legislating on the subject of abortion, as limited by the woman's right the Court restated and again guaranteed. *Planned Parenthood of Southeastern Pa. v. Casey* (1992). The political processes of the State are not to be foreclosed from enacting laws to promote the life of the unborn and to ensure respect for all human life and its potential. The State's constitutional authority is a vital means for citizens to address these grave and serious issues, as they must if we are to progress in knowledge and understanding and in the attainment of some degree of consensus.

The Court's decision today, in my submission, repudiates this understanding by invalidating a statute advancing critical state interests, even though the law denies no woman the right to choose an abortion and places no undue burden upon the right. The legislation is well within the State's competence to enact. Having concluded Nebraska's law survives the scrutiny dictated by a proper understanding of *Casey*, I dissent from the judgment invalidating it.

Scalia, in contrast, continued his assault on *Casey* (and, implicitly, *Roe*):

Today's decision, that the Constitution of the United States prevents the prohibition of a horrible mode of abortion, will be greeted by a firestorm of criticism—as well it should. I cannot understand why those who *acknowledge* that "[t]he issue of abortion is one of the most contentious and controversial in contemporary American society," persist in the belief that this Court, armed with neither constitutional text nor accepted tradition, can resolve that contention and controversy rather than be consumed by it. If only for the sake of its own preservation, the Court should return this matter to the people—where the Constitution, by its silence on the subject, left it—and let *them* decide, State by State, whether this practice should be allowed. *Casey* must be overruled.

Despite these dissents, the joint *Casey* opinion, which expressed some level of commitment to *Roe*, carried the day. Indeed, as Justice Stevens noted in a concurring opinion in *Carhart*, "During the past 27 years, the central holding of *Roe v. Wade* (1973), has been endorsed by all but 4 of the 17 Justices who have addressed the issue." But will *Casey* and *Carhart* be the last words on abortion? Can we now expect the justices to use the undue burden standard to assess regulations on abortion? On the one

TABLE 9-6 Approaches to Abortion: The 2000 Supreme Court

Justice	Favored Approach
Breyer	Undue burden
Ginsburg	Undue burden or equal protection analysis (?)[a]
Kennedy	Undue burden(?)
O'Connor	Undue burden
Rehnquist	Rational basis
Scalia	Rational basis
Souter	Undue burden
Stevens	*Roe*'s strict scrutiny
Thomas	Rational basis

a. In a 1985 law review article, Judge Ginsburg urged courts to acknowledge a "women's equality aspect" to the abortion issue. See Ruth Bader Ginsburg, "Some Thoughts on Autonomy and Equality in Relation to *Roe v. Wade*," *North Carolina Law Review* 63 (1985): 375–386.

hand, the pro-choice justices seem satisfied with that standard, along with the idea of keeping the central right proclaimed in *Roe* alive. Moreover, the *Casey* approach appears to meet the approval of the American public. Polls taken immediately after the decision found that a large majority of Americans (more than 80 percent) favor legalized abortion, but significant numbers also support restrictions on that right *(see Figure 9-2)*.

On the other hand, as Table 9-6 indicates, as of 2000 the justices remained divided over legal approaches to abortion. In addition, a justice can have a change of heart: for example, Kennedy signed Rehnquist's opinion in *Webster*, yet provided crucial support for O'Connor's undue burden approach in *Casey*. In *Carhart*, he dissented. Does his dissent signal a retreat on Kennedy's part from the opinion he helped write in *Casey?* Or does it instead shore up the undue burden standard? Only time will tell.

Justice Ginsburg, who replaced White, a *Roe* critic, also complicates the picture. Although Ginsburg supports a woman's right to choose, she has been critical of the *Roe* framework. In a 1985 law review article, she argued that abortion rights should be framed in equal protection terms; that is, the Court should consider whether laws restricting the right discriminate against women. Had the Court adopted this approach, Ginsburg assert-

BOX 9-4   ABORTION IN GLOBAL PERSPECTIVE

PRIOR TO THE U.S. Supreme Court's 1973 decision in *Roe v. Wade*, several nations—including China, India, the former Soviet Union, and the United Kingdom—already had liberalized their abortion laws. But the vast majority of change has come in the post-*Roe* period, and today more than 60 percent of the world's population lives in the sixty-four countries that permit abortion at the woman's request or with the approval of medical practitioners on broad social and economic grounds. For the other nearly 40 percent (living in 127 countries), abortion is still illegal under most circumstances.

Below we provide a sampling of laws governing abortion. As you read them, keep in mind that even in those countries granting women the right to obtain abortions, controversies have ensued—just have they had in the United States. The issue has been particularly contentious in nations with large Roman Catholic populations, such as Italy and France. Also bear in mind that the exercise of the abortion right is controlled not only by laws or court decisions but also by how officials interpret and execute these laws and by public attitudes, among other factors. So, for example, in some countries that permit abortion to save the woman's life or in case of rape or incest, virtually no abortions are performed because public opinion is overwhelmingly pro-life. In contrast are countries, such as Denmark, that attempt to make abortions freely and safely available to all women who want them by ensuring that public hospitals perform them and by paying for them.

EXAMPLES OF COUNTRIES WITH LIBERAL ABORTION LAWS

Canada

In 1988 the Canadian Supreme Court struck down the nation's criminal abortion law, and no federal law has replaced it. Some provinces have attempted to restrict abortion, but those laws probably would be struck down as an unconstitutional infringement on the federal government's exclusive power to enact criminal law. In 1993, for example, the court struck down a provincial law that prohibited abortions from being performed in facilities other than hospitals.

France

By law, a woman may obtain an abortion during the first twelve weeks of pregnancy if she declares herself to be in "distress." Because the woman is the judge of whether she is in "distress," abortion is effectively available on request. After twelve weeks, abortion is permitted only when two physi-

cians determine that the procedure is necessary to prevent a grave risk to woman's health or when there is a strong likelihood of fetal defect.

South Africa

Prior to 1996 South Africa permitted abortions only in case of rape, incest, or danger to the woman's physical or mental health. In that year, the country enacted the Choice on Termination of Pregnancy Act, which is among the world's most liberal. The act allows abortion on demand during the first twelve weeks of pregnancy and within twenty weeks on many grounds, including if a physician determines continuation of pregnancy would pose a risk to the woman's physical or mental health, if it would significantly affect the woman's social or economic circumstances, if the fetus has a severe defect, or in cases of rape or incest. It permits abortions at any point during the pregnancy if there is a risk to the woman's life or of severe fetal defect.

Sweden

Sweden enacted a liberal abortion law in 1974. Abortion is legal at the woman's request through the eighteenth week of pregnancy. Abortions after the eighteenth week are permitted for medical, socioeconomic, and legal reasons when approved by the National Board of Health and Welfare. Approval for abortions after viability of the fetus will be granted only when the pregnancy gravely threatens the woman's life or health or in the case of severe fetal impairment.

Turkey

Turkey's 1983 Population Planning Law permits abortion during the first twelve weeks of pregnancy. If the woman is married, her husband must consent to the termination of the pregnancy. After twelve weeks, an abortion may be performed (with physician approval) if the woman's health or when there is a strong likelihood of fetal defect.

EXAMPLES OF COUNTRIES WITH RESTRICTIVE LAWS

Chile

In 1989 Chile repealed a health code provision that permitted abortion on "therapeutic" grounds; abortion is currently illegal on all grounds. According to some reports, the government often prosecutes women who have obtained abortions, particularly low-income women.

(continued)

(Box 9-4 continued)

Colombia

In a 1994 case challenging Colombia's restrictive abortion law, the Constitutional Court held that the right to life is constitutionally protected from the moment of conception.

El Salvador

Under a previous law, abortion was permitted when necessary to protect a woman's life, when pregnancy resulted from rape, and when there was substantial risk of fetal defect. In 1997 El Salvador amended the law to eliminate all exceptions to its prohibition of abortion.

Ireland

Despite a 1992 decision by the Irish Supreme Court that a constitutional provision protecting the right to life of the unborn did not prevent a fourteen-year-old rape victim from legally traveling to England to obtain an abortion, abortions are virtually unavailable in Ireland.

Nepal

Abortion is illegal under all circumstances in Nepal and is punishable by imprisonment of both the patient and the physician performing the abortion. In 1997 an estimated 75 percent of all the women incarcerated in Nepal were imprisoned for having had an abortion.

Nigeria

Abortion in Nigeria is a criminal offense, unless performed to save a woman's life.

Poland

After the overthrow of the existing communist regime, which allowed abortions on demand, Poland in 1993 banned almost all abortions. It later liberalized its law, allowing abortions until the twelfth week of pregnancy "if women are financially or personally unprepared for childbirth." It requires a three-day waiting period. In 1997 Poland's Constitutional Court invalidated the law, finding that it violated the constitution's protection of the right to life of the "conceived child." Abortions in Poland are now available only when the pregnancy threatens the life and health of the woman, when there is justified suspicion that the pregnancy resulted from a "criminal act," and in instances of fetal defect.

SOURCES: *http://www.crlp.org/010798internation.html;* Anika Rahman, Laura Katzive, and Stanley K. Henshaw, "A Global Review of Laws on Induced Abortion, 1985–1997," *International Family Planning Perspectives* 24 (1998): 56–64. Available at: *http:// www.crlp.org/0698abortionlaws_1.html.*

---

ed, it would have struck down many state laws, including those that restricted funding for abortions. As she put it, "If the Court had acknowledged a woman's equality aspect [and] not simply a patient-physician autonomy constitutional dimension to the abortion issue, a majority perhaps might have seen the public assistance cases as instances in which . . . the [government] had violated its duty to govern impartially."[22] In *Carhart,* Ginsburg did not press this position on her colleagues, opting instead in a brief concurrence to explain her understanding of the undue burden standard: Whether Ginsburg will press the equal protection approach at some later date is unknown. What we do know is that future personnel changes could alter the Court's ideological balance, tip-

ping it in one direction or another. In addition, advances in medical technology may cause the public to reconsider the current state of the law, and actions by Congress or state legislatures could ignite additional rounds of litigation.

Finally, it is worth noting that although many Americans may be comfortable with the existing state of legal doctrine, women wishing to obtain abortions may be less so. "Five years after *Roe,*" Susan Hansen noted in 1980, "changes in access to abortion have been apparent throughout the U.S. The trend over time has been toward greater equalization of access with the largest increases in abortion rates in the most restrictive states."[23] But Gerald N. Rosenberg, writing in 1995, shows that the

22. Ruth Bader Ginsburg, "Some Thoughts on Autonomy and Equality in Relation to *Roe v. Wade,*" *University of North Carolina Law Review* 63 (1985): 382.

23. "State Implementation of Supreme Court Decisions: Abortion Rates Since *Roe v. Wade,*" *Journal of Politics* 42 (1980): 372.

number of doctors ready to perform abortions declined precipitously between 1982 and 1995.[24] The number of abortions also has decreased markedly over the past decade. Whether these changes are due to harassment of abortion clinics (see Chapter 5), the Court's retreat from *Roe*, moral concern among doctors about performing the procedure, or some combination of these and other factors is unclear. What is evident is that the lack of providers makes it difficult for women in many states, even populous states, to exercise what the Supreme Court has said is their constitutional right.

It seems inevitable that Americans (and the Court) will continue to debate the abortion issue, with no easy answers apparent. But Americans are not alone. While, as Box 9-4 describes, about 60 percent of the world's population lives in the sixty-four nations that now permit abortion without severe restrictions, the issue continues to generate controversy—years, even decades, after the right was articulated.

PRIVATE ACTIVITIES AND THE APPLICATION OF *GRISWOLD*

Little doubt exists that many Americans now equate the right to privacy, first established in *Griswold v. Connecticut*, with reproductive freedom, especially the right to abortion, but the right to privacy has implications for many other activities. Indeed, one of the first important applications of *Griswold* came in a criminal procedure case, *Katz v. United States* (1967).[25] FBI agents suspected Charles Katz of engaging in illegal bookmaking activity; in particular, they thought he was "transmitting wagering information by telephone from Los Angeles to Miami and Boston." To gather evidence, they placed listening and recording devices outside the telephone booth where Katz made his calls and used the transcripts of his conversations to obtain an eight-count indictment.

Katz challenged the use of the transcripts as evidence against him, asserting that his conversations were private and that the government had violated his rights under the Fourth Amendment. The government argued

that in previous Fourth Amendment search and seizure cases, the justices permitted the use of bugs and mikes so long as agents did not "physically penetrate" an individual's space. Because the FBI had attached listening devices to the *outside* of the booth, it claimed that it did not invade Katz's space.

The Court disagreed. In his majority opinion, Justice Stewart dealt primarily with existing precedent governing searches and seizures, a topic covered in Chapter 10. Stewart also touched on the privacy issue, asserting, "What a person knowingly exposes to the public, even in his own home or office, is not a subject of Fourth Amendment protection. But what he seeks to preserve as private, even in an area accessible to the public, may be constitutionally protected." Justice Harlan, in a concurring opinion, put it in these terms: if a person has "exhibited an actual (subjective) expectation of privacy," and "the expectation . . . [is] one that society is prepared to recognize as 'reasonable,'" then he or she comes under the protection of the Fourth Amendment. In other words, the justices—even Stewart, who dissented in *Griswold*—were willing to apply the right to privacy to searches and seizures. If citizens expect privacy, as Charles Katz did when he entered the telephone booth, then they are entitled to it. This position was not wholly different from what Justice Brandeis had advocated in *Olmstead v. United States* about forty years before *Katz*.

Two years later, in *Stanley v. Georgia* (1969), the Court had another occasion to examine the privacy doctrine and its relationship to searches and seizures. While police were investigating Robert Stanley for illegal bookmaking, they obtained a warrant to search his home. Authorities found little evidence of gambling activity, but they did find three reels of film. They watched the movies and arrested Stanley for possessing obscene material. Stanley's attorney challenged the seizure and arrest on the ground that the law should not "punish mere private possession of obscene material"—that his client had a right of privacy to view whatever he wished in his own home. The state argued that it had the right to seize obscene materials because they are illegal to possess. Indeed, in previous decisions, the Court had said that states could regulate the dissemination of obscene movies, magazines, and so forth.

24. Gerald N. Rosenberg, "The Real World of Constitutional Rights: The Supreme Court and the Implementation of the Abortion Decisions," in *Contemplating Courts*, Lee Epstein, ed. (Washington, D.C.: CQ Press, 1995).

25. An excerpt of *Katz* appears in Chapter 10.

In an unanimous opinion for the Court, Justice Marshall accepted Stanley's argument. Taking a lesson from Brandeis's dissent in *Olmstead*, he asserted: "If the First Amendment means anything, it means that a State has no business telling a man, sitting alone in his house, what books he may read or films he may watch." Put somewhat differently, states can regulate obscenity, but cannot prohibit such activity inside someone's house. The First Amendment and privacy rights simply prohibit this kind of intrusion into the home.

This point is important: *Stanley* hinged on a violation of a fundamental liberty—in this instance, the First Amendment. Marshall made this clear in a footnote to his opinion:

What we have said in no way infringes upon the power of the State or Federal Government to make possession of other items, such as narcotics, firearms, or stolen goods, a crime. Our holding in the present case turns upon the Georgia statute's infringement of fundamental liberties protected by the First Amendment. No First Amendment rights are involved in most statutes making mere possession a crime.

But would the Court apply *Stanley* to activities forbidden by the state that did not fall under the First Amendment? In *Bowers v. Hardwick* (1986) the Court considered the constitutionality of a man's conviction for engaging in sodomy.[26] As you read *Bowers* think about how the Court applied *Stanley* to the dispute. Some scholars allege that the Court virtually gutted the underpinnings of *Stanley*. Is this assertion accurate? Or did the Court merely seek to limit its application and that of the *Griswold* right to privacy, more generally?

Bowers v. Hardwick

478 U.S. 186 (1986)
laws.findlaw.com/US/478/186.html
Vote: 5 (Burger, O'Connor, Powell, Rehnquist, White)
*   4 (Blackmun, Brennan, Marshall, Stevens)*
Opinion of the Court: White
Concurring opinions: Burger, Powell
Dissenting opinions: Blackmun, Stevens

26. For oral arguments, navigate to: *oyez.nwu.edu.*

Michael Hardwick was arrested for violating the Georgia sodomy statute in 1982. With help from the American Civil Liberties Union, Hardwick sued the state, claiming the law violated his constitutional rights. In *Bowers v. Hardwick* (1986) the Supreme Court rejected Hardwick's privacy argument and upheld the Georgia law.

In August 1982 a police officer appeared at Michael Hardwick's residence to serve him with an arrest warrant for failure to keep a court date. According to the officer, one of Hardwick's housemates answered the door. He told the officer that he did not know if Hardwick was home, but that the officer was free to enter and look for him. As the officer walked down the hallway, he passed a partially open bedroom door and observed Hardwick engaged in sodomy with another man.[27] The officer arrested Hardwick for violating a Georgia law that prohibited the practice of oral or anal sex.[28] The district attorney decided not to pursue the matter, but Hardwick and his ACLU attorneys challenged the law, asserting that it violated the fundamental right to privacy as articulated in *Griswold* and should be subject to strict constitutional scrutiny. After the court of appeals ruled in Hardwick's

27. For more on this case, see Peter Irons, *The Courage of Their Convictions* (New York: Free Press, 1988).
28. The majority opinion dealt exclusively with "consensual homosexual sodomy," expressing "no opinion . . . on other acts of sodomy."

favor, the state asked the Supreme Court to review the case.

At first, the Supreme Court could not muster the necessary four votes to hear the case. But, after Justice White circulated an opinion to his colleagues, dissenting from the denial of certiorari, a sufficient number of justices agreed to review it. In particular, they granted certiorari to address this question: Did the court of appeals err in concluding that Georgia's sodomy statute infringes upon the fundamental rights of homosexuals and in requiring the state to demonstrate a compelling interest to support the constitutionality of the statute?

JUSTICE WHITE delivered the opinion of the Court.

The issue presented is whether the Federal Constitution confers a fundamental right upon homosexuals to engage in sodomy and hence invalidates the laws of the many States that still make such conduct illegal and have done so for a very long time. The case also calls for some judgment about the limits of the Court's role in carrying out its constitutional mandate.

We first register our disagreement . . . with respondent that the Court's prior cases have construed the Constitution to confer a right of privacy that extends to homosexual sodomy and for all intents and purposes have decided this case. . . .

. . . [N]one of the rights announced in . . . [past] cases bears any resemblance to the claimed constitutional right of homosexuals to engage in acts of sodomy. . . .

Precedent aside, however, respondent would have us announce . . . a fundamental right to engage in homosexual sodomy. This we are quite unwilling to do. It is true that despite the language of the Due Process Clauses of the Fifth and Fourteenth Amendments, which appears to focus only on the processes by which life, liberty, or property is taken, the cases are legion in which those Clauses have been interpreted to have substantive content, subsuming rights that to a great extent are immune from federal or state regulation or proscription. Among such cases are those recognizing rights that have little or no textual support in the constitutional language. . . .

Striving to assure itself and the public that announcing rights not readily identifiable in the Constitution's text involves much more than the imposition of the Justices' own choice of values on the States and the Federal Government, the Court has sought to identify the nature of the rights qualifying for heightened judicial protection. . . . [I]t was said that this category includes those fundamental liberties that are "implicit in the concept of ordered liberty," such that "neither liberty nor justice would exist if [they] were sacrificed.". . . [F]undamental liberties . . . are characterized as those . . . that are "deeply rooted in this Nation's history and tradition."

It is obvious to us that neither of these formulations would extend a fundamental right to homosexuals to engage in acts of consensual sodomy. Proscriptions against that conduct have ancient roots. Sodomy was a criminal offense at common law and was forbidden by the laws of the original thirteen States when they ratified the Bill of Rights. . . . In fact, until 1961, all 50 States outlawed sodomy, and today 24 States and the District of Columbia continue to provide criminal penalties for sodomy performed in private and between consenting adults. Against this background, to claim that a right to engage in such conduct is "deeply rooted in this Nation's history and tradition" or "implicit in the concept of ordered liberty" is, at best, facetious.

Nor are we inclined to take a more expansive view of our authority to discover new fundamental rights imbedded in the Due Process Clause. The Court is most vulnerable and comes nearest to illegitimacy when it deals with judge-made constitutional law having little or no cognizable roots in the language or design of the Constitution. That this is so was painfully demonstrated by the face-off between the Executive and the Court in the 1930's, which resulted in the repudiation of much of the substantive gloss that the Court had placed on the Due Process Clause of the Fifth and Fourteenth Amendments. There should be, therefore, great resistance to expand the substantive reach of those Clauses, particularly if it requires redefining the category of rights deemed to be fundamental. Otherwise, the Judiciary necessarily takes to itself further authority to govern the country without express constitutional authority. The claimed right pressed on us today falls far short of overcoming this resistance.

Respondent, however, asserts that the result should be different where the homosexual conduct occurs in the privacy of the home. He relies on *Stanley v. Georgia* (1969), where the Court held that the First Amendment prevents conviction for possessing and reading obscene material in the privacy of his home. . . .

Stanley did protect conduct that would not have been protected outside the home, and it partially prevented the enforcement of state obscenity laws; but the decision was firmly grounded in the First Amendment. The right pressed upon us here has no similar support in the text of the Constitution, and it does not qualify for recognition under the prevailing principles for construing the Fourteenth Amendment. Its limits are also difficult to discern. Plainly enough, otherwise illegal conduct is not always immunized whenever it occurs in the home. Victimless crimes, such as the possession and use of illegal drugs, do not escape the law where they are committed at home. *Stanley* itself recognized that its holding offered no protection for the possession in the home of drugs, firearms, or stolen goods. And if respondent's submission is limited to the voluntary sexual conduct between consenting adults, it would be difficult, except by fiat, to limit the claimed right to homosexual conduct while leaving exposed to prosecution adultery, incest, and other sexual crimes even though they are committed in the home. We are unwilling to start down that road. . . .

Accordingly, the judgment of the Court of Appeals is

Reversed.

CHIEF JUSTICE BURGER, concurring.

I join the Court's opinion, but I write separately to underscore my view that in constitutional terms there is no such thing as a fundamental right to commit homosexual sodomy.

As the Court notes, the proscriptions against sodomy have very "ancient roots." Decisions of individuals relating to homosexual conduct have been subject to state intervention throughout the history of Western civilization. Condemnation of those practices is firmly rooted in Judaeo-Christian moral and ethical standards. Homosexual sodomy was a capital crime under Roman law. During the English Reformation when powers of the ecclesiastical courts were transferred to the King's Courts, the first English statute criminalizing sodomy was passed. Blackstone described "the infamous crime against nature" as an offense of "deeper malignity" than rape, a heinous act "the very mention of which is a disgrace to human nature," and "a crime not fit to be named." The common law of England, including its prohibition of sodomy, became the received

law of Georgia and the other Colonies. In 1816 the Georgia Legislature passed the statute at issue here, and that statute has been continuously in force in one form or another since that time. To hold that the act of homosexual sodomy is somehow protected as a fundamental right would be to cast aside millennia of moral teaching.

This is essentially not a question of personal "preferences" but rather of the legislative authority of the State. I find nothing in the Constitution depriving a State of the power to enact the statute challenged here.

JUSTICE POWELL, concurring.

I join the opinion of the Court. I agree with the Court that there is no fundamental right—*i.e.,* no substantive right under the Due Process Clause—such as that claimed by respondent Hardwick, and found to exist by the Court of Appeals. This is not to suggest, however, that respondent may not be protected by the Eighth Amendment of the Constitution. The Georgia statute at issue in this case authorizes a court to imprison a person for up to 20 years for a single private, consensual act of sodomy. In my view, a prison sentence for such conduct—certainly a sentence of long duration—would create a serious Eighth Amendment issue. Under the Georgia statute a single act of sodomy, even in the private setting of a home, is a felony comparable in terms of the possible sentence imposed to serious felonies such as aggravated battery, first-degree arson, and robbery.

In this case, however, respondent has not been tried, much less convicted and sentenced. Moreover, respondent has not raised the Eighth Amendment issue below. For these reasons this constitutional argument is not before us.

JUSTICE BLACKMUN, with whom JUSTICE BRENNAN, JUSTICE MARSHALL, and JUSTICE STEVENS join, dissenting.

This case is no more about "a fundamental right to engage in homosexual sodomy," as the Court purports to declare, than *Stanley v. Georgia* (1969) was about a fundamental right to watch obscene movies, or *Katz v. United States* (1967) was about a fundamental right to place interstate bets from a telephone booth. Rather, this case is about "the most comprehensive of rights and the right most valued by civilized men," namely, "the right to be let alone." *Olmstead v. United States* (1928) (Brandeis, J., dissenting). . . .

In its haste to reverse the Court of Appeals and hold that

the Constitution does not "confe[r] a fundamental right upon homosexuals to engage in sodomy," the Court relegates the actual statute being challenged to a footnote and ignores the procedural posture of the case before it. A fair reading of the statute and of the complaint clearly reveals that the majority has distorted the question this case presents.

First, the Court's almost obsessive focus on homosexual activity is particularly hard to justify in light of the broad language Georgia has used. Unlike the Court, the Georgia Legislature has not proceeded on the assumption that homosexuals are so different from other citizens that their lives may be controlled in a way that would not be tolerated if it limited the choices of those other citizens. . . . The sex or status of the persons who engage in the act is irrelevant as a matter of state law. . . . Michael Hardwick's standing may rest in significant part on Georgia's apparent willingness to enforce against homosexuals a law it seems not to have any desire to enforce against heterosexuals. But his claim that . . . [the law] involves an unconstitutional intrusion into his privacy and his right of intimate association does not depend in any way on his sexual orientation.

Second, I disagree with the Court's refusal to consider whether . . . [the law] runs afoul of the . . . Ninth Amendment. . . . Respondent's complaint expressly invoked the Ninth Amendment and he relied heavily before this Court on *Griswold v. Connecticut* (1965), which identifies that Amendment as one of the specific constitutional provisions giving "life and substance" to our understanding of privacy. . . . I believe that Hardwick has stated a cognizable claim that . . . [the law] interferes with constitutionally protected interests in privacy and freedom of intimate association. . . .

The Court concludes today that none of our prior cases dealing with various decisions that individuals are entitled to make free of governmental interference "bears any resemblance to the claimed constitutional right of homosexuals to engage in acts of sodomy that is asserted in this case.". . .

In a variety of circumstances we have recognized that a necessary corollary of giving individuals freedom to choose how to conduct their lives is acceptance of the fact that different individuals will make different choices. For example, in holding that the clearly important state interest in public education should give way to a competing claim by the

Amish to the effect that extended formal schooling threatened their way of life, the Court declared: "There can be no assumption that today's majority is 'right' and the Amish and others like them are 'wrong.' A way of life that is odd or even erratic but interferes with no rights or interests of others is not to be condemned because it is different." *Wisconsin v. Yoder* (1972). The Court claims that its decision today merely refuses to recognize a fundamental right to engage in homosexual sodomy; what the Court really has refused to recognize is the fundamental interest all individuals have in controlling the nature of their intimate associations with others.

The behavior for which Hardwick faces prosecution occurred in his own home, a place to which the Fourth Amendment attaches special significance. The Court's treatment of this aspect of the case is symptomatic of its overall refusal to consider the broad principles that have informed our treatment of privacy in specific cases. Just as the right to privacy is more than the mere aggregation of a number of entitlements to engage in specific behavior, so too, protecting the physical integrity of the home is more than merely a means of protecting specific activities that often take place there. . . .

The Court's interpretation of the pivotal case of *Stanley v. Georgia* (1969) is entirely unconvincing. *Stanley* held that Georgia's undoubted power to punish the public distribution of constitutionally unprotected, obscene material did not permit the State to punish the private possession of such material. According to the majority here, *Stanley* relied entirely on the First Amendment, and thus, it is claimed, sheds no light on cases not involving printed materials. But that is not what *Stanley* said. Rather, the *Stanley* Court anchored its holding in the Fourth Amendment's special protection for the individual in his home. . . .

The central place that *Stanley* gives Justice Brandeis' dissent in *Olmstead*, a case raising no First Amendment claim, shows that Stanley rested as much on the Court's understanding of the Fourth Amendment as it did on the First. . . . [T]hus I cannot agree with the Court's statement that "[t]he right pressed upon us here has no . . . support in the text of the Constitution." Indeed, the right of an individual to conduct intimate relationships in the intimacy of his or her own home seems to me to be the heart of the Constitution's protection of privacy. . . .

It took but three years for the Court to see the error in its analysis in *Minersville School District v. Gobitis* and to recognize that the threat to national cohesion posed by a refusal to salute the flag was vastly outweighed by the threat to those same values posed by compelling such a salute. See *West Virginia Board of Education v. Barnette* (1943). I can only hope that here, too, the Court soon will reconsider its analysis and conclude that depriving individuals of the right to choose for themselves how to conduct their intimate relationships poses a far greater threat to the values most deeply rooted in our Nation's history than tolerance of nonconformity could ever do. Because I think the Court today betrays those values, I dissent.

JUSTICE STEVENS, with whom JUSTICE BRENNAN and JUSTICE MARSHALL join, dissenting.

Because the Georgia statute expresses the traditional view that sodomy is an immoral kind of conduct regardless of the identity of the persons who engage in it, I believe that a proper analysis of its constitutionality requires consideration of two questions: First, may a State totally prohibit the described conduct by means of a neutral law applying without exception to all persons subject to its jurisdiction? If not, may the State save the statute by announcing that it will only enforce the law against homosexuals? The two questions merit separate discussion.

Our prior cases make two propositions abundantly clear. First, the fact that the governing majority in a State has traditionally viewed a particular practice as immoral is not a sufficient reason for upholding a law prohibiting the practice; neither history nor tradition could save a law prohibiting miscegenation from constitutional attack. Second, individual decisions by married persons, concerning the intimacies of their physical relationship, even when not intended to produce offspring, are a form of "liberty" protected by the Due Process Clause of the Fourteenth Amendment. *Griswold v. Connecticut* (1965). Moreover, this protection extends to intimate choices by unmarried as well as married persons. . . .

. . . The essential "liberty" that animated the development of the law in cases like *Griswold* . . . surely embraces the right to engage in nonreproductive, sexual conduct that others may consider offensive or immoral.

Paradoxical as it may seem, our prior cases thus establish that a State may not prohibit sodomy within "the sacred precincts of marital bedrooms," *Griswold* or, indeed, between unmarried heterosexual adults. . . .

If the Georgia statute cannot be enforced as it is written—if the conduct it seeks to prohibit is a protected form of liberty for the vast majority of Georgia's citizens—the State must assume the burden of justifying a selective application of its law. Either the persons to whom Georgia seeks to apply its statute do not have the same interest in "liberty" that others have, or there must be a reason why the State may be permitted to apply a generally applicable law to certain persons that it does not apply to others.

The first possibility is plainly unacceptable. Although the meaning of the principle that "all men are created equal" is not always clear, it surely must mean that every free citizen has the same interest in "liberty" that the members of the majority share. From the standpoint of the individual, the homosexual and the heterosexual have the same interest in deciding how he will live his own life, and, more narrowly, how he will conduct himself in his personal and voluntary associations with his companions. State intrusion into the private conduct of either is equally burdensome.

The second possibility is similarly unacceptable. A policy of selective application must be supported by a neutral and legitimate interest—something more substantial than a habitual dislike for, or ignorance about, the disfavored group. Neither the State nor the Court has identified any such interest in this case. The Court has posited as a justification for the Georgia statute "the presumed belief of a majority of the electorate in Georgia that homosexual sodomy is immoral and unacceptable." But the Georgia electorate has expressed no such belief—instead, its representatives enacted a law that presumably reflects the belief that *all sodomy* is immoral and unacceptable. Unless the Court is prepared to conclude that such a law is constitutional, it may not rely on the work product of the Georgia Legislature to support its holding. For the Georgia statute does not single out homosexuals as a separate class meriting special disfavored treatment. . . .

Both the Georgia statute and the Georgia prosecutor thus completely fail to provide the Court with any support for the conclusion that homosexual sodomy, *simpliciter*, is considered unacceptable conduct in that State, and that the burden of justifying a selective application of the generally applicable law has been met.

BOX 9-5   AFTERMATH . . . *BOWERS V. HARDWICK*

BY A SINGLE VOTE the Supreme Court rejected Michael Hardwick's arguments that the Constitution bars state regulation of consensual homosexual activity between adults in the privacy of their own homes. Crucial to the outcome was the vote of Justice Lewis F. Powell Jr., who initially joined the four justices who favored striking down the Georgia antisodomy law, but changed his mind. Four years after the decision, while speaking to law students at New York University, Powell said he "probably made a mistake" in voting to uphold the Georgia law. Although Powell admitted that "the dissent had the better of the argument," he thought the case was "not very important" and was somewhat "frivolous" because Hardwick was never prosecuted.

In 1998, in another challenge to the state's anti-sodomy law, the Georgia Supreme Court struck down the statute on state constitutional grounds, saying, "We cannot think of any other activity that reasonable persons would rank as more private and more deserving of protection from government interference than consensual, private adult sexual activity." Although the case arose from sexual relations between a man and a woman, the justices found that the privacy protections in the state constitution made no distinction between homosexuals and heterosexuals.

Even before the Supreme Court handed down its decision in *Bowers v. Hardwick,* Michael Hardwick moved from Atlanta to Miami, where he made a living tending bar. He died of an AIDS-related illness in 1991 at the age of thirty-seven.

SOURCES: *Washington Post,* August 21, 1986; *St. Louis Post Dispatch,* November 7, 1990; *San Francisco Chronicle,* January 14, 1991; *New Orleans Times-Picayune,* July 3, 1996; and New York Times, November 25, 1998.

Both the majority and dissenting opinions in *Bowers* dealt with privacy concerns. White's opinion found fault with a due process approach to privacy or, at the very least, of using it to "discover" a new "fundamental right to engage in homosexual sodomy." Nor was he interested in using *Stanley* to find in favor of Hardwick. He read *Stanley* narrowly: it protected the performance of some otherwise illegal activity only if the First Amendment was implicated. Because *Bowers* did not raise a First Amendment objection to sodomy laws, *Stanley* was not applicable. The dissenters (including Marshall, the author of *Stanley*) called this interpretation "unconvincing." In their view, *Stanley* took its cues from Brandeis's dissent in *Olmstead* and, accordingly, rested as much on the Fourth Amendment as on the First.

Did the Burger Court in *Bowers* begin to dismantle the Warren Court's rulings in *Stanley* and *Griswold,* or did it merely draw sensible limits around them? For most Americans, the latter would be true. In surveys conducted during the 1980s and 1990s, about 75 percent of respondents said they believed "sexual relations between two adults of the same sex" are wrong. We shall return to this subject in Chapter 12, which considers the Court's treatment of gays and lesbians. Here we note that in *Bowers* the justices showed less consensus than the public: the case was decided by a one-vote margin, and, after he retired, Justice Powell said that he "probably made a mistake" in voting to uphold the Georgia laws *(see Box 9-5).*

Powell's remark provides some indication of the difficulty involved in resolving disputes touching on the amorphous right to privacy. The disputes have become even more complex over time. Indeed, during the Rehnquist Court years, the justices have struggled with two of the more troublesome of all privacy issues: the right to die and drug testing. And we suspect that others may soon reach the Court's doorstep, namely, issues associated with the "information age." In what follows, we consider all three.

The Right to Die

Right-to-die cases present many different kinds of questions. The Court first examined whether and under what circumstances the family or guardian of an incapacitated individual can make the decision to end life. In the 1970s and 1980s, most state courts allowed various forms of what are called "substituted judgments"; that is, they

FIGURE 9-3 Percentage of Respondents Supporting an Individual's Right to Die

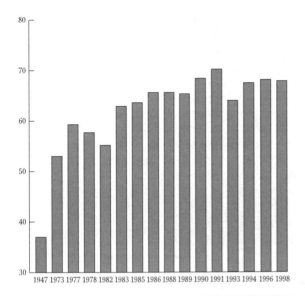

SOURCE: Lee Epstein, Jeffrey A. Segal, Harold J. Spaeth, and Thomas G. Walker, *The Supreme Court Compendium: Data, Decisions, and Developments*, 2d ed. (Washington, D.C.: Congressional Quarterly, 1996), Table 8-24; and General Social Survey.

NOTE: The question was: Do you believe that doctors should be allowed by law to end an incurable patient's life if the patient and his family request it?

permitted relatives or guardians to "surmise" what the patient would have wanted or to act in the "best interest" of the patient. A frequently cited example of the use of substituted judgment is the New Jersey Supreme Court's ruling in *In re Quinlan* (1976). As twenty-two-year-old Karen Ann Quinlan lay in a coma, her parents sought to have the respirator that was sustaining her life removed. When Karen's doctors refused, the Quinlans went to court. The state supreme court decided that the right to privacy is broad enough to allow a patient to decline medical treatment under certain circumstances. Because Karen could not make that decision for herself, the "only practical way to prevent the destruction of the right [to privacy] is to permit the guardian and family of Karen to render their best judgment as to whether she would exercise it in these circumstances."

Under this decision, the Quinlans could (and did) have Karen's respirator removed without intervention

from the state and its courts. Although most state courts endorsed *Quinlan*, the Missouri Supreme Court took a different stance.[29] Viewing the state's interest in preserving life as controlling, it asserted that the family must provide "clear and convincing" evidence that the patient would have wanted medical care terminated. This kind of standard is often difficult for families to meet because they must provide direct evidence about the patient's desires.

In any event, rules that permit patients and the families to end treatment have garnered public support. As Figure 9-3 shows, in the 1940s only about 37 percent of the citizenry agreed that doctors should be allowed to end a terminal patient's life if that patient or the family request it. The most recent polls show that the number has grown to nearly 70 percent.

Would the Supreme Court agree with the public? Would it allow even competent patients to end their medical treatment? If so, would it also permit families to make these decisions? What kind of proof would it require? These were the questions the Court dealt with in its first right-to-die case.[30]

Cruzan v. Director, Missouri Department of Health

497 U.S. 261 (1990)
laws.findlaw.com/US/497/261.html
Vote: 5 (Kennedy, O'Connor, Rehnquist, Scalia, White)
4 (Blackmun, Brennan, Marshall, Stevens)
Opinion of the Court: Rehnquist
Concurring opinions: O'Connor, Scalia
Dissenting opinions: Brennan, Stevens

In January 1983 Nancy Beth Cruzan was in a serious car accident. When paramedics found her, she was "lying face down in a ditch without detectable respiratory or cardiac function." Although they were able to restore her

29. See Henry R. Glick, "Policy Making and State Supreme Courts," in *The American Courts: A Critical Assessment*, ed. John B. Gates and Charles A. Johnson (Washington, D.C.: CQ Press, 1990, 108–110), for a list of state right-to-die cases that predate *Cruzan*.

30. For oral arguments, navigate to: *oyez.nwu.edu*.

breathing and heartbeat, Cruzan remained unconscious and was taken to a hospital. Both short- and long-term medical efforts failed, and, as a result, Cruzan degenerated to a persistent vegetative state, "a condition in which a person exhibits motor reflexes but evinces no indications of significant cognitive function." She required feeding and hydration tubes to stay alive. When Cruzan's case was before the Court, some experts suggested that she might live another thirty years, but no one predicted any improvement in her condition.

Her parents, Lester and Joyce Cruzan, asked doctors to remove her feeding tubes, a step that would lead to Nancy's death. The hospital staff refused, and the Cruzans sought permission from a state court. They argued that "a person in Nancy's condition had a fundamental right to refuse or direct the withdrawal of 'death prolonging procedures.'" The Cruzans presented as evidence that when Nancy was twenty-five, she had told a friend that "she would not wish to continue her life unless she could live it at least halfway normally."

The trial court ruled in their favor, but the state supreme court reversed. It found no support in common law for a right to die, and it refused to apply privacy doctrines to the Cruzan situation. It also held that because the state had a strong interest in preserving life, the Cruzans would have to provide "clear and convincing evidence" that Nancy would have wanted her feeding tubes withdrawn.

CHIEF JUSTICE REHNQUIST delivered the opinion of the Court.

We granted certiorari to consider the question of whether Cruzan has a right under the United States Constitution which would require the hospital to withdraw life-sustaining treatment from her under these circumstances. . . .

The Fourteenth Amendment provides that no state shall "deprive any person of life, liberty, or property, without due process of law." The principle that a competent person has a constitutionally protected liberty interest in refusing unwanted medical treatment may be inferred from our prior decisions. . . .

But determining that a person has a "liberty interest" under the Due Process Clause does not end the inquiry; "whether respondent's constitutional rights have been violated must be determined by balancing his liberty interests against the relevant state interests."

Petitioners insist that under the general holdings of our cases, the forced administration of life-sustaining medical treatment, and even of artificially-delivered food and water essential to life, would implicate a competent person's liberty interest. Although we think the logic of the cases . . . would embrace such a liberty interest, the dramatic consequences involved in refusal of such treatment would inform the inquiry as to whether the deprivation of that interest is constitutionally permissible. But for purposes of this case, we assume that the United States Constitution would grant a competent person a constitutionally protected right to refuse lifesaving hydration and nutrition.

Petitioners go on to assert that an incompetent person should possess the same right in this respect as is possessed by a competent person. . . .

The difficulty with petitioners' claim is that in a sense it begs the question: an incompetent person is not able to make an informed and voluntary choice to exercise a hypothetical right to refuse treatment or any other right. Such a "right" must be exercised for her, if at all, by some sort of surrogate. Here, Missouri has in effect recognized that under certain circumstances a surrogate may act for the patient in electing to have hydration and nutrition withdrawn in such a way as to cause death, but it has established a procedural safeguard to assure that the action of the surrogate conforms as best it may to the wishes expressed by the patient while competent. Missouri requires that evidence of the incompetent's wishes as to the withdrawal of treatment be proved by clear and convincing evidence. The question, then, is whether the United States Constitution forbids the establishment of this procedural requirement by the State. We hold that it does not.

Whether or not Missouri's clear and convincing evidence requirement comports with the United States Constitution depends in part on what interests the State may properly seek to protect in this situation. Missouri relies on its interest in the protection and preservation of human life, and there can be no gainsaying this interest. As a general matter, the States—indeed, all civilized nations—demonstrate their commitment to life by treating homicide as a serious crime. Moreover, the majority of States in this country have laws imposing criminal penalties on one who assists another to commit suicide. We do not think a State is required to remain neutral in the face of an informed and voluntary decision by a physically-able adult to starve to death.

But in the context presented here, a State has more particular interests at stake. The choice between life and death is a deeply personal decision of obvious and overwhelming finality. We believe Missouri may legitimately seek to safeguard the personal element of this choice through the imposition of heightened evidentiary requirements. It cannot be disputed that the Due Process Clause protects an interest in life as well as an interest in refusing life-sustaining medical treatment. Not all incompetent patients will have loved ones available to serve as surrogate decision-makers. And even where family members are present, "there will, of course, be some unfortunate situations in which family members will not act to protect a patient." A State is entitled to guard against potential abuses in such situations. Similarly, a State is entitled to consider that a judicial proceeding to make a determination regarding an incompetent's wishes may very well not be an adversarial one, with the added guarantee of accurate factfinding that the adversary process brings with it. Finally, we think a State may properly decline to make judgments about the "quality" of life that a particular individual may enjoy, and simply assert an unqualified interest in the preservation of human life to be weighed against the constitutionally protected interests of the individual.

In our view, Missouri has permissibly sought to advance these interests through the adoption of . . . "an intermediate standard of proof—'clear and convincing evidence'— when the individual interests at stake in a state proceeding are both 'particularly important' and 'more substantial than mere loss of money.'"

We think it self-evident that the interests at stake in the instant proceedings are more substantial, both on an individual and societal level, than those involved in a run-of-the-mine civil dispute. But not only does the standard of proof reflect the importance of a particular adjudication, it also serves as "a societal judgment about how the risk of error should be distributed between the litigants." The more stringent the burden of proof a party must bear, the more that party bears the risk of an erroneous decision. We believe that Missouri may permissibly place an increased risk of an erroneous decision on those seeking to terminate an incompetent individual's life-sustaining treatment. An erroneous decision not to terminate results in a maintenance of the status quo; the possibility of subsequent developments such as advancements in medical science, the discovery of new evidence regarding the patient's intent, changes in the law, or simply the unexpected death of the patient despite the administration of life-sustaining treatment, at least create the potential that a wrong decision will eventually be corrected or its impact mitigated. An erroneous decision to withdraw life-sustaining treatment, however, is not susceptible of correction. . . .

It is also worth noting that most, if not all, States simply forbid oral testimony entirely in determining the wishes of parties in transactions which, while important, simply do not have the consequences that a decision to terminate a person's life does. At common law and by statute in most States, the parole evidence rule prevents the variations of the terms of a written contract by oral testimony. The statute of frauds makes unenforceable oral contracts to leave property by will, and statutes regulating the making of wills universally require that those instruments be in writing. There is no doubt that statutes requiring wills to be in writing, and statutes of frauds which require that a contract to make a will be in writing, on occasion frustrate the effectuation of the intent of a particular decedent, just as Missouri's requirement of proof in this case may have frustrated the effectuation of the not-fully-expressed desires of Nancy Cruzan. But the Constitution does not require general rules to work faultlessly; no general rule can.

In sum, we conclude that a State may apply a clear and convincing evidence standard in proceedings where a guardian seeks to discontinue nutrition and hydration of a person diagnosed to be in a persistent vegetative state. . . .

The Supreme Court of Missouri held that in this case the testimony adduced at trial did not amount to clear and convincing proof of the patient's desire to have hydration and nutrition withdrawn. In so doing, it reversed a decision of the Missouri trial court which had found that the evidence "suggest[ed]" Nancy Cruzan would not have desired to continue such measures, but which had not adopted the standard of "clear and convincing evidence" enunciated by the Supreme Court. The testimony adduced at trial consisted primarily of Nancy Cruzan's statements made to a housemate about a year before her accident that she would not want to live should she face life as a "vegetable," and other observations to the same effect. The observations did not deal in terms with withdrawal of medical treatment or of hydration and nutrition. We cannot say that the Supreme Court of Missouri committed constitutional error in reaching the conclusion that it did.

Petitioners alternatively contend that Missouri must accept the "substituted judgment" of close family members even in the absence of substantial proof that their views reflect the views of the patient. . . . Here again petitioners would seek to turn a decision which allowed a State to rely on family decisionmaking into a constitutional requirement that the State recognize such decisionmaking. But constitutional law does not work that way.

No doubt is engendered by anything in this record but that Nancy Cruzan's mother and father are loving and caring parents. If the State were required by the United States Constitution to repose a right of "substituted judgment" with anyone, the Cruzans would surely qualify. But we do not think the Due Process Clause requires the State to repose judgment on these matters with anyone but the patient herself. Close family members may have a strong feeling—a feeling not at all ignoble or unworthy, but not entirely disinterested, either—that they do not wish to witness the continuation of the life of a loved one which they regard as hopeless, meaningless, and even degrading. But there is no automatic assurance that the view of close family members will necessarily be the same as the patient's would have been had she been confronted with the prospect of her situation while competent. All of the reasons previously discussed for allowing Missouri to require clear and convincing evidence of the patient's wishes lead us to conclude that the State may choose to defer only to those wishes, rather than confide the decision to close family members.

The judgment of the Supreme Court of Missouri is

Affirmed.

JUSTICE O'CONNOR, concurring.

I agree that a protected liberty interest in refusing unwanted medical treatment may be inferred from our prior decisions . . . and that the refusal of artificially delivered food and water is encompassed within that liberty interest. . . .

I . . . write separately to emphasize that the Court does not today decide the issue whether a State must also give ef-

fect to the decisions of a surrogate decisionmaker. In my view, such a duty may well be constitutionally required to protect the patient's liberty interest in refusing medical treatment. Few individuals provide explicit oral or written instructions regarding their intent to refuse medical treatment should they become incompetent. States which decline to consider any evidence other than such instructions may frequently fail to honor a patient's intent. Such failures might be avoided if the State considered an equally probative source of evidence: the patient's appointment of a proxy to make health care decisions on her behalf. Delegating the authority to make medical decisions to a family member or friend is becoming a common method of planning for the future. Several States have recognized the practical wisdom of such a procedure by enacting durable power of attorney statutes that specifically authorize an individual to appoint a surrogate to make medical treatment decisions. Some state courts have suggested that an agent appointed pursuant to a general durable power of attorney statute would also be empowered to make health care decisions on behalf of the patient. Other States allow an individual to designate a proxy to carry out the intent of a living will. These procedures for surrogate decisionmaking, which appear to be rapidly gaining in acceptance, may be a valuable additional safeguard of the patient's interest in directing his medical care. Moreover, as patients are likely to select a family member as a surrogate, giving effect to a proxy's decisions may also protect the "freedom of personal choice in matters of . . . family life."

Today's decision, holding only that the Constitution permits a State to require clear and convincing evidence of Nancy Cruzan's desire to have artificial hydration and nutrition withdrawn, does not preclude a future determination that the Constitution requires the States to implement the decisions of a patient's duly appointed surrogate. Nor does it prevent States from developing other approaches for protecting an incompetent individual's liberty interest in refusing medical treatment. . . . [N]o national consensus has yet emerged on the best solution for this difficult and sensitive problem. Today we decide only that one State's practice does not violate the Constitution; the more challenging task of crafting appropriate procedures for safeguarding incompetents' liberty interests is entrusted to the "laboratory" of the States.

JUSTICE SCALIA, concurring.

The various opinions in this case portray quite clearly the difficult, indeed agonizing, questions that are presented by the constantly increasing power of science to keep the human body alive for longer than any reasonable person would want to inhabit it. The States have begun to grapple with these problems through legislation. I am concerned, from the tenor of today's opinions, that we are poised to confuse that enterprise as successfully as we have confused the enterprise of legislating concerning abortion—requiring it to be conducted against a background of federal constitutional imperatives that are unknown because they are being newly crafted from Term to Term. That would be a great misfortune.

While I agree with the Court's analysis today, and therefore join in its opinion, I would have preferred that we announce, clearly and promptly, that the federal courts have no business in this field; that American law has always accorded the State the power to prevent, by force if necessary, suicide—including suicide by refusing to take appropriate measures necessary to preserve one's life; that the point at which life becomes "worthless," and the point at which the means necessary to preserve it become "extraordinary" or "inappropriate," are neither set forth in the Constitution nor known to the nine Justices of this Court any better than they are known to nine people picked at random from the Kansas City telephone directory; and hence, that even when it is demonstrated by clear and convincing evidence that a patient no longer wishes certain measures to be taken to preserve her life, it is up to the citizens of Missouri to decide, through their elected representatives, whether that wish will be honored. It is quite impossible (because the Constitution says nothing about the matter) that those citizens will decide upon a line less lawful than the one we would choose; and it is unlikely (because we know no more about "life-and-death" than they do) that they will decide upon a line less reasonable.

The text of the Due Process Clause does not protect individuals against deprivations of liberty *simpliciter*. It protects them against deprivations of liberty "without due process of law." To determine that such a deprivation would not occur if Nancy Cruzan were forced to take nourishment against her will, it is unnecessary to reopen the historically recurrent debate over whether "due process" includes substan-

tive restrictions. It is at least true that no "substantive due process" claim can be maintained unless the claimant demonstrates that the State has deprived him of a right historically and traditionally protected against State interference. That cannot possibly be established here. . . .

What I have said above is not meant to suggest that I would think it desirable, if we were sure that Nancy Cruzan wanted to die, to keep her alive by the means at issue here. I assert only that the Constitution has nothing to say about the subject. To raise up a constitutional right here we would have to create out of nothing (for it exists neither in text nor tradition) some constitutional principle whereby, although the State may insist that an individual come in out of the cold and eat food, it may not insist that he take medicine; and although it may pump his stomach empty of poison he has ingested, it may not fill his stomach with food he has failed to ingest. Are there, then, no reasonable and humane limits that ought not to be exceeded in requiring an individual to preserve his own life? There obviously are, but they are not set forth in the Due Process Clause. What assures us that those limits will not be exceeded is the same constitutional guarantee that is the source of most of our protection—what protects us, for example, from being assessed a tax of 100% of our income above the subsistence level, from being forbidden to drive cars, or from being required to send our children to school for 10 hours a day, none of which horribles is categorically prohibited by the Constitution. Our salvation is the Equal Protection Clause, which requires the democratic majority to accept for themselves and their loved ones what they impose on you and me. This Court need not, and has no authority to, inject itself into every field of human activity where irrationality and oppression may theoretically occur, and if it tries to do so it will destroy itself.

JUSTICE BRENNAN, with whom JUSTICE MARSHALL and JUSTICE BLACKMUN join, dissenting.

"Medical technology has effectively created a twilight zone of suspended animation where death commences while life, in some form, continues. Some patients, however, want no part of a life sustained only by medical technology. Instead, they prefer a plan of medical treatment that allows nature to take its course and permits them to die with dignity."

Nancy Cruzan has dwelt in that twilight zone for six years. She is oblivious to her surroundings and will remain so. . . .

Today the Court, while tentatively accepting that there is some degree of constitutionally protected liberty interest in avoiding unwanted medical treatment, including life-sustaining medical treatment such as artificial nutrition and hydration, affirms the decision of the Missouri Supreme Court. The majority opinion, as I read it, would affirm that decision on the ground that a State may require "clear and convincing" evidence of Nancy Cruzan's prior decision to forgo life-sustaining treatment under circumstances such as hers in order to ensure that her actual wishes are honored. Because I believe that Nancy Cruzan has a fundamental right to be free of unwanted artificial nutrition and hydration, which right is not outweighed by any interests of the State, and because I find that the improperly biased procedural obstacles imposed by the Missouri Supreme Court impermissibly burden that right, I respectfully dissent. Nancy Cruzan is entitled to choose to die with dignity. . . .

The question before this Court is a relatively narrow one: whether the Due Process Clause allows Missouri to require a now-incompetent patient in an irreversible persistent vegetative state to remain on life-support absent rigorously clear and convincing evidence that avoiding the treatment represents the patient's prior, express choice. . . .

Although the right to be free of unwanted medical intervention, like other constitutionally protected interests, may not be absolute, no State interest could outweigh the rights of an individual in Nancy Cruzan's position. Whatever a State's possible interests in mandating life-support treatment under other circumstances, there is no good to be obtained here by Missouri's insistence that Nancy Cruzan remain on life-support systems if it is indeed her wish not to do so. Missouri does not claim, nor could it, that society as a whole will be benefited by Nancy's receiving medical treatment. No third party's situation will be improved and no harm to others will be averted.

The only state interest asserted here is a general interest in the preservation of life. But the State has no legitimate general interest in someone's life, completely abstracted from the interest of the person living that life, that could outweigh the person's choice to avoid medical treatment. . . . Thus, the State's general interest in life must accede to Nancy Cruzan's particularized and intense interest in self-determination in her choice of medical treatment. There is simply nothing legitimately within the State's purview to be gained by superseding her decision. . . .

I do not suggest that States must sit by helplessly if the choices of incompetent patients are in danger of being ignored. Even if the Court had ruled that Missouri's rule of decision is unconstitutional, as I believe it should have, States would nevertheless remain free to fashion procedural protections to safeguard the interests of incompetents under these circumstances. The Constitution provides merely a framework here: protections must be genuinely aimed at ensuring decisions commensurate with the will of the patient, and must be reliable as instruments to that end. Of the many States which have instituted such protections, Missouri is virtually the only one to have fashioned a rule that lessens the likelihood of accurate determinations. In contrast, nothing in the Constitution prevents States from reviewing the advisability of a family decision, by requiring a court proceeding or by appointing an impartial guardian ad litem.

There are various approaches to determining an incompetent patient's treatment choice in use by the several States today and there may be advantages and disadvantages to each and other approaches not yet envisioned. The choice, in largest part, is and should be left to the States, so long as each State is seeking, in a reliable manner, to discover what the patient would want. But with such momentous interests in the balance, States must avoid procedures that will prejudice the decision. . . .

Finally, I cannot agree with the majority that where it is not possible to determine what choice an incompetent patient would make, a State's role as *parens patriae* permits the State automatically to make that choice itself. Under fair rules of evidence, it is improbable that a court could not determine what the patient's choice would be. Under the rule of decision adopted by Missouri and upheld today by this Court, such occasions might be numerous. But in neither case does it follow that it is constitutionally acceptable for the State invariably to assume the role of deciding for the patient. A State's legitimate interest in safeguarding a patient's choice cannot be furthered by simply appropriating it.

The majority justifies its position by arguing that, while close family members may have a strong feeling about the question, "there is no automatic assurance that the view of close family members will necessarily be the same as the patient's would have been had she been confronted with the prospect of her situation while competent." I cannot quarrel with this observation. But it leads only to another question: Is there any reason to suppose that a State is more likely to make the choice that the patient would have made than someone who knew the patient intimately? To ask this is to answer it. . . .

As many as 10,000 patients are being maintained in persistent vegetative states in the United States, and the number is expected to increase significantly in the near future. Medical technology, developed over the past 20 or so years, is often capable of resuscitating people after they have stopped breathing or their hearts have stopped beating. Some of those people are brought fully back to life. Two decades ago, those who were not and could not swallow and digest food, died. Intravenous solutions could not provide sufficient calories to maintain people for more than a short time. Today, various forms of artificial feeding have been developed that are able to keep people metabolically alive for years, even decades. In addition, in this century, chronic or degenerative ailments have replaced communicable diseases as the primary causes of death. The 80% of Americans who die in hospitals are "likely to meet their end . . . 'in a sedated or comatose state; betubed nasally, abdominally and intravenously; and far more like manipulated objects than like moral subjects.'" A fifth of all adults surviving to age 80 will suffer a progressive dementing disorder prior to death.

. . . The new medical technology can reclaim those who would have been irretrievably lost a few decades ago and restore them to active lives. For Nancy Cruzan, it failed, and for others with wasting incurable disease it may be doomed to failure. In these unfortunate situations, the bodies and preferences and memories of the victims do not escheat to the State; nor does our Constitution permit the State or any other government to commandeer them. No singularity of feeling exists upon which such a government might confidently rely as *parens patriae*. . . . Missouri and this Court have displaced Nancy's own assessment of the processes associated with dying. They have discarded evidence of her will, ignored her values, and deprived her of the right to a decision as closely approximating her own choice as humanly possible. They have done so disingenuously in her name, and openly in Missouri's own. That Missouri and

this Court may truly be motivated only by concern for incompetent patients makes no matter. . . .

I respectfully dissent.

In August 1990, two months after the Court's decision, the Cruzans petitioned a Missouri court for a new hearing. Three of Nancy's former co-workers testified that she had said she would not want to live "like a vegetable." Despite protests from pro-life groups, a state court judge ruled December 14 that the Cruzans could have Nancy's feeding tube removed. She died December 26.

For the Cruzans the battle was over, but, as Brennan's dissent points out, there are approximately 10,000 "Nancy Cruzans" in the United States, a figure that may increase tenfold as medical technology advances. Does the Court's opinion provide guidance for them and their families? Yes and no. On the one hand, the Court clearly ruled that the Fourteenth Amendment's Due Process Clause permits a competent individual to terminate medical treatment. As to incompetent patients, the majority of the justices suggested that states may fashion their own standards, including those that require "clear and convincing evidence" of the patient's interests. Living wills, as O'Connor's concurrence suggests, may be the best form of such evidence *(see Box 9-6)*.

On the other hand, the case did not call for the Court to address another dimension of the right-to-die question—suicides or "assisted suicides" for the terminally ill. May a person take his own life or arrange an assisted suicide when suffering from an incurable illness? In the 1990s this question took on unusual importance, with the media full of accounts of people with progressively debilitating diseases seeking to end their lives and of the assisted suicides conducted by Dr. Jack Kevorkian and others. Some of the justices' opinions provided hints as to how they would rule on "mercy killings," assisted suicides, and so forth. In a 1996 speech, Justice Scalia did more than provide a hint: he asserted his belief that the Constitution plainly provides "no right to die."[31]

---

31. Antonin Scalia, "A Theory of Constitutional Interpretation," Remarks at the Catholic University Law School, Washington, D.C., October 18, 1996. Available at: *http://www.courttv.com/old/library/rights/scalia.html.*

BOX 9-6   LIVING WILLS

I N 1976 California became the first state to adopt living will legislation. Since then almost all the other states have followed suit. Living wills permit individuals various types of control over the use of heroic, life-sustaining medical treatment in the event of a terminal illness. Demand for living will laws is a product of increased social concern with the ability and tendency of modern medicine to keep elderly, terminally ill, and permanently comatose patients alive beyond the natural course of death from age or infirmity. Respirators, cardiac resuscitation, artificial feeding and hydration, drug treatment, and other procedures may prevent a natural and easy death, often from pneumonia, known widely in the past as the "old man's friend." Living will laws—and the broader issue of the right to die—affect all age and social groups, although the growing elderly population is disproportionately affected. The issue is similar to abortion because it concerns the preservation of life, but at the opposite end of the life cycle.

NATURAL DEATH ACT DECLARATION
("LIVING WILL")

Virginia's Natural Death Act was enacted in 1983 to permit Virginians to record their wishes regarding extraordinary care in the event of terminal illness. The declaration below is the suggested form developed by the state legislators to implement the Act. Fill out this form and give it to your physician and any relatives and friends you would like to have a copy. You must sign in the presence of two witnesses, and both witnesses must sign in your presence. Blood relatives or spouse may not be witnesses.

DECLARATION

In accordance with the Virginia Natural Death Act, this Declaration was made on _____.
_{Month/Day/Year}

I, _____, willfully and voluntarily make known my desire and do here-
Name of person making declaration

by declare:

You must choose between the following two paragraphs. PARAGRAPH ONE designates a person to make a decision for you. In PARAGRAPH TWO, you make the decision. Cross through the paragraph you do NOT want.

PARAGRAPH ONE:

If at any time I should have a terminal condition and I am comatose, incompetent or otherwise mentally or physically incapable of communication, I designate _____ to make a decision on my behalf as to whether life-prolonging procedures shall be withheld or withdrawn. In the event that my designee decides that such procedures should be withheld or withdrawn, I wish to be permitted to die naturally with only the administration of medication or the performance of any medical procedure deemed necessary to provide me with comfort care or to alleviate pain. (OPTION: I specifically direct that the following procedures or treatments be provided to me:

OR

PARAGRAPH TWO:

If at any time I should have a terminal condition where the application of life-prolonging procedures would serve only to artificially prolong the dying process, I direct that such procedures be withheld or withdrawn, and that I be permitted to die naturally with only the administration of medication or the performance of any medical procedure deemed necessary to provide me with comfort care or to alleviate pain. (OPTION: I specifically direct that the following procedures or treatments be provided to me:

_____

_____

But it was not until seven years after *Cruzan* that the Court considered whether the right to privacy or "liberty interest" is broad enough to encompass assisted suicides. That consideration came in two 1997 cases, *Washington v. Glucksberg* and *Vacco v. Quill*, both involving state laws making it a crime to assist another to commit suicide. By 9–0 votes, the justices rejected claims that such statutes violate the Due Process and Equal Protection Clauses. In addition to identifying long-standing traditions against suicide, the Court found that the states had legitimate interests in preserving human life, protecting the integrity and ethics of the medical profession, safeguarding the vulnerable from coercion, and ensuring the value of life even of the elderly and terminally ill.

What should we take away from these decisions? On the one hand, the justices made it crystal clear that states may maintain their existing bans on assisted suicides. On the other, they did not foreclose the possibility of future constitutional claims. In a concurring opinion, Justice O'Connor, for example, left open the possibility that the Court might respond positively to the question of "whether a mentally competent person who is experiencing great suffering has a constitutionally cognizable interest in controlling the circumstances of his or her imminent death." Even Rehnquist's majority opinion in *Glucksberg* noted that "throughout the Nation, Americans are engaged in an earnest and profound debate about the morality, legality, and practicality of physician-assisted suicide" and that the decision "permits this debate to continue, as it should in a democratic society."

Drug Testing

As the Court and the public continue to wrestle with the right to die, another privacy-related issue has moved to the forefront: drug testing. Many public and private employers have initiated drug screening or testing programs for job applicants or employees; some schools have started them for students. Under many of these programs, individuals must have their urine tested even if the examiner has no reason to suspect illegal drug use.

Those who support drug testing assert that the nation has a legitimate concern with drug abuse and the social problems that flow from illegal drug operations. Drug testing, they argue, is an effective method of identifying individuals who have consumed illegal substances. Finally, proponents suggest that a urinalysis is a minor intrusion into an individual's privacy rights and a minor incursion into the body.

Opponents respond that, under *Katz v. United States*, employers may be intruding into their employees' reasonable privacy expectations. They assert that employers order tests without reason to believe that a specific employee has committed a crime. In other words, opponents allege that drug-testing programs violate the right to privacy.

Beginning in 1989 the Court began to sort through these competing claims. We cover this topic in Chapter 9 but note here that the Court upheld the programs at issue in three of its first four major rulings *(see Table 9-7)*. In those cases, the justices took the position that government interests outweigh individuals' expectations of privacy. In *Chandler v. Miller* (1997), however, the Court held that a Georgia law requiring drug screening of all candidates for public office went too far, that it "diminishes personal privacy for a symbol's sake."

Privacy in the Information Age

Drug-testing programs touch on privacy issues related to the body. If employers require you to submit to a urinalysis, they obtain information about your physical state. What about other information such as the Web sites you visit, the books you check out of the library, the amount of money you owe in school loans, and the content of your e-mail messages and cellular phone conversations? Do you have the right to privacy over what others can find out about you?

In the not-so-distant past, no one would have raised these questions because communication devices like e-mail and Web sites did not exist. In addition, obtaining personal data was difficult and expensive. But, with the growth of computer recordkeeping and the Internet, such information is readily available—and available to those with whom you may not want to share it. This was certainly the case for Michael A. Smyth, who, in an e-mail to a co-worker, called his employers "back-stabbing bastards." Smyth's bosses monitored his e-mail and fired

TABLE 9-7 The Supreme Court and Drug-Testing Programs

Case	Program	Court's Holding
Skinner v. Railway Labor Executives' Association (1989)	Requirement of the Federal Railroad Administration that employees take a breath or urine test if they were involved in a train accident or other serious incident.	In a 7–2 decision, the justices ruled that while "federal regulations requiring employees of private railroads to produce urine samples for chemical testing implicate the Fourth Admendment, as those tests invade reasonable expectations of privacy," the program at issue was not unreasonable. On the Court's logic, the government has a strong interest in preventing train accidents, some of which had been caused by drug and alcohol use by employees.
National Treasury Union v. Von Raab (1989)	Requirement of the U.S. Custom's Bureau that all job applicants be screened for drugs, as well as those seeking promotions to positions that (1) involve direct drug "interdiction," (2) require employees to carry weapons, and (3) require employees to handle classified material.	In a 5–4 decision, the justices upheld the program, even though it was a suspicionless program that authorized drug testing in the absence of any evidence that a crime had been committed. According to the majority the program was a reasonable one because "[t]he Government's compelling interests in preventing the promotion of drug users to positions where they might endanger the integrity of our Nation's borders or the life of the citizenry outweigh the privacy interests of those who seek promotion of these positions, who enjoy a diminished expectation of privacy by virtue of the special, and obvious, physical and ethical demands of those positions."
Vernonia School District 47J v. Acton (1995)	School system requirement that students wishing to play sports sign a form giving consent to drug testing. The school tests all athletes at the beginning of each season of their sport and randomly thereafter.	In a 6–3 decision, the Court held that random, suspicionless drug testing of students by public school officials does not violate the Constitution. The majority asserted that students have reduced privacy expectations, and that "[l]egitimate privacy expectations are even less with regard to student athletes. School sports are not for the bashful. They require 'suiting up' before each practice or event, and showering and changing afterwards. . . . There is an additional respect in which school athletes have a reduced expectation of privacy. By choosing to 'go out for the team,' they voluntarily subject themselves to a degree of regulation even higher than that imposed on students generally."
Chandler v. Miller (1997)	Law passed by Georgia requiring all candiates for public office to take a urine test as a condition for appearing on the ballot.	In an 8–1 decision, the justices held that the law violated the Constitution. Writing for the majority, Justice Ginsburg noted that the Court had upheld drug-testing programs for which the government presented some "special need," such as the protection of public safety. Here, Georgia was seeking to protect its "image," which is insufficient to justify the law. "However well-meant, the candidate drug test Georgia has devised diminishes personal privacy for a symbol's sake. The Fourth Amendment shields society against that state action," Ginsburg wrote.

him. Not only individuals, but society as a whole may bear high costs for the ability to gather data quickly, as an experiment conducted by a Los Angeles television reporter vividly shows. Using the name of convicted child killer Richard Allen Davis, the reporter contacted one of the country's largest compilers of consumer data. For $277 the company sent her a list of more than five thousand children's names, ages, addresses, and phone numbers.[32]

The larger problem is that "we are living in a time

32. Children are not the only ones at risk. Undoubtedly, if you applied for a credit card, subscribed to a magazine, or made a purchase through the Web, your name appears on some marketer's list, and that list is available to virtually anyone for a price.

when the law has not caught up with technology."[33] Although many bills are now pending in Congress, to date the government has passed only a few to limit the dissemination of information.[34] The Supreme Court has yet to decide a Smyth-like case. In addition, there are fundamental disagreements over possible remedies and even their desirability. On the one hand, an individual may not want the titles of books checked out of the library widely known, and we as a society do not want the names and addresses of five thousand children to fall in the hands of a convicted killer. On the other, many individuals enjoy their unfettered freedom to use the Internet, e-mail, and so forth as they wish, and view with great skepticism government attempts at regulation.

It remains to be seen on which side of this debate the justices will fall. There is little doubt, however, that these and other issues relating to privacy in our age of information will eventually make their way up to the Court; in fact, at least one—the Communications Decency Act *(see pages 373–377)*—already has. But that ruling hinged on First Amendment concerns rather than privacy. It seems clear, however, that cases centering on privacy and the Internet will follow and become a major part of the Court's docket in the twenty-first century.

READINGS

Bennett, Colin J., and Rebecca Grant, eds. *Visions of Privacy: Policy Choices for the Digital Age.* Toronto: University of Toronto Press, 1999.

Bond, Jon R., and Charles A. Johnson. "Implementing a Permissive Policy: Hospital Abortion Services after Roe v. Wade." *American Journal of Political Science* 26 (1982): 1–24.

Burgess, Susan R. *Contest for Constitutional Authority: The Abortion and War Powers Debate.* Lawrence: University Press of Kansas, 1992.

Canon, Bradley C., and Charles A. Johnson. *Judicial Policies: Implementation and Impact,* 2d ed. Washington, D.C.: CQ Press, 1998.

Cate, Fred H. *Privacy in the Information Age.* Washington, D.C.: Brookings, 1997.

Craig, Barbara Hinkson, and David M. O'Brien. *Abortion and American Politics.* Chatham, N.J.: Chatham House, 1993.

Decew, Judith Wagner. *In Pursuit of Privacy: Law, Ethics, and the Rise of Technology.* Ithaca, N.Y.: Cornell University Press, 1997.

Ely, John Hart. "The Wages of Crying Wolf: A Comment on *Roe v. Wade." Yale Law Journal* 82 (1973): 920–949.

Emerson, Thomas I. "Nine Justices in Search of a Doctrine." *Michigan Law Review* 64 (1965): 219–234.

Epstein, Lee, and Joseph F. Kobylka. *The Supreme Court and Legal Change: Abortion and the Death Penalty.* Chapel Hill: University of North Carolina Press, 1992.

Epstein, Richard A. "Substantive Due Process by Any Other Name." *Supreme Court Review* (1973): 159–186.

Etzioni, Amitai. *The Limits of Privacy.* New York: Basic Books, 1999.

Faux, Marian. *Roe v. Wade.* New York: Macmillan, 1988.

Franklin, Charles H., and Liane C. Kosaki. "Republican Schoolmaster: The U.S. Supreme Court, Public Opinion, and Abortion." *American Political Science Review* 83 (1989): 751–771.

Garrow, David. J. *Liberty and Sexuality: The Right to Privacy and the Making of Roe v. Wade.* Berkeley: University of California Press, 1998.

Gilliom, John. *Surveillance, Privacy, and the Law: Employee Drug Testing and the Politics of Social Control.* Ann Arbor: University of Michigan Press, 1994.

Glick, Henry R. *The Right to Die: Policy Innovation and Its Consequences.* New York: Columbia University Press, 1992.

Graber, Mark A. *Rethinking Abortion: Equal Choice, the Constitution, and Reproductive Politics.* Princeton: Princeton University Press, 1996.

Griffiths, John, Alex Bood, and Helen Weyers. *Euthanasia and Law in the Netherlands.* Amsterdam: Amsterdam University Press, 1998.

Hansen, Susan B. "State Implementation of Supreme Court Decisions: Abortion Rates Since *Roe v. Wade." Journal of Politics* 42 (1980): 372.

Humphry, Derek, and Mary Clement. *Freedom to Die: People, Politics and the Right-to-Die Movement.* New York: St. Martin's Press, 1998.

Lader, Lawrence. *Abortion II.* Boston: Beacon Press, 1973.

———. *Abortion.* Indianapolis: Bobbs-Merrill, 1966.

Luker, Kristen. *Abortion and the Politics of Motherhood.* Berkeley: University of California Press, 1984.

McDonagh, Eileen L. *Breaking the Abortion Deadlock.* New York: Oxford University Press, 1996.

McWhirter, Darien A., and Jon D. Bible. *Privacy as a Constitutional Right: Sex, Drugs, and the Right to Life.* Westport, Conn.: Greenwood Publishing Group, 1992.

Mohr, James C. *Abortion in America.* New York: Oxford University Press, 1978.

Mooney, Christopher Z., and Mei-Hsien Lee. "Legislative Morality in the American States: The Case of Pre-Roe Abortion Regulation Reform." *American Journal of Political Science* 39 (1995): 599–627.

O'Connor, Karen. *No Neutral Ground? Abortion Politics in an Age of Absolutes.* Boulder, Colo.: Westview Press, 1996.

---

33. The Cyberspace Law Institute at: *www.cli.org.* See also Colin J. Bennett and Rebecca Grant, eds., *Visions of Privacy: Policy Choices for the Digital Age* (Toronto: University of Toronto Press, 1999).

34. The Video Protection Act of 1988, for example, makes it illegal to release information about the videos a person rents or buys. Congress passed this law in response to concern over the publication of video titles Robert Bork rented, while his nomination was pending in the Senate.

Plasencia, Madeline, and Paul Finkelman, eds. *Right to Privacy and the Constitution*. New York: Garland, 1999.

Reagan, Leslie J. *When Abortion was a Crime: Women, Medicine and Law in the United States, 1867–1973*. Berkeley: University of California Press, 1997.

Rosenberg, Gerald N. "The Real World of Constitutional Rights: The Supreme Court and the Implementation of Abortion Decisions," in *Contemplating Courts*, ed. Lee Epstein. Washington, D.C.: CQ Press, 1995.

Rubin, Eva R. *Abortion, Politics, and the Courts*. Westport, Conn.: Greenwood Press, 1987.

Scherer, Jennifer M., and Rita J. Simon. *Euthanasia and the Right to Die: A Comparative View*. Lanham, Md.: Rowman and Littlefield, 1999.

Simon, J. Rita. *Abortion: Statutes, Policies, and Public Attitudes the World Over*. Westport, Conn.: Praeger, 1998.

Strum, Philippa. *Privacy: The Debate in the United States Since 1945*. Fort Worth, Texas: Harcourt Brace College Publishers, 1998.

Tribe, Laurence H. *Abortion: The Clash of Absolutes*. New York: W.W. Norton, 1990.

Uhlmann, Michael M., ed. *Last Rights? Assisted Suicide and Euthanasia Debated*. Published jointly by Ethics and Policy Center, Washington, D.C., and William B. Eerdmans Publishing, Grand Rapids, 1998.

Wardle, Lynn D., and Mary A. Wood. *A Lawyer Looks at Abortion*. Provo, Utah: Brigham Young University Press, 1982.

Yarnold, Barbara M. *Abortion Politics in the Federal Courts: Right Versus Right*. Westport, Conn.: Praeger, 1995.

Zucker, Marjorie B. *The Right to Die Debate: A Documentary History*. Westport, Conn.: Greenwood Press, 1999.

PART III

THE RIGHTS OF THE CRIMINALLY ACCUSED

THE CRIMINAL JUSTICE SYSTEM AND CONSTITUTIONAL RIGHTS

W E AMERICANS regard the Bill of Rights as an enumeration of our most cherished freedoms. The right to speak freely and to worship (or not) without undue interference from government are the guarantees to which politicians and citizens refer most often when they describe the unique character of the United States. We may need to be reminded, therefore, that four of the first eight amendments guarantee rights for the *criminally accused*. The Framers of the Constitution placed great emphasis on criminal rights because they had grown to despise the abusive practices of British criminal procedure. The Founders believed that agents of government should not enter private homes or search personal property without proper justification and that the accused should not be tried without the benefit of public scrutiny.

Consequently, the Fourth Amendment protects us from unreasonable searches and prescribes the procedures by which law enforcement officials can obtain search warrants. The Fifth Amendment prohibits self-incrimination and double jeopardy and provides for grand juries and due process of law. The Sixth Amendment governs trial proceedings. It calls for speedy and public jury trials during which defendants can call witnesses and face their accusers. It also provides for the assistance of counsel. The Eighth Amendment prohibits excessive bail and monetary fines and any punishments that are cruel and unusual. The Framers insisted on constitutional guarantees that would protect the guilty as

well as the innocent against the potentially abusive prosecutorial powers of the government.

Just because these rights are not the first that come to mind when we think about the Bill of Rights does not mean that they are any less important or less relevant to society. At least once during your life, you are likely to participate in the criminal justice system. You may be the victim of a crime. You may serve as a juror in a criminal trial or become involved as a witness. You may even be accused of a crime. As citizens we should understand the rights accorded us and the procedures that invoke such guarantees.

The two chapters that follow explore the constitutional rights of the criminally accused and the Supreme Court's interpretation of them. To appreciate their importance, however, we first take a brief look at the stages of the criminal justice process. Following that discussion, we describe trends in Supreme Court decisionmaking in this area.

OVERVIEW OF THE CRIMINAL JUSTICE SYSTEM

Figure III-1 provides a general overview of the criminal justice system and the constitutional rights effective at each stage. Two points should be kept in mind. First, because the states are given a degree of latitude in developing their criminal justice systems, these procedures vary from jurisdiction to jurisdiction. Second, fewer than 10 percent of all criminal cases actually proceed through

FIGURE III-1 The American Criminal Justice System

Stage	Governing Amendment[a]
Reported or suspected crime	
↓	
Investigation by law enforcement officials	Fourth Amendment search and seizure rights
↓	Fifth Amendment self-incrimination clause
Arrest	
↓	Sixth Amendment right to counsel clause
Booking	
↓	
Decision to prosecute	
↓	
Pretrial hearings (initial appearance, bail hearing, preliminary hearing, arraignment)	Fifth Amendment grand jury clause
	Sixth Amendment notification clause
	Eighth Amendment bail clause
↓	
	Fifth Amendment self-incrimination clause
Trial	Sixth Amendment speedy and public trial, jury, confrontation, and compulsory process clauses
↓	
Sentencing	Eighth Amendment cruel and unusual punishment clause
↓	
Appeals, postconviction stages	Fifth Amendment double jeopardy clause

a. The right to due process of law is in effect throughout the process.

every stage of the system. At some point during the process, most criminal defendants plead guilty, thereby waiving their right to a jury trial, and proceed directly to sentencing. Most of these guilty pleas are the result of plea-bargaining arrangements in which the accused agrees to admit guilt in exchange for reduced charges or a lenient sentence.

This qualification noted, the criminal process begins with the response of law enforcement officials to a suspected violation of a state or federal law. Many scholars and lawyers consider this part of the process to be of the utmost importance. The way police conduct their investigation and gather evidence affects all subsequent decisions made by lawyers, judges, and juries. The police are also significant actors because of the conflicting roles society asks them to play. We expect police officers to act lawfully, within the confines of the Constitution. We do not want them to break down our doors and search our

houses without proper cause. But society also expects effective law enforcement, with the police using reasonable discretion to make arrests and apply the laws. We do not want a heinous crime to go unpunished because constitutional guarantees have unreasonably tied the hands of police. Law enforcement officers must understand the rules well enough to act without violating them because when they make mistakes the consequences can be enormous.

Once police make an arrest and take an individual into custody, the prosecuting attorney joins the process. The prosecutor of state crimes, commonly known as the district attorney, is an elected official having jurisdiction over criminal matters in a given local jurisdiction, usually a county. Prosecutors of federal offenses, who are appointed by the president and confirmed by the Senate, are called United States attorneys. Their assignments correspond to the geographical jurisdiction of the federal district courts, and they serve at the president's pleasure. State and federal prosecutors decide whether the government will bring charges against the accused. Among other factors, prosecutors consider whether police acted properly in gathering evidence and making the arrest. If the prosecutor decides not to press charges, the police must release the suspect, and the process ends. If prosecution is indicated, the government brings the individual before a judge, who ensures that the accused has legal representation and understands the charges. The judge also must verify that police had adequate justification for holding the accused. Further, the judge may also set bail, a monetary guarantee that the accused will appear for trial.

The system next provides a step to ensure that the prosecutor is not abusing the power to charge persons with crimes. This check on prosecutorial discretion takes place in one of two ways. Individuals accused of committing federal offenses or of violating the laws of some states will receive grand jury hearings in accordance with the Fifth Amendment. Composed of lay persons, grand juries, without the accused being present, examine the strength of the prosecutor's case to determine whether the government's evidence is strong enough to support formal charges. If the grand jury decides that the prosecutor has satisfied the legal requirements, it issues a formal document, known as an *indictment*, ordering the accused to stand trial on specified charges. If the grand jury concludes that the prosecutor's case is insufficient, the defendant is released.

Because the right to a grand jury hearing is not one of the incorporated provisions of the Bill of Rights, states are free to develop other methods of checking the prosecutor. Several states use preliminary hearings, which more closely resemble trials than does the grand jury process. Both prosecution and defense may present their cases to a judge who evaluates the adequacy of the government's evidence. If the judge agrees that the prosecutor's case justifies a trial, the prosecutor issues an *information*. Roughly the equivalent of an indictment, the information is a formal document that orders the accused to stand trial on certain specified violations of the criminal code. If the prosecutor's case is found inadequate to justify a trial, the judge may order the release of the defendant.

Once formally charged, the defendant proceeds to the arraignment stage. At arraignment, a judge reads the indictment or information to ensure that the defendant understands the charges and the applicable constitutional rights. The judge also asks if the defendant is represented by counsel. Because the specific criminal accusations may have changed in seriousness or number of counts since the defendant's initial appearance, the judge reviews and perhaps modifies the bail amount. Finally, the judge accepts the defendant's plea: guilty, nolo contendere (no contest), or not guilty. Should the defendant plead guilty or no contest, a trial is not necessary, and the accused proceeds to sentencing.

A plea of not guilty normally leads to a full trial governed by constitutional provisions found in the Fifth and Sixth Amendments. The accused is entitled to a fair, public, and speedy trial by jury. The judge presides over the trial, and the two opposing lawyers question witnesses and summarize case facts. When both sides have presented their cases, the jury deliberates to reach a verdict. If the individual is found guilty, the judge issues a sentence, which under Eighth Amendment protections may not be cruel and unusual.

If the defendant is found not guilty, the process ends. Fifth Amendment prohibition against double jeopardy bars the government from putting an acquitted defendant on trial a second time for the same offense. The prosecution has no right to appeal an acquittal verdict reached by the trial court. Should the verdict be guilty, however, the defendant has the right to appeal the conviction to a higher court. The appeals court reviews the trial procedures to determine if any significant errors in law or procedure occurred. If dissatisfied with the findings of the appeals court, either side—the government or the defense—may try for a review by an even higher court. These requests may be denied because the system generally provides for only one appeal as a matter of right. Subsequent appeals are left to the discretion of the appellate courts.

TRENDS IN COURT DECISIONMAKING

In the next two chapters, we examine each stage in the criminal justice system vis-à-vis the constitutional rights of the criminally accused. While reading the narrative and opinions, keep in mind that the four amendments governing criminal proceedings do not work in isolation. Rather, they fit into a larger scheme that includes law, politics, local custom, and the practical necessities of coping with crime in a contemporary society.

The rights accorded the criminally accused by the four amendments set limits that, in tandem with the legal system, define the criminal justice process. The system depends heavily upon Supreme Court interpretation of the several clauses contained in those amendments. As we

have seen in other legal areas, however, the way the Court interprets constitutional rights is not determined exclusively by traditional legal factors such as precedent, the plain language of the law, or the intent of the Framers. Historical circumstances, ideological stances, and pressure from other institutions and private groups also affect the course of law, which explains why jurisprudence varies from one Supreme Court era to the next or even from term to term.

Perhaps no issue illustrates this intersection of law and politics better than criminal rights. In the 1960s, with Chief Justice Earl Warren at the helm, the Supreme Court revolutionized criminal law by expanding the protections accorded those charged with crimes *(see Box III-1)*. The extent to which the Warren Court altered existing law will become clear as you read the cases to come. For now, note the high percentage of decisions favoring the criminally accused during the 1960s, as depicted in Figure III-2.

The liberal trend did not go unnoticed. President Richard Nixon was among the first to recognize that expanded rights for the criminally accused upset a majority of Americans. During his presidential campaign of 1968 and once he was elected, Nixon emphasized the law and order theme, proclaiming to the voters that the liberal Warren Court had gone too far.

In a 1968 speech Nixon said, "It's time for some honest talk about the problem of order in the United States. Let us always respect, as I do, our courts and those who serve on them, but let us also recognize that some of our courts in their decisions have gone too far in weakening the peace forces as against the criminal forces in this country." All who heard these words knew that Nixon was referring only to the Warren Court. Apparently, many voters agreed with the future president. Public opinion polls taken in 1968 show that nearly two-thirds of Americans believed that the courts were not dealing with criminals harshly enough, compared with about 50 percent just three years earlier.[1] In short, Nixon had hit a nerve with U.S. citizens; he placed crime on the public agenda, where it remains.

FIGURE III-2 Percentage of Supreme Court Criminal Rights Cases Decided in Favor of the Accused, 1953–1998

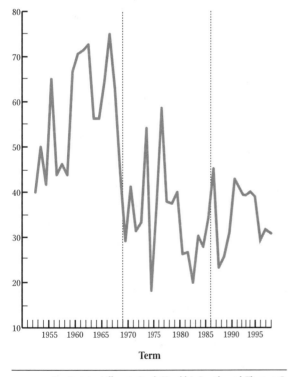

SOURCE: Lee Epstein, Jeffrey A. Segal, Harold J. Spaeth, and Thomas G. Walker, *The Supreme Court Compendium: Data, Decisions, and Developments,* 2d ed. (Washington, D.C.: Congressional Quarterly, 1996), Table 3-8. Updated by the authors.

1. Harold W. Stanley and Richard G. Niemi, *Vital Statistics on American Politics, 1999–2000* (Washington, D.C.: CQ Press, 2000), 158.

BOX III-1   EARL WARREN (1953-1969)

EARL WARREN, the son of Scandinavian immigrant parents, was born on March 19, 1891, in Los Angeles, California. Soon after his birth, the family moved to Bakersfield, where his father worked as a railroad car repairman.

Warren worked his way through college and law school at the University of California. After graduating in 1914, he worked in law offices in San Francisco and Oakland, the only time in his career that he engaged in private practice.

Warren married Nina P. Meyers, October 14, 1925. They had three daughters and three sons.

In 1938, after Warren had become active in politics, his father was bludgeoned to death in a crime that was never solved.

FROM 1919 UNTIL his resignation from the Supreme Court in 1969, Warren served without interruption in public office. His first post was deputy city attorney for Oakland. Then he was named a deputy district attorney for Alameda County, which embraces the cities of Oakland, Alameda, and Berkeley.

In 1925 Warren was appointed district attorney when the incumbent resigned. He won election to the post in his own right in 1926, 1930, and 1934. During his fourteen years as district attorney, Warren developed a reputation as a crime fighter, sending a city manager and several councilmen to jail on graft charges and smashing a crooked deal on garbage collection.

A Republican, Warren decided in 1938 to run for state attorney general. He cross-filed and won three primaries—his own party's as well as the Democratic and Progressive party contests.

In 1942 Warren ran for governor of California. Although he was an underdog, he wound up defeating incumbent Democratic governor Culbert Olson by a margin of 342,000, winning 57.1 percent of the total votes cast. He was twice reelected, winning the Democratic as well as the Republican nomination in 1946 and defeating Democrat James Roosevelt, son of President Franklin D. Roosevelt, by an almost two-to-one margin in 1950.

At first viewed as a conservative governor—he denounced "communist radicals" and supported the wartime federal order to move all persons of Japanese ancestry away from the West Coast—Warren developed a progressive image after the war. In 1945 he proposed a state program of prepaid medical insurance and later championed liberal pension and welfare benefits.

Warren made two bids for national political office. In 1948 he ran for vice president on the Republican ticket with Gov. Thomas E. Dewey of New York. In 1952 he sought the Republican presidential nomination. But with little chance to win he threw his support at a crucial moment behind Gen. Dwight D. Eisenhower, helping him win the battle with Sen. Robert A. Taft of Ohio for the nomination.

That support resulted in Eisenhower's political indebtedness to Warren, which the president repaid in 1953 with a recess appointment to the Supreme Court. Warren replaced Chief Justice Fred M. Vinson, who had died. Warren was confirmed by the Senate March 1, 1954, by a voice vote. Eisenhower, reflecting on his choice years later in the light of the Warren Court's liberal record, called the appointment "the biggest damn-fool mistake I ever made."

In addition to his work on the Court, Warren headed the commission that investigated the assassination of President John F. Kennedy.

In 1968 Warren submitted his resignation, conditional on confirmation of a successor. But the Senate got bogged down in the fight to confirm President Lyndon B. Johnson's nomination of Justice Abe Fortas to succeed Warren, so Warren agreed to serve another year. In 1969, when Richard Nixon assumed office, he chose Warren E. Burger as the new chief justice, and Warren stepped down. He died July 9, 1974.

SOURCE: Adapted from Joan Biskupic and Elder Witt, *Guide to the U.S. Supreme Court*, 3d ed. (Washington, D.C.: Congressional Quarterly, 1990), 869–870.

Nixon also had the opportunity to keep his promise to restore law and order to American communities by changing the composition of the Supreme Court. One year before Nixon took office Earl Warren had resigned to give President Lyndon Johnson the chance to appoint his successor. When Johnson's choice for that position, Associate Justice Abe Fortas, failed to obtain Senate confirmation, the chief justiceship remained vacant for Nixon to fill. His choice was Warren Burger, a court of appeals judge who agreed with Nixon's stance on criminal law.

During the 1970s those who sympathized with the liberal decisions of the Warren Court watched in horror as Nixon appointed three more justices to the Court. The American Civil Liberties Union and various legal aid societies predicted that this new Court would not only stop any expansion of criminal rights, but also begin to overturn Warren Court precedents. Figure III-2 shows there may be some truth to this view. The Court was far less supportive of criminal rights under Burger's leadership than under Warren's. This trend continued when William Rehnquist replaced Burger as chief justice in 1986.

But the data depicted in the figure present only an aggregated view of Court behavior. To understand whether, in fact, the Burger and Rehnquist Courts managed to alter existing precedent, we must examine the changes in particular areas of criminal law and procedure. As you read the chapters, note the date of each decision. Cases decided between 1953 and 1969 are Warren Court decisions, those between 1970 and 1986, Burger Court opinions, and all subsequent cases belong to the Rehnquist Court. Are there identifiable differences in interpretation? Did the Burger and Rehnquist Courts weaken the pro-defendant precedents set by the Warren Court as many civil libertarians predicted? If so, did this reaction impose a reasonable balance between effective law enforcement and the rights of the accused, or did it go too far in favoring the prosecution of criminal defendants?

CHAPTER 10

INVESTIGATIONS AND EVIDENCE

O N DECEMBER 21, 1911, police officers, acting on a tip, arrested Freemont Weeks at Union Station in Kansas City, where he worked for an express company. They charged him with using the U.S. mails to transport lottery tickets, a violation of federal law. Simultaneously, other police officers went to the accused's home and learned from neighbors where Weeks hid the key to his house. The officers entered the house and conducted a search without a search warrant and without the owner's permission. In his room they found various papers and articles, which they seized and turned over to the United States marshal.

Believing that additional investigation would yield more promising evidence, the marshal returned to the Weeks home later that day accompanied by police officers. A boarder who lived there allowed the officers to enter after they knocked. Once again, police entered the house without a search warrant. This search yielded documents and other articles, including books, letters, money, papers, notes, evidence of indebtedness, stock certificates, insurance policies, bonds, deeds, candy, and clothes. When federal authorities carefully examined what had been seized, they found some letters, lottery tickets, and other written statements that were used as evidence against Weeks, but most of the materials taken were not relevant to the criminal charges.

Over objections that the police had violated the search and seizure provisions of the Fourth Amendment, the government used the evidence against Weeks at his trial and obtained a conviction. Weeks was fined and

sentenced to prison. He challenged the conviction on appeal, ultimately taking his case to the Supreme Court. The justices found that the police had violated the Fourth Amendment and that, because the evidence had been unconstitutionally obtained, it should not have been used in court to establish the defendant's guilt. The conviction was overturned, and Weeks went free.

How is it possible that Weeks could avoid criminal penalties? The evidence showed, without doubt, that he was guilty of the charges. The answer is simple: proof that a crime was committed is a necessary but insufficient condition for a successful prosecution. The government must also show that the proof (or evidence) was obtained in a way that respected the rights of the accused.

The decision in *Weeks v. United States* (1914) represents one of the Court's earliest attempts to grapple with the issues of constitutional violations by police while gathering evidence and what to do when such violations occur. This area of the law has not yielded easy answers. In each term of the modern Court, the justices have heard cases in which individuals convicted of crimes claim that police acted improperly in gathering evidence. The stakes in these cases are great. They affect not only law enforcement procedures and criminal punishments, but also establish constitutional rules that protect all of us against unreasonable government intrusion into our lives.

In broad terms, when police seek to gather physical evidence, they are bound to respect the guarantees accorded to the criminally accused in the two clauses of the Fourth Amendment:

[1] The right of the people to be secure in their persons, houses, papers, and effects, against unreasonable searches and seizures, shall not be violated, and

[2] no Warrants shall issue, but upon probable cause, supported by Oath or affirmation, and particularly describing the place to be searched, and the persons or things to be seized.

In short, the first clause requires that searches be reasonable, and the second clause prescribes the procedures by which warrants can be obtained.

At first glance, these clauses seem to suggest that police may not conduct searches and seizures without warrants and that is why the Court turned down the government's case against Weeks. That interpretation is not correct. The Supreme Court, as we shall see, has said the Fourth Amendment does not always require that searches and seizures be authorized by a warrant to be valid. Instead, the justices have developed rules to determine when warrants are not required.

Physical evidence is not the only kind presented in court; there is also verbal evidence. Indeed, from the government's perspective, the most convincing proof that an accused person committed the crime is a confession—a form of verbal evidence. But, here too, law enforcement officials are not free to obtain confessions, or other kinds of verbal evidence, in just any fashion. They are bound to respect the privilege against self-incrimination contained in the Fifth Amendment: "No person . . . shall be compelled in any criminal case to be a witness against himself."

In this chapter we shall have a good deal to say about the Court's interpretation of the Fifth Amendment's self-incrimination provision, along with its decisions regarding the Fourth Amendment. Here we note that these guarantees, like most provisions of the Constitution, permit various interpretations. To understand why, we have only to remember that the men who wrote the Fourth Amendment in 1789 could not envision electronic surveillance, fingerprinting, DNA testing, or dogs trained to sniff out illegal drugs. Moreover, the terms used in the Fourth and Fifth Amendments, like many others in the Constitution, are vague and require interpretation. For example, in Clause 1 of the Fourth Amendment, what

does the word *unreasonable* mean? What separates a *reasonable* search from an *unreasonable* search? In Clause 2 what is the meaning of *probable cause?* The answers to these questions are of critical importance if the Fourth Amendment is to have any force. As you read the cases, keep in mind the material we reviewed in the Part III essay and consider how different Supreme Courts and justices have approached the rights of the criminally accused.

THE FOURTH AMENDMENT: HISTORICAL NOTES

Like many of the constitutional guarantees accorded the criminally accused, the Fourth Amendment has its genesis in the Framers' resentment of an English institution—the writs of assistance. These writs were general search warrants that did not impose limits on the places or things to be searched. The Crown authorized them beginning in the mid-1600s; by the early 1700s the writs were used in the colonies primarily to allow customs officials to conduct unrestricted searches. By authorizing these searches, Britain hoped to discourage smuggling by colonial merchants and to enforce existing restrictions on colonial trade.[1]

As general searches became more common, some colonists began to express their distaste for what they felt were major intrusions on their personal privacy and political liberty. James Otis, a Massachusetts lawyer, summed up the situation in a now famous statement. In 1761, when customs officials asked a Massachusetts court for writs of assistance to enforce the "hated Stamp Act," Otis mounted a legal challenge.[2] He argued that the writs went "against the fundamental principles of law," not because the government lacked the power to conduct searches but because it should not be permitted to conduct the open-ended searches—those that did not specify the places and things to be searched—authorized by the writs. In his view, a "man's house is his castle; and whilst he is quiet, he is well guarded as a prince in his

---

1. For more, see Melvin I. Urofsky, *A March of Liberty* (New York: Knopf, 1988), 36–42.

2. Marvin Zalman and Larry Siegel, *Criminal Procedure,* 2d ed. (St. Paul, Minn.: West Publishing, 1997), 24, 62, 118.

castle." He thought the general warrants, to put it in modern-day terms, intruded on personal privacy.

The Massachusetts court ignored Otis's plea and continued to issue the writs. But his concerns were echoed in England by William Pitt. In a speech delivered in the House of Commons, Pitt uttered these equally famous words:

The poorest may, in his cottage, bid defiance to all the forces of the Crown. It may be frail; its roof may shake; the wind may blow through it; the storm may enter; the rain may enter; but the King of England may not enter.

Unlike Otis, Pitt was successful: in 1766 the House of Commons invalidated general warrants.

Still, the damage had been done. Right before the Declaration of Independence was issued, Samuel Adams said that opposition over the general searches was the "Commencement of the Controversy between Great Britain and America."[3] And, by the time James Madison proposed the Bill of Rights to Congress, it was clear that most Americans agreed with the position Otis had advocated: almost all of the newly adopted state constitutions restricted government searches and seizures. In other words, they outlawed use of general warrants in favor of those that provided for limited searches. It is not surprising that such restrictions in the federal Constitution met with little opposition.

THE SUPREME COURT AND THE FOURTH AMENDMENT

Even though Madison's version of the Fourth Amendment caused little public or political controversy, the Supreme Court has not had an easy time interpreting it. To the contrary, since the early twentieth century, the justices have struggled to develop rules to govern searches and seizures. The crux of the problem is that the Court needs to be true to the spirit of the Fourth Amendment, providing protection for all citizens against abusive intrusions by the government but not restricting police in ways that render effective law enforcement impossible.

In grappling with these often conflicting goals, the Court has reached decisions that sometimes appear con-

tradictory, but it has been guided by one important principle: the Fourth Amendment requires that searches be *reasonable.* Clearly, the Court has preferred that searches and seizures be conducted pursuant to a validly issued search warrant. Yet the justices have realized that obtaining a search warrant is often not practical. Therefore, the Court has developed rules, consistent with the goals of the Fourth Amendment, that allow exceptions to the warrant procedure.

Searches with Warrants

The Constitution mentions only one search authorization method: how to obtain a warrant. Clause 2 of the Fourth Amendment outlines the steps to be followed. A police officer must go before a judge or magistrate and swear under oath that there is reason to believe that a crime has been committed and that evidence of the crime is located in a particular place. This information often is presented in a sworn statement called an affidavit. The judge then must determine whether there is probable cause to issue the warrant. If such cause is present, the judge authorizes a search by issuing a warrant that carefully describes the area to be searched and the items that may be seized. Police are then permitted to execute the search in a way that does not extend beyond the boundaries described in the warrant.

Probable Cause. Although obtaining a search warrant sounds like a straightforward procedure, searches conducted with warrants occur less frequently than we might expect, and the reason is the elusive nature of probable cause. The rationale behind the probable cause requirement is easy to understand: individuals are deserving of security in their private lives, and government intrusion should not be allowed unless there is substantial reason for it. But what is probable cause, and how do police know when they have it?

In *Brinegar v. United States* (1949) the Supreme Court explained that when police, or even judges, deal "with probable cause . . . as the very name implies, [they] deal with probabilities. These are not technical; they are the factual and practical considerations of everyday life on which reasonable and prudent men, not legal technicians, act." But does this statement provide police with

3. Ira Glasser, *Visions of Liberty* (New York: Arcade, 1991), 166.

any guidance? For example, assume that a number of credible witnesses inform police that a certain man is operating as a fence, buying and reselling stolen goods out of a particular apartment. One of these witnesses provides police with a stolen wristwatch the witness claims to have purchased at the apartment. Under these conditions police clearly have probable cause to believe that crimes have been committed and a sufficient factual basis to persuade a judge to issue a warrant to search the apartment. Much police work, however, is not so simple. Officers frequently are forced to investigate on the basis of informants' tips, anonymous letters, and the like. Do these items constitute sufficient probable cause to allow a judge to issue a search warrant?

In *Aguilar v. Texas* (1964) the Supreme Court, under Earl Warren's leadership, articulated a stringent two-pronged test to determine whether informants' tips or letters could be used as probable cause to obtain search warrants. First, the tip had to "reveal adequately" the informant's "basis of knowledge." How did the individual come to possess the information given to the police? Second, the tip "had to provide facts sufficiently establishing either the veracity of the affiant's informant, or, alternatively, the 'reliability' of the informant's report." The Court later developed the test more fully in *Spinelli v. United States* (1969) and thereafter referred to it as the Aguilar-Spinelli test.

In the years following *Aguilar,* police and law enforcement organizations complained that this test made it almost impossible for them to use any letter or tip as the basis for probable cause. These criticisms, coupled with changes in Supreme Court personnel, created an atmosphere in which the Court would reevaluate Aguilar-Spinelli. The opportunity came in *Illinois v. Gates* (1983).[4] Justice Rehnquist's opinion not only analyzes the concept of probable cause, but also provides an interesting example of how the Court deals with precedent it no longer feels to be prudent policy.

4. For oral arguments in this case, navigate to: *oyez.nwu.edu.*

Illinois v. Gates

462 U.S. 213 (1983)
laws.findlaw.com/US/462/213.html
Vote: 6 (Blackmun, Burger, O'Connor, Powell, Rehnquist, White)
    3 (Brennan, Marshall, Stevens)
Opinion of the Court: Rehnquist
Concurring opinion: White
Dissenting opinions: Brennan, Stevens

On May 3, 1978, police in a Chicago suburb received the following anonymous letter:

This letter is to inform you that you have a couple in your town who strictly make their living on selling drugs. They are Sue and Lance Gates, they live on Greenway, off Bloomingdale Rd. in the condominiums. Most of their buys are done in Florida. Sue his wife drives their car to Florida, where she leaves it to be loaded up with drugs, then Lance flies down and drives it back. Sue flies back after she drops the car off in Florida. May 3 she is driving down there again and Lance will be flying down in a few days to drive it back. At the time Lance drives the car back he has the trunk loaded with over $100,000.00 in drugs. Presently they have over $100,000.00 worth of drugs in their basement.

They brag about the fact they never have to work, and make their entire living on pushers.

I guarantee if you watch them carefully you will make a big catch. They are friends with some big drug dealers, who visit their house often.

A precinct detective partially verified the information in the note and went to a judge to obtain a search warrant based on probable cause. Warrant in hand, the police waited for the couple to return from Florida to search their car. The search turned up 350 pounds of marijuana.

The Gateses' attorney argued that the judge should exclude this evidence from trial because police, under the Aguilar test, lacked sufficient probable cause. Specifically, the letter failed to state how the writer came upon the information, a requirement mandated by Aguilar-Spinelli. At a pretrial hearing the judge agreed that the evidence could not be used at the trial. The prosecution appealed the ruling, but the Illinois Supreme Court affirmed it.

The state, along with several amicus curiae, asked the Supreme Court to review the decision. Illinois argued, "Probable cause to justify issuance of a search warrant exists when the facts and circumstances presented to the magistrate are sufficient to warrant a prudent person to believe that the described items are in the indicated locale." The U.S. Supreme Court, therefore, addressed this question: May a judge issue a search warrant on the basis of a "partially corroborated anonymous informant's tip"?

JUSTICE REHNQUIST delivered the opinion of the Court.

We granted certiorari to consider the application of the Fourth Amendment to a magistrate's issuance of a search warrant on the basis of a partially corroborated anonymous informant's tip. . . .

The Illinois Supreme Court concluded—and we are inclined to agree—that standing alone, the anonymous letter sent to the Bloomingdale Police Department would not provide the basis for a magistrate's determination that there was probable cause to believe contraband would be found in the Gateses' car and home. The letter provides virtually nothing from which one might conclude that its author is either honest or his information reliable; likewise, the letter gives absolutely no indication of the basis for the writer's predictions regarding the Gateses' criminal activities. Something more was required, then, before a magistrate could conclude that there was probable cause to believe that contraband would be found in the Gateses' home and car.

The Illinois Supreme Court also properly recognized that Detective Mader's affidavit might be capable of supplementing the anonymous letter with information sufficient to permit a determination of probable cause. In holding that the affidavit in fact did not contain sufficient additional information to sustain a determination of probable cause, the Illinois court applied a "two-pronged test," derived from our decision in *Spinelli v. United States* (1969). The Illinois Supreme Court, like some others, apparently understood *Spinelli* as requiring that the anonymous letter satisfy each of two independent requirements before it could be relied on. According to this view, the letter, as supplemented by Mader's affidavit, first had to adequately reveal the "basis of knowledge" of the letterwriter—the particular means by which he came by the information given in his report. Second, it had to provide facts sufficiently establishing either the "veracity" of the affiant's informant, or, alternatively, the "reliability" of the informant's report in this particular case. The Illinois court, alluding to an elaborate set of legal rules that have developed among various lower courts to enforce the "two-pronged test," found that the test had not been satisfied. First, the "veracity" prong was not satisfied because, "[t]here was simply no basis [for] concluding that the anonymous person [who wrote the letter to the Bloomingdale Police Department] was credible." The court indicated that corroboration by police of details contained in the letter might never satisfy the "veracity" prong, and in any event, could not do so if, as in the present case, only "innocent" details are corroborated. In addition, the letter gave no indication of the basis of its writer's knowledge of the Gateses' activities. The Illinois court understood *Spinelli* as permitting the detail contained in a tip to be used to infer that the informant had a reliable basis for his statements, but it thought that the anonymous letter failed to provide sufficient detail to permit such an inference. Thus, it concluded that no showing of probable cause had been made.

We agree with the Illinois Supreme Court that an informant's "veracity," "reliability," and "basis of knowledge" are all highly relevant in determining the value of his report. We do not agree, however, that these elements should be understood as entirely separate and independent requirements to be rigidly exacted in every case, which the opinion of the Supreme Court of Illinois would imply. Rather, as detailed below, they should be understood simply as closely intertwined issues that may usefully illuminate the commonsense, practical question whether there is "probable cause" to believe that contraband or evidence is located in a particular place.

This totality-of-the-circumstances approach is far more consistent with our prior treatment of probable cause than is any rigid demand that specific "tests" be satisfied by every informant's tip. Perhaps the central teaching of our decisions bearing on the probable-cause standard is that it is a "practical, nontechnical conception." "In dealing with probable cause, . . . as the very name implies, we deal with probabilities. These are not technical; they are the factual and practical considerations of everyday life on which reasonable and prudent men, not legal technicians, act.". . .

As these comments illustrate, probable cause is a fluid concept—turning on the assessment of probabilities in particular factual contexts—not readily, or even usefully, reduced to a neat set of legal rules. Informants' tips doubtless come in many shapes and sizes from many different types of persons. . . .

Moreover, the "two-pronged test" directs analysis into two largely independent channels—the informant's "veracity" or "reliability" and his "basis of knowledge." There are persuasive arguments against according these two elements such independent status. Instead, they are better understood as relevant considerations in the totality-of-the-circumstances analysis that traditionally has guided probable-cause determinations: a deficiency in one may be compensated for, in determining the overall reliability of a tip, by a strong showing as to the other, or by some other indicia of reliability. . . .

We . . . have recognized that affidavits "are normally drafted by nonlawyers in the midst and haste of a criminal investigation. Technical requirements of elaborate specificity once exacted under common law pleadings have no proper place in this area." Likewise, search and arrest warrants long have been issued by persons who are neither lawyers nor judges, and who certainly do not remain abreast of each judicial refinement of the nature of "probable cause." The rigorous inquiry into the *Spinelli* prongs and the complex superstructure of evidentiary and analytical rules that some have seen implicit in our *Spinelli* decision, cannot be reconciled with the fact that many warrants are, quite properly, issued on the basis of nontechnical, commonsense judgments of laymen applying a standard less demanding than those used in more formal legal proceedings. Likewise, given the informal, often hurried context in which it must be applied, the "built-in subtleties" of the "two-pronged test" are particularly unlikely to assist magistrates in determining probable cause.

Similarly, we have repeatedly said that after-the-fact scrutiny by courts of the sufficiency of an affidavit should not take the form of *de novo* review. . . .

If the affidavits submitted by police officers are subjected to the type of scrutiny some courts have deemed appropriate, police might well resort to warrantless searches, with the hope of relying on consent or some other exception to the Warrant Clause that might develop at the time of the search. . . .

Finally, the direction taken by decisions following *Spinelli* poorly serves "the most basic function of any government": "to provide for the security of the individual and of

his property." The strictures that inevitably accompany the "two-pronged test" cannot avoid seriously impeding the task of law enforcement. . . .

For all these reasons, we conclude that it is wiser to abandon the "two-pronged test" established by our decisions in *Aguilar* and *Spinelli*. In its place we reaffirm the totality-of-the-circumstances analysis that traditionally has informed probable-cause determinations. The task of the issuing magistrate is simply to make a practical, commonsense decision whether, given all the circumstances set forth in the affidavit before him, including the "veracity" and "basis of knowledge" of persons supplying hearsay information, there is a fair probability that contraband or evidence of a crime will be found in a particular place. And the duty of a reviewing court is simply to ensure that the magistrate had a "substantial basis for . . . concluding" that probable cause existed. We are convinced that this flexible, easily applied standard will better achieve the accommodation of public and private interests that the Fourth Amendment requires than does the approach that has developed from *Aguilar* and *Spinelli*. . . .

The showing of probable cause in the present case . . . [is] compelling. . . . Even standing alone, the facts obtained through the independent investigation of Mader and the DEA [Drug Enforcement Administration] at least suggested that the Gateses were involved in drug trafficking. In addition to being a popular vacation site, Florida is well-known as a source of narcotics and other illegal drugs. Lance Gates' flight to West Palm Beach, his brief, overnight stay in a motel, and apparent immediate return north to Chicago in the family car, conveniently awaiting him in West Palm Beach, is as suggestive of a prearranged drug run, as it is of an ordinary vacation trip.

In addition, the judge could rely on the anonymous letter, which had been corroborated in major part. . . . The corroboration of the letter's predictions that the Gateses' car would be in Florida, that Lance Gates would fly to Florida in the next day or so, and that he would drive the car north toward Bloomingdale all indicated, albeit not with certainty, that the informant's other assertions also were true. . . .

Finally, the anonymous letter contained a range of details relating not just to easily obtained facts and conditions existing at the time of the tip, but to future actions of third parties ordinarily not easily predicted. The letterwriter's accurate information as to the travel plans of each of the Gateses was of a character likely obtained only from the Gateses themselves, or from someone familiar with their not entirely ordinary travel plans. If the informant had access to accurate information of this type, a magistrate could properly conclude that it was not unlikely that he also had access to reliable information of the Gateses' alleged illegal activities. Of course, the Gateses' travel plans might have been learned from a talkative neighbor or travel agent; under the "two-pronged test" developed from *Spinelli,* the character of the details in the anonymous letter might well not permit a sufficiently clear inference regarding the letterwriter's "basis of knowledge." But, as discussed previously, probable cause does not demand the certainty we associate with formal trials. It is enough that there was a fair probability that the writer of the anonymous letter had obtained his entire story either from the Gateses or someone they trusted. And corroboration of major portions of the letter's predictions provides just this probability. It is apparent, therefore, that the judge issuing the warrant had a "substantial basis for . . . concluding" that probable cause to search the Gateses' home and car existed. The judgment of the Supreme Court of Illinois therefore must be

Reversed.

JUSTICE BRENNAN, with whom JUSTICE MARSHALL joins, dissenting.

I write separately to dissent from the Court's unjustified and ill-advised rejection of the two-prong test for evaluating the validity of a warrant based on hearsay announced in *Aguilar v. Texas* (1964) and refined in *Spinelli v. United States* (1969). . . .

In recognition of the judiciary's role as the only effective guardian of Fourth Amendment rights, this Court has developed over the last half century a set of coherent rules governing a magistrate's consideration of a warrant application and the showings that are necessary to support a finding of probable cause. We start with the proposition that a neutral and detached magistrate, and not the police, should determine whether there is probable cause to support the issuance of a warrant. . . .

In order to emphasize the magistrate's role as an independent arbiter of probable cause and to insure that searches or seizures are not effected on less than probable cause, the Court has insisted that police officers provide magis-

trates with the underlying facts and circumstances that support the officers' conclusions. . . .

At the heart of the Court's decision to abandon *Aguilar* and *Spinelli* appears to be its belief that "the direction taken by decisions following *Spinelli* poorly serves '[t]he most basic function of any government': 'to provide for the security of the individual and of his property.'" This conclusion rests on the judgment that *Aguilar* and *Spinelli* "seriously imped[e] the task of law enforcement" and render anonymous tips valueless in police work. Surely, the Court overstates its case. But of particular concern to all Americans must be that the Court gives virtually no consideration to the value of insuring that findings of probable cause are based on information that a magistrate can reasonably say has been obtained in a reliable way by an honest or credible person. . . .

The Court's complete failure to provide any persuasive reason for rejecting *Aguilar* and *Spinelli* doubtlessly reflects impatience with what it perceives to be "overly technical" rules governing searches and seizures under the Fourth Amendment. Words such as "practical," "nontechnical," and "common sense," as used in the Court's opinion, are but code words for an overly permissive attitude towards police practices in derogation of the rights secured by the Fourth Amendment. Everyone shares the Court's concern over the horrors of drug trafficking, but under our Constitution, only measures consistent with the Fourth Amendment may be employed by government to cure this evil. We must be ever mindful of Justice Stewart's admonition in *Coolidge v. New Hampshire* (1971): "[I]n times of unrest, whether caused by crime or racial conflict or fear of internal subversion, this basic law and the values that it represents may appear unrealistic or 'extravagant' to some. But the values were those of the authors of our fundamental constitutional concepts.". . .

Rights secured by the Fourth Amendment are particularly difficult to protect, because their "advocates are usually criminals." *Draper v. United States* [1959] (Douglas, J., dissenting). But the rules "we fashion [are] for the innocent and guilty alike." *Ibid.* By replacing *Aguilar* and *Spinelli* with a test that provides no assurance that magistrates, rather than the police, or informants, will make determinations of probable cause; imposes no structure on magistrates' probable-cause inquiries; and invites the possibility that intrusions may be justified on less than reliable information from an honest or credible person, today's decision threatens to "obliterate one of the most fundamental distinctions between our form of government, where officers are under the law, and the police-state, where they are the law." *Johnson v. United States* [1948].

The "totality-of-the-circumstances" standard established in *Illinois v. Gates* clearly facilitates police efforts to obtain search warrants. But, in addition to establishing probable cause, police must (1) specify the area to be searched and the things to be seized; (2) execute the warrant in an orderly and timely fashion;[5] and (3) seize only things specifically listed in the warrant unless they find items whose very possession is a crime, for example, contraband.

Warrants and Electronic Surveillance. As you can see, police face several legal and political obstacles in obtaining search warrants. Perhaps no other area of law illustrates this point as well as that involving wiretapping and electronic eavesdropping, where special statutory warrant requirements have been developed. Careful study of this line of cases also provides us with some insight into the myriad problems the Court has faced more generally in its Fourth Amendment jurisprudence.

As is typical in Fourth Amendment cases, the Court's initial forays involved situations in which law enforcement officials failed to obtain warrants to eavesdrop on conversations. For example, *Olmstead v. United States* (1928) centered on the ability of federal agents to place wiretaps on outside telephone lines without warrants. Roy Olmstead, who was accused of importing and selling alcohol in violation of the National Prohibition Act, alleged that even though agents had not entered his home or office, they had, through the wiretaps, "seized" his conversations in violation of the Fourth Amendment. The government maintained that wiretapping was not a search and seizure within the meaning of the Fourth Amendment.

The Court ruled in favor of the government. After reviewing the general history of the amendment, the Court concluded that the Fourth Amendment did not protect

Olmstead's conversations because it only covers searches of "material things—the person, the house, his papers or his effects." Therefore, "[t]he Amendment does not forbid what was done here. There was no searching. There was no seizure. The evidence was secured by the use of the sense of hearing and that only. There was no entry of the houses or offices of the defendants." Certainly, the majority stated, Congress may "protect the secrecy of telephone messages by making them, when intercepted, inadmissible in evidence in federal criminal trials, by direct legislation. . . . But the courts may not adopt such a policy by attributing an enlarged and unusual meaning to the Fourth Amendment."

The Court's logic was lost on four justices, who wrote dissenting opinions. Perhaps the best remembered was by Justice Brandeis. He echoed the words of Otis, Pitt, and the others who had fought against the general warrants when he wrote:

The makers of our Constitution undertook to secure conditions favorable to the pursuit of happiness. . . . They conferred, as against the Government, the right to be left alone—the most comprehensive of rights and the right most valued by civilized men. To protect that right, every unjustifiable intrusion by the Government upon the privacy of the individual, whatever the means employed, must be deemed a violation of the Fourth Amendment.

To Brandeis, it was "immaterial" that agents had not needed to enter Olmstead's home or office to place the wiretaps; it was equally unimportant that "the intrusion was in aid of law enforcement." He declared, "The greatest dangers to liberty lurk in insidious encroachment by men of zeal, well-meaning but without understanding."

The Brandeis position, however, did not prevail. Instead, the majority interpreted the Fourth Amendment to protect only against physical intrusions into constitutionally protected areas. This line of reasoning became known as the "physical penetration" rule. As long as the police did not physically encroach on an individual's "person, houses, papers, or effects" incriminating statements overheard electronically or otherwise could be gathered without a warrant and used as evidence in court.

The Court continued to apply this test in subsequent

---

5. See *Wilson v. Arkansas* (1995) and *Richards v. Wisconsin* (1997) for rules pertaining to the orderly execution of a search warrant.

cases. For example, in *Goldman v. United States* (1942) the justices allowed as evidence incriminating statements overheard by police through the warrantless use of a listening device attached to a wall adjoining the defendant's office. Because police had not entered Goldman's constitutionally protected space (his office), no warrant was required.

In response to public demands, Congress offered a degree of protection from police abuse of this rule by imposing significant limitations on telephone wiretapping in the Federal Communications Act of 1934. Many states followed suit, passing laws to eliminate the bugging of telephone lines.[6] However, as more sophisticated technology developed, police acquired increasingly effective methods of overhearing private conversations without tapping telephone lines and without physically intruding into a constitutionally protected space.

Growing dissatisfaction caused the Court to reevaluate the physical penetration rule in 1967 in *Katz v. United States*.[7] The political environment at the time sent mixed signals to the justices. Americans generally believed that the judicial system had become too soft on crime. On the other hand, public opinion polls showed that an overwhelming majority of the people disapproved of electronic surveillance.

How would the generally liberal Warren Court respond in a political environment that presented such conflicting messages? Would it retain the physical penetration rule or replace it with one that imposed greater restraints on law enforcement? Keep these questions in mind as you read *Katz*. Pay attention also to the dissenting opinion of Justice Black, in which he forcefully argues against judicial interpretations that stray too far from the original meaning of the words as written by the Framers.

6. Zalman and Siegel, *Criminal Procedure*, 2d ed., 206–207.
7. For oral arguments in this case, navigate to: *oyez.nwu.edu*.

Katz v. United States

389 U.S. 347 (1967)
laws.findlaw.com/US/389/347.html
Vote: 7 (Brennan, Douglas, Fortas, Harlan, Stewart, Warren, White)
1 (Black)
Opinion of the Court: Stewart
Concurring opinions: Douglas, Harlan, White
Dissenting opinion: Black
Not participating: Marshall

FBI agents suspected Charles Katz of engaging in illegal bookmaking activity; in particular, they thought he was placing bets and transmitting other wagering information by telephone from Los Angeles to Miami and Boston. To gather evidence, they placed listening and recording devices outside the telephone booth Katz used to make his calls. (Keep in mind that back then public telephones were often housed in glass booths.) Despite the fact that law enforcement officials had listened in on Katz's conversations without a warrant, federal attorneys used the transcripts of those conversations to obtain an eight-count indictment.

Both sides believed that the Court would use the physical penetration test; therefore, Katz and the government centered their arguments on the nature of the place where the conversations occurred. Katz challenged the use of the transcripts as evidence against him on the ground that the telephone booth was a "constitutionally protected area." In making this argument, which was not so different from Olmstead's nearly forty years earlier, Katz may have been on somewhat stronger ground. In the 1965 case of *Griswold v. Connecticut (see Chapter 9)*, the Supreme Court had created a constitutional right to privacy. Although *Griswold* involved birth control, some observers believed it was applicable to Katz's situation, as well. In other words, police could not invade his privacy unless they obtained a search warrant.

The government argued that in previous Fourth Amendment cases the justices permitted the warrantless use of bugs and recording devices so long as agents did not "physically penetrate" an individual's space. Here, the FBI attached the listening device to the *outside* of the booth; it never invaded Katz's space.

Should the Court be unwilling to follow this precedent—and, given the general liberal inclination of this Court, there were good reasons to suspect that it would not—then the government urged a back-up position: that the justices create an exception to the warrant rule to cover this case. It urged the Court to rule that "surveillance of a telephone booth . . . be exempted from the usual requirement" to obtain a search warrant.

MR. JUSTICE STEWART delivered the opinion of the Court.

We granted certiorari in order to consider the constitutional questions thus presented.

The petitioner has phrased those questions as follows:

"A. Whether a public telephone booth is a constitutionally protected area so that evidence obtained by attaching an electronic listening recording device to the top of such a booth is obtained in violation of the right to privacy of the user of the booth.

"B. Whether physical penetration of a constitutionally protected area is necessary before a search and seizure can be said to be violative of the Fourth Amendment to the United States Constitution."

We decline to adopt this formulation of the issues. In the first place, the correct solution of Fourth Amendment problems is not necessarily promoted by incantation of the phrase "constitutionally protected area." Secondly, the Fourth Amendment cannot be translated into a general constitutional "right to privacy." That Amendment protects individual privacy against certain kinds of governmental intrusion, but its protections go further, and often have nothing to do with privacy at all. Other provisions of the Constitution protect personal privacy from other forms of governmental invasion. But the protection of a person's *general* right to privacy—his right to be let alone by other people—is, like the protection of his property and of his very life, left largely to the law of the individual States.

Because of the misleading way the issues have been formulated, the parties have attached great significance to the characterization of the telephone booth from which the petitioner placed his calls. The petitioner has strenuously argued that the booth was a "constitutionally protected area."

The Government has maintained with equal vigor that it was not. But this effort to decide whether or not a given "area," viewed in the abstract, is "constitutionally protected" deflects attention from the problem presented by this case. For the Fourth Amendment protects people, not places. What a person knowingly exposes to the public, even in his own home or office, is not a subject of Fourth Amendment protection. But what he seeks to preserve as private, even in an area accessible to the public, may be constitutionally protected.

The Government stresses the fact that the telephone booth from which the petitioner made his calls was constructed partly of glass, so that he was as visible after he entered it as he would have been if he had remained outside. But what he sought to exclude when he entered the booth was not the intruding eye—it was the uninvited ear. He did not shed his right to do so simply because he made his calls from a place where he might be seen. No less than an individual in a business office, in a friend's apartment, or in a taxicab, a person in a telephone booth may rely upon the protection of the Fourth Amendment. One who occupies it, shuts the door behind him, and pays the toll that permits him to place a call is surely entitled to assume that the words he utters into the mouthpiece will not be broadcast to the world. To read the Constitution more narrowly is to ignore the vital role that the public telephone has come to play in private communication.

The Government contends, however, that the activities of its agents in this case should not be tested by Fourth Amendment requirements, for the surveillance technique they employed involved no physical penetration of the telephone booth from which the petitioner placed his calls. It is true that the absence of such penetration was at one time thought to foreclose further Fourth Amendment inquiry, *Olmstead v. United States; Goldman v. United States*, for that Amendment was thought to limit only searches and seizures of tangible property. But "the premise that property interests control the right of the Government to search and seize has been discredited.". . . Indeed, we have expressly held that the Fourth Amendment governs not only the seizure of tangible items, but extends as well to the recording of oral statements, overheard without any "technical trespass under . . . local property law." Once this much is acknowledged, and once it is recognized that the Fourth Amendment protects people—and not simply "areas"—against unreasonable searches and seizures, it becomes clear that the reach of that Amendment cannot turn upon the presence or absence of a physical intrusion into any given enclosure.

We conclude that the underpinnings of *Olmstead* and *Goldman* have been so eroded . . . [that they] can no longer be regarded as controlling. The Government's activities in electronically listening to and recording the petitioner's words violated the privacy upon which he justifiably relied while using the telephone booth and thus constituted a "search and seizure" within the meaning of the Fourth Amendment. The fact that the electronic device employed to achieve that end did not happen to penetrate the wall of the booth can have no constitutional significance.

The question remaining for decision, then, is whether the search and seizure conducted in this case complied with constitutional standards. In that regard, the Government's position is that its agents acted in an entirely defensible manner: They did not begin their electronic surveillance until investigation of the petitioner's activities had established a strong probability that he was using the telephone in question to transmit gambling information to persons in other States, in violation of federal law. Moreover, the surveillance was limited, both in scope and in duration, to the specific purpose of establishing the contents of the petitioner's unlawful telephonic communications. The agents confined their surveillance to the brief periods during which he used the telephone booth, and they took great care to overhear only the conversations of the petitioner himself.

Accepting this account of the Government's actions as accurate, it is clear that this surveillance was so narrowly circumscribed that a duly authorized magistrate, properly notified of the need for such investigation, specifically informed of the basis on which it was to proceed, and clearly apprised of the precise intrusion it would entail, could constitutionally have authorized, with appropriate safeguards, the very limited search and seizure that the Government asserts in fact took place. Only last Term we sustained the validity of such an authorization, holding that, under sufficiently "precise and discriminate circumstances," a federal court may empower government agents to employ a concealed electronic device "for the narrow and particularized purpose of ascertaining the truth of the . . . allegations" of a "detailed factual affidavit alleging the commis-

sion of a specific criminal offense.". . . Here, too, a similar judicial order could have accommodated "the legitimate needs of law enforcement" by authorizing the carefully limited use of electronic surveillance.

The Government urges that, because its agents relied upon the decisions in *Olmstead* and *Goldman*, and because they did no more here than they might properly have done with prior judicial sanction, we should retroactively validate their conduct. That we cannot do. It is apparent that the agents in this case acted with restraint. Yet the inescapable fact is that this restraint was imposed by the agents themselves, not by a judicial officer. They were not required, before commencing the search, to present their estimate of probable cause for detached scrutiny by a neutral magistrate. They were not compelled, during the conduct of the search itself, to observe precise limits established in advance by a specific court order. Nor were they directed, after the search had been completed, to notify the authorizing magistrate in detail of all that had been seized. In the absence of such safeguards, this Court has never sustained a search upon the sole ground that officers reasonably expected to find evidence of a particular crime and voluntarily confined their activities to the least intrusive means consistent with that end. Searches conducted without warrants have been held unlawful "notwithstanding facts unquestionably showing probable cause," for the Constitution requires "that the deliberate, impartial judgment of a judicial officer . . . be interposed between the citizen and the police. . . ." "Over and again this Court has emphasized that the mandate of the [Fourth] Amendment requires adherence to judicial processes," and that searches conducted outside the judicial process, without prior approval by judge or magistrate, are per se unreasonable under the Fourth Amendment—subject only to a few specifically established and well-delineated exceptions.

It is difficult to imagine how any of those exceptions could ever apply to the sort of search and seizure involved in this case. Even electronic surveillance substantially contemporaneous with an individual's arrest could hardly be deemed an "incident" of that arrest. . . . And, of course, the very nature of electronic surveillance precludes its use pursuant to the suspect's consent.

The Government does not question these basic principles. Rather, it urges the creation of a new exception to cover this case. It argues that surveillance of a telephone booth should be exempted from the usual requirement of advance authorization by a magistrate upon a showing of probable cause. We cannot agree. Omission of such authorization "bypasses the safeguards provided by an objective predetermination of probable cause, and substitutes instead the far less reliable procedure of an after-the-event justification for the . . . search, too likely to be subtly influenced by the familiar shortcomings of hindsight judgment." And bypassing a neutral predetermination of the scope of a search leaves individuals secure from Fourth Amendment violations "only in the discretion of the police."

These considerations do not vanish when the search in question is transferred from the setting of a home, an office, or a hotel room to that of a telephone booth. Wherever a man may be, he is entitled to know that he will remain free from unreasonable searches and seizures. The government agents here ignored "the procedure of antecedent justification . . . that is central to the Fourth Amendment," a procedure that we hold to be a constitutional precondition of the kind of electronic surveillance involved in this case. Because the surveillance here failed to meet that condition, and because it led to the petitioner's conviction, the judgment must be reversed.

MR. JUSTICE HARLAN, concurring.

I join the opinion of the Court, which I read to hold only (a) that an enclosed telephone booth is an area where, like a home . . . a person has a constitutionally protected reasonable expectation of privacy; (b) that electronic as well as physical intrusion into a place that is in this sense private may constitute a violation of the Fourth Amendment; and (c) that the invasion of a constitutionally protected area by federal authorities is, as the Court has long held, presumptively unreasonable in the absence of a search warrant.

As the Court's opinion states, "the Fourth Amendment protects people, not places." The question, however, is what protection it affords to those people. Generally, as here, the answer to that question requires reference to a "place." My understanding of the rule that has emerged from prior decisions is that there is a twofold requirement, first that a person have exhibited an actual (subjective) expectation of privacy and, second, that the expectation be one that society is prepared to recognize as "reasonable." Thus a man's home is, for most purposes, a place where he expects privacy, but

objects, activities, or statements that he exposes to the "plain view" of outsiders are not "protected" because no intention to keep them to himself has been exhibited. On the other hand, conversations in the open would not be protected against being overheard, for the expectation of privacy under the circumstances would be unreasonable.

The critical fact in this case is that "[o]ne who occupies it, [a telephone booth] shuts the door behind him, and pays the toll that permits him to place a call is surely entitled to assume" that his conversation is not being intercepted. The point is not that the booth is "accessible to the public" at other times, but that it is a temporarily private place whose momentary occupants' expectations of freedom from intrusion are recognized as reasonable. . . .

This case requires us to reconsider *Goldman,* and I agree that it should now be overruled. Its limitation on Fourth Amendment protection is, in the present day, bad physics as well as bad law, for reasonable expectations of privacy may be defeated by electronic as well as physical invasion.

Finally, I do not read the Court's opinion to declare that no interception of a conversation one-half of which occurs in a public telephone booth can be reasonable in the absence of a warrant. As elsewhere under the Fourth Amendment, warrants are the general rule, to which the legitimate needs of law enforcement may demand specific exceptions. It will be time enough to consider any such exceptions when an appropriate occasion presents itself, and I agree with the Court that this is not one.

MR. JUSTICE BLACK, dissenting.

If I could agree with the Court that eavesdropping carried on by electronic means (equivalent to wiretapping) constitutes a "search" or "seizure," I would be happy to join the Court's opinion. . . .

My basic objection is two-fold: (1) I do not believe that the words of the Amendment will bear the meaning given them by today's decision, and (2) I do not believe that it is the proper role of this Court to rewrite the Amendment in order "to bring it into harmony with the times," and thus reach a result that many people believe to be desirable.

While I realize that an argument based on the meaning of words lacks the scope, and no doubt the appeal, of broad policy discussions and philosophical discourses on such nebulous subjects as privacy, for me, the language of the

Amendment is the crucial place to look in construing a written document such as our Constitution. The Fourth Amendment says that

"The right of the people to be secure in their persons, houses, papers, and effects, against unreasonable searches and seizures, shall not be violated, and no Warrants shall issue, but upon probable cause, supported by Oath or affirmation, and particularly describing the place to be searched and the persons or things to be seized."

The first clause protects "persons, houses, papers, and effects against unreasonable searches and seizures. . . ." These words connote the idea of tangible things with size, form, and weight, things capable of being searched, seized, or both. The second clause of the Amendment still further establishes its Framers' purpose to limit its protection to tangible things by providing that no warrants shall issue but those "particularly describing the place to be searched, and the persons or things to be seized." A conversation overheard by eavesdropping, whether by plain snooping or wiretapping, is not tangible and, under the normally accepted meanings of the words, can neither be searched nor seized. In addition the language of the second clause indicates that the Amendment refers not only to something tangible so it can be seized but to something already in existence so it can be described. Yet the Court's interpretation would have the Amendment apply to overhearing future conversations which by their very nature are nonexistent until they take place. How can one "describe" a future conversation, and, if one cannot, how can a magistrate issue a warrant to eavesdrop one in the future? It is argued that information showing what is expected to be said is sufficient to limit the boundaries of what later can be admitted into evidence; but does such general information really meet the specific language of the Amendment which says "particularly describing"? Rather than using language in a completely artificial way, I must conclude that the Fourth Amendment simply does not apply to eavesdropping.

Tapping telephone wires, of course, was an unknown possibility at the time the Fourth Amendment was adopted. But eavesdropping (and wiretapping is nothing more than eavesdropping by telephone) was . . . "an ancient practice which, at common law, was condemned as a nuisance" 4 Blackstone, Commentaries, 168. "In those days, the eavesdropper listened by naked ear under the eaves of houses or their windows, or beyond their walls seeking out private dis-

course." [*Berger v. New York* (1967).] There can be no doubt that the Framers were aware of this practice, and, if they had desired to outlaw or restrict the use of evidence obtained by eavesdropping, I believe that they would have used the appropriate language to do so in the Fourth Amendment. They certainly would not have left such a task to the ingenuity of language-stretching judges. No one, it seems to me, can read the debates on the Bill of Rights without reaching the conclusion that its Framers and critics well knew the meaning of the words they used, what they would be understood to mean by others, their scope and their limitations. Under these circumstances it strikes me as a charge against their scholarship, their common sense and their candor to give to the Fourth Amendment's language the eavesdropping meaning the Court imputes to it today.

I do not deny that common sense requires and that this Court often has said that the Bill of Rights' safeguards should be given a liberal construction. This principle, however, does not justify construing the search and seizure amendment as applying to eavesdropping or the "seizure" of conversations. The Fourth Amendment was aimed directly at the abhorred practice of breaking in, ransacking and searching homes and other buildings and seizing people's personal belongings without warrants issued by magistrates. The Amendment deserves, and this Court has given it, a liberal construction in order to protect against warrantless searches of buildings and seizures of tangible personal effects. But, until today, this Court has refused to say that eavesdropping comes within the ambit of Fourth Amendment restrictions. See, *e.g., Olmstead v. United States* (1928) and *Goldman v. United States* (1942). . . .

Since I see no way in which the words of the Fourth Amendment can be construed to apply to eavesdropping, that closes the matter for me. In interpreting the Bill of Rights, I willingly go as far as a liberal construction of the language takes me, but I simply cannot in good conscience give a meaning to words which they have never before been thought to have and which they certainly do not have in common ordinary usage. I will not distort the words of the Amendment in order to "keep the Constitution up to date" or "to bring it into harmony with the times." It was never meant that this Court have such power, which, in effect, would make us a continuously functioning constitutional convention. . . .

The Fourth Amendment protects privacy only to the

extent that it prohibits unreasonable searches and seizures of "persons, houses, papers, and effects." No general right is created by the Amendment so as to give this Court the unlimited power to hold unconstitutional everything which affects privacy. Certainly the Framers, well acquainted as they were with the excesses of governmental power, did not intend to grant this Court such omnipotent lawmaking authority as that. The history of governments proves that it is dangerous to freedom to repose such powers in courts.

For these reasons, I respectfully dissent.

Katz is an important, perhaps landmark, ruling for the following reasons. First, the Court applied the right of privacy to searches and seizures. If citizens have a reasonable "expectation of privacy," as Justice Harlan's concurrence noted, then they are entitled to it. It is not the place that is protected, but the person occupying that place. Brandeis had advocated this position in his *Olmstead* dissent forty years earlier.

Second, and more relevant here, is the Court's statement about the Fourth Amendment's warrant requirement. Although the justices noted their preference for searches conducted pursuant to warrants, they acknowledged that they had created exceptions—special circumstances under which police did not need to obtain warrants to conduct searches. They found, however, that electronic surveillance did not fall under any of those exceptions, and they declined to create a new one. The clear holding of *Katz* is if police want to engage in electronic surveillance, they must obtain search warrants.

Although most Americans agree with this position, it was seen in some circles as a hindrance to state and federal law enforcement efforts. In 1968 Congress responded to these divergent concerns with legislation designed to "retain eavesdropping while maintaining the Constitution."[8] Under Title III of the Federal Omnibus Crime Control and Safe Streets Act, agents may "intercept a wire, oral, or electronic communication" without a warrant if one of the parties to the conversation has consented. The act also spells out the procedures by which agents can obtain warrants to intercept conversations.[9]

The Warren Court's decision in *Katz* may have precipitated the need for Title III, but resolving cases that emanated from it fell to more conservative Courts. Generally, the Burger and Rehnquist Courts interpreted the statute broadly, typically upholding law enforcement agents when they are challenged on appeal.[10] In *United States v. White* (1971), for example, the Court found no constitutional defect in permitting agents to wear body mikes to record conversations with the criminally suspect. The majority ruled that when people make incriminating statements during the course of open conversations, they have no reasonable expectation of privacy under *Katz.* Moreover, the Court noted that Title III allowed agents to tape conversations if one party had given consent. To the majority, this provision meant that an undercover police officer wearing a wire could be the consenting party.

Exceptions to the Warrant Requirement

Although warrants are the constitutionally preferred way for searches and seizures to be authorized, the search warrant procedure is cumbersome. It requires police to seek out and convince a judge that there is probable cause to justify a search and seizure. Often, adhering to such procedural requirements is not practical. The Supreme Court has recognized this fact and as a consequence has designated certain circumstances under which obtaining a warrant is not required. Here we will discuss seven such "exceptions" to the warrant requirement: (1) searches incident to a valid arrest; (2) searches to ensure that evidence is not lost; (3) searches based on consent; (4) searches to ensure the safety of law enforcement official; (5) searches done in "hot pursuit"; (6) searches conducted under the plain view doctrine; and (7) searches conducted in specified places that merit low levels of protection. Although these exceptions to the warrant requirement have expanded the authority of the

---

8. Zalman and Siegel, *Criminal Procedure,* 2d ed., 209.

9. In 1978 Congress created a court to deal with special eavesdropping issues. Called the Foreign Intelligence Surveillance Court, this tribunal has jurisdiction over requests for warrants by the executive branch to engage in domestic electronic surveillance for the purposes of gathering foreign intelligence. Unlike other courts, the FISC meets in secret and all its decisions are classified.

10. Zalman and Siegel, *Criminal Procedure,* 2d ed., 212.

police to search, the justices have placed constraints on each: they are limited in scope based on the initial justification the Court used to create them.

As you read the material to come, ask yourself these questions: Why did the Court create exceptions to the warrant requirement? What are the limits placed on them? Keep in mind the ideological propensities of the various Courts. Have the justices of the Burger and Rehnquist Courts eradicated the constitutional protections for the criminally accused devised by the Warren Court? If so, have they merely sought to rebalance the scales of justice?

Searches Incident to a Valid Arrest. As a general principle of law, police may conduct a search when placing a suspect under a valid arrest *(see Box 10-1).* For example, if a law enforcement official checks a lawfully apprehended suspect for weapons, the officer is engaging in a search incident to a valid arrest. The Supreme Court has allowed such searches for three reasons: to protect the safety of the police officer in case the suspect is armed, to remove any means of escape, and to prevent the suspect from disposing of evidence.

The Court also has imposed two types of limits—temporal and spatial—on searches incident to a valid arrest. The temporal limit means that police can conduct such a search only at the time of the arrest. If the arresting officers forget to check something or someone at the time of arrest, they cannot later return to conduct a search unless they have some other justification to do so. This rule makes sense in light of the original purposes for allowing searches incident to arrest: an individual can place a police officer in jeopardy or attempt escape at the time of an arrest, but no danger exists once police remove the individual from the scene. The spatial limitation means that searches made incident to a valid arrest may go no further than searching the arrested suspect and the area under the suspect's immediate control. Such searches are allowed so that police can respond to any immediate threats to safety and security. They are not designed to be full, evidentiary searches such as those authorized by a warrant.

An example of the spatial limitation is provided by *Chimel v. California* (1969). With an arrest warrant in hand, police apprehended Ted Steven Chimel, suspected

BOX 10-1 ARREST AND ARREST WARRANTS

MOST COURT CASES centering on warrants deal with searches and seizures, not arrests. Still, in many of the opinions excerpted in this chapter you will come across the terms *arrest* and *arrest warrant.* Here we answer some questions associated with these terms.

What is an arrest? Although many citizens think of an arrest as police taking a person into custody, it is—for legal purposes—something less. An arrest takes place when a legal authority deprives an individual of his or her freedom of movement and rights of personal privacy for some period of time.

What is required for police to make an arrest? An arrest, which is a seizure of a person, is subject to constitutional strictures under the Fourth Amendment. In particular, before they can make an arrest, police must have probable cause to show that a crime has been committed and that the individual they wish to arrest is the perpetrator.

Under what circumstances may police make an arrest? Police may make an arrest with or without an arrest warrant. In both instances, they must meet the probable cause requirement.

For an arrest with a warrant, police appear before a magistrate and present sworn evidence in support of probable cause. If such evidence exists, the magistrate will issue the warrant.

For a warrantless arrest, police can establish probable cause on the basis of things they observe, smell, hear, taste, or touch. Police can also establish probable cause on the basis of reliable hearsay—secondhand evidence or what persons say they have heard other persons say.

SOURCE: Marvin Zalman and Larry Siegel, *Criminal Procedure,* 2d ed. (St. Paul, Minn.: West Publishing, 1997), 348–350.

of a coin shop burglary, in the living room of his home. Over his objections, police then conducted a search of the entire three-bedroom house, including attic, garage, and workshop. During the course of the search police found incriminating evidence that was used to convict Chimel.[11] By a 6–2 margin, the Supreme Court reversed the conviction. Justice Stewart, for the majority, found that the

11. For a more detailed account of this case, see Richard C. Cortner, *The Supreme Court and Civil Liberties Policy* (Palo Alto, Calif.: Mayfield, 1974).

police simply went too far, extending the search well beyond that which is permissible. Stewart concluded:

Application of sound Fourth Amendment principles to the facts of this case produces a clear result. The search here went far beyond the petitioner's person and the area from within which he might have obtained either a weapon or something that could have been used as evidence against him. There was no constitutional justification, in the absence of a search warrant, for extending the search beyond that area. The scope of the search was, therefore, "unreasonable" under the Fourth and Fourteenth Amendments and the petitioner's conviction cannot stand.

Loss of Evidence Searches. As a general principle of law, police can conduct warrantless searches and seizures to prevent the loss of evidence. Frequently, officers come upon situations in which they must act quickly to preserve evidence that is in danger of being destroyed by, for example, a drug dealer about to flush narcotics down the toilet or an armed robber intent on throwing the weapon into the river. It would not be reasonable to require an officer faced with such a situation to find a judge to issue a search warrant. By the time the law enforcement official complied with this requirement, the evidence would be gone. Therefore, the Supreme Court has allowed police considerable latitude in acting without a warrant under such circumstances. But like other searches and seizures, evidence-loss searches are limited: the search and seizure may extend no further than necessary to preserve the evidence from loss or destruction. Searches justified under evidence-loss conditions, therefore, may not be full evidence-seeking procedures, but must focus exclusively on the evidence at risk.

Cupp v. Murphy (1973) provides an example of such a search and seizure. In this case, the police, without any other justification, acted quickly to secure possible evidence of a murder, fearing that any delay would allow the suspect to dispose of the material.

The case began when the body of Daniel Murphy's wife was discovered in her Portland, Oregon, home. She had been strangled to death, and abrasions and lacerations were found on her neck and throat. There was no evidence of a break-in or robbery. When word of the murder reached Murphy, who was not living with his wife, he telephoned Portland police and volunteered to come to the police station for questioning. He was met there by his attorney. A police officer noticed a dark spot on Murphy's finger and a dark residue under his fingernails. The officer suspected the stains were dried blood and asked Murphy if he would allow police to take scrapings from his nails. Murphy refused. During the rest of his time at the police station, Murphy kept his hands behind his back or in his pockets where they could not be seen. Police suspected that he was using his keys or some coins to rub his fingers clean. In reaction to this, over Murphy's protests and without a warrant, police took the scrapings. The procedure yielded traces of blood and skin cells from the victim and fibers from her nightgown. On the basis of this and other evidence, Murphy was convicted of second-degree murder. He challenged the evidence as a violation of his Fourth Amendment rights.

The Supreme Court upheld the conviction. The justices reasoned that Murphy knew he was a suspect in the killing of his wife, and he knew police suspected that evidence of the crime was under his fingernails. If police had allowed Murphy to leave following his refusal to consent to a nail scraping, he would have quickly cleaned his nails, destroying the evidence. Under these conditions, police had no time to secure a warrant. They had to act quickly to preserve the evidence. Therefore, the Court held that "considering the existence of probable cause, the very limited intrusion undertaken incident to the station house detention, and the ready destructibility of the evidence, we cannot say that this search violated the Fourth and Fourteenth Amendments."

A more complicated set of issues is involved when the evidence about to be destroyed has been ingested, which can happen when the offense is related to drug possession or alcohol consumption. Because it is inevitable that the body's natural processes will, with time, eliminate all traces of the drugs or alcohol, may the police act quickly without judicial authorization to retrieve such evidence? Intrusions into the human body are certainly more invasive than those into a home or office, and the privacy concerns discussed in Chapter 9 also come into play, but the government does have an interest in obtaining evidence for the prosecution of crime.

Rochin v. California, decided by the Supreme Court in 1952, provided a foundation for many cases in this area. With information that Rochin was selling drugs, three deputy sheriffs went to his house, where he lived with his common-law wife, mother, and siblings. The officers, finding the front door ajar, went in, walked upstairs to Rochin's bedroom, and forced open the closed door. Rochin was sitting, partly dressed, on his bed where his wife was reclining. Noticing two capsules on the night-stand, the police asked Rochin about them, but, instead of answering, Rochin stuffed the capsules into his mouth. The officers jumped on him, trying to remove the capsules from his throat. When that failed, they hand-cuffed him and took him to a hospital. Following police orders, but over Rochin's protests, doctors forced an emetic solution through a tube into the suspect's stomach to induce vomiting. The doctors found the partially digested capsules, which contained morphine, a controlled substance. Largely on the basis of this evidence, Rochin was convicted and sentenced to sixty days in jail.

Was this an appropriate way for police to obtain evidence? Grounding their decision in principles of due process of law, the justices expressed obvious disgust with the police procedures used here. This sense of outrage was so overwhelming that it led to the formulation of the "shocked-conscience" rule, the legal test frequently used by the Court to judge the validity of investigatory procedures. Simply stated, if the way police obtain evidence shocks civilized people or causes unreasonable pain and discomfort, the principles of due process of law are violated. While *Rochin* articulated the standard to be used in such cases, it provided little guidance for assessing the constitutionality of intrusions into the human body that are less shocking and violent than inducing vomiting.

Schmerber v. California (1966) offered a partial answer to this question. The Court ruled that a blood sample taken in a hospital without a warrant over the objections of a suspected drunk driver could be used as evidence. The procedure did not violate the *Rochin* shocked-conscience standard because a blood test (unlike a stomach pumping) is a relatively painless, routine procedure constituting a minor intrusion into the suspect's body. Additional-ly, the test was conducted in the safety of a hospital by trained medical staff. Nor did police violate the Fourth Amendment in ordering that the blood test be taken. The officers had probable cause because they had observed that Schmerber exhibited symptoms of drunkenness and the loss-of-evidence exception was in effect. If police had taken the time to obtain a warrant to sample Schmerber's blood, the evidence would have vanished.

Together, *Schmerber* and *Rochin* hold that law enforcement officials may, with good cause but without a warrant, order minor and safe intrusions into the human body to obtain evidence that would otherwise be destroyed. But in attempting to follow this mandate, police faced a problem: besides forcibly obtaining the contents of a suspect's stomach, what constitutes a major intrusion?

The Court addressed this issue in *Winston v. Lee* (1985). After running wounded from the scene of an armed robbery where shots had been exchanged, Rudolph Lee collapsed on the street and was taken to the hospital for treatment. X-rays showed that a bullet had entered Lee's chest and was lodged near his collarbone. Removal was not medically necessary, but prosecutors sought a court order to have Lee undergo surgery because the bullet might link him to the robbery attempt. Lee's attorneys objected to the procedure. The Supreme Court unanimously concluded that the compulsory surgery (even with a court order) would constitute an unreasonable search and seizure in violation of the Fourth Amendment. They had several reasons. First, the operation would be a severe intrusion on Lee's privacy interests. Second, the uncertain dangers of an operation under general anesthesia made the procedure presumptively unreasonable. Third, the state, while able to show that obtaining the bullet would be helpful to a prosecution, was unable to demonstrate that it was absolutely necessary. Still, the Court made clear that it would not always strike down such incursions into the body; it was just that it did not find the procedure at issue here to be reasonable.

Despite the differences of the degree of intrusion into the body, *Rochin*, *Schmerber*, and *Lee* share a common feature. In each case the government was attempting to secure evidence from the body of someone suspected of criminal activity. More recently, however, the Court has dealt with similar searches where no criminal accusation was involved. The challenged programs, usually drug testing, require the taking of evidence from the body where little or no probable cause is present. As we noted in our discussion of privacy rights, the justices have handed down four major decisions in response to these challenges.

First, in *Skinner v. Railway Labor Executives' Association* (1989), the justices upheld a federal rule mandating blood and urine testing of rail employees involved in major train accidents or found in violation of certain safety rules. There was no requirement that there be cause to believe that a specific employee had abused drugs or alcohol. Involvement in an accident or safety violation alone was sufficient to trigger the testing. The Railway Labor Executives' Association, representing union interests, challenged the regulations, arguing that the Fourth Amendment requires particularized suspicion. The government's concern with safety in commercial transportation and the evidence of drug abuse causing many accidents made the drug testing provisions reasonable. The justices refused to impose a warrant requirement in part because evidence of drug or alcohol ingestion may be destroyed quickly by the body. The Court also refused to require individualized suspicion on the grounds that a railroad employee's performance would be impaired, which placed the traveling public in jeopardy, long before there might be sufficient observable evidence to establish suspicion.

Second, in *National Treasury Employees Union v. Von Raab* (1989) the Court gave constitutional approval to federal regulations requiring drug screening of U.S. Customs Service employees involved in the interdiction and seizure of illegal drugs. By a 5–4 vote the justices found that the program was reasonable given that the Customs Service is the nation's first line of defense against the illegal importation of drugs. The agents were often exposed to criminals who might tempt them with bribes or access to illegal drugs. Since the government has a compelling interest in protecting the integrity of the service, the drug testing program is reasonable, even without warrant requirements or individualized suspicion.

Six years later the Court handed down its third major drug testing decision. In *Vernonia School District 47J v. Acton* the justices confronted a difficult question: Does random, suspicionless drug testing of students by public school officials violate the Constitution?[12]

Vernonia School District 47J v. Acton

515 U. S. 646 (1995)
supct.law.cornell.edu/supct/html/94-590.ZS.html
Vote: 6 (Breyer, Ginsburg, Kennedy, Rehnquist, Scalia,
        Thomas)
        3 (O'Connor, Souter, Stevens)
Opinion of the Court: Scalia
Concurring Opinion: Ginsburg
Dissenting opinion: O'Connor

Vernonia is a small logging community of about three thousand residents in western Oregon. School District 47J operates one high school and three elementary schools, serving about seven hundred students. As in many rural areas, high school athletics are an important part of the town's life, with a high level of student participation and community involvement.

During the 1980s school officials became worried about disciplinary problems in the schools, and many of the incidents appeared to be drug related. In addition, students began to speak out about their attraction to the drug culture and boast about their drug involvement. Teachers and administrators became convinced that some student athletes were leaders in the local drug culture, which gave rise to fears about an increased risk of sports-related injuries. The first response of the school district was to institute drug and alcohol education and counseling programs. When these proved ineffective, a drug testing program was introduced.

The drug testing program applied only to students participating in interscholastic athletics. Students wishing to play sports were required to sign a form giving consent to drug testing. All athletes were tested at the beginning of each season of their sport, and, thereafter, 10

---

12. For oral arguments in this case, navigate to: *oyez.nwu.edu.*

James Acton, center, a high school student from Vernonia, Oregon, leaves the Supreme Court with friends and family members following oral arguments. From left are Kathy Armstrong of the American Civil Liberties Union, brother Simon, and parents Judy and Wayne Acton.

percent were selected at random to undergo testing. Students' urine samples were sent to an independent laboratory that screened them for amphetamines, cocaine, and marijuana. The results were carefully controlled, and confidentiality was generally observed. If a test was positive, a second test was taken immediately. If the second test was negative, no further action was taken. If positive, however, the student was required to spend six weeks in an assistance program with weekly testing or suspension from athletics for the current and next seasons. Second and third offenses called for longer suspensions from school athletics.

In 1991 James Acton, a seventh-grader, signed up to play football. He was denied participation when he and his parents refused to sign the testing consent forms. The Acton family filed suit, challenging the drug policy as a violation of the Oregon and U.S. Constitutions. The district court ruled against them, but the court of appeals reversed. The school district requested Supreme Court review.

JUSTICE SCALIA delivered the opinion of the Court.

The Fourth Amendment to the United States Constitution provides that the Federal Government shall not violate "[t]he right of the people to be secure in their persons, houses, papers, and effects, against unreasonable searches and seizures. . . ." We have held that the Fourteenth Amendment extends this constitutional guarantee to searches and seizures by state officers, including public school officials, *New Jersey v. T. L. O.* (1985). In *Skinner v. Railway Labor Executives' Assn.* (1989) we held that state-compelled collection and testing of urine, such as that required by the Student Athlete Drug Policy, constitutes a "search" subject to the demands of the Fourth Amendment. See also *Treasury Employees v. Von Raab* (1989).

As the text of the Fourth Amendment indicates, the ultimate measure of the constitutionality of a governmental search is "reasonableness." At least in a case such as this, where there was no clear practice, either approving or disapproving the type of search at issue, at the time the constitutional provision was enacted, whether a particular search meets the reasonableness standard "'is judged by balancing its intrusion on the individual's Fourth Amendment interests against its promotion of legitimate governmental interests.'" *Skinner.* Where a search is undertaken by law enforcement officials to discover evidence of criminal wrongdoing, this Court has said that reasonableness generally requires the obtaining of a judicial warrant, *Skinner.* Warrants cannot be issued, of course, without the showing of probable cause required by the Warrant Clause. But a warrant is not required to establish the reasonableness of *all* government searches; and when a warrant is not required (and the Warrant Clause therefore not applicable), probable cause is not invariably required either. A search unsupported by probable cause can be constitutional, we have said, "when special needs, beyond the normal need for law enforcement, make the warrant and probable-cause requirement impracticable." *Griffin v. Wisconsin* (1987).

We have found such "special needs" to exist in the public-school context. There, the warrant requirement "would unduly interfere with the maintenance of the swift and informal disciplinary procedures [that are] needed," and "strict adherence to the requirement that searches be based upon probable cause" would undercut "the substantial need of teachers and administrators for freedom to maintain order in the schools." *T. L. O.* The school search we approved in *T. L. O.,* while not based on probable cause, *was* based on individualized *suspicion* of wrongdoing. As we explicitly acknowledged, however, "'the Fourth Amendment imposes no irreducible requirement of such suspicion.'" We have upheld suspicionless searches and seizures to conduct drug testing of railroad personnel involved in train accidents, see *Skinner;* to conduct random drug testing of federal customs officers who carry arms or are involved in drug interdiction, see *Von Raab;* and to maintain automobile checkpoints looking for illegal immigrants and contraband, [*United States v.*] *Martinez-Fuerte* [1976], and drunk drivers, *Michigan Dept. of State Police v. Sitz* (1990).

The first factor to be considered is the nature of the privacy interest upon which the search here at issue intrudes. . . . Central, in our view, to the present case is the fact that the subjects of the Policy are (1) children, who (2) have been committed to the temporary custody of the State as schoolmaster.

Traditionally at common law, and still today, unemancipated minors lack some of the most fundamental rights of self-determination—including even the right of liberty in its narrow sense, *i.e.,* the right to come and go at will. They are subject, even as to their physical freedom, to the control of their parents or guardians. . . .

Fourth Amendment rights, no less than First and Fourteenth Amendment rights, are different in public schools than elsewhere; the "reasonableness" inquiry cannot disregard the schools' custodial and tutelary responsibility for children. For their own good and that of their classmates, public school children are routinely required to submit to various physical examinations, and to be vaccinated against various diseases. . . .

Legitimate privacy expectations are even less with regard to student athletes. School sports are not for the bashful. They require "suiting up" before each practice or event, and showering and changing afterwards. Public school locker rooms, the usual sites for these activities, are not notable for the privacy they afford. The locker rooms in Vernonia are typical: no individual dressing rooms are provided; shower heads are lined up along a wall, unseparated by any sort of partition or curtain; not even all the toilet stalls have doors. . . .

There is an additional respect in which school athletes have a reduced expectation of privacy. By choosing to "go out for the team," they voluntarily subject themselves to a degree of regulation even higher than that imposed on students generally. In Vernonia's public schools, they must submit to a preseason physical exam (James testified that his included the giving of a urine sample), they must acquire adequate insurance coverage or sign an insurance waiver, maintain a minimum grade point average, and comply with any "rules of conduct, dress, training hours and related matters as may be established for each sport by the head coach and athletic director with the principal's approval.". . .

Having considered the scope of the legitimate expectation of privacy at issue here, we turn next to the character of the intrusion that is complained of. We recognized in *Skinner* that collecting the samples for urinalysis intrudes upon "an excretory function traditionally shielded by great privacy." We noted, however, that the degree of intrusion depends upon the manner in which production of the urine sample is monitored. Under the District's Policy, male students produce samples at a urinal along a wall. They remain fully clothed and are only observed from behind, if at all.

Female students produce samples in an enclosed stall, with a female monitor standing outside listening only for sounds of tampering. These conditions are nearly identical to those typically encountered in public restrooms, which men, women, and especially school children use daily. Under such conditions, the privacy interests compromised by the process of obtaining the urine sample are in our view negligible.

The other privacy-invasive aspect of urinalysis is, of course, the information it discloses concerning the state of the subject's body, and the materials he has ingested. In this regard it is significant that the tests at issue here look only for drugs, and not for whether the student is, for example, epileptic, pregnant, or diabetic. Moreover, the drugs for which the samples are screened are standard, and do not vary according to the identity of the student. And finally, the results of the tests are disclosed only to a limited class of school personnel who have a need to know; and they are not turned over to law enforcement authorities or used for any internal disciplinary function. . . .

Finally, we turn to consider the nature and immediacy of the governmental concern at issue here, and the efficacy of this means for meeting it. In both *Skinner* and *Von Raab*, we characterized the government interest motivating the search as "compelling.". . . It is a mistake, however, to think that the phrase "compelling state interest," in the Fourth Amendment context, describes a fixed, minimum quantum of governmental concern, so that one can dispose of a case by answering in isolation the question: Is there a compelling state interest here? Rather, the phrase describes an interest which appears *important enough* to justify the particular search at hand, in light of other factors which show the search to be relatively intrusive upon a genuine expectation of privacy. Whether that relatively high degree of government concern is necessary in this case or not, we think it is met.

That the nature of the concern is important—indeed, perhaps compelling—can hardly be doubted. Deterring drug use by our Nation's schoolchildren is at least as important as enhancing efficient enforcement of the Nation's laws against the importation of drugs, which was the governmental concern in *Von Raab*, or deterring drug use by engineers and trainmen, which was the governmental concern in *Skinner*. School years are the time when the physical, psychological, and addictive effects of drugs are most severe.

. . . And of course the effects of a drug infested school are visited not just upon the users, but upon the entire student body and faculty, as the educational process is disrupted. In the present case, moreover, the necessity for the State to act is magnified by the fact that this evil is being visited not just upon individuals at large, but upon children for whom it has undertaken a special responsibility of care and direction. Finally, it must not be lost sight of that this program is directed more narrowly to drug use by school athletes, where the risk of immediate physical harm to the drug user or those with whom he is playing his sport is particularly high. . . .

As for the immediacy of the District's concerns: We are not inclined to question—indeed, we could not possibly find clearly erroneous—the District Court's conclusion that "a large segment of the student body, particularly those involved in interscholastic athletics, was in a state of rebellion," that "[d]isciplinary actions had reached 'epidemic proportions,'" and that "the rebellion was being fueled by alcohol and drug abuse as well as by the student's misperceptions about the drug culture." That is an immediate crisis of greater proportions than existed in *Skinner*, where we upheld the Government's drug testing program based on findings of drug use by railroad employees nationwide, without proof that a problem existed on the particular railroads whose employees were subject to the test. And of much greater proportions than existed in *Von Raab*, where there was no documented history of drug use by any customs officials.

As to the efficacy of this means for addressing the problem: It seems to us self-evident that a drug problem largely fueled by the "role model" effect of athletes' drug use, and of particular danger to athletes, is effectively addressed by making sure that athletes do not use drugs. . . .

Taking into account all the factors we have considered above—the decreased expectation of privacy, the relative unobtrusiveness of the search, and the severity of the need met by the search—we conclude Vernonia's Policy is reasonable and hence constitutional.

We caution against the assumption that suspicionless drug testing will readily pass constitutional muster in other contexts. The most significant element in this case is the first we discussed: that the Policy was undertaken in furtherance of the government's responsibilities, under a public school system, as guardian and tutor of children entrusted to its care. . . .

We may note that the primary guardians of Vernonia's schoolchildren appear to agree. The record shows no objection to this districtwide program by any parents other than the couple before us here—even though . . . a public meeting was held to obtain parents' views. We find insufficient basis to contradict the judgment of Vernonia's parents, its school board, and the District Court, as to what was reasonably in the interest of these children under the circumstances.

. . . We therefore vacate the judgment, and remand the case to the Court of Appeals for further proceedings consistent with this opinion.

It is so ordered.

JUSTICE O'CONNOR, with whom JUSTICE STEVENS and JUSTICE SOUTER join, dissenting.

The population of our Nation's public schools, grades 7 through 12, numbers around 18 million. By the reasoning of today's decision, the millions of these students who participate in interscholastic sports, an overwhelming majority of whom have given school officials no reason whatsoever to suspect they use drugs at school, are open to an intrusive bodily search.

In justifying this result, the Court dispenses with a requirement of individualized suspicion on considered policy grounds. First, it explains that precisely because *every* student athlete is being tested, there is no concern that school officials might act arbitrarily in choosing who to test. Second, a broad-based search regime, the Court reasons, dilutes the accusatory nature of the search. In making these policy arguments, of course, the Court sidesteps powerful, countervailing privacy concerns. Blanket searches, because they can involve "thousands or millions" of searches, "pos[e] a greater threat to liberty" than do suspicion-based ones, which "affec[t] one person at a time," *Illinois v. Krull* (1987) (O'CONNOR, J., dissenting). Searches based on individualized suspicion also afford potential targets considerable control over whether they will, in fact, be searched because a person can avoid such a search by not acting in an objectively suspicious way. And given that the surest way to avoid acting suspiciously is to avoid the underlying wrongdoing, the costs of such a regime, one would think, are minimal.

But whether a blanket search is "better" than a regime based on individualized suspicion is not a debate in which we should engage. In my view, it is not open to judges or government officials to decide on policy grounds which is better and which is worse. For most of our constitutional history, mass, suspicionless searches have been generally considered *per se* unreasonable within the meaning of the Fourth Amendment. And we have allowed exceptions in recent years only where it has been clear that a suspicion-based regime would be ineffectual. Because that is not the case here, I dissent. . . .

. . . One searches today's majority opinion in vain for recognition that history and precedent establish that individualized suspicion is "usually required" under the Fourth Amendment (regardless of whether a warrant and probable cause are also required) and that, in the area of intrusive personal searches, the only recognized exception is for situations in which a suspicion-based scheme would be likely ineffectual. Far from acknowledging anything special about individualized suspicion, the Court treats a suspicion-based regime as if it were just any run-of-the-mill, less intrusive alternative—that is, an alternative that officials may bypass if the lesser intrusion, in their reasonable estimation, is outweighed by policy concerns unrelated to practicability. . . .

But having misconstrued the fundamental role of the individualized suspicion requirement in Fourth Amendment analysis, the Court never seriously engages the practicality of such a requirement in the instant case. And that failure is crucial because nowhere is it *less* clear that an individualized suspicion requirement would be ineffectual than in the school context. In most schools, the entire pool of potential search targets—students—is under constant supervision by teachers and administrators and coaches, be it in classrooms, hallways, or locker rooms.

The record here indicates that the Vernonia schools are no exception. The great irony of this case is that most (though not all) of the evidence the District introduced to justify its suspicionless drug testing program consisted of first- or second-hand stories of particular, identifiable students acting in ways that plainly gave rise to reasonable suspicion of in-school drug use—and thus that would have justified a drug related search under our *T. L. O.* decision. . . .

In light of all this evidence of drug use by particular students, there is a substantial basis for concluding that a vigorous regime of suspicion-based testing (for which the District appears already to have rules in place) would have gone a long way toward solving Vernonia's school drug problem while preserving the Fourth Amendment rights of James Acton and others like him. And were there any doubt about such a conclusion, it is removed by indications in the record that suspicion-based testing could have been supplemented by an equally vigorous campaign to have Vernonia's parents encourage their children to submit to the District's *voluntary* drug testing program. In these circumstances, the Fourth Amendment dictates that a mass, suspicionless search regime is categorically unreasonable. . . .

On this record, then, it seems to me that the far more reasonable choice would have been to focus on the class of students found to have violated published school rules against severe disruption in class and around campus—disruption that had a strong nexus to drug use, as the District established at trial. Such a choice would share two of the virtues of a suspicion-based regime: testing dramatically fewer students, tens as against hundreds, and giving students control, through their behavior, over the likelihood that they would be tested. . . .

It cannot be too often stated that the greatest threats to our constitutional freedoms come in times of crisis. But we must also stay mindful that not all government responses to such times are hysterical overreactions; some crises are quite real, and when they are, they serve precisely as the compelling state interest that we have said may justify a measured intrusion on constitutional rights. The only way for judges to mediate these conflicting impulses is to do what they should do anyway: stay close to the record in each case that appears before them, and make their judgments based on that alone. Having reviewed the record here, I cannot avoid the conclusion that the District's suspicionless policy of testing all student-athletes sweeps too broadly, and too imprecisely, to be reasonable under the Fourth Amendment.

Taken along with *Skinner* and *Von Raab*, *Vernonia School District 47J v. Acton* appears to be a powerful decision. The justices for the third time approved a drug testing program imposed on a class of persons without requiring warrants or individualized suspicion. Yet the majority in *Acton* argues that the ruling is limited. The Court approved a program of suspicionless testing only for stu-

dents in public schools who voluntarily elected to participate in athletics.

The final decision among the Court's four major drug testing cases concerned a different group of people. *Chandler v. Miller* (1997) involved a challenge to a 1990 Georgia statute requiring that each candidate for certain state offices provide evidence from an approved laboratory that the candidate was tested for illegal drugs (marijuana, cocaine, opiates, amphetamines, and phencyclidines) and that the results were negative. If a candidate failed to supply the drug-free certification, his or her name could not appear on the ballot. Georgia was the only state to pass such a law.

Responding to legal actions filed by three Libertarian Party candidates for office, seven justices joined a majority opinion written by Justice Ginsburg striking down the Georgia drug testing requirement as a violation of the Fourth Amendment. Only Chief Justice Rehnquist voted to uphold the law. The Court held that the drug testing program constituted a search under the meaning of the Fourth Amendment, and, therefore, must be reasonable. Suspicionless searches, even noninvasive ones, generally fail the test of reasonableness except under very narrow circumstances. The Court previously allowed such searches when vital interests were at stake, especially if a generalized drug problem had been identified. Unlike in *Skinner*, *Vernonia*, and *Von Raab*, the justices were unable to find any special circumstances surrounding the Georgia drug testing law. The state failed to present any evidence that illegal drugs had been a general problem affecting candidates for state office. The Court found the Georgia law to be an ineffective response to an undocumented problem. The law did not meet the test of reasonableness.

Consent Searches. As a rule, law enforcement officials can conduct warrantless searches upon consent. Like most general principles of law, however, the Court has placed constraints on such searches. To be considered valid, consent searches must satisfy two criteria. First, permission must be freely and voluntarily granted. Second, the individual granting consent must have the authority to do so.

The requirement that consent to a search be voluntary means that permission cannot be coerced. If police engage in actual or threatened physical violence in order to obtain permission, the search fails the voluntary consent requirement. In addition, consent is not considered valid if the police lie or use trickery to extract permission. For example, *Bumper v. North Carolina* (1968) concerned the investigation of a rape in which Bumper was the primary suspect. Police went to his house and told his grandmother, with whom he lived, that they had a search warrant when in fact they did not. Believing the police, Bumper's grandmother granted her permission for the search, which yielded a .22-caliber rifle used in the rape. The state asserted a trial that the search and seizure were valid because permission was granted. Bumper's attorney argued otherwise, noting that police tricked and, in essence, coerced the grandmother into giving consent. The U.S. Supreme Court agreed. The justices found that the grant of consent was coercive and therefore not voluntary.

The second requirement restricts the number of people who are legally eligible to authorize a police search. The owner-occupant of a house, for example, has the authority to allow police to enter the home and search it. Similar authority extends to the person who leases an apartment, the proprietor of a shop, or the driver of an automobile. In each of these cases, the person has legal control over the area and can grant permission for a search.[13]

If consent is voluntarily given by a person with authority, police may search without first obtaining a warrant. However, the search may only extend so far as the permission grant allows.

Safety Searches. As the Warren Court expanded the rights of the criminally accused during the 1960s, police throughout the United States complained not only that the justices hampered their ability to conduct investigations, but also that the new rules placed their lives in jeopardy—they could no longer conduct full searches unless they made an arrest. To comply with existing law

while ensuring their own safety, police began using "stop-and-frisk" searches. Rather than doing a full search, police "patted down" individuals they thought to be dangerous. Did such activity fall beyond the purview of the Fourth Amendment? In *Terry v. Ohio* the Warren Court addressed this issue.[14]

Terry v. Ohio

392 U.S. 1 (1968)
laws.findlaw.com/US/392/1.html
Vote: 8 (Black, Brennan, Fortas, Harlan, Marshall, Stewart, Warren, White)
    1 (Douglas)
Opinion of the Court: Warren
Concurring opinions: Black, Harlan, White
Dissenting opinion: Douglas

While Officer-Detective Martin McFadden, a thirty-nine-year veteran of the police force, patrolled in plainclothes in downtown Cleveland one afternoon, he observed two men he had never seen before. He watched as the two paced along the street, "pausing to stare in the same store window roughly 24 times." After each pass by the window, the two individuals conferred. McFadden also observed a third man join the two briefly. Acting on his suspicion that the men were casing the store for a robbery, McFadden approached the trio and identified himself as a police officer and asked them to identify themselves. The suspects began whispering to each other, and Terry mumbled a response to McFadden. The officer then spun Terry around, patted down his outside clothing, and found a pistol in his overcoat pocket. He ordered the others to face the wall with their hands raised and patted them down as well. McFadden also found a gun on another man and arrested them on concealed weapons charges.

In trial court, the prosecuting attorney argued that McFadden's warrantless search was incident to arrest. While the judge rejected that plea, noting that no probable cause existed, he held for the state, ruling that

---

13. This position was further broadened by the Court in *Illinois v. Rodriguez* (1990). The Court ruled that consent searches may be valid when police reasonably believe the person granting consent has common authority over the premises, but in fact does not.

14. For oral arguments in this case, navigate to: *oyez.nwu.edu.*

officers have the right to stop and frisk when they believe their lives are in jeopardy.

MR. CHIEF JUSTICE WARREN delivered the opinion of the Court.

This case presents serious questions concerning the role of the Fourth Amendment in the confrontation on the street between the citizen and the policeman investigating suspicious circumstances. . . .

. . . We have recently held that "the Fourth Amendment protects people, not places," and wherever an individual may harbor a reasonable "expectation of privacy," he is entitled to be free from unreasonable governmental intrusion. . . . Unquestionably petitioner was entitled to the protection of the Fourth Amendment as he walked down the street in Cleveland. The question is whether in all the circumstances of this on-the-street encounter, his right to personal security was violated by an unreasonable search and seizure.

We would be less than candid if we did not acknowledge that this question thrusts to the fore difficult and troublesome issues regarding a sensitive area of police activity—issues which have never before been squarely presented to this Court. Reflective of the tensions involved are the practical and constitutional arguments pressed with great vigor on both sides of the public debate over the power of the police to "stop and frisk"—as it is sometimes euphemistically termed—suspicious persons.

On the one hand, it is frequently argued that in dealing with the rapidly unfolding and often dangerous situations on city streets the police are in need of an escalating set of flexible responses, graduated in relation to the amount of information they possess. For this purpose it is urged that distinctions should be made between a "stop" and an "arrest" (or a "seizure" of a person), and between a "frisk" and a "search." Thus, it is argued, the police should be allowed to "stop" a person and detain him briefly for questioning upon suspicion that he may be connected with criminal activity. Upon suspicion that the person may be armed, the police should have the power to "frisk" him for weapons. If the "stop" and the "frisk" give rise to probable cause to believe that the suspect has committed a crime, then the police should be empowered to make a formal "arrest," and a full incident "search" of the person. This scheme is justified in part upon the notion that a "stop" and a "frisk" amount to a mere "minor inconvenience and petty indignity," which can properly be imposed upon the citizen in the interest of effective law enforcement on the basis of a police officer's suspicion.

On the other side the argument is made that the authority of the police must be strictly circumscribed by the law of arrest and search as it has developed to date in the traditional jurisprudence of the Fourth Amendment. It is contended with some force that there is not—and cannot be—a variety of police activity which does not depend solely upon the voluntary cooperation of the citizen and yet which stops short of an arrest based upon probable cause to make such an arrest. The heart of the Fourth Amendment, the argument runs, is a severe requirement of specific justification for any intrusion upon protected personal security, coupled with a highly developed system of judicial controls to enforce upon the agents of the State the commands of the Constitution. Acquiescence by the courts in the compulsion inherent in the field interrogation practices at issue here, it is urged, would constitute an abdication of judicial control over, and indeed an encouragement of, substantial interference with liberty and personal security by police officers whose judgment is necessarily colored by their primary involvement in "the often competitive enterprise of ferreting out crime." This, it is argued, can only serve to exacerbate police-community tensions in the crowded centers of our Nation's cities. . . .

Having thus roughly sketched the perimeters of the constitutional debate over the limits on police investigative conduct in general and the background against which this case presents itself, we turn our attention to the quite narrow question posed by the facts before us: whether it is always unreasonable for a policeman to seize a person and subject him to a limited search for weapons unless there is probable cause for an arrest. Given the narrowness of this question, we have no occasion to canvass in detail the constitutional limitations upon the scope of a policeman's power when he confronts a citizen without probable cause to arrest him.

Our first task is to establish at what point in this encounter the Fourth Amendment becomes relevant. That is, we must decide whether and when Officer McFadden "seized" Terry and whether and when he conducted a "search." There is some suggestion in the use of such terms as "stop" and "frisk" that such police conduct is outside the purview of the Fourth Amendment because neither action rises to the level of a "search" or "seizure" within the meaning of the Constitution. We emphatically reject this notion. It is quite plain that the Fourth Amendment governs "seizures" of the person which do not eventuate in a trip to the station house and prosecution for crime—"arrests" in traditional terminology. It must be recognized that whenever a police officer accosts an individual and restrains his freedom to walk away, he has "seized" that person. And it is nothing less than sheer torture of the English language to suggest that a careful exploration of the outer surfaces of a person's clothing all over his or her body in an attempt to find weapons is not a "search." Moreover, it is simply fantastic to urge that such a procedure performed in public by a policeman while the citizen stands helpless, perhaps facing a wall with his hands raised, is a "petty indignity." It is a serious intrusion upon the sanctity of the person, which may inflict great indignity and arouse strong resentment, and it is not to be undertaken lightly.

The danger in the logic which proceeds upon distinctions between a "stop" and an "arrest," or "seizure" of the person, and between a "frisk" and a "search" is twofold. It seeks to isolate from constitutional scrutiny the initial stages of the contact between the policeman and the citizen. And by suggesting a rigid all-or-nothing model of justification and regulation under the Amendment, it obscures the utility of limitations upon the scope, as well as the initiation, of police action as a means of constitutional regulation. This Court has held in the past that a search which is reasonable at its inception may violate the Fourth Amendment by virtue of its intolerable intensity and scope. . . .

The distinctions of classical "stop-and-frisk" theory thus serve to divert attention from the central inquiry under the Fourth Amendment—the reasonableness in all the circumstances of the particular governmental invasion of a citizen's personal security. "Search" and "seizure" are not talismans. We therefore reject the notions that the Fourth Amendment does not come into play at all as a limitation upon police conduct if the officers stop short of something called a "technical arrest" or a "full-blown search."

In this case there can be no question, then, that Officer McFadden "seized" petitioner and subjected him to a "search" when he took hold of him and patted down the outer surfaces of his clothing. We must decide whether at that point it was reasonable for Officer McFadden to have interfered with petitioner's personal security as he did. . . .

. . . In order to assess the reasonableness of Officer McFadden's conduct as a general proposition, it is necessary "first to focus upon the governmental interest which allegedly justifies official intrusion upon the constitutionally protected interests of the private citizen," for there is "no ready test for determining reasonableness other than by balancing the need to search or seize against the invasion which the search or seizure entails." And in justifying the particular intrusion the police officer must be able to point to specific and articulable facts which, taken together with rational inferences from those facts, reasonably warrant that intrusion. The scheme of the Fourth Amendment becomes meaningful only when it is assured that at some point the conduct of those charged with enforcing the laws can be subjected to the more detached, neutral scrutiny of a judge who must evaluate the reasonableness of a particular search or seizure in light of the particular circumstances. And in making that assessment it is imperative that the facts be judged against an objective standard: would the facts available to the officer at the moment of the seizure or the search "warrant a man of reasonable caution in the belief" that the action taken was appropriate? . . .

Applying these principles to this case, we consider first the nature and extent of the governmental interests involved. One general interest is of course that of effective crime prevention and detection; it is this interest which underlies the recognition that a police officer may in appropriate circumstances and in an appropriate manner approach a person for purposes of investigating possibly criminal behavior even though there is no probable cause to make an arrest. It was this legitimate investigative function Officer McFadden was discharging when he decided to approach petitioner and his companions. He had observed Terry, Chilton, and Katz go through a series of acts, each of them perhaps innocent in itself, but which taken together warranted further investigation. There is nothing unusual in two men standing together on a street corner, perhaps waiting for someone. Nor is there anything suspicious about people in such circumstances strolling up and down the street, singly or in pairs. Store windows, moreover, are made to be looked in. But the story is quite different where, as here, two men hover about a street corner for an extended period of time, at the end of which it becomes apparent that they are not waiting for anyone or anything; where these men pace alternately along an identical route, pausing to stare in the same store window roughly 24 times; where each completion of this route is followed immediately by a conference between the two men on the corner; where they are joined in one of these conferences by a third man who leaves swiftly; and where the two men finally follow the third and rejoin him a couple of blocks away. It would have been poor police work indeed for an officer of 30 years' experience in the detection of thievery from stores in this same neighborhood to have failed to investigate this behavior further.

The crux of this case, however, is not the propriety of Officer McFadden's taking steps to investigate petitioner's suspicious behavior, but rather, whether there was justification for McFadden's invasion of Terry's personal security by searching him for weapons in the course of that investigation. We are now concerned with more than the governmental interest in investigating crime; in addition, there is the more immediate interest of the police officer in taking steps to assure himself that the person with whom he is dealing is not armed with a weapon that could unexpectedly and fatally be used against him. Certainly it would be unreasonable to require that police officers take unnecessary risks in the performance of their duties. American criminals have a long tradition of armed violence, and every year in this country many law enforcement officers are killed in the line of duty, and thousands more are wounded. . . .

In view of these facts, we cannot blind ourselves to the need for law enforcement officers to protect themselves and other prospective victims of violence in situations where they may lack probable cause for an arrest. When an officer is justified in believing that the individual whose suspicious behavior he is investigating at close range is armed and presently dangerous to the officer or to others, it would appear to be clearly unreasonable to deny the officer the power to take necessary measures to determine whether the person is in fact carrying a weapon and to neutralize the threat of physical harm. . . .

We conclude that the revolver seized from Terry was properly admitted in evidence against him. At the time he seized petitioner and searched him for weapons, Officer McFadden had reasonable grounds to believe that petitioner was armed and dangerous, and it was necessary for the protection of himself and others to take swift measures to discover the true facts and neutralize the threat of harm if it materialized. The policeman carefully restricted his search to what was appropriate to the discovery of the particular items which he sought. Each case of this sort will, of course, have to be decided on its own facts. We merely hold today that where a police officer observes unusual conduct which leads him reasonably to conclude in light of his experience that criminal activity may be afoot and that the persons with whom he is dealing may be armed and presently dangerous, where in the course of investigating this behavior he identifies himself as a policeman and makes reasonable inquiries, and where nothing in the initial stages of the encounter serves to dispel his reasonable fear for his own or others' safety, he is entitled for the protection of himself and others in the area to conduct a carefully limited search of the outer clothing of such persons in an attempt to discover weapons which might be used to assault him.

Such a search is a reasonable search under the Fourth Amendment, and any weapons seized may properly be introduced in evidence against the person from whom they were taken.

Affirmed.

MR. JUSTICE HARLAN, concurring.

The facts of this case are illustrative of a proper stop and an incident frisk. Officer McFadden had no probable cause to arrest Terry for anything, but he had observed circumstances that would reasonably lead an experienced, prudent policeman to suspect that Terry was about to engage in burglary or robbery. His justifiable suspicion afforded a proper constitutional basis for accosting Terry, restraining his liberty of movement briefly, and addressing questions to him, and Officer McFadden did so. When he did, he had no reason whatever to suppose that Terry might be armed, apart from the fact that he suspected him of planning a violent crime. McFadden asked Terry his name, to which Terry "mumbled something." Whereupon McFadden, without asking Terry to speak louder and without giving him any chance to explain his presence or his actions, forcibly frisked him.

I would affirm this conviction for what I believe to be the same reasons the Court relies on. I would, however, make explicit what I think is implicit in affirmance on the present facts. Officer McFadden's right to interrupt Terry's freedom of movement and invade his privacy arose only because circumstances warranted forcing an encounter with Terry in an effort to prevent or investigate a crime. Once that forced encounter was justified, however, the officer's right to take suitable measures for his own safety followed automatically.

Upon the foregoing premises, I join the opinion of the Court.

MR. JUSTICE DOUGLAS, dissenting.

The infringement on personal liberty of any "seizure" of a person can only be "reasonable" under the Fourth Amendment if we require the police to possess "probable cause" before they seize him. Only that line draws a meaningful distinction between an officer's mere inkling and the presence of facts within the officer's personal knowledge which would convince a reasonable man that the person seized has committed, is committing, or is about to commit a particular crime. "In dealing with probable cause, . . . as the very name implies, we deal with probabilities. These are not technical; they are the factual and practical considerations of everyday life on which reasonable and prudent men, not legal technicians, act." *Brinegar v. United States.*

To give the police greater power than a magistrate is to take a long step down the totalitarian path. Perhaps such a step is desirable to cope with modern forms of lawlessness. But if it is taken, it should be the deliberate choice of the people through a constitutional amendment. Until the Fourth Amendment, which is closely allied with the Fifth, is rewritten, the person and the effects of the individual are beyond the reach of all government agencies until there are reasonable grounds to believe (probable cause) that a criminal venture has been launched or is about to be launched.

There have been powerful hydraulic pressures throughout our history that bear heavily on the Court to water down constitutional guarantees and give the police the upper hand. That hydraulic pressure has probably never been greater than it is today.

Yet if the individual is no longer to be sovereign, if the police can pick him up whenever they do not like the cut of his jib, if they can "seize" and "search" him in their discretion, we enter a new regime. The decision to enter it should be made only after a full debate by the people of this country.

Scholars, lawyers, judges, and others concerned with the process of criminal justice regard *Terry v. Ohio* as one of the Supreme Court's more significant decisions. It is interesting to note that *Terry* was decided by the Warren Court, and, as such, represents one of its few significant departures from its generally liberal stances.

The Court continues to confront cases involving Terry stop issues. Frequently these cases hinge on the question of what constitutes sufficient cause to stop and frisk a suspect. Comparing the outcomes of two cases, both decided in 2000, illustrates the position the Court has generally taken on such questions. The first dispute, *Illinois v. Wardlow* (2000), arose when a caravan of four police cars converged on an area of Chicago known for high levels of drug trafficking. Two police officers noticed William Wardlow standing next to a building holding a bag. When Wardlow saw the uniformed officers, he ran. The officers gave chase, caught him, and patted him down. When they squeezed the bag, they could tell that it contained a gun. Wardlow was arrested on weapons charges. Police justified their search on Terry stop grounds. The Supreme Court upheld the search, concluding that running from a high crime area upon seeing the police created sufficient suspicion to authorize a stop and frisk.

Florida v. J. L. (2000) had a different outcome. Police received an anonymous telephone tip that a teenager standing at a particular bus stop and wearing a plaid shirt was carrying a gun. When police officers arrived at the bus stop, they found three young black males just "hanging out" there. One was wearing a plaid shirt. Apart from the anonymous tip, police had no reason to suspect any wrongdoing. The three teenagers were engaged in no suspicious behavior and did nothing to threaten the officers. The police approached the three young men, told them to put their hands up, and frisked them. The search of J. L., the fifteen-year-old with the plaid shirt, yielded a pistol. The Supreme Court held that the stop and frisk was illegal. An unsubstantiated anonymous tip alone is not sufficient to justify a Terry stop. The suspect in question had done nothing to indicate that he was carrying a weapon or that he was engaged in any illegal activity.

These two cases illustrate that although *Terry* gives

police discretion to act when confronted with a potentially dangerous situation, the suspicious actions of the suspect are the key to triggering that discretion.

Hot Pursuit. Suppose a police officer witnesses a mugging on a city street and chases the perpetrators, who run into an apartment building and close the door.[15] Must the police officer obtain a warrant to enter the building? As a general rule of law, the answer is no, and the reason is that the Supreme Court has carved out yet another exception to the Fourth Amendment's warrant requirement: "hot pursuit." In other words, the Court has said that it would be reasonable for the police officer to enter the apartment without a search warrant because evidence could be destroyed and lives could be endangered. And, if the officer found evidence of a crime—for example, the wallet of the person the officer saw being mugged—under the hot pursuit exception, the evidence could be used against the defendant.

As with all other exceptions to the warrant requirement, the Court has placed limits on the hot pursuit exception—limits that, as always, reflect the original justifications for permitting the exception. These limits were laid out by the justices in *Warden v. Hayden* (1967), a Warren Court case that provides an important example of the hot pursuit exception. Hayden robbed a taxi company and fled on foot. Hearing yells of "Holdup!" from company employees, two cab drivers followed Hayden and saw him enter a house. One of the drivers radioed the cab dispatcher with a description of Hayden and where he was hiding. The police arrived immediately, entered the house, and found Hayden in a bedroom pretending to be asleep. In the meantime, another officer found—in an adjoining bathroom—two guns and the clothing that matched what witnesses had said the robber was wearing. These and other items were introduced as evidence against Hayden.

Even though police officers had entered the house without a warrant, the Supreme Court ruled that the search was constitutional on the grounds that they were in hot pursuit of a suspect. It is reasonable to allow warrantless searches in such circumstances, as Justice Brennan put it for the majority, because the "Fourth Amendment does not require police officers to delay in the course of an investigation if to do so would gravely endanger their lives or the lives of others. Speed here was essential, and only a thorough search of the house for persons and weapons could have ensured that Hayden was the only man present and the police had control of all weapons which could be used against them or to effect an escape." The "exigencies of the situation"—the fact that lives were in danger, that evidence could have been lost, and so forth—made the warrantless entry into Hayden's house "imperative."

The Court was careful to note that the hot pursuit exception was limited to those circumstances that warranted its creation in the first place. Police may not, for example, conduct a warrantless search and expect courts to admit seized evidence under the hot pursuit exception unless the officers have probable cause to believe that the individual they are pursuing committed a crime or is likely to endanger lives. In general, the Court is willing to tolerate only a short delay between the observed crime and the warrantless search, a limitation that makes sense given the reason for creating the exception—that police must act quickly.

Even the more conservative Burger Court stressed the importance of these limits. In *Welsh v. Wisconsin* (1984) the justices considered whether the Fourth Amendment "prohibits the police from making a warrantless night entry of a person's home in order to arrest him for a violation of a nonjailable traffic offense." One rainy night an apparently drunk Welsh drove his car off the road. Another driver pulled over, blocked Welsh's car with his truck, and had someone call the police. He also suggested to Welsh that he wait in the car, but Welsh walked off. The police arrived at Welsh's house at about 9:00 p.m. Welsh's stepdaughter answered the door and, without gaining her consent, police entered the house. They found Welsh in bed and arrested him. At the police station, Welsh would not submit to a breath analysis. This refusal led authorities to revoke his license.

The state tried to use the hot pursuit exception to justify the officers' warrantless entry into Welsh's home. It

15. We adopt this discussion from Zalman and Siegel, *Criminal Procedure*, 2d ed., 284–285.

suggested that police need to act with speed to prevent the loss of evidence and to prevent the threat to public safety posed by drunk drivers. But the Supreme Court did not agree. Writing for the majority, Justice Brennan found the hot pursuit claim "unconvincing because there was no immediate or continuous pursuit of the petitioner from the scene of the crime. Moreover, because the petitioner had already arrived home, and had abandoned his car at the scene of the accident, there was little remaining threat to the public safety." As for the state's claim that the hot pursuit exception was activated by the need to test Welsh for the presence of alcohol before the substance left his body, Brennan had this to say: "A warrantless home arrest cannot be upheld simply because evidence of the petitioner's blood-alcohol level might have dissipated while police obtained a warrant. To allow [it] on these facts would be to approve unreasonable police behavior that the principles of the Fourth Amendment will not sanction."

Welsh reinforced existing limits on the hot pursuit exception, but it also created yet another restriction—the gravity of the offense. As the majority noted, "We . . . hold that an important factor to be considered when determining whether any exigency exists is the gravity of the underlying offense for which the arrest is being made." In short, the Court is unwilling to apply the hot pursuit exception "when there is probable cause to believe that only a minor offense . . . has been committed," as was the case in *Welsh*.

Plain View Doctrine. Our discussion so far has described circumstances under which police may search and the guidelines the Court has established to determine reasonableness. Under each justification for a search there are limitations: searches based on a warrant must be confined to the place specified in the document; consent searches may go no farther than the grant of permission stipulates; and safety searches can extend only far enough to discover or remove the possible danger. But what if, while conducting a valid search, police come upon seizable articles that are outside the scope of the search authorization? For example, suppose law enforcement officials have a valid warrant to search a house for stolen goods and, in the course of their investigation,

come across illegal narcotics. What should they do? Must they ignore such items? Or may they seize the drugs? These questions are addressed by the plain view doctrine, a controversial rule that expands the powers of police to gather evidence. This doctrine holds that if police officers are lawfully present and items subject to seizure are openly visible, the officers may take possession of those articles without any additional authorization.

Some analysts refer to the plain view doctrine as yet another exception to the Fourth Amendment's warrant requirement. This interpretation is reasonable because the doctrine provides police with some freedom to seize contraband and other evidence of a crime, without necessarily having a warrant. Still, it is important to understand that, at the heart of the doctrine, is the requirement that police must be acting lawfully when seizable items come into plain view. Accordingly, the plain view doctrine often supplements other searches. Imagine that two officers come to a student's apartment and the student allows them to enter. Walking into the apartment, police spot marijuana on a table. Under the plain view doctrine, the officers could seize the marijuana because the student *consented* to the search. Had the student denied the officers permission and they entered anyway, the plain view doctrine would not apply unless the officers had some other legitimate reason for conducting a search or they had a search warrant.

This hypothetical case brings to light yet another important aspect of the doctrine: to qualify, the items must clearly be in plain view. In *Arizona v. Hicks* (1987) police lawfully entered an apartment looking for weapons thought to have been used in a shooting. The officers found some very expensive stereo equipment in the otherwise squalid apartment. Suspecting that the stereo equipment had been stolen, one of the officers moved some of the components to get the serial numbers. A check against police records confirmed that the items had been reported stolen, and the occupant of the apartment was convicted of robbery. The Supreme Court, however, found the actions of the officers to be in violation of the Fourth Amendment. The justices reasoned that, although the police had a legitimate reason for entering the apartment, they had violated the plain view doctrine when the officer moved the stereo components to find the serial numbers. Unlike the marijuana in our hypothetical case, those serial numbers were not in plain view, and moving the components was not part of the legitimate search for weapons. The plain view doctrine clearly expands the opportunities of police to seize evidence.

In spite of this expansion, there are limits to the plain view doctrine. In *Bond v. United States* (2000), for example, the justices evaluated the actions of a border patrol agent in Texas who entered a Greyhound bus to check the immigration status of the passengers. As he walked through the bus, he squeezed the soft luggage that passengers had placed in the overhead storage space above the seats. In one bag he felt a brick-like object that he suspected to be illegal drugs. He received the consent of the bag's owner to open it and found a brick of illegal methamphetamine. The Supreme Court ruled the search illegal. Although the officer was lawfully present, his squeezing of the bags to check for possible contraband was not the same as viewing an openly visible illegal substance. Passengers, the justices held, have an expectation that their baggage will not be handled in such an exploratory manner.

Place Searches. All the cases we have examined so far have dealt with police procedure, addressing the questions of when and under what circumstances police could conduct searches and seizures. The Court, under the leadership of Warren Burger, examined a number of cases that asked different questions: Where can law enforcement officials search and seize without a warrant? Do certain places require special consideration? These questions assume that not all places deserve equal levels of Fourth Amendment protection. In some places we have a higher expectation of privacy than in others. The home, for example, merits the highest degree of protection. Other places, such as automobiles, open fields, and prisons, have not fared as well in the decisions of the Court.

The issue of place search exceptions originates in modern jurisprudence with automobile searches. With the appearance of automobiles on the American scene in

the early 1900s, the Supreme Court has been forced to address the following question: Should the law treat cars the same as houses, in which case traditional search and seizure rules would apply, or as something different? Since its first car search case in 1925, *Carroll v. United States,* the Court has always decided that cars do not deserve the same degree of protection as people, houses, papers, and the like. In general, the Court has given the police broad latitude in searching cars without warrants because (1) cars are mobile and can quickly leave the jurisdiction of the police; (2) automobile windows allow outsiders to look in, and drivers have a lower expectation of privacy inside a car than they do in their homes; and (3) the government has a pervasive interest in regulating cars.

Even though the doctrine that automobiles deserve little constitutional protection from warrantless searches was well established, the Court was confronted with many car search questions beginning in the 1970s. How far may such searches extend? May police search only the area where driver and passengers sit? What about the glove compartment and trunk? Are baggage or boxes in a car fair game? What degree of justification or cause does a law enforcement official need before a warrantless search can be conducted? If an automobile is impounded, may police search and inventory the contents?

In *Knowles v. Iowa* (1998) the justices ruled that a routine traffic stop culminating in the issuing of a citation is insufficient to justify a full search of an automobile. Generally, however, the Supreme Court has given police great latitude in searching vehicles. If an officer has probable cause to believe a crime has been committed or if the police have grounds to impound an automobile, a comprehensive, warrantless search of the vehicle is normally permitted. Table 10-1 briefly summarizes the Court's decisions that have created the automobile exception to the warrant requirement. A quick reading of this information will underscore the minimal protections offered by the Fourth Amendment to vehicles, their passengers, and contents.

Automobiles are not the only place exceptions to the Fourth Amendment. Since *Hester v. United States* (1924) the Supreme Court adhered to an open fields doctrine

TABLE 10-1 The Automobile Exception

Case	Facts	Ruling
Carroll v. United States (1925)	Federal agents suspect individuals are transporting illegal liquor. They stop and search car, finding evidence of the crime.	Automobiles merit low levels of protection. Their mobility often makes obtaining a search warrant impractical.
Chambers v. Maroney (1970)	Robbery suspects are pulled over and arrested. Their impounded automobile is searched and evidence is found in trunk.	To secure its contents, protect against liability claims, and remove any potential dangers, police may conduct an inventory search of an impounded automobile when its occupants have been arrested.
South Dakota v. Opperman (1976)	Illegally parked car is impounded. While conducting an inventory search, police find illegal drugs in glove compartment.	Police may conduct inventory searches of automobiles impounded for parking violations.
New York v. Belton (1981)	Police stop car for speeding. Officer smells marijuana, arrests suspects, and searches car, finding cocaine in the zipped pocket of a jacket in the back seat.	After police have made a lawful arrest of an occupant of an automobile, they may search, incident to the arrest, the entire passenger compartment and the contents of any container therein.
United States v. Ross (1982)	Based on a reliable informant's tip that he sold drugs out of his car trunk, police stop Ross. They search the car, finding a pistol in the glove compartment and illegal drugs contained in a brown paper bag in the trunk.	With probable cause police may search every part of a vehicle and any contents that may conceal the object of the search.
United States v. Johns (1985)	Police search impounded truck three days after driver was arrested on marijuana charges.	There is no requirement that contents of impounded vehicle must be searched contemporaneous with the arrest.
Michigan State Police v. Sitz (1990)	Police stop all passing cars pursuant to a sobriety checkpoint program.	Brief stops, where police do not use discretion to determine who will be stopped, reasonably advance the state's interest in preventing drunk driving.
California v. Alcevdo (1991)	Police observe suspect leaving a house with a package they had reason to believe contains marijuana. Suspect places package in trunk of car. Police stop car, open trunk, and seize the evidence.	Police may search an automobile and the containers within it where they have probable cause to believe contraband or evidence is contained.
Whren v. United States (1996)	After stopping a driver for a traffic violation, police observe and seize two plastic bags of what appeared to be cocaine in the passenger's hands.	There was probable cause for the traffic stop allowing the police to observe what appeared to be illegal drugs. Seizure is valid.
Ohio v. Robinette (1996)	Suspect is pulled over for speeding. Officer asks for and obtains permission to search car. Illegal drugs are found.	Police are not required to inform suspect that he is free to go prior to requesting permission to search.
Maryland v. Wilson (1997)	Police stop car for speeding. When passengers act nervous, officer orders them out of the car. As one steps out of the car, cocaine drops to the ground.	An officer making a traffic stop may order passengers (as well as the driver) out of the car.
Wyoming v. Houghton (1999)	Police officer stops a car for a faulty brake light and sees a hypodermic syringe in the driver's pocket. The driver admits to drug use. The officer searches the car and finds illegal drugs in a passenger's purse.	If probable cause justifies a search of a lawfully stopped vehicle, it justifies the search of every part of the vehicle and every article or container therein that might conceal the object of the search.

that allowed police to enter and search a field without a warrant. The status of the open field doctrine, however, was brought into question following the Court's ruling in *Katz v. United States*, which held that Fourth Amendment requirements apply whenever an individual has a reasonable expectation of privacy. Some civil libertarians argued that the open field exception to the Fourth Amendment warrant requirement would be nullifed if the owner of the field took steps to declare an expectation of privacy, perhaps by installing a fence or posting No Trespassing signs.

The Supreme Court dashed any hopes for a major change in the open field exception in *Oliver v. United States* (1984). The justices upheld a warrantless search of a field of marijuana in spite of the fact that the field was bordered by fencing, an earthen embankment, and trees; and that the owner had posted No Trespassing signs. According to the justices, these obvious attempts to hide the field from outsiders were not enough to create a legitimate expectation of privacy in the sense required by the Fourth Amendment.

Since *Oliver*, the Court has continued to narrow privacy expectations concerning open fields. In *Florida v. Riley* (1988) the issue was the validity of a warrantless aerial observation. From a helicopter flying four hundred feet above ground, law enforcement officials viewed marijuana growing in a greenhouse. Quoting from an earlier decision, Justice White asserted, "In an age where private and commercial flight in the public airways is routine, it is unreasonable for [Riley] to expect that his marijuana plants were constitutionally protected from being observed with the naked eye."

In addition to automobiles and open fields, police and other officials may conduct warrantless searches of prisoners. In *Hudson v. Palmer* (1984) the Court ruled that, although some constitutional guarantees apply to prisoners, others do not. Imprisonment by its very nature necessitates the loss of rights, among them the guarantees contained in the Fourth Amendment. If the law accorded prisoners such rights, Chief Justice Burger's opinion for the majority reasoned, it would "undermine the effectiveness of prison operations," an important element of which involves "surprise searches" for weapons

and narcotics. Burger argued that prisons are "volatile communities," lacking any expectations of privacy, and therefore lie beyond full Fourth Amendment protection.

ENFORCING THE FOURTH AMENDMENT: THE EXCLUSIONARY RULE

So far, our discussion has focused on the constitutional rules governing searches and seizures. We learned that the Court has carved out numerous exceptions to the general principle that police should obtain warrants to conduct searches. At the same time, we saw that the Court has placed limits on those exceptions. For example, if police use the "incident to arrest" exception to conduct the warrantless search of an individual, they must conduct that search *at the time* the individual is arrested. As we discussed, the Court justified this exception on the grounds that the suspect may be carrying weapons that could endanger the lives of police officers. If police returned to the crime scene after the suspect was removed and conducted a warrantless search, the Court would not allow them to use the "incident to arrest" exception to justify their search. After all, police could not be harmed by an individual who was no longer there.

But suppose that is precisely what police did? They went back to the scene of the crime a day later, found evidence, and tried to justify the search under the incident to arrest exception. We know that this would be an illegal search, but what is to prevent police from doing it anyway? In England, if police conduct an illegal search and seizure, the evidence they obtain *may* be used in court against the accused, but the person whose privacy rights have been violated can sue the police for damages. This system of police liability enables the British to enforce search and seizure rights.

The United States imposes a different remedy for police infractions.[16] The Fourth Amendment is enforced through the application of the exclusionary rule, a judicially created principle that reduces the incentive police might otherwise have for violating search and seizure

16. It is true, however, that in the United States civil suits can be initiated against officers for violations of Fourth Amendment rights. The discussion that follows focuses on the exclusionary rule, the major remedy used in criminal proceedings.

rights. The exclusionary rule holds that evidence gathered illegally may not be admitted into court. It is excluded from use by prosecutors in attempting to establish the suspect's guilt. The rationale behind the rule is straightforward: if police know that evidence produced by an illegal search will be of no use, they have no motive for violating the Constitution.

Development of the Exclusionary Rule

At one time, law enforcement officials faced no federal punitive measures for conducting illegal searches and seizures. Unless the individual states imposed some form of redress, the police were not held liable for their activities and unconstitutionally obtained evidence was not excluded from trials. The law began to change in 1914 when the Court handed down *Weeks v. United States,* the case with which we began this chapter. Recall that police officers and a U.S. marshal went to Weeks's house and, without a warrant, carried off boxes of his papers, documents, and other possessions. These materials were not narrowly selected for their relevance; rather, they were voluminous business records that authorities could search in hopes of finding possible incriminating evidence. Should the documents be used as evidence against *Weeks,* even though gathered in an illegal manner? Writing for the Court, Justice William R. Day proclaimed:

If letters and private documents can thus be seized and held and used as evidence against a citizen accused of an offense, the protection of the Fourth Amendment declaring his right to be secure against such searches and seizures is of no value, and, so far as those thus placed are concerned, might as well be stricken from the Constitution.

With this conclusion, the Court, through Justice Day, created the exclusionary rule: judges must exclude from trial any evidence gathered in violation of the Fourth Amendment.

Although *Weeks* constituted a major decision, it was limited in scope, applying only to *federal* agents and *federal* judges in *federal* criminal cases. It was clear, however, that eventually the Court would be asked to apply the exclusionary rule to the states because that is where most criminal prosecutions take place. But it was also the case that many states or their judges resisted adopting an exclusionary rule. *People v. Defore* (1926) provides perhaps

the best-known example. In that case, Benjamin Cardozo, then a judge on the New York Court of Appeals, rejected adoption of *Weeks* to New York. He wrote the now-famous lines disparaging the exclusionary rule: "The criminal is to go free because the constable has blundered. . . . A room is searched against the law, and the body of a murdered man is found. . . . The privacy of the home has been infringed, and the murderer goes free."

The issue first reached the Supreme Court in 1949 in *Wolf v. Colorado.* This case involved a Colorado physician who was suspected of performing illegal abortions. Because the police were unable to obtain any solid evidence against him, a deputy sheriff surreptitiously took Wolf's appointment book and followed up on the names in it. The police gathered enough evidence to convict him. Wolf's attorney argued that because the case against his client rested on illegally obtained evidence, the Court should dismiss it. To implement his arguments, however, the justices would have to apply or incorporate the Fourth Amendment and impose the exclusionary rule on the states *(see Chapter 3).*

Writing for the Court, Justice Frankfurter agreed to incorporate the Fourth Amendment. The right to be secure against unreasonable searches and seizures was deemed a fundamental right, "basic to a free society," and the provisions of the amendment applied to the states through the Due Process Clause of the Fourteenth Amendment. However, the Court refused to hold that the exclusionary rule was a necessary part of the Fourth Amendment. The rule was one method of enforcing search and seizure rights, but not the only one. In other words, although state law enforcement officials must abide by the guarantees contained in the Fourth Amendment, judges need not use a particular mechanism, such as the exclusionary rule, to ensure compliance. Frankfurter noted that the law in England, where there was no exclusionary rule, and in the states, the majority of which rejected the rule, proved that justice could be served without this check on police behavior. States were left free to adopt whatever procedures they wished to enforce search and seizure rights. The exclusionary rule was not mandatory.

Growing conflicts between state and federal search and seizure rules, coupled with changes in Court person-

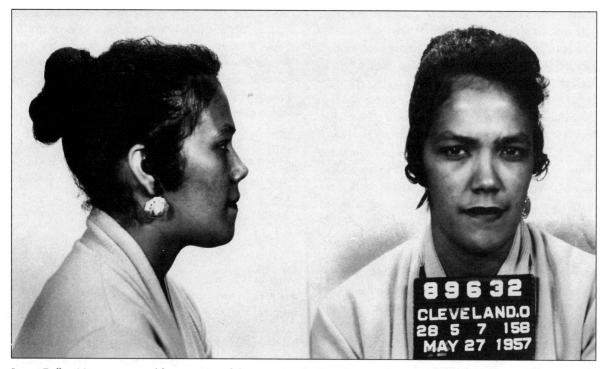

In 1957 Dollree Mapp was arrested for possession of obscene materials. The police seized vital evidence against her during an unconstitutional search. In *Mapp v. Ohio* (1961) the Supreme Court reversed her conviction holding that evidence obtained through an illegal search could not be admitted in court.

nel, caused the Court to reconsider the applicability of the exclusionary rule to states in *Mapp v. Ohio* (1961).[17] As you read *Mapp*, can you discern why it is such a significant, yet controversial, opinion? Does Justice Clark's majority opinion leave any room for exceptions? This question arose during the 1980s and continues into the current Supreme Court era.

Mapp v. Ohio

367 U.S. 643 (1961)
laws.findlaw.com/US/367/643.html
Vote: 6 *(Black, Brennan, Clark, Douglas, Stewart, Warren)*
   3 *(Frankfurter, Harlan, Whittaker)*
Opinion of the Court: Clark
Concurring opinions: Black, Douglas, Stewart
Dissenting opinion: Harlan

Dollree Mapp, a woman in her early twenties, was involved in a number of illegal activities that she carried on in her Cleveland home. For several months the police had attempted to shut down her operations, but apparently Mapp was tipped off because each time police planned a raid, she managed to elude them.

On May 23, 1957, police officers, led by Sgt. Carl Delau, tried to enter Mapp's house, this time on the grounds that she was harboring a fugitive from justice. (The fugitive was suspected of bombing the house of an alleged Cleveland numbers racketeer, Don King, who was later to become a prominent boxing promoter.)[18] When the police arrived, Mapp refused to let them in because they did not have a search warrant. Delau returned to his car, radioed for a search warrant, and kept the house under surveillance. Three hours later, and with additional police

17. For oral arguments in this case, navigate to: *oyez.nwu.edu.*

18. See Fred W. Friendly and Martha J. H. Elliott, *The Constitution—That Delicate Balance* (New York: Random House, 1984), 128–133.

officers, Delau again tried to enter. This time Mapp did not come to the door, so police forced it open.

At this point several events occurred almost simultaneously. Mapp's attorney, whom she had called when police first appeared, arrived and tried to see her. Police would not let him in. Hearing the police break in, Mapp came downstairs and began arguing with them. Delau held up a piece of paper, which he claimed was a search warrant. Mapp grabbed it and stuffed it down her blouse. A fight broke out, during which police handcuffed Mapp, retrieved the paper, and searched the house. The police seized some allegedly obscene pictures, which were illegal to possess under Ohio law. The state was never able to establish the existence of a valid search warrant. Mapp was found guilty of possession of obscene materials and sentenced to prison. Her attorney appealed to the U.S. Supreme Court, asking the justices to review Mapp's claim on First Amendment grounds, but the justices were more interested in exploring the search and seizure issue.[19]

MR. JUSTICE CLARK delivered the opinion of the Court.

Seventy-five years ago, in *Boyd v. United States* . . . [t]he Court noted that

"constitutional provisions for the security of person and property should be liberally construed. . . . It is the duty of courts to be watchful for the constitutional rights of the citizen, and against any stealthy encroachments thereon."

In this jealous regard for maintaining the integrity of individual rights, the Court gave life to Madison's prediction that "independent tribunals of justice . . . will be naturally led to resist every encroachment upon rights expressly stipulated for in the Constitution by the declaration of rights.". . .

Less than 30 years after *Boyd*, this Court, in *Weeks v.*

19. Indeed, both Mapp's and the state's lawyers argued this case on First Amendment grounds because she was convicted for possessing obscene material. The ACLU, in an amicus curiae brief, raised the Fourth Amendment issue on which the Court ultimately decided the case. *Mapp*, therefore, presents an excellent illustration of how amicus curiae briefs can influence the justices. It also serves as an example of the uneven quality of state attorneys general. During oral argument, a justice asked Ohio's attorney about the applicability of *Wolf* to *Mapp*. The attorney responded that he did not know anything about *Wolf*, even though it was the leading case in the area.

United States, 1914, . . . stated that use of the seized evidence involved "a denial of the constitutional rights of the accused." Thus, in the year 1914, in the *Weeks* case, this Court "for the first time" held that "in a federal prosecution the Fourth Amendment barred the use of evidence secured through an illegal search and seizure." This Court has ever since required of federal law officers a strict adherence to that command which this Court has held to be a clear, specific, and constitutionally required—even if judicially implied—deterrent safeguard without insistence upon which the Fourth Amendment would have been reduced to "a form of words." It meant, quite simply, that "conviction by means of unlawful seizures and enforced confessions . . . should find no sanction in the judgments of the courts . . . ," that such evidence "shall not be used at all."

There are in the cases of this Court some passing references to the *Weeks* rule as being one of evidence. But the plain and unequivocal language of *Weeks*—and its later paraphrase in *Wolf*—to the effect that the *Weeks* rule is of constitutional origin, remains entirely undisturbed. . . .

In 1949, 35 years after *Weeks* was announced, this Court, in *Wolf v. Colorado,* again for the first time, discussed the effect of the Fourth Amendment upon the states through the operation of the Due Process Clause of the Fourteenth Amendment. It said:

"[W]e have no hesitation in saying that were a State affirmatively to sanction such police incursion into privacy it would run counter to the guaranty of the Fourteenth Amendment."

Nevertheless, after declaring that the "security of one's privacy against arbitrary intrusion by the police" is "implicit in 'the concept of ordered liberty' and as such enforceable against the States through the Due Process Clause," and announcing that it "stoutly adhere[d]" to the *Weeks* decision, the Court decided that the *Weeks* exclusionary rule would not then be imposed upon the States as "an essential ingredient of the right." The Court's reasons for not considering essential to the right to privacy, as a curb imposed upon the States by the Due Process Clause, that which decades before had been posited as part and parcel of the Fourth Amendment's limitation upon federal encroachment of individual privacy, were bottomed on factual considerations.

While they are not basically relevant to a decision that the exclusionary rule is an essential ingredient of the Fourth

Amendment as the right it embodies is vouchsafed against the States by the Due Process Clause, we will consider the current validity of the factual grounds upon which *Wolf* was based.

The Court in *Wolf* first stated that "[t]he contrariety of views of the States" on the adoption of the exclusionary rule of *Weeks* was "particularly impressive" and, in this connection that it could not "brush aside the experience of States which deem the incidence of such conduct by the police too slight to call for a deterrent remedy . . . by overriding the [States'] relevant rules of evidence." While in 1949, prior to the *Wolf* case, almost two-thirds of the States were opposed to the use of the exclusionary rule, now, despite the *Wolf* case, more than half of those since passing upon it, by their own legislative or judicial decision, have wholly or partly adopted or adhered to the *Weeks* rule. Significantly, among those now following the rule is California, which, according to its highest court, was "compelled to reach that conclusion because other remedies have completely failed to secure compliance with the constitutional provisions. . . ." In connection with this California case, we note that the second basis elaborated in *Wolf* in support of its failure to enforce the exclusionary doctrine against the States was that "other means of protection" have been afforded "the right to privacy." The experience of California that such other remedies have been worthless and futile is buttressed by the experience of other States. . . .

Likewise, time has set its face against . . . *Wolf*. . . . [T]he force of that reasoning has been largely vitiated by later decisions of this Court. These include the recent discarding of the "silver platter" doctrine which allowed federal judicial use of evidence seized in violation of the Constitution by state agents; the relaxation of the formerly strict requirements as to standing to challenge the use of evidence thus seized, so that now the procedure of exclusion, "ultimately referable to constitutional safeguards," is available to anyone even "legitimately on [the] premises" unlawfully searched; and finally, the formulation of a method to prevent state use of evidence unconstitutionally seized by federal agents. Because there can be no fixed formula, we are admittedly met with "recurring questions of the [r]easonableness of searches," but less is not to be expected when dealing with a Constitution, and, at any rate, "reasonableness is in the first instance for the [trial court] to determine."

It, therefore, plainly appears that the factual considerations supporting the failure of the *Wolf* Court to include the *Weeks* exclusionary rule when it recognized the enforceability of the right to privacy against the States in 1949, while not basically relevant to the constitutional consideration, could not, in any analysis, now be deemed controlling.

Some five years after *Wolf*, in answer to a plea made here Term after Term that we overturn its doctrine on applicability of the *Weeks* exclusionary rule, this Court indicated that such should not be done until the States had "adequate opportunity to adopt or reject the [*Weeks*] rule.". . . Today we once again examine *Wolf*'s constitutional documentation of the right to privacy free from unreasonable state intrusion, and, after its dozen years on our books, are led by it to close the only courtroom door remaining open to evidence secured by official lawlessness in flagrant abuse of that basic right, reserved to all persons as a specific guarantee against that very same unlawful conduct. We hold that all evidence obtained by searches and seizures in violation of the Constitution is, by that same authority, inadmissible in a state court.

Since the Fourth Amendment's right of privacy has been declared enforceable against the States through the Due Process Clause of the Fourteenth, it is enforceable against them by the same sanction of exclusion as is used against the Federal Government. Were it otherwise, then just as without the *Weeks* rule the assurance against unreasonable federal searches and seizures would be "a form of words," valueless and undeserving of mention in a perpetual charter of inestimable human liberties, so too, without that rule the freedom from state invasions of privacy would be so ephemeral and so neatly severed from its conceptual nexus with the freedom from all brutish means of coercing evidence as not to merit this Court's high regard as a freedom "implicit in 'the concept of ordered liberty.'" At the time that the Court held in *Wolf* that the Amendment was applicable to the States through the Due Process Clause, the cases of this Court, as we have seen, had steadfastly held that as to federal officers the Fourth Amendment included the exclusion of the evidence seized in violation of its provisions. Even *Wolf* "stoutly adhered" to that proposition. The right to privacy, when conceded operatively enforceable against the States, was not susceptible of destruction by avulsion of the sanction upon which its protection and enjoyment had always been deemed dependent. . . . Therefore, in extending the substantive protections of due process to all consti-tutionally unreasonable searches—state or federal—it was logically and constitutionally necessary that the exclusion doctrine—an essential part of the right to privacy—be also insisted upon as an essential ingredient of the right newly recognized by the *Wolf* case. In short, the admission of the new constitutional right by *Wolf* could not consistently tolerate denial of its most important constitutional privilege, namely, the exclusion of the evidence which an accused had been forced to give by reason of the unlawful seizure. To hold otherwise is to grant the right but in reality to withhold its privilege and enjoyment. Only last year the Court itself recognized that the purpose of the exclusionary rule "is to deter—to compel respect for the constitutional guaranty in the only effectively available way—by removing the incentive to disregard it."

Indeed, we are aware of no restraint, similar to that rejected today, conditioning the enforcement of any other basic constitutional right. The right to privacy, no less important than any other right carefully and particularly reserved to the people, would stand in marked contrast to all other rights declared as "basic to a free society." This Court has not hesitated to enforce as strictly against the States as it does against the Federal Government the rights of free speech and of a free press, the rights to notice and to a fair, public trial, including, as it does, the right not to be convicted by use of a coerced confession, however logically relevant it be, and without regard to its reliability. And nothing could be more certain than that when a coerced confession is involved, "the relevant rules of evidence" are overridden without regard to "the incidence of such conduct by the police," slight or frequent. Why should not the same rule apply to what is tantamount to coerced testimony by way of unconstitutional seizure of goods, papers, effects, documents, etc.? We find that, as to the Federal Government, the Fourth and Fifth Amendments and, as to the States, the freedom from unconscionable invasions of privacy and the freedom from convictions based upon coerced confessions do enjoy an "intimate relation" in their perpetuation of "principles of humanity and civil liberty [secured] . . . only after years of struggle." The philosophy of each Amendment and of each freedom is complementary to, although not dependent upon, that of the other in its sphere of influence—the very least that together they assure in either sphere is that no man is to be convicted on unconstitutional evidence.

Moreover, our holding that the exclusionary rule is an essential part of both the Fourth and Fourteenth Amendments is not only the logical dictate of prior cases, but it also makes very good sense. There is no war between the Constitution and common sense. Presently, a federal prosecutor may make no use of evidence illegally seized, but a State's attorney across the street may, although he supposedly is operating under the enforceable prohibitions of the same Amendment. Thus the State, by admitting evidence unlawfully seized, serves to encourage disobedience to the Federal Constitution which it is bound to uphold. Moreover, "[t]he very essence of a healthy federalism depends upon the avoidance of needless conflict between state and federal courts." Such a conflict, hereafter needless, arose this very Term, in *Wilson v. Schnettler,* in which . . . we gave full recognition to our practice in this regard by refusing to restrain a federal officer from testifying in a state court as to evidence unconstitutionally seized by him in the performance of his duties. Yet the double standard recognized until today hardly put such a thesis into practice. In non-exclusionary States, federal officers, being human, were by it invited to and did, as our cases indicate, step across the street to the State's attorney with their unconstitutionally seized evidence. Prosecution on the basis of that evidence was then had in a state court in utter disregard of the enforceable Fourth Amendment. If the fruits of an unconstitutional search had been inadmissible in both state and federal courts, this inducement to evasion would have been sooner eliminated. There would be no need to reconcile such cases as . . . *Schnettler,* pointing up the hazardous uncertainties of our heretofore ambivalent approach. . . .

There are those who say, as did Justice (then Judge) Cardozo, that under our constitutional exclusionary doctrine "[t]he criminal is to go free because the constable has blundered." *People v. Defore.* In some cases this will undoubtedly be the result. But . . . "there is another consideration—the imperative of judicial integrity." The criminal goes free, if he must, but it is the law that sets him free. Nothing can destroy a government more quickly than its failure to observe its own laws, or worse, its disregard of the character of its own existence. Nor can it lightly be assumed that, as a practical matter, adoption of the exclusionary rule fetters law enforcement. Only last year this Court expressly considered that contention and found that "pragmatic evidence of a sort" to the contrary was not wanting. . . . Moreover, the experience of the states is impressive. . . . The movement towards the rule of exclusion has been halting but seemingly inexorable.

The ignoble shortcut to conviction left open to the State tends to destroy the entire system of constitutional restraints on which the liberties of the people rest. Having once recognized that the right to privacy embodied in the Fourth Amendment is enforceable against the States, and that the right to be secure against rude invasions of privacy by state officers is, therefore, constitutional in origin, we can no longer permit that right to remain an empty promise. Because it is enforceable in the same manner and to like effect as other basic rights secured by the Due Process Clause, we can no longer permit it to be revocable at the whim of any police officer who, in the name of law enforcement itself, chooses to suspend its enjoyment. Our decision, founded on reason and truth, gives to the individual no more than that which the Constitution guarantees him, to the police officer no less than that to which honest law enforcement is entitled, and, to the courts, that judicial integrity so necessary in the true administration of justice.

The judgment of the Supreme Court of Ohio is reversed and the cause remanded for further proceedings not inconsistent with this opinion.

Reversed and remanded.

MR. JUSTICE BLACK, concurring.

I am still not persuaded that the Fourth Amendment, standing alone, would be enough to bar the introduction into evidence against an accused of papers and effects seized from him in violation of its commands. For the Fourth Amendment does not itself contain any provision expressly precluding the use of such evidence, and I am extremely doubtful that such a provision could properly be inferred from nothing more than the basic command against unreasonable searches and seizures. Reflection on the problem, however, in the light of cases coming before the Court since *Wolf,* has led me to conclude that when the Fourth Amendment's ban against unreasonable searches and seizures is considered together with the Fifth Amendment's ban against compelled self-incrimination, a constitutional basis emerges which not only justifies but actually requires the exclusionary rule.

The close interrelationship between the Fourth and Fifth amendments, as they apply to this problem, has long been recognized and, indeed, was expressly made the ground for this Court's holding in *Boyd v. United States* [1866]. There the Court fully discussed this relationship and declared itself "unable to perceive that the seizure of a man's private books and papers to be used in evidence against him is substantially different from compelling him to be a witness against himself." It was upon this ground that Mr. Justice Rutledge largely relied in his dissenting opinion in the *Wolf* case. And, although I rejected the argument at that time, its force has, for me at least, become compelling with the more thorough understanding of the problem brought on by recent cases. In the final analysis, it seems to me that the *Boyd* doctrine, though perhaps not required by the express language of the Constitution strictly construed, is amply justified from an historical standpoint, soundly based in reason, and entirely consistent with what I regard to be the proper approach to interpretation of our Bill of Rights.

MR. JUSTICE DOUGLAS, concurring.

We held in *Wolf v. People of State of Colorado* that the Fourth Amendment was applicable to the states by reason of the due process clause of the Fourteenth Amendment. But a majority held that the exclusionary rule of the *Weeks* case was not required of the states, that they could apply such sanctions as they chose. That position had the necessary votes to carry the day. But with all respect it was not the voice of reason or principle.

As stated in the *Weeks* case, if evidence seized in violation of the Fourth Amendment can be used against an accused, "his right to be secure against such searches and seizures is of no value, and . . . might as well be stricken from the Constitution."

When we allowed States to give constitutional sanction to the "shabby business" of unlawful entry into a home (to use an expression of Mr. Justice Murphy), we did indeed rob the Fourth Amendment of much meaningful force.

MR. JUSTICE HARLAN, whom MR. JUSTICE FRANKFURTER and MR. JUSTICE WHITTAKER join, dissenting.

In overruling the *Wolf* case the Court, in my opinion, has forgotten the sense of judicial restraint which, with due regard for *stare decisis,* is one element that should enter into deciding whether a past decision of this Court should be overruled. Apart from that I also believe that the *Wolf* rule represents sounder Constitutional doctrine than the new rule which now replaces it. . . .

I would not impose upon the States this federal exclusionary remedy. The reasons given by the majority for now suddenly turning its back on *Wolf* seem to me notably unconvincing.

First, it is said that "the factual grounds upon which *Wolf* was based" have since changed, in that more States now follow the *Weeks* exclusionary rule than was so at the time *Wolf* was decided. While that is true, a recent survey indicates that at present one-half of the States still adhere to the common-law non-exclusionary rule, and one, Maryland, retains the rule as to felonies. But in any case surely all this is beside the point, as the majority itself indeed seems to recognize. Our concern here, as it was in *Wolf,* is not with the desirability of that rule but only with the question whether the States are Constitutionally free to follow it or not as they may themselves determine, and the relevance of the disparity of views among the States on this point lies simply in the fact that the judgment involved is a debatable one. Moreover, the very fact on which the majority relies, instead of lending support to what is now being done, points away from the need of replacing voluntary state action with federal compulsion.

The preservation of a proper balance between state and federal responsibility in the administration of criminal justice demands patience on the part of those who might like to see things move faster among the States in this respect. Problems of criminal law enforcement vary widely from State to State. One State, in considering the totality of its legal picture, may conclude that the need for embracing the *Weeks* rule is pressing because other remedies are unavailable or inadequate to secure compliance with the substantive Constitutional principle involved. Another, though equally solicitous of Constitutional rights, may choose to pursue one purpose at a time, allowing all evidence relevant to guilt to be brought into a criminal trial, and dealing with Constitutional infractions by other means. Still another may consider the exclusionary rule too rough-and-ready a remedy, in that it reaches only unconstitutional intrusions which eventuate in criminal prosecution of the victims. Further, a State after experimenting with the *Weeks* rule for a time may, because of unsatisfactory experience with it, decide to revert to a non-exclusionary rule. And so on. From the standpoint of Constitutional permissibility in pointing a State in one direction or another, I do not see at all why "time has set its face against" the considerations which led Mr. Justice Cardozo, then chief judge of the New York Court of Appeals, to reject for New York in *People v. Defore,* the *Weeks* exclusionary rule. For us the question remains, as it has always been, one of state power, not one of passing judgment on the wisdom of one state course or another. In my view this Court should continue to forbear from fettering the States with an adamant rule which may embarrass them in coping with their own peculiar problems in criminal law enforcement.

Further, we are told that imposition of the *Weeks* rule on the States makes "very good sense," in that it will promote recognition by state and federal officials of their "mutual obligation to respect the same fundamental criteria" in their approach to law enforcement, and will avoid "'needless conflict between state and federal courts.'" . . .

An approach which regards the issue as one of achieving procedural symmetry or of serving administrative convenience surely disfigures the boundaries of this Court's functions in relation to the state and federal courts. Our role in promulgating the *Weeks* rule . . . was quite a different one than it is here. There, in implementing the Fourth Amendment, we occupied the position of a tribunal having the ultimate responsibility for developing the standards and procedures of judicial administration within the judicial system over which it presides. Here we review state procedures whose measure is to be taken not against the specific substantive commands of the Fourth Amendment but under the flexible contours of the Due Process Clause. I do not believe that the Fourteenth Amendment empowers this Court to mould state remedies effectuating the right to freedom from "arbitrary intrusion by the police" to suit its own notions of how things should be done. . . .

In conclusion, it should be noted that the majority opinion in this case is in fact an opinion only for the *judgment* overruling *Wolf,* and not for the basic rationale by which four members of the majority have reached that result. For my Brother BLACK is unwilling to subscribe to their view that the *Weeks* exclusionary rule derives from the Fourth Amendment itself. . . .

I regret that I find so unwise in principle and so inexpedient in policy a decision motivated by the high purpose of increasing respect for Constitutional rights. But in the last analysis I think this Court can increase respect for the Constitution only if it rigidly respects the limitations which the Constitution places upon it, and respects as well the principles inherent in its own processes. In the present case I think we exceed both, and that our voice becomes only a voice of power, not of reason.

The application of the exclusionary rule provides yet another example of the Warren Court's revolutionary treatment of the rights of the criminally accused. It also illustrates the highly politicized nature of criminal law. Since 1961, when the Court informed states that they must adopt it, the rule has been attacked and defended by scholars, lawyers, and judges. Opponents argue that letting a guilty person go free is too great a price for society to pay just because a police officer violated search and seizure guidelines. Supporters fear that if the exclusionary rule is eliminated, police will have no incentive to respect the law.

Exceptions to the Exclusionary Rule

The disagreement over the exclusionary rule, expressed in academic circles and the public, was also evident among the justices. Six voted to overturn Mapp's conviction, but only five expressed full support for the exclusionary rule. Justice Stewart voted with the majority, but on other grounds. When Chief Justice Warren left the Court and was replaced by the law-and-order–minded Warren Burger in 1969, legal scholars predicted that the Court might well overrule *Mapp*. With each additional Court appointment by Richard Nixon, Ronald Reagan, and George Bush, speculation increased about the end of the exclusionary rule.

Between 1969 and 1974, however, the justices made no significant move to alter the applicability of the exclusionary rule, even though Chief Justice Burger made no attempts to hide his disdain for it. As early as 1971, in a dissenting opinion in *Bivens v. Six Unknown Named Agents of Federal Bureau of Narcotics,* he provided a clear indication of his views about the exclusionary rule. He began by rejecting part of the Court's rationale for creating the rule—the so-called "sporting thesis" under which the government must "play the game fairly" and cannot be

---

BOX 10-2   AFTERMATH . . . DOLLREE MAPP

DOLLREE MAPP was a free woman following the Supreme Court's reversal of her obscenity conviction in 1961. As a consequence of the decision, state courts were obliged to use the exclusionary rule as a means of enforcing Fourth Amendment search and seizure rights.

In 1968 Mapp moved from Cleveland to New York City. She did not give up her life of crime. In November 1970 police arrested Mapp on charges of possession of and trafficking in stolen property. Pursuing the investigation, detectives obtained a warrant to search her home. They found stolen goods valued at more than $100,000 and 50,000 envelopes of heroin. Although she claimed that the search warrant was defective, New York courts did not agree. After her trial she was sentenced to a term of twenty years to life in the New York Correctional Institution for Women.

On New Year's Eve 1980, Gov. Hugh Carey of New York commuted Mapp's sentence to time served, and she became eligible for release on parole.

SOURCES: *New York Times,* May 27, 1971, December 15, 1975, January 1, 1981; and James A. Inciardi, *Criminal Justice,* 4th ed. (Fort Worth: Harcourt Brace Jovanovich, 1993).

---

permitted to "profit from its own illegal acts." Instead, he claimed that the only reasonable justification for the rule was that it might deter "law enforcement authorities from using improper methods to obtain evidence." Yet he questioned whether, in fact, the exclusionary rule had accomplished this objective:

Although I would hesitate to abandon it until some meaningful substitute is developed, the history of the [exclusionary rule] demonstrates that it is both conceptually sterile and practically ineffective in accomplishing its stated objective. . . .

Some clear demonstration of the benefits and effectiveness of the exclusionary rule is required to justify it in view of the high price it extracts from society—the release of countless guilty criminals. But there is no empirical evidence to support the claim that the rule actually deters illegal conduct of law enforcement officials.

To some scholars, Burger's opinion was disingenuous. They reasoned that Burger selected the deterrence rationale on which to rest the exclusionary rule because he knew that it would provide the greatest leeway to narrow and eventually abolish it; after all, it is difficult to demonstrate that any particular measure—including the exclusionary rule—deters crime, but it is always true that the exclusionary rule makes the government, or should make the government, "play the game fairly." If this was Burger's plan, would he succeed? This question was present in many minds when, in 1974, much to the elation of law enforcement interests and the horror of civil libertarians, the Court decided to hear oral arguments in *United States v. Calandra*, a case involving the applicability of the exclusionary rule to grand jury proceedings. Many observers expected the Court to use this case to overrule *Mapp;* instead, the Court ruled solely on the issue of grand jury hearings, stating that *Mapp* did not apply to them. Civil libertarians breathed a sigh of relief.

However, even though *Calandra* did not overrule *Mapp*, it narrowed *Mapp*'s reach—the exclusionary rule would not apply to grand jury hearings—and it moved a step closer to embracing Burger's deterrence theory as the sole rationale for the exclusionary rule. As Justice Powell wrote for the majority:

In deciding whether to extend the exclusionary rule to grand jury proceedings, we must weigh the potential injury to the historic role and functions of the grand jury against the potential benefits of the rule as applied in this context. It is evident that this extension of the exclusionary rule would seriously impede the grand jury. . . . Permitting witnesses to invoke the exclusionary rule before a grand jury would precipitate adjudication of issues hitherto reserved for the trial on the merits and would delay and disrupt grand jury proceedings. . . .

Against this potential damage to the role and functions of the grand jury, we must weight the benefits to be derived from this proposed extension of the exclusionary rule. . . . Any incremental deterrent effect which might be achieved by extending the rule to grand jury proceedings is uncertain at best. Whatever deterrence of police misconduct may result from the exclusion of illegally seized evidence from criminal trials, it is unrealistic to assume that application of the rule to grand jury proceedings would significantly further that goal.

Can you see how reliance solely on a deterrence theory can lead to the narrowing of the exclusionary rule? Think about it this way: Had the Court adopted the sporting thesis, would it have decided this case the same way?

As the Court continued to rely on the deterrence rationale and to neglect other justifications, such as the sporting approach, some scholars remained convinced that the exclusionary rule's days were numbered. But with the passage of time, other analysts began to believe that the Court would let *Mapp* stand. That prediction has turned out to be the more accurate; the Court still has not overruled *Mapp*. During the 1980s, however, it created certain exceptions to the use of the rule, exceptions that, according to some justices, are so pervasive as to undermine its usefulness.

The most important of these is called the good faith exception, which the Court created in *United States v. Leon.*[20] Why did the Court authorize this exception to *Mapp?* Justice Brennan, who dissented, was the sole remaining member of the five-person majority who agreed to Clark's opinion in *Mapp.* Why did he object to the Court's decision in *Leon?* Note that he points to *Calandra* and its adoption of the deterrence rationale as the beginning of the demise of the rule.

United States v. Leon

468 U.S. 897 (1984)
laws.findlaw.com/US/468/897.html
Vote: 6 (Blackmun, Burger, O'Connor, Powell, Rehnquist, White)
    3 (Brennan, Marshall, Stevens)
Opinion of the Court: White
Concurring opinion: Blackmun
Dissenting opinions: Brennan, Stevens

In 1981 Burbank police received a tip from a person of unproven reliability, identifying two individuals, Patsy Stewart and Armando Sanchez, as drug dealers. Apparently, the pair kept small quantities of drugs in their

20. For oral arguments in this case, navigate to: *oyez.nwu.edu.*

house and the remainder at another residence in Burbank. Police began a comprehensive investigation, including surveillance of the houses. Following leads based on the cars that frequented the homes, the police expanded the scope of the investigation. At one point in this process, police identified Ricardo Del Castillo and his friend Alberto Leon as participating in the operation. Both individuals were known to be active in the drug trade. Based on observation, continued surveillance of the residences, and information from a second informant, a veteran detective drew up an affidavit to obtain a search warrant, which a judge issued. With the warrant, police searched the several residences and automobiles, seized illegal substances, and arrested Leon, Stewart, Sanchez, and Del Castillo.

At the trial stage, attorneys for the defendants argued that the warrant was invalid because the detective lacked sufficient probable cause to sign an affidavit and the judge should not have issued it. The defect was the lack of established credibility of the original tip. The government's lawyers admitted that the defendants had a valid point, but argued that the courts should decline to throw out the entire case because of a defective warrant. They claimed that the officers had acted in "good faith"; the police believed they had a legitimate warrant and acted accordingly.

JUSTICE WHITE delivered the opinion of the Court.

This case presents the question whether the Fourth Amendment exclusionary rule should be modified so as not to bar the use in the prosecution's case-in-chief of evidence obtained by officers acting in reasonable reliance on a search warrant issued by a detached and neutral magistrate but ultimately found to be unsupported by probable cause. To resolve this question, we must consider once again the tension between the sometimes competing goals of, on the one hand, deterring official misconduct and removing inducements to unreasonable invasions of privacy and, on the other, establishing procedures under which criminal defendants are "acquitted or convicted on the basis of all the evidence which exposes the truth.". . .

The Fourth Amendment contains no provision expressly precluding the use of evidence obtained in violation of its commands, and an examination of its origin and purposes makes clear that the use of fruits of a past unlawful search or seizure "work[s] no new Fourth Amendment wrong." The wrong condemned by the Amendment is "fully accomplished" by the unlawful search or seizure itself, and the exclusionary rule is neither intended nor able to "cure the invasion of the defendant's rights which he has already suffered." The rule thus operates as "a judicially created remedy designed to safeguard Fourth Amendment rights generally through its deterrent effect, rather than a personal constitutional right of the person aggrieved."

Whether the exclusionary sanction is appropriately imposed in a particular case, our decisions make clear, is "an issue separate from the question whether the Fourth Amendment rights of the party seeking to invoke the rule were violated by police conduct." Only the former question is currently before us, and it must be resolved by weighing the costs and benefits of preventing the use in the prosecution's case-in-chief of inherently trustworthy tangible evidence obtained in reliance on a search warrant issued by a detached and neutral magistrate that ultimately is found to be defective.

The substantial social costs exacted by the exclusionary rule for the vindication of Fourth Amendment rights have long been a source of concern. "Our cases have consistently recognized that unbending application of the exclusionary sanction to enforce ideals of governmental rectitude would impede unacceptably the truth-finding functions of judge and jury." An objectionable collateral consequence of this interference with the criminal justice system's truth-finding function is that some guilty defendants may go free or receive reduced sentences as a result of favorable plea bargains. Particularly when law enforcement officers have acted in objective good faith or their transgressions have been minor, the magnitude of the benefit conferred on such guilty defendants offends basic concepts of the criminal justice system. Indiscriminate application of the exclusionary rule, therefore, may well "generat[e] disrespect for the law and the administration of justice." Accordingly, "[a]s with any remedial device, the application of the rule has been restricted to those areas where its remedial objectives are thought most efficaciously served."

Close attention to those remedial objectives has characterized our recent decisions concerning the scope of the Fourth Amendment exclusionary rule. The Court has, to be sure, not seriously questioned, "in the absence of a more efficacious sanction, the continued application of the rule to suppress evidence from the [prosecution's] case where a Fourth Amendment violation has been substantial and deliberate. . . ." Nevertheless, the balancing approach that has evolved in various contexts—including criminal trials—"forcefully suggest[s] that the exclusionary rule be more generally modified to permit the introduction of evidence obtained in the reasonable good-faith belief that a search or seizure was in accord with the Fourth Amendment.". . .

The same attention to the purposes underlying the exclusionary rule also has characterized decisions not involving the scope of the rule itself. We have not required suppression of the fruits of a search incident to an arrest made in good-faith reliance on a substantive criminal statute that subsequently is declared unconstitutional. Similarly, although the Court has been unwilling to conclude that new Fourth Amendment principles are always to have only prospective effect, no Fourth Amendment decision marking a "clear break with the past" has been applied retroactively. . . .

As yet, we have not recognized any form of good-faith exception to the Fourth Amendment exclusionary rule. But the balancing approach that has evolved during the years of experience with the rule provides strong support for the modification currently urged upon us. As we discuss below, our evaluation of the costs and benefits of suppressing reliable physical evidence seized by officers reasonably relying on a warrant issued by a detached and neutral magistrate leads to the conclusion that such evidence should be admissible in the prosecution's case-in-chief.

Because a search warrant "provides the detached scrutiny of a neutral magistrate, which is a more reliable safeguard against improper searches than the hurried judgment of a law enforcement officer 'engaged in the often competitive enterprise of ferreting out crime,'" we have expressed a strong preference for warrants and declared that "in a doubtful or marginal case a search under a warrant may be sustainable where without one it would fail." Reasonable minds frequently may differ on the question whether a particular affidavit establishes probable cause, and we have thus concluded that the preference for warrants is most appropriately effectuated by according "great deference" to a magistrate's determination.

Deference to the magistrate, however, is not boundless.

It is clear, first, that the deference accorded to a magistrate's finding of probable cause does not preclude inquiry into the knowing or reckless falsity of the affidavit on which that determination was based. Second, the courts must also insist that the magistrate purport to "perform his 'neutral and detached' function and not serve merely as a rubber stamp for the police.". . .

Third, reviewing courts will not defer to a warrant based on an affidavit that does not "provide the magistrate with a substantial basis for determining the existence of probable cause.". . . Even if the warrant application was supported by more than a "bare bones" affidavit, a reviewing court may properly conclude that, notwithstanding the deference that magistrates deserve, the warrant was invalid because the magistrate's probable-cause determination reflected an improper analysis of the totality of the circumstances or because the form of the warrant was improper in some respect.

Only in the first of these three situations, however, has the Court set forth a rationale for suppressing evidence obtained pursuant to a search warrant; in the other areas, it has simply excluded such evidence without considering whether Fourth Amendment interests will be advanced. To the extent that proponents of exclusion rely on its behavioral effects on judges and magistrates in these areas, their reliance is misplaced. First, the exclusionary rule is designed to deter police misconduct rather than to punish the errors of judges and magistrates. Second, there exists no evidence suggesting that judges and magistrates are inclined to ignore or subvert the Fourth Amendment or that lawlessness among these actors requires application of the extreme sanction of exclusion.

Third, and most important, we discern no basis, and are offered none, for believing that exclusion of evidence seized pursuant to a warrant will have a significant deterrent effect on the issuing judge or magistrate. Many of the factors that indicate that the exclusionary rule cannot provide an effective "special" or "general" deterrent for individual offending law enforcement officers apply as well to judges or magistrates. And, to the extent that the rule is thought to operate as a "systemic" deterrent on a wider audience, it clearly can have no such effect on individuals empowered to issue search warrants. Judges and magistrates are not adjuncts to the law enforcement team; as neutral judicial officers, they have no stake in the outcome of particular criminal prosecutions. The threat of exclusion thus cannot be expected significantly to deter them. Imposition of the exclusionary sanction is not necessary meaningfully to inform judicial officers of their errors, and we cannot conclude that admitting evidence obtained pursuant to a warrant while at the same time declaring that the warrant was somehow defective will in any way reduce judicial officers' professional incentives to comply with the Fourth Amendment, encourage them to repeat their mistakes, or lead to the granting of all colorable warrant requests.

If exclusion of evidence obtained pursuant to a subsequently invalidated warrant is to have any deterrent effect, therefore, it must alter the behavior of individual law enforcement officers or the policies of their departments. One could argue that applying the exclusionary rule in cases where the police failed to demonstrate probable cause in the warrant application deters future inadequate presentations or "magistrate shopping" and thus promotes the ends of the Fourth Amendment. Suppressing evidence obtained pursuant to a technically defective warrant supported by probable cause also might encourage officers to scrutinize more closely the form of the warrant and to point out suspected judicial errors. We find such arguments speculative and conclude that suppression of evidence obtained pursuant to a warrant should be ordered only on a case-by-case basis and only in those unusual cases in which exclusion will further the purposes of the exclusionary rule.

We have frequently questioned whether the exclusionary rule can have any deterrent effect when the offending officers acted in the objectively reasonable belief that their conduct did not violate the Fourth Amendment. . . . But even assuming that the rule effectively deters some police misconduct and provides incentives for the law enforcement profession as a whole to conduct itself in accord with the Fourth Amendment, it cannot be expected, and should not be applied, to deter objectively reasonable law enforcement activity. . . .

We conclude that the marginal or nonexistent benefits produced by suppressing evidence obtained in objectively reasonable reliance on a subsequently invalidated search warrant cannot justify the substantial costs of exclusion. We do not suggest, however, that exclusion is always inappropriate in cases where an officer has obtained a warrant and abided by its terms. "[S]earches pursuant to a warrant will rarely require any deep inquiry into reasonableness," for "a

warrant issued by a magistrate normally suffices to establish" that a law enforcement officer has "acted in good faith in conducting the search." Nevertheless, the officer's reliance on the magistrate's probable-cause determination and on the technical sufficiency of the warrant he issues must be objectively reasonable, and it is clear that in some circumstances the officer will have no reasonable grounds for believing that the warrant was properly issued.

Suppression therefore remains an appropriate remedy if the magistrate or judge in issuing a warrant was misled by information in an affidavit that the affiant knew was false or would have known was false except for his reckless disregard of the truth. The exception we recognize today will also not apply in cases where the issuing magistrate wholly abandoned his judicial role. . . . [I]n such circumstances, no reasonably well-trained officer should rely on the warrant. Nor would an officer manifest objective good faith in relying on a warrant based on an affidavit "so lacking in indicia of probable cause as to render official belief in its existence entirely unreasonable." Finally, depending on the circumstances of the particular case, a warrant may be so facially deficient—*i.e.,* in failing to particularize the place to be searched or the things to be seized—that the executing officers cannot reasonably presume it to be valid.

In so limiting the suppression remedy, we leave untouched the probable-cause standard and the various requirements for a valid warrant. Other objections to the modification of the Fourth Amendment exclusionary rule we consider to be insubstantial. The good-faith exception for searches conducted pursuant to warrants is not intended to signal our unwillingness strictly to enforce the requirements of the Fourth Amendment, and we do not believe that it will have this effect. As we have already suggested, the good-faith exception, turning as it does on objective reasonableness, should not be difficult to apply in practice. . . .

When the principles we have enunciated today are applied to the facts of this case, it is apparent that the judgment of the Court of Appeals cannot stand. The Court of Appeals applied the prevailing legal standards to Officer Rombach's warrant application and concluded that the application could not support the magistrate's probable-cause determination. In so doing, the court clearly informed the magistrate that he had erred in issuing the challenged warrant. This aspect of the court's judgment is not under attack in this proceeding. . . .

In the absence of an allegation that the magistrate abandoned his detached and neutral role, suppression is appropriate only if the officers were dishonest or reckless in preparing their affidavit or could not have harbored an objectively reasonable belief in the existence of probable cause. . . . Under these circumstances, the officers' reliance on the magistrate's determination of probable cause was objectively reasonable, and application of the extreme sanction of exclusion is inappropriate.

Accordingly, the judgment of the Court of Appeals is

Reversed.

JUSTICE BRENNAN, with whom JUSTICE MARSHALL joins, dissenting.

Ten years ago in *United States v. Calandra* (1974), I expressed the fear that the Court's decision "may signal that a majority of my colleagues have positioned themselves to reopen the door [to evidence secured by offical lawlessness] still further and abandon altogether the exclusionary rule in search-and-seizure cases." (BRENNAN, J., dissenting.) Since then, in case after case, I have witnessed the Court's gradual but determined strangulation of the rule. It now appears that the Court's victory over the Fourth Amendment is complete. That today's decision represents the *pièce de resistance* of the Court's past efforts cannot be doubted, for today the Court sanctions the use in the prosecution's case-in-chief of illegally obtained evidence against the individual whose rights have been violated—a result that had previously been thought to be foreclosed.

The Court seeks to justify this result on the ground that the "costs" of adhering to the exclusionary rule in cases like those before us exceed the "benefits." But the language of deterrence and of cost/benefit analysis, if used indiscriminately, can have a narcotic effect. It creates an illusion of technical precision and ineluctability. It suggests that not only constitutional principle but also empirical data support the majority's result. When the Court's analysis is examined carefully, however, it is clear that we have not been treated to an honest assessment of the merits of the exclusionary rule, but have instead been drawn into a curious world where the "costs" of excluding illegally obtained evidence loom to exaggerated heights and where the "benefits" of such exclusion are made to disappear with a mere wave of the hand.

The majority ignores the fundamental constitutional importance of what is at stake here. While the machinery of law enforcement and indeed the nature of crime itself have changed dramatically since the Fourth Amendment became part of the Nation's fundamental law in 1791, what the Framers understood then remains true today—that the task of combating crime and convicting the guilty will in every era seem of such critical and pressing concern that we may be lured by the temptations of expediency into forsaking our commitment to protecting individual liberty and privacy. It was for that very reason that the Framers of the Bill of Rights insisted that law enforcement efforts be permanently and unambiguously restricted in order to preserve personal freedoms. In the constitutional scheme they ordained, the sometimes unpopular task of ensuring that the government's enforcement efforts remain within the strict boundaries fixed by the Fourth Amendment was entrusted to the courts. . . . If those independent tribunals lose their resolve, however, as the Court has done today, and give way to the seductive call of expediency, the vital guarantees of the Fourth Amendment are reduced to nothing more than a "form of words.". . .

A proper understanding of the broad purposes sought to be served by the Fourth Amendment demonstrates that the principles embodied in the exclusionary rule rest upon a far firmer constitutional foundation than the shifting sands of the Court's deterrence rationale. But even if I were to accept the Court's chosen method of analyzing the question posed by these cases, I would still conclude that the Court's decision cannot be justified. . . .

At bottom, the Court's decision turns on the proposition that the exclusionary rule is merely a "'judicially created remedy designed to safeguard Fourth Amendment rights generally through its deterrent effect, rather than a personal constitutional right.'". . . The germ of that idea is found in *Wolf v. Colorado* (1949), and although I had thought that such a narrow conception of the rule had been forever put to rest by our decision in *Mapp v. Ohio* (1961), it has been revived by the present Court and reaches full flower with today's decision. . . .

I submit that such a crabbed reading of the Fourth Amendment casts aside the teaching of those Justices who first formulated the exclusionary rule, and rests ultimately on an impoverished understanding of judicial responsibility in our constitutional scheme. For my part, "[t]he right of the people to be secure in their persons, houses, papers, and effects, against unreasonable searches and seizures" comprises a personal right to exclude all evidence secured by means of unreasonable searches and seizures. . . .

When the public, as it quite properly has done in the past as well as in the present, demands that those in government increase their efforts to combat crime, it is all too easy for those government officials to seek expedient solutions. . . . In the long run, however, we as a society pay a heavy price for such expediency, because as Justice Jackson observed, the rights guaranteed in the Fourth Amendment "are not mere second-class rights but belong in the catalog of indispensable freedoms." Once lost, such rights are difficult to recover. There is hope, however, that in time this or some later Court will restore these precious freedoms to their rightful place as a primary protection for our citizens against overreaching officialdom.

I dissent.

As you can see, Justice White's opinion rests on the view that the exclusionary rule is not a constitutionally protected right, but serves as a deterrent against police misbehavior. When police act in good faith, as they did in this case, the punitive aspect of the exclusionary rule becomes irrelevant.

In his dissent, Justice Brennan called *Leon* the *pièce de resistance* for those opposed to the rule. Unlike White, he believed that *Leon* erodes the rule's deterrent function because it can lead to all sorts of illegal police behavior. For example, he predicted that police would attempt to secure warrants on only minimal information, knowing full well that if they can obtain one, whatever evidence is seized will stand up in court.

Brennan was expressing his fear that the Supreme Court would blunt the effectiveness of the exclusionary rule by creating exceptions to it. To him, the Court, while stating its allegiance to *Mapp*, weakened the precedent in decisions such as *Leon* and another 1984 case, *Nix v. Williams.* In *Nix* the Court established an additional exception to the exclusionary rule, the inevitable discovery exception. This ruling holds that evidence discovered as the result of an illegal search can still be introduced in court if it can be shown that the evidence would have been found anyway. Was Brennan correct in fearing that

the Court is effectively overruling *Mapp* without explicitly doing so?

THE FIFTH AMENDMENT AND SELF-INCRIMINATION

As we now know, the Fourth Amendment governs the procedures by which police obtain evidence—generally physical evidence. But evidence used in criminal investigations is not always physical or material. Very often arrests, and ultimately convictions, hinge on verbal evidence—testimony, confessions, and the like—the gathering of which is governed by the Fifth Amendment's Self-incrimination Clause: "No person . . . shall be compelled in any criminal case to be a witness against himself." Taken together, the Fourth (physical) and Fifth (verbal) Amendments dictate the procedures police use to gather most evidence against individuals.

The Self-incrimination Clause is violated by the presence of two elements. First, there must be some form of testimonial evidence that incriminates the person who provides it, and, second, the testimonial evidence must somehow be compelled by the government. Given these standards, self-incrimination violations occur most commonly during police interrogations and government hearings. Of the two, the police interrogations have presented the more difficult questions of constitutional interpretation.

The Self-Incrimination Clause and Police Interrogations

Even before the 1960s when the courts became the most sensitive to defendants' rights, the Supreme Court had established certain guidelines for police interrogations. For the most part, these guidelines dealt with the concept of coercion. Principles of self-incrimination and due process of law are violated, the Court held, when confessions are coerced from a suspect. Such illegal coercion may be either physical or psychological.

The issue of the use of physical force to obtain confessions was raised at the Supreme Court as early as 1936 in *Brown v. Mississippi.*[21] Law enforcement officers, with the

---

21. For more details, see Richard C. Cortner, *A Scottsboro Case in Mississippi: The Supreme Court and Brown v. Mississippi* (Jackson: University of Mississippi Press, 1986).

assistance of other racist citizens, stripped, whipped, hanged until near death, and otherwise physically tortured African American suspects to force them into confessing to a murder. Writing for the Court, Chief Justice Charles Evans Hughes claimed, "It would be difficult to conceive of methods more revolting to the sense of justice than those taken to procure the confessions of these petitioners."

More than twenty years later, in *Spano v. New York* (1959), the Court struck a blow against the use of psychological coercion. Vincent Joseph Spano, an Italian immigrant with little formal education and a history of emotional instability, was drinking in a bar one night when another man, a former professional boxer, took some of his money. Spano followed him out of the bar, and a fight ensued. The boxer left Spano on the street with severe head lacerations. Spano went to his apartment for a gun and, in a candy store the boxer was known to patronize, Spano shot and killed him in front of an eyewitness. After the shooting Spano disappeared. A grand jury returned an indictment and a warrant was issued for his arrest. Several days later, Spano telephoned a close friend, Gaspar Bruno, who was in the police academy. Bruno agreed with Spano that he should hire a lawyer and turn himself in. Spano gave himself up, and Bruno told the whole story to his superiors.

Spano's attorney told him not to answer any questions, and, following this advice, Spano refused to explain to the police his fight with the boxer. Frustrated by Spano's refusal to talk, police called Bruno and told him to lie to Spano by telling him that his job with the police was in danger if Spano did not confess. Bruno carried out the orders, playing on Spano's sympathies by explaining that the loss of his job would be disastrous to his three children, his wife, and his unborn child. After repeated pleas from Bruno, Spano gave in. Based on this confession as a primary piece of evidence, the jury sentenced Spano to death.

May police use such psychological coercion to obtain confessions? The justices unanimously agreed that police behavior in *Spano* violated the accused's rights: psychological torture has no place in a modern criminal justice system. Three members of the Court felt that Chief Jus-

tice Warren's majority opinion did not go far enough toward protecting the privilege against self-incrimination. In their concurring opinion, Justices Brennan, Douglas, and Black argued that attorneys should be present during interrogations to protect unsuspecting and naive defendants against unscrupulous police behavior.

In 1964 and 1966 the Supreme Court was asked two new questions regarding police interrogations. First, in *Escobedo v. Illinois*, the justices grappled with the issue raised by the concurring opinions in *Spano:* If a person under arrest wants an attorney to be present during police questioning, must that request be honored?[22] And, because the Court answered this question affirmatively, how should this right be enforced? The Court answered that question in *Miranda v. Arizona.*

The decisions in *Escobedo* and *Miranda* are two of the most important in criminal law. Consider the following questions as you read these decisions: first, and most critical, what does the Court argue about the privilege against self-incrimination? Second, how does the Court safeguard that right? Finally, why do scholars and lawyers consider these decisions and the cases that follow them to be so significant, and why are they so controversial?

Escobedo v. Illinois

378 U.S. 478 (1964)
laws.findlaw.com/US/378/478.html
Vote: 5 (Black, Brennan, Douglas, Goldberg, Warren)
*   4 (Clark, Harlan, Stewart, White)*
Opinion of the Court: Goldberg
Dissenting opinions: Harlan, Stewart, White

At 2:30 a.m. on January 20, 1960, police arrested Danny Escobedo, a twenty-two-year-old of Mexican extraction, for the murder of his brother-in-law. They attempted to interrogate him, but, on the advice of his counsel, Escobedo refused to make any statements and was released. A week or so later, Benedict DiGerlando, who was in police custody and considered another sus-

---

22. For oral arguments in this case, navigate to: *oyez.nwu.edu.*

pect, told police that Escobedo had indeed shot his brother-in-law because he had mistreated his sister. Based on DiGerlando's story, police again arrested Escobedo, as well as his sister.

As police transported the pair to the station they explained that DiGerlando had told them the whole story so they might as well confess. Escobedo again declined. At the station, Escobedo asked to see his attorney, but the police refused. His attorney came to the police station and repeatedly asked to see his client, but he was refused access. Instead, police and prosecutors questioned Escobedo for fourteen and a half hours until he made damaging statements. Found guilty of murder, Escobedo appealed, claiming that he was denied his right to counsel and that counsel should have been present during the interrogation.

MR. JUSTICE GOLDBERG delivered the opinion of the Court.

The critical question in this case is whether, under the circumstances, the refusal by the police to honor petitioner's request to consult with his lawyer during the course of an interrogation constitutes a denial of "the Assistance of Counsel" in violation of the Sixth Amendment to the Constitution as "made obligatory upon the States by the Fourteenth Amendment," and thereby renders inadmissible in a state criminal trial any incriminating statement elicited by the police during the interrogation. . . .

. . . We granted a writ of certiorari to consider whether the petitioner's statement was constitutionally admissible at his trial. We conclude, for the reasons stated below, that it was not and, accordingly, we reverse the judgment of conviction. . . .

The interrogation here was conducted before petitioner was formally indicted. But in the context of this case, that fact should make no difference. When petitioner requested, and was denied, an opportunity to consult with his lawyer, the investigation had ceased to be a general investigation of "an unsolved crime." Petitioner had become the accused, and the purpose of the interrogation was to "get him" to confess his guilt despite his constitutional right not to do so. At the time of his arrest and throughout the course of the interrogation, the police told petitioner that they had

Danny Escobedo's 1960 arrest and conviction for the murder of his brother-in-law led to a Supreme Court decision that expanded constitutional protections for criminal defendants during police interrogations. This photograph of Escobedo was taken as he awaited processing on charges of burglarizing a hot dog stand not long after the Supreme Court issued its landmark ruling in *Escobedo v. Illinois* in 1964.

convincing evidence that he had fired the fatal shots. Without informing him of his absolute right to remain silent in the face of this accusation, the police urged him to make a statement. . . .

Petitioner, a layman, was undoubtedly unaware that under Illinois law an admission of "mere" complicity in the murder plot was legally as damaging as an admission of firing of the fatal shots. The "guiding hand of counsel" was essential to advise petitioner of his rights in this delicate situation. This was the "stage when legal aid and advice" were most critical to petitioner. [I]t was a stage surely as critical as . . . arraignment and preliminary hearing. What happened at this interrogation could certainly "affect the whole trial," since rights "may be as irretrievably lost, if not then and there asserted, as they are when an accused represented by counsel waives a right for strategic purposes." It would exalt form over substance to make the right to counsel, under these circumstances, depend on whether at the time of the interrogation, the authorities had secured a formal indictment. Petitioner had, for all practical purposes, already been charged with murder. . . .

. . . In *Gideon v. Wainwright* we held that every person accused of a crime, whether state or federal, is entitled to a lawyer at trial. . . .

It is argued that if the right to counsel is afforded prior to indictment, the number of confessions obtained by the police will diminish significantly, because most confessions are obtained during the period between arrest and indictment, and "any lawyer worth his salt will tell the suspect in no uncertain terms to make no statement to police under any circumstances." This argument, of course, cuts two ways. The fact that many confessions are obtained during this period points up its critical nature as a "stage when legal aid and advice" are surely needed. The right to counsel would indeed be hollow if it began at a period when few confessions were obtained. There is necessarily a direct relationship between the importance of a stage to the police in their quest for a confession and the criticalness of that stage to the accused in his need for legal advice. Our Constitution, unlike some others, strikes the balance in favor of the right of the accused to be advised by his lawyer of his privilege against self-incrimination.

We have learned the lesson of history, ancient and modern, that a system of criminal law enforcement which comes to depend on the "confession" will, in the long run, be less reliable and more subject to abuses than a system which depends on extrinsic evidence independently secured through skillful investigation. . . . This Court also has recognized that "history amply shows that confessions have often been extorted to save law enforcement officials the trouble and effort of obtaining valid and independent evidence. . . ."

We have also learned the companion lesson of history that no system of criminal justice can, or should, survive if it comes to depend for its continued effectiveness on the citizens' abdication through unawareness of their constitutional rights. No system worth preserving should have to fear that if an accused is permitted to consult with a lawyer, he will become aware of, and exercise, these rights. If the exercise of constitutional rights will thwart the effectiveness of a system of law enforcement, then there is something very wrong with that system.

We hold, therefore, that where, as here, the investigation is no longer a general inquiry into an unsolved crime but has begun to focus on a particular suspect, the suspect has been taken into police custody, the police carry out a process of interrogations that lends itself to eliciting incriminating statements, the suspect has requested and been denied an opportunity to consult with his lawyer, and the police have not effectively warned him of his absolute constitutional right to remain silent, the accused has been denied "the Assistance of Counsel" in violation of the Sixth Amendment to the Constitution as "made obligatory upon the States by the Fourteenth Amendment," and that no statement elicited by the police during the interrogation may be used against him at a criminal trial. . . .

Nothing we have said today affects the powers of the police to investigate "an unsolved crime" by gathering information from witnesses and by other "proper investigative efforts." We hold only that when the process shifts from investigatory to accusatory—when its focus is on the accused and its purpose is to elicit a confession—our adversary system begins to operate, and, under the circumstances here, the accused must be permitted to consult with his lawyer.

The judgment of the Illinois Supreme Court is reversed and the case remanded for proceedings not inconsistent with this opinion.

Reversed and remanded.

MR. JUSTICE WHITE, with whom MR. JUSTICE CLARK and MR. JUSTICE STEWART join, dissenting.

In *Massiah v. United States* [1964] the Court held that as of the date of the indictment the prosecution is disentitled to secure admissions from the accused. The Court now moves that date back to the time when the prosecution begins to "focus" on the accused. . . . At the very least the Court holds that once the accused becomes a suspect and, presumably, is arrested, any admission made to the police thereafter is inadmissible evidence unless the accused has waived his right to counsel. The decision is thus another major step in the direction of the goal which the Court seemingly has in mind—to bar from evidence all admissions obtained from an individual suspected of crime, whether involuntarily made or not. . . . I reject this step and the invitation to go farther which the Court has now issued. . . .

By abandoning the voluntary-involuntary test for admissibility of confessions, the Court seems driven by the notion that it is uncivilized law enforcement to use an accused's own admissions against him at his trial. It attempts to find a home for this new and nebulous rule of due process by attaching it to the right to counsel guaranteed in the federal system by the Sixth Amendment and binding upon the States by virtue of the due process guarantee of the Fourteenth Amendment. The right to counsel now not only entitles the accused to counsel's advice and aid in preparing for trial but stands as an impenetrable barrier to any interrogation once the accused has become a suspect. From that very moment apparently his right to counsel attaches, a rule wholly unworkable and impossible to administer unless police cars are equipped with public defenders and undercover agents and police informants have defense counsel at their side. I would not abandon the Court's prior cases defining with some care and analysis the circumstances requiring the presence or aid of counsel and substitute the amorphous and wholly unworkable principle that counsel is constitutionally required whenever he would or could be helpful. . . .

It is incongruous to assume that the provision for counsel in the Sixth Amendment was meant to amend or supersede the self-incrimination provision of the Fifth Amendment, which is now applicable to the States. *Malloy v. Hogan* [1964]. That amendment addresses itself to the very issue of incriminating admissions of an accused and resolves it by proscribing only compelled statements. . . .

Today's decision cannot be squared with other provisions of the Constitution which, in my view, define the system of criminal justice this Court is empowered to administer. . . .

I do not suggest for a moment that law enforcement will be destroyed by the rule announced today. The need for peace and order is too insistent for that. But it will be crippled and its task made a great deal more difficult, all in my opinion, for unsound, unstated reasons, which can find no home in any of the provisions of the Constitution.

Danny Escobedo had been denied his right to counsel, and the majority found this right to be a primary defense against violations of the Self-incrimination Clause. If an attorney is present, it is unlikely that police will use even subtle methods to coerce confessions from suspects. The *Escobedo* majority held that the right to counsel begins at the accusatory stage of the process, defined as the point at which the investigation ceases to be general and focuses on a specific individual. The right is in effect for every critical stage of the process, which includes all interrogations. But once the Court ruled this way, it was faced, in *Miranda v. Arizona*, with a more difficult and far-reaching question. How should this new right be enforced?[23]

Miranda v. Arizona

384 U.S. 436 (1966)
laws.findlaw.com/US/384/436.html
Vote: 5 (Black, Brennan, Douglas, Fortas, Warren)
        4 (Clark, Harlan, Stewart, White)
Opinion of the Court: Warren
Opinion dissenting in part: Clark
Dissenting opinions: Harlan, White

Ernesto Miranda, a twenty-three-year-old indigent, nearly illiterate truck driver, allegedly kidnapped and raped a young woman outside of Phoenix, Arizona. Ten days after the incident, police arrested him, took him to the station, and interrogated him. After two hours of questioning, Miranda confessed. There was no evidence of any police misbehavior during the interrogation, and at no point during questioning did Miranda request an attorney. Because of the decision in *Gideon v. Wainwright* (1963) *(see Chapter 11)*, which mandated that all indigent criminal defendants receive a defense attorney at government expense, the trial judge appointed a lawyer to defend Miranda against the charges. By most accounts, that attorney provided an inadequate defense—he hoped to prove Miranda mentally defective or insane—and Miranda received a sentence of twenty to thirty years. The conviction was based not only on the confession but also on other evidence, including the victim's positive identification of Miranda as her assailant.

Miranda obtained new attorneys, who presented wholly different arguments to the Supreme Court, where Miranda's appeal was combined with three others presenting similar issues. The attorneys claimed that because the entire interrogation process is so inherently coercive that any individual will eventually break down, the Court should affirmatively protect the right against self-incrimination by adding to those protections already extended in *Escobedo.*

MR. CHIEF JUSTICE WARREN delivered the opinion of the Court.

The cases* before us raise questions which go to the roots of our concepts of American criminal jurisprudence: the restraints society must observe consistent with the Federal Constitution in prosecuting individuals for crime. More specifically, we deal with the admissibility of statements obtained from an individual who is subjected to custodial police interrogation and the necessity for procedures which assure that the individual is accorded his privilege under the Fifth Amendment to the Constitution not to be compelled to incriminate himself.

We dealt with certain phases of this problem recently in *Escobedo v. State of Illinois* (1964). . . .

This case has been the subject of judicial interpretation and spirited legal debate since it was decided two years ago. Both state and federal courts, in assessing its implications, have arrived at varying conclusions. A wealth of scholarly material has been written tracing its ramifications and underpinnings. Police and prosecutor have speculated on its range and desirability. We granted certiorari in these cases in order further to explore some facets of the problems, thus exposed, of applying the privilege against self-incrimination to in-custody interrogation, and to give concrete constitutional guidelines for law enforcement agencies and courts to follow.

We start here, as we did in *Escobedo,* with the premise that our holding is not an innovation in our jurisprudence, but is an application of principles long recognized and applied in other settings. We have undertaken a thorough re-examination of the *Escobedo* decision and the principles it

---

*[Authors' note]: Along with *Miranda,* the Court decided *Vignera v. New York, Westover v. United States,* and *California v. Stewart.*

Ernesto Miranda, right, pictured with his defense attorney, John L. Flynn, was convicted of kidnapping and rape after he confessed to the crimes while in police custody. In a landmark ruling, *Miranda v. Arizona* (1966), the Supreme Court reversed the conviction because Miranda had not been told he had the right to remain silent and to have an attorney present during questioning.

announced, and we reaffirm it. That case was but an explication of basic rights that are enshrined in our Constitution—that "No person . . . shall be compelled in any criminal case to be a witness against himself," and that "the accused shall . . . have the Assistance of Counsel"—rights which were put in jeopardy in that case through official overbearing. . . .

It was necessary in *Escobedo,* as here, to insure that what was proclaimed in the Constitution had not become but a "form of words" in the hands of government officials. And it is in this spirit, consistent with our role as judges, that we adhere to the principles of *Escobedo* today.

Our holding will be spelled out with some specificity in the pages which follow but briefly stated it is this: the prosecution may not use statements, whether exculpatory or inculpatory, stemming from custodial interrogation of the defendant unless it demonstrates the use of procedural safeguards effective to secure the privilege against self-incrimination. By custodial interrogation, we mean questioning initiated by law enforcement officers after a person has been taken into custody or otherwise deprived of his freedom of action in any significant way. As for the procedural safeguards to be employed, unless other fully effective means are devised to inform accused persons of their right of silence and to assure a continuous opportunity to exercise it, the following measures are required. Prior to any question-

ing, the person must be warned that he has a right to remain silent, that any statement he does make may be used as evidence against him, and that he has a right to the presence of an attorney, either retained or appointed. The defendant may waive effectuation of these rights, provided the waiver is made voluntarily, knowingly and intelligently. If, however, he indicates in any manner and at any stage of the process that he wishes to consult with an attorney before speaking there can be no questioning. Likewise, if the individual is alone and indicates in any manner that he does not wish to be interrogated, the police may not question him. The mere fact that he may have answered some questions or volunteered some statements on his own does not deprive him of the right to refrain from answering any further inquiries until he has consulted with an attorney and thereafter consents to be questioned.

The constitutional issue we decide in each of these cases is the admissibility of statements obtained from a defendant questioned while in custody or otherwise deprived of his freedom of action in any significant way. . . .

An understanding of the nature and setting of this incustody interrogation is essential to our decisions today. The difficulty in depicting what transpires at such interrogations stems from the fact that in this country they have largely taken place incommunicado. From extensive factual studies undertaken in the early 1930's, including the famous

Wickersham Report to Congress by a Presidential Commission, it is clear that police violence and the "third degree" flourished at that time. In a series of cases decided by this Court long after these studies, the police resorted to physical brutality—beatings, hanging, whipping—and to sustained and protracted questioning incommunicado in order to extort confessions. The Commission on Civil Rights in 1961 found much evidence to indicate that "some policemen still resort to physical force to obtain confessions. . . ." Only recently in Kings County, New York, the police brutally beat, kicked and placed lighted cigarette butts on the back of a potential witness under interrogation for the purpose of securing a statement incriminating a third party.

The examples given above are undoubtedly the exception now, but they are sufficiently widespread to be the object of concern. Unless a proper limitation upon custodial interrogation is achieved—such as these decisions will advance—there can be no assurance that practices of this nature will be eradicated in the foreseeable future. . . .

Again we stress that the modern practice of in-custody interrogation is psychologically rather than physically oriented. As we have stated before, "[T]his Court has recognized that coercion can be mental as well as physical, and that the blood of the accused is not the only hallmark of an unconstitutional inquisition." *Blackburn v. State of Alabama* (1960). Interrogation still takes place in privacy. Privacy results in secrecy and this in turn results in a gap in our knowledge as to what in fact goes on in the interrogation rooms. A valuable source of information about present police practices, however, may be found in various police manuals and texts which document procedures employed with success in the past, and which recommend various other effective tactics. These texts are used by law enforcement agencies themselves as guides. It should be noted that these texts professedly present the most enlightened and effective means presently used to obtain statements through custodial interrogation. By considering these texts and other data, it is possible to describe the procedures observed and noted around the country.

The officers are told by the manuals that the "principal psychological factor contributing to a successful interrogation is privacy—being alone with the person under interrogation.". . .

To highlight the isolation and unfamiliar surroundings, the manuals instruct the police to display an air of confidence in the suspect's guilt and from outward appearance to maintain only an interest in confirming certain details. The guilt of the subject is to be posited as a fact. The interrogator should direct his comments toward the reasons why the subject committed the act, rather than court failure by asking the subject whether he did it. Like other men, perhaps the subject has had a bad family life, had an unhappy childhood, had too much to drink, had an unrequited desire for women. The officers are instructed to minimize the moral seriousness of the offense, to cast blame on the victim or on society. These tactics are designed to put the subject in a psychological state where his story is but an elaboration of what the police purport to know already—that he is guilty. Explanations to the contrary are dismissed and discouraged.

The texts thus stress that the major qualities an interrogator should possess are patience and perseverance. . . .

The manuals suggest that the suspect be offered legal excuses for his actions in order to obtain an initial admission of guilt. . . .

When the techniques described above prove unavailing, the texts recommend they be alternated with a show of some hostility. . . .

The interrogators sometimes are instructed to induce a confession out of trickery. . . .

Even without employing brutality, the "third degree" or the specific stratagems described above, the very fact of custodial interrogation exacts a heavy toll on individual liberty and trades on the weakness of individuals. . . .

In the cases before us today, given this background, we concern ourselves primarily with this interrogation atmosphere and the evils it can bring. In No. 759, *Miranda v. Arizona*, the police arrested the defendant and took him to a special interrogation room where they secured a confession. In No. 760, *Vignera v. New York*, the defendant made oral admissions to the police after interrogation in the afternoon and then signed an inculpatory statement upon being questioned by an assistant district attorney later the same evening. In No. 761, *Westover v. United States*, the defendant was handed over to the Federal Bureau of Investigation by local authorities after they had detained and interrogated him for a lengthy period, both at night and the following morning. After some two hours of questioning, the federal officers had obtained signed statements from the defendant. Lastly, in No. 584, *California v. Stewart*, the local police held the defendant five days in the station and interrogated him on nine separate occasions before they secured his inculpatory statement.

In these cases, we might not find the defendants' statements to have been involuntary in traditional terms. Our concern for adequate safeguards to protect precious Fifth Amendment rights is, of course, not lessened in the slightest. In each of the cases, the defendant was thrust into an unfamiliar atmosphere and run through menacing police interrogation procedures. The potentiality for compulsion is forcefully apparent, for example, in *Miranda*, where the indigent Mexican defendant was a seriously disturbed individual with pronounced sexual fantasies. . . . To be sure, the records do not evince overt physical coercion or patent psychological ploys. The fact remains that in none of these cases did the officers undertake to afford appropriate safeguards at the outset of the interrogation to insure that the statements were truly the product of free choice.

It is obvious that such an interrogation environment is created for no purpose other than to subjugate the individual to the will of his examiner. This atmosphere carries its own badge of intimidation. To be sure, this is not physical intimidation, but it is equally destructive of human dignity. The current practice of incommunicado interrogation is at odds with one of our Nation's most cherished principles—that the individual may not be compelled to incriminate himself. Unless adequate protective devices are employed to dispel the compulsion inherent in custodial surroundings, no statement obtained from the defendant can truly be the product of his free choice.

From the foregoing, we can readily perceive an intimate connection between the privilege against self-incrimination and police custodial questioning. . . .

Today, then, there can be no doubt that the Fifth Amendment privilege is available outside of criminal court proceedings and serves to protect persons in all settings in which their freedom of action is curtailed in any significant way from being compelled to incriminate themselves. We have concluded that without proper safeguards the process of in-custody interrogation of persons suspected or accused of crime contains inherently compelling pressures which work to undermine the individual's will to resist and to compel him to speak where he would not otherwise do so freely. In order to combat these pressures and to permit a full opportunity to exercise the privilege against self-incrim-

ination, the accused must be adequately and effectively apprised of his rights and the exercise of those rights must be fully honored. . . .

At the outset, if a person in custody is to be subjected to interrogation, he must first be informed in clear and unequivocal terms that he has the right to remain silent. For those unaware of the privilege, the warning is needed simply to make them aware of it—the threshold requirement for an intelligent decision as to its exercise. More important, such a warning is an absolute prerequisite in overcoming the inherent pressures of the interrogation atmosphere. . . . Further, the warning will show the individual that his interrogators are prepared to recognize his privilege should he choose to exercise it.

The Fifth Amendment privilege is so fundamental to our system of constitutional rule and the expedient of giving an adequate warning as to the availability of the privilege so simple, we will not pause to inquire in individual cases whether the defendant was aware of his rights without a warning being given. Assessments of the knowledge the defendant possessed, based on information as to his age, education, intelligence, or prior contact with authorities, can never be more than speculation; a warning is a clear-cut fact. More important, whatever the background of the person interrogated, a warning at the time of the interrogation is indispensable to overcome its pressures and to insure that the individual knows he is free to exercise the privilege at that point in time.

The warning of the right to remain silent must be accompanied by the explanation that anything said can and will be used against the individual in court. This warning is needed in order to make him aware not only of the privilege, but also of the consequences of forgoing it. It is only through an awareness of these consequences that there can be any assurance of real understanding and intelligent exercise of the privilege. Moreover, this warning may serve to make the individual more acutely aware that he is faced with a phase of the adversary system—that he is not in the presence of persons acting solely in his interest.

The circumstances surrounding in-custody interrogation can operate very quickly to overbear the will of one merely made aware of his privilege by his interrogators. Therefore, the right to have counsel present at the interrogation is indispensable to the protection of the Fifth Amendment privilege under the system we delineate today.

Our aim is to assure that the individual's right to choose between silence and speech remains unfettered throughout the interrogation process. A once-stated warning, delivered by those who will conduct the interrogation, cannot itself suffice to that end among those who most require knowledge of their rights. A mere warning given by the interrogators is not alone sufficient to accomplish that end. Prosecutors themselves claim that the admonishment of the right to remain silent without more "will benefit only the recidivist and the professional." Even preliminary advice given to the accused by his own attorney can be swiftly overcome by the secret interrogation process. Thus, the need for counsel to protect the Fifth Amendment privilege comprehends not merely a right to consult with counsel prior to questioning, but also to have counsel present during any questioning if the defendant so desires.

The presence of counsel at the interrogation may serve several significant subsidiary functions as well. If the accused decides to talk to his interrogators, the assistance of counsel can mitigate the dangers of untrustworthiness. With a lawyer present the likelihood that the police will practice coercion is reduced, and if coercion is nevertheless exercised the lawyer can testify to it in court. The presence of a lawyer can also help to guarantee that the accused gives a fully accurate statement to the police and that the statement is rightly reported by the prosecution at trial.

An individual need not make a pre-interrogation request for a lawyer. While such request affirmatively secures his right to have one, his failure to ask for a lawyer does not constitute a waiver. No effective waiver of the right to counsel during interrogation can be recognized unless specifically made after the warnings we here delineate have been given. The accused who does not know his rights and therefore does not make a request may be the person who most needs counsel. . . .

Accordingly we hold that an individual held for interrogation must be clearly informed that he has the right to consult with a lawyer and to have the lawyer with him during interrogation under the system for protecting the privilege we delineate today. As with the warnings of the right to remain silent and that anything stated can be used in evidence against him, this warning is an absolute prerequisite to interrogation. No amount of circumstantial evidence that the person may have been aware of this right will suffice to stand in its stead. Only through such a warning is there ascertainable assurance that the accused was aware of this right.

If an individual indicates that he wishes the assistance of counsel before any interrogation occurs, the authorities cannot rationally ignore or deny his request on the basis that the individual does not have or cannot afford a retained attorney. The financial ability of the individual has no relationship to the scope of the rights involved here. The privilege against self-incrimination secured by the Constitution applies to all individuals. The need for counsel in order to protect the privilege exists for the indigent as well as the affluent. In fact, were we to limit these constitutional rights to those who can retain an attorney, our decisions today would be of little significance. The cases before us as well as the vast majority of confession cases with which we have dealt in the past involve those unable to retain counsel. While authorities are not required to relieve the accused of his poverty, they have the obligation not to take advantage of indigence in the administration of justice. Denial of counsel to the indigent at the time of interrogation while allowing an attorney to those who can afford one would be no more supportable by reason or logic than the similar situation at trial and on appeal struck down in *Gideon v. Wainwright* (1963).

In order fully to apprise a person interrogated of the extent of his rights under this system then, it is necessary to warn him not only that he has the right to consult with an attorney, but also that if he is indigent a lawyer will be appointed to represent him. Without this additional warning, the admonition of the right to consult with counsel would often be understood as meaning only that he can consult with a lawyer if he has one or has the funds to obtain one. The warning of a right to counsel would be hollow if not couched in terms that would convey to the indigent—the person most often subjected to interrogation—the knowledge that he too has a right to have counsel present. As with the warnings of the right to remain silent and of the general right to counsel, only by effective and express explanation to the indigent of this right can there be assurance that he was truly in a position to exercise it.

Once warnings have been given, the subsequent procedure is clear. If the individual indicates in any manner, at any time prior to or during questioning, that he wishes to remain silent, the interrogation must cease. At this point he has shown that he intends to exercise his Fifth Amendment privilege; any statement taken after the person invokes his privilege cannot be other than the product of compulsion, subtle or otherwise. Without the right to cut off questioning, the setting of in-custody interrogation operates on the individual to overcome free choice in producing a statement after the privilege has been once invoked. If the individual states that he wants an attorney, the interrogation must cease until an attorney is present. At that time, the individual must have an opportunity to confer with the attorney and to have him present during any subsequent questioning. If the individual cannot obtain an attorney and he indicates that he wants one before speaking to police, they must respect his decision to remain silent. . . .

If the interrogation continues without the presence of an attorney and a statement is taken, a heavy burden rests on the government to demonstrate that the defendant knowingly and intelligently waived his privilege against self-incrimination and his right to retained or appointed counsel. . . .

The warnings required and the waiver necessary in accordance with our opinion today are, in the absence of a fully effective equivalent, prerequisites to the admissibility of any statement made by a defendant. No distinction can be drawn between statements which are direct confessions and statements which amount to "admissions" of part or all of an offense. The privilege against self-incrimination protects the individual from being compelled to incriminate himself in any manner; it does not distinguish degrees of incrimination. . . .

To summarize, we hold that when an individual is taken into custody or otherwise deprived of his freedom by the authorities in any significant way and is subjected to questioning, the privilege against self-incrimination is jeopardized. Procedural safeguards must be employed to protect the privilege and unless other fully effective means are adopted to notify the person of his right of silence and to assure that the exercise of the right will be scrupulously honored, the following measures are required. He must be warned prior to any questioning that he has the right to remain silent, that anything he says can be used against him in a court of law, that he has the right to the presence of an attorney, and that if he cannot afford an attorney one will be appointed for him prior to any questioning if he so desires. Opportunity to exercise these rights must be afforded to him throughout the interrogation. After such warnings

have been given, and such opportunity afforded him, the individual may knowingly and intelligently waive these rights and agree to answer questions or make a statement. But unless and until such warnings and waiver are demonstrated by the prosecution at trial, no evidence obtained as a result of interrogation can be used against him.

A recurrent argument made in these cases is that society's need for interrogation outweighs the privilege. This argument is not unfamiliar to this Court. The whole thrust of our foregoing discussion demonstrates that the Constitution has prescribed the rights of the individual when confronted with the power of government when it provided in the Fifth Amendment that an individual cannot be compelled to be a witness against himself. That right cannot be abridged. . . .

In announcing these principles, we are not unmindful of the burdens which law enforcement officials must bear, often under trying circumstances. We also fully recognize the obligation of all citizens to aid in enforcing the criminal laws. This Court, while protecting individual rights, has always given ample latitude to law enforcement agencies in the legitimate exercise of their duties. The limits we have placed on the interrogation process should not constitute an undue interference with a proper system of law enforcement. . . . [O]ur decision does not in any way preclude police from carrying out their traditional investigatory functions. Although confessions may play an important role in some convictions, the cases before us present graphic examples of the overstatement of the "need" for confessions. . . .

Over the years the Federal Bureau of Investigation has compiled an exemplary record of effective law enforcement while advising any suspect or arrested person, at the outset of an interview, that he is not required to make a statement, that any statement may be used against him in court, that the individual may obtain the services of an attorney of his own choice and, more recently, that he has a right to free counsel if he is unable to pay. . . .

The practice of the FBI can readily be emulated by state and local enforcement agencies. The argument that the FBI deals with different crimes than are dealt with by state authorities does not mitigate the significance of the FBI experience. . . .

Judicial solutions to problems of constitutional dimension have evolved decade by decade. As courts have been presented with the need to enforce constitutional rights, they have found means of doing so. That was our responsibility when *Escobedo* was before us and it is our responsibility today. Where rights secured by the Constitution are involved, there can be no rule making or legislation which would abrogate them.

Reversed.

MR. JUSTICE WHITE, with whom MR. JUSTICE HARLAN and MR. JUSTICE STEWART join, dissenting.

The obvious underpinning of the Court's decision is a deep-seated distrust of all confessions. As the Court declares that the accused may not be interrogated without counsel present, absent a waiver of the right to counsel, and as the Court all but admonishes the lawyer to advise the accused to remain silent, the result adds up to a judicial judgment that evidence from the accused should not be used against him in any way, whether compelled or not. This is the not so subtle overtone of the opinion—that it is inherently wrong for the police to gather evidence from the accused himself. And this is precisely the nub of this dissent. I see nothing wrong or immoral, and certainly nothing unconstitutional, in the police's asking a suspect whom they have reasonable cause to arrest whether or not he killed his wife or in confronting him with the evidence on which the arrest was based, at least where he has been plainly advised that he may remain completely silent. Until today, "the admissions or confessions of the prisoner, when voluntarily and freely made, have always ranked high in the scale of incriminating evidence." Particularly when corroborated, as where the police have confirmed the accused's disclosure of the hiding place of implements or fruits of the crime, such confessions have the highest reliability and significantly contribute to the certitude with which we may believe the accused is guilty. Moreover, it is by no means certain that the process of confessing is injurious to the accused. To the contrary it may provide psychological relief and enhance the prospects for rehabilitation.

This is not to say that the value of respect for the inviolability of the accused's individual personality should be accorded no weight or that all confessions should be indiscriminately admitted. This Court has long read the Constitution to proscribe compelled confessions, a salutary rule from which there should be no retreat. But I see no sound basis, factual or otherwise, and the Court gives none, for concluding that the present rule against the receipt of co-erced confessions is inadequate for the task of sorting out inadmissible evidence and must be replaced by the per se rule which is now imposed. Even if the new concept can be said to have advantages of some sort over the present law, they are far outweighed by its likely undesirable impact on other very relevant and important interests.

The most basic function of any government is to provide for the security of the individual and of his property. These ends of society are served by the criminal laws which for the most part are aimed at the prevention of crime. Without the reasonably effective performance of the task of preventing private violence and retaliation, it is idle to talk about human dignity and civilized values.

The modes by which the criminal laws serve the interest in general security are many. First the murderer who has taken the life of another is removed from the streets, deprived of his liberty and thereby prevented from repeating his offense. In view of the statistics on recidivism in this country and of the number of instances in which apprehension occurs only after repeated offenses, no one can sensibly claim that this aspect of the criminal law does not prevent crime or contribute significantly to the personal security of the ordinary citizen.

Secondly, the swift and sure apprehension of those who refuse to respect the personal security and dignity of their neighbor unquestionably has its impact on others who might be similarly tempted. That the criminal law is wholly or partly ineffective with a segment of the population or with many of those who have been apprehended and convicted is a very faulty basis for concluding that it is not effective with respect to the great bulk of our citizens or for thinking that without the criminal laws, or in the absence of their enforcement, there would be no increase in crime. Arguments of this nature are not borne out by any kind of reliable evidence that I have seen to this date.

Thirdly, the law concerns itself with those whom it has confined. The hope and aim of modern penology, fortunately, is as soon as possible to return the convict to society a better and more law-abiding man than when he left. Sometimes there is success, sometimes failure. But at least the effort is made, and it should be made to the very maximum extent of our present and future capabilities.

The rule announced today will measurably weaken the ability of the criminal law to perform these tasks. It is a deliberate calculus to prevent interrogations, to reduce the incidence of confessions and pleas of guilty and to increase the number of trials. Criminal trials, no matter how efficient the police are, are not sure bets for the prosecution, nor should they be if the evidence is not forthcoming. Under the present law, the prosecution fails to prove its case in about 30% of the criminal cases actually tried in the federal courts. But it is something else again to remove from the ordinary criminal case all those confessions which heretofore have been held to be free and voluntary acts of the accused and to thus establish a new constitutional barrier to the ascertainment of truth by the judicial process. There is, in my view, every reason to believe that a good many criminal defendants who otherwise would have been convicted on what this Court has previously thought to be the most satisfactory kind of evidence will now, under this new version of the Fifth Amendment, either not be tried at all or will be acquitted if the State's evidence, minus the confession, is put to the test of litigation.

I have no desire whatsoever to share the responsibility for any such impact on the present criminal process.

Chief Justice Warren's majority opinion in *Miranda* is a *tour de force* on self-incrimination, creating the so-called Miranda warnings that police must read to suspects before any custodial interrogation. But the opinion left open a number of questions. In fact, the majority of self-incrimination cases after 1966 are the fallout from *Miranda*, seeking to fill three gaps it left open: (1) What is custody? (2) What constitutes interrogation? and (3) Must statements made in absence of Miranda warnings be excluded from evidence?

The first two questions are of the utmost importance for police. The *Miranda* ruling provided little guidance to police questioning individuals outside of the traditional interrogation room setting. Nor did the decision discuss situations in which police question individuals in a nonaccusatory fashion. Under such circumstances, must police advise individuals of their rights?

As you read about the Court's answers to these questions, keep another point in mind: immediately after *Miranda*, law enforcement officials condemned the decision. They—as did the dissenters—thought it would seriously hamper their ability to investigate and solve

---

BOX 10-4 AFTERMATH . . . ERNESTO MIRANDA

IN FEBRUARY 1967, following the Supreme Court's decision overturning his conviction on kidnapping and rape charges, Ernesto Miranda was retried, this time with his incriminating statements excluded. To mask his identity from the jurors, Miranda stood trial as "José Gomez." He was convicted and sentenced to twenty to thirty years in prison. Most damning was the testimony of his common-law wife who claimed that Miranda had admitted to her that he had kidnapped and raped the victim. He was also convicted of an unrelated robbery of a woman at knifepoint and was sentenced to a concurrent term of twenty to twenty-five years.

In December 1972 Miranda was released on parole. Only two years later he was arrested on drug and firearms charges after being stopped on a routine traffic violation. These charges were dropped because of Fourth Amendment violations and insufficient evidence. In 1975 he returned to prison for a short time on a parole violation.

Miranda's life ended in 1976. While drinking and playing cards in a Phoenix skid row bar, he became involved in a fight with two illegal aliens. Miranda got the best of the fight and went to the rest room to wash his bloodied hands. When he returned, the two attacked him with a knife. Miranda was stabbed once in the chest and once in the abdomen. He collapsed and died. Miranda was thirty-four years old. Upon arresting his assailants, police read them their Miranda warnings.

SOURCES: *New York Times*, October 12, 1974; *Atlanta Journal*, December 13, 1972, February 1, 1976, February 2, 1976; and James A. Inciardi, *Criminal Justice*, 4th ed. (Fort Worth: Harcourt Brace Jovanovich, 1993).

---

crimes. Some analysts thought Chief Justice Burger—who generally supported the government in criminal cases and whose Court was largely responsible for filling *Miranda*'s gaps—would be sympathetic to the concerns of law enforcement officials. Was he? Moreover, has *Miranda* created the burden on law enforcement that some suspected?

What Is Custody? The first post-*Miranda* case heard

PD 47
Rev. 8/73

METROPOLITAN POLICE DEPARTMENT
WARNING AS TO YOUR RIGHTS

You are under arrest. Before we ask you any questions, you must understand what your rights are.

You have the right to remain silent. You are not required to say anything to us at any time or to answer any questions. Anything you say can be used against you in court.

You have the right to talk to a lawyer for advice before we question you and to have him with you during questioning.

If you cannot afford a lawyer and want one, a lawyer will be provided for you.

If you want to answer questions now without a lawyer present you will still have the right to stop answering at any time. You also have the right to stop answering at any time until you talk to a lawyer.

WAIVER

1. Have you read or had read to you the warning as to your rights?

2. Do you understand these rights?

3. Do you wish to answer any questions?

4. Are you willing to answer questions without having an attorney present?

5. Signature of defendant on line below.

6. Time   Date

7. Signature of Officer

8. Signature of Witness

by the justices dealt with custody. In *Orozco v. Texas* (1969) the Court determined that "custodial interrogations," regardless of where they occur, require Miranda warnings. In this instance, police questioned an alleged murderer in his boardinghouse room at four o'clock in the morning, while he was in bed. They did not read him his rights, believing that they must do so only when they take individuals out of their environment, that is, into police headquarters. But, as Justice Black noted,

The State has argued here that since Orozco was interrogated on his own bed, in familiar surroundings, our *Miranda* holding should not apply. . . . But the opinion iterated and reiterated the absolute necessity for officers interrogating people "in custody" to give the described warnings. According to the officers' testimony, petitioner was under arrest and not free to leave. . . . The *Miranda* opinion declared that the warnings were required when the person being interrogated was in custody at the station *or otherwise deprived of his freedom of action in any significant way.*

Orozco v. Texas was the Warren Court's only major post-*Miranda* decision on custody. Although it sent a clear signal to law enforcement officials that they must provide the required warnings to all individuals deprived of their freedom, regardless of where that deprivation occurs, it created more gaps for the Burger Court to fill in. For example, must police warn an individual who voluntarily accedes to police questioning? Is interrogation of a person suspected of certain kinds of crimes exempt from *Miranda?*

In several cases, the more conservative Burger Court moved away from the spirit of the *Orozco* decision. In *Beckwith v. United States* (1976), for example, the Court held that Miranda warnings were not required when IRS agents questioned a man in a congenial and noncoercive manner at the man's residence, even though the investigation later could lead to criminal tax fraud violations. In *Oregon v. Mathiason* (1977) the Court held that a noncoercive custodial interrogation, in which an individual voluntarily appears at a police station for questioning, does not require Miranda warnings. As the Burger Court gradually narrowed the circumstances under which police had to inform suspects of their rights, many thought that the Court would overrule *Miranda,* and *Berkemer v. McCarty* (1984) seemed the perfect vehicle.

This case had its beginnings when an Ohio highway patrol officer saw Richard McCarty's car weaving in and out of traffic lanes. The officer pulled McCarty over and asked him to step out of his car. McCarty had difficulty standing up. The officer asked McCarty if he had taken anything, and McCarty said that he had drunk two beers and smoked two joints of marijuana. The officer arrested him and drove him to the police station. At no point was he given full Miranda warnings. Even though McCarty's blood test showed no alcohol, police interrogated him further, and he made additional incriminating statements. McCarty was charged with driving while intoxicated, a misdemeanor, for which he received ten days in jail and a fine.

On appeal, the Supreme Court confronted two important questions. First, does the Miranda rule apply to minor infractions such as misdemeanor traffic offenses or only to more serious crimes? And second, if the Miranda rule does apply to minor crimes, at what point should McCarty have been advised of his rights—at the initial roadside stop or later, when he was formally arrested and taken to the station?

With a unanimous vote, the justices responded that Miranda rights apply to anyone accused of a crime, regardless of the nature or severity of the alleged offense. If an accused individual is taken into custody, Miranda warnings must be given before any interrogation. However, the justices also held that the common roadside stop of a motorist does not constitute "custody" for Miranda purposes. Unlike arrests for more significant charges, the roadside stop does not create an overwhelmingly coercive environment. The Court offers three justifications. First, the roadside stop is a routine procedure that almost all drivers experience sooner or later. Second, the common roadside stop is short in duration. Third, the roadside stop takes place in public where police are not likely to abuse their authority without being observed. The justices ruled that because a roadside stop is not a custodial situation for Miranda purposes, the officer had no obligation to provide Miranda warnings when he initially questioned McCarty, and McCarty's responses to those questions could be used as evidence. However, once the officer formally arrested McCarty and placed him in the patrol car for transport to the police station, the conditions of a routine roadside stop had changed and a custodial condition had begun. Miranda warnings, therefore, should have been given prior to any questioning from that point forward. As a result, McCarty's incriminating statements at the police station, made without the benefit of Miranda warnings, were inadmissible.

The Court's opinion in *Berkemer v. McCarty* provides additional instructions on the issue of custody. Police must read Miranda warnings only when some element of coercion exists during custodial questioning. If an individual is interrogated in a noncoercive atmosphere, such as in a routine, public, roadside stop, the possibility for police abuse is dramatically diminished.

Although *Berkemer v. McCarty* may have reduced police confusion over the issue of custody, we must consider its compatibility with the Warren Court's mandate in *Miranda* and *Orozco.* Did *Berkemer* merely clarify those opinions, as some have suggested, or did it undermine their intent? If you believe the latter, how else could the Court have ruled? Would the reading of Miranda rights at all roadside stops, even for relatively minor offenses such as speeding, have been a viable alternative?

What Constitutes Interrogation? Based on *Escobedo* and *Miranda,* police must inform individuals of their rights before they question them in an accusatory fashion. But both of these decisions dealt with traditional interrogations, occurring within the confines of a police station. What about questioning in the guise of conversation? That is, must police read Miranda warnings before they engage in any dialogue with a suspect?

The Burger Court grappled with this question in *Brewer v. Williams* (1977). This case involved Robert Williams, a deeply religious man with severe psychological problems, who allegedly kidnapped and killed a ten-year-old girl in Des Moines, Iowa, on Christmas Eve, in 1968. Two days later Williams turned himself in to police in Davenport, some 170 miles away, after apparently dumping the child's body somewhere along the way. Williams telephoned an attorney in Des Moines, who told him to remain silent, talking neither to the Davenport police nor to the Des Moines detectives who were to take him back.

As the detectives drove Williams to Des Moines, they engaged the suspect in a wide-ranging conversation. At one point they began reciting what has become known as the "Christian burial speech." Recognizing Williams's religious convictions, one of the detectives addressed him as Reverend, and said:

I want to give you something to think about while we're traveling down the road. . . . Number one, I want you to observe the weather conditions, it's raining, it's sleeting, it's freezing, driving is very treacherous, visibility is poor, it's going to be dark early this evening. They are predicting several inches of snow for tonight, and I feel that you yourself are the only person that knows where this little girl's body is, that you yourself have only been there once, and if you get a snow on top of it you yourself may be unable to find it. And, since we will be going right past the area on the way into Des Moines, I feel that we could stop and locate the body, that the parents of this little girl should be entitled to a Christian burial for the little girl who was snatched away from them on Christmas Eve and murdered. And I feel we should stop and locate it on the way in rather than waiting until morning and trying to come back out after a snow storm and possibly not being able to find it at all. . . . I do not want you to answer me. I don't want to discuss it any further. Just think about it as we're riding down the road.

Williams promptly directed police to the girl's body.

At his trial, Williams's attorney argued that the statements made by him in the car should be excluded as evidence, as should any evidence—the body—resulting from those statements. The statements, the attorney argued, were inadmissible because they had been obtained by illegal means. By playing on Williams's weaknesses, police had tricked him. Their conversation, therefore, amounted to an interrogation, prior to which Williams should have been advised of his rights.

In a 5–4 vote the U.S. Supreme Court agreed. Writing for the majority, Justice Stewart said:

There can be no serious doubt . . . that [the detective] deliberately and designedly set out to elicit information from Williams just as surely as . . . if he had formally interrogated him. [He] was fully aware before departing . . . that Williams was being represented [by counsel]. Yet, he purposely sought during Williams' isolation from his lawyers to obtain as much incriminating evidence as possible.

The importance of the *Williams* case is the Court's acknowledgement that for Miranda purposes an interrogation may take many forms. It is not confined to a traditional question and answer session in a police interrogation room. Regardless of the form it takes, any attempt to obtain incriminating statements from a suspect in custody triggers the need to give Miranda warnings.

This does not mean, however, that police are prohibited from making statements or having conversations that can be overheard by the suspect. In *Rhode Island v. Innis* (1980), for example, police officers in a patrol car engaged in a short conversation about safety considerations surrounding a missing gun that may have been used in a murder and a robbery. During this conversation they noted that the gun may have been discarded in

an area near a school for handicapped children. The suspect who was sitting in the back of the patrol car interrupted the conversation and showed them where he had left the gun. Tests later indicated that this was the same gun that had been involved in the crimes.

The Supreme Court held in *Innis* that the suspect had not been interrogated. An interrogation occurs, according to Court, when police use "any words or actions" that they should know "are reasonably likely to elicit an incriminating response from the suspect." The "Christian burial speech" in *Williams* met that definition; however, the police conversation in *Innis*, although it might have created some "subtle compulsion," did not.

Exceptions to the Miranda Rule and its Continuing Viability. The Warren Court premised its decision in *Miranda* on the inevitable power imbalance between the accused and the police during custodial interrogations. Without some procedure to safeguard the rights of the accused, suspects too often would forgo their privilege against self-incrimination under intense and ultimately coercive police. Arguably, the justices operated under the assumption that incriminating statements made in the absence of Miranda warnings would automatically violate the Fifth Amendment and that such evidence should be excluded from court.

Beginning in 1971 and continuing thorugh the 1990s, however, the Burger and Rehnquist Courts began applying *Miranda* in a narrower fashion and even created exceptions to the rule. These holdings often stemmed from cases presenting unusual circumstances in which prosecutors argued that *Miranda*'s ban on the use of self-incriminating statements should not apply. Table 10-2 summarizes the rulings from a number of these cases. Some Court observers speculated that the cumulative effect of these various exceptions to *Miranda* had watered down the rule to the point that it lacked any real meaning. Others guessed that if this trend continued a formal overruling of *Miranda* was inevitable.

Although no additional exceptions to the rule were imposed during the latter half of the 1990s, interest in the fate of *Miranda* was intensified in 1999 when the Fourth Circuit Court of Appeals ruled that the Miranda warnings were not constitutionally required. The case,

TABLE 10-2 Exceptions to *Miranda*

Case	Facts	Ruling
Harris v. New York (1971)	Arrested drug suspect made incriminating statements without the benefit of Miranda warnings. At trial he delivered an alibi at odds with his earlier statements. To impeach his credibility, the prosecutor introduced the suspect's initial statements.	Statements made without Miranda warnings may be used for the narrow purpose of counteracting perjury.
Michigan v. Tucker (1974)	Rape suspect who had not been given Miranda warnings claims he was with a friend at the time of the crime. Police question friend who does not corroborate the story, and testimony is used as evidence.	Although police were led to the witness by the defendant's statements made without the required warnings, the reliability of the witness's testimony is not affected and may be used.
New York v. Quarles (1984)	Rape suspect is apprehended after a chase through a supermarket. Police discover an empty holster and ask, "Where's the gun?" Suspect reveals where he dropped it. Police then read Miranda warnings.	When there is a danger to public safety, police may ask questions to remove that danger prior to reading Miranda warnings. Answers to such questions may be used as evidence.
Oregon v. Elstad (1985)	Burglary suspect makes incriminating statement prior to receiving Miranda warnings. He is given his warnings at the police station and confesses. The confession is used in court over his attorney's objection that the initial self-incriminating statement taints all future interrogations.	Confession may be used as evidence because it was preceded by Miranda warnings. Initial statements made prior to warnings may not be used, but failure to give warnings immediately does not preclude the validity of later interrogations.
Moran v. Burbine (1985)	Murder suspect in custody makes incriminating statements after receiving Miranda warnings and waiving his right to have an attorney present during questioning. Suspect's lawyer had previously contacted police and indicated a desire to advise his client. Police did not inform suspect of his lawyer's wishes.	Statements may be used as evidence. Defendant knew he had a right to an attorney and a right to remain silent. His waiver of these rights was not coerced.
Illinois v. Perkins (1990)	Undercover police agent enters prison in hope of obtaining evidence that an inmate had committed a murder prior to incarceration on other charges. Suspect, without Miranda warnings, makes incriminating statements to the undercover officer.	The statements may be used as evidence. Miranda warnings are not required when suspect is unaware he is speaking to a law enforcement official and gives a voluntary statement.
New York v. Harris (1990)	Police unlawfully enter the home of a murder suspect without a warrant and without permission. They arrest the suspect and take him to the police station. He is read his Miranda warnings and subsequently signs a written confession. The statement is used as evidence against him.	The fact that police enter a home illegally to make an arrest does not taint a subsequent confession at the police station that takes place after Miranda warnings are given.
Arizona v. Fulminante (1991)	An inmate, also a suspected child murderer, was under threat of physical attack from other prisoners. A fellow inmate, in reality a federal informant, said he would protect the suspect in return for the truth about the murder charge. The suspect confessed.	The confession was coerced by the threat of physical attack. But if such tainted testimony is erroneously admitted as evidence, a conviction need not be overturned if sufficient independent evidence supporting a guilty verdict is also introduced.

Dickerson v. United States, was immediately appealed to the Supreme Court. Would the Rehnquist Court with its conservative record on criminal rights issues use *Dickerson* as an opportunity to overrule *Miranda?* Or would the justices be reluctant to alter a precedent that had become such an entrenched part of American culture and jurisprudence?

Dickerson v. United States

530 U.S. — (2000)
supct.law.cornell.edu/supct/html/99-5525.ZS.html
Vote: 7 (Breyer, Ginsburg, Kennedy, O'Connor, Rehnquist,
    Souter, Stevens)
    2 (Scalia, Thomas)
Opinion of the Court: Rehnquist
Dissenting Opinion: Scalia

When *Miranda v. Arizona* was handed down in 1966, the reaction in Congress was quite negative. To blunt the effect of the decision, Congress enacted 18 U.S.C. §3501, a provision declaring that any confession "shall be admissible in evidence if it is voluntarily given." The statute listed several factors relevant to determining whether a confession is voluntary, and one factor was compliance with the *Miranda* decision. However, the law made clear that the absence of any particular factor "need not be conclusive on the issue of voluntariness of the confession." In short, the law said that a confession could be voluntary, and thus admissible, even if Miranda warnings were not given. The Justice Department, assuming that the law was unconstitutional, never made use of it. Consequently the law remained virtually dormant until resurrected by the Fourth Circuit Court of Appeals 1999.

Charles Thomas Dickerson was picked up by FBI agents for questioning about a bank robbery in Alexandria, Virginia. He was interviewed twice and gave statements to the agents. The first questioning took place without Miranda warnings. There was a dispute over whether Dickerson was advised of his rights prior to the second interview. The statements he made led officers to search his apartment (with a warrant) where additional evidence was seized.

Prior to his trial, Dickerson moved to suppress the statements he made and the items seized from his apartment on the grounds that this evidence was all based on comments he made without being informed of his constitutional rights. The trial court judge granted the motion to suppress. The trial was postponed while the United States appealed the suppression ruling. The Court of Appeals for the Fourth Circuit reversed, holding that the statements and physical evidence could be admitted as evidence because Dickerson's comments had been made voluntarily, despite the fact that his rights under *Miranda* had been violated. The appeals court based its decision on Section 3501, even though the United States refused to rely on that provision and asserted that the law was unconstitutional.

Dickerson appealed to the Supreme Court. Because the Justice Department remained opposed to the reasoning behind the Fourth Circuit's decision to admit the evidence, the Supreme Court appointed University of Utah law professor Paul Cassell, a longtime critic of the *Miranda* ruling, as a special friend of the court to argue in favor of the Fourth Circuit's position.

CHIEF JUSTICE REHNQUIST delivered the opinion of the Court.

In *Miranda v. Arizona* (1966) we held that certain warnings must be given before a suspect's statement made during custodial interrogation could be admitted in evidence. In the wake of that decision, Congress enacted 18 U.S.C. §3501 which in essence laid down a rule that the admissibility of such statements should turn only on whether or not they were voluntarily made. We hold that *Miranda*, being a constitutional decision of this Court, may not be in effect overruled by an Act of Congress, and we decline to overrule *Miranda* ourselves. We therefore hold that *Miranda* and its progeny in this Court govern the admissibility of statements made during custodial interrogation in both state and federal courts. . . .

Given §3501's express designation of voluntariness as the touchstone of admissibility, its omission of any warning requirement, and the instruction for trial courts to consider a nonexclusive list of factors relevant to the circumstances of a confession, we agree with the Court of Appeals that Congress intended by its enactment to overrule *Miranda.* . . . Because of the obvious conflict between our decision in *Miranda* and §3501, we must address whether Congress has constitutional authority to thus supersede *Miranda.* If Congress has such authority, §3501's totality-of-the-circumstances approach must prevail over *Miranda*'s requirement of warnings; if not, that section must yield to *Miranda*'s more specific requirements.

The law in this area is clear. This Court has supervisory authority over the federal courts, and we may use that authority to prescribe rules of evidence and procedure that are binding in those tribunals. However, the power to judicially create and enforce nonconstitutional "rules of procedure and evidence for the federal courts exists only in the absence of a relevant Act of Congress." *Palermo v. United States* (1959) and *Gordon v. United States* (1953). Congress retains the ultimate authority to modify or set aside any judicially created rules of evidence and procedure that are not required by the Constitution.

But Congress may not legislatively supersede our decisions interpreting and applying the Constitution. See, *e.g., City of Boerne v. Flores* (1997). This case therefore turns on whether the *Miranda* Court announced a constitutional rule or merely exercised its supervisory authority to regulate evidence in the absence of congressional direction. Recognizing this point, the Court of Appeals surveyed *Miranda* and its progeny to determine the constitutional status of the *Miranda* decision. Relying on the fact that we have created several exceptions to *Miranda*'s warnings requirement and that we have repeatedly referred to the *Miranda* warnings as "prophylactic" and "not themselves rights protected by the Constitution," the Court of Appeals concluded that the protections announced in *Miranda* are not constitutionally required.

We disagree with the Court of Appeals' conclusion, although we concede that there is language in some of our opinions that supports the view taken by that court. But first and foremost of the factors on the other side—that *Miranda* is a constitutional decision—is that both *Miranda* and two of its companion cases applied the rule to proceedings in state courts—to wit, Arizona, California, and New York. Since that time, we have consistently applied *Miranda*'s rule to prosecutions arising in state courts. . . . It is beyond dispute that we do not hold a supervisory power over the courts of the several States. With respect to proceedings in state courts, our "authority is limited to enforcing the commands of the United States Constitution.". . .

The *Miranda* opinion itself begins by stating that the Court granted certiorari "to explore some facets of the problems . . . of applying the privilege against self-incrimination to in-custody interrogation, *and to give concrete constitutional guidelines for law enforcement agencies and courts to follow*" (emphasis added). In fact, the majority opinion is replete with statements indicating that the majority thought it was announcing a constitutional rule. Indeed, the Court's ultimate conclusion was that the unwarned confessions obtained in the four cases before the Court in *Miranda* "were obtained from the defendant under circumstances that did not meet constitutional standards for protection of the privilege.". . .

The dissent argues that it is judicial overreaching for this Court to hold §3501 unconstitutional unless we hold that the *Miranda* warnings are required by the Constitution, in the sense that nothing else will suffice to satisfy constitutional requirements. But we need not go farther than *Miranda* to decide this case. In *Miranda*, the Court noted that reliance on the traditional totality-of-the-circumstances test raised a risk of overlooking an involuntary custodial confession, a risk that the Court found unacceptably great when the confession is offered in the case in chief to prove guilt. The Court therefore concluded that something more than the totality test was necessary. As discussed above, §3501 reinstates the totality test as sufficient. Section 3501 therefore cannot be sustained if *Miranda* is to remain the law.

Whether or not we would agree with *Miranda*'s reasoning and its resulting rule, were we addressing the issue in the first instance, the principles of *stare decisis* weigh heavily against overruling it now. While "*stare decisis* is not an inexorable command," *State Oil Co. v. Khan* (1997), particularly when we are interpreting the Constitution, *Agostini v. Felton* (1997), "even in constitutional cases, the doctrine carries such persuasive force that we have always required a departure from precedent to be supported by some 'special justification.'" *United States v. International Business Machines Corp.* (1996).

We do not think there is such justification for overruling *Miranda. Miranda* has become embedded in routine police practice to the point where the warnings have become part of our national culture. . . . While we have overruled our precedents when subsequent cases have undermined their doctrinal underpinnings, . . . we do not believe that this has happened to the *Miranda* decision. If anything, our subsequent cases have reduced the impact of the *Miranda* rule on legitimate law enforcement while reaffirming the decision's core ruling that unwarned statements may not be used as evidence in the prosecution's case in chief.

The disadvantage of the *Miranda* rule is that statements which may be by no means involuntary, made by a defendant who is aware of his "rights," may nonetheless be excluded and a guilty defendant go free as a result. But experience suggests that the totality-of-the-circumstances test which §3501 seeks to revive is more difficult than *Miranda* for law enforcement officers to conform to, and for courts to apply in a consistent manner. . . . The requirement that Miranda warnings be given does not, of course, dispense with the voluntariness inquiry. But as we said in *Berkemer v. McCarty* (1984), "[c]ases in which a defendant can make a colorable argument that a self-incriminating statement was 'compelled' despite the fact that the law enforcement authorities adhered to the dictates of *Miranda* are rare."

In sum, we conclude that *Miranda* announced a constitutional rule that Congress may not supersede legislatively. Following the rule of *stare decisis*, we decline to overrule *Miranda* ourselves. The judgment of the Court of Appeals is therefore

Reversed.

JUSTICE SCALIA, with whom JUSTICE THOMAS joins, dissenting.

[W]hile I agree with the Court that §3501 cannot be upheld without also concluding that *Miranda* represents an illegitimate exercise of our authority to review state-court judgments, I do not share the Court's hesitation in reaching that conclusion. For while the Court is also correct that the doctrine of *stare decisis* demands some "special justification" for a departure from longstanding precedent—even precedent of the constitutional variety—that criterion is more than met here. . . . Despite the Court's Orwellian assertion to the contrary, it is undeniable that later cases . . . have "undermined [*Miranda*'s] doctrinal underpinnings," denying constitutional violation and thus stripping the holding of its only constitutionally legitimate support. *Miranda*'s critics and supporters alike have long made this point. . . .

The Court cites *Patterson v. McLean Credit Union* (1989) as accurately reflecting our standard for overruling, which I am pleased to accept, even though *Patterson* was speaking of overruling statutory cases and the standard for constitutional decisions is somewhat more lenient. What is set forth there reads as though it was written precisely with the current status of *Miranda* in mind:

"In cases where statutory precedents have been overruled, the primary reason for the Court's shift in position has been the intervening development of the law, through either the growth of judicial doctrine or further action taken by Congress. Where such changes have removed or weakened the conceptual underpinnings from the prior decision, . . . or where the later law has rendered the decision irreconcilable with competing legal doctrines or policies, . . . the Court has not hesitated to overrule an earlier decision."

Neither am I persuaded by the argument for retaining *Miranda* that touts its supposed workability as compared with the totality-of-the-circumstances test it purported to replace. *Miranda*'s proponents cite *ad nauseam* the fact that the Court was called upon to make difficult and subtle distinctions in applying the "voluntariness" test in some 30-odd due process "coerced confessions" cases in the 30 years between *Brown v. Mississippi* (1936) and *Miranda*. It is not immediately apparent, however, that the judicial burden has been eased by the "bright-line" rules adopted in *Miranda*. In fact, in the 34 years since *Miranda* was decided, this Court has been called upon to decide nearly 60 cases involving a host of *Miranda* issues, most of them predicted with remarkable prescience by Justice White in his *Miranda* dissent.

Moreover, it is not clear why the Court thinks that the "totality-of-the-circumstances test . . . is more difficult than *Miranda* for law enforcement officers to conform to, and for courts to apply in a consistent manner.". . .

Finally, I am not convinced by petitioner's argument that *Miranda* should be preserved because the decision occupies a special place in the "public's consciousness." As far as I am aware, the public is not under the illusion that we are infallible. I see little harm in admitting that we made a mistake in taking away from the people the ability to decide for themselves what protections (beyond those required by the Constitution) are reasonably affordable in the criminal investigatory process. And I see much to be gained by reaffirming for the people the wonderful reality that they

---

BOX 10-5 *MIRANDA* **IN GLOBAL PERSPECTIVE**

ALTHOUGH MANY Americans may think that Miranda warnings are a unique feature of the U.S. criminal justice system, this is not the case. Indeed, in his opinion for the Court in *Miranda*, Chief Justice Earl Warren noted that "Scottish judicial decisions bar use in evidence of most confessions obtained through police interrogation. In India, confessions made to police not in the presence of a magistrate have been excluded by rule of evidence since 1872, at a time when it operated under British law."

Warren also pointed to the Judges' Rules of 1912, operative in England at the time of *Miranda*:

"II. As soon as a police officer has evidence which would afford reasonable grounds for suspecting that a person has committed an offence, he shall caution that person or cause him to be cautioned before putting to him any questions, or further questions, relating to that offence. The caution shall be in the following terms:

"'You are not obliged to say anything unless you wish to do so but what you say may be put into writing and given in evidence.'

"When after being cautioned a person is being questioned, or elects to make a statement, a record shall be kept of the time and place at which any such questioning or statement began and ended and of the persons present."

The Judges' Rules also provided:

"That every person at any stage of an investigation should be able to communicate and to consult privately with a solic-

itor. This is so even if he is in custody provided that in such a case no unreasonable delay or hindrance is caused to the processes of investigation or the administration of justice by his doing so."

Some scholars claim that today British practice even more closely resembles *Miranda*. During the 1980s Parliament passed several acts to safeguard the rights of the criminally accused, including a provision that allowed suspects to have an attorney present during questioning. And, under the 1994 Criminal Justice and Public Order Act, police officers are required to read the following warning:

You do not have to say anything. But if you do not mention now something which you later use in your defence, the court may decide that your failure to mention it now strengthens the case against you. A record will be made of anything you say and it may be given in evidence if you are brought to trial.

Note the similarity to *Miranda:* police must tell suspects that they have the right to remain silent. The difference, however, is equally striking: whereas *Miranda* suggests that only statements suspects make can be used against them, the British rule indicates that silence may be invoked against them as well.

SOURCES: William E. Schmidt, "Silence May Speak Against the Accused in Britain," *New York Times*, November 11, 1994, 10; Paul G. Cassell, "Miranda's Social Costs: An Empirical Reassessment," *Northwestern University Law Review* 90 (1996): 387–440.

---

govern themselves—which means that "[t]he powers not delegated to the United States by the Constitution" that the people adopted, "nor prohibited . . . to the States" by that Constitution, "are reserved to the States respectively, or to the people," U.S. Const., Amdt. 10.

Today's judgment converts *Miranda* from a milestone of judicial overreaching into the very Cheops' Pyramid (or perhaps the Sphinx would be a better analogue) of judicial arrogance. In imposing its Court-made code upon the States, the original opinion at least *asserted* that it was demanded by the Constitution. Today's decision does not pretend that it is—and yet *still* asserts the right to impose it against the will of the people's representatives in Congress. Far from believing that *stare decisis* compels this result, I believe we can-

not allow to remain on the books even a celebrated decision—*especially* a celebrated decision—that has come to stand for the proposition that the Supreme Court has power to impose extraconstitutional constraints upon Congress and the States. This is not the system that was established by the Framers, or that would be established by any sane supporter of government by the people.

I dissent from today's decision, and, until §3501 is repealed, will continue to apply it in all cases where there has been a sustainable finding that the defendant's confession was voluntary.

In *Dickerson* the Court, with only Scalia and Thomas in dissent, rejected the opportunity to overrule *Miranda*.

BOX 10-6   THE AFRICAN QUEEN STORY

The following was told to a reporter by two New York police officers:

Powerful as the internal pressure is, the *Miranda* rule and other constraints on questioning suspects have placed some limits on a detective's ability to exploit it. Nonetheless, there's one ancient technique that still has a place in the modern detective's repertory: trickery.

"We can still deceive them," Weidenbaum tells me. "We can use trickery as long as it doesn't violate their rights."

He then proceeds to give me a classic instance of what he called permissible deception in a case he and Cachie worked on, a case they called "the African Queen."

"She cut her husband's head off," Weidenbaum begins. "What happened was, this man was, well . . ."

"Retarded," says Cachie.

"He was a veteran from World War II with 100 percent disability. She was an immigrant from . . ."

"The Cameroons," supplies Cachie.

"In any case, she met him and decided she's going to get his Government insurance. And one day she calls the police and says, 'Look what happened to my husband.' And the police come there, and there he is, a bloody mess on the floor, the only thing holding his head onto the body is maybe a little piece of skin. You lift him, the head's going to roll right off. And so how do we investigate this? We start talking with her, and she thinks she's smart enough to fool everybody. Every day she comes to the precinct to talk to us."

The more she talked to them, the more suspicious they became. The blackberry brandy story was the last straw for the two detectives.

She had set the table in the apartment as if to show there were four people up there drinking the night of the murder,

a night she claimed she was "away." She had put out an empty bottle of blackberry brandy and four glasses.

The problem was, the glasses in which the four people were supposed to have downed the blackberry brandy "were sparkling clean," says Weidenbaum. "She hadn't thought through her deception very thoroughly."

Convinced now that she'd murdered her husband, but handicapped by the lack of any witnesses or conclusive evidence, the detectives decided to use some deception of their own.

"I explain to her that when a person is murdered the last thing a person sees is the person who killed them. And this image remains on the lens of their eyes after they die, and with all this modern technology that we have, at the time of the autopsy we have the eyes removed and they are sent to a special lab, and in this lab they develop them like you would develop film, and we get a picture back of the murderer."

"That isn't true, is it?" I say, almost gulled by his deceptively sincere recitation.

"No, this is what I'm telling her," Weidenbaum clarifies for my benefit. "And she's sitting there listening to the story, and then she says to me, 'I guess you're going to find my picture.' The next day she goes back to the morgue and asks somebody at the morgue, 'Can you do this with the eyes?' And they thought she was crazy. She insisted on having the body immediately cremated with the eyes in it."

Her guilty reaction to the detectives' ruse helped convince a grand jury to indict the woman, Weidenbaum says. She subsequently pleaded guilty.

SOURCE: Ron Rosenbaum, "Crack Murder," *New York Times Magazine*, February 15, 1987. Copyright © 1987 by the New York Times Company. Reprinted by permission.

The decision appears to put *Miranda* on solid ground, with little likelihood that the Court will alter the basic tenets of that decision in the foreseeable future.

But how do we account for this outcome? How do we explain conservative justices such as Rehnquist, O'Connor, and Kennedy joining with the more moderate justices to retain the precedent most associated with the

protection of the rights of the criminally accused? Perhaps, as we saw with the exclusionary rule, the justices have reached an appropriate compromise: the more liberal justices are pleased that the conservatives have not succeeded in overturning *Miranda*, and the conservatives are satisfied that they have made enough changes in the application of the doctrine to make it acceptable.

Now that you have a good understanding of how the Fifth Amendment's Self-incrimination Clause governs out-of-court "testimony," let us return to the question we posed earlier in this section: Why does *Miranda* continue to be so controversial? After all, the Miranda doctrine is not particularly novel. As Box 10-5 illustrates, similar rules were developed in other nations long before the Supreme Court issued its decision in 1966. And as the Court acknowledged, the FBI had been successfully following Miranda-like guidelines for many years prior to the Supreme Court's ruling. Moreover, the doctrine has been in place for more than three decades and has become embedded in our political and legal culture.

Some continue to argue that the decision binds the hands of police to an intolerable degree. They also point to cases in which criminals go free simply because their confessions were not preceded by a correct recitation of the Miranda warnings. That a criminal who confessed could be released is precisely what concerned Justice White and the others who dissented in *Miranda*. *Miranda*'s supporters make equally strong arguments. As Marvin Zalman and Larry Siegel point out, *Miranda* has not, in fact, made it more difficult for police to obtain incriminating statements. Empirical investigations into *Miranda*'s effect in cities, both large and small, indicate that "equivalent proportions of confessions were obtained in the post-*Miranda* period as before and that police effectiveness did not appear to suffer."[24]

Others, however, claim that *Miranda* has done little to reduce the coercion that actually occurs when police question suspects. In practice, large numbers of suspects, even after being informed of their constitutional rights, agree to answer police questions without an attorney present. Such individuals are at the mercy of police investigators whose interrogation techniques are well honed and very effective. Critics of police practices claim that especially skillful interrogators can easily extract incriminating statements even from innocent suspects. Occasionally, such tactics include various forms of trickery. Read Box 10-6, the African Queen story, which details the

procedures New York detectives used to obtain evidence against a murder suspect. The officers said their tactics were perfectly legitimate under Supreme Court precedent. Their view may have received some general support from Justice Kennedy, who, writing for the majority in *Illinois v. Perkins* (1990), which concerned a jailed defendant who implicated himself in a murder by talking to an undercover agent placed in his cell. Kennedy stated: "*Miranda* forbids coercion, not mere strategic deception."

Thus, while *Dickerson v. United States* reaffirmed the viability of the *Miranda* ruling, the debate over its meaning and impact continues. On which side of the controversy do you stand?

The Self-Incrimination Clause and Testimony

In addition to governing custodial interrogations, the Fifth Amendment's Self-incrimination Clause covers testimony in all government hearings. Individuals called to testify in a court of law or before a legislative committee or other government body can refuse to answer any questions on the grounds that the answers may incriminate or implicate them in some unlawful activity. Journalists and other observers call this "taking the Fifth."

History is full of important investigations during which witnesses refused to cooperate by asserting their Fifth Amendment privilege. During the red scare of the 1950s, many called before Sen. Joseph R. McCarthy's committee investigating communist activities refused to testify on those grounds. In 1987 the Fifth Amendment was invoked when Congress investigated the sale of arms to Iran in exchange for hostages. Several of those directly involved in the scandal refused to testify on the grounds that their statements would implicate them.

If a witness refuses to answer questions on Fifth Amendment grounds, no inference of guilt may be made. Judges may not instruct jurors to consider a defendant's refusal to take the witness stand and deny guilt under oath; nor may prosecutors argue that a defendant's decision not to testify is evidence of wrongdoing. Such actions by prosecutors or judges would be clear violations of the Fifth Amendment. An individual's decision to invoke the Fifth Amendment privilege and not answer

---

24. Zalman and Siegel, *Criminal Procedure*, 2d ed., 518. For a review of some of these studies, see Welsh S. White, "Defending *Miranda*: A Reply to Professor Caplan," *Vanderbilt Law Review* 39 (1986): 1–22.

questions can be interpreted as nothing more than a decision to remain silent.

Furthermore, individuals must be free to exercise their Fifth Amendment rights. Governments may not coerce a person to testify. A prosecutor, for example, may not threaten a defendant that if he or she does not take the witness stand, the government will ask for a more severe sentence. Nor may the government use economic pressure to coerce an individual to waive the Fifth Amendment privilege. In *Garrity v. New Jersey* (1967) and *Gardner v. Broderick* (1968) the Supreme Court ruled that public employees could not be threatened with the loss of their jobs if they did not testify in government investigations of corruption and wrongdoing. Citizens must be given the choice of exercising their rights against self-incrimination.

Although taking the Fifth is rarely challenged (only those asserting their right can know with certainty whether their statements would be incriminating), the right is not absolute. There are at least two situations in which a person may not legitimately claim a Fifth Amendment privilege. The first situation involves a grant of immunity, and the second occurs after a person accused of a crime has been tried.

Under a grant of immunity, the prosecution agrees that it will not use any of the testimony against the witness. In return, the witness provides information that the prosecution believes will result in the convictions of other criminals, usually more dangerous or more important than the immune witness. Because a grant of immunity means that nothing the witness says may be used against him or her, it is a direct substitute for the Fifth Amendment. As a consequence, the immune witness may not take the Fifth Amendment.

When a defendant has been tried for a criminal offense, he or she may be asked to testify about the crime in other legal proceedings and normally may not avoid doing so by claiming Fifth Amendment protection. This situation may occur when prosecutors believe, for example, that two men committed a crime. They might put the first defendant on trial for the offense. If a conviction results, the prosecutors can then try the second defendant and call the first to testify. The first man may not invoke the Fifth Amendment because he has already been found guilty and cannot further incriminate himself with respect to that particular crime.

Another example of this principle occurred in the 1994–1997 legal actions against O. J. Simpson, an actor and former professional football star, who was accused of the 1994 killing of his former wife and an acquaintance of hers. After a criminal court jury found Simpson not guilty of the murders, the victims' families filed a civil suit asking that Simpson be found responsible for the deaths and that he be ordered to pay compensation. Because Simpson had already been found not guilty of the murders, he could never be tried again on those criminal charges and therefore could not incriminate himself with respect to the killings. When he was called as a witness in the civil trial, he could not avoid taking the stand by invoking the privilege against self-incrimination. In fact, Simpson was called as a witness by the plaintiffs, and he was required to testify.

Now that you have an understanding of the constitutional rights designed to protect the criminally accused during the evidence-gathering stages of the process, we now turn to Chapter 11, which deals with what the Constitution requires during the trial and punishment phases.

READINGS

Baker, Liva. *Miranda: Crime, Law, and Politics.* New York: Atheneum, 1983.

Bradley, Craig M. *The Failure of the Criminal Procedure Revolution.* Philadelphia: University of Pennsylvania Press, 1993.

Casper, Jonathan D. *American Criminal Justice: The Defendant's Perspective.* Englewood Cliffs, N.J.: Prentice-Hall, 1972.

Creamer, J. Shane. *The Law of Arrest, Search and Seizure.* New York: Holt, Rinehart, and Winston, 1980.

Eisenstein, James, Roy B. Fleming, and Peter F. Nardulli. *The Contours of Justice: Communities and Their Courts.* Boston: Little, Brown, 1988.

Helmholz, R. H., Charles M. Gray, John H. Langbein, Eben Moglen, Henry E. Smith, and Albert W. Alschuler. *The Privilege Against Self-Incrimination: Its Origins and Development.* Chicago: University of Chicago Press, 1997.

Jacob, Herbert. *Law and Politics in the United States.* Boston: Little, Brown, 1988.

Kamisar, Yale. "The Warren Court (Was it Really so Defense-Minded?), the Burger Court (Was it Really so Prosecution Oriented?) and Police Investigatory Procedures." In *The Burger Court*, ed. Vincent Blasi. New Haven: Yale University Press, 1983.

Landynski, Jacob W. *Search and Seizure and the Supreme Court.* Baltimore: Johns Hopkins University Press, 1966.

Levy, Leonard W. *Against the Law: The Nixon Court and Criminal Justice.* New York: Harper & Row, 1974.

McWhirter, Darien A. *Search, Seizure, and Privacy: Exploring the Constitution.* Phoenix: Oryx Press, 1994.

Medalie, Richard J. *From Escobedo to Miranda.* Washington, D.C.: Lerner Law Books, 1966.

Myren, Richard A. *Law and Justice.* Pacific Grove, Calif.: Brooks/Cole, 1987.

Neubauer, David W. *America's Courts and the Criminal Justice System.* 3d ed. Pacific Grove, Calif.: Brooks/Cole, 1988.

Scheingold, Stuart. *The Politics of Law and Order.* New York: Longman, 1984.

CHAPTER 11
ATTORNEYS, TRIALS, AND PUNISHMENTS

THE FRAMERS clearly understood the importance of fairness in evidence gathering; they also understood the need to ensure the integrity of the more formal stages of the criminal process. Consequently, the Bill of Rights included specific guarantees to prohibit the government from abusing prosecuted defendants. These rights are among those we hold most dear, such as the right to be represented by counsel, to be tried by an impartial jury of our peers, and to be protected against punishments that are cruel and unusual. Other guarantees, less well known but no less important, also enjoy constitutional status—the right to a speedy and public trial, to confront our accusers in open court, to have access to evidence favorable to our defense, and to have a reasonable opportunity for bail. Taken as a whole, these rights were designed to help achieve a universally valued goal—fundamentally fair criminal trials. In this chapter we discuss what the Constitution says about these important procedural guarantees and how they have evolved through Supreme Court interpretations over the years.

THE RIGHT TO COUNSEL

The Sixth Amendment states, "In all criminal prosecutions, the accused shall enjoy the right . . . to have the Assistance of Counsel for his defence." At the time these words were written, the law was relatively uncomplicated, and lawyers in the new nation were scarce. Some individuals charged with crimes sought the advice of counsel, but most handled their own cases. Still, the Framers

understood the importance of legal representation well enough to include the right to counsel in the Bill of Rights.

Today, probably no other right guaranteed to the criminally accused is more important than the right to counsel. Until recently, a lawyer representing a criminal client could do the job by appearing at trial and dealing with well-established principles of evidence and procedure. Appearing at the trial is now only a small part of what a criminal defense attorney must do. As we saw in the fifth Amendment cases reviewed in Chapter 10, the Supreme Court has emphasized repeatedly that the role of the defense attorney begins when police first interrogate a suspect. From arrest through appeal, there are critical and complicated stages during which a defendant's rights might be violated. It is the responsibility of counsel to ensure that the interests of the defendant are not jeopardized. The defense attorney, therefore, is the primary guarantee that all of the other rights of criminal due process are observed.

The provisions of the Sixth Amendment are sufficiently clear that there has been little controversy over the right of an individual to have legal representation throughout the various stages of the criminal process. Historically, however, it has always been the responsibility of the accused to secure a lawyer and to pay for the services. The most prolonged controversy over legal representation in criminal matters has centered on the rights of those who do not have the money to pay for legal assistance.

The plight of the nine "Scottsboro boys," arrested in rural Alabama in 1931 for raping two white females, spawned numerous legal actions including *Powell v. Alabama* (1932), which expanded the rights of indigents to legal representation. Samuel Leibowitz, a prominent attorney and later a judge, handled the defendants' cases after their original conviction. He is shown here conferring with his clients.

Indigents and the Right to Counsel: Foundations

As the U.S. system of justice became increasingly complex, more people retained lawyers to handle their cases. But as soon as this practice took hold, people began to complain of economic discrimination. Civil libertarians and reformers throughout the country argued that only those who could afford it were guaranteed the right to counsel; indigent defendants were denied their constitutional guarantee. Reformers claimed that the only way to eliminate this injustice was a Supreme Court decision that would force governments to appoint free counsel for poor defendants.

In *Powell v. Alabama* (1932) the Supreme Court scrutinized this claim for the first time. Justice George Sutherland's opinion for the majority does not adopt the view that states must assign counsel to indigents in *all* cases, but does he completely shut the door on such an interpretation of the Constitution?

Powell v. Alabama (The Scottsboro Boys Case)

287 U.S. 45 (1932)
laws.findlaw.com/US/287/45.html
Vote: 7 *(Brandeis, Cardozo, Hughes, Roberts, Stone,*
    Sutherland, Van Devanter)
    2 *(Butler, McReynolds)*
Opinion of the Court: Sutherland
Dissenting opinion: Butler

Riding in an open car on a freight train traveling from Chattanooga through Alabama on March 25, 1931, were nine young black men, seven young white men, and two white women.[1] During the journey, the young men got into a fight, which ended with the white youths being thrown off the train and the women claiming they had been raped by the blacks. Word of the alleged rape spread, and, when the train reached Paint Rock, a sheriff's posse arrested the blacks, who ranged in age from twelve to twenty, and jailed them in the county seat of Scottsboro. A hostile, racist crowd gathered to harass the alleged assailants, and extra security personnel were needed to prevent a lynching.

When the youths appeared at the courthouse, it was obvious they were frightened. They were young, uneducated, and away from home, with no friends or family to help them. Under Alabama law, the judge was supposed to appoint counsel to assist them because they were charged with a capital offense. Instead, he assigned all the town's members of the bar to represent the accused.[2] No single lawyer took responsibility for their defense. Moreover, the judge set the trial date for April 6, just six days after they had been indicted.

On the morning of April 6 a Tennessee lawyer named Stephen R. Roddy appeared to represent the defendants. Roddy had been sent by people interested in their plight. He had not yet prepared a case and was not familiar with Alabama law and procedure. The judge authorized Milo Moody, a local attorney, to work with Roddy. In rapid succession the nine defendants were tried in a series of four trials. Given the hostile environment in which they were tried, it should come as no surprise that eight of the nine "Scottsboro boys" were found guilty and sentenced to death.

The main question emerging from this case was this: Do indigents have the right to counsel at government expense?

1. For more on this case, see Dan T. Carter, *Scottsboro—A Tragedy of the American South* (New York: Oxford University Press, 1969).
2. Many states had laws mandating the appointment of counsel for capital crimes such as rape. In *Coker v. Georgia* (1977) the Supreme Court outlawed the use of the death penalty in rape cases.

MR. JUSTICE SUTHERLAND delivered the opinion of the Court.

It is hardly necessary to say that the right to counsel being conceded, a defendant should be afforded a fair opportunity to secure counsel of his own choice. Not only was that not done here, but such designation of counsel as was attempted was either so indefinite or so close upon the trial as to amount to a denial of effective and substantial aid in that regard. . . .

. . . [U]ntil the very morning of the trial no lawyer had been named or definitely designated to represent the defendants. Prior to that time, the trial judge had "appointed all the members of the bar" for the limited "purpose of arraigning the defendants." Whether they would represent the defendants thereafter, if no counsel appeared in their behalf, was a matter of speculation only, or, as the judge indicated, of mere anticipation on the part of the court. Such a designation, even if made for all purposes, would, in our opinion, have fallen far short of meeting, in any proper sense, a requirement for the appointment of counsel. How many lawyers were members of the bar does not appear; but, in the very nature of things, whether many or few, they would not, thus collectively named, have been given that clear appreciation of responsibility or impressed with that individual sense of duty which should and naturally would accompany the appointment of a selected member of the bar, specifically named and assigned.

That this action of the trial judge in respect of appointment of counsel was little more than an expansive gesture, imposing no substantial or definite obligation upon any one, is borne out by the fact that prior to the calling of the case for trial on April 6, a leading member of the local bar accepted employment on the side of the prosecution and actively participated in the trial. . . . This the lawyer in question, of his own accord, frankly stated to the court; and no doubt he acted with the utmost good faith. Probably other members of the bar had a like understanding. In any event, the circumstance lends emphasis to the conclusion that during perhaps the most critical period of the proceedings against these defendants, that is to say, from the time of their arraignment until the beginning of their trial, when consultation, thoroughgoing investigation and preparation were vitally important, the defendants did not have the aid of counsel in any real sense, although they were as much entitled to such aid during that period as at the trial itself. . . .

The defendants, young, ignorant, illiterate, surrounded by hostile sentiment, haled back and forth under guard of soldiers, charged with an atrocious crime regarded with especial horror in the community where they were to be tried, were thus put in peril of their lives within a few moments after counsel for the first time charged with any degree of responsibility began to represent them.

It is not enough to assume that counsel thus precipitated into the case thought there was no defense, and exercised their best judgment in proceeding to trial without preparation. Neither they nor the court could say what a prompt and thoroughgoing investigation might disclose as to the facts. No attempt was made to investigate. No opportunity to do so was given. . . .

. . . [W]e think the failure of the trial court to give them reasonable time and opportunity to secure counsel was a clear denial of due process.

But passing that, and assuming their inability, even if opportunity had been given, to employ counsel, as the trial court evidently did assume, we are of opinion that, under the circumstances just stated, the necessity of counsel was so vital and imperative that the failure of the trial court to make an effective appointment of counsel was likewise a denial of due process within the meaning of the Fourteenth Amendment. Whether this would be so in other criminal prosecutions, or under other circumstances, we need not determine. All that is necessary now to decide, as we do decide, is that in a capital case, where the defendant is unable to employ counsel, and is incapable adequately of making his own defense because of ignorance, feeblemindedness, illiteracy, or the like, it is the duty of the court, whether requested or not, to assign counsel for him as a necessary requisite of due process of law; and that duty is not discharged by an assignment at such a time or under such circumstances as to preclude the giving of effective aid in the preparation and trial of the case. To hold otherwise would be to ignore the fundamental postulate, already adverted to, "that there are certain immutable principles of justice which inhere in the very idea of free government which no member of the Union may disregard." In a case such as this, whatever may be the rule in other cases, the right to have counsel appointed, when necessary, is a logical corollary from the constitutional right to be heard by counsel. . . .

Judgments reversed

MR. JUSTICE BUTLER, dissenting.

The Court . . . grounds its opinion and judgment upon a single assertion of fact. It is that petitioners "were denied the right of counsel, with the accustomed incidents of consultation and opportunity of preparation for trial." If that is true, they were denied due process of law and are entitled to have the judgments against them reversed.

But no such denial is shown by the record.

Nine defendants . . . were accused in one indictment. . . . Instead of trying them *en masse,* the State gave four trials and so lessened the danger of mistake and injustice that inevitably attends an attempt in a single trial to ascertain the guilt or innocence of many accused. . . .

. . . It must be inferred from the record that Mr. Roddy at all times was in touch with the defendants and the people who procured him to act for them. Mr. Moody and others of the local bar also acted for defendants at the time of the first arraignment, and . . . thereafter proceeded in the discharge of their duty, including conferences with the defendants. There is not the slightest ground to suppose that Roddy or Moody were by fear or in any manner restrained from full performance of their duties. Indeed, it clearly appears that the State, by proper and adequate show of its purpose and power to preserve order, furnished adequate protection to them and the defendants.

When the first case was called for trial, defendants' attorneys had already prepared, and then submitted, a motion for change of venue, together with supporting papers. They were ready to, and did at once, introduce testimony of witnesses to sustain that demand. . . .

If there had been any lack of opportunity for preparation, trial counsel would have applied to the court for postponement. No such application was made. There was no suggestion, at the trial or in the motion for a new trial which they made, that Mr. Roddy or Mr. Moody was denied such opportunity, or that they were not, in fact, fully prepared. The amended motion for new trial, by counsel who succeeded them, contains the first suggestion that defendants were denied counsel or opportunity to prepare for trial. But neither Mr. Roddy nor Mr. Moody has given any support to that claim. Their silence requires a finding that the claim is groundless, for if it had any merit they would be bound to support it. And no one has come to suggest any lack of zeal or good faith on their part.

If correct, the ruling that the failure of the trial court to give petitioners time and opportunity to secure counsel was denial of due process is enough, and with this the opinion should end. But the Court goes on to declare that "the failure of the trial court to make an effective appointment of counsel was likewise a denial of due process within the meaning of the Fourteenth Amendment." This is an extension of federal authority into a field hitherto occupied exclusively by the several States. Nothing before the Court calls for a consideration of the point. It was not suggested below, and petitioners do not ask for its decision here. The Court, without being called upon to consider it, adjudges without a hearing an important constitutional question concerning criminal procedure in state courts. . . .

The record wholly fails to reveal that petitioners have been deprived of any right guaranteed by the Federal Constitution, and I am of opinion that the judgment should be affirmed.

MR. JUSTICE MCREYNOLDS concurs in this opinion.

The Court declined to decide if the Sixth Amendment guarantees the right to counsel for every defendant. But, writing for the majority, Justice Sutherland recognized that cases involving unusual situations (capital offenses, intense public pressure, or young, uneducated, and inexperienced defendants) would necessitate a lawyer's participation to secure fundamental fairness for defendants. Although the Court in *Powell* made no sweeping statements about the Sixth Amendment, it mandated for the first time the appointment of counsel.

Given the pervasive racism in southern criminal justice systems, the extent to which this ruling helped the defendants in *Powell* may have been negligible *(see Box 11-1)*. But, just six years after *Powell*, the Court went one step further. In *Johnson v. Zerbst* it ruled that indigent defendants involved in federal criminal prosecutions must be represented by counsel. Although *Johnson* was a major ruling, like *Powell*, its scope was limited. As we saw with the line of cases leading to the universal application of the exclusionary rule, decisions applying only to the fed-

eral government affect an insignificant number of defendants because most prosecutions occur in the states. Criminal defense attorneys, therefore, pushed the Court to apply *Johnson* to the states in the same way they argued in *Wolf v. Colorado* (1949) that *Weeks v. United States* (1914), which established the exclusionary rule, ought to govern state investigations. But just as the *Wolf* attempt failed to convince a majority of the Court to apply certain Fourth Amendment guarantees to the states, so too did *Betts v. Brady* (1942), the first attempt after *Johnson*.

Indicted for robbery in Maryland, Betts—a poor, uneducated, but literate, white man—wanted an attorney at government expense. Like many states, Maryland provided indigents with counsel only in rape and murder cases. Betts conducted his own defense and was convicted. On appeal he asked the Supreme Court to apply *Johnson* to the states, thereby incorporating the Sixth Amendment guarantee. The Court refused, 6–3. Writing for the majority, Justice Owen Roberts claimed that the Framers never intended that the right to counsel be defined as a fundamental guarantee, just that it apply to extreme situations as in *Powell*. When Roberts compared Betts's claim to that of the Scottsboro defendants, he found that it came up short because Betts was not helpless or illiterate, and he was in no danger of the death penalty for his offense.

Justice Black dissented. He wrote:

Denial to the poor of the request for counsel in proceedings based on charges of serious crime has been long regarded as shocking to the "universal sense of justice" throughout this country. . . . Most . . . states have shown their agreement [and] assure that no man shall be deprived of counsel merely because of his poverty. Any other practice seems to me to defeat the promise of our democratic society to provide equal justice under law.

Twenty-one years later, a Court more sympathetic to the rights of the criminally accused reevaluated the wisdom of *Betts v. Brady*. As you read the famous case of *Gideon v. Wainwright*, think about these questions: Why did the Court extend the right to government-provided attorneys to indigents accused of state crimes? Did something distinguish *Gideon* from *Betts*, or did other factors come into play?

BOX 11-1   AFTERMATH . . . THE SCOTTSBORO BOYS

THEIR CONVICTIONS were reversed by the Supreme Court in 1932, but the subsequent lives of the nine defendants, known as the "Scottsboro Boys," were filled with tragedy and additional criminal accusations. Even though one of the alleged rape victims later admitted that she had not been raped, the defendants were convicted following their second trial. This time the convictions were overturned by the Supreme Court in *Norris v. Alabama* (1935) because of racial discrimination in jury selection. Between 1936 and 1937, additional retrials took place leading to the conviction of four of the original defendants, with sentences ranging from seventy-five years in prison to death.

In 1937 the rape charges were dropped against Olen Montgomery, Willie Roberson, and Eugene Williams. They subsequently fell into obscurity.

Charges against Roy Wright also were dismissed. In 1959 Wright stabbed his wife to death and then took his own life.

Rape charges against Ozie Powell were dropped. He was later convicted of shooting a law enforcement officer in the head. He received a long prison sentence, but was paroled in 1946.

Charlie Weems, Andrew Wright, Haywood Patterson, and Clarence Norris were convicted of the rape charges on retrial. Weems and Patterson were sentenced to seventy-five years in prison, Wright to a term of ninety-nine years, and Norris to death.

Three of the convicted men were subsequently released from prison, and one escaped. Weems was paroled in 1943. Wright was paroled in 1944, but was returned to prison three times for parole violations. In 1951 Wright was accused of raping a thirteen-year-old girl, but was acquitted and released. Patterson escaped from prison and fled to Michigan. In 1951 he was convicted of manslaughter and sentenced to prison. Shortly thereafter he died of lung cancer.

Norris had his death sentence commuted to life in prison in 1938. He was paroled in 1944, but was sent back to prison for leaving the state in violation of his parole agreement. Norris was paroled again in 1946, and almost immediately fled the state in violation of parole a second time. He lived undercover in New York City for many years. In 1976 the attorney general of Alabama acknowledged that subsequent studies of the case had concluded that Norris was not guilty of the original rape charge, and Gov. George Wallace pardoned him. A bill to compensate Norris for wrongful conviction was defeated in the Alabama legislature. Norris died in 1989 at the age of seventy-six.

SOURCE: James A. Inciardi, *Criminal Justice*, 4th ed. (Fort Worth: Harcourt Brace Jovanovich, 1993), 372.

Gideon v. Wainwright

372 U.S. 335 (1963)

laws.findlaw.com/US/372/335.html

Vote: 9 (Black, Brennan, Clark, Douglas, Goldberg, Harlan,
    Stewart, Warren, White)

    0

Opinion of the Court: Black
Concurring opinions: Clark, Douglas, Harlan

Florida officials charged Clarence Earl Gideon with breaking and entering a poolroom.[3] The trial court refused to appoint counsel for him because Florida did not provide free lawyers to those charged with anything less than a capital offense. Gideon, like Betts, a poor, uneducated white man, tried to defend himself, but failed. After studying the law in the prison library and attempting a number of lower court actions, Gideon filed a petition for a writ of certiorari with the U.S. Supreme Court.[4] The petition was handwritten on prison notepaper, but the justices granted it a review.

Because Gideon was without counsel, the Court appointed Abe Fortas, a well-known attorney (and future

---

3. For oral arguments in this case, navigate to: *oyez.nwu.edu.*

4. See Anthony Lewis, *Gideon's Trumpet* (New York: Vintage Books, 1964).

DIVISION OF CORRECTIONS
CORRESPONDENCE REGULATIONS

MAIL WILL NOT BE DELIVERED WHICH DOES NOT CONFORM WITH THESE RULES

No. 1 -- Only 2 letters each week, not to exceed 2 sheets letter-size 8 1/2 x 11" and written *on one side only,* and if ruled paper, do not write between lines. *Your complete name* must be signed at the close of your letter. *Clippings, stamps, letters* from other people, *stationery* or *cash must not be enclosed* in your letters.
No. 2 -- All *letters* must be addressed in the *complete prison name* of the inmate. *Cell number,* where applicable, and *prison number* must be placed in lower left corner of envelope, with your complete name and address in the upper left corner.
No. 3 -- *Do not send any packages without a Package Permit.* Unauthorized *packages* will be destroyed.
No. 4 -- *Letters* must be written in English only.
No. 5 -- *Books, magazines, pamphlets,* and *newspapers* of reputable character will be delivered *only if* mailed direct from the publisher.
No. 6 -- *Money* must be sent in the form of *Postal Money Orders* only, in the inmate's complete prison name and prison number.

INSTITUTION _____   CELL NUMBER _____

NAME _____   NUMBER _____

In The Supreme Court of The United States
Washington D.C.
clarence Earl Gideon
*   Petitioner-*   *Petition for a writ*
vs.   *of Certiorari Directed*
H.G. Cochran, Jr, as   to The Supreme Court
Director, Divisions   State of Florida.
of corrections State
of Florida.   No. 890 Misc.
                            OCT. TERM 1961
To: The Honorable Earl Warren, Chief   U.S. Supreme Court
Justice of the United States
*   Comes now The petitioner, Clarence*
Earl Gideon, a citizen of The United States
of America, in proper person, and appearing
as his own counsel. Who petitions this
Honorable Court for a Writ of Certiorari
directed to The Supreme Court of The State
of Florida. To review the order and Judge-
ment of the court below denying The
petitioner a writ of Habeus Corpus.
*   Petitioner submits That The Supreme*
Court of The United States has The authority
and jurisdiction to review The final Judge-
ment of The Supreme Court of The State
of Florida The highest court of The State
Under sec. 344 (B) Title 28 U.S.C.A. and
Because The "Due process clause" of the

(left) Clarence Earl Gideon's handwritten petition to the Supreme Court. The Court ruled unanimously that indigent defendants must be provided counsel in state trials.

(above) Clarence Earl Gideon.

Supreme Court justice), to represent him. Twenty-two states filed an amicus curiae brief, which was written by Walter Mondale (then the attorney general of Minnesota and later a senator and U.S. vice president), supporting Gideon's argument. Clarence Gideon went from being a poor convict facing a lonely court battle to a man represented by some of the country's finest legal minds.

MR. JUSTICE BLACK delivered the opinion of the Court.

Since 1942, when *Betts v. Brady* was decided by a divided Court, the problem of a defendant's federal constitutional

right to counsel in a state court has been a continuing source of controversy and litigation in both state and federal courts. To give this problem another review here, we granted certiorari. Since Gideon was proceeding *in forma pauperis,* we appointed counsel to represent him and requested both sides to discuss in their briefs and oral arguments the following: "Should this Court's holding in *Betts v. Brady* be reconsidered?"

The facts upon which Betts claimed that he had been unconstitutionally denied the right to have counsel appointed to assist him are strikingly like the facts upon which Gideon here bases his federal constitutional claim. . . . Since the facts and circumstances of the two cases are so nearly indistinguishable, we think the *Betts v. Brady* holding if left standing would require us to reject Gideon's claim that the Constitution guarantees him the assistance of counsel. Upon full reconsideration we conclude that *Betts v. Brady* should be overruled.

The Sixth Amendment provides, "In all criminal prosecutions, the accused shall enjoy the right . . . to have the Assistance of Counsel for his defence." We have construed this to mean that in federal courts counsel must be provided for defendants unable to employ counsel unless the right is competently and intelligently waived. Betts argued that this right is extended to indigent defendants in state courts by the Fourteenth Amendment. In response the Court stated that, while the Sixth Amendment laid down "no rule for the conduct of the states, the question recurs whether the constraint laid by the amendment upon the national courts expresses a rule so fundamental and essential to a fair trial, and so, to due process of law, that it is made obligatory upon the states by the Fourteenth Amendment." In order to decide whether the Sixth Amendment's guarantee of counsel is of this fundamental nature, the Court in *Betts* set out and considered "[r]elevant data on the subject . . . afforded by constitutional and statutory provisions subsisting in the colonies and the states prior to the inclusion of the Bill of Rights in the national Constitution, and in the constitutional, legislative, and judicial history of the states to the present date." On the basis of this historical data the Court concluded that "appointment of counsel is not a fundamental right, essential to a fair trial.". . .

We accept *Betts v. Brady*'s assumption, based as it was on our prior cases, that a provision of the Bill of Rights which is "fundamental and essential to a fair trial" is made obligatory upon the States by the Fourteenth Amendment. We think the Court in *Betts* was wrong, however, in concluding that the Sixth Amendment's guarantee of counsel is not one of these fundamental rights. Ten years before *Betts v. Brady*, this Court, after full consideration of all the historical data examined in *Betts*, had unequivocally declared that "the right to the aid of counsel is of this fundamental character." *Powell v. Alabama* (1932). While the Court at the close of its *Powell* opinion did by its language, as this Court frequently does, limit its holding to the particular facts and circumstances of that case, its conclusions about the fundamental nature of the right to counsel are unmistakable. Several

years later, in 1936, the Court reemphasized what it had said about the fundamental nature of the right to counsel in this language:

"We concluded that certain fundamental rights, safeguarded by the first eight amendments against federal action, were also safeguarded against state action by the due process of law clause of the Fourteenth Amendment, and among them the fundamental right of the accused to the aid of counsel in a criminal prosecution." *Grosjean v. American Press Co.* (1936). . . .

In light of these and many other prior decisions of the Court, it is not surprising that the *Betts* Court, when faced with the contention that "one charged with crime, who is unable to obtain counsel, must be furnished counsel by the state," conceded that "[e]xpressions in the opinions of this court lend color to the argument. . . ." The fact is that in deciding as it did—that "appointment of counsel is not a fundamental right, essential to a fair trial"—the Court in *Betts v. Brady* made an abrupt break with its own well-considered precedents. In returning to these old precedents, sounder we believe than the new, we but restore constitutional principles established to achieve a fair system of justice. Not only these precedents but also reason and reflection require us to recognize that in our adversary system of criminal justice, any person haled into court, who is too poor to hire a lawyer, cannot be assured a fair trial unless counsel is provided for him. This seems to us to be an obvious truth. Governments, both state and federal, quite properly spend vast sums of money to establish machinery to try defendants accused of crime. Lawyers to prosecute are everywhere deemed essential to protect the public's interest in an orderly society. Similarly, there are few defendants charged with crime, few indeed, who fail to hire the best lawyers they can get to prepare and present their defenses. That government hires lawyers to prosecute and defendants who have the money hire lawyers to defend are the strongest indications of the widespread belief that lawyers in criminal courts are necessities, not luxuries. The right of one charged with crime to counsel may not be deemed fundamental and essential to fair trials in some countries, but it is in ours. From the very beginning, our state and national constitutions and laws have laid great emphasis on procedural and substantive safeguards designed to assure fair trials before impartial tribunals in which every defendant stands equal before the law. This noble ideal cannot be realized if the poor man charged with crime has to face his accusers without a lawyer to assist him. A defendant's need for a lawyer is nowhere better stated than in the moving words of Mr. Justice Sutherland in *Powell v. Alabama:*

"The right to be heard would be, in many cases, of little avail if it did not comprehend the right to be heard by counsel. Even the intelligent and educated layman has small and sometimes no skill in the science of law. If charged with crime, he is incapable, generally, of determining for himself whether the indictment is good or bad. He is unfamiliar with the rules of evidence. Left without the aid of counsel he may be put on trial without a proper charge, and convicted upon incompetent evidence, or evidence irrelevant to the issue or otherwise inadmissible. He lacks both the skill and knowledge adequately to prepare his defense, even though he have a perfect one. He requires the guiding hand of counsel at every step in the proceedings against him. Without it, though he be not guilty, he faces the danger of conviction because he does not know how to establish his innocence."

The Court in *Betts v. Brady* departed from the sound wisdom upon which the Court's holding in *Powell v. Alabama* rested. Florida, supported by two other States, has asked that *Betts v. Brady* be left intact. Twenty-two States, as friends of the Court, argue that *Betts* was "an anachronism when handed down" and that it should now be overruled. We agree. The judgment is reversed and the cause is remanded to the Supreme Court of Florida for further action not inconsistent with this opinion.

Reversed.

MR. JUSTICE HARLAN, concurring.

I agree that *Betts v. Brady* should be overruled, but consider it entitled to a more respectful burial than has been accorded. . . .

I cannot subscribe to the view that *Betts v. Brady* represented "an abrupt break with its own well-considered precedents." In 1932, in *Powell v. Alabama,* a capital case, this Court declared that under the particular facts there presented—"the ignorance and illiteracy of the defendants, their youth, the circumstances of public hostility . . . and above all that they stood in deadly peril of their lives"—the state court had a duty to assign counsel for the trial as a necessary requisite of due process of law. It is evident that these limiting facts were not added to the opinion as an afterthought; they were repeatedly emphasized and were clearly regarded as important to the result.

Thus when this Court, a decade later, decided *Betts v. Brady,* it did no more than to admit of the possible existence of special circumstances in noncapital as well as capital trials, while at the same time insisting that such circumstances be shown in order to establish a denial of due process. . . . The declaration that the right to appointed counsel in state prosecutions, as established in *Powell v. Alabama,* was not limited to capital cases was in truth not a departure from, but an extension of, existing precedent.

The principles declared in *Powell* and in *Betts,* however, have had a troubled journey throughout the years. . . .

In noncapital cases, the "special circumstances" rule has continued to exist in form while its substance has been substantially and steadily eroded. . . . The Court has come to recognize, in other words, that the mere existence of a serious criminal charge constituted in itself special circumstances requiring the services of counsel at trial. In truth the *Betts v. Brady* rule is no longer a reality. . . .

The special circumstances rule has been formally abandoned in capital cases, and the time has now come when it should be similarly abandoned in noncapital cases, at least as to offenses which, as the one involved here, carry the possibility of a substantial prison sentence. (Whether the rule should extend to *all* criminal cases need not now be decided.) This indeed does no more than to make explicit something that has long since been foreshadowed in our decisions. . . .

On these premises I join in the judgment of the Court.

Beyond its legal significance, *Gideon* is interesting for several reasons. First, the case provides another example of the Warren Court's revolution in criminal rights. The Court of 1963 took a carbon copy of *Betts* and came up with a radically different solution. *Gideon* completed a process of constitutional evolution in which the Court first applied a rule of law to the federal government, refused to extend that rule to the states, and then reversed its position and brought the states under the rule's applicability. As indicated in Table 11-1, this historical pattern is the same as in the battle over applicability of the exclusionary rule, considered in Chapter 10.

Second, *Gideon* is a classic example of the importance of dissents. In considering cases applying the Bill of

TABLE 11-1 Comparison of the Development of the Exclusionary Rule and the Right to Counsel for Indigents

Doctrine	Exclusionary Rule	Right to Counsel for Indigents
Establishment of right for federal prosecutions	*Weeks v. United States* (1918)	*Johnson v. Zerbst* (1938)
Refusal to apply to states	*Wolf v. Colorado* (1949)	*Betts v. Brady* (1942)
Application to states	*Mapp v. Ohio* (1961)	*Gideon v. Wainwright* (1963)

Rights to the states, we saw how Justice Harlan's minority views in the incorporation cases were adopted by later justices. Here, however, we see an even more unusual event: Justice Black, who wrote the dissenting opinion in *Betts,* wrote the majority opinion in *Gideon.*

Finally, *Gideon v. Wainwright* has had a tremendous impact on the U.S. criminal justice system, in which 75 percent of the criminally accused are indigent. To comply with the Court's ruling, states had to alter their defender systems, creating mechanisms to provide lawyers for the accused. Many localities have created a public defender office that mirrors the prosecuting attorney's office. In other words, the state hires lawyers to represent indigents. Other areas use court-appointed attorney systems in which judges assign members of the legal community to represent the underprivileged.

Despite its importance, *Gideon* left several questions unanswered. What crimes does the ruling cover? Does it apply only to felonies, as in Gideon's case, or to lesser crimes as well? Through what stages in the criminal system does *Gideon* apply? That is, when does the right to counsel end? After trial? After the first appeal?

For the most part, these fallout questions were left to the Burger Court to answer. As you read further, think again about whether the Burger Court followed the Warren Court's mandate or if it tried to blunt the impact of the Warren era decisions.

Applying Gideon: *The Nature of the Offense*

Whether *Gideon* should be applied to offenses less serious than a breaking and entering charge was addressed in *Argersinger v. Hamlin* (1972), an appeal from a man sentenced to serve ninety days in jail for weapons violations. Writing for the majority, Justice Douglas developed a rule known as the loss of liberty rule: whoever is deprived of liberty even for one day is entitled to an attorney. By articulating such a standard, the Court rejected the argument of several states (including Florida once again) that only indigents facing jail sentences of more than six months are entitled to a lawyer at public expense.

Argersinger's loss of liberty standard provided an important answer to the question of which indigent defendants are eligible for counsel at government expense under the *Gideon* ruling. If the crime carries a sentence of imprisonment for even one day, the defendant is entitled to representation at state expense. If the crime is punishable by only a fine or other nonimprisonment penalty, the indigent defendant does not have the right to a government-provided attorney. What remained unanswered was how *Gideon* might apply to suspects charged with crimes punishable by imprisonment *or* a lesser penalty.[5]

The justices settled this final issue in *Scott v. Illinois* (1979). The defendant, Aubrey Scott, was charged with the crime of theft, punishable by a maximum sentence of one year in prison and/or a $500 fine. Prior to the trial, the prosecutor announced that he had no intention of asking for a sentence of imprisonment if Scott were convicted. Because the defendant faced no real threat of imprisonment, the trial court judge ruled that he had no

5. The justices were aware that this argument would likely arise. In *Argersinger* Justice Powell's concurring opinion pressed the point that Douglas's "loss of liberty" analysis failed to consider the serious consequences resulting from some misdemeanor convictions even if a jail sentence is not imposed.

right under *Gideon* to an attorney at state expense. Scott was tried, convicted, and fined $50. He appealed, claiming that he should have had a lawyer.

The Supreme Court ruled in favor of the state, holding that actual imprisonment, not the threat of such a penalty, was the relevant factor in applying *Argersinger's* loss of liberty rule. Put another way, regardless of the range of penalties available to a judge, indigent criminal defendants may not be sentenced to incarceration unless they have been offered legal representation at government expense.

Gideon *and the Appellate Stage*

Justice Black's opinion in *Gideon* said that an indigent accused of a criminal offense must be represented by counsel at trial. What Black did not address was whether that right extended through the appellate process. And if so, did such a right apply only to obligatory appeals (usually the first appeal after a trial) or also to discretionary appeals (subsequent appeals that the appellate court may or may not agree to hear)?

In *Douglas v. California* (1963) the Court answered part of this question, holding that the right indeed extended through the first obligatory appeal. Writing for the Court, Justice Douglas proclaimed:

[W]here the merits of *the one and only appeal* an indigent has as of right are decided without benefit of counsel, we think an unconstitutional line has been drawn between rich and poor. . . . There is lacking that equality demanded by the Fourteenth Amendment where the rich man, who appeals as of right, enjoys the benefit of the counsel's examination into the record, research of the law, and marshaling of arguments on his behalf, while the indigent . . . is forced to shift for himself.

Justice Douglas's opinion, however, left open the question of whether the Sixth Amendment right extends to the discretionary review stages, an issue the Burger Court took up in *Ross v. Moffitt* (1974).

Moffitt involved two separate cases from two counties in North Carolina for forgery offenses. In both, Moffitt, an indigent, pleaded not guilty, received court-appointed counsel, and was convicted. An intermediate state appellate court affirmed both convictions. Moffitt then sought review in the North Carolina Supreme Court and asked that his attorney represent him at government expense. The court denied this request. Moffitt also sought the same objective in the federal courts. Here, he was more successful: the Fourth Circuit Court of Appeals ordered the state to appoint him counsel to prepare an appeal to the U.S. Supreme Court. By accepting this case, the Court could address the following question for both state and federal courts: Does *Douglas v. California* require the appointment of counsel at discretionary review stages?

Writing for the Court, Justice Rehnquist concluded that it did not. He stated:

We do not believe . . . that a defendant in respondent's circumstances is denied meaningful access to the North Carolina Supreme Court simply because the State does not appoint counsel to aid him in seeking review. At that stage he will have, at the very least, a transcript or other record of the trial proceedings, a brief on his behalf in the Court of Appeals setting forth his error, and in many cases an opinion by the court of appeals disposing of his case. . . .

We do not mean by this opinion to in any way discourage those States which have, as a matter of legislative choice, made counsel available . . . at all stages of judicial review. . . . Our reading [of the Constitution] leaves these choices to the State.

The justices of the Burger Court failed to overrule revolutionary Warren Court decisions, but, as *Ross v. Moffitt* shows, they shut the door on further expansions of rights.

Money, Representation, and Justice

The purpose of the *Gideon* line of decisions was to reduce the disparity between rich and poor in the criminal process. Prior to *Gideon*, indigent defendants had no constitutional right to legal representation. If the state did not provide legal aid, the accused often was forced to rely on self-representation. For Justice Black and others this system was indefensible because the quality of justice depended on the financial resources of the defendant. The government employed a prosecuting attorney whose job it was to obtain a conviction, and the indigent accused was left defenseless. *Gideon* changed that imbalance. After its implementation, the poor were represented in court. They had the services of an attorney to prepare a defense and to ensure that their procedural rights were fully observed.

The impact of *Gideon* was to bring a minimum level of legal representation to indigents. Today, most poor people accused of crimes are represented by attorneys appointed by the trial court judge or by public defenders. The services provided these defendants are certainly adequate in most cases, but *Gideon* cannot be said to have totally reduced the gap between rich and poor. Those individuals with substantial resources are still able to hire the very best lawyers, investigators, and experts to advance a defense against criminal charges.

Many people cite the 1994–1995 O. J. Simpson criminal trial as a case in point. Simpson, an actor and former professional football star, was accused of killing his ex-wife, Nicole Brown, and Ronald Goldman, an acquaintance of hers. The trial proceedings were televised nationwide and held the country's attention for months. Because Simpson was wealthy, he was able to assemble a group of defense lawyers more formidable perhaps than in any previous criminal trial. Dubbed the Dream Team, it included prominent criminal lawyers Johnnie Cochran, F. Lee Bailey, Robert Shapiro, Alan Dershowitz, and Barry Scheck. After months of legal maneuvering, the Simpson defense team was successful at combating the prosecution's evidence and persuading the jury to return a not guilty verdict. To many commentators, money made the difference. An indigent facing similar charges and evidence would have been represented by a single public defender, and most experts agree that someone in that situation probably would be convicted.

Gideon, then, is a decision of extraordinary importance. It brought legal representation to a class of defendants who previously did not enjoy the services of an attorney. Yet, as significant as *Gideon* is, financial resources remain an important influence on how someone fares when charged with a crime.

THE PRETRIAL PERIOD AND THE RIGHT TO BAIL

The defense attorney must protect the accused's rights during every stage of the criminal process, starting with interrogation and investigation and the formal stages of the pretrial period. If already retained or appointed, counsel represents the accused at the initial appearance and is present at the preliminary hearing and arraignment. The defense attorney negotiates with the prosecuting attorney over the exact charges to be brought. Pretrial motions may be made for judicial rulings on questions of evidence and procedure. The defense attorney also begins preparing the case to be presented in court should the defendant go to trial.

Of all the pretrial stages, the setting of bail is perhaps the most important to the defendant. Bail is a monetary guarantee ensuring that the accused will show up for the trial. Defendants who are not eligible for bail and those who cannot raise the money must wait in jail until their trial date. Defendants who can "make bail" are released, pending their trial.

How does a judge decide who is eligible for release? How is the bail amount determined? Individuals charged with misdemeanors are automatically eligible for bail, and the amount is usually set according to a specific fee schedule. For those charged with felonies, a judge sets bail on a case-by-case basis. Among the factors the judge considers are the seriousness of the offense, the trustworthiness of the individual, and the Eighth Amendment's prohibition against excessive bail. Until 1987 the Supreme Court had not decided a major dispute over what factors a judge may appropriately consider in making bail determinations; that year *United States v. Salerno* challenged the Bail Reform Act of 1984.[6]

United States v. Salerno

481 U.S. 739 (1987)
laws.findlaw.com/US/481/739.html
Vote: 6 (Blackmun, O'Connor, Powell, Rehnquist, Scalia, White)
    3 (Brennan, Marshall, Stevens)
Opinion of the Court: Rehnquist
Dissenting opinions: Marshall, Stevens

In 1986 the Justice Department brought racketeering charges against Anthony Salerno, the boss of the Genovese crime family. At Salerno's bail hearing, U.S. attor-

6. For oral arguments in this case, navigate to: *oyez.nwu.edu.*

neys urged the judge to deny bail on the grounds that the accused would continue to engage in criminal activity if released. Before 1984 judges probably would not have considered such a factor in their decision-making processes because bail had always been used only to ensure a defendant's presence at trial. But in 1984 Congress passed the Bail Reform Act, authorizing judges to deny bail to defendants to "assure . . . the safety of any other person and the community." After federal prosecutors presented evidence suggesting that Salerno would commit murder if let out, the judge denied bail. Salerno successfully appealed to the U.S. court of appeals, which declared the 1984 act unconstitutional. The federal government then asked the Supreme Court to reverse.

CHIEF JUSTICE REHNQUIST delivered the opinion of the Court.

The Bail Reform Act of 1984 allows a federal court to detain an arrestee pending trial if the government demonstrates by clear and convincing evidence after an adversary hearing that no release conditions "will reasonably assure . . . the safety of any other person and the community." The United States Court of Appeals for the Second Circuit struck down this provision of the Act as facially unconstitutional, because, in that court's words, this type of pretrial detention violates "substantive due process." We granted certiorari because of a conflict among the Courts of Appeals regarding the validity of the Act. We hold that, as against the facial attack mounted by these respondents, the Act fully comports with constitutional requirements. We therefore reverse.

Responding to "the alarming problem of crimes committed by persons on release," Congress formulated the Bail Reform Act of 1984 as the solution to the bail crisis in the federal courts. The Act represents the National Legislature's considered response to numerous perceived deficiencies in the federal bail process. By providing for sweeping changes in both the way federal courts consider bail applications and the circumstances under which bail is granted, Congress hoped to "give the courts adequate authority to make release decisions that give appropriate recognition to the danger a person may pose to others if released.". . .

A facial challenge to a legislative Act is, of course, the most difficult challenge to mount successfully, since the challenger must establish that no set of circumstances exists

under which the Act would be valid. . . . We think respondents have failed to shoulder their heavy burden to demonstrate that the Act is "facially" unconstitutional.

Respondents present two grounds for invalidating the Bail Reform Act's provisions permitting pretrial detention on the basis of future dangerousness. First, they rely upon the Court of Appeals' conclusion that the Act exceeds the limitations placed upon the Federal Government by the Due Process Clause of the Fifth Amendment. Second, they contend that the Act contravenes the Eighth Amendment's proscription against excessive bail. We treat these contentions in turn.

The Due Process Clause of the Fifth Amendment provides that "No person shall . . . be deprived of life, liberty, or property, without due process of law. . . ." This Court has held that the Due Process Clause protects individuals against two types of government action. So-called "substantive due process" prevents the government from engaging in conduct that "shocks the conscience" or interferes with rights "implicit in the concept of ordered liberty." When government action depriving a person of life, liberty, or property survives substantive due process scrutiny, it must still be implemented in a fair manner. This requirement has traditionally been referred to as "procedural" due process.

Respondents first argue that the Act violates substantive due process because the pretrial detention it authorizes constitutes impermissible punishment before trial. The Government, however, has never argued that pretrial detention could be upheld if it were "punishment." The Court of Appeals assumed that pretrial detention under the Bail Reform Act is regulatory, not penal, and we agree that it is.

As an initial matter, the mere fact that a person is detained does not inexorably lead to the conclusion that the government has imposed punishment. To determine whether a restriction on liberty constitutes impermissible punishment or permissible regulation, we first look to legislative intent. Unless Congress expressly intended to impose punitive restrictions, the punitive/regulatory distinction turns on "'whether an alternative purpose to which the restriction may rationally be connected is assignable for it, and whether it appears excessive in relation to the alternative purpose assigned [to it].'"

We conclude that the detention imposed by the Act falls on the regulatory side of the dichotomy. The legislative history of the Bail Reform Act clearly indicates that Congress did not formulate the pretrial detention provisions as punishment for dangerous individuals. Congress instead perceived pretrial detention as a potential solution to a pressing societal problem. There is no doubt that preventing danger to the community is a legitimate regulatory goal.

Nor are the incidents of pretrial detention excessive in relation to the regulatory goal Congress sought to achieve. The Bail Reform Act carefully limits the circumstances under which detention may be sought to the most serious of crimes. The arrestee is entitled to a prompt detention hearing, and the maximum length of pretrial detention is limited by the stringent time limitations of the Speedy Trial Act. Moreover, . . . the conditions of confinement envisioned by the Act "appear to reflect the regulatory purposes relied upon by the" government. . . . We conclude, therefore, that the pretrial detention contemplated by the Bail Reform Act is regulatory in nature, and does not constitute punishment before trial in violation of the Due Process Clause.

The Court of Appeals nevertheless concluded that "the Due Process Clause prohibits pretrial detention on the ground of danger to the community as a regulatory measure, without regard to the duration of the detention." Respondents characterize the Due Process Clause as erecting an impenetrable "wall" in this area that "no governmental interest—rational, important, compelling or otherwise— may surmount."

We do not think the Clause lays down any such categorical imperative. We have repeatedly held that the government's regulatory interest in community safety can, in appropriate circumstances, outweigh an individual's liberty interest. For example, in times of war or insurrection, when society's interest is at its peak, the government may detain individuals whom the government believes to be dangerous. Even outside the exigencies of war, we have found that sufficiently compelling governmental interests can justify detention of dangerous persons. Thus, we have found no absolute constitutional barrier to detention of potentially dangerous resident aliens pending deportation proceedings. We have also held that the government may detain mentally unstable individuals who present a danger to the public and dangerous defendants who become incompetent to stand trial. We have approved of post-arrest regulatory detention of juveniles when they present a continuing danger to the community. . . .

Respondents characterize all of these cases as exceptions to the "general rule" of substantive due process that the government may not detain a person prior to a judgment of guilt in a criminal trial. Such a "general rule" may freely be conceded, but we think that these cases show a sufficient number of exceptions to the rule that the congressional action challenged here can hardly be characterized as totally novel. Given the well-established authority of the government, in special circumstances, to restrain individuals' liberty prior to or even without criminal trial and conviction, we think that the present statute providing for pretrial detention on the basis of dangerousness must be evaluated in precisely the same manner that we evaluated the laws in the cases discussed above.

The government's interest in preventing crime by arrestees is both legitimate and compelling. . . . The Bail Reform Act . . . narrowly focuses on a particularly acute problem in which the government interests are overwhelming. The Act operates only on individuals who have been arrested for a specific category of extremely serious offenses. Congress specifically found that these individuals are far more likely to be responsible for dangerous acts in the community after arrest. . . .

On the other side of the scale, of course, is the individual's strong interest in liberty. We do not minimize the importance and fundamental nature of this right. But, as our cases hold, this right may, in circumstances where the government's interest is sufficiently weighty, be subordinated to the greater needs of society. We think that Congress' careful delineation of the circumstances under which detention will be permitted satisfies this standard. When the government proves by clear and convincing evidence that an arrestee presents an identified and articulable threat to an individual or the community, we believe that, consistent with the Due Process Clause, a court may disable the arrestee from executing that threat. Under these circumstances, we cannot categorically state that pretrial detention "offends some principle of justice so rooted in the traditions and conscience of our people as to be ranked as fundamental.". . .

Respondents also contend that the Bail Reform Act violates the Excessive Bail Clause of the Eighth Amendment. The Court of Appeals did not address this issue because it found that the Act violates the Due Process Clause. We think that the Act survives a challenge founded upon the Eighth Amendment.

The Eighth Amendment addresses pretrial release by providing merely that "Excessive bail shall not be required." This Clause, of course, says nothing about whether bail shall be available at all. Respondents nevertheless contend that this Clause grants them a right to bail calculated solely upon considerations of flight. They rely on *Stack v. Boyle* (1951) in which the Court stated that "Bail set at a figure higher than an amount reasonably calculated [to ensure the defendant's presence at trial] is 'excessive' under the Eighth Amendment." In respondents' view, since the Bail Reform Act allows a court essentially to set bail at an infinite amount for reasons not related to the risk of flight, it violates the Excessive Bail Clause. Respondents concede that the right to bail they have discovered in the Eighth Amendment is not absolute. A court may, for example, refuse bail in capital cases. And, as the Court of Appeals noted and respondents admit, a court may refuse bail when the defendant presents a threat to the judicial process by intimidating witnesses. Respondents characterize these exceptions as consistent with what they claim to be the sole purpose of bail—to ensure integrity of the judicial process.

While we agree that a primary function of bail is to safeguard the courts' role in adjudicating the guilt or innocence of defendants, we reject the proposition that the Eighth Amendment categorically prohibits the government from pursuing other admittedly compelling interests through regulation of pretrial release. The above-quoted *dicta* in *Stack v. Boyle* is far too slender a reed on which to rest this argument. The Court in *Stack* had no occasion to consider whether the Excessive Bail Clause requires courts to admit all defendants to bail, because the statute before the Court in that case in fact allowed the defendants to be bailed. Thus, the Court had to determine only whether bail, admittedly available in that case, was excessive if set at a sum greater than that necessary to ensure the arrestees' presence at trial. . . .

Nothing in the text of the Bail Clause limits permissible government considerations solely to questions of flight. The only arguable substantive limitation of the Bail Clause is that the government's proposed conditions of release or detention not be "excessive" in light of the perceived evil. Of course, to determine whether the government's response is excessive, we must compare that response against the interest the government seeks to protect by means of that response. Thus, when the government has admitted that its only interest is in preventing flight, bail must be set by a court at a sum designed to ensure that goal, and no more. We believe that when Congress has mandated detention on the basis of a compelling interest other than prevention of flight, as it has here, the Eighth Amendment does not require release on bail.

In our society liberty is the norm, and detention prior to trial or without trial is the carefully limited exception. We hold that the provisions for pretrial detention in the Bail Reform Act of 1984 fall within that carefully limited exception. The Act authorizes the detention prior to trial of arrestees charged with serious felonies who are found after an adversary hearing to pose a threat to the safety of individuals or to the community which no condition of release can dispel. The numerous procedural safeguards detailed above must attend this adversary hearing. We are unwilling to say that this congressional determination, based as it is upon that primary concern of every government—a concern for the safety and indeed the lives of its citizens—on its face violates either the Due Process Clause of the Fifth Amendment or the Excessive Bail Clause of the Eighth Amendment.

The judgment of the Court of Appeals is therefore

Reversed.

JUSTICE MARSHALL, with whom JUSTICE BRENNAN joins, dissenting.

This case brings before the Court for the first time a statute in which Congress declares that a person innocent of any crime may be jailed indefinitely, pending the trial of allegations which are legally presumed to be untrue, if the Government shows to the satisfaction of a judge that the accused is likely to commit crimes, unrelated to the pending charges, at any time in the future. Such statutes, consistent with the usages of tyranny and the excesses of what bitter experience teaches us to call the police state, have long been thought incompatible with the fundamental human rights protected by our Constitution. Today a majority of this Court holds otherwise. Its decision disregards basic principles of justice established centuries ago and enshrined beyond the reach of governmental interference in the Bill of Rights. . . .

The logic of the majority's Eighth Amendment analysis is . . . unsatisfactory. The Eighth Amendment, as the majority notes, states that "[e]xcessive bail shall not be required." The majority then declares, as if it were undeniable, that: "[t]his Clause, of course, says nothing about whether bail shall be available at all." If excessive bail is imposed the defendant stays in jail. The same result is achieved if bail is denied altogether. Whether the magistrate sets bail at $1 billion or refuses to set bail at all, the consequences are indistinguishable. It would be mere sophistry to suggest that the Eighth Amendment protects against the former decision, and not the latter. Indeed, such a result would lead to the conclusion that there was no need for Congress to pass a preventive detention measure of any kind; every federal magistrate and district judge could simply refuse, despite the absence of any evidence of risk of flight or danger to the community, to set bail. This would be entirely constitutional, since, according to the majority, the Eighth Amendment "says nothing about whether bail shall be available at all.". . .

The essence of this case may be found, ironically enough, in a provision of the Act to which the majority does not refer. Title 18 U.S.C. §3142(j) (1982 ed., Supp. III) provides that "[n]othing in this section shall be construed as modifying or limiting the presumption of innocence." But the very pith and purpose of this statute is an abhorrent limitation of the presumption of innocence. The majority's untenable conclusion that the present Act is constitutional arises from a specious denial of the role of the Bail Clause and the Due Process Clause in protecting the invaluable guarantee afforded by the presumption of innocence. . . .

It is not a novel proposition that the Bail Clause plays a vital role in protecting the presumption of innocence. Reviewing the application for bail pending appeal by members of the American Communist Party convicted under the Smith Act, Justice Jackson wrote:

"Grave public danger is said to result from what [the defendants] may be expected to do, in addition to what they have done since their conviction. If I assume that defendants are disposed to commit every opportune disloyal act helpful to Communist countries, it is still difficult to reconcile with traditional American law the jailing of persons by the courts because of anticipated but as yet uncommitted crimes. Imprisonment to protect society from predicted but unconsummated offenses is . . . unprecedented in this country and . . . fraught with danger of excesses and injustice. . . ." *Williamson v. United States* (1950).

As Chief Justice Vinson wrote for the Court in *Stack v. Boyle:* "Unless th[e] right to bail before trial is preserved, the presumption of innocence, secured only after centuries of struggle, would lose its meaning.". . .

I dissent.

By upholding this federal law, the Supreme Court gave implicit assent to the statutes of twenty-four states that allowed the denial of bail on similar bases.

Unlike Salerno, the majority of defendants will be eligible for bail. The job of their attorneys is to convince the judges to set bail at affordable levels. Most criminal defendants cannot put up the entire bail amount, even if set at modest levels. Many seek the services of a bail bondsman, who, for a significant and nonrefundable fee, files a bail bond with the court. The bond substitutes for cash bail and allows the defendant to be free, pending trial.

Because the bail procedure discriminates against the poor and the bail bonding industry has often been linked to unsavory practices, many criminal justice experts regard the bail stage as one of the weakest links in the system. Many jurisdictions have developed programs under which some worthy defendants may be allowed to go free without putting up bail, but overall there has been little support for bail reform. Most citizens lack sympathy for those accused of crimes. Many law-and-order–minded Americans believe that the criminally accused should not be released. As a result, the bail system operates today much as it did a hundred years ago.

THE SIXTH AMENDMENT AND FAIR TRIALS

From a quantitative perspective, trials are insignificant; only about 5 percent to 10 percent of all criminal prosecutions go to trial. In the other cases, the defendant pleads guilty, usually after arriving at a plea-bargaining agreement with the prosecutor. In such arrangements, the defendant waives the right to a jury trial and agrees to plead guilty in return for certain concessions made by the prosecutor. These concessions normally involve a reduction in the seriousness of the crimes charged, a reduction in the number of counts, or a recommendation for a lenient sentence. Although many citizens look at such arrangements unfavorably, the Supreme Court has sanctioned the practice, and it remains the most common way criminal prosecutions are settled.[7]

Qualitatively, however, trials are significant; the most serious crimes go to trial. In addition, trials serve a symbolic function and educate the public about crime and justice in the community. And they embody what Americans treasure so much—openness and fundamental and objective fairness.

The Framers of the Constitution clearly intended American trials to be the epitome of justice. They drafted the Sixth Amendment to correct the weaknesses they had observed in the English justice system, weaknesses that included closed proceedings, long delays, and few safeguards for defendants. Specifically, Sixth Amendment provisions governing trials state that:

In all criminal prosecutions, the accused shall enjoy the right to a speedy and public trial, by an impartial jury of the State and district wherein the crime shall have been committed, . . . to be confronted with the witnesses against him; to have compulsory process for obtaining witnesses in his favor.

In short, the Sixth Amendment provides strict guidelines for trial proceedings. The next pages examine how the Supreme Court has interpreted each right and the overall impact of its decisions on the trial process.

Speedy Trials

Before the late 1960s the speedy trial provision of the Sixth Amendment was seldom invoked. Most cases proceeded from arrest to trial in a timely fashion. Then backlogs of cases began to build up at the trial court level. The Supreme Court was asked to interpret the Speedy Trial Clause, and, because very little legal doctrine existed, the cases coming to the Court raised basic issues about its meaning. In one of the first, *United States v. Marion* (1971), the justices were asked to determine what stages of the criminal process the Speedy Trial Clause governed. Some lawyers argued that the constitutional ban against unreasonable delays covered the period from the commission of the crime to the beginning of the trial. Others held that the provision governed only the period from formal charges (arrest, indictment, or information) to the beginning of the trial.

Marion originated with a series of articles published in the *Washington Post* in October 1967. The pieces alleged fraudulent practices by home improvement firms, including a company called Allied Enterprises. One of the articles quoted a U.S. attorney as saying that indictments against an unnamed business would be forthcoming. Sure enough, during the summer of 1968, federal prosecutors conducted interviews with Allied officials. In the fall a grand jury was impaneled, and in April 1970 it handed down indictments against Allied officials.

Before their trial, Allied employees argued that their Sixth Amendment right to a speedy trial had been violated because of the three-year lapse between the commission of the alleged offense and the grand jury indictment. During this prolonged period, they claimed, witnesses had forgotten certain events and bias against them had grown. They asked the Court to rule that the delay between the commission of the crime and arrest or indictment was unreasonable.

In a unanimous decision, the Court refused to do so, but not on the grounds that the delay had been too long. Rather, Justice White's opinion said that the Speedy Trial Clause does not apply to the time before the formal charges are issued. The intent of the provision was to keep those publicly charged with a criminal offense from suffering unreasonable delays before they had their day in court. In so concluding, *Marion* gave clear notice that the Court would be unwilling to find violations of the Speedy Trial Clause unless unreasonable delays occurred after arrest or formal charges had been made.

The next year, in *Barker v. Wingo* (1972), the Court confronted the question left unanswered in *Marion*: What criteria are to be used to determine if there has been unreasonable postindictment delay? In this case, two individuals, Barker and Manning, were charged with beating an elderly Kentucky couple to death with a tire iron. The prosecutor had a strong case against Manning, but not against Barker. To convict Barker, the prosecutor needed Manning to testify, but Manning refused on Fifth Amendment grounds. The prosecutor devised the following strategy: he would put Manning on trial first, and, after obtaining a conviction against him, he would try Barker and call Manning as a major witness. Manning would no longer be able to refuse to testify on Fifth

---

7. See, for example, *North Carolina v. Alford* (1970).

Amendment grounds because, once he was convicted of murder, he could not further incriminate himself.

This strategy was theoretically sound, but ran into difficulties. Getting Manning convicted took longer than the prosecutor had anticipated. In fact, because of hung juries, successful appeals, and subsequent retrials, it took several years. Prosecutors had to ask the court to postpone Barker's trial sixteen times. Beginning with the twelfth continuance request, Barker's attorneys started asserting that the speedy trial provision of the Sixth Amendment was being violated. Finally, five years after he was indicted for murder, Barker was tried, found guilty, and sentenced to life in prison.

Barker's attorneys appealed the conviction on the grounds that the five-year delay was a violation of the Sixth Amendment. A unanimous Supreme Court, through an opinion by Justice Powell, refused to designate a specific length of time that would constitute unreasonable delay. Instead, the justices recognized that this period could vary from case to case. However, the Court established four criteria that should be considered in deciding questions of unreasonable delay: the length of the delay; the reason for the delay; the point at which the defendant begins asserting a Sixth Amendment violation; and whether the delay prejudiced the defendant's case.

As applied to Barker, the Court found no constitutional violation. While the five-year delay was admittedly long, the reason for the delay—the unavailability of an important witness—was sound. Furthermore, the defendant did not register objections to the delay until well into the process. Finally, the Court was unable to see that the defendant suffered any prejudice caused by the delay. Under Justice Powell's balancing test, defendants have a great deal to prove before the Court finds a violation of the speedy trial provision.

The general reaction to *Barker* was that criminal defendants deserved greater speedy trial right protections than the Court's interpretation of the Sixth Amendment allowed. Consequently, in 1974 Congress passed the Speedy Trial Act, requiring indictment within thirty days of arrest, arraignment ten days after indictment, and trial sixty days after arraignment. Moreover, every state has enacted speedy trial laws of various sorts.

Jury Trials

Like many other aspects of law and procedure, the Framers incorporated the British jury system into the U.S. Constitution. The Sixth Amendment states in part, "In all criminal prosecutions, the accused shall enjoy the right to a . . . trial, by an impartial jury." But what did the term *jury* mean to the Framers? We can speculate that they had in mind at least three aspects of the British system: that a jury be composed of the defendant's peers, that it consist of twelve persons, and that it reach unanimous verdicts. Today, none of these three guarantees is fully operative in criminal proceedings.

Jury Members. Presumably, in England being tried by a jury of one's peers meant that one would face members of one's social class. In other words, a commoner would be tried by a jury of commoners and a nobleman by a jury of noblemen. In the United States such class distinctions are not recognized; rather, a jury of one's peers means a jury that represents a cross-section of the community. To put together representative panels, most jurisdictions follow a procedure that works this way:

1. Individuals living within a specified geographical area are called for jury duty. Most localities use voter registration, property tax, or driver's license lists from which to select names.

2. Those selected form the jury pool or venire, the group from which attorneys choose the jury.

3. The judge may conduct initial interviews excusing certain classes of people (felons, illiterates, the mentally ill) and certain occupational groups, as allowed under the laws of the particular jurisdiction.

4. The remaining individuals are available to be chosen to serve on a trial (petit) jury. In the final selection phase, the opposing attorneys interview the prospective jurors. This process is called *voir dire*. During *voir dire* attorneys can dismiss those individuals they believe would not vote in the best interests of their clients. The attorneys, therefore, select the jury.

During *voir dire*, attorneys use two mechanisms or challenges to eliminate potential jurors. When a prospective juror appears to be unqualified to carry out the obligations of service, attorneys can *challenge for cause.* To do so, they must explain to the judge their reasons for requesting the disqualification of that individual (for example, conflict of interest or expressions of extreme prejudice), and the judge must agree. Challenges for cause are unlimited. Attorneys also have a fixed number of *peremptory challenges*, which they may use to excuse jurors without stating a reason.

The objective of this long-standing process is to form a petit jury representing a cross-section of the community. Does the process work? This question has been the subject of numerous scholarly analyses and is still debated. Many argue that the system is the best among myriad inferior alternatives. Others claim that it is plagued with problems from beginning to end, resulting in unacceptable biases. For example, because most localities now draw their jury pools from voter registration lists, juries reflect the average voter—white, middle-aged, and middle class. Another criticism comes from the practice of "jury-stacking." Lawyers have always tried to use their challenges to eliminate jurors likely to be unsympathetic to their side, but they have generally proceeded only on the basis of their personal experience, professional judgment, and idiosyncratic hunches. More recently—and more expensively—lawyers have engaged firms that sample public opinion in a community to map the backgrounds of ideal jurors. They also have hired social psychologists to sit in the courtroom during the *voir dire* and observe potential jurors to predict their attitudes more accurately.

Another concern is that attorneys, specifically prosecutors, may use their peremptory challenges systematically to excuse blacks from juries. This action is based on the belief that black jurors are reluctant to convict black defendants. Although trial court judges have long recognized that prosecutors engaged in this practice, they could do little about it because peremptory challenges do not require the approval of the judge. Most courts refused to interfere with the traditional privilege of attorneys to excuse jurors for no specific reason, viewing it as part of a litigation strategy. The U.S. Supreme Court, in *Swain v. Alabama* (1965), reinforced this sentiment by making it very difficult for judges to prohibit prosecutors

from using the peremptory challenge to remove prospective jurors for reasons of race. (The *Batson* excerpt below contains a full discussion of *Swain*.)

In *Batson v. Kentucky* (1986), however, the Court reevaluated *Swain* and startled the legal community by holding that even peremptory challenges are subject to court scrutiny. As you read this case, note that all but two of the Burger Court justices agreed with a ruling that clearly flew in the face of well-established custom and precedent. *Batson* is an interesting (and unusual) example of a decision in which the Burger Court modified a Warren Court precedent and replaced it with a decision more favorable to the rights of the criminally accused.[8]

Batson v. Kentucky

476 U.S. 79 (1986)
laws.findlaw.com/US/476/79.html
Vote: 7 (Blackmun, Brennan, Marshall, O'Connor, Powell, Stevens, White)
    2 (Burger, Rehnquist)
Opinion of the Court: Powell
Concurring opinions: Marshall, O'Connor, Stevens, White
Dissenting opinions: Burger, Rehnquist

James Batson, a black man, was indicted for second-degree burglary. Although his venire had four blacks, the prosecutor used his peremptory challenges to eliminate them, leaving Batson with an all-white jury. Batson's attorney challenged this outcome, claiming that it denied his client equal protection of the laws and his Sixth Amendment right to an impartial jury representing a cross-section of the community. The trial court and the Kentucky Supreme Court denied this claim in part because of the sanctity of peremptory challenges.

The U.S. Supreme Court was asked to address this question: May prosecutors use their peremptory challenges to eliminate prospective jurors of a specific racial group? Naturally, such an issue drew many opinions in the form of amicus curiae briefs from organized interest groups. The NAACP Legal Defense Fund, for instance,

---

8. For oral arguments in this case, navigate to: *oyez.nwu.edu.*

argued, "The exclusion of Blacks from juries not only stigmatizes them and deprives them of their right . . . to participate in the criminal justice system. It destroys the appearance of justice." The National Legal Aid and Defender Association, representing the public defender offices and legal aid societies, framed its argument a bit differently: "No significant state interest exists in allowing unrestricted use of the peremptory challenge . . . because it is not essential to the ability of the prosecutor to select fair and impartial jurors."

JUSTICE POWELL delivered the opinion of the Court.

This case requires us to reexamine that portion of *Swain v. Alabama* concerning the evidentiary burden placed on a criminal defendant who claims that he has been denied equal protection through the State's use of peremptory challenges to exclude members of his race from the petit jury. . . .

In *Swain v. Alabama,* this Court recognized that a "State's purposeful or deliberate denial to Negroes on account of race of participation as jurors in the administration of justice violates the Equal Protection Clause." This principle has been "consistently and repeatedly" reaffirmed, in numerous decisions of this Court both preceding and following *Swain.* We reaffirm the principle today.

More than a century ago, the Court decided that the State denies a black defendant equal protection of the laws when it puts him on trial before a jury from which members of his race have been purposefully excluded. *Strauder v. West Virginia* (1880). That decision laid the foundation for the Court's unceasing efforts to eradicate racial discrimination in the procedures used to select the venire from which individual jurors are drawn. In *Strauder,* the Court explained that the central concern of the recently ratified Fourteenth Amendment was to put an end to governmental discrimination on account of race. Exclusion of black citizens from service as jurors constitutes a primary example of the evil the Fourteenth Amendment was designed to cure.

In holding that racial discrimination in jury selection offends the Equal Protection Clause, the Court in *Strauder* recognized, however, that a defendant has no right to a "petit jury composed in whole or in part of persons of his own race." But the defendant does have the right to be tried by a jury whose members are selected pursuant to nondiscrimi-

natory criteria. The Equal Protection Clause guarantees the defendant that the State will not exclude members of his race from the jury venire on account of race or on the false assumption that members of his race as a group are not qualified to serve as jurors.

Purposeful racial discrimination in selection of the venire violates a defendant's right to equal protection because it denies him the protection that a trial by jury is intended to secure. "The very idea of a jury is a body . . . composed of the peers or equals of the person whose rights it is selected or summoned to determine; that is, of his neighbors, fellows, associates, persons having the same legal status in society as that which he holds.". . .

Racial discrimination in selection of jurors harms not only the accused whose life or liberty they are summoned to try. Competence to serve as a juror ultimately depends on an assessment of individual qualifications and ability impartially to consider evidence presented at a trial. A person's race simply "is unrelated to his fitness as a juror." As long ago as *Strauder,* therefore, the Court recognized that by denying a person participation in jury service on account of his race, the State unconstitutionally discriminated against the excluded juror. . . .

In *Strauder,* the Court invalidated a state statute that provided that only white men could serve as jurors. We can be confident that no state now has such a law. The Constitution requires, however, that we look beyond the face of the statute defining juror qualifications and also consider challenged selection practices to afford "protection against action of the State through its administrative officers in effecting the prohibited discrimination.". . .

Accordingly, the component of the jury selection process at issue here, the State's privilege to strike individual jurors through peremptory challenges, is subject to the commands of the Equal Protection Clause. Although a prosecutor ordinarily is entitled to exercise permitted peremptory challenges "for any reason at all, as long as that reason is related to his view concerning the outcome" of the case to be tried, the Equal Protection Clause forbids the prosecutor to challenge potential jurors solely on account of their race or on the assumption that black jurors as a group will be unable impartially to consider the State's case against a black defendant.

The principles announced in *Strauder* never have been questioned in any subsequent decision of this Court.

Rather, the Court has been called upon repeatedly to review the application of those principles to particular facts. A recurring question in these cases, as in any case alleging a violation of the Equal Protection Clause, was whether the defendant had met his burden of proving purposeful discrimination on the part of the State. That question also was at the heart of the portion of *Swain v. Alabama* we reexamine today.

Swain required the Court to decide, among other issues, whether a black defendant was denied equal protection by the State's exercise of peremptory challenges to exclude members of his race from the petit jury. The record in *Swain* showed that the prosecutor had used the State's peremptory challenges to strike the six black persons included on the petit jury venire. While rejecting the defendant's claim for failure to prove purposeful discrimination, the Court nonetheless indicated that the Equal Protection Clause placed some limits on the State's exercise of peremptory challenges.

The Court sought to accommodate the prosecutor's historical privilege of peremptory challenge free of judicial control, and the constitutional prohibition on exclusion of persons from jury service on account of race. While the Constitution does not confer a right to peremptory challenges, those challenges traditionally have been viewed as one means of assuring the selection of a qualified and unbiased jury. To preserve the peremptory nature of the prosecutor's challenge, the Court in *Swain* declined to scrutinize his actions in a particular case by relying on a presumption that he properly exercised the State's challenges.

The Court went on to observe, however, that a state may not exercise its challenges in contravention of the Equal Protection Clause. It was impermissible for a prosecutor to use his challenges to exclude blacks from the jury "for reasons wholly unrelated to the outcome of the particular case on trial" or to deny to blacks "the same right and opportunity to participate in the administration of justice enjoyed by the white population." Accordingly, a black defendant could make out a prima facie case of purposeful discrimination on proof that the peremptory challenge system was "being perverted" in that manner. For example, an inference of purposeful discrimination would be raised on evidence that a prosecutor, "in case after case, whatever the circumstances, whatever the crime and whoever the defendant or the victim may be, is responsible for the removal of Negroes who have been selected as qualified jurors by the jury commissioners and who have survived challenges for cause, with the result that no Negroes ever serve on petit juries." Evidence offered by the defendant in *Swain* did not meet that standard. While the defendant showed that prosecutors in the jurisdiction had exercised their strikes to exclude blacks from the jury, he offered no proof of the circumstances under which prosecutors were responsible for striking black jurors beyond the facts of his own case.

A number of lower courts following the teaching of *Swain* reasoned that proof of repeated striking of blacks over a number of cases was necessary to establish a violation of the Equal Protection Clause. Since this interpretation of *Swain* has placed on defendants a crippling burden of proof, prosecutors' peremptory challenges are now largely immune from constitutional scrutiny. . . . [We] reject this evidentiary formulation as inconsistent with standards that have been developed since *Swain* for assessing a prima facie case under the Equal Protection Clause. . . .

The standards for assessing a prima facie case in the context of discriminatory selection of the venire have been fully articulated since *Swain*. These principles support our conclusion that a defendant may establish a prima facie case of purposeful discrimination in selection of the petit jury solely on evidence concerning the prosecutor's exercise of peremptory challenges at the defendant's trial. To establish such a case, the defendant first must show that he is a member of a cognizable racial group and that the prosecutor has exercised peremptory challenges to remove from the venire members of the defendant's race. Second, the defendant is entitled to rely on the fact, as to which there can be no dispute, that peremptory challenges constitute a jury selection practice that permits "those to discriminate who are of a mind to discriminate." Finally, the defendant must show that these facts and any other relevant circumstances raise an inference that the prosecutor used that practice to exclude the veniremen from the petit jury on account of their race. This combination of factors in the empanelling of the petit jury, as in the selection of the venire, raises the necessary inference of purposeful discrimination.

In deciding whether the defendant has made the requisite showing, the trial court should consider all relevant circumstances. For example, a "pattern" of strikes against black jurors included in the particular venire might give rise to an inference of discrimination. Similarly, the prosecutor's questions and statements during *voir dire* examination and in exercising his challenges may support or refute an inference of discriminatory purpose. These examples are merely illustrative. We have confidence that trial judges, experienced in supervising *voir dire,* will be able to decide if the circumstances concerning the prosecutor's use of peremptory challenges creates a prima facie case of discrimination against black jurors.

Once the defendant makes a prima facie showing, the burden shifts to the State to come forward with a neutral explanation for challenging black jurors. Though this requirement imposes a limitation in some cases on the full peremptory character of the historic challenge, we emphasize that the prosecutor's explanation need not rise to the level justifying exercise of a challenge for cause. But the prosecutor may not rebut the defendant's prima facie case of discrimination by stating merely that he challenged jurors of the defendant's race on the assumption—or his intuitive judgment—that they would be partial to the defendant because of their shared race. Just as the Equal Protection Clause forbids the States to exclude black persons from the venire on the assumption that blacks as a group are unqualified to serve as jurors, so it forbids the States to strike black veniremen on the assumption that they will be biased in a particular case simply because the defendant is black. The core guarantee of equal protection, ensuring citizens that their State will not discriminate on account of race, would be meaningless were we to approve the exclusion of jurors on the basis of such assumptions, which arise solely from the jurors' race. Nor may the prosecutor rebut the defendant's case merely by denying that he had a discriminatory motive or "affirming his good faith in individual selections." If these general assertions were accepted as rebutting a defendant's prima facie case, the Equal Protection Clause "would be but a vain and illusory requirement." The prosecutor therefore must articulate a neutral explanation related to the particular case to be tried. The trial court then will have the duty to determine if the defendant has established purposeful discrimination.

The State contends that our holding will eviscerate the fair trial values served by the peremptory challenge. Conceding that the Constitution does not guarantee a right to peremptory challenges and that *Swain* did state that their use ultimately is subject to the strictures of equal protection, the State argues that the privilege of unfettered exercise of the challenge is of vital importance to the criminal justice system.

While we recognize, of course, that the peremptory challenge occupies an important position in our trial procedures, we do not agree that our decision today will undermine the contribution the challenge generally makes to the administration of justice. The reality of practice, amply reflected in many state and federal court opinions, shows that the challenge may be, and unfortunately at times has been, used to discriminate against black jurors. By requiring trial courts to be sensitive to the racially discriminatory use of peremptory challenges, our decision enforces the mandate of equal protection and furthers the ends of justice. In view of the heterogeneous population of our nation, public respect for our criminal justice system and the rule of law will be strengthened if we ensure that no citizen is disqualified from jury service because of his race. . . .

In this case, petitioner made a timely objection to the prosecutor's removal of all black persons on the venire. Because the trial court flatly rejected the objection without requiring the prosecutor to give an explanation for his action, we remand this case for further proceedings. If the trial court decides that the facts establish, prima facie, purposeful discrimination and the prosecutor does not come forward with a neutral explanation for his action, our precedents require that petitioner's conviction be reversed.

It is so ordered.

JUSTICE MARSHALL, concurring.

I join JUSTICE POWELL's eloquent opinion for the Court, which takes a historic step toward eliminating the shameful practice of racial discrimination in the selection of juries. The Court's opinion cogently explains the pernicious nature of the racially discriminatory use of peremptory challenges, and the repugnancy of such discrimination to the Equal Protection Clause. The Court's opinion also ably demonstrates the inadequacy of any burden of proof for racially discriminatory use of peremptories that requires that "justice . . . sit supinely by" and be flouted in case after case before a remedy is available. I nonetheless write separately to express my views. The decision today will not end the racial discrimination that peremptories inject into the jury-selection process. That goal can be accomplished only by eliminating peremptory challenges entirely. . . .

Misuse of the peremptory challenge to exclude black jurors has become both common and flagrant. Black defendants rarely have been able to compile statistics showing the extent of that practice, but the few cases setting out such figures are instructive. See *United States v. Carter* (CA8 [Court of Appeals] 1975) (in 15 criminal cases in 1974 in the Western District of Missouri involving black defendants, prosecutors peremptorily challenged 81% of black jurors), cert. denied (1976); *United States v. McDaniels* (ED La. 1974) (in 53 criminal cases in 1972–1974 in the Eastern District of Louisiana involving black defendants, federal prosecutors used 68.9% of their peremptory challenges against black jurors, who made up less than one-quarter of the venire). . . . An instruction book used by the prosecutor's office in Dallas County, Texas, explicitly advised prosecutors that they conduct jury selection so as to eliminate "'any member of a minority group.'" In 100 felony trials in Dallas County in 1983–1984, prosecutors peremptorily struck 405 out of 467 eligible black jurors; the chance of a qualified black sitting on a jury was one-in-ten, compared to one-in-two for a white. . . .

Much ink has been spilled regarding the historic importance of defendants' peremptory challenges. . . . [T]he *Swain* Court emphasized the "very old credentials" of the peremptory challenge and cited the "long and widely held belief that peremptory challenge is a necessary part of trial by jury." But this Court has also repeatedly stated that the right of peremptory challenge is not of constitutional magnitude, and may be withheld altogether without impairing the constitutional guarantee of impartial jury and fair trial. The potential for racial prejudice, further, inheres in the defendant's challenge as well. If the prosecutor's peremptory challenge could be eliminated only at the cost of eliminating the defendant's challenge as well, I do not think that would be too great a price to pay.

I applaud the Court's holding that the racially discriminatory use of peremptory challenges violates the Equal Protection Clause, and I join the Court's opinion. However, only by banning peremptories entirely can such discrimination be ended.

JUSTICE REHNQUIST, with whom THE CHIEF JUSTICE joins, dissenting.

I cannot subscribe to the Court's unprecedented use of the Equal Protection Clause to restrict the historic scope of the peremptory challenge, which has been described as "a necessary part of trial by jury." *Swain.* In my view, there is simply nothing "unequal" about the State's using its peremptory challenges to strike blacks from the jury in cases involving black defendants, so long as such challenges are also used to exclude whites in cases involving white defendants, Hispanics in cases involving Hispanic defendants, Asians in cases involving Asian defendants, and so on. This case-specific use of peremptory challenges by the State does not single out blacks, or members of any other race for that matter, for discriminatory treatment. Such use of peremptories is at best based upon seat-of-the-pants instincts, which are undoubtedly crudely stereotypical and may in many cases be hopelessly mistaken. But as long as they are applied across the board to jurors of all races and nationalities, I do not see—and the Court most certainly has not explained—how their use violates the Equal Protection Clause.

Nor does such use of peremptory challenges by the State infringe upon any other constitutional interests. The Court does not suggest that exclusion of blacks from the jury through the State's use of peremptory challenges results in a violation of either the fair cross-section or impartiality component of the Sixth Amendment. And because the case-specific use of peremptory challenges by the State does not deny blacks the right to serve as jurors in cases involving nonblack defendants, it harms neither the excluded jurors nor the remainder of the community.

The use of group affiliations, such as age, race, or occupation, as a "proxy" for potential juror partiality, based on the assumption or belief that members of one group are more likely to favor defendants who belong to the same group, has long been accepted as a legitimate basis for the State's exercise of peremptory challenges. See *Swain.* Indeed, given the need for reasonable limitations on the time devoted to *voir dire*, the use of such "proxies" by both the State and the defendant may be extremely useful in eliminating from the jury persons who might be biased in one way or another. The Court today holds that the State may not use its peremptory challenges to strike black prospective jurors on this basis without violating the Constitution. But I do not believe there is anything in the Equal Protection Clause, or any other constitutional provision, that justifies such a departure from the substantive holding contained in Part II of *Swain.* Petitioner in the instant case failed to make a sufficient showing to overcome the presumption announced in *Swain* that the State's use of peremptory challenges was related to the context of the case. I would therefore affirm the judgment of the court below.

Batson represents an important turn in Supreme Court doctrine governing jury selection. Prior to this case, the justices *generally* refused to interfere with attorney exercise of peremptory challenges, even in the face of evidence that prosecutors often used them to exclude blacks from juries. In *Batson* the justices reevaluated their approach and established a framework by which defendants could challenge prosecutors who appeared to be using their peremptory challenges in a racially discriminatory way.

Batson, however, was just the beginning of the Court's reevaluation of the peremptory challenge system. In *Powers v. Ohio* (1991) it ruled that criminal defendants may object to race-based exclusion of jurors through peremptory challenges whether or not the defendant and the excluded jurors are the same race. The same term, in *Edmonson v. Leesville Concrete Co.*, it also applied the *Batson* framework to civil cases, holding that private litigants may not use their peremptory challenges in a racially biased manner. In *Georgia v. McCollum* (1992) the Court ruled that the *prosecution* can stop the *defense* from exercising its peremptories to eliminate blacks from a jury. In other words, they ruled that the *Batson* framework applies to both sides of criminal cases, the prosecution *and the defense.* Why? Justice Blackmun addressed this question in an opinion for the majority:

Be it at the hands of the State or the defense, if a court allows jurors to be excluded because of group bias, it is a willing participant in a scheme that could only undermine the very foundation of our system of justice—our citizens' confidence in it. Just as public confidence in criminal justice is undermined by a conviction in a trial where racial discrimination has occurred in jury selection, so is public confidence undermined where a defendant, assisted by racially discriminatory peremptory strikes, obtains an acquittal.

Even Chief Justice Rehnquist—a dissenter in *Batson* and in other cases extending its reach—concurred in *McCollum.* In explaining his vote, Rehnquist noted:

I was in dissent in *Edmonson v. Leesville Concrete Co.* (1991) and continue to believe that case to have been wrongly decided. But so long as it remains the law, I believe that it controls the disposition of this case. . . . I therefore join the opinion of the Court.

With the justices handing down decisions such as *Batson* and *McCollum* it was inevitable that the Court soon would be asked to extend the restrictions on the use of peremptory challenges to other groups as well. In fact, just two years after *McCollum*, the justices were urged to extend this line of reasoning to jury challenges based on sex. In *J. E. B. v. Alabama ex rel. T. B.* (1994), they accepted this invitation and applied *Batson* to intentional sex discrimination in selecting jurors. Or, as Justice Blackmun put it for the majority: "Today we reaffirm what, by now, should be axiomatic: Intentional discrimination on the basis of gender by state actors violates the Equal Protection Clause, particularly where, as here, the discrimination serves to ratify and perpetuate invidious, archaic, and overbroad stereotypes about the relative abilities of men and women."

According to some observers, the decisions in *McCollum* and *J. E. B.* were not unexpected; rather, they represent logical extensions of *Batson* and related Court decisions that opened up to judicial scrutiny the exercise of peremptory challenges. But others argue that the Court has gone too far, that it has moved perilously close to the position advocated by Justice Marshall in his *Batson* concurrence: the eradication of peremptory challenges altogether. As Justice Scalia, a critic of Court doctrine in this area, put it in his *McCollum* dissent:

Today's decision gives the lie once again to the belief that an activist, "evolutionary" constitutional jurisprudence always evolves in the direction of greater individual rights. In the interest of promoting the supposedly greater good of race relations in the society as a whole (make no mistake that that is what underlies all of this), we use the Constitution to destroy the ages-old right of criminal defendants to exercise peremptory challenges as they wish, to secure a jury that they consider fair.

Do you agree? Or do you think the Court has taken appropriate steps to ensure fairness in the jury selection process?

Jury Size. Another long-standing tradition Americans

adopted from the British is jury size. Since the four-teenth century all English juries had twelve people, a number of disputed origin. Some suggest that it repre-sents the twelve apostles; others claim it emanates from the twelve tribes of Israel. A point on which all agree is that the Framers accepted twelve as the proper number for a jury.

Beginning in the mid-1960s, however, many states be-gan to abandon this practice, substituting six-person ju-ries in noncapital cases. These states reasoned that six-person juries would be more economical, faster, and more likely to reach a verdict. Was the use of fewer than twelve people consistent with the demands of the Sixth Amendment? The Court answered this question in *Williams v. Florida,* a 1970 appeal from a robbery convic-tion. For the Court, Justice White explained that the number twelve had no special constitutional significan-ce. The traditional twelve-person jury was basically the result of historical accident. All the Constitution re-quires, according to the Court, is a jury sufficiently large to allow actual deliberation and to represent a cross-section of the community. The six-person jury used to convict Williams was sufficiently large to meet these standards.

In the wake of *Williams,* a number of states followed Florida's lead and now use juries smaller than twelve for some offenses. Nonetheless, White's reasoning has been closely scrutinized by legal scholars, and numerous em-pirical investigations have tried to determine whether six-person juries reach conclusions significantly different from their twelve-person counterparts. Although the scholarly verdict is far from unanimous, many now agree that "research on the effects of panel size on jury perfor-mance indicates that the use of six-member juries does not result in significant differences in either trial out-come or deliberation quality."[9] On the other hand, stud-ies have confirmed the obvious: the fewer the jurors, the less time it takes for the panel to read a verdict.

Jury Verdicts. Following the English tradition, the Framers thought juries should reach unanimous verdicts or none at all. If a jury cannot reach a unanimous verdict, the judge declares the jury "hung," and the prosecutor ei-ther schedules a retrial or releases the defendant. For the sake of efficient justice, some states altered the unanimi-ty rule for twelve-person juries, requiring instead the agreement of nine or ten of the twelve.

Two cases, *Johnson v. Louisiana* and *Apodaca v. Oregon,* decided together in 1972, tested the constitutionality of non-unanimous juries. The side in support of non-una-nimity claimed that the alternative was excessive and ob-solete in modern society, that because hung juries oc-curred more frequently, it often led to miscarriages of justice. The other side pointed out that the very essence of jury decisionmaking is that verdicts are based on doubt. If no reasonable doubt exists about a person's guilt, the jury is supposed to reach a guilty verdict; if doubt is present, the jury should come to the opposite conclusion. But if a jury is split 9–3 or 10–2, does that not indicate a reasonable doubt? According to Justice White, writing for the Court, less than unanimous verdicts do not violate the Sixth Amendment. A lack of unanimity is not the equivalent of doubt. He concluded:

[T]he fact of three dissenting votes to acquit raises no question of institutional substance about either the integrity or the accu-racy of the majority vote of guilt. . . . [By obtaining] nine [votes] to convict, the State satisfied its burden of proving guilt beyond any reasonable doubt.

Impartial Juries

As we have seen, Supreme Court decisions have led to jury practices that differ substantially from the vision of the Framers. These decisions have been controversial, but they pale in comparison to the furor over the notion of impartial juries.[10] Given the constitutional guarantees of a public trial and freedom of the press, how can judges see to it that defendants receive fair, impartial jury trials? This question has major constitutional importance be-cause it forces courts to deal with conflicting rights. The Sixth Amendment requires judges to regulate trials, en-

9. Reid Hastie, Steven D. Penrod, and Nancy Pennington, *Inside the Jury* (Cambridge: Harvard University Press, 1983), 38. Other scholars have found differences between large and small juries, but agree that "regardless of which jury type is chosen some desirable features of the unchosen type are lost." Michael J. Saks, *Jury Verdicts* (Lexington, Mass.: Lexington Books, 1977), 107.

10. See *Patton v. Yount* (1984).

suring, among other things, that jury members have not prejudged the outcome. In a highly publicized case, the judge's task can become arduous. The judge must deal with the media exercising their constitutional guarantee of a free press. How can judges keep trials fair without interfering with the rights of the press and the public?

The cases that follow deal with the controversies surrounding impartial juries. Has the Court struck a reasonable balance between competing constitutional rights? Is such a balance even possible?

Press v. Jury: The Warren Court. Before the mid-1960s no balance existed between freedom of the press and the right to an impartial jury—the former far outweighed the latter. In cases involving well-known individuals or otherwise of interest to the public, the press descended on courtrooms. Because there were no well-defined rules, reporters, accompanied by crews carrying bulky, noisy equipment, simply showed up and interviewed and photographed witnesses and other participants at will.

Not surprisingly, the Warren Court placed limitations on the media. Although this issue is not one that can be placed on an ideological continuum, the Warren Court clearly favored the rights of the criminally accused. *Sheppard v. Maxwell* (1966) is the Warren Court's strongest statement on this clash of rights. This case provided an excellent vehicle for the Court because it was the most widely publicized case of its day and illustrates the ill effects media pressure can produce.[11]

Sheppard v. Maxwell

384 U.S. 333 (1966)
laws.findlaw.com/US/384/333.html
Vote: 8 (Brennan, Clark, Douglas, Fortas, Harlan, Stewart,
    Warren, White)
    1 (Black)
Opinion of the Court: Clark

On July 4, 1954, Marilyn Sheppard, the pregnant wife of Dr. Sam Sheppard, a well-known osteopath, was mur-

---

[11]. For oral arguments in *Sheppard,* navigate to: *oyez.nwu.edu.* Several movies were based on this case, including *The Lawyer* and *The Fugitive,* as well as a television series with the latter name.

dered. According to Sheppard, he and his wife had entertained friends and watched television in their lakefront home the night before. He fell asleep on the couch, and Marilyn went upstairs to bed. In the early morning, he awoke to her screams. He ran upstairs where he struggled with a "form," who knocked him unconscious. Returning to consciousness, he heard noises outside, ran to the lake's edge, and unsuccessfully wrestled with this "form" on the beach. Then he went back into the house, found his wife dead, and called his neighbor, the village mayor. These events touched off a month-long investigation, coupled with an avalanche of negative publicity, that culminated in Sheppard's arrest.

The adverse publicity began on July 7, the day of Marilyn's funeral, when a newspaper story criticized the Sheppard family for refusing to cooperate with the investigation. It continued for the rest of the month. Accusations against Sheppard and demands that he be prosecuted for the murder appeared in the local press almost daily. The coroner's inquest became a media circus, swarming with print and broadcast journalists. Sheppard was denied access to his attorney at various critical stages of the process. He was arrested on the night of July 30, the same day a front page editorial asked, "Why Isn't Sam Sheppard in Jail?" and portrayed him as a liar and an unfaithful husband. The arrest did not quiet the press; instead, the massive publicity continued.

Sheppard's trial began on October 18. Both the judge and chief prosecutor were running for public office, and the election was just two weeks later. All three Cleveland newspapers published the names and addresses of people called for jury service. As a result, prospective jurors received numerous messages from people wanting to express their views on the case. During jury selection a Cleveland newspaper ran a two-inch, front-page headline, "But Who Will Speak for Marilyn?"

Hundreds of reporters were in Cleveland to cover the trial. The courtroom, filled with journalists from all media and the equipment they needed to report on the trial, was so noisy that much of the testimony could not be heard despite a newly installed loud-speaker system. Photographs of the jury appeared more than forty times in Cleveland newspapers. Local officials failed to monitor the jurors, who made numerous telephone calls during deliberations with no records kept regarding who they called or what was said. After five days of deliberations, the jury returned a verdict of guilty.

Later, represented by defense attorney F. Lee Bailey, Sheppard filed for federal habeas corpus relief, claiming he was denied a fair trial due to the excessive activity by the news media.[12] Unsuccessful in the lower courts, Sheppard appealed to the Supreme Court.

MR. JUSTICE CLARK delivered the opinion of the Court.

The principle that justice cannot survive behind walls of silence has long been reflected in the "Anglo-American distrust for secret trials." A responsible press has always been regarded as the handmaiden of effective judicial administration, especially in the criminal field. Its function in this regard is documented by an impressive record of service over several centuries. The press does not simply publish information about trials but guards against the miscarriage of justice by subjecting the police, prosecutors, and judicial processes to extensive public scrutiny and criticism. This Court has, therefore, been unwilling to place any direct limitations on the freedom traditionally exercised by the news media for "[w]hat transpires in the court room is public property.". . .

But the Court has also pointed out that "[l]egal trials are not like elections, to be won through the use of the meeting-hall, the radio, and the newspaper." And the Court has insisted that no one be punished for a crime without "a charge fairly made and fairly tried in a public tribunal free of prejudice, passion, excitement, and tyrannical power.". . .

Only last Term in *Estes v. State of Texas* (1965) we set aside a conviction despite the absence of any showing of prejudice. We said there:

"It is true that in most cases involving claims of due process deprivations we require a showing of identifiable prejudice to the accused. Nevertheless, at times a procedure employed by the State involves such a probability that prejudice will result that it is deemed inherently lacking in due process."

And we cited with approval the language of MR. JUS-

12. Bailey credits the Sheppard case with launching his career. See F. Lee Bailey, *The Defense Never Rests* (New York: Signet, 1971), chap. 2. See also Cynthia Cooper, *Mockery of Justice: The True Story of the Sheppard Murder Case* (Boston: Northeastern University Press, 1995).

TICE BLACK . . . that "our system of law has always endeavored to prevent even the probability of unfairness."

It is clear that the totality of circumstances in this case also warrants such an approach. Unlike Estes, Sheppard was not granted a change of venue to a locale away from where the publicity originated; nor was his jury sequestered. . . . [T]he Sheppard jurors were subjected to newspaper, radio and television coverage of the trial while not taking part in the proceedings. They were allowed to go their separate ways outside of the courtroom, without adequate directions not to read or listen to anything concerning the case. . . . At intervals during the trial, the judge simply repeated his "suggestions" and "requests" that the jurors not expose themselves to comment upon the case. Moreover, the jurors were thrust into the role of celebrities by the judge's failure to insulate them from reporters and photographers. The numerous pictures of the jurors, with their addresses, which appeared in the newspapers before and during the trial itself, exposed them to expressions of opinion from both cranks and friends. The fact that anonymous letters had been received by prospective jurors should have made the judge aware that this publicity seriously threatened the jurors' privacy.

The press coverage of the Estes trial was not nearly as massive and pervasive as the attention given by the Cleveland newspapers and broadcasting stations to Sheppard's prosecution. Sheppard stood indicted for the murder of his wife; the State was demanding the death penalty. For months the virulent publicity about Sheppard and the murder had made the case notorious. Charges and countercharges were aired in the news media besides those for which Sheppard was called to trial. In addition, only three months before trial, Sheppard was examined for more than five hours without counsel during a three-day inquest which ended in a public brawl. The inquest was televised live from a high school gymnasium seating hundreds of people. Furthermore, the trial began two weeks before a hotly contested election at which both Chief Prosecutor Mahon and Judge Blythin were candidates for judgeships.

While we cannot say that Sheppard was denied due process by the judge's refusal to take precautions against the influence of pretrial publicity alone, the court's later rulings must be considered against the setting in which the trial was held. In light of this background, we believe that the arrangements made by the judge with the news media caused Sheppard to be deprived of that "judicial serenity and calm to which [he] was entitled." The fact is that bedlam reigned at the courthouse during the trial and newsmen took over practically the entire courtroom, hounding most of the participants in the trial, especially Sheppard. . . .

There can be no question about the nature of the publicity which surrounded Sheppard's trial. . . . Indeed, every court that has considered this case, save the court that tried it, has deplored the manner in which the news media inflamed and prejudiced the public. . . .

Nor is there doubt that this deluge of publicity reached at least some of the jury. On the only occasion that the jury was queried, two jurors admitted in open court to hearing the highly inflammatory charge that a prison inmate claimed Sheppard as the father of her illegitimate child. Despite the extent and nature of the publicity to which the jury was exposed during trial, the judge refused defense counsel's other requests that the jurors be asked whether they had read or heard specific prejudicial comment about the case, including the incidents we have previously summarized. In these circumstances, we can assume that some of this material reached members of the jury.

The court's fundamental error is compounded by the holding that it lacked power to control the publicity about the trial. From the very inception of the proceedings the judge announced that neither he nor anyone else could restrict prejudicial news accounts. And he reiterated this view on numerous occasions. Since he viewed the news media as his target, the judge never considered other means that are often utilized to reduce the appearance of prejudicial material and to protect the jury from outside influence. We conclude that these procedures would have been sufficient to guarantee Sheppard a fair trial and so do not consider what sanctions might be available against a recalcitrant press nor the charges of bias now made against the state trial judge.

The carnival atmosphere at trial could easily have been avoided since the courtroom and courthouse premises are subject to the control of the court. . . . [T]he presence of the press at judicial proceedings must be limited when it is apparent that the accused might otherwise be prejudiced or disadvantaged. Bearing in mind the massive pretrial publicity, the judge should have adopted stricter rules governing the use of the courtroom by newsmen, as Sheppard's counsel requested. The number of reporters in the courtroom itself could have been limited at the first sign that their pres-

ence would disrupt the trial. They certainly should not have been placed inside the bar. Furthermore, the judge should have more closely regulated the conduct of newsmen in the courtroom. For instance, the judge belatedly asked them not to handle and photograph trial exhibits lying on the counsel table during recesses.

. . . [T]he court should have insulated the witnesses. All of the newspapers and radio stations apparently interviewed prospective witnesses at will, and in many instances disclosed their testimony. . . .

. . . [T]he court should have made some effort to control the release of leads, information, and gossip to the press by police officers, witnesses, and the counsel for both sides. Much of the information thus disclosed was inaccurate, leading to groundless rumors and confusion. . . .

The fact that many of the prejudicial news items can be traced to the prosecution, as well as the defense, aggravates the judge's failure to take any action. Effective control of these sources—concededly within the court's power— might well have prevented the divulgence of inaccurate information, rumors, and accusations that made up much of the inflammatory publicity, at least after Sheppard's indictment.

More specifically, the trial court might well have proscribed extrajudicial statements by any lawyer, party, witness, or court official which divulged prejudicial matters, such as the refusal of Sheppard to submit to interrogation or take any lie detector tests; any statement made by Sheppard to officials; the identity of prospective witnesses or their probable testimony; any belief in guilt or innocence; or like statements concerning the merits of the case. . . .

From the cases coming here we note that unfair and prejudicial news comment on pending trials has become increasingly prevalent. Due process requires that the accused receive a trial by an impartial jury free from outside influences. Given the pervasiveness of modern communications and the difficulty of effacing prejudicial publicity from the minds of the jurors, the trial courts must take strong measures to ensure that the balance is never weighed against the accused. And appellate tribunals have the duty to make an independent evaluation of the circumstances. Of course, there is nothing that proscribes the press from reporting events that transpire in the courtroom. But where there is a reasonable likelihood that prejudicial news prior to trial will prevent a fair trial, the judge should continue

BOX 11-2   AFTERMATH . . . SAM SHEPPARD

DR. SAM SHEPPARD was convicted for the 1954 murder of his wife, Marilyn, and spent ten years in an Ohio prison. Following the Su-preme Court's reversal of the conviction in 1966, Sheppard was retried for the offense and found not guilty due to a lack of sufficient evidence. In spite of the acquittal, many people remained convinced that Sheppard was guilty. No other person was ever arrested for the crime. Unable to restart his medical career, Sheppard fell into a life of alcohol abuse and died of liver disease in 1970 at the age of forty-six. His son, Sam Reese Sheppard, who was seven years old at the time of the murder, spent much of his adult life attempting to clear his father's name.

Sam Sheppard embraces his son and his second wife Ariane as they leave the courthouse following his acquittal in September 1966. At right is F. Lee Bailey, Sheppard's attorney.

An alternative suspect surfaced in 1959 when Richard Eberling, who had worked at the Sheppard home as a window washer, was arrested for burglary. During the course of their investigation, police found a ring belonging to Marilyn Sheppard in Eberling's home. Eberling later was convicted of murdering a ninety-year-old widow, Ethel May Durdin, and sentenced to life in prison. A woman who had worked with Eberling claimed that he had boasted of killing Marilyn Sheppard. Eberling, who later denied any involvement in the Sheppard murder, died in prison in 1998.

Certain evidence at the Sheppard murder scene was never fully explained. Blood was spattered throughout the house. Given her wounds, it would have been nearly impossible for that blood to have come from Marilyn, and no cuts were found on Sam. This gave rise to the theory that a third person was there that night. Marilyn's two broken teeth allowed speculation that she had bitten her assailant, causing the blood loss.

Sam Reese Sheppard filed suit against the state of Ohio for the wrongful imprisonment of his father. To win the case and a subsequent damage award, he would have to convince a jury that his father was innocent. DNA evidence was taken from Eberling before his death, and the bodies of Sam and Marilyn Sheppard were exhumed for DNA samples. The results showed that the blood found at the crime scene was not from either Sam or Marilyn Sheppard, but that Eberling could not be excluded as the source of the blood.

The wrongful imprisonment trial took place in 2000. Sheppard's case was largely based on the DNA evidence. Attorneys for Ohio, who earlier made private statements hinting at Sheppard's probable innocence, aggressively defended against the lawsuit, claiming that the state had prosecuted the right man in the first place. They branded the DNA evidence as "mumbo jumbo" and portrayed Sam Sheppard as an adulterous playboy who killed his pregnant wife to get out of an unhappy marriage. After a trial taking two months, the jury returned a verdict in favor of the state. Sam Reese Sheppard had lost the battle to clear his father's name.

SOURCES: *New York Times,* March 26, 1996, February 5, 1997, April 13, 2000; and *USA Today,* April 13, 2000.

---

the case until the threat abates, or transfer it to another county not so permeated with publicity. In addition, sequestration of the jury was something the judge should have raised *sua sponte* with counsel. If publicity during the proceedings threatens the fairness of the trial, a new trial should be ordered. But we must remember that reversals are but palliatives; the cure lies in those remedial measures that will prevent the prejudice at its inception. The courts must take such steps by rule and regulation that will protect their processes from prejudicial outside interferences. Neither prosecutors, counsel for defense, the accused, witnesses, court staff nor enforcement officers coming under the jurisdiction of the court should be permitted to frustrate its function. Collaboration between counsel and the press as to information affecting the fairness of a criminal trial is not only subject to regulation, but is highly censurable and worthy of disciplinary measures.

Since the state trial judge did not fulfill his duty to protect Sheppard from the inherently prejudicial publicity which saturated the community and to control disruptive influences in the courtroom, we must reverse the denial of the habeas petition. The case is remanded to the District Court with instructions to issue a writ and order that Sheppard be released from custody unless the State puts him to its charges again within a reasonable time.

It is so ordered.

The Supreme Court's ruling ordered Sheppard, who had already spent ten years behind bars, released from prison. He was retried for the murder of his wife in 1966 and found not guilty. But even that did not end the saga of Sam Sheppard, as Box 11-2 details.

As for other defendants, *Sheppard* provides lower court judges with real ammunition to combat the dangers of an overzealous press. In Justice Clark's view, judges can take a variety of actions to prevent trials from becoming carnivals, mockeries of justice, as the Sheppard trial did.

Press v. Juries: The 1980s and Beyond. As trial court judges continued to limit the role and presence of the media at criminal proceedings, critics began to question the new balance between rights. This time the criticism was that the courts were excessively favoring the rights of the defendant. In a 1979 case, *Gannett Company v. DePasquale,* the Burger Court had the opportunity to "rebalance" the scales. A newspaper company asked the Court to prohibit a judge from closing the pretrial hearings for a highly publicized case. Writing for a majority of the Court, however, Justice Stewart declined to do so. Adopting the Warren Court's reasoning in *Sheppard,* he claimed that adverse publicity can endanger proceedings, a problem particularly acute at the pretrial stages. Stewart wrote,

This Court has long recognized that adverse publicity can endanger the ability of a defendant to receive a fair trial. . . . To

safeguard the due process rights of the accused, a trial judge has an affirmative constitutional duty to minimize the effects of prejudicial pretrial publicity. . . . And because of the Constitution's pervasive concern for these due process rights, a trial judge may surely take protective measures even when they are not strictly and inescapably necessary.

He also dealt with the company's assertion of a First Amendment right by stating that "any denial of access in this case was not absolute but only temporary."

But a year later, in *Richmond Newspapers v. Virginia,* the Court ruled in favor of a First Amendment claim over a Sixth Amendment claim, modifying the balance between these rights.[13] In this case, the justices addressed what some consider the bottom-line issue in this kind of dispute: May a judge completely close a trial? The justices ruled against such a practice, but why? What distinguishes trials from pretrial hearings?

Richmond Newspapers v. Virginia

448 U.S. 555 (1980)
laws.findlaw.com/US/448/555.html
Vote: 7 (Blackmun, Brennan, Burger, Marshall, Stevens,
        Stewart, White)
        1 (Rehnquist)

Opinion announcing the judgment of the Court: Burger
*Concurring opinions: Blackmun, Brennan, Stevens, Stewart,
        White*
Dissenting opinion: Rehnquist
Not participating: Powell

In July 1976 a Virginia court convicted a man named Stevenson for stabbing a hotel manager to death. An appellate court reversed the conviction on a procedural error, and a new trial occurred before the same court. But that proceeding and one other ended in mistrials. By the time the fourth trial date was set for 1978, the case had garnered a great deal of public and media interest. Because such attention could interfere with jury selection, Stevenson's attorney asked the judge to close the trial to the public. When the prosecutor voiced no objection, the judge granted the request, a privilege judges had under Virginia law.

---

13. For oral arguments in this case, navigate to: *oyez.nwu.edu.*

Reporters covering the case brought suit against the state, arguing that its law violated the First Amendment. This claim received legal support from numerous civil liberties and media organizations. They not only agreed with the appellants, but also asked the Court to overrule *Gannett*. The Reporters Committee for Freedom of the Press, on behalf of several media associations, said, "Great confusion has arisen as to what *Gannett* means, and the case is being used as grounds for closing all types of criminal proceedings." The ACLU stated, "The public and press have a constitutionally protected right of access to criminal pretrial and trial proceedings."

MR. CHIEF JUSTICE BURGER announced the judgment of the Court.

The narrow question presented in this case is whether the right of the public and press to attend criminal trials is guaranteed under the United States Constitution. . . .

We begin consideration of this case by noting that the precise issue presented here has not previously been before this Court for decision. In *Gannett Co. v. DePasquale* [1979], the Court was not required to decide whether a right of access to *trials*, as distinguished from hearings on *pre*trial motions, was constitutionally guaranteed. The Court held that the Sixth Amendment's guarantee to the accused of a public trial gave neither the public nor the press an enforceable right of access to a pretrial suppression hearing. . . .

In prior cases the Court has treated questions involving conflicts between publicity and a defendant's right to a fair trial. But here for the first time the Court is asked to decide whether a criminal trial itself may be closed to the public upon the unopposed request of a defendant, without any demonstration that closure is required to protect the defendant's superior right to a fair trial, or that some other overriding consideration requires closure.

The origins of the proceeding which has become the modern criminal trial in Anglo-American justice can be traced back beyond reliable historical records. . . . What is significant for present purposes is that throughout its evolution, the trial has been open to all who care to observe. . . .

. . . [T]he historical evidence demonstrates conclusively that at the time when our organic laws were adopted, criminal trials both here and in England had long been presumptively open. This is no quirk of history; rather, it has long

been recognized as an indispensable attribute to an Anglo-American trial. . . .

From this unbroken, uncontradicted history, supported by reasons as valid today as in centuries past, we are bound to conclude that a presumption of openness inheres in the very nature of a criminal trial under our system of justice. This conclusion is hardly novel; without a direct holding on the issue, the Court has voiced its recognition of it in a variety of contexts over the years. . . .

Despite the history of criminal trials being presumptively open since long before the Constitution, the State presses its contention that neither the Constitution nor the Bill of Rights contains any provision which by its terms guarantees to the public the right to attend criminal trials. Standing alone, this is correct, but there remains the question whether, absent an explicit provision, the Constitution affords protection against exclusion of the public from criminal trials.

The First Amendment, in conjunction with the Fourteenth, prohibits governments from "abridging the freedom of speech, or of the press; or the right of the people peaceably to assemble, and to petition the Government for a redress of grievances." These expressly guaranteed freedoms share a common core purpose of assuring freedom of communication on matters relating to the functioning of government. Plainly it would be difficult to single out any aspect of government of higher concern and importance to the people than the manner in which criminal trials are conducted; . . . recognition of this pervades the centuries-old history of open trials and the opinions of this Court.

The Bill of Rights was enacted against the backdrop of the long history of trials being presumptively open. Public access to trials was then regarded as an important aspect of the process itself; the conduct of trials "before as many of the people as chuse to attend" was regarded as one of "the inestimable advantages of a free English constitution of government." In guaranteeing freedoms such as those of speech and press, the First Amendment can be read as protecting the right of everyone to attend trials so as to give meaning to those explicit guarantees. . . . What this means in the context of trials is that the First Amendment guarantees of speech and press, standing alone, prohibit government from summarily closing courtroom doors which had long been open to the public at the time that Amendment was adopted. . . .

It is not crucial whether we describe this right to attend criminal trials to hear, see, and communicate observations concerning them as a "right of access" or a "right to gather information," for we have recognized that "without some protection for seeking out the news, freedom of the press could be eviscerated." The explicit, guaranteed rights to speak and to publish concerning what takes place at a trial would lose much meaning if access to observe the trial could, as it was here, be foreclosed arbitrarily. . . .

The State argues that the Constitution nowhere spells out a guarantee for the right of the public to attend trials, and that accordingly no such right is protected. The possibility that such a contention could be made did not escape the notice of the Constitution's draftsmen; they were concerned that some important rights might be thought disparaged because not specifically guaranteed. It was even argued that because of this danger no Bill of Rights should be adopted. . . .

But arguments such as the State makes have not precluded recognition of important rights not enumerated. Notwithstanding the appropriate caution against reading into the Constitution rights not explicitly defined, the Court has acknowledged that certain unarticulated rights are implicit in enumerated guarantees. For example, the rights of association and of privacy, the right to be presumed innocent, and the right to be judged by a standard of proof beyond a reasonable doubt in a criminal trial, as well as the right to travel, appear nowhere in the Constitution or Bill of Rights. Yet these important but unarticulated rights have nonetheless been found to share constitutional protection in common with explicit guarantees. . . .

We hold that the right to attend criminal trials is implicit in the guarantees of the First Amendment; without the freedom to attend such trials, which people have exercised for centuries, important aspects of freedom of speech and "of the press could be eviscerated."

Having concluded there was a guaranteed right of the public under the First and Fourteenth Amendments to attend the trial of Stevenson's case, we return to the closure order challenged by appellants. The Court in *Gannett* made clear that although the Sixth Amendment guarantees the accused a right to a public trial, it does not give a right to a private trial. Despite the fact that this was the fourth trial of the accused, the trial judge made no findings to support closure; no inquiry was made as to whether alternative solu-

tions would have met the need to ensure fairness; there was no recognition of any right under the Constitution for the public or press to attend the trial. In contrast to the pretrial proceeding dealt with in *Gannett,* there exist in the context of the trial itself various tested alternatives to satisfy the constitutional demands of fairness. There was no suggestion that any problems with witnesses could not have been dealt with by their exclusion from the courtroom or their sequestration during the trial. Nor is there anything to indicate that sequestration of the jurors would not have guarded against their being subjected to any improper information. All of the alternatives admittedly present difficulties for trial courts, but none of the factors relied on here was beyond the realm of the manageable. Absent an overriding interest articulated in findings, the trial of a criminal case must be open to the public. Accordingly, the judgment under review is

Reversed.

MR. JUSTICE BRENNAN, with whom MR. JUSTICE MARSHALL joins, concurring in the judgment.

[R]esolution of First Amendment public access claims in individual cases must be strongly influenced by the weight of historical practice and by an assessment of the specific structural value of public access in the circumstances. With regard to the case at hand, our ingrained tradition of public trials and the importance of public access to the broader purposes of the trial process, tip the balance strongly toward the rule that trials be open. What countervailing interests might be sufficiently compelling to reverse this presumption of openness need not concern us now, for the statute at stake here authorizes trial closures at the unfettered discretion of the judge and parties. Accordingly, Va. Code §19.2-266 (Supp. 1980) violates the First and Fourteenth Amendments, and the decision of the Virginia Supreme Court to the contrary should be reversed.

MR. JUSTICE REHNQUIST, dissenting.

For the reasons stated in my separate concurrence in *Gannett Co. v. DePasquale* (1979), I do not believe that either the First or Sixth Amendment, as made applicable to the States by the Fourteenth, requires that a State's reasons for denying public access to a trial, where both the prosecuting attorney and the defendant have consented to an order of closure approved by the judge, are subject to any additional constitutional review at our hands. And I most certainly do not believe that the Ninth Amendment confers upon us any such power to review orders of state trial judges closing trials in such situations.

We have, at present, 50 state judicial systems and one federal judicial system in the United States, and our authority to reverse a decision by the highest court of the State is limited to only those occasions when the state decision violates some provision of the United States Constitution. And that authority should be exercised with a full sense that the judges whose decisions we review are making the same effort as we to uphold the Constitution. As said by Mr. Justice Jackson, concurring in the result in *Brown v. Allen* (1953), "We are not final because we are infallible, but we are infallible only because we are final.". . .

The issue here is not whether the "right" to freedom of the press conferred by the First Amendment to the Constitution overrides the defendant's "right" to a fair trial conferred by other Amendments to the Constitution; it is, instead, whether any provision in the Constitution may fairly be read to prohibit what the trial judge in the Virginia state-court system did in this case. Being unable to find any such prohibition in the First, Sixth, Ninth, or any other Amendment to the United States Constitution, or in the Constitution itself, I dissent.

In finding the balance between defendants' rights and those of the press, the Court said that judges can pursue a variety of strategies to protect the accused, but they cannot completely close trial proceedings to the public and press. In recent years, however, judges have become more sympathetic to press coverage of criminal trials. One reason is that audio and video equipment is not as noisy and disruptive as it was when *Sheppard* was decided. Trials may be recorded or televised without violating the conditions necessary for the dispassionate consideration of evidence. Some new courtrooms are constructed with videotaping facilities fully incorporated into the building's plans. Court TV, a network dedicated to covering trials, is now one of the more popular channels on cable television.

Juries and the American Criminal Justice System: Some Concluding Observations

In spite of this increased exposure, broadcast coverage of important trials remains a controversial issue. The Simpson murder trial touched off another national debate on the ways televising trials may alter criminal proceedings and outcomes, especially in jury trials.[14]

But this is not the only controversy surrounding American juries. We have already mentioned two practices—the use of experts to advise lawyers on jury selection and peremptory challenges to eliminate undesirable jurors—that raise questions about the degree to which juries conform to the Sixth Amendment's mandate that they be impartial. Many judges, prosecutors, and scholars also have severely criticized the jury system for its expense and its slowness in administering justice. Perhaps it was in response to such criticisms that the Supreme Court permitted experimentation with two historic features of juries under the common law, that they consist of twelve persons and reach a unanimous verdict.

Although these decisions may have helped quicken the pace of justice, they have not mitigated other criticisms of the American jury system. Concerns with the process of selecting jurors, whether centered on biases within the process or the plight of prospective jurors who often spend days waiting to be called, continue to provoke intense debates. At the same time, the problem of jury nullification—the refusal of a jury to convict for reasons that may have nothing to do with the strength of the evidence—has emerged as a pressing issue within the American system of criminal justice.

Despite these concerns, few scholars, lawyers, or judges argue for the total elimination of the jury. To the contrary, most seem to agree with Tracy Weiss: "Although the jury system is far from being perfect, it acts as a great democratizing principle which brings the people of our country directly into the government system."[15]

14. We adopt some of the discussion this section from Walter F. Murphy, C. Herman Pritchett, and Lee Epstein, *Courts, Judges, and Politics*, 5th ed. (New York: McGraw-Hill, forthcoming).

15. Tracy Gilstrap Weiss, "The Great Democratizing Principle: The Effect on South Africa of Planning a Democracy with a Jury System," *Temple International and Comparative Law Journal* 11 (1997): 107.

TRIAL PROCEEDINGS

Once attorneys complete the *voir dire* and select the petit jury, the trial begins. Almost all trials follow the same format. First, attorneys make opening statements. Each side, beginning with the prosecution because it must prove guilt beyond a reasonable doubt, presents an opening argument, explaining the crime and what it must prove to obtain a guilty or not guilty verdict.

Next, each side presents its case, again beginning with the prosecution. At this point, attorneys call witnesses who testify for their side and then are cross-examined by the opposing attorney. This stage is the heart of the trial, and here, as in all other important parts of the criminal justice system, the Constitution affords defendants a great many rights. For example, a Sixth Amendment clause states that the accused shall "be confronted with the witnesses against him." This provision, often called the Confrontation Clause, means that defendants have the right to be present during their own trials and to cross-examine prosecution witnesses, who must appear in court to testify.

The right to confrontation generally prohibits trials *in absentia*, but there are limits to this right. In *Illinois v. Allen* (1970), for example, the Supreme Court considered the actions of a trial judge in response to a defendant's misbehavior in the courtroom. Allen, on trial for armed robbery, verbally abused the judge and others in the courtroom, threw papers, continually talked loudly, and interrupted witnesses. After ample warning, the judge ordered Allen removed, and the trial continued in his absence. Allen was convicted, and he appealed on the grounds that he was not allowed to be present during his trial. A unanimous Supreme Court rejected his appeal. Writing for the Court, Justice Black explained that the right to confrontation can be waived by the defendant's own abusive behavior. As a response to such disruptive action, a trial court judge may find the accused in contempt of court or remove him, as the judge did with Allen. Black indicated that in extreme cases a judge may order the defendant to be bound and gagged.

A controversial question is whether the Confrontation Clause confers an absolute right on all defendants to face their accusers in open court. In rape or child abuse trials, such meetings can cause emotional stress or damage, especially for children. In response to this situation, several states devised ways for children to testify under oath without being in the presence of the defendant. Some states have used closed-circuit television systems so that a child could testify and be cross-examined in another room and the session transmitted into the courtroom. Other states have screened the child witness so that he or she cannot see the defendant. Are these alternatives constitutional? The Court has had difficulty answering this question.

For example, in *Coy v. Iowa* (1988) the Court struck down a system in which the child witness testified behind a screen. The child could not see the defendant, but the defendant could see the dim outline of the witness and hear the testimony. This arrangement, according to a six-justice majority, was insufficient to satisfy the Confrontation Clause.

Two years later, however, in *Maryland v. Craig* the justices, 5–4, upheld the conviction of a woman on child abuse charges after a trial in which a six-year-old witness testified on closed circuit television. Justice O'Connor, for the majority, explained that the state's interest in child welfare could justify these procedural modifications:

[W]here necessary to protect a child witness from trauma that would be caused by testifying in the physical presence of the defendant, at least where such trauma would impair the child's ability to communicate, the Confrontation Clause does not prohibit use of a procedure that, despite the absence of face-to-face confrontation, ensures the reliability of the evidence by subjecting it to rigorous adversarial testing and thereby preserves the essence of effective confrontation.

In dissent Justice Scalia scolded the majority for ignoring the plain meaning of the Sixth Amendment:

Seldom has this Court failed so conspicuously to sustain a categorical guarantee of the Constitution against the tide of prevailing current opinion. The Sixth Amendment provides, with unmistakable clarity, that "[i]n all criminal prosecutions, the accused shall enjoy the right . . . to be confronted with the witnesses against him." The purpose of enshrining this protection in the Constitution was to assure that none of the many policy interests from time to time pursued by statutory law could overcome a defendant's right to face his or her accusers in court.

In addition to specific Sixth Amendment guarantees, defendants also have the right to a fair trial, generally guaranteed by the Due Process Clauses of the Fifth and Fourteenth Amendments. As we have seen, this rather vague term—*due process*—has been used to ensure that police obtain evidence by fair means and as a way to apply constitutional guarantees to the states. The Court also has used it to guarantee that defendants receive fair treatment from prosecutors and courts.

One of the most important manifestations of due process in criminal proceedings is what is known in civil cases as discovery. This long-standing legal tradition allows both sides of a civil dispute to have access to each other's cases. Until 1963 *mandated* discovery was not a part of most criminal proceedings. Instead, each side prepared its case in relative isolation, knowing little of the evidence the other side had. That year, however, the Supreme Court in *Brady v. Maryland* radically changed criminal procedure by creating the so-called Brady request. Upon the request of the defense, prosecutors must divulge all relevant information about the case. The defense, however, does not have to provide any information to the prosecutor unless specifically mandated under state law. The Supreme Court viewed the Brady request as a necessary mechanism to preserve the fundamental fairness of the trial process. "We now hold that the suppression by the prosecution of evidence favorable to an accused upon request violates due process where the evidence is material either to guilt or to punishment, irrespective of the good faith or bad faith of the prosecution," the Court said.

In 1976 the Court greatly expanded the Brady request procedure. The case, *United States v. Agurs,* evolved from charges against Linda Agurs for stabbing to death James Sewell after a brief interlude in a motel room. Agurs claimed self-defense, but the jury returned a guilty verdict after less than twenty-five minutes of deliberation. Agurs's defense attorney later discovered that Sewell had a history of violent behavior, a fact the attorney believed could have been used to establish self-defense. The prosecutor knew Sewell's history, but had not told it to the defense because the defense had made no Brady request. Agurs's attorney claimed that this information should have been disclosed even without a specific request. The Supreme Court held that the Constitution requires the prosecutor to disclose everything relevant to the case that might establish a reasonable doubt of the defendant's guilt that would not otherwise exist. This obligation rests on the prosecutor even when the defense makes no request for information. With respect to Agurs, however, the Court held that Sewell's violent history would not have created a reasonable doubt that was not already apparent from information at the disposal of the defendant, and, therefore, the prosecutor had not committed a constitutional violation for failing to volunteer the information.

FINAL TRIAL STAGE: AN OVERVIEW OF SENTENCING

Judges run trials in fairly standardized ways and in accordance with an established set of rules based on constitutional guarantees. The end stages are no exception. Once both sides have presented their cases, the attorneys make closing arguments in which they summarize their cases and try to convince the jury that they have proved them. Next, the judge makes a charge to the jury, providing the members with instructions and guidelines upon which to base a decision of guilt or innocence. The jury then deliberates to reach a verdict. What goes on in the jury room is private and known only to the jurors. Once the jury reaches a verdict, it announces its decision in open court. If it finds the defendant not guilty, the accused goes free. If it finds the defendant guilty, the judge pronounces sentence.[16]

In general, sentencing is a highly discretionary process. Within limits for various crimes, judges—particularly those in state courts—enjoy wide latitude in selecting an appropriate penalty. On any given day in the United States, defendants convicted of the same crime in different localities may receive vastly different sentences. Why do disparities exist? A partial explanation is that a judge considers all kinds of information before pronouncing sentence, including the nature of the crime

16. In six states juries sentence defendants. However, in cases involving the death penalty, juries often determine whether the convicted should be executed.

BOX 11-3   A SUMMARY OF THE FEDERAL SENTENCING GUIDELINES

1. In imposing a sentence, a district judge must consider the guidelines of the Sentencing Commission, a body established by the statute. Under these guidelines, the possible sentence ranges are based on 43 offense level categories (determined from the offense, adjusted for factors such as the type of victim and the defendant's role in the offense) and six criminal history categories (determined primarily from the number and characteristics of past convictions). For each combination of offense and criminal history categories, a range of possible imprisonment lengths (for instance, 57 to 71 months) is indicated. Other guidelines indicate when probation may be substituted for a prison sentence and the amounts of monetary fines appropriate for each offense level.

2. In each case the judge must impose a sentence within the range established by the Sentencing Commission unless the judge finds a relevant aggravating or mitigating circumstance that the Commission did not adequately take into account. Not ordinarily relevant are such personal characteristics as age, education, employment record, and family and community ties; never relevant are race, sex, religion, and socio-economic status. A judge can depart from the guidelines if the prosecution states that the defendant has provided substantial assistance in the investigation or prosecution of another offender.

3. If the sentence is above the range established by the Sentencing Commission, the defendant may appeal the sentence; if it is below the range, the prosecution may appeal. If the court of appeals finds that the sentence is unreasonable, it may return the case to the district judge for resentencing or amend the sentence itself.

SOURCE: Lawrence Baum, *American Courts*, 3d ed. (Boston: Houghton Mifflin, 1994).

committed; the individual's job prospects, family situation, prior criminal record, history of alcohol or drug abuse; and any presentencing reports supplied by social workers or other state agents. In addition, under the Supreme Court's decision in *Wisconsin v. Mitchell* (1993) *(see pages 278–280)*, judges may "enhance" sentences for racially motivated crimes. Mitchell was convicted of battery—a crime carrying a maximum sentence of two years. When it was determined that Mitchell "intentionally" selected his victim because of his race, his sentence was "enhanced" to four years.

By considering various kinds of information about convicted defendants, judges assert that they can form a more complete picture of them and hand down appropriate sentences. Discretionary sentencing has its share of detractors. Some scholars argue that irrelevant factors enter the process. Just as partisanship and ideology seem to play a role in Supreme Court decisionmaking, they also may influence the sentences lower court judges reach. Another serious charge is that discrimination pervades sentencing decisions, with some research suggesting that white judges are likely to deal more harshly with convicted blacks than with whites.[17]

Given these complaints, it is not surprising that Congress has tried to limit judges' discretion by creating the United States Sentencing Commission. The commission's task is to establish sentencing guidelines that federal judges must follow. The guidelines are designed to reduce the opportunity for discrimination to influence sentencing, but preserve enough flexibility so that a judge can tailor a penalty to the individual defendant based upon legally relevant criteria *(see Box 11-3)*.

THE EIGHTH AMENDMENT

In addition to statutory attempts to limit judicial discretion in sentencing, there is an important constitutional limit: the clause in the Eighth Amendment that bans

17. See Susan Welch, Michael Combs, and John Gruhl, "Do Black Judges Make a Difference?" *American Journal of Political Science* 32 (1988): 126–136. Other studies, however, have not found much evidence of racially based sentencing. In general, a reasonable conclusion is that "[d]iscrimination appears to exist in some places, for some types of crimes, and for some judges, but not universally." Lawrence Baum, *American Courts*, 3d ed. (Boston: Houghton Mifflin, 1994), 209.

cruel and unusual punishments. The meaning of this clause has plagued generations of justices, with no issue more perplexing than the constitutionality of the death penalty.

The justices' opinions in the death penalty cases tell us a great deal about what cruel and unusual punishment means and what it does not. Since 1947 the Court has held that the death penalty is inherently neither cruel nor unusual.[18] Never has a *majority* of the justices agreed that it is, but why not? The answer lies with the intent of the Framers (at the time of ratification, death penalties were in use) and with the Due Process Clauses of the Fifth and Fourteenth Amendments, which state that no person can be deprived of life without due process of law. Presumably, if due process is observed, life *can* be deprived.

The majority of Americans also support use of the death penalty (*see Figure 11-1, page 601*), but many interest groups are working to eliminate it. These groups believe that the death penalty constitutes cruel and unusual punishment, but, recognizing the Court's unwillingness to agree, they have tried to convince the justices that the way the death penalty is applied violates due process norms.

One of the first attempts to implement a due process strategy was undertaken by the NAACP Legal Defense and Educational Fund in *Furman v. Georgia* (1972). William Furman, a black man, was accused of murdering a white man, the father of five children. Under Georgia law, the jury determined whether a convicted murderer should be put to death. This system, the LDF argued, led to unacceptable disparities in sentencing: blacks convicted of murdering whites were far more likely to receive the death penalty than whites convicted of the same crime.

A divided Supreme Court agreed with the LDF. In a short *per curiam* opinion, deciding *Furman* and two companion cases, the justices said, "The Court holds that the imposition and carrying out of the death penalty in these cases constitutes cruel and unusual punishment." Following this terse statement, however, were nine separate opinions (five for the LDF and four against), running 243 pages (50,000 words)—the longest in Court history.[19]

The views presented in the opinions of the five-member majority varied considerably—three justices (Douglas, Stewart, and White) thought capital punishment, *as currently imposed*, violated the Constitution, and two (Brennan and Marshall) said it was unconstitutional in all circumstances. Beyond these general groupings, the five justices agreed on only one major point of law: that those states using capital punishment do so in an arbitrary manner, particularly with regard to race. However, they framed even this statement in divergent terms. Douglas said arbitrariness led to discriminatory sentencing. Brennan used arbitrariness as part of a four-part test designed to determine whether the death penalty is acceptable punishment. He found that it was degrading, arbitrary, unacceptable to contemporary society, and excessive. Marshall adopted a similar approach, but explained that arbitrariness was but one reason why capital punishment was cruel and unusual and "morally unacceptable." To Stewart, arbitrariness in sentencing meant that the death penalty was imposed in a "wanton" and "freak[ish] manner," akin to being struck by lightening. For White, arbitrariness led to the infrequency of imposition, which in turn made death a less than credible deterrent.

The dissenters, Blackmun, Burger, Powell, and Rehnquist (the four Nixon appointees), were more uniform in their critiques. To a lesser or greater extent, all expressed the view that the Court was encroaching on legislative turf and that Americans had not "repudiated" the death penalty. Justice Blackmun also lambasted the majority for expressing views wholly inconsistent with past precedent. In particular, he noted that Stewart and White had previously found that it would be virtually impossible to create sentencing standards, but now they were striking laws in part because of the absence of such standards.

Chief Justice Burger's opinion raised a unique issue: he noted that the plurality (Douglas, Stewart, and White) had not ruled that capital punishment under all circumstances was unconstitutional and that it may be possible for states to rewrite their laws to meet their objections. As he asserted: "It is clear that if state legisla-

---

18. See *Louisiana ex rel. Frances v. Resweber* (1947).
19. We adopt this discussion from Lee Epstein and Joseph F. Kobylka,

The Supreme Court and Legal Change: Abortion and the Death Penalty (Chapel Hill: University of North Carolina Press, 1992), 78–80.

tures and the Congress wish to maintain the availability of capital punishment, significant statutory changes will have to be made. . . . [L]egislative bodies may seek to bring their laws into compliance with the Court's ruling by providing standards for juries and judges to follow . . . or by more narrowly defining crimes for which the penalty is imposed." Privately, however, Burger thought his suggestion futile, lamenting later, "There will never be another execution in this country."[20]

This view was echoed in many quarters. A University of Washington law professor wrote, "My hunch is that *Furman* spells the complete end of capital punishment in this country."[21] LDF attorneys were ecstatic. One called it "the biggest step forward criminal justice has taken in 1,000 years."[22]

As it turned out, the abolitionists celebrated a bit too soon because the Supreme Court was not finished with the death penalty. Just three years after *Furman*, the Court agreed to hear *Gregg v. Georgia* to consider the constitutionality of a new breed of death penalty laws written to overcome the defects of the old laws. Did these new laws reduce the chance for "wanton and freakish" punishment of the sort the Court found so distasteful in *Furman?* Consider this question as you read the facts and opinions in *Gregg v. Georgia.*[23]

Gregg v. Georgia

428 U.S. 153 (1976)
laws.findlaw.com/US/428/153.html
Vote: 7 (Blackmun, Burger, Powell, Rehnquist, Stevens, Stewart, White)
2 (Brennan, Marshall)
Opinion announcing the judgment of the Court: Stewart
Concurring opinions: Blackmun, Burger and Rehnquist, White
Dissenting opinions: Brennan, Marshall

20. Bob Woodward and Scott Armstrong, *The Brethren* (New York: Simon and Schuster, 1979), 219.

21. John M. Junker, "The Death Penalty Cases: A Preliminary Comment," *Washington Law Review* 48 (1972): 109.

22. Quoted in Frederick Mann, "Anthony Amsterdam," *Juris Doctor* 3 (1973): 31–32.

23. For oral arguments in this case, navigate to: *oyez.nwu.edu.*

Taking cues from *Furman*, many states set out to revise their death penalty laws. Among the new plans was one proposed by Georgia (and other states). At the heart of this law was the "bifurcated trial," which consisted of two stages—the trial and the sentencing phase. The trial would proceed as usual, with a jury finding the defendant guilty or not guilty. If the verdict was guilty, the prosecution could seek the death penalty at the sentencing stage, in which the defense attorney presents the mitigating facts and the prosecution presents the aggravating facts. Mitigating facts include the individual's record, family responsibility, psychiatric reports, chances for rehabilitation, and age.[24] Such data are not specified in law. The prosecution, however, has to demonstrate that at least one codified aggravating factor was present.

The Georgia law specified ten aggravating factors, including murders committed "while the offender was engaged in the commission of another capital offense," the murder of "a judicial officer . . . or . . . district attorney because of the exercise of his official duty," and murders that are "outrageously or wantonly vile, horrible, or inhumane." After hearing both sides, the jury determines whether the individual receives the death penalty. By spelling out the conditions that must be present before a death penalty can be imposed, the law sought to reduce the jury's discretion and eliminate the arbitrary application of the death penalty that the Court found unacceptable in *Furman*. As a further safeguard, the Georgia Supreme Court was to review all jury determinations of death. This new law was applied to Troy Gregg and quickly challenged by abolitionist interests.

Gregg and a friend were hitchhiking north in Florida. Two men picked them up, and the foursome was later joined by another passenger who rode with them as far as Atlanta. The four then continued to a rest stop on the highway. The next day, the bodies of the two drivers were found in a nearby ditch. The individual let off in Atlanta identified Gregg and his friend as possible assailants.

24. In 1982 in *Eddings v. Oklahoma* the Court agreed that age constituted a mitigating factor, which does not mean that minors cannot receive the death penalty—just that juries and judges may consider age during the sentencing stage. In fact, the Court has held that someone as young as sixteen at the time the crime was committed can be executed. See *Thompson v. Oklahoma* (1988) and *Sanford v. Kentucky* (1989).

Gregg was tried under Georgia's new death penalty system. He was convicted of murder and sentenced to death, a penalty the state's highest court upheld.

Judgment of the Court, and opinions of MR. JUSTICE STEWART, MR. JUSTICE POWELL, and MR. JUSTICE STEVENS announced by MR. JUSTICE STEWART.

The issue in this case is whether the imposition of the sentence of death for the crime of murder under the law of Georgia violates the Eighth and Fourteenth Amendments. . . .

We address initially the basic contention that the punishment of death for the crime of murder is, under all circumstances, "cruel and unusual" in violation of the Eighth and Fourteenth Amendments of the Constitution. . . . [W]e . . . [also] consider the sentence of death imposed under the Georgia statutes at issue in this case.

The Court on a number of occasions has both assumed and asserted the constitutionality of capital punishment. In several cases that assumption provided a necessary foundation for the decision, as the Court was asked to decide whether a particular method of carrying out a capital sentence would be allowed to stand under the Eighth Amendment. But until *Furman v. Georgia* (1972), the Court never confronted squarely the fundamental claim that the punishment of death always, regardless of the enormity of the offense or the procedure followed in imposing the sentence, is cruel and unusual punishment in violation of the Constitution. Although this issue was presented and addressed in *Furman*, it was not resolved by the Court. Four Justices would have held that capital punishment is not unconstitutional *per se;* two Justices would have reached the opposite conclusion; and three Justices, while agreeing that the statutes then before the Court were invalid as applied, left open the question whether such punishment may ever be imposed. We now hold that the punishment of death does not invariably violate the Constitution.

The history of the prohibition of "cruel and unusual" punishment already has been reviewed at length. The phrase first appeared in the English Bill of Rights of 1689, which was drafted by Parliament at the accession of William and Mary. The English version appears to have been directed against punishments unauthorized by statute and beyond the jurisdiction of the sentencing court, as well as those disproportionate to the offense involved. The American draftsmen, who adopted the English phrasing in drafting the Eighth Amendment, were primarily concerned, however, with proscribing "tortures" and other "barbarous" methods of punishment.

In the earliest cases raising Eighth Amendment claims, the Court focused on particular methods of execution to determine whether they were too cruel to pass constitutional muster. The constitutionality of the sentence of death itself was not at issue, and the criterion used to evaluate the mode of execution was its similarity to "torture" and other "barbarous" methods.

But the Court has not confined the prohibition embodied in the Eighth Amendment to "barbarous" methods that were generally outlawed in the 18th century. Instead, the Amendment has been interpreted in a flexible and dynamic manner. The Court early recognized that "a principle to be vital must be capable of wider application than the mischief which gave it birth." *Weems v. United States* (1910). Thus the Clause forbidding "cruel and unusual" punishments "is not fastened to the obsolete but may acquire meaning as public opinion becomes enlightened by a humane justice.". . .

It is clear from . . . these precedents that the Eighth Amendment has not been regarded as a static concept. As Mr. Chief Justice Warren said, in an oft-quoted phrase, "[t]he Amendment must draw its meaning from the evolving standards of decency that mark the progress of a maturing society." Thus, an assessment of contemporary values concerning the infliction of a challenged sanction is relevant to the application of the Eighth Amendment. As we develop below more fully, this assessment does not call for a subjective judgment. It requires, rather, that we look to objective indicia that reflect the public attitude toward a given sanction.

But our cases also make clear that public perceptions of standards of decency with respect to criminal sanctions are not conclusive. A penalty also must accord with "the dignity of man," which is the "basic concept underlying the Eighth Amendment." This means, at least, that the punishment not be "excessive." When a form of punishment in the abstract (in this case, whether capital punishment may ever be imposed as a sanction for murder) rather than in the particular (the propriety of death as a penalty to be applied to a specific defendant for a specific crime) is under consideration, the inquiry into "excessiveness" has two aspects. First, the punishment must not involve the unnecessary and wanton infliction of pain. Second, the punishment must not be grossly out of proportion to the severity of the crime.

Of course, the requirements of the Eighth Amendment must be applied with an awareness of the limited role to be played by the courts. This does not mean that judges have no role to play, for the Eighth Amendment is a restraint upon the exercise of legislative power. . . .

But, while we have an obligation to insure that constitutional bounds are not overreached, we may not act as judges as we might as legislators. . . .

Therefore, in assessing a punishment selected by a democratically elected legislature against the constitutional measure, we presume its validity. We may not require the legislature to select the least severe penalty possible so long as the penalty selected is not cruelly inhumane or disproportionate to the crime involved. And a heavy burden rests on those who would attack the judgment of the representatives of the people. . . .

In the discussion to this point we have sought to identify the principles and considerations that guide a court in addressing an Eighth Amendment claim. We now consider specifically whether the sentence of death for the crime of murder is a *per se* violation of the Eighth and Fourteenth Amendments to the Constitution. We note first that history and precedent strongly support a negative answer to this question.

The imposition of the death penalty for the crime of murder has a long history of acceptance both in the United States and in England. . . .

It is apparent from the text of the Constitution itself that the existence of capital punishment was accepted by the Framers. At the time the Eighth Amendment was ratified, capital punishment was a common sanction in every State. . . . The Fifth Amendment, adopted at the same time as the Eighth, contemplated the continued existence of the capital sanction by imposing certain limits on the prosecution of capital cases:

"No person shall be held to answer for a capital, or otherwise infamous crime, unless on a presentment or indictment of a Grand Jury . . . ; nor shall any person be subject for the same offense to be twice put in jeopardy of life or limb; . . . nor be deprived of life, liberty, or property, without due process of law. . . ."

And the Fourteenth Amendment, adopted over three quarters of a century later, similarly contemplates the existence of the capital sanction in providing that no State shall deprive any person of "life, liberty, or property" without due process of law.

For nearly two centuries, this Court, repeatedly and often expressly, has recognized that capital punishment is not invalid *per se*. . . .

Four years ago, the petitioners in *Furman* and its companion cases predicated their argument primarily upon the asserted proposition that standards of decency had evolved to the point where capital punishment no longer could be tolerated. The petitioners in those cases said, in effect, that the evolutionary process had come to an end, and that standards of decency required that the Eighth Amendment be construed finally as prohibiting capital punishment for any crime regardless of its depravity and impact on society. This view was accepted by two Justices. Three other Justices were unwilling to go so far; focusing on the procedures by which convicted defendants were selected for the death penalty rather than on the actual punishment inflicted, they joined in the conclusion that the statutes before the Court were constitutionally invalid.

The petitioners in the capital cases before the Court today renew the "standards of decency" argument, but developments during the four years since *Furman* have undercut substantially the assumptions upon which their argument rested. Despite the continuing debate, dating back to the 19th century, over the morality and utility of capital punishment, it is now evident that a large proportion of American society continues to regard it as an appropriate and necessary criminal sanction.

The most marked indication of society's endorsement of the death penalty for murder is the legislative response to *Furman*. The legislatures of at least 35 States have enacted new statutes that provide for the death penalty for at least some crimes that result in the death of another person. And the Congress of the United States, in 1974, enacted a statute providing the death penalty for aircraft piracy that results in death. These recently adopted statutes have attempted to address the concerns expressed by the Court in *Furman* primarily (i) by specifying the factors to be weighed and the procedures to be followed in deciding when to impose a capital sentence, or (ii) by making the death penalty mandatory for specified crimes. But all of the post-*Furman* statutes make clear that capital punishment itself has not been rejected by the elected representatives of the people.

In the only statewide referendum occurring since *Furman* and brought to our attention, the people of California adopted a constitutional amendment that authorized capital punishment, in effect negating a prior ruling by the Supreme Court of California that the death penalty violated the California Constitution.

The jury also is a significant and reliable objective index of contemporary values because it is so directly involved. . . . It may be true that evolving standards have influenced juries in recent decades to be more discriminating in imposing the sentence of death. But the relative infrequency of jury verdicts imposing the death sentence does not indicate rejection of capital punishment *per se.* Rather, the reluctance of juries in many cases to impose the sentence may well reflect the humane feeling that this most irrevocable of sanctions should be reserved for a small number of extreme cases. Indeed, the actions of juries in many States since *Furman* are fully compatible with the legislative judgments, reflected in the new statutes, as to the continued utility and necessity of capital punishment in appropriate cases. At the close of 1974 at least 254 persons had been sentenced to death since *Furman,* and by the end of March 1976, more than 460 persons were subject to death sentences.

As we have seen, however, the Eighth Amendment demands more than that a challenged punishment be acceptable to contemporary society. The Court also must ask whether it comports with the basic concept of human dignity at the core of the Amendment. Although we cannot "invalidate a category of penalties because we deem less severe penalties adequate to serve the ends of penology," the sanction imposed cannot be so totally without penological justification that it results in the gratuitous infliction of suffering.

The death penalty is said to serve two principal social purposes: retribution and deterrence of capital crimes by prospective offenders.

In part, capital punishment is an expression of society's moral outrage at particularly offensive conduct. This function may be unappealing to many, but it is essential in an ordered society that asks its citizens to rely on legal processes rather than self-help to vindicate their wrongs. . . . "Retribution is no longer the dominant objective of the criminal law," but neither is it a forbidden objective nor one inconsistent with our respect for the dignity of men. . . .

Statistical attempts to evaluate the worth of the death penalty as a deterrent to crimes by potential offenders have occasioned a great deal of debate. The results simply have been inconclusive. . . .

Although some of the studies suggest that the death penalty may not function as a significantly greater deterrent than lesser penalties, there is no convincing empirical evidence either supporting or refuting this view. We may nevertheless assume safely that there are murderers, such as those who act in passion, for whom the threat of death has little or no deterrent effect. But for many others, the death penalty undoubtedly is a significant deterrent. There are carefully contemplated murders, such as murder for hire, where the possible penalty of death may well enter into the cold calculus that precedes the decision to act. And there are some categories of murder, such as murder by a life prisoner, where other sanctions may not be adequate.

The value of capital punishment as a deterrent of crime is a complex factual issue the resolution of which properly rests with the legislatures, which can evaluate the results of statistical studies in terms of their own local conditions and with a flexibility of approach that is not available to the courts. Indeed, many of the post-*Furman* statutes reflect just such a responsible effort to define those crimes and those criminals for which capital punishment is most probably an effective deterrent.

In sum, we cannot say that the judgment of the Georgia Legislature that capital punishment may be necessary in some cases is clearly wrong. Considerations of federalism, as well as respect for the ability of a legislature to evaluate, in terms of its particular State, the moral consensus concerning the death penalty and its social utility as a sanction, require us to conclude, in the absence of more convincing evidence, that the infliction of death as a punishment for murder is not without justification and thus is not unconstitutionally severe.

Finally, we must consider whether the punishment of death is disproportionate in relation to the crime for which it is imposed. There is no question that death as a punishment is unique in its severity and irrevocability. When a defendant's life is at stake, the Court has been particularly sensitive to insure that every safeguard is observed. But we are concerned here only with the imposition of capital punishment for the crime of murder, and when a life has been taken deliberately by the offender, we cannot say that the punishment is invariably disproportionate to the crime. It is an extreme sanction, suitable to the most extreme of crimes.

We hold that the death penalty is not a form of punishment that may never be imposed, regardless of the circumstances of the offense, regardless of the character of the offender, and regardless of the procedure followed in reaching the decision to impose it.

We now consider whether Georgia may impose the death penalty on the petitioner in this case.

While *Furman* did not hold that the infliction of the death penalty *per se* violates the Constitution's ban on cruel and unusual punishments, it did recognize that the penalty of death is different in kind from any other punishment imposed under our system of criminal justice. Because of the uniqueness of the death penalty, *Furman* held that it could not be imposed under sentencing procedures that created a substantial risk that it would be inflicted in an arbitrary and capricious manner. . . .

Furman mandates that where discretion is afforded a sentencing body on a matter so grave as the determination of whether a human life should be taken or spared, that discretion must be suitably directed and limited so as to minimize the risk of wholly arbitrary and capricious action. . . .

Jury sentencing has been considered desirable in capital cases in order "to maintain a link between contemporary community values and the penal system—a link without which the determination of punishment could hardly reflect 'the evolving standards of decency that mark the progress of a maturing society.'" But it creates special problems. Much of the information that is relevant to the sentencing decision may have no relevance to the question of guilt, or may even be extremely prejudicial to a fair determination of that question. This problem, however, is scarcely insurmountable. Those who have studied the question suggest that a bifurcated procedure—one in which the question of sentence is not considered until the determination of guilt has been made—is the best answer. . . . When a human life is at stake and when the jury must have information prejudicial to the question of guilt but relevant to the question of penalty in order to impose a rational sentence, a bifurcated system is more likely to ensure elimination of the constitutional deficiencies identified in *Furman*.

But the provision of relevant information under fair procedural rules is not alone sufficient to guarantee that the information will be properly used in the imposition of punishment, especially if sentencing is performed by a jury. Since the members of a jury will have had little, if any, previous experience in sentencing, they are unlikely to be skilled in dealing with the information they are given. To the extent that this problem is inherent in jury sentencing, it may not be totally correctable. It seems clear, however, that the problem will be alleviated if the jury is given guidance regarding the factors about the crime and the defendant that the State, representing organized society, deems particularly relevant to the sentencing decision.

The idea that a jury should be given guidance in its decisionmaking is also hardly a novel proposition. Juries are invariably given careful instructions on the law and how to apply it before they are authorized to decide the merits of a lawsuit. It would be virtually unthinkable to follow any other course in a legal system that has traditionally operated by following prior precedents and fixed rules of law. When erroneous instructions are given, retrial is often required. It is quite simply a hallmark of our legal system that juries be carefully and adequately guided in their deliberations.

While some have suggested that standards to guide a capital jury's sentencing deliberations are impossible to formulate, the fact is that such standards have been developed. . . . While such standards are by necessity somewhat general, they do provide guidance to the sentencing authority and thereby reduce the likelihood that it will impose a sentence that fairly can be called capricious or arbitrary. Where the sentencing authority is required to specify the factors it relied upon in reaching its decision, the further safeguard of meaningful appellate review is available to ensure that death sentences are not imposed capriciously or in a freakish manner.

In summary, the concerns expressed in *Furman* that the penalty of death not be imposed in an arbitrary or capricious manner can be met by a carefully drafted statute that ensures that the sentencing authority is given adequate information and guidance. As a general proposition these concerns are best met by a system that provides for a bifurcated proceeding at which the sentencing authority is apprised of the information relevant to the imposition of sentence and provided with standards to guide its use of the information.

We do not intend to suggest that only the above-described procedures would be permissible under *Furman* or that any sentencing system constructed along these general lines would inevitably satisfy the concerns of *Furman*, for each distinct system must be examined on an individual basis. Rather, we have embarked upon this general exposition to make clear that it is possible to construct capital-sentencing systems capable of meeting *Furman's* constitutional concerns.

We now turn to consideration of the constitutionality of Georgia's capital-sentencing procedures. In the wake of *Furman*, Georgia amended its capital punishment statute, but chose not to narrow the scope of its murder provisions. Thus, now as before *Furman*, in Georgia "[a] person commits murder when he unlawfully and with malice aforethought, either express or implied, causes the death of another human being." All persons convicted of murder "shall be punished by death or by imprisonment for life."

Georgia did act, however, to narrow the class of murderers subject to capital punishment by specifying 10 statutory aggravating circumstances, one of which must be found by the jury to exist beyond a reasonable doubt before a death sentence can ever be imposed. In addition, the jury is authorized to consider any other appropriate aggravating or mitigating circumstances. The jury is not required to find any mitigating circumstance in order to make a recommendation of mercy that is binding on the trial court, but it must find a *statutory* aggravating circumstance before recommending a sentence of death.

These procedures require the jury to consider the circumstances of the crime and the criminal before it recommends sentence. No longer can a Georgia jury do as *Furman's* jury did: reach a finding of the defendant's guilt and then, without guidance or direction, decide whether he should live or die. Instead, the jury's attention is directed to the specific circumstances of the crime. . . . In addition, the jury's attention is focused on the characteristics of the person who committed the crime. . . . As a result, while some jury discretion still exists, "the discretion to be exercised is controlled by clear and objective standards so as to produce nondiscriminatory application."

As an important additional safeguard against arbitrariness and caprice, the Georgia statutory scheme provides for automatic appeal of all death sentences to the State's Supreme Court. That court is required by statute to review each sentence of death and determine whether it was imposed under the influence of passion or prejudice, whether the evidence supports the jury's finding of a statutory aggravating circumstance, and whether the sentence is disproportionate compared to those sentences imposed in similar cases.

In short, Georgia's new sentencing procedures require as a prerequisite to the imposition of the death penalty, specific jury findings as to the circumstances of the crime or the character of the defendant. Moreover, to guard further against a situation comparable to that presented in *Furman*, the Supreme Court of Georgia compares each death sentence with the sentences imposed on similarly situated defendants to ensure that the sentence of death in a particular case is not disproportionate. On their face these procedures seem to satisfy the concerns of *Furman*. No longer should there be "no meaningful basis for distinguishing the few cases in which [the death penalty] is imposed from the many cases in which it is not.". . .

The basic concern of *Furman* centered on those defendants who were being condemned to death capriciously and arbitrarily. Under the procedures before the Court in that case, sentencing authorities were not directed to give attention to the nature or circumstances of the crime committed or to the character or record of the defendant. Left unguided, juries imposed the death sentence in a way that could only be called freakish. The new Georgia sentencing procedures, by contrast, focus the jury's attention on the particularized nature of the crime and the particularized characteristics of the individual defendant. While the jury is permitted to consider any aggravating or mitigating circumstances, it must find and identify at least one statutory aggravating factor before it may impose a penalty of death. In this way the jury's discretion is channeled. No longer can a jury wantonly and freakishly impose the death sentence; it is always circumscribed by the legislative guidelines. In addition, the review function of the Supreme Court of Georgia affords additional assurance that the concerns that prompted our decision in *Furman* are not present to any significant degree in the Georgia procedure applied here.

For the reasons expressed in this opinion, we hold that the statutory system under which Gregg was sentenced to death does not violate the Constitution. Accordingly, the judgment of the Georgia Supreme Court is affirmed.

MR. JUSTICE WHITE, with whom THE CHIEF JUSTICE and MR. JUSTICE REHNQUIST join, concurring in the judgment.

Petitioner's argument that there is an unconstitutional amount of discretion in the system which separates those suspects who receive the death penalty from those who receive life imprisonment, a lesser penalty, or are acquitted or never charged, seems to be in final analysis an indictment of our entire system of justice. Petitioner has argued, in effect, that no matter how effective the death penalty may be as a punishment, government, created and run as it must be by humans, is inevitably incompetent to administer it. This cannot be accepted as a proposition of constitutional law. Imposition of the death penalty is surely an awesome responsibility for any system of justice and those who participate in it. Mistakes will be made and discriminations will occur which will be difficult to explain. However, one of society's most basic tasks is that of protecting the lives of its citizens and one of the most basic ways in which it achieves the task is through criminal laws against murder. I decline to interfere with the manner in which Georgia has chosen to enforce such laws on what is simply an assertion of lack of faith in the ability of the system of justice to operate in a fundamentally fair manner.

MR. JUSTICE BRENNAN, dissenting.

My opinion in *Furman v. Georgia* concluded that . . . the punishment of death, for whatever crime and under all circumstances, is "cruel and unusual" in violation of the Eighth and Fourteenth Amendments of the Constitution. I shall not again canvass the reasons that led to that conclusion. I emphasize only that foremost among the "moral concepts" recognized in our cases and inherent in the Clause is the primary moral principle that the State, even as it punishes, must treat its citizens in a manner consistent with their intrinsic worth as human beings—a punishment must not be so severe as to be degrading to human dignity. A judicial determination whether the punishment of death comports with human dignity is therefore not only permitted but compelled by the Clause.

I do not understand that the Court disagrees that "[i]n comparison to all other punishments today . . . the deliberate extinguishment of human life by the State is uniquely degrading to human dignity." For three of my Brethren hold today that mandatory infliction of the death penalty constitutes the penalty cruel and unusual punishment. I perceive no principled basis for this limitation. Death for whatever crime and under all circumstances "is truly an awesome punishment. The calculated killing of a human being by the State involves, by its very nature, a denial of the executed person's humanity. . . . An executed person has indeed 'lost the right to have rights.'" Death is not only an unusually severe punishment, unusual in its pain, in its finality, and in its enormity, but it serves no penal purpose more effectively than a less severe punishment; therefore the principle inherent in the Clause that prohibits pointless infliction of excessive punishment when less severe punishment can adequately achieve the same purposes invalidates the punishment.

The fatal constitutional infirmity in the punishment of death is that it treats "members of the human race as nonhumans, as objects to be toyed with and discarded. [It is] thus inconsistent with the fundamental premise of the Clause that even the vilest criminal remains a human being possessed of common human dignity." As such it is a penalty that "subjects the individual to a fate forbidden by the principle of civilized treatment guaranteed by the [Clause]." I therefore would hold, on that ground alone, that death is today a cruel and unusual punishment prohibited by the Clause.

MR. JUSTICE MARSHALL, dissenting.

In *Furman v. Georgia* (1972) (concurring opinion), I set forth at some length my views on the basic issue presented to the Court in these cases. The death penalty, I concluded, is a cruel and unusual punishment prohibited by the Eighth and Fourteenth Amendments. That continues to be my view.

I have no intention of retracing the "long and tedious journey" that led to my conclusion in *Furman.* My sole purposes here are to consider the suggestion that my conclusion in *Furman* has been undercut by developments since then, and briefly to evaluate the basis for my Brethren's holding that the extinction of life is a permissible form of punishment under the Cruel and Unusual Punishments Clause.

In *Furman* I concluded that the death penalty is constitutionally invalid for two reasons. First, the death penalty is excessive. And second, the American people, fully informed as to the purposes of the death penalty and its liabilities, would in my view reject it as morally unacceptable.

Since the decision in *Furman*, the legislatures of 35 States have enacted new statutes authorizing the imposition of the death sentence for certain crimes, and Congress has enacted a law providing the death penalty for air piracy resulting in death. I would be less than candid if I did not acknowledge that these developments have a significant bearing on a realistic assessment of the moral acceptability of the death penalty to the American people. But if the constitutionality of the death penalty turns, as I have urged, on the opinion of an informed citizenry, then even the enactment of new death statutes cannot be viewed as conclusive. In *Furman*, I observed that the American people are largely unaware of the information critical to a judgment on the morality of the death penalty, and concluded that if they were better informed they would consider it shocking, unjust, and unacceptable. A recent study, conducted after the enactment of the post-*Furman* statutes, has confirmed that the American people know little about the death penalty, and that the opinions of an informed public would differ significantly from those of a public unaware of the consequences and effects of the death penalty.

Even assuming, however, that the post-*Furman* enactment of statutes authorizing the death penalty renders the prediction of the views of an informed citizenry an uncertain basis for a constitutional decision, the enactment of those statutes has no bearing whatsoever on the conclusion that the death penalty is unconstitutional because it is excessive. An excessive penalty is invalid under the Cruel and Unusual Punishments Clause "even though popular sentiment may favor" it. The inquiry here, then, is simply whether the death penalty is necessary to accomplish the legitimate legislative purposes in punishment, or whether a less severe penalty—life imprisonment—would do as well.

The two purposes that sustain the death penalty as nonexcessive in the Court's view are general deterrence and retribution. In *Furman*, I canvassed the relevant data on the deterrent effect of capital punishment. . . . The available evidence, I concluded in *Furman*, was convincing that "capital punishment is not necessary as a deterrent to crime in our society.". . .

The evidence I reviewed in *Furman* remains convincing, in my view, that "capital punishment is not necessary as a

deterrent to crime in our society." The justification for the death penalty must be found elsewhere.

The other principal purpose said to be served by the death penalty is retribution. The notion that retribution can serve as a moral justification for the sanction of death finds credence in the opinion of my Brothers STEWART, POWELL, and STEVENS, and that of my Brother WHITE. . . . See also *Furman v. Georgia* (BURGER, C.J., dissenting). It is this notion that I find to be the most disturbing aspect of today's unfortunate decisions.

The concept of retribution is a multifaceted one, and any discussion of its role in the criminal law must be undertaken with caution. On one level, it can be said that the notion of retribution or reprobation is the basis of our insistence that only those who have broken the law be punished, and in this sense the notion is quite obviously central to a just system of criminal sanctions. But our recognition that retribution plays a crucial role in determining who may be punished by no means requires approval of retribution as a general justification for punishment. It is the question whether retribution can provide a moral justification for punishment—in particular, capital punishment—that we must consider.

My Brothers STEWART, POWELL, and STEVENS offer the following explanation of the retributive justification for capital punishment:

"'The instinct for retribution is part of the nature of man, and channeling that instinct in the administration of criminal justice serves an important purpose in promoting the stability of a society governed by law. When people begin to believe that organized society is unwilling or unable to impose upon criminal offenders the punishment they "deserve," then there are sown the seeds of anarchy—of self-help, vigilante justice, and lynch law.'"

This statement is wholly inadequate to justify the death penalty. As my Brother BRENNAN stated in *Furman*, "[t]here is no evidence whatever that utilization of imprisonment rather than death encourages private blood feuds and other disorders." It simply defies belief to suggest that the death penalty is necessary to prevent the American people from taking the law into their own hands. . . .

The death penalty, unnecessary to promote the goal of deterrence or to further any legitimate notion of retribution, is an excessive penalty forbidden by the Eighth and Fourteenth Amendments. I respectfully dissent from the

Court's judgment upholding the sentences of death imposed upon the petitioners in these cases.

Despite the plethora of opinions in *Gregg*, the majority of justices agreed that the Georgia law was constitutional; indeed, some members of the Court referred to it as a model death penalty scheme. But what accounts for the abrupt change in the law between *Furman* and *Gregg?* Given that some scholars and even justices thought that *Furman* had brought an end to capital punishment, this about-face is all the more puzzling. Analysts offer several explanations. Some point to the membership change on the Court that occurred between the two cases: William Douglas, who had voted with the five-person *Furman* majority, had been replaced by John Paul Stevens, who voted with the seven-person *Gregg* majority.

Other explanations center on the turn in the political environment between 1972 and 1976. As Figure 11-1 shows, public opinion became more supportive of capital punishment. Around the time of the *Furman* decision, Americans were relatively divided on the issue. By November 1972 those in favor of capital punishment had jumped by seven percentage points; by 1974, roughly two-thirds of Americans supported legal executions. Given this trend in public opinion, state legislators could barely wait to reconvene after *Furman* and pass new laws designed to limit arbitrariness in sentencing. Indeed, almost every state that had a death penalty prior to *Furman* had reinstated it by 1976. The national government even got into the act. The day after *Furman* came down, President Nixon seized on Burger's dissent in noting that the Court had not completely ruled out capital punishment. He subsequently sent to Congress a bill calling for the death penalty in certain federal crimes.

Some scholars suggest that the Court succumbed to public pressure in this area: Americans wanted the death penalty and the justices caved in, the argument goes. Even Justice Marshall, in his *Gregg* dissent, acknowledged that post-*Furman* "developments have a significant bearing on a realistic assessment of the moral acceptability of the death penalty to the American people." (But recall that he also maintained that "the American people are largely unaware of the information critical to a judgment

FIGURE 11-1 Support for Capital Punishment, Even Years, 1972–1998

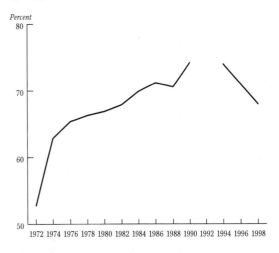

DATA SOURCE: Lee Epstein, Jeffrey A. Segal, Harold J. Spaeth, and Thomas G. Walker, *The Supreme Court Compendium: Data, Decisions, and Developments*, 2d ed. (Washington, D.C.: Congressional Quarterly, 1996), 682. Updated by the authors; no data available for 1992.

on the morality of the death penalty, and . . . if they were better informed they would consider it shocking, unjust, and unacceptable.") Although there is probably no systematic evidence to support this claim, we do know that Americans respond differently to questions according to how they are worded. For example, when surveyers asked in 1994, "In your view, what should be the penalty for murder—the death penalty or life imprisonment with absolutely no possiblity of parole," respondents' support for the death penalty dropped to 50 percent, with 32 percent favoring prison without parole.[25]

Yet another explanation centers on the new laws themselves and the way attorneys tried to challenge them. To put it simply, abolitionist lawyers may have overestimated the degree of their victory in *Furman*. In their arguments to the Court, they asserted that "death is different." But this view was held by only two justices in *Furman*—Brennan and Marshall. The others, especially

25. See Brian Doan, "Death Penalty Policy, Statistics, and Public Opinion," *Focus on Law Studies* 7 (1997). Available at: *www.abanet.org/publiced/focus/spr97pol.html.*

FIGURE 11-2 Executions, 1976–1999

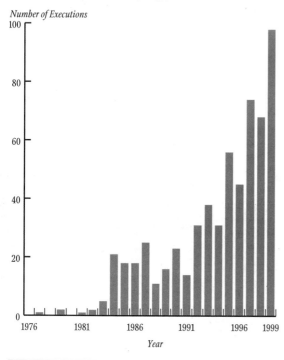

DATA SOURCE: Death Penalty Information Center, *http://www.deathpenaltyinfo.org.*

Stewart and White, were more concerned with the arbitrariness of death penalty sentencing and not with the constitutionality of the death penalty. In the end, as Justice White's concurrence in *Gregg* indicates, abolitionist attorneys were unable to convince the majority that the new laws—which explicitly sought to eliminate arbitrariness in sentencing by limiting jury discretion—were unconstitutional.

Whatever the explanation for the Court's change of heart, the results were clear. Many states adopted a variation of Georgia's death penalty law (currently thirty-eight states have death penalty laws on their books), and executions increased accordingly, as Figure 11-2 shows. During the 1970s, only three people were legally executed in the United States; in the 1990s, that figure was more than 470. In 1999 alone a record ninety-eight individuals were executed and, as of January 2000 nearly four thousand waited on death rows.

In the Aftermath of Gregg

In some ways, *Gregg* settled the death penalty issue: the Court asserted that capital punishment did not violate the Constitution, a position to which it still adheres. But opponents of the death penalty did not give up. In the immediate aftermath of *Gregg,* they continued to bring lawsuits, many of which were aimed at narrowing the application of capital punishment. In other words, this litigation challenged procedural practices adopted by the states, and not the constitutionality of the death penalty.

A good number of these procedural cases involved this question: What factors should sentencers consider in their deliberations? Occasionally, the Court has ruled for defendants in these disputes. In *Eddings v. Oklahoma* (1982), for example, it held that a trial court judge could not refuse to hear mitigating evidence pointing to the defendant's youth, troubled childhood, and history of mental problems. But the Court generally has taken a pro–death penalty posture. A prime example is *McCleskey v. Kemp* (1987), which some observers consider the most significant capital punishment case since *Gregg.*[26] Why was *McCleskey* so important? Can you square the Court's opinion in this case with the logic of *Furman?*

McCleskey v. Kemp

481 U.S. 279 (1987)
laws.findlaw.com/US/481/279.html
Vote: 5 (O'Connor, Powell, Rehnquist, Scalia, White)
    4 (Blackmun, Brennan, Marshall, Stevens)
Opinion of the Court: Powell
Dissenting opinions: Blackmun, Brennan, Stevens

On May 13, 1978, Warren McCleskey, a black man, and three accomplices attempted to rob a furniture store in Atlanta, Georgia. One of the employees hit a silent alarm button, which was answered by a white, thirty-one-year-old police officer. As the officer entered the store, he was shot and killed. Several weeks later, when police arrested McCleskey on another charge, he con-

---

26. For oral arguments in this case, navigate to: *oyez.nwu.edu.*

fessed to the robbery. At his trial, McCleskey was identified by one of the accomplices as the individual who
killed the officer. The prosecution also entered evidence
indicating that McCleskey had bragged about the
shooting.

Three months after the robbery, a jury of eleven
whites and one black convicted McCleskey and sentenced him to death. At that point, the NAACP LDF took
over his defense. The LDF based its appeal in the federal
courts on a 1986 study showing that blacks convicted of
murdering whites received death sentences at disproportionately high rates. The study centered on a statistical
examination by several professors of the application of
Georgia's death penalty. Named for one of the researchers, David Baldus, the study examined 2,484 Georgia murder cases from 1973 to 1979, coded for some 230
variables. To analyze this mammoth amount of data, Baldus used a multivariate technique, which allows researchers to demonstrate the effects of possible explanatory variables (such as the race of the defendant or victim) on outcomes (such as the decision to sentence to
death).[27]

Baldus's conclusions were dramatic. Among the most
noteworthy were the following:

• The chances of receiving a death sentence were 4.3
times greater for defendants whose victims were white
than for defendants whose victims were black.

• Of the 128 cases in which death was imposed, 108 or
87 percent involved white victims.

• Prosecutors sought the death penalty in 70 percent
of cases involving black defendants and white victims,
but in only 32 percent in which both the defendant and
victim were white.

• Black defendants were 1.1 times more likely than
other defendants to receive death sentences.

Armed with this study the LDF tried to convince the
justices once and for all that the disparate application of
death penalty laws led to unacceptable violations of the
Equal Protection, Due Process, and Cruel and Unusual
Punishment Clauses.

27. For more on this study, see David Baldus, George Woodruff, and
Charles Pulaski, *Equal Justice and the Death Penalty* (Boston: Northeastern
University Press, 1990).

Warren McCleskey based the appeal of his death sentence on a
study showing that someone convicted of killing a white person
was four times more likely to receive the death penalty than
someone convicted of killing a black person. His appeal was rejected in *McCleskey v. Kemp* (1987), and he was executed in 1991.

JUSTICE POWELL delivered the opinion of the Court.

This case presents the question whether a complex statistical study that indicates a risk that racial considerations
enter into capital sentencing determinations proves that petitioner McCleskey's capital sentence is unconstitutional
under the Eighth or Fourteenth Amendment. . . .

Our analysis begins with the basic principle that a defendant who alleges an equal protection violation has the burden of proving "the existence of purposeful discrimination."
A corollary to this principle is that a criminal defendant
must prove that the purposeful discrimination "had a discriminatory effect" on him. Thus, to prevail under the Equal
Protection Clause, McCleskey must prove that the decisionmakers in *his* case acted with discriminatory purpose. He
offers no evidence specific to his own case that would support an inference that racial considerations played a part in

his sentence. Instead, he relies solely on the Baldus study. McCleskey argues that the Baldus study compels an inference that his sentence rests on purposeful discrimination. McCleskey's claim that these statistics are sufficient proof of discrimination, without regard to the facts of a particular case, would extend to all capital cases in Georgia, at least where the victim was white and the defendant is black.

The Court has accepted statistics as proof of intent to discriminate in certain limited contexts. First, this Court has accepted statistical disparities as proof of an equal protection violation in the selection of the jury venire in a particular district. Although statistical proof normally must present a "stark" pattern to be accepted as the sole proof of discriminatory intent under the Constitution, "[b]ecause of the nature of the jury-selection task, . . . we have permitted a finding of constitutional violation even when the statistical pattern does not approach [such] extremes." Second, this Court has accepted statistics in the form of multiple regression analysis to prove statutory violations under Title VII.[28]

But the nature of the capital sentencing decision, and the relationship of the statistics to that decision, are fundamentally different from the corresponding elements in the venire-selection or Title VII cases. Most importantly, each particular decision to impose the death penalty is made by a petit jury selected from a properly constituted venire. Each jury is unique in its composition, and the Constitution requires that its decision rest on consideration of innumerable factors that vary according to the characteristics of the individual defendant and the facts of the particular capital offense. Thus, the application of an inference drawn from the general statistics to a specific decision in a trial and sentencing simply is not comparable to the application of an inference drawn from general statistics to a specific venire-selection or Title VII case. In those cases, the statistics relate to fewer entities, and fewer variables are relevant to the challenged decisions.

Another important difference between the cases in which we have accepted statistics as proof of discriminatory intent and this case is that, in the venire-selection and Title VII contexts, the decisionmaker has an opportunity to explain the statistical disparity. Here, the State has no practical opportunity to rebut the Baldus study. . . .

Finally, McCleskey's statistical proffer must be viewed in the context of his challenge. McCleskey challenges decisions at the heart of the State's criminal justice system. "[O]ne of society's most basic tasks is that of protecting the lives of its citizens and one of the most basic ways in which it achieves the task is through criminal laws against murder." Implementation of these laws necessarily requires discretionary judgments. Because discretion is essential to the criminal justice process, we would demand exceptionally clear proof before we would infer that the discretion has been abused. The unique nature of the decisions at issue in this case also counsel against adopting such an inference from the disparities indicated by the Baldus study. Accordingly, we hold that the Baldus study is clearly insufficient to support an inference that any of the decisionmakers in McCleskey's case acted with discriminatory purpose. . . .

McCleskey also argues that the Baldus study demonstrates that the Georgia capital sentencing system violates the Eighth Amendment. . . .

Two principal decisions guide our resolution of McCleskey's Eighth Amendment claim. In *Furman v. Georgia* (1972), the Court concluded that the death penalty was so irrationally imposed that any particular death sentence could be presumed excessive. . . .

In *Gregg*, the Court specifically addressed the question left open in *Furman*—whether the punishment of death for murder is "under all circumstances, 'cruel and unusual' in violation of the Eighth and Fourteenth Amendments of the Constitution.". . . We noted that any punishment might be unconstitutionally severe if inflicted without penological justification, but concluded:

"Considerations of federalism, as well as respect for the ability of a legislature to evaluate, in terms of its particular State, the moral consensus concerning the death penalty and its social utility as a sanction, require us to conclude, in the absence of more convincing evidence, that the infliction of death as a punishment for murder is not without justification and thus is not unconstitutionally severe.". . .

In light of our precedents under the Eighth Amendment, McCleskey cannot argue successfully that his sentence is "disproportionate to the crime in the traditional sense." He does not deny that he committed a murder in the course of a planned robbery, a crime for which this Court has deter-

28. Authors' note: Title VII of the Civil Rights Act prohibits employers from engaging in discrimination based on race, color, religion, sex, or national origin.

mined that the death penalty constitutionally may be imposed. His disproportionality claim "is of a different sort." McCleskey argues that the sentence in his case is disproportionate to the sentences in other murder cases.

On the one hand, he cannot base a constitutional claim on an argument that his case differs from other cases in which defendants did receive the death penalty. On automatic appeal, the Georgia Supreme Court found that McCleskey's death sentence was not disproportionate to other death sentences imposed in the State. . . .

On the other hand, absent a showing that the Georgia capital punishment system operates in an arbitrary and capricious manner, McCleskey cannot prove a constitutional violation by demonstrating that other defendants who may be similarly situated did not receive the death penalty. In *Gregg,* the Court confronted the argument that "the opportunities for discretionary action that are inherent in the processing of any murder case under Georgia law," specifically, the opportunities for discretionary leniency, rendered the capital sentences imposed arbitrary and capricious. We rejected this contention. . . .

Because McCleskey's sentence was imposed under Georgia's sentencing procedures that focus discretion "on the particularized nature of the crime and the particularized characteristics of the individual defendant," we lawfully may presume that McCleskey's death sentence was not "wantonly and freakishly" imposed, and thus that the sentence is not disproportionate within any recognized meaning under the Eighth Amendment.

Although our decision in *Gregg* as to the facial validity of the Georgia capital punishment statute appears to foreclose McCleskey's disproportionality argument, he further contends that the Georgia capital punishment system is arbitrary and capricious in *application,* and therefore his sentence is excessive, because racial considerations may influence capital sentencing decisions in Georgia. We now address this claim.

To evaluate McCleskey's challenge, we must examine exactly what the Baldus study may show. Even Professor Baldus does not contend that his statistics prove that race enters into any capital sentencing decisions or that race was a factor in McCleskey's particular case. Statistics at most may show only a likelihood that a particular factor entered into some decisions. There is, of course, some risk of racial prejudice influencing a jury's decision in a criminal case. There

are similar risks that other kinds of prejudice will influence other criminal trials. The question "is at what point that risk becomes constitutionally unacceptable." McCleskey asks us to accept the likelihood allegedly shown by the Baldus study as the constitutional measure of an unacceptable risk of racial prejudice influencing capital sentencing decisions. This we decline to do.

Because of the risk that the factor of race may enter the criminal justice process, we have engaged in "unceasing efforts" to eradicate racial prejudice from our criminal justice system. Our efforts have been guided by our recognition that "the inestimable privilege of trial by jury . . . is a vital principle, underlying the whole administration of criminal justice." Specifically, a capital sentencing jury representative of a criminal defendant's community assures a "'diffused impartiality'" in the jury's task of "express[ing] the conscience of the community on the ultimate question of life or death."

Individual jurors bring to their deliberations "qualities of human nature and varieties of human experience, the range of which is unknown and perhaps unknowable." The capital sentencing decision requires the individual jurors to focus their collective judgment on the unique characteristics of a particular criminal defendant. It is not surprising that such collective judgments often are difficult to explain. But the inherent lack of predictability of jury decisions does not justify their condemnation. . . .

McCleskey's argument that the Constitution condemns the discretion allowed decisionmakers in the Georgia capital sentencing system is antithetical to the fundamental role of discretion in our criminal justice system. Discretion in the criminal justice system offers substantial benefits to the criminal defendant. Not only can a jury decline to impose the death sentence, it can decline to convict, or choose to convict of a lesser offense. Whereas decisions against a defendant's interest may be reversed by the trial judge or on appeal, these discretionary exercises of leniency are final and unreviewable. Similarly, the capacity of prosecutorial discretion to provide individualized justice is "firmly entrenched in American law." As we have noted, a prosecutor can decline to charge, offer a plea bargain, or decline to seek a death sentence in any particular case. Of course, "the power to be lenient [also] is the power to discriminate," but a capital-punishment system that did not allow for discretionary acts of leniency "would be totally alien to our notions of criminal justice."

At most, the Baldus study indicates a discrepancy that appears to correlate with race. Apparent disparities in sentencing are an inevitable part of our criminal justice system. . . . Despite these imperfections, our consistent rule has been that constitutional guarantees are met when "the mode [for determining guilt or punishment] itself has been surrounded with safeguards to make it as fair as possible." Where the discretion that is fundamental to our criminal process is involved, we decline to assume that what is unexplained is invidious. In light of the safeguards designed to minimize racial bias in the process, the fundamental value of jury trial in our criminal justice system, and the benefits that discretion provides to criminal defendants, we hold that the Baldus study does not demonstrate a constitutionally significant risk of racial bias affecting the Georgia capital-sentencing process.

Two additional concerns inform our decision in this case. First, McCleskey's claim, taken to its logical conclusion, throws into serious question the principles that underlie our entire criminal justice system. The Eighth Amendment is not limited in application to capital punishment, but applies to all penalties. Thus, if we accepted McCleskey's claim that racial bias has impermissibly tainted the capital sentencing decision, we could soon be faced with similar claims as to other types of penalty. Moreover, the claim that his sentence rests on the irrelevant factor of race easily could be extended to apply to claims based on unexplained discrepancies that correlate to membership in other minority groups, and even to gender. Similarly, since McCleskey's claim relates to the race of his victim, other claims could apply with equally logical force to statistical disparities that correlate with the race or sex of other actors in the criminal justice system, such as defense attorneys or judges. Also, there is no logical reason that such a claim need be limited to racial or sexual bias. If arbitrary and capricious punishment is the touchstone under the Eighth Amendment, such a claim could—at least in theory—be based upon any arbitrary variable, such as the defendant's facial characteristics, or the physical attractiveness of the defendant or the victim, that some statistical study indicates may be influential in jury decisionmaking. As these examples illustrate, there is no limiting principle to the type of challenge brought by McCleskey. The Constitution does not require that a State eliminate any demonstrable disparity that correlates with a potentially irrelevant factor in order to operate a criminal justice system that includes capital punishment. As we have stated specifically in the context of capital punishment, the Constitution does not "plac[e] totally unrealistic conditions on its use." Second, McCleskey's arguments are best presented to the legislative bodies. It is not the responsibility—or indeed even the right—of this Court to determine the appropriate punishment for particular crimes. . . . Legislatures also are better qualified to weigh and "evaluate the results of statistical studies in terms of their own local conditions and with a flexibility of approach that is not available to the courts." Capital punishment is now the law in more than two thirds of our States. It is the ultimate duty of courts to determine on a case-by-case basis whether these laws are applied consistently with the Constitution. Despite McCleskey's wide ranging arguments that basically challenge the validity of capital punishment in our multiracial society, the only question before us is whether in his case the law of Georgia was properly applied. We agree with the District Court and the Court of Appeals for the Eleventh Circuit that this was carefully and correctly done in this case.

Accordingly, we affirm the judgment of the Court of Appeals for the Eleventh Circuit.

It is so ordered.

JUSTICE BRENNAN, with whom JUSTICE MARSHALL, . . . JUSTICE BLACKMUN and JUSTICE STEVENS join . . . dissenting.

At some point in this case, Warren McCleskey doubtless asked his lawyer whether a jury was likely to sentence him to die. A candid reply to this question would have been disturbing. First, counsel would have to tell McCleskey that few of the details of the crime or of McCleskey's past criminal conduct were more important than the fact that his victim was white. Furthermore, counsel would feel bound to tell McCleskey that defendants charged with killing white victims in Georgia are 4.3 times as likely to be sentenced to death as defendants charged with killing blacks. In addition, frankness would compel the disclosure that it was more likely than not that the race of McCleskey's victim would determine whether he received a death sentence: 6 of every 11 defendants convicted of killing a white person would not have received the death penalty if their victims had been black, while, among defendants with aggravating and mitigating factors comparable to McCleskey's, 20 of every 34 would not have been sentenced to die if their victims had been black. Finally, the assessment would not be complete without the information that cases involving black defendants and white victims are more likely to result in a death sentence than cases featuring any other racial combination of defendant and victim. The story could be told in a variety of ways, but McCleskey could not fail to grasp its essential narrative line: there was a significant chance that race would play a prominent role in determining if he lived or died.

The Court today holds that Warren McCleskey's sentence was constitutionally imposed. It finds no fault in a system in which lawyers must tell their clients that race casts a large shadow on the capital sentencing process. . . .

The Court's decision today will not change what attorneys in Georgia tell other Warren McCleskeys about their chances of execution. Nothing will soften the harsh message they must convey, nor alter the prospect that race undoubtedly will continue to be a topic of discussion. McCleskey's evidence will not have obtained judicial acceptance, but that will not affect what is said on death row. However many criticisms of today's decision may be rendered, these painful conversations will serve as the most eloquent dissents of all.

JUSTICE BLACKMUN, with whom JUSTICE MARSHALL . . . JUSTICE STEVENS and . . . JUSTICE BRENNAN join . . . dissenting.

The Court today sanctions the execution of a man despite his presentation of evidence that establishes a constitutionally intolerable level of racially based discrimination leading to the imposition of his death sentence. I am disappointed with the Court's action not only because of its denial of constitutional guarantees to petitioner McCleskey individually, but also because of its departure from what seems to me to be well-developed constitutional jurisprudence.

JUSTICE BRENNAN has thoroughly demonstrated that, if one assumes that the statistical evidence presented by petitioner McCleskey is valid, as we must in light of the Court of Appeals' assumption, there exists in the Georgia capital sentencing scheme a risk of racially based discrimination that is so acute that it violates the Eighth Amendment. His analysis of McCleskey's case in terms of the Eighth Amendment is consistent with this Court's recognition that, because capital cases involve the State's imposition of a punishment that is unique both in kind and degree, the decision in such cases must reflect a heightened degree of reliability under the Amendment's prohibition of the infliction of cruel and unusual punishments. . . .

Yet McCleskey's case raises concerns that are central not only to the principles underlying the Eighth Amendment, but also to the principles underlying the Fourteenth Amendment. Analysis of his case in terms of the Fourteenth Amendment is consistent with this Court's recognition that racial discrimination is fundamentally at odds with our constitutional guarantee of equal protection. The protections afforded by the Fourteenth Amendment are not left at the courtroom door. Nor is equal protection denied to persons convicted of crimes. The Court in the past has found that racial discrimination within the criminal justice system is particularly abhorrent: "Discrimination on the basis of race, odious in all aspects, is especially pernicious in the administration of justice." *Rose v. Mitchell* (1979). Disparate enforcement of criminal sanctions "destroys the appearance of justice, and thereby casts doubt on the integrity of the judicial process."

JUSTICE STEVENS, with whom JUSTICE BLACKMUN joins, dissenting.

The Court's decision appears to be based on a fear that the acceptance of McCleskey's claim would sound the death knell for capital punishment in Georgia. If society were indeed forced to choose between a racially discriminatory death penalty (one that provides heightened protection against murder "for whites only") and no death penalty at all, the choice mandated by the Constitution would be plain. But the Court's fear is unfounded. One of the lessons of the Baldus study is that there exist certain categories of extremely serious crimes for which prosecutors consistently seek, and juries consistently impose, the death penalty without regard to the race of the victim or the race of the offender. If Georgia were to narrow the class of death-eligible defendants to those categories, the danger of arbitrary and discriminatory imposition of the death penalty would be significantly decreased, if not eradicated. . . . [S]uch a restructuring of the sentencing scheme is surely not too high a price to pay.

The Current State of the Death Penalty

Before the Court handed down *McCleskey,* some observers speculated that if the justices agreed with the LDF, they might have found that capital punishment was an inherently arbitrary form of punishment that could never be imposed fairly. Such a decision would have, in effect, resurrected *Furman.* But it was not to be. Although *McCleskey* caused great division among the justices, the majority of the Court upheld the constitutionality of the death penalty. In short, the LDF's ace in the hole, the Baldus study, failed.

For abolitionists, Court decisions in the wake of *Mc-Cleskey* generally have not been encouraging. The Court grew less tolerant of the long procedural delays and appeals processes often involved in capital punishment cases. In 1991 the justices restricted the use of habeas corpus petitions by state prisoners, making it difficult for lower federal court judges to accept second petitions in all but the rarest of circumstances. By coincidence, this ruling came in *McCleskey v. Zant,* a case brought by attorneys representing Warren McCleskey. In this particular petition—McCleskey filed many over the years, including the one that led to the ruling in *McCleskey v. Kemp*—McCleskey alleged that police had violated his rights when they used a prison informant to "coerce" a confession from him.

This case was a significant setback for death penalty opponents because most death-row inmates, like McCleskey, file successive *habeas corpus* petitions, raising different constitutional claims, with the goal of having their sentences overturned. Limiting the ability of courts to consider such petitions enables states to impose death more quickly. This was obviously the case for McCleskey: in September 1991, shortly after the Court's decision in *Zant,* the State of Georgia executed him—thirteen years after he shot a police officer.

Challenging the death penalty became even more difficult in 1996 when President Clinton signed into law the Antiterrorism and Effective Death Penalty Act. This statute directed that habeas corpus petitions presenting claims that had already been presented in earlier petitions should be dismissed. It also directed that second or subsequent habeas corpus petitions that presented new claims should be dismissed unless the claims could not have been made previously because of a subsequent change in the law or the discovery of facts not knowable at the time of the earlier petition. This act severely restricted the opportunities for death row inmates to challenge their sentences in federal court. Shortly after passage of the act, the Supreme Court upheld its constitutionality in *Felker v. Turpin* (1996), denying relief to a Georgia death-row inmate.

Should we conclude from these decisions that opponents of the death penalty have lost their cause? After all, public support for capital punishment remains strong; politicians rarely take public stances against it (in fact, the most recent presidents have all supported the death penalty); and the Court has made its position quite clear. Yet the future may not be completely devoid of hope for abolitionists. First, early in 1994 Justice Blackmun—a member of the minority in *Furman* and of the majority in *Gregg*—expressed a change of heart on the death penalty. In a dissent from the Court's refusal to hear a Texas death penalty appeal, he stated that he thought "no sentence of death may be constitutionally imposed." *(See Box 11-4.)* Blackmun's dissent provoked an interesting response from Justice Scalia, a capital punishment supporter. Blackmun was not the only justice to change his mind on the death penalty. In 1994 the press reported that Lewis Powell, the author of the original *McKleskey* opinion and an important vote in capital punishment cases of the 1980s, expressed regret over supporting Georgia's claims in the 1987 case. Justice Brennan, who left the Court in 1990, continued to campaign against the death penalty in his retirement.[29]

Blackmun's and Powell's changed positions on the death penalty are interesting, but former justices cannot influence future decisions, except by the moral suasion of their writings. But what of the current justices? Justices Souter, Stevens, and Ginsburg, while not explicitly advocating the abolition of capital punishment, have taken more moderate stances than Justices Scalia, Thomas, and the other members of the pro–death penalty wing of the Court. Justice Breyer had little firsthand experience in

29. See William J. Brennan Jr., "What the Constitution Requires," *New York Times,* April 28, 1996.

BOX 11-4   JUSTICES BLACKMUN AND SCALIA ON THE
DEATH PENALTY

BELOW ARE EXCERPTS from Justice Blackmun's dissent from the Court's denial of review in *Callins v. Collins* (1994) and Justice Scalia's response.

JUSTICE BLACKMUN

On February 23, 1994, at approximately 1:00 A.M., Bruce Edwin Callins will be executed by the State of Texas. Intravenous tubes attached to his arms will carry the instrument of death, a toxic fluid designed specifically for the purpose of killing human beings. The witnesses, standing a few feet away, will behold Callins, no longer a defendant, an appellant or a petitioner, but a man, strapped to a gurney, and seconds away from extinction.

Within days, or perhaps hours, the memory of Callins will begin to fade. The wheels of justice will churn again, and somewhere, another jury or another judge will have the unenviable task of determining whether some human being is to live or die. We hope, of course, that the defendant whose life is at risk will be represented by competent counsel—someone who is inspired by the awareness that a less-than-vigorous defense truly could have fatal consequences for the defendant. We hope that the attorney will investigate all aspects of the case, follow all evidentiary and procedural rules, and appear before a judge who is still committed to the protection of defendants' rights—even now, as the prospect of meaningful judicial oversight has diminished. In the same vein, we hope that the prosecution, in urging the penalty of death, will have exercised its discretion wisely, free from bias, prejudice, or political motive, and will be humbled, rather than emboldened, by the awesome authority conferred by the State.

But even if we can feel confident that these actors will fulfill their roles to the best of their human ability, our collective conscience will remain uneasy. Twenty years have passed since this Court declared that the death penalty must be imposed fairly, and with reasonable consistency, or not at all, see *Furman v. Georgia* (1972), and, despite the effort of the States and courts to devise legal formulas and procedural rules to meet this daunting challenge, the death penalty remains fraught with arbitrariness, discrimination, caprice, and mistake....

... Having virtually conceded that both fairness and rationality cannot be achieved in the administration of the death penalty, see *McCleskey v. Kemp* (1987), the Court has chosen to deregulate the entire enterprise, replacing, it would seem, substantive constitutional requirements with mere aesthetics, and abdicating its statutorily and constitutionally imposed duty to provide meaningful judicial oversight to the administration of death by the States.

From this day forward, I no longer shall tinker with the machinery of death. For more than 20 years I have endeavored—indeed, I have struggled—along with a majority of this Court, to develop procedural and substantive rules that would lend more than the mere appearance of fairness to the death penalty endeavor. Rather than continue to coddle the Court's delusion that the desired level of fairness has been achieved and the need for regulation eviscerated, I feel morally and intellectually obligated simply to concede that the death penalty experiment has failed. It is virtually self-evident to me now that no combination of procedural rules or substantive regulations ever can save the death penalty from its inherent constitutional deficiencies. The basic question—does the system accurately and consistently determine which defendants "deserve" to die?—cannot be answered in the affirmative.... The problem is that the inevitability of factual, legal, and moral error gives us a system that we know must wrongly kill some defendants, a system that fails to deliver the fair, consistent, and reliable sentences of death required by the Constitution....

There is little doubt now that *Furman*'s essential holding was correct. Although most of the public seems to desire, and the Constitution appears to permit, the penalty of death, it surely is beyond dispute that if the death penalty cannot be administered consistently and rationally, it may not be administered at all....

Delivering on the *Furman* promise, however, has proved to be another matter. *Furman* aspired to eliminate the vestiges of racism and the effects of poverty in capital sentencing; it deplored the "wanton" and "random" infliction of death by a government with constitutionally limited power. *Furman* demanded that the sentencer's discretion be directed and limited by procedural rules and objective standards in order to minimize the risk of arbitrary and capricious sentences of death.

In the years following *Furman*, serious efforts were made to comply with its mandate. State legislatures and appellate courts struggled to provide judges and juries with

(box continues)

(Box 11-4 continued)

sensible and objective guidelines for determining who should live and who should die....

Unfortunately, all this experimentation and ingenuity yielded little of what *Furman* demanded. It soon became apparent that discretion could not be eliminated from capital sentencing without threatening the fundamental fairness due a defendant when life is at stake....

Perhaps one day this Court will develop procedural rules or verbal formulas that actually will provide consistency, fairness, and reliability in a capital-sentencing scheme. I am not optimistic that such a day will come. I am more optimistic, though, that this Court eventually will conclude that the effort to eliminate arbitrariness while preserving fairness "in the infliction of (death) is so plainly doomed to failure that it and the death penalty must be abandoned altogether." I may not live to see that day, but I have faith that eventually it will arrive. The path the Court has chosen lessens us all. I dissent.

JUSTICE SCALIA

Convictions in opposition to the death penalty are often passionate and deeply held. That would be no excuse for reading them into a Constitution that does not contain them, even if they represented the convictions of a majority of Americans. Much less is there any excuse for using that course to thrust a minority's views upon the people. JUSTICE BLACKMUN begins his statement by describing with poignancy the death of a convicted murderer by lethal injection. He chooses, as the case in which to make that statement, one of the less brutal of the murders that regularly come before us—the murder of a man ripped by a bullet suddenly and unexpectedly, with no opportunity to prepare himself and his affairs, and left to bleed to death on the floor of a tavern. The death-by-injection which JUSTICE BLACKMUN describes looks pretty desirable next to that. It looks even better next to some of the other cases currently before us, which JUSTICE BLACKMUN did not select as the vehicle for his announcement that the death penalty is always unconstitutional—for example, the case of the 11-year-old girl raped by four men and then killed by stuffing her panties down her throat.... How enviable a quiet death by lethal injection compared with that! If the people conclude that such more brutal deaths may be deterred by capital punishment; indeed, if they merely conclude that justice requires such brutal deaths to be avenged by capital punishment; the creation of false, untextual and unhistorical contradictions within "the Court's Eighth Amendment jurisprudence" should not prevent them.

---

this area; before joining the Supreme Court he served on the U.S. Court of Appeals for the First Circuit, which hears virtually no death penalty cases.[30] During his confirmation hearings Breyer was asked his views on the death penalty in light of Blackmun's dissent. Breyer replied, "[T]hat there are some circumstances in which the death penalty is consistent with the Cruel and Unusual Punishment Clause . . . is, in my opinion, settled law. At this point it is settled." Does his last statement mean that at some point it could become unsettled?

This question takes on added meaning at the beginning of the twenty-first century, when lawyers are making use of DNA tests and other technologies to prove that some death-row inmates were wrongfully convicted.

In Illinois at least twelve men on death row were proven innocent, a situation so extreme that the governor called for a moratorium on executions.

The Eighth Amendment and Noncapital Cases

In the future, opponents of the death penalty may win their war. Perhaps, as Justice Brennan wrote in 1986, "a majority of the Supreme Court will one day accept that when the state punishes with death, it denies the humanity and dignity of the victim and transgresses the prohibition against cruel and unusual punishment."[31] For now, the Court remains committed to the position that the Cruel and Unusual Punishments Clause of the Eighth Amendment does not prohibit the death penalty—a

---

30. With the exception of New Hampshire, none of the states in the First Circuit permit capital punishment, and New Hampshire has not had an inmate on death row since the 1930s.

31. William J. Brennan Jr., "Constitutional Adjudication and the Death Penalty: A View from the Court," *Harvard Law Review* 100 (1986): 331.

BOX 11-5   CAPITAL PUNISHMENT IN GLOBAL PERSPECTIVE

WHILE THE NUMBER of legal executions in the United States is reaching all-time highs, those in other nations are declining markedly—primarily because more than half have abolished the death penalty in law or in practice. These countries include Australia, Canada, and most West European democracies.

Many newly fledged democracies also have eradicated capital punishment. Estonia's parliament voted to ratify an international treaty that obliges the country to end its death penalty. Azerbaijan's parliament approved a proposal by its president to abolish the death penalty. All 128 inmates currently on death row will be given long prison terms. Likewise, in 1999 the head of the presidential pardons commission in Moscow announced that all of Russia's death row inmates would have their sentences commuted. Finally, the constitutional courts in Lithuania and South Africa have found their death penalties to be unconstitutional. The South African court's decision was particularly interesting because the justices reviewed but ultimately rejected U.S. Supreme Court doctrine and rationale.

Ninety countries retain the death penalty, but not many of them use it with any regularity. For example, 1,625 of the *known* executions occurring in 1998 took place in only thirty-

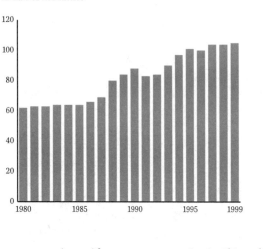

Number of Countries That Have Abolished the Death Penalty in Law or in Practice

seven countries—with 80 percent occurring in China, the Democratic Republic of Congo, the United States, and Iran.

SOURCES: Death Penalty Information Center: *http://www.deathpenaltyinfo.org;* Amnesty International: *http://www.amnesty.org/ailib/intcam/dp.*

stance that contrasts with the positions other democratic societies have adopted *(see Box 11-5)*.

But are there other kinds of punishments that may be cruel and unusual? Has the Court provided us with any definition of that concept? Indeed, in *Solem v. Helm* (1983), it attempted to do just that.

By 1979 South Dakota courts had convicted Jerry Helm for the commission of six nonviolent felonies. That year he was charged with yet another offense—writing bad checks. Normally, that crime carries with it a maximum sentence of five years in prison and/or a $5,000 fine. But because of Helm's previous record, a South Dakota judge invoked a state recidivism law: if an individual is convicted of three felonies, the sentence can be the same as for a Class 1 felony, which includes life in prison with no parole and/or a $25,000 fine. Believing that Helm was beyond rehabilitation, the judge sen-

tenced him to life. After two years of trying to get the governor to commute his sentence, Helm appealed to the Supreme Court, claiming that his punishment was cruel and unusual.

By a 5–4 vote, the justices found the life sentence violated the Cruel and Unusual Punishment Clause. Justice Powell's majority opinion held that the Eighth Amendment proscribes not only barbaric punishments, but also sentences that are disproportionate to the crime committed. The justices held that this concept of proportionality could be traced back to the earliest development of English law. As applied in this case, life in prison was out of proportion to the bad check charges.[32] Finally, after years of death penalty litigation, the Court provided attorneys

32. The Court's decision in *Solem v. Helm* provides a basis to question the constitutional validity of the many "three strikes and you're out" laws passed by anticrime state legislatures in the 1990s.

with a working definition of cruel and unusual, ironically using a noncapital case to do so. The Court seemed to abide by the old adage—let the punishment fit the crime.

Individuals who have been fully prosecuted for criminal offenses retain certain procedural protections during the post-trial period. Convicted defendants have the right to challenge the validity of their trials, usually through an appeal. Under the concept of due process of law, those convicted of crimes may ask a higher court to review what transpired during the trial to determine if there was any significant procedural error. If the appeals court finds that a reversible error occurred—an error significant enough to have affected the outcome of the trial—the conviction may be declared invalid or a new trial may be ordered. Convicted criminals have the right to have their cases heard on appeal once; any subsequent appeals take place at the discretion of the appellate court.

Another way of challenging a conviction is to file a motion for a new trial. If new evidence comes to light that brings a trial's outcome into question, a convicted defendant can ask for a new trial. Such motions are rarely granted: the defendant must show that the new evidence could not have been known or presented at the first trial and that the evidence is strong enough to cast serious doubt on the original verdict.

THE DOUBLE JEOPARDY CLAUSE

An entirely different set of post-trial protections is accorded by the Double Jeopardy Clause of the Fifth Amendment: "nor shall any person be subject for the same offence to be twice put in jeopardy of life or limb." The right against double jeopardy is one of the least understood provisions governing the criminal process. This lack of understanding is due both to the unusual wording of the clause and to some confusing rulings from the Supreme Court.

The Double Jeopardy Clause includes three basic protections. First, an individual tried for an offense and found not guilty cannot be prosecuted a second time for the same offense. This guarantee was designed to ensure that someone would not be subjected to multiple prose-

cutions for the same crime. Without this restraint, a powerful government could conduct prosecution after prosecution until a conviction was finally obtained. With each successive prosecution the defendant's resources would be decreased, leaving the individual more vulnerable in subsequent trials. It seemed only fair to the Framers to restrict the government to one attempt to convict a defendant on a single offense. Furthermore, this right prohibits the government from appealing a trial court's verdict of not guilty. Once a not guilty verdict is announced, the defendant is forever free from criminal prosecutions based on that offense.

But what is meant by the term "same offense"? The Supreme Court answered part of the question in *Ashe v. Swenson* (1970). Bob Fred Ashe, along with others, was charged with breaking into a house and robbing its owner and five others who were playing poker. The prosecutor tried Ashe for robbing one of the poker players. That trial ended in a not guilty verdict due to insufficient evidence. Six weeks later the prosecutor charged Ashe with robbing another member of the poker party and this time got a conviction. Ashe claimed on appeal that the second trial violated his double jeopardy rights. The Supreme Court agreed, holding that the robbery was a single offense, although there were multiple victims. Except for the name of the victim, the second trial involved exactly the same incident and circumstances as the first. Therefore, to be found not guilty in the first trial precluded a second. In Justice Stewart's words, the Fifth Amendment "surely protects a man who has been acquitted from having to 'run the gauntlet' a second time."

The Double Jeopardy Clause, however, does not bar separate governments from prosecuting an individual based on the same incident. In *Heath v. Alabama* (1985) the Court applied this dual sovereignty doctrine to Larry Gene Heath, who had arranged to have his wife, who was nine months pregnant, kidnapped and killed. The hired killers took Rebecca Heath from her home in Alabama and murdered her in Georgia. Heath was arrested in Georgia and pleaded guilty to murder charges as part of a plea bargain arrangement to avoid the death penalty. Alabama authorities, independently investigating the crime, then indicted Heath for kidnapping and murder.

Heath objected on double jeopardy grounds, but the Supreme Court held that the Fifth Amendment did not prohibit prosecution by Alabama. An act that offends the criminal laws of two jurisdictions may be punished by both.

The same doctrine can be applied to an action that violates both state and federal criminal codes. An example is the infamous 1992 Rodney King incident. A state jury acquitted Los Angeles police officers who had been accused of beating King following a high-speed chase. The verdict was reached despite a damaging and frequently televised videotape account of the incident. Federal prosecutors later won convictions by convincing a different jury that the officers' actions constituted a criminal violation of King's civil rights.

A second protection of the Double Jeopardy Clause is the ban against prosecuting someone a second time for an offense on which a guilty verdict has already been returned. Suppose a woman is convicted of killing a coworker and receives a long prison sentence. The prosecution may consider the penalty too lenient, but the Double Jeopardy Clause prohibits prosecutors from trying her a second time to obtain a more severe sentence. However, as early as 1896, in *United States v. Ball*, the Supreme Court held that a second trial is not necessarily prohibited if the defendant appeals the trial court decision and an appellate court reverses the conviction. Nor is a second trial prohibited if the first ends in a hung jury, which means the jurors are deadlocked and cannot reach a verdict. The justices came to this conclusion in the earliest double jeopardy case, *United States v. Perez* (1824).

Third, the Double Jeopardy Clause bars multiple punishments for the same offense, the central issue in two 1996 cases, *United States v. Ursery* and *United States v. $405,089.23*, which the Court decided together. These cases challenged the property forfeiture actions taken by the federal government against certain criminals. This aggressive law enforcement strategy allows the government to make a two-pronged attack on crime. The government not only charges the accused with actual criminal offenses but also institutes a separate legal action requesting the forfeiture of any property used in the crime or purchased with the fruits of the crime. Property forfei-

ture is a civil, not criminal, action. In the *Ursery* case, federal authorities found evidence of marijuana production in Guy Ursery's house and marijuana plants growing on adjacent land. The government prosecuted criminal drug charges against him and moved to have his house and land forfeited to the government. In *$404,089.23* the government charged two individuals with illegal drug distribution and in a separate legal action moved to seize cash, silver, boats, aircraft, and automobiles on the grounds that they were purchased with illegal money or used in the criminal activity.

The defendants in these cases claimed that the criminal prosecutions and the civil property forfeiture actions constituted double penalties for the same offense in violation of the Fifth Amendment. In an 8–1 decision, the justices disagreed. The Court concluded that Congress in drafting the property forfeiture statutes intended such actions to be civil matters and not a criminal punishment. Furthermore, the justices found that property forfeitures are not "so punitive in form or effect as to render them criminal in spite of Congress' intent to the contrary." The Court's decision was a major victory for law enforcement authorities. Property seizures, particularly against those engaged in highly profitable crimes such as drug dealing, allow the government to attack crime much more vigorously than using criminal sentences alone.

In *Kansas v. Hendricks* (1997) the justices continued to take a narrow view of the Double Jeopardy Clause. This case involved a challenge to a statute that permitted the state to keep certain sexual offenders in custody even after they had served their sentences. According to the law, violent sexual predators who have mental abnormalities that prohibit them from controlling their unlawful sexual conduct may be committed to a mental health facility after completion of their criminal sentences. Such civil commitments, involuntary and indeterminate in length, can take place only after strict procedural safeguards are observed, including a jury trial.

Leroy Hendricks was a pedophile with a forty-year history of sexually molesting young boys and girls. In 1984 he was convicted of sexually assaulting two teenage boys. As his prison sentence was about to be completed in 1994, Kansas authorities, who believed Hendricks was a danger to society, initiated proceedings to commit him to a mental institution. A jury found beyond a reasonable doubt that he should be committed. Hendricks appealed, claiming that the commitment constituted a second punishment for his offense in violation of the Double Jeopardy and Due Process Clauses. A closely divided Supreme Court upheld the law, finding that the civil commitment was not a second criminal punishment, but a separate civil procedure allowing the state to protect the public from sexual predators who are unable to control their behavior. With double jeopardy doubts erased by the Court, lawmakers in several other states proposed adopting legislation modeled on the Kansas statute.

ATTORNEYS, TRIALS, AND PUNISHMENTS: (RE)EMERGING ISSUES

The amendments covered in this chapter—the Fifth, Sixth, and Eighth—have confronted the Supreme Court with complex questions. Must a defendant be able to directly confront his or her accuser? Should trial court judges be able to close proceedings to the press and public? Under what circumstances, if any, can states impose capital punishment? Although the justices have given decisive answers to some of these questions and others of equal importance, it is possible that new Court members will supplant those answers in the years and decades to come.

Underlying many of the issues we have covered in this and the previous chapters is one with which the justices have not fully come to terms: allegations from many quarters that rampant racism infects the criminal justice system. The following types of facts often motivate such allegations:

• Reports that police engage in various forms of racial profiling, most predominately singling out black and Hispanic drivers for highway drug searches;

• Studies indicating the disparate impact of harsher sentences for the use of crack cocaine, which is more available in the black community, than for drugs preferred by whites;

• The huge imbalances existing between whites and minorities in U.S. prisons, with one in three African-

American males between twenty and twenty-nine years of age within the criminal justice system; and

• More studies demonstrating bias in applying the death penalty at both state and federal levels, by prosecutors, judges, and juries.[33]

To be sure, some of these charges may be beyond the Court's purview; others, the Court has heard before in cases such as *Batson* and *McCleskey.* But with nearly 60 percent of Americans believing that racial and ethnic minorities do not receive equitable treatment in the justice system, with scores of interest groups studying the issue, and states creating task forces, it is inevitable that the justices will be asked to take a harder look at the problem.[34]

READINGS

Abramson, Jeffrey. *We, the Jury: The Jury System and the Ideal of Democracy.* New York: Basic Books, 1994.

Adler, Stephen J. *The Jury: Trial and Error in the American Courtroom.* New York: Times Books, 1994.

Alschuler, Andrew W., and Albert G. Deiss. "A Brief History of the Criminal Jury in the United States." *University of Chicago Law Review* 61 (1994): 867–875.

Baldus, David C., George G. Woodworth, and Charles A. Pulaski Jr. *Equal Justice and the Death Penalty.* Boston: Northeastern University Press, 1990.

Butler, Paul. "Racially Based Jury Nullification: Black Power in the Criminal Justice System." *Yale Law Journal* 105 (1995): 677.

Eisenstein, James, and Herbert Jacob. *Felony Justice.* Boston: Little, Brown, 1977.

Epstein, Lee, and Joseph F. Kobylka. *The Supreme Court and Legal Change: Abortion and the Death Penalty.* Chapel Hill: University of North Carolina Press, 1992.

Gerber, Rudolph J. *Cruel and Usual: Our Criminal Injustice System.* Westport: Praeger, 1999.

Goldfarb, Ronald. *Ransom: A Critique of the American Bail System.* New York: Harper & Row, 1965.

Haines, Herbert H. 1996. *Against Capital Punishment: The Anti–Death Penalty Movement in America, 1972–1994.* New York: Oxford University Press.

Hastie, Reid, Steven D. Penrod, and Nancy Pennington. *Inside the Jury.* Cambridge: Harvard University Press, 1983.

Heumann, Milton. *Plea Bargaining.* Chicago: University of Chicago Press, 1978.

Hurwitz, Jon, and Mark Peffley. "Public Perceptions of Race and

33. We obtained some of this information from the National Association of Criminal Defense Lawyers (*www.criminaljustice.org*) and the American Bar Association (*abanet.org*).

34. This figure comes from a 1999 ABA survey on public perceptions of the justice systems.

Crime: The Role of Racial Stereoptypes." *American Journal of Political Science* 41 (1997): 375–401.

Kalven, Harry, Jr., and Hans Zeisel. *The American Jury.* Boston: Little, Brown, 1966.

Levine, James P. *Juries and Politics.* Pacific Grove, Calif.: Brooks/Cole, 1992.

Lewis, Anthony. *Gideon's Trumpet.* New York: Vintage Books, 1964.

Meltsner, Michael. *Cruel and Unusual: The Supreme Court and Capital Punishment.* New York: Random House, 1973.

Russell, Gregory D. *The Death Penalty and Racial Bias: Overturning Supreme Court Assumptions.* Westport, Conn.: Greenwood Press, 1994.

Sigler, Jay A. *Double Jeopardy: The Development of Legal and Social Policy.* Ithaca, N.Y.: Cornell University Press, 1969.

Thaler, Paul. *The Watchful Eye: American Justice in the Age of the Television Trial.* Westport, Conn.: Praeger, 1994.

Tonry, Michael. *Malign Neglect: Race, Crime and Punishment.* New York: Oxford University Press, 2000.

Walker, Sam, Cassia Spohn, and Miriam DeLone. *The Color of Justice.* Belmont, Calif.: Wadsworth, 1996.

PART IV
CIVIL RIGHTS

CIVIL RIGHTS AND THE CONSTITUTION

IN MARKED CONTRAST to the colonial period, when most Americans came from British roots, U.S. citizens today are from many different backgrounds. Immigration has diversified the population, and this trend is expected to continue. Americans are a people of wide-ranging religions, races, ethnic backgrounds, and levels of wealth. Given this diversity, the slogan "e pluribus unum" or "one from many" sometimes appears to be more of a challenge than a statement of fact. In spite of the differences, however, the nation has pledged itself to fairness and equality. All Americans are to be free from unconstitutional discrimination, to have equal opportunity, and to participate fully in the political process.

Even so, at times people feel they have been mistreated by their government, not because of what they have done but because of who they are. They claim that discrimination has occurred because of race, creed, national origin, sex, economic status, or some other characteristic that government should not use as a basis for policy. When disputes over such charges arise, the court system provides a venue for their resolution. In this part, we discuss the civil rights of Americans and how the Supreme Court has interpreted them. By civil rights we mean those legal provisions emanating from the concept of equality. Unlike civil liberties issues, which focus on personal freedoms protected by the Bill of Rights, civil rights issues involve the status of persons with shared characteristics who historically have been disadvantaged in

some way. Civil rights laws attempt to guarantee full and equal citizenship for such persons and to protect them from arbitrary and capricious treatment. Chapter 12 examines discrimination, and Chapter 13 explores the rights of political participation. Before we confront those subjects, however, a review of some basic concepts of history and law might be useful.

Today, we are used to hearing not only about charges of discrimination but also about Supreme Court rulings on the proper meaning of the Constitution governing such issues. These phenomena are comparatively recent. Although "equality" in the United States was relatively advanced for the period, colonial Americans discriminated in a number of ways that we now consider abhorrent. The most significant breach of fundamental equality was the institution of slavery. In spite of the Declaration of Independence, which proclaimed that all men were created equal, the enslavement of Africans brought to North America against their will was politically accepted, although not universally supported. The Constitution recognized this form of inequality, stipulating in Article I that a slave would be counted as three-fifths of a person for representation purposes; it also gave slavery a degree of protection by prohibiting any federal restrictions on the importation of slaves until 1808. Other forms of discrimination also were common. Voting qualifications, for example, were quite restrictive: only men could vote, and in some states only men who owned property could vote.

Guarantees of equality did not officially become part

of the Constitution until after the Civil War. When the Radical Republicans took control of the legislative branch, three constitutional amendments, generally referred to as the Civil War Amendments, were proposed and ratified. They incorporated into the Constitution what had been won on the battlefield and dramatically changed the concept of civil rights in the United States. The Thirteenth Amendment, ratified in 1865, unambiguously ended the institution of slavery. Although there have been some disputes over the involuntary servitude prohibition (in relation, for example, to the military draft), the slavery issue, over which the nation had been divided since the Constitutional Convention, finally was put to rest. The other two amendments, the Fourteenth and Fifteenth, have generated a great deal of litigation and many Supreme Court cases, and we discuss them in turn.

THE FOURTEENTH AMENDMENT

The Fourteenth Amendment, ratified in 1868, is unlike the other two because of its length and complexity. The first section is the most significant: it states that U.S. citizenship is superior to state citizenship, constitutionally reinforcing the Civil War outcome of national superiority over states' rights. This idea was a dramatic change from the pre–Civil War concept that national citizenship was dependent upon state citizenship. The first section also includes the Due Process Clause and Privileges or Immunities Clause we discussed in earlier chapters, as well as the Equal Protection Clause. Because this last clause forms the basis of constitutional protections against discrimination, we describe it in some detail. The remaining parts of the Fourteenth Amendment require the former slaves to be fully counted for representational purposes, impose universal adult male suffrage, restrict the civil rights of certain participants in the rebellion, and guarantee the public debt resulting from the war. The amendment was ratified in 1868.

The Supreme Court and Equal Protection of the Laws

An analysis of the wording of the Equal Protection Clause helps us to understand what it covers and what its limitations are. It says, "[N]or shall any State . . . deny to any person within its jurisdiction the equal protection of the laws."

The first significant element of the clause is the word *state*. The members of Congress who drafted the Fourteenth Amendment were concerned primarily with the danger of the states (especially those in the South) imposing discriminatory laws. With the Radical Republicans, who were deeply committed to an abolition ideology, in control of Congress and the White House, the legislators had little fear that the federal government would impose discriminatory policies. Consequently, the prohibitions of the clause apply only to the states and their political subdivisions, such as counties and cities.

Second, the amendment protects *all* persons within a state's jurisdiction, not just former slaves. In an early dispute over the amendment, the Supreme Court acknowledged its broad applicability. *Yick Wo v. Hopkins* (1886) concerned the discriminatory enforcement of fire safety regulations in San Francisco. The Court held that the Equal Protection Clause applies to persons other than black Americans, also protecting noncitizens who are the target of discrimination by the state.

Finally, the clause outlaws a denial of equal protection of the laws; in other words, it prohibits discrimination. Any person within a state's jurisdiction is constitutionally entitled to be treated equitably, to be free from arbitrary and unreasonable treatment at the hands of the state government.

The wording of the Equal Protection Clause means that before an individual can legitimately assert a claim of its violation, two important elements must be demonstrated. First, the aggrieved party must prove some form of unequal treatment or discrimination. Second, there must be state action; that is, the discrimination must have been initiated or supported by the state or its local governments. These two requirements have undergone substantial interpretation by the justices of the Supreme Court, and we need to understand what is included in each requirement.

Discrimination. Discrimination simply means to distinguish between people or things. It occurs in many forms, not all of which are prohibited by the Constitution. For example, in administering an admissions program, a state university must discriminate among its applicants. It admits some, rejects others. Decisions usually are based on an applicant's high school grades, standardized test scores, and letters of recommendation. The university admits those who, based on valid predictors of performance, have the best chance to succeed. Those who are rejected usually accept the decision because the university's admissions criteria appear reasonable. But the reaction would be quite different if an applicant received a letter that said, "In spite of your demonstrated potential for college studies, we cannot admit you because of our policy not to accept students of your ethnic background." In this case, the rejected applicant would rightly feel victimized by unreasonable discrimination.

What rule of law distinguishes acceptable discrimination from that which violates the Constitution? The Supreme Court answered this question by declaring that the Equal Protection Clause goes no further than prohibiting "invidious discrimination."[1] By invidious discrimination, the Court means discrimination that is arbitrary and capricious, unequal treatment that has no rational basis. Reasonable discrimination, on the other hand, is not unconstitutional. When the state treats two individuals differently, we need to ask upon what criteria the state is distinguishing them. If two surgeons perform heart operations on patients and one is thrown in jail and the other is not, we might feel that the imprisoned person has not been treated fairly. Our opinion would change, however, if we learned that the jailed person had never been to medical school and was not licensed. Here the state would be discriminating on the basis of legitimate, reasonable criteria. The Equal Protection Clause demands that similarly situated persons be treated equally. The two surgeons, because of their vastly different qualifications, are not similarly situated, and consequently the Constitution does not require that they be treated the same.

Almost every government action involves some form of discrimination. Most are perfectly legitimate, although all those affected might not agree. For example, when a state government passes an income tax law that

imposes a higher rate on the wealthy than it does on the poor, the rich may feel they are the target of unconstitutional discrimination. When individuals believe they have been denied equal protection at the hands of the state, the courts must decide if the government's discrimination runs afoul of the Fourteenth Amendment. When it comes to taxes, the courts have ruled that progressive rate structures are not invidious, but reasonable.

To assist the judiciary in deciding such disputes, the Supreme Court has developed three basic tests of the Equal Protection Clause. Which test is applied in any given case is determined by the alleged discrimination and the government interests at stake.

The traditional test used to decide discrimination cases is the *rational basis* test. When using this approach to the Constitution, the justices ask: Is the challenged discrimination rational? Or is it arbitrary and capricious? If a state passes a law that says a person must be at least eighteen years old to enter a legally binding contract, it is imposing an age-based discrimination. Individuals under eighteen are not granted the right to consummate legal agreements; those over eighteen are. If a dispute over the validity of this law were brought to court, the judge would have to decide whether the state had acted reasonably to achieve a legitimate government objective.[2] Using the rational basis test, the Court generally defers to the state and presumes the validity of the government's action. The burden of proof rests with the party challenging the law to establish that the statute is irrational. Unless the Court has determined otherwise, discrimination claims proceed according to the rules of the rational basis test.

The second test is called the *suspect class* or *strict scrutiny* test. This test is used when the state discriminates on the basis of a criterion that the Supreme Court has declared to be inherently suspect or when there is a claim that a fundamental right has been violated. A suspect classification is based on characteristics assumed to be irrational. The Supreme Court has ruled, for example, that race is a suspect class. Laws that discriminate on racial grounds are given strict scrutiny by the courts. The

1. See *Williamson v. Lee Optical* (1955).

2. See *McGowan v. Maryland* (1961).

TABLE IV-1 Equal Protection Tests

Test	Examples of Applicability	Validity Standard
Rational basis test	General discrimination claims	The law must be a *reasonable* measure designed to achieve a *legitimate* government purpose.
Intermediate ("heightened") scrutiny test	Sex discrimination	The law must be *substantially related* to the achievement of an *important* objective.
Suspect class (strict scrutiny) test	Racial discrimination; cases involving fundamental rights (e.g., voting)	The law must be the *least restrictive* means available to achieve a *compelling* state interest.

reason for moving racial discrimination from the rational basis test to the suspect class test is that the Supreme Court has concluded that racial criteria are inherently arbitrary, that compelling state interests are rarely (if ever) served by treating people differently according to race. For a law to be valid under strict scrutiny, it must be found to advance a compelling state interest by the least restrictive means available. When the suspect class test is used, the Court presumes that the state action is unconstitutional, and the burden of proof is on the government to demonstrate that the law is rational.

Given the rules associated with these two tests, it should be obvious that it is much easier to establish that a violation of the Constitution has occurred if the suspect class test is used. Therefore, many cases before the Supreme Court have been filed by attorneys representing groups seeking that classification. The Court has ruled that suspect class status should be accorded only to those groups that constitute discrete and insular minorities that have experienced a history of unequal treatment and a lack of political power.[3] Applying such criteria is difficult and has given rise to sharp divisions of opinion among the justices.

Legal battles over what rules should apply to sex discrimination cases were particularly difficult for the Court to resolve.[4] A majority could not agree to elevate sex to suspect class status, but there was substantial opinion

that the rational basis test was also inappropriate for dealing with sex discrimination. This conflict gave rise to a third test of the Equal Protection Clause, the *intermediate* (or *heightened*) *scrutiny* test. This test holds that to be valid the unequal treatment must serve important government objectives and must be substantially related to the achievement of those objectives.[5] As such, this test falls squarely between the rational basis test and the suspect class test *(see Table IV-1)*.

This three-tiered approach can be confusing, and the Supreme Court has been neither clear nor consistent in applying the principles. Justice Marshall in *Dunn v. Blumstein* (1972) acknowledged that the tests do not have the "precision of mathematical formulas." Justice White hinted that in reality the Court may be using a spectrum of tests rather than three separate tests. Frustration over the status of the Equal Protection Clause tests prompted Justice Stevens to claim in his concurring opinion in *Cleburne v. Cleburne Living Center* (1985) that a continuum of standards was being used. Not persuaded of the wisdom of the Court's approach, Stevens has argued that a single test should be adopted for all equal protection claims. In spite of these criticisms, the Court has stuck to the three-tiered approach, which reflects the belief that the more historically disadvantaged and politically powerless a class of people has been, the greater justification government must provide for any state action that discriminates against the members of that class.

3. See *United States v. Carolene Products* (1938); *San Antonio Independent School District v. Rodriguez* (1973).

4. See, for example, *Frontiero v. Richardson* (1973).

5. *Craig v. Boren* (1976).

State Action. As noted, the Equal Protection Clause specifically prohibits discrimination by any state. The Supreme Court has interpreted this concept to include a wide array of state actions—statutes, their enforcement and administration, and the actions of state officials. We have already mentioned *Yick Wo v. Hopkins,* in which the Court struck down a fire safety regulation that was racially neutral as written but enforced in a discriminatory manner against Chinese laundry operators. State action includes the policies of political subdivisions such as towns, cities, counties, or special purpose agencies. The states are prohibited from engaging in invidious discrimination either directly or indirectly. A city, for instance, may not run its municipal swimming pools in a racially segregated manner, nor may it donate the pools to a private organization that will restrict pool use to a particular racial group. In whatever form, however, some element of state action supporting invidious discrimination must be shown before a violation of the Equal Protection Clause occurs.

This requirement means that discrimination by purely private individuals or organizations is not prohibited by the Equal Protection Clause. A white apartment house owner who refuses to rent to a black family is not in violation of the Constitution; neither is a restaurant manager who will not serve Hispanics, a private club that will not admit women, nor an employer who will not hire applicants over forty years of age. In each of these cases there is ample evidence of irrational discrimination, but no state action. The discrimination is conducted by private individuals or organizations. These forms of discrimination may well be in violation of any number of state or federal statutes, but they do not offend the Equal Protection Clause of the Fourteenth Amendment.

Moreover, because it is restricted to the states, the Equal Protection Clause does not prohibit the federal government from engaging in discrimination. The Supreme Court, therefore, faced a difficult situation in 1954 in the school desegregation cases. The best-known case is *Brown v. Board of Education of Topeka, Kansas,* but *Brown* was only one of several cases involving the same basic issue. In *Bolling v. Sharpe* the Court faced the thorny issue of racial segregation in the Washington, D.C., pub-lic schools. The District of Columbia is not a state. In the 1950s Congress was the ultimate authority over Washington, as it is today. The Equal Protection Clause was not applicable there. Given the political situation at the time, the Court had to find a way to declare all segregated schools unconstitutional.

The justices found a solution in the Due Process Clause of the Fifth Amendment, which states, "No person shall . . . be deprived of life, liberty, or property, without due process of law." This guarantee of essential fairness applies to the federal government and was used by the justices in *Bolling* as a bar against racial discrimination. Chief Justice Warren explained for a unanimous Court:

The Fifth Amendment, which is applicable in the District of Columbia, does not contain an equal protection clause as does the Fourteenth Amendment which applies only to the states. But the concepts of equal protection and due process, both stemming from our American ideal of fairness, are not mutually exclusive. The "equal protection of the laws" is a more explicit safeguard of prohibited unfairness than "due process of law," and, therefore, we do not imply that the two are always interchangeable phrases. But, as this Court has recognized, discrimination may be so unjustifiable as to be violative of due process.

Although Warren cautioned that the Due Process Clause and the Equal Protection Clause could not be used interchangeably, the Court consistently has ruled that both provisions stand for the same general principles. In most areas of discrimination law (but not all), the justices have applied the same standards to both state and federal governments by using these two constitutional provisions. As a rule, any discriminatory action by a state found to be in violation of the Equal Protection Clause would also be a violation of the Fifth Amendment if engaged in by the federal government. However, we should understand which provision of the Constitution is offended when invidious discrimination is practiced by either state governments or the federal government. If the U.S. National Park Service were to require racially segregated campgrounds at Yellowstone, it would violate the Due Process Clause of the Fifth Amendment; if a state imposed the same restriction at a state park, it would violate the Equal Protection Clause of the Fourteenth Amendment.

BOX IV-1   MAJOR CIVIL RIGHTS ACTS

CIVIL RIGHTS ACTS OF 1866, 1870, 1871, AND 1875

Laws passed by Congress after the Civil War to guarantee the rights of blacks. The public accommodation provisions of the 1875 law were declared unconstitutional by the Supreme Court in the *Civil Rights Cases* (1883), as a federal invasion of private rights. Other provisions of these laws were struck down by the courts or repealed by Congress. Today, a few major provisions remain from the acts of 1866 and 1871. One makes it a federal crime for any person acting under the authority of a state law to deprive another of any rights protected by the Constitution or by laws of the United States. Another authorizes suits for civil damages against state or local officials by persons whose rights are abridged. Others permit actions against persons who conspire to deprive people of their rights.

CIVIL RIGHTS ACT OF 1957

The first civil rights law passed by Congress since Reconstruction, designed to secure the right to vote for blacks. Its major feature empowers the Department of Justice to seek court injunctions against any deprivation of voting rights, and authorizes criminal prosecutions for violations of an injunction. In addition, the act established a Civil Rights Division, headed by an Assistant Attorney General in the Department of Justice, and created a bipartisan Civil Rights Commission to investigate civil rights violations and to recommend legislation.

CIVIL RIGHTS ACT OF 1960

A law designed to further secure the right to vote for blacks and to meet the problems arising from racial upheavals in the South in the late 1950s. The major provision authorizes federal courts to appoint referees who will help blacks to register after a voter-denial conviction is obtained under the 1957 Civil Rights Act, and after a court finding of a "pattern or practice" of discrimination against qualified voters. Other provisions: (1)

authorize punishment for persons who obstruct any federal court order, such as a school desegregation order, by threats or force; (2) authorize criminal penalties for transportation of explosives for the purpose of bombing a building; (3) require preservation of voting records for twenty-two months, and authorize the Attorney General to inspect the records; and (4) provide for schooling of children of armed forces personnel in the event that a school closes because of an integration dispute.

CIVIL RIGHTS ACT OF 1964

A major enactment designed to erase racial discrimination in most areas of American life. Major provisions of the act: (1) outlaw arbitrary discrimination in voter registration and expedite voting rights suits; (2) bar discrimination in public accommodations, such as hotels and restaurants, that have a substantial relation to interstate commerce; (3) authorize the national government to bring suits to desegregate public facilities and schools; (4) extend the life and expand the power of the Civil Rights Commission; (5) provide for the withholding of federal funds from programs administered in a discriminatory manner; (6) establish the right to equality in employment opportunities; and (7) establish a Community Relations Service to help resolve civil rights problems. The act forbids discrimination based on race, color, religion, national origin, and, in the case of employment, sex. Techniques for gaining voluntary compliance are stressed in the act, and the resolution of civil rights problems through state and local action is encouraged. Discrimination in housing is not covered by the law, but is prohibited by the Civil Rights Act of 1968.

Significance. The Civil Rights Act of 1964 is the most far-reaching civil rights legislation since Reconstruction. It was passed after the longest debate in Senate history (eighty-three days) and only after cloture was invoked for the first time to cut off a civil rights filibuster. Compliance with the act's controversial provisions on public accommodations and equal employment opportunities has been widespread. Title VI of the

Congressional Enforcement of the Fourteenth Amendment

The civil rights of Americans are defined and protected by more than just the Constitution. Over the years Congress has passed laws designed to enforce and extend constitutional guarantees *(see Box IV-1)*. These laws ex-

pand prohibitions against discriminatory behavior, give the federal executive branch authority to enforce civil rights protections, and enlarge the opportunities for aggrieved parties to seek redress in the courts. The rules of evidence and procedure in some of these laws make it easier for litigants to prevail by proving a violation of act, which authorizes the cutoff of federal funds to state and local programs practicing discrimination, proved to be the most effective provision of the act. For example, a dramatic jump in southern school integration took place when the national government threatened to withhold federal funds from schools failing to comply with desegregation orders. All agencies receiving federal funds are required to submit assurance of compliance with the 1964 act. Hundreds of grant-in-aid programs are involved, amounting to 20 percent of all state and local revenues.

CIVIL RIGHTS ACT OF 1968

A law which prohibits discrimination on the advertising, financing, sale, or rental of housing, based on race, religion, or national origin and, as of 1974, sex, but provided limited and ineffective enforcement powers. A major amendment to the act in 1988 extended coverage to the handicapped and to families with children and added enforcement machinery through either administrative enforcement by the Department of Housing and Urban Development (HUD) or by suits filed in federal court, with the choice of forums left to either party in the dispute. The law covers about 80 percent of all housing. Major exclusions are owner-occupied dwellings of four units or less and those selling without services of a broker.

VOTING RIGHTS ACT

A major law enacted by Congress in 1965 and renewed and expanded in 1970, 1975, and 1982 that has sought to eliminate restrictions on voting that have been used to discriminate against blacks and other minority groups. A major provision of the 1965 act suspended the use of literacy and other tests used to discriminate. The act also authorized registration by federal registrars in any state or county where such tests had been used and where less than 50 percent of eligible voters were registered. Seven southern states were mainly affected by these provisions. The act also authorized a legal test of poll

taxes in state elections, and the Supreme Court in 1966 declared payment of poll taxes as a condition of voting to be unconstitutional. Major provisions of the 1965 act were upheld by the Court as a valid exercise of power under the Fifteenth Amendment. The Voting Rights Act of 1970: (1) extended the 1965 act for five years; (2) lowered the minimum age for all elections from twenty-one to eighteen; (3) prohibited the states from disqualifying voters in presidential elections because of their failure to meet state residence requirements beyond thirty days; and (4) provided for uniform national rules for absentee registration and voting in presidential elections. In 1970 the Court upheld the eighteen-year-old vote for national elections but found its application to state and local elections unconstitutional. In 1975 the act was continued for seven years. Federal voting protection was extended to all parts of ten additional states, bilingual ballots were required, election law changes in states covered by the act were required to be approved by either a United States attorney or a federal court, and legal protection of voting rights was extended to Spanish-Americans, Alaskan Natives, American Indians, and Asian-Americans. The 1982 act extends the law for twenty-five years, authorizes a "bailout" for covered states showing a clear record for ten years, and provides the intent to discriminate need not be proven if the results demonstrate otherwise.

CIVIL RIGHTS ACT OF 1991

A reaffirmation and expansion of protection against discrimination in employment. The main purpose of the legislation was to overturn several 1989 Supreme Court decisions that made it harder for employees to challenge or prove discrimination, that narrowly interpreted the scope of civil rights laws, and that limited access to the courts.

SOURCE: Jack C. Plano and Milton Greenberg, *The American Political Dictionary* (Fort Worth: Harcourt Brace Jovanovich, 1993).

a civil rights statute rather than a constitutional violation.

The authority for Congress to pass such laws can be found in several constitutional provisions. Each Civil War Amendment contains a section granting Congress the power to enforce the amendment with appropriate

legislation. Consequently, these amendments have had considerable impact not only because of their basic substantive content, but also because they gave Congress new legislative power. Immediately following the Civil War, Congress used this authority to pass laws intended to give the new amendments teeth. For example, the

Civil Rights Act of 1866, passed over the veto of President Andrew Johnson, guaranteed blacks the right to purchase, lease, and use real property. The Supreme Court upheld the law, ruling that the Thirteenth Amendment's enforcement section gave Congress the power not only to outlaw slavery but also to legislate against the "badges and incidents of slavery."[6] Much of the federal regulation on fair housing is based on this authority.

Congress learned by trial and error to ground legislation in the correct Civil War Amendment. In 1883 the Supreme Court handed down its decisions in the *Civil Rights Cases*, which involved challenges to the Civil Rights Act of 1875, a statute based on the Fourteenth Amendment that made discrimination in public accommodations unlawful. Because the law covered privately owned businesses, the owners of hotels, entertainment facilities, and transportation companies claimed that Congress had exceeded the authority granted to it by the amendment. The Court, with only one justice dissenting, struck down the statute, holding that any legislation based on the Fourteenth Amendment could regulate only discrimination promoted by state action. Discrimination by private individuals was not covered by the amendment and, therefore, Congress could not prohibit it through an enforcement statute.

Congress eventually was able to pierce the private discrimination veil by finding a different constitutional grant of power upon which to base the Civil Rights Act of 1964. The most comprehensive civil rights statute ever, the law regulated discrimination in employment, education, and public accommodations. It placed restrictions on federal appropriations and programs to ensure that nondiscrimination principles were followed in any activity supported by the U.S. government. The act outlawed discrimination based not only on race but also on other factors as well, such as sex, national origin, and religion. Much of what was regulated by the statute was private behavior, including prohibitions of discrimination by restaurants, hotels, and other privately run public accommodations. Rather than the Fourteenth Amendment, Congress used the Commerce Clause of Article I.

That clause gives the national legislature the power to regulate interstate commerce, and the provisions of the 1964 Civil Rights Act apply to all activities in interstate commerce. The Supreme Court upheld the constitutionality of the law and gave it increased effectiveness by broadly defining what is considered to be within interstate commerce.[7]

Since then, Congress has expanded the scope of federal regulation over civil rights by passing amendments to the 1964 act and by enacting additional legislation *(see Box IV-1)*. For example, the Civil Rights Act of 1968 attempted to remove discrimination in the sale, rental, or financing of housing, and the Americans with Disabilities Act of 1990 extended federal protections to the disabled in employment, public services, and access to public places. As a result of such legislative actions, a large portion of federal civil rights law is based on congressional statutes rather than constitutional provisions.

Federal civil rights laws provide great opportunities for those who wish to challenge discriminatory behavior. Not only do these statutes regulate private-sector discrimination, but also they frequently impose thresholds of proof that are easier to satisfy than those the Supreme Court requires for constitutional challenges. For example, under the civil rights laws a worker claiming employment discrimination based on race may not have to establish discriminatory intent (a requirement for a violation of the Constitution), but may instead submit statistical evidence that the employer treats racial groups differently. Because of the growth of civil rights laws, the federal courts today hear many more cases involving alleged violations of civil rights statutes than those claiming a violation of the Constitution.

THE FIFTEENTH AMENDMENT

The Fifteenth Amendment removed race as a condition by which the right to vote could be denied. Unlike the Thirteenth Amendment, which was almost self-executing, the policy expressed so clearly in the Fifteenth

---

6. *Jones v. Alfred Mayer, Inc.* (1968).

7. In *Heart of Atlanta Motel v. United States* (1964) the Supreme Court upheld the public accommodations provisions of the law, thereby giving constitutional approval for Congress to expand civil rights protections by using the commerce power.

Amendment in 1870 did not become a reality until almost a century later. Stubborn resistance by the southern states denied black citizens full participatory rights. It was not until the 1960s, when the nation renewed its commitment to civil rights, that equality in voting rights was substantially achieved.

The long delay in implementing the principles of the Fifteenth Amendment has several explanations. Although the nation's leaders seemed unshakably committed to equality right after the Civil War, they soon turned their attention to other matters. Issues ranging from political corruption to the nation's industrialization moved to the top of the political agenda. At the same time, the white power structure of the prewar South began to reassert itself. Although forced to accept the Civil War Amendments as a condition of rejoining the union, the southern states survived Reconstruction and, once freed from the direct supervision of their victors, began to reinstitute discriminatory laws. Slavery was never again seriously considered, but, in its place, racial segregation became the official policy. For years the federal legislative and executive branches showed little interest in pursuing civil rights issues. And, even though the Supreme Court issued several important rulings, the nation did not turn its attention to freedom from discrimination and full participatory rights for all until the civil rights movement gained momentum in the 1960s.

The Fifteenth Amendment extended significant powers to the federal government to preserve fairness and equality in the political process. So too have the Nineteenth, Twenty-fourth, and Twenty-sixth Amendments, which, respectively, expanded the electorate by limiting state discrimination based on sex and the ability to pay a tax and by lowering the voting age. From the enforcement provisions of these four voting rights amendments, Congress has passed a number of statutes ensuring the integrity of the election process. The most important of these is the Voting Rights Act of 1965, which has been strengthened by amendment over the years. This statute provided the machinery for federal enforcement and prosecution of voting rights violations. Its provisions have been the catalyst for significant growth in voter registration rates among segments of the population where political participation historically has been depressed.

Because this volume deals with constitutional law, our discussion of the various forms of discrimination focuses on the civil rights guarantees provided in the three Civil War amendments. As you read the cases and narrative to follow, however, keep in mind that in many areas Congress has passed statutes that extend those constitutional provisions to create various legal rights that go well beyond protections included in the Constitution itself.

CHAPTER 12
DISCRIMINATION

I N A 1987 ADDRESS, delivered amid the planning for the bicentennial celebration of the Constitution, Justice Thurgood Marshall said the document was "defective from the start," that its first words—"We the People"—left out the majority of Americans because the phrase did not include women and blacks. He further alleged:

These omissions were intentional. . . . The record of the Framers' debates on the slave question is especially clear: The Southern states acceded to the demands of the New England states for giving Congress broad power to regulate commerce in exchange for the right to continue the slave trade. The economic interests of the regions coalesced.

One does not have to agree with Marshall to believe that discrimination has been a difficult and persistent problem for the United States since its beginnings. Although our Founders were considered the vanguard of enlightened politics, different treatment based on race, economic status, religious affiliation, and sex was the rule in the colonies. And, since those early years of nationhood, issues of discrimination have persisted on the country's political agenda. During the nineteenth century, slavery eroded national unity. Although officially settled by the Civil War and the constitutional amendments that followed, racial inequity did not disappear. Rather, it continued through the Jim Crow era, the organized civil rights struggle, and it persists today.

During the twentieth century, the national spotlight was turned on claims of unfair treatment based on sex,

sexual orientation, economic status, and physical ability. Attempts to force government to address these claims have given rise to counterclaims by those who fear that a government overly sensitive to the needs of minorities will deprive the majority of its rights. With each new argument, the issues become more complex. This chapter explores the kinds of discrimination that have occurred (and continue to occur) in American society and how the Supreme Court has responded. We also consider contemporary remedies that have been offered to blunt the effects of past discrimination.

RACIAL DISCRIMINATION

The institution of slavery is a blight on the record of a nation that otherwise has led the way in protecting individual rights. From 1619, when the first slaves were brought to Jamestown, to the ratification of the Civil War Amendments 250 years later, people of African ancestry were considered an inferior race; they could be bought, sold, and used as personal property. Although some states extended various civil and political rights to emancipated slaves and their descendants, the national Constitution did not recognize black Americans as full citizens. In *Scott v. Sandford* (1857), Chief Justice Roger B. Taney, delivering the opinion of the Court, described the prevailing view of blacks when the Constitution was written:

They had for more than a century before been regarded as beings of an inferior order, and altogether unfit to associate with the white race, either in social or political relations; and so far inferior, that they had no rights which the white man was bound to respect; and that the negro might justly and lawfully be reduced to slavery for his benefit. He was bought and sold, and treated as an ordinary article of merchandise and traffic, whenever a profit could be made by it. This opinion was at that time fixed and universal in the civilized portion of the white race.

The Court's decision in *Scott* interpreted the Constitution in a way consistent with this view and helped set the stage for the Civil War. The ruling, which held that a black slave could not become a full member of the political community and be entitled to the constitutional privileges of citizens, undermined the legitimacy of the Court and damaged Taney's reputation forever. Union victories on the battlefield reunited the country, and the Constitution was amended to end slavery and confer full national citizenship on black Americans.

Congress moved with dispatch to give force to the new amendments, but the Supreme Court did not act with the same level of zeal. Although the justices supported the claims of the newly emancipated black Americans in some cases, they did not construe the new amendments broadly, nor did they support new legislation designed to enforce them. In the *Slaughterhouse Cases* (1873), for example, the Court interpreted the Fourteenth Amendment's Privileges and Immunities Clause quite narrowly. A broader view might have provided opportunities for women and blacks to bring cases based on this clause to the Court. In *United States v. Harris* and the *Civil Rights Cases,* both decided in 1883, the justices nullified major provisions of the Ku Klux Klan Act of 1871 and the Civil Rights Act of 1875 for attempting to prevent discriminatory actions by private institutions. It was clear that the battle for legal equality of the races was far from over.

The "Separate but Equal" Era

By the end of the nineteenth century, the Supreme Court still had not answered what was perhaps the most important question arising from the Fourteenth Amendment: What is equal protection? As the vitality of the Reconstruction Acts and federal efforts to enforce them gradually waned, the political forces of the old order began to reassert control in the South. During this period, known as the Jim Crow era, what progress had been made to achieve racial equality not only came to a halt but began to run in reverse. The South, where 90 percent of the minority population lived, began to enact laws that reimposed an inferior legal status on blacks and commanded a strict separation of the races. Northern liberals were of little help. With the battle against slavery won, they turned their attention to other issues.

Although the Constitution made it clear that slavery was dead and the right to vote could not be denied on the basis of race, the validity of many other racially based state actions remained unresolved. With more conservative political forces gaining power in Congress, it was left to the Court, still smarting from the *Scott* debacle, to give meaning to the phrase *equal protection of the laws.*

The most important case of this period was *Plessy v. Ferguson* (1896), in which the justices were forced to confront directly the meaning of equality under the Constitution. At odds were the Equal Protection Clause of the Fourteenth Amendment and a host of segregation statutes by then in force in the southern and border states. While reading *Plessy,* note that the Court uses the reasonableness standard (rational basis test) to interpret the Equal Protection Clause. Ironically, Justice Henry B. Brown, a Lincoln Republican, a New Englander who supported the abolitionist movement, wrote the majority opinion upholding the separation standards of the South. Justice John Marshall Harlan (I), an aristocratic Kentuckian, whose family had owned slaves, wrote the lone dissent. The dissent is considered a classic and one of the most prophetic ever registered.

Plessy v. Ferguson

163 U.S. 537 (1896)
laws.findlaw.com/US/163/537.html
Vote: 7 (Brown, Field, Fuller, Gray, Peckham, Shiras, White)
    1 (Harlan)
Opinion of the Court: Brown
Dissenting opinion: Harlan
Not participating: Brewer

Following the lead of Florida, Mississippi, and Texas, in 1890 Louisiana passed a statute ordering the separation of the races on all railroads. An organized group of

Attorney and equal rights activist Albion Tourgée, who argued Homer Plessy's case and lost in the Supreme Court. Justice Harlan's lone dissent said that the Constitution must be color-blind, a phrase suggested by Tourgée's brief.

New Orleans residents of black and mixed-race heritage, with the support of the railroads, opposed the act. Attempts to have the judiciary invalidate the statute were partially successful when the Louisiana Supreme Court struck down the law as it applied to passengers crossing state lines because it placed an unconstitutional burden on interstate commerce. This decision, however, left unanswered the question of segregated travel wholly within the state's borders.

On June 7, 1892, as part of the litigation strategy, Homer Adolph Plessy, who described himself as "of seven-eighths Caucasian and one-eighth African blood," bought a first-class rail ticket from New Orleans to Covington, Louisiana. He took a seat in a car reserved for white passengers. The conductor demanded that Plessy, under pain of ejection and imprisonment, move to a car for black passengers. Plessy refused. With the help of a police officer, he was taken off the train and held in a New Orleans jail to await trial.

His lawyer moved to block the trial on the grounds that the segregation law was in violation of the U.S. Constitution. Judge John Ferguson denied the motion, and appeal was taken to the Louisiana Supreme Court. The state high court, under the leadership of Chief Justice Francis Tillou Nicholls, who, as governor two years earlier, had signed the segregation statute into law, denied Plessy's petition, and the case moved to the U.S. Supreme Court.

MR. JUSTICE BROWN delivered the opinion of the Court.

This case turns upon the constitutionality of an act of the General Assembly of the State of Louisiana, passed in 1890, providing for separate railway carriages for the white and colored races. . . .

By the Fourteenth Amendment, all persons born or naturalized in the United States, and subject to the jurisdiction thereof, are made citizens of the United States and of the State wherein they reside; and the States are forbidden from making or enforcing any law which shall abridge the privileges or immunities of citizens of the United States, or shall deprive any person of life, liberty or property without due process of law, or deny to any person within their jurisdiction the equal protection of the laws. . . .

The object of the amendment was undoubtedly to enforce the absolute equality of the two races before the law, but in the nature of things it could not have been intended to abolish distinctions based upon color, or to enforce social, as distinguished from political equality, or a commingling of the two races upon terms unsatisfactory to either. Laws permitting, and even requiring, their separation in places where they are liable to be brought into contact do not necessarily imply the inferiority of either race to the other, and have been generally, if not universally, recognized as within the competency of the state legislatures in the exercise of their police power. The most common instance of this is connected with the establishment of separate schools for white and colored children, which has been held to be a valid exercise of the legislative power even by courts of States where the political rights of the colored race have been longest and most earnestly enforced.

One of the earliest of these cases is that of *Roberts v. City of Boston* [1849], in which the Supreme Judicial Court of Massachusetts held that the general school committee of Boston had power to make provision for the instruction of colored children in separate schools established exclusively for them, and to prohibit their attendance upon the other schools. . . .

Laws forbidding the intermarriage of the two races may be said in a technical sense to interfere with the freedom of contract, and yet have been universally recognized as within the police power of the State.

The distinction between laws interfering with the political equality of the negro and those requiring the separation of the two races in schools, theatres and railway carriages has been frequently drawn by this court. Thus in *Strauder v. West Virginia* [1880] it was held that a law of West Virginia limiting to white male persons, 21 years of age and citizens of the State, the right to sit upon juries, was a discrimination which implied a legal inferiority in civil society, which lessened the security of the right of the colored race, and was a step toward reducing them to a condition of servility. Indeed, the right of a colored man that, in the selection of jurors to pass upon his life, liberty, and property, there shall be no exclusion of his race, and no discrimination against them because of color, has been asserted in a number of cases. . . .

So far, then, as a conflict with the Fourteenth Amendment is concerned, the case reduces itself to the question whether the statute of Louisiana is a reasonable regulation, and with respect to this there must necessarily be a large discretion on the part of the legislature. In determining the question of reasonableness it is at liberty to act with reference to the established usages, customs and traditions of the people, and with a view to the promotion of their comfort, and the preservation of the public peace and good order. Gauged by this standard, we cannot say that a law which authorizes or even requires the separation of the two races in public conveyances is unreasonable, or more obnoxious to the Fourteenth Amendment than the acts of Congress requiring separate schools for colored children in the District of Columbia, the constitutionality of which does not seem to have been questioned, or the corresponding acts of state legislatures.

We consider the underlying fallacy of the plaintiff's argument to consist in the assumption that the enforced separation of the two races stamps the colored race with a badge of inferiority. If this be so, it is not by reason of anything found in the act, but solely because the colored race chooses to put that construction upon it. The argument necessarily assumes that if, as has been more than once the case, and is not unlikely to be so again, the colored race should become the dominant power in the state legislature, and should enact a law in precisely similar terms, it would thereby relegate the white race to an inferior position. We imagine that the white race, at least, would not acquiesce in this assumption. The argument also assumes that social prejudices may be overcome by legislation, and that equal rights cannot be secured to the negro except by an enforced commingling of the two races. We cannot accept this proposition. If the two races are to meet upon terms of social equality, it must be the result of natural affinities, a mutual appreciation of each other's merits and a voluntary consent of individuals. . . . Legislation is powerless to eradicate racial instincts or to abolish distinctions based upon physical differences, and the attempt to do so can only result in accentuating the difficulties of the present situation. If the civil and political rights of both races be equal one cannot be inferior to the other civilly or politically. If one race be inferior to the other socially, the Constitution of the United States cannot put them upon the same plane. . . .

The judgment of the court below is, therefore,

Affirmed.

MR. JUSTICE HARLAN dissenting.

In respect of civil rights, common to all citizens, the Constitution of the United States does not, I think, permit any public authority to know the race of those entitled to be protected in the enjoyment of such rights. Every true man has pride of race, and under appropriate circumstances when the rights of others, his equals before the law, are not to be affected, it is his privilege to express such pride and to take such action based upon it as to him seems proper. But I deny that any legislative body or judicial tribunal may have regard to the race of citizens when the civil rights of those citizens are involved. Indeed, such legislation, as that herein question, is inconsistent not only with that equality of rights which pertains to citizenship, National and State, but with the personal liberty enjoyed by every one within the United States.

The Thirteenth Amendment does not permit the withholding or the deprivation of any right necessarily inhering in freedom. It not only struck down the institution of slavery as previously existing in the United States, but it prevents the imposition of any burdens or disabilities that constitute badges of slavery or servitude. It decreed universal civil freedom in this country. This court has so adjudged. But that amendment having been found inadequate to the protection of the rights of those who had been in slavery, it was followed by the Fourteenth Amendment, which added greatly to the dignity and glory of American citizenship, and to the security of personal liberty. . . . These two amendments, if enforced according to their true intent and meaning, will protect all the civil rights that pertain to freedom and citizenship. Finally, and to the end that no citizen should be denied, on account of his race, the privilege of participating in the political control of his country, it was declared by the Fifteenth Amendment that "the right of citizens of the United States to vote shall not be denied or abridged by the United States or by any State on account of race, color or previous condition of servitude."

These notable additions to the fundamental law were welcomed by the friends of liberty throughout the world. They removed the race line from our governmental systems. They had, as this court has said, a common purpose, namely, to secure "to a race recently emancipated, a race that through many generations have been held in slavery, all the civil rights that the superior race enjoy.". . .

If a State can prescribe, as a rule of civil conduct, that whites and blacks shall not travel as passengers in the same railroad coach, why may it not so regulate the use of the streets of its cities and towns as to compel white citizens to keep on one side of a street and black citizens to keep on the other? Why may it not, upon like grounds, punish whites and blacks who ride together in street cars or in open vehicles on a public road or street? Why may it not require sheriffs to assign whites to one side of a courtroom and blacks to the other? And why may it not also prohibit the commingling of the two races in the galleries of legislative halls or in public assemblages convened for the consideration of the political questions of the day? Further, if this statute of Louisiana is consistent with the personal liberty of citizens, why may not the State require the separation in railroad coaches of native and naturalized citizens of the United States, or of Protestants and Roman Catholics? . . .

The white race deems itself to be the dominant race in this country. And so it is, in prestige, in achievements, in education, in wealth and in power. So, I doubt not, it will continue to be for all time, if it remains true to its great heritage and holds fast to the principles of constitutional liberty. But in view of the Constitution, in the eye of the law, there is in this country no superior, dominant, ruling class of citizens. There is no caste here. Our Constitution is colorblind, and neither knows nor tolerates classes among citizens. In respect of civil rights, all citizens are equal before the law. The humblest is the peer of the most powerful. The law regards man as man, and takes no account of his surroundings or of his color when his civil rights as guaranteed by the supreme law of the land are involved. It is, therefore, to be regretted that this high tribunal, the final expositor of the fundamental law of the land, has reached the conclusion that it is competent for a State to regulate the enjoyment by citizens of their civil rights solely upon the basis of race.

In my opinion, the judgment this day rendered will, in time, prove to be quite as pernicious as the decision made by this tribunal in the *Dred Scott* case. . . .

I am of opinion that the statute of Louisiana is inconsistent with the personal liberty of citizens, white and black, in that State, and hostile to both the spirit and letter of the Constitution of the United States. If laws of like character should be enacted in the several States of the Union, the effect would be in the highest degree mischievous. Slavery, as an institution tolerated by law would, it is true, have disappeared from our country, but there would remain a power in the States, by sinister legislation, to interfere with the full enjoyment of the blessings of freedom; to regulate civil rights, common to all citizens, upon the basis of race; and to place in a condition of legal inferiority a large body of American citizens, now constituting a part of the political community called the People of the United States, for whom, and by whom through representatives, our government is administered. Such a system is inconsistent with the guarantee given by the Constitution to each State of a republican form of government, and may be stricken down by Congressional action, or by the courts in the discharge of their solemn duty to maintain the supreme law of the land, anything in the constitution or laws of any State to the contrary notwithstanding.

For the reasons stated, I am constrained to withhold my assent from the opinion and judgment of the majority.

Under the rule of law established in *Plessy v. Ferguson* (1896), states could require racial separation if facilities for blacks and whites were of equal quality. In public education black schools were not always equal to those reserved for whites.

The *Plessy* decision's separate but equal doctrine ushered in full-scale segregation in the southern and border states. According to the Court, separation did not constitute inequality under the Fourteenth Amendment; if the facilities and opportunities were somewhat similar, the Equal Protection Clause permitted the separation of the races. Encouraged by the ruling, the legislatures of the South passed a wide variety of statutes to keep blacks segregated from the white population. The segregation laws affected transportation, schools, hospitals, parks, public restrooms and water fountains, libraries, cemeteries, recreational facilities, hotels, restaurants, and almost every other public and commercial facility.

Early Battles for Equality

Laws passed in the wake of *Plessy*, coupled with segregated private lives, resulted in two separate societies in America; they also led to unequal public facilities. Although this disparity extended to almost every area of life, education became the center of attention. Whites and blacks were given access to public schools, but the black schools, at all levels, received support and funding far inferior to that of white institutions. Moreover, the degree of segregation was stunning. According to a 1935 article written by the prominent scholar and social activist W. E. B. DuBois:

There are in the United States some four million Negroes of school age, of whom two million are in school, and of these, four-fifths are taught by forty-eight thousand Negro teachers in separate schools. Less than a half million are in mixed schools in the North, where they are taught almost exclusively by white teachers.[1]

1. W. E. B. DuBois, "Does the Negro Need Separate Schools?" *Journal of Negro Education* 4 (1935): 328.

During the 1930s, the black community seriously debated whether it should fight for the eradication of the existing system of separate public schools.[2] Some, like DuBois, pointed out the dangers of integrated public schools; for example, because black students might be ostracized by white students and teachers, they would be unable to excel academically. In DuBois's words:

[T]heoretically, the Negro needs neither segregated schools nor mixed schools. What he needs is Education. What he must remember is that there is no magic either in mixed schools or in segregated schools. A mixed school with poor and unsympathetic teachers, with hostile public opinion, and no teaching of truth concerning black folk, is bad. A segregated school with ignorant placeholders, inadequate equipment, poor salaries, and wretched housing, is equally bad. Other things being equal, the mixed school is the broader, more natural basis for the education of all youth. It gives wider contacts; it inspires greater self-confidence; and suppresses the inferiority complex. But other things seldom are equal, and in that case, Sympathy, Knowledge, and the Truth, outweigh all that the mixed school can offer.[3]

Many others, including Charles Thompson, the dean of Howard University Graduate School of Education, understood DuBois's position but thought integrated education was a desirable goal. In their view, "to *segregate* is to *stigmatize*, however much we try to rationalize." Besides, Thompson, argued:

Not only is the separate school uneconomical and undemocratic but it results in the *mis*-education of both races. Separation of the two racial groups, at an early age, when they should be learning to know and respect each other, develops anti-racial and provincial attitudes in both, and necessitates, in adulthood, reeducation against tremendous odds. . . . The Negro develops an almost ineradicable inferiority complex . . . ; the white child develops an unwarranted sense of superiority—if not actual contempt for or an indifference towards the Negro.[4]

As we shall see, debates over public education are not limited to race—they reappeared in contemporary America when the Court took up the issue of sex-segregated schools. But in the 1930s and 1940s, the premier civil rights organization of the day, the National Association for the Advancement of Colored People (NAACP) and its affiliate, the Legal Defense and Educational Fund (LDF), thought that Thompson made the better argument. Accordingly, their attorneys, including Thurgood Marshall, initiated a twenty-year campaign in the courts to eradicate the separate but equal doctrine as it applied to public education and to all other aspects of American life *(see Box 12-1)*.

Not surprisingly, one of the NAACP's earliest legal victories came in public education, in the 1938 case of *Missouri ex rel. Gaines v. Canada.* Lloyd Gaines, a Missouri resident, had graduated from the all-black Lincoln University and applied for admission to the University of Missouri's law school. He was denied admission because of his race. Missouri did not have a law school for its black citizens, so the state offered to send qualified black students to law school in a neighboring state that did not have segregationist policies. The Supreme Court, 7–2, concluded that the Missouri plan to pay out-of-state tuition did not meet the obligations imposed by the Equal Protection Clause. The state then moved to establish a law school for blacks at Lincoln.

Although *Gaines* imposed little substantive change, it served notice that segregation policies were about to undergo close evaluation. At the time, this idea had little popular support. Polls showed that two-thirds of Americans believed that blacks and whites should attend separate schools. By the late 1940s, however, change was in the air. Some of the impetus for change grew out of the nation's experiences during World War II. With the support and approval of Presidents Roosevelt and Truman, strict separation in the armed forces was reduced, and black and white soldiers fought together on the battlefields. At home, workers of both races joined to produce the arms and equipment necessary to support the war effort.

When the war was over, black soldiers returned to the United States intent on pursuing a better life for themselves and their families. Once they had experienced something different, there was little likelihood that blacks would be satisfied with a segregated society. Many whites, having had their first substantial contacts with

2. For a full discussion of this debate, see Jack Greenberg, *Judicial Process and Social Change* (St. Paul: West Publishing, 1977).

3. DuBois, "Does the Negro Need Separate Schools?"

4. Charles Thompson, "Court Action the Only Reasonable Alternative to Remedy Immediate Abuses of the Negro Separate School," *Journal of Negro Education* 4 (1935): 419.

BOX 12-1   THURGOOD MARSHALL (1967–1991)

THURGOOD MARSHALL was born July 2, 1908, in Baltimore, Maryland. He was the son of a primary school teacher and a club steward. In 1926 he left Baltimore to attend the all-black Lincoln University in Chester, Pennsylvania, where he developed a reputation as an outstanding debater. He graduated cum laude in 1930 and decided to study law and entered Howard University in Washington, D.C.

During his law school years, Marshall developed an interest in civil rights. After graduating first in his class in 1933, he began a long and historic involvement with the National Association for the Advancement of Colored People (NAACP). In 1940 he became the head of the newly formed NAACP Legal Defense and Educational Fund, a position he held for more than twenty years.

Over those two decades, Marshall coordinated the fund's attack on segregation in voting, housing, public accommodations, and education. The culmination of his career as a civil rights attorney came in 1954 as chief counsel in a series of cases grouped under the title *Brown v. Board of Education*. In that historic case, civil rights advocates convinced the Supreme Court to declare segregation in public schools unconstitutional.

Marshall married Vivian Burey, September 4, 1929. Vivian Marshall died in February 1955, and Marshall married Cecilia Suyat, December 17, 1955. They had two sons.

IN 1961 Marshall was appointed by President John F. Kennedy to the Second Circuit Court of Appeals, but because of heated opposition from southern Democratic senators, he was not confirmed for a year.

Four years after he was named to the appeals court, Marshall was chosen by President Lyndon B. Johnson to be solicitor general. Marshall was the first black to serve in that capacity. During his years as the government's chief advocate before the Supreme Court, Marshall scored impressive victories in the areas of civil and constitutional rights. He won Supreme Court approval of the 1965 Voting Rights Act, voluntarily informed the Court that the government had used eavesdropping devices in two cases, and joined a suit that successfully overturned a California constitutional amendment that prohibited open housing legislation.

On June 13, 1967, President Johnson nominated Marshall to the seat vacated by Justice Tom C. Clark, who had retired. Marshall was confirmed by the Senate, 69–11, August 30, 1967. Marshall, the first black justice of the Supreme Court, retired on October 1, 1991. He died January 24, 1993.

SOURCE: Adapted from Joan Biskupic and Elder Witt, *Guide to the U.S. Supreme Court*, 3d ed. (Washington, D.C.: Congressional Quarterly, 1996), 950.

---

blacks during the war, began questioning the wisdom of segregation.

It was in this new political climate that the LDF achieved some of its most impressive victories to date. One of those came in the *Sweatt v. Painter* (1950), in which Marshall and his staff launched a frontal attack on the separate but equal doctrine in public school education.[5] They hoped the Court would do away with *Plessy*,

but at a minimum demanded that the justices ensure that facilities and opportunities were truly equal. Although the Court's decision was not everything civil rights advocates had hoped, it marked another significant step in the development of race relations law. As you read Chief Justice Vinson's opinion for the Court, note the emphasis he places on the importance of equal facilities for black and white students.

---

5. Another came in *Shelley v. Kraemer* (1948), involving restrictive covenants, which prevented private property owners from selling their

homes to nonwhites. We consider that case in the section on state action in race discrimination.

Sweatt v. Painter

339 U.S. 629 (1950)

laws.findlaw.com/US/339/629.html

Vote: 9 *(Black, Burton, Clark, Douglas, Frankfurter, Jackson,*
Minton, Reed, Vinson)

0

Opinion of the Court: Vinson

In 1946 H. M. Sweatt, a Texas postal worker, applied for admission to the racially segregated University of Texas law school. His application was rejected on the exclusive ground that he was black. Because there was no Texas law school that admitted blacks, Sweatt filed suit demanding that the University of Texas admit him. Given the *Gaines* precedent, the trial court judge was aware that Sweatt had a strong case. Rather than grant Sweatt's motion, however, he continued the case for six months to allow the state time to address the problem. The state hastily established an interim law school for blacks in Austin that was to open in February 1947. A permanent black law school, part of the Texas State University for Negroes, was later to open in Houston.

When the six-month period ended in December 1946, the judge dismissed Sweatt's complaint on the grounds that the state was meeting its obligations under the Equal Protection Clause. Sweatt served notice of appeal, refusing to attend the new school. Supported by the NAACP and the LDF, Sweatt challenged the school as substantially inferior to the University of Texas law school. The Texas courts concluded that the two schools were "substantially equivalent," and appeal was taken to the U.S. Supreme Court, where Sweatt asked the justices to reconsider *Plessy's* separate but equal principle. Sweatt's appeal was supported by amicus curiae briefs submitted by the U.S. government as well as a number of organizations such as the American Federation of Teachers and the American Jewish Committee. Eleven southern and border states filed briefs supporting Texas.

MR. CHIEF JUSTICE VINSON delivered the opinion of the Court.

The University of Texas Law School, from which petitioner was excluded, was staffed by a faculty of sixteen full-time and three part-time professors, some of whom are nationally recognized authorities in their field. Its student body numbered 850. The library contained over 65,000 volumes. Among the other facilities available to the students were a law review, moot court facilities, scholarship funds, and Order of the Coif affiliation. The school's alumni occupy the most distinguished positions in the private practice of the law and in the public life of the State. It may properly be considered one of the nation's ranking law schools.

The law school for Negroes which was to have opened in February, 1947, would have had no independent faculty or library. The teaching was to be carried on by four members of the University of Texas Law School faculty, who were to maintain their offices at the University of Texas while teaching at both institutions. Few of the 10,000 volumes ordered for the library had arrived; nor was there any full-time librarian. The school lacked accreditation.

Since the trial of this case, respondents report the opening of a law school at the Texas State University for Negroes. It is apparently on the road to full accreditation. It has a faculty of five full-time professors; a student body of 23; a library of some 16,500 volumes serviced by a full-time staff; a practice court and legal aid association; and one alumnus who has become a member of the Texas Bar.

Whether the University of Texas Law School is compared with the original or the new law school for Negroes, we cannot find substantial equality in the educational opportunities offered white and Negro law students by the State. In terms of number of the faculty, variety of courses and opportunity for specialization, size of student body, scope of the library, availability of law review and similar activities, the University of Texas Law School is superior. What is more important, the University of Texas Law School possesses to a far greater degree those qualities which are incapable of objective measurement but which make for greatness in a law school. Such qualities, to name but a few, include reputation of the faculty, experience of the administration, position and influence of the alumni, standing in the community, traditions and prestige. It is difficult to believe that one who had a free choice between these law schools would consider the question close.

Moreover, although the law is a highly learned profession, we are well aware that it is an intensely practical one. The law school, the proving ground for legal learning and practice, cannot be effective in isolation from the individuals and institutions with which the law interacts. Few students and no one who has practiced law would choose to study in an academic vacuum, removed from the interplay of ideas and the exchange of views with which the law is concerned. The law school to which Texas is willing to admit petitioner excludes from its student body members of the racial groups which number 85% of the population of the State and include most of the lawyers, witnesses, jurors, judges and other officials with whom petitioner will inevitably be dealing when he becomes a member of the Texas Bar. With such a substantial and significant segment of society excluded, we cannot conclude that the education offered petitioner is substantially equal to that which he would receive if admitted to the University of Texas Law School.

It may be argued that excluding petitioner from that school is no different from excluding white students from the new law school. This contention overlooks realities. It is unlikely that a member of a group so decisively in the majority, attending a school with rich traditions and prestige which only a history of consistently maintained excellence could command, would claim that the opportunities afforded him for legal education were unequal to those held open to petitioner. That such a claim, if made, would be dishonored by the State, is no answer.

It is fundamental that these cases concern rights which are personal and present. This Court has stated unanimously that "The State must provide [legal education] for [petitioner] in conformity with the equal protection clause of the Fourteenth Amendment and provide it as soon as it does for applicants of any other group.". . . In *Missouri ex rel. Gaines v. Canada* (1938), the Court, speaking through Chief Justice Hughes, declared that "petitioner's right was a personal one. It was as an individual that he was entitled to the equal protection of the laws, and the State was bound to furnish him within its borders facilities for legal education substantially equal to those which the State there afforded for persons of the white race, whether or not other negroes sought the same opportunity." These are the only cases in this Court which present the issue of the constitutional validity of race distinctions in state-supported graduate and professional education.

In accordance with these cases, petitioner may claim his full constitutional right: legal education equivalent to that offered by the State to students of other races. Such education is not available to him in a separate law school as offered by the State. We cannot, therefore, agree with respondents that the doctrine of *Plessy v. Ferguson* (1896) requires affirmance of the judgment below. Nor need we reach petitioner's contention that *Plessy v. Ferguson* should be reexamined in the light of contemporary knowledge respecting the purposes of the Fourteenth Amendment and the effects of racial segregation.

We hold that the Equal Protection Clause of the Fourteenth Amendment requires that petitioner be admitted to the University of Texas Law School. The judgment is reversed and the cause is remanded for proceedings not inconsistent with this opinion.

Reversed.

The same day the Court decided *Sweatt*, it also handed the LDF a victory in *McLaurin v. Oklahoma State Regents* (1950), which took another step toward racial equality in higher education. *McLaurin* highlights an interesting aspect of the desegregation battle—the fear held by many segregationists that blacks and whites in school together would lead to interracial dating and marriage.[6] To comply with judicial decisions, the University of Oklahoma admitted black graduate students when these students could not obtain the desired degrees at minority schools. However, to protect against the possibilities of interracial marriage, the university restricted blacks to segregated areas of classrooms, libraries, and dining halls. Fraternization between the races was almost impossible.

To neutralize this fear of interracial marriage, the LDF chose George W. McLaurin to challenge the university's segregationist policies. McLaurin was a black graduate student, already holding a master's degree, who was pursuing a doctorate in education. What made him perfect to challenge the separatist regulations was that McLaurin

6. For a discussion of this issue, see Richard Kluger, *Simple Justice* (New York: Random House, 1975), especially chap. 12.

was sixty-eight years old and unlikely to marry. Although McLaurin's suit was unsuccessful in the lower courts, the Supreme Court unanimously found Oklahoma's system in violation of the Equal Protection Clause.

Race Discrimination and the Warren Court: The Demise of Plessy

As the nation entered the 1950s, conditions were ripe for a final assault on the half-century-old separate but equal doctrine. Civil rights groups continued to marshal legal arguments and political support to eliminate segregation. Legal challenges to a wide array of discriminatory laws were filed throughout the country, and the Justice Department under President Truman supported these efforts. The Supreme Court, through its unanimous rulings in favor of racial equality in higher education, appeared on the verge of seriously considering an end to *Plessy*. In addition, a significant leadership change took place on the Court. Chief Justice Vinson died September 8, 1953, and was replaced by Earl Warren, a former governor of California, who was much more comfortable with activist judicial policies than was his predecessor.

All of these factors combined to produce *Brown v. Board of Education of Topeka, Kansas* (1954), which many consider to be the Supreme Court's most significant decision of the twentieth century. Unlike earlier civil rights cases that involved relatively small professional and graduate education programs, the *Brown* case challenged official racial segregation in the nation's primary and secondary public schools. The decision affected thousands of school districts concentrated primarily in the southern and border states. Moreover, it was apparent to all that the precedent to be set for public education would be extended to other areas as well.

As you read Warren's opinion for a unanimous Court, note how the concept of equality has changed. No longer does the Court examine only physical facilities and tangible items such as buildings, libraries, teacher qualifications, and funding levels; instead it emphasizes the intangible negative impact of racial segregation on children. Warren's opinion includes a footnote listing social science references as authorities for his arguments. The opinion was criticized for citing sociological and psychological studies to support the Court's conclusions rather than confining the analysis to legal arguments. Are these criticisms valid? Should the Court take social science evidence into account in arriving at constitutional decisions? Note how similar Warren's opinion is to Justice Harlan's lone dissent in *Plessy*.

Brown v. Board of Education (I)

347 U.S. 483 (1954)
laws.findlaw.com/US/347/483.html
Vote: 9 (Black, Burton, Clark, Douglas, Frankfurter, Jackson, Minton, Reed, Warren)
0
Opinion of the Court: Warren

The Court consolidated five cases involving similar issues consideration at the same time; *Brown v. Board of Education* was one of these cases. Part of the total deseg-

Linda Brown at age nine. Her father joined the suit that led to the desegregation of the nation's public schools. Oliver Brown was upset that Linda had to travel two and half miles to school even though the family lived close to Sumner, a white school. Despite their victory, Linda never went to Sumner School; by the time the decision was rendered, she was old enough for the junior high, a school that had been integrated since 1879.

Pictured on the steps of the U.S. Supreme Court are the NAACP Legal Defense Fund lawyers who argued the school segregation cases that resulted in the *Brown v. Board of Education* precedent. Left to right: Howard Jenkins, James M. Nabrit Jr., Spottswood W. Robinson III, Frank Reeves, Jack Greenberg, Special Counsel Thurgood Marshall, Louis Redding, U. Simpson Tate, and George E. C. Hayes. Missing is Robert L. Carter, who argued the Topeka case.

regation litigation strategy orchestrated by Marshall and funded by the NAACP, these cases challenged the segregated public schools of Delaware, South Carolina, Virginia, and the District of Columbia, in addition to Topeka, Kansas. The most prominent lawyers in the civil rights movement, Spottswood Robinson III, Louis Redding, Jack Greenberg, Constance Baker Motley, Robert Carter, and James Nabrit Jr., prepared them. As Marshall had expected, the suits were unsuccessful at the trial level, with the lower courts relying on *Plessy* as precedent. The leading lawyer for the states was John W. Davis, a prominent constitutional attorney who had been a Democratic candidate for president in 1924. (Davis had reportedly once been offered a nomination to the Court by President Warren G. Harding.)

Linda Carol Brown was an eight-year-old black girl, whose father, Oliver Brown, was an assistant pastor of a Topeka church. The Browns lived in a predominantly white neighborhood only a short distance from an elementary school. Under state law, cities with populations over fifteen thousand were permitted to administer racially segregated schools, and the Topeka Board of Education required its elementary schools to be racially divided. The Browns did not want their daughter to be sent to the school reserved for black students. It was far from home, and they considered the trip dangerous. In addition, their neighborhood school was a good one, and the Browns wanted their daughter to receive an integrated education. They filed suit challenging the segregated school system as violating their daughter's rights under the Equal Protection Clause of the Fourteenth Amendment.

The Brown appeal was joined by those from the other four suits, and the cases were argued in December 1952. The following June the Court asked the cases to be reargued in December 1953 with special emphasis to be placed on a series of questions dealing with the history and meaning of the Fourteenth Amendment. This delay also allowed the newly appointed Earl Warren to participate fully in the decision. Six months later, on May 17, 1954, the Court issued its ruling.

MR. CHIEF JUSTICE WARREN delivered the opinion of the Court.

In each of the cases, minors of the Negro race, through their legal representatives, seek the aid of the courts in obtaining admission to the public schools of their community on a nonsegregated basis. In each instance, they had been denied admission to schools attended by white children under laws requiring or permitting segregation according to race. This segregation was alleged to deprive the plaintiffs of the equal protection of the laws under the Fourteenth Amendment. . . .

The plaintiffs contend that segregated public schools are not "equal" and cannot be made "equal," and that hence they are deprived of the equal protection of the laws. Because of the obvious importance of the question presented, the Court took jurisdiction. Argument was heard in the 1952 Term, and reargument was heard this Term on certain questions propounded by the Court.

Reargument was largely devoted to the circumstances surrounding the adoption of the Fourteenth Amendment in 1868. It covered exhaustively consideration of the Amendment in Congress, ratification by the states, then existing practices in racial segregation, and the views of proponents and opponents of the Amendment. This discussion and our own investigation convince us that, although these sources cast some light, it is not enough to resolve the problem with which we are faced. At best, they are inconclusive. . . .

An additional reason for the inconclusive nature of the Amendment's history, with respect to segregated schools, is the status of public education at that time. In the South, the movement toward free common schools, supported by general taxation, had not yet taken hold. Education of white children was largely in the hands of private groups. Education of Negroes was almost nonexistent, and practically all of the race were illiterate. In fact, any education of Negroes was forbidden by law in some states. Today, in contrast, many Negroes have achieved outstanding success in the arts and sciences as well as in the business and professional world. It is true that public school education at the time of the Amendment had advanced further in the North, but the effect of the Amendment on Northern States was generally ignored in the congressional debates. Even in the North, the conditions of public education did not approximate those existing today. The curriculum was usually rudimentary; ungraded schools were common in rural areas; the school term was but three months a year in many states; and compulsory school attendance was virtually unknown. As a consequence, it is not surprising that there should be so little in the history of the Fourteenth Amendment relating to its intended effect on public education.

In the first cases in this Court construing the Fourteenth

Amendment, decided shortly after its adoption, the Court interpreted it as proscribing all state-imposed discriminations against the Negro race. The doctrine of "separate but equal" did not make its appearance in this Court until 1896 in the case of *Plessy v. Ferguson*, involving not education but transportation. American courts have since labored with the doctrine for over half a century. . . .

Here, unlike *Sweatt v. Painter*, there are findings below that the Negro and white schools involved have been equalized, or are being equalized, with respect to buildings, curricula, qualifications and salaries of teachers, and other "tangible" factors. Our decision, therefore, cannot turn on merely a comparison of these tangible factors in the Negro and white schools involved in each of the cases. We must look instead to the effect of segregation itself on public education.

In approaching this problem, we cannot turn the clock back to 1868 when the Amendment was adopted, or even to 1896 when *Plessy v. Ferguson* was written. We must consider public education in the light of its full development and its present place in American life throughout the Nation. Only in this way can it be determined if segregation in public schools deprives these plaintiffs of the equal protection of the laws.

Today, education is perhaps the most important function of state and local governments. Compulsory school attendance laws and the great expenditures for education both demonstrate our recognition of the importance of education to our democratic society. It is required in the performance of our most basic public responsibilities, even service in the armed forces. It is the very foundation of good citizenship. Today it is a principal instrument in awakening the child to cultural values, in preparing him for later professional training, and in helping him to adjust normally to his environment. In these days, it is doubtful that any child may reasonably be expected to succeed in life if he is denied the opportunity of an education. Such an opportunity, where the state has undertaken to provide it, is a right which must be made available to all on equal terms.

We come then to the question presented: Does segregation of children in public schools solely on the basis of race, even though the physical facilities and other "tangible" factors may be equal, deprive the children of the minority group of equal educational opportunities? We believe that it does.

In *Sweatt v. Painter*, in finding that a segregated law school of Negroes could not provide them equal educational opportunities, this Court relied in large part on "those qualities which are incapable of objective measurement but which make for greatness in a law school." In *McLaurin v. Oklahoma State Regents*, the Court, in requiring that a Negro admitted to a white graduate school be treated like all other students, again resorted to intangible considerations: ". . . his ability to study, to engage in discussions and exchange views with other students, and, in general, to learn his profession." Such considerations apply with added force to children in grade and high schools. To separate them from others of similar age and qualifications solely because of their race generates a feeling of inferiority as to their status in the community that may affect their hearts and minds in a way unlikely ever to be undone. The effect of this separation on their educational opportunities was well stated by a finding in the Kansas case by a court which nevertheless felt compelled to rule against the Negro plaintiffs:

"Segregation of white and colored children in public schools has a detrimental effect upon the colored children. The impact is greater when it has the sanction of the law; for the policy of separating the races is usually interpreted as denoting the inferiority of the negro group. A sense of inferiority affects the motivation of a child to learn. Segregation with the sanction of law, therefore, has a tendency to [retard] the educational and mental development of negro children and to deprive them of some of the benefits they would receive in a racial[ly] integrated school system."

Whatever may have been the extent of psychological knowledge at the time of *Plessy v. Ferguson*, this finding is amply supported by modern authority.* Any language in *Plessy v. Ferguson* contrary to this finding is rejected.

We conclude that in the field of public education the doctrine of "separate but equal" has no place. Separate educational facilities are inherently unequal. Therefore, we hold that the plaintiffs and others similarly situated for whom

the actions have been brought are, by reason of the segregation complained of, deprived of the equal protection of the laws guaranteed by the Fourteenth Amendment. . . .

Because these are class actions, because of the wide applicability of this decision, and because of the great variety of local conditions, the formulation of decrees in these cases presents problems of considerable complexity. On reargument, the consideration of appropriate relief was necessarily subordinated to the primary question—the constitutionality of segregation in public education. We have now announced that such segregation is a denial of the equal protection of the laws. In order that we may have the full assistance of the parties in formulating decrees, the cases will be restored to the docket, and the parties are requested to present further argument on Questions 4 and 5 previously propounded by the Court for the reargument this Term.* The Attorney General of the United States is again invited to participate. The Attorneys General of the states requiring or permitting segregation in public education will also be permitted to appear as amici curiae upon request to do so by September 15, 1954, and submission of briefs by October 1, 1954.

It is so ordered.

Note the final paragraph of the Court's unanimous decision in *Brown*: It asks the attorneys to return the next year and argue the issue of remedies. The justices recognized that agreeing that racial separation in the public

*K. B. Clark, *Effect of Prejudice and Discrimination On Personality Development* (Midcentury White House Conference on Children and Youth, 1950); Witmer and Kotinsky, *Personality in the Making* (1952), C. Vi; Deutscher and Chein, *The Psychological Effects of Enforced Segregation: A Survey of Social Science Opinion*, 26 J. Psychol. 259 (1948); Chein, *What are the Psychological Effects of Segregation Under Conditions Of Equal Facilities?*, 3 Int. J. Opinion and Attitude Res. 229 (1949); Brameld, *Educational Costs, In Discrimination and National Welfare* (Maciver, Ed.), 1949), 44–48; Frazier, *The Negro in the United States* (1949), 674–681. And see generally Myrdal, *An American Dilemma* (1944).

*4. Assuming it is decided that segregation in public schools violates the Fourteenth Amendment

(a) would a decree necessarily follow providing that, within the limits set by normal geographic school districting, Negro children should forthwith be admitted to schools of their choice, or

(b) may this Court, in the exercise of its equity powers, permit an effective gradual adjustment to be brought about from existing segregated systems to a system not based on color distinctions?

5. On the assumption on which questions 4(a) and (b) are based, and assuming further that this Court will exercise its equity powers to the end described in question 4(b),

(a) should this Court formulate detailed decrees in these cases;

(b) if so, what specific issues should the decrees reach;

(c) should this Court appoint a special master to hear evidence with a view to recommending specific terms for such decrees;

(d) should this Court remand to the courts of first instance with directions to frame decrees in these cases and, if so, what general directions should the decrees of this Court include and what procedures should the courts of first instance follow in arriving at the specific terms of more detailed decrees?

schools was unconstitutional was not the same as deciding how to end the practice and what would replace it.

The result of the Court's request, commonly referred to as *Brown II* (1955), set the stage for public school desegregation battles that were to dominate the national agenda for the next decade and still linger in some districts. As you read *Brown II*, consider how the justices dealt with two basic questions: Who was to be responsible for implementing school desegregation and on what kind of schedule?

Brown v. Board of Education (II)

349 U.S. 294 (1955)
laws.findlaw.com/US/349/294.html
Vote: 9 (Black, Burton, Clark, Douglas, Frankfurter, Harlan,
    Minton, Reed, Warren)
        0
Opinion of the Court: Warren

In *Brown I* the Court restored the cases to the docket and requested further arguments on the question of remedies. The justices invited the U.S. attorney general and the attorneys general of all states that maintained segregated schools, in addition to the parties, to present their views.

As we might have expected, the NAACP asked the Court to order an immediate end to racial separation. Representatives of the federal government recommended a specific timetable for local governments to develop their desegregation plans. Attorneys for the southern states cited substantial difficulties standing in the way of compliance with *Brown I* and requested its gradual implementation. In *Brown II*, therefore, the Court had to struggle with these competing claims over the schedule for desegregation, as well as the question of who would be responsible for implementing the plan.

MR. CHIEF JUSTICE WARREN delivered the opinion of the Court.

These cases were decided on May 17, 1954. The opinions of that date, declaring the fundamental principle that racial discrimination in public education is unconstitutional, are incorporated herein by reference. All provisions of federal, state, or local law requiring or permitting such discrimination must yield to this principle. There remains for consideration the manner in which relief is to be accorded. . . .

Full implementation of these constitutional principles may require solution of varied local school problems. School authorities have the primary responsibility for elucidating, assessing, and solving these problems; courts will have to consider whether the action of school authorities constitutes good faith implementation of the governing constitutional principles. Because of their proximity to local conditions and the possible need for further hearings, the courts which originally heard these cases can best perform this judicial appraisal. Accordingly, we believe it appropriate to remand the cases to those courts.

In fashioning and effectuating the decrees, the courts will be guided by equitable principles. Traditionally, equity has been characterized by a practical flexibility in shaping its remedies and by a facility for adjusting and reconciling public and private needs. These cases call for the exercise of these traditional attributes of equity power. At stake is the personal interest of the plaintiffs in admission to public schools as soon as practicable on a nondiscriminatory basis. To effectuate this interest may call for elimination of a variety of obstacles in making the transition to school systems operated in accordance with the constitutional principles set forth in our May 17, 1954, decision. Courts of equity may properly take into account the public interest in the elimination of such obstacles in a systematic and effective manner. But it should go without saying that the vitality of these constitutional principles cannot be allowed to yield simply because of disagreement with them.

While giving weight to these public and private considerations, the courts will require that the defendants make a prompt and reasonable start toward full compliance with our May 17, 1954, ruling. Once such a start has been made, the courts may find that additional time is necessary to carry out the ruling in an effective manner. The burden rests upon the defendants to establish that such time is necessary in the public interest and is consistent with good faith compliance at the earliest practicable date. To that end, the courts may consider problems related to administration, arising from the physical condition of the school plant, the school transportation system, personnel, revision of school districts and attendance areas into compact units to achieve a system of determining admission to the public schools on a nonracial basis, and revision of local laws and regulations which may be necessary in solving the foregoing problems. They will also consider the adequacy of any plans the defendants may propose to meet these problems and to effectuate a transition to a racially nondiscriminatory school system. During this period of transition, the courts will retain jurisdiction of these cases.

The judgments below . . . are accordingly reversed, and the cases are remanded to the District Courts to take such proceedings and enter such orders and decrees consistent with this opinion as are necessary and proper to admit to public schools on a racially nondiscriminatory basis with all deliberate speed the parties to these cases. . . .

It is so ordered.

Brown I and *Brown II* are extraordinary Court opinions, true landmarks in American legal history. In *Brown I,* Chief Justice Warren, while not explicitly overturning *Plessy,* effectively gutted it. At least "in the field of education," Warren wrote, "the doctrine of 'separate but equal' has no place. Separate educational facilities are inherently unequal." In *Brown II* he laid out a plan for the implementation of that constitutional principle. On the question of who should be responsible for implementation, the justices held that the primary duty for ending segregation rested with local school boards. These political bodies carried out the general administration of the schools, and they should be responsible for implementing desegregation. The Court, however, was aware that many school boards would resist the change. In most states, board members were elected by the people, and desegregation was not popular with the electorate. To ensure that the school boards acted properly, the Court gave oversight responsibilities to the federal district courts, the trial courts of general jurisdiction for the federal system. Because they are the federal courts closest to the people, their judges understand local conditions. In addition, district court judges enjoy life tenure; they are appointed, not elected. If school boards failed to live up to the expectation of *Brown I,* district judges were in-

structed to use their equity jurisdiction to fashion whatever remedies were necessary to achieve desegregation. This grant of authority allowed the judges to impose plans especially tailored to meet the specific conditions of the district's schools.

The Court sidestepped the question of the desegregation schedule. It did not set a timetable, but instead ordered that desegregation take place "with all deliberate speed." This standard acknowledged that the situation in each district would determine how rapidly desegregation could progress. It also may have been a necessary compromise among the justices to achieve a unanimous ruling.[7]

The next section deals with the impact of *Brown II* on American society and on the remedies contemporary Courts have fashioned in the school desegregation area. Here we consider two aspects of the *Brown* rulings that are not necessarily apparent from the opinions. The first concerns public reaction. Realizing that the decisions would be controversial and generate resistance, especially in the South, and that the Court had no way to enforce them, Chief Justice Warren went to great pains to unite the Court. He believed unanimous opinions, written by him, would encourage voluntary compliance. He was wrong, as was Thurgood Marshall, who predicted that segregated schools would be eliminated within five years of the *Brown* decision.[8] The unanimous decisions did not impress southern politicians, who did little to implement them. In fact, during the 1950s, they adopted the strategy that "as long as we can legislate, we can segregate" and enacted hundreds of laws designed to thwart integration. "Impeach Earl Warren" posters and billboards became a common sight on southern roads. The U.S. Congress and the president did little to counter this trend. As one scholar characterized Eisenhower's position, "Thurgood Marshall got his decision, now let him enforce it."[9] Some members of Congress were so outraged by *Brown* and

7. Bernard Schwartz, *Super Chief* (New York: New York University Press, 1983).

8. We adopt the material in this paragraph and the next from Gerald N. Rosenberg, *The Hollow Hope* (Chicago: University of Chicago Press, 1991), chap. 3.

9. Jack Peltason, *Fifty-Eight Lonely Men* (Urbana: University of Illinois Press, 1971), 54.

TABLE 12-1 Percentage of Black Students Attending School with Whites, Southern and Border States, 1954–1972

Year	Percent	Year	Percent
1954	0.001	1962	0.45
1955	0.12	1963	1.2
1956	0.14	1964	2.3
1957	0.15	1965	6.1
1958	0.13	1966	16.9
1959	0.16	1968	32.0
1960	0.16	1970	85.9
1961	0.24	1972	91.3

SOURCE: Lee Epstein, Jeffrey A. Segal, Harold J. Spaeth, and Thomas G. Walker, *The Supreme Court Compendium: Data, Decisions, and Developments*, 2d ed. (Washington, D.C.: Congressional Quarterly, 1996), Table 9-4.

other liberal decisions that they introduced more than fifty Court-curbing bills during the period.

What was the upshot of the lack of federal support and defiance in the South? One result was that through the 1950s, *Brown* had little impact on public education in the United States. As Table 12-1 shows, in 1954, 0.001 percent of all southern black school children attended schools with whites; by 1960 that figure was only 0.16 percent. Segregated education remained a fact of American life.

This is not to say that *Brown* was an insignificant decision. To the contrary, many point to *Brown*'s substantial long-term effects. By placing civil rights on the political agenda, it may have spurred the civil rights movement of the 1960s, which in turn generated significant federal action. Congress finally passed civil rights legislation with some teeth *(see Box IV-1, pages 624–625)*. And, under the administration of President Lyndon Johnson, the Justice Department became an active participant in school desegregation litigation. As a result, as Table 12-1 depicts, by 1972 the percentage of black school children in southern and border states attending schools with whites increased to more than 90 percent.

A second interesting aspect of the *Brown* decision concerns the Court itself. Perhaps as a result of the reaction to *Brown*, the Court avoided the issue of school desegregation and civil rights, more generally. Three years passed before it again took up school desegregation. In *Cooper v. Aaron* (1958), the Court responded firmly to

popular resistance in Arkansas by declaring that violence or threats of violence would not be allowed to slow the progress toward full desegregation. And nearly seven years elapsed before it decided another major civil rights case, *Burton v. Wilmington Parking Authority* (1961), which we discuss in the section on race discrimination and state action *(see pages 664–666)*.

School Desegregation in the Post-Brown Era

Although the Warren Court justices did not decide many of the cases that followed *Brown II*, they held steadfast in their desegregation goals in those they heard. *Cooper* is one example; *Griffin v. Prince Edward County School Board* (1964) is another. There, the Court stopped a Virginia plan to close down public schools rather than integrate them. Also, in *Green v. School Board of New Kent County* (1968) the justices struck down a "freedom of choice" plan as failing to bring about a nondiscriminatory school system. By the mid-1960s the justices had begun to lose patience. Justice Black remarked in his opinion for the Court in *Griffin* that "there has been entirely too much deliberation and not enough speed" in enforcing *Brown*'s desegregation mandate.

In short, the justices of the Warren Court tried to make it clear that dilatory tactics would not be tolerated.[10] But the resistance continued. The freedom given to district judges to approve desegregation plans led to a wide variety of schemes, some of which were criticized by school officials for going too far, and some by civil rights advocates for not going far enough. The specific methods of integration commonly were attacked for exceeding the powers of the district courts.

Clearing up the confusion was left to the Burger Court. In 1971 it accepted an appeal that it saw as a vehicle for the declaration of authoritative rules to govern the desegregation process. The case, *Swann v. Charlotte-Mecklenburg Board of Education*, involved challenges to a desegregation plan imposed by a district judge on North Carolina's largest city.[11] As you read Chief Justice Burger's opinion for a unanimous Court, note the wide range of powers the Court approves for imposing remedies once a violation of the Constitution has been demonstrated.

10. See *Alexander v. Holmes Board of Education* (1969).
11. For oral arguments in this case, navigate to: *oyez.nwu.edu*.

Would Chief Justice Warren and the members of his Court have approved?

Swann v. Charlotte-Mecklenburg Board of Education

402 U.S. 1 (1971)
laws.findlaw.com/US/402/1.html
Vote: 9 (Black, Blackmun, Brennan, Burger, Douglas, Harlan, Marshall, Stewart, White)
    0
Opinion of the Court: Burger

This case resulted from a long-standing legal dispute over the desegregation of schools in Charlotte, North Carolina. As part of the efforts to bring the district into compliance, the Charlotte schools were consolidated with the surrounding Mecklenburg County schools. The combined district covered 550 square miles, with 107 schools and an enrollment of 84,000 children. Seventy-one percent of the students were white, and 29 percent black.

As a result of a plan imposed by the courts in 1965, desegregation began in earnest, but the results were not satisfactory. Two-thirds of the 21,000 black students in Charlotte attended schools that were at least 99 percent black. All parties agreed that the plan was not working, but there was considerable controversy over what to do. When the school board failed to submit a suitable plan, the district court appointed John Finger, an educational consultant, to devise one. The minority members of the school board and the U.S. Department of Health, Education and Welfare (now Health and Human Services) also offered plans. After considerable legal maneuvering, the district court imposed the Finger plan, part of which was later approved by the court of appeals. Both the plaintiffs and the school board appealed to the Supreme Court.

MR. CHIEF JUSTICE BURGER delivered the opinion of the Court.

Nearly 17 years ago this Court held, in explicit terms, that state-imposed segregation by race in public schools de-

nies equal protection of the laws. At no time has the Court deviated in the slightest degree from that holding or its constitutional underpinnings. . . .

Over the 16 years since *Brown II*, many difficulties were encountered in implementation of the basic constitutional requirement that the State not discriminate between public school children on the basis of their race. Nothing in our national experience prior to 1955 prepared anyone for dealing with changes and adjustments of the magnitude and complexity encountered since then. Deliberate resistance of some to the Court's mandates has impeded the good-faith efforts of others to bring school systems into compliance. The detail and nature of these dilatory tactics have been noted frequently by this Court and other courts. . . .

The problems encountered by the district courts and courts of appeals make plain that we should now try to amplify guidelines, however incomplete and imperfect, for the assistance of school authorities and courts. The failure of local authorities to meet their constitutional obligations aggravated the massive problem of converting from the state-enforced discrimination of racially separate school systems. This process has been rendered more difficult by changes since 1954 in the structure and patterns of communities, the growth of student population, movement of families, and other changes, some of which had marked impact on school planning, sometimes neutralizing or negating remedial action before it was fully implemented. Rural areas accustomed for half a century to the consolidated school systems implemented by bus transportation could make adjustments more readily than metropolitan areas with dense and shifting population, numerous schools, congested and complex traffic patterns.

The objective today remains to eliminate from the public schools all vestiges of state-imposed segregation. Segregation was the evil struck down by *Brown I* as contrary to the equal protection guarantees of the Constitution. That was the violation sought to be corrected by the remedial measures of *Brown II*. That was the basis for the holding in *Green* [*v. School Board of New Kent County*, 1968] that school authorities are "clearly charged with the affirmative duty to take whatever steps might be necessary to convert to a unitary system in which racial discrimination would be eliminated root and branch."

If school authorities fail in their affirmative obligations under these holdings, judicial authority may be invoked.

Once a right and a violation have been shown, the scope of a district court's equitable powers to remedy past wrongs is broad, for breadth and flexibility are inherent in equitable remedies. . . .

This allocation of responsibility once made, the Court attempted from time to time to provide some guidelines for the exercise of the district judge's discretion and for the reviewing function of the courts of appeals. However, a school desegregation case does not differ fundamentally from other cases involving the framing of equitable remedies to repair the denial of a constitutional right. The task is to correct, by a balancing of the individual and collective interests, the condition that offends the Constitution.

In seeking to define even in broad and general terms how far this remedial power extends it is important to remember that judicial powers may be exercised only on the basis of a constitutional violation. Remedial judicial authority does not put judges automatically in the shoes of school authorities whose powers are plenary. Judicial authority enters only when local authority defaults.

School authorities are traditionally charged with broad power to formulate and implement educational policy and might well conclude, for example, that in order to prepare students to live in a pluralistic society each school should have a prescribed ratio of Negro to white students reflecting the proportion for the district as a whole. To do this as an educational policy is within the broad discretionary powers of school authorities; absent a finding of a constitutional violation, however, that would not be within the authority of a federal court. As with any equity case, the nature of the violation determines the scope of the remedy. In default by the school authorities of their obligation to proffer acceptable remedies, a district court has broad power to fashion a remedy that will assure a unitary school system. . . .

We turn now to the problem of defining with more particularity the responsibilities of school authorities in desegregating a state-enforced dual school system in light of the Equal Protection Clause. Although the several related cases before us are primarily concerned with problems of student assignment, it may be helpful to begin with a brief discussion of other aspects of the process.

In *Green*, we pointed out that existing policy and practice with regard to faculty, staff, transportation, extracurricular activities, and facilities were among the most important indicia of a segregated system. Independent of student assignment, where it is possible to identify a "white school" or a "Negro school" simply by reference to the racial composition of teachers and staff, the quality of school buildings and equipment, or the organization of sports activities, a prima facie case of violation of substantive constitutional rights under the Equal Protection Clause is shown.

When a system has been dual in these respects, the first remedial responsibility of school authorities is to eliminate invidious racial distinctions. . . .

The construction of new schools and the closing of old ones are two of the most important functions of local school authorities and also two of the most complex. . . .

In ascertaining the existence of legally imposed school segregation, the existence of a pattern of school construction and abandonment is thus a factor of great weight. In devising remedies where legally imposed segregation has been established, it is the responsibility of local authorities and district courts to see to it that future school construction and abandonment are not used and do not serve to perpetuate or reestablish the dual system. When necessary, district courts should retain jurisdiction to assure that these responsibilities are carried out.

The central issue in this case is that of student assignment, and there are essentially four problem areas:

(1) to what extent racial balance or racial quotas may be used as an implement in a remedial order to correct a previously segregated system;

(2) whether every all-Negro and all-white school must be eliminated as an indispensable part of a remedial process of desegregation;

(3) what the limits are, if any, on the rearrangement of school districts and attendance zones, as a remedial measure; and

(4) what the limits are, if any, on the use of transportation facilities to correct state-enforced racial school segregation.

(1) Racial Balances or Racial Quotas.

The constant theme and thrust of every holding from Brown I to date is that state-enforced separation of races in public schools is discrimination that violates the Equal Protection Clause. The remedy commanded was to dismantle dual school systems. . . .

Our objective in dealing with the issues presented by

these cases is to see that school authorities exclude no pupil of a racial minority from any school, directly or indirectly, on account of race; it does not and cannot embrace all the problems of racial prejudice, even when those problems contribute to disproportionate racial concentrations in some schools.

In this case it is urged that the District Court has imposed a racial balance requirement of 71%–29% on individual schools. . . .

As the voluminous record in this case shows, the predicate for the District Court's use of the 71%–29% ratio was twofold: first, its express finding, approved by the Court of Appeals and not challenged here, that a dual school system had been maintained by the school authorities at least until 1969; second, its finding, also approved by the Court of Appeals, that the school board had totally defaulted in its acknowledged duty to come forward with an acceptable plan of its own, notwithstanding the patient efforts of the District Judge who, on at least three occasions, urged the board to submit plans. As the statement of facts shows, these findings are abundantly supported by the record. . . .

We see therefore that the use made of mathematical ratios was no more than a starting point in the process of shaping a remedy, rather than an inflexible requirement. From that starting point the District Court proceeded to frame a decree that was within its discretionary powers, as an equitable remedy for the particular circumstances. As we said in Green, a school authority's remedial plan or a district court's remedial decree is to be judged by its effectiveness. Awareness of the racial composition of the whole school system is likely to be a useful starting point in shaping a remedy to correct past constitutional violations. In sum, the very limited use made of mathematical ratios was within the equitable remedial discretion of the District Court.

(2) One-race Schools.

The record in this case reveals the familiar phenomenon that in metropolitan areas minority groups are often found concentrated in one part of the city. In some circumstances certain schools may remain all or largely of one race until new schools can be provided or neighborhood patterns change. Schools all or predominantly of one race in a district of mixed population will require close scrutiny to de-

termine that school assignments are not part of state-enforced segregation.

In light of the above, it should be clear that the existence of some small number of one-race, or virtually one-race, schools within a district is not in and of itself the mark of a system that still practices segregation by law. The district judge or school authorities should make every effort to achieve the greatest possible degree of actual desegregation and will thus necessarily be concerned with the elimination of one-race schools. No per se rule can adequately embrace all the difficulties of reconciling the competing interests involved, but in a system with a history of segregation the need for remedial criteria of sufficient specificity to assure a school authority's compliance with its constitutional duty warrants a presumption against schools that are substantially disproportionate in their racial composition. Where the school authority's proposed plan for conversion from a dual to a unitary system contemplates the continued existence of some schools that are all or predominately of one race, they have the burden of showing that such school assignments are genuinely nondiscriminatory. The court should scrutinize such schools, and the burden upon the school authorities will be to satisfy the court that their racial composition is not the result of present or past discriminatory action on their part. . . .

(3) Remedial Altering of Attendance Zones.

The maps submitted in these cases graphically demonstrate that one of the principal tools employed by school planners and by courts to break up the dual school system has been a frank—and sometimes drastic—gerrymandering of school districts and attendance zones. An additional step was pairing, "clustering," or "grouping" of schools with attendance assignments made deliberately to accomplish the transfer of Negro students out of formerly segregated Negro schools and transfer of white students to formerly all-Negro schools. More often than not, these zones are neither compact nor contiguous; indeed they may be on opposite ends of the city. As an interim corrective measure, this cannot be said to be beyond the broad remedial powers of a court.

Absent a constitutional violation there would be no basis for judicially ordering assignment of students on a racial basis. All things being equal, with no history of discrimination, it might well be desirable to assign pupils to schools nearest their homes. But all things are not equal in a system that has been deliberately constructed and maintained to enforce racial segregation. The remedy for such segregation may be administratively awkward, inconvenient, and even bizarre in some situations and may impose burdens on some; but all awkwardness and inconvenience cannot be avoided in the interim period when remedial adjustments are being made to eliminate the dual school systems. . . .

We hold that the pairing and grouping of noncontiguous school zones is a permissible tool and such action is to be considered in light of the objectives sought. . . . Conditions in different localities will vary so widely that no rigid rules can be laid down to govern all situations.

(4) Transportation of Students.

The scope of permissible transportation of students as an implement of a remedial decree has never been defined by this Court and by the very nature of the problem it cannot be defined with precision. No rigid guidelines as to student transportation can be given for application to the infinite variety of problems presented in thousands of situations. Bus transportation has been an integral part of the public education system for years, and was perhaps the single most important factor in the transition from the one-room schoolhouse to the consolidated school. Eighteen million of the Nation's public school children, approximately 39%, were transported to their schools by bus in 1969–1970 in all parts of the country. . . .

The importance of bus transportation as a normal and accepted tool of educational policy is readily discernible in this . . . case. . . . The Charlotte school authorities did not purport to assign students on the basis of geographically drawn attendance zones until 1965 and then they allowed almost unlimited transfer privileges. The District Court's conclusion that assignment of children to the school nearest their home serving their grade would not produce an effective dismantling of the dual system is supported by the record.

Thus the remedial techniques used in the District Court's order were within that court's power to provide equitable relief; implementation of the decree is well within the capacity of the school authority.

The decree provided that the buses used to implement the plan would operate on direct routes. Students would be picked up at schools near their homes and transported to the schools they were to attend. The trips for elementary school pupils average about seven miles and the District Court found that they would take "not over 35 minutes at the most." This system compares favorably with the transportation plan previously operated in Charlotte under which each day 23,600 students on all grade levels were transported an average of 15 miles one way for an average trip requiring over an hour. In these circumstances, we find no basis for holding that the local school authorities may not be required to employ bus transportation as one tool of school desegregation. Desegregation plans cannot be limited to the walk-in school.

An objection to transportation of students may have validity when the time or distance of travel is so great as to either risk the health of the children or significantly impinge on the educational process. District courts must weigh the soundness of any transportation plan in light of what is said in subdivisions (1), (2), and (3) above. It hardly needs stating that the limits on time of travel will vary with many factors, but probably with none more than the age of the students. The reconciliation of competing values in a desegregation case is, of course, a difficult task with many sensitive facets but fundamentally no more so than remedial measures courts of equity have traditionally employed.

The Court of Appeals, searching for a term to define the equitable remedial power of the district courts, used the term "reasonableness.". . . On the facts of this case, we are unable to conclude that the order of the District Court is not reasonable, feasible and workable. However, in seeking to define the scope of remedial power or the limits on remedial power of courts in an area as sensitive as we deal with here, words are poor instruments to convey the sense of basic fairness inherent in equity. Substance, not semantics, must govern, and we have sought to suggest the nature of limitations without frustrating the appropriate scope of equity. . . .

. . . The order of the District Court . . . is . . . affirmed.

It is so ordered.

The Court's decision in *Swann* reaffirmed the broad powers of district courts in implementing desegregation. Plans imposed by the courts can affect teacher placement, school construction and maintenance, staff assignment, and funding equalization among schools within the district. Judges may use the overall racial composition of the district's students to set goals for racial balance in individual schools. Courts are empowered to use a wide arsenal of student placement strategies, including rearrangement of attendance zones and the politically unpopular imposition of forced busing.

In spite of the generally sweeping powers given to the district judges, a careful reading of Burger's opinion reveals certain limits. First, this judicial authority can be used only when the courts have determined that a particular district has violated the Constitution— that is to say, when black schools are the result of past or continuing *de jure* (by law) discrimination. In these instances, district courts should presume that government actors intended to create the segregation, and the courts' powers to address the situation are remedial. Questions of school administration are to be left to local school officials unless unconstitutional discrimination has occurred and the districts have not made the necessary corrections. Second, the remedy imposed must be tailored to compensate for the violation. In Burger's terms, "The nature of the violation determines the scope of the remedy."

These limits have at times been obstacles to achieving effective integration, especially in large metropolitan areas in the North where many independent school districts may be in operation, and some may be composed of one race. True integration can take place only if multiple districts are brought into a single plan. But before a desegregation plan can be imposed, unconstitutional discrimination must be found to have occurred within that particular district. Violations are difficult to prove in northern cities where segregation laws never were in effect and segregated neighborhoods grew up without obvious government involvement. In these cases the segregation may exist in fact (*de facto*) but may not be the result of past or continuing *de jure* discrimination.

That description fit Detroit, Michigan, in 1972. A district judge ordered a desegregation plan embracing Detroit and fifty-three suburban school districts. To achieve the integration of the predominantly black central city schools with the largely white suburbs, the judge ordered massive busing. The plan required the purchase of about three hundred school buses and the appropriation of

millions of dollars to fund the transportation system. On appeal, the Supreme Court ruled in *Millikin v. Bradley* (1974) by a 5–4 vote that the district court had exceeded its authority by imposing a desegregation plan on school districts for which there had been no finding of constitutional violations. According to the Court, the school segregation in Detroit resulted from housing patterns rather than from any intent to discriminate on the part of government actors.

The scope and limits of judicial authority to impose remedies for racial segregation remain open and controversial. The desegregation of contemporary metropolitan areas may require overwhelming dislocation and staggering sums of money. District judges often are forced to impose orders that jurisdictions can ill afford. When judges see such desegregation plans as the only way to comply with the Constitution, disputes are likely.

A case in point is the 1989 Rehnquist Court decision in *Missouri v. Jenkins*. This suit arose out of attempts to attain satisfactory desegregation levels in the public schools of Kansas City, Missouri. The long-standing controversy focused on implementation of the district court's desegregation plan, at the heart of which was an expensive magnet school program. At various times the district judge had imposed spending orders to activate the plan, including $142.7 million for the magnet schools and $187.5 million for capital improvements. Because the state's law imposed certain property tax ceilings, the Kansas City school district could not raise its share of the money. The district judge, therefore, doubled the property tax rate. The state challenged his order, claiming that the district judge had abused his powers. The Supreme Court agreed that the district judge had exceeded his proper discretion, that he could not raise the taxes himself, but he could order city authorities to raise them.

Many school districts came under court supervision shortly after *Brown*. Judges monitored all significant actions taken by these districts to ensure that desegregation efforts continued and that resegregation was not encouraged. How long should such judicial supervision continue, and what standards must school districts meet to be free of it?

The Supreme Court provided a partial answer to these questions in *Board of Education of Oklahoma City*

Public Schools v. Dowell (1991). The Oklahoma City schools had been under various levels of judicial supervision since the 1970s. As the 1980s drew to a close, it looked as if the school district was becoming resegregated. The supervising district judge ruled that the court's desegregation decree should be dissolved because the district was in compliance; any resegregation was due to residential patterns, not intentional actions taken by school officials. The court of appeals reversed, and the controversy over the appropriate standard came to the Supreme Court. A five-justice majority held that judicial supervision would be ended when, after considering every facet of school operations, the court finds that the elements of state-sanctioned discrimination have been removed "as far as practicable." This standard was attacked by the dissenters (Marshall, Blackmun, and Stevens) as too lenient; they thought districts should remain under court control until all feasible means of removing racial concentrations have been exhausted.

To many observers, the Oklahoma City case was an indication that the Rehnquist Court was gradually reducing or perhaps eliminating close judicial supervision over the public schools on desegregation matters. This conclusion was reinforced one year later when the justices issued their ruling in *Freeman v. Pitts* (1992), a dispute concerning the extent to which the federal courts should maintain supervision over the public schools in DeKalb County, Georgia. The schools in this suburban Atlanta district had been under court supervision since 1969. In 1986 school officials petitioned the district court to release the school system from judicial supervision on the grounds that the county had made sufficient progress toward desegregation. The district court held that the county had achieved satisfactory desegregation in the areas of student assignments, transportation, physical facilities, and extracurricular activities.

The judge noted that the schools were becoming resegregated because of changing residential patterns, but found that such racial imbalances were the result of independent demographic changes unrelated to actions taken by the county. From these findings, the judge declared that no additional remedial actions would be necessary in the areas where satisfactory progress had been made. However, the judge found inadequate progress in the areas of faculty assignments and resource allocation. Here, the district court refused to relinquish control and ordered additional remedial steps. The court of appeals reversed, holding that until full compliance is reached the district court must continue supervision of the entire school system.

On appeal, the Supreme Court upheld the authority of the district court to reduce supervision over desegregation efforts on an incremental basis. It was within the trial court judge's discretion to reduce or eliminate judicial control over areas in which the district had attained compliance with the principles of *Brown*, and retain control over those areas where compliance had not yet been achieved. The Court, therefore, rejected the more stringent enforcement called for by the appeals court. The vote in the case was unanimous, although in a strongly worded concurring opinion three justices, Blackmun, O'Connor, and Stevens, cautioned that the judiciary must not abdicate its responsibility to ensure that all state-sponsored racial segregation in the public schools be eliminated.

The decision in *Freeman v. Pitts* was another example of the Rehnquist justices' backing away from the Court's long-standing commitment to racial equality—or so some argued. But just three months later, in *United States v. Fordice* (1992), the Court served notice that it was not removing itself from segregation controversies.[12] In *Fordice* the Court confronted racial separation in Mississippi's public university system, which various parties alleged had failed to take the necessary steps to dismantle segregation.

United States v. Fordice

505 U.S. 717 (1992)
laws.findlaw.com/US/505.717.html
Vote: 8 (Blackmun, Kennedy, O'Connor, Rehnquist, Souter,
    Stevens, Thomas, White)
    1 (Scalia)
Opinion of the Court: White
Concurring opinions: O'Connor, Thomas
Opinion concurring in part and dissenting in part: Scalia

---

12. For oral arguments in this case, navigate to: *oyez.nwu.edu.*

Mississippi founded its public university system in 1848 with the establishment of the University of Mississippi and over the years added seven institutions to the system. The universities were racially segregated. Five schools, University of Mississippi, Mississippi State University, Mississippi University for Women, University of Southern Mississippi, and Delta State University, enrolled white students. Three institutions, Alcorn State University, Jackson State University, and Mississippi Valley State University, enrolled black students.

The state did not respond to the Supreme Court's decision in *Brown v. Board of Education.* The first black student did not enroll in the University of Mississippi until 1962, and then only under court order. Over the next twelve years, no meaningful desegregation occurred. For example, no white students attended Jackson State or Mississippi Valley, and only five whites enrolled at Alcorn State. The white schools remained almost totally white.

In 1969 the Department of Health, Education and Welfare began efforts to force the state to desegregate its universities. After several years of controversy, the University of Mississippi system's board of trustees developed a desegregation plan, but the federal government found it inadequate. When no significant progress was made, private parties, later joined by the United States, filed suit in 1975 claiming that the university system was in violation of the Equal Protection Clause and the Civil Rights Act of 1964. For twelve years thereafter the parties attempted to reach consensus on a desegregation plan, but they were unsuccessful. In the mid-1980s, 99 percent of Mississippi's white college students attended the five "white" universities. Those schools were 80 percent to 91 percent white. The three "black" universities were 92 percent to 99 percent black.

Failing to reach an out-of-court agreement, the parties took the case to trial in 1987. Seventy-one witnesses testified, and the record included 56,700 pages of exhibits. The district court ruled in favor of the state, finding that it had imposed desegregation policies in good faith and had not violated federal law. The court of appeals affirmed, and the United States appealed to the Supreme Court.

JUSTICE WHITE delivered the opinion of the Court.

The District Court, the Court of Appeals, and respondents recognize and acknowledge that the State of Mississippi had the constitutional duty to dismantle the dual school system that its laws once mandated. Nor is there any dispute that this obligation applies to its higher education system. If the State has not discharged this duty, it remains in violation of the Fourteenth Amendment. *Brown v. Board of Education* and its progeny clearly mandate this observation. Thus, the primary issue in this case is whether the State has met its affirmative duty to dismantle its prior dual university system. . . .

Like the United States, we do not disagree with the Court of Appeals' observation that a state university system is quite different in very relevant respects from primary and secondary schools. Unlike attendance at the lower level schools, a student's decision to seek higher education has been a matter of choice. The State historically has not assigned university students to a particular institution. . . .

We do not agree with the Court of Appeals or the District Court, however, that the adoption and implementation of race-neutral policies alone suffice to demonstrate that the State has completely abandoned its prior dual system. That college attendance is by choice and not by assignment does not mean that a race-neutral admissions policy cures the constitutional violation of a dual system. In a system based on choice, student attendance is determined not simply by admissions policies, but also by many other factors. Although some of these factors clearly cannot be attributed to State policies, many can be. Thus, even after a State dismantles its segregative *admissions* policy, there may still be state action that is traceable to the State's prior *de jure* segregation and that continues to foster segregation. . . . If policies traceable to the *de jure* system are still in force and have discriminatory effects, those policies too must be reformed to the extent practicable and consistent with sound educational practices. We also disagree with respondents that the Court of Appeals and District Court properly relied on our decision in *Bazemore v. Friday* (1986). *Bazemore* neither requires nor justifies the conclusions reached by the two courts below.

Bazemore raised the issue whether the financing and operational assistance provided by a state university's extension service to voluntary 4-H and Homemaker Clubs was inconsistent with the Equal Protection Clause because of the existence of numerous all-white and all-black clubs. Though prior to 1965 the clubs were supported on a segregated basis, the District Court had found that the policy of segregation had been completely abandoned and that no evidence existed of any lingering discrimination in either services or membership; any racial imbalance resulted from the wholly voluntary and unfettered choice of private individuals. In this context, we held inapplicable the *Green* [*v. New Kent County School Board*, 1968] Court's judgment that a voluntary choice program was insufficient to dismantle a *de jure* dual system in public primary and secondary schools, but only after satisfying ourselves that the State had not fostered segregation by playing a part in the decision of which club an individual chose to join.

Bazemore plainly does not excuse inquiry into whether Mississippi has left in place certain aspects of its prior dual system that perpetuate the racially segregated higher education system. If the State perpetuates policies and practices traceable to its prior system that continue to have segregative effects—whether by influencing student enrollment decisions or by fostering segregation in other facets of the university system—and such policies are without sound educational justification and can be practically eliminated, the State has not satisfied its burden of proving that it has dismantled its prior system. Such policies run afoul of the Equal Protection Clause, even though the State has abolished the legal requirement that whites and blacks be educated separately and has established racially neutral policies not animated by a discriminatory purpose. Because the standard applied by the District Court did not make these inquiries, we hold that the Court of Appeals erred in affirming the District Court's ruling that the State had brought itself into compliance with the Equal Protection Clause in the operation of its higher education system.

Had the Court of Appeals applied the correct legal standard, it would have been apparent from the undisturbed factual findings of the District Court that there are several surviving aspects of Mississippi's prior dual system which are constitutionally suspect; for even though such policies may be race-neutral on their face, they substantially restrict a person's choice of which institution to enter and they contribute to the racial identifiability of the eight public universities. Mississippi must justify these policies or eliminate them.

It is important to state at the outset that we make no effort to identify an exclusive list of unconstitutional remnants of Mississippi's *de jure* system. . . . With this caveat in mind, we address four policies of the present system: admission standards, program duplication, institutional mission assignments, and continued operation of all eight public universities.

We deal first with the current admissions policies of Mississippi's public universities. As the District Court found, the three flagship historically white universities in the system—University of Mississippi, Mississippi State University, and University of Southern Mississippi—enacted policies in 1963 requiring all entrants to achieve a minimum composite score of 15 on the American College Testing Program (ACT). The court described the "discriminatory taint" of this policy, an obvious reference to the fact that, at the time, the average ACT score for white students was 18 and the average for blacks was 7. The District Court concluded, and the en banc Court of Appeals agreed, that present admissions standards derived from policies enacted in the 1970's to redress the problem of student unpreparedness. Obviously, this mid-passage justification for perpetuating a policy enacted originally to discriminate against black students does not make the present admissions standards any less constitutionally suspect.

The present admission standards are not only traceable to the *de jure* system and were originally adopted for a discriminatory purpose, but they also have present discriminatory effects. Every Mississippi resident under 21 seeking admission to the university system must take the ACT. Any applicant who scores at least 15 qualifies for automatic admission to any of the five historically white institutions except Mississippi University for Women, which requires a score of 18 for automatic admission unless the student has a 3.0 high school grade average. Those scoring less than 15 but at least 13 automatically qualify to enter Jackson State University, Alcorn State University, and Mississippi Valley State University. Without doubt, these requirements restrict the range of choices of entering students as to which institution they may attend in a way that perpetuates segregation. . . .

The segregative effect of this automatic entrance standard is especially striking in light of the differences in minimum automatic entrance scores among the regional universities in Mississippi's system. The minimum score for automatic admission to Mississippi University for Women

(MUW) is 18; it is 13 for the historically black universities. Yet MUW is assigned the same institutional mission as two other regional universities, Alcorn State and Mississippi Valley—that of providing quality undergraduate education. The effects of the policy fall disproportionately on black students who might wish to attend MUW; and though the disparate impact is not as great, the same is true of the minimum standard ACT score of 15 at Delta State University—the other "regional" university—as compared to the historically black "regional" universities where a score of 13 suffices for automatic admission. The courts below made little if any effort to justify in educational terms those particular disparities in entrance requirements or to inquire whether it was practicable to eliminate them.

We also find inadequately justified by the courts below or by the record before us the differential admissions requirements between universities with dissimilar programmatic missions. We do not suggest that absent a discriminatory purpose different programmatic missions accompanied by different admissions standards would be constitutionally suspect simply because one or more schools are racially identifiable. But here the differential admission standards are remnants of the dual system with a continuing discriminatory effect, and the mission assignments "to some degree follow the historical racial assignments." Moreover, the District Court did not justify the differing admission standards based on the different mission assignments. It observed only that in the 1970's, the Board of Trustees justified a minimum ACT score of 15 because too many students with lower scores were not prepared for the historically white institutions and that imposing the 15 score requirement on admissions to the historically black institutions would decimate attendance at those universities. The District Court also stated that the mission of the regional universities had the more modest function of providing quality undergraduate education. Certainly the comprehensive universities are also, among other things, educating undergraduates. But we think the 15 ACT test score for automatic admission to the comprehensive universities, as compared with a score of 13 for the regionals, requires further justification in terms of sound educational policy.

Another constitutionally problematic aspect of the State's use of the ACT test scores is its policy of denying automatic admission if an applicant fails to earn the minimum ACT score specified for the particular institution,

without also resorting to the applicant's high school grades as an additional factor in predicting college performance. The United States produced evidence that the American College Testing Program (ATCP), the administering organization of the ACT, discourages use of ACT scores as the sole admissions criterion on the ground that it gives an incomplete "picture" of the student applicant's ability to perform adequately in college. . . . The record also indicated that the disparity between black and white students' high school grade averages was much narrower than the gap between their average ACT scores, thereby suggesting that an admissions formula which included grades would increase the number of black students eligible for automatic admission to all of Mississippi's public universities. . . .

A second aspect of the present system that necessitates further inquiry is the widespread duplication of programs. "Unnecessary" duplication refers, under the District Court's definition, "to those instances where two or more institutions offer the same nonessential or noncore program. Under this definition, all duplication at the bachelor's level of nonbasic liberal arts and sciences course work and all duplication at the master's level and above are considered to be unnecessary." The District Court found that 34.6 percent of the 29 undergraduate programs at historically black institutions are "unnecessarily duplicated" by the historically white universities, and that 90 percent of the graduate programs at the historically black institutions are unnecessarily duplicated at the historically white institutions. In its conclusions of law on this point, the District Court nevertheless determined that "there is no proof" that such duplication "is directly associated with the racial identifiability of institutions," and that "there is no proof that the elimination of unnecessary program duplication would be justifiable from an educational standpoint or that its elimination would have a substantial effect on student choice."

The District Court's treatment of this issue is problematic from several different perspectives. First, the court appeared to impose the burden of proof on the plaintiffs to meet a legal standard the court itself acknowledged was not yet formulated. It can hardly be denied that such duplication was part and parcel of the prior dual system of higher education—the whole notion of "separate but equal" required duplicative programs in two sets of schools—and that the present unnecessary duplication is a continuation of that practice. *Brown* and its progeny, however, established that the burden of proof falls on the *State*, and not the aggrieved plaintiffs, to establish that it has dismantled its prior *de jure* segregated system. The court's holding that petitioners could not establish the constitutional defect of unnecessary duplication, therefore, improperly shifted the burden away from the State. Second, implicit in the District Court's finding of "unnecessary" duplication is the absence of any educational justification and the fact that some if not all duplication may be practicably eliminated. Indeed, the District Court observed that such duplication "cannot be justified economically or in terms of providing quality education." Yet by stating that "there is no proof" that elimination of unnecessary duplication would decrease institutional racial identifiability, affect student choice, and promote educationally sound policies, the court did not make clear whether it had directed the parties to develop evidence on these points, and if so, what that evidence revealed. Finally, by treating this issue in isolation, the court failed to consider the combined effects of unnecessary program duplication with other policies, such as differential admissions standards, in evaluating whether the State had met its duty to dismantle its prior *de jure* segregated system.

We next address Mississippi's scheme of institutional mission classification, and whether it perpetuates the State's formerly *de jure* dual system. The District Court found that, throughout the period of *de jure* segregation, University of Mississippi, Mississippi State University, and University of Southern Mississippi were the flagship institutions in the state system. They received the most funds, initiated the most advanced and specialized programs, and developed the widest range of curricular functions. At their inception, each was restricted for the education solely of white persons. The missions of Mississippi University for Women and Delta State University (DSU), by contrast, were more limited than their other all-white counterparts during the period of legalized segregation. MUW and DSU were each established to provide undergraduate education solely for white students in the liberal arts and such other fields as music, art, education, and home economics. When they were founded, the three exclusively black universities were more limited in their assigned academic missions than the five all-white institutions. Alcorn State, for example, was designated to serve as "an agricultural college for the education of Mississippi's black youth.". . .

In 1981, the State assigned certain missions to Mississip-

pi's public universities as they then existed. It classified University of Mississippi, Mississippi State, and Southern Mississippi as "comprehensive" universities having the most varied programs and offering graduate degrees. Two of the historically white institutions, Delta State University and Mississippi University for Women, along with two of the historically black institutions, Alcorn State University and Mississippi Valley State University, were designated as "regional" universities with more limited programs and devoted primarily to undergraduate education. Jackson State University was classified as an "urban" university whose mission was defined by its urban location.

The institutional mission designations adopted in 1981 have as their antecedents the policies enacted to perpetuate racial separation during the *de jure* segregated regime. . . . That different missions are assigned to the universities surely limits to some extent an entering student's choice as to which university to seek admittance. . . . We do not suggest that absent discriminatory purpose the assignment of different missions to various institutions in a State's higher education system would raise an equal protection issue where one or more of the institutions become or remain predominantly black or white. But here the issue is whether the State has sufficiently dismantled its prior dual system; and when combined with the differential admission practices and unnecessary program duplication, it is likely that the mission designations interfere with student choice and tend to perpetuate the segregated system. On remand, the court should inquire whether it would be practicable and consistent with sound educational practices to eliminate any such discriminatory effects of the State's present policy of mission assignments.

Fourth, the State attempted to bring itself into compliance with the Constitution by continuing to maintain and operate all eight higher educational institutions. The existence of eight instead of some lesser number was undoubtedly occasioned by State laws forbidding the mingling of the races. And as the District Court recognized, continuing to maintain all eight universities in Mississippi is wasteful and irrational. The District Court pointed especially to the facts that Delta State and Mississippi Valley are only 35 miles apart and that only 20 miles separate Mississippi State and Mississippi University for Women. It was evident to the District Court that "the defendants undertake to fund more institutions of higher learning than are justified by the amount of financial resources available to the state," but the court concluded that such fiscal irresponsibility was a policy choice of the legislature rather than a feature of a system subject to constitutional scrutiny.

Unquestionably, a larger rather than a smaller number of institutions from which to choose in itself makes for different choices, particularly when examined in the light of other factors present in the operation of the system, such as admissions, program duplication, and institutional mission designations. Though certainly closure of one or more institutions would decrease the discriminatory effects of the present system, based on the present record we are unable to say whether such action is constitutionally required. Elimination of program duplication and revision of admissions criteria may make institutional closure unnecessary. However, on remand this issue should be carefully explored by inquiring and determining whether retention of all eight institutions itself affects student choice and perpetuates the segregated higher education system, whether maintenance of each of the universities is educationally justifiable, and whether one or more of them can be practically closed or merged with other existing institutions.

Because the former *de jure* segregated system of public universities in Mississippi impeded the free choice of prospective students, the State in dismantling that system must take the necessary steps to ensure that this choice now is truly free. The full range of policies and practices must be examined with this duty in mind. That an institution is predominantly white or black does not in itself make out a constitutional violation. But surely the State may not leave in place policies rooted in its prior officially segregated system that serve to maintain the racial identifiability of its universities if those policies can practicably be eliminated without eroding sound educational policies. . . .

Because the District Court and the Court of Appeals failed to reconsider the State's duties in their proper light, the cases must be remanded. To the extent that the State has not met its affirmative obligation to dismantle its prior dual system, it shall be adjudged in violation of the Constitution and Title VI and remedial proceedings shall be conducted. The decision of the Court of Appeals is vacated, and the cases are remanded for further proceedings consistent with this opinion.

It is so ordered.

Vacated and remanded.

In *Fordice* the Court clarified the standard states must meet to bring their school systems into compliance with the Fourteenth Amendment. Some have argued that *Fordice* may be too little too late. Researchers at the Harvard Graduate School of Education found that federal court decisions of the 1990s, such as *Freeman*, have made it easier for districts to abandon school desegregation plans. As a result, the number of minority children enrolled in schools with whites has fallen precipitously. As the researchers put it, "In American race relations, the bridge from the 20th century may be leading back to the 19th century. We may be deciding to bet the future of the country once more on separate but equal. There is no evidence that separate but equal today works better than it did a century ago."[13]

Expanding the Application of Brown

The death of the separate but equal doctrine brought about by *Brown* had widespread ramifications for American society because of the huge number of state laws and local ordinances that mandated segregation in areas other than schools. Although the Court generally declined to resolve challenges to these practices in the immediate aftermath of *Brown*, once Congress and the Justice Department entered the fray, the Court again became an active participant in the struggle for equality.

In these post-*Brown* disputes the justices faithfully applied the 1954 precedent. The Court presumed that racial classifications used to discriminate against black Americans violated the Equal Protection Clause, and states attempting to justify such actions faced a heavy burden of proof. As members of a suspect class, black litigants enjoyed the advantages of the strict scrutiny test. These factors made it difficult for the states to withstand the attacks made against discriminatory policies and practices. One by one the legal barriers between the races fell.

An illustration of the Warren Court's approach to racial equality is the ruling in *Loving v. Virginia* (1967), which concerned the part of life segregationist forces least wanted to see integrated—marriage—and which the Court had ducked since *Brown*. When *Loving* came to

13. Peter Applebome, "Schools See Re-emergence of 'Separate but Equal,'" *New York Times*, April 8, 1997, A8.

the Court, sixteen states, all of them southern or border, had miscegenation statutes that made interracial marriages unlawful. Other states, including Arizona, California, Colorado, Indiana, and Oregon, only recently had repealed similar laws. The *Loving* case presents an interesting twist to the equality issue. Virginia argued that the Equal Protection Clause was not violated because whites and blacks were treated with absolute equality: members of both races were equally prohibited from marrying outside their race. If violations occurred, whites and blacks were subject to the same criminal penalties. How does Chief Justice Warren's opinion respond to this argument? Note the Court's discussion of the heavy burden carried by a state attempting to justify any racial classification.[14]

Loving v. Virginia

388 U.S. 1 (1967)
laws.findlaw.com/US/388/1.html
Vote: 9 *(Black, Brennan, Clark, Douglas, Fortas, Harlan,*
Stewart, Warren, White)

    0

Opinion of the Court: Warren
Concurring opinion: Stewart

In June 1958 two Virginia residents, Mildred Jeter, a black woman, and Richard Loving, a white man, were married in Washington, D.C. *(see Box 12-2).* They returned to Virginia to live and later that year were charged with violating Virginia's miscegenation law, which made interracial marriages unlawful and punished offenders with up to five years in the state penitentiary. They pleaded guilty to the charge and were sentenced to one year in jail. The judge suspended the sentences on condition that the Lovings leave Virginia and not return for twenty-five years. In handing down the sentence, the judge said, "Almighty God created the races white, black, yellow, malay and red, and he placed them on separate continents. And but for the interference with his arrangement there would be no cause for such mar-

14. For oral arguments in this case, navigate to: *oyez.nwu.edu.*

riages. The fact that he separated the races shows that he did not intend for the races to mix."

The Lovings moved to Washington. In 1963, with the help of an ACLU attorney, they initiated a suit to have the sentence set aside on the grounds that it violated their rights under the Equal Protection Clause of the Fourteenth Amendment. The Virginia Supreme Court upheld the constitutionality of the law and affirmed the original convictions.

MR. CHIEF JUSTICE WARREN delivered the opinion of the Court.

This case presents a constitutional question never addressed by this Court: whether a statutory scheme adopted by the State of Virginia to prevent marriages between persons solely on the basis of racial classifications violates the Equal Protection and Due Process Clauses of the Fourteenth Amendment. For reasons which seem to us to reflect the central meaning of those constitutional commands, we conclude that these statutes cannot stand consistently with the Fourteenth Amendment. . . .

While the state court is no doubt correct in asserting that marriage is a social relation subject to the State's police power, the State does not contend in its argument before this Court that its powers to regulate marriage are unlimited notwithstanding the commands of the Fourteenth Amendment. Instead, the State argues that the meaning of the Equal Protection Clause, as illuminated by the statements of the Framers, is only that state penal laws containing an interracial element as part of the definition of the offense must apply equally to whites and Negroes in the sense that members of each race are punished to the same degree. Thus, the State contends that, because its miscegenation statutes punish equally both the white and the Negro participants in an interracial marriage, these statutes, despite their reliance on racial classifications do not constitute an invidious discrimination based upon race. The second argument advanced by the State assumes the validity of its equal application theory. The argument is that, if the Equal Protection Clause does not outlaw miscegenation statutes because of their reliance on racial classifications, the question of constitutionality would thus become whether there was any rational basis for a State to treat interracial marriages differently from other marriages. On this question, the

BOX 12-2   INTERMARRIAGE BROKEN UP BY DEATH

MILDRED JETER LOVING is part of history, but she doesn't like a lot of fuss about it. She is alone now. Her husband, Richard, died in 1975. Their three children are grown. Her life is quiet, slowed by rheumatoid arthritis. Of publicity, she says politely, "It's not my style."

Mildred, who is black, and Richard, who was white, married in 1958. She was seventeen and he was twenty-four. She did not even know the marriage was illegal. Maybe her husband did; she isn't sure. She thought they took their vows in the District because there was less red tape to go through there than in Virginia.

They were caught, convicted, exiled, then allowed to return home a few years later while their case rose to the Supreme Court, which in 1967 ruled in *Loving v. Virginia* that the state's antimiscegenation law was unconstitutional and the Lovings could no longer be hounded by authorities. Fifteen other southern states had such laws and they too were dealt a death blow that day.

Her church in Central Point, Virgina, presented her with a plaque earlier this year to commemorate what the Lovings had done. "The preacher at my church classified me with Rosa Parks," she said, referring to the woman credited with starting the Montgomery, Alabama, bus boycott. "I don't feel like that. Not at all. What happened, we really didn't intend for it to happen. What we wanted, we wanted to come home."

The nine-year court battle began at 2 a.m. one day in July 1958, when a Caroline County, Virginia, sheriff roused the Lovings from sleep and took them to the Bowling Green jail house.

"Somebody had to tell, but I have no idea who it could have been," Loving says, laughing softly. "I guess we had one enemy."

They were sentenced several months later to a year in jail each, which Judge Leon M. Bazile said would be suspended if they agreed to stay out of Virginia for twenty-five years.

They moved to the District, where they lived with one of Mildred's cousins on Neal Street, N.E. Richard worked as an auto mechanic. All three of their children were born here. They missed Virginia all the while.

Richard and Mildred Loving in 1965 during court fight to overturn Virginia's law prohibiting interracial marriage.

Mildred Loving, now fifty-two, wrote for help to then-U.S. Attorney General Robert F. Kennedy. Bernard S. Cohen, an attorney with the American Civil Liberties Union, wound up with the case.

Cohen was eager to take it, viewing it as a clear shot at the last legal vestiges of *de jure* racism: the antimiscegenation laws, once prevalent in more than half the states, remained while other official forms of racism had fallen. Justice Harry L. Carrico of the state supreme court wrote the 1966 opinion upholding the law, saying there were no "sound judicial reasons" to overturn it. A year later, the U.S. Supreme Court disagreed.

Reflecting on the case, Cohen said it was filled with ironies. "It was ironical that her husband was killed in an auto accident just a few years after they finally got peace. And the irony that the justice of the Virginia Supreme Court who wrote the decision upholding the constitutionality of the law is now the chief justice" of the high court. "And another irony is that I am now a member of that legislature."

SOURCE: Lynne Duke, *Washington Post*, June 12, 1992. Reprinted by permission.

State argues, the scientific evidence is substantially in doubt and, consequently, this Court should defer to the wisdom of the state legislature in adopting its policy of discouraging interracial marriages.

Because we reject the notion that the mere "equal application" of a statute containing racial classifications is enough to remove the classifications from the Fourteenth Amendment's proscription of all invidious racial discriminations, we do not accept the State's contention that these statutes should be upheld if there is any possible basis for concluding that they serve a rational purpose. . . . In the case at bar, we deal with statutes containing racial classifications, and the fact of equal application does not immunize the statute from the very heavy burden of justification which the Fourteenth Amendment has traditionally required of state statutes drawn according to race. . . .

The State finds support for its "equal application" theory in the decision of the Court in *Pace v. Alabama* (1883). In that case, the Court upheld a conviction under an Alabama statute forbidding adultery or fornication between a white person and a Negro which imposed a greater penalty than that of a statute proscribing similar conduct by members of the same race. The Court reasoned that the statute could not be said to discriminate against Negroes because the punishment for each participant in the offense was the same. However, as recently as the 1964 Term, in rejecting the reasoning of that case, we stated *"Pace* represents a limited view of the Equal Protection Clause which has not withstood analysis in the subsequent decisions of this Court." As we there demonstrated, the Equal Protection Clause requires the consideration of whether the classifications drawn by any statute constitute an arbitrary and invidious discrimination. The clear and central purpose of the Fourteenth Amendment was to eliminate all official state sources of invidious racial discrimination in the States.

There can be no question but that Virginia's miscegenation statutes rest solely upon distinctions drawn according to race. The statutes proscribe generally accepted conduct if engaged in by members of different races. Over the years, this Court has consistently repudiated "[d]istinctions between citizens solely because of their ancestry" as being "odious to a free people whose institutions are founded upon the doctrine of equality." *Hirabayashi v. United States* (1943). At the very least, the Equal Protection Clause de-

mands that racial classifications, especially suspect in criminal statutes, be subjected to the "most rigid scrutiny," *Korematsu v. United States* (1944), and, if they are ever to be upheld, they must be shown to be necessary to the accomplishment of some permissible state objective, independent of the racial discrimination which it was the object of the Fourteenth Amendment to eliminate. . . .

There is patently no legitimate overriding purpose independent of invidious racial discrimination which justifies this classification. The fact that Virginia prohibits only interracial marriages involving white persons demonstrates that the racial classifications must stand on their own justification, as measures designed to maintain White Supremacy. We have consistently denied the constitutionality of measures which restrict the rights of citizens on account of race. There can be no doubt that restricting the freedom to marry solely because of racial classifications violates the central meaning of the Equal Protection Clause.

These statutes also deprive the Lovings of liberty without due process of law in violation of the Due Process Clause of the Fourteenth Amendment. The freedom to marry has long been recognized as one of the vital personal rights essential to the orderly pursuit of happiness by free men.

Marriage is one of the "basic civil rights of man," fundamental to our very existence and survival. To deny this fundamental freedom on so unsupportable a basis as the racial classifications embodied in these statutes, classifications so directly subversive of the principle of equality at the heart of the Fourteenth Amendment, is surely to deprive all the State's citizens of liberty without due process of law. The Fourteenth Amendment requires that the freedom of choice to marry not be restricted by invidious racial discriminations. Under our Constitution, the freedom to marry or not marry a person of another race resides with the individual and cannot be infringed by the State.

These convictions must be reversed. It is so ordered.

Reversed.

The *Loving* decision illustrates the Warren Court's rejection of discriminatory racial classifications. Government policies that allocated benefits or imposed penalties exclusively on the basis of race rarely survived Supreme Court scrutiny, especially when such laws or programs placed minorities at a disadvantage or were based on racial stereotypes.

What of subsequent Courts? Did the justices of the Burger and Rehnquist Courts followed their predecessor's lead? Or did they depart from the principles established during the 1950s and 1960s? If the issue is blatant racial discrimination by a government, the contemporary situation is easy to summarize: the justices of the Burger and Rehnquist Court eras have been just as willing as their predecessors to reject it. *Palmore v. Sidoti* (1984) provides a good example.

A Florida couple, Linda and Anthony J. Sidoti, both Caucasian, divorced in May 1980. The court awarded custody of the couple's three-year-old daughter, Melanie, to Linda Sidoti. In September 1981 Anthony Sidoti filed a petition requesting a change in the custody arrangement because of new conditions. He objected to his former wife cohabiting with a black man, Clarence Palmore Jr., whom she married two months after the court action was initiated. Sidoti also made several allegations of improper child care. A court counselor investigated the child care situation. Although there was no evidence of serious neglect, the counselor recommended a change in custody on the grounds that the child would be forced to suffer significant environmental pressures stemming from the mother's choice of a life style "unacceptable to the father and to society." The judge agreed, concluding that the best interests of the child would be served by awarding custody to the father. He gave the following reason for his decision:

The father's evident resentment of the mother's choice of a black partner is not sufficient to wrest custody from the mother. It is of some significance, however, that the mother did see fit to bring a man into her home and carry on a sexual relationship with him without being married to him. Such action tended to place gratification of her own desires ahead of her concern for the child's future welfare. This Court feels that despite the strides that have been made in bettering relations between the races in this country, it is inevitable that Melanie will, if allowed to remain in her present situation and attains school age and [is] thus more vulnerable to peer pressures, suffer from the social stigmatization that is sure to come.

A Florida appellate court upheld the judge's custody ruling, but the Supreme Court reversed. Chief Justice Burger's opinion for the Court was short, direct, and endorsed unanimously by the other justices.

The court [below] correctly stated that the child's welfare was the controlling factor. But that court was entirely candid and made no effort to place its holding on any ground other than race. Taking the court's findings and rationale at face value, it is clear that the outcome would have been different had petitioner married a Caucasian male of similar respectability. A core purpose of the Fourteenth Amendment was to do away with all governmentally imposed discrimination based on race. Classifying persons according to their race is more likely to reflect racial prejudice than legitimate public concerns; the race, not the person, dictates the category. Such classifications are subject to the most exacting scrutiny; to pass constitutional muster, they must be justified by a compelling governmental interest and must be "necessary . . . to the accomplishment" of their legitimate purpose. See *Loving v. Virginia* (1967).

The State, of course, has a duty of the highest order to protect the interests of minor children, particularly those of tender years. . . . It would ignore reality to suggest that racial and ethnic prejudices do not exist or that all manifestations of those prejudices have been eliminated. There is a risk that a child living with a stepparent of a different race may be subject to a variety of pressures and stresses not present if the child were living with parents of the same racial or ethnic origin.

The question, however, is whether the reality of private biases and the possible injury they might inflict are permissible considerations for removal of an infant child from the custody of its natural mother. We have little difficulty concluding that they are not. The Constitution cannot control such prejudices but neither can it tolerate them. Private biases may be outside the reach of the law, but the law cannot, directly or indirectly, give them effect.

Palmore, Brown, and *Loving* involve challenges to laws or regulations that show racial bias in their wording or in their application. In dealing with this kind of case, contemporary Courts have had little trouble finding a violation of the Constitution and striking down the discriminatory policies. The intent to discriminate, however, is not always so evident. Some laws are written in a language that is racially neutral, but the impact of the statute disproportionately disadvantages a particular racial group. What about a law that is passed to accomplish a legitimate governmental purpose, with no racially discriminatory intent? Are such laws unconstitutional?

Washington v. Davis (1976) presented this question to

the Court. At issue was a standard examination that all applicants to the police force in Washington, D.C., were required to take. Unsuccessful black applicants challenged the exam, pointing out that it had a disproportionately negative effect on black candidates; in fact, four times as many blacks as whites failed. A federal appeals court agreed. It held that the disproportionate impact of the test, standing alone and without regard to proof of discriminatory intent, was sufficient to invalidate it on constitutional grounds. But, in a 7–2 decision, the Supreme Court reversed. Writing for the Court, Justice White noted that past cases "have not embraced the proposition that a law or other official act, without regard to whether it reflects a racially discriminatory purpose, is unconstitutional solely because it has a racially disproportionate impact." He went on to say that while a disproportionate impact is not "irrelevant," it is not "the sole touchstone of an invidious racial discrimination forbidden by the Constitution. Standing alone, it does not trigger the rule that racial classifications are to be subjected to the strictest scrutiny and are justifiable only by the weightiest of considerations." White justified this conclusion in part on the grounds that applying the compelling interest approach to laws designed to serve neutral ends "would raise serious questions, and perhaps invalidate, a whole range of tax, welfare, public service, regulatory, and licensing statutes that may be more burdensome to the poor and to the average black than to the more affluent white."

The State Action Requirement

The Court's decision in *Washington v. Davis* was a blow to civil rights groups. By requiring that a racially discriminatory intent (not just a disproportionate impact) must be shown to demonstrate a constitutional violation, the Burger Court made it more difficult for such groups to prevail in litigation.[15] Still, we should not ignore a more general point brought out by the cases we have discussed, especially *Palmore.* The Burger and Rehn-

---

15. In his *Washington v. Davis* opinion, Justice White pointed out that under some federal civil rights statutes disproportionate impact is enough to trigger a violation of the law. Therefore, it may be easier for civil rights advocates to win suits under congressional statutes than to claim a violation of the Constitution.

quist Courts remained true to the core holding of *Brown:* the Constitution does not permit government classifications that penalize historically disadvantaged racial minorities or impose distinctions that imply the racial inferiority of any group. Where some commentators suggest that the Burger and Rehnquist Courts have parted company with the more liberal Warren Court is on remedies for discrimination (a subject examined at the end of the chapter) and on the state action requirement of the Fourteenth Amendment.

To see why some level this charge and, more generally, why state action is such an important issue, consider a common form of race discrimination in many areas of the country during the first half of the twentieth century: restrictive covenants. These convenants were private contractual arrangements, covering whole neighborhoods or subdivisions, that prohibited individual homeowners from selling their property to nonwhites. The agreements were binding on all subsequent owners of the property. Racially restrictive covenants were a response to black migration into northern cities and to a 1917 Supreme Court decision, *Buchanan v. Warley,* striking down state laws that mandated racial segregation in housing. Whites opposed to residential integration viewed restrictive covenants as a way to keep blacks from moving into their neighborhoods.

The covenants were so effective that the civil rights groups, especially the NAACP LDF, considered their elimination, along with school segregation a top priority. But they posed a vexing problem for the organization because the state was not responsible for passing or maintaining them; in other words, there did not *seem* to be the "state" action necessary to create a violation of the Fourteenth Amendment's Equal Protection Clause. The clause states that it provides protection against actions taken by the government, not by private individuals. Indeed, as early as 1883, in the *Civil Rights Cases,* the Supreme Court confirmed that the provisions of the Fourteenth Amendment do not extend beyond actions by the state. Consequently, establishing a violation of the Fourteenth Amendment requires proof that the discrimination was initiated, sponsored, or supported by a state government. Violations of the Due Process Clause of the

Fifth Amendment demand a showing that the federal government was somehow involved in the discriminatory action.

The state action requirement posed no obstacle for civil rights litigants seeking to challenge public school segregation because that was clearly the result of action by the government or its officials. The state action requirement was, however, a serious problem for legal challenges to private discrimination. Blacks often were denied access to public accommodations such as restaurants and hotels. Restrictive covenants and other "gentlemen's agreements" kept them from buying or renting the property of their choice. In all these cases, private enterprises and the individuals who owned properties simply refused to do business with blacks. Such discrimination, without any government involvement, appeared beyond the reach of the Constitution.

Even so, LDF attorneys pushed forward, developing imaginative arguments to convince judges that state action was present in these seemingly private cases. *Shelley v. Kraemer* (1948) was among their first attempts to do so before the Supreme Court. In this case, the Court found the presence of state action in an essentially private matter, the purchase of a house. Some have criticized the *Shelley* case for adopting an inappropriately broad definition of what constitutes state action. Those who drafted and ratified the Equal Protection Clause, it is argued, had no intention of prohibiting such indirect government involvement. Were the justices wrong in their interpretation of the concept of state action? Or did the Court appropriately condemn a form of discrimination that could not have existed without state support?

Shelley v. Kraemer

334 U.S. 1 (1948)
laws.findlaw.com/US/334/1.html
Vote: 6 (Black, Burton, Douglas, Frankfurter, Murphy, Vinson)
*   0*
Opinion of the Court: Vinson
Not participating: Jackson, Reed, Rutledge

J. D. and Ethel Lee Shelley, a black couple, moved from Mississippi to Missouri just before World War II.

When their family grew to six children, the Shelleys decided to move from their poor, predominantly black neighborhood to a more desirable location. On August 11, 1945, the Shelleys bought a house in the Grand Prairie neighborhood of St. Louis, a white residential area, with only a few houses occupied by blacks.[16]

Two months later, on October 9, Louis and Fern Kraemer, along with other property owners in the neighborhood, filed suit asking the court to divest the Shelleys of their property. Their suit was based on a violation of a restrictive covenant signed in 1911. This covenant was a legal contract signed by thirty neighborhood property owners who agreed that for fifty years they would not allow their respective properties to be occupied by any person not of the Caucasian race. This restriction was binding upon subsequent owners of the properties as well as the original parties. The Shelley house was covered by the agreement, and the white property owners demanded that it be enforced.

The Missouri Supreme Court ruled that the covenant should be enforced. The Shelleys, represented by Thurgood Marshall and the LDF staff, appealed to the U.S. Supreme Court, and the case was combined with a similar one from Michigan. Marshall argued that when the courts of Missouri enforced the agreement the state became party to the discrimination. The Justice Department and a host of civil rights organizations submitted briefs supporting Marshall's position.

MR. CHIEF JUSTICE VINSON delivered the opinion of the Court.

Whether the equal protection clause of the Fourteenth Amendment inhibits judicial enforcement by state courts of restrictive covenants based on race or color is a question which this Court has not heretofore been called upon to consider. . . . Here the particular patterns of discrimination and the areas in which the restrictions are to operate, are determined, in the first instance, by the terms of agreements among private individuals. Participation of the State consists in the enforcement of the restrictions so defined. The crucial issue with which we are here confronted is whether this distinction removes these cases from the oper-

16. For more on this case, see Clement E. Vose, *Caucasians Only* (Berkeley: University of California Press, 1959).

In 1948 the Supreme Court held that the state of Missouri had engaged in unconstitutional discrimination when it enforced a restrictive covenant that prevented J. D. and Ethel Lee Shelley and their six children from retaining ownership of their newly purchased home in St. Louis.

ation of the prohibitory provisions of the Fourteenth Amendment.

Since the decision of this Court in the *Civil Rights Cases* (1883), the principle has become firmly embedded in our constitutional law that the action inhibited by the first section of the Fourteenth Amendment is only such action as may fairly be said to be that of the States. That Amendment erects no shield against merely private conduct, however discriminatory or wrongful.

We conclude, therefore, that the restrictive agreements standing alone cannot be regarded as violative of any rights guaranteed to petitioners by the Fourteenth Amendment. So long as the purposes of those agreements are effectuated by voluntary adherence to their terms, it would appear clear that there has been no action by the State and the provisions of the Amendment have not been violated.

But here there was more. These are cases in which the purposes of the agreements were secured only by judicial enforcement by state courts of the restrictive terms of the

agreements. The respondents urge that judicial enforcement of private agreements does not amount to state action; or, in any event, the participation of the State is so attenuated in character as not to amount to state action within the meaning of the Fourteenth Amendment. . . .

That the action of state courts and judicial officers in their official capacities is to be regarded as action of the State within the meaning of the Fourteenth Amendment, is a proposition which has long been established by decisions of this Court. That principle was given expression in the earliest cases involving the construction of the terms of the Fourteenth Amendment. . . .

The short of the matter is that from the time of the adoption of the Fourteenth Amendment until the present, it has been the consistent ruling of this Court that the action of the States to which the Amendment has reference includes action of state courts and state judicial officials. Although, in construing the terms of the Fourteenth Amendment, differences have from time to time been expressed as to whether particular types of state action may be said to offend the Amendment's prohibitory provisions, it has never been suggested that state court action is immunized from the operation of those provisions simply because the act is that of the judicial branch of the state government.

Against this background of judicial construction, extending over a period of some three-quarters of a century, we are called upon to consider whether enforcement by state courts of the restrictive agreements in these cases may be deemed to be the acts of those States; and, if so, whether that action has denied these petitioners the equal protection of the laws which the Amendment was intended to insure.

We have no doubt that there has been state action in these cases in the full and complete sense of the phrase. The undisputed facts disclose that petitioners were willing purchasers of properties upon which they desired to establish homes. The owners of the properties were willing sellers; and contracts of sale were accordingly consummated. It is clear that but for the active intervention of the state courts, supported by the full panoply of state power, petitioners would have been free to occupy the properties in question without restraint.

These are not cases, as has been suggested, in which the States have merely abstained from action, leaving private individuals free to impose such discriminations as they see fit. Rather, these are cases in which the States have made available to such individuals the full coercive power of government to deny to petitioners, on the grounds of race or color, the enjoyment of property rights in premises which petitioners are willing and financially able to acquire and which the grantors are willing to sell. The difference between judicial enforcement and nonenforcement of the restrictive covenants is the difference to petitioners between being denied rights of property available to other members of the community and being accorded full enjoyment of those rights on an equal footing. . . .

State action, as that phrase is understood for the purposes of the Fourteenth Amendment, refers to exertions of state power in all forms. And when the effect of that action is to deny rights subject to the protection of the Fourteenth Amendment, it is the obligation of this Court to enforce the constitutional commands.

We hold that in granting judicial enforcement of the restrictive agreements in these cases, the States have denied petitioners the equal protection of the laws and that, therefore, the action of the state courts cannot stand. We have noted that freedom from discrimination by the States in the enjoyment of property rights was among the basic objectives sought to be effectuated by the framers of the Fourteenth Amendment. That such discrimination has occurred in these cases is clear. Because of the race or color of these petitioners they have been denied rights of ownership or occupancy enjoyed as a matter of course by other citizens of different race or color. . . .

The problem of defining the scope of the restrictions which the Federal Constitution imposes upon exertions of power by the States has given rise to many of the most persistent and fundamental issues which this Court has been called upon to consider. That problem was foremost in the minds of the framers of the Constitution, and, since that early day, has arisen in a multitude of forms. The task of determining whether the action of a State offends constitutional provisions is one which may not be undertaken lightly. Where, however, it is clear that the action of the State violates the terms of the fundamental charter, it is the obligation of this Court so to declare.

The historical context in which the Fourteenth Amendment became a part of the Constitution should not be forgotten. Whatever else the framers sought to achieve, it is clear that the matter of primary concern was the establishment of equality in the enjoyment of basic civil and political rights and the preservation of those rights from discriminatory action on the part of the States based on considerations of race or color. Seventy-five years ago this Court announced that the provisions of the Amendment are to be construed with this fundamental purpose in mind. Upon full consideration, we have concluded that in these cases the States have acted to deny petitioners the equal protection of the laws guaranteed by the Fourteenth Amendment.

Reversed.

In *Shelley* the Vinson Court adopted the LDF's broad approach to the state action requirement of the Fourteenth Amendment—at least in the area of restrictive covenants. In *Burton v. Wilmington Parking Authority* (1961), the Warren Court revisited *Shelley v. Kraemer,* and more generally, the state action requirement of the Fourteenth Amendment. In this case a black man was discriminated against by a privately owned and operated business, and, therefore, the Equal Protection Clause did not seem to apply. But the attorneys representing William Burton argued that the state was indeed a participant in the discrimination. Was the Court's ruling a natural application of *Shelley?* Or was the involvement of the state government too remote to warrant an application of the Fourteenth Amendment?

Burton v. Wilmington Parking Authority

365 U.S. 715 (1961)

laws.findlaw.com/US/365/715.html

Vote: 6 (Black, Brennan, Clark, Douglas, Stewart, Warren)

  3 (Frankfurter, Harlan, Whittaker)

Opinion of the Court: Clark

Concurring opinion: Stewart

Dissenting opinions: Frankfurter, Harlan

In August 1958 Burton parked his car in a downtown parking garage in Wilmington, Delaware, and went to the Eagle Coffee Shoppe, a restaurant located within the parking structure. Burton was denied service in the restaurant because he was black.

The parking garage was built, owned, and operated by the Wilmington Parking Authority, a city agency. Before the structure was completed, it had become clear that parking revenues alone would be insufficient to repay the loans and bonds that had financed the construction. To increase revenues, the parking authority leased space in the building to private business ventures, including the Eagle Coffee Shoppe, which had a thirty-year lease to operate a restaurant in the garage. The Eagle Corporation invested some $220,000 of its own money to convert the space for restaurant use. The parking authority, under the terms of the lease, provided certain materials and services for the operation, and the city collected more than $28,000 in annual rent from Eagle.

Burton filed suit claiming that his rights under the Equal Protection Clause had been violated. The parking authority disagreed, arguing that the discrimination was purely private with the state having no substantive involvement. The trial court ruled in favor of Burton, find-

ing that the lease arrangement did not insulate the parking authority from the discrimination of its tenant. The Delaware Supreme Court, however, reversed, holding that Eagle was operating in a purely private capacity.

MR. JUSTICE CLARK delivered the opinion of the Court.

It is clear, as it always has been since the *Civil Rights Cases* [1883], that "Individual invasion of individual rights is not the subject-matter of the [Fourteenth] amendment," and that private conduct abridging individual rights does no violence to the Equal Protection Clause unless to some significant extent the State in any of its manifestations has been found to have become involved in it. Because the virtue of the right to equal protection of the laws could lie only in the breadth of its application, its constitutional assurance was reserved in terms whose imprecision was necessary if the right were to be enjoyed in the variety of individual-state relationships which the Amendment was designed to embrace. For the same reason, to fashion and apply a precise formula for recognition of state responsibility under the Equal Protection Clause is an "impossible task" which "This Court has never attempted."

The trial court's disposal of the issues on summary judgment has resulted in a rather incomplete record, but the opinion of the Supreme Court as well as that of the Chancellor presents the facts in sufficient detail for us to determine the degree of state participation in Eagle's refusal to serve petitioner. In this connection the Delaware Supreme Court seems to have placed controlling emphasis on its conclusion, as to the accuracy of which there is doubt, that only some 15% of the total cost of the facility was "advanced" from public funds; that the cost of the entire facility was allocated three-fifths to the space for commercial leasing and two-fifths to parking space; that anticipated revenue from parking was only some 30.5% of the total income, the balance of which was expected to be earned by the leasing; that the Authority had no original intent to place a restaurant in the building, it being only a happenstance resulting from the bidding; that Eagle expended considerable moneys on furnishings; that the restaurant's main and marked public entrance is on Ninth Street without any public entrance direct from the parking area; and that "the only connection Eagle has with the public facility . . . is the furnishing of the sum of $28,700 annually in the form of rent which is used by the Authority to defray a portion of the operating expense of an otherwise unprofitable enterprise." While these factual considerations are indeed validly accountable aspects of the enterprise upon which the State has embarked, we cannot say that they lead inescapably to the conclusion that state action is not present. Their persuasiveness is diminished when evaluated in the context of other factors which must be acknowledged.

The land and building were publicly owned. As an entity, the building was dedicated to "public uses" in performance of the Authority's "essential governmental functions." The costs of land acquisition, construction, and maintenance are defrayed entirely from donations by the City of Wilmington, from loans and revenue bonds and from the proceeds of rentals and parking services out of which the loans and bonds were payable. Assuming that the distinction would be significant, the commercially leased areas were not surplus state property, but constituted a physically and financially integral and, indeed, indispensable part of the State's plan to operate its project as a self-sustaining unit. Upkeep and maintenance of the building, including necessary repairs, were responsibilities of the Authority and were payable out of public funds. It cannot be doubted that the peculiar relationship of the restaurant to the parking facility in which it is located confers on each an incidental variety of mutual benefits. Guests of the restaurant are afforded a convenient place to park their automobiles, even if they cannot enter the restaurant directly from the parking area. Similarly, its convenience for diners may well provide additional demand for the Authority's parking facilities. Should any improvements effected in the leasehold by Eagle become part of the realty, there is no possibility of increased taxes being passed on to it since the fee is held by a tax-exempt government agency. Neither can it be ignored, especially in view of Eagle's affirmative allegation that for it to serve Negroes would injure its business, that profits earned by discrimination not only contribute to, but also are indispensable elements in, the financial success of a governmental agency.

Addition of all these activities, obligations and responsibilities of the Authority, the benefits mutually conferred, together with the obvious fact that the restaurant is operated as an integral part of a public building devoted to a public parking service, indicates that degree of state participation and involvement in discriminatory action which it was the design of the Fourteenth Amendment to condemn. It is irony amounting to grave injustice that in one part of a single building, erected and maintained with public funds by an agency of the State to serve a public purpose, all persons have equal rights, while in another portion, also serving the public, a Negro is a second-class citizen, offensive because of his race, without rights and unentitled to service, but at the same time fully enjoys equal access to nearby restaurants in wholly privately owned buildings. As the Chancellor pointed out, in its lease with Eagle the Authority could have affirmatively required Eagle to discharge the responsibilities under the Fourteenth Amendment imposed upon the private enterprise as a consequence of state participation. But no State may effectively abdicate its responsibilities by either ignoring them or by merely failing to discharge them whatever the motive may be. It is of no consolation to an individual denied the equal protection of the laws that it was done in good faith. . . . By its inaction, the Authority, and through it the State, has not only made itself a party to the refusal of service, but has elected to place its power, property and prestige behind the admitted discrimination. The State has so far insinuated itself into a position of interdependence with Eagle that it must be recognized as a joint participant in the challenged activity, which, on that account, cannot be considered to have been so "purely private" as to fall without the scope of the Fourteenth Amendment.

Because readily applicable formulae may not be fashioned, the conclusions drawn from the facts and circumstances of this record are by no means declared as universal truths on the basis of which every state leasing agreement is to be tested. Owing to the very "largeness" of government, a multitude of relationships might appear to some to fall within the Amendment's embrace, but that, it must be remembered, can be determined only in the framework of the peculiar facts or circumstances present. Therefore respondents' prophecy of nigh universal application of a constitutional precept so peculiarly dependent for its invocation upon appropriate facts fails to take into account "Differences in circumstances which beget appropriate differences in law." Specifically defining the limits of our inquiry, what we hold today is that when a State leases public property in the manner and for the purpose shown to have been the case here, the proscriptions of the Fourteenth Amendment must be complied with by the lessee as certainly as though they were binding covenants written into the agreement itself. . . .

Reversed and remanded.

Burton demonstrates the Warren Court's willingness to impose an expansive view of state action, even in the face of lingering hostility toward its *Brown* decision. But, as we shall soon discover, *Burton* did not eliminate the public/private distinction.

Along those lines is the Burger Court's decision in *Moose Lodge 107 v. Irvis* (1972), which suggests that the definition of state action has its limits.[17] Note how Justice Rehnquist distinguishes the state's involvement here from Delaware's relationship with the Eagle Coffee Shoppe. Is his argument that the *Burton* precedent is inapplicable convincing? Would finding state action in this case blur any meaningful state/private distinction? Or is Justice Brennan more persuasive when he argues that the state was involved in racial discrimination? If the Court had taken the dissenters' position, what implications would it have had for other private organizations, such as country clubs or fraternal organizations?

Moose Lodge No. 107 v. Irvis

407 U.S. 163 (1972)
laws.findlaw.com/US/407/163.html
Vote: 6 (Blackmun, Burger, Powell, Rehnquist, Stewart, White)
3 (Brennan, Douglas, Marshall)
Opinion of the Court: Rehnquist
Dissenting opinions: Brennan, Douglas

A white member in good standing of the Harrisburg, Pennsylvania, Moose Lodge, accompanied by a guest, entered the lodge's dining room and bar and requested service. The lodge employees refused to serve him because his guest, K. Leroy Irvis, was black. Irvis was also a member of the Pennsylvania state legislature. Lodge 107, part of the national Moose organization, was subject to the rules of its Supreme Lodge, which limited membership

17. For oral arguments in this case, navigate to: *oyez.nwu.edu.*

to Caucasians and permitted members to entertain only Caucasian guests on the premises. Irvis sued the lodge, claiming that he had been denied his rights under the Equal Protection Clause of the Fourteenth Amendment. His suit was based on the theory that by granting the Moose Lodge a liquor license the state of Pennsylvania was approving the organization's racially discriminatory policies. A federal court ruled in favor of Irvis, declaring that the lodge's liquor license would be invalid until such time as the discriminatory practices ceased. The lodge appealed.

MR. JUSTICE REHNQUIST delivered the opinion of the Court.

Moose Lodge is a private club in the ordinary meaning of that term. It is a local chapter of a national fraternal organization having well-defined requirements for membership. It conducts all of its activities in a building that is owned by it. It is not publicly funded. Only members and guests are permitted in any lodge of the order; one may become a guest only by invitation of a member or upon invitation of the house committee.

Appellee, while conceding the right of private clubs to choose members upon a discriminatory basis, asserts that the licensing of Moose Lodge to serve liquor by the Pennsylvania Liquor Control Board amounts to such state involvement with the club's activities as to make its discriminatory practices forbidden by the Equal Protection Clause of the Fourteenth Amendment. . . . We conclude that Moose Lodge's refusal to serve food and beverages to a guest by reason of the fact that he was a Negro does not, under the circumstances here presented, violate the Fourteenth Amendment.

In 1883, this Court in *The Civil Rights Cases* set forth the essential dichotomy between discriminatory action by the State, which is prohibited by the Equal Protection Clause, and private conduct, "however discriminatory or wrongful," against which that clause "erects no shield." That dichotomy has been subsequently reaffirmed in *Shelley v. Kraemer* and in *Burton v. Wilmington Parking Authority.*

While the principle is easily stated, the question of whether particular discriminatory conduct is private, on the one hand, or amounts to "state action," on the other hand, frequently admits of no easy answer. "Only by sifting facts and weighing circumstances can the nonobvious involvement of the State in private conduct be attributed its true significance."

Our cases make clear that the impetus for the forbidden discrimination need not originate with the State if it is state action that enforces privately originated discrimination. *Shelley v. Kraemer.* The Court held in *Burton v. Wilmington Parking Authority* that a private restaurant owner who refused service because of a customer's race violated the Fourteenth Amendment, where the restaurant was located in a building owned by a state-created parking authority and leased from the authority. The Court, after a comprehensive review of the relationship between the lessee and the parking authority concluded that the latter had "so far insinuated itself into a position of interdependence with Eagle [the restaurant owner] that it must be recognized as a joint participant in the challenged activity, which, on that account, cannot be considered to have been so 'purely private' as to fall without the scope of the Fourteenth Amendment."

The Court has never held, of course, that discrimination by an otherwise private entity would be violative of the Equal Protection Clause if the private entity receives any sort of benefit or service at all from the State, or if it is subject to state regulation in any degree whatever. Since state-furnished services include such necessities of life as electricity, water, and police and fire protection, such a holding would utterly emasculate the distinction between private as distinguished from state conduct set forth in *The Civil Rights Cases* and adhered to in subsequent decisions. Our holdings indicate that where the impetus for the discrimination is private, the State must have "significantly involved itself with invidious discriminations" in order for the discriminatory action to fall within the ambit of the constitutional prohibition. . . .

Here there is nothing approaching the symbiotic relationship between lessor and lessee that was present in *Burton*, where the private lessee obtained the benefit of locating in a building owned by the state-created parking authority, and the parking authority was enabled to carry out its primary public purpose of furnishing parking space by advantageously leasing portions of the building constructed for that purpose to commercial lessees such as the owner of the Eagle Restaurant. Unlike *Burton*, the Moose Lodge building is located on land owned by it, not by any public authority. Far from apparently holding itself out as a place of public

accommodation, Moose Lodge quite ostentatiously proclaims the fact that it is not open to the public at large. Nor is it located and operated in such surroundings that although private in name, it discharges a function or performs a service that would otherwise in all likelihood be performed by the State. In short, while Eagle was a public restaurant in a public building, Moose Lodge is a private social club in a private building.

With the exception hereafter noted, the Pennsylvania Liquor Control Board plays absolutely no part in establishing or enforcing the membership or guest policies of the club that it licenses to serve liquor. There is no suggestion in this record that Pennsylvania law, either as written or as applied, discriminates against minority groups either in their right to apply for club licenses themselves or in their right to purchase and be served liquor in places of public accommodation. The only effect that the state licensing of Moose Lodge to serve liquor can be said to have on the right of any other Pennsylvanian to buy or be served liquor on premises other than those of Moose Lodge is that for some purposes club licenses are counted in the maximum number of licenses that may be issued in a given municipality. . . .

The District Court was at pains to point out in its opinion what it considered to be the "pervasive" nature of the regulation of private clubs by the Pennsylvania Liquor Control Board. As that court noted, an applicant for a club license must make such physical alterations in its premises as the board may require, must file a list of the names and addresses of its members and employees, and must keep extensive financial records. The board is granted the right to inspect the licensed premises at any time when patrons, guests, or members are present.

However detailed this type of regulation may be in some particulars, it cannot be said to in any way foster or encourage racial discrimination. Nor can it be said to make the State in any realistic sense a partner or even a joint venturer in the club's enterprise. The limited effect of the prohibition against obtaining additional club licenses when the maximum number of retail licenses allotted to a municipality has been issued, when considered together with the availability of liquor from hotel, restaurant, and retail licensees, falls far short of conferring upon club licensees a monopoly in the dispensing of liquor in any given municipality or in the State as a whole. We therefore hold that . . . the operation of the regulatory scheme enforced by the Pennsylvania

Liquor Control Board does not sufficiently implicate the State in the discriminatory guest policies of Moose Lodge to make the latter "state action" within the ambit of the Equal Protection Clause of the Fourteenth Amendment.

Reversed.

MR. JUSTICE BRENNAN . . . dissenting.

When Moose Lodge obtained its liquor license, the State of Pennsylvania became an active participant in the operation of the Lodge bar. Liquor licensing laws are only incidentally revenue measures; they are primarily pervasive regulatory schemes under which the State dictates and continually supervises virtually every detail of the operation of the licensee's business. Very few, if any, other licensed businesses experience such complete state involvement. Yet the Court holds that such involvement does not constitute "state action" making the Lodge's refusal to serve a guest liquor solely because of his race a violation of the Fourteenth Amendent. The vital flaw in the Court's reasoning is its complete disregard of the fundamental value underlying the "state action" concept. . . .

Plainly, the State of Pennsylvania's liquor regulations intertwine the State with the operation of the Lodge bar in a "significant way [and] lend [the State's] authority to the sordid business of racial discrimination." The opinion of the late Circuit Judge Freedman, for the three-judge District Court, most persuasivey demonstrates the "state action" present in this case:

"We believe the decisive factor is the uniqueness and the all-pervasiveness of the regulation by the Commonwealth of Pennsylvania of the dispensing of liquor under licenses granted by the state. The regulation inherent in the grant of a state liquor license is so different in nature and extent from the ordinary licenses issued by the state that it is different in quality.". . .

This is thus a case requiring application of the principle that until today has governed our determinations of the existence of "state action": "Our prior decisions leave no doubt that the mere existence of efforts by the State, through legislation or otherwise, to authorize, encourage, or otherwise support racial discrimination in a particular facet of life constitutes illegal state involvement in those pertinent private acts of discrimination that subsequently occur."

I therefore dissent and would affirm the final decree entered by the District Court.

Did the Burger Court retreat from *Shelley* and *Burton* or did it merely draw a sensible distinction between private and public discrimination for purposes of the Fourteenth Amendment? We leave these questions to you to address, but note that the three dissenters in *Moose Lodge No. 107*—Brennan, Marshall, and Douglas—had been members of the Warren Court's liberal majority responsible for expanding the rights of racial minorities.

Remember that victims of invidious discrimination may find recourse in federal or state statutes that outlaw private forms of discrimination when state action is not present or is difficult to prove. Governments enjoy a number of powers, especially those over commercial activities, that permit regulating certain forms of private discriminatory behavior. Although the Supreme Court ruled in *Moose Lodge No. 107* that state action had not contributed to the discrimination, several states have used the power to regulate alcoholic beverages as a means of combating racial bias. For example, in 1973 the Supreme Court upheld a Maine regulation that made the granting of a liquor license contingent on nondiscriminatory service policies.[18]

Civil Rights Statutes and Race Discrimination in the Contemporary Era

Whether it seemed that the Burger and Rehnquist Courts were retreating from the letter and spirit of Warren Court decisions (or not), the battles over racial discrimination continued.[19] Legal confrontations occurred over housing, employment, and admission policies in higher education. In most of these areas, federal civil rights statutes (rather than the Fourteenth Amendment's Equal Protection Clause) and the government's enforcement of them have provided the basis for the Court's decisionmaking.

As we noted in the introduction to this section, these laws historically have offered great opportunities for those who wish to challenge discriminatory behavior

18. *B. P. O. E. Lodge No. 2043 v. Ingraham* (1973).

19. In housing, see *Village of Arlington Heights v. Metropolitan Housing Development Corporation* (1977), *Hills v. Gautreaux* (1976), and *Spallone v. United States* (1990). In employment, see *Sheet Metal Workers v. EEOC* (1986), *Wards Cove Packing Co. v. Atonio* (1989), *Martin v. Wilks* (1989), and *Patterson v. McLean Credit Union* (1989). For admissions policy in higher education, see *Regents of the University of California v. Bakke* (1978).

and, historically, the Supreme Court has supported congressional legislation to extend fair treatment to racial minorities. During the 1980s and 1990s, however, Congress and the Court often clashed over statutory interpretations of civil rights laws—with the justices handing down some rulings that members of Congress saw as excessively limiting the opportunities of blacks and other disadvantaged groups to assert their statutory rights. In response, Congress has passed or amended laws to counteract the Court's decisions.

Three cases decided in 1989 (*Wards Cove Packing Co. v. Atonio*, *Martin v. Wilks*, and *Lorance v. AT&T Technologies*) provide good examples. These decisions made it more difficult for civil rights claimants to win employment discrimination suits, and, in response, Congress passed the Civil Rights Act of 1991, which nullified the Supreme Court's interpretation of these statutory provisions. Not to be outdone, the Court in *Rivers v. Roadway Express* (1994) and *Landgraf v. USI Film Products* (1994) refused to apply the new law retroactively.

SEX DISCRIMINATION

Before *Brown v. Board of Education*, groups and individuals challenging practices as racially discriminatory had a major obstacle to overcome: *Plessy v. Ferguson.* Lawsuits based claims of sex discrimination were also handicapped and for an even longer period of time. Indeed, before the 1970s, the few sex discrimination cases that reached the Supreme Court often ended in decisions that reinforced traditional views of sex roles. In *Bradwell v. Illinois* (1873), for example, the Court heard a challenge to an action by the Illinois Supreme Court denying Myra Bradwell a license to practice law solely because of her sex. The Court, with only Chief Justice Salmon P. Chase dissenting, upheld the state action. Justice Joseph P. Bradley's concurring opinion, which Justices Noah H. Swayne and Stephen J. Field joined, illustrates the attitude of the legal community toward women. Bradley said that he gave his "heartiest concurrence" to contemporary society's "multiplication of avenues for women's advancement." But he added, "The natural and proper timidity and delicacy which belongs to the female sex evidently unfits it for many of the occupations of civil life."

Myra Bradwell studied law with her husband, a judge, and edited and published the *Chicago Legal News*, the most important legal publication in the Midwest. Although she passed the bar exam, the Illinois Supreme Court refused to admit her to the state bar because of her sex. She appealed to the U.S. Supreme Court, but lost.

This condition, according to Bradley, was the product of divine ordinance. Two years later, in *Minor v. Happersett* (1875), the Court upheld Missouri's denial of voting rights to women, a precedent in effect until ratification of the Nineteenth Amendment in 1920.

Similar decisions came early in the next century. The majority opinion in the 1908 case of *Muller v. Oregon*, in which the Court upheld a maximum work hour law that covered only women, echoed Justice Bradley's view of women.[20] Writing for the Court, Justice David J. Brewer noted:

20. At the time of their implementation, statutes such as the one at issue in *Muller* were seen as a progressive step to protect women in the workforce. Today, this kind of law is considered paternalistic, based on an assumption of the inferiority of women.

BOX 12-3   MAJOR CONGRESSIONAL ACTION ON WOMEN'S RIGHTS

1960S

• Title VII of the Civil Rights Act of 1964 makes it unlawful for an employer "to refuse to hire . . . any individual . . . because of such individual's race, color, religion, sex, or national origin" except where "religion, sex, or national origin" is a bona fide occupational qualification necessary to the normal operation of that particular business.

• Equal Pay Act of 1963 requires employers to pay men and women performing equal work an equal salary.

1970S

• Equal Rights Amendment sent to the states for ratification in 1972. This amendment would have declared that "Equality of rights under the law shall not be denied or abridged by the United States or by any State on account of sex."

• Expansion of Title VII's ban on employment discrimination to cover employees of state and local governments.

• Title IX of the education amendments (passed in 1972) states that "No person in the United States shall, on the basis of sex, be excluded from participation in, be denied benefits of, or be subjected to discrimination under any educational program or activity receiving Federal financial assistance."

• Pregnancy Discrimination Act of 1978 forbids employment discrimination on grounds of pregnancy.

• Application in 1974 of the Civil Rights Act of 1968 to sex discrimination. The act prohibits discrimination on the advertising, financing, sale, or rental of housing.

1980S

• Civil Rights Restoration Act of 1988 extends Title IX coverage to all operations of state or local units and to private organizations if federal aid is given to the enterprise as a whole or if the enterprise is "principally engaged" in providing education, housing, health care, parks, or social services.

• An attempt to repropose the ERA falls short of the two-thirds requirement.

1990S

• Civil Rights Act of 1991 reaffirms and expands protections against discrimination in employment.

• The Family and Medical Leave Act of 1993 allows individuals who work for employers with fifty or more employees to take up to twelve weeks of unpaid leave to stay home with a new baby or sick parent, child, or spouse or to recover from an illness.

• Violence Against Women Act of 1994 makes, among other things, crossing a state line to assault a spouse or domestic partner a federal crime punishable by a sentence of up to twenty years or life in prison.

SOURCES: Leslie Friedman Goldstein, *The Constitutional Rights of Women* (Madison: University of Wisconsin Press, 1988); Susan Gluck Mezey, *In Pursuit of Equality* (New York: St. Martin's, 1992); and National Organization for Women, *Legislative Updates*, http://www.now.org/issues/legislat/index.html.

That woman's physical structure and the performance of maternal functions place her at a disadvantage in the struggle for subsistence is obvious. This is especially true when the burdens of motherhood are upon her. Even when they are not, by abundant testimony of the medical fraternity continuance for a long time on her feet at work, repeating this from day to day, tends to injurious effects upon her body, and, as healthy mothers are essential to vigorous offspring, the physical well-being of women becomes an object of public interest and care in order to preserve the strength and vigor of the race.

As late as 1948, the Court upheld the right of the state to ban women from certain occupations. In *Goesaert v. Cleary,* decided that year, the justices declared valid a Michigan law that barred a woman from becoming a bartender unless she was a member of the bar owner's immediate family. In explaining the ruling, Justice Frankfurter wrote, "The fact that women may now have achieved the virtues that men have long claimed as their prerogatives and now indulge in vices that men have long practiced, does not preclude the States from drawing a sharp line between the sexes, certainly in such matters as the regulation of the liquor traffic." In a comparatively modern case, *Hoyt v. Florida* (1961), the justices upheld a Florida law that automatically exempted women from jury duty unless they asked to serve.

While the Court continued to articulate a traditional view of women, the growing strength of the women's movement in the 1960s prompted legislatures to act. Congress passed a number of federal statutes extending equal rights to women, among them the Equal Pay Act of 1963, which requires equal pay for equal work, and the 1964 Civil Rights Act, which forbids discrimination based on sex in the area of employment *(see Box 12-3)*. Many states passed similar laws to eliminate discriminatory conditions in the marketplace and in state legal codes. In addition to these legislative actions, in 1972 Congress proposed an amendment to the Constitution. Known as the Equal Rights Amendment, it declared, "Equality of rights under the law shall not be denied or abridged by the United States or by any State on account of sex." Although the amendment ultimately failed to attain support of the required number of states, the very fact that Congress proposed it (and later extended the deadline for ratification) provides some indication of changing views toward women.

Standard of Scrutiny

While continuing to press for the ERA, women's rights organizations also turned to the courts for redress of their grievances. Like the advocates for black Americans, many in the women's movement believed that the Due Process and Equal Protection Clauses held the same potential for ensuring women's rights, and they began organizing to assert their claims in court.

One of the first cases to reach the contemporary Supreme Court was *Reed v. Reed* (1971).[21] In this case, the justices considered the validity of an Idaho inheritance statute that used sex classifications, which ACLU attorneys, including Ruth Bader Ginsburg, challenged as a violation of the Equal Protection Clause of the Fourteenth Amendment *(see Box 12-4)*.

It was clear from the outset that the same requirements that had developed in race relations cases would apply here; that is, the statute's challenger would have to demonstrate both invidious discrimination and state action before a violation could be found. What was not so

21. For oral arguments in this case, navigate to: *oyez.nwu.edu.*

clear was the standard of scrutiny the justices would use. In the racial discrimination cases, the Court had declared strict scrutiny the appropriate standard. Racial minorities were considered a suspect class, and, therefore, classifications based on race were presumed to be unconstitutional. The state had a heavy burden of proof if it wished to show that a law based on race was the least restrictive means to achieve a compelling state interest. Much of the success enjoyed by civil rights groups was due to this favorable legal status. Ginsburg and other advocates of equal rights for women hoped the Court would adopt the same standard for sex discrimination claims. Did the justices go along?

Reed v. Reed

404 U.S. 71 (1971)
laws.findlaw.com/US/404/71.html
Vote: 7 (Blackmun, Brennan, Burger, Douglas, Marshall,
     Stewart, White)
     0
Opinion of the Court: Burger

Richard Reed was Sally and Cecil Reed's adopted son. He died March 29, 1967, in Ada County, Idaho, leaving no will. The Reeds, who had separated before Richard's death, became involved in a legal dispute over who should administer his estate. The estate was insignificant, consisting of a few personal items and a small savings account. The total value was less than $1,000. The probate court judge appointed Cecil Reed administrator of the estate, in accordance with Idaho law. Section 15-312 of the Idaho Code stipulated that when a person died intestate (without a will) an administrator would be appointed according to a list of priority relationships. First priority went to a surviving spouse, second priority to children, third to parents, and so forth. Section 15-314 of the statute stated that in the case of competing petitions from otherwise qualified individuals of the same priority relationship, "males must be preferred to females."

Sally Reed challenged the law as a violation of the Equal Protection Clause of the Fourteenth Amendment. The state district court agreed with her argument, but

BOX 12-4   RUTH BADER GINSBURG (1993–)

WHEN PRESIDENT Bill Clinton nominated Ruth Bader Ginsburg in 1993 to fill the vacancy left by retiring justice Byron White, the president was enjoying the first such opportunity for a Democrat in more than a quarter century. Ginsburg became the second woman to sit on the Court and the first Jewish justice since the resignation of Abe Fortas in 1969. She brought to the Court a sterling record as a law professor, advocate, and federal judge. She earned a reputation as the "Thurgood Marshall of sex discrimination law" for her pioneering work in that field.

GINSBURG WAS BORN in Brooklyn, New York, in 1933 to Nathan and Celia Bader. In 1950 she began her undergraduate studies at Cornell University, where she met her future husband, Martin Ginsburg. After her graduation in 1954, the Ginsburgs lived briefly in Oklahoma where Martin was stationed in the army and Ruth worked for the Social Security Administration. In 1956 they moved to Cambridge, Massachusetts, to attend Harvard Law School. After graduation Martin accepted a job in New York City and Ruth transferred to Columbia Law School to finish her legal training. She graduated from Columbia in 1959, tied for first in her class and having the distinction of serving on the law review staffs at both Harvard and Columbia.

In spite of her academic credentials, Ginsburg's attempts to obtain employment in a major law firm were unsuccessful. She later explained these rejections by noting: "To be a woman, a Jew and a mother to boot, that combination was a bit much." She secured a clerkship with federal district judge Edmund Palmieri, where she worked from 1959 to 1961. She then joined a Columbia University research project on civil law procedures in other countries and became an expert on the Swedish legal system. Ginsburg joined the law faculty at Rutgers University where she worked up the ranks from assistant professor to full professor. In 1972 she returned to Columbia University as professor of law and became the first woman to be awarded tenure at that school.

While on the faculty at Columbia, Ginsburg served as general counsel for the American Civil Liberties Union, heading the Women's Rights Project. In that capacity she was in the vanguard of sex discrimination cases of the 1970s. Her legal arguments before the Supreme Court had a profound impact on the development of sex discrimination law. Of the six cases she argued before the justices, she was successful in five. She participated in *Reed v. Reed* (1971), *Frontiero v. Richardson* (1973), *Kahn v. Shevin* (1974), *Weinberger v. Wiesenfeld* (1975), and *Craig v. Boren* (1976).

In 1980 President Jimmy Carter nominated Ginsburg for the Court of Appeals for the District of Columbia. She was later joined on that court by Clarence Thomas and Antonin Scalia who would precede her to the Supreme Court. In thirteen years as a federal appellate judge, Ginsburg developed a reputation as an intelligent, highly competent jurist with a moderate political ideology.

Ginsburg's nomination to the Supreme Court met with broad, bipartisan approval. She received the highest rating of the American Bar Association. On August 3, 1993, by a vote of 96–3 the Senate confirmed Ruth Bader Ginsburg as the Supreme Court's 107th justice.

SOURCE: "Ruth Ginsburg: Carving a Career Path Through a Male-Dominated Legal World," *Congressional Quarterly Weekly Report,* July 17, 1993, 1876–7.

the Idaho Supreme Court reversed. With assistance of Ginsburg and other ACLU lawyers, Sally Reed took her case to the U.S. Supreme Court. There, her attorneys asked the justices to adopt a strict scrutiny approach to sex discrimination cases, but also suggested that the law was unconstitutional even under a less rigorous standard.

MR. CHIEF JUSTICE BURGER delivered the opinion of the Court.

Having examined the record and considered the briefs and oral arguments of the parties, we have concluded that the arbitrary preference established in favor of males by §15-314 of the Idaho Code cannot stand in the face of the Fourteenth Amendment's command that no State deny the equal protection of the laws to any person within its jurisdiction.

Idaho does not, of course, deny letters of administration to women altogether. Indeed, under §15-312, a woman whose spouse dies intestate has a preference over a son, father, brother, or any other male relative of the decedent. Moreover, we can judicially notice that in this country, presumably due to the greater longevity of women, a large proportion of estates, both intestate and under wills of decedents, are administered by surviving widows.

Section 15-314 is restricted in its operation to those situations where competing applications for letters of administration have been filed by both male and female members of the same entitlement class established by §15-312. In such situations, §15-314 provides that different treatment be accorded to the applicants on the basis of their sex; it thus establishes a classification subject to scrutiny under the Equal Protection Clause.

In applying that clause, this Court has consistently recognized that the Fourteenth Amendment does not deny to States the power to treat different classes of persons in different ways. The Equal Protection Clause of that amendment does, however, deny to States the power to legislate that different treatment be accorded to persons placed by a statute into different classes on the basis of criteria wholly unrelated to the objective of that statute. A classification "must be reasonable, not arbitrary, and must rest upon some ground of difference having a fair and substantial relation to the object of the legislation, so that all persons similarly circumstanced shall be treated alike." The question

presented by this case, then, is whether a difference in the sex of competing applicants for letters of administration bears a rational relationship to a state objective that is sought to be advanced by the operation of §§15-312 and 15-314.

In upholding the latter section, the Idaho Supreme Court concluded that its objective was to eliminate one area of controversy when two or more persons, equally entitled under §15-312, seek letters of administration and thereby present the probate court "with the issue of which one should be named." The court also concluded that where such persons are not of the same sex, the elimination of females from consideration "is neither an illogical nor arbitrary method devised by the legislature to resolve an issue that would otherwise require a hearing as to the relative merits . . . of the two or more petitioning relatives. . . ."

Clearly the objective of reducing the workload on probate courts by eliminating one class of contests is not without some legitimacy. The crucial question, however, is whether §15-314 advances that objective in a manner consistent with the command of the Equal Protection Clause. We hold that it does not. To give a mandatory preference to members of either sex over members of the other, merely to accomplish the elimination of hearings on the merits, is to make the very kind of arbitrary legislative choice forbidden by the Equal Protection Clause of the Fourteenth Amendment; and whatever may be said as to the positive values of avoiding intrafamily controversy, the choice in this context may not lawfully be mandated solely on the basis of sex.

We note finally that if §15-314 is viewed merely as a modifying appendage to §15-312 and aimed at the same objective, its constitutionality is not thereby saved. The objective of §15-312 clearly is to establish degrees of entitlement of various classes of persons in accordance with their varying degrees and kinds of relationship to the intestate. Regardless of their sex, persons within any one of the enumerated classes of that section are similarly situated with respect to that objective. By providing dissimilar treatment for men and women who are thus similarly situated, the challenged section violates the Equal Protection Clause. The judgment of the Idaho Supreme Court is reversed and the case remanded for further proceedings not inconsistent with this opinion.

Reversed and remanded.

The Court's unanimous decision in *Reed* applied two important principles to sex discrimination. First, the Court refused to accept Idaho's defense of its statute. The state had contended that it was inefficient to hold full court hearings on the relative merits of competing candidates to administer estates, especially small estates. Imposing arbitrary criteria saved court time and avoided intrafamily squabbles. The Supreme Court held that administrative convenience is no justification for violating the Constitution. Second, defenders of the Idaho law argued that the arbitrary favoring of males over females made sense because, in most cases, the male will have had more education and experience in financial matters than the competing female. In rejecting this argument, the justices said that laws containing overbroad, sex-based assumptions violate the Equal Protection Clause.

The *Reed* case also signaled that the justices were receptive to sex discrimination claims and would not hesitate to strike down state laws that imposed arbitrary sex classifications. While this was certainly good news for women's rights advocates, the standard used in the case was not. Chief Justice Burger invoked the rational basis test (rather than strict scrutiny), holding that laws based on gender classifications must be reasonable and have a rational relationship to a state objective. The Idaho law was sufficiently arbitrary to fail the rational basis test, but other laws and policies might well survive it.

Two years later, the Court heard another sex discrimination case, *Frontiero v. Richardson*, in which Ginsburg and her ACLU colleagues, in an amicus curiae brief, attempted to convince the Court to adopt the strict scrutiny test.[22] The case provided the first opportunity for two newly appointed justices, Powell and Rehnquist, to rule on a sex discrimination case. Note how the justices divide on which test is appropriate for sex discrimination cases. Also, keep in mind that, because this case involves a challenge to a U.S. military regulation, the governing constitutional provision is the Due Process Clause of the Fifth Amendment.

22. For oral arguments in this case, navigate to: *oyez.nwu.edu.*

Frontiero v. Richardson

411 U.S. 677 (1973)
laws.findlaw.com/US/411/677.html
Vote: 8 (Blackmun, Brennan, Burger, Douglas, Marshall,
      Powell, Stewart, White)
   1 (Rehnquist)
Opinion announcing the judgment of the Court: Brennan
Concurring opinion: Powell
Statement concurring in the judgment: Stewart

Sharron Frontiero was a lieutenant in the U.S. Air Force, and her husband, Joseph Frontiero, was a full-time student at Huntingdon College in Montgomery, Alabama. Sharron applied for certain dependent benefits for her husband, including medical and housing allowances. These benefits were part of the package the military offered to be competitive with private employers. To receive the benefits for her spouse, Sharron had to prove that Joseph was financially dependent upon her, which meant that she provided at least half of her husband's support.

According to the facts agreed to by the parties, Joseph's expenses amounted to $354 per month. He received $205 (58 percent of his monthly expenses) from his own veterans' benefits. Consequently, Joseph was not considered financially dependent on his wife, and the benefits were denied. Sharron Frontiero objected to this treatment because male officers did not have to prove that their wives were financially dependent on them; such dependence was presumed.

Supported by Ginsburg's amicus arguments for the ACLU, Frontiero challenged the regulations as a violation of the Due Process Clause on two grounds. First, females were required to provide evidence that males were not. Second, as a consequence, male officers could receive dependent benefits for their wives even if their spouses were not financially dependent, and female officers could not.

MR. JUSTICE BRENNAN announced the judgment of the Court. . . .

At the outset, appellants contend that classifications based upon sex, like classifications based upon race, alienage, and national origin, are inherently suspect and must therefore be subjected to close judicial scrutiny. We agree and, indeed, find at least implicit support for such an approach in our unanimous decision only last Term in *Reed v. Reed* (1971).

In *Reed*, the Court considered the constitutionality of an Idaho statute providing that, when two individuals are otherwise equally entitled to appointment as administrator of an estate, the male applicant must be preferred to the female. . . .

The Court noted that the Idaho statute "provides that different treatment be accorded to the applicants on the basis of their sex; it thus establishes a classification subject to scrutiny under the Equal Protection Clause." Under "traditional" equal protection analysis, a legislative classification must be sustained unless it is "patently arbitrary" and bears no rational relationship to a legitimate governmental interest.

In an effort to meet this standard, appellee contended that the statutory scheme was a reasonable measure designed to reduce the workload on probate courts by eliminating one class of contests. Moreover, appellee argued that the mandatory preference for male applicants was in itself reasonable since "men [are] as a rule more conversant with business affairs than . . . women." Indeed, appellee maintained that "it is a matter of common knowledge, that women still are not engaged in politics, the professions, business or industry to the extent that men are." And the Idaho Supreme Court, in upholding the constitutionality of this statute, suggested that the Idaho Legislature might reasonably have "concluded that in general men are better qualified to act as an administrator than are women."

Despite these contentions, however, the Court held the statutory preference for male applicants unconstitutional. In reaching this result, the Court implicitly rejected appellee's apparently rational explanation of the statutory scheme, and concluded that, by ignoring the individual qualifications of particular applications, the challenged statute provided "dissimilar treatment for men and women who are . . . similarly situated." The Court therefore held that, even though the State's interest in achieving administrative efficiency "is not without some legitimacy," "[t]o give a mandatory preference to members of either sex over members of the other, merely to accomplish the elimination of hearings on the merits, is to make the very kind of arbi-

trary legislative choice forbidden by the Constitution. . . ." This departure from "traditional" rational-basis analysis with respect to sex-based classifications is clearly justified.

There can be no doubt that our Nation has had a long and unfortunate history of sex discrimination. Traditionally, such discrimination was rationalized by an attitude of "romantic paternalism" which, in practical effect, put women, not on a pedestal, but in a cage. . . . Our statute books gradually became laden with gross, stereotyped distinctions between the sexes and, indeed, throughout much of the 19th century the position of women in our society was, in many respects, comparable to that of blacks under the pre–Civil War slave codes. Neither slaves nor women could hold office, serve on juries, or bring suit in their own names, and married women traditionally were denied the legal capacity to hold or convey property or to serve as legal guardians of their own children. And although blacks were guaranteed the right to vote in 1870, women were denied even that right—which is itself "preservative of other basic civil and political rights"—until adoption of the Nineteenth Amendment half a century later.

It is true, of course, that the position of women in America has improved markedly in recent decades. Nevertheless, it can hardly be doubted that, in part because of the high visibility of the sex characteristic, women still face pervasive, although at times more subtle, discrimination in our educational institutions, in the job market and, perhaps most conspicuously, in the political arena.

Moreover, since sex, like race and national origin, is an immutable characteristic determined solely by the accident of birth, the imposition of special disabilities upon the members of a particular sex because of their sex would seem to violate "the basic concept of our system that legal burdens should bear some relationship to individual responsibility. . . ." And what differentiates sex from such nonsuspect statuses as intelligence or physical disability, and aligns it with the recognized suspect criteria, is that the sex characteristic frequently bears no relation to ability to perform or contribute to society. As a result, statutory distinctions between the sexes often have the effect of invidiously relegating the entire class of females to inferior legal status without regard to the actual capabilities of its individual members.

We might also note that, over the past decade, Congress has itself manifested an increasing sensitivity to sex-based classifications. In Title VII of the Civil Rights Act of 1964, for example, Congress expressly declared that no employer, labor union, or other organization subject to the provisions of the Act shall discriminate against any individual on the basis of "race, color, religion, sex, or national origin." Similarly, the Equal Pay Act of 1963 provides that no employer covered by the Act "shall discriminate . . . between employees on the basis of sex." And §1 of the Equal Rights Amendment, passed by Congress on March 22, 1972, and submitted to the legislatures of the States for ratification, declares that "[e]quality of rights under the law shall not be denied or abridged by the United States or by any State on account of sex." Thus, Congress itself has concluded that classifications based upon sex are inherently invidious, and this conclusion of a coequal branch of Government is not without significance to the question presently under consideration.

With these considerations in mind, we can only conclude that classifications based upon sex, like classifications based upon race, alienage, or national origin, are inherently suspect, and must therefore be subjected to strict judicial scrutiny. Applying the analysis mandated by that stricter standard of review, it is clear that the statutory scheme now before us is constitutionally invalid.

The sole basis of the classification established in the challenged statutes is the sex of the individuals involved. Thus . . . a female member of the uniformed services seeking to obtain housing and medical benefits for her spouse must prove his dependency in fact, whereas no such burden is imposed upon male members. In addition, the statutes operate so as to deny benefits to a female member, such as appellant Sharron Frontiero, who provides less than one-half of her spouse's support, while at the same time granting such benefits to a male member who likewise provides less than one-half of his spouse's support. Thus, to this extent at least, it may fairly be said that these statutes command "dissimilar treatment for men and women who are . . . similarly situated."

Moreover, the Government concedes that the differential treatment accorded men and women under these statutes serves no purpose other than mere "administrative convenience." In essence, the Government maintains that, as an empirical matter, wives in our society frequently are dependent upon their husbands, while husbands rarely are dependent upon their wives. Thus, the Government argues that Congress might reasonably have concluded that it would be both cheaper and easier simply conclusively to presume that wives of male members are financially dependent upon their husbands, while burdening female members with the task of establishing dependency in fact.

The Government offers no concrete evidence, however, tending to support its view that such differential treatment in fact saves the Government any money. In order to satisfy the demands of strict judicial scrutiny, the Government must demonstrate, for example, that it is actually cheaper to grant increased benefits with respect to *all* male members, than it is to determine which male members are in fact entitled to such benefits and to grant increased benefits only to those members whose wives actually meet the dependency requirement. Here, however, there is substantial evidence that, if put to the test, many of the wives of male members would fail to qualify for benefits. And in light of the fact that the dependency determination with respect to the husbands of female members is presently made solely on the basis of affidavits rather than through the more costly hearing process, the Government's explanation of the statutory scheme is, to say the least, questionable.

In any case, our prior decisions make clear that, although efficacious administration of governmental programs is not without some importance, "the Constitution recognizes higher values than speed and efficiency." And when we enter the realm of "strict judicial scrutiny," there can be no doubt that "administrative convenience" is not a shibboleth, the mere recitation of which dictates constitutionality. On the contrary, any statutory scheme which draws a sharp line between the sexes, *solely* for the purpose of achieving administrative convenience, necessarily commands "dissimilar treatment for men and women who are . . . similarly situated," and therefore involves the "very kind of arbitrary legislative choice forbidden by the [Constitution]. . . ." We therefore conclude that, by according differential treatment to male and female members of the uniformed services for the sole purpose of achieving administrative convenience, the challenged statutes violate the Due Process Clause of the Fifth Amendment insofar as they require a female member to prove the dependency of her husband.

Reversed.

MR. JUSTICE POWELL, with whom THE CHIEF JUSTICE and MR. JUSTICE BLACKMUN join, concurring in the judgment.

I agree that the challenged statutes constitute an unconstitutional discrimination against servicewomen in violation of the Due Process Clause of the Fifth Amendment, but I cannot join the opinion of MR. JUSTICE BRENNAN, which would hold that all classifications based upon sex, "like classifications based upon race, alienage, and national origin, are inherently suspect and must therefore be subjected to close judicial scrutiny." It is unnecessary for the Court in this case to characterize sex as a suspect classification, with all of the far-reaching implications of such a holding. *Reed v. Reed* (1971), which abundantly supports our decision today, did not add sex to the narrowly limited group of classifications which are inherently suspect. In my view, we can and should decide this case on the authority of *Reed* and reserve for the future any expansion of its rationale.

There is another, and I find compelling, reason for deferring a general categorizing of sex classifications as invoking the strictest test of judicial scrutiny. The Equal Rights Amendment, which if adopted will resolve the substance of this precise question, has been approved by the Congress and submitted for ratification by the States. If this Amendment is duly adopted, it will represent the will of the people accomplished in the manner prescribed by the Constitution. By acting prematurely and unnecessarily, as I view it, the Court has assumed a decisional responsibility at the very time when state legislatures, functioning within the traditional democratic process, are debating the proposed Amendment. It seems to me that this reaching out to preempt by judicial action a major political decision which is currently in process of resolution does not reflect appropriate respect for duly prescribed legislative processes.

There are times when this Court, under our system, cannot avoid a constitutional decision on issues which normally should be resolved by the elected representatives of the people. But democratic institutions are weakened, and confidence in the restraint of the Court is impaired, when we appear unnecessarily to decide sensitive issues of broad social and political importance at the very time they are under consideration within the prescribed constitutional processes.

The *Frontiero* ruling was a victory for the supporters of equality of the sexes. The Court again condemned the imposition of sex classifications for administrative convenience, as well as the practice of incorporating overly broad, sex-based assumptions into the law. These two principles now seemed solidly woven into the fabric of constitutional law. But the result in *Frontiero* disappointed those who wanted the strict scrutiny test to be applied to such cases. Justice Brennan's opinion was a strong defense of such a position, but only three of his colleagues supported him. Blackmun, Burger, and Powell explicitly opposed the application of the strict scrutiny test, although they found the military regulation unconstitutional even under the rational basis test. To their number we can add Rehnquist, who dissented from the Court's judgment. With four justices in favor of the traditional rational basis test, and four supporting elevation to the strict scrutiny test, Justice Potter Stewart held the deciding vote. But he failed to make his preferences known. In one line, Stewart indicated that he found the Air Force regulation unconstitutional without saying what standard he applied.

The question of an appropriate standard for sex discrimination cases was finally answered in *Craig v. Boren* (1976). On what standard did the Court settle? Why did Rehnquist, in dissent, reject it?

Craig v. Boren

429 U.S. 190 (1976)
laws.findlaw.com/US/429/190.html
Vote: 7 (Blackmun, Brennan, Marshall, Powell, Stevens, Stewart, White)
    2 (Burger, Rehnquist)
Opinion of the Court: Brennan
Concurring opinions: Powell, Stevens
Opinion concurring in judgment: Stewart
Opinion concurring in part: Blackmun
Dissenting opinions: Burger, Rehnquist

In 1972 Oklahoma passed a statute setting the age of legal majority for both males and females at eighteen. Before then, females reached legal age at eighteen and males at twenty-one.[23] The equalization statute, however, contained one exception. Males could not purchase beer, even with the low 3.2 percent alcohol level, until they reached twenty-one; females could buy beer at eighteen. The state differentiated between the sexes in response to statistical evidence indicating a much greater tendency for males ages eighteen to twenty-one to be involved in alcohol-related traffic accidents, including fatalities.

Viewing the Oklahoma law as a form of sex discrimination Curtis Craig, a twenty-year-old male who wanted to buy beer, and Carolyn Whitener, a licensed vendor who wanted to sell it, brought suit in a federal trial court. Among the arguments they made was that laws discriminating on the basis of sex should be, at least according to the U.S. Supreme Court, subject to the strict scrutiny test. Under this test, they argued, the justices should strike down the Oklahoma law because a compelling governmental interest was not achieved by establishing different drinking ages for men and women.

In response, the state argued that the U.S. Supreme Court had never explicitly applied the strict scrutiny test to laws discriminating on the basis of sex. Rather, the justices had ruled that such laws ought to be subject to the rational basis standard. Surely, Oklahoma contended, its law met this test because statistical studies indicated that men "drive more, drink more, and commit more alcohol-related offenses."

Acknowledging that the U.S. Supreme Court decisions were murky, the trial court held for the state. The court felt that the weight of the case law supported the state's reliance on the lower-level standard and that the state had met its obligation of establishing a "rational basis" for the law: given the statistical evidence, Oklahoma's goal of reducing drunk-driving incidents seemed legitimate.

Refusing to give up the battle, Craig and Whitener appealed to the U.S. Supreme Court. Although both they and the state continued to press the same claims that they had at trial (with Craig and Whitener arguing for strict scrutiny and the state advocating rational basis), ACLU attorneys, including Ginsburg, advanced a some-

what different approach. Entering the case as an amicus curiae on behalf of Craig, they argued that the Oklahoma law "could not survive review whatever the appropriate test," whether it was strict scrutiny or rational basis or "something in between." This was an interesting argument in two regards: it suggested that the Court could apply the lower rational basis standard and still hold for Craig or the Court might consider developing a standard "in between" strict scrutiny and rational basis.

MR. JUSTICE BRENNAN delivered the opinion of the Court.

Analysis may appropriately begin with the reminder that *Reed* [*v. Reed*, 1971] emphasized that statutory classifications that distinguish between males and females are "subject to scrutiny under the Equal Protection Clause." To withstand constitutional challenge, previous cases establish that classifications by gender must serve important governmental objectives and must be substantially related to achievement of those objectives. Thus, in *Reed*, the objectives of "reducing the workload on probate courts" and "avoiding intrafamily controversy" were deemed of insufficient importance to sustain use of an overt gender criterion in the appointment of administrators of intestate decedents' estates. Decisions following *Reed* similarly have rejected administrative ease and convenience as sufficiently important objectives to justify gender-based classifications. . . .

Reed v. Reed has also provided the underpinning for decisions that have invalidated statutes employing gender as an inaccurate proxy for other, more germane bases of classification. Hence, "archaic and overbroad" generalizations could not justify use of a gender line in determining eligibility for certain governmental entitlements. Similarly, increasingly outdated misconceptions concerning the role of females in the home rather than in the "marketplace and world of ideas" were rejected as loose-fitting characterizations incapable of supporting state statutory schemes that were premised upon their accuracy. In light of the weak congruence between gender and the characteristic or trait that gender purported to represent, it was necessary that the legislatures choose either to realign their substantive laws in a gender-neutral fashion, or to adopt procedures for identifying those instances where the sex-centered generalization actually comported with fact.

In this case, too, *"Reed*, we feel, is controlling. . . ." We

---

23. For more on this case, see Lee Epstein and Jack Knight, *The Choices Justices Make* (Washington, D.C.: CQ Press, 1998).

turn then to the question whether, under *Reed*, the difference between males and females with respect to the purchase of 3.2% beer warrants the differential in age drawn by the Oklahoma statute. We conclude that it does not.

The District Court recognized that *Reed v. Reed* was controlling. In applying the teachings of that case, the court found the requisite important governmental objective in the traffic-safety goal proffered by the Oklahoma Attorney General. It then concluded that the statistics introduced by the appellees established that the gender-based distinction was substantially related to achievement of that goal.

. . . Clearly, the protection of public health and safety represents an important function of state and local governments. However, appellees' statistics in our view cannot support the conclusion that the gender-based distinction closely serves to achieve that objective and therefore the distinction cannot under *Reed* withstand equal protection challenge.

The appellees introduced a variety of statistical surveys. First, an analysis of arrest statistics for 1973 demonstrated that 18–20-year-old male arrests for "driving under the influence" and "drunkenness" substantially exceeded female arrests for that same age period. Similarly, youths aged 17–21 were found to be overrepresented among those killed or injured in traffic accidents, with males again numerically exceeding females in this regard. Third, a random roadside survey in Oklahoma City revealed that young males were more inclined to drive and drink beer than were their female counterparts. Fourth, Federal Bureau of Investigation nationwide statistics exhibited a notable increase in arrests for "driving under the influence." Finally, statistical evidence gathered in other jurisdictions, particularly Minnesota and Michigan, was offered to corroborate Oklahoma's experience by indicating the pervasiveness of youthful participation in motor vehicle accidents following the imbibing of alcohol. . . .

Even were this statistical evidence accepted as accurate, it nevertheless offers only a weak answer to the equal protection question presented here. The most focused and relevant of the statistical surveys, arrests of 18–20-year-olds for alcohol-related driving offenses, exemplifies the ultimate unpersuasiveness of this evidentiary record. Viewed in terms of the correlation between sex and the actual activity that Oklahoma seeks to regulate—driving while under the influence of alcohol—the statistics broadly establish that .18% of females and 2% of males in that age group were ar-

rested for that offense. While such a disparity is not trivial in a statistical sense, it hardly can form the basis for employment of a gender line as a classifying device. Certainly if maleness is to serve as a proxy for drinking and driving, a correlation of 2% must be considered an unduly tenuous "fit." Indeed, prior cases have consistently rejected the use of sex as a decisionmaking factor even though the statutes in question certainly rested on far more predictive empirical relationships than this.

Moreover, the statistics exhibit a variety of other shortcomings that seriously impugn their value to equal protection analysis. Setting aside the obvious methodological problems, the surveys do not adequately justify the salient features of Oklahoma's gender-based traffic-safety law. None purports to measure the use and dangerousness of 3.2% beer as opposed to alcohol generally, a detail that is of particular importance since, in light of its low alcohol level, Oklahoma apparently considers the 3.2% beverage to be "nonintoxicating." Moreover, many of the studies, while graphically documenting the unfortunate increase in driving while under the influence of alcohol, make no effort to relate their findings to age-sex differentials as involved here. Indeed, the only survey that explicitly centered its attention upon young drivers and their use of beer—albeit apparently not of the diluted 3.2% variety—reached results that hardly can be viewed as impressive in justifying either a gender or age classification.

There is no reason to belabor this line of analysis. It is unrealistic to expect either members of the judiciary or state officials to be well versed in the rigors of experimental or statistical technique. But this merely illustrates that proving broad sociological propositions by statistics is a dubious business, and one that inevitably is in tension with the normative philosophy that underlies the Equal Protection Clause. Suffice to say that the showing offered by the appellees does not satisfy us that sex represents a legitimate, accurate proxy for the regulation of drinking and driving. In fact, when it is further recognized that Oklahoma's statute prohibits only the selling of 3.2% beer to young males and not their drinking the beverage once acquired (even after purchase by their 18–20-year-old female companions), the relationship between gender and traffic safety becomes far too tenuous to satisfy *Reed*'s requirement that the gender-based difference be substantially related to achievement of the statutory objective.

We hold, therefore, that under *Reed*, Oklahoma's 3.2% beer statute invidiously discriminates against males 18–20 years of age.

Reversed.

MR. JUSTICE REHNQUIST, dissenting.

The Court's disposition of this case is objectionable on two grounds. First is its conclusion that men challenging a gender-based statute which treats them less favorably than women may invoke a more stringent standard of judicial review than pertains to most other types of classifications. Second is the Court's enunciation of this standard, without citation to any source, as being that "classification by gender must serve *important* governmental objectives and must be *substantially* related to achievement of those objectives." (Emphasis added.) The only redeeming feature of the Court's opinion, to my mind, is that it apparently signals a retreat by those who joined the plurality opinion in *Frontiero v. Richardson* (1973) from their view that sex is a "suspect" classification for purposes of equal protection analysis. I think the Oklahoma statute challenged here need pass only the "rational basis" equal protection analysis expounded in cases such as *McGowan v. Maryland* (1961) and *Williamson v. Lee Optical Co.* (1955), and I believe that it is constitutional under that analysis.

In *Frontiero v. Richardson*, the opinion for the plurality sets forth the reasons of four Justices for concluding that sex should be regarded as a suspect classification for purposes of equal protection analysis. These reasons center on our Nation's "long and unfortunate history of sex discrimination," which has been reflected in a whole range of restrictions on the legal rights of women, not the least of which have concerned the ownership of property and participation in the electoral process. Noting that the pervasive and persistent nature of the discrimination experienced by women is in part the result of their ready identifiability, the plurality rested its invocation of strict scrutiny largely upon the fact that "statutory distinctions between the sexes often have the effect of invidiously relegating the entire class of females to inferior legal status without regard to the actual capabilities of its individual members."

Subsequent to *Frontiero*, the Court has declined to hold that sex is a suspect class, and no such holding is imported by the Court's resolution of this case. However, the Court's application here of an elevated or "intermediate" level scrutiny, like that invoked in cases dealing with discrimination against females, raises the question of why the statute here should be treated any differently from countless legislative classifications unrelated to sex which have been upheld under a minimum rationality standard.

Most obviously unavailable to support any kind of special scrutiny in this case, is a history or pattern of past discrimination, such as was relied on by the plurality in *Frontiero* to support its invocation of strict scrutiny. There is no suggestion in the Court's opinion that males in this age group are in any way peculiarly disadvantaged, subject to systematic discriminatory treatment, or otherwise in need of special solicitude from the courts.

The Court does not discuss the nature of the right involved, and there is no reason to believe that it sees the purchase of 3.2% beer as implicating any important interest, let alone one that is "fundamental" in the constitutional sense of invoking strict scrutiny. Indeed, the Court's accurate observation that the statute affects the selling but not the drinking of 3.2% beer further emphasizes the limited effect that it has on even those persons in the age group involved. There is, in sum, nothing about the statutory classification involved here to suggest that it affects an interest, or works against a group, which can claim under the Equal Protection Clause that it is entitled to special judicial protection.

It is true that a number of our opinions contain broadly phrased dicta implying that the same test should be applied to all classifications based on sex, whether affecting females or males. However, before today, no decision of this Court has applied an elevated level of scrutiny to invalidate a statutory discrimination harmful to males, except where the statute impaired an important personal interest protected by the Constitution. There being no such interest here, and there being no plausible argument that this is a discrimination against females, the Court's reliance on our previous sex-discrimination cases is ill-founded. It treats gender classification as a talisman which—without regard to the rights involved or the persons affected—calls into effect a heavier burden of judicial review.

The Court's conclusion that a law which treats males less favorably than females "must serve important governmental objectives and must be substantially related to achievement of those objectives" apparently comes out of thin air. The Equal Protection Clause contains no such language, and none of our previous cases adopt that standard. I would think we have had enough difficulty with the two standards of review which our cases have recognized—the norm of "rational basis," and the "compelling state interest" required where a "suspect classification" is involved—so as to counsel weightily against the insertion of still another "standard" between those two. How is this Court to divine what objectives are important? How is it to determine whether a particular law is "substantially" related to the achievement of such objective, rather than related in some other way to its achievement? Both of the phrases used are so diaphanous and elastic as to invite subjective judicial preferences or prejudices relating to particular types of legislation, masquerading as judgments whether such legislation is directed at "important" objectives or, whether the relationship to those objectives is "substantial" enough.

I would have thought that if this Court were to leave anything to decision by the popularly elected branches of the Government, where no constitutional claim other than that of equal protection is invoked, it would be the decision as to what governmental objectives to be achieved by law are "important," and which are not. As for the second part of the Court's new test, the Judicial Branch is probably in no worse position than the Legislative or Executive Branches to determine if there is any rational relationship between a classification and the purpose which it might be thought to serve. But the introduction of the adverb "substantially" requires courts to make subjective judgments as to operational effects, for which neither their expertise nor their access to data fits them. And even if we manage to avoid both confusion and the mirroring of our own preferences in the development of this new doctrine, the thousands of judges in other courts who must interpret the Equal Protection Clause may not be so fortunate.

The heightened scrutiny test—requiring that laws that classify on the basis of sex be substantially related to an important government objective—was adopted by a narrow margin. Although six justices joined the opinion, Powell's and Stevens's concurring views indicated that their agreement with Brennan's new standard was qualified *(see Table 12-2)*. Nevertheless, *Craig v. Boren* established the elevated level of scrutiny standard that has been used in sex discrimination cases ever since. The bat-

TABLE 12-2 Court Division on Equal Protection Standards in Sex Discrimination Cases

Frontiero v. Richardson (1973)

Rational basis test:	Blackmun
	Burger
	Powell
	Rehnquist
Strict scrutiny test:	Brennan
	Douglas
	Marshall
	White
Undeclared:	Stewart

Craig v. Boren (1976)

Heightened scrutiny test:	Blackmun
	Brennan
	Marshall
	Powell (with reservations)
	Stevens (with qualifications)
	White
Rational basis test:	Burger
	Rehnquist
Undeclared:	Stewart

tle between strict scrutiny advocates and rational basis proponents thus ended with neither side able to claim victory. The strict scrutiny justices were forced to moderate their position just enough to capture sufficient votes to adopt an intermediate level test.

Heightened scrutiny was a compromise solution that pleased neither those who preferred strict scrutiny nor those who favored the rational basis approach. Under these circumstances, the compromise may be temporary, lasting only as long as neither side has sufficient votes to adopt its preferences. In the sexual harassment case of *Harris v. Forklift Systems, Inc.* (1993) Justice Ginsburg signaled that the battle over appropriate standards for sex discrimination cases may be fought again.[24] Consider the following statement contained in a footnote of Ginsburg's concurring opinion:

24. In *United States v. Virginia* (1996) *(see pages 683–689)* Ginsburg also attempted to interpret the intermediate scrutiny standard the way she suggests in *Harris:* to require governments to provide an "exceedingly persuasive justification" for gender classification.

Indeed, even under the Court's equal protection jurisprudence, which requires "an exceedingly persuasive justification" for a gender-based classification, it remains an open question whether "classifications based on gender are inherently suspect."

Her assertion that gender classification standards remain an *open question* is a clear indication that at least for Ginsburg the issue is not yet settled. That she included this statement in her first published opinion as a Supreme Court justice may well reflect the continuing importance of this issue to her—as a prominent sex discrimination litigator prior to her appointment as a federal judge, Justice Ginsburg had worked on most of the major cases of the 1970s.

The Court's Application of Heightened Scrutiny

Ginsburg may continue to press for the adoption of a strict scrutiny approach to sex discrimination cases, but at this point the majority of her colleagues seemed satisfied with the intermediate scrutiny standard. Under this approach, the Court sometimes voids sex-based classifications and occasionally upholds them. In the next two sections, we consider cases that show these different results. Are there common features of laws that the justices have voided or upheld? Or has the Court applied the midlevel standard in haphazard fashion?

Gender-Based Classifications the Court Has Voided. The sex discrimination cases we have examined so far— *Reed, Frontiero,* and *Craig*—are what some legal scholars refer to as "easy" cases.[25] The practices under review were based on old-fashioned, stereotypical generalizations about sex differences that typically assume that women are inferior. The law at issue in *Reed,* for example, was based on the outdated assumption that men were better than women in business matters. Such laws cannot withstand even a minimal level of review, much less the stricter standard articulated in *Craig.* In other words, the Court has made it clear that governments cannot base sex distinctions on out-dated presumptions about the "proper" role of women in American society.

Decisions in the area of sex-segregated education nice-

25. We adapt this discussion from Susan Gluck Mezey, *In Pursuit of Equality* (New York: St. Martin's, 1992), 20–27.

ly illustrate the point. The Court's first full-fledged ruling on the subject came in *Mississippi University for Women v. Hogan* (1982). This suit, filed by a male who was denied admission to a nursing program, challenged state-operated single-sex schools. Although the state expanded the choices and opportunities for females by creating a women's college, critics charged that the program was based on an outmoded notion that women need an environment protected from men to succeed academically.

Mississippi University for Women provided an opportunity for Justice O'Connor, the first woman appointed to the Supreme Court, to express her legal views on laws that classify according to sex. She started her majority opinion by reiterating the Court's approach to sex discrimination:

We begin our analysis aided by several firmly established principles. Because the challenged policy expressly discriminates among applicants on the basis of gender, it is subject to scrutiny under the Equal Protection Clause of the Fourteenth Amendment. *Reed v. Reed* (1971). That this statutory policy discriminates against males rather than against females does not exempt it from scrutiny or reduce the standard of review. Our decisions also establish that the party seeking to uphold a statute that classifies individuals on the basis of their gender must carry the burden of showing an "exceedingly persuasive justification" for the classification. The burden is met only by showing at least that the classification serves "important governmental objectives and that the discriminatory means employed" are "substantially related to the achievement of those objectives."

Although the test for determining the validity of a gender-based classification is straightforward, it must be applied free of fixed notions concerning the roles and abilities of males and females. Care must be taken in ascertaining whether the statutory objective itself reflects archaic and stereotypic notions. Thus, if the statutory objective is to exclude or "protect" members of one gender because they are presumed to suffer from an inherent handicap or to be innately inferior, the objective itself is illegitimate.

O'Connor then firmly asserted that the Mississippi program was repugnant to the Fourteenth Amendment because of its presumptions of the inferiority of women:

Rather than compensate for discriminatory barriers faced by women, MUW's policy of excluding males from admission to the School of Nursing tends to perpetuate the stereotyped view of nursing as an exclusively woman's job. By assuring that Mississippi allots more openings in its state-supported nursing schools to women than it does to men, MUW's admissions policy lends credibility to the old view that women, not men, should become nurses, and makes the assumption that nursing is a field for women a self-fulfilling prophecy. Thus, we conclude that, although the State recited a "benign, compensatory purpose," it failed to establish that the alleged objective is the actual purpose underlying the discriminatory classification.

The dissenting justices, through an opinion by Justice Powell, took issue with O'Connor's analysis. They suggested that the majority imposed an unwise uniformity and deprived women of educational choices and alternatives:

The Court's opinion bows deeply to conformity. Left without honor—indeed, held unconstitutional—is an element of diversity that has characterized much of American education and enriched much of American life. The Court in effect holds today that no State now may provide even a single institution of higher learning open only to women students. It gives no heed to the efforts of the State of Mississippi to provide abundant opportunities for young men and young women to attend co-educational institutions, and none to the preferences of the more than 40,000 young women who over the years have evidenced their approval of an all-women's college by choosing Mississippi University for Women (MUW) over seven coeducational universities within the State. The Court decides today that the Equal Protection Clause makes it unlawful for the State to provide women with a traditionally popular and respected choice of educational environment. It does so in a case instituted by one man, who represents no class, and whose primary concern is personal convenience.

Despite these words, the *Mississippi University for Women* decision *seemed* to settle the matter of government-operated single-sex schools—they violate the Constitution. By the time of the decision, most single-sex public colleges, including the U.S. military academies, had initiated coeducational admissions policies. However, state schools in Virginia (Virginia Military Institute) and South Carolina (The Citadel) resolutely resisted compliance with *MUW*. Both schools had long traditions of offering a military-style education to all-male student bodies. When female applicants sued the schools claiming a violation of the Constitution and federal law, the schools responded with a spirited legal defense of their traditions. They asserted that the military nature of their institutions distinguished them from other colleges and universities and that introducing coeducational instruction would require changes that would alter the nature of the schools. When the case involving VMI reached the Supreme Court, the Clinton Justice Department asked the Court to abandon the use of intermediate scrutiny and adopt the suspect class test as the appropriate standard for use in sex discrimination cases.[26]

United States v. Virginia

518 U.S. 515 (1996)
supct.law.cornell.edu/supct/html/94-1941.ZS.html
Vote: 7 (Breyer, Ginsburg, Kennedy, O'Connor, Rehnquist, Souter, Stevens)
1 (Scalia)
Opinion of the Court: Ginsburg
Concurring opinion: Rehnquist
Dissenting opinion: Scalia
Not participating: Thomas

The Virginia Military Institute (VMI), founded in 1839, was the only one among Virginia's fifteen public supported institutions of higher learning with a single-sex admissions policy. VMI's distinctive mission is to produce "citizen-soldiers," men prepared to take leadership positions in military and civilian life. VMI trains its 1,300 cadets by an "adversative" model of education that emphasizes physical rigor, mental stress, absolute equality of treatment, absence of privacy, minute regulation of behavior, and indoctrination in desirable values. The cadets live in spartan barracks where surveillance is constant and privacy is nonexistent. They are required to wear military uniforms, eat together in the mess hall, and participate in military drills. There is a hierarchical class system with freshmen, known as "rats," accorded the lowest status.

In 1990, in response to a letter of complaint from a female high school student, the United States sued the Commonwealth of Virginia and VMI, alleging that VMI's

26. For oral arguments in this case, navigate to: *oyez.nwu.edu.*

Women were admitted to Virginia Military Institute following the Supreme Court's decision in *United States v. Virginia* (1996). Mia Utz transferred to VMI in 1999 as an upperclassman. "I don't think the rats [freshmen] are thinking about the fact that I'm a woman," she remarked. "They are thinking that I'm an upperclassman and I'm getting in their faces."

men-only admissions policy was in violation of the Equal Protection Clause of the Fourteenth Amendment. The district court ruled in favor of the state, concluding that single-sex education yielded substantial benefits and that having a single-sex institution added diversity of opportunity to the range of educational options offered by the state. The court of appeals reversed, holding that the state could not justify offering a unique educational opportunity to men but not to women.

In response, the state created the Virginia Women's Institute for Leadership (VWIL) to operate as a parallel program for women. The VWIL was located on the campus of Mary Baldwin College, a private women's college a short distance from the VMI campus. This new state-supported program was designed to provide an education that would train female "citizen-soldiers" to take leadership positions in American society, but many acknowledged that the funding, facilities, and educational programs at VWIL were inferior to the resources at VMI.

Once the VWIL was established, the state returned to the district court for judicial approval of the continuation of the all-male VMI admissions policy. The district court supported the state's position, and the court of appeals generally affirmed by a divided vote. The United States and the state asked the Supreme Court to review various aspects of the case. The United States argued that

the VWIL was an insufficient remedy to compensate for VMI's violation of the Equal Protection Clause. The state countered that removing the single-sex nature of the VMI would destroy the institution. Justice Thomas, whose son, Jamal, was attending VMI when the Court heard this appeal, did not participate in the decision.

JUSTICE GINSBURG delivered the opinion of the Court.

Virginia's public institutions of higher learning include an incomparable military college, Virginia Military Institute (VMI). The United States maintains that the Constitution's equal protection guarantee precludes Virginia from reserving exclusively to men the unique educational opportunities VMI affords. We agree. . . .

The cross-petitions in this case present two ultimate issues. First, does Virginia's exclusion of women from the educational opportunities provided by VMI—extraordinary opportunities for military training and civilian leadership development—deny to women "capable of all of the individual activities required of VMI cadets" the equal protection of the laws guaranteed by the Fourteenth Amendment? Second, if VMI's "unique" situation—as Virginia's sole single-sex public institution of higher education—offends the Constitution's equal protection principle, what is the remedial requirement?

We note, once again, the core instruction of this Court's

pathmarking decisions in *J. E. B. v. Alabama ex rel. T. B.* (1994), and *Mississippi Univ. for Women* [*v. Hogan* (1982)]: Parties who seek to defend gender-based government action must demonstrate an "exceedingly persuasive justification" for that action.

Today's skeptical scrutiny of official action denying rights or opportunities based on sex responds to volumes of history. As a plurality of this Court acknowledged a generation ago, "our Nation has had a long and unfortunate history of sex discrimination." *Frontiero v. Richardson* (1973). . . .

In 1971, for the first time in our Nation's history, this Court ruled in favor of a woman who complained that her State had denied her the equal protection of its laws. *Reed v. Reed.* Since *Reed*, the Court has repeatedly recognized that neither federal nor state government acts compatibly with the equal protection principle when a law or official policy denies to women, simply because they are women, full citizenship stature—equal opportunity to aspire, achieve, participate in and contribute to society based on their individual talents and capacities.

Without equating gender classifications, for all purposes, to classifications based on race or national origin, the Court, in post-*Reed* decisions, has carefully inspected official action that closes a door or denies opportunity to women (or to men). To summarize the Court's current directions for cases of official classification based on gender: Focusing on the differential treatment or denial of opportunity for which relief is sought, the reviewing court must determine whether the proffered justification is "exceedingly persuasive." The burden of justification is demanding and it rests entirely on the State. See *Mississippi Univ. for Women.* The State must show "at least that the [challenged] classification serves 'important governmental objectives and that the discriminatory means employed' are 'substantially related to the achievement of those objectives.'" The justification must be genuine, not hypothesized or invented *post hoc* in response to litigation. And it must not rely on overbroad generalizations about the different talents, capacities, or preferences of males and females.

The heightened review standard our precedent establishes does not make sex a proscribed classification. Supposed "inherent differences" are no longer accepted as a ground for race or national origin classifications. See *Loving v. Virginia* (1967). Physical differences between men and women, however, are enduring: "[T]he two sexes are not fungible; a community made up exclusively of one [sex] is different from a community composed of both." *Ballard v. United States* (1946).

"Inherent differences" between men and women, we have come to appreciate, remain cause for celebration, but not for denigration of the members of either sex or for artificial constraints on an individual's opportunity. . . . [S]uch classifications may not be used, as they once were, to create or perpetuate the legal, social, and economic inferiority of women.

Measuring the record in this case against the review standard just described, we conclude that Virginia has shown no "exceedingly persuasive justification" for excluding all women from the citizen-soldier training afforded by VMI. We therefore affirm the Fourth Circuit's initial judgment, which held that Virginia had violated the Fourteenth Amendment's Equal Protection Clause. Because the remedy proffered by Virginia—the Mary Baldwin VWIL program—does not cure the constitutional violation, *i.e.*, it does not provide equal opportunity, we reverse the Fourth Circuit's final judgment in this case.

The Fourth Circuit initially held that Virginia had advanced no state policy by which it could justify, under equal protection principles, its determination "to afford VMI's unique type of program to men and not to women." Virginia challenges that "liability" ruling and asserts two justifications in defense of VMI's exclusion of women. First, the Commonwealth contends, "single-sex education provides important educational benefits" and the option of single-sex education contributes to "diversity in educational approaches." Second, the Commonwealth argues, "the unique VMI method of character development and leadership training," the school's adversative approach, would have to be modified were VMI to admit women. We consider these two justifications in turn.

Single-sex education affords pedagogical benefits to at least some students, Virginia emphasizes, and that reality is uncontested in this litigation. Similarly, it is not disputed that diversity among public educational institutions can serve the public good. But Virginia has not shown that VMI was established, or has been maintained, with a view to diversifying, by its categorical exclusion of women, educational opportunities within the State. In cases of this genre, our precedent instructs that "benign" justifications proffered in defense of categorical exclusions will not be accepted automatically; a tenable justification must describe actual state purposes, not rationalizations for actions in fact differently grounded.

Mississippi Univ. for Women is immediately in point. There the State asserted, in justification of its exclusion of men from a nursing school, that it was engaging in "educational affirmative action" by "compensat[ing] for discrimination against women." Undertaking a "searching analysis," the Court found no close resemblance between "the alleged objective" and "the actual purpose underlying the discriminatory classification." Pursuing a similar inquiry here, we reach the same conclusion. . . .

[W]e find no persuasive evidence in this record that VMI's male-only admission policy "is in furtherance of a state policy of 'diversity.'" No such policy, the Fourth Circuit observed, can be discerned from the movement of all other public colleges and universities in Virginia away from single-sex education. That court also questioned "how one institution with autonomy, but with no authority over any other state institution, can give effect to a state policy of diversity among institutions." A purpose genuinely to advance an array of educational options, as the Court of Appeals recognized, is not served by VMI's historic and constant plan—a plan to "affor[d] a unique educational benefit only to males." However "liberally" this plan serves the State's sons, it makes no provision whatever for her daughters. That is not *equal* protection.

Virginia next argues that VMI's adversative method of training provides educational benefits that cannot be made available, unmodified, to women. Alterations to accommodate women would necessarily be "radical," so "drastic," Virginia asserts, as to transform, indeed "destroy," VMI's program. Neither sex would be favored by the transformation, Virginia maintains: Men would be deprived of the unique opportunity currently available to them; women would not gain that opportunity because their participation would "eliminat[e] the very aspects of [the] program that distinguish [VMI] from . . . other institutions of higher education in Virginia."

The District Court forecast from expert witness testimony, and the Court of Appeals accepted, that coeducation would materially affect "at least these three aspects of VMI's program—physical training, the absence of privacy, and the adversative approach." And it is uncontested that women's admission would require accommodations, primarily in ar-

ranging housing assignments and physical training programs for female cadets. It is also undisputed, however, that "the VMI methodology could be used to educate women." The District Court even allowed that some women may prefer it to the methodology a women's college might pursue. "[S]ome women, at least, would want to attend [VMI] if they had the opportunity," the District Court recognized, and "some women," the expert testimony established, "are capable of all of the individual activities required of VMI cadets." The parties, furthermore, agree that *"some* women can meet the physical standards [VMI] now impose[s] on men." In sum, as the Court of Appeals stated, "neither the goal of producing citizen soldiers," VMI's *raison d'être,* "nor VMI's implementing methodology is inherently unsuitable to women.". . .

The United States does not challenge any expert witness estimation on average capacities or preferences of men and women. Instead, the United States emphasizes that time and again since this Court's turning point decision in *Reed v. Reed* (1971), we have cautioned reviewing courts to take a "hard look" at generalizations or "tendencies" of the kind pressed by Virginia, and relied upon by the District Court. State actors controlling gates to opportunity, we have instructed, may not exclude qualified individuals based on "fixed notions concerning the roles and abilities of males and females." *Mississippi Univ. for Women; J. E. B.*. . .

Women's successful entry into the federal military academies, and their participation in the Nation's military forces, indicate that Virginia's fears for the future of VMI may not be solidly grounded. The State's justification for excluding all women from "citizen-soldier" training for which some are qualified, in any event, cannot rank as "exceedingly persuasive," as we have explained and applied that standard. . . .

In the second phase of the litigation, Virginia presented its remedial plan—maintain VMI as a male-only college and create VWIL as a separate program for women. . . .

A remedial decree, this Court has said, must closely fit the constitutional violation; it must be shaped to place persons unconstitutionally denied an opportunity or advantage in "the position they would have occupied in the absence of [discrimination]." See *Milliken v. Bradley* (1977). The constitutional violation in this case is the categorical exclusion of women from an extraordinary educational opportunity afforded men. A proper remedy for an unconstitutional exclusion, we have explained, aims to "eliminate [so far as possible] the discriminatory effects of the past" and to "bar like discrimination in the future." *Louisiana v. United States* (1965).

Virginia chose not to eliminate, but to leave untouched, VMI's exclusionary policy. For women only, however, Virginia proposed a separate program, different in kind from VMI and unequal in tangible and intangible facilities. Having violated the Constitution's equal protection requirement, Virginia was obliged to show that its remedial proposal "directly address[ed] and relate[d] to" the violation, *i.e.*, the equal protection denied to women ready, willing, and able to benefit from educational opportunities of the kind VMI offers. Virginia described VWIL as a "parallel program," and asserted that VWIL shares VMI's mission of producing "citizen-soldiers" and VMI's goals of providing "education, military training, mental and physical discipline, character . . . and leadership development." If the VWIL program could not "eliminate the discriminatory effects of the past," could it at least "bar like discrimination in the future"? A comparison of the programs said to be "parallel" informs our answer. . . .

VWIL affords women no opportunity to experience the rigorous military training for which VMI is famed. . . .

VWIL students participate in ROTC and a "largely ceremonial" Virginia Corps of Cadets, but Virginia deliberately did not make VWIL a military institute. The VWIL House is not a military-style residence and VWIL students need not live together throughout the 4-year program, eat meals together, or wear uniforms during the school day. VWIL students thus do not experience the "barracks" life "crucial to the VMI experience," the spartan living arrangements designed to foster an "egalitarian ethic." "[T]he most important aspects of the VMI educational experience occur in the barracks," the District Court found, yet Virginia deemed that core experience nonessential, indeed inappropriate, for training its female citizen-soldiers.

VWIL students receive their "leadership training" in seminars, externships, and speaker series, episodes and encounters lacking the "[p]hysical rigor, mental stress, . . . minute regulation of behavior, and indoctrination in desirable values" made hallmarks of VMI's citizen-soldier training. . . .

In myriad respects other than military training, VWIL does not qualify as VMI's equal. VWIL's student body, facul-

ty, course offerings, and facilities hardly match VMI's. Nor can the VWIL graduate anticipate the benefits associated with VMI's 157-year history, the school's prestige, and its influential alumni network.

Mary Baldwin College, whose degree VWIL students will gain, enrolls first-year women with an average combined SAT score about 100 points lower than the average score for VMI freshmen. The Mary Baldwin faculty holds "significantly fewer Ph.D.'s," and receives substantially lower salaries than the faculty at VMI.

Mary Baldwin does not offer a VWIL student the range of curricular choices available to a VMI cadet. . . .

Although Virginia has represented that it will provide equal financial support for in-state VWIL students and VMI cadets, and the VMI Foundation has agreed to endow VWIL with $5.4625 million, the difference between the two schools' financial reserves is pronounced. Mary Baldwin's endowment, currently about $19 million, will gain an additional $35 million based on future commitments; VMI's current endowment, $131 million—the largest per-student endowment in the Nation—will gain $220 million.

The VWIL student does not graduate with the advantage of a VMI degree. Her diploma does not unite her with the legions of VMI "graduates [who] have distinguished themselves" in military and civilian life. . . .

Virginia, in sum, while maintaining VMI for men only, has failed to provide any "comparable single-gender women's institution." Instead, the Commonwealth has created a VWIL program fairly appraised as a "pale shadow" of VMI in terms of the range of curricular choices and faculty stature, funding, prestige, alumni support and influence. . . .

. . . [W]e rule here that Virginia has not shown substantial equality in the separate educational opportunities the State supports at VWIL and VMI. . . .

VMI . . . offers an educational opportunity no other Virginia institution provides, and the school's "prestige"—associated with its success in developing "citizen-soldiers"—is unequaled. Virginia has closed this facility to its daughters and, instead, has devised for them a "parallel program," with a faculty less impressively credentialed and less well paid, more limited course offerings, fewer opportunities for military training and for scientific specialization. VMI, beyond question, "possesses to a far greater degree" than the VWIL program "those qualities which are incapable of objective measurement but which make for greatness in a . . . school," including "position and influence of the alumni, standing in the community, traditions and prestige." Women seeking and fit for a VMI-quality education cannot be offered anything less, under the State's obligation to afford them genuinely equal protection. . . .

For the reasons stated, the initial judgment of the Court of Appeals is affirmed, the final judgment of the Court of Appeals is reversed, and the case is remanded for further proceedings consistent with this opinion.

It is so ordered.

Reversed and remanded.

CHIEF JUSTICE REHNQUIST, concurring in judgment.

The Court holds first that Virginia violates the Equal Protection Clause by maintaining the Virginia Military Institute's (VMI's) all-male admissions policy, and second that establishing the Virginia Women's Institute for Leadership (VWIL) program does not remedy that violation. While I agree with these conclusions, I disagree with the Court's analysis and so I write separately.

Two decades ago in *Craig v. Boren* (1976), we announced that "[t]o withstand constitutional challenge, . . . classifications by gender must serve important governmental objectives and must be substantially related to achievement of those objectives." We have adhered to that standard of scrutiny ever since. While the majority adheres to this test today, it also says that the State must demonstrate an "'exceedingly persuasive justification'" to support a gender-based classification. It is unfortunate that the Court thereby introduces an element of uncertainty respecting the appropriate test.

While terms like "important governmental objective" and "substantially related" are hardly models of precision, they have more content and specificity than does the phrase "exceedingly persuasive justification." That phrase is best confined, as it was first used, as an observation on the difficulty of meeting the applicable test, not as a formulation of the test itself. To avoid introducing potential confusion, I would have adhered more closely to our traditional, "firmly established" standard that a gender-based classification "must bear a close and substantial relationship to important governmental objectives."

JUSTICE SCALIA, dissenting.

Today the Court shuts down an institution that has served the people of the Commonwealth of Virginia with pride and distinction for over a century and a half. To achieve that desired result, it rejects (contrary to our established practice) the factual findings of two courts below, sweeps aside the precedents of this Court, and ignores the history of our people. As to facts: it explicitly rejects the finding that there exist "gender-based developmental differences" supporting Virginia's restriction of the "adversative" method to only a men's institution, and the finding that the all-male composition of the Virginia Military Institute (VMI) is essential to that institution's character. As to precedent: it drastically revises our established standards for reviewing sex-based classifications. And as to history: it counts for nothing the long tradition, enduring down to the present, of men's military colleges supported by both States and the Federal Government.

Much of the Court's opinion is devoted to deprecating the closed-mindedness of our forebears with regard to women's education, and even with regard to the treatment of women in areas that have nothing to do with education. Closed-minded they were—as every age is, including our own, with regard to matters it cannot guess, because it simply does not consider them debatable. The virtue of a democratic system with a First Amendment is that it readily enables the people, over time, to be persuaded that what they took for granted is not so, and to change their laws accordingly. That system is destroyed if the smug assurances of each age are removed from the democratic process and written into the Constitution. So to counterbalance the Court's criticism of our ancestors, let me say a word in their praise: they left us free to change. The same cannot be said of this most illiberal Court, which has embarked on a course of inscribing one after another of the current preferences of the society (and in some cases only the counter-majoritarian preferences of the society's law-trained elite) into our Basic Law. Today it enshrines the notion that no substantial educational value is to be served by an all-men's military academy—so that the decision by the people of Virginia to maintain such an institution denies equal protection to women who cannot attend that institution but can attend others. Since it is entirely clear that the Constitution of the United States—the old one—takes no sides in this educational debate, I dissent. . . .

To reject the Court's disposition today, however, it is not necessary to accept my view that the Court's made-up tests cannot displace long-standing national traditions as the primary determinant of what the Constitution means. It is only necessary to apply honestly the test the Court has been applying to sex-based classifications for the past two decades. It is well settled, as JUSTICE O'CONNOR stated some time ago for a unanimous Court, that we evaluate a statutory classification based on sex under a standard that lies "[b]etween th[e] extremes of rational basis review and strict scrutiny." Clark v. Jeter (1988). We have denominated this standard "intermediate scrutiny" and under it have inquired whether the statutory classification is "substantially related to an important governmental objective.". . .

Although the Court in two places recites the test as stated in [Mississippi University for Women v.] Hogan [1982], which asks whether the State has demonstrated "that the classification serves important governmental objectives and that the discriminatory means employed are substantially related to the achievement of those objectives," the Court never answers the question presented in anything resembling that form. When it engages in analysis, the Court instead prefers the phrase "exceedingly persuasive justification" from Hogan. The Court's nine invocations of that phrase and even its fanciful description of that imponderable as "the core instruction" of the Court's decisions in J. E. B. v. Alabama ex rel. T. B. (1994) and Hogan would be unobjectionable if the Court acknowledged that whether a "justification" is "exceedingly persuasive" must be assessed by asking "[whether] the classification serves important governmental objectives and [whether] the discriminatory means employed are substantially related to the achievement of those objectives." Instead, however, the Court proceeds to interpret "exceedingly persuasive justification" in a fashion that contradicts the reasoning of Hogan and our other precedents. . . .

Justice Brandeis said it is "one of the happy incidents of the federal system that a single courageous State may, if its citizens choose, serve as a laboratory; and try novel social and economic experiments without risk to the rest of the country." New State Ice Co. v. Liebmann (1932) (dissenting opinion). But it is one of the unhappy incidents of the federal system that a self-righteous Supreme Court, acting on its Members' personal view of what would make a "more perfect Union," (a criterion only slightly more restrictive than a "more perfect world"), can impose its own favored social and economic dispositions nationwide. As today's disposition, and others this single Term, show, this places it beyond the power of a "single courageous State," not only to introduce novel dispositions that the Court frowns upon, but to reintroduce, or indeed even adhere to, disfavored dispositions that are centuries old. See, e.g., BMW of North America, Inc. v. Gore (1996); Romer v. Evans (1996). The sphere of self-government reserved to the people of the Republic is progressively narrowed.

Although the Court struck down VMI's single-sex admissions policy, the justices still did not adopt the strict scrutiny standard for sex discrimination cases. Officially, they remained wedded to the intermediate scrutiny standard. However, both the concurring and dissenting opinions criticized the majority for interpreting intermediate scrutiny in a new way. Whether the "exceedingly persuasive justification" element signals a real change in the Court's approach to gender issues, as Rehnquist and Scalia suggest, will be answered in future cases.

United States v. Virginia demonstrates the limits of the Supreme Court to generate compliance with its decisions. On paper, the case was a bitter defeat for both VMI and The Citadel, which had spent millions of dollars defending their all-male policies and now had to admit women. But women cadets have not had an easy time of it. Of the four women who initially enrolled in The Citadel, two dropped out after alleging that they were assaulted, hazed, and sexually harassed. Several male cadets accused of the hazing resigned, and others were disciplined.

Both schools promised to remedy the problems of assimilating women into their environments, and some progress has been made. As of 2000, 61 of the 1,650 cadets at The Citadel are women and well over 100 more have applied for admission. The school has even appointed its first woman with voting power to its Board of Visitors. But the incidents at The Citadel clearly show the limitations of formal Court decisions. Simply because the justices render a decision does not mean that barriers between the sexes—just like those between the races—will fall over night.

Gender-Based Classifications the Court Has Upheld.
The cases in the previous section suggest that the Court, in applying the heightened scrutiny standard, has been unwilling to tolerate government actions that are based on outmoded stereotypes of women. On the whole, that is true: data show that in the years since *Reed*, the justices have ruled in favor of the sex discrimination claim in more than half their cases.

There is at least one category of litigation, however, in which the Court has been less willing to strike down sex-based laws: cases involving physical differences between men and women.[27] In contrast to the "easy" cases you just read, these are "difficult" because they center on basic societal views about women's roles rather than on outmoded stereotypes. Moreover, because we can trace most of those views to physical differences between men and women (only women can become pregnant), the "difficult" cases raise a fundamental problem for the Court, which is that in all discrimination cases (regardless of what standard of scrutiny courts impose) claims of unequal treatment must be based only on comparisons of persons "similarly situated."

To see this problem, consider *Michael M. v. Superior Court of Sonoma County* (1981). This case had its origins in June 1978, when Michael M., a seventeen-year-old boy, and two friends approached Sharon, who was sixteen, and her sister at a bus stop. It was around midnight and both Michael and Sharon had been drinking. During the course of their encounter, Michael and Sharon split off from the others. First they went into some bushes, where they hugged and kissed. Later, after Sharon's sister had left, Sharon and Michael walked to a nearby park, laid down on a bench, and continued kissing. Michael tried to convince Sharon to remove her clothes and have sexual relations. When Sharon refused, Michael hit her in the face. Then, in Sharon's words, "I let him do what he wanted to do."

Michael M. was charged with a violation of Section 261.5 of the California penal code, which prohibits "an act of sexual intercourse accomplished with a female not the wife of the perpetrator, where the female is under the age of 18 years." This statutory rape law makes males alone criminally liable for the act of sexual intercourse. Michael M. moved to have the criminal prosecution dropped on the grounds that §261.5 invidiously discriminates on the basis of sex and therefore violates the Equal Protection Clause. California courts upheld the validity of the law.

Although the opinion that the Supreme Court issued lacked majority support, the Court also upheld the law. Writing for the plurality, Justice Rehnquist began by noting the Court's adherence to the standard articulated in *Craig* and in other cases. He then wrote:

Underlying these decisions is the principle that a legislature may not "make overbroad generalizations based on sex which are entirely unrelated to any differences between men and women or which demean the ability or social status of the affected class." But because the Equal Protection Clause does not "demand that a statute necessarily apply equally to all persons" or require "'things which are different in fact . . . to be treated in law as though they were the same,'" this Court has consistently upheld statutes where the gender classification is not invidious, but rather realistically reflects the fact that the sexes are not similarly situated in certain circumstances. . . .

We are satisfied not only that the prevention of illegitimate pregnancy is at least one of the "purposes" of the statute, but also that the State has a strong interest in preventing such pregnancy. At the risk of stating the obvious, teenage pregnancies, which have increased dramatically over the last two decades, have significant social, medical, and economic consequences for both the mother and her child, and the State. Of particular concern to the State is that approximately half of all teenage pregnancies end in abortion. And of those children who are born, their illegitimacy makes them likely candidates to become wards of the State.

We need not be medical doctors to discern that young men and young women are not similarly situated with respect to the problems and the risks of sexual intercourse. Only women may become pregnant, and they suffer disproportionately the profound physical, emotional and psychological consequences of sexual activity. The statute at issue here protects women from sexual intercourse at an age when those consequences are particularly severe.

The question thus boils down to whether a State may attack the problem of sexual intercourse and teenage pregnancy directly by prohibiting a male from having sexual intercourse with a minor female. We hold that such a statute is sufficiently related to the State's objectives to pass constitutional muster.

27. Mezey, *In Pursuit of Equality*, 25–27.

Four justices (Brennan, Marshall, Stevens, and White) registered a spirited dissent. Indeed, in Justice Brennan's view, it was "disturbing to find the Court so splintered on a case that presents such a straightforward issue: Whether the admittedly gender-based classification bears a sufficient relationship to the State's asserted goal of preventing teenage pregnancies to survive the midlevel constitutional scrutiny mandated by *Craig v. Boren* (1976)."

Straightforward or not, Rehnquist's decision takes us back to the requirement in all discrimination cases that claims of unequal treatment be based only on comparisons of persons "similarly situated." In *Michael M.*, the Court found that men and women were not similarly situated because only women can become pregnant.

Seen in this way, *Michael M.* shores up the point we made at the beginning of the section: disputes involving physical differences between men and women have been more difficult for the Court to resolve (and to resolve in favor of the litigant claiming discrimination) than those involving outdated views about women. Another 1981 case, decided just three months after *Michael M.*, also illustrates the point. *Rostker v. Goldberg* involved military service. Historically, males have had the primary responsibility and opportunity to serve in the armed forces. Physical differences between men and women led to this custom, which has been reinforced by the way society views sex roles.

The federal legislation challenged in this case continued the policy of distinguishing men and women with respect to military matters. The case also involved Congress's constitutional power to raise and regulate the armed forces. Traditionally, when the legislature has acted under this authority, the Court has accorded it great deference. In light of the subsequent military actions taken by the United States in Grenada, Panama, and the Persian Gulf, does the Court's position on the draft as expressed in *Rostker* have more or less validity than it did when it was announced?[28]

28. For oral arguments in this case, navigate to: *oyez.nwu.edu*.

Rostker v. Goldberg

453 U.S. 57 (1981)
laws.findlaw.com/US/453/57.html
Vote: 6 (*Blackmun, Burger, Powell, Rehnquist, Stevens, Stewart*)
    3 (*Brennan, Marshall, White*)
Opinion of the Court: Rehnquist
Dissenting opinions: Marshall, White

Under the Military Selective Service Act (MSSA) the president can require every male citizen and resident alien between the ages of eighteen and twenty-six to register for the draft. In 1971 several draft-age men filed suit in federal court in Pennsylvania against the director of the Selective Service System challenging the constitutionality of the registration law. Because draft registration was suspended in 1975, the suit became dormant. However, in 1980, in reaction to the Soviet invasion of Afghanistan, President Jimmy Carter reactivated the draft registration program. With 150,000 women already serving in the military, Carter also asked Congress to amend the law to require females, as well as males, to register.

Congress refused to change the law and appropriated only enough money to administer the registration of males. The long-dormant suit was reactivated, and on July 18, 1980, three days before registration was to begin, the district court declared the law unconstitutional because its single-sex provisions violated the Due Process Clause of the Fifth Amendment. Bernard Rostker, director of Selective Service, appealed to the Supreme Court.

JUSTICE REHNQUIST delivered the opinion of the Court.

Whenever called upon to judge the constitutionality of an Act of Congress—"the gravest and most delicate duty that this Court is called upon to perform," the Court accords "great weight to the decisions of Congress.". . .

This is not, however, merely a case involving the customary deference accorded congressional decisions. The case arises in the context of Congress' authority over national defense and military affairs, and perhaps in no other area has the Court accorded Congress greater deference. In rejecting the registration of women, Congress explicitly relied upon its constitutional powers under Art. I, §8, cls. 12–14. . . . This Court has consistently recognized Congress' "broad constitutional power" to raise and regulate armies and navies. As the Court noted in considering a challenge to the selective service laws: "The constitutional power of Congress to raise and support armies and to make all laws necessary and proper to that end is broad and sweeping."

Not only is the scope of Congress' constitutional power in this area broad, but the lack of competence on the part of the courts is marked. . . .

None of this is to say that Congress is free to disregard the Constitution when it acts in the area of military affairs. In that area, as any other, Congress remains subject to the limitations of the Due Process Clause, but the tests and limitations to be applied may differ because of the military context. We of course do not abdicate our ultimate responsibility to decide the constitutional question, but simply recognize that the Constitution itself requires such deference to congressional choice. In deciding the question before us we must be particularly careful not to substitute our judgment of what is desirable for that of Congress, or our own evaluation of evidence for a reasonable evaluation by the Legislative Branch. . . .

In this case the courts are called upon to decide whether Congress, acting under an explicit constitutional grant of authority, has by that action transgressed an explicit guarantee of individual rights which limits the authority so conferred. Simply labeling the legislative decision "military" on the one hand or "gender-based" on the other does not automatically guide a court to the correct constitutional result.

No one could deny that under the test of *Craig v. Boren*, the Government's interest in raising and supporting armies is an "important governmental interest." Congress and its Committees carefully considered and debated two alternative means of furthering that interest: the first was to register only males for potential conscription, and the other was to register both sexes. Congress chose the former alternative. When that decision is challenged on equal protection grounds, the question a court must decide is not which alternative it would have chosen, had it been the primary decisionmaker, but whether that chosen by Congress denies equal protection of the laws. . . .

This case is quite different from several of the gender-based discrimination cases we have considered in that, despite appellees' assertions, Congress did not act "unthinkingly" or "reflexively and not for any considered reason." The question of registering women for the draft not only received considerable national attention and was the subject of wide-ranging public debate, but also was extensively considered by Congress in hearings, floor debate, and in committee. Hearings held by both Houses of Congress in response to the President's request for authorization to register women adduced extensive testimony and evidence concerning the issue. These hearings built on other hearings held the previous year addressed to the same question. . . .

While proposals to register women were being rejected in the course of transferring funds to register males, Committees in both Houses which had conducted hearings on the issue were also rejecting the registration of women. . . .

. . . [T]he decision to exempt women from registration was not the "'accidental by-product of a traditional way of thinking about females.'" In *Michael M.*, we rejected a similar argument because of action by the California Legislature considering and rejecting proposals to make a statute challenged on discrimination grounds gender-neutral. The cause for rejecting the argument is considerably stronger here. The issue was considered at great length, and Congress clearly expressed its purpose and intent.

Women as a group, . . . unlike men as a group, are not eligible for combat. The restrictions on the participation of women in combat in the Navy and Air Force are statutory. Under 10 U.S.C. §6015 (1976 ed., Supp. III), "women may not be assigned to duty on vessels or in aircraft that are engaged in combat missions," and under 10 U.S.C. §8549 female members of the Air Force "may not be assigned to duty in aircraft engaged in combat missions." The Army and Marine Corps preclude the use of women in combat as a matter of established policy. Congress specifically recognized and endorsed the exclusion of women from combat in exempting women from registration. . . .

The existence of the combat restrictions clearly indicates the basis for Congress' decision to exempt women from registration. The purpose of registration was to prepare for a draft of combat troops. Since women are excluded from combat, Congress concluded that they would not be needed in the event of a draft, and therefore decided not to register them. . . . This is not a case of Congress arbitrarily choosing to burden one of two similarly situated groups, such as would be the case with an all-black or all-white, or an all-Catholic or all-Lutheran, or an all-Republican or all-Democratic registration. Men and women, because of the combat restrictions on women, are simply not similarly situated for purposes of a draft or registration for a draft.

Congress' decision to authorize the registration of only men, therefore, does not violate the Due Process Clause. The exemption of women from registration is not only sufficiently but also closely related to Congress' purpose in authorizing registration. The fact that Congress and the Executive have decided that women should not serve in combat fully justifies Congress in not authorizing their registration, since the purpose of registration is to develop a pool of potential combat troops. . . . "[T]he gender classification is not invidious, but rather realistically reflects the fact that the sexes are not similarly situated" in this case. The Constitution requires that Congress treat similarly situated persons similarly, not that it engage in gestures of superficial equality. . . .

. . . [W]e conclude that Congress acted well within its constitutional authority when it authorized the registration of men, and not women, under the Military Selective Service Act. The decision of the District Court holding otherwise is accordingly

Reversed.

JUSTICE MARSHALL, with whom JUSTICE BRENNAN joins, dissenting.

The Court today places its imprimatur on one of the most potent remaining public expressions of "ancient canards about the proper role of women." It upholds a statute that requires males but not females to register for the draft, and which thereby categorically excludes women from a fundamental civic obligation. Because I believe the Court's decision is inconsistent with the Constitution's guarantee of equal protection of the laws, I dissent. . . .

By now it should be clear that statutes like the MSSA, which discriminate on the basis of gender, must be examined under the "heightened" scrutiny mandated by *Craig v. Boren.* Under this test, a gender-based classification cannot withstand constitutional challenge unless the classification

is substantially related to the achievement of an important governmental objective. . . .

[A]lthough the Court purports to apply the *Craig v. Boren* test, the "similarly situated" analysis the Court employs is in fact significantly different from the *Craig v. Boren* approach. The Court essentially reasons that the gender classification employed by the MSSA is constitutionally permissible because nondiscrimination is not necessary to achieve the purpose of registration to prepare for a draft of combat troops. In other words, the majority concludes that women may be excluded from registration because they will not be needed in the event.

This analysis, however, focuses on the wrong question. The relevant inquiry under the *Craig v. Boren* test is not whether a gender-neutral classification would substantially advance important governmental interests. Rather, the question is whether the gender-based classification is itself substantially related to the achievement of the asserted governmental interest. Thus, the Government's task in this case is to demonstrate that excluding women from registration substantially furthers the goal of preparing for a draft of combat troops. Or to put it another way, the Government must show that registering women would substantially impede its efforts to prepare for such a draft. Under our precedents, the Government cannot meet this burden without showing that a gender-neutral statute would be a less effective means of attaining this end. . . .

In this case, the Government makes no claim that preparing for a draft of combat troops cannot be accomplished just as effectively by registering both men and women but drafting only men if only men turn out to be needed. Nor can the Government argue that this alternative entails the additional cost and administrative inconvenience of registering women. This Court has repeatedly stated that the administrative convenience of employing a gender classification is not an adequate constitutional justification under the *Craig v. Boren* test. . . .

. . . "[W]hen it appears that an Act of Congress conflicts with [a constitutional] provisio[n], we have no choice but to enforce the paramount commands of the Constitution. We are sworn to do no less. We cannot push back the limits of the Constitution merely to accommodate challenged legislation." In some 106 instances since this Court was established it has determined that congressional action exceeded the bounds of the Constitution. I believe the same is true of this statute. In an attempt to avoid its constitutional obligation, the Court today "pushes back the limits of the Constitution" to accommodate an Act of Congress.

What do we learn from *Rostker* and the other constitutional sex discrimination cases in this section? We observe that Court decisions have paralleled society's changing views on women's roles. In 1974 more than a third of Americans believed that a "woman's job is to take care of the home"; today that figure is about 13 percent.[29] As the public changed, so did the Court, evincing little hesitation (since the 1970s) in striking down laws that prefer men to women as executors of wills or state policies that maintain male-only institutions. In addition, the justices have generally, but not always, interpreted congressional legislation in ways that have advanced the cause of sexual equality, especially in the workplace. Even the Court's adoption of a midlevel scrutiny standard, however, has not prevented it from upholding legislation based on the presumption that men and women are not similarly situated—generally legislation based on physical differences. In fact, in *Rostker*, Rehnquist essentially took the position that the *Craig* test should not be applied when the sexes are not similarly situated. As Susan Gluck Mezey points out, this problem may have been created by the early women's rights litigators, who argued that the Court should treat similarly situated men and women equally. But, "unfortunately . . . embracing the theory of 'sameness' means that any sign of difference between women and men could be used to justify treating women differently than men."[30] Such was the case in *Michael M.* and *Rostker*.

Trends in Sex Discrimination Litigation

These observations pertain to constitutional cases. But, as is true for claims of race discrimination, litigants alleging sex discrimination now tend to bring their claims under federal civil rights statutes *(see Box 12-3)*. How have they fared? The answer is somewhat mixed.

On the one hand, the justices have been sensitive to certain problems that women face on the job more often than men—with sexual harassment providing a good example. Title VII of the 1964 Civil Rights Act prohibits sex discrimination in employment. The law originally contemplated making it illegal for an employer to deny tangible benefits such as a job, a promotion, or fair compensation because of the employee's sex. With the rising number of complaints of sexual harassment on the job, however, standards of appropriate behavior began to evolve. As a result, courts were asked to include the existence of a sex-based "hostile" or "abusive" job environment as a form of discrimination. Even the generally conservative Burger and Rehnquist Courts supported expanding the definition of illegal discrimination to encompass various forms of harassing behavior *(see Box 12-5)*. By interpreting the Civil Rights Act as prohibiting sexual harassment in the workplace, the Supreme Court encouraged additional complaints to be filed in federal court and signaled to the lower courts that such claims should be treated seriously. Faced with public disapproval and the possibility of costly lawsuits, employers began adopting more comprehensive policies to combat sexual harassment on the job.

On the other hand, during the 1980s and 1990s the Court issued several statutory decisions that were more conservative than both women's rights litigators and Congress found acceptable. For example, in *Grove City College v. Bell* (1984) the Court narrowly interpreted the sex discrimination provision of a federal statute pertaining to educational assistance programs. Protests from civil rights groups prompted the legislature to respond by passing the Civil Rights Restoration Act of 1988, which for most purposes reversed the *Grove City* ruling.

---

29. See Lee Epstein, Jeffrey A. Segal, Harold J. Spaeth, and Thomas G. Walker, *The Supreme Court Compendium: Data, Decisions, and Developments,* 2d ed. (Washington, D.C.: Congressional Quarterly, 1996), Table 8-14.

30. Mezey, *In Pursuit of Equality,* 27.

CONGRESS has passed legislation to protect citizens against discrimination where constitutional prohibitions do not reach. An example is Title VII of the Civil Rights Act of 1964 that makes it "an unlawful employment practice for an employer . . . to discriminate against any individual with respect to his compensation, terms, conditions, or privileges of employment, because of such individual's race, color, religion, sex, or national origin." When workers believe that their civil rights have been violated they may file lawsuits demanding that the situation be remedied. But the federal civil rights laws are only effective if the courts are willing to enforce them. Applying Title VII to discriminatory harassment has been one of the more controversial civil rights issues. Although the Burger and Rehnquist Courts have been criticized for failing to apply civil rights statutes vigorously, the justices have demonstrated special consideration for sexual harassment claimants. Here we summarize the two most important Supreme Court actions.

Meritor Savings Bank v. Vinson (1986)

Facts: In 1974 Mechelle Vinson began working for the Meritor Savings Bank. Her supervisor was bank vice president Sidney Taylor. Over a four-year period Vinson was promoted up the ranks from teller-trainee to assistant branch manager. All agree that these were merit-based promotions. In September 1978 Vinson took sick leave for an indefinite period, and two months later she was fired for abusing the leave policy. Vinson brought legal action against Taylor and the bank. She claimed she had been subject to constant sexual harassment. She said Taylor demanded sexual favors. After first resisting, she agreed because she feared losing her job. She estimated that she had sexual relations with Taylor between thirty and forty times. She also testified that Taylor fondled her in front of other employees, followed her into the restroom, where he exposed himself to her, and forcibly raped her on several occasions. Vinson did not report Taylor's advances to any of his supervisors or make use of established complaint procedures. The district court ruled in favor of the employer finding that much of the sexual relationship was voluntary, but the court of appeals reversed.

Outcome: By unanimous vote the justices supported Mechelle Vinson's claim. Justice Rehnquist wrote the majority opinion.

Ruling: The Court held that sexual harassment constitutes sex discrimination and is actionable under the 1964 Civil Rights Act. Sexual harassment litigants do not have to prove loss of any tangible or economic benefit. Noneco-nomic injury also violates the law. Harassment that creates a hostile work environment is sufficient cause to bring legal action. Sexual harassment may occur even if sexual activity is voluntary. The employer is not automatically immune nor automatically liable for the behavior of its supervising personnel. The question of employer responsibility must be considered separately in each case.

Harris v. Forklift Systems, Inc. (1993)

Facts: Teresa Harris worked as a manager at Forklift Systems, an equipment rental company in Tennessee, from 1985 to 1987. Charles Hardy was the company president. Throughout Harris's employment at Forklift, Hardy often insulted her because she was a woman and made her the target of unwanted sexual innuendos. He would make statements such as, "You're a woman, what do you know" and "We need a man as the rental manager." He referred to her as "a dumb ass woman," and suggested that they "go to the Holiday Inn to negotiate [a] raise." Hardy would occasionally ask female employees to get coins from his front pocket. He threw objects on the ground in front of women and asked them to pick the objects up. He made sexually oriented comments about the clothing female employees wore. When Harris complained to Hardy about this conduct, he expressed surprise that she was offended and said that he was only joking. He apologized and promised to stop, but he soon returned to his former ways. Harris then sued Forklift, claiming that Hardy had created an abusive environment based on sex in violation of Title VII. The district court concluded that Hardy had engaged in offensive behavior, but not to the extent that he created an abusive environment that would interfere with job performance. The judge emphasized that Hardy's behavior was not so severe as to affect seriously Harris's psychological well-being. The court of appeals affirmed.

Outcome: By unanimous vote the justices supported Teresa Harris. Justice O'Connor wrote the majority opinion.

Ruling: A violation of Title VII occurs when the workplace is permeated with discriminatory behavior that is sufficiently severe or pervasive to create a hostile or abusive working environment. Harris need not prove that the offensive conduct seriously affected her psychological well-being. Whether an environment is "hostile" or "abusive" must be determined by examining all the circumstances rather than any single factor. Courts may look at the frequency of the offensive behavior, its severity, whether it was physically threatening or humiliating, and whether it reasonably interfered with an employee's work performance.

FIGURE 12-1 Responses to Questions About Interracial
Marriage, Women's Role, and Sexual Orientation

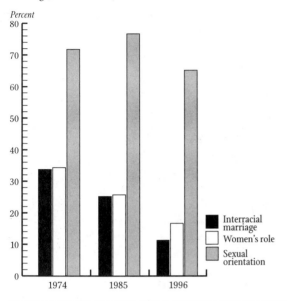

DATA SOURCE: Lee Epstein, Jeffrey A. Segal, Harold J. Spaeth, and Thomas
G. Walker, *The Supreme Court Compendium: Data, Decisions, and Developments*,
2d ed. (Washington, D.C.: Congressional Quarterly, 1996), Tables 8-10, 8-14,
8-20. Updated by the authors.

NOTE: Interracial marriage = percentage of respondents favoring laws
against interracial marriage; Women's role = percentage of respondents believing that a woman's job is to take care of the home; Sexual orientation = percentage of respondents believing that homosexual behavior is wrong.

DISCRIMINATION BASED ON SEXUAL ORIENTATION

Discrimination against gays and lesbians differs in at least two important ways from race and sex discrimination. First, although federal laws prohibit various forms of discrimination based on race and sex, no law explicitly protects homosexuals. In fact, the U.S. government maintains policies that discriminate on the basis of sexual preference. For example, in 1996 Congress passed the Defense of Marriage Act, which denies federal recognition of same-sex marriages and permits the states to refuse to recognize same-sex marriages performed in other states. Also in 1996 Congress refused to prohibit job discrimination based on sexual orientation by extending the remedies of the 1964 Civil Rights Act to sexual orientation.

Second, while Americans' views about blacks and

women have changed since the early 1970s, they have remained remarkably consistent (and negative) toward gays and lesbians. Figure 12-1, which compares attitudes about women, blacks, and homosexuals, makes this point crystal clear. In 1974, more than a third of the population believed that interracial marriages should be prohibited and that a woman's job is to take care of the home. By 1996 those figures fell to under 15 percent. Now consider Americans' views about gays and lesbians. In 1974, 71.8 percent believed that homosexual behavior is wrong. Twenty years later, the number was only slightly lower, 65.6 percent.

These data may help explain the actions of Congress and many states. They also may shed light on the Supreme Court's posture toward gays and lesbians, which brings up a third difference between race and sex discrimination and discrimination against homosexuals. The Supreme Court has issued many decisions regarding race and sex classifications, but it has very little to say about the rights of gays and lesbians. Moreover, the few decisions it has issued have been decidedly mixed.

We have already discussed the privacy case of *Bowers v. Hardwick* (1986), in which the justices upheld Georgia's sodomy law *(see pages 458–462)*. It is no surprise that the gay community was deeply critical of *Bowers*. Did gays fare better in *Romer v. Evans* (1996), in which the Court turned its attention to a Fourteenth Amendment claim? Because this was the first major gay discrimination case to be heard by the justices, Court observers were interested not only in whether the challenged state law would fall but also which standard of scrutiny the justices would use to adjudicate claims of discrimination based on sexual orientation.[31]

Romer v. Evans

517 U.S. 620 (1996)
supct.law.cornell.edu/supct/html/94-1039.ZS.html
Vote: 6 (Breyer, Ginsburg, Kennedy, O'Connor, Souter, Stevens)
    3 (Rehnquist, Scalia, Thomas)
Opinion of the Court: Kennedy
Dissenting opinion: Scalia

31. For oral arguments in this case, navigate to: *oyez.nwu.edu.*

Attorney Jean Dubofsky hugs Priscilla Inkpen, one of the plaintiffs who challenged Colorado's antigay rights initiative, after the Supreme Court ruled the measure unconstitutional. Richard Evans, the first named plantiff in the case, is at left.

This case involved a challenge to an amendment to the Colorado state constitution, which had been adopted by statewide initiative. The initiative arose in response to local laws passed by communities such as Boulder, Aspen, and Denver making sexual orientation an impermissible ground upon which to discriminate. In effect, the local laws gave sexual orientation the same status as race, sex, and other protected categories. To reverse this trend and remove the possibility of future legislation, a sufficient number of citizens signed a petition to place a proposed constitutional amendment on the ballot for the November 1992 elections. Known as Amendment 2, it passed with the support of 53.4 percent of those voting. The amendment states:

Neither the State of Colorado, through any of its branches or departments, nor any of its agencies, political subdivisions, municipalities or school districts, shall enact, adopt or enforce any statute, regulation, ordinance or policy whereby homosexual, lesbian or bisexual orientation, conduct, practices or relationships shall constitute or otherwise be the basis of or entitle any person or class of persons to have or claim any minority status, quota preferences, protected status or claim of discrimination. This Section of the Constitution shall be in all respects self-executing.

Almost immediately Richard G. Evans, a gay employee in the office of the mayor of Denver, other citizens, and several Colorado local governments sued Gov. Roy Romer and the state of Colorado, claiming that the new amendment was in violation of the Fourteenth Amendment's Equal Protection Clause. The Colorado Supreme Court, 6–1, struck down the amendment, and the state appealed to the U.S. Supreme Court.

JUSTICE KENNEDY delivered the opinion of the Court.

One century ago, the first Justice Harlan admonished this Court that the Constitution "neither knows nor tolerates classes among citizens." *Plessy v. Ferguson* (1896) (dissenting opinion). Unheeded then, those words now are understood to state a commitment to the law's neutrality where the rights of persons are at stake. The Equal Protection Clause enforces this principle and today requires us to hold invalid a provision of Colorado's Constitution. . . .

Soon after Amendment 2 was adopted, this litigation to declare its invalidity and enjoin its enforcement was commenced in the District Court for the City and County of Denver. . . .

The trial court granted a preliminary injunction to stay enforcement of Amendment 2, and an appeal was taken to the Supreme Court of Colorado. Sustaining the interim injunction and remanding the case for further proceedings, the State Supreme Court held that Amendment 2 was subject to strict scrutiny under the Fourteenth Amendment because it infringed the fundamental right of gays and lesbians to participate in the political process. . . . On remand, the State advanced various arguments in an effort to show that Amendment 2 was narrowly tailored to serve compelling interests, but the trial court found none sufficient. It enjoined enforcement of Amendment 2, and the Supreme Court of Colorado, in a second opinion, affirmed the ruling. We granted certiorari and now affirm the judgment, but on a rationale different from that adopted by the State Supreme Court.

The State's principal argument in defense of Amendment 2 is that it puts gays and lesbians in the same position as all other persons. So, the State says, the measure does no more than deny homosexuals special rights. This reading of the amendment's language is implausible. We rely not upon our own interpretation of the amendment but upon the authoritative construction of Colorado's Supreme Court. The state court, deeming it unnecessary to determine the full extent of the amendment's reach, found it invalid even on a modest reading of its implications. The critical discussion of the amendment, set out . . . [by the Colorado Supreme Court], is as follows:

"The immediate objective of Amendment 2 is, at a minimum, to repeal existing statutes, regulations, ordinances, and policies of state and local entities that barred discrimination based on sexual orientation. . . .

The "ultimate effect" of Amendment 2 is to prohibit any governmental entity from adopting similar, or more protective statutes, regulations, ordinances, or policies in the future unless the state constitution is first amended to permit such measures."

Sweeping and comprehensive is the change in legal status effected by this law. So much is evident from the ordinances that the Colorado Supreme Court declared would be void by operation of Amendment 2. Homosexuals, by state decree, are put in a solitary class with respect to transactions and relations in both the private and governmental spheres. The amendment withdraws from homosexuals, but no others, specific legal protection from the injuries caused by discrimination, and it forbids reinstatement of these laws and policies.

The change that Amendment 2 works in the legal status of gays and lesbians in the private sphere is far-reaching, both on its own terms and when considered in light of the structure and operation of modern anti-discrimination laws. That structure is well illustrated by contemporary statutes and ordinances prohibiting discrimination by providers of public accommodations. . . .

Amendment 2 bars homosexuals from securing protection against the injuries that these public-accommodations laws address. That in itself is a severe consequence, but there is more. Amendment 2, in addition, nullifies specific legal protections for this targeted class in all transactions in housing, sale of real estate, insurance, health and welfare services, private education, and employment.

Not confined to the private sphere, Amendment 2 also operates to repeal and forbid all laws or policies providing specific protection for gays or lesbians from discrimination by every level of Colorado government. . . . The repeal of these measures and the prohibition against their future reenactment demonstrates that Amendment 2 has the same force and effect in Colorado's governmental sector as it does elsewhere and that it applies to policies as well as ordinary legislation.

Amendment 2's reach may not be limited to specific laws passed for the benefit of gays and lesbians. It is a fair, if not necessary, inference from the broad language of the amendment that it deprives gays and lesbians even of the protection of general laws and policies that prohibit arbitrary discrimination in governmental and private settings. . . .

. . . [W]e cannot accept the view that Amendment 2's prohibition on specific legal protections does no more than deprive homosexuals of special rights. To the contrary, the amendment imposes a special disability upon those persons alone. Homosexuals are forbidden the safeguards that others enjoy or may seek without constraint. They can obtain specific protection against discrimination only by enlisting the citizenry of Colorado to amend the state constitution or perhaps, on the State's view, by trying to pass helpful laws of general applicability. This is so no matter how local or discrete the harm, no matter how public and widespread the injury. We find nothing special in the protections Amendment 2 withholds. These are protections taken for granted by most people either because they already have them or do not need them; these are protections against exclusion from an almost limitless number of transactions and endeavors that constitute ordinary civic life in a free society.

The Fourteenth Amendment's promise that no person shall be denied the equal protection of the laws must coexist with the practical necessity that most legislation classifies for one purpose or another, with resulting disadvantage to various groups or persons. We have attempted to reconcile the principle with the reality by stating that, if a law neither burdens a fundamental right nor targets a suspect class, we will uphold the legislative classification so long as it bears a rational relation to some legitimate end. See, *e.g., Heller v. Doe* (1993).

Amendment 2 fails, indeed defies, even this conventional inquiry. First, the amendment has the peculiar property of imposing a broad and undifferentiated disability on a single named group, an exceptional and, as we shall explain, invalid form of legislation. Second, its sheer breadth is so discontinuous with the reasons offered for it that the amendment seems inexplicable by anything but animus toward the class that it affects; it lacks a rational relationship to legitimate state interests.

Taking the first point, even in the ordinary equal protection case calling for the most deferential of standards, we insist on knowing the relation between the classification adopted and the object to be attained. The search for the link between classification and objective gives substance to the Equal Protection Clause; it provides guidance and discipline for the legislature, which is entitled to know what sorts of laws it can pass; and it marks the limits of our own authority. In the ordinary case, a law will be sustained if it can be said to advance a legitimate government interest, even if the law seems unwise or works to the disadvantage of a particular group, or if the rationale for it seems tenuous. . . . By requiring that the classification bear a rational relationship to an independent and legitimate legislative end, we ensure that classifications are not drawn for the purpose of disadvantaging the group burdened by the law.

Amendment 2 confounds this normal process of judicial review. It is at once too narrow and too broad. It identifies persons by a single trait and then denies them protection across the board. The resulting disqualification of a class of persons from the right to seek specific protection from the law is unprecedented in our jurisprudence. . . .

It is not within our constitutional tradition to enact laws of this sort. Central both to the idea of the rule of law and to our own Constitution's guarantee of equal protection is the principle that government and each of its parts remain open on impartial terms to all who seek its assistance. . . .

Respect for this principle explains why laws singling out a certain class of citizens for disfavored legal status or general hardships are rare. A law declaring that in general it shall be more difficult for one group of citizens than for all others to seek aid from the government is itself a denial of equal protection of the laws in the most literal sense. . . .

. . . [L]aws of the kind now before us raise the inevitable inference that the disadvantage imposed is born of animosity toward the class of persons affected. . . . Even laws enacted for broad and ambitious purposes often can be explained by reference to legitimate public policies which justify the incidental disadvantages they impose on certain persons. Amendment 2, however, in making a general announcement that gays and lesbians shall not have any particular protections from the law, inflicts on them immediate, continuing, and real injuries that outrun and belie any legitimate justifications that may be claimed for it. We conclude that, in addition to the far-reaching deficiencies of Amendment 2 that we have noted, the principles it offends, in another sense, are conventional and venerable; a law must bear a rational relationship to a legitimate governmental purpose, and Amendment 2 does not.

The primary rationale the State offers for Amendment 2 is respect for other citizens' freedom of association, and in particular the liberties of landlords or employers who have personal or religious objections to homosexuality. Colorado also cites its interest in conserving resources to fight discrimination against other groups. The breadth of the Amendment is so far removed from these particular justifications that we find it impossible to credit them. We cannot say that Amendment 2 is directed to any identifiable legitimate purpose or discrete objective. It is a status-based enactment divorced from any factual context from which we could discern a relationship to legitimate state interests; it is a classification of persons undertaken for its own sake, something the Equal Protection Clause does not permit.

We must conclude that Amendment 2 classifies homosexuals not to further a proper legislative end but to make them unequal to everyone else. This Colorado cannot do. A State cannot so deem a class of persons a stranger to its laws. Amendment 2 violates the Equal Protection Clause, and the judgment of the Supreme Court of Colorado is affirmed.

It is so ordered.

JUSTICE SCALIA, with whom THE CHIEF JUSTICE and JUSTICE THOMAS join, dissenting.

The Court has mistaken a Kulturkampf for a fit of spite. The constitutional amendment before us here is not the manifestation of a "'bare . . . desire to harm'" homosexuals, but is rather a modest attempt by seemingly tolerant Coloradans to preserve traditional sexual mores against the efforts of a politically powerful minority to revise those mores through use of the laws. That objective, and the means chosen to achieve it, are not only unimpeachable under any constitutional doctrine hitherto pronounced (hence the opinion's heavy reliance upon principles of righteousness rather than judicial holdings); they have been specifically approved by the Congress of the United States and by this Court.

In holding that homosexuality cannot be singled out for disfavorable treatment, the Court contradicts a decision, unchallenged here, pronounced only 10 years ago, see *Bowers v. Hardwick* (1986), and places the prestige of this institution behind the proposition that opposition to homosexuality is as reprehensible as racial or religious bias. Whether it is or not is *precisely* the cultural debate that gave rise to the Colorado constitutional amendment (and to the preferential laws against which the amendment was directed). Since the Constitution of the United States says nothing about this subject, it is left to be resolved by normal democratic means, including the democratic adoption of provisions in state constitutions. This Court has no business imposing upon all Americans the resolution favored by the elite class from which the Members of this institution are selected, pronouncing that "animosity" toward homosexuality is evil. I vigorously dissent.

Let me first discuss Part II of the Court's opinion, its longest section, which is devoted to rejecting the State's arguments that Amendment 2 "puts gays and lesbians in the same position as all other persons," and "does no more than deny homosexuals special rights.". . .

. . . [T]he principle underlying the Court's opinion is that one who is accorded equal treatment under the laws, but cannot as readily as others obtain *preferential* treatment under the laws, has been denied equal protection of the laws. If merely stating this alleged "equal protection" violation does not suffice to refute it, our constitutional jurisprudence has achieved terminal silliness. . . .

I turn next to whether there was a legitimate rational ba-

sis for the substance of the constitutional amendment—for the prohibition of special protection for homosexuals. It is unsurprising that the Court avoids discussion of this question, since the answer is so obviously yes. The case most relevant to the issue before us today is not even mentioned in the Court's opinion: In *Bowers v. Hardwick* (1986), we held that the Constitution does not prohibit what virtually all States had done from the founding of the Republic until very recent years—making homosexual conduct a crime. That holding is unassailable, except by those who think that the Constitution changes to suit current fashions. But in any event it is a given in the present case: Respondents' briefs did not urge overruling *Bowers*, and at oral argument respondents' counsel expressly disavowed any intent to seek such overruling. If it is constitutionally permissible for a State to make homosexual conduct criminal, surely it is constitutionally permissible for a State to enact other laws merely *disfavoring* homosexual conduct. . . .

But assuming that, in Amendment 2, a person of homosexual "orientation" is someone who does not engage in homosexual conduct but merely has a tendency or desire to do so, *Bowers* still suffices to establish a rational basis for the provision. If it is rational to criminalize the conduct, surely it is rational to deny special favor and protection to those with a self-avowed tendency or desire to engage in the conduct. Indeed, where criminal sanctions are not involved, homosexual "orientation" is an acceptable stand-in for homosexual conduct. . . .

. . . The Court's opinion contains grim, disapproving hints that Coloradans have been guilty of "animus" or "animosity" toward homosexuality, as though that has been established as Unamerican. Of course it is our moral heritage that one should not hate any human being or class of human beings. But I had thought that one could consider certain conduct reprehensible—murder, for example, or polygamy, or cruelty to animals—and could exhibit even "animus" toward such conduct. Surely that is the only sort of "animus" at issue here: moral disapproval of homosexual conduct, the same sort of moral disapproval that produced the centuries-old criminal laws that we held constitutional in *Bowers*. . . .

But though Coloradans are, as I say, *entitled* to be hostile toward homosexual conduct, the fact is that the degree of hostility reflected by Amendment 2 is the smallest conceivable. The Court's portrayal of Coloradans as a society fallen victim to pointless, hate-filled "gay-bashing" is so false as to be comical. Colorado not only is one of the 25 States that have repealed their antisodomy laws, but was among the first to do so. But the society that eliminates criminal punishment for homosexual acts does not necessarily abandon the view that homosexuality is morally wrong and socially harmful; often, abolition simply reflects the view that enforcement of such criminal laws involves unseemly intrusion into the intimate lives of citizens. . . .

When the Court takes sides in the culture wars, it tends to be with the knights rather than the villeins—and more specifically with the Templars, reflecting the views and values of the lawyer class from which the Court's Members are drawn. How that class feels about homosexuality will be evident to anyone who wishes to interview job applicants at virtually any of the Nation's law schools. The interviewer may refuse to offer a job because the applicant is a Republican; because he is an adulterer; because he went to the wrong prep school or belongs to the wrong country club; because he eats snails; because he is a womanizer; because she wears real-animal fur; or even because he hates the Chicago Cubs. But if the interviewer should wish not to be an associate or partner of an applicant because he disapproves of the applicant's homosexuality, *then* he will have violated the pledge which the Association of American Law Schools requires all its member-schools to exact from job interviewers: "assurance of the employer's willingness" to hire homosexuals. This law-school view of what "prejudices" must be stamped out may be contrasted with the more plebeian attitudes that apparently still prevail in the United States Congress, which has been unresponsive to repeated attempts to extend to homosexuals the protections of federal civil rights laws, and which took the pains to exclude them specifically from the Americans With Disabilities Act of 1990.

Today's opinion has no foundation in American constitutional law, and barely pretends to. The people of Colorado have adopted an entirely reasonable provision which does not even disfavor homosexuals in any substantive sense, but merely denies them preferential treatment. Amendment 2 is designed to prevent piecemeal deterioration of the sexual morality favored by a majority of Coloradans, and is not only an appropriate means to that legitimate end, but a means that Americans have employed before. Striking it down is an act, not of judicial judgment, but of political will. I dissent.

The majority's opinion is a strong statement against laws that single out homosexuals for discriminatory treatment. But the ruling is also important for other reasons. The justices explicitly distanced themselves from the "strict scrutiny" approach of the Colorado Supreme Court and did not even engage in a full discussion of the relative merits of the three equal protections tests as applied to gay rights. Instead, the Court concluded that Amendment 2 offends even the lowest level of scrutiny (rational basis), leaving little necessity to engage in additional argument regarding an appropriate test. The Court struck down Amendment 2, but created no new rights or protections for homosexuals.

So, despite *Romer*'s importance, it will not be the Court's last word on the rights of gays and lesbians. While some states are following Congress's lead and passing legislation that bans same-sex marriages, others are moving in the opposite direction. For example, in response to a state supreme court decision upholding the right of lesbian and gay couples to obtain the same benefits as opposite-sex couples, but leaving it to the legislature to determine whether those benefits would accrue through a marriage or domestic partnership law, the Vermont legislature opted for the latter route. Vermont became the first state to give gay and lesbian couples the benefits of marriage, though in the form of civil unions certified by a justice of the peace, judge, or member of the clergy. But what if other states go a step further and enable same-sex couples to marry? Under the Defense of Marriage Act, their marriages would not be recognized in states that do not have such legislation. What will the Supreme Court have to say about this? Will the justices permit states not to recognize marriages legally performed in another state? Or will they strike down the act?

Larger questions loom as well: Will the Court ever accord gays and lesbians with the same level of protection as women, for example, enjoy under the Fourteenth Amendment? How would such a decision affect a range of laws that classify on the basis of sexual orientation? Unfortunately, the Court's most recent foray into the area, *Boy Scouts of America v. Dale (see pages 303–308)* does not provide much help in answering these questions. The Court framed the case largely in First Amend-

BOX 12-6   SEXUAL ORIENTATION IN GLOBAL PERSPECTIVE

IN MANY AREAS, law scholars agree, the United States differs from other democracies in its legal treatment of gays and lesbians. For example, with the exception of several former republics of the Soviet Union, no country in Europe prohibits private consensual homosexual relations. The European Court of Human Rights has held that laws prohibiting sodomy violate the "right to privacy" under the European Convention for the Protection of Human Rights. In addition, in 1994 the United Nations Human Rights Committee ruled that the anti-sodomy law passed by the Australian state of Tasmania violated the privacy and nondiscrimination provisions of the International Covenant on Civil and Political Rights (ICCPR). These rulings stand in marked contrast to the U.S. Supreme Court's approach to sodomy in *Bowers v. Hardwick (see Chapter 9).*

Moreover, at a time when U.S. law denies recognition of same-sex marriages, some countries are reconsidering their bans or at least legislation that would recognize gay and lesbian partnerships. The current list includes Brazil, Latvia, and Portugal. Other nations, such as Canada, Denmark, Hungary, Iceland, the Netherlands, Norway, and Sweden, have moved or are moving in the direction of providing benefits to same-sex couples traditionally enjoyed by those legally married.

Many countries provide various protections against discrimination based on sexual orientation. Some of these protections are laws, such as Costa Rica's, which reads: "Whoever practices any form of discrimination, based on race, nationality, gender, age, political opinion, sexual orientation, social position, economic situation, marriage status, or diseases will be sanctioned by the law with twenty to sixty days in jail." Other protections have come in the form of constitutional provisions or court interpretations of those provisions. South Africa was the first country, in 1996, to explicitly prohibit discrimination based on sexual orientation in its constitution (bans discrimination on the basis of "race, gender, sex, pregnancy, marital status, ethnic or social origin, colour, sexual orientation, age, disability, religion, conscience, belief, culture, language and birth"). Others, including Ecuador and Fiji, have followed suit. Courts in some nations have read their constitutional documents to accomplish similar ends. So, for example, in 1995 the Canadian Supreme Court read the relevant clause in its country's charter—"Every individual is equal before and under the law and has the right to the equal protection and equal benefit of the law without discrimination and, in particular, without discrimination based on race, national or ethnic origin, colour, religion, sex, age, or mental or physical disability"—to cover sexual orientation.

Despite these steps, gays and lesbians still remain the targets of discrimination throughout the world. In 1993 Romania agreed to decriminalize homosexual acts to conform to the European Convention for the Protection of Human Rights and Fundamental Freedoms, but failed to do so. Although Fiji's constitution prohibits discrimination on the basis of sexual orientation, the prime minister has proposed to amend it to ban same-sex marriages. Poland explicitly rejected national and international attempts to include sexual orientation as a ground for nondiscrimination in its new constitution. Moreover, violence against gays and lesbians continues throughout the world, as it does in the United States.

SOURCES: James D. Wilets, "Using International Law to Vindicate the Civil Rights of Gays and Lesbians in United States Courts," *Columbia Human Rights Law Review* 27 (1995): 33–56; Edward H. Sadtler, "A Right to Same-Sex Marriage Under International Law: Can It Be Vindicated in the United States?" *Virginia Journal of International Law* 40 (1999): 405–447; Martha Bailey, "How Will Canada Respond to Foreign Same-Sex Marriages?" *Creighton Law Review* 32 (1998): 105–119; and International Gay and Lesbian Human Rights Commission, *http://www.iglhrc.org.*

ment terms, accepting the Boy Scouts' argument that its right to freedom of association prohibits it from being forced to accept homosexual members. But another way to get some perspective on these questions is to consider developments in other countries regarding the treatment of gays and lesbians. Box 12-6 provides a sampling.

OTHER FORMS OF DISCRIMINATION

Discrimination based on race, sex, and—more recently—sexual preference occupy high places in the national dialogue. But we should not forget that other categories of people face discrimination in our society. As you read the narrative and case materials that follow, note the level of scrutiny that the Court has applied to each classification, because, as we have learned, the standard the justices adopt can have an important impact on the ultimate resolution of particular disputes.

Discrimination Based on Economic Status

As with matters of race and gender, society's views on economic status have changed. In the early days of our nation, wealth was considered a reflection of individual worth. The poor were thought to be less deserving. The free enterprise philosophy that emphasized personal economic responsibility discouraged public policies designed to help them. The fact that people could be imprisoned for failure to pay debts—a contrast with today's more lenient treatment under the bankruptcy laws—reflects that period's hardline approach to economic failure. Even a sitting Supreme Court justice, James Wilson, was imprisoned in 1796 because of a failure to satisfy his creditors. In *City of New York v. Miln* (1837) the Court supported the power of the state to take "precautionary measures against the moral pestilence of paupers."

As our society has evolved, the plight of the poor has become a major public policy concern. Although opinions differ widely on the proper role of government in handling poverty, housing, and health care, our political system has developed social programs that would have been inconceivable to leaders during the nation's formative years. Moreover, economic disadvantage, at least according to the Supreme Court, is no longer a justification for denying a person full political and social rights. We have already seen, for example, that the Court has extended certain rights, such as government-provided attorneys, to indigent criminal defendants. It has also ruled on government policies discriminating against the poor, including welfare programs that require individuals to live in a particular state for a specified amount of time before receiving benefits and public education.

When the Court examines such policies, what standard of review does it use? The standard varies depending on the nature of the right in question. If the classification burdens a "fundamental" right, the justices apply strict scrutiny; if not, they invoke the rational basis standard.

Two cases decided during the Burger Court years illustrate the point. The first, *Shapiro v. Thompson* (1969), involved the kind of law we just mentioned, that is, to obtain welfare benefits, some states required applicants to live in the state for one year. The states argued that the residency requirement was needed for fiscal reasons. They claimed that those who require welfare assistance when they first move to a state are likely to become continuing burdens. If a state can deter such people from moving there in the first place by denying them welfare benefits during the first year, the state can continue to provide aid to long-time residents.

Writing for the Court, Justice Brennan disagreed. He concluded that the "states do not use and have no need to use the one-year requirement for the governmental purposes suggested. Thus, even under traditional equal protection tests a classification of welfare applicants according to whether they have lived in the State for one year would seem irrational and unconstitutional." But he went on to say:

The traditional criteria do not apply in these cases. Since the classification here touches on the fundamental right of interstate movement, its constitutionality must be judged by the stricter standard of whether it promotes a compelling state interest. Under this standard, the waiting-period requirement clearly violates the Equal Protection Clause.

In other words, while a rational basis standard normally would be appropriate in cases involving classifications based on wealth, when a fundamental right also is involved—here, the right to interstate travel—the standard is elevated. The Court invoked the same logic in *Harper v. Virginia State Board of Elections* (1966), in which it struck down poll taxes as infringing on the fundamental right to vote *(see Chapter 13)*.

When a fundamental right is not involved, however, the justices have tended to stick with the rational basis standard. An example is *San Antonio Independent School District v. Rodriguez* (1973), a case of enormous importance. First, it involved the right of children to receive a public education, the surest way for the disadvantaged to improve their prospects for economic and social advancement. Second, it questioned the constitutionality of the way Texas funded public schools. Education is the most expensive of all state programs, and any change in the method of distributing these funds can have a tremendous impact. Third, the Texas system challenged here was similar to schemes used by most states in determining the allocation of education dollars. Whatever the Court decided, this case was going to be significant economically and socially.

At its heart was the contention that the Texas system for funding schools discriminated against the poor. It was undeniable that children who lived in wealthy school districts had access to a higher quality education than children in poor districts. But does this difference violate the Constitution? In large measure, the answer depends on which equal protection standard is used. Under strict scrutiny the Texas funding system almost certainly would fall. But before strict scrutiny can be applied, as we now know, one of two requirements has to be met. Either the poor, like black Americans in the racial discrimination cases, would have to be declared a suspect class, a step the Court refused to take in *Shapiro*, or the right to an education would have to be declared a fundamental right, as was the right to travel in *Shapiro*. If the Court failed to support one of these positions, the rational basis test would control, and the state plan likely would stand. As you read Justice Powell's decision, think about his reasoning and conclusions on these two points.[32]

San Antonio Independent School District v. Rodriguez

411 U.S. 1 (1973)
laws.findlaw.com/US/411/1.html
Vote: 5 (Blackmun, Burger, Powell, Rehnquist, Stewart)
        4 (Brennan, Douglas, Marshall, White)
Opinion of the Court: Powell
Concurring opinion: Stewart
Dissenting opinions: Brennan, Marshall, White

Demetrio Rodriguez and other Mexican-American parents whose children attended the public schools of the Edgewood Independent School District in San Anto-

nio, Texas, were concerned about the quality of the local schools. The Edgewood district was about 90 percent Mexican-American and quite poor. Efforts to improve their children's schools were unsuccessful due to insufficient funding. Because the state formula for distributing education funds resulted in low levels of financial support for economically depressed districts, the parents filed suit to declare the state funding system in violation of the Equal Protection Clause. The funding program guaranteed each child in the state a minimum basic education by appropriating funds to local school districts through a complex formula designed to take into account economic variations across school districts. Local districts levied property taxes to meet their assigned contributions to the state program but could use the property taxing power to obtain additional funds.

The Edgewood district had an assessed property value per pupil of $5,960, the lowest in the San Antonio area. It taxed its residents at a rate of $1.05 per $100 in assessed valuation, the area's highest rate. This local tax yielded $26 per pupil above the contributions that had to be made to the state for the 1967–1968 school year. Funds from the state added $222 per pupil, and federal programs contributed $108. These sources combined for a total of $356 per pupil for the year. In the nearby Alamo Heights district, property values amounted to $49,000 per pupil, which was taxed at a rate of $.85 per $100 of assessed valuation. These property taxes yielded $333 additional available revenues per pupil. Combined with $225 from state funds and $36 from federal sources, Alamo Heights enjoyed a total funding level of $594 per pupil.

The suit filed by Rodriguez and the other parents was based on these disparities. Although the residents of Edgewood taxed themselves at a much higher rate, the yield from local taxes in Alamo Heights was almost thirteen times greater. To achieve equal property tax dollars with Alamo Heights, Edgewood would have had to raise its tax rate to $13 per $100 in assessed valuation, but state law placed a $1.50 ceiling on such taxes. There was no way for the Edgewood parents to achieve funding equality.

A three-judge federal court agreed with the Rodriguez suit, finding that the Texas funding program invidiously discriminated against children on the basis of economic status. According to the federal court, the poor were a suspect class, and education was a fundamental right. The state appealed to the Supreme Court. Twenty-five states filed amicus curiae briefs supporting the Texas funding system. Groups such as the NAACP, the American Civil Liberties Union, and the American Education Association filed briefs backing Rodriguez.

MR. JUSTICE POWELL delivered the opinion of the Court.

Texas virtually concedes that its historically rooted dual system of financing education could not withstand the strict judicial scrutiny that this Court has found appropriate in reviewing legislative judgments that interfere with fundamental constitutional rights or that involve suspect classifications. If, as previous decisions have indicated, strict scrutiny means that the State's system is not entitled to the usual presumption of validity, that the State rather than the complainants must carry a "heavy burden of justification," that the State must demonstrate that its educational system has been structured with "precision," and is "tailored" narrowly to serve legitimate objectives and that it has selected the "less drastic means" for effectuating its objectives, the Texas financing system and its counterpart in virtually every other State will not pass muster. The State candidly admits that "[n]o one familiar with the Texas system would contend that it has yet achieved perfection." Apart from its concession that educational financing in Texas has "defects" and "imperfections," the State defends the system's rationality with vigor and disputes the District Court's finding that it lacks a "reasonable basis."

This, then, establishes the framework for our analysis. We must decide, first, whether the Texas system of financing public education operates to the disadvantage of some suspect class or impinges upon a fundamental right explicitly or implicitly protected by the Constitution, thereby requiring strict judicial scrutiny. If so, the judgment of the District Court should be affirmed. If not, the Texas scheme must still be examined to determine whether it rationally furthers some legitimate, articulated state purpose and therefore does not constitute an invidious discrimination in violation of the Equal Protection Clause of the Fourteenth Amendment. . . .

Demetrio Rodriguez and other Mexican-American parents challenged the Texas public school financing system as discriminatory on the basis of economic status, but in 1973 the Supreme Court ruled against them.

. . . For the several reasons that follow, we find neither the suspect-classification nor the fundamental-interest analysis persuasive.

The wealth discrimination discovered by the District Court in this case, and by several other courts that have recently struck down school-financing laws in other States, is quite unlike any of the forms of wealth discrimination heretofore reviewed by this Court. Rather than focusing on the unique features of the alleged discrimination, the courts in these cases have virtually assumed their findings of a suspect classification through a simplistic process of analysis: since, under the traditional systems of financing public schools, some poorer people receive less expensive educations than other more affluent people, these systems discriminate on the basis of wealth. This approach largely ignores the hard threshold questions, including whether it makes a difference for purposes of consideration under the

Constitution that the class of disadvantaged "poor" cannot be identified or defined in customary equal protection terms, and whether the relative—rather than absolute—nature of the asserted deprivation is of significant consequence. Before a State's laws and the justification for the classifications they create are subjected to strict judicial scrutiny, we think these threshold considerations must be analyzed more closely than they were in the court below. . . .

. . . First, in support of their charge that the system discriminates against the "poor," appellees have made no effort to demonstrate that it operates to the peculiar disadvantage of any class fairly definable as indigent, or as composed of persons whose incomes are beneath any designated poverty level. Indeed, there is reason to believe that the poorest families are not necessarily clustered in the poorest property districts. A recent and exhaustive study of school districts in Connecticut concluded that . . . the poor were clustered around commercial and industrial areas—those same areas that provide the most attractive sources of property tax income for school districts. Whether a similar pattern would be discovered in Texas is not known, but there is no basis on the record in this case for assuming that the poorest people—defined by reference to any level of absolute impecunity—are concentrated in the poorest districts.

Second, neither appellees nor the District Court addressed the fact that, unlike each of the foregoing cases, lack of personal resources has not occasioned an absolute deprivation of the desired benefit. The argument here is not that the children in districts having relatively low assessable property values are receiving no public education; rather, it is that they are receiving a poorer quality education than that available to children in districts having more assessable wealth. Apart from the unsettled and disputed question whether the quality of education may be determined by the amount of money expended for it, a sufficient answer to appellees' argument is that, at least where wealth is involved, the Equal Protection Clause does not require absolute equality or precisely equal advantages. . . .

For these two reasons—the absence of any evidence that the financing system discriminates against any definable category of "poor" people or that it results in the absolute deprivation of education—the disadvantaged class is not susceptible of identification in traditional terms.

. . . Appellees and the District Court may have embraced a second or third approach, the second of which might be characterized as a theory of relative or comparative discrimination based on family income. Appellees sought to prove that a direct correlation exists between the wealth of families within each district and the expenditures therein for education. That is, along a continuum, the poorer the family the lower the dollar amount of education received by the family's children.

The principal evidence adduced in support of this comparative-discrimination claim is an affidavit submitted by Professor Joel S. Berke of Syracuse University's Educational Finance Policy Institute. The District Court, relying in major part upon this affidavit and apparently accepting the substance of appellees' theory, noted, first, a positive correlation between the wealth of school districts, measured in terms of assessable property per pupil, and their levels of per-pupil expenditures. Second, the court found a similar correlation between district wealth and the personal wealth of its residents, measured in terms of median family income.

If, in fact, these correlations could be sustained, then it might be argued that expenditures on education—equated by appellees to the quality of education—are dependent on personal wealth. Appellees' comparative-discrimination theory would still face serious unanswered questions, including whether a bare positive correlation or some higher degree of correlation is necessary to provide a basis for concluding that the financing system is designed to operate to the peculiar disadvantage of the comparatively poor, and whether a class of this size and diversity could ever claim the special protection accorded "suspect" classes. These questions need not be addressed in this case, however, since appellees' proof fails to support their allegations or the District Court's conclusions. . . .

This brings us, then, to the third way in which the classification scheme might be defined—district wealth discrimination. Since the only correlation indicated by the evidence is between district property wealth and expenditures, it may be argued that discrimination might be found without regard to the individual income characteristics of district residents. Assuming a perfect correlation between district property wealth and expenditures from top to bottom, the disadvantaged class might be viewed as encompassing every child in every district except the district that has the most assessable wealth and spends the most on education. Alternatively, . . . the class might be defined more restrictively to include children in districts with assessable property which falls below the statewide average, or median, or below some other artificially defined level.

However described, it is clear that appellees' suit asks this Court to extend its most exacting scrutiny to review a system that allegedly discriminates against a large, diverse, and amorphous class, unified only by the common factor of residence in districts that happen to have less taxable wealth than other districts. The system of alleged discrimination and the class it defines have none of the traditional indicia of suspectness: the class is not saddled with such disabilities, or subjected to such a history of purposeful unequal treatment, or relegated to such a position of political powerlessness as to command extraordinary protection from the majoritarian political process.

We thus conclude that the Texas system does not operate to the peculiar disadvantage of any suspect class. But in recognition of the fact that this Court has never heretofore held that wealth discrimination alone provides an adequate basis for invoking strict scrutiny, appellees have not relied solely on this contention. They also assert that the State's system impermissibly interferes with the exercise of a "fundamental" right and that accordingly the prior decisions of this Court require the application of the strict standard of judicial review. It is this question—whether education is a fundamental right, in the sense that it is among the rights and liberties protected by the Constitution—which has so consumed the attention of courts and commentators in recent years. . . .

Nothing this Court holds today in any way detracts from our historic dedication to public education. We are in complete agreement with the conclusion of the three-judge panel below that "the grave significance of education both to the individual and to our society" cannot be doubted. But the importance of a service performed by the State does not determine whether it must be regarded as fundamental for purposes of examination under the Equal Protection Clause. Mr. Justice Harlan, dissenting from the Court's application of strict scrutiny to a law impinging upon the right of interstate travel, admonished that "[v]irtually every state statute affects important rights." *Shapiro v. Thompson*. In his view, if the degree of judicial scrutiny of state legislation fluctuated, depending on a majority's view of the impor-

tance of the interest affected, we would have gone "far toward making this Court a 'super-legislature.'" We would, indeed, then be assuming a legislative role and one for which the Court lacks both authority and competence. But MR. JUSTICE STEWART's response in *Shapiro* to Mr. Justice Harlan's concern correctly articulates the limits of the fundamental-rights rationale employed in the Court's equal protection decisions:

"The Court today does *not* 'pick out particular human activities, characterize them as "fundamental," and give them added protection. . . .' To the contrary, the Court simply recognizes, as it must, an established constitutional right, and gives to that right no less protection than the Constitution itself demands." (Emphasis in original.)

MR. JUSTICE STEWART's statement serves to underline what the opinion of the Court in *Shapiro* makes clear. In subjecting to strict judicial scrutiny state welfare eligibility statutes that imposed a one-year durational residency requirement as a precondition to receiving [welfare] benefits, the Court explained:

"[I]n moving from State to State . . . appellees were exercising a constitutional right, and any classification which serves to penalize the exercise of that right, unless shown to be necessary to promote a *compelling* governmental interest, is unconstitutional." (Emphasis in original.)

The right to interstate travel had long been recognized as a right of constitutional significance, and the Court's decision, therefore, did not require an ad hoc determination as to the social or economic importance of that right.

Lindsey v. Normet (1972), decided only last Term, firmly reiterates that social importance is not the critical determinant for subjecting state legislation to strict scrutiny. The complainants in that case, involving a challenge to the procedural limitations imposed on tenants in suits brought by landlords under Oregon's Forcible Entry and Wrongful Detainer Law, urged the Court to examine the operation of the statute under "a more stringent standard than mere rationality." The tenants argued that the statutory limitations implicated "fundamental interests which are particularly important to the poor," such as the "'need for decent shelter'" and the "'right to retain peaceful possession of one's home.'" MR. JUSTICE WHITE's analysis, in his opinion for the Court, is instructive:

"We do not denigrate the importance of decent, safe, and sanitary housing. But the Constitution does not provide judicial remedies for every social and economic ill. We are unable to perceive in that document any constitutional guarantee of access to dwellings of a particular quality or any recognition of the right of a tenant to occupy the real property of his landlord beyond the term of his lease, without the payment of rent. . . . *Absent constitutional mandate,* the assurance of adequate housing and the definition of landlord-tenant relationships are legislative, not judicial, functions." (Emphasis supplied.). . . .

The lesson of these cases in addressing the question now before the Court is plain. It is not the province of this Court to create substantive constitutional rights in the name of guaranteeing equal protection of the laws. Thus, the key to discovering whether education is "fundamental" is not to be found in comparisons of the relative societal significance of education as opposed to subsistence or housing. Nor is it to be found by weighing whether education is as important as the right to travel. Rather, the answer lies in assessing whether there is a right to education explicitly or implicitly guaranteed by the Constitution.

Education, of course, is not among the rights afforded explicit protection under our Federal Constitution. Nor do we find any basis for saying it is implicitly so protected. As we have said, the undisputed importance of education will not alone cause this Court to depart from the usual standard for reviewing a State's social and economic legislation. It is appellees' contention, however, that education is distinguishable from other services and benefits provided by the State because it bears a peculiarly close relationship to other rights and liberties accorded protection under the Constitution. Specifically, they insist that education is itself a fundamental personal right because it is essential to the effective exercise of First Amendment freedoms and to intelligent utilization of the right to vote. In asserting a nexus between speech and education, appellees urge that the right to speak is meaningless unless the speaker is capable of articulating his thoughts intelligently and persuasively. The "marketplace of ideas" is an empty forum for those lacking basic communicative tools. Likewise, they argue that the corollary right to receive information becomes little more than a hollow privilege when the recipient has not been taught to read, assimilate, and utilize available knowledge. . . .

We need not dispute any of these propositions. The Court has long afforded zealous protection against unjustifiable governmental interference with the individual's rights to speak and to vote. Yet we have never presumed to possess either the ability or the authority to guarantee to the citizenry the most *effective* speech or the most *informed* electoral choice. That these may be desirable goals of a system of freedom of expression and of a representative form of government is not to be doubted. These are indeed goals to be pursued by a people whose thoughts and beliefs are freed from governmental interference. But they are not values to be implemented by judicial intrusion into otherwise legitimate state activities.

Even if it were conceded that some identifiable quantum of education is a constitutionally protected prerequisite to the meaningful exercise of either right, we have no indication that the present levels of educational expenditures in Texas provide an education that falls short. . . .

We have carefully considered each of the arguments supportive of the District Court's finding that education is a fundamental right or liberty and have found those arguments unpersuasive. . . .

The foregoing considerations buttress our conclusion that Texas' system of public school finance is an inappropriate candidate for strict judicial scrutiny. These same considerations are relevant to the determination whether that system, with its conceded imperfections, nevertheless bears some rational relationship to a legitimate state purpose. It is to this question that we next turn our attention.

The basic contours of the Texas school finance system have been traced at the outset of this opinion. We will now describe in more detail that system and how it operates, as these facts bear directly upon the demands of the Equal Protection Clause.

Apart from federal assistance, each Texas school receives its funds from the State and from its local school district. . . .

In its reliance on state as well as local resources, the Texas system is comparable to the systems employed in virtually every other State. The power to tax local property for educational purposes has been recognized in Texas at least since 1883. When the growth of commercial and industrial centers and accompanying shifts in population began to create disparities in local resources, Texas undertook a program calling for a considerable investment of state funds. . . .

. . . While assuring a basic education for every child in the State, it permits and encourages a large measure of participation in and control of each district's schools at the local level. In an era that has witnessed a consistent trend toward centralization of the functions of government, local sharing of responsibility for public education has survived. . . .

The persistence of attachment to government at the lowest level where education is concerned reflects the depth of commitment of its supporters. In part, local control means . . . the freedom to devote more money to the education of one's children. Equally important, however, is the opportunity it offers for participation in the decisionmaking process that determines how those local tax dollars will be spent. Each locality is free to tailor local programs to local needs. Pluralism also affords some opportunity for experimentation, innovation, and a healthy competition for educational excellence. An analogy to the Nation-State relationship in our federal system seems uniquely appropriate. Mr. Justice Brandeis identified as one of the peculiar strengths of our form of government each State's freedom to "serve as a laboratory; and try novel social and economic experiments." No area of social concern stands to profit more from a multiplicity of viewpoints and from a diversity of approaches than does public education.

Appellees do not question the propriety of Texas' dedication to local control of education. To the contrary, they attack the school-financing system precisely because, in their view, it does not provide the same level of local control and fiscal flexibility in all districts. Appellees suggest that local control could be preserved and promoted under other financing systems that resulted in more equality in educational expenditures. While it is no doubt true that reliance on local property taxation for school revenues provides less freedom of choice with respect to expenditures for some districts than for others, the existence of "some inequality" in the manner in which the State's rationale is achieved is not alone a sufficient basis for striking down the entire system. . . .

In sum, to the extent that the Texas system of school financing results in unequal expenditures between children who happen to reside in different districts, we cannot say that such disparities are the product of a system that is so irrational as to be invidiously discriminatory. Texas has acknowledged its shortcomings and has persistently endeavored—not without some success—to ameliorate the differences in levels of expenditures without sacrificing the benefits of local participation. The Texas plan is not the result of hurried, ill-conceived legislation. It certainly is not

the product of purposeful discrimination against any group or class. On the contrary, it is rooted in decades of experience in Texas and elsewhere, and in major part is the product of responsible studies by qualified people. . . .

These practical considerations, of course, play no role in the adjudication of the constitutional issues presented here. But they serve to highlight the wisdom of the traditional limitations on this Court's function. The consideration and initiation of fundamental reforms with respect to state taxation and education are matters reserved for the legislative processes of the various States, and we do no violence to the values of federalism and separation of powers by staying our hand. We hardly need add that this Court's action today is not to be viewed as placing its judicial imprimatur on the status quo. The need is apparent for reform in tax systems which may well have relied too long and too heavily on the local property tax. And certainly innovative thinking as to public education, its methods, and its funding is necessary to assure both a higher level of quality and greater uniformity of opportunity. These matters merit the continued attention of the scholars who already have contributed much by their challenges. But the ultimate solutions must come from the lawmakers and from the democratic pressures of those who elect them.

Reversed.

MR. JUSTICE MARSHALL . . . dissenting.

The Court today decides, in effect, that a State may constitutionally vary the quality of education which it offers its children in accordance with the amount of taxable wealth located in the school districts within which they reside. The majority's decision represents an abrupt departure from the mainstream of recent state and federal court decisions concerning the unconstitutionality of state educational financing schemes dependent upon taxable local wealth. More unfortunately, though, the majority's holding can only be seen as a retreat from our historic commitment to equality of educational opportunity and as unsupportable acquiescence in a system which deprives children in their earliest years of the chance to reach their full potential as citizens. The Court does this despite the absence of any substantial justification for a scheme which arbitrarily channels educational resources in accordance with the fortuity of the amount of taxable wealth within each district.

In my judgment, the right of every American to an equal

start in life, so far as the provision of a state service as important as education is concerned, is far too vital to permit state discrimination on grounds as tenuous as those presented by this record. Nor can I accept the notion that it is sufficient to remit these appellees to the vagaries of the political process which, contrary to the majority's suggestion, has proved singularly unsuited to the task of providing a remedy for this discrimination. I, for one, am unsatisfied with the hope of an ultimate "political" solution sometime in the indefinite future while, in the meantime, countless children unjustifiably receive inferior educations that "may affect their hearts and minds in a way unlikely ever to be undone." I must therefore respectfully dissent. . . .

. . . I must . . . voice my disagreement with the Court's rigidified approach to equal protection analysis. The Court apparently seeks to establish today that equal protection cases fall into one of two neat categories which dictate the appropriate standard of review—strict scrutiny or mere rationality. But this Court's decisions in the field of equal protection defy such easy categorization. A principled reading of what this Court has done reveals that it has applied a spectrum of standards in reviewing discrimination allegedly violative of the Equal Protection Clause. This spectrum clearly comprehends variations in the degree of care with which the Court will scrutinize particular classifications, depending, I believe, on the constitutional and societal importance of the interest adversely affected and the recognized invidiousness of the basis upon which the particular classification is drawn. I find in fact that many of the Court's recent decisions embody the very sort of reasoned approach to equal protection analysis for which I previously argued— that is, an approach in which "concentration [is] placed upon the character of the classification in question, the relative importance to individuals in the class discriminated against of the governmental benefits that they do not receive, and the asserted state interests in support of the classification."

I therefore cannot accept the majority's labored efforts to demonstrate that fundamental interests, which call for strict scrutiny of the challenged classification, encompass only established rights which we are somehow bound to recognize from the text of the Constitution itself. To be sure, some interests which the Court has deemed to be fundamental for purposes of equal protection analysis are themselves constitutionally protected rights. . . . But it will not do to suggest that the "answer" to whether an interest is fundamental for purposes of equal protection analysis is always determined by whether that interest "is a right . . . explicitly or implicitly guaranteed by the Constitution."

I would like to know where the Constitution guarantees the right to procreate, *Skinner v. Oklahoma* (1942), or the right to vote in state elections, *e.g., Reynolds v. Sims* (1964), or the right to an appeal from a criminal conviction, *e.g., Griffin v. Illinois* (1956). These are instances in which, due to the importance of the interests at stake, the Court has displayed a strong concern with the existence of discriminatory state treatment. But the Court has never said or indicated that these are interests which independently enjoy full-blown constitutional protection. . . .

The majority is, of course, correct when it suggests that the process of determining which interests are fundamental is a difficult one. But I do not think the problem is insurmountable. And I certainly do not accept the view that the process need necessarily degenerate into an unprincipled, subjective "picking-and-choosing" between various interests or that it must involve this Court in creating "substantive constitutional rights in the name of guaranteeing equal protection of the laws." Although not all fundamental interests are constitutionally guaranteed, the determination of which interests are fundamental should be firmly rooted in the text of the Constitution. The task in every case should be to determine the extent to which constitutionally guaranteed rights are dependent on interests not mentioned in the Constitution. As the nexus between the specific constitutional guarantee and the nonconstitutional interest draws closer, the nonconstitutional interest becomes more fundamental and the degree of judicial scrutiny applied when the interest is infringed on a discriminatory basis must be adjusted accordingly. Thus, it cannot be denied that interests such as procreation, the exercise of the state franchise, and access to criminal appellate processes are not fully guaranteed to the citizen by our Constitution. But these interests have nonetheless been afforded special judicial consideration in the face of discrimination because they are, to some extent, interrelated with constitutional guarantees. Procreation is now understood to be important because of its interaction with the established constitutional right of privacy. The exercise of the state franchise is closely tied to basic civil and political rights inherent in the First Amendment. And access to criminal appellate processes enhances the integrity of the range of rights implicit in the Fourteenth Amendment guarantee of due process of law. Only if we closely protect the related interests from state discrimination do we ultimately ensure the integrity of the constitutional guarantee itself. This is the real lesson that must be taken from our previous decisions involving interests deemed to be fundamental. . . .

. . . [I]f the discrimination inherent in the Texas scheme is scrutinized with the care demanded by the interest and classification present in this case, the unconstitutionality of that scheme is unmistakable.

The Rehnquist Court and Economic Discrimination

The decision in *Rodriguez* was a blow to civil rights advocates. It had a substantial impact on education by validating financing systems that perpetuated inequity. Several states, however, reacted by adjusting their financing schemes to reduce funding disparities, and a few state supreme courts even found unequal funding systems to be in violation of state constitutional provisions.

In terms of constitutional development, the ruling introduced problems for future litigation. The Court expressly held that the poor were not a suspect class. Unlike other groups, such as black Americans and aliens, that were granted such status, the poor were neither an easily identified group nor politically powerless; as a group they did not have a history of overt discrimination. The decision not to elevate the poor to suspect class status meant that a rational basis test would be used in economic discrimination cases in which a fundamental right was not at issue. This test provides the government with an advantage in demonstrating that challenged laws are valid. As the Court became more dominated by Reagan and Bush appointees, it continued to refrain from expanding constitutional protections for the poor.

In addition, the Court in *Rodriguez* held that education, unlike the right to interstate travel, was not a fundamental right under the Constitution. This holding also created potential problems for future cases. Advocates of the poor have concentrated their efforts on education because of its crucial role in human development. By not according it fundamental right status, the Court made successful legal action on behalf of the disadvantaged much more difficult.

But it is important to keep in mind that when economic discrimination compromises a fundamental right, a higher standard is used and a state finds it much more difficult to justify distinguishing people on the basis of their economic status. We saw this in the 1969 case of *Shapiro v. Thompson* (discussed on pages 703–704) involving the fundamental right to interstate travel. Because the right at stake was "fundamental" the Court ruled that the state needed to show that its law—denying welfare assistance to residents who had lived in their jurisdictions for less than one year—was necessary to promote a compelling governmental interest. In *Shapiro,* no such showing was made and the Court struck down the law.

To what extent has the Rehnquist Court gone along with this approach? One way to consider that question is to look at a 1999 case, *Saenz v. Roe,* which seems to raise an issue similar to *Shapiro.* The majority cites *Shapiro,* but did the justices invoke its logic to answer it? One of the more interesting aspects of the case is the Court's use of the "previously dormant" Privileges or Immunities Clause of the Fourteenth Amendment *(see Chapter 3).* Does the majority make a compelling case for its reliance on this clause, or do you agree with the dissenters who argue that it may not have the meaning the Court ascribes to it?

Saenz v. Roe

526 U.S. — (1999)
supct.law.cornell.edu/supct/html/98-97.ZS.html
Vote: 7 (Breyer, Ginsburg, Kennedy, O'Connor, Scalia, Souter, Stevens)
2 (Rehnquist, Thomas)
Opinion of the Court: Stevens
Dissenting Opinions: Rehnquist, Thomas

In 1992 the California Legislature enacted §11450.03 of the state Welfare and Institutions Code. That section, which sought to reduce the state's budget, limited new residents, for the first year they live in California, to the welfare benefits they would have received in the state of their prior residence. In other words, the state established a two-tier welfare system: residents of a year or more received California's standard (and generous) benefits, but newcomers got a different amount, depending on where they had lived before.

The statute was challenged by several new California residents. Among them were two women known as Brenda Roe, who had moved with her husband to Long Beach, California, from Oklahoma and Anna Doe, who had moved from Washington, D.C., when six months pregnant. Under the California statute, the Roes would have received $307 per month rather than the $565 benefit given to in-state residents; for Doe, those figures were $330 and $454, respectively.

California did not dispute the contention that §11450.03 would create significant disparities between newcomers and welfare recipients who have resided in the state for more than one year. Rather, it relied on the undisputed fact that the statute would save some $10.9 million in annual welfare costs. It argued that this cost saving was an appropriate exercise of budgetary authority as long as the residency requirement did not penalize the right to travel.

A district court judge disagreed. Relying primarily on the Supreme Court's decision in *Shapiro v. Thompson* (1969), he concluded that the statute placed "a penalty on the decision of new residents to migrate to the State and be treated on an equal basis with existing residents."

JUSTICE STEVENS delivered the opinion of the Court.

The word "travel" is not found in the text of the Constitution. Yet the "constitutional right to travel from one State to another" is firmly embedded in our jurisprudence. Indeed, as Justice Stewart reminded us in *Shapiro v. Thompson* (1969), the right is so important that it is "assertable against private interference as well as governmental action . . . a virtually unconditional personal right, guaranteed by the Constitution to us all."

In *Shapiro*, we reviewed the constitutionality of three statutory provisions that denied welfare assistance to residents of Connecticut, the District of Columbia, and Pennsylvania, who had resided within those respective jurisdictions less than one year immediately preceding their applications for assistance. Without pausing to identify the specific source of the right, we began by noting that the Court had long "recognized that the nature of our Federal

Union and our constitutional concepts of personal liberty unite to require that all citizens be free to travel throughout the length and breadth of our land uninhibited by statutes, rules, or regulations which unreasonably burden or restrict this movement." We squarely held that it was "constitutionally impermissible" for a State to enact durational residency requirements for the purpose of inhibiting the migration by needy persons into the State. We further held that a classification that had the effect of imposing a penalty on the exercise of the right to travel violated the Equal Protection Clause "unless shown to be necessary to promote a *compelling* governmental interest," and that no such showing had been made.

In this case California argues that §11450.03 was not enacted for the impermissible purpose of inhibiting migration by needy persons and that, unlike the legislation reviewed in *Shapiro*, it does not penalize the right to travel because new arrivals are not ineligible for benefits during their first year of residence. California submits that, instead of being subjected to the strictest scrutiny, the statute should be upheld if it is supported by a rational basis and that the State's legitimate interest in saving over $10 million a year satisfies that test. . . . The debate about the appropriate standard of review, together with the potential relevance of the federal statute, persuades us that it will be useful to focus on the source of the constitutional right on which respondents rely.

The "right to travel" discussed in our cases embraces at least three different components. It protects the right of a citizen of one State to enter and to leave another State, the right to be treated as a welcome visitor rather than an unfriendly alien when temporarily present in the second State, and, for those travelers who elect to become permanent residents, the right to be treated like other citizens of that State.

It was the right to go from one place to another, including the right to cross state borders while en route, that was vindicated in *Edwards v. California* (1941), which invalidated a state law that impeded the free interstate passage of the indigent. . . . Given that §11450.03 imposed no obstacle to respondents' entry into California, we think the State is correct when it argues that the statute does not directly impair the exercise of the right to free interstate movement. For the purposes of this case, therefore, we need not identify the source of that particular right in the text of the Constitution. . . .

The second component of the right to travel is, however, expressly protected by the text of the Constitution. The first sentence of Article IV, §2, provides:

"The Citizens of each State shall be entitled to all Privileges and Immunities of Citizens in the several States."

Thus, by virtue of a person's state citizenship, a citizen of one State who travels in other States, intending to return home at the end of his journey, is entitled to enjoy the "Privileges and Immunities of Citizens in the several States" that he visits. This provision removes "from the citizens of each State the disabilities of alienage in the other States." It provides important protections for nonresidents who enter a State whether to obtain employment, to procure medical services, or even to engage in commercial shrimp fishing. Those protections are not "absolute," but the Clause "does bar discrimination against citizens of other States where there is no substantial reason for the discrimination beyond the mere fact that they are citizens of other States." There may be a substantial reason for requiring the nonresident to pay more than the resident for a hunting license or to enroll in the state university, see *Vlandis v. Kline* (1973), but our cases have not identified any acceptable reason for qualifying the protection afforded by the Clause for "the 'citizen of State A who ventures into State B' to settle there and establish a home." Permissible justifications for discrimination between residents and nonresidents are simply inapplicable to a nonresident's exercise of the right to move into another State and become a resident of that State.

What is at issue in this case, then, is this third aspect of the right to travel—the right of the newly arrived citizen to the same privileges and immunities enjoyed by other citizens of the same State. That right is protected not only by the new arrival's status as a state citizen, but also by her status as a citizen of the United States. That additional source of protection is plainly identified in the opening words of the Fourteenth Amendment:

"All persons born or naturalized in the United States, and subject to the jurisdiction thereof, are citizens of the United States and of the State wherein they reside. No State shall make or enforce any law which shall abridge the privileges or immunities of citizens of the United States; . . . ."

Despite fundamentally differing views concerning the coverage of the Privileges or Immunities Clause of the Fourteenth Amendment, most notably expressed in the majority and dissenting opinions in the *Slaughter-House Cases* (1873),

it has always been common ground that this Clause protects the third component of the right to travel. Writing for the majority in the *Slaughter-House Cases,* Justice Miller explained that one of the privileges conferred by this Clause "is that a citizen of the United States can, of his own volition, become a citizen of any State of the Union by a *bona fide* residence therein, with the same rights as other citizens of that State." Justice Bradley, in dissent, used even stronger language to make the same point:

"The states have not now, if they ever had, any power to restrict their citizenship to any classes or persons. A citizen of the United States has a perfect constitutional right to go to and reside in any State he chooses, and to claim citizenship therein, and an equality of rights with every other citizen; and the whole power of the nation is pledged to sustain him in that right. He is not bound to cringe to any superior, or to pray for any act of grace, as a means of enjoying all the rights and privileges enjoyed by other citizens."

That newly arrived citizens "have two political capacities, one state and one federal," adds special force to their claim that they have the same rights as others who share their citizenship. Neither mere rationality nor some intermediate standard of review should be used to judge the constitutionality of a state rule that discriminates against some of its citizens because they have been domiciled in the State for less than a year. The appropriate standard may be more categorical than that articulated in *Shapiro,* but it is surely no less strict.

Because this case involves discrimination against citizens who have completed their interstate travel, the State's argument that its welfare scheme affects the right to travel only "incidentally" is beside the point. Were we concerned solely with actual deterrence to migration, we might be persuaded that a partial withholding of benefits constitutes a lesser incursion on the right to travel than an outright denial of all benefits. But since the right to travel embraces the citizen's right to be treated equally in her new State of residence, the discriminatory classification is itself a penalty. . . .

The classifications challenged in this case—and there are many—are defined entirely by (a) the period of residency in California and (b) the location of the prior residences of the disfavored class members. The favored class of beneficiaries includes all eligible California citizens who have resided there for at least one year, plus those new arrivals who last resided in another country or in a State that provides benefits at least as generous as California's. Thus, within the broad category of citizens who resided in California for less than a year, there are many who are treated like lifetime residents. And within the broad sub-category of new arrivals who are treated less favorably, there are many smaller classes whose benefit levels are determined by the law of the States from whence they came. To justify §11450.03, California must therefore explain not only why it is sound fiscal policy to discriminate against those who have been citizens for less than a year, but also why it is permissible to apply such a variety of rules within that class.

These classifications may not be justified by a purpose to deter welfare applicants from migrating to California for three reasons. First, although it is reasonable to assume that some persons may be motivated to move for the purpose of obtaining higher benefits, the empirical evidence reviewed by the District Judge, which takes into account the high cost of living in California, indicates that the number of such persons is quite small—surely not large enough to justify a burden on those who had no such motive. Second, California has represented to the Court that the legislation was not enacted for any such reason. Third, even if it were, as we squarely held in *Shapiro v. Thompson* (1969), such a purpose would be unequivocally impermissible.

Disavowing any desire to fence out the indigent, California has instead advanced an entirely fiscal justification for its multitiered scheme. The enforcement of §11450.03 will save the State approximately $10.9 million a year. The question is not whether such saving is a legitimate purpose but whether the State may accomplish that end by the discriminatory means it has chosen. An evenhanded, across-the-board reduction of about 72 cents per month for every beneficiary would produce the same result. But our negative answer to the question does not rest on the weakness of the State's purported fiscal justification. It rests on the fact that the Citizenship Clause of the Fourteenth Amendment expressly equates citizenship with residence: "That Clause does not provide for, and does not allow for, degrees of citizenship based on length of residence." It is equally clear that the Clause does not tolerate a hierarchy of 45 subclasses of similarly situated citizens based on the location of their prior residence. Thus §11450.03 is doubly vulnerable: Neither the duration of respondents' California residence, nor the identity of their prior States of residence, has any relevance to their need for benefits. Nor do those factors bear

any relationship to the State's interest in making an equitable allocation of the funds to be distributed among its needy citizens. As in *Shapiro*, we reject any contributory rationale for the denial of benefits to new residents:

"But we need not rest on the particular facts of these cases. Appellants' reasoning would logically permit the State to bar new residents from schools, parks, and libraries or deprive them of police and fire protection. Indeed it would permit the State to apportion all benefits and services according to the past tax contributions of its citizens."

In short, the State's legitimate interest in saving money provides no justification for its decision to discriminate among equally eligible citizens. . . .

Citizens of the United States, whether rich or poor, have the right to choose to be citizens "of the State wherein they reside." The States, however, do not have any right to select their citizens. The Fourteenth Amendment, like the Constitution itself, was, as Justice Cardozo put it, "framed upon the theory that the peoples of the several states must sink or swim together, and that in the long run prosperity and salvation are in union and not division."

The judgment of the Court of Appeals is affirmed.

It is so ordered.

CHIEF JUSTICE REHNQUIST, with whom JUSTICE THOMAS joins, dissenting.

The Court today breathes new life into the previously dormant Privileges or Immunities Clause of the Fourteenth Amendment—a Clause relied upon by this Court in only one other decision, *Colgate v. Harvey* (1935), overruled five years later by *Madden v. Kentucky* (1940). It uses this Clause to strike down what I believe is a reasonable measure falling under the head of a "good-faith residency requirement." Because I do not think any provision of the Constitution—and surely not a provision relied upon for only the second time since its enactment 130 years ago—requires this result, I dissent.

JUSTICE THOMAS, with whom THE CHIEF JUSTICE joins, dissenting.

I join THE CHIEF JUSTICE's dissent. I write separately to address the majority's conclusion that California has violated "the right of the newly arrived citizen to the same privileges and immunities enjoyed by other citizens of the same State." In my view, the majority attributes a meaning to the Privileges or Immunities Clause that likely was unintended when the Fourteenth Amendment was enacted and ratified. . . .

AS THE CHIEF JUSTICE points out, it comes as quite a surprise that the majority relies on the Privileges or Immunities Clause at all in this case. That is because the *Slaughter-House Cases* sapped the Clause of any meaning. Although the majority appears to breathe new life into the Clause today, it fails to address its historical underpinnings or its place in our constitutional jurisprudence. Because I believe that the demise of the Privileges or Immunities Clause has contributed in no small part to the current disarray of our Fourteenth Amendment jurisprudence, I would be open to reevaluating its meaning in an appropriate case. Before invoking the Clause, however, we should endeavor to understand what the framers of the Fourteenth Amendment thought that it meant. We should also consider whether the Clause should displace, rather than augment, portions of our equal protection and substantive due process jurisprudence. The majority's failure to consider these important questions raises the specter that the Privileges or Immunities Clause will become yet another convenient tool for inventing new rights, limited solely by the "predilections of those who happen at the time to be Members of this Court."

I respectfully dissent.

Discrimination Against Aliens

The Supreme Court generally has sympathized with the rights of noncitizens, a position consistent with the country's relatively generous immigration and naturalization policies. Although aliens do not enjoy the full range of rights and liberties granted to American citizens, they are entitled to certain protections under the Constitution. The Court has a history of striking down state laws that unnecessarily discriminate against aliens. As early as *Yick Wo v. Hopkins* (1886) the justices held that a resident alien was entitled to equal protection guarantees. Since then, the Court has nullified laws that prohibit resident aliens from obtaining civil service employment, receiving financial aid for college, becoming a member of the bar, or even getting a fishing license.[33] In fact, the Court in *Graham v. Richardson* (1971), a challenge to the denial of public assistance to an alien, accorded suspect class status to noncitizens, explaining that:

[C]lassifications based on alienage, like those based on nationality or race, are inherently suspect and subject to close judicial scrutiny. Aliens as a class are a prime example of a "discrete and insular" minority . . . for whom such heightened judicial solicitude is appropriate.

This position is based on the recognition that aliens who lawfully reside in the United States are politically powerless because they can neither vote nor hold office. Yet they pay taxes, support the economy, serve in the military, and contribute to society in other ways, and, if they otherwise qualify for government benefits or opportunities, they should not be denied them on the basis of noncitizenship alone.

Has the Court been faithful to *Graham?* The answer is mixed or, as Justice Powell once put it, "The decisions of this Court regarding the permissibility of statutory classifications involving aliens have not formed an unwavering line."[34] In some instances, such as *Nyquist v. Mauclet* (1977)—involving a New York policy that barred certain resident aliens from state financial assistance for higher education—the justices reiterated the lesson of *Graham* and held that state classifications based on alienage are "inherently suspect and subject to close judicial scrutiny." At the opposite end of the spectrum is *Foley v. Connelie* (1978), in which a divided Court concluded that the Constitution is not violated when a state denies an alien a job in law enforcement. The justices held that it is not necessary to apply strict scrutiny when a government can demonstrate that its confinement of the performance of a duty to U.S. citizens is based on furthering some important public function. Somewhere in the middle is the important case of *Plyler v. Doe* (1982). At issue was a 1975 Texas law that withheld from local school districts any state funds for the education of children who were not legal residents of the United States (undocumented aliens). The law also allowed local school districts to deny enrollment to any student who was an undocumented alien (§21.031 of the Texas Education Code). The trial court, however, was not convinced by these arguments, con-

---

33. *Sugarman v. Dougall* (1973), *Nyquist v. Mauclet* (1977), *In re Griffiths* (1973), and *Takahashi v. Fish and Game Commission* (1948), respectively.

34. *Ambach v. Norwick* (1979).

cluding instead that the state law violated the Equal Protection Clause of the Fourteenth Amendment.

Writing for a divided Court, Justice Brennan agreed. But he did not apply the strict scrutiny standard, opting instead to invoke a midlevel approach to discrimination against illegal aliens:

Undocumented aliens cannot be treated as a suspect class because their presence in this country in violation of federal law is not a "constitutional irrelevancy." Nor is education a fundamental right; a State need not justify by compelling necessity every variation in the manner in which education is provided to its population. But more is involved in these cases than the abstract question whether §21.031 discriminates against a suspect class, or whether education is a fundamental right. Section 21.031 imposes a lifetime hardship on a discrete class of children not accountable for their disabling status. The stigma of illiteracy will mark them for the rest of their lives. By denying these children a basic education, we deny them the ability to live within the structure of our civic institutions, and foreclose any realistic possibility that they will contribute in even the smallest way to the progress of our Nation. In determining the rationality of §21.031, we may appropriately take into account its costs to the Nation and to the innocent children who are its victims. In light of these countervailing costs, the discrimination contained in §21.031 can hardly be considered rational unless it furthers some substantial goal of the State.

Under this approach, Brennan found that Texas had not offered a "substantial state interest" for denying "a discrete group of children the free public education that it offers to the other children residing within its borders." Four members of the Court vehemently disagreed with this conclusion. Writing for himself and Justices O'Connor, Rehnquist, and White, Chief Justice Burger believed that the majority had overstepped its bounds:

Were it our business to set the Nation's social policy, I would agree without hesitation that it is senseless for an enlightened society to deprive any children—including illegal aliens—of an elementary education. I fully agree that it would be folly—and wrong—to tolerate creation of a segment of society made up of illiterate persons, many having a limited or no command of our language. However, the Constitution does not constitute us as "Platonic Guardians" nor does it vest in this Court the authority to strike down laws because they do not meet our standards of desirable social policy, "wisdom," or "common sense." We trespass on the assigned function of the political branches

under our structure of limited and separated powers when we assume a policymaking role as the Court does today.

The Court makes no attempt to disguise that it is acting to make up for Congress' lack of "effective leadership" in dealing with the serious national problems caused by the influx of uncountable millions of illegal aliens across our borders. The failure of enforcement of the immigration laws over more than a decade and the inherent difficulty and expense of sealing our vast borders have combined to create a grave socioeconomic dilemma. It is a dilemma that has not yet even been fully assessed, let alone addressed. However, it is not the function of the Judiciary to provide "effective leadership" simply because the political branches of government fail to do so.

How the Court treats future claims of discrimination against aliens remains to be seen. What is beyond dispute is that, as legal and illegal immigration patterns change and new residents place additional burdens on states for government services, new questions of discrimination based on alien status are bound to arise.

Discrimination Against Illegitimate Children

Although the Supreme Court has decided a number of cases centering on discrimination against children born out of wedlock, this area remains relatively underdeveloped and, in some important ways, inconsistent. On the one hand, the Court has held that laws that discriminate against illegitimate children would be held to a higher standard than mere rational basis. For example, in *Trimble v. Gordon* (1977) the Court struck down an Illinois law that allowed illegitimate children to inherit by intestate (without a will) succession only from their mothers—under the state's law, legitimate children may inherit by intestate succession from both parents—on the ground that the law was not "substantially related to permissible state interests."[35] The majority rejected the argument that classifications based on illegitimacy are "suspect," so that any justifications must survive the

---

35. The Court makes this point about *Trimble* in *Lalli v. Lalli* (1978). In *Trimble* the majority wrote that "illegitimacy is analogous in many respects to the personal characteristics that have been held to be suspect when used as the basis of statutory differentiations. We nevertheless concluded that the analogy was not sufficient to require 'our most exacting scrutiny.' Despite the conclusion that classifications based on illegitimacy fall in a 'realm of less than strictest scrutiny,' [that level of scrutiny] 'is not a toothless one.'"

"most exacting scrutiny." But it went on to apply "more far-reaching scrutiny" than the rational basis test would require. On the other hand, because the justices have applied this standard to strike some classifications and uphold others, seemingly contradictory rulings have resulted. Just a year after *Trimble*, in *Lalli v. Lalli* (1978), the justices upheld a law that prohibited illegitimate children from inheriting from fathers who died intestate unless paternity had been established while the father was still alive. In this case, the justices found that the law, unlike the one at issue in *Trimble*, was substantially related to permissible state interests.

Such rulings, along with the decision in *Michael H. v. Gerald D.* (1989),[36] have led some scholars to conclude that the justices, while concerned about ending blatant forms of discrimination against illegitimate children, are equally concerned about reinforcing societal norms against bringing illegitimate children into the world. The majority opinion in *Trimble* exemplifies the rationale behind this conclusion:

The status of illegitimacy has expressed through the ages society's condemnation of irresponsible liaisons beyond the bonds of marriage. But visiting this condemnation on the head of an infant is illogical and unjust. Moreover, imposing disabilities on the illegitimate child is contrary to the basic concept of our system that legal burdens should bear some relationship to individual responsibility or wrongdoing. Obviously, no child is responsible for his birth, and penalizing the illegitimate child is an ineffectual—as well as an unjust—way of deterring the parent. The parents have the ability to conform their conduct to societal norms, but their illegitimate children can affect neither their parents' conduct nor their own status.

Discrimination Based on Age

Unlike its rulings in the cases involving discrimination against illegitimate children, Court decisions on age classifications are relatively clear. First, the justices have held that laws discriminating on the basis of age are not subject to the strict scrutiny standard. The majority explained why in *Massachusetts Bd. of Retirement v. Murgia* (1976), involving a Massachusetts state law making it mandatory for uniformed state police officers to retire at age fifty.

[*San Antonio School District v.*] *Rodriguez* observed that a suspect class is one "saddled with such disabilities, or subjected to such a history of purposeful unequal treatment, or relegated to such a position of political powerlessness as to command extraordinary protection from the majoritarian political process." While the treatment of the aged in this Nation has not been wholly free of discrimination, such persons, unlike, say, those who have been discriminated against on the basis of race or national origin, have not experienced a "history of purposeful unequal treatment" or been subjected to unique disabilities on the basis of stereotyped characteristics not truly indicative of their abilities. The class subject to the compulsory retirement feature of the Massachusetts statute consists of uniformed state police officers over the age of 50. It cannot be said to discriminate only against the elderly. Rather, it draws the line at a certain age in middle life. But even old age does not define a "discrete and insular" group in need of "extraordinary protection from the majoritarian political process." Instead, it marks a stage that each of us will reach if we live out our normal span. Even if the statute could be said to impose a penalty upon a class defined as the aged, it would not impose a distinction sufficiently akin to those classifications that we have found suspect to call for strict judicial scrutiny.

The Court's invocation of the rational basis approach has worked to the detriment of litigants claiming age discrimination. For example, in *Gregory v. Ashcroft* (1991) the issue was a provision of the Missouri constitution that forced public officials to retire when they reached age seventy. Above objections that the law violated the federal Age Discrimination in Employment Act (making it unlawful for an employer "to discharge any individual" who is at least forty years old "because of such individual's age") and the Equal Protection Clause of the Fourteenth Amendment, the justices upheld the requirement.

In her opinion for the majority, Justice O'Connor reiterated the lesson of *Murgia*: the Court would use the rational basis test to adjudicate age claims. From there, she held that the state had met its obligation:

The people of Missouri have a legitimate, indeed compelling, interest in maintaining a judiciary fully capable of performing the demanding tasks that judges must perform. It is an unfor-

36. In this case a plurality of the Court upheld a California law that presumed that children born to a married woman who was living with her husband are children of the marriage. This decision makes it difficult for a biological father to establish paternity and to obtain visitation rights, and so forth.

tunate fact of life that physical and mental capacity sometimes diminish with age. The people may therefore wish to replace some older judges. Voluntary retirement will not always be sufficient. Nor may impeachment—with its public humiliation and elaborate procedural machinery—serve acceptably the goal of a fully functioning judiciary.

The election process may also be inadequate. Whereas the electorate would be expected to discover if their governor or state legislator were not performing adequately and vote the official out of office, the same may not be true of judges. Most voters never observe state judges in action, nor read judicial opinions. State judges also serve longer terms of office than other public officials, making them—deliberately—less dependent on the will of the people. . . . The people of Missouri rationally could conclude that retention elections—in which state judges run unopposed at relatively long intervals—do not serve as an adequate check on judges whose performance is deficient. Mandatory retirement is a reasonable response to this dilemma. . . .

The Missouri mandatory retirement provision, like all legal classifications, is founded on a generalization. It is far from true that all judges suffer significant deterioration in performance at age 70. It is probably not true that most do. It may not be true at all. But a State "'does not violate the Equal Protection Clause merely because the classifications made by its laws are imperfect.'"

Would O'Connor have struck down the provision under a strict scrutiny approach? Her words—"The people of Missouri have a legitimate, indeed *compelling*, interest"—suggest that she would not. But, given the fact that the justices almost never uphold classifications when they apply that high level of scrutiny, the question remains open to speculation, as does whether the Court will ever consider adopting a heightened or even suspect approach to age. As the as the baby boom generation ages, creating the largest number of senior citizens in American history, age discrimination lawsuits are likely to be filed at significant rates.

REMEDYING THE EFFECTS OF DISCRIMINATION: AFFIRMATIVE ACTION

Creating appropriate standards for interpreting the equal protection principles of the Constitution and determining when governments have engaged in impermissible discrimination are, as we now know, exceedingly

difficult tasks. But even when they have been accomplished, the Court's business is not finished. In addition to condemning unconstitutional discrimination, the Court confronts the problem of remedies, which entails consideration of acceptable ways to eliminate the discrimination, to implement nondiscriminatory policies, and to compensate the victims of discrimination.

For some discrimination issues remedial action is minimal: often striking down a statute is sufficient. For example, nullifying Idaho's discriminatory inheritance statute in *Reed v. Reed* required no remedial action. The state simply had to decide future estate administration issues without regard to sex. Declaring Virginia's miscegenation law in violation of the Equal Protection Clause in the *Loving* decision also needed no follow-up action. Virginia was plainly barred from any future prosecutions of such cases.

For other discrimination issues, however, the enforcement of the Court's orders can be a lengthy, complex process. Timetables for change, compliance standards, and methods of implementation pose troublesome choices, and conditions are exacerbated when the affected population resists the change. The integration of the public schools is an obvious and painful example.

The Supreme Court not only has created rules for implementing its own equal protection decisions, but also has heard cases challenging the antidiscrimination policies imposed by Congress and the state legislatures. Beginning in the late 1960s, many political bodies asserted that the Fifth and Fourteenth Amendments demanded more than the elimination of overt discrimination; they also required positive actions taken by government to ensure that equality is achieved and the effects of past discrimination are eliminated. This policy gave rise to affirmative action and minority set-aside programs, which have been attacked as unconstitutional reverse discrimination. Questions of just how far Congress and state governments can go in developing remedies without violating the Constitution show up regularly on the Supreme Court's docket.

In this section, we examine the Court's response to these questions. As you read the narrative and opinions, note just how much difficulty the Court has had in addressing them. The justices, like the nation generally, have been deeply divided over the appropriate actions to take. There is little agreement on what the Constitution requires and what it prohibits. It is not surprising that the Court to date has not succeeded in building a consistent and coherent rule of law.

The Origins of Affirmative Action

Few issues of constitutional law have prompted as much controversy as affirmative action. Based on the notion that the principles of the Equal Protection Clause cannot be achieved by simply terminating illegal discrimination, affirmative action programs direct government and private institutions to take positive measures to ensure that equality becomes a reality.

Affirmative action programs have their roots in presidential orders, issued as early as the 1940s, that expanded government employment opportunities for blacks. These programs received their most significant boost in 1965 when President Johnson issued Executive Order 11246 instructing the Labor Department to ensure that businesses contracting with the federal government were nondiscriminatory. To meet the requirements, government contractors altered their employment policies and recruited minority workers.

Over the years, these requirements were strengthened and expanded. Failure to comply with the government's principles of nondiscriminatory employment was grounds for stripping a business or institution of its federal contract or appropriated funds. Moreover, some state and local governments adopted similar programs, many aggressively establishing numerical standards for minority participation. Private businesses also began to adopt programs to increase the numbers of women and minorities, especially in positions where their numbers historically had been low. Are these programs desirable? Constitutional? Such questions have generated debates in both political and legal circles. Those supporting affirmative action marshal a number of arguments.

First, taking issue with Justice Harlan's assertion in his *Plessy v. Ferguson* dissent that the Constitution is "color-blind," supporters hold that characteristics associated with disadvantaged status must be considered and taken into account. Special programs and incentives for people from disadvantaged groups are warranted to eradicate and compensate for the effects of past discrimination. As Justice Marshall said in 1978:

After several hundred years of class-based discrimination against Negroes . . . a class-based remedy is permissible. . . . Negroes have been discriminated against, not as individuals, but rather solely because of the color of their skin. . . . [T]he racism of our society has been so pervasive that none, regardless of wealth or position, has managed to escape it. The experience of Negroes has been different in kind, not just in degree, from that of other ethnic groups. It is not merely the history of slavery alone but also that a whole people were marked as inferior by the law. And that mark has endured. The dream of America as the great melting pot has not been realized for the Negro; because of his skin color he never even made it into the pot.

These experiences of the Negro make it difficult for me to accept that Negroes cannot be afforded greater protection under the Fourteenth Amendment where it is necessary to remedy the effects of past discrimination.[37]

Second, advocates suggest that affirmative action plans do not benefit just one or two groups in society; rather, they benefit the entire community. Without these plans, many members of society would remain shut out of certain careers, returning us to the days of white male domination. Finally, supporters suggest that affirmative action plans are fully consistent with the Fourteenth Amendment's Equal Protection Clause. Justice Marshall remarked about the plan of a medical school that gave preference to minority applicants, "Neither [the Fourteenth Amendment's] history nor our past cases lend any support to the conclusion that a university may not remedy the cumulative effects of society's discrimination by giving consideration to race in an effort to increase the number and percentage of Negro doctors." In fact, based on an analysis of circumstances surrounding the amendment's adoption, Marshall concluded that it "would pervert the intent of [its] Framers by substituting abstract equality for the genuine equality the Amendment was intended to achieve."[38]

Opponents of special programs, however, see things

37. *Regents of the University of California v. Bakke* (1978).
38. Ibid.

very differently. Many valued goods and opportunities in society—jobs, promotions, and admission to education and training programs—are scarce at times. When, instead of merit alone, factors such as race and sex are used to determine who obtains these opportunities, the losers may feel themselves victimized and claim reverse discrimination. The principles of equal protection, affirmative action opponents assert, should prohibit discrimination against whites and males just as they prohibit discrimination against blacks and women. Those who have been negatively affected by it view affirmative action as inconsistent with the nation's commitment to equal opportunity. Opponents also claim that it stigmatizes its beneficiaries. Justice O'Connor made this point in *City of Richmond v. J. A. Croson Co.* (1989): "Classifications based on race carry a danger of stigmatic harm. Unless they are strictly reserved for remedial settings, they may in fact promote notions of racial inferiority and lead to a politics of racial hostility."

Finally, opponents note two legal obstacles to affirmative action programs: the Constitution and the Civil Rights Act of 1964. In contrast to Marshall's thinking, opponents claim that the Equal Protection Clause of the Fourteenth Amendment and the Due Process Clause of the Fifth prohibit the government from giving special consideration to individuals because of their race, sex, or national origin. As Justice Stewart once wrote, "The Fourteenth Amendment was adopted to ensure that every person must be treated equally by each State regardless of the color of his skin. The Amendment promised to carry to its necessary conclusion a fundamental principle upon which this Nation had been founded—that the law would honor no preference based on lineage."[39] The Civil Rights Act of 1964, specifically Title VII, states, with respect to private employment, that race, color, religion, sex, and national origin cannot be used to discriminate against any employee. It further holds:

It shall be an unlawful employment practice for an employer . . . to limit, segregate, or classify his employees or applicants for employment in any way which would deprive or tend to deprive any individual of employment opportunities or otherwise adversely affect his status as an employee, because of such individual's race, color, religion, sex, or national origin.

Title VI of the same statute contains similar provisions for state and local government programs that receive federal funding. These provisions were originally intended to prohibit discrimination against members of groups that historically have been the victims of prejudice. Whether giving preference to such individuals, at the possible expense of others, also violates these constitutional or statutory provisions remained for the Supreme Court to determine.

The Supreme Court Enters the Fray

Which side of this debate would the Court favor? This question was very much on the minds of civil rights groups, scholars, and the public when the justices agreed to hear *Regents of the University of California v. Bakke* (1978), an Equal Protection Clause challenge to a public university's policy to admit a specific number of minority applicants.[40]

The stakes were high. For civil rights groups, the case represented a threat to the best way yet devised to eliminate the effects of past discrimination and promote minority students into professional positions. For opponents of affirmative action, it was an opportunity to overturn the growing burden of paying for the sins of the past and return to a system based on merit. Fifty-seven friend of the court briefs were filed by various organizations and interested parties.

The Supreme Court was deeply divided over this case. Four justices gave strong support to affirmative action programs, four others had serious reservations about them, and Justice Powell found himself in the middle. Portions of his opinion announcing the judgment of the Court were supported by one set of four justices, and other parts were joined by an entirely different group of four. As the "swing" justice in this case, Powell was effectively able to determine what the Constitution means with respect to affirmative action programs. What did he conclude?

39. *Fullilove v. Klutznick* (1980).

40. For oral arguments in this case, navigate to: *oyez.nwu.edu.*

Regents of the University of California v. Bakke

438 U.S. 265 (1978)

laws.findlaw.com/US/438/265.html

Vote: 5 (Burger, Powell, Rehnquist, Stevens, Stewart)
*   4 (Blackmun, Brennan, Marshall, White)*

Opinion announcing the judgment of the Court: Powell

Opinion concurring in part and dissenting in part: Blackmun,
*   Brennan, Marshall, White (jointly authored)*

Separate opinion: White

Separate opinion: Marshall

Separate opinion: Blackmun

Opinion concurring in part and dissenting in part: Stevens

The medical school of the University of California at Davis began operations in 1968. In its first two years, it admitted only three minority students, all Asians. To improve minority participation, the school developed two admissions programs to fill the one hundred seats in its entry class—a regular admissions program and a special admissions program. The regular admissions program worked in the customary way: applicants were evaluated on the basis of undergraduate grades, standardized test scores, letters of recommendation, extracurricular activities, and an interview. The special admissions program was for applicants who indicated that they were economically or educationally disadvantaged, or were black, Chi-

cano, Asian, or Native American. Such applicants could choose to go through the regular admissions process or to be referred to a special admissions committee. Special admissions applicants were judged on the same characteristics as the regular applicants, but they competed only against each other. The school reserved sixteen seats to be filled from the special admissions pool. Many white applicants, claiming poverty, indicated a desire to be considered by the special admissions committee, but none was admitted. All specially admitted students were members of the designated minority groups.

Allan Bakke was a white male of Scandinavian descent. He graduated with honors in engineering from the University of Minnesota and was a Vietnam veteran. He worked for the National Aeronautics and Space Administration and received his master's degree in engineering from Stanford. Developing an interest in a medical career, Bakke took extra science courses and did volunteer work in a local hospital. At age thirty-three, he applied for admission to the 1973 entry class of the medical school at Davis. He was rejected. He applied in 1974 and was again rejected. Because applicants admitted under the special admissions program were, at least statistically, less qualified than he *(see Table 12-3)*, Bakke sued for admission, claiming that the university's dual admissions program violated the Equal Protection Clause of the Fourteenth Amendment.

TABLE 12-3 Admissions Data for the Entering Class of the Medical School of the University of California at Davis, 1973 and 1974

	SGPA[a]	OGPA[b]	MCAT (Percentiles)			
			Verbal	Quantitative	Science	Gen. Infor.
Class Entering in 1973						
Bakke	3.44	3.46	96	94	97	72
Average of regular admittees	3.51	3.49	81	76	83	69
Average of special admittees	2.62	2.88	46	24	35	33
Class Entering in 1974						
Bakke	3.44	3.46	96	94	97	72
Average of regular admittees	3.36	3.29	69	67	82	72
Average of special admittees	2.42	2.62	34	30	37	18

SOURCE: *Regents of the University of California v. Bakke* (1978).
   NOTES: a. Science grade point average.
       b. Overall grade point average.

Twice rejected for admission to the medical school of the University of California at Davis, Allan Bakke (center) filed suit challenging school policy that admitted minority students with grades and test scores lower than his. Bakke's suit led to the Supreme Court's first major statement on the constitutionality of affirmative action programs. Bakke was awarded his medical degree from the university in 1982.

The state trial court struck down the special program, declaring that race could not be constitutionally taken into account in deciding who would be admitted, but the court refused to order Bakke's admission. Both Bakke and the university appealed. The California Supreme Court found the special admissions program unconstitutional, holding that "no applicant may be rejected because of his race, in favor of another who is less qualified, as measured by standards applied without regard to race." The state supreme court's order to admit Bakke was stayed, pending the university's appeal to the U.S. Supreme Court.

MR. JUSTICE POWELL announced the judgment of the Court.

Petitioner does not deny that decisions based on race or ethnic origin by faculties and administrations of state universities are reviewable under the Fourteenth Amendment. For his part, respondent does not argue that all racial or ethnic classifications are *per se* invalid. The parties do disagree as to the level of judicial scrutiny to be applied to the special admissions program. Petitioner argues that the court below erred in applying strict scrutiny, as this inexact term has been applied in our cases. That level of review, petitioner asserts, should be reserved for classifications that disadvantage "discrete and insular minorities." Respondent, on the other hand, contends that the California court correctly rejected the notion that the degree of judicial scrutiny accorded a particular racial or ethnic classification hinges upon membership in a discrete and insular minority and duly recognized that the "rights established [by the Fourteenth Amendment] are personal rights."

En route to this crucial battle over the scope of judicial review, the parties fight a sharp preliminary action over the proper characterization of the special admissions program. Petitioner prefers to view it as establishing a "goal" of minority representation in the Medical School. Respondent, echoing the courts below, labels it a racial quota.

This semantic distinction is beside the point: The special admissions program is undeniably a classification based on race and ethnic background. To the extent that there existed a pool of at least minimally qualified minority applicants to fill the 16 special admissions seats, white applicants could compete only for 84 seats in the entering class, rather than the 100 open to minority applicants. Whether this limitation is described as a quota or a goal, it is a line drawn on the basis of race and ethnic status.

The guarantees of the Fourteenth Amendment extend to all persons. Its language is explicit: "No State shall . . . deny to any person within its jurisdiction the equal protection of the laws." It is settled beyond question that the "rights created by the first section of the Fourteenth Amendment are, by its terms, guaranteed to the individual. The rights established are personal rights." The guarantee of equal protection cannot mean one thing when applied to one individual and something else when applied to a person of another color. If both are not accorded the same protection, then it is not equal. . . .

Racial and ethnic distinctions of any sort are inherently suspect and thus call for the most exacting judicial examination. . . .

Although many of the Framers of the Fourteenth Amendment conceived of its primary function as bridging the vast distance between members of the Negro race and the white "majority," the Amendment itself was framed in universal terms, without reference to color, ethnic origin, or condition of prior servitude. . . .

Petitioner urges us to adopt for the first time a more restrictive view of the Equal Protection Clause and hold that discrimination against members of the white "majority" cannot be suspect if its purpose can be characterized as "benign." The clock of our liberties, however, cannot be turned back to 1868. It is far too late to argue that the guarantee of equal protection to *all* persons permits the recognition of special wards entitled to a degree of protection greater than that accorded others. "The Fourteenth Amendment is not directed solely against discrimination due to a 'two-class theory'—that is, based upon differences between 'white' and Negro.". . .

If it is the individual who is entitled to judicial protection against classifications based upon his racial or ethnic background because such distinctions impinge upon personal rights, rather than the individual only because of his membership in a particular group, then constitutional standards may be applied consistently. Political judgments regarding the necessity for the particular classification may be weighed in the constitutional balance, but the standard of justification will remain constant. This is as it should be, since those political judgments are the product of rough compromise struck by contending groups within the democratic process. When they touch upon an individual's race or ethnic background, he is entitled to a judicial determination that the burden he is asked to bear on that basis is precisely tailored to serve a compelling governmental interest. The Constitution guarantees that right to every person regardless of his background. . . .

We have held that in "order to justify the use of a suspect classification, a State must show that its purpose or interest is both constitutionally permissible and substantial, and that its use of the classification is 'necessary . . . to the accomplishment' of its purpose or the safeguarding of its interest." The special admissions program purports to serve the purposes of: (i) "reducing the historic deficit of traditionally disfavored minorities in medical schools and in the medical profession"; (ii) countering the effects of societal discrimination; (iii) increasing the number of physicians who will practice in communities currently underserved; and (iv) obtaining the educational benefits that flow from an ethnically diverse student body. It is necessary to decide which, if any, of these purposes is substantial enough to support the use of a suspect classification.

If petitioner's purpose is to assure within its student body some specified percentage of a particular group merely because of its race or ethnic origin, such a preferential purpose must be rejected not as insubstantial but as facially invalid. Preferring members of any one group for no reason other than race or ethnic origin is discrimination for its own sake. This the Constitution forbids.

The State certainly has a legitimate and substantial interest in ameliorating, or eliminating where feasible, the disabling effects of identified discrimination. The line of school desegregation cases, commencing with *Brown*, attests to the importance of this state goal and the commitment of the judiciary to affirm all lawful means toward its attainment. In the school cases, the States were required by court order to redress the wrongs worked by specific instances of racial discrimination. That goal was far more focused than the remedying of the effects of "societal discrimination," an amorphous concept of inquiry that may be ageless in its reach into the past.

We have never approved a classification that aids persons perceived as members of relatively victimized groups at the expense of other innocent individuals in the absence of judicial, legislative, or administrative findings of constitutional or statutory violations. After such findings have been made, the governmental interest in preferring members of the injured groups at the expense of others is substantial, since the legal rights of the victims must be vindicated. In such a case, the extent of the injury and the consequent remedy will have been judicially, legislatively, or administratively defined. Also, the remedial action usually remains subject to continuing oversight to assure that it will work the least harm possible to other innocent persons competing for the benefit. Without such findings of constitutional or statutory violations, it cannot be said that the government has any greater interest in helping one individual than in refraining from harming another. Thus, the government has no compelling justification for inflicting such harm.

Petitioner does not purport to have made, and is in no position to make, such findings. Its broad mission is education, not the formulation of any legislative policy or the adjudication of particular claims of illegality. . . . Before relying upon these sorts of findings in establishing a racial classification, a governmental body must have the authority and capability to establish, in the record, that the classification is responsive to identified discrimination. Lacking this capability, petitioner has not carried its burden of justification on this issue.

Hence, the purpose of helping certain groups whom the faculty of the Davis Medical School perceived as victims of "societal discrimination" does not justify a classification that imposes disadvantages upon persons like respondent, who bear no responsibility for whatever harm the beneficiaries of the special admissions program are thought to have suffered. To hold otherwise would be to convert a remedy heretofore reserved for violations of legal rights into a privilege that all institutions throughout the Nation could grant at their pleasure to whatever groups are perceived as victims of societal discrimination. That is a step we have never approved.

Petitioner identifies, as another purpose of its program, improving the delivery of health-care services to communities currently underserved. It may be assumed that in some situations a State's interest in facilitating the health care of its citizens is sufficiently compelling to support the use of a suspect classification. But there is virtually no evidence in the record indicating that petitioner's special admissions program is either needed or geared to promote that goal. . . .

Petitioner simply has not carried its burden of demonstrating that it must prefer members of particular ethnic groups over all other individuals in order to promote better health-care delivery to deprived citizens. Indeed, petitioner has not shown that its preferential classification is likely to have any significant effect on the problem.

The fourth goal asserted by petitioner is the attainment of a diverse student body. This clearly is a constitutionally permissible goal for an institution of higher education. Academic freedom, though not a specifically enumerated constitutional right, long has been viewed as a special concern of the First Amendment. The freedom of a university to make its own judgments as to education includes the selection of its student body. . . .

The atmosphere of "speculation, experiment and creation"—so essential to the quality of higher education—is widely believed to be promoted by a diverse student body. As the Court noted in *Keyishian* [*v. Board of Regents of the University of the State of New York,* 1967] it is not too much to say that the "nation's future depends upon leaders trained through wide exposure" to the ideas and mores of students as diverse as this Nation of many peoples.

Thus, in arguing that its universities must be accorded the right to select those students who will contribute the most to the "robust exchange of ideas," petitioner invokes a countervailing constitutional interest, that of the First Amendment. In this light, petitioner must be viewed as seeking to achieve a goal that is of paramount importance in the fulfillment of its mission.

It may be argued that there is greater force to these views at the undergraduate level than in a medical school where the training is centered primarily on professional competency. But even at the graduate level, our tradition and experience lend support to the view that the contribution of diversity is substantial. . . . Physicians serve a heterogeneous population. An otherwise qualified medical student with a particular background—whether it be ethnic, geographic, culturally advantaged or disadvantaged—may bring to a professional school of medicine experiences, outlooks, and ideas that enrich the training of its student body and better equip its graduates to render with understanding their vital service to humanity.

Ethnic diversity, however, is only one element in a range of factors a university properly may consider in attaining the goal of a heterogeneous student body. Although a university must have wide discretion in making the sensitive judgments as to who should be admitted, constitutional limitations protecting individual rights may not be disregarded. Respondent urges—and the courts below have held—that petitioner's dual admissions program is a racial classification that impermissibly infringes his rights under the Fourteenth Amendment. As the interest of diversity is compelling in the context of a university's admissions program, the question remains whether the program's racial classification is necessary to promote this interest. . . .

It may be assumed that the reservation of a specified number of seats in each class for individuals from the preferred ethnic groups would contribute to the attainment of considerable ethnic diversity in the student body. But petitioner's argument that this is the only effective means of serving the interest of diversity is seriously flawed. In a most fundamental sense the argument misconceives the nature of the state interest that would justify consideration of race or ethnic background. It is not an interest in simple ethnic diversity, in which a specified percentage of the student body is in effect guaranteed to be members of selected ethnic groups, with the remaining percentage an undifferentiated aggregation of students. The diversity that furthers a compelling state interest encompasses a far broader array of qualifications and characteristics of which racial or ethnic origin is but a single though important element. Petitioner's special admissions program, focused solely on ethnic diversity, would hinder rather than further attainment of genuine diversity.

Nor would the state interest in genuine diversity be served by expanding petitioner's two-track system into a multitrack program with a prescribed number of seats set aside for each identifiable category of applicants. Indeed, it is conceivable that a university would thus pursue the logic of petitioner's two-track program to the illogical end of insulating each category of applicants with certain desired qualifications from competition with all other applicants. . . .

In such an admissions program, race or ethnic background may be deemed a "plus" in a particular applicant's file, yet it does not insulate the individual from comparison with all other candidates for the available seats. The file of a particular black applicant may be examined for his potential contribution to diversity without the factor of race being decisive when compared, for example, with that of an applicant identified as an Italian-American if the latter is thought to exhibit qualities more likely to promote beneficial educational pluralism. Such qualities could include exceptional personal talents, unique work or service experience, leadership potential, maturity, demonstrated compassion, a history of overcoming disadvantage, ability to communicate with the poor, or other qualifications deemed important. In short, an admissions program operated in this way is flexible enough to consider all pertinent elements of diversity in light of the particular qualifications of each applicant, and to place them on the same footing for consideration, although not necessarily according them the same weight. Indeed, the weight attributed to a particular quality may vary from year to year depending upon the "mix" both of the student body and the applicants for the incoming class.

This kind of program treats each applicant as an individual in the admissions process. The applicant who loses out on the last available seat to another candidate receiving a "plus" on the basis of ethnic background will not have been foreclosed from all consideration for that seat simply because he was not the right color or had the wrong surname. It would mean only that his combined qualifications, which may have included similar nonobjective factors, did not outweigh those of the other applicant. His qualifications would have been weighed fairly and competitively, and he would have no basis to complain of unequal treatment under the Fourteenth Amendment. . . .

In summary, it is evident that the Davis special admissions program involves the use of an explicit racial classification never before countenanced by this Court. It tells applicants who are not Negro, Asian, or Chicano that they are totally excluded from a specific percentage of the seats in an entering class. No matter how strong their qualifications, quantitative and extracurricular, including their own potential for contribution to educational diversity, they are never afforded the chance to compete with applicants from the preferred groups for the special admissions seats. At the same time, the preferred applicants have the opportunity to compete for every seat in the class.

The fatal flaw in petitioner's preferential program is its disregard of individual rights as guaranteed by the

Fourteenth Amendment. Such rights are not absolute. But when a State's distribution of benefits or imposition of burdens hinges on ancestry or the color of a person's skin, that individual is entitled to a demonstration that the challenged classification is necessary to promote a substantial state interest. Petitioner has failed to carry this burden. For this reason, that portion of the California court's judgment holding petitioner's special admissions program invalid under the Fourteenth Amendment must be affirmed.

In enjoining petitioner from ever considering the race of any applicant, however, the courts below failed to recognize that the State has a substantial interest that legitimately may be served by a properly devised admissions program involving the competitive consideration of race and ethnic origin. For this reason, so much of the California court's judgment as enjoins petitioner from any consideration of the race of any applicant must be reversed.

With respect to respondent's entitlement to an injunction directing his admission to the Medical School, petitioner has conceded that it could not carry its burden of proving that, but for the existence of its unlawful special admissions program, respondent still would not have been admitted. Hence, respondent is entitled to the injunction, and that portion of the judgment must be affirmed.

Affirmed in part and reversed in part.

Opinion of MR. JUSTICE BRENNAN, MR. JUSTICE WHITE, MR. JUSTICE MARSHALL, and MR. JUSTICE BLACKMUN, concurring in the judgment in part and dissenting in part.

The Court today, in reversing in part the judgment of the Supreme Court of California, affirms the constitutional power of Federal and State Governments to act affirmatively to achieve equal opportunity for all. The difficulty of the issue presented—whether government may use race-conscious programs to redress the continuing effects of past discrimination—and the mature consideration which each of our Brethren has brought to it have resulted in many opinions, no single one speaking for the Court. But this should not and must not mask the central meaning of today's opinions: Government may take race into account when it acts not to demean or insult any racial group, but to remedy disadvantages cast on minorities by past racial prejudice, at least when appropriate findings have been made

by judicial, legislative, or administrative bodies with competence to act in this area. . . .

We agree with MR. JUSTICE POWELL that . . . the effect of the California Supreme Court's affirmance of the judgment of the Superior Court of California would be to prohibit the University from establishing in the future affirmative-action programs that take race into account. Since we conclude that the affirmative admissions program at the Davis Medical School is constitutional, we would reverse the judgment below in all respects. MR. JUSTICE POWELL agrees that some uses of race in university admissions are permissible and, therefore, he joins with us to make five votes reversing the judgment below insofar as it prohibits the University from establishing race-conscious programs in the future. . . .

Respondent argues that racial classifications are always suspect, and, consequently, that this Court should weigh the importance of the objectives served by Davis' special admissions program to see if they are compelling. In addition, he asserts that this Court must inquire whether, in its judgment, there are alternatives to racial classifications which would suit Davis' purposes. Petitioner, on the other hand, states that our proper role is simply to accept petitioner's determination that the racial classifications used by its program are reasonably related to what it tells us are its benign purposes. We reject petitioner's view, but, because our prior cases are in many respects inapposite to that before us now, we find it necessary to define with precision the meaning of that inexact term, "strict scrutiny."

Unquestionably we have held that a government practice or statute which restricts "fundamental rights" or which contains "suspect classifications" is to be subjected to "strict scrutiny," and can be justified only if it furthers a compelling government purpose and, even then, only if no less restrictive alternative is available. But no fundamental right is involved here. Nor do whites, as a class, have any of the "traditional indicia of suspectness: the class is not saddled with such disabilities, or subjected to such a history of purposeful unequal treatment, or relegated to such a position of political powerlessness as to command extraordinary protection from the majoritarian political process."

Moreover, if the University's representations are credited, this is not a case where racial classifications are "irrelevant, and therefore prohibited." Nor has anyone suggested that the University's purposes contravene the cardinal principle that racial classifications that stigmatize—because they are drawn on the presumption that one race is inferior to another or because they put the weight of government behind racial hatred and separatism—are invalid without more.

On the other hand, the fact that this case does not fit neatly into our prior analytic framework for race cases does not mean that it should be analyzed by applying the very loose rational-basis standard of review that is the very least that is always applied in equal protection cases. . . . Instead, a number of considerations—developed in gender-discrimination cases but which carry even more force when applied to racial classifications—lead us to conclude that racial classifications designed to further remedial purposes "'must serve important governmental objectives, and must be substantially related to achievement of those objectives.'"

First, race, like, "gender-based classifications, too often [has] been inexcusably utilized to stereotype and stigmatize politically powerless segments of society." While a carefully tailored statute designed to remedy past discrimination could avoid these vices, we nonetheless have recognized that the line between honest and thoughtful appraisal of the effects of past discrimination and paternalistic stereotyping is not so clear, and that a statute based on the latter is patently capable of stigmatizing all women with a badge of inferiority. State programs designed ostensibly to ameliorate the effects of past racial discrimination obviously create the same hazard of stigma, since they may promote racial separatism and reinforce the views of those who believe that members of racial minorities are inherently incapable of succeeding on their own.

Second, race, like gender and illegitimacy, is an immutable characteristic which its possessors are powerless to escape or set aside. While a classification is not per se invalid because it divides classes on the basis of an immutable characteristic, it is nevertheless true that such divisions are contrary to our deep belief that "legal burdens should bear some relationship to individual responsibility or wrongdoing" and that advancement sanctioned, sponsored, or approved by the State should ideally be based on individual merit or achievement, or at the least on factors within the control of an individual.

Because this principle is so deeply rooted it might be supposed that it would be considered in the legislative process and weighed against the benefits of programs preferring individuals because of their race. But this is not necessarily so: The natural consequence of our governing processes [may well be] that the most "discrete and insular" of whites . . . will be called upon to bear the immediate, direct costs of benign discrimination. Moreover, it is clear from our cases that there are limits beyond which majorities may not go when they classify on the basis of immutable characteristics. Thus, even if the concern for individualism is weighed by the political process, that weighing cannot waive the personal rights of individuals under the Fourteenth Amendment.

In sum, because of the significant risk that racial classifications established for ostensibly benign purposes can be misused, causing effects not unlike those created by invidious classifications, it is inappropriate to inquire only whether there is any conceivable basis that might sustain such a classification. Instead, to justify such a classification, an important and articulated purpose for its use must be shown. In addition, any statute must be stricken that stigmatizes any group or that singles out those least well represented in the political process to bear the brunt of a benign program. Thus, our review under the Fourteenth Amendment should be strict—not "'strict' in theory and fatal in fact," because it is stigma that causes fatality—but strict and searching nonetheless.

Davis' articulated purpose of remedying the effects of past societal discrimination is, under our cases, sufficiently important to justify the use of race-conscious admissions programs where there is a sound basis for concluding that minority underrepresentation is substantial and chronic, and that the handicap of past discrimination is impeding access of minorities to the Medical School.

Justice Stevens wrote an opinion concurring in the judgment in part and dissenting in part. He was joined by Burger, Rehnquist, and Stewart. Stevens's opinion dealt almost exclusively with the statutory issue of whether the university's admission program violated Title VI of the Civil Rights Act of 1964: "No person in the United States shall, on the ground of race, color, or national origin, be excluded from participation in, be denied the benefits of, or be subjected to discrimination under any program or activity receiving Federal financial assistance." Stevens explains why he focused on the act and the conclusion he reached:

In this case, we are presented with a constitutional question of undoubted and unusual importance. Since, however, a dispositive statutory claim was raised at the very inception of this case, and squarely decided in the portion of the trial court judgment affirmed by the California Supreme Court, it is our plain duty to confront it. Only if petitioner should prevail on the statutory issue would it be necessary to decide whether the University's admissions program violated the Equal Protection Clause of the Fourteenth Amendment.

The University, through its special admissions policy, excluded Bakke from participation in its program of medical education because of his race. The University also acknowledges that it was, and still is, receiving federal financial assistance. The plain language of the statute therefore requires affirmance of the judgment below. A different result cannot be justified unless that language misstates the actual intent of the Congress that enacted the statute or the statute is not enforceable in a private action. Neither conclusion is warranted.

Affirmative Action Following Bakke

The *Bakke* decision held that absent a history of racial discrimination demanding a strong remedy, affirmative action programs that set quotas for particular racial or ethnic groups violate the Equal Protection Clause. But minority status may play a role in the admissions process. Universities may seek a diverse student body by giving minority applicants special consideration. Race and ethnic background may permissibly be deemed a plus, but they cannot be the only factor determining admissions outcomes.

Even so, *Bakke* left many questions unaddressed. First, does the Constitution or federal law prohibit the use of racial classifications as a means of correcting a situation in which a history of racial discrimination exists? Second, does the rationale of *Bakke* apply to women—another group that historically has faced discrimination? Finally, would the Court apply *Bakke* to other types of affirmative action programs, such as minority set-asides? Let us consider the justices' responses to each of these and then turn to the current state of affirmative action debate.

Use of Racial Classifications. An answer to the first question was provided by *United Steelworkers of America v. Weber* (1979), decided just one year after *Bakke.* The case stemmed from an agreement between the union and Kaiser Aluminum and Chemical Company. The agreement set up a training program for a Kaiser plant in Gramercy, Louisiana, for which half of the positions were reserved for blacks. The plan was voluntary, temporary, and a response to a history of discrimination against blacks in the craft unions. Almost no blacks worked in the skilled trades: in the area around the Gramercy plant, for example, 39 percent of the workforce was black, but only 1.83 percent of the skilled force was black. Using lists of senior white workers and senior black workers, the union determined who would be offered positions in the training program, but only within racial groups.

Brian Weber, a white union member, was denied a position in the program, while black workers with less seniority were admitted. He filed suit to declare the program in violation of Title VII of the Civil Rights Act. The Supreme Court found no violations of the law, holding that this voluntary program, designed to remove discrimination from the workplace, was consistent with the spirit of the Civil Rights Act to "break down old patterns of racial segregation and hierarchy." The majority also cited the temporary nature of the plan and the fact that no white workers were discharged or absolutely barred from entering the training program. The minority thought the plan ran contrary to the act, a literal reading of which prohibited discrimination on the basis of race in job training programs, and contrary to the intent of Congress as expressed in legislative debates on the statute.

In *United States v. Paradise* (1987) the Court upheld the use of racial quotas to combat the effects of long-standing discrimination. This dispute centered on the hiring practices of the Alabama Department of Public Safety. In 1972 a district judge found the department in violation of the Equal Protection Clause: in the thirty-seven years since its inception, the department had never hired a black state trooper. Blacks had been employed only as laborers. The district court imposed a strict 50 percent black hiring quota for all troopers and instructed the department to rid itself of all discriminatory practices, including those involving promotions. During the next twelve years, however, the department failed to achieve that goal. By 1984 only four blacks had been promoted to corporal, and none had been promoted to a higher rank. In response to the lack of progress, the district court imposed a temporary 50 percent black quota for promotion to corporal and a similar, though conditioned, quota for promotions to the higher ranks.

The Reagan administration, opposed to the imposition of strict racial quotas, objected to the district court's order. Attempts to block the plan were unsuccessful at the court of appeals level, and the government asked the Supreme Court for review. In a 5–4 vote, the Court upheld the promotion quotas. The plurality opinion, issued by Justice Brennan, stressed the long history of discrimination by Alabama officials and the lack of progress made since the district court's first finding of constitutional violations. The remedy imposed here, according to the majority, was necessary given the extreme nature of the violations. The plan was temporary, flexible, and did not overly burden innocent parties. Writing for the dissenters, Justice O'Connor said that less extreme plans might have been just as effective and should have been considered before the imposition of quotas.

Affirmative Action and Sex Discrimination. The affirmative action plan at issue in *Bakke* was for applicants who indicated that they were economically or educationally disadvantaged or black, Chicano, Asian, or Native American; it was not designed to provide special consideration to women. How would the Court treat a challenge to affirmative action designed to remedy the effects of sex discrimination?

That was one of the questions at issue in *Johnson v. Transportation Agency of Santa Clara County, California* (1987), which presented the justices with their first opportunity to examine preferential treatment for women. The plan at issue imposed no rigid quotas, but carried an expectation that measurable progress would be made in the employment of women. Unlike the plans that had passed Supreme Court muster, this one was not explicitly temporary. The dispute arose when two people, a man and a woman, tried for the same job. The male applicant scored slightly higher on the competitive examination, but both were judged to be qualified. When affirmative action considerations were applied, the woman got the job.[41]

Johnson v. Transportation Agency of Santa Clara County, California

480 U.S. 616 (1987)
laws.findlaw.com/US/480/616.html
Vote: 6 (Blackmun, Brennan, Marshall, O'Connor, Powell,
    Stevens)
    3 (Rehnquist, Scalia, White)
Opinion of the Court: Brennan
Concurring opinion: Stevens
Opinion concurring in judgment: O'Connor
Dissenting opinions: Scalia, White

In 1978 the Santa Clara County Transportation Agency adopted an affirmative action plan designed to attain equitable representation in its workforce for minorities, women, and the handicapped. The plan allowed sex to be taken into account in deciding on promotions to positions in which women were significantly underrepresented. Women constituted 36.4 percent of the area labor market, but they occupied significantly lower percentages of the administrative, professional, and skilled craft positions in the agency. At 76 percent, females were overrepresented in office and clerical jobs. The agency's plan was designed to achieve "statistically measurable yearly improvement in hiring, training and promotion of minorities and women throughout the Agency in all major job classifications where they are underrepresented."

In December 1979 the agency announced a vacancy for a road dispatcher, a craftworker position. Of the 238 jobs in the craftworker category, none was held by a woman. Twelve employees applied for the promotion, including Paul Johnson and Diane Joyce. Both had sufficient training and experience to qualify for the position. After an evaluation of their records and two rounds of interviews, Johnson's score was 75 and Joyce's was 73. The

---

41. For oral arguments in this case, navigate to: *oyez.nwu.edu.*

selection panel recommended that Johnson receive the promotion. In the meantime, Joyce contacted the agency's affirmative action office and expressed a concern that her candidacy would not be treated fairly. After intervention by the affirmative action coordinator, Joyce got the job.

Johnson filed a complaint under the Civil Rights Act. He claimed that he had been denied promotion on account of sex. The federal district court ruled in his favor, finding that sex had been the determining factor in filling the position and that the agency's plan was defective because it was not temporary. The district court further found that although women were statistically underrepresented in various job categories, there was no evidence of agency discrimination as the cause of that imbalance. The court of appeals reversed, holding that the agency was free to correct the imbalances in its workforce. The appeals court also held that the lack of a specific termination date for the plan was not sufficiently important to invalidate it, especially in the absence of strict quotas. Johnson then appealed to the Supreme Court.

JUSTICE BRENNAN delivered the opinion of the Court.

As a preliminary matter, we note that petitioner bears the burden of establishing the invalidity of the Agency's Plan. Only last term in *Wygant v. Jackson Board of Education* (1986), we held that "[t]he ultimate burden remains with the employees to demonstrate the unconstitutionality of an affirmative-action program," and we see no basis for a different rule regarding a plan's alleged violation of Title VII. . . . Once a plaintiff establishes a prima facie case that race or sex has been taken into account in an employer's employment decision, the burden shifts to the employer to articulate a nondiscriminatory rationale for its decision. The existence of an affirmative action plan provides such a rationale. If such a plan is articulated as the basis for the employer's decision, the burden shifts to the plaintiff to prove that the employer's justification is pretextual and the plan is invalid. . . .

The assessment of the legality of the Agency Plan must be guided by our decision in [*United Steelworkers of America v.*] *Weber* [1979]. In that case, the Court addressed the ques-

tion whether the employer violated Title VII by adopting a voluntary affirmative action plan designed to "eliminate manifest racial imbalances in traditionally segregated job categories.". . .

We upheld the employer's decision to select less senior black applicants over the white respondent, for we found that taking race into account was consistent with Title VII's objective of "breaking down old patterns of racial segregation and hierarchy.". . .

We noted that the plan did not "unnecessarily trammel the interests of the white employees," since it did not require "the discharge of white workers and their replacement with new black hires." Nor did the plan create "an absolute bar to the advancement of white employees," since half of those trained in the new program were to be white. Finally, we observed that the plan was a temporary measure, not designed to maintain racial balance, but to "eliminate a manifest racial imbalance.". . . Our decision was grounded in the recognition that voluntary employer action can play a crucial role in furthering Title VII's purpose of eliminating the effects of discrimination in the workplace, and that Title VII should not be read to thwart such efforts.

In reviewing the employment decision at issue in this case, we must first examine whether that decision was made pursuant to a plan prompted by concerns similar to those of the employer in *Weber*. Next, we must determine whether the effect of the plan on males and non-minorities is comparable to the effect of the plan in that case.

The first issue is therefore whether consideration of the sex of applicants for skilled craft jobs was justified by the existence of a "manifest imbalance" that reflected underrepresentation of women in "traditionally segregated job categories." In determining whether an imbalance exists that would justify taking sex or race into account, a comparison of the percentage of minorities or women in the employer's workforce with the percentage in the area labor market or general population is appropriate in analyzing jobs that require no special expertise or training programs designed to provide expertise. Where a job requires special training, however, the comparison should be with those in the labor force who possess the relevant qualifications. The requirement that the "manifest imbalance" relate to a "traditionally segregated job category" provides assurance both that sex or race will be taken into account in a manner consistent with Title VII's purpose of eliminating the effects of employment discrimination, and that the interests of those employees not benefitting from the plan will not be unduly infringed. . . .

It is clear that the decision to hire Joyce was made pursuant to an Agency plan that directed that sex or race be taken into account for the purpose of remedying underrepresentation. The Agency Plan acknowledged the "limited opportunities that have existed in the past" for women to find employment in certain job classifications "where women have not been traditionally employed in significant numbers." As a result, observed the Plan, women were concentrated in traditionally female jobs in the Agency, and represented a lower percentage in other job classifications than would be expected if such traditional segregation had not occurred. . . . The Plan sought to remedy these imbalances through "hiring, training and promotion of . . . women throughout the Agency in all major job classifications where they are underrepresented."

As an initial matter, the Agency adopted as a benchmark for measuring progress in eliminating underrepresentation the long-term goal of a workforce that mirrored in its major job classifications the percentage of women in the area labor market. Even as it did so, however, the Agency acknowledged that such a figure could not by itself necessarily justify taking into account the sex of applicants for positions in all job categories. . . . The Plan therefore directed that annual short-term goals be formulated that would provide a more realistic indication of the degree to which sex should be taken into account in filling particular positions. The Plan stressed that such goals "should not be construed as 'quotas' that must be met," but as reasonable aspirations in correcting the imbalance in the Agency's workforce. . . .

As the Agency Plan recognized, women were most egregiously underrepresented in the Skilled Craft job category, since *none* of the 238 positions was occupied by a woman. . . .

The Agency's Plan emphasized that the long-term goals were not to be taken as guides for actual hiring decisions, but that supervisors were to consider a host of practical factors in seeking to meet affirmative action objectives, including the fact that in some job categories women were not qualified in numbers comparable to their representation in the labor force. . . .

Given the obvious imbalance in the Skilled Craft category, and given the Agency's commitment to eliminating such

imbalances, it was plainly not unreasonable for the Agency to determine that it was appropriate to consider as one factor the sex of Ms. Joyce in making its decision. The promotion of Joyce thus satisfies the first requirement enunciated in *Weber*, since it was undertaken to further an affirmative action plan designed to eliminate Agency workforce imbalances in traditionally segregated job categories.

We next consider whether the Agency Plan unnecessarily trammeled the rights of male employees or created an absolute bar to their advancement. In contrast to the plan in *Weber*, which provided that 50% of the positions in the craft training program were exclusively for blacks, the Plan sets aside no positions for women. The Plan expressly states that "[t]he 'goals' established for each Division should not be construed as 'quotas' that must be met." Rather, the Plan merely authorizes that consideration be given to affirmative action concerns when evaluating qualified applicants. As the Agency Director testified, the sex of Joyce was but one of numerous factors he took into account in arriving at his decision. . . . Similarly, the Agency Plan requires women to compete with all other qualified applicants. No persons are automatically excluded from consideration; *all* are able to have their qualifications weighed against those of other applicants.

In addition, petitioner had no absolute entitlement to the road dispatcher position. Seven of the applicants were classified as qualified and eligible, and the Agency Director was authorized to promote any of the seven. Thus, denial of the promotion unsettled no legitimate firmly rooted expectation on the part of the petitioner. Furthermore, while the petitioner in this case was denied a promotion, he retained his employment with the Agency, at the same salary and with the same seniority, and remained eligible for other promotions.

Finally, the Agency's Plan was intended to *attain* a balanced workforce, not to maintain one. The Plan contains ten references to the Agency's desire to "attain" such a balance, but no reference whatsoever to a goal of maintaining it. . . .

The Agency acknowledged the difficulties that it would confront in remedying the imbalance in its workforce, and it anticipated only gradual increases in the representation of minorities and women. It is thus unsurprising that the Plan contains no explicit end date, for the Agency's flexible, case-by-case approach was not expected to yield success in a brief period of time. Express assurance that a program is only temporary may be necessary if the program actually sets aside positions according to specific numbers. . . . In this case, however, substantial evidence shows that the Agency has sought to take a moderate, gradual approach to eliminating the imbalance in its workforce, one which establishes realistic guidance for employment decisions, and which visits minimal intrusion on the legitimate expectations of other employees. Given this fact, as well as the Agency's express commitment to "attain" a balanced workforce, there is ample assurance that the Agency does not seek to use its Plan to maintain a permanent racial and sexual balance. . . .

We therefore hold that the Agency appropriately took into account as one factor the sex of Diane Joyce in determining that she should be promoted to the road dispatcher position. The decision to do so was made pursuant to an affirmative action plan that represents a moderate, flexible, case-by-case approach to effecting a gradual improvement in the representation of minorities and women in the Agency's workforce. Such a plan is fully consistent with Title VII, for it embodies the contribution that voluntary employer action can make in eliminating the vestiges of discrimination in the workplace. Accordingly, the judgment of the Court of Appeals is

Affirmed.

JUSTICE SCALIA . . . dissenting.

With a clarity which, had it not proven so unavailing, one might well recommend as a model of statutory draftsmanship, Title VII of the Civil Rights Act of 1964 declares:

"It shall be an unlawful employment practice for an employer—

"(1) to fail or refuse to hire or to discharge any individual, or otherwise to discriminate against any individual with respect to his compensation, terms, conditions, or privileges of employment, because of such individual's race, color, religion, sex, or national origin; or

"(2) to limit, segregate, or classify his employees or applicants for employment in any way which would deprive or tend to deprive any individual of employment opportunities or otherwise adversely affect his status as an employee, because of such individual's race, color, religion, sex, or national origin." 42 U.S.C. §2000e-2(a).

The Court today completes the process of converting this from a guarantee that race or sex will *not* be the basis for employment determinations, to a guarantee that it often *will*. Ever so subtly, without even alluding to the last obstacles preserved by earlier opinions that we now push out of our path, we effectively replace the goal of a discrimination-free society with the quite incompatible goal of proportionate representation by race and by sex in the workplace. . . .

It is unlikely that today's result will be displeasing to politically elected officials, to whom it provides the means of quickly accommodating the demands of organized groups to achieve concrete, numerical improvement in the economic status of particular constituencies. Nor will it displease the world of corporate and governmental employers (many of whom have filed briefs as *amici* in the present case, all on the side of Santa Clara) for whom the cost of hiring less qualified workers is often substantially less—and infinitely more predictable—than the cost of litigating Title VII cases and of seeking to convince federal agencies by nonnumerical means that no discrimination exists. In fact, the only losers in the process are the Johnsons of the country, for whom Title VII has been not merely repealed but actually inverted. The irony is that these individuals—predominantly unknown, unaffluent, unorganized—suffer this injustice at the hands of a Court fond of thinking itself the champion of the politically impotent.

I dissent.

Minority Set-Asides. Minority set-aside programs are closely related to affirmative action plans and share underlying philosophies and goals. Minority set-asides attempt to enhance the prospects of disadvantaged groups by granting them special considerations in the awarding of government contracts and benefits. The justification for such programs is the long history of discrimination against minority-owned businesses in general commercial activity and in providing goods and services for the government. Set-asides are based on the idea that just eliminating discrimination in the letting of government contracts will not result in more business for minority-owned firms. Because of past discrimination, many minority businesses lack capital, management experience, and bonding eligibility. They cannot compete successfully with more solid, better-financed white firms. Consequently, minority set-aside programs propose for a time to reserve a percentage of government business and contracts for minority-owned enterprises.

Set-aside programs received their first significant review by the Court in 1980 in *Fullilove v. Klutznick.* The Court's deliberations reveal that the justices were no more able to reach consensus here than they had on affirmative action issues. *Fullilove* concerned the Public Works Employment Act passed by Congress in 1977. A provision of that law directed that in federally financed state public works projects, 10 percent of the goods and services had to be procured from minority-owned businesses. A minority-owned business was defined as a company at least 50 percent owned by citizens of the United States who were black, Spanish-speaking, Asian, Native American, Eskimo, or Aleut. The constitutionality of the statute was attacked by a group of contractors who claimed economic injury due to its enforcement.

The Supreme Court upheld the validity of the law as a remedial action to correct a history of discrimination in government contracting. Although the vote was 6 to 3, the divisions among the justices were many and deep. Five different opinions were written, and no opinion garnered the support of more than three justices. Burger, Powell, and White held that the law was constitutional as a necessary means of advancing a compelling government interest. In their view, the law was a narrow and carefully tailored measure to eliminate a particular type of discrimination. Blackmun, Brennan, and Marshall also supported the law's validity. They adhered to their views expressed in *Bakke* giving strong support for the use of quotas as a means to alleviate discrimination. Rehnquist, Stewart, and Stevens dissented. Stewart wrote a strong opinion arguing that the Constitution should be hostile to all racial classifications.

Despite the divisions, six justices voted in *Fullilove* to uphold the federal set-aside program. This decision encouraged state and local governments that wanted to use the same kind of remedial approach. But in *City of Richmond v. J. A. Croson Co.* (1989) the Court reviewed a particular plan enacted by Richmond, Virginia.[42] This plan, like the federal program, set aside a certain proportion of

city construction contracting business for minority-owned enterprises. The law's expressed purpose was to correct the effects of past discrimination in the letting of city contracts and in the construction industry generally. In spite of its shared traits with the program approved in *Fullilove*, a majority of the justices found constitutional defects in the Richmond plan. As you read this case, consider whether the *Fullilove* precedent should control. Do the elements of the Richmond plan sufficiently distinguish it from the federal program to justify the Court's treating it differently?

City of Richmond v. J. A. Croson Co.

488 U.S. 469 (1989)
laws.findlaw.com/US/488/469.html
Vote: 6 (Kennedy, O'Connor, Rehnquist, Scalia, Stevens, White)
　　　3 (Blackmun, Brennan, Marshall)
Opinion of the Court: O'Connor
Concurring opinions: Kennedy, Stevens
Opinion concurring in the judgment: Scalia
Dissenting opinions: Blackmun, Marshall

In 1983 the Richmond City Council, consisting of five black and four white members, adopted the Minority Utilization Plan, which required the city's prime contractors to award subcontracts of at least 30 percent of the dollar amount of the total contract to one or more minority business enterprises (MBEs). Minority contractors were defined as businesses at least 51 percent owned by persons who were black, Spanish-speaking, Asian, Native American, Eskimo, or Aleut. The minority business did not have to be located in Richmond.

The plan was developed to correct the effects of racial discrimination. Richmond's population was 50 percent black, but between 1978 and 1983 only .678 percent of the city's construction business had been awarded to minority contractors. There was no specific finding that the city had discriminated in awarding contracts to minority businesses; rather, the problem stemmed largely from a lack of minority-owned contracting businesses in the Richmond area.

The Croson company was the only bidder on a project

---

42. For oral arguments in this case, navigate to: *oyez.nwu.edu.*

to install plumbing fixtures at the city jail, but the company had difficulty finding a minority subcontractor to supply the materials. Once Croson located a qualified company willing to participate, the projected price was too high. Croson requested a waiver from the set-aside requirements or permission to raise the cost of the project. The city refused and elected to rebid the contract. Croson sued to have the set-aside program declared unconstitutional as a violation of the Equal Protection Clause of the Fourteenth Amendment. The company argued that set-aside programs should be allowed only to combat discrimination by the government. A plurality of the Court had supported such a position three years earlier in *Wygant v. Jackson Board of Education* (1986). Richmond, on the other hand, argued that *Fullilove v. Klutznick* should be interpreted to give state and local governments broad authority to combat the effects of discrimination.

JUSTICE O'CONNOR delivered the opinion of the Court. . . .

In this case, we confront once again the tension between the Fourteenth Amendment's guarantee of equal treatment to all citizens, and the use of race-based measures to ameliorate the effects of past discrimination on the opportunities enjoyed by members of minority groups in our society. . . .

The Equal Protection Clause of the Fourteenth Amendment provides that "[N]o State shall . . . deny to *any person* within its jurisdiction the equal protection of the laws" (emphasis added). As this Court has noted in the past, the "rights created by the first section of the Fourteenth Amendment are, by its terms, guaranteed to the individual. The rights established are personal rights." The Richmond Plan denies certain citizens the opportunity to compete for a fixed percentage of public contracts based solely upon their race. To whatever racial group these citizens belong, their "personal rights" to be treated with equal dignity and respect are implicated by a rigid rule erecting race as the sole criterion in an aspect of public decisionmaking.

Absent searching judicial inquiry into the justification for such race-based measures, there is simply no way of determining what classifications are "benign" or "remedial" and what classifications are in fact motivated by illegitimate notions of racial inferiority or simple racial politics. Indeed,

the purpose of strict scrutiny is to "smoke out" illegitimate uses of race by assuring that the legislative body is pursuing a goal important enough to warrant use of a highly suspect tool. The test also ensures that the means chosen "fit" this compelling goal so closely that there is little or no possibility that the motive for the classification was illegitimate racial prejudice or stereotype.

Classifications based on race carry a danger of stigmatic harm. Unless they are strictly reserved for remedial settings, they may in fact promote notions of racial inferiority and lead to a politics of racial hostility. We thus reaffirm the view expressed by the plurality in *Wygant* [*v. Jackson Board of Education*, 1986] that the standard of review under the Equal Protection Clause is not dependent on the race of those burdened or benefited by a particular classification. . . .

In *Wygant*, four Members of the Court applied heightened scrutiny to a race-based system of employee layoffs. Justice Powell, writing for the plurality, again drew the distinction between "societal discrimination" which is an inadequate basis for race-conscious classifications, and the type of identified discrimination that can support and define the scope of race-based relief. The challenged classification in that case tied the layoff of minority teachers to the percentage of minority students enrolled in the school district. The lower courts had upheld the scheme, based on the theory that minority students were in need of "role models" to alleviate the effects of prior discrimination in society. This Court reversed, with a plurality of four Justices reiterating the view expressed by Justice Powell in [*Regents of the University of California v.*] *Bakke* [1978] that "[s]ocietal discrimination, without more, is too amorphous a basis for imposing a racially classified remedy.". . .

Like the "role model" theory employed in *Wygant*, a generalized assertion that there has been past discrimination in an entire industry provides no guidance for a legislative body to determine the precise scope of the injury it seeks to remedy. It "has no logical stopping point.". . .

Appellant argues that it is attempting to remedy various forms of past discrimination that are alleged to be responsible for the small number of minority businesses in the local contracting industry. Among these the city cites the exclusion of blacks from skilled construction trade unions and training programs. This past discrimination has prevented them "from following the traditional path from laborer to entrepreneur." The city also lists a host of nonracial factors which would seem to face a member of any racial group attempting to establish a new business enterprise, such as deficiencies in working capital, inability to meet bonding requirements, unfamiliarity with bidding procedures, and disability caused by an inadequate track record.

While there is no doubt that the sorry history of both private and public discrimination in this country has contributed to a lack of opportunities for black entrepreneurs, this observation, standing alone, cannot justify a rigid racial quota in the awarding of public contracts in Richmond, Virginia. Like the claim that discrimination in primary and secondary schooling justifies a rigid racial preference in medical school admissions, an amorphous claim that there has been past discrimination in a particular industry cannot justify the use of an unyielding racial quota.

It is sheer speculation how many minority firms there would be in Richmond absent past societal discrimination, just as it was sheer speculation how many minority medical students would have been admitted to the medical school at Davis absent past discrimination in educational opportunities. Defining these sorts of injuries as "identified discrimination" would give local governments license to create a patchwork of racial preferences based on statistical generalizations about any particular field of endeavor.

These defects are readily apparent in this case. The 30% quota cannot in any realistic sense be tied to any injury suffered by anyone. The District Court relied upon five predicate "facts" in reaching its conclusion that there was an adequate basis for the 30% quota: (1) the ordinance declares itself to be remedial; (2) several proponents of the measure stated their views that there had been past discrimination in the construction industry; (3) minority businesses received .67% of prime contracts from the city while minorities constituted 50% of the city's population; (4) there were very few minority contractors in local and state contractors' associations; and (5) in 1977, Congress made a determination that the effects of past discrimination had stifled minority participation in the construction industry nationally.

None of these "findings," singly or together, provide the city of Richmond with a "strong basis in evidence for its conclusion that remedial action was necessary." There is nothing approaching a prima facie case of a constitutional or statutory violation by anyone in the Richmond construction industry.

The District Court accorded great weight to the fact that the city council designated the Plan as "remedial." But the mere recitation of a "benign" or legitimate purpose for a racial classification is entitled to little or no weight. Racial classifications are suspect, and that means that simple legislative assurances of good intention cannot suffice. The District Court also relied on the highly conclusionary statement of a proponent of the Plan that there was racial discrimination in the construction industry "in this area, and the State, and around the nation." It also noted that the city manager had related his view that racial discrimination still plagued the construction industry in his home city of Pittsburgh. These statements are of little probative value in establishing identified discrimination in the Richmond construction industry. The fact-finding process of legislative bodies is generally entitled to a presumption of regularity and deferential review by the judiciary. But when a legislative body chooses to employ a suspect classification, it cannot rest upon a generalized assertion as to the classification's relevance to its goals. . . . The history of racial classifications in this country suggests that blind judicial deference to legislative or executive pronouncements of necessity has no place in equal protection analysis.

Reliance on the disparity between the number of prime contracts awarded to minority firms and the minority population of the city of Richmond is similarly misplaced. There is no doubt that "[w]here gross statistical disparities can be shown, they alone in a proper case may constitute prima facie proof of a pattern or practice of discrimination" under Title VII. But it is equally clear that "[w]hen special qualifications are required to fill particular jobs, comparisons to the general population (rather than to the smaller group of individuals who possess the necessary qualifications) may have little probative value."

In the employment context, we have recognized that for certain entry level positions or positions requiring minimal training, statistical comparisons of the racial composition of an employer's workforce to the racial composition of the relevant population may be probative of a pattern of discrimination. But where special qualifications are necessary, the relevant statistical pool for purposes of demonstrating discriminatory exclusion must be the number of minorities qualified to undertake the particular task.

In this case, the city does not even know how many MBEs in the relevant market are qualified to undertake prime or subcontracting work in public construction projects. Nor does the city know what percentage of total city construction dollars minority firms now receive as subcontractors on prime contracts let by the city. . . .

The city and the District Court also relied on evidence that MBE membership in local contractors' associations was extremely low. Again, standing alone this evidence is not probative of any discrimination in the local construction industry. There are numerous explanations for this dearth of minority participation, including past societal discrimination in education and economic opportunities as well as both black and white career and entrepreneurial choices. Blacks may be disproportionately attracted to industries other than construction. The mere fact that black membership in these trade organizations is low, standing alone, cannot establish a prima facie case of discrimination.

For low minority membership in these associations to be relevant, the city would have to link it to the number of local MBEs eligible for membership. If the statistical disparity between eligible MBEs and MBE membership were great enough, an inference of discriminatory exclusion could arise. In such a case, the city would have a compelling interest in preventing its tax dollars from assisting these organizations in maintaining a racially segregated construction market.

Finally, the city and the District Court relied on Congress' finding in connection with the set-aside approved in *Fullilove* [v. *Klutznick,* 1980] that there had been nationwide discrimination in the construction industry. The probative value of these findings for demonstrating the existence of discrimination in Richmond is extremely limited. By its inclusion of a waiver procedure in the national program addressed in *Fullilove,* Congress explicitly recognized that the scope of the problem would vary from market area to market area.

Moreover, as noted above, Congress was exercising its powers under §5 of the Fourteenth Amendment in making a finding that past discrimination would cause federal funds to be distributed in a manner which reinforced prior patterns of discrimination. While the States and their subdivisions may take remedial action when they possess evidence that their own spending practices are exacerbating a pattern of prior discrimination, they must identify that discrimination, public or private, with some specificity before they may use race-conscious relief. . . .

In sum, none of the evidence presented by the city points to any identified discrimination in the Richmond construction industry. We, therefore, hold that the city has failed to demonstrate a compelling interest in apportioning public contracting opportunities on the basis of race. To accept Richmond's claim that past societal discrimination alone can serve as the basis for rigid racial preferences would be to open the door to competing claims for "remedial relief" for every disadvantaged group. The dream of a Nation of equal citizens in a society where race is irrelevant to personal opportunity and achievement would be lost in a mosaic of shifting preferences based on inherently unmeasurable claims of past wrongs. . . . We think such a result would be contrary to both the letter and spirit of a constitutional provision whose central command is equality.

The foregoing analysis applies only to the inclusion of blacks within the Richmond set-aside program. There is *absolutely no evidence* of past discrimination against Spanish-speaking, Oriental, Indian, Eskimo, or Aleut persons in any aspect of the Richmond construction industry. The District Court took judicial notice of the fact that the vast majority of "minority" persons in Richmond were black. It may well be that Richmond has never had an Aleut or Eskimo citizen. The random inclusion of racial groups that, as a practical matter, may never have suffered from discrimination in the construction industry in Richmond, suggests that perhaps the city's purpose was not in fact to remedy past discrimination.

If a 30% set-aside was "narrowly tailored" to compensate black contractors for past discrimination, one may legitimately ask why they are forced to share this "remedial relief" with an Aleut citizen who moves to Richmond tomorrow? The gross overinclusiveness of Richmond's racial preference strongly impugns the city's claim of remedial motivation.

As noted by the court below, it is almost impossible to assess whether the Richmond Plan is narrowly tailored to remedy prior discrimination since it is not linked to identified discrimination in any way. We limit ourselves to two observations in this regard.

First, there does not appear to have been any consideration of the use of race-neutral means to increase minority business participation in city contracting. Many of the barriers to minority participation in the construction industry relied upon by the city to justify a racial classification appear to be race-neutral. If MBEs disproportionately lack capital or cannot meet bonding requirements, a race-neutral program of city financing for small firms would, *a fortiori,* lead to greater minority participation. The principal opinion in *Fullilove* found that Congress had carefully examined and rejected race-neutral alternatives before enacting the MBE set-aside. There is no evidence in this record that the Richmond City Council has considered any alternatives to a race-based quota.

Second, the 30% quota cannot be said to be narrowly tailored to any goal, except perhaps outright racial balancing. It rests upon the "completely unrealistic" assumption that minorities will choose a particular trade in lockstep proportion to their representation in the local population.

Since the city must already consider bids and waivers on a case-by-case basis, it is difficult to see the need for a rigid numerical quota. As noted above, the congressional scheme upheld in *Fullilove* allowed for a waiver of the set-aside provision where an MBE's higher price was not attributable to the effects of past discrimination. Based upon proper findings, such programs are less problematic from an equal protection standpoint because they treat all candidates individually, rather than making the color of an applicant's skin the sole relevant consideration. Unlike the program upheld in *Fullilove,* the Richmond Plan's waiver system focuses solely on the availability of MBEs; there is no inquiry into whether or not the particular MBE seeking a racial preference has suffered from the effects of past discrimination by the city or prime contractors. . . .

Under Richmond's scheme, a successful black, Hispanic, or Oriental entrepreneur from anywhere in the country enjoys an absolute preference over other citizens based solely on their race. We think it obvious that such a program is not narrowly tailored to remedy the effects of prior discrimination.

Nothing we say today precludes a state or local entity from taking action to rectify the effects of identified discrimination within its jurisdiction. If the city of Richmond had evidence before it that nonminority contractors were systematically excluding minority businesses from subcontracting opportunities, it could take action to end the discriminatory exclusion. Where there is a significant statistical disparity between the number of qualified minority contractors willing and able to perform a particular service and the number of such contractors actually engaged by the lo-

cality or the locality's prime contractors, an inference of discriminatory exclusion could arise. Under such circumstances, the city could act to dismantle the closed business system by taking appropriate measures against those who discriminate on the basis of race or other illegitimate criteria. In the extreme case, some form of narrowly tailored racial preference might be necessary to break down patterns of deliberate exclusion. . . .

Even in the absence of evidence of discrimination, the city has at its disposal a whole array of race-neutral devices to increase the accessibility of city contracting opportunities to small entrepreneurs of all races. Simplification of bidding procedures, relaxation of bonding requirements, and training and financial aid for disadvantaged entrepreneurs of all races would open the public contracting market to all those who have suffered the effects of past societal discrimination or neglect. Many of the formal barriers to new entrants may be the product of bureaucratic inertia more than actual necessity, and may have a disproportionate effect on the opportunities open to new minority firms. Their elimination or modification would have little detrimental effect on the city's interests and would serve to increase the opportunities available to minority business without classifying individuals on the basis of race. The city may also act to prohibit discrimination in the provision of credit or bonding by local suppliers and banks. Business as usual should not mean business pursuant to the unthinking exclusion of certain members of our society from its rewards.

In the case at hand, the city has not ascertained how many minority enterprises are present in the local construction market nor the level of their participation in city construction projects. The city points to no evidence that qualified minority contractors have been passed over for city contracts or subcontracts, either as a group or in any individual case. Under such circumstances, it is simply impossible to say that the city has demonstrated "a strong basis in evidence for its conclusion that remedial action was necessary."

Proper findings in this regard are necessary to define both the scope of the injury and the extent of the remedy necessary to cure its effects. Such findings also serve to assure all citizens that the deviation from the norm of equal treatment of all racial and ethnic groups is a temporary matter, a measure taken in the service of the goal of equality itself. Absent such findings, there is a danger that a racial classification is merely the product of unthinking stereotypes or a form of racial politics. "[I]f there is no duty to attempt either to measure the recovery by the wrong or to distribute that recovery within the injured class in an evenhanded way, our history will adequately support a legislative preference for almost any ethnic, religious, or racial group with the political strength to negotiate 'a piece of the action' for its members." Because the city of Richmond has failed to identify the need for remedial action in the awarding of its public construction contracts, its treatment of its citizens on a racial basis violates the dictates of the Equal Protection Clause. Accordingly, the judgment of the Court of Appeals for the Fourth Circuit is

Affirmed.

JUSTICE MARSHALL . . . dissenting.

It is a welcome symbol of racial progress when the former capital of the Confederacy acts forthrightly to confront the effects of racial discrimination in its midst. In my view, nothing in the Constitution can be construed to prevent Richmond, Virginia, from allocating a portion of its contracting dollars for businesses owned or controlled by members of minority groups. Indeed, Richmond's set-aside program is indistinguishable in all meaningful respects from— and in fact was patterned upon—the federal set-aside plan which this Court upheld in *Fullilove v. Klutznick.*

A majority of this Court holds today, however, that the Equal Protection Clause of the Fourteenth Amendment blocks Richmond's initiative. The essence of the majority's position is that Richmond has failed to catalogue adequate findings to prove that past discrimination has impeded minorities from joining or participating fully in Richmond's construction contracting industry. I find deep irony in second-guessing Richmond's judgment on this point. As much as any municipality in the United States, Richmond knows what racial discrimination is; a century of decisions by this and other federal courts has richly documented the city's disgraceful history of public and private racial discrimination. In any event, the Richmond City Council has supported its determination that minorities have been wrongly excluded from local construction contracting. Its proof includes statistics showing that minority-owned businesses have received virtually no city contracting dollars and rarely if ever belonged to area trade associations; testimony by

municipal officials that discrimination has been widespread in the local construction industry; and the same exhaustive and widely publicized federal studies relied on in *Fullilove,* studies which showed that pervasive discrimination in the Nation's tight-knit construction industry had operated to exclude minorities from public contracting. These are precisely the types of statistical and testimonial evidence which, until today, this Court had credited in cases approving of race-conscious measures designed to remedy past discrimination.

More fundamentally, today's decision marks a deliberate and giant step backward in this Court's affirmative action jurisprudence. Cynical of one municipality's attempt to redress the effects of past racial discrimination in a particular industry, the majority launches a grapeshot attack on race-conscious remedies in general. The majority's unnecessary pronouncements will inevitably discourage or prevent governmental entities, particularly States and localities, from acting to rectify the scourge of past discrimination. This is the harsh reality of the majority's decision, but it is not the Constitution's command. . . .

The majority today sounds a full-scale retreat from the Court's long-standing solicitude to race-conscious remedial efforts "directed toward deliverance of the century-old promise of equality of economic opportunity." The new and restrictive tests it applies scuttle one city's effort to surmount its discriminatory past, and imperil those of dozens more localities. I, however, profoundly disagree with the cramped vision of the Equal Protection Clause which the majority offers today and with its application of that vision to Richmond, Virginia's, laudable set-aside plan. The battle against pernicious racial discrimination or its effects is nowhere near won. I must dissent.

The Court's condemnation of Richmond's minority set-aside program was a clear signal to other state and local governments that any plan to increase business for minority-owned enterprises was going to be difficult to justify. A plan must be shown to be narrowly tailored to meet a compelling government interest. The decision also gave encouragement to majority-owned businesses that wanted to challenge such plans.

Yet the very next year in *Metro Broadcasting v. Federal*

Communications Commission the Court approved the FCC's use of minority preferences. The purpose of the FCC plan was to encourage minority ownership of radio and television stations. Unlike most forms of commercial activity, the number of radio and television stations that can operate in a particular market is limited. Because of this constraint and the fact that broadcasters use the public air waves, the federal government—through the FCC—decides who is to be granted a license to broadcast. The process of obtaining a license can be highly competitive.

Writing for the five-person majority, Justice Brennan held the federal government to more lenient standards than the states: "We hold that the FCC minority ownership policies pass muster under the test we announce today. First, we find that they serve the important governmental objective of broadcast diversity. Second, we conclude that they are substantially related to the achievement of that objective." To this, Justice O'Connor, who wrote the majority opinion in *City of Richmond,* registered a strong dissent:

At the heart of the Constitution's guarantee of equal protection lies the simple command that the Government must treat citizens "as individuals, not 'as simply components of a racial, religious, sexual or national class.'" Social scientists may debate how peoples' thoughts and behavior reflect their background, but the Constitution provides that the Government may not allocate benefits and burdens among individuals based on the assumption that race or ethnicity determines how they act or think. To uphold the challenged programs, the Court departs from these fundamental principles and from our traditional requirement that racial classifications are permissible only if necessary and narrowly tailored to achieve a compelling interest. This departure marks a renewed toleration of racial classifications and a repudiation of our recent affirmation that the Constitution's equal protection guarantees extend equally to all citizens. The Court's application of a lessened equal protection standard to congressional actions finds no support in our cases or in the Constitution. I respectfully dissent.

The gap between *City of Richmond* and *Metro Broadcasting* added more confusion to this area of the law. Would the Court continue to hold the federal government and the states to different standards? This question became all the more important because, by the time the justices heard a 1995 affirmative action case, *Adarand*

Constructors, Inc. v. Peña, the Court had changed substantially. Justice Brennan's majority opinion in *Metro Broadcasting* was his last after an illustrious career of thirty-four years on the Court. During that time, he had been a steadfast defender of liberal principles in constitutional interpretation. Brennan's 1990 retirement was followed the next year by Thurgood Marshall's. Like Brennan, Marshall had consistently supported affirmative action programs.

President Bush appointed David Souter to Brennan's seat and Clarence Thomas to Marshall's. Given the close vote on most affirmative action appeals and the nearly even division between liberal and conservative justices on an appropriate rule of law to govern these issues, the Brennan and Marshall retirements were a significant blow to those who supported affirmative action. However, President Clinton's appointment of Justices Ginsburg and Breyer (replacing White and Blackmun) put two new Democrats on the bench. Would they provide the Court with enough votes to uphold affirmative action programs or would the worst fears of supporters of preferential treatment be realized in *Adarand?*[43]

Adarand Constructors, Inc. v. Peña

515 U. S. 200 (1995)
supct.law.cornell.edu/supct/html/93-1841.ZS.html
Vote: 5 (Kennedy, O'Connor, Rehnquist, Scalia, Thomas)
    4 (Breyer, Ginsburg, Souter, Stevens)
Opinion of the Court: O'Connor
Concurring opinions: Scalia, Thomas
Dissenting opinions: Ginsburg, Souter, Stevens

This case involves the validity of minority preferences in federal construction projects. What is challenged is a clause in Federal Highway Division contracts issued under the Federal Construction Procurement Program. These contracts are authorized by two statutes: the Small Business Act (SBA) and the Surface Transportation and Uniform Relocation Assistance Act of 1987 (STURAA). The preference policy calls for the prime contractor to be

43. For oral arguments in this case, navigate to: *oyez.nwu.edu.*

Randy Pech, owner of a guardrail installation company in Colorado Springs, challenged a federal minority set-aside program in *Adarand Constructors, Inc. v. Peña.*

paid a bonus if at least 10 percent of the overall contract amount is subcontracted to "disadvantaged business enterprises" (DBEs), small businesses that are minority owned and operated.

In 1989 the Federal Highway Division awarded a prime contract for highway work in Colorado to Mountain Gravel and Construction Company. Adarand Constructors, owned and operated by a white male, submitted the lowest subcontract bid to do guardrail work on the project. However, the guardrail contract was issued to Gonzales Construction, a minority-owned firm. Because Mountain Gravel awarded the subcontract to a DBE, it received a $10,000 bonus.

Adarand filed suit against Secretary of Transportation Federico Peña, claiming that the preference policy violated the Due Process Clause of the Fifth Amendment. The

federal program was upheld at the trial level. The Tenth Circuit Court of Appeals affirmed, holding that Supreme Court precedent allowed more latitude to the federal government in implementing race-conscious programs (*Metro Broadcasting*) than was permitted the states (*Croson*). Adarand requested Supreme Court review.

JUSTICE O'CONNOR announced the judgment of the Court and delivered an opinion . . . which is for the Court except insofar as it might be inconsistent with the views expressed in JUSTICE SCALIA'S concurrence. . . .

Adarand's claim arises under the Fifth Amendment to the Constitution, which provides that "No person shall . . . be deprived of life, liberty, or property, without due process of law." Although this Court has always understood that Clause to provide some measure of protection against arbitrary treatment by the Federal Government, it is not as explicit a guarantee of equal treatment as the Fourteenth Amendment, which provides that "No State shall . . . deny to any person within its jurisdiction the equal protection of the laws." Our cases have accorded varying degrees of significance to the difference in the language of those two Clauses. We think it necessary to revisit the issue here. . . .

In *Bolling v. Sharpe* (1954), the Court for the first time explicitly questioned the existence of any difference between the obligations of the Federal Government and the States to avoid racial classifications. . . . *Bolling's* facts concerned school desegregation, but its reasoning was not so limited. The Court's observations that "[d]istinctions between citizens solely because of their ancestry are by their very nature odious," *Hirabayashi* [*v. United States*, 1943], and that "all legal restrictions which curtail the civil rights of a single racial group are immediately suspect," *Korematsu* [*v. United States*, 1944], carry no less force in the context of federal action than in the context of action by the States—indeed, they first appeared in cases concerning action by the Federal Government. . . .

Later cases in contexts other than school desegregation did not distinguish between the duties of the States and the Federal Government to avoid racial classifications. Consider, for example, the following passage from *McLaughlin v. Florida*, a 1964 case that struck down a race-based state law:

"[W]e deal here with a classification based upon the race of the participants, which must be viewed in light of the historical fact that the central purpose of the Fourteenth Amendment was to eliminate racial discrimination emanating from official sources in the States. This strong policy renders racial classifications 'constitutionally suspect,' *Bolling v. Sharpe;* and subject to the 'most rigid scrutiny,' *Korematsu v. United States;* and 'in most circumstances irrelevant' to any constitutionally acceptable legislative purpose, *Hirabayashi v. United States.*"

McLaughlin's reliance on cases involving federal action for the standards applicable to a case involving state legislation suggests that the Court understood the standards for federal and state racial classifications to be the same.

Cases decided after *McLaughlin* continued to treat the equal protection obligations imposed by the Fifth and the Fourteenth Amendments as indistinguishable. . . . *Loving v. Virginia* [1967], which struck down a race-based state law, cited *Korematsu* for the proposition that "the Equal Protection Clause demands that racial classifications . . . be subjected to the 'most rigid scrutiny.'" The various opinions in *Frontiero v. Richardson* (1973), which concerned sex discrimination by the Federal Government, took their equal protection standard of review from *Reed v. Reed* (1971), a case that invalidated sex discrimination by a State, without mentioning any possibility of a difference between the standards applicable to state and federal action. Thus, in 1975, the Court stated explicitly that "[t]his Court's approach to Fifth Amendment equal protection claims has always been precisely the same as to equal protection claims under the Fourteenth Amendment." *Weinberger v. Wiesenfeld;* see also *Buckley v. Valeo* (1976); *United States v. Paradise* (1987) . . . .

Most of the cases discussed above involved classifications burdening groups that have suffered discrimination in our society. In 1978, the Court confronted the question whether race-based governmental action designed to benefit such groups should also be subject to "the most rigid scrutiny." *Regents of Univ. of California v. Bakke* involved an equal protection challenge to a state-run medical school's practice of reserving a number of spaces in its entering class for minority students. The petitioners argued that "strict scrutiny" should apply only to "classifications that disadvantage 'discrete and insular minorities.'" *Bakke* did not produce an opinion for the Court, but Justice Powell's opinion announcing the Court's judgment rejected the argument. . . .

Two years after *Bakke,* the Court faced another challenge to remedial race-based action, this time involving action un-

dertaken by the Federal Government. In *Fullilove v. Klutznick* (1980), the Court upheld Congress' inclusion of a 10% set-aside for minority-owned businesses in the Public Works Employment Act of 1977. As in *Bakke,* there was no opinion for the Court. Chief Justice Burger, in an opinion joined by Justices White and Powell, observed that "[a]ny preference based on racial or ethnic criteria must necessarily receive a most searching examination to make sure that it does not conflict with constitutional guarantees.". . .

In *Wygant v. Jackson Board of Ed.* (1986), the Court considered a Fourteenth Amendment challenge to another form of remedial racial classification. The issue in *Wygant* was whether a school board could adopt race-based preferences in determining which teachers to lay off. Justice Powell's plurality opinion observed that "the level of scrutiny does not change merely because the challenged classification operates against a group that historically has not been subject to governmental discrimination.". . . In other words, "racial classifications of any sort must be subjected to 'strict scrutiny.'" (O'CONNOR, J., concurring in part and concurring in judgment) . . . .

The Court's failure to produce a majority opinion in *Bakke, Fullilove,* and *Wygant* left unresolved the proper analysis for remedial race-based governmental action. . . .

The Court resolved the issue, at least in part, in 1989. *Richmond v. J. A. Croson Co.* concerned a city's determination that 30% of its contracting work should go to minority-owned businesses. A majority of the Court in *Croson* held that "the standard of review under the Equal Protection Clause is not dependent on the race of those burdened or benefited by a particular classification," and that the single standard of review for racial classifications should be "strict scrutiny.". . .

With *Croson,* the Court finally agreed that the Fourteenth Amendment requires strict scrutiny of all race-based action by state and local governments. But *Croson* of course had no occasion to declare what standard of review the Fifth Amendment requires for such action taken by the Federal Government. . . .

Despite lingering uncertainty in the details, however, the Court's cases through *Croson* had established three general propositions with respect to governmental racial classifications. First, skepticism: "'[a]ny preference based on racial or ethnic criteria must necessarily receive a most searching examination,'" *Wygant, Fullilove, McLaughlin, Hirabayashi.* . . .

Second, consistency: "the standard of review under the Equal Protection Clause is not dependent on the race of those burdened or benefited by a particular classification," *Croson, Bakke.* . . . And third, congruence: "[e]qual protection analysis in the Fifth Amendment area is the same as that under the Fourteenth Amendment," *Buckley v. Valeo, Weinberger v. Wiesenfeld, Bolling v. Sharpe.* Taken together, these three propositions lead to the conclusion that any person, of whatever race, has the right to demand that any governmental actor subject to the Constitution justify any racial classification subjecting that person to unequal treatment under the strictest judicial scrutiny. . . .

A year later, however, the Court took a surprising turn. *Metro Broadcasting, Inc. v. FCC* (1990) involved a Fifth Amendment challenge to two race-based policies of the Federal Communications Commission. In *Metro Broadcasting,* the Court repudiated the long-held notion that "it would be unthinkable that the same Constitution would impose a lesser duty on the Federal Government" than it does on a State to afford equal protection of the laws, *Bolling.* It did so by holding that "benign" federal racial classifications need only satisfy intermediate scrutiny, even though *Croson* had recently concluded that such classifications enacted by a State must satisfy strict scrutiny. . . .

By adopting intermediate scrutiny as the standard of review for congressionally mandated "benign" racial classifications, *Metro Broadcasting* departed from prior cases in two significant respects. First, it turned its back on *Croson's* explanation of why strict scrutiny of all governmental racial classifications is essential. . . .

Second, *Metro Broadcasting* squarely rejected one of the three propositions established by the Court's earlier equal protection cases, namely, congruence between the standards applicable to federal and state racial classifications, and in so doing also undermined the other two—skepticism of all racial classifications, and consistency of treatment irrespective of the race of the burdened or benefited group. Under *Metro Broadcasting,* certain racial classifications ("benign" ones enacted by the Federal Government) should be treated less skeptically than others; and the race of the benefited group is critical to the determination of which standard of review to apply. *Metro Broadcasting* was thus a significant departure from much of what had come before it.

The three propositions undermined by *Metro Broadcasting* all derive from the basic principle that the Fifth and Fourteenth Amendments to the Constitution protect persons, not groups. It follows from that principle that all governmental action based on race—a group classification long recognized as "in most circumstances irrelevant and therefore prohibited," *Hirabayashi*—should be subjected to detailed judicial inquiry to ensure that the personal right to equal protection of the laws has not been infringed. These ideas have long been central to this Court's understanding of equal protection, and holding "benign" state and federal racial classifications to different standards does not square with them. "[A] free people whose institutions are founded upon the doctrine of equality," *ibid.,* should tolerate no retreat from the principle that government may treat people differently because of their race only for the most compelling reasons. Accordingly, we hold today that all racial classifications, imposed by whatever federal, state, or local governmental actor, must be analyzed by a reviewing court under strict scrutiny. In other words, such classifications are constitutional only if they are narrowly tailored measures that further compelling governmental interests. To the extent that *Metro Broadcasting* is inconsistent with that holding, it is overruled. . . .

Because our decision today alters the playing field in some important respects, we think it best to remand the case to the lower courts for further consideration in light of the principles we have announced. . . .

It is so ordered.

JUSTICE SCALIA, concurring in part and concurring in the judgment.

I join the opinion of the Court . . . except insofar as it may be inconsistent with the following: In my view, government can never have a "compelling interest" in discriminating on the basis of race in order to "make up" for past racial discrimination in the opposite direction. Individuals who have been wronged by unlawful racial discrimination should be made whole; but under our Constitution there can be no such thing as either a creditor or a debtor race. That concept is alien to the Constitution's focus upon the individual. . . . To pursue the concept of racial entitlement—even for the most admirable and benign of purposes—is to reinforce and preserve for future mischief the way of thinking that produced race slavery, race privilege and race hatred. In the eyes of government, we are just one race here. It is American.

It is unlikely, if not impossible, that the challenged program would survive under this understanding of strict scrutiny, but I am content to leave that to be decided on remand.

JUSTICE THOMAS, concurring in part and concurring in the judgment.

That these programs may have been motivated, in part, by good intentions cannot provide refuge from the principle that under our Constitution, the government may not make distinctions on the basis of race. As far as the Constitution is concerned, it is irrelevant whether a government's racial classifications are drawn by those who wish to oppress a race or by those who have a sincere desire to help those thought to be disadvantaged. There can be no doubt that the paternalism that appears to lie at the heart of this program is at war with the principle of inherent equality that underlies and infuses our Constitution.

These programs not only raise grave constitutional questions, they also undermine the moral basis of the equal protection principle. Purchased at the price of immeasurable human suffering, the equal protection principle reflects our Nation's understanding that such classifications ultimately have a destructive impact on the individual and our society. Unquestionably, "[i]nvidious [racial] discrimination is an engine of oppression." It is also true that "[r]emedial" racial preferences may reflect "a desire to foster equality in society." But there can be no doubt that racial paternalism and its unintended consequences can be as poisonous and pernicious as any other form of discrimination. So-called "benign" discrimination teaches many that because of chronic and apparently immutable handicaps, minorities cannot compete with them without their patronizing indulgence. Inevitably, such programs engender attitudes of superiority or, alternatively, provoke resentment among those who believe that they have been wronged by the government's use of race. These programs stamp minorities with a badge of inferiority and may cause them to develop dependencies or to adopt an attitude that they are "entitled" to preferences. . . .

In my mind, government-sponsored racial discrimina-

tion based on benign prejudice is just as noxious as discrimination inspired by malicious prejudice. In each instance, it is racial discrimination, plain and simple.

JUSTICE STEVENS, with whom JUSTICE GINSBURG joins, dissenting.

The Court's concept of "consistency" assumes that there is no significant difference between a decision by the majority to impose a special burden on the members of a minority race and a decision by the majority to provide a benefit to certain members of that minority notwithstanding its incidental burden on some members of the majority. In my opinion that assumption is untenable. There is no moral or constitutional equivalence between a policy that is designed to perpetuate a caste system and one that seeks to eradicate racial subordination. Invidious discrimination is an engine of oppression, subjugating a disfavored group to enhance or maintain the power of the majority. Remedial race-based preferences reflect the opposite impulse: a desire to foster equality in society. No sensible conception of the Government's constitutional obligation to "govern impartially," *Hampton v. Mow Sun Wong* (1976), should ignore this distinction. . . .

The Court's concept of "congruence" assumes that there is no significant difference between a decision by the Congress of the United States to adopt an affirmative-action program and such a decision by a State or a municipality. In my opinion that assumption is untenable. It ignores important practical and legal differences between federal and state or local decisionmakers. . . .

Ironically, after all of the time, effort, and paper this Court has expended in differentiating between federal and state affirmative action, the majority today virtually ignores the issue. It provides not a word of direct explanation for its sudden and enormous departure from the reasoning in past cases. Such silence, however, cannot erase the difference between Congress' institutional competence and constitutional authority to overcome historic racial subjugation and the States' lesser power to do so. . . .

In my judgment, the Court's novel doctrine of "congruence" is seriously misguided. Congressional deliberations about a matter as important as affirmative action should be accorded far greater deference than those of a State or municipality.

The Court's concept of stare decisis treats some of the language we have used in explaining our decisions as though it were more important than our actual holdings. In my opinion that treatment is incorrect.

This is the third time in the Court's entire history that it has considered the constitutionality of a federal affirmative-action program. On each of the two prior occasions, the first in 1980, *Fullilove v. Klutznick,* and the second in 1990, *Metro Broadcasting, Inc. v. FCC,* the Court upheld the program. Today the Court explicitly overrules *Metro Broadcasting* (at least in part), and undermines *Fullilove* by recasting the standard on which it rested and by calling even its holding into question. . . .

The Court's holding in *Fullilove* surely governs the result in this case. . . . In no meaningful respect is the current scheme more objectionable than the 1977 Act. Thus, if the 1977 Act was constitutional, then so must be the SBA and STURAA. Indeed, even if my dissenting views in *Fullilove* had prevailed, this program would be valid. . . .

My skeptical scrutiny of the Court's opinion leaves me in dissent. The majority's concept of "consistency" ignores a difference, fundamental to the idea of equal protection, between oppression and assistance. The majority's concept of "congruence" ignores a difference, fundamental to our constitutional system, between the Federal Government and the States. And the majority's concept of stare decisis ignores the force of binding precedent. I would affirm the judgment of the Court of Appeals.

JUSTICE SOUTER, with whom JUSTICE GINSBURG and JUSTICE BREYER join, dissenting.

I agree with JUSTICE STEVENS's conclusion that stare decisis compels the application of *Fullilove.* Although *Fullilove* did not reflect doctrinal consistency, its several opinions produced a result on shared grounds that petitioner does not attack: that discrimination in the construction industry had been subject to government acquiescence, with effects that remain and that may be addressed by some preferential treatment falling within the congressional power under section 5 of the Fourteenth Amendment. Once *Fullilove* is applied, as Justice Stevens points out, it follows that the statutes in question here (which are substantially better tailored to the harm being remedied than the statute endorsed in *Fullilove*) pass muster under Fifth Amendment due process and Fourteenth Amendment equal protection. . . .

. . . The Court has long accepted the view that constitutional authority to remedy past discrimination is not limited to the power to forbid its continuation, but extends to eliminating those effects that would otherwise persist and skew the operation of public systems even in the absence of current intent to practice any discrimination. This is so whether the remedial authority is exercised by a court, the Congress, or some other legislature. Indeed, a majority of the Court today reiterates that there are circumstances in which Government may, consistently with the Constitution, adopt programs aimed at remedying the effects of past invidious discrimination.

When the extirpation of lingering discriminatory effects is thought to require a catch-up mechanism, like the racially preferential inducement under the statutes considered here, the result may be that some members of the historically favored race are hurt by that remedial mechanism, however innocent they may be of any personal responsibility for any discriminatory conduct. When this price is considered reasonable, it is in part because it is a price to be paid only temporarily; if the justification for the preference is eliminating the effects of a past practice, the assumption is that the effects will themselves recede into the past, becoming attenuated and finally disappearing. Thus, Justice Powell wrote in his concurring opinion in *Fullilove* that the "temporary nature of this remedy ensures that a race-conscious program will not last longer than the discriminatory effects it is designed to eliminate."

JUSTICE GINSBURG, with whom JUSTICE BREYER joins, dissenting.

The divisions in this difficult case should not obscure the Court's recognition of the persistence of racial inequality and a majority's acknowledgment of Congress' authority to act affirmatively, not only to end discrimination, but also to counteract discrimination's lingering effects. Those effects, reflective of a system of racial caste only recently ended, are evident in our workplaces, markets, and neighborhoods. . . . Bias both conscious and unconscious, reflecting traditional and unexamined habits of thought, keeps up barriers that must come down if equal opportunity and nondiscrimination are ever genuinely to become this country's law and practice.

Given this history and its practical consequences, Congress surely can conclude that a carefully designed affirmative action program may help to realize, finally, the "equal protection of the laws" the Fourteenth Amendment has promised since 1868.

The Court's decision to apply the same strict standards to the federal government as to state and local governments is an important one. While the ruling does not strike down all affirmative action programs, it holds them to very exacting standards (see Box 12-7). The decision also demonstrates that the more conservative members of the Court continue to have a controlling influence over affirmative action policy. Note, however, that the case was decided by a 5–4 vote, which means that the Court's doctrine on affirmative action issues is not indelibly written, but may fluctuate with a single vote. Any personnel changes could result in a shift in the Court's position.

CONTEMPORARY DEVELOPMENTS IN DISCRIMINATION LAW

After nearly twenty years of political and legal debate, affirmative action remains high on the public agenda. Americans are deeply divided over the issue, but less than a majority favor racial preferences in hiring even where there has been past discrimination. Indeed, over the last few years a backlash has developed against such programs (see Box 12-8).

The continuing debate over *Bakke* shores up an important point: As they have since the Fourteenth Amendment was ratified in 1868, discrimination issues continue to evolve. Immigration brings new groups of people to the United States, and groups that once were silent begin to organize and make their demands heard. Americans continually rethink concepts of equality and fair treatment, sometimes concluding that previously acceptable practices have discriminatory effects. Fluctuations in economic and political power alter the methods used to pursue equality demands. As such changes occur, the nature of the discrimination *issues* brought to the courts also changes, and so may the legal *fora* used to pursue claims.

BOX 12-7 AFFIRMATIVE ACTION/MINORITY SET-ASIDE PRINCIPLES

THE SUPREME COURT'S affirmative action and minority set-aside decisions have been criticized for failing to develop a consistent and coherent set of legal principles. The unstable majorities that have controlled these cases surely have contributed to this result. The justices have not provided a rule of law in one clear test that would allow a reasonably accurate indicator of what is constitutionally defective. While there are no absolutes, there are certain characteristics that clearly make minority enhancement plans more acceptable.

An affirmative action or minority set-aside program is more likely to be found constitutional if it:

1. is enacted as a response to clear and demonstrable acts of unconstitutional or illegal discrimination;
2. is narrowly tailored to respond to acts of illegal discrimination or to the continuing effects of that illegal discrimination;
3. is designed to assist only those groups who have been the victim of illegal discrimination;
4. is not based on racial, ethnic, or gender stereotypes, or presumes the inferiority of such groups;
5. avoids the use of quotas and does not absolutely bar any group from competing or participating;
6. is temporary, with clear indicators of plan termination when certain thresholds are met;
7. seeks to eliminate racial imbalance, not maintain racial balance;
8. is based on data from relevant labor pools or other appropriate statistical comparisons;
9. does not trammel the rights of the majority;
10. seeks to achieve balance by providing new benefits to minorities rather than taking already earned benefits away from the majority; and
11. is imposed by a federal court as a remedy for demonstrated constitutional violations.

BOX 12·8   IN THE AFTERMATH OF *BAKKE*

At the time of his retirement, Lewis F. Powell Jr. said that *Regents of the University of California v. Bakke* was the most important opinion he had written as a justice on the Supreme Court.[1] There is no doubt that *Bakke* was important, but it also created controversy from the moment the opinion came down. Even now, as *Bakke* approaches its twenty-fifth anniversary, the fervor it created shows no signs of abating. To be sure, many universities continue to adopt affirmative action criteria in making their admissions decisions, but it is fair to say that a backlash of sorts has developed. In November 1996 voters in California approved a ballot initiative, known as Proposition 209, that says: "The State shall not discriminate against, or grant preferential treatment to, any individual or group on the basis of race, sex, color, ethnicity, or national origin in the operation of public employment, public education, or public contracting."

The same year, a federal courts of appeals, in *Hopwood v. Texas,* took the unusual step of rejecting the Supreme Court's conclusion in *Bakke* that race may be taken into account in university admissions' decisions and, accordingly, invalidated the University of Texas's preferential admissions program. It held "that the University of Texas School of Law may not use race as a factor in deciding which applicants to admit in order to achieve a diverse student body, to combat the perceived effects of a hostile environment at the law school, to alleviate the law school's poor reputation in the minority community, or to eliminate any present effects of past discrimination by actors other than the law school."

With these words, the lower court took a nearly unprecedented step—it virtually overruled a U.S. Supreme Court case. At the very least, seven circuit judges, dissenting from their court's failure to grant rehearing en banc in *Hopwood v. Texas,* accused their colleagues of overturning *Bakke:*

---

1. Reported in Bernard Schwartz, *Behind* Bakke (New York: New York University Press, 1988).

The label "judicial activism" is usually found in the lexicon of those voicing concern about judges whom they perceive to be "liberal," fashioning remedies beyond the scope of what is deemed to be appropriate under the law. Such judicial legislating is generally excoriated as a "bad thing." *Hopwood v. State of Texas* is a textbook example of judicial activism. Here, two members of the three-judge panel determined to bar any consideration of race in the Law School's admission process. This "injunction" is wholly unnecessary to the disposition of the matter appealed and thus is clearly dictum; yet dictum that is a frontal assault on contrary Supreme Court precedent and thus not the kind of dictum we can ignore. By tenuously stringing together pieces and shards of recent Supreme Court opinions that have dealt with race in such diverse settings as minority set asides for government contractors, broadcast licenses, redistricting, and the like, the panel creates a gossamer chain which it proffers as a justification for overruling *Bakke.*

How has the Court responded to these challenges to affirmative action? *Adarand Constructors, Inc. v. Peña* (1995), at the very least, suggests that the justices are badly divided over the issue, as does their action over the *Hopwood* dispute: they refused to review the appellate court's decision. In denying petitions for writs of certiorari, the Court typically does not explain its logic, but in this case Justice Ginsburg issued a short opinion (also signed by Justice Souter). She said that the Court was rejecting the case because the controversy was no longer a live one. "Accordingly, we must await a final judgment on a program genuinely in controversy before addressing the important question raised in this petition."

Whether you take Ginsburg's explanation at face value or believe some legal and scholarly commentary that suggests that the Court was evading the affirmative action issue, one thing is clear: the *Hopwood* decision, along with Proposition 209, has created still more confusion for universities that maintain affirmative action programs—confusion that the

Court may eventually need to clarify. As for the University of Texas, the *Hopwood* lower court ruling is already having a major impact. For its class of 2001, the law school has said that its enrollment of blacks will go from about thirty to three and of Hispanics from about forty to twenty. The freshman class of 2002 at some of the University of California schools also looks quite different from the way it did in the past, as the table below reveals.

What direction the Court will take is a matter of speculation. But it is true that President Clinton's two appointments to the Court have given affirmative action supporters more hope than they have had in years. At the very least, it is safe to say that the Court has not heard its last minority preference case.

The Freshman Class of 2002. The racial breakdown of students who have been accepted by the University of California for fall 1998, post–affirmative action. Students may ultimately decide to enroll elsewhere.

		Black	Asian	American Indian	Filipino*	White/ other	Hispanic**	Did not report
Berkeley	'97	598	3,866	77	—	3,831	1,411	627
	'98	255	3,861	47	—	3,635	852	1,586
	Pct. chg.	**–57**	**+0**	**–38**	**—**	**–5**	**–40**	**+153**
Los Angeles	'97	488	4,154	81	—	3,456	1,497	569
	'98	280	4,187	46	—	3,334	1,001	1,463
	Pct. chg.	**–43**	**+1**	**–43**	**—**	**+4**	**–33**	**+157**
San Diego	'97	373	4,071	105	477	5,309	1,427	1,541
	'98	203	3,928	66	472	4,790	979	2,603
	Pct. chg.	**–46**	**–4**	**–37**	**–1**	**–10**	**–31**	**+69**
Davis	'97	518	3,380	122	433	6,305	1,626	692
	'98	332	3,630	100	500	5,640	1,302	1,915
	Pct. chg.	**–36**	**+7**	**–18**	**+15**	**–11**	**–20**	**+177**
Irvine	'97	303	4,611	66	778	3,770	1,412	442
	'98	246	4,490	57	819	3,375	1,291	1,423
	Pct. chg.	**–19**	**–3**	**–14**	**+5**	**–10**	**–9**	**+222**
Riverside	'97	257	3,706	29	—	1,816	1,071	197
	'98	345	4,140	51	—	2,027	1,536	816
	Pct. chg.	**+34**	**+12**	**+76**	**—**	**+12**	**+43**	**+314**
Santa Barbara	'97	438	3,075	149	—	7,933	2,215	725
	'98	375	2,871	111	—	6,433	1,701	2,060
	Pct. chg.	**–14**	**–7**	**–26**	**—**	**–19**	**–23**	**+184**
Santa Cruz	'97	223	2,021	82	295	4,915	1,159	562
	'98	219	2,169	96	347	4,448	1,245	1,709
	Pct. chg.	**–2**	**+7**	**+17**	**+18**	**–10**	**+7**	**+204**

SOURCE: *New York Times*, April 1, 1998.
   *Data not available at all schools.
   **May be of any race.

Emerging Issues

With the possible exception of race, all of the forms of discrimination we have considered in this chapter are, in some sense, emerging. A few justices continue to push to make sex a suspect class, and the law governing discrimination against illegitimate children remains unsettled, as do policies that distinguish on the basis of sexual orientation. Questions regarding equitable treatment of the poor with respect to education and other government services continue to arise. As legal and illegal immigration patterns change, new questions of discrimination based on alien status and national origin are inevitable. When these new residents place additional burdens on the states for government services, budget-conscious officials may adopt policies perceived as discriminatory. In addition, the Court's handling of affirmative action questions has resulted in a confusing body of law that begs for clarification.

While it deals with these issues, the Court will face new questions. The disabled are politicized and have demanded reforms from both the legislative and judicial branches. Claims of discrimination based on physical disability, mental handicap, and disease (cancer, AIDS, alcoholism, drug addiction) have become common and promise to escalate in number.

Issue evolution, in other words, characterizes the history of discrimination law, and there is no evidence that the process will stop. Rather, it is inevitable that the Supreme Court's docket will include appeals asking the justices to consider new questions that arise from the changing sociopolitical environment.

Legal Fora

During the early years of the civil rights movement, its leaders and sympathizers saw the federal courts as a reliable defender of minority interests, the most sympathetic agency of government on discrimination matters. State governments were perceived as the enemy. After all, the states had enacted and enforced most of the laws that women and minorities found objectionable. The term *states' rights* was considered a code word for discrimination.

After 1969 these perceptions began to change. As more conservative jurists replaced justices from the Warren era, observers noted that the Supreme Court was becoming more hostile to civil rights. In addition, conservative Reagan and Bush appointees to lower court judgeships transformed the image of the federal judiciary from accepting of discrimination claims to unsympathetic. These perceptions were not altogether unjustified. During the Burger and Rehnquist years, the courts handed down a number of civil rights decisions that gave little encouragement to parties bringing such lawsuits.

Concerned about possible unfavorable rulings from the federal courts, civil rights organizations and other liberal interest groups found a more sympathetic audience at the state level. Some states passed statutes that expanded civil rights protections. A number of the cases we have discussed in this chapter—such as *Regents of the University of California v. Bakke* and *City of Richmond v. J. A. Croson Co.*—address state and local laws intended to enhance the rights of minorites and women. *Roberts v. United States Jaycees* (1984) provides yet another example. The Supreme Court held that the state's interest in eradicating discrimination was sufficiently compelling to outweigh the Jaycees' associational rights, specifically, their desire to limit full membership to men.

Using the states to advance the civil rights agenda has its drawbacks. Obviously, not all states favor expanded civil rights policies, as the passage of Proposition 209 in California makes abundantly clear *(see Box 12-8)*. Even if a state legislature or judiciary is amenable to discrimination claimants, the impact of any favorable action is confined to that state alone. Nevertheless, one strategy of civil rights groups is to turn to the states for help rather than risk unfavorable decisions in the federal courts. This trend likely will continue until the ideological complexion of the federal judiciary changes.

READINGS

Baer, Judith A. *Our Lives Before The Law: Constructing a Feminist Jurisprudence.* Princeton: Princeton University Press, 1999.
———. *Women in American Law: The Struggle Toward Equality From the New Deal to the Present.* New York: Holmes and Meier, 1991.

———. *Equality Under the Constitution*. Ithaca, N.Y.: Cornell University Press, 1983.

Banton, Michael P. *International Action against Racial Discrimination*. New York: Oxford University Press, 1996.

Bok, Derek, and William Bowen. *The Shape of the River: Long Term Consequences of Considering Race in College and University Admissions*. Princeton: Princeton University Press, 1998.

Davis, Abraham L., and Barbara Luck Graham. *The Supreme Court, Race, and Civil Rights: From Marshall to Rehnquist*. Thousand Oaks, Calif.: Sage Publications, 1995.

Delgado, Richard, and Jean Stefancic, eds. *Critical Race Theory: The Cutting Edge*, 2d ed. Philadelphia: Temple University Press, 2000.

DuBois, W. E. B. "Does the Negro Need Separate Schools?" *Journal of Negro Education* 4 (1935): 328.

Eskridge, William N. Jr. *Gaylaw: Challenging the Apartheid of the Closet*. Cambridge: Harvard University Press, 1999.

Eskridge, William N., Jr., and Nan D. Hunter. *Sexuality, Gender, and the Law*. Westbury, N.Y.: Foundation Press, 1998.

Glazer, Nathan. *Affirmative Discrimination*. New York: Basic Books, 1975.

Goldstein, Leslie Friedman. *Feminist Jurisprudence: The Difference Debate*. Lanham, Md.: Rowman & Littlefield, 1992.

———. *The Constitutional Rights of Women*. 2d ed. Madison: University of Wisconsin Press, 1988.

Graglia, Lino A. *Disaster by Decree: The Supreme Court's Decisions on Race and the Schools*. Ithaca, N.Y.: Cornell University Press, 1976.

Greenberg, Jack. *Judicial Process and Social Change*. St. Paul: West Publishing, 1977.

Halpern, Stephen C. *On the Limits of the Law: The Ironic Legacy of Title VI of the 1964 Civil Rights Act*. Baltimore: Johns Hopkins University Press, 1995.

Higginbotham, A. Leon. *In the Matter of Color: Race and the American Legal Process: The Colonial Period*. New York: Oxford University Press, 1989.

Kluger, Richard. *Simple Justice*. New York: Knopf, 1976.

Kull, Andrew. *The Color-Blind Constitution*. Cambridge: Harvard University Press, 1994.

Mezey, Susan Gluck. *Children in Court: Public Policymaking and Federal Court Decisions*. Albany: State University of New York Press, 1996.

———. *In Pursuit of Equality*. New York: St. Martin's Press, 1992.

Orfield, Gary. *Must We Bus? Segregated Schools and National Policy*. Washington, D.C.: Brookings Institution, 1978.

Otten, Laura. *Women's Rights and the Law*. Westport, Conn.: Praeger, 1993.

Peltason, Jack. *Fifty-Eight Lonely Men*. Urbana: University of Illinois Press, 1971.

Perry, Michael J. *The People: The Fourteenth Amendment and the Supreme Court*. New York: Oxford University Press, 1999.

Peters, Anne. *Women, Quotas and Constitutions: A Comparative Study of Affirmative Action for Women under American, German, EC and International Law*. The Hague; Boston: Kluwer Law International, 1999.

Peterson, Paul E., ed. *Classifying by Race*. Princeton: Princeton University Press, 1996.

Pratt, Carla D. "In the Wake of Hopwood: An Update on Affirmative Action in the Education Arena." *Howard Law Journal* 42 (1999): 451–467.

Rhode, Deborah L. *Justice and Gender*. Cambridge: Harvard University Press, 1989.

Rosenberg, Gerald N. *The Hollow Hope*. Chicago: University of Chicago Press, 1991.

Ross, Susan Deller, and Ann Barcher. *The Rights of Women*. New York: Bantam Books, 1984.

Sarat, Austin, ed. *Race, Law, and Culture: Reflections on Brown v. Board of Education*. New York: Oxford University Press, 1997.

Schwartz, Bernard. *Behind Bakke*. New York: New York University Press, 1988.

———. *Swann's Way: The School Busing Case and the Supreme Court*. New York: Oxford University Press, 1986.

Selmi, Michael. "The Life of Bakke: An Affirmative Action Retrospective." *Georgetown Law Journal* 87 (1999): 981–1022.

Sindler, Allan P. *Bakke, DeFunis, and Minority Admissions*. New York: Longman, 1978.

Skaggs, Jason. "Justifying Gender-Based Affirmative Action under United States v. Virginia's 'Exceedingly Persuasive Justification' Standard." *California Law Review* 86 (1998): 1169–1210.

Smith, Christopher E. *The Courts and the Poor*. Chicago: Nelson-Hall Publishers, 1991.

Spann, Girardeau A. *Race Against the Court: The Supreme Court and Minorities in Contemporary America*. New York: New York University Press, 1993.

Strasser, Mark. *The Challenge of Same-Sex Marriage: Federalist Principles and Constitutional Protections*. Westport, Conn.: Praeger Publishers, 1999.

Thompson, Charles. "Court Action the Only Reasonable Alternative to Remedy Immediate Abuses of the Negro Separate School," *Journal of Negro Education* 4 (1935): 419.

Urofsky, Melvin I. *Affirmative Action on Trial: Sex Discrimination in Johnson v. Santa Clara*. Lawrence: University Press of Kansas, 1997.

Vose, Clement E. *Caucasians Only: The Supreme Court, the NAACP, and the Restrictive Covenant Cases*. Berkeley: University of California Press, 1959.

Wasby, Stephen L. *Race Relations Litigation in an Age of Complexity*. Charlottesville: University Press of Virginia, 1995.

Wilkinson, J. Harvie. *From Brown to Bakke: The Supreme Court and School Integration 1954–1978*. New York: Oxford University Press, 1979.

FOR ANY GOVERNMENT built on a foundation of popular sovereignty, voting and representation are of critical importance. Through these mechanisms, the people express their political will and ultimately control the institutions of government. Representative democracy can function properly only when the citizenry has full rights to regular and meaningful elections and when the system is structured so that public officials act on behalf of their constituents. If any segment of society is denied the right to vote or is denied legitimate representation, the ideals of a republican form of government are not completely realized. Because elections and representation are the primary links between the people and their government, it is not surprising that the history of American constitutional law is replete with disputes over rights of political participation.

VOTING RIGHTS

When the Framers met in Philadelphia in 1787, the thirteen states already had elections systems, with their own voter qualification requirements and procedures for selecting state and local officials. By European standards, the states were quite liberal in extending the right to vote.[1] But suffrage was not universal. Ballot access generally was granted only to free adult males, and in several states only to those men who owned sufficient property. Women, slaves, Indians, minors, and the poor could not vote. Some states prohibited Jews and Catholics from voting.

1. Melvin I. Urofsky, *A March of Liberty: A Constitutional History of the United States* (New York: Knopf, 1988), 294.

With state systems in place, the Framers saw no reason to create a separate set of qualifications for participating in federal elections. Because there was little uniformity from state to state and qualifications often changed, the addition of a new body of federal voting requirements could cause conflict. Moreover, under the Constitution, only one agency of the new national government, the House of Representatives, was to be elected directly by the people, further reason why the federal government need not develop its own voter rolls. The Constitution therefore left voting qualifications to the states. Specifically, in Article I, Section 2, the Constitution says with respect to House elections that "the Electors in each State shall have the Qualifications requisite for Electors of the most numerous Branch of the State Legislature." If citizens were qualified to cast ballots in their state's legislative elections, they were also qualified to vote in congressional elections.

Only one constitutional provision gave the federal government any regulatory authority over elections. Section 4 of Article I stipulates, "The Times, Places and Manner of holding Elections for Senators and Representatives, shall be prescribed in each State by the Legislature thereof; but the Congress may at any time by Law make or alter such Regulations, except as to the Places of chusing Senators." Congress took only modest advantage of this authority. In 1842 it passed a law requiring representatives to be elected from specific constituencies, rather than from the state at large; and in 1866 it clarified the procedures to be used in the selection of senators by the state legislatures. These statutes dealt essentially with procedural matters; they did not speak to the question of voter qualifications. Prior to the Civil War, this authority also remained in the hands of the states, where the electorate was expanding and barriers to suffrage gradually were being reformed. Following the war, however, power over voting rights began a steady shift toward the federal government.

Ratification of four constitutional amendments substantially limited the states' authority to restrict the right to vote. The first was the Fifteenth Amendment in 1870. Part of the Reconstruction package initiated by the Radical Republicans after the Civil War, the Fifteenth Amendment removed from the states the power to deny voting rights on the basis of race, color, or previous condition of servitude. It prohibits such discrimination by either the federal government or the states, but the obvious target was the South. Most members of the reconstructionist Congress reasoned that unless some action was taken to protect the political rights of the newly freed slaves, the majority white southerners would reinstitute measures to deny black citizens full participation.

Fifty years later the Constitution was again amended to expand the electorate. The Nineteenth Amendment, ratified in 1920, stipulated that the right to vote could not be denied on account of sex. Its acceptance represented decades of effort by supporters of female suffrage. Although a number of states had already modified their laws to allow women to vote, a change in the Constitution was necessary to extend the right uniformly across the nation. This amendment effectively nullified the Supreme Court's unanimous 1875 decision in *Minor v. Happersett,* in which the justices rejected Virginia Minor's contention that the Missouri Constitution's granting of voting rights only to males violated the Privileges or Immunities Clause of the Fourteenth Amendment.

The third voter qualification amendment went into effect in 1964. The Twenty-fourth Amendment denied the federal government and the states the power to impose a poll tax as a voter qualification for federal elections. The levying of a tax on the right to vote was a common practice in the South and was identified by Congress as one of many tactics used to keep blacks from voting, and thereby circumventing the clear intent of the Fifteenth Amendment.

In 1971 the last of the voting rights amendments, the Twenty-sixth, was ratified. It set eighteen years as the minimum voting age for all state and federal elections. Before 1971 individual states determined the minimum voting age, which ranged from eighteen to twenty-one. Earlier, Congress had attempted to impose the eighteen-year minimum through legislation. The constitutionality of that act was challenged in *Oregon v. Mitchell* (1970). In a 5–4 vote, the justices held that Congress had the power under Article I to set a minimum age for voting in federal elections, but could not impose an age standard on state and local elections. Rather than face the possible confusion of conflicting sets of qualifications, Congress abrogated the impact of the *Mitchell* ruling by proposing the Twenty-sixth Amendment.

Each of these four constitutional changes altered the balance of authority over the establishment of voter qualifications. The states retained the basic right to set such qualifications, but with restrictions. States may no longer abridge voting rights by denying access to the ballot on the basis of race, sex, age, or ability to pay a tax; any actions by the states affecting voting rights also are constrained by the Fourteenth Amendment's guarantee of the equal protection of the laws. In addition to limiting state power, the voting rights amendments increased congressional authority. The Fourteenth, Fifteenth, Nineteenth, Twenty-fourth, and Twenty-sixth Amendments declare: "The Congress shall have the power to enforce this article by appropriate legislation." These enforcement clauses grant Congress authority over an area that had been left entirely to the states.

Congress has not been reluctant to use its enforcement authority. Shortly after ratification of the Fourteenth and Fifteenth Amendments, it demonstrated the federal government's interest in extending the franchise to blacks by passing the Enforcement Act of 1870. This statute made it unlawful for state election officials to discriminate against blacks in the application of state voting regulations. It also made acts of electoral corruption, including bribery, violence, and intimidation, federal crimes. The following year Congress passed the Enforcement Act of 1871, which allowed for federal supervision of congressional elections. The federal government also intervened to stem the growing incidence of private indation of black voters with the Ku Klux Klan Act of 1671, giving the president broad powers to combat conspiracies against voting rights.

The Supreme Court's response to these post–Civil War enforcement statutes was mixed. In some of its decisions the justices questioned the breadth of the congressional actions that regulated state elections beyond the specific racial purposes of the Fifteenth Amendment. For example, in *United States v. Reese* (1876) the justices declined to uphold the indictment of a Kentucky election official who refused to register a qualified black voter for a state election. The Court justified its conclusion on the ground that the Enforcement Act of 1870 was too broadly drawn. On the same day as *Reese,* and for the same reason, the Court in *United States v. Cruikshank* dismissed the federal indictments of ninety-six Louisiana whites who were charged with intimidating potential black voters by shooting them. The Court was also reluctant to approve sanctions under the Ku Klux Klan Act when the prosecution centered on purely private behavior (*United States v. Harris,* 1883). However, in *Ex parte Yarbrough* (1884) the justices gave strong support to federal enforcement actions against even private behavior when the right to vote in national elections was abridged. Similarly, in *Ex parte Clark* (1880), *Ex parte Siebold* (1880), and *United States v. Gale* (1883) the Court approved criminal charges against state officials who compromised the integrity of federal elections.

Although these enforcement measures had an impact on the South, their influence was short-lived. By the 1890s the zeal behind the Reconstruction efforts had waned. White southerners had regained control of their home states and began passing measures to restrict black participation in state and federal elections. The Jim Crow era had begun. The Civil War amendments officially had reduced the power of the states to discriminate and given regulatory authority to the federal government, but full voting rights were not a reality until after the civil rights movement of the mid–twentieth century.

Throughout the years, however, the Supreme Court was called upon to settle a number of important disputes over the constitutional right to vote. The specific issues brought to the Court involved state-imposed restrictions based on race, economics, residency, and criminal behav-

ior. In spite of the wide-ranging subject matter, the underlying question remained the same: To what extent are the states free to determine voting qualifications?

Racial Restrictions on Voting

In 1869, during the congressional debate over the Fifteenth Amendment, Sen. Waitman T. Willey, a Republican from West Virginia, proclaimed from the Senate floor:

This amendment, when adopted, will settle the question for all time of negro suffrage in the insurgent States, where it has lately been extended under the pressure of congressional legislation, and will preclude the possibility of any future denial of this privilege by any change in the constitutions of those States.

In retrospect, it would be hard to imagine a more overly optimistic prediction of the impact of the Fifteenth Amendment. Although ratification meant that the states were constitutionally prohibited from engaging in racial discrimination in extending the right to vote, the southern states, once out from under the policies of Reconstruction, acted to keep blacks out of the voting booth.

These states used many tactics to limit black participation in voting, including white-only voting in Democratic Party primary elections, poll taxes, difficult registration requirements, literacy and understanding tests, and outright intimidation. These strategies worked. Black participation at the ballot box in the South was negligible well into the middle of the twentieth century.

Those who favored restricting black voting participation interpreted the Constitution to prohibit the federal government from interfering in state electoral affairs. Specifically, the southern states held that political parties were private organizations that could discriminate on the basis of race without running afoul of the Fourteenth Amendment's Equal Protection Clause, that primary elections were essentially private affairs not falling under the Fifteenth Amendment, and that the administration of elections (including registration of voters) was a state government function. Because the Democratic Party had dominated the South since the end of Reconstruction, all meaningful political decisions were made inside the party and in the Democratic primaries. If the Civil War

Prior to the 1970s southern states engaged in a number of tactics to keep black citizens from voting. In spite of threats and legal obstacles, black voters turned out in large numbers when given an opportunity. Blacks in Cobb County, Georgia, endured long lines to cast their ballots in the July 1946 Democratic primary elections.

amendments and the authority of the federal government did not extend to these critical stages of the electoral process, there was little chance that black political participation would increase.

At first the southern states were successful in advancing their legal position. For example, in *Newberry v. United States* (1921) the Court held that primary elections *were* the private affairs of political parties and not included under the constitutional meaning of elections; and in *Grovey v. Townsend* (1935) the justices unanimously ruled that a political party that discriminated on the basis of race, without state government support, did not violate the Constitution. Such decisions muted serious attempts to change the political conditions in the South.

The Court's position on these matters began to change with two important decisions in the 1940s. The first was *United States v. Classic* (1941), which involved federal charges against a Louisiana election commissioner for deliberately changing the ballots of Democratic voters in a primary election. Classic's defense, successful in the lower courts, was that the federal government had no authority to regulate what occurred in a primary elec-

tion. The Supreme Court rejected this argument, holding that Louisiana statutes had made the primary election an integral part of selecting candidates for congressional seats and that the outcome of the primary election effectively determined who would be sent to Washington. Under these conditions, the justices ruled, the United States had the right to protect the integrity of the election and to ensure that the ballot of each voter is properly counted.

The second significant decision was *Smith v. Allwright* (1944). This case involved a challenge to the way Texas ran party primaries. Texas permitted the political parties to select their memberships and thereby to determine who would vote in the primaries. The Texas Democratic Party allowed only whites to join and vote. Black voters, supported by the NAACP Legal Defense Fund, challenged this system as a violation of the Fifteenth Amendment. Consistent with the *Classic* ruling, the justices held that the primary was an essential step in deciding who would be placed on the general election ballot. The state's support of an election system that allowed a racially discriminatory primary to affect the selection of candidates for public office violated the Fifteenth Amendment. The Court explicitly overruled *Grovey v. Townsend.*

Decisions such as *Classic* and *Smith* expanded the reach of the Civil War amendments and gave the federal government increased authority to regulate elections, authority that the government began to exercise in the 1960s. All three branches were involved: Congress passed legislation to enforce voting rights and remove legal barriers to the ballot box; the executive branch brought suits against state governments and election officials who deprived blacks of their rights; and the judiciary heard legal disputes over claims of voting discrimination. As you read Justice Black's opinion for the Court in *Louisiana v. United States* (1965), a dispute over the use of "understanding tests," pay close attention to his account of the many obstacles the state placed in the way of suffrage and how effective they were.

Louisiana v. United States

380 U.S. 145 (1965)
laws.findlaw.com/US/380/145.html
Vote: 9 (Black, Brennan, Clark, Douglas, Goldberg, Harlan,
    Stewart, Warren, White)
        o
Opinion of the Court: Black
Concurring opinion: Harlan

The U.S. government brought suit in the federal District Court for the Eastern District of Louisiana against the state of Louisiana and members of the state Board of Registration. The government charged the defendants with enforcing state laws denying black citizens the right to vote in violation of the Fourteenth and Fifteenth Amendments. The suit centered on the use of "interpretation" or "understanding tests." These devices, commonly used throughout the South, required any citizen applying for voter registration to pass a test demonstrating a proper understanding of any section of the Louisiana or U.S. Constitution. The test had no objective standards: the local voting registrar selected the passage to be interpreted by the potential voter and determined whether sufficient understanding had been demonstrat-

ed. The state justified this requirement as a means of ensuring a well-informed, qualified electorate. The fact that the Board of Registration developed the interpretation test in cooperation with the state Segregation Committee indicated that other goals also were intended. The test was effective in denying blacks, even those with graduate and professional degrees, the right to vote. The district court ruled in favor of the federal government, and the state appealed.

MR. JUSTICE BLACK delivered the opinion of the Court.

The complaint alleged, and the District Court found, that beginning with the adoption of the Louisiana Constitution of 1898, when approximately 44 percent of all the registered voters in the State were Negroes, the State had put into effect a successful policy of denying Negro citizens the right to vote because of their race. The 1898 constitution adopted what was known as a "grandfather clause," which imposed burdensome requirements for registration thereafter but exempted from these future requirements any person who had been entitled to vote before January 1, 1867, or who was the son or grandson of such a person. Such a transparent expedient for disfranchising Negroes, whose ancestors had been slaves until 1863 and not entitled to vote in Louisiana before 1867, was held unconstitutional in 1915 as a violation of the Fifteenth Amendment, in a case involving a similar Oklahoma constitutional provision. *Guinn v. United States.* Soon after that decision Louisiana, in 1921, adopted a new constitution replacing the repudiated "grandfather clause" with what the complaint calls an "interpretation test," which required that an applicant for registration be able to "give a reasonable interpretation" of any clause in the Louisiana Constitution or the Constitution of the United States. From the adoption of the 1921 interpretation test until 1944, the District Court's opinion stated, the percentage of registered voters in Louisiana who were Negroes never exceeded one percent. Prior to 1944 Negro interest in voting in Louisiana had been slight, largely because the State's white primary law kept Negroes from voting in the Democratic Party primary election, the only election that mattered in the political climate of that State. In 1944, however, this Court invalidated the substantially identical white primary law of Texas, and with the explicit statutory bar to their voting in the primary removed and because of a generally heightened political interest, Negroes in increasing numbers began to register in Louisiana. The white primary system had been so effective in barring Negroes from voting that the "interpretation test" as a disfranchising device had been ignored over the years. Many registrars continued to ignore it after 1944, and in the next dozen years the proportion of registered voters who were Negroes rose from two-tenths of one percent to approximately 15% by March 1956. This fact, coupled with this Court's 1954 invalidation of laws requiring school segregation, prompted the State to try new devices to keep the white citizens in control. The Louisiana Legislature created a committee which became known as the "Segregation Committee" to seek means of accomplishing this goal. The chairman of this committee also helped to organize a semiprivate group called the Association of Citizens Councils, which thereafter acted in close cooperation with the legislative committee to preserve white supremacy. The legislative committee and the Citizens Councils set up programs, which parish voting registrars were required to attend, to instruct the registrars on how to promote white political control. The committee and the Citizens Councils also began a wholesale challenging of Negro names already on the voting rolls, with the result that thousands of Negroes, but virtually no whites, were purged from the rolls of voters. Beginning in the middle 1950's registrars of at least 21 parishes began to apply the interpretation test. In 1960 the State Constitution was amended to require every applicant thereafter to "be able to understand" as well as "give a reasonable interpretation" of any section of the State or Federal Constitution "when read to him by the registrar." The State Board of Registration in cooperation with the Segregation Committee issued orders that all parish registrars must strictly comply with the new provisions.

The interpretation test, the court found, vested in the voting registrars a virtually uncontrolled discretion as to who should vote and who should not. Under the State's statutes and constitutional provisions the registrars, without any objective standard to guide them, determine the manner in which the interpretation test is to be given, whether it is to be oral or written, the length and complexity of the sections of the State or Federal Constitution to be understood and interpreted, and what interpretation is to be considered correct. There was ample evidence to support the District Court's finding that registrars in the 21 parishes where the test was found to have been used had exercised their broad powers to deprive otherwise qualified Negro citizens of their right to vote; and that the existence of the test as a hurdle to voter qualification has in itself deterred and will continue to deter Negroes from attempting to register in Louisiana.

Because of the virtually unlimited discretion vested by the Louisiana laws in the registrars of voters, and because in the 21 parishes where the interpretation test was applied that discretion had been exercised to keep Negroes from voting because of their race, the District Court held the interpretation test invalid on its face and as applied, as a violation of the Fourteenth and Fifteenth Amendments to the United States Constitution and of 42 U.S.C. §1971(a). The District Court enjoined future use of the test in the State, and with respect to the 21 parishes where the invalid interpretation test was found to have been applied, the District Court also enjoined use of a newly enacted "citizenship" test, which did not repeal the interpretation test and the validity of which was not challenged in this suit, unless a reregistration of all voters in those parishes is ordered, so that there would be no voters in those parishes who had not passed the same test.

We have held this day in *United States v. Mississippi* that the Attorney General has power to bring suit against a State and its officials to protect the voting rights of Negroes guaranteed by 42 U.S.C. §1971(a) and the Fourteenth and Fifteenth Amendments. There can be no doubt from the evidence in this case that the District Court was amply justified in finding that Louisiana's interpretation test, as written and as applied, was part of a successful plan to deprive Louisiana Negroes of their right to vote. This device for accomplishing unconstitutional discrimination has been little if any less successful than was the "grandfather clause" invalidated by this Court's decision in *Guinn v. United States* 50 years ago, which when that clause was adopted in 1898 had seemed to the leaders of Louisiana a much preferable way of assuring white political supremacy. The Governor of Louisiana stated in 1898 that he believed that the "grandfather clause" solved the problem of keeping Negroes from voting "in a much more upright and manly fashion" than the method adopted previously by the States of Mississippi and South Carolina, which left the qualification of applicants to vote "largely to the arbitrary discretion of the officers administering the law." A delegate to the 1898

Louisiana Constitutional Convention also criticized an interpretation test because the "arbitrary power, lodged with the registration officer, practically places his decision beyond the pale of judicial review; and he can enfranchise or disfranchise voters at his own sweet will and pleasure without let or hindrance."

But Louisianans of a later generation did place just such arbitrary power in the hands of election officers who have used it with phenomenal success to keep Negroes from voting in the State. The State admits that the statutes and provisions of the state constitution establishing the interpretation test "vest discretion in the registrars of voters to determine the qualifications of applicants for registration" while imposing "no definite and objective standards upon registrars of voters for the administration of the interpretation test." And the District Court found that "Louisiana . . . provides no effective method whereby arbitrary and capricious action by registrars of voters may be prevented or redressed." The applicant facing a registrar in Louisiana thus has been compelled to leave his voting fate to that official's uncontrolled power to determine whether the applicant's understanding of the Federal or State Constitution is satisfactory. As the evidence showed, colored people, even some with the most advanced education and scholarship, were declared by voting registrars with less education to have an unsatisfactory understanding of the Constitution of Louisiana or of the United States. This is not a test but a trap, sufficient to stop even the most brilliant man on his way to the voting booth. The cherished right of people in a country like ours to vote cannot be obliterated by the use of laws like this, which leave the voting fate of a citizen to the passing whim or impulse of an individual registrar. Many of our cases have pointed out the invalidity of laws so completely devoid of standards and restraints. Squarely in point is *Schnell v. Davis,* in which we affirmed a district court judgment striking down as a violation of the Fourteenth and Fifteenth Amendments an Alabama constitutional provision restricting the right to vote in that State to persons who could "understand and explain any article of the Constitution of the United States" to the satisfaction of voting registrars. We likewise affirm here the District Court's holding that the provisions of the Louisiana Constitution and statutes which require voters to satisfy registrars of their ability to "understand and give a reasonable interpretation of any section" of the Federal or Louisiana Constitution vio-

late the Constitution. And we agree with the District Court that it specifically conflicts with the prohibitions against discrimination in voting because of race found both in the Fifteenth Amendment and 42 U.S.C. §1971(a) to subject citizens to such an arbitrary power as Louisiana has given its registrars under these laws.

Affirmed.

Although decisions such as *Louisiana v. United States* defined the constitutional rights of minority voters and condemned efforts by the states to depress black voting participation, court rulings alone were insufficient to bring about major changes. Too many alternative measures, many of them informal, were available to block or delay the effective exercise of the right to vote. Registration numbers in the southern states highlight the fact that court victories did not necessarily translate into social change. According to Justice Department statistics, between 1958 and 1964 black voter registration in Alabama rose to 19.4 percent from 14.2 percent. From 1956 to 1965 Louisiana black registration increased only to 31.8 percent from 31.7 percent. And in Mississippi the ten years from 1954 to 1964 saw black registration rates rise to only 6.4 percent from 4.4 percent. In each of these states the white registration rates were fifty or more percentage points higher than black rates. These figures convinced Congress that its strategy of passing legislation to expand opportunities for taking civil rights claims to court had been ineffective and that a more aggressive policy was required. President Lyndon Johnson is reported to have instructed Attorney General Nicholas Katzenbach to "write the god-damnedest, toughest voting rights act that you can devise."[2] The result was the Voting Rights Act of 1965, the most comprehensive statute ever enacted by Congress to enforce the guarantees of the Fifteenth Amendment.

The provisions of the Voting Rights Act did not apply equally to all sections of the country, but targeted certain areas. The coverage formula stipulated that the most stringent provisions of the statute would govern all states

2. Howard Ball, "The Voting Rights Act of 1965," in *The Oxford Companion to the Supreme Court of the United States,* ed. Kermit L. Hall, James W. Ely Jr., Joel B. Grossman, and William M. Wiecek (New York: Oxford University Press, 1992), 903.

President Lyndon B. Johnson signing into law the Voting Rights Act on August 6, 1965.

or counties that met the following two criteria: a discriminatory test or device was in operation in November 1964 and fewer than 40 percent of the voting-age population was registered to vote or had voted in the 1964 presidential general election.

In 1965 the states covered were Alabama, Alaska, Georgia, Louisiana, Mississippi, South Carolina, and Virginia, as well as portions of Arizona, Hawaii, Idaho, and North Carolina. A state could be removed from coverage by convincing the District Court for the District of Columbia that no discrimination had been practiced for five years. The act's most significant provision authorized the U.S. attorney general to appoint federal examiners to supervise registration and voting procedures when the Justice Department determined that low black participation rates were likely due to racial discrimination. The law prohibited literacy tests and stipulated that any changes in state election laws had to be approved by the attorney general before they could take effect. The 1965 Voting Rights Act was Congress's most comprehen-

sive intervention into the states' traditional powers over voter qualifications, and it was not surprising that it was almost immediately challenged as exceeding constitutional limits on federal power.[3]

South Carolina v. Katzenbach

383 U.S. 301 (1966)
laws.findlaw.com/US/383/301.html
Vote: 8 (Brennan, Clark, Douglas, Fortas, Harlan, Stewart, Warren, White)
    1 (Black)
Opinion of the Court: Warren
Opinion concurring in part and dissenting in part: Black

To gain a review of the Voting Rights Act, South Carolina instituted legal action against Attorney General Katzenbach, asking that he be enjoined from enforcing

3. For oral arguments in this case, navigate to: *oyez.nwu.edu.*

the act's provisions. Because the dispute involved a state suing a citizen of another state and because of the importance of the issues involved, the Supreme Court accepted the case under its original jurisdiction. The hearing before the Supreme Court involved not only South Carolina and the federal government but also other states invited by the Court to participate. Five states (all southern) appeared in support of South Carolina, and twenty-one states submitted legal arguments urging the Court to approve the act.

MR. CHIEF JUSTICE WARREN delivered the opinion of the Court.

The Voting Rights Act was designed by Congress to banish the blight of racial discrimination in voting, which has infected the electoral process in parts of our country for nearly a century. The Act creates stringent new remedies for voting discrimination where it persists on a pervasive scale, and in addition the statute strengthens existing remedies for pockets of voting discrimination elsewhere in the country. Congress assumed the power to prescribe these remedies from §2 of the Fifteenth Amendment, which authorizes the National Legislature to effectuate by "appropriate" measures the constitutional prohibition against racial discrimination in voting. We hold that the sections of the Act which are properly before us are an appropriate means for carrying out Congress' constitutional responsibilities and are consonant with all other provisions of the Constitution. We therefore deny South Carolina's request that enforcement of these sections of the Act be enjoined.

The constitutional propriety of the Voting Rights Act of 1965 must be judged with reference to the historical experience which it reflects. Before enacting the measure, Congress explored with great care the problem of racial discrimination in voting. The House and Senate Committees on the Judiciary each held hearings for nine days and received testimony from a total of 67 witnesses. More than three full days were consumed discussing the bill on the floor of the House, while the debate in the Senate covered 26 days in all. At the close of these deliberations, the verdict of both chambers was overwhelming. The House approved the bill by a vote of 328–74, and the measure passed the Senate by a margin of 79–18.

Two points emerge vividly from the voluminous legisla-

tive history of the Act contained in the committee hearings and floor debates. First: Congress felt itself confronted by an insidious and pervasive evil which had been perpetuated in certain parts of our country through unremitting and ingenious defiance of the Constitution. Second: Congress concluded that the unsuccessful remedies which it had prescribed in the past would have to be replaced by sterner and more elaborate measures in order to satisfy the clear commands of the Fifteenth Amendment. . . .

The Voting Rights Act of 1965 reflects Congress' firm intention to rid the country of racial discrimination in voting. The heart of the Act is a complex scheme of stringent remedies aimed at areas where voting discrimination has been most flagrant. Section 4(a)–(d) lays down a formula defining the States and political subdivisions to which these new remedies apply. The first of the remedies, contained in §4(a), is the suspension of literacy tests and similar voting qualifications for a period of five years from the last occurrence of substantial voting discrimination. Section 5 prescribes a second remedy, the suspension of all new voting regulations pending review by federal authorities to determine whether their use would perpetuate voting discrimination. The third remedy, covered in §§6(b), 7, 9, and 13(a), is the assignment of federal examiners on certification by the Attorney General to list qualified applicants who are thereafter entitled to vote in all elections.

Other provisions of the Act prescribe subsidiary cures for persistent voting discrimination. Section 8 authorizes the appointment of federal poll-watchers in places to which federal examiners have already been assigned. Section 10(d) excuses those made eligible to vote in sections of the country covered by §4(b) of the Act from paying accumulated past poll taxes for state and local elections. Section 12(e) provides for balloting by persons denied access to the polls in areas where federal examiners have been appointed.

The remaining remedial portions of the Act are aimed at voting discrimination in any area of the country where it may occur. Section 2 broadly prohibits the use of voting rules to abridge exercise of the franchise on racial grounds. Sections 3, 6(a), and 13(b) strengthen existing procedures for attacking voting discrimination by means of litigation. Section 4(e) excuses citizens educated in American schools conducted in a foreign language from passing English-language literacy tests. Section 10(a)–(c) facilitates constitutional litigation challenging the imposition of all poll taxes for state and local elections. Sections 11 and 12(a)–(d) authorize civil and criminal sanctions against interference with the exercise of rights guaranteed by the Act. . . .

These provisions of the Voting Rights Act of 1965 are challenged on the fundamental ground that they exceed the powers of Congress and encroach on an area reserved to the States by the Constitution. . . .

The ground rules for resolving this question are clear. The language and purpose of the Fifteenth Amendment, the prior decisions construing its several provisions, and the general doctrines of constitutional interpretation, all point to one fundamental principle. As against the reserved powers of the States, Congress may use any rational means to effectuate the constitutional prohibition of racial discrimination in voting. . . .

Section 1 of the Fifteenth Amendment declares that "[t]he right of citizens of the United States to vote shall not be denied or abridged by the United States or by any State on account of race, color, or previous condition of servitude." This declaration has always been treated as self-executing and has repeatedly been construed, without further legislative specification, to invalidate state voting qualifications or procedures which are discriminatory on their face or in practice. . . . [T]he Fifteenth Amendment expressly declares that "Congress shall have power to enforce this article by appropriate legislation.". . . Accordingly, in addition to the courts, Congress has full remedial powers to effectuate the constitutional prohibition against racial discrimination in voting.

Congress has repeatedly exercised these powers in the past, and its enactments have repeatedly been upheld. . . . On the rare occasions when the Court has found an unconstitutional exercise of these powers, in its opinion Congress had attacked evils not comprehended by the Fifteenth Amendment.

The basic test to be applied in a case involving §2 of the Fifteenth Amendment is the same as in all cases concerning the express powers of Congress with relation to the reserved powers of the States. Chief Justice Marshall laid down the classic formulation, 50 years before the Fifteenth Amendment was ratified:

"Let the end be legitimate, let it be within the scope of the constitution, and all means which are appropriate, which are plainly adapted to that end, which are not prohibited, but consist with the letter and spirit of the constitution, are constitutional." *McCulloch v. Maryland.*

The Court has subsequently echoed his language in describing each of the Civil War Amendments:

"Whatever legislation is appropriate, that is, adapted to carry out the objects the amendments have in view, whatever tends to enforce submission to the prohibitions they contain, and to secure to all persons the enjoyment of perfect equality of civil rights and the equal protection of the laws against State denial or invasion, if not prohibited, is brought within the domain of congressional power." *Ex parte Virginia.*

. . . We therefore reject South Carolina's argument that Congress may appropriately do no more than to forbid violations of the Fifteenth Amendment in general terms—that the task of fashioning specific remedies or of applying them to particular localities must necessarily be left entirely to the courts. Congress is not circumscribed by any such artificial rules under §2 of the Fifteenth Amendment. . . .

Congress exercised its authority under the Fifteenth Amendment in an inventive manner when it enacted the Voting Rights Act of 1965. First: The measure prescribes remedies for voting discrimination which go into effect without any need for prior adjudication. This was clearly a legitimate response to the problem, for which there is ample precedent under other constitutional provisions. . . .

Second: The Act intentionally confines these remedies to a small number of States and political subdivisions which in most instances were familiar to Congress by name. This, too, was a permissible method of dealing with the problem. Congress had learned that substantial voting discrimination presently occurs in certain sections of the country, and it knew no way of accurately forecasting whether the evil might spread elsewhere in the future. In acceptable legislative fashion, Congress chose to limit its attention to the geographic areas where immediate action seemed necessary. . . .

After enduring nearly a century of widespread resistance to the Fifteenth Amendment, Congress has marshalled an array of potent weapons against the evil, with authority in the Attorney General to employ them effectively. Many of the areas directly affected by this development have indicated their willingness to abide by any restraints legitimately imposed upon them. We here hold that the portions of the Voting Rights Act properly before us are a valid means for carrying out the commands of the Fifteenth Amendment. Hopefully, millions of nonwhite Americans will now be able to participate for the first time on an equal basis in the government under which they live. We may finally look forward to the day when truly "[t]he right of citizens of the United States to vote shall not be denied or abridged by the United States or by any State on account of race, color, or previous condition of servitude."

The bill of complaint is

Dismissed.

MR. JUSTICE BLACK, concurring and dissenting.

Though . . . I agree with most of the Court's conclusions, I dissent from its holding that every part of §5 of the Act is constitutional. . . . I think this section is unconstitutional on at least two grounds.

(a) The Constitution gives federal courts jurisdiction over cases and controversies only. If it can be said that any case or controversy arises under this section which gives the District Court for the District of Columbia jurisdiction to approve or reject state laws or constitutional amendments, then the case or controversy must be between a State and the United States Government. But it is hard for me to believe that a justiciable controversy can arise in the constitutional sense from a desire by the United States Government or some of its officials to determine in advance what legislative provisions a State may enact or what constitutional amendments it may adopt. If this dispute between the Federal Government and the States amounts to a case or controversy it is a far cry from the traditional constitutional notion of a case or controversy as a dispute over the meaning of enforceable laws or the manner in which they are applied. . . .

(b) My second and more basic objection to §5 is that Congress has here exercised its power under §2 of the Fifteenth Amendment through the adoption of means that conflict with the most basic principles of the Constitution. . . . Section 5, by providing that some of the States cannot pass state laws or adopt state constitutional amendments without first being compelled to beg federal authorities to approve their policies, so distorts our constitutional structure of government as to render any distinction drawn in the Constitution between state and federal power almost meaningless. One of the most basic premises upon which our structure of government was founded was that the Federal Government was to have certain specific and limited powers and no others, and all other power was to be reserved either "to the States respectively, or to the people." Certainly if all the provisions of our Constitution which lim-

TABLE 13-1 Percentage of Eligible Blacks Registered to Vote, Selected Years, 1940–1984

Year	South	Peripheral South	Deep South
1940	3%	5%	1%
1947	12	17	8
1956	25	29	21
1964	43	52	30
1966	52	58	46
1968	62	67	57
1976	63	62	64
1984	59	58	59

SOURCE: Earl Black and Merle Black, *Politics and Society in the South* (Cambridge: Harvard University Press, 1987), 137. Reprinted by permission.
NOTE: South: the eleven Peripheral and Deep South States. Peripheral South: Arkansas, Florida, North Carolina, Tennessee, Texas, Virginia. Deep South: Alabama, Georgia, Louisiana, Mississippi, South Carolina.

it the power of the Federal Government and reserve other power to the States are to mean anything, they mean at least that the States have power to pass laws and amend their constitutions without first sending their officials hundreds of miles away to beg federal authorities to approve them. Moreover, it seems to me that §5, which gives federal officials power to veto state laws they do not like is in direct conflict with the clear command of our Constitution that "The United States shall guarantee to every State in this Union a Republican Form of Government." I cannot help but believe that the inevitable effect of any such law which forces any one of the States to entreat federal authorities in far-away places for approval of local laws before they can become effective is to create the impression that the State or States treated in this way are little more than conquered provinces. . . .

. . . I would hold §5 invalid for the reasons stated above with full confidence that the Attorney General has ample power to give vigorous, expeditious and effective protection to the voting rights of all citizens.

With the Court's approval of the Voting Rights Act, the federal government was free to launch a vigorous campaign to make the goals of the Fifteenth Amendment a reality. The executive branch actively enforced the law, and Congress periodically strengthened and extended its provisions. These efforts, coupled with large-scale voter registration drives conducted by civil rights organizations, have resulted in southern blacks being registered to vote at rates only slightly below that of whites. As the data in Table 13-1 depict, it took about a century after the ratification of the Fifteenth Amendment for the voting participation of minority citizens in the South to become widespread.

Property, Taxation, and Residency

In addition to race, states have imposed other kinds of prerequisites, such as owning property, paying a poll tax, or establishing residency, on voting participation. Inevitably, such requirements have been challenged, usually as violations of the Equal Protection Clause. As a rule the Supreme Court has been skeptical of any limitation placed on voting rights.

In the past it had been common for suffrage to be tied to property ownership, but the states over time gradually eliminated these requirements. In the 1960s, however, property qualifications again became an issue. With the postwar baby boom in full force and a growing need to improve education and other social programs, governments greatly expanded public services and raised taxes to pay for them. At the local level, the primary means of increasing revenue was to raise the property tax, and many states required voter approval. Citizens opposed to tax increases were dismayed that individuals who would not have to pay the higher property taxes were allowed to vote in these elections. Clearly, people who did not own property would tend to favor increased facilities and services because the cost would be borne by others. Property owners considered this situation unfair, and some states passed laws restricting the right to vote in property tax and related elections to those who owned or rented real property. In *Kramer v. Union Free School District* (1969), however, the Supreme Court struck down such laws, finding that property ownership as a voting requirement violated the Equal Protection Clause of the Fourteenth Amendment.

Another form of the voting/economics relationship was the state-imposed tax on the privilege of casting a ballot. Even though the poll tax was small, the states that levied it claimed that the tax improved the quality of the electorate by weeding out those who did not sufficiently

appreciate the right to vote and who probably would not be well informed on the issues and the candidates. In 1937, in *Breedlove v. Suttles,* the Supreme Court heard a challenge to the constitutionality of the poll tax and rejected the idea that the Georgia poll tax violated the Equal Protection Clause of the Fourteenth Amendment.

With the rise of the civil rights movement two decades later, the poll tax began to attract increasing criticism. The poll-tax states were in the South, and many saw the tax as just another way of depressing black voting participation. Although large numbers of whites also forfeited the right to vote by not paying the poll tax, proportionately, the requirement hit blacks harder. Civil rights as well as other interest groups targeted the poll tax for elimination. In response, Congress proposed the Twenty-fourth Amendment outlawing the poll tax as a requirement for voting in any federal election. The amendment did not cover state elections because opposition by southerners in Congress and a number of states was judged sufficient to jeopardize its passage. Those who proposed the elimination of the tax were confident that once it was removed as a condition for voting in federal elections, state elections would likely follow. It would be too costly and cumbersome, they reasoned, for the states to maintain two separate voting rolls. The amendment was ratified in 1964.

Shortly thereafter, all but four states rescinded the poll tax on state elections. Alabama, Texas, and Virginia retained their poll taxes of $1.50, and Mississippi continued its $2 tax. Poll-tax opponents sought relief in the courts. In *Harper v. Virginia State Board of Elections* (1966) the Supreme Court invalidated state taxes on the privilege to vote in state and local elections. As Justice Douglas summarized, "We conclude that a State violates the Fourteenth Amendment whenever it makes the affluence of the voter or payment of any fee an electoral standard."

Traditionally, the states have had the authority to restrict voting to individuals who were truly citizens and residents of the community, and state legislatures usually require individuals to be residents for a certain period of time before they can vote. States also normally require potential voters to register prior to election day. These restrictions have been based on the principle that only bona fide residents should have a voice in making politi-

BOX 13-1   VOTING IN GLOBAL PERSPECTIVE

ALTHOUGH Americans have fought hard to remove legal barriers to the vote—property requirements, literacy tests, and laws prohibiting women from voting—many of us do not exercise that right. For the 1996 presidential election, less than 50 percent of Americans eligible to register and vote did so; for the 1998 congressional elections the turnout was 36 percent.

These figures are quite low compared with other Western-type democracies. Even if we consider turnout among registered voters only (rather than by the entire voting age population), as the table below indicates, the United States ranks near the bottom of the list.

Country	Year	Type of Election	% Turnout of Registered Voters
Australia	1998	Parliamentary	95.2
Belgium	1999	Parliamentary	90.5
Sweden	1994	Parliamentary	87.3
Iceland	1999	Parliamentary	84.1
	1996	Presidential	85.9
Austria	1995	Parliamentary	82.7
	1998	Presidential	74.4
Italy	1995	Regional	77.4
Greece	1996	Parliamentary	76.3
Canada	1993	Prime Ministerial	73.0
	1997	General	67.0
Germany	1996	Parliamentary	67.5
Portugal	1995	Parliamentary	67.2
	1996	Presidential	66.3
United States	1996	Presidential	66.0
	1998	Congressional	51.5
Ireland	1997	Presidential	47.6

SOURCE: United States Federal Election Commission (www.fec.gov).

status, the Supreme Court has taken steps to ensure that they do not unreasonably deny the right to vote.

The Court, for example, has ruled that individuals moving into a community must have a reasonable opportunity to obtain resident status. *Carrington v. Rash* (1965) provides a good illustration. The Court struck down a Texas regulation that imposed too great a burden on military personnel. Texas, home to numerous military bases, feared that the large numbers of armed services personnel transferred into the state for relatively short assignments would have a disproportionate impact on local elections. The state argued that it was difficult to determine whether these individuals were bona fide residents. Texas therefore imposed a blanket exclusion on service personnel, stipulating that members of the armed forces who moved into Texas could not vote so long as they remained in the military. The Court refused to accept such a burden being placed on an entire class of individuals, holding that the Equal Protection Clause demands a more precise test to determine those whose residence in the state is bona fide.

But the Court has never seriously questioned the authority of the state to limit voting to bona fide residents, and, in fact, many states require that individuals live in the state and the local community for a minimum period of time before they are eligible to vote. In 1970 Congress amended the Voting Rights Act to outlaw residency requirements longer than thirty days for voting in presidential elections. This change was based on the rationale that the length of time one lived in a particular state or locality had no reasonable connection to being qualified to vote for the federal executive. However, many states retained their time requirements for state and local elections. In 1972, however, the Court's decision in *Dunn v. Blumstein* sharply curtailed the ability of the state to impose lengthy residency requirements. Here the justices struck down Tennessee's requirement that an individual live in the state for at least one year and in the county for a minimum of three months before being eligible to vote. The Court ruled that these minimums were entirely too long and suggested that the state could accomplish its goals by reducing the residency requirement to no more than thirty days.

cal decisions for the community. They also prevent voter fraud: candidates cannot recruit large numbers of nonresident supporters to present themselves on election day and demand the right to vote. Although these limitations do not have the same connotations as restricting access to the ballot box on the basis of race or economic

The combined effects of constitutional amendments, federal enforcement legislation, and judicial decisions have taken away most of the states' discretion to determine qualifications for voting. The states retain responsibility for administering the voting process, but contemporary political and legal notions of universal suffrage have left them little else. The state may still deny individuals the right to vote if for legitimate reasons (for example, mental illness) they are unqualified. The Court also has ruled that states may strip convicted felons of the right to vote. In some states, such bans last only until the convicted criminals complete all aspects of their sentences. In *Richardson v. Ramirez* (1974), however, the justices upheld a California law that forever disenfranchised individuals found guilty of felonies.

The history of voting rights in America has been a steady expanion of the electorate. The barriers of race, sex, economic status, and residency that once blocked millions of Americans from participating in the electoral process have been torn down. Few legitimate reasons currently exist for the government to deny someone the right to vote. Voter education projects and registration drives have encouraged individuals to participate in the political process. Reformed registration laws make it easier than ever to qualify to vote. In spite of these legal and constitutional reforms, American elections are characterized by relatively low voter turnout. As Box 13-1 illustrates, the electoral participation rates of Americans do not compare well to those of other western democracies.

State Authority over Elections and Political Parties

As we have seen, litigation over voting rights has been dominated by challenges to state actions that restrict the right to participate in the selection of public officials based on factors such as race, sex, property ownership, and residence. The Supreme Court's decisions generally have expanded voting rights. These decisions, as well as the ratification of constitutional amendments pertaining to voting, have steadily moved authority over the regulation of voting and elections from the states to the federal government. However, the states retain the authority to administer the elections process.

In 2000 the Supreme Court heard *California Demo-* *cratic Party v. Jones*, which involved state attempts to expand rather than restrict electoral participation. At issue was a California law, enacted by popular initiative, which removed party membership limitations in primary elections. A coalition of political parties, both large and small, challenged the new system as a violation of political association rights.

California Democratic Party v. Jones

530 U.S. — (2000)
supct.law.cornell.edu/supct/html/99-401.ZS.html
Vote: 7 (Breyer, Kennedy, O'Connor, Rehnquist, Scalia, Souter, Thomas)
    2 (Ginsburg, Stevens)
Opinion of the Court: Scalia
Dissenting Opinion: Stevens

To gain access to the California general election ballot, a candidate running as a member of a political party must win that party's primary election. Under California law the primaries were closed, meaning that only voters who were registered members of a political party could vote in that party's primary. In 1996 California voters passed Proposition 198, which replaced the closed primary system with a "blanket" primary. In a blanket primary, the voters are given a ballot containing the names of all candidates for office, regardless of party affiliation, and they may vote for any single candidate for any office. Thus, a voter might cast a ballot for a Republican candidate for governor and at the same time select a Democratic candidate for state senate. The candidate from each party receiving the highest number of votes becomes the nominee of the party for that office. Consequently, participation in the selection of a party's nominee is not restricted to members of that party. The states of Alaska and Washington have similar blanket primary systems. Proponents of the blanket primary argue that it encourages increased voting participation and greater freedom of choice among voters who are not restricted to candidates from a single party.

Four political parties in California (the Democratic Party, the Republican Party, the Libertarian Party, and the Peace and Freedom Party) filed suit to have the blanket primary law declared unconstitutional as a violation of the freedom of association. Each party operated under organizational rules restricting voting in their party primaries to its own members. The state defended the law based on its authority to regulate voting and elections. Both the federal district court and the court of appeals upheld the law as a means of enhancing the democratic nature of the election process and the representativeness of elected officials.

JUSTICE SCALIA delivered the opinion of the Court.

This case presents the question whether the State of California may, consistent with the First Amendment to the United States Constitution, use a so-called "blanket" primary to determine a political party's nominee for the general election. . . .

Respondents rest their defense of the blanket primary upon the proposition that primaries play an integral role in citizens' selection of public officials. As a consequence, they contend, primaries are public rather than private proceedings, and the States may and must play a role in ensuring that they serve the public interest. Proposition 198, respondents conclude, is simply a rather pedestrian example of a State's regulating its system of elections.

We have recognized, of course, that States have a major role to play in structuring and monitoring the election process, including primaries. See *Burdick v. Takushi* (1992); *Tashjian v. Republican Party of Conn.* (1986). We have considered it "too plain for argument," for example, that a State may require parties to use the primary format for selecting their nominees, in order to assure that intraparty competition is resolved in a democratic fashion. . . .

What we have not held, however, is that the processes by which political parties select their nominees are, as respondents would have it, wholly public affairs that States may regulate freely. To the contrary, we have continually stressed that when States regulate parties' internal processes they must act within limits imposed by the Constitution. In this regard, respondents' reliance on *Smith v. Allwright* (1944) and *Terry v. Adams* (1953) is misplaced. In *Allwright*, we invalidated the Texas Democratic Party's rule limiting participation in its primary to whites; in *Terry*, we invalidated the same rule promulgated by the Jaybird Democratic Associa-

tion, a "self-governing voluntary club.". . . They do not stand for the proposition that party affairs are public affairs, free of First Amendment protections—and our later holdings make that entirely clear. See, *e.g., Tashjian.*

Representative democracy in any populous unit of governance is unimaginable without the ability of citizens to band together in promoting among the electorate candidates who espouse their political views. The formation of national political parties was almost concurrent with the formation of the Republic itself. Consistent with this tradition, the Court has recognized that the First Amendment protects "the freedom to join together in furtherance of common political beliefs," *Tashjian,* which "necessarily presupposes the freedom to identify the people who constitute the association, and to limit the association to those people only," [*Democratic Party v. Wisconsin ex rel.*] *La Follette* [1981]. That is to say, a corollary of the right to associate is the right not to associate. "'Freedom of association would prove an empty guarantee if associations could not limit control over their decisions to those who share the interests and persuasions that underlie the association's being.'"

In no area is the political association's right to exclude more important than in the process of selecting its nominee. That process often determines the party's positions on the most significant public policy issues of the day, and even when those positions are predetermined it is the nominee who becomes the party's ambassador to the general electorate in winning it over to the party's views. . . .

Unsurprisingly, our cases vigorously affirm the special place the First Amendment reserves for, and the special protection it accords, the process by which a political party "select[s] a standard bearer who best represents the party's ideologies and preferences.". . .

. . . Proposition 198 forces political parties to associate with—to have their nominees, and hence their positions, determined by—those who, at best, have refused to affiliate with the party, and, at worst, have expressly affiliated with a rival. In this respect, it is qualitatively different from a closed primary. Under that system, even when it is made quite easy for a voter to change his party affiliation the day of the primary, and thus, in some sense, to "cross over," at least he must formally *become a member of the party;* and once he does so, he is limited to voting for candidates of that party.

The evidence in this case demonstrates that under California's blanket primary system, the prospect of having a party's nominee determined by adherents of an opposing party is far from remote—indeed, it is a clear and present danger. For example, in one 1997 survey of California voters 37 percent of Republicans said that they planned to vote in the 1998 Democratic gubernatorial primary, and 20 percent of Democrats said they planned to vote in the 1998 Republican United States Senate primary. Those figures are comparable to the results of studies in other States with blanket primaries. . . . The impact of voting by nonparty members is much greater upon minor parties, such as the Libertarian Party and the Peace and Freedom Party. . . .

The record also supports the obvious proposition that these substantial numbers of voters who help select the nominees of parties they have chosen not to join often have policy views that diverge from those of the party faithful. The 1997 survey of California voters revealed significantly different policy preferences between party members and primary voters who "crossed over" from another party. . . .

In concluding that the burden Proposition 198 imposes on petitioners' rights of association is not severe, the Ninth Circuit cited testimony that the prospect of malicious crossover voting, or raiding, is slight, and that even though the numbers of "benevolent" crossover voters were significant, they would be determinative in only a small number of races. But a single election in which the party nominee is selected by nonparty members could be enough to destroy the party. In the 1860 presidential election, if opponents of the fledgling Republican Party had been able to cause its nomination of a pro-slavery candidate in place of Abraham Lincoln, the coalition of intraparty factions forming behind him likely would have disintegrated, endangering the party's survival and thwarting its effort to fill the vacuum left by the dissolution of the Whigs. Ordinarily, however, being saddled with an unwanted, and possibly antithetical, nominee would not destroy the party but severely transform it. . . .

In any event, the deleterious effects of Proposition 198 are not limited to altering the identity of the nominee. Even when the person favored by a majority of the party members prevails, he will have prevailed by taking somewhat different positions—and, should he be elected, will continue to take somewhat different positions in order to be *re*nominated. . . .

In sum, Proposition 198 forces petitioners to adulterate their candidate-selection process—the "basic function of a political party"—by opening it up to persons wholly unaffiliated with the party. Such forced association has the likely outcome—indeed, in this case the *intended* outcome—of changing the parties' message. We can think of no heavier burden on a political party's associational freedom. Proposition 198 is therefore unconstitutional unless it is narrowly tailored to serve a compelling state interest. It is to that question which we now turn.

Respondents proffer seven state interests they claim are compelling. Two of them—producing elected officials who better represent the electorate and expanding candidate debate beyond the scope of partisan concerns—are simply circumlocution for producing nominees and nominee positions other than those the parties would choose if left to their own devices. Indeed, respondents admit as much. . . . Both of these supposed interests, therefore, reduce to nothing more than a stark repudiation of freedom of political association: Parties should not be free to select their own nominees because those nominees, and the positions taken by those nominees, will not be congenial to the majority. . . .

Respondents' third asserted compelling interest is that the blanket primary is the only way to ensure that disenfranchised persons enjoy the right to an effective vote. By "disenfranchised," respondents do not mean those who cannot vote; they mean simply independents and members of the minority party in "safe" districts. These persons are disenfranchised, according to respondents, because under a closed primary they are unable to participate in what amounts to the determinative election—the majority party's primary; the only way to ensure they have an "effective" vote is to force the party to open its primary to them. This also appears to be nothing more than reformulation of an asserted state interest we have already rejected—recharacterizing nonparty members' keen desire to participate in selection of the party's nominee as "disenfranchisement" if that desire is not fulfilled. We have said, however, that a "nonmember's desire to participate in the party's affairs is overborne by the countervailing and legitimate right of the party to determine its own membership qualifications." *Tashjian*. . . .

Respondents' remaining four asserted state interests—promoting fairness, affording voters greater choice, increasing voter participation, and protecting privacy—are not, like the others, automatically out of the running; but nei-ther are they, *in the circumstances of this case,* compelling. That determination is not to be made in the abstract, by asking whether fairness, privacy, etc., are highly significant values; but rather by asking whether the *aspect* of fairness, privacy, etc., addressed by the law at issue is highly significant. And for all four of these asserted interests, we find it not to be. . . .

. . . The burden Proposition 198 places on petitioners' rights of political association is both severe and unneces-sary. The judgment for the Court of Appeals for the Ninth Circuit is reversed.

It is so ordered.

JUSTICE STEVENS, with whom JUSTICE GINSBURG joins . . . , dissenting.

Today the Court construes the First Amendment as a limitation on a State's power to broaden voter participation in elections conducted by the State. The Court's holding is novel and, in my judgment, plainly wrong. I am convinced that California's adoption of a blanket primary pursuant to Proposition 198 does not violate the First Amendment, and that its use in primary elections for state offices is therefore valid. . . .

A State's power to determine how its officials are to be elected is a quintessential attribute of sovereignty. This case is about the State of California's power to decide who may vote in an election conducted, and paid for, by the State. The United States Constitution imposes constraints on the States' power to limit access to the polls, but we have never before held or suggested that it imposes any constraints on States' power to authorize additional citizens to participate in any state election for a state office. In my view, principles of federalism require us to respect the policy choice made by the State's voters in approving Proposition 198. . . .

The so-called "right not to associate" that the Court re-lies upon, then, is simply inapplicable to participation in a state election. A political party, like any other association, may refuse to allow non-members to participate in the party's decisions when it is conducting its own affairs; Cali-fornia's blanket primary system does not infringe this prin-ciple. But an election, unlike a convention or caucus, is a public affair. Although it is true that we have extended First Amendment protection to a party's right to invite indepen-dents to participate in its primaries, *Tashjian v. Republican*

Party of Conn. (1986), neither that case nor any other has held or suggested that the "right not to associate" imposes a limit on the State's power to open up its primary elections to all voters eligible to vote in a general election. . . .

In my view, the First Amendment does not mandate that a putatively private association be granted the power to dic-tate the organizational structure of state-run, state-financed primary elections. It is not this Court's constitutional func-tion to choose between the competing visions of what makes democracy work—party autonomy and discipline versus progressive inclusion of the entire electorate in the process of selecting their public officials—that are held by the litigants in this case. . . .

. . . I respectfully dissent.

POLITICAL REPRESENTATION

Voting rights alone do not guarantee that people share equally in political influence. The United States is not a direct democracy; consequently, few public policy decisions are made in the voting booth. In a republican form of government, most political decisions are made by officials elected by the people from defined geographi-cal districts. The duty of these officials is to represent the interests of their constituencies in the policy-making process.

How well and how equitably this representational process works depends in part on how the boundary lines of political units are drawn. These issues are not easy to resolve, as the history of our nation shows. Much of the debate at the Constitutional Convention centered on representation. The smaller states wanted representa-tion in Congress based on statehood, with each of the thirteen states having equal voting powers. The larger states argued for legislative representation based on size of population. The convention compromised by accept-ing both ideas in a bicameral Congress.

Because district lines determine political representa-tion, the authority to draw those boundaries carries with it a great deal of political power. Skillful construction of political subdivisions can be used to great advantage, and politicians have never been reluctant to use this power to advance their own interests. Since 1812 the art of structuring legislative districts to ensure political success has been known as gerrymandering. The term refers to the political maneuverings of Gov. Elbridge Gerry of Massachusetts, who convinced the state legislature to draw district lines so that his partisan supporters would have a high probability of reelection. Gerrymandered districts frequently are characterized by the rather strange geographical configurations necessary to achieve the desired political ends.

Establishing or modifying the district lines historically has been a political matter. Battles over drawing the boundaries of political subdivisions usually are fought within the halls of the state legislatures. However, serious legal or even constitutional questions may arise when officials use inappropriate criteria for drawing boundaries, or when the process results in the discriminatory treatment of certain groups of voters. In such cases the courts may be called upon to intervene in what is otherwise a legislative duty.

Gomillion v. Lightfoot (1960) is an example. C. G. Gomillion and other black citizens of Alabama filed suit against Phil Lightfoot, the mayor of Tuskegee, over a legislative act that redrew the city boundaries. Before 1957 Tuskegee city limits were in the shape of a square that covered the entire urban area. With the growing civil rights activism of the time and the increasing tendency of black citizens to vote, the white establishment in Tuskegee feared a loss of political control. Sympathetic members of the Alabama legislature successfully sponsored a bill that changed the boundary lines. Instead of a square, the altered city limits formed, in Justice Frankfurter's words, "an uncouth twenty-eight-sided figure." The effect of the redistricting was phenomenal. The law removed from the city all but four or five of its four hundred black voters, but no white voters. The black plaintiffs, now former residents of Tuskegee, claimed that their removal from the city denied them the right to vote on the basis of race and, therefore, violated their Fifteenth Amendment rights. The city did not deny that race was at issue, but claimed that the state of Alabama had an unrestricted right to draw city boundaries as it saw fit and that the courts could not intervene to limit that authority. A unanimous Supreme Court ruled to the contrary, holding that when an otherwise lawful exercise

In 1812 Elkanah Tinsdale lampooned the political maneuverings of Gov. Elbridge Gerry of Massachusetts, who deftly engineered the construction of constituency boundaries to aid in the election of a member of his own party. Because the district resembled a salamander in the cartoonist's illustration, the term *gerrymander* has come to mean the drawing of political district lines for partisan advantage.

of state power is used to circumvent a federally protected right, the courts may indeed intervene. A legislative act that removes citizens from the municipal voting rolls in a racially discriminatory fashion violates the Fifteenth Amendment.

The power to define political constituencies has given rise to a number of important legal questions. Under what conditions are the courts entitled to intervene in an activity normally left to the political process? Does the Constitution place limits on the relative size of representational districts? What criteria may a legislature take into account in deciding where to draw the boundaries of a political subdivision? How does the Constitution limit the legislature's freedom in shaping political units? Beginning in the 1960s the Supreme Court issued rulings on these and related issues of political representation.

The Reapportionment Controversy

In drafting Article I of the Constitution, the Framers clearly intended that representation in the lower house of Congress would be based upon population. Each state was allotted at least one representative, with additional seats based upon the number of persons residing within its boundaries.[4]

The Constitutional Convention wisely anticipated that the population would grow and that people would move from one state to another. The Framers determined that the number of congressional seats allocated to each state would be reformulated every ten years following the national census. States that grew in population would gain increased congressional representation, and those that lost population would lose representation. This process remains relatively unchanged today. The number of seats in the House of Representatives is fixed by federal law, currently at 435. Every ten years, when the Census Bureau completes its work, the allocation of those 435 seats among the states must be recalculated to reflect changes since the previous population count.

Following the census, each state is told the number of representatives it will have for the next decade. The state legislature then geographically divides the state into separate congressional districts, each of which elects a member of Congress. This scheme is known as the single-member constituency system of representation.[5] Political representation is equitable only if the state legislature constructs its congressional districts so that each contains approximately the same number of residents.

The process of devising legislative districts is called apportionment. When the legislature creates equally populated districts, the system is properly apportioned. But when the districts are not in proper balance, when some districts are substantially larger than others, they are said to be malapportioned. A state can be malapportioned if the legislature does not draw the district lines properly or fails to adjust boundaries to keep pace with population shifts.

Representational districts are used not only for congressional seats but also for other government units. The state legislatures, for example, generally are based on a single-member constituency system, as are many county commissions and city councils. Even special purpose commissions, such as boards of education and public utility districts, often follow the same scheme. In each case, a legislative body must create districts from which representatives will be selected. The same apportionment concepts apply to these bodies as to congressional districts.

The constitutional issues regarding apportionment rose to the surface after World War II. Spurred by industrialization, two major wars, and an economic depression, large population shifts from rural areas and small towns into urban centers had occurred during the first half of the twentieth century. Cities grew rapidly and agricultural areas declined, but state legislatures failed to respond adequately to these migration patterns by reapportioning their congressional and state legislative districts. The more state legislatures came to be dominated by rural interests, the less incumbent legislators wished to consider redistricting. To apportion the districts properly would mean fewer legislative seats for the rural areas, and that meant abolishing some seats held by incumbents. At the midpoint of the century, many states had not reapportioned since the 1900 Census.

The first major apportionment case to come before the Supreme Court was *Colegrove v. Green* (1946). Kenneth Colegrove and two others filed suit to challenge the constitutionality of the Illinois congressional district system. These plaintiffs lived in districts with large populations. They argued, among other points, that the Illinois districts were so badly malapportioned that they violated the constitutional guarantee of a republican form of government specified in Article IV, Section 4. Colegrove's factual case was strong. The Illinois legislature had not reapportioned its congressional districts since 1901, even though four census counts had documented major popu-

---

4. Originally, population was determined by the number of free persons, including indentured servants, but excluding Indians not taxed, plus three-fifths of the slaves. This formula was changed with ratification of the Fourteenth Amendment in 1868 to define population as the whole number of persons, excluding Indians not taxed.

5. During the first half-century of the nation's history, it was common for the states to select their delegates to the House of Representatives on an at-large basis rather than using the single-member constituency plan.

lation shifts into urban centers. When the plaintiffs filed their suit, the largest Illinois district had 914,053 residents and the smallest only 112,116. A resident in the smallest district had eight times more congressional representation than a citizen living in the largest district. In spite of these population disparities and legal provisions supporting redistricting, the Supreme Court, by a 4–3 vote, ruled that the question of reapportionment was a political, not legal, issue. The authority to draw district boundaries for congressional seats belonged to the state legislatures, and the federal courts had no power to intervene. Justice Frankfurter, for the plurality, served notice that the Court "ought not to enter this political thicket," instead informing the complaining parties that their remedy was through the ballot box and legislative process rather than the courts.

The Court's admonishment presented an insurmountable problem for urban residents living in disproportionately large districts. Many states were so badly malapportioned, and the dominant rural interests so opposed to change, that electing enough state legislators sympathetic to reapportionment was almost impossible. But the Court maintained its position that reapportionment questions were outside the purview of judicial scrutiny. Meanwhile, the census figures for 1950 and 1960 indicated that the malapportionment problem was growing.

As the nation entered the 1960s, the Supreme Court's position began to soften. This change was prompted by a greater awareness of the problems associated with malapportionment and by significant personnel changes on the Court. Of the four justices who had voted against Colegrove, only Frankfurter remained on the bench. The Court, now under the leadership of Earl Warren, expressed a much greater willingness to accept rights violations claims.

In 1962 the Court decided *Baker v. Carr,* in which a group of urban residents from Tennessee challenged the way their state legislative districts were drawn. Although this case involved representation in the state assembly rather than in Congress, there were significant factual parallels between *Baker* and *Colegrove.* The central question in *Baker* was whether the federal courts have jurisdiction over apportionment cases. Rather than basing their jurisdictional claim on the Constitution's republican form of government guarantee, as Colegrove had done, the plaintiffs in *Baker* argued that the malapportioned Tennessee legislature violated the Fourteenth Amendment's Equal Protection Clause. If the Court did not alter its position that apportionment was a political question over which the federal courts had no say, urban residents would continue to find their representational voice diluted by legislatures dominated by rural interests. But a decision that granted federal court jurisdiction undoubtedly would set off an avalanche of litigation throughout the nation.

The justices considered the *Baker* case with extreme care.[6] The Court heard six hours of oral argument on two separate occasions. The justices deliberated at length in conference. The opinions took up 163 pages in *U.S. Reports* and covered a wide range of subjects such as the political question doctrine, the Guarantee and Equal Protection Clauses, standing, and justiciability. In the excerpt of the *Baker* opinion reprinted here, the Court discusses the power of the federal judiciary to hear reapportionment cases when a claim is made that legislative districting violates equal protection of the laws.[7]

Baker v. Carr

369 U.S. 186 (1962)
laws.findlaw.com/US/369/186.html
Vote: 6 (Black, Brennan, Clark, Douglas, Stewart, Warren)
   2 (Frankfurter, Harlan)
Opinion of the Court: Brennan
Concurring opinions: Clark, Douglas, Stewart
Dissenting opinions: Frankfurter, Harlan
Not participating: Whittaker

Tennessee had experienced massive population migration to its urban areas during the first half of the twentieth century, but the state legislature had not redistricted since 1901. The result was a malapportioned state

6. See J. W. Peltason, "Baker v. Carr," in *The Oxford Companion,* 56–59.
7. For oral arguments in this case, navigate to: *oyez.nwu.edu.*

legislature in which the smallest district had nineteen times the representational power of the largest district. Charles Baker and other residents from Memphis, Nashville, and Knoxville sued Joseph C. Carr, the state secretary of state, requesting that the court declare the apportionment law unconstitutional and prohibit the state from conducting future elections under it. Feeling bound by the precedent of *Colegrove v. Green*, the district court dismissed the suit on grounds that legislative apportionment issues presented political questions over which the judiciary had no jurisdiction. The plaintiffs appealed to the U.S. Supreme Court.

MR. JUSTICE BRENNAN delivered the opinion of the Court.

Article III, §2, of the Federal Constitution provides that "The judicial Power shall extend to all Cases, in Law and Equity, arising under this Constitution, the Laws of the United States, and Treaties made, or which shall be made, under their Authority. . . ." It is clear that the cause of action is one which "arises under" the Federal Constitution. The complaint alleges that the 1901 statute effects an apportionment that deprives the appellants of the equal protection of the laws in violation of the Fourteenth Amendment. Dismissal of the complaint upon the ground of lack of jurisdiction of the subject matter would, therefore, be justified only if that claim were "so attenuated and unsubstantial as to be absolutely devoid of merit," or "frivolous." That the claim is unsubstantial must be "very plain." Since the District Court obviously and correctly did not deem the asserted federal constitutional claim unsubstantial and frivolous, it should not have dismissed the complaint for want of jurisdiction of the subject matter. And of course no further consideration of the merits of the claim is relevant to a determination of the court's jurisdiction of the subject matter. We said in an earlier voting case from Tennessee: "It is obvious . . . that the court, in dismissing for want of jurisdiction, was controlled by what it deemed to be the want of merit in the arguments which were made in the complaint as to the violation of the Federal right. But as the very nature of the controversy was Federal, and, therefore, jurisdiction existed, whilst the opinion of the court as to the want of merit in the cause of action might have furnished ground for dismissing for that reason, it afforded no sufficient ground for deciding

that the action was not one arising under the Constitution and laws of the United States." *Swafford v. Templeton* [1902]. "For it is well settled that the failure to state a proper cause of action calls for a judgment on the merits and not for a dismissal for want of jurisdiction." *Bell v. Hood* [1946].

Since the complaint plainly sets forth a case arising under the Constitution, the subject matter is within the federal judicial power defined in Art. III, §2, and so within the power of Congress to assign to the jurisdiction of the District Courts. . . .

An unbroken line of our precedents sustains the federal courts' jurisdiction of the subject matter of federal constitutional claims of this nature. The first cases involved the redistricting of States for the purpose of electing Representatives to the Federal Congress. When the Ohio Supreme Court sustained Ohio legislation against an attack for repugnancy to Art. I, §4, of the Federal Constitution, we affirmed on the merits and expressly refused to dismiss for want of jurisdiction "In view . . . of the subject-matter of the controversy and the Federal characteristics which inhere in it. . . ." *Ohio ex rel. Davis v. Hildebrant* [1916]. When the Minnesota Supreme Court affirmed the dismissal of a suit to enjoin the Secretary of State of Minnesota from acting under Minnesota redistricting legislation, we reviewed the constitutional merits of the legislation and reversed the State Supreme Court. *Smiley v. Holm* [1932]. . . . When a three-judge District Court, exercising jurisdiction under the predecessor of 28 U.S.C. §1343 (3), permanently enjoined officers of the State of Mississippi from conducting an election of Representatives under a Mississippi redistricting act, we reviewed the federal questions on the merits and reversed the District Court. *Wood v. Broom* [1932]. A similar decree of a District Court, exercising jurisdiction under the same statute, concerning a Kentucky redistricting act, was reviewed and the decree reversed. *Mahan v. Hume* [1932].

The appellees refer to *Colegrove v. Green* [1946] as authority that the District Court lacked jurisdiction of the subject matter. Appellees misconceive the holding of that case. The holding was precisely contrary to their reading of it. Seven members of the Court participated in the decision. Unlike many other cases in this field which have assumed without discussion that there was jurisdiction, all three opinions filed in *Colegrove* discussed the question. Two of the opinions expressing the views of four of the Justices, a majority, flatly held that there was jurisdiction of the subject matter.

MR. JUSTICE BLACK joined by MR. JUSTICE DOUGLAS and Mr. Justice Murphy stated: "It is my judgment that the District Court had jurisdiction . . .," citing the predecessor of 28 U.S.C. §1343 (3), and *Bell v. Hood* [1946]. Mr. Justice Rutledge, writing separately, expressed agreement with this conclusion. Indeed, it is even questionable that the opinion of MR. JUSTICE FRANKFURTER, joined by Justices Reed and Burton, doubted jurisdiction of the subject matter. . . .

Several subsequent cases similar to *Colegrove* have been decided by the Court in summary *per curiam* statements. None was dismissed for want of jurisdiction of the subject matter.

Two cases decided with opinions after *Colegrove* likewise plainly imply that the subject matter of this suit is within District Court jurisdiction. In *McDougall v. Green* [1948] the District Court dismissed for want of jurisdiction, which had been invoked under 28 U.S.C. §1343 (3), a suit to enjoin enforcement of the requirement that nominees for state-wide elections be supported by a petition signed by a minimum number of persons from at least 50 of the State's 102 counties. This Court's disagreement with that action is clear since the Court affirmed the judgment after a review of the merits and concluded that the particular claim there was without merit. In *South v. Peters* [1950] we affirmed the dismissal of an attack on the Georgia "county unit" system but founded our action on a ground that plainly would not have been reached if the lower court lacked jurisdiction of the subject matter, which allegedly existed under 28 U.S.C. §1343 (3). The express words of our holding were that "Federal courts consistently refuse to exercise their equity powers in cases posing political issues arising from a state's geographical distribution of electoral strength among its political subdivisions."

We hold that the District Court has jurisdiction of the subject matter of the federal constitutional claim asserted in the complaint.

We come, finally, to the ultimate inquiry whether our precedents as to what constitutes a nonjusticiable "political question" bring the case before us under the umbrella of that doctrine. A natural beginning is to note whether any of the common characteristics which we have been able to identify and label descriptively are present. We find none: The question here is the consistency of state action with the Federal Constitution. We have no question decided, or to be decided, by a political branch of government coequal with this Court. Nor do we risk embarrassment of our government abroad, or grave disturbance at home if we take issue with Tennessee as to the constitutionality of her action here challenged. Nor need the appellants, in order to succeed in this action, ask the Court to enter upon policy determinations for which judicially manageable standards are lacking. Judicial standards under the Equal Protection Clause are well developed and familiar, and it has been open to courts since the enactment of the Fourteenth Amendment to determine, if on the particular facts they must, that a discrimination reflects *no* policy, but simply arbitrary and capricious action.

This case does, in one sense, involve the allocation of political power within a State, and the appellants might conceivably have added a claim under the Guaranty Clause. Of course, as we have seen, any reliance on that clause would be futile. But because any reliance on the Guaranty Clause could not have succeeded it does not follow that appellants may not be heard on the equal protection claim which in fact they tender. True, it must be clear that the Fourteenth Amendment claim is not so enmeshed with those political question elements which render Guaranty Clause claims nonjusticiable as actually to present a political question itself. But we have found that not to be the case here. . . .

We conclude that the complaint's allegations of a denial of equal protection present a justiciable constitutional cause of action upon which appellants are entitled to a trial and a decision. The right asserted is within the reach of judicial protection under the Fourteenth Amendment.

The judgment of the District Court is reversed and the cause is remanded for further proceedings consistent with this opinion.

Reversed and remanded.

MR. JUSTICE DOUGLAS, concurring.

I agree with my Brother CLARK that, if the allegations in the complaint can be sustained, a case for relief is established. We are told that a single vote in Moore County, Tennessee, is worth 19 votes in Hamilton County, that one vote in Stewart or in Chester County is worth nearly eight times a single vote in Shelby or Knox County. The opportunity to prove that an "invidious discrimination" exists should therefore be given the appellants.

It is said that any decision in cases of this kind is beyond the competence of courts. Some make the same point as regards the problem of equal protection in cases involving racial segregation. Yet the legality of claims and conduct is a traditional subject for judicial determination. Adjudication is often perplexing and complicated. . . . The constitutional guide is often vague, as the decisions under the Due Process and Commerce Clauses show. The problem under the Equal Protection Clause is no more intricate.

MR. JUSTICE CLARK, concurring.

Although I find the Tennessee apportionment statute offends the Equal Protection Clause, I would not consider intervention by this Court into so delicate a field if there were any other relief available to the people of Tennessee. But the majority of the people of Tennessee have no "practical opportunities for exerting their political weight at the polls" to correct the existing "invidious discrimination." Tennessee has no initiative and referendum. I have searched diligently for other "practical opportunities" present under the law. I find none other than through the federal courts. The majority of the voters have been caught up in a legislative strait jacket. Tennessee has an "informed, civically militant electorate" and "an aroused popular conscience," but it does not sear "the conscience of the people's representatives." This is because the legislative policy has riveted the present seats in the Assembly to their respective constituencies, and by the votes of their incumbents a reapportionment of any kind is prevented. The people have been rebuffed at the hands of the Assembly; they have tried the constitutional convention route, but since the call must originate in the Assembly it, too, has been fruitless. They have tried Tennessee courts with the same result, and Governors have fought the tide only to flounder. It is said that there is recourse in Congress, and perhaps that may be, but, from a practical standpoint, this is without substance. To date, Congress has never undertaken such a task in any State. We therefore must conclude that the people of Tennessee are stymied, and, without judicial intervention, will be saddled with the present discrimination in the affairs of their state government.

MR. JUSTICE FRANKFURTER, whom MR. JUSTICE HARLAN joins, dissenting.

The Court today reverses a uniform course of decision established by a dozen cases, including one by which the very claim now sustained was unanimously rejected only five years ago. The impressive body of rulings thus cast aside reflected the equally uniform course of our political history regarding the relationship between population and legislative representation—a wholly different matter from denial of the franchise to individuals because of race, color, religion or sex. Such a massive repudiation of the experience of our whole past in asserting destructively novel judicial power demands a detailed analysis of the role of this Court in our constitutional scheme. Disregard of inherent limits in the effective exercise of the Court's "judicial Power" not only presages the futility of judicial intervention in the essentially political conflict of forces by which the relation between population and representation has time out of mind been, and now is, determined. It may well impair the Court's position as the ultimate organ of "the supreme Law of the Land" in that vast range of legal problems, often strongly entangled in popular feeling, on which this Court must pronounce. The Court's authority—possessed of neither the purse nor the sword—ultimately rests on sustained public confidence in its moral sanction. Such feeling must be nourished by the Court's complete detachment, in fact and in appearance, from political entanglements and by abstention from injecting itself into the clash of political forces in political settlements. . . .

Although the District Court had jurisdiction in the very restricted sense of power to determine whether it could adjudicate the claim, the case is of that class of political controversy which, by the nature of its subject, is unfit for federal judicial action. The judgment of the District Court, in dismissing the complaint for failure to state a claim on which relief can be granted, should therefore be affirmed.

Dissenting opinion of MR. JUSTICE HARLAN, whom MR. JUSTICE FRANKFURTER joins.

I can find nothing in the Equal Protection Clause or elsewhere in the Federal Constitution which expressly or impliedly supports the view that state legislatures must be so structured as to reflect with approximate equality the voice of every voter. Not only is that proposition refuted by history . . . but it strikes deep into the heart of our federal system. Its acceptance would require us to turn our backs on the regard which this Court has always shown for the judgment of state legislatures and courts on matters of basically local concern.

In the last analysis, what lies at the core of this controversy is a difference of opinion as to the function of representative government. It is surely beyond argument that those who have the responsibility for devising a system of representation may permissibly consider that factors other than bare numbers should be taken into account. The existence of the United States Senate is proof enough of that. To consider that we may ignore the Tennessee Legislature's judgment in this instance because that body was the product of an asymmetrical electoral apportionment would, in effect, be to assume the very conclusion here disputed. Hence, we must accept the present form of the Tennessee Legislature as the embodiment of the State's choice, or, more realistically, its compromise, between competing political philosophies. The federal courts have not been empowered by the Equal Protection Clause to judge whether this resolution of the State's internal political conflict is desirable or undesirable, wise or unwise. . . .

In conclusion, it is appropriate to say that one need not agree, as a citizen, with what Tennessee has done or failed to do in order to deprecate, as a judge, what the majority is doing today. Those observers of the Court who see it primarily as the last refuge for the correction of all inequality or injustice, no matter what its nature or source, will no doubt applaud this decision and its break with the past. Those who consider that continuing national respect for the Court's authority depends in large measure upon its wise exercise of self-restraint and discipline in constitutional adjudication will view the decision with deep concern.

I would affirm.

In *Baker v. Carr,* with only Frankfurter and Harlan in dissent, the Court held that the federal judiciary has authority to hear challenges to state districting systems and that equal protection arguments present justiciable issues not barred by the political question doctrine. Although the Court confined itself to these jurisdictional issues, the ruling in *Baker* opened the Supreme Court's doors to reapportionment cases; and there was little doubt that the justices were prepared to initiate significant changes in the nation's system of political representation.

The next major reapportionment case was *Wesberry v. Sanders* (1964), which involved a challenge to the way

Georgia apportioned its congressional districts. Although this case involved only Georgia, the malapportionment there was typical of most states following the 1960 Census and the 1962 congressional elections.

This suit was filed by James P. Wesberry and other qualified voters of Georgia's Fifth Congressional District against Gov. Carl Sanders and other state officials. The plaintiffs claimed that the state's congressional districting system violated the federal Constitution. The Fifth (metropolitan Atlanta) was the largest of Georgia's ten congressional districts, with a population of 823,680. By comparison the Ninth District had only 272,154 residents, and the population of the average district was 394,312. This inequality meant that the Fifth District's legislator represented two to three times as many people as the other members of Congress from Georgia. The districting scheme had been enacted by the state legislature in 1931, and no effort to bring the districts into balance had occurred since then.

The justices held that this condition of significant malapportionment violated Article I, Section 2, of the Constitution, which says, "The House of Representatives shall be composed of Members chosen every second Year by the People of the several States." To satisfy that constitutional provision, the Court ruled, the congressional districts within a state must be as equal in population as practicably possible. The decision required the state legislature to redraw its congressional districts to meet this standard.

Wesberry, however, did not resolve the reapportionment controversy. A more difficult and politically charged issue centered on malapportionment within the state legislatures. It was one thing to command the state legislators to alter the boundaries of congressional districts, but still another to require them to reapportion their own legislative districts. Many states would regard such an action as an infringement of their sovereignty. In addition, the wholesale alteration of state legislative districts would mean that many state representatives would lose their districts or become politically vulnerable, and legislative power would shift from rural to urban interests. That the state legislatures were less than enthusiastic about such prospects is hardly surprising.

It did not take the Supreme Court long to address the

dilemma of the state legislatures. Only four months after the *Wesberry* ruling, the Court announced its decision in *Reynolds v. Sims.*[8] While *Reynolds* shares with *Wesberry* questions of representational equality, the legal basis for the two cases is very different. Article I, Section 2, of the Constitution, upon which the *Wesberry* outcome rested, deals only with the U.S. House of Representatives. Consequently, a challenge to state representational schemes had to be based on other grounds. In addition, all state legislatures except Nebraska's are bicameral, leaving open for dispute whether both houses of the state assembly must be population based. Notice in Chief Justice Warren's majority opinion in *Reynolds* how the Court reaches a conclusion consistent with *Wesberry* while using entirely different constitutional grounds. Is the Court's holding on bicameralism reasonable? Or should the states be allowed to base representation in one house of the legislature on interests other than population alone? How compelling is Justice Harlan's dissent?

Reynolds v. Sims

377 U.S. 533 (1964)
laws.findlaw.com/US/377/533.html
Vote: 8 (Black, Brennan, Clark, Douglas, Goldberg, Stewart,
    Warren, White)
    1 (Harlan)
Opinion of the Court: Warren
Concurring opinions: Clark, Stewart
Dissenting opinion: Harlan

Alabama's 1901 constitution authorized a state legislature of 106 House members and 35 senators. These legislators were to represent districts created generally on the basis of population equality. Although obliged to reapportion following each national census, the legislature had never altered the districts that were originally drawn following the 1900 Census. Because of population shifts and a state constitutional requirement that each county, regardless of size, have at least one representative, Alabama had become severely malapportioned. In

8. For oral arguments in this case, navigate to: *oyez.nwu.edu.*

the state House of Representatives, the most populous legislative district had sixteen times the people as the least populous. Conditions in the state Senate were even more inequitable. The largest senatorial district had a population forty-one times greater than the smallest. As was the case in other states, rural areas enjoyed representation levels far in excess of what their populations warranted. For example, rural Lowndes County had one senator for its 15,417 citizens, while urban Jefferson County's single senator represented more than 600,000 residents.

Voters in urban counties filed suit to have the Alabama system declared unconstitutional as a violation of the Equal Protection Clause of the Fourteenth Amendment. Pressured by the threat of legal action in light of the Supreme Court's decision in *Baker v. Carr,* the state legislature offered two reapportionment plans to improve the situation. A three-judge district court declared the existing system unconstitutional and the proposed reforms inadequate. A temporary reapportionment plan was imposed by the trial court judges, and the state appealed to the Supreme Court. The *Reynolds* case was one of six state legislative reapportionment disputes the Supreme Court heard at the same time. The others came from Colorado, Delaware, Maryland, New York, and Virginia. The justices used the opinion in *Reynolds* as the primary vehicle for articulating the Court's position on the state redistricting issue.

MR. CHIEF JUSTICE WARREN delivered the opinion of the Court.

Legislators represent people, not trees or acres. Legislators are elected by voters, not farms or cities or economic interests. As long as ours is a representative form of government, and our legislatures are those instruments of government elected directly by and directly representative of the people, the right to elect legislators in a free and unimpaired fashion is a bedrock of our political system. It could hardly be gainsaid that a constitutional claim had been asserted by an allegation that certain otherwise qualified voters had been entirely prohibited from voting for members of their state legislature. And, if a State should provide that the votes of citizens in one part of the State should be given two times, or five times, or 10 times the weight of votes of citizens in another part of the State, it could hardly be contended that the right to vote of those residing in the disfavored areas had not been effectively diluted. It would appear extraordinary to suggest that a State could be constitutionally permitted to enact a law providing that certain of the State's voters could vote two, five, or 10 times for their legislative representatives, while voters living elsewhere could vote only once. And it is inconceivable that a state law to the effect that, in counting votes for legislators, the votes of citizens in one part of the State would be multiplied by two, five, or 10 while the votes of persons in another area would be counted only at face value, could be constitutionally sustainable. Of course, the effect of state legislative districting schemes which give the same number of representatives to unequal numbers of constituents is identical. Overweighting and overvaluation of the votes of those living here has the certain effect of dilution and undervaluation of the votes of those living there. The resulting discrimination against those individual voters living in disfavored areas is easily demonstrable mathematically. Their right to vote is simply not the same right to vote as that of those living in a favored part of the State. Two, five, or 10 of them must vote before the effect of their voting is equivalent to that of their favored neighbor. Weighting the votes of citizens differently, by any method or means, merely because of where they happen to reside, hardly seems justifiable. One must be ever aware that the Constitution forbids "sophisticated as well as simple-minded modes of discrimination.". . .

Logically, in a society ostensibly grounded on representative government, it would seem reasonable that a majority of the people of a State could elect a majority of that State's legislators. To conclude differently, and to sanction minority control of state legislative bodies, would appear to deny majority rights in a way that far surpasses any possible denial of minority rights that might otherwise be thought to result. Since legislatures are responsible for enacting laws by which all citizens are to be governed, they should be bodies which are collectively responsive to the popular will. And the concept of equal protection has been traditionally viewed as requiring the uniform treatment of persons standing in the same relation to the governmental action questioned or challenged. With respect to the allocation of legislative representation, all voters, as citizens of a State, stand in the same relation regardless of where they live. Any suggested criteria for the differentiation of citizens are insufficient to justify any discrimination, as to the weight of their votes, unless relevant to the permissible purposes of legislative apportionment. Since the achieving of fair and effective representation for all citizens is concededly the basic aim of legislative apportionment, we conclude that the Equal Protection Clause guarantees the opportunity for equal participation by all voters in the election of state legislators. Diluting the weight of votes because of place of residence impairs basic constitutional rights under the Fourteenth Amendment just as much as invidious discriminations based upon factors such as race or economic status. . . .

We are told that the matter of apportioning representation in a state legislature is a complex and many-faceted one. We are advised that States can rationally consider factors other than population in apportioning legislative representation. We are admonished not to restrict the power of the States to impose differing views as to political philosophy on their citizens. We are cautioned about the dangers of entering into political thickets and mathematical quagmires. Our answer is this: a denial of constitutionally protected rights demands judicial protection; our oath and our office require no less of us. . . . To the extent that a citizen's right to vote is debased, he is that much less a citizen. The fact that an individual lives here or there is not a legitimate reason for overweighting or diluting the efficacy of his vote. The complexions of societies and civilizations change, often with amazing rapidity. A nation once primarily rural in character becomes predominantly urban. Representation schemes once fair and equitable become archaic and outdated. But the basic principle of representative government remains, and must remain, unchanged—the weight of a citizen's vote cannot be made to depend on where he lives. Population is, of necessity, the starting point for consideration and the controlling criterion for judgment in legislative apportionment controversies. A citizen, a qualified voter, is no more nor no less so because he lives in the city or on the farm. This is the clear and strong command of our Constitution's Equal Protection Clause. This is an essential part of the concept of a government of laws and not men. This is at the heart of Lincoln's vision of "government of the people, by the people, [and] for the people." The Equal Protection Clause demands no less than substantially equal state legislative representation for all citizens, of all places as well as of all races.

We hold that, as a basic constitutional standard, the

Equal Protection Clause requires that the seats in both houses of a bicameral state legislature must be apportioned on a population basis. Simply stated, an individual's right to vote for state legislators is unconstitutionally impaired when its weight is in a substantial fashion diluted when compared with votes of citizens living in other parts of the State. . . .

Legislative apportionment in Alabama is signally illustrative and symptomatic of the seriousness of this problem in a number of the States. At the time this litigation was commenced, there had been no reapportionment of seats in the Alabama Legislature for over 60 years. Legislative inaction, coupled with the unavailability of any political or judicial remedy, had resulted, with the passage of years, in the perpetuated scheme becoming little more than an irrational anachronism. Consistent failure by the Alabama Legislature to comply with state constitutional requirements as to the frequency of reapportionment and the bases of legislative representation resulted in a minority stranglehold on the State Legislature. Inequality of representation in one house added to the inequality in the other. . . . Since neither of the houses of the Alabama Legislature, under any of the three plans considered by the District Court, was apportioned on a population basis, we would be justified in proceeding no further. However, one of the proposed plans, that contained in the so-called 67-Senator Amendment, at least superficially resembles the scheme of legislative representation followed in the Federal Congress. Under this plan, each of Alabama's 67 counties is allotted one senator, and no counties are given more than one Senate seat. Arguably, this is analogous to the allocation of two Senate seats, in the Federal Congress, to each of the 50 States, regardless of population. Seats in the Alabama House, under the proposed constitutional amendment, are distributed by giving each of the 67 counties at least one, with the remaining 39 seats being allotted among the more populous counties on a population basis. This scheme, at least at first glance, appears to resemble that prescribed for the Federal House of Representatives, where the 435 seats are distributed among the States on a population basis, although each State, regardless of its population, is given at least one Congressman. Thus, although there are substantial differences in underlying rationale and results, the 67-Senator Amendment, as proposed by the Alabama Legislature, at least arguably presents for consideration a scheme analogous to that used for apportioning seats in Congress. . . .

We agree with the District Court, and find the federal analogy inapposite and irrelevant to state legislative districting schemes. Attempted reliance on the federal analogy appears often to be little more than an after-the-fact rationalization offered in defense of maladjusted state apportionment arrangements. The original constitutions of 36 of our States provided that representation in both houses of the state legislatures would be based completely, or predominantly, on population. And the Founding Fathers clearly had no intention of establishing a pattern or model for the apportionment of seats in state legislatures when the system of representation in the Federal Congress was adopted. . . .

The system of representation in the two Houses of the Federal Congress is one ingrained in our Constitution, as part of the law of the land. It is one conceived out of compromise and concession indispensable to the establishment of our federal republic. Arising from unique historical circumstances, it is based on the consideration that in establishing our type of federalism a group of formerly independent States bound themselves together under one national government. . . .

Political subdivisions of States—counties, cities, or whatever—never were and never have been considered as sovereign entities. Rather, they have been traditionally regarded as subordinate governmental instrumentalities created by the State to assist in the carrying out of state governmental functions. . . . The relationship of the States to the Federal Government could hardly be less analogous.

Thus, we conclude that the plan contained in the 67-Senator Amendment for apportioning seats in the Alabama Legislature cannot be sustained by recourse to the so-called federal analogy. Nor can any other inequitable state legislative apportionment scheme be justified. . . .

By holding that as a federal constitutional requisite both houses of a state legislature must be apportioned on a population basis, we mean that the Equal Protection Clause requires that a State make an honest and good faith effort to construct districts, in both houses of its legislature, as nearly of equal population as is practicable. We realize that it is a practical impossibility to arrange legislative districts so that each one has an identical number of residents, or citizens, or voters. Mathematical exactness or precision is hardly a workable constitutional requirement. . . .

A State may legitimately desire to maintain the integrity of various political subdivisions, insofar as possible, and provide for compact districts of contiguous territory in designing a legislative apportionment scheme. Valid considerations may underlie such aims. Indiscriminate districting, without any regard for political subdivision or natural or historical boundary lines, may be little more than an open invitation to partisan gerrymandering. Single-member districts may be the rule in one State, while another State might desire to achieve some flexibility by creating multi-member or floterial districts. Whatever the means of accomplishment, the overriding objective must be substantial equality of population among the various districts, so that the vote of any citizen is approximately equal in weight to that of any other citizen in the State.

History indicates, however, that many States have deviated, to a greater or lesser degree, from the equal-population principle in the apportionment of seats in at least one house of their legislatures. So long as the divergences from a strict population standard are based on legitimate considerations incident to the effectuation of a rational state policy, some deviations from the equal-population principle are constitutionally permissible with respect to the apportionment of seats in either or both of the two houses of a bicameral state legislature. But neither history alone, nor economic or other sorts of group interests, are permissible factors in attempting to justify disparities from population-based representation. Citizens, not history or economic interests, cast votes. Considerations of area alone provide an insufficient justification for deviations from the equal population principle. . . .

We find, therefore, that the action taken by the District Court in this case, in ordering into effect a reapportionment of both houses of the Alabama Legislature for purposes of the 1962 primary and general elections, by using the best parts of the two proposed plans which it had found, as a whole, to be invalid, was an appropriate and well-considered exercise of judicial power. Admittedly, the lower court's ordered plan was intended only as a temporary and provisional measure and the District Court correctly indicated that the plan was invalid as a permanent apportionment. In retaining jurisdiction while deferring a hearing on the issuance of a final injunction in order to give the provisionally reapportioned legislature an opportunity to act effectively, the court below proceeded in a proper fashion. . . .

Affirmed and remanded.

MR. JUSTICE HARLAN, dissenting.

In these cases the Court holds that seats in the legislatures of six States are apportioned in ways that violate the Federal Constitution. Under the Court's ruling it is bound to follow that the legislature in all but a few of the other 44 States will meet the same fate. These decisions, with *Wesberry v. Sanders,* involving congressional districting by the States, and *Gray v. Sanders,* relating to elections for statewide office, have the effect of placing basic aspects of state political systems under the pervasive overlordship of the federal judiciary. Once again, I must register my protest.

Today's holding is that the Equal Protection Clause of the Fourteenth Amendment requires every State to structure its legislature so that all the members of each house represent substantially the same number of people; other factors may be given play only to the extent that they do not significantly encroach on this basic "population" principle. Whatever may be thought of this holding as a piece of political ideology—and even on that score the political history and practices of this country from its earliest beginnings leave wide room for debate . . . —I think it demonstrable that the Fourteenth Amendment does not impose this political tenet on the States or authorize this Court to do so.

The Court's constitutional discussion, found in its opinion in the Alabama cases, is remarkable . . . for its failure to address itself at all to the Fourteenth Amendment as a whole or to the legislative history of the Amendment pertinent to the matter at hand. Stripped of aphorisms, the Court's argument boils down to the assertion that appellees' right to vote has been invidiously "debased" or "diluted" by systems of apportionment which entitle them to vote for fewer legislators than other voters, an assertion which is tied to the Equal Protection Clause only by the constitutionally frail tautology that "equal" means "equal."

Had the Court paused to probe more deeply into the matter, it would have found that the Equal Protection Clause was never intended to inhibit the States in choosing any democratic method they pleased for the apportionment of their legislatures. This is shown by the language of the Fourteenth Amendment taken as a whole, by the understanding of those who proposed and ratified it, and by the political practices of the States at the time the Amendment was adopted. It is confirmed by numerous state and congressional actions since the adoption of the Fourteenth

Amendment, and by the common understanding of the Amendment as evidenced by subsequent constitutional amendments and decisions of this Court before *Baker v. Carr* made an abrupt break with the past in 1962.

The failure of the Court to consider any of these matters cannot be excused or explained by any concept of "developing" constitutionalism. It is meaningless to speak of constitutional "development" when both the language and history of the controlling provisions of the Constitution are wholly ignored. Since it can, I think, be shown beyond doubt that state legislative apportionments, as such, are wholly free of constitutional limitations, save such as may be imposed by the Republican Form of Government Clause (Const., Art. IV, §4), the Court's action now bringing them within the purview of the Fourteenth Amendment amounts to nothing less than an exercise of the amending power by this Court.

So far as the Federal Constitution is concerned, the complaints in these cases should all have been dismissed below for failure to state a cause of action because what has been alleged or proved shows no violation of any constitutional right.

Harlan's dissent in *Reynolds* predicting that the legislatures of all the states would be affected by the Court's one person, one vote principle proved to be accurate. At first, there was some disagreement with the Court's ruling. State advocates began a movement to amend the Constitution to provide states the authority to have at least one house of their legislatures based on factors other than population, but the proposal failed to garner sufficient support. As the states began the Court-imposed reapportionment process, opposition started to wane. Today, reapportionment of congressional and state legislative districts occurs each decade following the national census. The impact of the reapportionment rulings initially was to shift a significant amount of political power from the rural areas to the cities. In more recent years, consistent with demographic changes, the suburbs have been the beneficiaries of the Court's redistricting policies. In the near future, increased representation for minority citizens, especially for the rapidly growing Hispanic population, undoubtedly will occur.

Upon his retirement, Chief Justice Warren said that, in his opinion, the reapportionment decisions were the most significant rulings rendered during his sixteen-year tenure. That statement was remarkable, considering that under his leadership the Court handed down landmark decisions on race relations, criminal justice, obscenity, libel, and school prayer. In spite of their significance, however, the initial redistricting decisions did not answer all of the relevant questions regarding the one person, one vote principle. For the next three decades, the Court faced additional perplexing constitutional issues flowing from *Baker*, *Wesberry*, and *Reynolds*.

Representational Equality: Applicability and Measurement

Although *Wesberry* and *Reynolds* made it clear that the Constitution demanded population-based representational units for the U.S. House of Representatives and both houses of state legislatures, the question of applying the one person, one vote principle to other governing bodies remained open. As early as 1963, when it struck down Georgia's county unit system of electing governors in *Gray v. Sanders*, the Supreme Court indicated a willingness to apply principles of population equality to political entities other than legislatures. It appeared quite possible that the justices would impose equal protection standards on the thousands of local government commissions, councils, and boards to which Americans regularly elect representatives. Most of these bodies were loosely based upon population, but they could not meet the exacting standards of the reapportionment rulings. Did the Constitution demand that these governing bodies be properly apportioned in the same manner as state legislatures? Supporters of representational equality sponsored numerous lawsuits asking the judiciary to extend one person, one vote to these local government units.

In *Avery v. Midland County* (1968) the Court ruled on a challenge to the representational system used to elect the county government. The seat of Midland County, Texas, contained more than 95 percent of the county's population but was only given 20 percent of the representatives on the governing commission. The Court struck down this scheme, holding that the equal protection principles that govern representation in the state legislature also control representation on elected local government bodies. In *Hadley v. Junior College District* (1970) the justices extended the same principles to elected special purpose boards that exercise legislative functions. As late as 1989, in *Board of Estimate of New York v. Morris,* the Supreme Court unanimously struck down the system used for selecting members of New York City's Board of Estimate, which gave equal representation to each of the five New York boroughs even though they had substantially unequal populations. The Court's position has been relatively clear: the Equal Protection Clause demands that the principle of one person, one vote applies to local governing bodies that are elected and exercise legislative or general governing powers. The basic rule was articulated well in *Hadley:*

[W]henever a state or local government decides to select persons by popular election to perform governmental functions, the Equal Protection Clause of the Fourteenth Amendment requires that each qualified voter must be given an equal opportunity to participate in that election, and when members of an elected body are chosen from separate districts, each district must be established on a basis that will insure, as far as is practicable, that equal numbers of voters can vote for proportionally equal numbers of officials.

Exceptions have been made when the governing board exercises essentially administrative rather than general or legislative powers (see *Sailors v. Board of Education of Kent County,* 1967) and when the substantive authority of the commission is so narrow and so specialized as to justify representation based on factors other than population (see *Sayler Land Company v. Tulare Lake Basin Water Storage District,* 1973).

In its early apportionment decisions, the Supreme Court emphasized the need for population-based representational schemes. The justices used phrases such as "one person, one vote," "substantial equality," and "as equal as practicably possible" to refer to this standard. But the Court did not define what is meant by such equality. Although the justices regularly acknowledged that mathematical precision could not be expected, they failed to say what variation among districts would be constitutionally tolerated. Redistricting is an exceedingly

An editorial cartoon showing the loss of political power suffered by rural interests because of decisions such as *Gray v. Sanders.*

complex process. Even with the assistance of sophisticated computer technology, drawing boundaries that create districts of nearly perfect equality is difficult. Adding to the burden are the demands of partisan, racial, ethnic, and economic interests for political power.

For the state legislatures involved in this process, it would be helpful for the Supreme Court to designate a minimum level of deviation that is constitutionally permissible. Such a *de minimis* standard would give legislators a guide as to what population equality means in practice. But in the Missouri congressional reapportionment case of *Kirkpatrick v. Preisler* (1969) the Supreme Court explicitly refused to provide any specified mathematical standard of equality. For the majority, Justice Brennan explained,

We reject Missouri's argument that there is a fixed numerical or percentage population variance small enough to be considered *de minimis* and to satisfy without question the "as nearly as practicable" standard. The whole thrust of the "as nearly as practicable" approach is inconsistent with adoption of fixed numerical standards which excuse population variances without regard to the circumstances of each particular case.

In this decision, the Court declared Missouri's reapportionment plan to be unconstitutional in spite of the relatively small 1.6 percent average deviation from the ideal. The state had failed to convince the Court's majority that it had made a good faith attempt to achieve equality.

The Court's policy of imposing exacting standards for congressional districts continued in *Karcher v. Daggett* (1983). This case involved the New Jersey legislature's redistricting scheme when the state lost one congressional seat following the 1980 Census. After fierce political battles, the legislature passed a reapportionment plan in which the difference between the largest and smallest districts was 3,674 or a disparity of 0.6984 percent. Before passing this plan, the legislature considered several alternatives that would have created an even smaller difference. The reapportionment law was challenged in court. Justice Brennan, for a five-justice majority, struck down the plan, finding that the legislature had not demonstrated a good faith attempt to achieve population equality. The state failed to show that there were convincing reasons why plans allowing greater equality were not adopted. Four justices in the minority, led by Byron White, attacked the majority for "unreasonable insistence on an unattainable perfection in the equalizing of congressional districts." Further, the minority argued that, absent extraordinary circumstances, plans with deviations of less than 5 percent from absolute equality ought to be considered close enough to meet constitutional standards.

It is important to keep in mind that in *Karcher v. Daggett* the Supreme Court is interpreting Article I, Section 2, of the Constitution, which deals with the election of members to the U.S. House. The majority's rather strict approach to equality standards for congressional districts is not necessarily applicable to the apportionment of state and local governments, which is governed by the Equal Protection Clause of the Fourteenth Amendment. In fact, the Supreme Court has allowed the states much greater latitude in devising reapportionment plans

and has tolerated much greater deviation from absolute equality than it has with creation of congressional constituencies.

For example, in *Mahan v. Howell* (1973) the justices examined a reapportionment plan for the Virginia State House of Delegates that had an average deviation from perfect equality of 3.89 percent and a 16.4 percent variance between the largest and smallest districts. These deviations were due, in part, to the state's preference for drawing legislative district lines that followed existing city and county political boundaries. In upholding the plan, the Court emphasized the ruling in *Reynolds v. Sims* that "so long as the divergences from a strict population standard are based on legitimate considerations incident to the effectuation of a rational state policy, some deviations from the equal-population principle are constitutionally permissible with respect to the apportionment of seats in either or both of the two houses of a bicameral state legislature." Respecting the integrity of political subdivision boundaries in constructing a reapportionment plan, the justices ruled, does advance a rational state policy.

In a number of decisions, the Court has continued to follow the guidelines set in *Mahan*. For example, in *Gaffney v. Cummings* (1973) the justices upheld a Connecticut state legislative redistricting plan with a maximum 7.83 percent deviation from ideal equality, in part because the state provided evidence that the particular plan preserved political fairness. In *White v. Regester* (1973) a Texas state reapportionment scheme with a 9.9 percent maximum variation from the ideal was upheld, with the Court concluding that the threshold for a prima facie case of invidious discrimination had not been passed. On the same day, almost as if to emphasize the differences, the Court struck down the Texas congressional redistricting plan that contained substantially less deviation from perfect equality than did the state scheme the justices had upheld (*White v. Weiser*, 1973).

In developing state apportionment rules under the Equal Protection Clause, the Supreme Court has even accepted the *de minimis* position that it explicitly rejected in a number of congressional redistricting cases. In *Brown v. Thomson* (1983) Justice Powell, speaking for the

Court, stated, "Our decisions have established, as a general matter, that an apportionment plan with a maximum population deviation under 10% falls within this category of minor deviations. . . . A plan with larger disparities in population, however, creates a prima facie case of discrimination and therefore must be justified by the State." The *Brown* case centered on a Wyoming redistricting plan that included a maximum deviation of 89 percent from perfect equality. This large variation was caused by the representation given to one isolated and sparsely populated county. The Court upheld the law, concluding that the state had provided convincing, nondiscriminatory reasons for allowing this exception to the one person, one vote rule. Ironically, *Brown* was handed down the same day that the Court in *Karcher v. Daggett* struck down New Jersey's congressional reapportionment with its maximum deviation of less than 1 percent and rejected a *de minimis* rationale for use in such cases.

Although the Court has been divided in its application of reapportionment rules developed since *Baker v. Carr*, there has been no turning back on the basic principle underlying these cases. That is, representational units must be based on the one person, one vote principle. With so much at stake, the way the government conducts the census and allocates congressional seats has been subject to constitutional challenges. Two cases highlight the recent litigation.

In *United States Department of Commerce v. Montana* (1992) the justices heard the appeal of the state of Montana, which lost one congressional seat following the 1990 Census, leaving it with a single representative. Montana's loss was due to the population explosion in California, Florida, and Texas. The reallocation of congressional seats meant that Montana's single member of Congress represented 803,655 people, a significant deviation from the average congressional district of 572,466. Giving Montana two seats in Congress would reduce each district to almost 402,000 citizens, a number much closer to the average size. Montana charged that the formula used to distribute congressional seats was constitutionally flawed. The justices rejected the state's challenge, holding that no formula for allocating House seats

among the states would result in equal districts across states and that the system in use was a rational one.

Another issue finding its way to the Court's door was undercounting, a problem that has plagued the Census Bureau for many years. The best estimates are that the census undercounts Americans by about 2.7 percent. Undercounting tends to be greatest among the African American and Hispanic communities. Systematic undercounting of these minorities may have a significant impact on their political representation. Responding to this problem, the Census Bureau developed statistical adjustment techniques for compensating for uncounted Americans. The bureau intended to have the systems in place by the 1990 Census. As the time for the census approached, however, the secretary of commerce, whose department oversees the Census Bureau, concluded that the accuracy of the statistical adjustment procedures had not yet been verified and that traditional counting methods would be used in 1990.

New York City led a coalition of groups challenging the secretary's decision, claiming that traditional methods resulted in the systematic undercounting of identifiable racial and ethnic minorities, which, in turn, led to political underrepresentation. In *Wisconsin v. City of New York* (1996), the Court rejected this constitutional attack. The justices held that Congress had legitimately delegated the authority to conduct the census to the Department of Commerce. The secretary's conclusion that traditional methods would lead to a more accurate count than the newly developed adjustment techniques was entirely reasonable.

In spite of a Supreme Court that has been ideologically divided, the *Montana* and *City of New York* cases were decided by unanimous votes. The opinions for the Court provoked not a single concurring opinion. Clearly, we can conclude from these decisions, both of which supported the government's discretion in deciding how to conduct a census and how to apportion representation based on its results, that the justices do not want to interfere in this rather technical area of governance. As a political matter, however, issues of undercounting and statistical estimation remain hotly debated. They resulted in political battles over the 2000 Census and will undoubtedly continue to be politically sensitive in future census efforts.

Political Representation and Minority Rights

So long as the one person, one vote principle is observed, the Supreme Court generally has allowed the states freedom in constructing representational districts. That latitude, however, is not without limit. The Court has always been aware that representational schemes that satisfy standards of numerical equality may still offend basic constitutional principles. Plans that discriminate on the basis of race or ethnicity have been of particular concern. The justices have served notice that boundary lines cannot be drawn in a way that dilutes the political power of minorities.

Reducing the political participation rights of minorities can take forms other than Alabama's crude deannexation methods struck down in *Gomillion v. Lightfoot*. One representational form, the multimember district, has received considerable scrutiny because of its potential for abusing the rights of minority groups. Under a multimember arrangement, the districts are larger in population than the average constituency and are represented by more than one officeholder. For example, the state legislature may construct a district that is three times larger than the average single-member district and authorize the election of three representatives from that constituency. Normally under such a plan, there are three separate legislative seats with each voter casting a ballot in each of the three races. Once elected, all three legislators serve the same large constituency.

The Supreme Court consistently has held that multimember districts are not constitutionally defective per se and the states retain the right to use them as long as the representation is properly weighted according to population (*Burns v. Richardson*, 1966; *Whitcomb v. Chavis*, 1971). However, such districts run afoul of the Equal Protection Clause if they are developed or maintained as intentional methods of minimizing, canceling out, or diluting the voting strength of racial or ethnic minorities. A multimember district can easily be designed to accomplish this purpose. Using our three-member legislative district example, assume that 40 percent of the district's popula-

tion is found in a compact residential section made up of a particular minority group. If the district were divided into three single-member constituencies, the minority population would likely control one of those districts and be relatively assured of electing one of their own to the state legislature. With the multimember district scheme, however, the votes of the minority citizens would likely be insufficient to win any of the three at-large races. In *White v. Regester* (1973), for example, the Court found the use of some multimember districts in Texas to have politically disadvantaged black and Mexican American voters in violation of the Equal Protection Clause.

Considerable controversy arose over what standards should be used in districting cases in which the diluting of minority voting power is alleged. In *Mobile v. Bolden* (1980) the Court ruled on claims that the at-large system for electing members of the Mobile, Alabama, city commission diluted the electoral strength of blacks to the extent that the Fourteenth and Fifteenth Amendments were violated. The Court held, 6–3, that to establish a violation of the Constitution the challengers must prove more than the fact that minority citizens were disadvantaged politically. It is required, the Court ruled, that racially discriminatory intent be demonstrated. If a governmental action is racially neutral on its face (as multimember districts and at-large election schemes almost always are), then a racially discriminatory purpose must be shown to prove a violation of the Constitution.

Proving discriminatory intent or purpose is quite difficult. Few government officials who want to implement racially discriminatory policies publicly admit it. Although the Court showed a willingness to infer discriminatory purpose when black political participation was especially muted,[9] Congress, at the urging of civil rights groups, concluded that additional legislative action was necessary.

Short of proposing a constitutional amendment, Con-

---

9. See, for example, *Rogers v. Lodge* (1982), in which the Court found discriminatory purpose in a county's representational system. Although 38 percent of the electorate was black, not a single black had been elected to the five-person county commission since the adoption of at-large elections in 1911.

gress could do little to reverse the Court's position that discriminatory purpose must be shown before a violation of the Fourteenth or Fifteenth Amendment could be declared. Congress, however, was empowered to enforce voting rights through the normal legislative process. Consequently, in 1982 it amended the 1965 Voting Rights Act so that violations could be proven by discriminatory effects alone. Congress made clear that a demonstration of discriminatory purpose was not required. Whether intended or not, if a government action resulted in diluting black voting strength, Congress wanted black litigants to be able to use the legal process to put an end to it. This change in the voting rights law has made it easier for minority groups to win representational discrimination cases. In 1986, for example, the Supreme Court in *Thornburg v. Gingles* struck down a North Carolina redistricting plan after minority voters were able to show the law's discriminatory effects. It is important to remember, however, that the amendment of the Voting Rights Act did not alter the requirements for providing a violation of the Constitution. To challenge the validity of a government act under the Fourteenth or Fifteenth Amendments, a party still must show discriminatory intent. Only with respect to alleged violations of the Voting Rights Act is the demonstration of discriminatory effects or results sufficient.

The need to ensure that a reapportionment effort does not have the effect of diluting the electoral strength of certain minority groups has made redistricting a more complex task. Increasing representation to one group almost always means decreasing the political influence of another. In a time when various racial and ethnic groups are competing for political power, no plan, even if drafted with good intentions, is likely to satisfy all parties.

In *United Jewish Organizations of Williamsburgh v. Carey* (1977) the Court was faced with just such a situation. Between 1972 and 1974 the state of New York grappled with reapportionment of the state legislature. Under pressure from the Justice Department to ensure that African Americans received adequate representation, the New York legislature ultimately passed a plan that created a number of legislative districts with nonwhite populations exceeding 65 percent. The clear purpose and ef-

fect of the revisions was to ensure black representation from these districts. The Justice Department approved the program. As a consequence of creating these majority-minority districts, however, the state legislature had to divide Williamsburgh, a community where about 30,000 Hasidic Jews lived, into two state Senate and two state Assembly districts. The effect was to make it virtually impossible for the Hasidic community to elect members of their community to the state legislature. The legislature had given preference to ensuring African American representation over the interests of the Hasidic Jews. The Supreme Court upheld the New York redistricting plan, holding that it was permissible to take race into account in order to attain the goals envisioned by the Voting Rights Act.

United Jewish Organizations and *Thornburg v. Gingles* gave constitutional approval to the process of constructing political districts with the expressed purpose of ensuring the election of minority candidates. Civil rights groups and other liberal organizations had been advocating this practice as the only meaningful way to guarantee blacks and other minorities a fair share of legislative seats.

In promoting this cause, advocates of increasing the political power of minorities received significant support from the Justice Department under Presidents Reagan and Bush. Why would a Republican administration back efforts to increase the number of black representatives, especially since these legislators probably would be Democrats? The answer is simple: when lines are drawn to create districts with high concentrations of black voters, the other districts become more white and more Republican. In other words, by creating a few districts that are dominated by minorities, the state legislatures also fashion districts that are more likely to elect Republicans.

In many states the reapportionment battles that followed the 1990 Census were not over one person, one vote issues; rather, they focused on drawing district boundary lines in a manner that would increase the number of minority officeholders. The successful creation of districts with heavy concentrations of racial and ethnic minorities had its intended effect. Following the 1992 congressional elections, the number of African

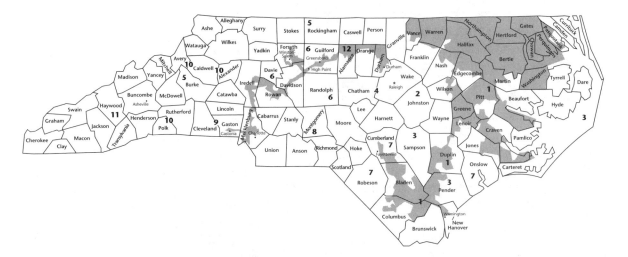

The irregular shapes of North Carolina's First and Twelfth Congressional Districts were challenged in *Shaw v. Reno*.

American House representatives increased from twenty-six to thirty-nine, and Hispanic representatives grew from eleven to seventeen.

To draw these new "majority-minority" districts, state legislatures often had to engage in very creative districting methods. Critics contended that legislators went too far, frequently establishing district boundaries that were highly irregular in shape and possessing little compactness. It was one thing, they argued, to create districts that did not purposefully dilute minority voting strength, but a much different thing to base representational boundaries exclusively on race. As a consequence, lawsuits filed in Florida, Georgia, Louisiana, North Carolina, and Texas challenged the constitutionality of many new districts. The first appeal to reach the Supreme Court was *Shaw v. Reno* (1993), a challenge to two majority-minority congressional districts in North Carolina.

North Carolina gained one congressional seat as a result of the 1990 Census, increasing its House membership to thirteen and requiring the state legislature to redraw the districts. Because of previous racial discrimination, North Carolina fell under the provisions of the 1965 Voting Rights Act, which mandated that any redistricting plan adopted by the state legislature be submitted to the Justice Department or the District Court for

the District of Columbia for approval. Approval would be forthcoming only if the plan did not jeopardize minority representation.

North Carolina's initial reapportionment effort included one district purposefully constructed to have a majority of black voters. The Bush administration's Justice Department rejected this plan on the grounds that it gave African Americans insufficient congressional representation. The state legislature then revised the plan to create two districts (the First and the Twelfth) that would have a majority of black voters. The Justice Department accepted this revision.

The shapes of the two majority-black districts were quite controversial. The First District was somewhat hook-shaped, beginning in the northeastern part of the state and tapering down with fingerlike extensions almost to the South Carolina border. It included all of or portions of twenty-eight counties. In the lower court record the district was said to resemble a Rorschach inkblot test, and the *Wall Street Journal* claimed the district looked like a "bug splattered on a windshield." The Twelfth District received even harsher criticism. It was 160 miles long and generally corresponded to the Interstate 85 corridor. One of the lower court judges described it as winding in a snakelike fashion through tobacco country, financial centers, and manufacturing areas until it gobbled up enough enclaves of black neighborhoods to create a majority-black district. At some points the district was no wider than Interstate 85, prompting one state legislator to remark that if "you drove down the interstate with both car doors open, you'd kill most of the people in the district." In spite of such criticisms, the redistricting accomplished its goal. In 1992 voters in both districts elected black representatives. They were the first blacks to represent North Carolina, a state with a 20 percent black population, since 1901.

Ruth Shaw and four other white North Carolina voters filed suit against the U.S. attorney general and various North Carolina officials, claiming that race-based redistricting violated, among other provisions, the Equal Protection Clause of the Fourteenth Amendment. A special three-judge district court dismissed the suit against both the attorney general and the state officials. Shaw appealed. Traditional civil rights groups—the NAACP Legal Defense Fund, Lawyers' Committee for Civil Rights Under Law, and the Mexican American Legal Defense Fund—submitted amicus curiae briefs in favor of the minority districts, and groups with long histories of opposition to quota programs—the Washington Legal Foundation and the American Jewish Congress—argued against them. True to their ideological positions (but perhaps in spite of obvious partisan implications), the Democratic National Committee maintained that the minority districts were constitutional, and the Republican National Committee argued that they were not.

The immediate task of the Supreme Court in *Shaw v. Reno* was to determine if the trial court had erred by dismissing the suit without a full hearing. The Court had to focus on whether the plaintiffs presented a legitimate constitutional claim for the courts to consider. In a 5–4 vote, the justices ruled that allegations of racial gerrymandering present a Fourteenth Amendment issue that courts have authority to decide. For the majority, Justice O'Connor explained that such claims must allege that the state reapportionment scheme is so irrational on its face that "it can be understood only as an effort to segregate voters into separate voting districts because of their race." If the allegation is proven or unanswered by the

state, the courts must decide if the state's plan is narrowly tailored to further a compelling government interest. If the state cannot demonstrate such a compelling interest, the reapportionment plan is in violation of the Equal Protection Clause of the Fourteenth Amendment. In so ruling, the Court applied the strict scrutiny standard to constitutional attacks on racially engineered representational districts. The *Shaw* case was sent back to the lower courts to be considered in light of the Court's newly articulated standard.

The *Shaw* decision sent shock waves throughout the civil rights community. Although the Court had not declared the North Carolina districts unconstitutional, O'Connor's opinion was a clear signal that the majority did not look with favor upon districting based primarily on race. The justices seemed to be turning away from previous rulings that had been sympathetic to plans designed to enhance minority representation.

Civil rights leaders received more bad news with two 1994 decisions interpreting the Voting Rights Act. In *Holder v. Hall* the justices, by a 5–4 vote, held that the act did not prohibit Bleckley County, Georgia, from using a single commissioner form of government in which one officeholder exercised both legislative and administrative authority. The county's population was 22 percent black, and no minority candidate had ever been elected commissioner. The Court ruled that the act did not compel the county to adopt a multimember commission to increase the probability of black representation. In the second case, *Johnson v. De Grandy*, the justices rejected an argument that the Voting Rights Act required a legislature to draw district lines to maximize minority representation. The dispute centered on newly drawn legislative districts in Miami-Dade County, Florida. The lines could have been drawn to create eleven House districts and four Senate districts with Hispanic majorities, but the final reapportionment act contained only nine House and three Senate majority Hispanic districts. The justices concluded that as long as minority voters form effective voting majorities in a number of districts roughly proportional to their respective share of the voting-age population, the Voting Rights Act is not violated.

The issue of majority-minority districts returned to

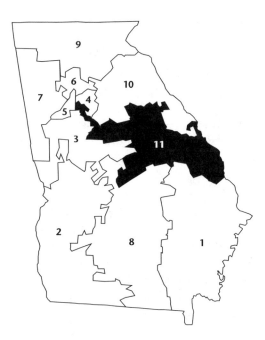

Georgia's Eleventh Congressional District was challenged in *Miller v. Johnson* (1995). Although its shape is not generally irregular, note the district's fingerlike extensions to the northwest, northeast, and west. These were designed to incorporate high concentrations of black voters in Savannah, Augusta, and Atlanta.

the Court in 1995. By this time the lower courts had heard several cases under the new standards articulated in *Shaw,* and these decisions had worked their way to the Supreme Court. The outcome was far from clear. Although the Court had ruled against the position of civil rights groups in several voting rights cases, the decisions often were by 5–4 votes. Much was at stake, and one vote could tip the balance. The first appeal reaching the justices was *Miller v. Johnson,* a challenge to congressional districting in Georgia.[10] This appeal provided an interesting test of the Court's new position. The challenged Georgia district, while clearly constructed to enhance chances of electing a minority representative, was not drawn in a manner as extreme as the North Carolina districts attacked in *Shaw.* Would the Court find the cre-

10. For oral arguments in this case, navigate to: *oyez.nwu.edu.*

ation of this district constitutionally defective for being excessively motivated by racial gerrymandering? Could Georgia justify its actions as responding to a compelling state interest?

Miller v. Johnson

515 U.S. 900 (1995)
supct.law.cornell.edu/supct/html/94-631.ZS.html
Vote: 5 (Kennedy, O'Connor, Rehnquist, Scalia, Thomas)
*   4 (Breyer, Ginsburg, Souter, Stevens)*
Opinion of the Court: Kennedy
Concurring opinion: O'Connor
Dissenting opinions: Ginsburg, Stevens

Following the 1990 Census it was necessary for the state of Georgia to redraw the lines of its eleven congressional districts. The state legislature passed a plan in 1991 that included two districts with a majority of black voters. Because Georgia is subject to the provisions of the Voting Rights Act, the plan went to the Justice Department for approval ("preclearance"). The Justice Department rejected the plan, holding that it did not give sufficient attention to black voting strength. The state revised its apportionment plan, but the new version also included only two majority black districts and also failed to receive approval. In 1992 the state passed a new districting plan that met with Justice Department approval. This legislation created three majority black districts: the Second (southwest Georgia), the Fifth (Atlanta), and the Eleventh, the district challenged in this case.

The Eleventh District ran diagonally across the state from the edge of Atlanta to the Atlantic Ocean. It included portions of urban Atlanta, Savannah, and Augusta, as well as sparsely populated, but overwhelmingly black, rural areas in the central part of the district. The Eleventh covered 6,784 square miles, splitting eight counties and five cities along the way. There were numerous, narrow land bridges used to incorporate areas with significant black populations into the district. The district was 60 percent black. In the 1992 and 1994 congressional elections district voters sent Cynthia McKinney, a black Democrat, to the House of Representatives. The other two majority-minority districts in Georgia also elected African American representatives.

In 1994 five white voters from the Eleventh District, including Davida Johnson, filed suit claiming that the legislature violated the Equal Protection Clause of the Fourteenth Amendment by adopting a redistricting plan driven primarily by considerations of race. A three-judge federal court, applying principles articulated in *Shaw v. Reno,* struck down the district. The Constitution was violated, the judges ruled, because race was the overriding, predominant factor employed to determine the lines of the district. Gov. Zell Miller, a Democrat, appealed to the Supreme Court on behalf of the state.

JUSTICE KENNEDY delivered the opinion of the Court.

The Equal Protection Clause of the Fourteenth Amendment provides that no State shall "deny to any person within its jurisdiction the equal protection of the laws." Its central mandate is racial neutrality in governmental decisionmaking. Though application of this imperative raises difficult questions, the basic principle is straightforward: "Racial and ethnic distinctions of any sort are inherently suspect and thus call for the most exacting judicial examination. . . . This perception of racial and ethnic distinctions is rooted in our Nation's constitutional and demographic history." *Regents of Univ. of California v. Bakke* (1978) (opinion of Powell, J.). This rule obtains with equal force regardless of "the race of those burdened or benefited by a particular classification." *Richmond v. J. A. Croson Co.* (1989) (plurality opinion). Laws classifying citizens on the basis of race cannot be upheld unless they are narrowly tailored to achieving a compelling state interest.

In *Shaw v. Reno* [1993] we recognized that these equal protection principles govern a State's drawing of congressional districts, though, as our cautious approach there discloses, application of these principles to electoral districting is a most delicate task. Our analysis began from the premise that "[l]aws that explicitly distinguish between individuals on racial grounds fall within the core of [the Equal Protection Clause's] prohibition." This prohibition extends not just to explicit racial classifications, but also to laws neutral on their face but "'unexplainable on grounds other than race.'" Applying this basic Equal Protection analysis in the voting rights context, we held that "redistricting legislation

Democratic representatives protesting the Court's decision in *Miller v. Johnson.* From left, Charles B. Rangel of New York; Cynthia McKinney of Georgia, who was reelected despite the redistricting; and Bobby Rush and Luis V. Gutierrez of Illinois.

that is so bizarre on its face that it is 'unexplainable on grounds other than race,' . . . demands the same close scrutiny that we give other state laws that classify citizens by race."

This case requires us to apply the principles articulated in *Shaw* to the most recent congressional redistricting plan enacted by the State of Georgia. . . .

. . . Just as the State may not, absent extraordinary justification, segregate citizens on the basis of race in its public parks, buses, golf courses, beaches, and schools, so did we recognize in *Shaw* that it may not separate its citizens into different voting districts on the basis of race. The idea is a simple one: "At the heart of the Constitution's guarantee of equal protection lies the simple command that the Government must treat citizens 'as individuals, not "as simply components of a racial, religious, sexual or national class."'" *Metro Broadcasting, Inc. v. FCC* (1990) (O'CON-

NOR, J., dissenting). When the State assigns voters on the basis of race, it engages in the offensive and demeaning assumption that voters of a particular race, because of their race, "think alike, share the same political interests, and will prefer the same candidates at the polls." Race-based assignments "embody stereotypes that treat individuals as the product of their race, evaluating their thoughts and efforts—their very worth as citizens—according to a criterion barred to the Government by history and the Constitution." They also cause society serious harm. As we concluded in *Shaw:*

"Racial classifications with respect to voting carry particular dangers. Racial gerrymandering, even for remedial purposes, may balkanize us into competing racial factions; it threatens to carry us further from the goal of a political system in which race no longer matters—a goal that the Fourteenth and Fifteenth Amendments embody, and to which the Nation continues to aspire. It is for these reasons that race-based districting by our state legislatures demands close judicial scrutiny."

Our observation in *Shaw* of the consequences of racial stereotyping was not meant to suggest that a district must be bizarre on its face before there is a constitutional violation. Nor was our conclusion in *Shaw* that in certain instances a district's appearance (or, to be more precise, its appearance in combination with certain demographic evidence) can give rise to an equal protection claim, a holding that bizarreness was a threshold showing, as appellants believe it to be. Our circumspect approach and narrow holding in *Shaw* did not erect an artificial rule barring accepted equal protection analysis in other redistricting cases. Shape is relevant not because bizarreness is a necessary element of the constitutional wrong or a threshold requirement of proof, but because it may be persuasive circumstantial evidence that race for its own sake, and not other districting principles, was the legislature's dominant and controlling rationale in drawing its district lines. The logical implication, as courts applying *Shaw* have recognized, is that parties may rely on evidence other than bizarreness to establish race-based districting.

Our reasoning in *Shaw* compels this conclusion. We recognized in *Shaw* that, outside the districting context, statutes are subject to strict scrutiny under the Equal Protection Clause not just when they contain express racial classifications, but also when, though race neutral on their face, they are motivated by a racial purpose or object. . . .

Shaw applied these same principles to redistricting. "In some exceptional cases, a reapportionment plan may be so highly irregular that, on its face, it rationally cannot be understood as anything other than an effort to 'segregat[e] . . . voters' on the basis of race." In other cases, where the district is not so bizarre on its face that it discloses a racial design, the proof will be more "difficul[t]." Although it was not necessary in *Shaw* to consider further the proof required in these more difficult cases, the logical import of our reasoning is that evidence other than a district's bizarre shape can be used to support the claim. . . .

In sum, we make clear that parties alleging that a State has assigned voters on the basis of race are neither confined in their proof to evidence regarding the district's geometry and makeup nor required to make a threshold showing of bizarreness. Today's case requires us further to consider the requirements of the proof necessary to sustain this equal protection challenge.

. . . Electoral districting is a most difficult subject for legislatures, and so the States must have discretion to exercise the political judgment necessary to balance competing interests. Although race-based decisionmaking is inherently suspect, until a claimant makes a showing sufficient to support that allegation the good faith of a state legislature must be presumed. The courts, in assessing the sufficiency of a challenge to a districting plan, must be sensitive to the complex interplay of forces that enter a legislature's redistricting calculus. Redistricting legislatures will, for example, almost always be aware of racial demographics; but it does not follow that race predominates in the redistricting process. The distinction between being aware of racial considerations and being motivated by them may be difficult to make. This evidentiary difficulty, together with the sensitive nature of redistricting and the presumption of good faith that must be accorded legislative enactments, requires courts to exercise extraordinary caution in adjudicating claims that a state has drawn district lines on the basis of race. The plaintiff's burden is to show, either through circumstantial evidence of a district's shape and demographics or more direct evidence going to legislative purpose, that race was the predominant factor motivating the legislature's decision to place a significant number of voters within or without a particular district. To make this showing, a plaintiff must prove that the legislature subordinated traditional race-neutral districting principles, including but not limited to compactness, contiguity, respect for political subdivisions or communities defined by actual shared interests, to racial considerations. Where these or other race-neutral considerations are the basis for redistricting legislation, and are not subordinated to race, a state can "defeat a claim that a district has been gerrymandered on racial lines." *Shaw.* These principles inform the plaintiff's burden of proof at trial. . . .

In our view, the District Court applied the correct analysis, and its finding that race was the predominant factor motivating the drawing of the Eleventh District was not clearly erroneous. The court found it was "exceedingly obvious" from the shape of the Eleventh District, together with the relevant racial demographics, that the drawing of narrow land bridges to incorporate within the District outlying appendages containing nearly 80% of the district's total black population was a deliberate attempt to bring black populations into the district. Although by comparison with other districts the geometric shape of the Eleventh District may not seem bizarre on its face, when its shape is considered in conjunction with its racial and population densities, the story of racial gerrymandering seen by the District Court becomes much clearer. Although this evidence is quite compelling, we need not determine whether it was, standing alone, sufficient to establish a *Shaw* claim that the Eleventh District is unexplainable other than by race. The District Court had before it considerable additional evidence showing that the General Assembly was motivated by a predominant, overriding desire to assign black populations to the Eleventh District and thereby permit the creation of a third majority-black district. . . .

The court found that "it became obvious," both from the Justice Department's objection letters and the three preclearance rounds in general, "that [the Justice Department] would accept nothing less than abject surrender to its maximization agenda." It further found that the General Assembly acquiesced and as a consequence was driven by its overriding desire to comply with the Department's maximization demands. . . .

In light of its well-supported finding, the District Court was justified in rejecting the various alternative explanations offered for the District. Although a legislature's compliance with "traditional districting principles such as compactness, contiguity, and respect for political subdivisions" may well suffice to refute a claim of racial gerrymandering, *Shaw,* appellants cannot make such a refutation

where, as here, those factors were subordinated to racial objectives. Georgia's Attorney General objected to the Justice Department's demand for three majority-black districts on the ground that to do so the State would have to "violate all reasonable standards of compactness and contiguity." This statement from a state official is powerful evidence that the legislature subordinated traditional districting principles to race when it ultimately enacted a plan creating three majority-black districts, and justified the District Court's finding that "every [objective districting] factor that could realistically be subordinated to racial tinkering in fact suffered that fate."

Nor can the State's districting legislation be rescued by mere recitation of purported communities of interest. The evidence was compelling "that there are no tangible 'communities of interest' spanning the hundreds of miles of the Eleventh District." A comprehensive report demonstrated the fractured political, social, and economic interests within the Eleventh District's black population. It is apparent that it was not alleged shared interests but rather the object of maximizing the District's black population and obtaining Justice Department approval that in fact explained the General Assembly's actions. A State is free to recognize communities that have a particular racial makeup, provided its action is directed toward some common thread of relevant interests. . . . But where the State assumes from a group of voters' race that they "think alike, share the same political interests, and will prefer the same candidates at the polls," it engages in racial stereotyping at odds with equal protection mandates.

Race was, as the District Court found, the predominant, overriding factor explaining the General Assembly's decision to attach to the Eleventh District various appendages containing dense majority-black populations. As a result, Georgia's congressional redistricting plan cannot be upheld unless it satisfies strict scrutiny, our most rigorous and exacting standard of constitutional review.

To satisfy strict scrutiny, the State must demonstrate that its districting legislation is narrowly tailored to achieve a compelling interest. There is a "significant state interest in eradicating the effects of past racial discrimination." *Shaw.* The State does not argue, however, that it created the Eleventh District to remedy past discrimination, and with good reason: there is little doubt that the State's true interest in designing the Eleventh District was creating a third majority-black district to satisfy the Justice Department's preclearance demands. . . . Whether or not in some cases compliance with the Voting Rights Act, standing alone, can provide a compelling interest independent of any interest in remedying past discrimination, it cannot do so here. As we suggested in *Shaw*, compliance with federal antidiscrimination laws cannot justify race-based districting where the challenged district was not reasonably necessary under a constitutional reading and application of those laws. The congressional plan challenged here was not required by the Voting Rights Act under a correct reading of the statute. . . .

We do not accept the contention that the State has a compelling interest in complying with whatever preclearance mandates the Justice Department issues. When a state governmental entity seeks to justify race-based remedies to cure the effects of past discrimination, we do not accept the government's mere assertion that the remedial action is required. Rather, we insist on a strong basis in evidence of the harm being remedied. "The history of racial classifications in this country suggests that blind judicial deference to legislative or executive pronouncements of necessity has no place in equal protection analysis." *Croson*. Our presumptive skepticism of all racial classifications prohibits us as well from accepting on its face the Justice Department's conclusion that racial districting is necessary under the Voting Rights Act. Where a State relies on the Department's determination that race-based districting is necessary to comply with the Voting Rights Act, the judiciary retains an independent obligation in adjudicating consequent equal protection challenges to ensure that the State's actions are narrowly tailored to achieve a compelling interest. See *Shaw*. Were we to accept the Justice Department's objection itself as a compelling interest adequate to insulate racial districting from constitutional review, we would be surrendering to the Executive Branch our role in enforcing the constitutional limits on race-based official action. We may not do so. . . .

The Voting Rights Act, and its grant of authority to the federal courts to uncover official efforts to abridge minorities' right to vote, has been of vital importance in eradicating invidious discrimination from the electoral process and enhancing the legitimacy of our political institutions. Only if our political system and our society cleanse themselves of that discrimination will all members of the polity share an equal opportunity to gain public office regardless of race. As a Nation we share both the obligation and the aspiration of working toward this end. The end is neither assured nor well served, however, by carving electorates into racial blocs. "If our society is to continue to progress as a multiracial democracy, it must recognize that the automatic invocation of race stereotypes retards that progress and causes continued hurt and injury." It takes a shortsighted and unauthorized view of the Voting Rights Act to invoke that statute, which has played a decisive role in redressing some of our worst forms of discrimination, to demand the very racial stereotyping the Fourteenth Amendment forbids.

The judgment of the District Court is affirmed, and the case is remanded for further proceedings consistent with this decision.

It is so ordered.

JUSTICE GINSBURG, with whom JUSTICES STEVENS, BREYER . . . and . . . SOUTER join, dissenting.

Legislative districting is highly political business. This Court has generally respected the competence of state legislatures to attend to the task. When race is the issue, however, we have recognized the need for judicial intervention to prevent dilution of minority voting strength. Generations of rank discrimination against African-Americans, as citizens and voters, account for that surveillance.

Two Terms ago, in *Shaw v. Reno* (1993), this Court took up a claim "analytically distinct" from a vote dilution claim. *Shaw* authorized judicial intervention in "extremely irregular" apportionments in which the legislature cast aside traditional districting practices to consider race alone—in the *Shaw* case, to create a district in North Carolina in which African-Americans would compose a majority of the voters.

Today the Court expands the judicial role, announcing that federal courts are to undertake searching review of any district with contours "predominantly motivated" by race: "strict scrutiny" will be triggered not only when traditional districting practices are abandoned, but also when those practices are "subordinated to"—given less weight than—race. Applying this new "race-as-predominant-factor" standard, the Court invalidates Georgia's districting plan even though Georgia's Eleventh District, the focus of today's dispute, bears the imprint of familiar districting practices. Because I do not endorse the Court's new standard and would not upset Georgia's plan, I dissent. . . .

Before *Shaw v. Reno* (1993), this Court invoked the Equal Protection Clause to justify intervention in the quintessentially political task of legislative districting in two circumstances: to enforce the one-person-one-vote requirement, see *Reynolds v. Sims* (1964); and to prevent dilution of a minority group's voting strength.

In *Shaw*, the Court recognized a third basis for an equal protection challenge to a State's apportionment plan. The Court wrote cautiously, emphasizing that judicial intervention is exceptional: "[S]trict [judicial] scrutiny" is in order, the Court declared, if a district is "so extremely irregular on its face that it rationally can be viewed only as an effort to segregate the races for purposes of voting."

"[E]xtrem[e] irregular[ity]" was evident in *Shaw*, the Court explained. . . .

The problem in *Shaw* was not the plan architects' consideration of race as relevant in redistricting. Rather, in the Court's estimation, it was the virtual exclusion of other factors from the calculus. Traditional districting practices were cast aside, the Court concluded, with race alone steering placement of district lines.

The record before us does not show that race similarly overwhelmed traditional districting practices in Georgia. Although the Georgia General Assembly prominently considered race in shaping the Eleventh District, race did not crowd out all other factors, as the Court found it did in North Carolina's delineation of the *Shaw* district.

In contrast to the snake-like North Carolina district inspected in *Shaw*, Georgia's Eleventh District is hardly "bizarre," "extremely irregular," or "irrational on its face." Instead, the Eleventh District's design reflects significant consideration of "traditional districting factors (such as keeping political subdivisions intact) and the usual political process of compromise and trades for a variety of nonracial reasons.". . .

Nor does the Eleventh District disrespect the boundaries of political subdivisions. Of the 22 counties in the District, 14 are intact and 8 are divided. That puts the Eleventh District at about the state average in divided counties. . . .

Evidence at trial similarly shows that considerations other than race went into determining the Eleventh District's boundaries. For a "political reason"—to accommodate the request of an incumbent State Senator regarding the placement of the precinct in which his son lived—the DeKalb County portion of the Eleventh District was drawn to include a particular (largely white) precinct. The corridor through Effingham County was substantially narrowed at the request of a (white) State Representative. In Chatham County, the District was trimmed to exclude a heavily black community in Garden City because a State Representative wanted to keep the city intact inside the neighboring First District. The Savannah extension was configured by "the narrowest means possible" to avoid splitting the city of Port Wentworth.

Georgia's Eleventh District, in sum, is not an outlier district shaped without reference to familiar districting techniques. . . .

The Court suggests that it was not Georgia's legislature, but the U.S. Department of Justice, that effectively drew the lines, and that Department officers did so with nothing but race in mind. . . .

And although the Attorney General refused preclearance to the first two plans approved by Georgia's legislature, the State was not thereby disarmed; Georgia could have demanded relief from the Department's objections by instituting a civil action in the United States District Court for the District of Columbia, with ultimate review in this Court. Instead of pursuing that avenue, the State chose to adopt the plan here in controversy—a plan the State forcefully defends before us. We should respect Georgia's choice by taking its position on brief as genuine.

Along with attention to size, shape, and political subdivisions, the Court recognizes as an appropriate districting principle, "respect for . . . communities defined by actual shared interests." The Court finds no community here, however, because a report in the record showed "fractured political, social, and economic interests within the Eleventh District's black population."

But ethnicity itself can tie people together, as volumes of social science literature have documented—even people with divergent economic interests. For this reason, ethnicity is a significant force in political life. . . .

To accommodate the reality of ethnic bonds, legislatures have long drawn voting districts along ethnic lines. Our Nation's cities are full of districts identified by their ethnic character—Chinese, Irish, Italian, Jewish, Polish, Russian, for example. . . .

To separate permissible and impermissible use of race in legislative apportionment, the Court orders strict scrutiny for districting plans "predominantly motivated" by race. No longer can a State avoid judicial oversight by giving—as in this case—genuine and measurable consideration to traditional districting practices. Instead, a federal case can be mounted whenever plaintiffs plausibly allege that other factors carried less weight than race. This invitation to litigate against the State seems to me neither necessary nor proper.

The Court derives its test from diverse opinions on the relevance of race in contexts distinctly unlike apportionment. The controlling idea, the Court says, is "'the simple command [at the heart of the Constitution's guarantee of equal protection] that the Government must treat citizens as individuals, not as simply components of a racial, religious, sexual or national class.'"

In adopting districting plans, however, States do not treat people as individuals. Apportionment schemes, by their very nature, assemble people in groups. States do not assign voters to districts based on merit or achievement, standards States might use in hiring employees or engaging contractors. Rather, legislators classify voters in groups—by economic, geographical, political, or social characteristics—and then "reconcile the competing claims of [these] groups." *Davis v. Bandemer* (1986) (O'CONNOR, J., concurring in judgment).

That ethnicity defines some of these groups is a political reality. Until now, no constitutional infirmity has been seen in districting Irish or Italian voters together, for example, so long as the delineation does not abandon familiar apportionment practices. If Chinese-Americans and Russian-Americans may seek and secure group recognition in the delineation of voting districts, then African-Americans should not be dissimilarly treated. Otherwise, in the name of equal protection, we would shut out "the very minority group whose history in the United States gave birth to the Equal Protection Clause." See *Shaw* (STEVENS, J., dissenting). . . .

Only after litigation—under either the Voting Rights Act, the Court's new *Miller* standard, or both—will States now be assured that plans conscious of race are safe. Federal judges in large numbers may be drawn into the fray. This enlargement of the judicial role is unwarranted. The reapportionment plan that resulted from Georgia's political process merited this Court's approbation, not its condemnation. Accordingly, I dissent.

With *Miller v. Johnson* the Court continued on its path of applying strict scrutiny standards to legislative redistricting designed to create majority-minority districts. Once again, the decision was the result of a 5–4 voting split. The more conservative justices (Kennedy, O'Connor, Rehnquist, Scalia, and Thomas) formed a solid bloc against districts whose boundaries are "unexplainable on grounds other than race" and where the legislature had "subordinated traditional race-neutral districting principles . . . to racial considerations." This same five-justice coalition had constituted the majority in *Shaw v. Reno* two years earlier. The more moderate justices (Breyer, Ginsburg, Souter, and Stevens) expressed much more sympathy for legislative and executive branch actions to enhance the representation of historically disadvantaged minorities.

The Supreme Court was called upon to settle similar disputes arising from other states. *Shaw v. Hunt* (1996) involved the continuing litigation against the First and Twelfth Districts of North Carolina, the same districts that had been the subject of *Shaw v. Reno* and had been sent back to the lower courts for reconsideration. The district court concluded that, although the legislative boundaries were deliberately drawn with racial representation goals in mind, the plan was narrowly tailored to further a compelling state interest and therefore constitutionally valid. The Supreme Court reversed, finding that the state had segregated voters on the basis of race. Furthermore, the state had subordinated to racial factors the traditional districting principles of compactness, contiguity, and respect for political subdivisions. Although North Carolina argued that the legislature had drawn the boundaries to ameliorate the effects of past discrimination and to avoid conflict with the provisions of the Voting Rights Act, the justices found these reasons insufficiently compelling to satisfy the requirements of strict scrutiny. The districts were found to be an unconstitutional racial gerrymander.

Another 1996 case, *Bush v. Vera*, arose from actions taken by the Texas legislature when the state gained three additional seats in Congress following the 1990 Census. After the state reconfigured its congressional constituencies, six Texas voters filed suit claiming that

BOX 13-2 AFTERMATH . . .
MILLER V. JOHNSON

THE IMMEDIATE impact of *Miller v. Johnson*, which struck down Georgia's redistricting plan, was to send the map back to the state legislature for revision. Despite numerous attempts, the lawmakers were unable to develop an acceptable plan, and the task of redesigning the congressional districts fell to the federal district court. After considering several plans, the court approved a scheme that included only one majority black district. This judicially imposed redistricting plan was challenged by civil rights advocates. The Supreme Court upheld the plan in *Abrams v. Johnson* (1997), with the justices divided into the same 5–4 voting blocs that occurred in *Shaw v. Reno* and *Miller v. Johnson*.

Despite this legal setback, Georgia's African American representatives held their positions in Congress. Rep. Cynthia McKinney, whose district was the primary target of the *Miller v. Johnson* litigation, found herself representing a district that was 58.4 percent white. She captured 58 percent of the vote in 1996 and 61 percent in 1998. Rep. Sanford Bishop's Second District became 59.5 percent white under the revised apportionment plan; he was reelected with 54 percent of the vote in 1996 and 57 percent in 1998. John Lewis, the lone representative of a majority black district, ran unopposed in 1996 and received 79 percent of the vote in 1998.

Data for the entire House of Representatives tend to replicate what happened in Georgia. The growth in African American representatives peaked in the mid-1990s and has leveled off since then.

Year	Hispanic Representatives	African American Representatives
1985	11	20
1987	11	22
1989	10	23
1991	11	26
1993	17	39
1995	17	39
1997	17	37
1999	19	37

SOURCES: Norman J. Ornstein, Thomas E. Mann, and Michael J. Malbin, *Vital Statistics on Congress 1999–2000* (Washington, D.C.: The AEI Press, 2000); and Michael Barone and Grant Ujifusa, with Richard E. Cohen and Charles E. Cook Jr., *The Almanac of American Politics 2000* (Washington, D.C.: National Journal, 1999).

twenty-four of the state's thirty congressional districts were unconstitutional racial gerrymanders. The district court struck down three districts as being in violation of the Equal Protection Clause; two favored African American voters and one had a Hispanic majority. The state appealed to the Supreme Court. The justices ruled that the three majority-minority districts failed to satisfy constitutional requirements. The Court found that the districts were "bizarrely shaped and far from compact," and that those characteristics were due to the state subordinating traditional districting factors to racial motives.

The Court's post-1993 decisions on minority districts have been remarkably consistent. Each of these decisions held against supporters of majority-minority districts, and each was decided by a 5–4 vote. The majority has uniformly included Chief Justice Rehnquist and Justices Kennedy, O'Connor, Scalia, and Thomas. They have strongly asserted their opposition to what they see as racial gerrymandering. The more liberal dissenting bloc, since 1995 consisting of Justices Breyer, Ginsburg, Souter, and Stevens, has been equally consistent and vigorous. The members of the Court appear committed to their respective positions. As a consequence, any changes in Court personnel could result in radically different outcomes.

READINGS

Alfange, Dean, Jr. "Gerrymandering and the Constitution: Into the Thorns of the Thicket at Last." *Supreme Court Review* (1986): 175–257.

Cortner, Richard C. *The Apportionment Cases.* Knoxville: University of Tennessee Press, 1970.

Davidson, Chandler, and Bernard Grofman, eds. *Quiet Revolution in the South: The Impact of the Voting Rights Act, 1965–1990.* Princeton: Princeton University Press, 1994.

Dixon, Robert G. *Democratic Representation: Reapportionment in Law and Politics.* New York: Oxford University Press, 1968.

Ely, John Hart. *Democracy and Distrust.* Cambridge: Harvard University Press, 1980.

Grofman, Bernard. *Political Gerrymandering and the Courts.* New York: Agathon Press, 1990.

Grofman, Bernard, and Chandler Davidson, eds. *Controversies in Minority Voting: The Voting Rights Act in Perspective.* Washington, D.C.: The Brookings Institution, 1992.

Hamilton, Charles V. *The Bench and Ballot: Southern Federal Judges and Black Voters.* New York: Oxford University Press, 1973.

Hudson, David Michael. *Along Racial Lines: Consequences of the 1965 Voting Rights Act.* New York: Peter Lang, 1998.

Lewinson, Paul. *Race, Class and Party: A History of Negro Suffrage and White Politics in the South.* New York: Grosset and Dunlap, 1959.

Maveety, Nancy. *Representation Rights and the Burger Court Years.* Ann Arbor: University of Michigan Press, 1991.

Norell, Robert J. *Reaping the Whirlwind: The Civil Rights Movement in Tuskegee.* Chapel Hill: University of North Carolina Press, 1998.

Peacock, Anthony A., ed. *Affirmative Action and Representation:* Shaw v. Reno *and the Future of Voting Rights.* Durham: Carolina Academic Press, 1997.

Scher, Richard K., Jon L. Mills, and John J. Hotaling. *Voting Rights and Democracy: The Law and Politics of Districting.* Chicago: Nelson-Hall Publishers, 1997.

Schuck, Peter H. "The Thickest Thicket: Partisan Gerrymandering and the Judicial Regulation of Politics." *Columbia Law Review* 87 (November 1987): 1325–84.

Taper, Bernard. Gomillion v. Lightfoot: *Apartheid in Alabama.* New York: McGraw-Hill, 1967.

Thernston, Abigail. *Whose Votes Count?* Cambridge: Harvard University Press, 1987.

REFERENCE MATERIAL

APPENDICES

1. CONSTITUTION OF THE UNITED STATES

2. FEDERALIST PAPER, NO. 78

3. U.S. PRESIDENTS

4. THUMBNAIL SKETCH OF THE
   SUPREME COURT'S HISTORY

5. THE JUSTICES

6. NATURAL COURTS

7. SUPREME COURT CALENDAR

8. BRIEFING SUPREME COURT CASES

9. GLOSSARY

CONSTITUTION OF THE UNITED STATES

We the People of the United States, in Order to form a more perfect Union, establish Justice, insure domestic Tranquility, provide for the common defence, promote the general Welfare, and secure the Blessings of Liberty to ourselves and our Posterity, do ordain and establish this Constitution for the United States of America.

ARTICLE I

Section 1. All legislative Powers herein granted shall be vested in a Congress of the United States, which shall consist of a Senate and House of Representatives.

Section 2. The House of Representatives shall be composed of Members chosen every second Year by the People of the several States, and the Electors in each State shall have the Qualifications requisite for Electors of the most numerous Branch of the State Legislature.

No Person shall be a Representative who shall not have attained to the age of twenty five Years, and been seven Years a Citizen of the United States, and who shall not, when elected, be an Inhabitant of that State in which he shall be chosen.

[Representatives and direct Taxes shall be apportioned among the several States which may be included within this Union, according to their respective Numbers, which shall be determined by adding to the whole Number of free Persons, including those bound to Service for a Term of Years, and excluding Indians not taxed, three fifths of all other Persons.][1] The actual Enumeration shall be made within three Years after the first Meeting of the Congress of the United States, and within every subsequent Term of ten Years, in such Manner as they shall by Law direct. The Number of Representatives shall not exceed one for every thirty Thousand, but each State shall have at Least one Representative; and until such enumeration shall be made, the State of New Hampshire shall be entitled to chuse three, Massachusetts eight,

Rhode-Island and Providence Plantations one, Connecticut five, New-York six, New Jersey four, Pennsylvania eight, Delaware one, Maryland six, Virginia ten, North Carolina five, South Carolina five, and Georgia three.

When vacancies happen in the Representation from any State, the Executive Authority thereof shall issue Writs of Election to fill such Vacancies.

The House of Representatives shall chuse their Speaker and other Officers; and shall have the sole Power of Impeachment.

Section 3. The Senate of the United States shall be composed of two Senators from each State, [chosen by the Legislature thereof,][2] for six Years; and each Senator shall have one Vote.

Immediately after they shall be assembled in Consequence of the first Election, they shall be divided as equally as may be into three Classes. The Seats of the Senators of the first Class shall be vacated at the Expiration of the second Year, of the second Class at the Expiration of the fourth Year, and of the third Class at the Expiration of the sixth Year, so that one third may be chosen every second Year; [and if Vacancies happen by Resignation, or otherwise, during the Recess of the Legislature of any State, the Executive thereof may make temporary Appointments until the next Meeting of the Legislature, which shall then fill such Vacancies.][3]

No Person shall be a Senator who shall not have attained to the Age of thirty Years, and been nine Years a Citizen of the United States, and who shall not, when elected, be an Inhabitant of that State for which he shall be chosen.

The Vice President of the United States shall be President of the Senate, but shall have no Vote, unless they be equally divided.

The Senate shall chuse their other Officers, and also a President pro tempore, in the Absence of the Vice President, or when he shall exercise the Office of President of the United States.

---

1. The part in brackets was changed by section 2 of the Fourteenth Amendment.

2. The part in brackets was changed by the first paragraph of the Seventeenth Amendment.

3. The part in brackets was changed by the second paragraph of the Seventeenth Amendment.

The Senate shall have the sole Power to try all Impeachments. When sitting for that Purpose, they shall be on Oath or Affirmation. When the President of the United States is tried, the Chief Justice shall preside: And no Person shall be convicted without the Concurrence of two thirds of the Members present.

Judgment in Cases of Impeachment shall not extend further than to removal from Office, and disqualification to hold and enjoy any Office of honor, Trust or Profit under the United States: but the Party convicted shall nevertheless be liable and subject to Indictment, Trial, Judgment and Punishment, according to Law.

Section 4. The Times, Places and Manner of holding Elections for Senators and Representatives, shall be prescribed in each State by the Legislature thereof; but the Congress may at any time by Law make or alter such Regulations, except as to the Places of chusing Senators.

The Congress shall assemble at least once in every Year, and such Meeting shall [be on the first Monday in December],[4] unless they shall by Law appoint a different Day.

Section 5. Each House shall be the Judge of the Elections, Returns and Qualifications of its own Members, and a Majority of each shall constitute a Quorum to do Business; but a smaller Number may adjourn from day to day, and may be authorized to compel the Attendance of absent Members, in such Manner, and under such Penalties as each House may provide.

Each House may determine the Rules of its Proceedings, punish its Members for disorderly Behaviour, and, with the Concurrence of two thirds, expel a Member.

Each House shall keep a Journal of its Proceedings, and from time to time publish the same, excepting such Parts as may in their Judgment require Secrecy; and the Yeas and Nays of the Members of either House on any question shall, at the Desire of one fifth of those Present, be entered on the Journal.

Neither House, during the Session of Congress, shall, without the Consent of the other, adjourn for more than three days, nor to any other Place than that in which the two Houses shall be sitting.

Section 6. The Senators and Representatives shall receive a Compensation for their Services, to be ascertained by Law, and paid out of the Treasury of the United States. They shall in all Cases, except Treason, Felony and Breach of the Peace, be privileged from Arrest during their Attendance at the Session of their respective Houses, and in going to and returning from the same; and for any Speech or Debate in either House, they shall not be questioned in any other Place.

No Senator or Representative shall, during the Time for which he was elected, be appointed to any civil Office under the Authority of the United States, which shall have been created, or the Emoluments whereof shall have been encreased during such time;

4. The part in brackets was changed by section 2 of the Twentieth Amendment.

and no Person holding any Office under the United States, shall be a Member of either House during his Continuance in Office.

Section 7. All Bills for raising Revenue shall originate in the House of Representatives; but the Senate may propose or concur with Amendments as on other Bills.

Every Bill which shall have passed the House of Representatives and the Senate, shall, before it become a Law, be presented to the President of the United States; If he approve he shall sign it, but if not he shall return it, with his Objections to that House in which it shall have originated, who shall enter the Objections at large on their Journal, and proceed to reconsider it. If after such Reconsideration two thirds of that House shall agree to pass the Bill, it shall be sent, together with the Objections, to the other House, by which it shall likewise be reconsidered, and if approved by two thirds of that House, it shall become a Law. But in all such Cases the Votes of both Houses shall be determined by Yeas and Nays, and the Names of the Persons voting for and against the Bill shall be entered on the Journal of each House respectively. If any Bill shall not be returned by the President within ten Days (Sundays excepted) after it shall have been presented to him, the Same shall be a Law, in like Manner as if he had signed it, unless the Congress by their Adjournment prevent its Return, in which Case it shall not be a Law.

Every Order, Resolution, or Vote to which the Concurrence of the Senate and House of Representatives may be necessary (except on a question of Adjournment) shall be presented to the President of the United States; and before the Same shall take Effect, shall be approved by him, or being disapproved by him, shall be repassed by two thirds of the Senate and House of Representatives, according to the Rules and Limitations prescribed in the Case of a Bill.

Section 8. The Congress shall have Power To lay and collect Taxes, Duties, Imposts and Excises, to pay the Debts and provide for the common Defence and general Welfare of the United States; but all Duties, Imposts and Excises shall be uniform throughout the United States;

To borrow Money on the credit of the United States;

To regulate Commerce with foreign Nations, and among the several States, and with the Indian Tribes;

To establish an uniform Rule of Naturalization, and uniform Laws on the subject of Bankruptcies throughout the United States;

To coin Money, regulate the Value thereof, and of foreign Coin, and fix the Standard of Weights and Measures;

To provide for the Punishment of counterfeiting the Securities and current Coin of the United States;

To establish Post Offices and post Roads;

To promote the Progress of Science and useful Arts, by securing for limited Times to Authors and Inventors the exclusive Right to their respective Writings and Discoveries;

To constitute Tribunals inferior to the supreme Court;

To define and punish Piracies and Felonies committed on the high Seas, and Offences against the Law of Nations;

To declare War, grant Letters of Marque and Reprisal, and make Rules concerning Captures on Land and Water;

To raise and support Armies, but no Appropriation of Money to that Use shall be for a longer Term than two Years;

To provide and maintain a Navy;

To make Rules for the Government and Regulation of the land and naval Forces;

To provide for calling forth the Militia to execute the Laws of the Union, suppress Insurrections and repel Invasions;

To provide for organizing, arming, and disciplining, the Militia, and for governing such Part of them as may be employed in the Service of the United States, reserving to the States respectively, the Appointment of the Officers, and the Authority of training the Militia according to the discipline prescribed by Congress;

To exercise exclusive Legislation in all Cases whatsoever, over such District (not exceeding ten Miles square) as may, by Cession of particular States, and the Acceptance of Congress, become the Seat of the Government of the United States, and to exercise like Authority over all Places purchased by the Consent of the Legislature of the State in which the Same shall be, for the Erection of Forts, Magazines, Arsenals, dock-Yards, and other needful Buildings;—And

To make all Laws which shall be necessary and proper for carrying into Execution the foregoing Powers, and all other Powers vested by this Constitution in the Government of the United States, or in any Department or Officer thereof.

Section 9. The Migration or Importation of such Persons as any of the States now existing shall think proper to admit, shall not be prohibited by the Congress prior to the Year one thousand eight hundred and eight, but a Tax or duty may be imposed on such Importation, not exceeding ten dollars for each Person.

The Privilege of the Writ of Habeas Corpus shall not be suspended, unless when in Cases of Rebellion or Invasion the public Safety may require it.

No Bill of Attainder or ex post facto Law shall be passed.

No Capitation, or other direct, Tax shall be laid, unless in Proportion to the Census or Enumeration herein before directed to be taken.[5]

No Tax or Duty shall be laid on Articles exported from any State.

No Preference shall be given by any Regulation of Commerce or Revenue to the Ports of one State over those of another; nor shall Vessels bound to, or from, one State, be obliged to enter, clear, or pay Duties in another.

No Money shall be drawn from the Treasury, but in Consequence of Appropriations made by Law; and a regular Statement and Account of the Receipts and Expenditures of all public Money shall be published from time to time.

No Title of Nobility shall be granted by the United States: And no Person holding any Office of Profit or Trust under them, shall, without the Consent of the Congress, accept of any present, Emolument, Office, or Title, of any kind whatever, from any King, Prince, or foreign State.

Section 10. No State shall enter into any Treaty, Alliance, or Confederation; grant Letters of Marque and Reprisal; coin Money; emit Bills of Credit; make any Thing but gold and silver Coin a Tender in Payment of Debts; pass any Bill of Attainder, ex post facto Law, or Law impairing the Obligation of Contracts, or grant any Title of Nobility.

No State shall, without the Consent of the Congress, lay any Imposts or Duties on Imports or Exports, except what may be absolutely necessary for executing it's inspection Laws: and the net Produce of all Duties and Imposts, laid by any State on Imports or Exports, shall be for the Use of the Treasury of the United States; and all such Laws shall be subject to the Revision and Controul of the Congress.

No State shall, without the Consent of Congress, lay any Duty of Tonnage, keep Troops, or Ships of War in time of Peace, enter into any Agreement or Compact with another State, or with a foreign Power, or engage in War, unless actually invaded, or in such imminent Danger as will not admit of delay.

ARTICLE II

Section 1. The executive Power shall be vested in a President of the United States of America. He shall hold his Office during the Term of four Years, and, together with the Vice President, chosen for the same Term, be elected, as follows

Each State shall appoint, in such Manner as the Legislature thereof may direct, a Number of Electors, equal to the whole Number of Senators and Representatives to which the State may be entitled in the Congress: but no Senator or Representative, or Person holding an Office of Trust or Profit under the United States, shall be appointed an Elector.

[The Electors shall meet in their respective States, and vote by Ballot for two Persons, of whom one at least shall not be an Inhabitant of the same State with themselves. And they shall make a List of all the Persons voted for, and of the Number of Votes for each; which List they shall sign and certify, and transmit sealed to the Seat of the Government of the United States, directed to the President of the Senate. The President of the Senate shall, in the Presence of the Senate and House of Representatives, open all the Certificates, and the Votes shall then be counted. The Person having the greatest Number of Votes shall be the President, if such Number be a Majority of the whole Number of Electors appointed; and if there be more than one who have such Majority, and have an equal Number of Votes, then the House of Represen-

5. The Sixteenth Amendment gave Congress the power to tax incomes.

tatives shall immediately chuse by Ballot one of them for President; and if no Person have a Majority, then from the five highest on the list the said House shall in like Manner chuse the President. But in chusing the President, the Votes shall be taken by States, the Representation from each State having one Vote; A quorum for this Purpose shall consist of a Member or Members from two thirds of the States, and a Majority of all the States shall be necessary to a Choice. In every Case, after the Choice of the President, the Person having the greatest Number of Votes of the Electors shall be the Vice President. But if there should remain two or more who have equal Votes, the Senate shall chuse from them by Ballot the Vice President.] [6]

The Congress may determine the Time of chusing the Electors, and the Day on which they shall give their Votes; which Day shall be the same throughout the United States.

No Person except a natural born Citizen, or a Citizen of the United States, at the time of the Adoption of this Constitution, shall be eligible to the Office of President; neither shall any Person be eligible to that Office who shall not have attained to the Age of thirty five Years, and been fourteen Years a Resident within the United States.

In Case of the Removal of the President from Office, or of his Death, Resignation, or Inability to discharge the Powers and Duties of the said Office,[7] the Same shall devolve on the Vice President, and the Congress may by Law provide for the Case of Removal, Death, Resignation or Inability, both of the President and Vice President, declaring what Officer shall then act as President, and such Officer shall act accordingly, until the Disability be removed, or a President shall be elected.

The President shall, at stated Times, receive for his Services, a Compensation, which shall neither be encreased nor diminished during the Period for which he shall have been elected, and he shall not receive within that Period any other Emolument from the United States, or any of them.

Before he enter on the Execution of his Office, he shall take the following Oath or Affirmation:—"I do solemnly swear (or affirm) that I will faithfully execute the Office of President of the United States, and will to the best of my Ability, preserve, protect and defend the Constitution of the United States."

Section 2. The President shall be Commander in Chief of the Army and Navy of the United States, and of the Militia of the several States, when called into the actual Service of the United States; he may require the Opinion, in writing, of the principal Officer in each of the executive Departments, upon any Subject relating to the Duties of their respective Offices, and he shall have Power to grant Reprieves and Pardons for Offences against the United States, except in Cases of Impeachment.

He shall have Power, by and with the Advice and Consent of the Senate, to make Treaties, provided two thirds of the Senators present concur; and he shall nominate, and by and with the Advice and Consent of the Senate, shall appoint Ambassadors, other public Ministers and Consuls, Judges of the supreme Court, and all other Officers of the United States, whose Appointments are not herein otherwise provided for, and which shall be established by Law: but the Congress may by Law vest the Appointment of such inferior Officers, as they think proper, in the President alone, in the Courts of Law, or in the Heads of Departments.

The President shall have Power to fill up all Vacancies that may happen during the Recess of the Senate, by granting Commissions which shall expire at the End of their next Session.

Section 3. He shall from time to time give to the Congress Information of the State of the Union, and recommend to their Consideration such Measures as he shall judge necessary and expedient; he may, on extraordinary Occasions, convene both Houses, or either of them, and in Case of Disagreement between them, with Respect to the Time of Adjournment, he may adjourn them to such Time as he shall think proper; he shall receive Ambassadors and other public Ministers; he shall take Care that the Laws be faithfully executed, and shall Commission all the Officers of the United States.

Section 4. The President, Vice President and all civil Officers of the United States, shall be removed from Office on Impeachment for, and Conviction of, Treason, Bribery, or other high Crimes and Misdemeanors.

ARTICLE III

Section 1. The judicial Power of the United States, shall be vested in one supreme Court, and in such inferior Courts as the Congress may from time to time ordain and establish. The Judges, both of the supreme and inferior Courts, shall hold their Offices during good Behaviour, and shall, at stated Times, receive for their Services, a Compensation, which shall not be diminished during their Continuance in Office.

Section 2. The judicial Power shall extend to all Cases, in Law and Equity, arising under this Constitution, the Laws of the United States, and Treaties made, or which shall be made, under their Authority;—to all Cases affecting Ambassadors, other public Ministers and Consuls;—to all Cases of admiralty and maritime Jurisdiction;—to Controversies to which the United States shall be a Party;—to Controversies between two or more States;—between a State and Citizens of another State;[8]—between Citizens of different States;—between Citizens of the same State claiming Lands under Grants of different States, and between a State, or the Citizens thereof, and foreign States, Citizens or Subjects.[8]

In all Cases affecting Ambassadors, other public Ministers and

---

6. The material in brackets has been superseded by the Twelfth Amendment.

7. This provision has been affected by the Twenty-fifth Amendment.

8. These clauses were affected by the Eleventh Amendment.

Consuls, and those in which a State shall be Party, the supreme Court shall have original Jurisdiction. In all the other Cases before mentioned, the supreme Court shall have appellate Jurisdiction, both as to Law and Fact, with such Exceptions, and under such Regulations as the Congress shall make.

The Trial of all Crimes, except in Cases of Impeachment, shall be by Jury; and such Trial shall be held in the State where the said Crimes shall have been committed; but when not committed within any State, the Trial shall be at such Place or Places as the Congress may by Law have directed.

Section 3. Treason against the United States, shall consist only in levying War against them, or in adhering to their Enemies, giving them Aid and Comfort. No Person shall be convicted of Treason unless on the Testimony of two Witnesses to the same overt Act, or on Confession in open Court.

The Congress shall have Power to declare the Punishment of Treason, but no Attainder of Treason shall work Corruption of Blood, or Forfeiture except during the Life of the Person attainted.

ARTICLE IV

Section 1. Full Faith and Credit shall be given in each State to the public Acts, Records, and judicial Proceedings of every other State. And the Congress may by general Laws prescribe the Manner in which such Acts, Records and Proceedings shall be proved, and the Effect thereof.

Section 2. The Citizens of each State shall be entitled to all Privileges and Immunities of Citizens in the several States.

A Person charged in any State with Treason, Felony, or other Crime, who shall flee from Justice, and be found in another State, shall on Demand of the executive Authority of the State from which he fled, be delivered up, to be removed to the State having Jurisdiction of the Crime.

[No Person held to Service or Labour in one State, under the Laws thereof, escaping into another, shall, in Consequence of any Law or Regulation therein, be discharged from such Service or Labour, but shall be delivered up on Claim of the Party to whom such Service or Labour may be due.][9]

Section 3. New States may be admitted by the Congress into this Union; but no new State shall be formed or erected within the Jurisdiction of any other State; nor any State be formed by the Junction of two or more States, or Parts of States, without the Consent of the Legislatures of the States concerned as well as of the Congress.

The Congress shall have Power to dispose of and make all needful Rules and Regulations respecting the Territory or other Property belonging to the United States; and nothing in this Constitution shall be so construed as to Prejudice any Claims of the United States, or of any particular State.

Section 4. The United States shall guarantee to every State in this Union a Republican Form of Government, and shall protect each of them against Invasion; and on Application of the Legislature, or of the Executive (when the Legislature cannot be convened) against domestic Violence.

ARTICLE V

The Congress, whenever two thirds of both Houses shall deem it necessary, shall propose Amendments to this Constitution, or, on the Application of the Legislatures of two thirds of the several States, shall call a Convention for proposing Amendments, which, in either Case, shall be valid to all Intents and Purposes, as Part of this Constitution, when ratified by the Legislatures of three fourths of the several States, or by Conventions in three fourths thereof, as the one or the other Mode of Ratification may be proposed by the Congress; Provided [that no Amendment which may be made prior to the Year One thousand eight hundred and eight shall in any Manner affect the first and fourth Clauses in the Ninth Section of the first Article; and][10] that no State, without its Consent, shall be deprived of its equal Suffrage in the Senate.

ARTICLE VI

All Debts contracted and Engagements entered into, before the Adoption of this Constitution, shall be as valid against the United States under this Constitution, as under the Confederation.

This Constitution, and the Laws of the United States which shall be made in Pursuance thereof; and all Treaties made, or which shall be made, under the Authority of the United States, shall be the supreme Law of the Land; and the Judges in every State shall be bound thereby, any Thing in the Constitution or Laws of any State to the Contrary notwithstanding.

The Senators and Representatives before mentioned, and the Members of the several State Legislatures, and all executive and judicial Officers, both of the United States and of the several States, shall be bound by Oath or Affirmation, to support this Constitution; but no religious Test shall ever be required as a Qualification to any Office or public Trust under the United States.

ARTICLE VII

The Ratification of the Conventions of nine States, shall be sufficient for the Establishment of this Constitution between the States so ratifying the Same. Done in Convention by the Unanimous Consent of the States present the Seventeenth Day of September in the Year of our Lord one thousand seven hundred and Eighty seven and of the Independence of the United States of America the Twelfth. IN WITNESS whereof We have hereunto subscribed our Names,

George Washington,
President and deputy from Virginia.

9. This paragraph has been superseded by the Thirteenth Amendment.

10. Obsolete.

New Hampshire:	John Langdon,
	Nicholas Gilman.
Massachusetts:	Nathaniel Gorham,
	Rufus King.
Connecticut:	William Samuel Johnson,
	Roger Sherman.
New York:	Alexander Hamilton.
New Jersey:	William Livingston,
	David Brearley,
	William Paterson,
	Jonathan Dayton.
Pennsylvania:	Benjamin Franklin,
	Thomas Mifflin,
	Robert Morris,
	George Clymer,
	Thomas FitzSimons,
	Jared Ingersoll,
	James Wilson,
	Gouverneur Morris.
Delaware:	George Read,
	Gunning Bedford Jr.,
	John Dickinson,
	Richard Bassett,
	Jacob Broom.
Maryland:	James McHenry,
	Daniel of St. Thomas Jenifer,
	Daniel Carroll.
Virginia:	John Blair,
	James Madison Jr.
North Carolina:	William Blount,
	Richard Dobbs Spaight,
	Hugh Williamson.
South Carolina:	John Rutledge,
	Charles Cotesworth Pinckney,
	Charles Pinckney,
	Pierce Butler.
Georgia:	William Few,
	Abraham Baldwin.

[The language of the original Constitution, not including the Amendments, was adopted by a convention of the states on September 17, 1787, and was subsequently ratified by the states on the following dates: Delaware, December 7, 1787; Pennsylvania, December 12, 1787; New Jersey, December 18, 1787; Georgia, January 2, 1788; Connecticut, January 9, 1788; Massachusetts, February 6, 1788; Maryland, April 28, 1788; South Carolina, May 23, 1788; New Hampshire, June 21, 1788.

Ratification was completed on June 21, 1788.

The Constitution subsequently was ratified by Virginia, June 25, 1788; New York, July 26, 1788; North Carolina, November 21, 1789; Rhode Island, May 29, 1790; and Vermont, January 10, 1791.]

AMENDMENTS

Amendment I
(First ten amendments ratified December 15, 1791.)

Congress shall make no law respecting an establishment of religion, or prohibiting the free exercise thereof; or abridging the freedom of speech, or of the press; or the right of the people peaceably to assemble, and to petition the Government for a redress of grievances.

Amendment II

A well regulated Militia, being necessary to the security of a free State, the right of the people to keep and bear Arms, shall not be infringed.

Amendment III

No Soldier shall, in time of peace be quartered in any house, without the consent of the Owner, nor in time of war, but in a manner to be prescribed by law.

Amendment IV

The right of the people to be secure in their persons, houses, papers, and effects, against unreasonable searches and seizures, shall not be violated, and no Warrants shall issue, but upon probable cause, supported by Oath or affirmation, and particularly describing the place to be searched, and the persons or things to be seized.

Amendment V

No person shall be held to answer for a capital, or otherwise infamous crime, unless on a presentment or indictment of a Grand Jury, except in cases arising in the land or naval forces, or in the Militia, when in actual service in time of War or public danger; nor shall any person be subject for the same offence to be twice put in jeopardy of life or limb; nor shall be compelled in any criminal case to be a witness against himself, nor be deprived of life, liberty, or property, without due process of law; nor shall private property be taken for public use, without just compensation.

Amendment VI

In all criminal prosecutions, the accused shall enjoy the right to a speedy and public trial, by an impartial jury of the State and district wherein the crime shall have been committed, which district shall have been previously ascertained by law, and to be informed of the nature and cause of the accusation; to be confronted with the witnesses against him; to have compulsory process for obtaining witnesses in his favor, and to have the Assistance of Counsel for his defence.

Amendment VII

In Suits at common law, where the value in controversy shall exceed twenty dollars, the right of trial by jury shall be preserved, and no fact tried by a jury, shall be otherwise re-examined in any Court of the United States, than according to the rules of the common law.

Amendment VIII

Excessive bail shall not be required, nor excessive fines imposed, nor cruel and unusual punishments inflicted.

Amendment IX

The enumeration in the Constitution, of certain rights, shall not be construed to deny or disparage others retained by the people.

Amendment X

The powers not delegated to the United States by the Constitution, nor prohibited by it to the States, are reserved to the States respectively, or to the people.

Amendment XI

(Ratified February 7, 1795)

The Judicial power of the United States shall not be construed to extend to any suit in law or equity, commenced or prosecuted against one of the United States by Citizens of another State, or by Citizens or Subjects of any Foreign State.

Amendment XII

(Ratified June 15, 1804)

The Electors shall meet in their respective states and vote by ballot for President and Vice-President, one of whom, at least, shall not be an inhabitant of the same state with themselves; they shall name in their ballots the person voted for as President, and in distinct ballots the person voted for as Vice-President, and they shall make distinct lists of all persons voted for as President, and of all persons voted for as Vice-President, and of the number of votes for each, which lists they shall sign and certify, and transmit sealed to the seat of the government of the United States, directed to the President of the Senate;—The President of the Senate shall, in the presence of the Senate and House of Representatives, open all the certificates and the votes shall then be counted;—The person having the greatest number of votes for President, shall be the President, if such number be a majority of the whole number of Electors appointed; and if no person have such majority, then from the persons having the highest numbers not exceeding three on the list of those voted for as President, the House of Representatives shall choose immediately, by ballot, the President. But in choosing the President, the votes shall be taken by states, the representation from each state having one vote; a quorum for this purpose shall consist of a member or members from two-thirds of the states, and a majority of all the states shall be necessary to a choice. [And if the House of Representatives shall not choose a President whenever the right of choice shall devolve upon them, before the fourth day of March next following, then the Vice-President shall act as President, as in the case of the death or other constitutional disability of the President.][11] The person hav-

ing the greatest number of votes as Vice-President, shall be the Vice-President, if such number be a majority of the whole number of Electors appointed, and if no person have a majority, then from the two highest numbers on the list, the Senate shall choose the Vice-President; a quorum for the purpose shall consist of two-thirds of the whole number of Senators, and a majority of the whole number shall be necessary to a choice. But no person constitutionally ineligible to the office of President shall be eligible to that of Vice-President of the United States.

Amendment XIII

(Ratified December 6, 1865)

Section 1. Neither slavery nor involuntary servitude, except as a punishment for crime whereof the party shall have been duly convicted, shall exist within the United States, or any place subject to their jurisdiction.

Section 2. Congress shall have power to enforce this article by appropriate legislation.

Amendment XIV

(Ratified July 9, 1868)

Section 1. All persons born or naturalized in the United States, and subject to the jurisdiction thereof, are citizens of the United States and of the State wherein they reside. No State shall make or enforce any law which shall abridge the privileges or immunities of citizens of the United States; nor shall any State deprive any person of life, liberty, or property, without due process of law; nor deny to any person within its jurisdiction the equal protection of the laws.

Section 2. Representatives shall be apportioned among the several States according to their respective numbers, counting the whole number of persons in each State, excluding Indians not taxed. But when the right to vote at any election for the choice of electors for President and Vice President of the United States, Representatives in Congress, the Executive and Judicial officers of a State, or the members of the Legislature thereof, is denied to any of the male inhabitants of such State, being twenty-one years of age,[12] and citizens of the United States, or in any way abridged, except for participation in rebellion, or other crime, the basis of representation therein shall be reduced in the proportion which the number of such male citizens shall bear to the whole number of male citizens twenty-one years of age in such State.

Section 3. No person shall be a Senator or Representative in Congress, or elector of President and Vice President, or hold any office, civil or military, under the United States, or under any State, who, having previously taken an oath, as a member of Congress, or as an officer of the United States, or as a member of any State legislature, or as an executive or judicial officer of any State, to support the Constitution of the United States, shall have engaged in insurrection or rebellion against the same, or given aid

---

11. The part in brackets has been superseded by section 3 of the Twentieth Amendment.

12. See the Nineteenth and Twenty-sixth Amendments.

or comfort to the enemies thereof. But Congress may by a vote of two-thirds of each House, remove such disability.

Section 4. The validity of the public debt of the United States, authorized by law, including debts incurred for payment of pensions and bounties for services in suppressing insurrection or rebellion, shall not be questioned. But neither the United States nor any State shall assume or pay any debt or obligation incurred in aid of insurrection or rebellion against the United States, or any claim for the loss or emancipation of any slave; but all such debts, obligations and claims shall be held illegal and void.

Section 5. The Congress shall have power to enforce, by appropriate legislation, the provisions of this article.

Amendment XV

(Ratified February 3, 1870)

Section 1. The right of citizens of the United States to vote shall not be denied or abridged by the United States or by any State on account of race, color, or previous condition of servitude.

Section 2. The Congress shall have power to enforce this article by appropriate legislation.

Amendment XVI

(Ratified February 3, 1913)

The Congress shall have power to lay and collect taxes on incomes, from whatever source derived, without apportionment among the several States, and without regard to any census or enumeration.

Amendment XVII

(Ratified April 8, 1913)

The Senate of the United States shall be composed of two Senators from each State, elected by the people thereof, for six years; and each Senator shall have one vote. The electors in each State shall have the qualifications requisite for electors of the most numerous branch of the State legislatures.

When vacancies happen in the representation of any State in the Senate, the executive authority of such State shall issue writs of election to fill such vacancies: *Provided,* That the legislature of any State may empower the executive thereof to make temporary appointments until the people fill the vacancies by election as the legislature may direct.

This amendment shall not be so construed as to affect the election or term of any Senator chosen before it becomes valid as part of the Constitution.

[Amendment XVIII

(Ratified January 16, 1919)

Section 1. After one year from the ratification of this article the manufacture, sale, or transportation of intoxicating liquors within, the importation thereof into, or the exportation thereof from the United States and all territory subject to the jurisdiction thereof for beverage purposes is hereby prohibited.

Section 2. The Congress and the several States shall have concurrent power to enforce this article by appropriate legislation.

Section 3. This article shall be inoperative unless it shall have been ratified as an amendment to the Constitution by the legislatures of the several States, as provided in the Constitution, within seven years from the date of the submission hereof to the States by the Congress.][13]

Amendment XIX

(Ratified August 18, 1920)

The right of citizens of the United States to vote shall not be denied or abridged by the United States or by any State on account of sex.

Congress shall have power to enforce this article by appropriate legislation.

Amendment XX

(Ratified January 23, 1933)

Section 1. The terms of the President and Vice President shall end at noon on the 20th day of January, and the terms of Senators and Representatives at noon on the 3d day of January, of the years in which such terms would have ended if this article had not been ratified; and the terms of their successors shall then begin.

Section 2. The Congress shall assemble at least once in every year, and such meeting shall begin at noon on the 3d day of January, unless they shall by law appoint a different day.

Section 3.[14] If, at the time fixed for the beginning of the term of the President, the President elect shall have died, the Vice President elect shall become President. If a President shall not have been chosen before the time fixed for the beginning of his term, or if the President elect shall have failed to qualify, then the Vice President elect shall act as President until a President shall have qualified; and the Congress may by law provide for the case wherein neither a President elect nor a Vice President elect shall have qualified, declaring who shall then act as President, or the manner in which one who is to act shall be selected, and such person shall act accordingly until a President or Vice President shall have qualified.

Section 4. The Congress may by law provide for the case of the death of any of the persons from whom the House of Representatives may choose a President whenever the right of choice shall have devolved upon them, and for the case of the death of any of the persons from whom the Senate may choose a Vice President whenever the right of choice shall have devolved upon them.

Section 5. Sections 1 and 2 shall take effect on the 15th day of October following the ratification of this article.

Section 6. This article shall be inoperative unless it shall have been ratified as an amendment to the Constitution by the legisla-

13. This Amendment was repealed by section 1 of the Twenty-first Amendment.

14. See the Twenty-fifth Amendment.

tures of three-fourths of the several States within seven years from the date of its submission.

Amendment XXI

(Ratified December 5, 1933)

Section 1. The eighteenth article of amendment to the Constitution of the United States is hereby repealed.

Section 2. The transportation or importation into any State, Territory, or possession of the United States for delivery or use therein of intoxicating liquors, in violation of the laws thereof, is hereby prohibited.

Section 3. This article shall be inoperative unless it shall have been ratified as an amendment to the Constitution by conventions in the several States, as provided in the Constitution, within seven years from the date of the submission hereof to the States by the Congress.

Amendment XXII

(Ratified February 27, 1951)

Section 1. No person shall be elected to the office of the President more than twice, and no person who has held the office of President, or acted as President, for more than two years of a term to which some other person was elected President shall be elected to the office of the President more than once. But this Article shall not apply to any person holding the office of President when this Article was proposed by the Congress, and shall not prevent any person who may be holding the office of President, or acting as President, during the term within which this Article become operative from holding the office of President or acting as President during the remainder of such term.

Section 2. This article shall be inoperative unless it shall have been ratified as an amendment to the Constitution by the legislatures of three-fourths of the several States within seven years from the date of its submission to the States by the Congress.

Amendment XXIII

(Ratified March 29, 1961)

Section 1. The District constituting the seat of Government of the United States shall appoint in such manner as the Congress may direct:

A number of electors of President and Vice President equal to the whole number of Senators and Representatives in Congress to which the District would be entitled if it were a State, but in no event more than the least populous State; they shall be in addition to those appointed by the States, but they shall be considered, for the purposes of the election of President and Vice President, to be electors appointed by a State; and they shall meet in the District and perform such duties as provided by the twelfth article of amendment.

Section 2. The Congress shall have power to enforce this article by appropriate legislation.

Amendment XXIV

(Ratified January 23, 1964)

Section 1. The right of citizens of the United States to vote in any primary or other election for President or Vice President, for electors for President or Vice President, or for Senator or Representative in Congress, shall not be denied or abridged by the United States or any State by reason of failure to pay any poll tax or other tax.

Section 2. The Congress shall have power to enforce this article by appropriate legislation.

Amendment XXV

(Ratified February 10, 1967)

Section 1. In case of the removal of the President from office or of his death or resignation, the Vice President shall become President.

Section 2. Whenever there is a vacancy in the office of the Vice President, the President shall nominate a Vice President who shall take office upon confirmation by a majority vote of both Houses of Congress.

Section 3. Whenever the President transmits to the President pro tempore of the Senate and the Speaker of the House of Representatives his written declaration that he is unable to discharge the powers and duties of his office, and until he transmits to them a written declaration to the contrary, such powers and duties shall be discharged by the Vice President as Acting President.

Section 4. Whenever the Vice President and a majority of either the principal officers of the executive departments or of such other body as Congress may by law provide, transmit to the President pro tempore of the Senate and the Speaker of the House of Representatives their written declaration that the President is unable to discharge the powers and duties of his office, the Vice President shall immediately assume the powers and duties of the office as Acting President.

Thereafter, when the President transmits to the President pro tempore of the Senate and the Speaker of the House of Representatives his written declaration that no inability exists, he shall resume the powers and duties of his office unless the Vice President and a majority of either the principal officers of the executive department or of such other body as Congress may by law provide, transmit within four days to the President pro tempore of the Senate and the Speaker of the House of Representatives their written declaration that the President is unable to discharge the powers and duties of his office. Thereupon Congress shall decide the issue, assembling within forty-eight hours for that purpose if not in session. If the Congress, within twenty-one days after receipt of the latter written declaration, or, if Congress is not in session, within twenty-one days after Congress is required to assemble, determines by two-thirds vote of both Houses that the President is unable to discharge the powers and duties of his office, the Vice

President shall continue to discharge the same as Acting President; otherwise, the President shall resume the powers and duties of his office.

Amendment XXVI

(Ratified July 1, 1971)

Section 1. The right of citizens of the United States, who are eighteen years of age or older, to vote shall not be denied or abridged by the United States or by any State on account of age.

Section 2. The Congress shall have power to enforce this article by appropriate legislation.

Amendment XXVII

(Ratified May 7, 1992)

No law varying the compensation for the services of the Senators and Representatives shall take effect, until an election of Representatives shall have intervened.

SOURCE: *United States Government Manual, 1993–94* (Washington, D.C.: Government Printing Office, 1993), 5–20.

FEDERALIST PAPER, NO. 78

A VIEW OF THE CONSTITUTION OF THE JUDICIAL DEPARTMENT IN RELATION TO THE TENURE OF GOOD BEHAVIOUR

We proceed now to an examination of the judiciary department of the proposed government.

In unfolding the defects of the existing Confederation, the utility and necessity of a federal judicature have been clearly pointed out. It is the less necessary to recapitulate the considerations there urged as the propriety of the institution in the abstract is not disputed; the only questions which have been raised being relative to the manner of constituting it, and to its extent. To these points, therefore, our observations shall be confined.

The manner of constituting it seems to embrace these several objects: 1st. The mode of appointing the judges. 2nd. The tenure by which they are to hold their places. 3rd. The partition of the judiciary authority between different courts and their relations to each other.

First. As to the mode of appointing the judges: this is the same with that of appointing the officers of the Union in general and has been so fully discussed in the two last numbers that nothing can be said here which would not be useless repetition.

Second. As to the tenure by which the judges are to hold their places: this chiefly concerns their duration in office, the provisions for their support, the precautions for their responsibility.

According to the plan of the convention, all judges who may be appointed by the United States are to hold their offices *during good behavior;* which is conformable to the most approved of the State constitutions, and among the rest, to that of the State. Its propriety having been drawn into question by the adversaries of that plan is no light symptom of the rage for objection which disorders their imaginations and judgments. The standard of good behavior for the continuance in office of the judicial magistracy is certainly one of the most valuable of the modern improvements in the practice of government. In a monarchy it is an excellent barrier to the despotism of the prince; in a republic it is a no less excellent barrier to the encroachments and oppressions of the representative body. And it is the best expedient which can be devised in any government to secure a steady, upright, and impartial administration of the laws.

Whoever attentively considers the different departments of power must perceive that, in a government in which they are separated from each other, the judiciary, from the nature of its functions, will always be the least dangerous to the political rights of the Constitution; because it will be least in a capacity to annoy or injure them. The executive not only dispenses the honors but holds the sword of the community. The legislature not only commands the purse but prescribes the rules by which the duties and rights of every citizen are to be regulated. The judiciary, on the contrary, has no influence over either the sword or the purse; no direction either of the strength or of the wealth of the society, and can take no active resolution whatever. It may truly be said to have neither FORCE nor WILL but merely judgment; and must ultimately depend upon the aid of the executive arm even for the efficacy of its judgments.

This simple view of the matter suggests several important consequences. It proves incontestably that the judiciary is beyond comparison the weakest of the three departments of power; that it can never attack with success either of the other two; and that all possible care is requisite to enable it to defend itself against their attacks. It equally proves that though individual oppression may now and then proceed from the courts of justice, the general liberty of the people can never be endangered from that quarter; I mean so long as the judiciary remains truly distinct from both the legislature and the executive. For I agree that "there is no liberty if the power of judging be not separated from the legislative and executive powers." And it proves, in the last place, that as liberty can have nothing to fear from the judiciary alone, but would have everything to fear from its union with either of the other departments; that as all the effects of such a union must ensue from a dependence of the former on the latter, notwithstanding a nominal and apparent separation; that as, from the natural feebleness of the judiciary, it is in continual jeopardy of being overpowered, awed, or influenced by its co-ordinate branches; and that as nothing can contribute so much to its firmness and independence as permanency in office, this quality may therefore be justly regarded as an indispensable ingredient in its constitution, and, in a great measure, as the citadel of the public justice and the public security.

The complete independence of the courts of justice is peculiarly essential in a limited Constitution. By a limited Constitution, I understand one which contains certain specified exceptions to the legislative authority; such, for instance, as that it shall pass no bills of attainder, no *ex post facto* laws, and the like. Limitations of this kind can be preserved in practice no other way than through the medium of courts of justice, whose duty it must be to declare all acts contrary to the manifest tenor of the Constitution void. Without this, all the reservations of particular rights or privileges would amount to nothing.

Some perplexity respecting the rights of the courts to pronounce legislative acts void, because contrary to the Constitution, has arisen from an imagination that the doctrine would imply a superiority of the judiciary to the legislative power. It is urged that the authority which can declare the acts of another void must necessarily be superior to the one whose acts may be declared void. As this doctrine is of great importance in all the American constitutions, a brief discussion of the grounds on which it rests cannot be unacceptable.

There is no position which depends on clearer principles than that every act of a delegated authority, contrary to the tenor of the commission under which it is exercised, is void. No legislative act, therefore, contrary to the Constitution, can be valid. To deny this would be to affirm that the deputy is greater than his principal; that the servant is above his master; that the representatives of the people are superior to the people themselves; that men acting by virtue of powers may do not only what their powers do not authorize, but what they forbid.

If it be said that the legislative body are themselves the constitutional judges of their own powers and that the construction they put upon them is conclusive upon the other departments it may be answered that this cannot be the natural presumption where it is not to be collected from any particular provisions in the Constitution. It is not otherwise to be supposed that the Constitution could intend to enable the representatives of the people to substitute their *will* to that of their constituents. It is far more rational to suppose that the courts were designed to be an intermediate body between the people and the legislature in order, among other things, to keep the latter within the limits assigned to their authority. The interpretation of the laws is the proper and peculiar province of the courts. A constitution is, in fact, and must be regarded by the judges as, a fundamental law. It therefore belongs to them to ascertain its meaning as well as the meaning of any particular act proceeding from the legislative body. If there should happen to be an irreconcilable variance between the two, that which has the superior obligation and validity ought, of course, to be preferred: or, in other words, the Constitution ought to be preferred to the statute, the intention of the people to the intention of their agents.

Nor does this conclusion by any means suppose a superiority of the judicial to the legislative power. It only supposes that the power of the people is superior to both, and that where the will of the legislature, declared in its statutes, stands in opposition to that of the people, declared in the Constitution, the judges ought to be governed by the latter rather than the former. They ought to regulate their decisions by the fundamental laws rather than by those which are not fundamental.

This exercise of judicial discretion in determining between two contradictory laws is exemplified in a familiar instance. It not uncommonly happens that there are two statutes existing at one time, clashing in whole or in part with each other and neither of them containing any repealing clause or expression. In such a case, it is the province of the courts to liquidate and fix their meaning and operation. So far as they can, by fair construction, be reconciled to each other, reason and law conspire to dictate that this should be done; where this is impracticable, it becomes a matter of necessity to give effect to one in exclusion of the other. The rule which has obtained in the courts for determining their relative validity is that the last in order of time shall be preferred to the first. But this is a mere rule of construction, not derived from any positive law but from the nature and reason of the thing. It is a rule not enjoined upon the courts by legislative provision but adopted by themselves, as consonant to truth and propriety, for the direction of their conduct as interpreters of the law. They thought it reasonable that between the interfering acts of an *equal* authority that which was the last indication of its will should have the preference.

But in regard to the interfering acts of a superior and subordinate authority of an original and derivative power, the nature and reason of the thing indicate the converse of that rule as proper to be followed. They teach us that the prior act of a superior ought to be preferred to the subsequent act of an inferior and subordinate authority; and that accordingly, whenever a particular statute contravenes the Constitution, it will be the duty of the judicial tribunals to adhere to the latter and disregard the former.

It can be of no weight to say that the courts, on the pretense of a repugnancy, may substitute their own pleasure to the constitutional intentions of the legislature. This might as well happen in the case of two contradictory statutes; or it might as well happen in every adjudication upon any single statute. The courts must declare the sense of the law; and if they should be disposed to exercise WILL instead of JUDGMENT, the consequence would equally be the substitution of their pleasure for that of the legislative body. The observation, if it proved anything, would prove that there ought to be no judges distinct from that body.

If, then, the courts of justice are to be considered as the bulwarks of a limited Constitution against legislative encroachments, this consideration will afford a strong argument for the permanent tenure of judicial offices, since nothing will contribute so much as this to that independent spirit in the judges which must be essential to the faithful performance of so arduous a duty.

This independence of the judges is equally requisite to guard the Constitution and the rights of individuals from the effects of those ill humors which the arts of designing men, or the influence of particular conjunctures, sometimes disseminate among the people themselves, and which, though they speedily give place to better information, and more deliberate reflection, have a tendency, in the meantime, to occasion dangerous innovations in the government, and serious oppressions of the minor party in the community. Though I trust the friends of the proposed Constitution will never concur with its enemies in questioning that fundamental principle of republican government which admits the right of the people to alter or abolish the established Constitution whenever they find it inconsistent with their happiness; yet it is not to be inferred from this principle that the representatives of the people, whenever a momentary inclination happens to lay hold of a majority of their constituents incompatible with the provisions in the existing Constitution, would, on that account, be justifiable in a violation of those provisions; or that the courts would be under a greater obligation to connive at infractions in this shape than when they had proceeded wholly from the cabals of the representative body. Until the people have, by some solemn and authoritative act, annulled or changed the established form, it is binding upon themselves collectively, as well as individually; and no presumption, or even knowledge, of their sentiment can warrant their representatives in a departure from it prior to such an act. But it is easy to see that it would require an uncommon portion of fortitude in the judges to do their duty as faithful guardians of the Constitution, where legislative invasions of it had been instigated by the major voice of the community.

But it is not with a view to infractions of the Constitution only that the independence of the judges may be an essential safeguard against the effects of occasional ill humors in the society. These sometimes extend no farther than to the injury of the private rights of particular classes of citizens, by unjust and partial laws. Here also the firmness of the judicial magistracy is of vast importance in mitigating the severity and confining the operation of such laws. It not only serves to moderate the immediate mischiefs of those which may have been passed but it operates as a check upon the legislative body in passing them; who, perceiving that obstacles to the success of an iniquitous intention are to be expected from the scruples of the courts, are in a manner compelled, by the very motives of the injustice they meditate, to qualify their attempts. This is a circumstance calculated to have more influence upon the character of our governments than but few may be aware of. The benefits of the integrity and moderation of the judi-

ciary have already been felt in more States than one; and though they may have displeased those whose sinister expectations they may have disappointed, they must have commanded the esteem and applause of all the virtuous and disinterested. Considerate men of every description ought to prize whatever will tend to beget or fortify that temper in the courts; as no man can be sure that he may not be tomorrow the victim of a spirit of injustice, by which he may be a gainer today. And every man must now feel that the inevitable tendency of such a spirit is to sap the foundations of public and private confidence and to introduce in its stead universal distrust and distress.

That inflexible and uniform adherence to the rights of the Constitution, and of individuals, which we perceive to be indispensable in the courts of justice, can certainly not be expected from judges who hold their offices by a temporary commission. Periodical appointments, however regulated, or by whomsoever made, would, in some way or other, be fatal to their necessary independence. If the power of making them was committed either to the executive or legislature there would be danger of an improper complaisance to the branch which possessed it; if to both, there would be an unwillingness to hazard the displeasure of either; if to the people, or to persons chosen by them for the special purpose, there would be too great a disposition to consult popularity to justify a reliance that nothing would be consulted but the Constitution and the laws.

There is yet a further and weighty reason for the permanency of the judicial offices which is deducible from the nature of the qualifications they require. It has been frequently remarked with great propriety that a voluminous code of laws is one of the inconveniences necessarily connected with the advantages of a free government. To avoid an arbitrary discretion in the courts, it is indispensable that they should be bound down by strict rules and precedents which serve to define and point out their duty in every particular case that comes before them; and it will readily be conceived from the variety of controversies which grow out of the folly and wickedness of mankind that the records of those precedents must unavoidably swell to a very considerable bulk and must demand long and laborious study to acquire a competent knowledge of them. Hence it is that there can be but few men in the society who will have sufficient skill in the laws to qualify them for the stations of judges. And making the proper deductions for the ordinary depravity of human nature, the number must be still smaller of those who unite the requisite integrity with the requisite knowledge. These considerations apprise us that the government can have no great option between fit characters; and that a temporary duration in office which would naturally discourage such characters from quitting a lucrative line of practice to accept a seat on the bench would have a tendency to throw the administration of justice into hands less able and less well qualified to conduct it with utility and dignity. In the present circumstances of this country and in those in which it is likely to be for a long time to come, the disadvantages on this score would be greater than they may at first sight appear; but it must be confessed that they are far inferior to those which present themselves under the other aspects of the subject.

Upon the whole, there can be no room to doubt that the convention acted wisely in copying from the models of those constitutions which have established *good behavior* as the tenure of their judicial offices, in the point of duration; and that so far from being blamable on this account, their plan would have been inexcusably defective if it had wanted this important feature of good government. The experience of Great Britain affords an illustrious comment on the excellence of the institution.

PUBLIUS [Hamilton]

APPENDIX 3
U.S. PRESIDENTS

President	Political Party	Term of Service
George Washington	Federalist	April 30, 1789–March 4, 1793
George Washington	Federalist	March 4, 1793–March 4, 1797
John Adams	Federalist	March 4, 1797–March 4, 1801
Thomas Jefferson	Democratic Republican	March 4, 1801–March 4, 1805
Thomas Jefferson	Democratic Republican	March 4, 1805–March 4, 1809
James Madison	Democratic Republican	March 4, 1809–March 4, 1813
James Madison	Democratic Republican	March 4, 1813–March 4, 1817
James Monroe	Democratic Republican	March 4, 1817–March 4, 1821
James Monroe	Democratic Republican	March 4, 1821–March 4, 1825
John Q. Adams	Democratic Republican	March 4, 1825–March 4, 1829
Andrew Jackson	Democrat	March 4, 1829–March 4, 1833
Andrew Jackson	Democrat	March 4, 1833–March 4, 1837
Martin Van Buren	Democrat	March 4, 1837–March 4, 1841
W. H. Harrison	Whig	March 4, 1841–April 4, 1841
John Tyler	Whig	April 6, 1841–March 4, 1845
James K. Polk	Democrat	March 4, 1845–March 4, 1849
Zachary Taylor	Whig	March 4, 1849–July 9, 1850
Millard Fillmore	Whig	July 10, 1850–March 4, 1853
Franklin Pierce	Democrat	March 4, 1853–March 4, 1857
James Buchanan	Democrat	March 4, 1857–March 4, 1861
Abraham Lincoln	Republican	March 4, 1861–March 4, 1865
Abraham Lincoln	Republican	March 4, 1865–April 15, 1865
Andrew Johnson	Republican	April 15, 1865–March 4, 1869
Ulysses S. Grant	Republican	March 4, 1869–March 4, 1873
Ulysses S. Grant	Republican	March 4, 1873–March 4, 1877
Rutherford B. Hayes	Republican	March 4, 1877–March 4, 1881
James A. Garfield	Republican	March 4, 1881–Sept. 19, 1881
Chester A. Arthur	Republican	Sept. 20, 1881–March 4, 1885
Grover Cleveland	Democrat	March 4, 1885–March 4, 1889

President	Political Party	Term of Service
Benjamin Harrison	Republican	March 4, 1889–March 4, 1893
Grover Cleveland	Democrat	March 4, 1893–March 4, 1897
William McKinley	Republican	March 4, 1897–March 4, 1901
William McKinley	Republican	March 4, 1901–Sept. 14, 1901
Theodore Roosevelt	Republican	Sept. 14, 1901–March 4, 1905
Theodore Roosevelt	Republican	March 4, 1905–March 4, 1909
William H. Taft	Republican	March 4, 1909–March 4, 1913
Woodrow Wilson	Democrat	March 4, 1913–March 4, 1917
Woodrow Wilson	Democrat	March 4, 1917–March 4, 1921
Warren G. Harding	Republican	March 4, 1921–Aug. 2, 1923
Calvin Coolidge	Republican	Aug. 3, 1923–March 4, 1925
Calvin Coolidge	Republican	March 4, 1925–March 4, 1929
Herbert Hoover	Republican	March 4, 1929–March 4, 1933
Franklin D. Roosevelt	Democrat	March 4, 1933–Jan. 20, 1937
Franklin D. Roosevelt	Democrat	Jan. 20, 1937–Jan. 20, 1941
Franklin D. Roosevelt	Democrat	Jan. 20, 1941–Jan. 20, 1945
Franklin D. Roosevelt	Democrat	Jan. 20, 1945–April 12, 1945
Harry S. Truman	Democrat	April 12, 1945–Jan. 20, 1949
Harry S. Truman	Democrat	Jan. 20, 1949–Jan. 20, 1953
Dwight D. Eisenhower	Republican	Jan. 20, 1953–Jan. 20, 1957
Dwight D. Eisenhower	Republican	Jan. 20, 1957–Jan. 20, 1961
John F. Kennedy	Democrat	Jan. 20, 1961–Nov. 22, 1963
Lyndon B. Johnson	Democrat	Nov. 22, 1963–Jan. 20, 1965
Lyndon B. Johnson	Democrat	Jan. 20, 1965–Jan. 20, 1969
Richard Nixon	Republican	Jan. 20, 1969–Jan. 20, 1973
Richard Nixon	Republican	Jan. 20, 1973–Aug. 9, 1974
Gerald R. Ford	Republican	Aug. 9, 1974–Jan. 20, 1977
Jimmy Carter	Democrat	Jan. 20, 1977–Jan. 20, 1981
Ronald Reagan	Republican	Jan. 20, 1981–Jan. 20, 1985
Ronald Reagan	Republican	Jan. 20, 1985–Jan. 20, 1989
George Bush	Republican	Jan. 20, 1989–Jan. 20, 1993
William J. Clinton	Democrat	Jan. 20, 1993–Jan. 20, 1997
William J. Clinton	Democrat	Jan. 20, 1997–Jan. 20, 2001

THUMBNAIL SKETCH OF THE SUPREME COURT'S HISTORY

Court Era	Chief Justices	Defining Characteristics	Major Court Cases
Developmental Period (1789–1800)	John Jay (1789–1795) John Rutledge (1795) Oliver Ellsworth (1796–1800)	Low prestige: spotty attendance by justices, resignations for more "prestigious positions," hears about fifty cases Business of the Court: largely admiralty and maritime disputes Use of seriatim opinion practice	*Chisholm v. Georgia* (1793) *Ware v. Hylton* (1796) *Hylton v. United States* (1796)
The Marshall Court (1801–1835)	John Marshall (1801–1835)	Establishment of Court's role in governmental process Strong Court support for national powers (especially commerce) over states' rights Use of "Opinions of the Court," rather than seriatim practice Beginning of systematic reporting of Court opinions Despite the importance of its opinions interpreting the Constitution, the business of the Court continues to involve private law issues (maritime, property, contracts)	*Marbury v. Madison* (1803) *Fletcher v. Peck* (1810) *Dartmouth College v. Woodward* (1819) *McCulloch v. Maryland* (1819) *Cohens v. Virginia* (1821) *Gibbons v. Ogden* (1824)
Taney and Civil War Courts (1836–1888)	Roger Taney (1836–1864) Salmon Chase (1864–1873) Morrison Waite (1874–1888)	Continued assertion of federal power over states (with some accommodation for state police powers) Growing North–South splits on the Court Court showdowns with Congress at the onset and conclusion of the Civil War Growth of Court's caseload, with the majority of post–Civil War cases involving private law issues and war litigation Congress fixes Court size at nine	*Charles River Bridge v. Warren Bridge* (1837) *New York v. Miln* (1837) *Luther v. Borden* (1849) *Scott v. Sandford* (1857) *Ex parte Milligan* (1866) *Ex parte McCardle* (1869) *Civil Rights Cases* (1883)
Conservative Court Eras (1889–1937)	Melville Fuller (1888–1910) Edward White (1910–1921) William Howard Taft (1921–1930) Charles Evans Hughes (1930–1937)	But for a brief period reflecting progressivism, the Courts of this era tended to protect business interests over governmental police powers Court sets "civil rights" policy of "separate but equal" Congress relieves justices of circuit-riding duty	*United States v. E. C. Knight* (1895) *Pollock v. Farmers' Loan* (1895) *Plessy v. Ferguson* (1896) *Allgeyer v. Louisiana* (1897) *Lochner v. New York* (1905) *Hammer v. Dagenhart* (1918)

Court Era	Chief Justices	Defining Characteristics	Major Court Cases
		Congress, in 1925 Judiciary Act, gives Court greater discretion over its docket Despite Judiciary Act, Court's docket continues to grow, with many cases reflecting economic issues (e.g., congressional power under the Commerce Clause) Some important construction of Bill of Rights guarantees (protection of rights increases after WW I) Showdown with FDR over New Deal legislation: Court continues to strike down New Deal leading the president to propose a Court-packing plan	*Schenck v. United States* (1919) *Adkins v. Children's Hospital* (1923) *Near v. Minnesota* (1931) *Powell v. Alabama* (1932) *Schechter Poultry v. United States* (1935)
The Roosevelt and World War II Court Eras (1937–1953)	Charles Evans Hughes (1937–1941) Harlan Fiske Stone (1941–1946) Fred Vinson (1946–1953)	With the "switch in time that saved nine" the Court begins to uphold federal regulations under the Commerce Clause, as well as state use of police powers Expansion of rights and liberties, until WW II and ensuing cold war Increases in nonconsensual behavior (dissents and concurrences) among the justices	*NLRB v. Jones & Laughlin Steel* (1937) *United States v. Carolene Products* (1938) *Korematsu v. United States* (1944) *Dennis v. United States* (1951) *Youngstown Sheet & Tube v. Sawyer* (1952)
The Warren Court Era (1953–1969)	Earl Warren (1953–1969)	Expansion of rights, liberties, and criminal justice Establishment of the right to privacy Emergence of Court as national policy maker Continued increase in Court's docket, with steady growth in the number of *in forma pauperis* petitions Growth in the percentage of constitutional cases on Court's plenary docket First black (Marshall, 1967) appointed to the Court	*Brown v. Board of Education* (1954) *Roth v. United States* (1957) *Mapp v. Ohio* (1961) *Baker v. Carr* (1962) *Abington School District v. Schempp* (1963) *Gideon v. Wainwright* (1963) *Heart of Atlanta Motel v. United States* (1964) *New York Times v. Sullivan* (1964) *Griswold v. Connecticut* (1965) *Miranda v. Arizona* (1966)
Republican Court Eras (1969–)	Warren Burger (1969–1986) William Rehnquist (1986–)	Attempts in some areas (e.g., criminal law) to limit or rescind Warren Court rulings Expansion of women's rights, including right to abortion Some attempt to increase state power Increased church/state accommodation Legitimation of affirmative action policies, with increasing restrictions in the 1990s Rejection of race-based legislative districting Increased attention to interbranch, separation of powers disputes Appointment of first woman (O'Connor, 1981) to the Court First justice (Ginsburg, 1993) appointed by a Democratic president since 1967	*Reed v. Reed* (1971) *Roe v. Wade* (1973) *Miller v. California* (1973) *United States v. Nixon* (1974) *Buckley v. Valeo* (1976) *Gregg v. Georgia* (1976) *Regents of the University of California v. Bakke* (1978) *United States v. Leon* (1984) *Garcia v. SAMTA* (1985) *Planned Parenthood of Southeastern Pennsylvania v. Casey* (1992) *United States v. Lopez* (1995) *Adarand Constructors, Inc. v. Peña* (1995) *Clinton v. Jones* (1997) *Alden v. Maine* (1999) *Mitchell v. Helms* (2000) *Boy Scouts of America v. Dale* (2000)

APPENDIX 5
THE JUSTICES

The justices of the Supreme Court are listed below in alphabetical order, with their birth and death years, state from which they were appointed, political party affiliation at time of appointment, educational institutions attended, appointing president, confirmation date and vote, date of service termination, and significant preappointment offices and activities.

Baldwin, Henry (1780–1844). Pennsylvania. Democrat. Yale. Nominated associate justice by Andrew Jackson; confirmed 1830 by 41–2 vote; died in office 1844. U.S. representative.

Barbour, Philip Pendleton (1783–1841). Virginia. Democrat. College of William and Mary. Nominated associate justice by Andrew Jackson; confirmed 1836 by 30–11 vote; died in office 1841. Virginia state legislator, U.S. representative, U.S. Speaker of the House, state court judge, federal district court judge.

Black, Hugo Lafayette (1886–1971). Alabama. Democrat. Birmingham Medical College, University of Alabama. Nominated associate justice by Franklin Roosevelt; confirmed 1937 by 63–16 vote; retired 1971. Alabama police court judge, county solicitor, U.S. senator.

Blackmun, Harry Andrew (1908–1999). Minnesota. Republican. Harvard. Nominated associate justice by Richard Nixon; confirmed 1970 by 94–0 vote; retired 1994. Federal appeals court judge.

Blair, John, Jr. (1732–1800). Virginia. Federalist. College of William and Mary; Middle Temple (England). Nominated associate justice by George Washington; confirmed 1789 by voice vote; resigned 1796. Virginia legislator, state court judge, delegate to Constitutional Convention.

Blatchford, Samuel (1820–1893). New York. Republican. Columbia. Nominated associate justice by Chester A. Arthur; confirmed 1882 by voice vote; died in office 1893. Federal district court judge, federal circuit court judge.

Bradley, Joseph P. (1813–1892). New Jersey. Republican. Rutgers. Nominated associate justice by Ulysses S. Grant; confirmed 1870 by 46–9 vote; died in office 1892. Private practice.

Brandeis, Louis Dembitz (1856–1941). Massachusetts. Republican. Harvard. Nominated associate justice by Woodrow Wilson; confirmed 1916 by 47–22 vote; retired 1939. Private practice.

Brennan, William Joseph, Jr. (1906–1997). New Jersey. Democrat. University of Pennsylvania, Harvard. Received recess appointment from Dwight Eisenhower to be associate justice 1956; confirmed 1957 by voice vote; retired 1990. New Jersey Supreme Court.

Brewer, David Josiah (1837–1910). Kansas. Republican. Wesleyan, Yale, Albany Law School. Nominated associate justice by Benjamin Harrison; confirmed 1889 by 53–11 vote; died in office 1910. Kansas state court judge, federal circuit court judge.

Breyer, Stephen G. (1938–). Massachusetts. Democrat. Stanford, Oxford, Harvard. Nominated associate justice by William Clinton; confirmed 1994 by 87–9 vote. Law professor; chief counsel, Senate Judiciary Committee; federal appeals court judge.

Brown, Henry B. (1836–1913). Michigan. Republican. Yale, Harvard. Nominated associate justice by Benjamin Harrison; confirmed 1890 by voice vote; retired 1906. Michigan state court judge, federal district court judge.

Burger, Warren Earl (1907–1995). Minnesota. Republican. University of Minnesota, St. Paul College of Law. Nominated chief justice by Richard Nixon; confirmed 1969 by 74–3 vote; retired 1986. Assistant U.S. attorney general, federal appeals court judge.

Burton, Harold Hitz (1888–1964). Ohio. Republican. Bowdoin College, Harvard. Nominated associate justice by Harry Truman; confirmed 1945 by voice vote; retired 1958. Ohio state legislator, mayor of Cleveland, U.S. senator.

Butler, Pierce (1866–1939). Minnesota. Republican. Carleton College.   Nominated associate justice by Warren G. Harding; confirmed 1922 by 61–8 vote; died in office 1939.   Minnesota county attorney, private practice.

Byrnes, James Francis (1879–1972).   South Carolina. Democrat.   Privately educated.   Nominated associate justice by Franklin Roosevelt; confirmed 1941 by voice vote; resigned 1942.   South Carolina local solicitor, U.S. representative, U.S. senator.

Campbell, John Archibald (1811–1889).   Alabama. Democrat.   Franklin College (University of Georgia), U.S. Military Academy.   Nominated associate justice by Franklin Pierce; confirmed 1853 by voice vote; resigned 1861.   Alabama state legislator.

Cardozo, Benjamin Nathan (1870–1938).   New York. Democrat.   Columbia.   Nominated associate justice by Herbert Hoover; confirmed 1932 by voice vote; died in office 1938.   State court judge.

Catron, John (1786–1865).   Tennessee. Democrat. Self-educated.   Nominated associate justice by Andrew Jackson; confirmed 1837 by 28–15 vote; died in office 1865.   Tennessee state court judge, state chief justice.

Chase, Salmon Portland (1808–1873).   Ohio.   Republican.   Dartmouth.   Nominated chief justice by Abraham Lincoln; confirmed 1864 by voice vote; died in office 1873.   U.S. senator, Ohio governor, U.S. secretary of the Treasury.

Chase, Samuel (1741–1811).   Maryland. Federalist.   Privately educated.   Nominated associate justice by George Washington; confirmed 1796 by voice vote; died in office 1811.   Maryland state legislator, delegate to Continental Congress, state court judge.

Clark, Tom Campbell (1899–1977).   Texas. Democrat.   University of Texas.   Nominated associate justice by Harry Truman; confirmed 1949 by 73–8 vote; retired 1967.   Texas local district attorney, U.S. attorney general.

Clarke, John Hessin (1857–1945).   Ohio. Democrat.   Western Reserve University.   Nominated associate justice by Woodrow Wilson; confirmed 1916 by voice vote; resigned 1922.   Federal district judge.

Clifford, Nathan (1803–1881).   Maine. Democrat. Privately educated.   Nominated associate justice by James Buchanan; confirmed 1858 by 26–23 vote; died in office 1881.   Maine state legislator, state attorney general, U.S. representative, U.S. attorney general, minister to Mexico.

Curtis, Benjamin Robbins (1809–1874).   Massachusetts. Whig.   Harvard.   Nominated associate justice by Millard Fillmore; confirmed 1851 by voice vote; resigned 1857.   Massachusetts state legislator.

Cushing, William (1732–1810).   Massachusetts. Federalist.   Harvard.   Nominated associate justice by George Wash-ington; confirmed 1789 by voice vote; died in office 1810.   Massachusetts state court judge, electoral college delegate.

Daniel, Peter Vivian (1784–1860).   Virginia. Democrat. Princeton.   Nominated associate justice by Martin Van Buren; confirmed 1841 by 22–5 vote; died in office 1860.   Virginia state legislator, state Privy Council, federal district court judge.

Davis, David (1815–1886).   Illinois. Republican. Kenyon College, Yale.   Nominated associate justice by Abraham Lincoln; confirmed 1862 by voice vote; resigned 1877.   Illinois state legislator, state court judge.

Day, William Rufus (1849–1923).   Ohio. Republican. University of Michigan.   Nominated associate justice by Theodore Roosevelt; confirmed 1903 by voice vote; resigned 1922. Ohio state court judge, U.S. secretary of state, federal court of appeals judge.

Douglas, William Orville (1898–1980).   Connecticut. Democrat.   Whitman College, Columbia.   Nominated associate justice by Franklin Roosevelt; confirmed 1939 by 62–4 vote; retired 1975.   Law professor, Securities and Exchange Commission.

Duvall, Gabriel (1752–1844).   Maryland. Democratic/Republican.   Privately educated.   Nominated associate justice by James Madison; confirmed 1811 by voice vote; resigned 1835. Maryland state legislator, U.S. representative, state court judge, presidential elector, comptroller of the U.S. Treasury.

Ellsworth, Oliver (1745–1807).   Connecticut. Federalist. Princeton.   Nominated chief justice by George Washington; confirmed 1796 by 21–1 vote; resigned 1800.   Connecticut state legislator, delegate to Continental Congress and Constitutional Convention, state court judge, U.S. senator.

Field, Stephen J. (1816–1899).   California. Democrat. Williams College.   Nominated associate justice by Abraham Lincoln; confirmed 1863 by voice vote; retired 1897.   California state legislator, California Supreme Court.

Fortas, Abe (1910–1982).   Tennessee. Democrat. Southwestern College, Yale.   Nominated associate justice by Lyndon Johnson; confirmed 1965 by voice vote; resigned 1969.   Counsel for numerous federal agencies, private practice.

Frankfurter, Felix (1882–1965).   Massachusetts. Independent.   College of the City of New York, Harvard.   Nominated associate justice by Franklin Roosevelt; confirmed 1939 by voice vote; retired 1962.   Law professor, War Department law officer, assistant to secretary of war, assistant to secretary of labor, War Labor Policies Board chairman.

Fuller, Melville Weston (1833–1910).   Illinois. Democrat. Bowdoin College, Harvard.   Nominated chief justice by Grover Cleveland; confirmed 1888 by 41–20 vote; died in office 1910. Illinois state legislator.

Ginsburg, Ruth Bader (1933–).   New York. Democrat. Columbia.   Nominated associate justice by William Clinton;

confirmed 1993 by 96–3 vote.   Professor, federal court of appeals judge.

Goldberg, Arthur J. (1908–1990).   Illinois.   Democrat. Northwestern.   Nominated associate justice by John Kennedy; confirmed 1962 by voice vote; resigned 1965.   Secretary of labor.

Gray, Horace (1828–1902).   Massachusetts.   Republican. Harvard.   Nominated associate justice by Chester A. Arthur; confirmed 1881 by 51–5 vote; died in office 1902.   Massachusetts Supreme Court.

Grier, Robert Cooper (1794–1870).   Pennsylvania. Democrat.   Dickinson College.   Nominated associate justice by James Polk; confirmed 1846 by voice vote; retired 1870.   Pennsylvania state court judge.

Harlan, John Marshall (1833–1911).   Kentucky.   Republican.   Centre College, Transylvania University.   Nominated associate justice by Rutherford B. Hayes; confirmed 1877 by voice vote; died in office 1911.   Kentucky attorney general.

Harlan, John Marshall (1899–1971).   New York.   Republican.   Princeton, Oxford, New York Law School.   Nominated associate justice by Dwight Eisenhower; confirmed 1955 by 71–11 vote; retired 1971.   Chief counsel for New York State Crime Commission, federal court of appeals.

Holmes, Oliver Wendell, Jr. (1841–1935).   Massachusetts. Republican.   Harvard.   Nominated associate justice by Theodore Roosevelt; confirmed 1902 by voice vote; retired 1932. Law professor; justice, Supreme Judicial Court of Massachusetts.

Hughes, Charles Evans (1862–1948).   New York. Republican.   Colgate, Brown, Columbia.   Nominated associate justice by William Howard Taft; confirmed 1910 by voice vote; resigned 1916; nominated chief justice by Herbert Hoover; confirmed 1930 by 52–26 vote; retired 1941.   New York governor, U.S. secretary of state, Court of International Justice judge.

Hunt, Ward (1810–1886).   New York.   Republican. Union College.   Nominated associate justice by Ulysses S. Grant; confirmed 1872 by voice vote; retired 1882.   New York state legislator, mayor of Utica, state court judge.

Iredell, James (1751–1799).   North Carolina.   Federalist. English schools.   Nominated associate justice by George Washington; confirmed 1790 by voice vote; died in office 1799.   Customs official, state court judge, state attorney general.

Jackson, Howell Edmunds (1832–1895).   Tennessee. Democrat.   West Tennessee College, University of Virginia, Cumberland University.   Nominated associate justice by Benjamin Harrison; confirmed 1893 by voice vote; died in office 1895. Tennessee state legislator, U.S. senator, federal circuit court judge, federal court of appeals judge.

Jackson, Robert Houghwout (1892–1954).   New York. Democrat.   Albany Law School.   Nominated associate justice by Franklin Roosevelt; confirmed 1941 by voice vote; died in office 1954.   Counsel for Internal Revenue Bureau and Securities and Exchange Commission, U.S. solicitor general, U.S. attorney general.

Jay, John (1745–1829).   New York.   Federalist.   King's College (Columbia University).   Nominated chief justice by George Washington; confirmed 1789 by voice vote; resigned 1795.   Delegate to Continental Congress, chief justice of New York, minister to Spain and Great Britain, secretary of foreign affairs.

Johnson, Thomas (1732–1819).   Maryland.   Federalist. Privately educated.   Nominated associate justice by George Washington; confirmed 1791 by voice vote; resigned 1793.   Delegate to Annapolis Convention and Continental Congress, governor, state legislator, state court judge.

Johnson, William (1771–1834).   South Carolina.   Democratic/Republican.   Princeton.   Nominated associate justice by Thomas Jefferson; confirmed 1804 by voice vote; died in office 1834.   South Carolina state legislator, state court judge.

Kennedy, Anthony McLeod (1936–).   California.   Republican.   Stanford, London School of Economics, Harvard. Nominated associate justice by Ronald Reagan; confirmed 1988 by 97–0 vote.   Federal appeals court judge.

Lamar, Joseph Rucker (1857–1916).   Georgia.   Democrat. University of Georgia, Bethany College, Washington and Lee. Nominated associate justice by William Howard Taft; confirmed 1910 by voice vote; died in office 1916.   Georgia state legislator, Georgia Supreme Court.

Lamar, Lucius Quintus Cincinnatus (1825–1893).   Mississippi.   Democrat.   Emory College.   Nominated associate justice by Grover Cleveland; confirmed 1888 by 32–28 vote; died in office 1893.   Georgia state legislator, U.S. representative, U.S. senator, U.S. secretary of the interior.

Livingston, Henry Brockholst (1757–1823).   New York. Democratic/Republican.   Princeton.   Nominated associate justice by Thomas Jefferson; confirmed 1806 by voice vote; died in office 1823.   New York state legislator, state court judge.

Lurton, Horace Harmon (1844–1914).   Tennessee.   Democrat.   University of Chicago, Cumberland.   Nominated associate justice by William Howard Taft; confirmed 1909 by voice vote; died in office 1914.   Tennessee Supreme Court, federal court of appeals judge.

McKenna, Joseph (1843–1926).   California.   Republican. Benicia Collegiate Institute.   Nominated associate justice by William McKinley; confirmed 1898 by voice vote; retired 1925. California state legislator, U.S. representative, federal court of appeals judge, U.S. attorney general.

McKinley, John (1780–1852).   Alabama.   Democrat.   Self educated.   Nominated associate justice by Martin Van Buren; confirmed 1837 by voice vote; died in office 1852.   Alabama state legislator, U.S. senator, U.S. representative.

McLean, John (1785–1861).   Ohio.   Democrat.   Privately educated.   Nominated associate justice by Andrew Jackson;

confirmed 1829 by voice vote; died in office 1861.   U.S. representative, Ohio Supreme Court, commissioner of U.S. General Land Office, U.S. postmaster general.

McReynolds, James Clark (1862–1946).   Tennessee. Democrat.   Vanderbilt, University of Virginia.   Nominated associate justice by Woodrow Wilson; confirmed 1914 by 44–6 vote; retired 1941.   U.S. attorney general.

Marshall, John (1755–1835).   Virginia.   Federalist.   Privately educated, College of William and Mary.   Nominated chief justice by John Adams; confirmed 1801 by voice vote; died in office 1835.   Virginia state legislator, minister to France, U.S. representative, U.S. secretary of state.

Marshall, Thurgood (1908–1993).   New York.   Democrat. Lincoln University, Howard University.   Nominated associate justice by Lyndon Johnson; confirmed 1967 by 69–11 vote; retired 1991.   NAACP Legal Defense Fund, federal court of appeals judge, U.S. solicitor general.

Matthews, Stanley (1824–1889).   Ohio.   Republican. Kenyon College.   Nominated associate justice by Rutherford B. Hayes; no Senate action on nomination; renominated associate justice by James A. Garfield; confirmed 1881 by 24–23 vote; died in office 1889.   Ohio state legislator, state court judge, U.S. attorney for southern Ohio, U.S. senator.

Miller, Samuel Freeman (1816–1890).   Iowa.   Republican. Transylvania University.   Nominated associate justice by Abraham Lincoln; confirmed 1862 by voice vote; died in office 1890. Medical doctor, private law practice, justice of the peace.

Minton, Sherman (1890–1965).   Indiana.   Democrat. Indiana University, Yale.   Nominated associate justice by Harry Truman; confirmed 1949 by 48–16 vote; retired 1956.   U.S. senator, federal court of appeals judge.

Moody, William Henry (1853–1917).   Massachusetts.   Republican.   Harvard.   Nominated associate justice by Theodore Roosevelt; confirmed 1906 by voice vote; retired 1910.   Massachusetts local district attorney, U.S. representative, secretary of the navy, U.S. attorney general.

Moore, Alfred (1755–1810).   North Carolina.   Federalist. Privately educated.   Nominated associate justice by John Adams; confirmed 1799 by voice vote; resigned 1804.   North Carolina legislator, state attorney general, state court judge.

Murphy, William Francis (Frank) (1880–1949).   Michigan.   Democrat.   University of Michigan, London's Inn (England), Trinity College (Ireland).   Nominated associate justice by Franklin Roosevelt; confirmed 1940 by voice vote; died in office 1949.   Michigan state court judge, mayor of Detroit, governor of the Philippines, governor of Michigan, U.S. attorney general.

Nelson, Samuel (1792–1873).   New York.   Democrat. Middlebury College.   Nominated associate justice by John Tyler; confirmed 1845 by voice vote; retired 1872.   Presidential elector, state court judge, New York Supreme Court chief justice.

O'Connor, Sandra Day (1930–   ).   Arizona.   Republican.

Stanford.   Nominated associate justice by Ronald Reagan; confirmed 1981 by 99–0 vote.   Arizona state legislator, state court judge.

Paterson, William (1745–1806).   New Jersey.   Federalist. Princeton.   Nominated associate justice by George Washington; confirmed 1793 by voice vote; died in office 1806.   New Jersey attorney general, delegate to Constitutional Convention, U.S. senator, governor.

Peckham, Rufus Wheeler (1838–1909).   New York. Democrat.   Albany Boys' Academy.   Nominated associate justice by Grover Cleveland; confirmed 1895 by voice vote; died in office 1909.   New York local district attorney, city attorney, state court judge.

Pitney, Mahlon (1858–1924).   New Jersey.   Republican. Princeton.   Nominated associate justice by William Howard Taft; confirmed 1912 by 50–26 vote; retired 1922.   U.S. representative, New Jersey state legislator, New Jersey Supreme Court, Chancellor of New Jersey.

Powell, Lewis Franklin, Jr. (1907–1998).   Virginia. Democrat.   Washington and Lee, Harvard.   Nominated associate justice by Richard Nixon; confirmed 1971 by 89–1 vote; retired 1987.   Private practice, Virginia State Board of Education, American Bar Association president, American College of Trial Lawyers president.

Reed, Stanley Forman (1884–1980).   Kentucky.   Democrat.   Kentucky Wesleyan, Yale, Virginia, Columbia, University of Paris.   Nominated associate justice by Franklin Roosevelt; confirmed 1938 by voice vote; retired 1957.   Federal Farm Board general counsel, Reconstruction Finance Corporation general counsel, U.S. solicitor general.

Rehnquist, William Hubbs (1924–   ).   Arizona.   Republican.   Stanford, Harvard.   Nominated associate justice by Richard Nixon; confirmed 1971 by 68–26 vote; nominated chief justice by Ronald Reagan; confirmed 1986 by 65–33 vote.   Private practice, assistant U.S. attorney general.

Roberts, Owen Josephus (1875–1955).   Pennsylvania.   Republican.   University of Pennsylvania.   Nominated associate justice by Herbert Hoover; confirmed 1930 by voice vote; resigned 1945.   Private practice, Pennsylvania local prosecutor, special U.S. attorney.

Rutledge, John (1739–1800).   South Carolina.   Federalist. Middle Temple (England).   Nominated associate justice by George Washington; confirmed 1789 by voice vote; resigned 1791. Nominated chief justice by George Washington August 1795 and served as recess appointment; confirmation denied and service terminated December 1795.   South Carolina legislator, state attorney general, governor, chief justice of South Carolina, delegate to Continental Congress and Constitutional Convention.

Rutledge, Wiley Blount (1894–1949).   Iowa.   Democrat. Maryville College, University of Wisconsin, University of Colorado.   Nominated associate justice by Franklin Roosevelt;

confirmed 1943 by voice vote; died in office 1949.   Law professor, federal court of appeals judge.

Sanford, Edward Terry (1865–1930).   Tennessee.   Republican.   University of Tennessee, Harvard.   Nominated associate justice by Warren G. Harding; confirmed 1923 by voice vote; died in office 1930.   Assistant U.S. attorney general, federal district court judge.

Scalia, Antonin (1936–   ).   District of Columbia.   Republican.   Georgetown, Harvard.   Nominated associate justice by Ronald Reagan; confirmed 1986 by 98–0 vote.   Assistant U.S. attorney general, federal court of appeals judge.

Shiras, George, Jr. (1832–1924).   Pennsylvania.   Republican.   Ohio University, Yale.   Nominated associate justice by Benjamin Harrison; confirmed 1892 by voice vote; retired 1903.   Private practice.

Souter, David Hackett (1939–   ).   New Hampshire.   Republican.   Harvard, Oxford.   Nominated associate justice by George Bush; confirmed 1990 by 90–9 vote.   New Hampshire attorney general, state court judge, federal appeals court judge.

Stevens, John Paul (1920–   ).   Illinois.   Republican.   Chicago, Northwestern.   Nominated associate justice by Gerald Ford; confirmed 1975 by 98–0 vote.   Federal court of appeals judge.

Stewart, Potter (1915–1985).   Ohio.   Republican.   Yale, Cambridge.   Received recess appointment from Dwight Eisenhower to be associate justice in 1958; confirmed 1959 by 70–17 vote; retired 1981.   Cincinnati city council, federal court of appeals judge.

Stone, Harlan Fiske (1872–1946).   New York.   Republican.   Amherst College, Columbia.   Nominated associate justice by Calvin Coolidge; confirmed 1925 by 71–6 vote; nominated chief justice by Franklin Roosevelt; confirmed 1941 by voice vote; died in office 1946.   Law professor, U.S. attorney general.

Story, Joseph (1779–1845).   Massachusetts.   Democratic/Republican.   Harvard.   Nominated associate justice by James Madison; confirmed 1811 by voice vote; died in office 1845.   Massachusetts state legislator, U.S. representative.

Strong, William (1808–1895).   Pennsylvania.   Republican.   Yale.   Nominated associate justice by Ulysses S. Grant; confirmed 1870 by voice vote; retired 1880.   U.S. representative, Pennsylvania Supreme Court.

Sutherland, George (1862–1942).   Utah.   Republican.   Brigham Young, University of Michigan.   Nominated associate justice by Warren G. Harding; confirmed 1922 by voice vote; retired 1938.   Utah state legislator, U.S. representative, U.S. senator.

Swayne, Noah Haynes (1804–1884).   Ohio.   Republican.   Privately educated.   Nominated associate justice by Abraham Lincoln; confirmed 1862 by 38–1 vote; retired 1881.   Ohio state legislator, local prosecutor, U.S. attorney for Ohio, Columbus city council.

Taft, William Howard (1857–1930).   Ohio.   Republican.   Yale, Cincinnati.   Nominated chief justice by Warren G. Harding; confirmed 1921 by voice vote; retired 1930.   Ohio local prosecutor, state court judge, U.S. solicitor general, federal court of appeals judge, governor of the Philippines, secretary of war, U.S. president.

Taney, Roger Brooke (1777–1864).   Maryland.   Democrat.   Dickinson College.   Nominated associate justice by Andrew Jackson; nomination not confirmed 1835; nominated chief justice by Andrew Jackson; confirmed 1836 by 29–15 vote; died in office 1864.   Maryland state legislator, state attorney general, acting secretary of war, secretary of the Treasury (nomination later rejected by Senate).

Thomas, Clarence (1948–   ).   Georgia.   Republican.   Holy Cross, Yale.   Nominated associate justice by George Bush; confirmed 1991 by 52–48 vote.   Department of Education, Equal Employment Opportunity Commission, federal appeals court judge.

Thompson, Smith (1768–1843).   New York.   Democratic/Republican.   Princeton.   Nominated associate justice by James Monroe; confirmed 1823 by voice vote; died in office 1843.   New York state legislator, state court judge, secretary of the navy.

Todd, Thomas (1765–1826).   Kentucky.   Democratic/Republican.   Liberty Hall (Washington and Lee).   Nominated associate justice by Thomas Jefferson; confirmed 1807 by voice vote; died in office 1826.   Kentucky state court judge, state chief justice.

Trimble, Robert (1776–1828).   Kentucky.   Democratic/Republican.   Kentucky Academy.   Nominated associate justice by John Quincy Adams; confirmed 1826 by 27–5 vote; died in office 1828.   Kentucky state legislator, state court judge, U.S. attorney, federal district court judge.

Van Devanter, Willis (1859–1941).   Wyoming.   Republican.   Indiana Asbury University, University of Cincinnati.   Nominated associate justice by William Howard Taft; confirmed 1910 by voice vote; retired 1937.   Cheyenne city attorney, Wyoming territorial legislature, Wyoming Supreme Court, assistant U.S. attorney general, federal court of appeals judge.

Vinson, Frederick Moore (1890–1953).   Kentucky.   Democrat.   Centre College.   Nominated chief justice by Harry Truman; confirmed 1946 by voice vote; died in office 1953.   U.S. representative, federal appeals court judge, director of Office of Economic Stabilization, secretary of the Treasury.

Waite, Morrison Remick (1816–1888).   Ohio.   Republican.   Yale.   Nominated chief justice by Ulysses S. Grant; confirmed 1874 by 63–0 vote; died in office 1888.   Private practice, Ohio state legislator.

Warren, Earl (1891–1974).   California.   Republican.   University of California.   Recess appointment as chief justice by Dwight Eisenhower 1953; confirmed 1954 by voice vote; retired

1969.   California local district attorney, state attorney general, governor.

Washington, Bushrod (1762–1829).   Virginia.   Federalist. College of William and Mary.   Nominated associate justice by John Adams; confirmed 1798 by voice vote; died in office 1829. Virginia state legislator.

Wayne, James Moore (1790–1867).   Georgia.   Democrat. Princeton.   Nominated associate justice by Andrew Jackson; confirmed 1835 by voice vote; died in office 1867.   Georgia state legislator, mayor of Savannah, state court judge, U.S. representative.

White, Byron Raymond (1917–   ).   Colorado.   Democrat.   University of Colorado, Oxford, Yale.   Nominated associate justice by John Kennedy; confirmed 1962 by voice vote; retired 1993.   Deputy U.S. attorney general.

White, Edward Douglass (1845–1921).   Louisiana.   Democrat.   Mount St. Mary's College, Georgetown.   Nominated associate justice by Grover Cleveland; confirmed 1894 by voice vote; nominated chief justice by William Howard Taft; confirmed 1910 by voice vote; died in office 1921.   Louisiana state legislator, Louisiana Supreme Court, U.S. senator.

Whittaker, Charles Evans (1901–1973).   Missouri.   Republican.   University of Kansas City.   Nominated associate justice by Dwight Eisenhower; confirmed 1957 by voice vote; retired 1962.   Federal district court judge, federal appeals court judge.

Wilson, James (1742–1798).   Pennsylvania.   Federalist. University of St. Andrews (Scotland).   Nominated associate justice by George Washington; confirmed 1789 by voice vote; died in office 1798.   Delegate to Continental Congress and Constitutional Convention.

Woodbury, Levi (1789–1851).   New Hampshire.   Democrat.   Dartmouth, Tapping Reeve Law School.   Nominated associate justice by James Polk; confirmed 1846 by voice vote; died in office 1851.   New Hampshire state legislator, state court judge, governor, U.S. senator, secretary of the navy, secretary of the Treasury.

Woods, William B. (1824–1887).   Georgia.   Republican. Western Reserve College, Yale.   Nominated associate justice by Rutherford B. Hayes; confirmed 1880 by 39–8 vote; died in office 1887.   Ohio state legislator, Alabama chancellor, federal circuit court judge.

APPENDIX 6
NATURAL COURTS

Natural Court[a]	Justices[b]	Dates	U.S. Reports[c]
Jay 1	Jay (*o* October 19, 1789), J. Rutledge (*o* February 15, 1790), Cushing (*o* February 2, 1790), Wilson (*o* October 5, 1789), Blair (*o* February 2, 1790)	October 5, 1789– May 12, 1790	2
Jay 2	Jay, Rutledge (*r* March 5, 1791), Cushing, Wilson, Blair, Iredell (*o* May 12, 1790)	May 12, 1790– August 6, 1792	2
Jay 3	Jay, Cushing, Wilson, Blair, Iredell, T. Johnson (*o* August 6, 1792; *r* January 16, 1793)	August 6, 1792– March 11, 1793	2
Jay 4	Jay (*r* June 29, 1795), Cushing, Wilson, Blair, Iredell, Paterson (*o* March 11, 1793)	March 11, 1793– August 12, 1795	2–3
Rutledge 1	J. Rutledge (*o* August 12, 1795; *rj* December 15, 1795), Cushing, Wilson, Blair (*r* January 27, 1796), Iredell, Paterson	August 12, 1795– February 4, 1796	3
No chief justice	Cushing, Wilson, Iredell, Paterson, S. Chase (*o* February 4, 1796)	February 4, 1796– March 8, 1796	3
Ellsworth 1	Ellsworth (*o* March 8, 1796), Cushing, Wilson (*d* August 21, 1798), Iredell, Paterson, S. Chase	March 8, 1796– February 4, 1799	3
Ellsworth 2	Ellsworth, Cushing, Iredell (*d* October 20, 1799), Paterson, S. Chase, Washington (*o* February 4, 1799)	February 4, 1799– April 21, 1800	3–4
Ellsworth 3	Ellsworth (*r* December 15, 1800), Cushing, Paterson, S. Chase, Washington, Moore (*o* April 21, 1800)	April 21, 1800– February 4, 1801	4
Marshall 1	Marshall (*o* February 4, 1801), Cushing, Paterson, S. Chase, Washington, Moore (*r* January 26, 1804)	February 4, 1801– May 7, 1804	5–6
Marshall 2	Marshall, Cushing, Paterson (*d* September 9, 1806), S. Chase, Washington, W. Johnson (*o* May 7, 1804)	May 7, 1804– January 20, 1807	6–7
Marshall 3	Marshall, Cushing, S. Chase, Washington, W. Johnson, Livingston (*o* January 20, 1807)	January 20, 1807– May 4, 1807	8
Marshall 4	Marshall, Cushing (*d* September 13, 1810), S. Chase (*d* June 19, 1811), Washington, W. Johnson, Livingston, Todd (*o* May 4, 1807)	May 4, 1807– November 23, 1811	8–10

Natural Court[a]	Justices[b]	Dates	U.S. Reports[c]
Marshall 5	Marshall, Washington, W. Johnson, Livingston, Todd, Duvall (o November 23, 1811)	November 23, 1811–February 3, 1812	11
Marshall 6	Marshall, Washington, W. Johnson, Livingston (d March 18, 1823), Todd, Duvall, Story (o February 3, 1812)	February 3, 1812–February 10, 1824	11–21
Marshall 7	Marshall, Washington, W. Johnson, Todd (d February 7, 1826), Duvall, Story, Thompson (o February 10, 1824)	February 10, 1824–June 16, 1826	22–24
Marshall 8	Marshall, Washington (d November 26, 1829), W. Johnson, Duvall, Story, Thompson, Trimble (o June 16, 1826; d August 25, 1828)	June 16, 1826–January 11, 1830	25–27
Marshall 9	Marshall, W. Johnson (d August 4, 1834), Duvall (r January 14, 1835), Story, Thompson, McLean (o January 11, 1830), Baldwin (o January 18, 1830)	January 11, 1830–January 14, 1835	28–33
Marshall 10	Marshall (d July 6, 1835), Story, Thompson, McLean, Baldwin, Wayne (o January 14, 1835)	January 14, 1835–March 28, 1836	34–35
Taney 1	Taney (o March 28, 1836), Story, Thompson, McLean, Baldwin, Wayne	March 28, 1836–May 12, 1836	35
Taney 2	Taney, Story, Thompson, McLean, Baldwin, Wayne, Barbour (o May 12, 1836)	May 12, 1836–May 1, 1837	35–36
Taney 3	Taney, Story, Thompson, McLean, Baldwin, Wayne, Barbour, Catron (o May 1, 1837)	May 1, 1837–January 9, 1838	36
Taney 4	Taney, Story, Thompson, McLean, Baldwin, Wayne, Barbour (d February 25, 1841), Catron, McKinley (o January 9, 1838)	January 9, 1838–January 10, 1842	37–40
Taney 5	Taney, Story, Thompson (d December 18, 1843), McLean, Baldwin (d April 21, 1844), Wayne, Catron, McKinley, Daniel (o January 10, 1842)	January 10, 1842–February 27, 1845	40–44
Taney 6	Taney, Story (d September 10, 1845), McLean, Wayne, Catron, McKinley, Daniel, Nelson (o February 27, 1845)	February 27, 1845–September 23, 1845	44
Taney 7	Taney, McLean, Wayne, Catron, McKinley, Daniel, Nelson, Woodbury (o September 23, 1845)	September 23, 1845–August 10, 1846	44–45
Taney 8	Taney, McLean, Wayne, Catron, McKinley, Daniel, Nelson, Woodbury (d September 4, 1851), Grier (o August 10, 1846)	August 10, 1846–October 10, 1851	46–52
Taney 9	Taney, McLean, Wayne, Catron, McKinley (d July 19, 1852), Daniel, Nelson, Grier, Curtis (o October 10, 1851)	October 10, 1851–April 11, 1853	53–55
Taney 10	Taney, McLean, Wayne, Catron, Daniel, Nelson, Grier, Curtis (r September 30, 1857), Campbell (o April 11, 1853)	April 11, 1853–January 21, 1858	56–61
Taney 11	Taney, McLean (d April 4, 1861), Wayne, Catron, Daniel (d May 31, 1860), Nelson, Grier, Campbell (r April 30, 1861), Clifford (o January 21, 1858)	January 21, 1858–January 27, 1862	61–66
Taney 12	Taney, Wayne, Catron, Nelson, Grier, Clifford, Swayne (o January 27, 1862)	January 27, 1862–July 21, 1862	66
Taney 13	Taney, Wayne, Catron, Nelson, Grier, Clifford, Swayne, Miller (o July 21, 1862)	July 21, 1862–December 10, 1862	67

Natural Court[a]	Justices[b]	Dates	U.S. Reports[c]
Taney 14	Taney, Wayne, Catron, Nelson, Grier, Clifford, Swayne, Miller, Davis (o December 10, 1862)	December 10, 1862–May 20, 1863	67
Taney 15	Taney (d October 12, 1864), Wayne, Catron, Nelson, Grier, Clifford, Swayne, Miller, Davis, Field (o May 20, 1863)	May 20, 1863–December 15, 1864	67–68
Chase 1	S. P. Chase (o December 15, 1864), Wayne (d July 5, 1867), Catron (d May 30, 1865), Nelson, Grier (r January 31, 1870), Clifford, Swayne, Miller, Davis, Field	December 15, 1864–March 14, 1870	69–76
Chase 2	S. P. Chase, Nelson (r November 28, 1872), Clifford, Swayne, Miller, Davis, Field, Strong (o March 14, 1870), Bradley (o March 23, 1870)	March 14, 1870–January 9, 1873	76–82
Chase 3	S. P. Chase (d May 7, 1873), Clifford, Swayne, Miller, Davis, Field, Strong, Bradley, Hunt (o January 9, 1873)	January 9, 1873–March 4, 1874	82–86
Waite 1	Waite (o March 4, 1874), Clifford, Swayne, Miller, Davis (r March 4, 1877), Field, Strong, Bradley, Hunt	March 4, 1874–December 10, 1877	86–95
Waite 2	Waite, Clifford, Swayne, Miller, Field, Strong (r December 14, 1880), Bradley, Hunt, Harlan I (o December 10, 1877)	December 10, 1877–January 5, 1881	95–103
Waite 3	Waite, Clifford, Swayne (r January 24, 1881), Miller, Field, Bradley, Hunt, Harlan I, Woods (o January 5, 1881)	January 5, 1881–May 17, 1881	103
Waite 4	Waite, Clifford (d July 25, 1881), Miller, Field, Bradley, Hunt, Harlan I, Woods, Matthews (o May 17, 1881)	May 17, 1881–January 9, 1882	103–104
Waite 5	Waite, Miller, Field, Bradley, Hunt (r January 27, 1882), Harlan I, Woods, Matthews, Gray (o January 9, 1882)	January 9, 1882–April 3, 1882	104–105
Waite 6	Waite, Miller, Field, Bradley, Harlan I, Woods (d May 14, 1887), Matthews, Gray, Blatchford (o April 3, 1882)	April 3, 1882–January 18, 1888	105–124
Waite 7	Waite (d March 23, 1888), Miller, Field, Bradley, Harlan I, Matthews, Gray, Blatchford, L. Lamar (o January 18, 1888)	January 18, 1888–October 8, 1888	124–127
Fuller 1	Fuller (o October 8, 1888), Miller, Field, Bradley, Harlan I, Matthews (d March 22, 1889), Gray, Blatchford, L. Lamar	October 8, 1888–January 6, 1890	128–132
Fuller 2	Fuller, Miller (d October 13, 1890), Field, Bradley, Harlan I, Gray, Blatchford, L. Lamar, Brewer (o January 6, 1890)	January 6, 1890–January 5, 1891	132–137
Fuller 3	Fuller, Field, Bradley (d January 22, 1892), Harlan I, Gray, Blatchford, L. Lamar, Brewer, Brown (o January 5, 1891)	January 5, 1891–October 10, 1892	137–145
Fuller 4	Fuller, Field, Harlan I, Gray, Blatchford, L. Lamar (d January 23, 1893), Brewer, Brown, Shiras (o October 10, 1892)	October 10, 1892–March 4, 1893	146–148
Fuller 5	Fuller, Field, Harlan I, Gray, Blatchford (d July 7, 1893), Brewer, Brown, Shiras, H. Jackson (o March 4, 1893)	March 4, 1893–March 12, 1894	148–151
Fuller 6	Fuller, Field, Harlan I, Gray, Brewer, Brown, Shiras, H. Jackson (d August 8, 1895), E. White (o March 12, 1894)	March 12, 1894–January 6, 1896	152–160

Natural Court[a]	Justices[b]	Dates	U.S. Reports[c]
Fuller 7	Fuller, Field (r December 1, 1897), Harlan I, Gray, Brewer, Brown, Shiras, E. White, Peckham (o January 6, 1896)	January 6, 1896– January 26, 1898	160–169
Fuller 8	Fuller, Harlan I, Gray (d September 15, 1902), Brewer, Brown, Shiras, E. White, Peckham, McKenna (o January 26, 1898)	January 26, 1898– December 8, 1902	169–187
Fuller 9	Fuller, Harlan I, Brewer, Brown, Shiras (r February 23, 1903), E. White, Peckham, McKenna, Holmes (o December 8, 1902)	December 8, 1902– March 2, 1903	187–188
Fuller 10	Fuller, Harlan I, Brewer, Brown (r May 28, 1906), E. White, Peckham, McKenna, Holmes, Day (o March 2, 1903)	March 2, 1903– December 17, 1906	188–203
Fuller 11	Fuller, Harlan I, Brewer, E. White, Peckham (d October 24, 1909), McKenna, Holmes, Day, Moody (o December 17, 1906)	December 17, 1906– January 3, 1910	203–215
Fuller 12	Fuller (d July 4, 1910), Harlan I, Brewer (d March 28, 1910), E. White, McKenna, Holmes, Day, Moody, Lurton (o January 3, 1910)	January 3, 1910– October 10, 1910	215–217
No chief justice	Harlan I, E. White (p December 18, 1910), McKenna, Holmes, Day, Moody (r November 20, 1910), Lurton, Hughes (o October 10, 1910)	October 10, 1910– December 19, 1910	218
White 1	E. White (o December 19, 1910), Harlan I (d October 14, 1911), McKenna, Holmes, Day, Lurton, Hughes, Van Devanter (o January 3, 1911), J. Lamar (o January 3, 1911)	December 19, 1910– March 18, 1912	218–223
White 2	E. White, McKenna, Holmes, Day, Lurton (d July 12, 1914), Hughes, Van Devanter, J. Lamar, Pitney (o March 18, 1912)	March 18, 1912– October 12, 1914	223–234
White 3	E. White, McKenna, Holmes, Day, Hughes, Van Devanter, J. Lamar (d January 2, 1916), Pitney, McReynolds (o October 12, 1914)	October 12, 1914– June 5, 1916	235–241
White 4	E. White, McKenna, Holmes, Day, Hughes (r June 10, 1916), Van Devanter, Pitney, McReynolds, Brandeis (o June 5, 1916)	June 5, 1916– October 9, 1916	241
White 5	E. White (d May 19, 1921), McKenna, Holmes, Day, Van Devanter, Pitney, McReynolds, Brandeis, Clarke (o October 9, 1916)	October 9, 1916– July 11, 1921	242–256
Taft 1	Taft (o July 11, 1921), McKenna, Holmes, Day, Van Devanter, Pitney, McReynolds, Brandeis, Clarke (r September 18, 1922)	July 11, 1921– October 2, 1922	257–259
Taft 2	Taft, McKenna, Holmes, Day (r November 13, 1922), Van Devanter, Pitney (r December 31, 1922), McReynolds, Brandeis, Sutherland (o October 2, 1922)	October 2, 1922– January 2, 1923	260
Taft 3	Taft, McKenna, Holmes, Van Devanter, McReynolds, Brandeis, Sutherland, Butler (o January 2, 1923)	January 2, 1923– February 19, 1923	260
Taft 4	Taft, McKenna (r January 5, 1925), Holmes, Van Devanter, McReynolds, Brandeis, Sutherland, Butler, Sanford (o February 19, 1923)	February 19, 1923– March 2, 1925	260–267
Taft 5	Taft (r February 3, 1930), Holmes, Van Devanter, McReynolds, Brandeis, Sutherland, Butler, Sanford, Stone (o March 2, 1925)	March 2, 1925– February 24, 1930	267–280
Hughes 1	Hughes (o February 24, 1930), Holmes, Van Devanter, McReynolds, Brandeis, Sutherland, Butler, Sanford (d March 8, 1930), Stone	February 24, 1930– June 2, 1930	280–281
Hughes 2	Hughes, Holmes (r January 12, 1932), Van Devanter, McReynolds, Brandeis, Sutherland, Butler, Stone, Roberts (o June 2, 1930)	June 2, 1930– March 14, 1932	281–285

Natural Court[a]	Justices[b]	Dates	U.S. Reports[c]
Hughes 3	Hughes, Van Devanter (r June 2, 1937), McReynolds, Brandeis, Sutherland, Butler, Stone, Roberts, Cardozo (o March 14, 1932)	March 14, 1932–August 19, 1937	285–301
Hughes 4	Hughes, McReynolds, Brandeis, Sutherland (r January 17, 1938), Butler, Stone, Roberts, Cardozo, Black (o August 19, 1937)	August 19, 1937 January 31, 1938	302–303
Hughes 5	Hughes, McReynolds, Brandeis, Butler, Stone, Roberts, Cardozo (d July 9, 1938), Black, Reed (o January 31, 1938)	January 31, 1938–January 30, 1939	303–305
Hughes 6	Hughes, McReynolds, Brandeis (r February 13, 1939), Butler, Stone, Roberts, Black, Reed, Frankfurter (o January 30, 1939)	January 30, 1939–April 17, 1939	306
Hughes 7	Hughes, McReynolds, Butler (d November 16, 1939), Stone, Roberts, Black, Reed, Frankfurter, Douglas (o April 17, 1939)	April 17, 1939–February 5, 1940	306–308
Hughes 8	Hughes (r July 1, 1941), McReynolds (r January 31, 1941), Stone (p July 2, 1941), Roberts, Black, Reed, Frankfurter, Douglas, Murphy (o February 5, 1940)	February 5, 1940–July 3, 1941	308–313
Stone 1	Stone (o July 3, 1941), Roberts, Black, Reed, Frankfurter, Douglas, Murphy, Byrnes (o July 8, 1941; r October 3, 1942), R. Jackson (o July 11, 1941)	July 3, 1941–February 15, 1943	314–318
Stone 2	Stone, Roberts (r July 31, 1945), Black, Reed, Frankfurter, Douglas, Murphy, R. Jackson, W. Rutledge (o February 15, 1943)	February 15, 1943–October 1, 1945	318–326
Stone 3	Stone (d April 22, 1946), Black, Reed, Frankfurter, Douglas, Murphy, R. Jackson, W. Rutledge, Burton (o October 1, 1945)	October 1, 1945–June 24, 1946	326–328
Vinson 1	Vinson (o June 24, 1946), Black, Reed, Frankfurter, Douglas, Murphy (d July 19, 1949), R. Jackson, W. Rutledge, Burton	June 24, 1946–August 24, 1949	329–338
Vinson 2	Vinson, Black, Reed, Frankfurter, Douglas, R. Jackson, W. Rutledge (d September 10, 1949), Burton, Clark (o August 24, 1949)	August 24, 1949–October 12, 1949	338
Vinson 3	Vinson (d September 8, 1953), Black, Reed, Frankfurter, Douglas, R. Jackson, Burton, Clark, Minton (o October 12, 1949)	October 12, 1949–October 5, 1953	338–346
Warren 1	Warren (o October 5, 1953), Black, Reed, Frankfurter, Douglas, R. Jackson (d October 9, 1954), Burton, Clark, Minton	October 5, 1953–March 28, 1955	346–348
Warren 2	Warren, Black, Reed, Frankfurter, Douglas, Burton, Clark, Minton (r October 15, 1956), Harlan II (o March 28, 1955)	March 28, 1955–October 16, 1956	348–352
Warren 3	Warren, Black, Reed (r February 25, 1957), Frankfurter, Douglas, Burton, Clark, Harlan II, Brennan (o October 16, 1956)	October 16, 1956–March 25, 1957	352
Warren 4	Warren, Black, Frankfurter, Douglas, Burton (r October 13, 1958), Clark, Harlan II, Brennan, Whittaker (o March 25, 1957)	March 25, 1957–October 14, 1958	352–358
Warren 5	Warren, Black, Frankfurter, Douglas, Clark, Harlan II, Brennan, Whittaker (r March 31, 1962), Stewart (o October 14, 1958)	October 14, 1958–April 16, 1962	358–369
Warren 6	Warren, Black, Frankfurter (r August 28, 1962), Douglas, Clark, Harlan II, Brennan, Stewart, B. White (o April 16, 1962)	April 16, 1962–October 1, 1962	369–370
Warren 7	Warren, Black, Douglas, Clark, Harlan II, Brennan, Stewart, B. White, Goldberg (o October 1, 1962; r July 25, 1965)	October 1, 1962–October 4, 1965	371–381

Natural Court[a]	Justices[b]	Dates	U.S. Reports[c]
Warren 8	Warren, Black, Douglas, Clark (r June 12, 1967), Harlan II, Brennan, Stewart, B. White, Fortas (o October 4, 1965)	October 4, 1965–October 2, 1967	382–388
Warren 9	Warren (r June 23, 1969), Black, Douglas, Harlan II, Brennan, Stewart, B. White, Fortas (r May 14, 1969), T. Marshall (o October 2, 1967)	October 2, 1967–June 23, 1969	389–395
Burger 1	Burger (o June 23, 1969), Black, Douglas, Harlan II, Brennan, Stewart, B. White, T. Marshall	June 23, 1969–June 9, 1970	395–397
Burger 2	Burger, Black (r September 17, 1971), Douglas, Harlan II (r September 23, 1971), Brennan, Stewart, B. White, T. Marshall, Blackmun (o June 9, 1970)	June 9, 1970–January 7, 1972	397–404
Burger 3	Burger, Douglas (r November 12, 1975), Brennan, Stewart, B. White, T. Marshall, Blackmun, Powell (o January 7, 1972), Rehnquist (o January 7, 1972)	January 7, 1972–December 19, 1975	404–423
Burger 4	Burger, Brennan, Stewart (r July 3, 1981), B. White, T. Marshall, Blackmun, Powell, Rehnquist, Stevens (o December 19, 1975)	December 19, 1975–September 25, 1981	423–453
Burger 5	Burger (r September 26, 1986), Brennan, B. White, T. Marshall, Blackmun, Powell, Rehnquist (p September 26, 1986), Stevens, O'Connor (o September 25, 1981)	September 25, 1981–September 26, 1986	453–478
Rehnquist 1	Rehnquist (o September 26, 1986), Brennan, B. White, T. Marshall, Blackmun, Powell (r June 26, 1987), Stevens, O'Connor, Scalia (o September 26, 1986)	September 26, 1986–February 18, 1988	478–484
Rehnquist 2	Rehnquist, Brennan (r July 20, 1990), B. White, T. Marshall, Blackmun, Stevens, O'Connor, Scalia, Kennedy (o February 18, 1988)	February 18, 1988–October 9, 1990	484–498
Rehnquist 3	Rehnquist, B. White, T. Marshall (r October 1, 1991), Blackmun, Stevens, O'Connor, Scalia, Kennedy, Souter (o October 9, 1990)	October 9, 1990–October 23, 1991	498–501
Rehnquist 4	Rehnquist, B. White (r July 1, 1993), Blackmun, Stevens, O'Connor, Scalia, Kennedy, Souter, Thomas (o October 23, 1991)	October 23, 1991–August 10, 1993	502–509
Rehnquist 5	Rehnquist, Blackmun (r August 3, 1994), Stevens, O'Connor, Scalia, Kennedy, Souter, Thomas, Ginsburg (o August 10, 1993)	August 10, 1993–August 3, 1994	510–512
Rehnquist 6	Rehnquist, Stevens, O'Connor, Scalia, Kennedy, Souter, Thomas, Ginsburg, Breyer (o August 3, 1994)	August 3, 1994–	513–

source: Lee Epstein, Jeffrey A. Segal, Harold J. Spaeth, and Thomas G. Walker, *The Supreme Court Compendium: Data, Decisions, and Developments,* 2d ed. (Washington, D.C.: Congressional Quarterly, 1996), Table 5-2.

note: The term *natural court* refers to a period of time during which the membership of the Court remains stable. There are a number of ways to determine the beginning and end of a natural court. Here a natural court begins when a new justice takes the oath of office and continues until the next new justice takes the oath. When two or more justices join the Court within a period of fifteen or fewer days, we treat it as the beginning of a single natural court (for example, Marshall 9, Chase 2, White 1, and Stone 1).

a. Numbered sequentially within the tenure of each chief justice.

b. The name of the chief justice appears first, with associate justices fol-

lowing in order of descending seniority. In addition, the date a justice left the Court, creating a vacancy for the next justice to be appointed, is given, as well as the date the new justice took the oath of office. *o* = oath of office taken, *d* = died, *r* = resigned or retired, *rj* = recess appointment rejected by Senate, *p* = promoted from associate justice to chief justice.

c. Volumes of *United States Reports* in which the actions of each natural court generally may be found. Because of the way decisions were published prior to the twentieth century, these volume numbers may not contain all of the decisions of a given natural court. They do, however, provide a general guide to the location of each natural court's published decisions. Natural courts of short duration may have little business published in the reports.

APPENDIX 7
SUPREME COURT CALENDAR

Activity	Time
Start of Term	First Monday in October
Oral Argument Cycle	October–April: Mondays, Tuesdays, Wednesdays in seven two-week sessions
Recess Cycle	October–April: two or more consecutive weeks after two weeks of oral argument; Christmas, Easter holidays
Conferences	Wednesday afternoon following Monday oral arguments (discussion of four Monday cases) Friday following Tuesday, Wednesday oral arguments (discussion of eight Tuesday–Wednesday cases; certiorari petitions) Friday before two-week oral argument period
Majority Opinion Assignment	Following oral arguments/conferences
Opinion Announcement	Throughout term with bulk coming in spring/summer
Summer Recess	Late June/early July until first Monday in October
Initial Conference	Late September (resolve old business, consider certiorari petitions from the summer)

APPENDIX 8
BRIEFING SUPREME COURT CASES

1. **What is the name of the case?**
   The name is important because it *generally* reveals which party is asking the Court to review the case. The name appearing first is usually (but not always) the appellant/petitioner, the party that lost in the court below.

2. **In what year did the Supreme Court decide the case?**
   The year is important because it will help to put the case into a legal and historical context. See Thumbnail Sketch of Supreme Court History for more detail.

3. **What circumstances triggered the dispute?**

4. **What statute or action triggered the dispute?**

5. **What provision of the Constitution is at issue?**

6. **What is the basic legal question(s) the Court is being asked to address?**

7. **What was the outcome of the dispute?**

8. **How did the majority reach its decision? What was its legal reasoning?**

9. **What legal doctrine, standards, or policy did the majority announce?**

10. **What other views (dissents, concurrences) were expressed?**

AN EXAMPLE: *Texas v. Johnson* (1989)

1. Case Name. *Texas v. Johnson*
2. Year Case Decided by Supreme Court. 1989
3. Facts that Triggered the Dispute. While the Republican National Convention was meeting in Dallas, Texas, in 1984, Gregory Johnson took part in a demonstration, protesting policies of the Reagan administration. During the demonstration, Johnson burned an American flag, and Dallas police arrested him.
4. Statute. Johnson was arrested and subsequently convicted under a Texas law that made it a criminal activity to desecrate a "venerable" object, including a state or a national flag.
5. Provision of the Constitution. Johnson alleged that his conviction, under the Texas state law, violated First Amendment guarantees of freedom of expression.
6. Legal Question. Is flag burning, in the context of this dispute, an activity protected by the First Amendment?
7. Outcome. In a 5–4 ruling, the Court held for Johnson.
8. Legal Reasoning of the Majority. In delivering the opinion of the Court, Justice William J. Brennan Jr. held that:

   a. Johnson's action constituted expressive conduct, allowing him to raise a First Amendment claim.
   b. Although governments have a "freer hand" in restricting "conduct" (as opposed to pure speech or writing), they still must demonstrate a sufficiently important governmental interest in regulating the activity in question.
   c. Texas's stated interests—preventing breaches of the peace and preserving the flag as a symbol of national unity—are insufficient to prohibit Johnson's expressive conduct.
9. Legal Doctrine. The majority:
   a. set policy in an area of the law that was previously murky. States may not "foster" their own view "of the flag by prohibiting expressive conduct relating to it."
   b. reaffirmed past precedents, suggesting that in such cases the Court will not only consider the nature of the expresion (whether it is verbal or nonverbal), but the governmental interest at stake.
   c. reaffirmed a general commitment to the fundamental nature of the First Amendment: "If there is a bedrock principle

underlying the First Amendment, it is that the Government may not prohibit the expression of an idea simply because society finds that idea itself offensive or disagreeable."

10. Other Points of View.

a. Justice Kennedy concurred: while the flag "holds a lonely place of honor," the Constitution mandates the outcome expressed by the majority. In short, sometimes justices "make decisions" they do not "like." But they make them "because they are right."

b. Chief Justice Rehnquist (joined by White and O'Connor) dissented: freedom of expression is not absolute: conduct may be prohibited in light of legitimate governmental interests. Here, those interests outweigh the expression.

i. Johnson's conduct had the tendency to incite a breach of the peace.

ii. the American flag is a "visible symbol embodying our Nation"; it does not represent a political idea or philosophy, nor is it just "another symbol."

c. Justice Stevens dissented: the question of flag desecration is unique. Cases involving other forms of symbolic expression are not dispositive of it. Our nation's flag symbolizes those values—liberty and equality—that "are worth fighting for." As such it cannot be "true that the flag . . . is not itself worthy of protection from unnecessary desecration."

GLOSSARY

Abstention A doctrine or policy of the federal courts to refrain from deciding a case so that the issues involved may first be definitively resolved by state courts.

Acquittal A decision by a court that a person charged with a crime is not guilty.

Advisory opinion An opinion issued by a court indicating how it would rule on a question of law should such a question come before it in an actual case. Federal courts do not hand down advisory opinions, but some state courts do.

Affidavit A written statement of facts voluntarily made under oath or affirmation.

Affirm To uphold a decision of a lower court.

A fortiori With greater force or reason.

Aggravating circumstances Conditions that increase the seriousness of a crime but are not a part of its legal definition.

Amicus curiae "Friend of the court." A person (or group), not a party to a case, who submits views (usually in the form of written briefs) on how the case should be decided.

Ante Prior to.

Appeal The procedure by which a case is taken to a superior court for a review of the lower court's decision.

Appellant The party dissatisfied with a lower court ruling who appeals the case to a superior court for review.

Appellate jurisdiction The legal authority of a superior court to review and render judgment on a decision by a lower court.

Appellee The party usually satisfied with a lower court ruling against whom an appeal is taken.

Arbitrary Unreasonable; capricious; not done in accordance with established principles.

Arguendo In the course of argument.

Arraignment A formal stage of the criminal process in which the defendants are brought before a judge, confronted with the charges against them, and they enter a plea to those charges.

Arrest Physically taking into custody or otherwise depriving freedom of a person suspected of violating the law.

Attainder, Bill of A legislative act declaring a person or easily identified group of people guilty of a crime and imposing punishments without the benefit of a trial. Such legislative acts are prohibited by the United States Constitution.

Attest To swear to; to be a witness.

Bail A security deposit, usually in the form of cash or bond, which allows those accused of crimes to be released from jail and guarantees their appearance at trial.

Balancing test A process of judicial decision making in which the court weighs the relative merits of the rights of the individual against the interests of the government.

Bench trial A trial, without a jury, conducted before a judge.

Bicameral A legislature, such as the U.S. Congress, with two houses.

Bona fide Good faith.

Brandeis brief A legal argument that stresses economic and sociological evidence along with traditional legal authorities. Named after Louis Brandeis, who pioneered its use.

Brief A written argument of law and fact submitted to the court by an attorney representing a party having an interest in a lawsuit.

Case A legal dispute or controversy brought to a court for resolution.

Case-in-chief The primary evidence offered by a party in a court case.

Case law Law that has evolved from past court decisions, as opposed to law created by legislative acts.

Case or controversy rule The constitutional requirement that courts may only hear real disputes brought by adverse parties.

Certification A procedure whereby a lower court requests that a superior court rule on specified legal questions so that the lower court may correctly apply the law.

Certiorari, Writ of An order of an appellate court to an inferior court to send up the records of a case that the appellate court has elected to review. The primary method by which the U.S. Supreme Court exercises its discretionary jurisdiction to accept appeals for a full hearing.

Civil law Law that deals with the private rights of individuals (e.g., property, contracts, negligence), as contrasted with criminal law.

Class action A lawsuit brought by one or more persons who represent themselves and all others similarly situated.

Collateral estoppel A rule of law that prohibits an already settled issue from being relitigated in another form.

Comity The principle by which the courts of one jurisdiction give respect and deference to the laws and legal decisions of another jurisdiction.

Common law Law that has evolved from usage and custom as reflected in the decisions of courts.

Compensatory damages A monetary award, equivalent to the loss sustained, to be paid to the injured party by the party at fault.

Concurrent powers Authority that may be exercised by both the state and federal governments.

Concurring opinion An opinion that agrees with the result reached by the majority, but disagrees as to the appropriate rationale for reaching that result.

Confrontation The right of a criminal defendant to see the testimony of prosecution witnesses and subject such witnesses to cross examination.

Consent decree A court-ratified agreement voluntarily reached by parties to settle a lawsuit.

Constitutional court A court created under authority of Article III of the Constitution. Judges serve for terms of good behavior and are protected against having their salaries reduced by the legislature.

Contempt A purposeful failure to carry out an order of a court (civil contempt) or a willful display of disrespect for the court (criminal contempt).

Contraband Articles that are illegal to possess.

Courts of appeals (federal) The intermediate level appellate courts in the federal system having jurisdiction over a particular region known as a circuit.

Criminal law Law governing the relationship between individuals and society. Deals with the enforcement of laws and the punishment of those who, by breaking laws, commit crimes.

Curtilage The land and outbuildings immediately adjacent to a home and regularly used by its occupants.

Declaratory judgment A court ruling determining a legal right or interpretation of the law, but not imposing any relief or remedy.

De facto In fact, actual.

Defendant A party at the trial level being sued in a civil case or charged with a crime in a criminal case.

De jure As a result of law or official government action.

De minimis Small or unimportant. A de minimis issue is considered one too trivial for a court to consider.

Demurrer A motion to dismiss a lawsuit in which the defendant admits to the facts alleged by the plaintiff but contends that those facts are insufficient to justify a legal cause of action.

De novo New, from the beginning.

Deposition Sworn testimony taken out of court.

Dicta; Obiter dicta Those portions of a judge's opinion that are not essential to deciding the case.

Directed verdict An action by a judge ordering a jury to return a specified verdict.

Discovery A pretrial procedure whereby one party to a lawsuit gains access to information or evidence held by the opposing party.

Dissenting opinion A formal written expression by a judge who disagrees with the result reached by the majority.

Distinguish A court's explanation of why a particular precedent is inapplicable to the case under consideration.

District courts The trial courts of general jurisdiction in the federal system.

Diversity jurisdiction The authority of federal courts to hear cases in which a party from one state is suing a party from another state.

Docket The schedule of cases to be heard by a court.

Double jeopardy The trying of a defendant a second time for the same offense. Prohibited by the Fifth Amendment to the Constitution.

Due process Government procedures that follow principles of essential fairness.

Eminent domain The authority of the government to take private property for public purpose.

En banc An appellate court hearing with all the judges of the court participating.

Enjoin An order from a court requiring a party to do or refrain from doing certain acts.

Entrapment Law enforcement officials inducing an otherwise innocent person into the commision of a criminal act.

Equity Law based on principles of fairness rather than strictly applied statutes.

Error, Writ of An order issued by an appeals court commanding a lower court to send up the full record of a case for review.

Exclusionary rule A principle of law that illegally gathered evidence may not be admitted in court.

Exclusive powers Powers reserved for either the federal government or the state governments, but not exercised by both.

Ex parte A hearing in which only one party to a dispute is present.

Ex post facto law A criminal law passed by the legislature and made applicable to acts committed prior to passage of the law. Prohibited by the U.S. Constitution.

Ex rel Upon information from. Used to designate a court case instituted by the government but instigated by a private party.

Ex vi termini From the force or very meaning of the term or expression.

Federal question A legal issue based on the U.S. Constitution, laws, or treaties.

Felony A serious criminal offense, usually punishable by incarceration of one year or more.

Gerrymander To construct political boundaries for the purpose of giving advantage to a particular political party or interest.

Grand jury A panel of twelve to twenty-three citizens who review prosecutorial evidence to determine if there are sufficient grounds to issue an indictment binding an individual over for trial on criminal charges.

Guilty A determination that a person accused of a criminal offense is legally responsible as charged.

Habeas corpus "You have the body." A writ issued to determine if a person held in custody is being unlawfully detained or imprisoned.

Harmless error An error occurring in a court proceeding that is insufficient in magnitude to justify the overturning of the court's final determination.

Hearsay Testimony not based on the personal knowledge of the witness, but a repetition of what the witness has heard others say.

Immunity An exemption from prosecution granted in exchange for testimony.

In camera A legal hearing held in the judge's chambers or otherwise in private.

Incorporation The process whereby provisions of the Bill of Rights are declared to be included in the due process guarantee of the Fourteenth Amendment and made applicable to state and local governments.

Indictment A document issued by a grand jury officially charging an individual with criminal violations and binding the accused over for trial.

In forma pauperis "In the form of a pauper." A special status granted to indigents that allows them to proceed without payment of court fees and to be exempt from certain procedural requirements.

Information A document, serving the same purpose as an indictment, but issued directly by the prosecutor.

Infra Below.

Injunction A writ prohibiting the person to whom it is directed from committing certain specified acts.

In pari materia On the same subject.

In re "In the matter of." The designation used in a judicial proceeding in which there are no formal adversaries.

In rem An act directed against a thing and not against a person.

Inter alia Among other things.

Interlocutory decree A provisional action that temporarily settles a legal question pending the final determination of a dispute.

Judgment of the court The final ruling of a court, independent of the legal reasoning supporting it.

Judicial activism A philosophy that courts should not be reluctant to review and if necessary strike down legislative and executive actions.

Judicial notice The recognition by a court of the truth of certain facts without requiring one of the parties to put them into evidence.

Judicial restraint A philosophy that courts should defer to the legislative and executive branches whenever possible.

Judicial review The authority of a court to determine the constitutionality of acts committed by the legislative and executive branches and to strike down acts judged to be in violation of the Constitution.

Jurisdiction The authority of a court to hear and decide legal disputes and to enforce its rulings.

Justiciable Capable of being heard and decided by a court.

Legislative court A court created by Congress under authority of Article I of the Constitution to assist in carrying out the powers of the legislature.

Litigant A party to a lawsuit.

Magistrate A low level judge with limited authority.

Mandamus "We command." A writ issued by a court commanding a public official to carry out a particular act or duty.

Mandatory jurisdiction A case that a court is required to hear.

Marque and reprisal An order from the government of one country requesting and legitimizing the seizure of persons and property of another country. Prohibited by the Constitution.

Merits The central issues of a case.

Misdemeanor A less serious criminal act, usually punishable by less than one year of incarceration.

Mistrial A trial that is prematurely ended by a judge because of procedural irregularities.

Mitigating circumstances Conditions that lower the moral blame of a criminal act, but do not justify or excuse it.

Moot Unsettled or undecided. A question presented in a lawsuit that cannot be answered by a court either because the issue has resolved itself or conditions have so changed that the court is unable to grant the requested relief.

Motion A request made to a court for a certain ruling or action.

Natural law Laws considered applicable to all persons in all nations because they are thought to be basic to human nature.

Nolle prosequi The decision of a prosecutor to drop criminal charges against an accused.

Nolo contendere No contest. A plea entered by a criminal defendant in which the accused does not admit guilt but submits to sentencing and punishment as if guilty.

Opinion of the court An opinion announcing the judgment and reasoning of a court endorsed by a majority of the judges participating.

Order A written command issued by a judge.

Original jurisdiction The authority of a court to try a case and to decide it, as opposed to appellate jurisdiction.

Per curiam An unsigned or collectively written opinion issued by a court.

Peremptory challenge Excusing a prospective juror without explaining the reasons for doing so.

Per se In and of itself.

Petitioner A party seeking relief in court.

Petit jury A trial court jury to decide criminal or civil cases.

Plaintiff The party who brings a legal action to court for resolution or remedy.

Plea bargain An arrangement in a criminal case in which the defendant agrees to plead guilty in return for the prosecutor reducing the criminal charges or recommending a lenient sentence.

Plurality opinion An opinion announcing the judgment of a court with supporting reasoning that is not endorsed by a majority of the justices participating.

Police powers The power of the state to regulate for the health, safety, morals, and general welfare of its citizens.

Political question An issue more appropriate for determination by the legislative or executive branch than the judiciary.

Precedent A previously decided case that serves as a guide for deciding a current case.

Preemption A doctrine under which an area of authority previously left to the states is, by act of Congress, brought into the exclusive jurisdiction of the federal government.

Prima facie "At first sight." A case that is sufficient to prevail unless effectively countered by the opposing side.

Pro bono publico "For the public good." Usually refers to legal representation done without fee for some charitable or public purpose.

Pro se A person who appears in court without an attorney.

Punitive damages A monetary award (separate from compensatory damages) imposed by a court for punishment purposes to be paid by the party at fault to the injured party.

Quash To annul, vacate, or totally do away with.

Ratio decidendi A court's primary reasoning for deciding a case the way it did.

Recuse The action of a judge not to participate in a case because of conflict of interest or other disqualifying condition.

Remand To send a case back to an inferior court for additional action.

Res judicata A legal issue that has been finally settled by a court judgment.

Respondent The party against whom a legal action is filed.

Reverse An action by an appellate court setting aside or changing a decision of a lower court.

Ripeness A condition in which a legal dispute has evolved to the point where the issues it presents can be effectively resolved by a court.

Selective incorporation The policy of the Supreme Court to decide incorporation issues on a case-by-case, right-by-right basis.

Show cause A judicial order commanding a party to appear in court and explain why the court should not take a proposed action.

Solicitor general Justice Department official whose office represents the federal government in all litigation before the U.S. Supreme Court.

Standing; standing to sue The right of parties to bring legal actions because they are directly affected by the legal issues raised.

Stare decisis "Let the decision stand." The doctrine that once a legal issue has been settled it should be followed as precedent in future cases presenting the same question.

State action An action taken by an agency or official of a state or local government.

Stay To stop or suspend.

Strict construction Narrow interpretation of the provisions of laws.

Subpoena ad testificandum An order compelling a person to testify before a court, legislative hearing, or grand jury.

Subpoena duces tecum An order compelling a person to produce a document or other piece of physical evidence that is relevant to issues pending before a court, legislative hearing, or grand jury.

Sub silentio "Under silence." A court action taken without explicit notice or indication.

Summary judgment A decision by a court made without a full hearing or without receiving briefs or oral arguments.

Supra Above.

Temporary restraining order A judicial order prohibiting certain challenged actions from being taken prior to a full hearing on the question.

Test A criterion or set of criteria used by courts to determine if certain legal thresholds have been met or constitutional provisions violated.

Three-judge court A special federal court made up of appellate and trial court judges created to expedite the processing of certain issues made eligible for such priority treatment by congressional statute.

Ultra vires Actions taken that exceed the legal authority of the person or agency performing them.

Usus loquendi The common usage of ordinary language.

Vacate To void or rescind.

Vel non "Or not."

Venireman A juror.

Venue The geographical jurisdiction in which a case is heard.

Voir dire "To speak the truth." The stage of a trial in which potential jurors are questioned to determine their competence to sit in judgment of a case.

Warrant A judicial order authorizing an arrest or search and seizure.

Writ A written order of a court commanding the recipient to perform or not to perform certain specified acts.

SUBJECT INDEX

CASE INDEX